WORLD LITERATURE CRITICISM

1500 to the Present

WORLD LITERATURE CRITICISM
Advisory Board

———

WORLD LITERATURE CRITICISM

1500 to the Present

*A Selection of
Major Authors from
Gale's Literary
Criticism Series*

**Stoker-Zola
INDEXES**

JAMES P. DRAPER, Editor

 Gale Research Inc. · *DETROIT · LONDON*

STAFF

James P. Draper, *Editor*

Laurie DiMauro, Tina Grant, Paula Kepos, Jelena Krstović, Daniel G. Marowski, Roger Matuz, James E. Person, Jr., Joann Prosyniuk, David Segal, Joseph C. Tardiff, Bridget Travers, Lawrence Trudeau, Thomas Votteler, Sandra L. Williamson, Robyn V. Young, *Contributing Editors*

Catherine Falk, Grace Jeromski, Michael W. Jones, Andrew M. Kalasky, David Kmenta, Marie Lazzari, Zoran Minderović, Sean René Pollock, Mark Swartz, *Contributing Associate Editors*

Jennifer Brostrom, David J. Engelman, Andrea Gacki, Judith Galens, Christopher Giroux, Ian A. Goodhall, Alan Hedblad, Elizabeth P. Henry, Christopher K. King, Kyung-Sun Lim, Elisabeth Morrison, Kristin Palm, Susan M. Peters, James Poniewozik, Eric Priehs, Bruce Walker, Debra A. Wells, Janet Witalec, Allyson J. Wylie, *Contributing Assistant Editors*

Jeanne A. Gough, *Permissions & Production Manager*

Linda M. Pugliese, *Production Supervisor*
Paul Lewon, Lorna Mabunda, Maureen Puhl, Camille Robinson, Jennifer VanSickle, *Editorial Associates*
Donna Craft, Brandy C. Johnson, Sheila Walencewicz, *Editorial Assistants*

Victoria B. Cariappa, *Research Manager*

Maureen Richards, *Research Supervisor*
Mary Beth McElmeel, Tamara C. Nott, *Editorial Associates*
Andrea B. Ghorai, Daniel J. Jankowski, Julie K. Karmazin, Robert S. Lazich, *Editorial Assistants*

Sandra C. Davis, *Permissions Supervisor (Text)*
Maria L. Franklin, Josephine M. Keene, Michele M. Lonoconus, Denise M. Singleton, Kimberly F. Smilay, *Permissions Associates*
Rebecca A. Hartford, Shalice Shah, Nancy K. Sheridan, *Permissions Assistants*

Margaret A. Chamberlain, *Permissions Supervisor (Pictures)*
Pamela A. Hayes, *Permissions Associate*
Amy Lynn Emrich, Karla Kulkis, Nancy M. Rattenbury, Keith Reed, *Permissions Assistants*

Mary Beth Trimper, *Production Manager*
Mary Winterhalter, *Production Assistant*

Arthur Chartow, *Art Director*
C. J. Jonik, *Keyliner*
Kathleen A. Hourdakis, Mary Krzewinski, *Graphic Designers*

∞™ This book is printed on acid-free paper that meets the minimum requirements of American National Standard for Information Sciences—Permanence Paper for Printed Library Materials, ANSI Z39.48-1984.

ISBN 0-8103-8361-6 (6-volume set)
A CIP catalogue record for this book is available from the British Library

Printed in the United States of America

Published simultaneously in the United Kingdom
by Gale Research International Limited
(An affiliated company of Gale Research Inc.)

Table of Contents

xiii

Introduction

A Comprehensive Information Source on World Literature

*W*orld Literature Criticism, 1500 to the Present (WLC) presents a broad selection of the best criticism of works by major writers of the past five hundred years. Among the authors included in *WLC* are sixteenth-century Spanish novelist Miguel de Cervantes and English dramatist William Shakespeare; seventeenth-century English poet John Milton and dramatist Aphra Behn; eighteenth-century Anglo-Irish novelist Jonathan Swift, English essayist Samuel Johnson, and French Enlightenment masters Jean-Jacques Rousseau and Voltaire; acclaimed nineteenth-century writers Jane Austen, William Blake, Emily Brontë, Lewis Carroll, Charles Dickens, Fyodor Dostoyevsky, Frederick Douglass, Gustave Flaubert, Edgar Allan Poe, Mary Shelley, Robert Louis Stevenson, William Wordsworth, and Emile Zola; and major twentieth-century authors W. H. Auden, James Baldwin, Albert Camus, Arthur Conan Doyle, Ralph Ellison, F. Scott Fitzgerald, Ernest Hemingway, James Joyce, Franz Kafka, Toni Morrison, Sylvia Plath, J. D. Salinger, Gertrude Stein, John Steinbeck, Virginia Woolf, and Richard Wright. The scope of *WLC* is wide: more than 225 writers representing dozens of nations, cultures, and time periods.

Coverage

This six-volume set is designed for high school, college, and university students, as well as for the general reader who wants to learn more about literature. *WLC* was developed in response to strong demand by students, librarians, and other readers for a one-stop, authoritative guide to the whole spectrum of world literature. No other compendium like it exists in the marketplace. About 95% of the entries in *WLC* were selected from Gale's acclaimed Literary Criticism Series and completely updated for publication here. Typically, the revisions are extensive, ranging from new author introductions to wide changes in the selection of criticism. A few entries—about 5%— were prepared especially for *WLC* in order to furnish the most comprehensive coverage possible.

Inclusion Criteria

Authors were selected for inclusion in *WLC* based on the advice of leading experts on world literature as well as on the recommendation of a specially formed advisory panel made up of high school teachers and high school and public librarians from throughout the United States. Additionally, the most recent major curriculum studies were closely examined, notably Arthur N. Applebee, *A Study of Book-Length Works Taught in High School English Courses* (1989); Arthur N. Applebee, *A Study of High School Literature Anthologies* (1991); and Doug Estel, Michele L. Satchwell, and Patricia S. Wright, *Reading Lists for College-Bound Students* (1990). All of these resources were collated and compared to produce a reference product that is strongly curriculum driven. To ensure that *WLC* will continue to meet the needs of students and general readers alike, an effort was made to identify a group of important new writers in addition to the most studied authors.

Scope

Each author entry in *WLC* presents a historical survey of critical response to the author's works. Typically, early criticism is offered to indicate initial responses, later selections document any rise or decline in literary reputations, and retrospective analyses provide modern views. Every endeavor has been made to include seminal essays on each author's work along with commentary providing current perspectives. Interviews and author statements are also included in many entries. Thus, *WLC* is both timely and comprehensive.

Organization of Author Entries

Information about authors and their works is presented through ten key access points:

■ The **Descriptive Table of Contents** guides readers through the range of world literature, offering summary sketches of authors' careers and achievements.

■ In each author entry, the **Author Heading** cites the name under which the author most commonly wrote, followed by birth and, where appropriate, death dates. Uncertain birth or death dates are indicated by question marks. Name variations, including full birth names when available, are given in parentheses in the caption below the **Author Portrait**.

■ The **Biographical and Critical Introduction** contains background information about the life and works of the author. Emphasis is given to four main areas: 1) biographical details that help reveal the life, character, and personality of the author; 2) overviews of the major literary interests of the author—for example, novel writing, autobiography, poetry, social reform, documentary, etc.; 3) descriptions and summaries of the author's best-known works; and 4) critical commentary about the author's achievement, stature, and importance. The concluding paragraph of the **Biographical and Critical Introduction** directs readers to other Gale series containing information about the author.

■ Every *WLC* entry includes an **Author Portrait**. Many entries also contain **Illustrations**—including holographs, title pages of works, letters, or pictures of important people, places, and events in the author's life—that document the author's career.

■ The **List of Principal Works** is chronological by date of first book publication and identifies the genre of each work. For non-English-language authors whose works have been translated into English, the title and date of the first English-language edition are given in brackets beneath the foreign-language listing. Unless otherwise indicated, dramas are dated by first performance rather than first publication.

■ **Criticism** is arranged chronologically in each author entry to provide a useful perspective on changes in critical evaluation over the years. Most entries contain a detailed, comprehensive study of the author's career as well as book reviews, studies of individual works, and comparative examinations. To ensure timeliness, current views are most often presented, but not to the exclusion of important early pieces. For the purpose of easy identification, the critic's name and the date of the critical work are given at the beginning of each piece of criticism. Unsigned criticism is preceded by the title of the source in which it appeared. Within the criticism, titles of works by the author are printed in boldface type. Publication information (such as publisher names and book prices) and certain numerical references (such as footnotes or page and line references to specific editions of works) have been deleted at the editor's discretion to provide smoother reading of the text.

- Critical essays are prefaced by **Explanatory Notes** as an additional aid to readers of *WLC*. These notes may provide several types of valuable information, including: 1) the reputation of the critic; 2) the importance of the work of criticism; 3) the commentator's approach to the author's work; 4) the purpose of the criticism; and 5) changes in critical trends regarding the author. In some cases, **Explanatory Notes** cross-reference the work of critics within an entry who agree or disagree with each other.

- A complete **Bibliographical Citation** of the original essay or book follows each piece of criticism.

- An annotated list of **Sources for Further Study** appears at the end of each entry and suggests resources for additional study. These lists were specially compiled to meet the needs of high school and college students. Additionally, most of the sources cited are available in typical small and medium-size libraries.

- Many entries contain a **Major Media Adaptations** section listing important non-print treatments and adaptations of the author's works, including feature films, TV mini-series, and radio broadcasts. This feature was specially conceived for *WLC* to meet strong demand from students for this type of information.

Other Features

WLC contains three distinct indexes to help readers find information quickly and easily:

- The **Author Index** lists all the authors appearing in *WLC*. To ensure easy access, name variations and changes are fully cross-indexed.

- The **Nationality Index** lists all authors featured in *WLC* by nationality. For expatriate authors and authors identified with more than one nation, multiple listings are offered.

- The **Title Index** lists in alphabetical order all individual works by the authors appearing in *WLC*. English-language translations of original foreign-language titles are cross-referenced to the foreign titles so that all references to a work are combined in one listing.

Citing *World Literature Criticism*

When writing papers, students who quote directly from *WLC* may use the following general forms to footnote reprinted criticism. The first example is for material drawn from periodicals, the second for material reprinted from books:

Gary Smith, "Gwendolyn Brooks's 'A Street in Bronzeville,' the Harlem Renaissance and the Mythologies of Black Women," *MELUS*, Vol. 10, No. 3 (Fall 1983), 33-46; excerpted and reprinted in *World Literature Criticism, 1500 to the Present*, ed. James P. Draper (Detroit: Gale Research, 1992), pp. 459-61.

Frederick R. Karl, *American Fictions, 1940/1980: A Comprehensive History and Critical Evaluation* (Harper & Row, 1983); excerpted and reprinted in *World Literature Criticism, 1500 to the Present*, ed. James P. Draper (Detroit: Gale Research, 1992), pp. 541-46.

Acknowledgments

The editor wishes to acknowledge the valuable contributions of the many librarians, authors, and scholars who assisted in the compilation of *WLC* with their responses to telephone and mail inquiries. Special thanks are offered to the members of *WLC*'s advisory board, whose names are listed opposite the title page.

Comments Are Welcome

The editor hopes that readers will find *WLC* to be a useful reference tool and welcomes comments about the work. Send comments and suggestions to: Editor, *World Literature Criticism, 1500 to the Present*, Gale Research Inc., Penobscot Building, Detroit, MI 48226-4094.

WORLD LITERATURE CRITICISM

1500 to the Present

Bram Stoker

1847-1912

(Born Abraham Stoker) Irish novelist, short story writer, biographer, essayist, and critic.

INTRODUCTION

Stoker is best known as the author of *Dracula* (1897), one of the most famous horror novels of all time. He also wrote adventure and romance novels, several other horror novels, short stories, and a laudatory biography of his long-time friend and employer, the Shakespearean actor Sir Henry Irving. Despite his contributions to other genres, however, Stoker's renown rests on his creation of the Transylvanian count whose name has become synonymous with vampirism.

Stoker was a sickly child, bedridden for much of his boyhood. As a student at Trinity College, however, he excelled in athletics as well as academics, and graduated with honors in mathematics in 1870. He worked for ten years in the Irish Civil Service, and during this time contributed drama criticism to the Dublin *Mail.* His glowing reviews of Henry Irving's performances encouraged the actor to seek him out. The two became friends, and in 1879 Stoker became Irving's manager. He also performed managerial, secretarial, and even directorial duties at London's Lyceum Theatre. Despite an active personal and professional life, he began writing and publishing novels, beginning with *The Snake's Pass* in 1890. *Dracula* appeared in 1897. Following Irving's death in 1905, Stoker was associated with the literary staff of the London *Telegraph* and wrote several more works of fiction, including the horror novels *The Lady of the Shroud* (1909) and *The Lair of the White Worm* (1911). He died in 1912.

Although most of Stoker's novels were favorably reviewed when they appeared, they are dated by their stereotyped characters and romanticized Gothic plots, and are rarely read today. Even the earliest reviews frequently decry the stiff characterization and tendency to melodrama that flaw Stoker's writing. Critics have universally praised, however, his beautifully precise place descriptions. Stoker's short stories, while sharing the faults of his novels, have fared better with modern readers. Anthologists frequently include Stoker's stories in collections of horror fiction. "Dracula's Guest," originally intended as a prefatory chapter to *Dracula*, is one of the best known.

Dracula is generally regarded as the culmination of the Gothic vampire story, preceded earlier in the nineteenth century by Dr. William Polidori's "The Vampyre," Thomas Prest's *Varney the Vampyre*, J. S. Le Fanu's *Carmilla*, and Guy de Maupassant's "Le Horla." A large part of the novel's initial success was due, however, not to its Gothicism but to the fact, noted by Daniel Farson, that "to the Victorian reader it must have seemed daringly modern." An early reviewer of *Dracula* in the *Spectator* commented that "the up-to-dateness of the book—the phonograph diaries, typewriters, and so on—hardly fits in with the mediaeval methods which ultimately secure the victory for Count Dracula's foes." Stoker utilized the epistolary style of narrative that was characteristic of Samuel Richardson and Tobias Smollett in the eighteenth century, and that Wilkie Collins further refined in the nineteenth. The narrative, comprising journal entries, letters, newspaper clippings, a ship's log, and phonograph recordings, allowed Stoker to contrast his characters' actions with their own explications of their acts.

Some early critics noted the "unnecessary number of hideous incidents" which could "shock and disgust" readers of *Dracula*. One critic even advised keeping the novel away from children and nervous adults. Initially, *Dracula* was interpreted as a straight-forward horror novel. Dorothy Scarborough indicated the direction of future criticism in 1916 when she wrote that "Bram Stoker furnished us with several interesting specimens of supernatural life always tangled with other uncanny motives." In 1931 Ernest Jones, in his *On the Nightmare*, drew attention to the theory that these "other uncanny motives" involve repressed sexuality. Critics have since tended to view *Dracula* from a Freudian psychosexual standpoint; however, the novel has also been interpreted from folkloric, political, feminist, medical, and religious points of view.

Today the name of Dracula is familiar to many people who may be wholly unaware of Stoker's identity, though the popularly held image of the vampire bears little resemblance to the demonic being that Stoker depicted. Adaptations of *Dracula* in plays and films have taken enormous liberties with Stoker's characterization. A resurgence of interest in traditional folklore has revealed that Stoker himself did not conform to established vampire legend. Yet *Dracula* has had tremendous impact on readers since its publication. Whether Stoker evoked a universal fear, or as some modern critics would have it, gave form to a universal fantasy, he created a powerful and lasting image that has become a part of popular culture.

(For further information about Stoker's life and works, see *Contemporary Authors*, Vol. 105; *Dictionary of Literary Biography*, Vols. 36, 70; *Something about the Author*, Vol. 28; and *Twentieth-Century Literary Criticism*, Vol. 8.)

CRITICAL COMMENTARY

THE ATHENAEUM
(essay date 1897)

[In the following review of *Dracula*, the anonymous critic comments on the horrific nature of the novel.]

Stories and novels appear just now in plenty stamped with a more or less genuine air of belief in the visibility of supernatural agency. The strengthening of a bygone faith in the fantastic and magical view of things in lieu of the purely material is a feature of the hour, a reaction—artificial, perhaps, rather than natural—against late tendencies in thought. Mr. Stoker is the purveyor of so many strange wares that *Dracula* reads like a determined effort to go, as were, "one better" than others in the same field. How far the author is himself a believer in the phenomena described is not for the reviewer to say. He can but attempt to gauge how far the general faith in witches, warlocks, and vampires—supposing it to exist in any general and appreciable measure—is likely to be stimulated by this story. The vampire idea is very ancient indeed, and there are in nature, no doubt, mysterious powers to account for the vague belief in such beings. Mr. Stoker's way of presenting his matter, and still more the matter itself, are of too direct and uncompromising a kind. They lack the

Principal Works

The Duties of Clerks of Petty Sessions in Ireland (handbook) 1879

Under the Sunset (short stories) 1882

A Glimpse of America (lecture) 1886

The Snake's Pass (novel) 1890

The Watter's Mou' (novel) 1895

Dracula (novel) 1897

Miss Betty (novel) 1898

The Mystery of the Sea (novel) 1902

The Jewel of Seven Stars (novel) 1903

The Man (novel) 1905

Personal Reminiscences of Henry Irving. 2 vols. (reminiscences) 1906

Snowbound (short stories) 1908

The Lady of the Shroud (novel) 1909

Famous Imposters (essays) 1910

The Lair of the White Worm (novel) 1911; also published as The Garden of Evil, 1966

Dracula's Guest, and Other Weird Stories (short stories) 1914

essential note of awful remoteness and at the same time subtle affinity that separates while it links our humanity with unknown beings and possibilities hovering on the confines of the known world. *Dracula* is highly sensational, but it is wanting in the constructive art as well as in the higher literary sense. It reads at times like a mere series of grotesquely incredible events; but there are better moments that show more power, though even these are never productive of the tremor such subjects evoke under the hand of a master. An immense amount of energy, a certain degree of imaginative faculty, and many ingenious and gruesome details are there. At times Mr. Stoker almost succeeds in creating the sense of possibility in impossibility; at others he merely commands an array of crude statements of incredible actions. The early part goes best, for it promises to unfold the roots of mystery and fear lying deep in human nature; but the want of skill and fancy grows more and more conspicuous. The people who band themselves together to run the vampire to earth have no real individuality or being. The German man of science is particularly poor, and indulges, like a German, in much weak sentiment. Still Mr. Stoker has got together a number of "horrid details," and his object, assuming it to be ghastliness, is fairly well fulfilled. Isolated scenes and touches are probably quite uncanny enough to please those for whom they are designed.

A review of "Dracula," in *The Athenaeum*, No. 3635, June 26, 1897, p. 235.

MONTAGUE SUMMERS
(essay date 1918)

[An author, theater historian, and critic, Summers was one of the foremost English scholars of Restoration drama and an authority on the occult, witchcraft, and the supernatural. In the following excerpt from a 1918 study collected in his *The Vampire: His Kith and Kin*, he offers a largely favorable review of *Dracula*, noting some weaknesses of construction but commending the fascination of the plot.]

[It] is well-nigh impossible for a story which deals with the supernatural or the horrible to be sustained to any great length. Elements which at first are almost unendurable will lose their effect if they are continued, for the reader's mind insensibly becomes inured to fresh emotions of awe and horror, and *Dracula* is by no means briefly told. . . . [It] extends to more than four hundred pages, nor does it escape the penalty of its prolixity. The first part, "Jonathan Harker's Journal," which consists of four chapters is most admirably done, and could the whole story have been sustained at so high a level we should have had a complete masterpiece. But that were scarcely possible. The description of the journey through Transylvania is interesting to a degree, and even has passages which attain to something like charm. "All day long we seemed to dawdle through a country which was full of beauty of every kind. Sometimes we saw little towns or castles on the top of steep hills such as we see in old missals; sometimes we ran by rivers and streams which seemed from the wide stony margin on each side of them to be subject to great floods. It takes a lot of water, and running strong, to sweep the outside edge of a river clear." Very effective is the arrival of the English traveller at the "vast ruined castle, from whose tall black windows came no ray of light, and whose broken battlements showed a jagged line against the moonlit sky." Very adroitly are the various incidents managed in their quick succession, those mysterious happenings which at last convince the matter-of-fact commonplace young solicitor of Exeter that he is a helpless prisoner in the power of a relentless and fearful being. The continual contrasts between business conversations, the most ordinary events of the dull listless days, and all the while the mantling of dark shadows in the background and the onrushing of some monstrous doom are in these opening chapters most excellently managed.

So tense a strain could not be preserved, and consequently when we are abruptly transported to Whitby and the rather tedious courtships of Lucy Westenra, who is a lay figure at best, we feel that a good deal of the interest has already begun to evaporate. I would hasten to add that before long it is again picked up, but it is never sustained in the same degree; and good sound sensational fare as we have set before us, fare which I have myself more than once thoroughly enjoyed, yet it is difficult not to feel that one's palate has been a little spoiled by the nonpareil of an antipast. This is not to say that the various complications are not sufficiently thrilling, but because of their very bounty now and again they most palpably fail of effect, and it can hardly escape notice that the author begins to avail himself of those more extravagant details of vampirism which frankly have no place outside the stories told round a winter's hearth. It would have been better had he confined himself to those particulars which are known and accepted, which indeed have been officially certified and definitely proved. But to have limited himself thus would have meant the shortening of his narrative, and here we return to the point which was made above.

If we review *Dracula* from a purely literary point of approach it must be acknowledged that there is much careless writing and many pages could have been compressed and something revised with considerable profit. It is hardly possible to feel any great interest in the characters, they are labels rather than individuals. As I have said, there are passages of graphic beauty, passages of graphic horror, but these again almost entirely occur within the first sixty pages. There are some capital incidents, for example the method by which Lord Godalming and his friend obtain admittance to No. 347 Piccadilly. Nor does this by any means stand alone.

However, when we have—quite fairly, I hope—thus criticized *Dracula,* the fact remains that it is a book of unwonted interest and fascination. Accordingly we are bound to acknowledge that the reason for the immense popularity of this romance,—the reason why, in spite of obvious faults it is read and reread—lies in the choice of subject and for this the author deserves all praise. (pp. 333-35)

Montague Summers, "The Vampire in Literature," in his *The Vampire: His Kith and Kin,* 1928. Reprint by University Books, 1960, pp. 271-340.

H. P. LOVECRAFT
(essay date 1927)

[One of the foremost modern authors of supernatural horror fiction, Lovecraft developed a type of horror tale that combines occult motifs, modern science, and the regional folklore of his native New England. He was well versed in the history of Gothic literature, and his *Supernatural Horror in Literature*

(1927) is one of the earliest and most comprehensive studies of this genre. In the following excerpt from an essay that first appeared in that work, he notes the archetypal and influential nature of Stoker's vampire novel *Dracula*.]

[The] ingenious Bram Stoker . . . created many starkly horrific conceptions in a series of novels whose poor technique sadly impairs their net effect. *The Lair of the White Worm,* dealing with a gigantic primitive entity that lurks in a vault beneath an ancient castle, utterly ruins a magnificent idea by a development almost infantile. *The Jewel of Seven Stars,* touching on a strange Egyptian resurrection, is less crudely written. But best of all is the famous *Dracula,* which has become almost the standard modern exploitation of the frightful vampire myth. Count Dracula, a vampire, dwells in a horrible castle in the Carpathians, but finally migrates to England with the design of populating the country with fellow vampires. How an Englishman fares within Dracula's stronghold of terrors, and how the dead fiend's plot for domination is at last defeated, are elements which unite to form a tale now justly assigned a permanent place in English letters. *Dracula* evoked many similar novels of supernatural horror, among which the best are perhaps *The Beetle,* by Richard Marsh, *Brood of the Witch-Queen,* by "Sax-Rohmer" (Arthur Sarsfield Ward), and *The Door of the Unreal,* by Gerald Bliss. (pp. 392-93)

H. P. Lovecraft, "Supernatural Horror in Literature," in his *Dagon and Other Macabre Tales,* edited by August Derleth, Arkham House Publishers, Inc., 1965, pp. 347-413.

LEONARD WOLF
(essay date 1972)

[Wolf is a Romanian-born author, editor, and critic. His *Wolf's Complete Book of Terror* (editor; 1979) has been characterized as featuring some of the most resolutely gruesome, violent, and obsessive horror stories ever collected. In the following excerpt from his *A Dream of Dracula: In Search of the Living Dead,* he pronounces *Dracula* a great book for its complex fusion of mythic, ancient, and modern themes, all only imperfectly comprehended by Stoker himself.]

[When] *Dracula* appeared, it was still recognizable as a Gothic novel in the tradition of Walpole, Lewis, Radcliffe and Maturin. There were the usual fearful dangers: a lustful villain, dark and mysterious mountains, crumbling architecture—a castle in Transylvania, a ruined chapel in London, a tumbling abbey in Whitby—the usual alarums and surprises along with vaults, stone walls and reverberating darkness in the holds of ships. A point of some importance is that the conflicts in the old fictions between antagonists were essentially physical and external. Stoker's achievement is that while he kept plenty of that machinery, thereby fulfilling an implied agreement with the literary past, he managed at the same time to make his vampire tale a gathering place for symbols of extraordinary internal meaning. In 1972, seventy-five years from the time of its publication, *Dracula* is fully visible as a visionary novel . . . whose allegorical power transcends the fairly narrow Christian work that Stoker made.

The Christian message is certainly there, but it is quiveringly entangled in matters that (sadly) seem to have more "modern" significance: the meaning of human energy; the concept of sanity; the nature of identity; and most intensively the awful powers of sexual repression and evasion. It is an entanglement, I hardly need add, that is probably unconscious on Stoker's part, and has been carefully unrecognized by a couple of generations of readers. For the most part, *Dracula* has been read as a rousing good thriller, rather than as the great contemporary allegory of blood it certainly is.

Even Montague Summers, who is prepared to dote on nearly anything vampiric, will only concede to Stoker the achievement of a brilliantly selected subject matter and occasionally "admirable" writing [see excerpt above]. But Summers, after praising the first four chapters, says of the book " . . . and could the whole story have been sustained at so high a level we should have had a complete masterpiece." In fact, we have a complete masterpiece. . . . (pp. 180-81)

A summary of the action of *Dracula,* useful as it is to remind us who does what to whom, can hardly explain why the story has domesticated itself in the contemporary imagination where, over a seventy-five-year period, it has taken on all the symbolic authority of a legend. How has this tale by a part-time hack writer managed to create in the minds of nearly three generations of readers a sense of an old memory recovered? Why does it inexhaustibly generate prose imitations of itself ? Even more to the point, how does it happen that the film industry of all the world has been unable to let Stoker's vampire achieve, finally, the rest the novel itself has given him?

I have already given a simple answer to these complex questions by claiming that *Dracula* is a great book, and I have suggested that its greatness lies in the ways in which Stoker fuses the Christian allegory of his vampire tale with the other matters he exposes even as he tries to avoid knowing what they mean. (p. 205)

Dracula squirms with . . . primordial, dark or forbidden news from the abyss. More than that, much of its artistic strength comes from the intensity with which Stoker evades what he guesses—while he decks it out in the safer Christian truths that he repeats. (p. 206)

[It is] a piece of triumphant restraint which makes Dracula move through the book, when he does appear with a cold, dry, sinister largeness that befits a creature who is a "man or shade, / Shade more than man, more image than a shade." From the first moment that we see him, he stirs up those matters with which the book deals. He is strong, feral and old. If Van Helsing has energy with grace abounding, then Dracula is charged with the grandeur of satanic power. Their struggle is allegorical and instinctual, but in either case, it turns on blood, because the blood as it flows in mortal veins is life, at the same time as it represents life everlasting. The struggle between Van Helsing and Dracula is, however, more than religious, though Van Helsing pursues him with crosses, the Host and prayers. Those aids belong to the Church, but Van Helsing also uses garlic flowers, the woodrose and the stake—remedies that do not depend upon Christ because the vampire is an evil beyond theology, rooted in instincts not yet recognized, much less controlled. (p. 220)

Dracula is considerably more than a sexual danger. Stoker insists on his brooding, primordial animality—he is antirational, childlike, instinctual. His evil is related to the animal heat of that Ugric tribe which "bore down from Iceland the fighting spirit which Thor and Wodin gave them, which their Berserkers displayed to such fell intent on the seaboards of Europe. . . . " The blood of such peoples, mingled with that of "the Huns, whose warlike fury had swept the earth like a living flame," is also in his veins. When he talks of his past, though he glows with his consciousness of inherited power, the vitality of which he boasts is above all bestial, as his features remind us. He is profusely hairy, with massive eyebrows, and hands that are "broad, with squat fingers" and pale pointed ears. . . . Even his cunning, slowly modifying itself toward intelligence, is the cunning of the animal that counts on swift physical motion to counter its errors in judgment. Van Helsing speaks of his "child-mind," and Dracula is dangerous because he is in the course of evolving it into a brain that will be devoted to the grandeur of evil.

So much for the beast. What sort of *person* is Dracula? The answer is that he is not a person—he is a presence; or, better, he is an absence that requires concealing. Stoker has not made Dracula's personality his problem, nor is trying to assess it ours. Beyond the physical descriptions of him that emphasize his power, there is little for us to turn to for character analysis, though I confess that there are a few sharp moments when something resembling a self passes before us; as, for instance, when we are given the suggestion that this quintessential monster whom the beasts and the very winds obey, sets the table, makes beds, cooks and cleans away the dishes in his castle. There is another moment when Van Helsing's band, searching Dracula's

Fenchurch Street house, comes upon the vampire's personal effects which include "also a clothes brush, a brush and comb, and a jug and basin—the latter containing dirty water which was reddened as if with blood." This find strikes a note of loneliness, but we are still far distant from a Dracula who might be a tormented figure, more acted upon than acting. Despite a few pious Christian remarks by Mina Harker that Dracula is to be pited, and the notation that in the moment of his death "there was in . . . [his] face a look of peace," Stoker has brilliantly avoided building *any* sympathy for him. He does nothing, ever, to entice compassion. Instead, he is a thoroughgoing evil creature who drinks the blood of his victims because he likes doing what, in any case, it is his destiny to do. Even in the instant before he is destroyed, his "red eyes glared with [a] horrible vindictive look. . . . " And, as "the eyes saw the sinking sun . . . the look of hate in them turned to triumph." We may well believe that Harker's great Kukri knife and Quincey Morris's bowie did not flash a moment too soon.

Dracula, then, is a novel that lurches toward greatness, stumbling over perceived and unperceived mysteries: Christianity, insanity, identity, a spectrum of incest possibilities, marriage, homosexuality, immortality and death. All of them are bound together in the inclusive meaning of blood. If I claim greatness for this strange book, it is because, after nearly three generations, it continues to pulse with sometimes coherent, more often dismembered symbolic material of the sort that makes up what Jung has called "primordial experience which surpasses man's understanding, and to which he is therefore in danger of succumbing." Stoker's achievement is that he put all this *stuff* into his book with such skill that a headlong reader as well as one capable of worrying over the signs and portents is always in the grip of the narrative line. To put it another way, Stoker, organizing the tale of the vampire and his enemies, did not create impediments to our appreciation of "the disturbing vision of monstrous and meaningless happenings that in every way exceed the grasp of human feeling." (pp. 220-22)

Leonard Wolf, "Dracula: The King Vampire," in his *A Dream of Dracula: In Search of the Living Dead,* 1972. Reprint by Popular Library, 1977, pp. 171-224.

ROBERT LIDSTON
(essay date 1980)

[In the following excerpt, Lidston compares *Dracula* with Stephen King's *'Salem's Lot,* demonstrating that Stoker's novel is the most successful of the two in its horrific presentation of its central vampire character.]

"Welcome to my house! Enter freely and of your own will!" He made no motion of stepping to meet me, but stood like a statue, as though his gesture of welcome had fixed him into stone. The instant, however, that I had stepped over the threshold, he moved impulsively forward, and holding out his hand grasped mine with a strength which made me wince, an effect which was not lessened by the fact that it seemed as cold as ice—more like the hand of a dead than a living man.

In this way Dracula beckons solicitor Jonathan Harker into his castle and into a horrifying adventure with the supernatural. In the same way millions of readers, uncoerced by professors and grades, have opened the covers of two novels and willingly suspended their disbelief to be captivated by stories of the undead. Neither Bram Stoker's *Dracula,* first published at the dawning of the twentieth century, nor Stephen King's *'Salem's Lot,* published just five years ago, can claim to be "great novels" by reason of their respective authors' adroit handling of theme, structure, symbol, and character development. Still, both have enjoyed enormous popular success far beyond that of most of their contemporary bestsellers.

Viewed under a harsh critical light, *Dracula* does not transcend the sensibilities of its age. Bram Stoker was a writer of Victorian potboilers. He often slips into the mawkishly sentimental and his characters, even when sufficiently developed, are period types. As a writer of dialogue, he has severe limitations. Dutch Professor Abraham Van Helsing, really the novel's hero, slips in and out of a laughable vaudeville dialect. Numerous small details, essential to verisimilitude, also often elude Stoker. In one scene a wolf crashes through a bedroom window—no small feat because Stoker placed the bedroom on the second floor. Even vampire chronicler Montague Summers admires the selection of subject matter and the first four chapters but laments: "The whole story [could] have been sustained at so high a level. Then we should have had a complete masterpiece" [*The Vampire: His Kith and Kin*].

Viewed in a similarly strict way, *'Salem's Lot* can be seen as no more likely to endure. The characterization of King's vampire, Kurt Barlow, obviously owes much to Stoker as does the device of frequently reminding the reader of the time and day to root him in reality. King's characters are superficially portrayed contemporary types, some of whom become involved in mild though now obligatory mass-audience sex scenes. Often they rather foolishly waste precious daylight fully aware of the undead's powers after dark. The novel is also too long, sometimes sacrificing the maintenance of tension to tell the stories of minor vampire victims. (p. 70)

Dracula has gone through twelve British and nineteen American editions. There have also been seven foreign language editions in Gaelic, French, Italian, Spanish, and German. Since first penned by Irish actor Hamilton Deane in 1923, the stage version has been revived frequently. As a Broadway hit in the 1920s, it launched the career of Bela Lugosi. As a Broadway hit in the 1970s, it launched the career of Frank Langella. Since F. W. Murnau's 1922 *Nosferatu,* dozens of films have retold Stoker's story. (p. 71)

'Salem's Lot has not had eighty years to establish such impressive credentials. Perhaps it never will carve out so widespread and lasting a place in popular culture. . . . [Yet it] has sold over three million copies and been turned into a CBS-TV mini-series with high ratings.

Dracula and *'Salem's Lot* are horror novels. They allow their readers to experience fear, one of man's deepest emotions, in the safety of their own homes. Both accomplish this feat by allowing them to imagine that distant horrors are present in their apparently understandable contemporary real world.

They are novels of horror rather than of terror. Both terms describe responses to a frightening person, act, or situation. Terror, however, is the extreme rational fear of some understandable form of reality. Horror is the extreme irrational fear of the unnatural or supernatural. As genres, novels of terror and novels of horror have their origins in the gothic romances flourishing in the late eighteenth and early nineteenth centuries.

Written in professed imitation of medieval romances, these novels emphasize gloomy settings, grotesque action, and a mood of decay. They usually feature a genteel, beautiful young woman menaced by an evil, dark man. After being threatened in various gloomy and mysterious settings, she is usually saved by a sexually unthreatening young man who vanquishes her tormentor.

Robert Walpole's *The Castle of Otranto* (1764) is, of course, generally cited as the "first" gothic romance. Other prominent examples of the genre, such as Ann Radcliffe's *The Mysteries of Udolpho* (1794), Matthew G. Lewis' *The Monk* (1796), and Charles Maturin's *Melmoth the Wanderer* (1820), helped establish a form today well represented in the paperback book industry. Though full of dungeons, young heroines, and frightening antagonists, none of these novels features the fear of the unnatural aroused by a vampire. Two nineteenth-century examples of the vampire sub-genre are worth noting here as likely influences on Stoker and, through his work, on King.

John Polidori's *The Vampyre* (1819) was a product of that same project to while away a rainy evening that generated Mary Shelley's *Frankenstein.* Rarely read any longer because of its weak style and defective plotting, Polidori's novel introduced the urbane, evil, and blood-sucking Lord Ruthven whose "dead grey eye" beguiled his female victims. Like its literary descendants with which we are concerned, *The Vampyre* became popular throughout Europe both as a novel and in a variety of theatrical productions.

William Presket Prest's *Varney the Vampyre* (1847) was also enormously popular in the nineteenth century and recent interest has brought about its reprinting. It is 868 double-columned pages of energetic prose with a wildly rambling plot. The villain here is another vampire nobleman, Sir Francis Varney. The existence of these two earlier works shows that *Dracula* and *'Salem's Lot* are heirs to a tradition, but it does not explain their popularity.

A look back beyond the advent of Gothic Romance reveals a long-established fascination with the horrible evident in works like *Beowulf* and *Gawain and the Green Knight.* Certainly, such interest can be explained partly as childish curiosity about death and the abnormal. Horror plays not only on our curiosities, however, but also on our anxieties. In every era man has had much in the explainable world around him about which to be anxious. On the surface it seems odd that he would seek things he cannot control to worry about. It seems odder still that the two novels we are considering here should have achieved their initial popularity during eras in which anxiety was rampant. But Stephen King suggests that such eras are quite understandably the times when horror stories are most appealing:

> When you've got a lot of free-floating anxieties, the horror story or movie helps to conceptualize them, shrink them down to size, make them concrete so they're manipulable. When you can do that, and then it's over at the end and it just sort of blows away, there's probably some minor catharsis involved.

There are, however, only a limited number of different things that can go bump in the night to serve as objectifications of our anxieties. For this reason, characterization is a major element that makes one horror novel stand out over others. In *Dracula* and *'Salem's Lot* it is the characterization of the antagonists. Though they appear but sparingly (Dracula on only 62 of 390 pages in the original edition . . .), perhaps *because* they seldom appear, the reader is weirdly attracted to them. They are figures of heroic dimension who call up the basic contests of good versus evil and the basic mysteries of blood, sex, and death. Their opponents (the ostensible heroes) are paler figures of their ages.

Though established as distinct individuals, the group confronting Dracula is composed of very typical Victorians. The women are morally strong, loving, and subservient. Lucy Westenra, an upper-class heiress who early falls prey to the vampire, receives three marriage proposals in one day from three perfect gentlemen. Her popularity, unencouraged by any loosening of her sexual stays, causes her to wonder, "Why are men so noble when we women are so little worthy of them?" Lucy's death leads to her similarly virtuous friend Mina Harker's nobly swearing herself to the pursuit of Dracula.

Very much a part of the Victorian middle class, Mina is a former school mistress who is training herself in secretarial skills so she can devote her energies to aiding her new, upwardly mobile husband. Though bitten by the vampire, she lives to see him dispatched, thus providing throughout the novel a proper object for his menace. In one of the work's most bathetic passages, psychiatrist John Seward provides this portrait of a Mina already scarred through her contact with Dracula:

> Oh that I could give an idea of the scene; of that sweet, sweet, good, good woman in all the radiant beauty of her youth and animation, with the red scar on her forehead of which she was conscious, and which we saw with grinding of our teeth— remembering whence and how it came; her loving kindness against our grim hate; her tender faith against all our fears and doubting; and we, knowing that so far as symbols went, she, with all her goodness and purity and faith, was outcast from God.

Lest the reader worry that Mina should end up outcast from God, it must be remembered that on preceding pages she establishes the kind of Victorian credentials that guarantee virtue will out. With forgivable sarcasm, she has earlier opined that "Some of the 'New Women' writers will some day start an idea that men and women should be allowed to see each other asleep before proposing or accepting." Even after she has married Jonathan she is concerned about his holding her arm as they walk down Piccadilly: "I felt it very improper."

The men who avenge Lucy, protect Mina, and finally destroy Dracula are no less representative of their age. Mina's beloved Jonathan is confused when a Transylvanian peasant offers him a vampire-chasing crucifix: "As an English Churchman, I have been taught to regard such things as in some measure idolatrous." Even when three female vampires are about to attack him, his class consciousness causes him to note they are "ladies by their dress and manner," but his repressed sexuality forces him to admit: "I felt in my heart a wicked, burning desire that they would kiss me with those red lips." The wealthy Arthur Holmwood, Lucy's fiancé, does not hesitate when asked to transfuse his blood to try to save her: "If you only knew how gladly I would die for her." Yet after Van Helsing compels him to drive a stake through her apparently dead body, the noble and generous Arthur tells the doctor: "God bless you that you have given my dear one her soul again."

The others who often join Jonathan and Arthur in oaths like those of medieval knights to destroy the evil of Dracula are no less Victorian. Lucy's disappoint-

ed suitor Dr. Seward possesses a trait common to the group: "He is one of the most resolute men. . . . He seems absolutely imperturbable." Quincey Morris, also disappointed by Lucy, is just the sort of rambunctious American a Victorian Briton would create: "A moral Viking. If America can go on breeding men like that, she will be a power in the world indeed." Even Van Helsing sounds like a product of Victorian England. He pledges: "I, too, have a duty to do, a duty to others, a duty to you, a duty to the dead; and, by God, I shall do it!" Still, he worries that a slackening of Victorian certitude will only encourage evil: "In this enlightened age, when men believe not even what they see, the doubting of wise men would be his [Dracula's] greatest strength." (pp. 71-4)

It is not such people who have made *Dracula* [a tremendously popular work]. . . . It is their antagonists who grip us. Readers become interested in, and finally attracted to, Count Dracula because he is much larger than the everyday life of one particular period.

Dracula is crafty and powerful. Unlike his merely mortal opponents and readers, he can defy even the laws of nature. He appears in the novel as a coachman, as himself, as the dog who leaps ashore from the *Demeter,* as a bat at various windows, and as a mist which creeps up the side of Dr. Seward's hospital. Besides ingeniously assuming these diverse physical forms, he devises a plan for spreading fifty coffin hiding places throughout England and frequently outsmarts his pursuers.

Dracula often proves Van Helsing's assertion that "he has the strength of twenty men." Not only possessing physical power, he also has the ability to control men's minds, as we see in his use of Seward's patient Renfield and in his reading of Mina's mind after forcing her to drink his blood. What is more, Mina finds him sexually powerful. In the midst of his bloodsucking attack, she sees "his eyes flamed red with devilish passion." Not surprisingly Van Helsing best summarizes the guile and power of his opponent:

> The *nosferatu* do not die like the bee when he sting once. He is only stronger. . . . He is of cunning more than mortal, for his cunning be the growth of ages; he have still the aids of necromancy, which is, as his etymology imply, the divination by the dead, and all the dead that he can come nigh to are for him at command; . . . he is devil in callous, and the heart of him is not; he can, within limitations, appear at will when, and where, and in any of the forms that are to him; he can, within his range, direct the elements: the storm, the fog, the thunder; he can command all the meaner things.

Simplistically viewed, romantic heroes are sympathetic figures who perform much better than we can. Sherlock Holmes is more logical, Superman much stronger, than mere mortals. Despite the fact that he is an evil force, we come to sympathize with Dracula. Like Satan in the first books of *Paradise Lost,* he is a noble figure who excites us far more than the novel's protagonists.

Besides possessing enviable abilities to change physical form, travel swiftly, and seduce virgins, Dracula is at home in the dark. Deep in his racial history man learned to be afraid of the dark. He could not produce food; he could not see his neighbors. Van Helsing may be a man who can turn the light of science on the world given us to understand, but Dracula flourishes in a world at once familiar yet very strange. Though Stoker shows us that Dracula can be abroad in the daylight, he is much less powerful and therefore more human. The Dracula who excites us does not need the Promethean gift of fire. His internal fires, visible through those hypnotic eyes, make him sufficient unto himself.

For these reasons and others, we admire Dracula. In addition, like Lucy and Mina, we find ourselves perversely attracted to him. Yet is that attraction so perverse? We are attracted to him because, Godlike, he promises eternal life through the replenishment of the life force. Women wear rouge and men and women sit for hours in the sun to give their bodies the look of a well-functioning circulatory system. For centuries people let blood to purge infirmities. Dracula offers the promise of new blood. Like us, he may grow older, but unlike us, he has found a fountain of youth.

It is the promise of life beyond the ultimate darkness of death which has propelled Christianity. Like Christ, Dracula has died and risen. This is the ultimate reason that readers have found a Victorian potboiler so engrossing for so long. *Dracula* is just another fairy tale, and yet what if we never had to die?

In *'Salem's Lot* it is Kurt Barlow who offers the temptation to eternal life. Another Dracula, he is an impressive man with whom communion is described as attractive. . . . (pp. 74-6)

Many of the qualities helping Barlow survive and prosper are those Stoker assigns to Dracula. His origins are every bit as ancient. He sneers at the antiquity of Father Callahan's Catholicism:

> I was old when it was young, when its members hid in the catacombs of Rome and painted fishes on their chests so they could tell one from another. I was strong when this simpering club of breadeaters and wine-drinkers who venerate the sheep-savior was weak. My rites were old when the rites of your church were unconceived. Yet I do not underestimate. I am wise in the ways of goodness as well as those of evil.

He too is a creature of the night, capable of controlling a shrewd assistant, and proficient, when he chooses, at

mesmerizing his prey. He too is physically strong and often one step ahead of his pursuers.

Despite possessing these and other of Dracula's traits, Barlow never becomes as grand a figure of evil. He is not seen moving about in the daylight and lacks Dracula's impressive ability to change his physical nature. He is frightening, and because of that, entertaining, but he never becomes the admirable and magnetic figure his model is. He is not sexually attractive and hardly seems a nobleman. He is all-too-reduceable to the FBI file that bears his name.

'Salem's Lot has been widely read for many of the same reasons that have allowed *Dracula* to survive so long, but its endurance may be limited by two factors. First of all, Stephen King dilutes Barlow as the center of all evil by mixing him up with the much more petty evils of bootlegger Hubie Marston. Through this connection King attempts to identify evil with Marston's house and with the town as a whole. At the novel's end, Barlow has been dispatched and a multitude of quite ordinary citizens turned vampires are about to be destroyed by a brush fire. This diffusion of evil may, in many ways, be a good device, but Barlow is proportionately reduced.

Secondly, *'Salem's Lot* is obviously a derivative book. King makes no secret of the fact Barlow as patterned after Dracula. Because he is derivative, Barlow would have paled next to the original even if King had created an equally impressive figure.

Bram Stoker was a minor writer who touched deep mysteries which trouble us all. Perhaps he would be flattered by a current author trying to match his performance. Because Stephen King has failed, it is not likely that Dracula will be dethroned as prince of darkness. (pp. 76-7)

Robert Lidston, "Dracula and 'Salem's Lot: Why the Monsters Won't Die," in *West Virginia University Philological Papers,* Vol. 28, 1980, pp. 70-7.

JOHN ALLEN STEVENSON
(essay date 1988)

[In the following excerpt, Stevenson examines themes of sexuality in *Dracula.*]

Near the end of *Dracula,* as the band of vampire hunters is tracking the count to his Carpathian lair, Mina Harker implores her husband to kill her if her partial transformation into a vampire should become complete. Her demand for this "euthanasia" (the phrase is Dr. Seward's) is itself extraordinary, but equally interesting is the way she defines her position and the duty of the men around her: "Think, dear, that there have been times when brave men have killed their wives and

Major Media Adaptations: Motion Pictures*

Nosferatu, Eine Symphonie des Grauens, 1922. [Silent; adaptation of *Dracula;* also released as *Nosferatu, the Vampire,* 1922.] Prana Co. Director: F. W. Murnau. Cast: Max Schreck, Alexander Granach, Greta Schroeder, Gustav von Wangenheim.

Dracula, 1931. Universal. Director: Tod Browning. Cast: Bela Lugosi, Dwight Frye, Edward Van Sloan, Helen Chandler.

Dracula's Daughter, 1936. Universal. Director: Lambert Hillyer. Cast: Gloria Holden, Otto Kruger, Edward Van Sloan, Irving Pichel, Nan Grey, Hedda Hopper.

Dracula, 1958. Hammer. Director: Terrence Fisher. Cast: Christopher Lee, Peter Cushing, Melissa Stribling, Carol Marsh.

Dracula, 1973. CBS Television. Director: Dan Curtis. Cast: Jack Palance, Simon Ward, Nigel Davenport, Fiona Lewis.

Andy Warhol's Dracula, 1974. Bryanston Pictures. Director: Paul Morrisey. Cast: Joe Dallesandro, Vittorio de Sica.

Dracula, 1979. Universal/Mirish. Director: John Badham. Cast: Laurence Olivier, Frank Langella, Donald Pleasence, Kate Nelligan, Trevor Eve.

Nosferatu, Phantom der nacht, 1979. Fox. [Adaptation of *Nosferatu, eine symphonie des grauens;* also released as *Nosferatu, the Vampire*] Director: Werner Herzog. Cast: Klaus Kinski, Isabelle Adjani, Bruno Ganz.

Major Media Adaptations: Recordings

Dracula, 1975. Caedmon. Excerpts from Stoker's novel read by David McCallum and Carole Shelley.

Dracula, 1976. Mark Records. Recording of Orson Welles's radio adaptation, first broadcast on *Mercury Theatre on the Air,* 1938, CBS Radio, featuring Orson Welles and Agnes Moorehead.

*Numerous motion pictures have used the character of the Transylvanian vampire Count Dracula without otherwise drawing directly from Stoker's 1897 novel.

---

womenkind, to keep them from falling into the hands of the enemy. . . . It is men's duty towards those whom they love, in such times of sore trial!" Why is this "duty" incumbent on "brave men"? Why are "wives and womenkind" a treasure better destroyed than lost to the "enemy"? In the context of Bram Stoker's novel, it is evident that the mercy implied by such euthanasia is not salvation from the loathsome embraces of a lewd foreigner. It is too late for that. Mina, after all, has already been the object of Dracula's attention. The problem is one of loyalty: the danger is not that she will be captured but that she will go willingly. She makes this clear: "this time, if it ever come, may come quickly . . . and . . . you must lose no time in using your opportunity. At such a time, I myself might be—nay! If the time ever comes, *shall be*——leagued with your enemy against you." Kill me, she says, before I can betray you.

That *Dracula* concerns competition between men for women can hardly be questioned—passages like these can be multiplied almost indefinitely. But what is the nature of that competition? Certainly, a number of readers have agreed on one interpretation. As they would have it, the horror we feel in contemplating Dracula is that his actions, when stripped of displacement and disguise, are fundamentally incestuous and that Stoker's novel is finally a rather transparent version of the "primal horde" theory Freud advanced—only about fifteen years after publication of the novel—in *Totem and Taboo.* According to this interpretation (as one adherent has it, "almost a donnée of *Dracula* criticism" [James Twitchell, *The Living Dead: A Study of the Vampire in Romantic Literature*]), the count, undeniably

long in the tooth, attempts to hoard all the available women, leaving the younger generation, his "sons," no recourse but to rise up and kill the wicked "father," thus freeing the women for themselves. The novel does concern how one old man ("centuries-old," he tells us) struggles with four young men (and another old, but good, man, Dr. Van Helsing) for the bodies and souls of two young women. But to call that strife intrafamilial [Twitchell, *Dreadful Pleasures: An Anatomy of Modern Horror*] or to say that all the characters, including Dracula, are linked "as members of one family" [Maurice Richardson, "The Psychoanalysis of Ghost Stories"] seems to be more of a tribute to the authority psychoanalysis enjoys among literary critics than it is an illuminating description of Stoker's narrative.

I would like to rethink the way sexual competition works in *Dracula* from the perspective of that frequent antagonist of psychoanalysis, anthropology. Nowhere is the gulf between these universalizing disciplines greater, perhaps, than it is on the subject that obsesses them both, incest. A good deal of recent anthropological work argues that, as one prominent scholar puts it, "human beings [do] not *want* to commit incest all that much" [Robin Fox, *Kinship and Marriage: An Anthropological Perspective*]. My intention in this essay is to apply this anti-incestuous model of human desire to *Dracula* in the place of the more customary Freudian model. As Mina's remarks above indicate, the novel insistently—indeed, obsessively—defines the vampire not as a monstrous father but as a foreigner, as someone who threatens and terrifies precisely because he is an outsider. In other words, it may be fruitful to reconsider Stoker's compelling and frequently retold story in terms of inter*racial* sexual competition rather than as intrafamilial strife. Dracula's pursuit of Lucy and Mina is motivated, not by the incestuous greed at the heart of Freud's scenario, but by an omnivorous appetite for difference, for novelty. His crime is not the hoarding of incest but a sexual theft, a sin we can term excessive exogamy. Although the old count has women of his own, he is exclusively interested in the women who belong to someone else. This reconsideration can yield a fresh appreciation of the appeal of Stoker's story and can suggest ways in which the novel embodies a quite powerful imagining of the nature of cultural and racial difference. (p. 139)

If most cultures have forbidden marriage within the family, they have also wanted to maintain the integrity of the group. *Group* is, admittedly, a vague term, an inherently cultural construct encompassing all manner of classifications: tribe, caste, class, race, religion, nation, and so on. But its vagueness does not diminish the importance of the distinction Fox speaks of, that boundary between "us" and "them," however artificially that line might be drawn. And according to these lights, marriage, or even a sexual relation, that crosses that boundary ceases to be a social act that simultaneously denies incest and affirms the group and becomes instead a threat, what I earlier called excessive exogamy. This was the problem worrying the Deuteronomist when he cautioned the Jews that intermarriage would "turn away thy sons . . . that they may serve other gods," and this was the kind of exogamy the great pioneer of the anthropology of marriage, Edward Westermarck, was thinking about when he coined the memorable phrase "social adultery" [*The History of Human Marriage*]. Here, then, is the real horror of Dracula, for he is the ultimate social adulterer, whose purpose is nothing if it is not to turn good Englishwomen like Lucy and Mina away from their own kind and customs. Mina's fear, we recall, is that she "*shall be . . . leagued with your enemy against you.*"

What sort of enemy, foreigner, stranger is Count Dracula? I have claimed that interracial sexual competition is fundamental to the energies that motivate this novel, but in what way are vampires another "race"? As a rigorous scientific concept, race enjoys little credence today, despite the many attempts—particularly as part of the nineteenth-century zeal for classification—to elevate it to a science involving physical criteria like jaws, cheekbones, cranial capacities, and so on. It is, however, a convenient metaphor to describe the undeniable human tendency to separate "us" from "them." An idea like race helps us grapple with human otherness—the fact that we do not all look alike or believe alike or act alike. Dracula is, above all, strange to those he encounters—strange in his habits, strange in his appearance, strange in his physiology. At one point, Van Helsing calls him "the other," and the competition

for women in the novel reflects a conflict between groups that define themselves as foreign to each other. My use of the term *interracial,* then, is a way to speak of what happens when any two groups set themselves at odds on the basis of what they see as differences in their fundamental identity, be that "racial," ethnic, tribal, religious, national, or whatever.

The problem of interracial competition would have probably had an especial resonance in 1897, the year *Dracula* appeared. For several decades, Great Britain had been engaged in an unprecedented program of colonial expansion: four and one quarter million square miles were added to the empire in the last thirty years of the century alone. British imperialism, of course, was not new, nor was suspicion of foreigners a novelty in a country where, as one eighteenth-century wit put it, "Before they learn there is a God to be worshipped, they learn there are Frenchmen to be detested." Yet the late nineteenth century saw the rise of that great vulgarization of evolution (and powerful racist rationalization), social Darwinism, and heard Disraeli say, "All is race; there is no other truth." *Dracula*'s insistence on the terror and necessity of racial struggle in an imperialist context (the count, after all, has invaded England and plans to take it over) must reflect that historical frame. My emphasis in this essay, however, is on Stoker's novel as a representation of fears that are more universal than a specific focus on the Victorian background would allow. Westermarck's comment about exogamy as social adultery is indeed contemporary with *Dracula* (his *History of Human Marriage* was first published in 1891), but the anthropologist was expressing nothing not on the mind of the Deuteronomist millennia before. And the difficulty facing the men who fight the vampire is not unlike that expressed by Roderigo to Brabantio, in lines first spoken at a much earlier time in British imperial history: Desdemona, he says, has made "a gross revolt, / Tying her duty, beauty, wit, and fortunes / In an extravagant and wheeling stranger. . . . " Let us look more specifically, then, at this stranger, Count Dracula.

First, appearances. Dracula is described repeatedly, always in the same way, with the same peculiar features emphasized. Take Mina's first sight of him:

> I knew him at once from the description of the others. The waxen face; the high aquiline nose, on which the light fell in a thin, white line; the parted red lips, with the sharp white teeth showing between; and the red eyes that I had seemed to see in the sunset on the windows of St. Mary's Church at Whitby. I knew, too, the red scar on his forehead where Jonathan had struck him.

Dracula is remarkable looking for his nose, for the color of his lips and eyes and skin, for the shape of his teeth, for the mark on his forehead; elsewhere, we learn also that he has a strange smell. Color, in fact, which is com-

Sir Henry Irving and Stoker leaving the Lyceum Theatre.

monly used in attempts at racial classification, is a key element in Stoker's creation of Dracula's foreignness. Here, and throughout the novel, the emphasis is on redness and whiteness. In a brief description, each color is mentioned three times (I count "waxen" as white), and the combination of the two colors is one of the count's most distinguishing racial features. That it is racial, and not personal, becomes clear when we note how Stoker consistently uses a combination of red and white to indicate either incipient or completed vampirism. The women Harker encounters at Castle Dracula, while one is blond and two are dark, are all primarily red and white ("All three had brilliant white teeth that shone like pearls against the ruby of their voluptuous lips"). More significant, Lucy and Mina take on this coloration as Dracula works his will on them. There is first of all the reiterated image of red blood on a white nightgown, a signature that Dracula leaves behind after one of his visits (and a traditional emblem of defloration). Even more striking is the scar left when Van Helsing, in a futile attempt at inoculation, presses the host into Mina's forehead to protect Mina against renewed attack. Harker calls it the "red scar on my poor darling's white forehead." The scar, a concentration of red and white that closely resembles the mark on Dracula's own forehead, thus becomes a kind of caste mark, a sign of membership in a homogeneous group—and a group that is foreign to the men to whom Mina supposedly belongs.

The scar shared by Dracula and Mina, one of the richest details in the novel, has a significance even beyond its function as a caste mark. After all, the wounds are not self-inflicted but given by members of the group of vampire hunters (Dracula's by Harker, Mina's by Van Helsing), so that they represent an attempt by the nonvampires to "mark off " the vampires—much as God puts a mark on Cain, the original type of an alien breed. But the caste mark is also a kind of venereal scar, not only because it results from the count's seduction of Mina but also because the echo of Hamlet's accusation against Gertrude is far too strong to be accidental: "Such an act / That blurs the grace and blush of modesty, / Calls virtue hypocrite, takes off the rose / From the fair forehead of an innocent love, / And sets a blister there. . . ." The scar is thus a sign of defilement (seeing it, Mina cries out, "Unclean! Unclean!"), of sexual possession by the outsider. Finally, it is curious to think of a scar on Dracula at all. He is remarkably protean, able to change his form (he leaves the shipwreck at Whitby as a dog) or even involve himself in rising mist. Why should he allow this disfigurement to remain? John Freccero, discussing the scar Dante describes on the purgatorial form of Manfred, insists that a mark like this on a supernatural being must be seen, not as literal and physical, but as a text, as something meant especially to be *read*. In that sense, the scars on the vampires serve a dense semiotic function, marking Dracula and Mina (potentially, anyway) as simultaneously untouchable, defiled, and damned—above all, different.

Red and white are, of course, the colors we associate with the typically "English" complexion, and I want to emphasize that vampire coloration is something different; at the same time, however, the coincidence of coloration is meaningful. On the one hand, a "rosy" English complexion is created by the perception of red *through* white—blood coursing beneath pale skin. The vampire inverts this order. He or she displays red *on* white, as with the scars or the effect of ruby lips against waxen skin. The result is rather like a mortician's makeup—a parody of what we expect and, as with a corpse, an effect that finally signals difference and not similarity. That is, the vampire has no rosy glow but presents what looks like dead flesh stained with blood (or drained flesh indicating the food it requires)—a grotesque inversion of good health. On the other hand, the vampire and his English competitors may have more in common than they wish to acknowledge. As we explore vampire sexuality, we will encounter a series of traits that initially assert themselves as foreign or strange but that are revealed as inversions (as in the coloration example), parodies, exaggerations, or even literalizations. Thus, the perception of otherness can be an accurate response to difference and, at the same time, an act that conceals or represses deeper connections.

The allies against the count are not described in comparable detail, and their descriptions tend to be moral rather than physical. Three of their qualities recur almost formulaically—*good, brave,* and *strong.* "Oh, thank God for good, brave men!" says Mina, and Van Helsing insists later, "You men are brave and strong." *Good* is also often attached to the women in their unvamped condition: "there are good women left still to make life happy." The distinction between the moral excellence of the insiders and the physical peculiarity of the foreigner underlines the outsider's inherent danger. As Mina puts it, "[T]he world seems full of good men—even if there *are* monsters in it." The familiar is the image of the good, while foreignness merges with monstrosity.

But looks are only one way to construct our im-

ages of the foreign, and, as we might expect, Dracula's habits are as bizarre as his appearance. The introductory section of the novel—Harker's diary account of his journey to Transylvania and of his stay at Castle Dracula—gradually reveals Dracula's distinctive customs, moving from the merely odd to the unequivocally horrifying. So, we learn early that Dracula lacks servants, that he is nocturnal, that he likes to eat alone, and that he despises mirrors, and only later do we watch him crawl down walls head first, feed small children to his women, and sleep in his coffin. All Dracula's peculiarities, however, reflect fundamental differences in the most basic human activities that signal group identity. Dracula is strange to Harker—and to us—because of what food he eats and how he obtains and prepares it, because of where and when he sleeps, because of his burial customs. To Harker as to so many, what is foreign is monstrous, even if it is only a matter of table manners.

In the structure of group identity, the regulation of sexuality has an especially privileged place, and *Dracula* is most fundamentally concerned with both distinguishing the differences between the way vampire "monsters" and "good, brave men" reproduce and identifying the threat those differences pose to Van Helsing and the other men. Our introduction to Dracula in the novel's first six chapters—what Christopher Craft calls the "admission" to monstrosity [" 'Kiss Me with Those Red Lips': Gender and Inversion in Bram Stoker's *Dracula,*" *Representations,* 1984]—establishes the count's foreignness; after that, the novel primarily shows us Dracula's attempts to reproduce and the struggle of the band of young men under Van Helsing to stop him. The tale horrifies because the vampire's manner of reproduction appears radically different and because it requires the women who already belong to these men.

Although the vampire reproduces differently, the ironic thing about vampire sexuality is that, for all its overt peculiarity, it is in many ways very like human sexuality, but human sexuality in which the psychological or metaphoric becomes physical or literal. It initially looks strange but quite often presents a distorted image of human tendencies and behavior. What is frightening about Dracula, then, is that his sexuality is simultaneously different and a parodic mirror. This seeming paradox probably reflects the full complexity of the way one group responds to the sexual customs of another.

We note first the remarkable economy at the heart of the vampire's survival instinct. Like human beings, Dracula has the need for self-preservation, which asserts itself in the drive to preserve both the life of the individual and the life of the species. The difference, of course, is that the vampire can satisfy the two needs simultaneously—the same action, vamping, answers the need for nourishment and procreation. But that equation of eating and sexual intercourse literalized by the vampire is a connection we all make metaphorically and one that, as Lévi-Strauss is fond of pointing out, a number of primitive tribes acknowledge by making the same verb do service for both actions (*Raw and Cooked* 269, *Savage Mind* 105). Dracula says he needs new women so that he can "feed" (312), but we know that is not all he means.

While the physiology of vampire sexuality literalizes a connection between sex and eating that, for human beings, operates metaphorically, the expression of that sexuality grotesquely exaggerates the typical human pattern of incest avoidance and exogamy. The vampire's "marriage" laws are first suggested when Harker is almost seduced by the three vampire women he encounters at Castle Dracula. Critical opinion about these women differs considerably, betraying how badly vampire sexuality has been misunderstood. The problem arises in part because the text does not explicitly define the women's relation to Dracula—who are they? Both Craft and Maurice Richardson call them Dracula's "daughters"; Carol Frye terms them "wives" ["Fictional Conventions and Sexuality in *Dracula, Victorian Newsletter,* 1972]; Leonard Wolf the count's "beautiful brides" [*The Annotated "Dracula"*]; and C. F. Bentley says that "they are either Dracula's daughters or his sisters" but insists that an "incestuous" relation existed between them in the past ["The Monster in the Bedroom: Sexual Symbolism in Bram Stoker's *Dracula,*" *Literature and Psychology,* 1972]. The difficulty here is a false either/or: these women must either be kin or be wives. What these readers ignore is the possibility that Dracula's relation to these women has, quite simply, changed, that they have occupied both roles—not simultaneously, as in incest, but sequentially, because of the way vampire reproduction works.

A speech Dracula makes to Mina late in the novel clarifies his relation to the women at the castle: "And you, their best beloved one, are now to me, flesh of my flesh; blood of my blood; kin of my kin; my bountiful wine-press for a while; and shall be later on my companion and helper." According to the count's description, he and Mina are like husband and wife (he uses the "flesh of my flesh" from Genesis and the marriage ceremony), but through the very fact of their union, they are also becoming "kin." Thus, because of the vampire's incest taboo, she can be his "wine-press" only for a "while," and in time, when her transformation from "good" Englishwoman to vampire is complete, she will become a daughterly "companion and helper." The vampire women at the castle have undergone a similar change. When one of them reproaches Dracula with the accusation, "You yourself never loved; you never love!" he can answer, "Yes, I too can love; you yourselves can tell it from the past. Is it not so?"

Dracula's relation to his women changes in this way because of another economy in vampire sexuality. Not only do vampires combine feeding with reproduction, they collapse the distinction between sexual partners and offspring. "Wives," that is, become daughters in an extraordinarily condensed procedure in which penetration, intercourse, conception, gestation, and parturition represent, not discrete stages, but one undifferentiated action. Dracula re-creates in his own image the being that he is simultaneously ravishing. But the transformation, once complete, is irreversible—Dracula makes it clear that once Mina becomes his daughter, his "companion and helper," she can never again be his "wine-press." We confront here one large inadequacy of the *Totem and Taboo* reading. In the primal horde, as female offspring mature, they fall under the sexual sway of their fathers—daughters become wives. In *Dracula,* this role transformation is reversed and is accompanied, moreover, by a powerful incest taboo that seems to preclude Dracula's further sexual interest in his onetime partners. In fact, unlike the greedy patriarch of the horde, Dracula encourages his women to seek other men. He tells the female vampires at his castle that, when Harker's usefulness to him is over, they can have their way with the Englishman: "Well, now I promise you that when I am done with him you shall kiss him at your will."

The inevitable question arises for vampires as well as for human beings: why is there an incest taboo? The answer, however, is not that incest avoidance has been ingrained in the vampire's conscience, if such a thing should exist; instead, vampires appear incapable of committing this particular crime, since they face a physical barrier to incest, not just a psychological one—another dramatic instance of vampire literalization. Such a barrier is an example of the many physical changes that mark the transformation into a vampire, as we learn on the day that Lucy dies to her old identity as Englishwoman and is reborn as one of Dracula's own kind. (Vampire victims, it seems, always die in childbirth.) Van Helsing and Seward examine her neck and discover, to their horror, that the punctures in her throat "had absolutely disappeared." Dracula could not commit incest even if he wanted to; he has no orifice to penetrate.

With the exaggeration of human tendencies characteristic of vampire sexuality, the vampire's incest taboo creates its own iron rule of exogamy. Just as there is a physical obstacle to vampire incest, so the vampire's need to marry out is not a matter of custom or of a long-term evolutionary benefit but an immediate and urgent biological necessity. Westermarck approvingly quotes another nineteenth-century anthropologist, who speaks of "mankind's instinctive hankering after foreign women." For Dracula, though, the need for "foreign women" is no mere hankering. Rather, because his sexual partner is also his food, the vampire must marry out or die. A world without foreign women would represent not only sterility but famine.

The vampire as a sexual being is thus strangely familiar—he avoids incest and he seeks sexual partners outside his family. But that sexuality is also a parody of human sexuality, a literalization that makes him seem very odd: he *cannot* commit incest, he *must* marry out. And that necessity, in turn, creates his primary danger. Since all vampires are kin, they cannot simultaneously seek likeness (i.e., marry within the confines of the group) and avoid incest, as human beings do. Dracula thus cannot respect group or racial boundaries with regard to women; his particular physiology demands instead that he take "foreign women" away from the men they already belong to, a theft that continues his own kind. Moreover, his physically insistent need to steal threatens the existence of the group on which he preys. As he tells Van Helsing and his allies, "Your girls that you all love are mine already; and through them you and others shall yet be mine." Dracula is thus doubly frightening—he is the the foreigner whose very strangeness renders him monstrous, and, more dangerous, he is an imperialist whose invasion seeks a specifically sexual conquest; he is a man who will take other men's women away and make them his own. [The critic adds in a footnote: "It is Dracula's status as an invader that sets him apart from other supernatural beings. Most of the terror ghosts create is bound up with the belief that dead people haunt the places they knew in life: houses are normally haunted by former residents, or at least by someone who had a significant relation to the place. Dracula, however, must leave his old home to do his dreadful work. This supernatural imperialism suggests again that the fear Dracula creates is linked to his strangeness, to his remote origins. In a sense, Dracula is a demonic version of Abraham, who also must leave his old home and go to another place to begin his new race."]

And Dracula will make "foreign women" his own in a radical way. He does not simply kidnap or alter cultural allegiances; his sexual union with women like Lucy and Mina physically deracinates them and recreates them as members of his own kind. This point will be clearer if we look at Stoker's manipulation of the novel's central image, that of blood. Blood means many things in *Dracula;* it is food, it is semen, it is a rather ghastly parody of the Eucharist, the blood of Christ that guarantees life eternal. But its meaning also depends on the way humanity has made blood a crucial metaphor for what it thinks of as racial identity. Blood is the essence that somehow determines all those other features—physical and cultural—that distinguish one race from another. And this connection of blood and

race explains most fully that fascinating sequence when each of the good, brave men in turn gives Lucy a transfusion. Ostensibly, they are replacing what the count has removed, so that she will not perish from loss of blood. But Dracula's action is not feeding, nor is it only a combination of feeding and copulation. The men are desperate to transfuse their blood into Lucy because they understand that sexual intercourse with a vampire deracinates. Dracula's threat is not miscegenation, the mixing of blood; instead, he gives his partners a new racial identity. And he can do this because the source of their original identity, their blood, has been taken away. In only one more of the remarkable literalizations that give this novel mythic power, the answer to the kind of genocide that the vampire threatens is to reinfuse Lucy with the "right" blood, "young and strong . . . and so pure," as Van Helsing says.

Such deracination is one effect of the economy we observed above, that of the vampire's sexual partners becoming his offspring. But what I have been calling the racial element needs emphasis here; not only do wives become daughters but brides who were originally foreign to Dracula become pure vampires. This is what the Deuteronomist understood: the problem with mixed marriages is that they produce new loyalties, not confused ones. As Mina says, "I . . . *shall be* . . . leagued with your enemy against you." And why? Because, with her own blood removed, she will be like Dracula, and it is that loss of women's loyalty that the good, brave men cannot abide. As Van Helsing explains it to Mina: "He have infect you in such a wise, that . . . in time, death . . . shall make you like to him. This must not be! We have sworn together that it must not. Thus are we ministers of God's own wish: that the world . . . will not be given over to monsters. . . . " The desperation these men feel about the threat from Dracula is suggested, perhaps, by the multiple transfusions they give Lucy. Van Helsing recognizes that these transfusions are sexual and that they imply a kind of promiscuity in Lucy; as he puts it in his distinctively incompetent English: "Ho, ho! then this so sweet maid is a polyandrist, and me, with my poor wife dead to me, but alive by Church's law, though no wits, all gone— even I, who am faithful husband to this now-no-wife, am bigamist." Lucy's promiscuity—her "polyandry," as the propriety of the Dutchman would have it—is forgivable, because finally her loyalty to her own kind is more vital than her absolute chastity. Clearly, it is more important that the group maintain its hold over her than that any one man has exclusive rights. In the face of such anxiety, too, there is always the option we began with, euthanasia, the killing by brave men of their women, to keep them from falling into the hands of the enemy.

In the light of all this, it is very hard to see as "incestuous" the competition for women that constitutes the primary action of the novel. *Dracula* does touch on primal fears and urges, but they are not the horror or allure of incest. Stoker's perdurable myth reflects the ancient fear that "they" will take away "our" women, and Dracula is at his most horrifying not when he drinks blood or travels in the form of a bat but when he, a man of palpable foreignness, can say, "Your girls that you all love are mine." An old black ram, he says, is tupping your white ewe. Richardson is right to find the count a figure of "huge potency," but Dracula's power is not that of the father, as Richardson suggests, but that of the "extravagant stranger," or, in Van Helsing's words, "the other." But such power raises a new set of questions. The men are anxious about losing their women, but what of the women themselves? How do they respond to Dracula's frightful glamour? What is this novel's attitude toward women?

Stoker's description of the first women we see in *Dracula*, the vampire women at the castle, strongly emphasizes their overt sexuality. The word *voluptuous* is repeated—they have "voluptuous lips" and a "deliberate voluptuousness" in their approach to Harker. And he, in turn, is quickly aroused by their seductive appeal, as he feels "a wicked, burning desire that they would kiss me with those red lips." They project themselves as sexualized beings and have power to inspire a sexual response in others. The pattern is exactly repeated when Lucy's transformation into a vampire is complete. Shortly after Van Helsing and Seward note the disappearance of the wounds in her neck, the young doctor reports that she speaks in a "soft, voluptuous voice, such as I had never heard from her lips"; and when the whole band confronts the undead Lucy outside her tomb, "we recognised the features of Lucy Westenra. Lucy Westenra, but yet how changed. The sweetness was turned to . . . cruelty, and the purity to voluptuous wantonness." Within the next three paragraphs, we hear that she has a "voluptuous smile" and a "wanton smile" and that she speaks with "a languorous, voluptuous grace." As is typical when Stoker discusses the characteristics of a group, his vocabulary shrinks, and he resorts to formulas—*good, brave,* and, for vampire females, *voluptuous.* And when the posse of racial purity hammers the stake through Lucy's heart, that merciful penetration which undoes the undead, the transformation is a return to her former state of desexualization: the "foul Thing" with its "voluptuous mouth" and its "carnal and unspiritual appearance" disappears, replaced with "Lucy as we had seen her in her life, with her face of unequalled sweetness and purity."

There are several ways to interpret the novel's attitude toward the sexuality these female vampires project. The first—developed by a number of critics—is that Stoker is expressing what have usually been regarded as typical Victorian attitudes about female sex-

uality. According to these readers, the violence against women in *Dracula,* most vividly rendered in the staking of Lucy, reflects a hostility toward female sexuality felt by the culture at large. Women should not be "wanton" or "voluptuous"; they should be "pure" and "spiritual." So, Phyllis Roth contends that "much of the novel's great appeal derives from its hostility to female sexuality" ["Suddenly Sexual Women in Bram Stoker's *Dracula,*" *Literature and Psychology,* 1977], Judith Weissman insists that *Dracula* "is an extreme version of the stereotypically Victorian attitudes toward sexual roles" ["Women and Vampires: *Dracula* as Victorian Novel," *Midwest Quarterly,* 1977], and Gail Griffin argues that, among other things, Dracula represents "a subliminal voice in our heros, whispering that, at heart, these girls . . . are potential vampires, that their angels are, in fact, whores" [" 'Your Girls that You Love Are Mine' " *Dracula* and the Victorian Male Sexual Imagination," *International Journal of Women's Studies,* 1980]. Very recently, Bram Dijkstra has renewed the charge, calling the book a "central document in the late nineteenth-century war on woman" [*Idols of Perversity: Fantasies of Evil in Fin-de-Siècle Culture*].

Undoubtedly, *Dracula* exhibits hostility toward female sexuality. Women who are "pure" are not only good, they are recognizable as members of the group—after the staking, Lucy again looks like "we had seen her in her life." By contrast, "voluptuous" women are monsters, loathsome creatures fit only for destruction. What interests me, however, is not the possibility that *Dracula* is yet another misogynist text but the way in which the novel incorporates its portrayal of women into its consideration of foreignness. A careful look at the women in *Dracula* reveals that the primary fear is a fear of the foreign and that women become terrifying insofar as they are associated with the kind of strangeness vampires represent. Lucy and those women at Castle Dracula are, as Van Helsing puts it, "like him," members of that "new order of beings" that the count wishes to "father." Two issues are important in this regard. First, there is the bisexuality of female vampires (and males, too), a consideration that complicates any attempt to generalize about the place of gender in this novel. Second, the women here do not transform themselves. The count is the indispensable catalyst for their alteration into sexual beings, a catalytic role that exposes again *Dracula*'s deep anxieties about excessive exogamy. I would like to look briefly at both these issues before concluding.

A famous psychoanalytic comment on vampirism occurs in Ernest Jones's *On the Nightmare:*

The explanation of these fantasies is surely not hard. A nightly visit from a beautiful or frightful being, who first exhausts the sleeper with passionate embraces and then withdraws from him a vital fluid; all this can point only to a natural and common process, namely to nocturnal emissions. . . . In the unconscious mind blood is commonly an equivalent for semen.

Dracula does indeed make blood and semen interchangeable fluids, and this equivalence may offer another clue why the combination of red and white is the vampire's distinct coloration. But the striking omission from Jones's rather condescending comment is that, in Stoker's novel, the "vital fluid" is being withdrawn from women, that the nightly visitor is a man. Vampirism may have something to do with nocturnal emissions, but surely it is important that in *Dracula* women have all the wet dreams. Clearly, in the vampire world traditional sexual roles are terribly confused. Dracula penetrates, but he receives the "vital fluid"; after Lucy becomes a vampire, she acts as a "penetrator" (and becomes sexually aggressive), but she now receives fluid from those she attacks. Nowhere is this confusion greater than at the moment the brave band interrupts Dracula's attack on Mina:

> With . . . his right hand [he] gripped her by the back of the neck, forcing her face down on his bosom. Her white nightdress was smeared with blood, and a thin stream trickled down the man's bare breast which was shown by his torn-open dress. The attitude of the two had a terrible resemblance to a child forcing a kitten's nose into a saucer of milk to compel it to drink.

As many have remarked, there is a powerful image of fellatio here (and there is also an exchange of fluids—a point not made clear in the description of Dracula's attack on Lucy); but in this scene Dracula, in a breathtaking transformation, is a mother as well, engaged in an act that has a "terrible resemblance" to breast-feeding. What is going on? Fellatio? Lactation? It seems that the vampire is sexually capable of everything.

Like Tiresias, the vampire has looked at sex from both sides, and that fact is significant for several reasons. First, it makes it difficult to say, simply, that the novel is hostile to female sexuality, when the nature of the "female" has itself been made problematic; it is more accurate to say that the primary fear is of vampire sexuality, a phenomenon in which "our" gender roles interpenetrate in a complicated way. Female vampires are not angels turned into whores but human women who have become something very strange, beings in whom traditional distinctions between male and female have been lost and traditional roles confusingly mixed. Moreover, we encounter again here the central paradox of *Dracula*'s representation of the foreign. For the bisexuality of the vampire is not only monstrously strange, it is also a very human impulse—an impulse that, once more, the vampire has made astonishingly literal. As we have seen throughout this essay, the sexuality of vampires—here their bisexuality—is both

strange and familiar, both an overt peculiarity to be seen and dreaded and a reflection to be repressed.

If female vampires are powerfully bisexual, they are also creatures who have been profoundly changed. The pure and spiritual become voluptuous, the passive become aggressive, and so on. As Van Helsing says, "Madame Mina, our poor dear Madame Mina, is changing." The novel makes it clear that these changes do not come from within—Dracula brings them about as part of that complex process of deracinative reproduction discussed above. In other words, the erotic energy of the female vampires is somehow the count's creation. And that, in turn, suggests another way in which he is terrifying to the band of good, brave men. What if the problem is not that women like Lucy and Mina have become sexual but that their sexuality has been released in the wrong way, by a foreigner, a foreigner who has achieved what the men fear they may be unable to accomplish? That is, the anxiety of Van Helsing and his band may be partly a fear of aggressive or demanding women, but it may also be a fear of superior sexual potency in the competition. The boy next door may be no match for an extravagant stranger.

The fear of excessive exogamy, so much a part of the terror that Dracula inspires, is thus both a racial and a sexual problem. As I suggested earlier, Dracula is a sexual imperialist, one who longs to be "the father or furtherer of a new order of beings." And he can beget this race only on the bodies of other men's women, imperilling the racial integrity of the West. The fear he inspires, however, is also personal, for his is not merely an imperialism that takes women, it is especially an imperialism of seduction—if he initially approaches these women through violence, in the end they are converts, "leagued with your enemy against you." Dracula threatens to destroy both the "good" men's race and their masculinity, to destroy them as a group and emasculate them as individuals. No wonder they are so desperate to stop him.

Dracula emerges, then, as a remarkable meditation on foreignness, in at least two ways. The surface of the tale is a memorable myth of interracial sexual competition, a struggle between men who wish to retain their control over women defined as members of their group and a powerful and attractive foreigner, who wishes to make the women his own. This battle, finally, is between two kinds of desire. The desire of the good, brave men is a force that must be called conservative, for it is an urge to protect possessions, to insist on the integrity of racial boundaries, to maintain unmixed the blood of their group. Hence, we see their xenophobic insistence that "the world"—meaning their world and their women—"not be given over to monsters." Dracula's desire is the antithesis of such conservatism: what the count has once possessed is useless to him in his continuing struggle for survival. His constantly renewed desire for difference may be "monstrous" in terms of the marriage practices of most cultures, but it is hardly the monstrosity of incest. The threat Dracula represents is not the desire of the father to hoard his own women; it is an urgent need to take, to violate boundaries, a desire that must incorporate foreign blood for the very survival of his kind. For the vampire, the blood he needs, both for sex and for food, always belongs to somebody else.

Dracula thus uncovers for us the kind of mind that sees excessive exogamy as a particularly terrifying threat. Such thinking is common in human experience: we tend to divide ourselves into groups and to fret about sexual contact across group lines. At the same time, such fears must have been acute in late nineteenth-century Britain, plump with imperial gain, but given perhaps to the bad dream that *Dracula* embodies: what if "they" should try to colonize *us*? *Dracula* is interesting, however, as something more than a representation of the xenophobic mind, in either its Victorian or its aboriginal avatar—fascinating as that representation is. For xenophobia requires, first of all, a concept of what is foreign, and the remarkable thing about Stoker's novel is the way it is able to undermine that very conception of the "foreign" on which so much of its narrative energy depends. That is, *Dracula* both exemplifies what Hannah Arendt [in *The Origins of Totalitarianism*] terms "race-thinking" and calls such thinking

radically into question. Again and again Stoker depicts vampire sexuality as a curiously doubled phenomenon—always overtly bizarre, but also somehow familiar. Such a paradox possibly is inherent in the enterprise by which foreignness, that ancient need to separate "us" from "them," is constructed in the human imagination. As *Dracula* represents that process, it is a simultaneous movement, in which differences are perceived and reified, while likenesses are repressed and denied. The refusal of some recognition may thus always be a part of the perception of foreignness—even (or maybe especially) the extreme foreignness of monstrosity.

Vampires, we all know, cast no reflection. Virtually the first frightening oddity that Harker notices at Castle Dracula is that "there was no reflection of [the count] in the mirror." In the light of this discussion, that missing image presents a striking metaphor. The vampire, "the other," "the monster"—everything that Dracula represents, and represents so powerfully—depends on our refusal to see the ways in which he is also a mirror. After all, it is Harker who can see nothing in the glass. When we say that the vampire is absent from the mirror, perhaps what we are saying is that we are afraid to see a reflection—however uneasy and strange—of ourselves. (pp. 140-47)

John Allen Stevenson, "A Vampire in the Mirror: The Sexuality of 'Dracula'," in *PMLA*, Vol. 103, No. 2, March, 1988, pp. 139-49.

SOURCES FOR FURTHER STUDY

Farson, Daniel. *The Man Who Wrote 'Dracula': A Biography of Bram Stoker.* New York: St. Martin's Press, 1975, 240 p.

Biography by Stoker's great-nephew, based largely on Harry Ludlam's 1962 *Biography of Dracula: The Life Story of Bram Stoker* and distinguished chiefly through the inclusion of anecdotal family accounts of Stoker.

Leatherdale, Clive. *"Dracula": The Novel and the Legend.* Wellingborough, England: Aquarian Press, 1985, 256 p.

Extensive study that presents the background of vampire mythology, discusses Stoker's life and other works, and offers sustained analyses of central characters and principal themes in *Dracula.*

McNally, Raymond T., and Florescu, Radu. "Bram Stoker and the Search for Dracula" and "Bram Stoker and the Vampire in Fiction and Film." In their *Dracula: A True History of Dracula and Vampire Legends*, pp. 18-33, 161-81. Greenwich, Conn.: New York Graphic Society, 1972.

Informal account of sources available to Stoker at the time he researched *Dracula.* The second chapter cited surveys appearances of Dracula and the vampire figure in film and literature.

Roth, Phyllis. *Bram Stoker.* Boston: Twayne, 1982, 167 p.

Critical overview of most of Stoker's work, including discussion of his adventure and romance novels but omitting discussion of his short stories. Roth focuses on *Dracula*, which she terms "Stoker's only unequivocal success." A biographical chapter and primary and secondary bibliographies are included.

Scarborough, Dorothy. "The Devil and His Allies." In her *The Supernatural in Modern Fiction*, pp. 130-73. 1916. Reprint. New York: Octagon Books, 1967.

Describes *Dracula* as "the tensest, most dreadful modern story of vampirism" and mentions that the book "loses in effect toward the last, for the mind cannot endure four hundred pages of vampiric outrage and respond to fresh impressions of terror."

Seed, David. "The Narrative Method of *Dracula.*" *Nineteenth-Century Fiction* 40, No. 1 (June 1985): 61-75.

Closely examines Stoker's "rigorous narrative method."

Tom Stoppard

1937-

(Born Tomas Straussler) Czechoslovakian-born English dramatist, novelist, short story writer, scriptwriter, critic, translator, and journalist.

INTRODUCTION

Stoppard is a leading playwright in contemporary theater. Like George Bernard Shaw and Oscar Wilde, with whom he is compared, Stoppard examines serious issues within the context of comedy, often conveying weighty moral and philosophical themes through such comedic devices as word games and slapstick. Stoppard addresses complex questions pertaining to authority, morality, the existence of God, the power of words to represent reality, and the role and function of art. His style of drama has thus been termed "philosophical farce." Stoppard's theater sometimes draws upon Shakespeare's plays for a framework in which to present modern concerns. His plays also reflect the influence of Samuel Beckett in their absurd view of existence; of Wilde in their use of comedy; and of the Italian playwright Luigi Pirandello in their use of drama as a means of probing the nature of illusion and reality. While some critics view Stoppard's theatrical devices as a smokescreen concealing a lack of profundity, most praise him for his wit and technical virtuosity.

As a young man, Stoppard worked as a journalist and critic while composing dramas that were performed on radio and television. With his first major play produced on the English stage, *Rosencrantz and Guildenstern Are Dead* (1966), Stoppard became an immediate critical and popular success. Exploring such themes as identity, chance, freedom, and death, the play centers on two minor characters from *Hamlet*. While waiting to act their roles in Shakespeare's tragedy, Rosencrantz and Guildenstern pass the time by telling jokes and musing upon reality, in the same way that the two tramps occupy themselves in Samuel Beckett's *Waiting for Godot*. *Rosencrantz and Guildenstern* depicts the absurdity of life through these two characters who have "bit parts" in a play not of their

3479

making and who are capable only of acting out their dramatic destiny. They are bewildered by their predicament and face death as they search for the meaning of their existence. While examining these themes, Stoppard makes extensive use of puns and paradox, which have become standard devices in his theater. *Rosencrantz and Guildenstern* was acclaimed by Harold Hobson as "the most important event in British professional theatre of the last nine years." The play won similar acclaim in America and was awarded the Antoinette Perry (Tony) Award as well as the New York Drama Critics Circle Award for best new play in 1968.

Jumpers (1972) reinforced Stoppard's reputation as a playwright who flamboyantly examines important questions. *Jumpers,* a parody of modern philosophy and the "thriller" genre, is filled with running gags, puns, and considerable verbal and visual wit. Farce is achieved by, among other things, a team of acrobatic philosophers whose physical gymnastics reflect their intellectual stunts. These philosophers are more intent on discussing the preoccupations of modern philosophy than on solving the mystery surrounding the death of one of their colleagues. Critics were most impressed by the pervading moral sense of the play and found the two protagonists especially moving. George Moore, a philosopher attempting to prove the existence of God and of moral absolutes, and his wife Dotty, a nightclub singer who believes in the sentimental songs she sings, are stripped of their moral ideals and romantic notions in the course of the play. However, unlike some of the characters in Stoppard's earlier plays who were trapped in a meaningless void, these characters continue to strive against the absurd.

Stoppard's next stage production, *Travesties* (1974), solidified his reputation as a major dramatist. Many critics began to rank Stoppard and Harold Pinter as England's foremost post-World War II playwrights. This play fictionally depicts Vladimir Ilyich Lenin, James Joyce, and Tristan Tzara residing in Zurich during World War I. By juxtaposing the theories of the three men—Lenin's Marxism, Joyce's Modernism, and Tzara's Dadaism—Stoppard offers observations on the purpose and significance of art. A play-within-a-play, *Travesties* is based on the memories of Henry Carr, a common man who claims to have come in contact with the three "revolutionaries." Mistaken identities, misunderstandings, and the faulty recollections of Carr are among the play's farcical elements. However, critics praised its intellectual depth and noted that Stoppard relies less on theatrics than in his previous plays. *Travesties* also marks a new development in Stoppard's career: it involves his most detailed political and ethical analysis, an increasingly important characteristic of his later drama. *Travesties* won a Tony Award in 1976.

Stoppard further examined political issues in his next four major plays, which have come to be known as his "dissident comedies." *Every Good Boy Deserves Favour* (1977), a play with orchestra written with the composer and conductor André Previn, is set in a prison hospital "somewhere in the Soviet Union." One of the inmates is being detained for psychiatric treatment because of his political beliefs. *Professional Foul* (1977) is set in Czechoslovakia and portrays the plight of dissidents in a totalitarian society. *Night and Day* (1978), set in a fictive African country during a rebellion against a dictatorial regime, examines the role of the press. In addition to dramatizing contradictory attitudes among journalists, ranging from responsible reporting to sensationalizing, Stoppard also presents the topics of marital infidelity, war, and government in the third world. The second of the interlocking plays *Dogg's Hamlet, Cahoot's Macbeth* (1979) is dedicated to the playwright Pavel Kohout. Kohout is one of several Czech dramatists and actors banned from the public stage during Stalinist rule in Czechoslovakia because of alleged subversive activities. *Cahoot's Macbeth* centers on a staging of *Macbeth* in a living room, recalling Kohout's Shakespearean "living-room theater." The performance is interrupted by a government inspector who has come to investigate the play's language to see if it is subversive. A character from *Dogg's Hamlet* enters *Cahoot's Macbeth* and introduces a new language, "Dogg," named after a professor in the first play. The actors then speak their lines in "Dogg" in order to befuddle the inspector. In general, the critical reaction to Stoppard's "dissident comedies" has been mixed. However, many critics have commended Stoppard for incorporating political themes into his work, thus extending the scope of his art.

Many critics suggest that in *The Real Thing* (1982) Stoppard continues the inclination toward more conventional comedy that they had noted in his dissident works. In this play, Stoppard further deemphasizes farcical action, concentrating instead on witty dialogue and autobiographical elements. While *The Real Thing* characteristically examines art, metaphysical issues, and political commitment, it also marks Stoppard's most significant treatment of the theme of love. Some critics consider *The Real Thing* a move toward high comedy and the comedy of manners. Critics have especially praised the characters of this play, finding them more realistic than those in Stoppard's previous plays. *The Real Thing* won a Tony Award in 1984.

Stoppard's theater has moved from depicting the absurd view of existence to attacks on absurdity through art and philosophy; from political detachment to commitment for personal and artistic freedom; and from wild, theatrical farce toward more conventional comedy. His ardent concern for truth and his willingness to present conflicting viewpoints have led critics to regard him as a moralistic playwright with a positive view of humanity.

(For further information about Stoppard's life and works, see *Contemporary Authors*, Vols. 81-84; *Contemporary Literary Criticism*, Vols. 1, 3, 4, 5, 8, 15, 29, 34, 64; *Dictionary of Literary Biography*, Vol. 13: *British Dramatists Since World War II*; and *Dictionary of Literary Biography Yearbook: 1985*.)

CRITICAL COMMENTARY

ENOCH BRATER

(essay date 1981)

[In the excerpt below, Brater reviews Stoppard's work, concluding that the atmosphere of utter chaos created by the playwright's seemingly uncontrolled verbal pyrotechnics eventually dissipates, leaving the reader face-to-face with some unavoidable questions concerning the human condition.]

Stoppard is that peculiar anomaly—a serious comic writer born in an age of tragicomedy and a renewed interest in theatrical realism. Such deviation from dramatic norms not only marks his original signature on the contemporary English stage, but has sometimes made it difficult for us to determine whether his unique posture of comic detachment has been "good," "bad," or simply "indifferent." "Seriousness compromised by frivolity" is not what we have been trained to value in the important theater of our time. Yet Stoppard's "high comedy of ideas" is a refreshing exception to the rule. Offering us "a funny play," Stoppard's world "makes coherent, in terms of theatre, a fairly complicated intellectual argument." That the argument is worth making, that it is constantly developing and sharpening its focus, and that it always seeks to engage an audience in a continuing dialogue, are the special characteristics of Stoppard's dramatic accomplishment. They are also the features which dignify and ultimately transform the comic tradition to which his work belongs.

It would be convenient to assume that Stoppard's first play, the rewriting of *A Walk on the Water* we now know as *Enter a Free Man,* already demonstrated some clear evidence of that discrete synthesis between "seriousness" and "frivolity" which has become the hallmark of his style. This is not, however, the case. . . . The play's hero, inventor George Riley, is the British cousin to Arthur Miller's Willy Loman. Complete with a long-suffering Linda (the daughter this time—the wife is now a dowdy English Persephone), *Enter a Free Man* tells the story of the generations who will never

make it. And Stoppard's play, like Miller's, is meant to be emblematic: each act opens to the tune of "Rule Britannia," enforcing the idea that the Riley syndrome is not so much eccentric as it is representative. The English hero dreams of sponge principles and re-usable envelopes, but the vacuum cleaner and the shilling-a-day (cribbed from Linda) are his true reality. . . . Time, place, and class, as much as his own inner weakness, block the entrance of Stoppard's free man.

But the thematic resemblance to Arthur Miller ends here—this is a *Flowering Death of a Salesman* after all. For the tone of *Enter a Free Man* is tragicomic and links Stoppard very conspicuously to his British contemporaries. This particular blend of outrageous humor in a tragicomic framework has its origins in a respectable tradition quite different from the one Stoppard has himself connected with Arthur Miller and the American drama. *Enter a Free Man,* a fanciful *tour-de-force* along the forget-me-not-lane, reminds us very much of the work of Peter Nichols, Joe Orton and, even earlier than that, N. F. Simpson. Here we see an early Stoppard at his most derivative: this is imitation, but it is good imitation. Stoppard, one-time theater critic in Bristol, has studied very carefully this particular style of playwriting. *Enter a Free Man* is the disciplined work of his apprenticeship and as such its form looks backward rather than forward. This is the play Stoppard wrote and then rewrote to get tragicomedy out of his system.

One must not, however, pass over *Enter a Free Man* too lightly. Though the tragicomic muse cramps the style we will later associate with vintage Stoppard in his other full-length plays, this early work contains in embryo an important element developed with greater precision in the comedy to come. The best moments in *Enter a Free Man* are the long passages of Riley's dialogue, comic verbosities which look ahead to those witty diatribes in *Jumpers* and *Travesties*. . . . (pp. 117-18)

The first signs of Stoppard's stylistic break-

Principal Works

A Walk on the Water (drama) 1963
  [Staged as Enter a Free Man, 1968]
Lord Malmquist and Mr. Moon: A Novel (novel) 1965
Rosencrantz and Guildenstern Are Dead (drama) 1966
The Real Inspector Hound (drama) 1968
After Magritte (drama) 1971
Jumpers (drama) 1972
Travesties (drama) 1974
Every Boy Deserves Favour (drama) 1977
Night and Day (drama) 1978
Dogg's Hamlet, Cahoot's Macbeth (drama) 1979
The Real Thing (drama) 1982
Squaring the Circle (drama) 1985
Hapgood (drama) 1988

through come with *Rosencrantz and Guildenstern Are Dead.* Here Stoppard discovers an objective comic vehicle which avoids any suggestion of sentimentality. . . . Turning *Hamlet* inside out gives Stoppard the opportunity to be simultaneously frivolous in conception but dead serious in execution. The heroes are Shakespeare's marginal men caught up in a stage reality of life and death they can never fully comprehend. But the tone here is deliberately cold and detached. It is only in this way that Stoppard can sustain for three acts his analytical perspective on what happens at Elsinore. The accent is on comedy, not psychology. Stoppard has caught us off guard: the surprise curtain raiser features a game of chance in place of Shakespeare's threatening apparition of a ghost. The coins keep landing on heads.

What is at stake here is not only a relaxed view of *Hamlet,* but a new kind of comic writing halfway between parody and travesty. (p. 119)

Because Stoppard has been so adept at treading a thin line between [parody and travesty], *Rosencrantz and Guildenstern* keeps us guessing. In certain respects this rewriting of *Hamlet* with Hamlet in a bit part is no mere travesty, but a rather ingenious parody of theatrical style. And Shakespeare is by no means the only butt of the joke. . . . Stoppard uses *Godot* as often as he relies on *Hamlet:* going conflicts with not-going, games are played to pass the time, the simile of leaves is the subject of considerable commentary, and pants fall down when the belt, not the center, cannot hold. Stoppard breathes new life into Rosencrantz and Guildenstern by making them dramatic ancestors of Beckett's Vladimir and Estragon. Their one-liners are the product of a verbal strategy designed to recycle Gogo and Didi's energetic "little canters." But Stoppard's parody of styles does not end here. Other playwrights will be called upon to strut and fret their hour upon this stage.

Stoppard uses the acting troupe of *The Murder of Gonzago,* Shakespeare's play-within-the-play, not only to insinuate the bleak subject of death, but to reflect the essence of tragedy in Pirandello's *teatro dello specchio.* What is theatrical death and what is real death? When does illusion end and reality begin? Are we responsible for our actions or are we merely manipulated stage characters predestined by some offstage hand? More particularly, are Rosencrantz and Guildenstern free to choose their own destiny or are they tied down to an Elizabethan script controlling the ultimate end of their action on the boards? Is Hamlet, too, impaled by the same fate? "There must have been a moment, at the beginning, where we could have said—no. But somehow we missed it," Guildenstern's exit lines, therefore make the irony cut deep. This is Stoppard parodying Shakespeare, Beckett, Pirandello, and existential philosophy all at once. The collage is still not complete. Oscar Wilde, too, must come momentarily out of the closet. A Player confronts us with a bitter paraphrase of Miss Prism's literary theory from *The Importance of Being Earnest:* "The bad end unhappily, the good unluckily. That is what tragedy means. . . . Positions!"

Suddenly the parody of theatrical styles has created a serious conflict of ideas on stage. Stoppard's technique has been to set in motion "a series of conflicting statements made by conflicting characters," then to let them play "a sort of infinite leap-frog. You know, an argument, a refutation, then a rebuttal of the refutation, then a counter-rebuttal, so that there is never any point in this intellectual leap-frog which I feel *that* is the speech to stop it on, *that* is the last word." The dramatic impact of such an imaginative "leap-frog" results in a verbal overkill which suggests that everything that can be said about the human condition appears to have already been said and—in the grand style of writers like Shakespeare, Beckett, Pirandello, or Wilde—said most persuasively. The only problem is that we, like Rosencrantz and Guildenstern, don't know which ideas still have a bearing on the present. . . . Stoppard therefore confronts us with the recognizable dilemma of the man who, having read much, can't be sure of anything. The more possibilities Stoppard's marginal man allows for, the less he understands. This is comedy of a high order, but it is a "comedy of incertitude." The hero of our time is not a romantic Hamlet, but a rather pathetic little fellow who can't even remember whether his name is dear Rosencrantz or gentle Guildenstern. We are all bit players at life. Because Stoppard has avoided giving us any "single, clear statement" in *Rosencrantz and Guildenstern Are Dead,* the determined confusion he fosters in this play succeeds in representing our own unenviable situation. The restraint has earned a crucial dividend. Just when we were having a really good laugh, the comedy has taken a serious turn indeed. (pp. 120-21)

In *The Real Inspector Hound* and *After Magritte* the difficulty of knowing precisely what is going on is similarly called into question. In the tradition of Ben Travers' highly successful Aldwych farces, Stoppard's one-acts show us what has happened to the comic-thriller once Shaftesbury Avenue has recovered from its flirtation with the theater of the absurd. A take-off on *The Mousetrap*, *The Real Inspector Hound* parodies the plot of Agatha Christie in the style of Luigi Pirandello. An establishment critic has unfortunately failed to remove himself from the set once the second act begins and is murdered for this breach of good form in forgetting his place. The distinction between "play" and "play-within-play" becomes as obscure as the obligatory mist surrounding Muldoon Manor. In this frolic, however, Stoppard's focus is on comedy, not ideas. No philosophical burden threatens to encumber the "nuts-and-bolts" of farce and fluff. . . . In *After Magritte* the comic emphasis is on visual as well as narrative ambiguity: when the curtain goes up the first prop to capture our attention is a light fixture on a counterweight system with a basket of fruit. In this extended parody of surrealist compositional technique, Stoppard takes Magritte out of the Tate and adapts for the stage his "eclectic" tricks with balance and perspective. Yet the special context of this staged Magritte is placed in a frame that makes perfect sense: what appears to be madness proves to be perfectly logical by the time the curtain comes down.

The comic style Stoppard masters in *After Magritte* and *The Real Inspector Hound* is crucial in understanding the strategy he uses to great advantage in his next two full-length plays. *Jumpers* and *Travesties* exploit the same devices of "nuts-and-bolts" comedy in order to sustain entirely different effects. The goal has changed; Stoppard has expanded his repertory. Having employed the punch of comedy and the timing of farce in *The Real Inspector Hound* and *After Magritte*, Stoppard will now use these methods to dramatize what might otherwise be dry philosophical debates. But while the one-acts never defile the purity of good comic romp, the longer plays confront us with more than one level of theatrical experience in more than one dimension of theatrical form. *Jumpers* and *Travesties* are farces *and* high comedies of ideas at one and the same time. In these plays parody and travesty no longer alternate in counterpoint, but rather reverberate in simultaneity. This is no Shavian "comedy" and "philosophy," but a new version of parody working in complicity with travesty.

In *Jumpers*, parody frequently masquerades as travesty. George Moore, professor of ethics, is Stoppard's contribution to the traditional figure of the stage pedant. But the three playing areas—the study, the bedroom, and the hall—are parts of an elaborate simultaneous set which suggests that there is far more here

than meets the eye. When we recognize that there is both a comic surface as well as a philosophical depth, the play begins to operate on more than one level. But Stoppard quickly sets out to short-circuit the connections between one level and the next. What appears to be philosophical debate turns into slapstick (Professor Moore will inadvertently crush poor Thumper) and what seems to be music hall innocence (a production number of "Shine on Harvest Moon") proves to be bitterly ironic. *Jumpers,* however, never fixes moral philosophy and musical comedy in any stable order, hierarchy, or progression. The play therefore implicates us in the process of making decisions. But as we try to distinguish the serious from the comic, the adventure of evaluation becomes far more complicated than we may have initially supposed. (pp. 121-23)

Travesties takes us several steps further in Stoppard's attempt to systematize confusion. In this piece the machinery of play-as-commentary-on-another-play used before in *Rosencrantz and Guildenstern Are Dead* is reassembled in a slightly different form. The tone has been altered to accommodate the levels of theatrical style which help set *Jumpers* in motion. Comedy is once again mismatched with ideology. But in this case Stoppard has us explore a serious relationship between art and revolution. This true history that never happened opens in Zurich and features Lenin, Joyce, and Tristan Tzara as dramatis personae. Each modern hero, however, has his own particular version of what constitutes modern heroism: Lenin's is a hammer and a sickle, Joyce's is art as a fire above all dogma, and Tzara's is a heart that belongs to Dada. Here is Stoppard's three-ring circus of twentieth-century alternatives. Which way should we turn? Where can authenticity be found? Does the artist need to justify himself in political terms? At what point do political realities begin to corrupt human values? When is "revolution" only a code word for crass materialism and bourgeois art? The philosophical debate, however, has been momentarily upstaged by that local aberration known as World War I. With military, ideological, and artistic warfare raging everywhere, the British Consular Office, stiff upper lip as always, opens rehearsals for *The Importance of Being Earnest.* Partisan politics must play second fiddle to drama.

Enter Henry Carr, very marginal man—but the real lead in Stoppard's play. The curtain discovers him as a seedy old man in the Zurich of today "recollecting, perhaps not with entire accuracy," what took place there in 1917-18. (pp. 124-25)

Juggling Joyce, Lenin, Tzara, Wilde's play, and Carr's memory, Stoppard counts on what the audience knows of the present to make a running commentary on the spectacle that unfolds in *Travesties.* For Stoppard's audience, no longer innocent, has seen every idea championed in this comedy developed, short-changed, and frequently prostituted by history. In the name of "art" or "revolution," the idealism expressed in *Travesties* has been seriously compromised by events since 1917. Hence the real impact of Stoppard's play: man can be a revolutionary, man can be an artist, man can even be a revolutionary artist—or man can be, like Henry Carr, absolutely nothing at all. Given what Stoppard's audience brings with it to the theater concerning the violent history of this century, the latter posture is not necessarily the least attractive.

Travesties therefore surprises us by offering something more than mere "clever nonsense." Making his elements of travesty reverberate with the density of parody, Stoppard tempts us to ask several questions simultaneously. The structure of this play has been carefully arranged to expose its many layers. This is, as the title suggests, a comedy of irreconcilable pluralities. Items which function on one level soon pass on to the next in swift dramatic tempo. Lenin's positive "Da, da," a Russian cry of yes to "revolutsia," is Tzara's nonsense word of artistic rebellion for its own sake and still another linguistic possibility for Joyce to forge in the smithy of his Irish soul. . . . Such rich allusive texture, however, can be deceptive. Rather than direct us to any one particular course of action, it dooms us instead to an endless circle of parts forever eluding a whole. The vast panorama that unfolds in this play, its scope and its extravagant vitality, has therefore been calculated to place us right in the center of its own fragmentation. Forcing us into a dramatic encounter with uncertainty when we least expected it, Stoppard's comedy rebounds on us.

Travesties, however, is both a beginning and an end. In terms of dramatic form it is the culmination of Stoppard's attempt to "marry" the play of ideas to comedy and farce. But in terms of theme the play demonstrates its author's increasing political consciousness. In questioning the compatibility of the revolutionary and artistic temperaments, Stoppard for the first time makes politics a central issue in his work. The subject has certainly been implied before: *Rosencrantz and Guildenstern Are Dead* situates its protagonists in the crossfire of Shakespearean power politics and *Jumpers* abandons its characters on the empty runway of radical liberalism. But wedded simultaneously to so many other considerations, the politics of these plays never succeeds in upstaging the spectacle of possibilities competing for our attention. Though in *Rosencrantz and Guildenstern Are Dead* and *Jumpers* politics makes for some rather strange bedfellows—as it does in the "nuts-and-bolts" of *Dirty Linen*—it commands only secondary interest when shaped by the hand of an accomplished farceur. *Travesties* signals a change, not only a shift in tone, this time in the direction of dramatic intention. With the shock of realism; politics begins to intrude a weary head into a theatrical merry-go-round previously free of any imperatives whatsoever. (pp. 125-26)

Stoppard's recent work has . . . been an attempt to adapt his own theater style to accommodate social and political issues far more identifiable than that motley of opposing values threatening to disturb the comic surface of his plays. In *Night and Day,* a work which, had it been written earlier, might have contrasted the lyrics of Cole Porter with the light/dark imagery of *Richard II* in a sophisticated parody of Noel Coward, Stoppard turns his attention to trade unionism, the price society must pay to ensure freedom of the press, and an African nation on the brink of civil war. Kenneth Tynan once called Tom Stoppard "a cool, apolitical stylist" and to illustrate the description quotes the playwright as having said that his favorite line of English drama comes from Christopher Hampton's *The Philanthropist:* "I'm a man of no convictions—at least, I think I am." But Stoppard's recent work displays a darkening tone, a focus on social responsibility, and the necessity—if not the inescapability—of taking a stand. It is impossible to say what role parody and travesty will ultimately take in Stoppard's continuing experimentation or whether they have any future at all in this sudden turn to theatrical naturalism. But what we can say about Tom Stoppard is that, unlike so many other fashionable playwrights, at least he has an authentic style he can develop and perhaps even depart from. In the past Stoppard has given us a new kind of comedy to capture the drama of contemporary ideas. Judging from the quality of his new work, there is no reason to suspect that this serious writer masquerading as a comedian has run out of ammunition. For style in Stoppard has always been a question of substance as well as technique. What he has found in his theater is not only a special way of saying something, but something, at least, that needed very much to be said. (pp. 128-29)

Enoch Brater, "Parody, Travesty, and Politics in the Plays of Tom Stoppard," in *Essays on Contemporary British Drama,* edited by Hedwig Bock and Albert Wertheim, Hueber, 1981, pp. 117-30.

HOWARD KISSEL

(essay date 1984)

[In the following excerpt, Kissel discusses Stoppard's 1984 play *The Real Thing*, concluding that the playwright, despite his mastery of language and artistic form, fails to develop a convincing story about love and betrayal.]

There is no more dazzling writer of English prose on either side of the Atlantic than Tom Stoppard, who, like

Vladimir Nabokov, was not born into the language (he is originally from Czechoslovakia), but embraced it with all the wonder and fervor of a convert. Stoppard is, of course, aware that his conversion came at a time of linguistic agnosticism—when other playwrights had become suspicious of words, chary of complicated sentences, nervous about language that exhibited any trace of musicality.

What has been in vogue is the space between the words, the awkward, pregnant, disturbing pauses. In *The Real Thing,* . . . Stoppard lets us know he realizes he has been bucking fashion and suggests he will try his high wire act without relying on words as a safety net. His central character could not capture his dilemma more adroitly or poignantly—he is a playwright who confesses, "I can't write love," who feels that "loving and being loved is unliterary."

When we first see the playwright's work, it is a scene from a play about infidelity brittle enough and almost witty enough to be a Stoppard parody of a conventional British drawing room comedy. We can well understand the writer's disappointment in his inability to deal with the most fundamental human emotions without betraying his high regard for language.

We get two more glimpses of his work. By the beginning of Act Two he has divorced his wife, and in order to meet alimony payments is writing a script of the Lucas-Spielberg sort, space drama so far removed from anything human that there can't possibly be any embarrassment about betraying literary styles. The last sample of his writing that we see is a doctoring job he has done or a dreadful script by a dimwitted political prisoner. The woman for whom the playwright has left his wife describes the cliched script as having something "real" to say. By the end of the second act she has been unfaithful to him—the closest he comes to understanding the power of love comes when she hurts him. The sacrifice he makes to prove his continuing love for her is to completely, knowingly compromise his convictions ("I don't think writers are sacred, but words are") by doctoring the stupid script so she can have it produced, subjugating his cherished principles for her naive ones.

Though the writer's professional use of words capitulates in the face of love, his conversation does not. Throughout the play he dazzles us with witty, telling disquisitions on the simplest subjects. But even if Stoppard convinces us that the writer's vulgarization of his art is his peculiar way of bowing to love, the play itself has only two moments when love becomes a palpable, rather than an intellectual or verbal matter. One is a tender moment where, saying farewell to a daughter whose gift for language is as great and even more belligerent than his own, he suddenly wraps his scarf around her, and, for the first time at a loss for words, starts quoting Polonius' advice to the departing Laertes.

The other is late in the play, when he puts on a Procol Harum record ("strange how potent cheap music is") that makes him cry at the possible loss of the woman he loves.

The paternal moment is convincing, the other (because it is surrounded with many witty associations set up from the beginning of the play) is less so. Moreover, when in the second act the characters are unfaithful to each other, the situations are all just like the ones in the playwright's brittle play, the one he himself found so unsatisfying—it is as if Stoppard is insisting "the real thing" really is banal and there's no use fighting it. Because the play is so ingeniously constructed, one can accept this argument while in the theater, but one becomes skeptical as soon as the curtain comes down.

Howard Kissel, "The Real Thing," in *Women's Wear Daily,* January 6, 1984, p. 16.

TIM BRASSELL
(essay date 1985)

[In the following excerpt, Brassell criticizes academic perceptions of Stoppard's works, explaining that underneath the dramatist's verbal acrobatics one finds a serious core.]

Tom Stoppard is unquestionably a major power in the contemporary theatre both in this country and, increasingly, in America. Ever since the first appearance of *Rosencrantz and Guildenstern are Dead* in 1966, his plays have enjoyed almost unrivalled box office success and the press reviewers have (as the first two quotations demonstrate) sung his praises to the skies. There has, however, been surprising indifference and at times outright hostility to his work in academic circles, as the [following] pair of quotations demonstrates. Or perhaps it is not so surprising, for Stoppard's plays continually testify to his enthusiasm for the world of theatre and showbusiness, a world with an often suspect connotation for those writing analytically about drama. When asked by Benedict Nightingale what he wanted his audiences to leave the theatre thinking and feeling after a performance of one of his plays, Stoppard replied:

> I'm sorry to tell you that my ambitions in that direction are very modest and possibly shameful. I don't wish them to think very much more than that it was money well spent.

Four years earlier, writing in the *Times Literary Supplement,* he had gone aggressively further, making such playful but unendearing swipes as:

> it is understandable that in seeking its own *raison d'être*, the vast oracular Lego set of Lit Crit with its chairs and lectureships, its colloquia and symposia, its presses, reprints, off-prints, monographs, reviews, footnotes and fireside chats, should come up with something better than that it beats working for a living.

The purpose of that article was to suggest that the analysis of drama was irrelevant to playwrights, directors, actors and, for the most part, audiences; that it was, in the main, aimed merely at fellow-theoreticians and thereby lacked 'the essential touch of reality which reassures the scientist that he is earning his keep.'

This general divergence of opinion about Stoppard between the 'theatre' world and the 'drama' world is curious in view of the indivisibility of the two in practice: drama is, after all, written to be performed and theatre is the act of its performance. The conflicting reactions to his work seem to reflect the crisis in our current cultural thinking about the theatre. As Stoppard implies, an over-literary attitude towards drama is a contradiction since it cannot sensibly exist in separation from the performing conditions that nurture it; that the words 'theatre' and more especially its derivative 'theatricality' should seem in danger of becoming semi-pejorative terms is therefore disturbing. The problem is partly an historical one. Raymond Williams has pointed out how little heed scholarship has generally taken of drama as a performance art and how one is restricted in its appreciation by the common adoption of the kind of literary approaches appropriate for poetry or novels. He stresses that

> the drama is, or can be, both literature and theatre, not the one at the expense of the other, but each *because* of the other.

What is wrong with much modern drama is that it is such poor theatre; a play which does not use its chosen medium well deserves to fail. Stoppard's plays, on the other hand, are brimful of theatricality and are always concerned, in the first instance, with entertaining their audiences. To believe that such an approach necessarily implies frivolity and superficiality is as unenlightened and culturally snobbish as to believe, for instance, that television drama, by definition, cannot be worth watching. What, after all, is unusual about 'playfulness' in a 'play'? I do not believe that those academics who have written about Stoppard in dismissive terms have penetrated beyond their own prejudices about theatre. Seeing only surface dazzle, self-conscious wit, verbal acrobatics and a 'toying' with ideas in his work, they have failed to recognise the unique manner in which each of his comedies is woven around a serious core.

Tim Brassell, in his *Tom Stoppard: An Assessment,* The Macmillan Press Ltd., 1985, 299 p.

ANTHONY JENKINS
(essay date 1989)

[In the following excerpt, Jenkins argues that Stoppard's plays, despite numerous technical, formal, and stylistic differences, all express a unified world view that is lucid and yet not despairing.]

Had *Lord Malquist and Mr Moon* become a best-seller in the autumn of 1966 and had *Rosencrantz and Guildenstern Are Dead* vanished—as Ros and Guil do—after that year's Fringe Festival at Edinburgh, the modern theatre could have lost its most adroit manipulator of stage pictures. I mention this not just as an interesting might-have-been but as a way of isolating Tom Stoppard's particular brand of theatricality. *Malquist* gives us the punster and word magician who skips from one chimera to the next with the same playfulness that animates his radio and stage scripts. The novel obviously comes from the centre of Stoppard's imagination. Its distorting mirrors and cartoon characters are fundamental to the way Stoppard perceives life, and must have an important place in any discussion of his theatre. Yet despite the theatricality of the novel's dialogue and illusory pictures, ultimately a relationship between reader, narrator and story cannot be likened to one which involves audience, performers and 'happening'. It is this idiomatic difference which Stoppard seizes upon to make things work on stage or in the sound studio.

In Stoppard's theatre, the stage is, first and foremost, a stage, just as the radio is a box of sounds. Two attendant lords tossing a coin on a bare stage create an immediacy which does not translate into a *description* of two coin-tossing attendants. The picture itself is an event and depends on the various rhythms at each spin of the coin, the actors' facial and bodily gestures, the speaking silences between them. More particularly, this image embodies the *play* which will follow and transport us into a chancy, bewildering, ominous world, at the same time that it stresses the fact that we watch two performers using all their skill as two bungling players. *Rosencrantz* explores the boundary between seductive reality and overt bravura. Its opening sequence also makes capital out of our subconscious feeling that, at any moment, something can go wrong with a performance. Stoppard flaunts that risk-taking in the first scene of *Jumpers* where things do go wrong with Dotty, the chanteuse, and might do so, in an unplanned way, for the actors who jump in from the wings, stumble about with a tray of glasses, or swing to and fro in an aerial striptease. Both episodes provide us with a means of looking at the rest of the evening's play, just as the elaborate sound picture which begins *Artist Descending a Staircase* affects our interpretation of every other episode. Should a scene seem realistic, Stoppard encourages us to forget we are in a theatre or listening to the radio and then subverts that convincing illusion with images which are equally convincing and disruptively contradictory.

This fascination with the way words and images convey meaning, connecting thought to speech or title to picture, shows Stoppard's temperamental affinity with Wittgenstein and Magritte. But it also has something to do with the fact that though he is supremely at home with the English language he does not take it for granted. He was eighteen months old when his family left Czechoslovakia. His father, Dr Eugene Straussler, worked as a medical officer for the Bata shoe company. Just before the Nazi invasion, the Strausslers were transferred from Zlin to Singapore, and in 1942, as the Japanese moved against Malaya, Mrs Straussler and her two sons were evacuated to India. Dr Straussler stayed behind and was killed some time after the Japanese occupation. In Darjeeling, Tom's mother met Kenneth Stoppard, a major with the British Army in India. They were married in 1946, and the boys took their stepfather's name. Soon after that, the Stoppards moved to England and, round about 1950, settled in Bristol. Surrounded by English in Singapore, Stoppard did not 'live' it until he went to his first school in India so that, like Wilde or Shaw, he came to the language not as a foreigner but as someone who was fractionally 'other', and so saw more clearly that words are signs. Samuel Beckett, born beyond the pale, cultivated that awareness by writing *Godot* in French and then translating it back into English; for Stoppard, that invigorating estrangement, however subliminal, remains an accident of history.

In *The Real Thing,* Henry says to Annie, "I don't think writers are sacred, but words are." To demonstrate that, Stoppard has him pick up a cricket bat and explain how pieces of wood have been put together with intricate simplicity. The analogy between writer and batsman could not be more English; it also combines elegance and play to serious intent. That same combination of stylish play worries some of Stoppard's critics. The most vociferous tend to be American, perhaps because they take less delight in elegant glances to silly mid-on and prefer words to be smacked into the stands by a no-nonsense baseball bat. Walter Kerr's *New York Times* review of *Dirty Linen* (1977) offers the most famous critique of Stoppard's games: "Intellectu-

ally restless as a hummingbird, and just as incapable of lighting anywhere, the playwright has a gift for making the randomness of his flights funny . . . Busy as Mr Stoppard's mind is, it is also lazy; he will settle for the first thing that pops into his head."

His detractors, at home and away, find him heartlessly intellectual, cold, obsessed with patterns. To them he seems an essentially frivolous dazzler who has little or nothing of substance to say. However, since *Every Good Boy Deserves Favour* (1977) ushered in a line of more obviously 'political' plays, that picture of him has changed. John Russell Taylor in his retrospective article, "From *Rosencrantz* to *The Real Thing*", for *Plays and Players* (1984) has fixed him with a neat, amusing pin: "Enfant Terrible shapes up as Grand Old Man, intellectual joker finds sense of responsibility, Tin Man welds heart to sleeve. It is neat, tidy, and dramatically satisfying as a progression." But Poor Tom is still a-cold, for Taylor adds that "one may be left with a sneaking feeling that one preferred the rake unreformed, the joker unsobered".

Stoppard's career seems to me to be all of a piece. Though his style has become more reticent and his statements more direct, he continues to exploit the play in plays. *Squaring the Circle* (1984) is as jokey about ways of looking and saying as *Rosencrantz* was. He has always been completely serious about frivolity and stylishness as ways to make ideas fly. And though his beliefs are surprisingly uncomplicated, they come from a benevolent, if sceptical mind. His assurance that, beneath their confusion and cruelties, human beings *are* worthwhile and that the proof of this lies in man's ongoing search for a just community may sound unfashionably optimistic but it generates the play in all his major works. There is no despair in Stoppard, yet to call *Rosencrantz* "Beckett without tears" (Robert Brustein: *New Republic,* 1967) ignores the very human bewilderment and terror that eventually overtake the jolly pair. It is this humanity which interests me in Stoppard, and it appears much earlier than most commentators allow.

The radio plays contain the essence of those qualities. Each achieves a delicate balance between form and content, play and pain. The medium's intimacy allows us to concentrate while words slither or somersault; without the distraction of visual pictures, we move steadily closer to the littleness behind his characters' desperate or jaunty loquacity. Yet the verbal ebullience never works loose from the supporting structure. Each of these plays, from *The Dissolution of Dominic Boot* to *The Dog It Was That Died,* is a miniature marvel. That balance is much harder to attain in the theatre because everything, including the central idea, has to be bigger, but it is by that union of form, idea, and human passion that the plays either stand, wobble or fall. *Jumpers* achieves a brilliant unity and, on a lesser scale as a sort of staged radio play, so does *Every Good*

Boy, while *Rosencrantz* (a mite too 'talky') and *The Real Thing* (problems with focus in the last two scenes) have a flawed splendour. It took Stoppard longer to translate his particular kind of theatricality into the vocabulary of the television cameras: his early farce, *Teeth,* is a one-shot triumph and *Professional Foul* and *Squaring the Circle* show him continuing to test himself and the medium.

Despite these verdicts, I [would not] rank the plays into leagues and divisions, like one of Stoppard's Dogg football results: "Tube Clock dock, Handbag dock; Haddock Clock quite, Haddock Foglamp trog". (pp. ix-xii)

Anthony Jenkins, in his *The Theatre of Tom Stoppard,* second edition, Cambridge University Press, 1989, 200 p.

PAUL DELANEY

(essay date 1990)

[In the following excerpt, Delaney discusses the moral philosophy underlying Stoppard's brilliant dramatic style.]

Tom Stoppard has a vision of life which permeates all of his major plays, a vision which has for the most part been misunderstood. Though thoroughly conversant with the currents of thought which prevail in his own day, Stoppard chooses to stand largely opposed to them. He accepts a direct connection between art and morality, between art and life, however distinctly unfashionable such a view may be. Even more importantly, he relegates politics to a secondary status, acknowledging that he is 'more interested in the metaphysical condition of man rather than the social position'. Simply and unequivocally Stoppard continues to declare, 'I'm not a moral relativist; I'm not a political relativist'. Stoppard's vision is of man as a moral being, a being subject to a moral order which is not contingent on intellectual fashion or political expedience or ideological imperatives or national interest. He writes of mankind as existing in a realm in which right and wrong are universal metaphysical absolutes.

Indeed, asserting that human beings are not just organisms, that 'there is more in me than meets the microscope' (as George says in *Jumpers*), Stoppard has from the first pitted himself against the whole gamut of materialist philosophy. Such a concern with the moral is not, Stoppard insists, a form of withdrawing with style from the chaos but of dealing most directly and honestly with reality: 'The truths which are important don't reside in particular events in the physical world. . . . On the contrary, the essential truths are much foggier things which we recognise instinctively rather than analyse and establish by demonstrative proof.' But if such truths may be apprehended by instinct, that does not mean—for Stoppard—that they can be altered either by individual will or by group consensus. 'The difference between moral rules and the rules of tennis', Stoppard declares, 'is that the rules of tennis can be changed.' 'I think it's a dangerous idea', Stoppard adds, 'that what constitutes "good behaviour" depends on social conventions—dangerous and unacceptable.' Indeed, consistency not of ideological doctrine but of moral vision is what Stoppard says he values pre-eminently. As opposed to such dangerous relativism, Stoppard affirms, 'I subscribe . . . to objective truth and to absolute morality'.

Whether such a moral order is of divine origin is a question Stoppard has pondered long and hard. Embracing a moral order derived from Christianity while finding it intellectually or spiritually impossible to embrace Christianity may contribute to Stoppard's much-vaunted uncertainty. But if he is not certain of the source of moral absolutes, his conviction is unshakeable that moral standards are certain. If a measure of indecision remains in his plays, there is a far greater level of certitude than has generally been recognised. Stoppard's plays clearly affirm that art reflects a real and objective world, even if a world more complex than we may have imagined; that social and political realities are subject to and derived from moral realities; that life is profoundly meaningful and ineluctably moral.

Yet the potential ponderousness of such moral perception is always alleviated in Stoppard by the ebullience of his wit. What emerges is less a numbing exposé of the forces of death than an exuberant celebration of the moral value of life. Stoppard writes with an *élan,* a verve, a *joie de vivre* which is as far removed from the turgid political propagandizing of some of Stoppard's fellow dramatists as from the numbingly existential *angst* of others. Indeed, after an extended exposure to the dark negations of much of modern drama, one may, upon discovering the work of Tom Stoppard, be dazzled not just by razzmatazz theatrics but by the light of moral illumination.

Tom Stoppard catapulted to international acclaim overnight with *Rosencrantz and Guildenstern are Dead.* Not only did he become the youngest playwright to have a play staged by the National Theatre, but that 1967 production was hailed as 'the most important event in the British professional theatre of the last nine years', that is, since the production of Harold Pinter's first play in 1958. Within a month of its London opening, productions of *Rosencrantz* were being mounted in Paris, Vienna, Berlin, Munich, Stockholm and The Hague; and young Stoppard's play became the first National Theatre production to cross the Atlantic for a production on Broadway. The hitherto unknown writer whose works had not received professional live production just six months earlier was hailed in New York as one of 'the finest English-speaking writers of our stage'.

Such unalloyed acclaim was to last but six months until Stoppard's next stage play, *The Real Inspector Hound,* began to prompt charges that his plays were detached cerebral exercises in wit which lacked a sense of felt life, that his humour was merely 'a grin without a cat'. The adulation and the disparagement have continued throughout Stoppard's career, with some praising him as the most brilliant playwright on either side of the Atlantic and others dismissing him as merely brilliant, some lauding his vaulting wit and others finding him too clever by half. Early on, the charges began to appear that he avoided social and political realities; that his work was, therefore, a stylish withdrawal from actualities; that his plays remained, essentially, unreal. From other quarters came the response that Stoppard was to be praised precisely for his unreality; for the supposedly absurdist or surrealistic quality of his work.

Attacking Stoppardian theatre for not seeking to alter 'the nature of the society of which it is a part', Philip Roberts disparages the plays as apolitical opportunities 'for wit, parody and metaphysical dalliance'. But if such detractors as Roberts dismiss Stoppard's plays as being merely playful, Thomas Whitaker takes the opposite tack of praising them for being merely playful. The 'single task' of all Stoppard's plays, Whitaker insists, has been that of 'exploring the playfulness to which he early committed himself '. Such a skewed view of Stoppard's dramatic universe leads Whitaker to praise such 'dandified' stylists as Lord Malquist, the Player in *Rosencrantz,* Archie in *Jumpers,* and Tzara in *Travesties.* At the same time Whitaker faults such characters as Mr Moon, Rosencrantz and Guildenstern, George, and Henry Carr because they 'have not known how to divorce themselves from the homely texture of our moral experience'—as if that were a separation devoutly to be wished!

Given his penchant for puns, Stoppard's plays are nothing if not playful. However such observers as Whitaker have toyed with the notion of playfulness in Stoppard until they reach the regrettable conclusion that Stoppard's plays are nothing but playful. Asserting that all Stoppard characters are stylists, Whitaker argues that 'all tacitly assume that style is our main clue to meaning' and that Stoppard himself seems to share that same assumption. Whitaker sees in the 'stylistic virtuosity' of *Lord Malquist and Mr Moon* a 'labyrinthine riddle' because for Stoppard 'fiction had now become a parodic and self-parodic game between writer and reader'. More recently Tim Brassell has given a much more satisfactory account of Stoppard's novel demonstrating that even at the very outset of his career 'the shortcomings of . . . verbal cleverness are ex-

posed'. Malquist's 'style', Brassell argues persuasively, is 'a thing of superficial brilliance which glosses over his outright irresponsibility'. Such later commentators as Kenneth Tynan would take Malquist's desire to 'withdraw with style from the chaos' as expressing Stoppard's own stance. Brassell aptly demonstrates that from the first 'such withdrawal is not only impossible but, as Stoppard is progressively concerned to reveal, implies a complete lack of concern with all human and social values'.

In response to the charge of being apolitical, as early as 1974 Stoppard voiced his 'belief that all political acts have a moral basis to them and are meaningless without it'. Acknowledging that such a belief 'goes against Marxist-Leninism in particular, and against all materialistic philosophy', Stoppard continued to declare . . . that 'I believe all political acts must be judged in moral terms' and that from such a moral framework the opposing political arguments of Leninism and Fascism may simply be 'restatements of each other':

> The repression which for better or worse turned out to be Leninism in action after 1917 was very much worse than anything which had gone on in Tsarist Russia. . . . But the point is not to compare one ruthless regime against another—it is to set each one up against a moral standard, a consistent idea of what constitutes good and bad in the way human beings treat each other regardless of class, colour or ideology.

Throughout his career, in other words, Stoppard has affirmed that human experience is inherently moral, and that a Marxist view of human beings as material objects is reprehensibly reductive. On that point he could scarcely have spoken more plainly for those who had ears to hear. In 1974 after acknowledging 'a sort of infinite leap-frog' in his plays—'you know, an argument, a refutation, then a rebuttal of the refutation, then a counter-rebuttal'—Stoppard proceeded to affirm with adamantine conviction the primacy of the moral, rather than the political, however much such an insistence on timeless criteria might run against the prevailing temper of the times. To eliminate any possibility of ambiguity Stoppard returned to the topic moments later: 'Few statements remain unrebutted. But I'm not going to rebut the things I have been saying just now. One thing I feel sure about is that a materialistic view of history is an insult to the human race'. Such unambiguous affirmations of the fundamentally moral nature of human experience have, for the most part, fallen on deaf ears.

To be sure, one may acknowledge that there is more to man 'than meets the microscope', may acknowledge a moral dimension to experience, without claiming that absolute, timeless, and immutable standards of right and wrong exist. Even the promulgation of 'a moral standard, a consistent idea of what constitutes good and bad in the way human beings treat each other' leaves open the possibility that such consistency might exist in the mind of the observer rather than being rooted in the essential nature of things.

Not until 1977 did Stoppard publicly affirm his belief in 'a moral order derived from Christian absolutes'. Such a moral order, he makes clear, is not merely contingent on social mores or some subjective sense of desirable behaviour but, in fact, exists outside of and apart from any human creation. In the same context Stoppard applauds 'the defence of objective truth from the attacks of Marxist relativists'. Affirming the existence of 'objectivity and truth in science, in nature and in logic', Stoppard offers a stinging refutation of relativists who would deny the existence of facts, truth and logic:

> These are now the quite familiar teachings of well-educated men and women holding responsible positions in respectable universities, and the thing to say about such teaching is not that it is 'radical' but that it is not true. What it is, is false. To claim the contrary is not 'interesting'. It is silly. Daft. Not very bright. Moreover, it is wicked.

It is, thus, to the pre-eminent existence of the moral realm that Stoppard recurs. What Stoppard publicly acknowledged in 1977 was his belief in a moral standard which is not merely consistent but timeless, immutable, and universal: 'I've always felt that whether or not "God-given" means anything, there has to be an ultimate external reference for our actions. Our view of good behaviour *must* not be relativist.'

Such a deep and abiding conviction of the reality of the moral realm impelled Stoppard, he acknowledged at the same time, to a belief in the reality not only of moral absolutes but of God. Rejection of a relativist view of behaviour, Stoppard confessed to an interviewer, 'led me to the conclusion, not reached all that willingly, that if our behaviour is open to absolute judgement, there must be an absolute judge'. Stoppard says he set out to reflect such a theistic conclusion in his writing for the stage: 'I felt that nobody was saying this and it tended to be assumed that nobody held such a view. So I wanted to write a theist play, to combat the arrogant view that anyone who believes in God is some kind of cripple, using God as a crutch. I wanted to suggest that atheists may be the cripples, lacking the strength to live with the idea of God.'

The significance of Stoppard's writing, however, has been as unrecognised, as misperceived as that of the early T. S. Eliot, or that of another writer Stoppard admires, Aleksandr Solzhenitsyn. In a 1979 interview Stoppard could declare: 'I'm a conservative in politics, literature, education and theatre.' Stoppard's comment to a *New York Times* reporter perhaps lacks the stately ca-

dences of T. S. Eliot's famous self-description as 'a royalist in politics, a classicist in literature, and an Anglo-Catholic in religion'. However, just as the 'absurd' juxtapositions within 'Prufrock' and *The Waste Land* provoked first bafflement and then misplaced praise for Eliot as a spokesman for the avant-garde before the traditional elements of his art were recognised and the spiritual quest embodied in his poetry was grasped, so Stoppard has been both wrongly denounced as an obscurantist and wrongly praised as an existentialist, an absurdist, and a surrealist. Indeed, recognising the inextricable rootedness of the individual talent within the context of tradition, Stoppard both transforms and preserves art and is thereby conservative artistically in the same sense as is Eliot or Joyce. Further, the informing impulse behind his art is profoundly moral and implicitly theistic.

Ironically, just such a concern for the timeless had previously pitted Stoppard against those who saw immediate social change as the sole reason or purpose for art and had, at times, seemed to pit him against any form of 'socially engaged' or 'committed' art. Indeed, the verbal texture and high wit of his plays have caused some who see reality in fundamentally political terms to conclude that Stoppard's art is frivolous, stylish nonsense. Even Kenneth Tynan, who was instrumental in bringing both *Rosencrantz and Guildenstern are Dead* and *Jumpers* into the National Theatre repertoire, charged more in sorrow than in anger that, because Stoppard did not focus primarily on immediate social and political issues, his plays constituted a form of 'withdrawing with style from the chaos'. Less charitably, Philip Roberts accused Stoppard of writing plays which are 'anodyne and anaesthetising', 'beloved by those for whom theatre is an end and not a means, diversionary and not central, a ramification and not a modifier of the *status quo*, a soother of worried minds and not an irritant'. Roberts would deny that Stoppard is a 'serious artist' because of the playwright's alleged 'refusal to believe in the efficacy, in any sense, of theatre to affect anything, including an audience'. Tynan concludes similarly that Stoppard rejects 'any pretensions that art might have to change, challenge, or criticize the world, or to modify, however marginally, our view of it'. The thing to say about such charges is not that they are radical but that they are not true.

Modifying our view of the world is, Stoppard asserts, precisely what art does adeptly: 'Art is very much better at laying down inch-by-inch a matrix for the sensibilities which we ultimately use to make our value-judgements on society, than in making an immediate value-judgement on an immediate situation. Particularly, much better at that than at changing a situation. . . . Art is intensely important for reasons other than writing angrily about this morning's headlines.' Such importance as art has, Stoppard insists, is inher-

Diana Rigg in a scene from the first production of *Jumpers.*

ently moral. Here Stoppard does indeed pit himself directly against the prevailing temper of the times by assuming a direct and open connection between art and morality. 'Art . . . is important', Stoppard asserts, 'because it provides the moral matrix, the moral sensibility, from which we make our judgments about the world'.

To illustrate his point Stoppard compares the work of Adam Raphael, a *Guardian* Journalist who has written on South Africa, and Athol Fugard, a South African playwright. While journalism may throw light on an immediate situation, art puts the immediate situation within a universal or timeless context. Thus, when Adam Raphael broke a story on wages in South Africa, Stoppard notes, 'within 48 hours the wages went up. Now Athol Fugard can't do that.' However, what the art of Athol Fugard can do is to demonstrate within a South African context that the difference between justice and injustice, between freedom and oppression, between decent treatment and indecent, is absolute and stands as a judgement on any regime which flouts the essential humanness of its citizens. 'The plain truth', Stoppard continues,

is that if you are angered or disgusted by a particular injustice or immorality, and you want to do something about it, *now, at once,* then you can hardly do worse than write a play about it. That's what art is bad at. But the less plain truth is that *without* that play and plays like it, without artists, the injustice will *never* be eradicated. In other words, because of Athol Fugard, to stretch a point, *The Guardian* understood that the Raphael piece was worth leading the paper with, worth printing'.

Thus what art can do most adeptly is to awaken, modify, refine our moral sensibilities. The editors of *The Guardian,* theatre audiences, members of civilised society can have their view of the world changed, challenged, criticised by art as it lays down inch-by-inch a moral matrix which demonstrates how in a new time and place the eternal verities converge.

Thus when Stoppard did begin to write plays which dealt more explicitly with social situations there was not the profound transformation, the wrenching metamorphosis in his work which many critics have supposed. 'There was', Stoppard insists, 'no sudden conversion on the road to Damascus', no epiphany in which he discovered that politics were what really mattered, that the body politic was the ultimate frame of reference. Indeed, Stoppard maintains, his concerns have not fundamentally changed. Both *Jumpers* and *Professional Foul,* for example, 'are about the way human beings are supposed to behave towards each other'.

The entire canon of Stoppard's major plays demonstrates just such a consistency, a consistency which has been largely ignored by most observers. Having seen only the glitter and sheen of the early theatrics, some critics were unprepared to recognise the naturalistic form of more recent plays as even 'identifiable as Stoppard's work'. Instead, his plays of the late 1970s prompted much talk of the 'politicization' of Tom Stoppard, talk which either praised Stoppard for finally getting it right by addressing political realities or faulted him for abandoning an exhilarating if vacuous realm of wit. But both praise and blame wrongly insist on a bifurcation in Stoppard's writing career, a Damascene conversion from the parodic to the prosaic, from mindless wit to earnest politics.

Critics who first labelled Stoppard an absurdist, a surrealist, an existentialist, have more recently been announcing a radical transformation, the 'politicization' of a 'cool, apolitical stylist'. At the same time they have essayed some wrenching convolutions of logic to try to cling to the validity of earlier misjudgements. 'We were right', Andrew K. Kennedy insists defensively, 'to stress the vertiginous interplay . . . surrealistic quasi-encounters, and self-breeding verbal games' in the early plays. But Kennedy proceeds to announce a 'remarkable change in Stoppard's comedy from a relativistic and parodic universe of wit'. Seldom have charges of leapfrogging in Stoppard been taken to such a cosmic degree. Indeed, rather than acknowledge the simple truth that Stoppard writes about moral behaviour in the real world and has been doing so for some while now, Kennedy persuades himself that the new Stoppard 'seems to be governed by a non-absurd vision of absurdity', whatever that may mean. However, *pace* Kennedy, reports that Stoppard has changed universes are greatly exaggerated.

That there is development in Stoppard is clear, but the development is from moral affirmation to moral application, from the assertion of moral principles to the enactment of moral practice. Such development from precept to praxis demonstrates organic growth rather than radical, or cosmic, metamorphosis. Failing to recognise the moral affirmation in Stoppard's early work, many critics have been unprepared to recognise the application of those moral affirmations in the more recent plays dealing overtly with socio-political situations. Some observers suppose Stoppard has shifted from uncommitted stylish wit to a committed political stance. They thereby miss the figure which Stoppard

from the first has been weaving in his theatrical tapestry. What separates Stoppard from the masses of current British playwrights writing about the masses is not a right-wing political stance as opposed to a left-wing stance, but a metaphysical perspective as opposed to a political perspective, a moral view of individuals and regimes as opposed to a materialistic or ideological view. Indeed, to ignore the affirmation of moral absolutes in the early plays and to ignore the application of moral absolutes in the more recent and more realistic plays is fundamentally to misconstrue Stoppard's entire canon.

Eric Salmon was the first to observe that Stoppard's self-proclaimed ' "lack of conviction" is more assumed than real'. Stoppard himself confirmed in 1981 that the earlier proclamations of indecision and leap-frogging were greatly exaggerated. Given a highly politicized climate in which 'theatre seemed to exist for the specific purpose of commenting on our own society directly', Stoppard explains, 'I took on a sort of "travelling pose" which exaggerated my insecurity'. But if he 'over-reacted with a bon mot about having "the courage of my lack of convictions" ', his truthful feeling even at that time, he says, was 'not that I had no convictions, but that a lot of my work connected with the same sort of areas of interest as more overtly social plays, but did so in much more generalised terms'. That connection, Stoppard insists, was always a matter of moral vision: 'I was always morally, if not politically, involved.'

Despite Stoppard's assertions that 'a lot' of his work was 'always morally . . . involved', attempts to see the figure in Stoppard's carpet are obscured in part by the amount of time he has devoted to weaving throw rugs. A craftsman as well as an artist, Stoppard has always found time to ply the tools of his trade on a variety of projects besides his major stage plays. In terms of sheer quantity, his scripts for radio and television plays, farces like *The Real Inspector Hound* and *Dirty Linen,* his adaptations and 'translations' for screen and stage together bulk larger than his serious plays (whether comic or not). The range of Stoppard's writing is not only impressive but has generated some confusion in assessments of the nature of his achievement and the continuity of his dramatic career.

Stoppard, however, clearly delineates between writing he has done 'for hire' and works he has written 'from pure choice' just as he further distinguishes between rompy farces designed for amusement and a different kind of play which, however amusing, is not merely amusing. He freely acknowledges how some might confuse the two quite different registers of his writing: 'All along I thought of myself as writing entertainments like *The Real Inspector Hound* and plays of ideas like *Jumpers.* The confusion arises because I treat plays of ideas in just about the same knockabout way as I treat the entertainments.' Yet the difference between the two is profound: '*Jumpers* is a serious play dealt with in the farcical terms which in *Hound* actually *constitute* the play'. Therefore, disregarding the vast bulk of his writing, Stoppard preferred to present himself in 1974 as 'the author of *Jumpers, Travesties,* and of my next unwritten unthought-of-play'. More than two years later Stoppard still regarded his dramatic canon in much the same terms: 'I haven't done a large play since *Travesties*. . . . I haven't got anywhere near . . . what would be for me a true successor to *Jumpers* and *Travesties,* i.e. stage plays with all the stops pulled out.' *Night and Day* (1978), although a full-length stage play, is in some ways a less satisfying successor to *Jumpers* and *Travesties* than is *Professional Foul* which Stoppard wrote for broadcast on the BBC in 1977. But if not previously, then assuredly with *The Real Thing* (1982) Stoppard pulled out all the stops to write such a successor. That masterwork was followed six years later by *Hapgood* (1988). If in *Jumpers* Stoppard came to terms with the ideas of Wittgenstein, Bertrand Russell and G. E. Moore, in *Hapgood* Stoppard deals with the ideas of Einstein and Heisenberg in a play which incorporates something of the mysteries of quantum mechanics.

Any attempt to assess the achievement or to recognise the continuity of Stoppard's dramatic career must focus on those major plays. The minor pieces have provided many diverting moments in the theatre and, as importantly, have provided a stage to Stoppard on which he could rehearse his art. But it is as fundamentally misleading to assess his canon as if such plays were of equal significance, Stoppard says, as it would be to 'use "Old Possum's Book of Practical Cats" to show that *The Waste Land* is essentially a frivolous work'. . . . Perhaps more problematic to consider as major plays are *Every Good Boy Deserves Favour* (1977) and *Dogg's Hamlet, Cahoot's Macbeth* (1979). The latter play is no longer than *Dirty Linen* and *New-Found-Land* (and not wholly unlike that work in being essentially two discrete one-act plays tenuously connected); the script of the former play bulks no larger than a brief one-act. But it is equally clear that these plays are more substantial in their concerns than such entertainments as *Dirty Linen* or even the full-length *On the Razzle* or *Rough Crossing,* which proved to be box office bonanzas for the National Theatre in 1981 and 1984. *Every Good Boy Deserves Favour* and *Dogg's Hamlet, Cahoot's Macbeth* are here grouped with Stoppard's remarkable television drama *Professional Foul* and the full-length *Night and Day* which also deal overtly with social issues. However, *The Real Thing* is the true successor to *Jumpers* and *Travesties.* As a magisterial refinement of many of Stoppard's concerns, *The Real Thing* should force recognition, however belatedly, that throughout his career Stoppard has set his major plays firmly within the realm of the real. Even *Hapgood,* with its focus on what one character calls 'the real world' of particle physics, also dramatises the moral obligations of human relationships in the real world.

Indeed, Stoppard's entire canon dramatises a movement towards incarnation, towards enfleshing the abstract word of moral precept in the corporeal realm of action. 'Words, words. They're all we have to go on', laments one of the title characters in *Rosencrantz and Guildenstern are Dead.* But the import of words in a text forever hidden from them remains unknown to Stoppard's courtiers. Hamlet is a planet out of their sphere; *Hamlet* a cosmos beyond their ken. In *Rosencrantz* the gulf is unbridgeable between the timeless stage world of *Hamlet* with its metaphysical resonances and the all too physical realm of Rosencrantz and Guildenstern who, by the end of things, *are Dead.* Apart from words, the rest is silence. In *Jumpers* Stoppard gives us the flesh and the words, the transcendent realm of moral absolutes and the sublunary sphere of musical comedy, the affirmation of moral precepts and a world of experience which can be quite remarkably without moral practice. We see the bifurcation, the lack of connection, the lack of incarnation: the flesh and the words. In such plays, Stoppard says, he is aiming for the perfect marriage of farce and the comedy of ideas. But thematically he is also concerned with marriages, unions, knowing and being known, becoming one flesh, the urge toward wholeness in union, the fusion of the flesh and the word. In *Travesties* the emphasis is on the way in which the passing world of the flesh can receive some permanence in art, how the mortal can be granted literary (if not literal) immortality, the mundane realities of life transmuted into the artifice of eternity, the flesh made words.

In his 'political' plays of the late 1970s, Stoppard's exploration proceeds in an opposite direction but the concerns are the same. Dealing with dissidents in a Soviet psychiatric prison, moral philosophers subject to a left-wing totalitarian Czech regime, journalists subject to a right-wing totalitarian African regime, artists and actors under Czech oppression, such plays as *Every Good Boy Deserves Favour, Professional Foul, Night and Day,* and *Dogg's Hamlet, Cahoot's Macbeth* question how the precepts of moral philosophy can be practised in the body politic, how timeless moral absolutes can be wed to action in the real world, how such words can be made flesh. From the body politic Stoppard turns his attention to the realm where the two should become one flesh, to the intimate confines of the relationship between one man and one woman. Stoppard continues to deal with the ethics of political action and the aesthetic possibility of achieving immortality in the words of art. But the focus of the moral vision in Stoppard's more recent work is on the ineluctably moral commitment of intimacy, on the responsibilities of personal commitment which turns out to be *The Real Thing.* And in *Hapgood* Stoppard pits the personal against the technical, an intuitive recognition of the worth of a person against an inhuman view of persons as objects to be used, the moral bond of parent and child against the value of a career, in a wrenching choice which remains inherently moral. (pp. 1-13)

Paul Delaney, in his *Tom Stoppard: The Moral Vision of the Major Plays,* St. Martin's Press, 1990, 202 p.

KATHERINE E. KELLY
(essay date 1991)

[In the excerpt below, Kelly traces Stoppard's creative development from his early, somewhat derivative works to mature comedies in which he tests the expressive capacities of language.]

Stoppard has consistently written plays from the vantage of consciously resisting an ideological position that would dictate the artist's choice of medium or matter, or that would restrict the space of the imagination by defining the kinds of operations literature should be allowed to perform. Stoppard's formalism is thus the product of an authentic engagement with his own past as a Czech emigré, with his experience as a journalist, and with his view of himself as a divided observer. For the other side of his political conservatism is expressed as a nagging—even obsessive—doubt concerning the right of the artist to exist both inside and outside society at once; to be both an active concerned citizen of his world and a detached observer of it; to create elegant dramatic structures of no immediate use to those contemplating them. One of the goals of this book is to document that doubt as it is expressed by Stoppard's virtuoso display of comic tropes, especially the trope of parody.

If we accept [Kenneth] Tynan's reading of the profound influence Stoppard's early flights from totalitarianism must have had in shaping his political values, then we can reasonably ask what effect his early childhood migrations have had on his artistic methods. One less obvious expression of Stoppard's hostility toward totalitarianism lies in his dislike of the declamatory in others' work and, by extension, his dread of the overly explicit in his own work. This dread has contributed, in the case of *Hapgood,* to the near failure of the play before audiences bewildered by a plot too convoluted and implicit to permit their ready comprehension. Another expression of his resistance to didacticism lies in Stoppard's insistent use of the open-ended debate

structure in several of his major plays, even when, as in *Travesties,* the implied playwright's position on the question under debate emerges in spite of a conceptual "tie." The obligation of artists to imagine a worldview hostile to their own is taken most seriously by this playwright, even when treated in a comic spirit.

Parody, another of Stoppard's formal expressions of aversion to the declamatory, gives him the means to engage the literary past in a particularly controlled way while avoiding didactic and explicit statements of his opinion of that past. In his plays up to and including *Travesties,* Stoppard solved his relation to dramatic and theatrical precursors in part by demonstrating that he could duplicate consciously their achievements. However, he also knew that virtuosity alone did not an artist make—that the ability to imitate what others before him had done forged a link between his own work and the cultural legacy, even in cases where his imitation mocked its model.

The second and more elusive attribute of the artist—talent—has always been for Stoppard a mysterious and forbidden subject of inquiry. As he told a New York audience in 1988, "Work informed by the subconscious is the most successful. . . . What you're working on can lose its force if you become too aware of your editorial stance . . . " (quoted in *Interview* with Leslie Bennetts 1988). He developed his writing skill gradually while working as a journalist and play reviewer for Bristol newspapers. As a drama and film critic, he began to learn the rules by which comedy works and became intrigued with the actor's mysterious and powerful art of presenting a role. From his earliest days as a playgoer, the theater presented him with both the formal challenge of deciphering the rules motivating comic art and the intriguing mystery by which that art can suggest both the real and the unreal, the expected event and the surprise event, the familiar text suddenly made strange. (pp. 3-5)

In his earliest stage works . . . Stoppard begins his customary borrowing from precursor texts. Ironically reworking the soap opera conventions of domestic melodrama, *Enter a Free Man* rewrites *Look Back in Anger* by placing greater emphasis on the unsinkable quality of the British character. *Rosencrantz and Guildenstern Are Dead* resists both *Hamlet* and *Waiting for Godot* by repeating its lines and gestures with difference. *The Real Inspector Hound* mocks the entire genre of whodunits, first flaunting and then circling back to reinforce its central clichés, while *After Magritte* mimics the verbal-visual play in the Belgian's *This Is Not a Pipe* by accompanying a bizarre visual tableau with banal domestic dialogue. The result is not Magrittean menace but a comic wink at the painter's evocative mysteries. *Jumpers* shows Stoppard reaching for a new comic synthesis by submitting the characters and situation of manners comedy to the extreme distortions of farce. As

Stoppard's first example of an extended mock-philosophical argument, *Jumpers* is important not for what it says about God or Bertrand Russell but for its interlacing of contrasts, situations, and character types that conditions our reception of the argument. *Travesties* is the fullest, most uninhibited example to date of Stoppard's play with specific texts. Hitching *Travesties* to *The Importance of Being Earnest* for practical and theoretical reasons, Stoppard both signals his affinity with and subverts Wilde's art-for-art's-sake ideology by insistently questioning the artist's role in politics. *Travesties* marked a watershed in Stoppard's play writing, after which he began to explore the conventions of psychological realism and nonverbal expression as a critique of his earlier practice. (pp. 5-6)

[Stoppard's plays about East European dissidents] are neither pure nor simple examples of a genre, but critical adaptations using standard genre markers. The essential feature of these satires is their clear definition of a target for ridicule: officials of totalitarian governments. But the moral norm essential to satire is implied, rather than militantly announced in these plays, by the heroes' resistance to official conformity. Stoppard's experiment with the "militant irony" of satire drove him toward nonverbal modes of expression in an effort to implicate his spectators in resisting monolithic texts and interpretations. Consequently, the eastern comedies make new use of gesture, music, and mime to signify artists' determination to express their reading of the world, especially when that reading conflicts with officially sanctioned versions of the real or the true. . . .

[Stoppard's newer plays also exemplify the] tendency, shared by many contemporary artists, to multiply the textual voices participating in and simultaneously commenting upon the dramatic event. In spite of their shift toward greater verisimilitude, both *Night and Day* and *The Real Thing* extend the use of parody as a method for evoking and remaking prior texts and their conventions. Further, they both expose the procedures by which art and life intersect and mimic one another. Parodic echoing in *Night and Day* serves to create the illusion of a relatively direct relation between events and newswriting, while parody in *The Real Thing* supports an indirect and metaphorical expression of the relation between art and life. *Hapgood* takes metaphor as its subject and method, foregrounding the "as if" make-believe of theater in an extended and rich comparison between particle-wave physics, the operations of double, triple, or even quadruple secret agents, and the interpretive efforts of spectators. (p. 6)

Katherine E. Kelly, in her *Tom Stoppard and the Craft of Comedy: Medium and Genre at Play*, The University of Michigan Press, 1991, 179 p.

SOURCES FOR FURTHER STUDY

Ayer, A. J. "Love among the Logical Positivists." *Sunday Times* (9 April 1972).

    The noted English philosopher, a leading logical positivist, discusses *Jumpers*.

Berlin, Norman. "*Rosencrantz and Guildenstern are Dead*: Theater of Criticism." *Modern Drama* 16 (December 1973): 269-77.

    Offers an interpretation of Stoppard's first dramatic success.

Cahn, Victor L. *Beyond Absurdity: The Plays of Tom Stoppard*. Rutherford, N.J.: Fairleigh Dickinson University Press, 1979, 169 p.

    Analyzes Stoppard's plays, placing them in the context of twentieth-century drama.

Ellmann, Richard. "The Zealots of Zurich." *Times Literary Supplement* (12 July 1974): 744.

    Comments on the literary and historical sources of *Travesties*.

Londre, Felicia H. *Tom Stoppard*. New York: Ungar, 1981, 192 p.

    Overview of Stoppard's works.

Rusinko, Susan. *Stoppard*. Boston: G.K. Hall, 1986, 184 p.

    Surveys Stoppard's career, literary accomplishments, and the critical reception of his works.

Harriet Beecher Stowe

1811-1896

(Full name Harriet Elizabeth Beecher Stowe; also wrote under pseudonym Christopher Crowfield) American novelist, essayist, and short story writer.

INTRODUCTION

Stowe stirred the conscience of the nation and the world with her famous novel, *Uncle Tom's Cabin; or, Life among the Lowly* (1852). Its strong humanitarian tone, melodramatic plot, religious themes, and controversial antislavery message combined to make *Uncle Tom's Cabin* one of the most popular and influential novels of the nineteenth century, and Stowe the most widely-known American woman writer of her time.

Born in Litchfield, Connecticut, in 1811, Harriet was the seventh of Lyman Beecher's nine children by his first wife, Roxana. Beecher, a famous evangelical Calvinist minister, was a demanding father who stressed strict adherence to Puritan values in the upbringing of his children. In 1824 Harriet began to attend the Hartford Female Academy, a school founded by her older sister Catharine, a pioneer in women's education. She gradually took on teaching responsibilities, working as a full-time instructor at the school from 1829 to 1832. In October of 1832, Lyman Beecher accepted the presidency of the newly-founded Lane Theological Seminary and moved with his family to Cincinnati, Ohio. There Catharine founded the Western Female Institute, and Harriet assisted her with the teaching duties. While a short trip to Kentucky in 1833 constituted her only direct experience with the South, Harriet would remain in Cincinnati for the next eighteen years, divided only by the Ohio River from a slaveholding community. She followed the debates about the institution of slavery in the Cincinnati press and was often in contact with friends who participated in the underground railroad.

In Cincinnati, Harriet became active in literary clubs and school life. She compiled a geography textbook in 1833 and began submitting short stories to the magazine *Western Monthly* that same year; in 1834 she was awarded fifty dollars for a short story entitled

"A New England Sketch." In 1836 she married Calvin Ellis Stowe, a respected biblical scholar and a theology professor at her father's seminary. She bore seven children over the next fifteen years, supplementing her husband's meager wages by continuing to write short stories and sketches for magazines, often using the pseudonym Christopher Crowfield. Some of her New England tales were collected and published in 1843 as *The Mayflower; or, Sketches of Scenes and Characters among the Descendants of the Pilgrims,* and the volume's modest success encouraged Stowe's hopes for a career as a writer. She returned to the east coast in 1850, when her husband accepted a professorship at Bowdoin College in Brunswick, Maine, but her experiences in Cincinnati left her resolved to document the horrors of American slavery.

The passage of the Fugitive Slave Law—which required northerners to assist In the return of escaped slaves to their masters in the South—provided the immediate impetus for her next work, the monumental *Uncle Tom's Cabin.* Originally published in serial form by the abolitionist magazine *The National Era,* the novel's first installment appeared on 5 June 1851; *Uncle Tom's Cabin* was published as a two-volume oot in March of 1852, before the serial was even completed. The success of the novel was phenomenal: within the first year, the book ran through 120 printings, and sales in America and England combined surpassed one million copies by early 1853. It was translated into twenty-three languages and inspired numerous popular dramatic adaptations. While faulty royalty and copyright agreements prevented Stowe from profiting from the book, it earned royalties beyond her greatest hopes and freed the family from financial burden. It also catapulted Stowe to worldwide prominence and placed her name squarely at the center of the abolitionist debate, which would climax in the Civil War less than a decade later. It is certain that *Uncle Tom's Cabin* did much to stir antislavery sentiment in the North: Abraham Lincoln, upon meeting Stowe in 1862, is said to have remarked, "So this is the little woman who brought on this big war." But aside from the abolitionist press, the initial reaction to the work was generally hostile. Stowe's name became anathema in the South, where her account was reviled, while critics in the North objected that the work romanticized the South and melodramatically represented slave life. Stowe defended herself and her work with *A Key to Uncle Tom's Cabin: Presenting the Original Facts and Documents on Which the Story is Founded* (1853), in which she cited retrospective accounts, court records, newspaper articles, state laws, and private letters to substantiate the veracity of the conditions depicted in *Uncle Tom's Cabin.*

In 1853, at the height of her fame, Stowe embarked on the first of three trips to Europe, where she emerged as a prominent spokesperson on American affairs; she recorded her experiences in *Sunny Memories of Foreign Lands* (1854). Stowe continued to explore the detrimental effects of slavery with her next novel, *Dred: A Tale of the Great Dismal Swamp* (1856), but *Dred* did not have the success of *Uncle Tom's Cabin,* and Stowe returned to depicting New England life. *The Minister's Wooing* (1859), a sentimental romance based on the life of her sister Catharine, is a study of the paradoxes and ironies inherent in Calvinism, a religion Stowe herself later abandoned when she converted to Episcopalianism. Other works, such as *The Pearl of Orr's Island* (1862) and *Oldtown Folks* (1869), remarkable as among the first to realistically record the New England dialect, increased Stowe's literary status as a local colorist. However, her reputation in England was greatly diminished with the publication of "The True Story of Lord Byron's Life" (1869), an article for *Atlantic Monthly* in which Stowe charged that Byron had an incestuous relationship with his sister. Stowe reinforced her view with *Lady Byron Vindicated: A History of the Byron Controversy, from Its Beginning in 1816 to the Present Time* (1870) and gradually regained her popularity abroad as her claim became more widely accepted. She completed her last novel, the semiautobiographical *Poganuc People. Their Loves and Lives,* in 1878, but continued to write short stories and give public readings for several years thereafter. She died in Connecticut on 1 July 1896.

Despite her many works, Stowe is principally remembered for one novel, *Uncle Tom's Cabin.* The story of a group of white Southern families and their slaves, the novel centers on the experiences of the virtuous slave Uncle Tom and his three successive owners. The raw emotional power and the historical significance of the work have brought it to the forefront of the American consciousness, and its characters—the saintly Uncle Tom, the angelic Little Eva, and the brutal Simon Legree—have achieved archetypal status. But long after its initially hostile reception, *Uncle Tom's Cabin* continues to be attacked as overly melodramatic and crudely didactic; critics point to its artificial language, contrived plot, and the intrusive use of Christian aphorisms as examples of its flaws. Yet others have countered that Stowe deftly manipulated the sentimental conventions common in her day to present not only a telling document in social realism, but a deceptively simple moral lesson in the tradition of Christian allegory. Stowe herself claimed that *Uncle Tom's Cabin* "was written by God" and constituted an apocalyptic judgment on America's sin of slavery. Commentators have asserted that Stowe attempted to engender sympathy for slaves by contrasting personal acts of conscience on the part of heroic women in the novel with the deeply flawed political and religious institutions dominated by white men. Many critics, however, also find much in the novel that is fiercely sympathetic to the traditions of the Old South and point out that the influence of Stowe's female characters is restricted to the sphere of the home. Furthermore, they maintain that her characters actually reinforce negative stereotypes of women and blacks; indeed, the term "Uncle Tom" now carries a strongly pejorative connotation. Yet the continuing debate about Stowe's depiction of the antebellum South affirms the significance of *Uncle Tom's Cabin* as both a literary phenomenon and a historical force in American culture.

(For further information about Stowe's life and works, see *Concise Dictionary of American Literary Biography, 1865-1917; Dictionary of Literary Biography*, Vols. 1, 12, 42, 74; and *Nineteenth-Century Literature Criticism*, Vol. 3.)

CRITICAL COMMENTARY

GEORGE SAND

(essay date 1852)

[Sand was a nineteenth-century French novelist, essayist, and playwright. Below, in a review that originally appeared in *La Presse* on 17 December 1852, she pays homage to Stowe and eulogizes *Uncle Tom's Cabin* as "a generous and pure work."]

To review a book, the very morrow after its appearance, in the very journal where it has just been published, is doubtless contrary to usage, but in [the case of *Uncle Tom's Cabin*] it is the most disinterested homage that can be rendered, since the immense success attained by this work at its publication does not need to be set forth.

This book is in all hands and in all journals. It has, and will have, editions in every form; people devour it, they cover it with tears. It is no longer permissible to those who can read not to have read it, and one mourns that there are so many souls condemned never to read it,—helots of poverty, slaves through ignorance, for whom society has been unable as yet to solve the double problem of uniting the food of the body with the food of the soul.

It is not, then, it cannot be, an officious and needless task to review this book of Mrs. Stowe. We repeat, it is a homage, and never did a generous and pure work merit one more tender and spontaneous. She is far from us; we do not know her who has penetrated our hearts with emotions so sad and yet so sweet. Let us thank her the more. Let the gentle voice of woman, the generous voice of man, with the voices of little children, so adorably glorified in this book, and those of the oppressed of this old world, let them cross the seas and hasten to say to her that she is esteemed and beloved!

If the best eulogy which one can make of the author is to love her, the truest that one can make of the book is to love its very faults. It has faults,—we need

not pass them in silence, we need not evade the discussion of them,—but you need not be disturbed about them, you who are rallied on the tears you have shed over the fortunes of the poor victims in a narrative so simple and true.

These defects exist only in relation to the conventional rules of art, which never have been and never will be absolute. If its judges, possessed with the love of what they call "artistic work," find unskillful treatment in the book, look well at them to see if their eyes are dry when they are reading this or that chapter.

They will recall to your mind that Ohio senator, who, having sagely demonstrated to his little wife that it is a political duty to refuse asylum and help to the fugitive slave, ends by taking two in his own carriage, in a dark night, over fearful roads, where he must from time to time plunge into mud to his waist to push on the vehicle. This charming episode in *Uncle Tom* (a digression, if you will) paints well the situation of most men placed between their prejudices and established modes of thought and the spontaneous and generous intuitions of their hearts.

It is the history, at the same time affecting and pleasing, of many independent critics. Whatever they may be in the matter of social or literary questions, those who pretend always to judge by strict rules are often vanquished by their own feelings, and sometimes vanquished when unwilling to avow it.

I have always been charmed by the anecdote of Voltaire, ridiculing and despising the fables of La Fontaine, seizing the book and saying, "Look here, now, you will see in the very first one"—he reads one. "Well, that is passable, but see how stupid this is!"—he reads a second, and finds after all that it is quite pretty; a third disarms him again, and at last he throws down the volume, saying, with ingenuous spite, "It's nothing but a collection of masterpieces." Great souls may be bilious

Principal Works

Primary Geography for Children on an Improved Plan [with Catharine Beecher] (nonfiction) 1833

"A New England Sketch" (short story) 1834; published in periodical Western Monthly

The Mayflower; or, Sketches of Scenes and Characters among the Descendants of the Pilgrims (short stories) 1843; also published as The Mayflower and Miscellaneous Writings, 1855

Uncle Tom's Cabin; or, Life among the Lowly (novel) 1852

A Key to Uncle Tom's Cabin: Presenting the Original Facts and Documents upon Which the Story is Founded (essays) 1853

Sunny Memories of Foreign Lands (travel essay) 1854

Dred: A Tale of the Great Dismal Swamp (novel) 1856

The Minister's Wooing (novel) 1859

Agnes of Sorrento (novel) 1862

The Pearl of Orr's Island: A Story of the Coast of Maine (novel) 1862

Oldtown Folks (novel) 1869

"The True Story of Lord Byron's Life" (essay) 1869; published in the periodical Atlantic Monthly

Lady Byron Vindicated: A History of the Byron Controversy, from Its Beginning in 1816 to the Present Time (essay) 1870

Sam Lawson's Oldtown Fireside Stories (short stories) 1872

Poganuc People: Their Loves and Lives (novel) 1878

and vindictive, but it is impossible for them to remain unjust and insensible.

It, however, should be said to people of culture, who profess to be able to give correct judgments, that if their culture is of the truest kind it will never resist a just and right emotion. Therefore it is that this book, defective according to the rules of the modern French romance, intensely interests everybody and triumphs over all criticisms in the discussions it causes in domestic circles.

For this book is essentially domestic and of the family,—this book, with its long discussions, its minute details, its portraits carefully studied. Mothers of families, young girls, little children, servants even, can read and understand them, and men themselves, even the most superior, cannot disdain them. We do not say that the success of the book is because its great merits redeem its faults; we say its success is because of these very alleged faults.

For a long time we have striven in France against the prolix explanations of Walter Scott. We have cried out against those of Balzac, but on consideration have

perceived that the painter of manners and character has never done too much, that every stroke of the pencil was needed for the general effect. Let us learn then to appreciate all kinds of treatment, when the effect is good, and when they bear the seal of a master hand.

Mrs. Stowe is all instinct; it is the very reason that she appears to some not to have talent. Has she not talent? What is talent? Nothing, doubtless, compared to genius; but has she genius? I cannot say that she has talent as one understands it in the world of letters, but she has genius, as humanity feels the need of genius,—the genius of goodness, not that of the man of letters, but of the saint. Yes,—a saint! Thrice holy the soul which thus loves, blesses, and consoles the martyrs. Pure, penetrating, and profound the spirit which thus fathoms the recesses of the human soul. Noble, generous, and great the heart which embraces in her pity, in her love, an entire race, trodden down in blood and mire under the whip of ruffians and the maledictions of the impious.

Thus should it be, thus should we value things ourselves. We should feel that genius is heart, that power is *faith*, that talent is *sincerity*, and, finally, *success is sympathy*, since this book overcomes us, since it penetrates the breast, pervades the spirit, and fills us with a strange sentiment of mingled tenderness and admiration for a poor negro lacerated by blows, prostrate in the dust, there gasping on a miserable pallet, his last sigh exhaled towards God.

In matters of art there is but one rule, to paint and to move. And where shall we find creations more complete, types more vivid, situations more touching, more original, than in *Uncle Tom,*—those beautiful relations of the slave with the child of his master, indicating a state of things unknown among us; the protest of the master himself against slavery during that innocent part of life when his soul belongs to God alone? Afterwards, when society takes him, the law chases away God, and interest deposes conscience. In coming to mature years the infant ceases to be *man* and become master. God dies in his soul.

What hand has ever drawn a type more fascinating and admirable than St. Clair,—this exceptional nature, noble, generous, and loving, but too soft and too nonchalant to be really great? Is it not man himself, human nature itself, with its innate virtues, its good aspirations, and its deplorable failures?—this charming master who loves and is beloved, who thinks and reasons, but concludes nothing and does nothing? He spends in his day treasures of indulgence, of consideration, of goodness; he dies without having accomplished anything. The story of his precious life is all told in a word,—"to aspire and to regret." He has never learned to *will*. Alas! is there not something of this even among the bravest and best of men?

The life and death of a little child and of a negro slave!—that is the whole book! This negro and this child are two saints of heaven! The affection that unites them, the respect of these two perfect ones for each other, is the only love-story, the only passion of the drama. I know not what other genius but that of sanctity itself could shed over this affection and this situation a charm so powerful and so sustained. The child reading the Bible on the knees of the slave, dreaming over its mysteries and enjoying them in her exceptional maturity; now covering him with flowers like a doll, and now looking to him as something sacred, passing from tender playfulness to tender veneration, and then fading away through a mysterious malady which seems to be nothing but the wearing of pity in a nature too pure, too divine, to accept earthly law; dying finally in the arms of the slave, and calling him after her to the bosom of God,—all this is so new, so beautiful, that one asks one's self in thinking of it whether the success which has attended the work is after all equal to the height of the conception.

Children are the true heroes of Mrs. Stowe's works. Her soul, the most motherly that could be, has conceived of these little creatures in a halo of grace. George Shelby, the little Harry, the cousin of Eva, the regretted babe of the little wife of the Senator, and Topsy, the poor, diabolic, excellent Topsy,—all the children that one sees, and even those that one does not see in this romance, but of whom one has only a few words from their desolate mothers, seem to us a world of little angels, white and black, where any mother may recognize some darling of her own, source of her joys and tears. In taking form in the spirit of Mrs. Stowe, these children, without ceasing to be children, assume ideal graces, and come at last to interest us more than the personages of an ordinary love-story.

Women, too, are here judged and painted with a master hand; not merely mothers who are sublime, but women who are not mothers either in heart or in fact, and whose infirmities are treated with indulgence or with rigor. By the side of the methodical Miss Ophelia, who ends by learning that duty is good for nothing without love, Marie St. Clair is a frightfully truthful portrait. One shudders in thinking that she exists, that she is everywhere, that each of us has met her and seen her, perhaps, not far from us, for it is only necessary that this charming creature should have slaves to torture, and we should see her revealed complete through her vapors and her nervous complaints.

The saints also have their claw! it is that of the lion. She buries it deep in the conscience, and a little of burning indignation and of terrible sarcasm does not, after all, misbecome this Harriet Stowe, this woman so gentle, so humane, so religious, and full of evangelical unction. Ah! yes, she is a very good woman, but not what we derisively call "goody good." Hers is a heart strong and courageous, which in blessing the unhappy and applauding the faithful, tending the feeble and succoring the irresolute, does not hesitate to bind to the pillory the hardened tyrant, to show to the world his deformity.

She is, in the true spirit of the word, consecrated. Her fervent Christianity sings the praise of the martyr, but permits no man the right to perpetuate the wrong. She denounces that strange perversion of Scripture which tolerates the iniquity of the oppressor because it gives opportunity for the virtues of the victims. She calls on God himself, and threatens in his name; she shows us human law on one side, and God on the other!

Let no one say that, because she exhorts to patient endurance of wrong, she justifies those who do the wrong. Read the beautiful page where George Harris, the white slave, embraces for the first time the shores of a free territory, and presses to his heart wife and child, who at last are *his own*. What a beautiful picture, that! What a large heart-throb! what a triumphant protest of the eternal and inalienable right of man to liberty!

Honor and respect to you, Mrs. Stowe! Some day your recompense, which is already recorded in heaven, will come also in this world. (pp. 3-6)

George Sand, in a review of "Uncle Tom's Cabin; or, Life Among the Lowly," in *Critical Essays on Harriet Beecher Stowe*, edited by Elizabeth Ammons, G. K. Hall & Co., 1980, pp. 3-6.

HARRIET BEECHER STOWE
(essay date 1852)

[Below, in remarks that appeared in the first edition of *Uncle Tom's Cabin*, Stowe details her motivations for writing the novel and asserts that the work accurately depicts life in the South during the 1850s.]

The writer has often been inquired of, by correspondents from different parts of the country, whether this narrative is a true one; and to these inquiries she will give one general answer.

The separate incidents that compose the narrative are, to a very great extent, authentic, occurring, many of them, either under her own observation or that of her personal friends. She or her friends have observed characters the counterpart of almost all that are here introduced; and many of the sayings are word for word as heard herself, or reported to her.

The personal appearance of Eliza, the characters ascribed to her, are sketches drawn from life. The incorruptible fidelity, piety, and honesty of Uncle Tom had more than one development, to her personal knowledge. Some of the most deeply tragic and romantic, some of the most terrible incidents, have also their parallel in reality. (p. 502)

The author hopes she has done justice to that nobility, generosity, and humanity, which in many cases characterize individuals at the South. Such instances save us from utter despair of our kind. But, she asks any person, who knows the world, are such characters *common,* anywhere?

For many years of her life, the author avoided all reading upon or allusion to the subject of slavery, considering it as too painful to be inquired into, and one which advancing light and civilization would certainly live down. But, since the legislative act of 1850, when she heard, with perfect surprise and consternation, Christian and humane people actually recommending the remanding escaped fugitives into slavery, as a duty binding on good citizens,—when she heard, on all hands, from kind, compassionate, and estimable people, in the free states of the North, deliberations and discussions as to what Christian duty could be on this head,—she could only think, These men and Christians cannot know what slavery is; if they did, such a question could never be open for discussion. And from this arose a desire to exhibit it in a *living dramatic reality.* She has endeavored to show it fairly, in its best and its worst phases. In its *best* aspect, she has, perhaps, been successful; but, oh! who shall say what yet remains untold in that valley and shadow of death, that lies the other side?

To you, generous, noble-minded men and women, of the South,—you, whose virtue, and magnanimity, and purity of character, are the greater for the severer trial it has encountered,—to you is her appeal. Have you not, in your own secret souls, in your own private conversings, felt that there are woes and evils, in this accursed system, far beyond what are here shadowed, or can be shadowed? Can it be otherwise? Is *man* ever a creature to be trusted with wholly irresponsible power? (pp. 504-05)

The writer has given only a faint shadow, a dim picture, of the anguish and despair that are, at this very moment, riving thousands of hearts, shattering thousands of families, and driving a helpless and sensitive race to frenzy and despair. There are those living who know the mothers whom this accursed traffic has driven to the murder of their children; and themselves seeking in death a shelter from woes more dreaded than death. Nothing of tragedy can be written, can be spoken, can be conceived, that equals the frightful reality of scenes daily and hourly acting on our shores, beneath the shadow of American law, and the shadow of the cross of Christ. (pp. 505-06)

This is an age of the world when nations are trembling and convulsed. A mighty influence is abroad, surging and heaving the world, as with an earthquake. And is America safe? Every nation that carries in its bosom great and unredressed injustice has in it the elements of this last convulsion.

For what is this mighty influence thus rousing in all nations and languages those groanings that cannot be uttered, for man's freedom and equality?

O, Church of Christ, read the signs of the times! Is not this power the spirit of HIM whose kingdom is yet to come, and whose will to be done on earth as it is in heaven? (p. 510)

A day of grace is yet held out to us. Both North and South have been guilty before God; and the *Christian Church* has a heavy account to answer. Not by combining together, to protect injustice and cruelty, and making a common capital of sin, is this Union to be saved,—but by repentance, justice, and mercy; for, not surer is the eternal law by which the millstone sinks in the ocean, than that stronger law, by which injustice and cruelty shall bring on nations the wrath of Almighty God! (pp. 510-11)

Harriet Beecher Stowe, "Concluding Remarks," in her *Uncle Tom's Cabin; or, Life Among the Lowly,* Collier-Macmillan, 1962, pp. 502-11.

JAMES BALDWIN
(essay date 1949)

[Baldwin was a twentieth-century American novelist, dramatist, and essayist. Here, he characterizes *Uncle Tom's Cabin* as a failure, maintaining that Stowe's account was motivated by "theological terror, the terror of damnation." This essay first appeared in *The Partisan Review* in 1949.]

In *Uncle Tom's Cabin,* that cornerstone of American social protest fiction, St. Clare, the kindly master, remarks to his coldly disapproving Yankee cousin, Miss Ophelia, that, so far as he is able to tell, the blacks have been turned over to the devil for the benefit of the whites in this world—however, he adds thoughtfully, it may turn out in the next. Miss Ophelia's reaction is, at least, vehemently right-minded: "This is perfectly horrible!" she exclaims. "You ought to be ashamed of yourselves!"

Miss Ophelia, as we may suppose, was speaking for the author; her exclamation is the moral, neatly framed, and incontestable like those improving mottoes sometimes found hanging on the walls of furnished rooms. And, like these mottoes, before which one invariably flinches, recognizing an insupportable, almost an indecent glibness, she and St. Clare are terribly in earnest. Neither of them questions the medieval morality from which their dialogue springs: black, white, the devil, the next world—posing its alternatives between heaven and the flames—were realities for them as, of course, they were for their creator. They spurned and were terrified of the darkness, striving mightily for the light; and considered from this aspect, Miss Ophelia's exclamation, like Mrs. Stowe's novel, achieves a bright, almost a lurid significance, like the light from a fire which consumes a witch. This is the more striking as one considers the novels of Negro oppression written in our own, more enlightened day, all of which say only: "This is perfectly horrible! You ought to be ashamed of yourselves!" (Let us ignore, for the moment, those novels of oppression written by Negroes, which add only a raging near-paranoiac postscript to this statement and actually reinforce as I hope to make clear later, the principles which activate the oppression they decry.)

Uncle Tom's Cabin is a very bad novel, having, in its self-righteous, virtuous sentimentality, much in common with *Little Women*. Sentimentality, the ostentatious parading of excessive and spurious emotion, is the mark of dishonesty, the inability to feel; the wet eyes of the sentimentalist betray his aversion to experience, his fear of life, his arid heart; and it is always, therefore, the signal of secret and violent inhumanity, the mask of cruelty. *Uncle Tom's Cabin*—like its multitudinous, hard-boiled descendants—is a catalogue of violence. This is explained by the nature of Mrs. Stowe's subject matter, her laudable determination to flinch from nothing in presenting the complete picture; an explanation which falters only if we pause to ask whether or not her picture is indeed complete; and what constriction or failure of perception forced her to do so depend on the description of brutality—unmotivated, senseless—and to leave unanswered and unnoticed the only important question: what it was, after all, that moved her people to such deeds.

But this, let us say, was beyond Mrs. Stowe's powers; she was not so much a novelist as an impassioned pamphleteer; her book was not intended to do anything more than prove that slavery was wrong; was, in fact, perfectly horrible. This makes material for a pamphlet but it is hardly enough for a novel; and the only question left to ask is why we are bound still within the same constriction. How is it that we are so loath to make a further journey than that made by Mrs. Stowe, to discover and reveal something a little closer to the truth?

But that battered word, truth, having made its appearance here, confronts one immediately with a series of riddles and has, moreover, since so many gospels are preached, the unfortunate tendency to make one belligerent. Let us say, then, that truth, as used here, is meant to imply a devotion to the human being, his freedom and fulfillment; freedom which cannot be legislated, fulfillment which cannot be charted. This is the prime concern, the frame of reference; it is not to be confused with a devotion to Humanity which is too easily equated with a devotion to a Cause; and Causes, as we know, are notoriously bloodthirsty. We have, as it seems to me, in this most mechanical and interlocking of civilizations, attempted to lop this creature down to the status of a timesaving invention. He is not, after all, merely a member of a Society or a Group or a deplorable conundrum to be explained by Science. He is—and how old-fashioned the words sound!—something more than that, something resolutely indefinable, unpredictable. In overlooking, denying, evading his complexity—which is nothing more than the disquieting complexity of ourselves—we are diminished and we perish; only within this web of ambiguity, paradox, this hunger, danger, darkness, can we find at once ourselves and the power that will free us from ourselves. It is this power of revelation which is the business of the novelist, this journey toward a more vast reality which must take precedence over all other claims. What is today parroted as his Responsibility—which seems to mean that he must make formal declaration that he is involved in, and affected by, the lives of other people and to say something improving about this somewhat self-evident fact—is, when he believes it, his corruption and our loss; moreover, it is rooted in, inter-locked with and intensifies this same mechanization. Both *Gentlemen's Agreement* and *The Postman Always Rings Twice* exemplify this terror of the human being, the determination to cut him down to size. And in *Uncle Tom's Cabin* we may find foreshadowing of both: the formula created by the necessity to find a lie more palatable than the truth has been handed down and memorized and persists yet with a terrible power.

It is interesting to consider one more aspect of Mrs. Stowe's novel, the method she used to solve the problem of writing about a black man at all. Apart from her lively procession of field-hands, house-niggers, Chloe, Topsy, etc.—who are the stock, lovable figures presenting no problem—she has only three other Negroes in the book. These are the important ones and two of them may be dismissed immediately, since we have only the author's word that they are Negro and they are, in all other respects, as white as she can make them. The two are George and Eliza, a married couple with a wholly adorable child—whose quaintness, incidentally, and whose charm, rather puts one in mind of a darky boot-black doing a buck and wing to the clatter of condescending coins. Eliza is a beautiful, pious hybrid, light enough to pass—the heroine of *Quality* might, indeed, be her reincarnation—differing from the genteel mistress who has overseered her education only in the respect that she is a servant. George is darker, but makes up for it by being a mechanical genius, and is, moreover, sufficiently un-Negroid to pass through town, a fugitive from his master, disguised as a Spanish gentleman, attracting no attention whatever beyond admiration. They are a race apart from Topsy. It transpires by the end of the novel, through one of those energetic, last-minute convolutions of the plot, that Eliza has some connection with French gentility. The figure from whom the novel takes its name, Uncle Tom, who is a figure of controversy yet, is jet-black, wooly-haired, illiterate; and he is phenomenally forbearing. He has to be; he is black; only through this forbearance can he survive or triumph. (Cf. Faulkner's preface to *The Sound and the Fury:* These others were not Compsons. They were black:—They endured.) His triumph is metaphysical, unearthly; since he is black, born without the light, it is only through humility, the incessant mortification of the flesh, that he can enter into communion with God or man. The virtuous rage of Mrs. Stowe is motivated by nothing so temporal as a concern for the relationship of men to one another—or, even, as she would have claimed, by a concern for their relationship to God—but merely by a panic of being hurled into the flames, of being caught in traffic with the devil. She embraced this merciless doctrine with all her heart, bargaining shamelessly before the throne of grace: God and salvation becoming her personal property, purchased with the coin of her virtue. Here, black equates with evil and white with grace; if, being mindful of the necessity of good works, she could not cast out the blacks—a wretched, huddled mass, apparently, claiming, like an obsession, her inner eye—she could not embrace them either without purifying them of sin. She must cover their intimidating nakedness, robe them in white, the garments of salvation; only thus could she herself be delivered from ever-present sin, only thus could she bury, as St. Paul demanded, "the carnal man, the man of the flesh." Tom, therefore, her only black man, has been robbed of his humanity and divested of his sex. It is the price for that darkness with which he has been branded.

Uncle Tom's Cabin, then, is activated by what might be called a theological terror, the terror of damnation; and the spirit that breathes in this book, hot, self-righteous, fearful, is not different from that spirit of medieval times which sought to exorcize evil by burning witches; and is not different from that terror which activates a lynch mob. One need not, indeed, search for examples so historic or so gaudy; this is a warfare waged daily in the heart, a warfare so vast, so relentless and so powerful that the interracial handshake or the interracial marriage can be as crucifying as the public hanging or the secret rape. This panic motivates our cruelty, this fear of the dark makes it impossible that our lives shall be other than superficial; this, interlocked with and feeding our glittering, mechanical,

inescapable civilization which has put to death our freedom. (pp. 92-5)

James Baldwin, "Everybody's Protest Novel," in *Critical Essays on Harriet Beecher Stowe,* edited by Elizabeth Ammons, G. K. Hall & Co., 1980, pp. 92-5.

LANGSTON HUGHES
(essay date 1952)

[An American poet, novelist, and dramatist, Hughes was a seminal figure of the Harlem Renaissance of the 1920s and early 1930s. Below, he chronicles the background and historical significance of *Uncle Tom's Cabin,* calling it "the most cussed and discussed book of its time." Hughes's remarks were first published in 1952 as the introduction to an illustrated edition of *Uncle Tom's Cabin.*]

The first publisher of *Uncle Tom's Cabin* was so fearful of not making his money back from the book that he wanted Harriet Beecher Stowe to share half of the expenses of publication, offering in return to give her half the income, if any. The author's husband, however, insisted on what he felt to be a more businesslike arrangement, a ten per cent royalty to his wife. Mrs. Stowe, happy to have her book published at all, since another publisher had unequivocally turned it down as being unlikely to sell, simply sighed, "I hope it will make enough so I may have a silk dress."

Two days after its publication in Boston on March 20, 1852, the entire first edition of 5000 copies had been exhausted. Four months after publication Mrs. Stowe's royalties amounted to $10,000. Within a year 300,000 copies had been sold in America and 150,000 in England. Six months after the book's appearance, George L. Aiken's dramatization of *Uncle Tom's Cabin* opened in Troy and ran for 100 performances in that small town, moving on to New York City for 350 performances at the National Theatre. At one time as many as four companies were performing it simultaneously in New York, sometimes giving three shows a day, so great were the crowds. It continued to be presented by various companies throughout the country, as America's most popular play, each season for the next eighty years. Meanwhile the book, translated into every civilized language from Welch to Bangali, became the world's second best seller, outranked only by the Bible.

Uncle Tom's Cabin was the most cussed and discussed book of its time. Tolstoy termed it a great work of literature "flowing from love of God and man." George Sand was so moved by it that she voluntarily offered to write the introduction to its first French edition. Longfellow, Dickens, Macaulay, Heine praised it. But others damned it as vicious propaganda, bad art, cheap melodrama, and factually a tissue of lies. The truth of the matter is that *Uncle Tom's Cabin* in 1852 was not merely a book. It was a flash, as Frederick Douglass put it, to "light a million camp fires in front of the embattled hosts of slavery." It was an appeal to the consciences of all free men to look upon bondage as a crime. It was a call to action as timely as a newly printed handbill or a newspaper headline. During the Civil War, when Abraham Lincoln met Harriet Beecher Stowe at the White House he said, "So this is the little lady who started this big war." No doubt he smiled, but Lincoln knew that thousands of men who had voted for him had read *Uncle Tom's Cabin,* and many a Union soldier must have remembered it as he marched, for the book was a moral battle cry.

But in addition *Uncle Tom's Cabin* also happened to be a good story, exciting in incident, sharp in characterization, and threaded with humor. That is why it still lives. No reader ever forgets Simon Legree, Little Eva, Miss Ophelia, Eliza, or Uncle Tom. And Topsy, who in cartoons and theatre later became a caricature, is in the book not only funny but human. Harriet Beecher Stowe, who had six children, created out of mother love her Eva, her Topsy, Eliza's baby, Harry, and the other unforgettable children in her book. And perhaps because her father, Lyman Beecher, was a Congregational minister and she had grown up in the Bible, her novel, as Carl Sandburg has described it, became in essence the story of a gentle black Christ who turned the other cheek, Uncle Tom, with Golgotha a place south of the Ohio River, a whipping post instead of the Cross, and a plantation as the background of the passion and the death. Once when asked how her book came into being, Harriet Beecher Stowe said, "God wrote it."

The book began in 1851 in a series of sketches in a paper called *The National Era.* With a baby to nurse, other children to attend, and a house to manage, Mrs. Stowe wrote by sheer determination. Her husband was Professor of Natural and Revealed Religion at Bowdoin College in Maine. They were poor. Her friends and neighbors looked askance upon a woman who aspired to any sort of career outside the home, who took sides in national controversies, or participated in political issues. Slavery was a political issue. But Harriet Beecher Stowe had grown up in Cincinnati where she had seen slavery at first hand just across the river in Kentucky. She had helped her brother, Henry Ward Beecher, edit a paper which was forbidden in some parts of the South. She had once aided a Negro woman to escape from a pursuing master. So she had already taken sides.

When she was almost forty she wrote a friend, "I feel now that the time is come when even a woman or a child who can speak a word for freedom and humanity is bound to speak. The Carthaginian women in the last peril of their state cut off their hair for bow-strings to give the defenders of their country, and such peril and shame as now hangs over this country is worse than Roman slavery. I hope every woman who can write will not be silent." So she began to write *Uncle Tom's Cabin.*

When the book appeared in England Queen Victoria wrote Mrs. Stowe a note of gratitude, and in London an overflow meeting of 5000 persons greeted the author at Exeter Hall on her first trip abroad. But our American Ambassador, James Buchanan, frowned upon such antislavery demonstrations and did not consider Mrs. Stowe's appearance at the London meeting in the best interests of our country. At home Northern papers such as the New York *Journal of Commerce* and Southern papers like the *Alabama Planter* denounced the book. A free Negro in Maryland received ten years in prison for possessing it. A book dealer in Mobile was hounded from the city for selling it. When Mrs. Stowe and her husband returned to Brunswick, Maine, from Europe, they found hundreds of scurrilous and even obscene letters attacking both the book and its author. And one day Mrs. Stowe opened a package that came in the mails, and a black human ear tumbled out.

In 1853 Mrs. Stowe published *A Key to Uncle Tom's Cabin* documenting and giving sources for the material relating to the horrors of slavery in her book. But readers around the world and throughout the years have not needed this "Key" to understand her book, nor to be moved by it to laughter and to tears. The love and warmth and humanity that went into its writing keep it alive a century later from Bombay to Boston. (pp. 102-04)

Langston Hughes, in an introduction to 'Uncle Tom's Cabin' in *Critical Essays on Harriet Beecher Stowe,* edited by Elizabeth Ammons, G. K. Hall & Co., 1980, pp. 102-04.

KENNETH S. LYNN
(essay date 1961)

[In the following excerpt from an essay written in 1961, Lynn describes *Uncle Tom's Cabin* as "the greatest tear-jerker of them all," arguing that Stowe skillfully exploited sentimental conventions to convey the reality of slavery.]

Uniting reality with fantasy, Mrs. Stowe [in *Uncle Tom's Cabin*] applied the standard, throat-catching examples of homely infelicity on which the sentimental novelists had battened for years to the one area of American experience where the sorrow could not be over-dreamed. Striking to the very heart of the slave's nightmare—and of the white South's guilt—she centered her novel on the helpless instability of the Negro's home life. In so doing she also tapped the richest emotional lode in the history of the American sentimental novel. Thus *Uncle Tom's Cabin* is the greatest tear-jerker of them all, but it is a tear-jerker with a difference: it did not permit its audience to escape reality. Instead, the novel's sentimentalism continually calls attention to the monstrous actuality which existed under the very noses of its readers. Mrs. Stowe aroused emotions not for emotion's sake alone—as the sentimental novelists notoriously did—but in order to facilitate the moral regeneration of an entire nation. Mrs. Stowe was deeply serious—a sentimentalist with a vengeance—and the clichés she invokes in *Uncle Tom's Cabin* are not an opiate, but a goad.

Throughout the book the horror of slavery is brought home to the reader in scenes of domestic anarchy . . . , while the moral degradation of the loathsome Legree is measured by the broken-down, ill-kept dwelling where he has set up housekeeping with his mulatto mistress—and explained by the fact that as a young man he had not had the moral guidance of a mother! Thus do the most time-hallowed situations of the sentimental tradition give form to a tragic story.

Mrs. Stowe's exploitation of the sentimental conventions was brilliantly conceived and brilliantly exe-

A daguerreotype portrait of Harriet Beecher Stowe, taken about 1850.

cuted; yet her use of these conventions is not the heart of her novel's vitality. *Uncle Tom's Cabin* is not merely a historical curiosity which sold half a million copies in the United States (and a million in Great Britain) in its first five years, stirred up the North, enraged the South, elicited numerous novelistic "answers" and started, as Lincoln half-jokingly said, the Civil War. It is also an unforgettable piece of American writing, and what makes it so is the penetrating and uncompromising realism of its portrayals of American character. If the plot of the novel and much of its diction derive from the sentimental tradition, only a small percentage of the characters do; for the most part, the dramatis personae of *Uncle Tom's Cabin*—black and white, Northern and Southern—are shockingly believable, no matter how factitious the dramatic situations may be in which they are placed. Augustine St. Clare, for example, is put through the paces of a deathbed act which may have moved nineteenth-century readers to tears but which strikes us today as hackneyed from beginning to end. . . . The personality of St. Clare, however, is so extraordinarily interesting, and so persuasively real, that the saccharine phoniness of his final scene simply washes off our memory of him. When we come away from *Uncle Tom's Cabin*, we cannot but recall its most celebrated sentimental scenes—Eliza fleeing across the ice, Uncle Tom and Little Eva talking about Christ, the death of Little Eva, and so on—for these histrionic moments are marvelous specimens of a confectionery art. But what really lives in our minds are the people we have met. Those critics who label *Uncle Tom's Cabin* good propaganda but bad art simply cannot have given sufficient time to the novel to meet its inhabitants. If they should ever linger over it long enough to take in the shrewdness, the energy, the truly Balzacian variousness of Mrs. Stowe's characterizations, they would surely cease to perpetuate one of the most unjust clichés in all of American criticism.

The Negroes in the novel constitute an amazing achievement. To be sure, some of them are comic stereotypes out of the minstrel shows, and one or two come perilously close to the "beautiful quadroon" type, but the majority are human beings, with all the individual differences one finds among the white people in the novel. The key to Mrs. Stowe's understanding of the Negro personality is her awareness of the destruction that the "peculiar institution" was wreaking on the slave's humanity. (pp. x-xi)

[No] American author before Mrs. Stowe had realized that the comic inefficiency of a Black Sam could constitute a studied insult to the white man's intelligence or comprehended that the unremitting gentleness of Uncle Tom was the most stirring defiance of all. In the age of Martin Luther King we can appreciate more fully than before the genius of such comprehension. She had an instinct, too, for the consolations that humor offered to the slave. The backstairs persiflage of the servants in the St. Clare household is at once funny and pathetic, a combination which has since become familiar to us in the Negro humor of a number of later writers, but which has rarely been handled more deftly. (p. xii)

Although Mrs. Stowe's studies of white character are no more powerful than her Negro portraits, they are more subtly drawn. . . . Although the New England spinster is one of the recurrent characters in American literature, never has she been "done" with more devastatingly accurate comic effect than Mrs. Stowe's Ophelia. (pp. xii-xiii)

[In] an era when American literature was still romantic and the great Balzac had a significant following only among the young and the unpublished, Mrs. Stowe had produced a work that throbbed with the spirit of realism. Instead of depicting Nature and the Self, she had portrayed character and society. . . . It is breath-taking enough to realize that an inexperienced writer, the author of a modest volume of stories and sketches entitled *The Mayflower* . . . , could bring to the sentimental novel such an unprecedented seriousness of purpose as to turn an escapist genre into an instrument of social upheaval. By the early 1850's, the greatest geniuses of American writing, Hawthorne and Melville, were taking drastic liberties with the formulas of the romance; *Uncle Tom's Cabin*, at its vital best, simply transcended them. (p. xv)

Kenneth S. Lynn, in an introduction to *Uncle Tom's Cabin; or, Life Among the Lowly* by Harriet Beecher Stowe, Cambridge, Mass.: The Belknap Press of Harvard University Press, 1962, pp. vii-xxiv.

LESLIE A. FIEDLER

(essay date 1966)

[In the following excerpt, Fiedler explores the underlying themes of love and death in *Uncle Tom's Cabin*, focusing on erotic and sadistic elements in the novel.]

The greatest of all novels of sentimental protest is . . . dedicated not to the problem of drink but to that of slavery, though its author was a total abstainer, who would appear at literary luncheons only if promised that no wine would be served. The novel, of course, is Harriet Beecher Stowe's *Uncle Tom's Cabin*. . . . It is an astonishingly various and complex book, simplified in the folk mind, which has remembered in its place the dramatic version in which Mrs. Stowe had no hand and which she saw, secretly, only once.

In *Uncle Tom's Cabin*, there are two contrasting studies of marriage: one between an opportunistic, morally lax husband and an enduring Christian wife; another between a hypochondriacal, self-pitying shrew—an acute but cruel caricature of the Southern lady—and a gentle, enduring husband. The latter relationship between the St. Clares, who are mother and father to Little Eva, is from a purely novelistic point of view the most skillfully executed section of the book; but it is scarcely remembered by *Uncle Tom's* admirers. No more do the really erotic episodes stick in the collective memory of America: neither Legree's passionate relationship with the half-mad slave girl, Cassy, nor his breathless, ultimately frustrated attempt to violate the fifteen-year-old quadroon, Emmeline. The story of the decline of Cassy from a protected Creole childhood, in which she is scarcely aware that she is a Negro, through her lush bondage to a chivalrous white New Orleans lover, in which she is scarcely aware she is a slave, to the point where she is pawed publicly in the slave market and degraded to the level of becoming Legree's unwilling mistress is fictional material of real interest; merely sketched in by Mrs. Stowe, it has recently been worked out in great detail by R. P. Warren in *Band of Angels.* Yet it fades from the mind even just after we have read *Uncle Tom.* It is not essential to the book which became part of our childhood. Of the complex novel created by Mrs. Stowe (or God!), America has chosen to preserve only the child's book.

Though we *know* Emmeline and Cassy are cowering in the attic at the moment that Quimbo and Sambo under Legree's direction are beating Uncle Tom to death, it is only the latter scene which we *feel.* We respond to the suffering and the triumph and the distressingly tearful arrival, just too late, of Marse George, the boy who has loved and remembered Tom and who is our surrogate in the book. All the conventional loves and romances of the book slip away, precisely because they are conventional, but also because they are irrelevant: the boy-girl all-white love of Eva and her cousin Henrique; and even, though it is a unifying thread joining the first volume of the novel to the second, the separation, the individual flights, and the joyous reunion in Canada of Eliza and George. We remember Eliza and the bloodhound, Eliza on the ice; we have to check the text to discover what happened to her after she left the floes behind, to remember that with her husband she emigrated to Liberia! Poor George—his existence is fictional only, not mythic. Unlettered Negroes to this day will speak of a pious compromiser of their own race, who urges Christian forbearance rather than militancy, as a "Tom" or "Uncle Tom"; it has become a standard term of contempt. But no one speaks of the advocate of force who challenges him as a "George," through Mrs. Stowe's protagonist of that name was a very model for the righteous use of force against force.

Only Uncle Tom and Topsy and Little Eva have archetypal stature; only the loves of the black man for the little white girl, of the white girl for the black, of the white boy for the slave live the lives of myths. Mrs. Stowe's laudable effort to establish a counter-stereotype to the image of the black rapist that haunts the mind of the South was a failure. We do not remember the turncoat puritan Legree squeezing the virginal breast of Emmeline, eyeing her lustfully; he is frozen forever, the last enduring myth of the book, in his role of slave-driver, at his purest moment of passion, himself the slave of his need to destroy the Christian slave Tom: "There was one hesitating pause, one irresolute relenting thrill, and the spirit of evil came back with sevenfold vehemence; and Legree, foaming with rage, smote his victim to the ground." It is at this moment that Legree seems the archetypal Seducer, ready for the final violation which the reader has all along feared and awaited with equal fervor.

For all the false rhetoric of Mrs. Stowe's description, that blow has an impact as wide in its significance as the assault of Lovelace, the attack of Cain; in it, the white man seals his guilt against the black, confesses his complicity in an act at once predestined and free. This is the moment that stays with us always, balanced against the counter-moment in which George grasps the hand of the dying Tom—*too late,* for Mrs. Stowe cannot help telling the truth—and weeps. The fact of brutality, the hope of forgiveness and mutual love: these are the twin images of guilt and reconciliation that represent for the popular mind of America the truth of slavery. How oddly they undercut the scenes of separated families, of baffled mother-love, at which Mrs. Stowe worked so hard—feeling perhaps that to her bourgeois readers slavery would stand condemned only if it were proved an offense against the sacred family and the suffering mother.

The chief pleasures of *Uncle Tom's Cabin* are, however, rooted not in the moral indignation of the reformer but in the more devious titillations of the sadist; not love but death is Mrs. Stowe's true Muse. For its potential readers, the death of Uncle Tom, the death of Little Eva, the almost-death of Eliza are the big scenes of *Uncle Tom's Cabin,* for they find in the fact and in the threat of death the thrill once provided by the fact or threat of sexual violation. Death is the supreme rapist who threatens when all other Seducers have been banished to the semi-pornographic pulps. And it is the sexless child who comes to seem his proper victim, after the nubile Maiden is considered too ambiguous and dangerous a subject for polite literature. (pp. 264-66)

Little Eva seemed the answer to a particularly vexing genteel dilemma. To save the female for polite readers who wanted women but not sex was not an easy matter. The only safe woman is a dead woman; but even she, if young and beautiful, is only half safe, as any American knows, recalling the necrophilia of Edgar Allan Poe. The only *safe,* safe female is a pre-adolescent girl dying or dead. But this, of course, is Little Eva, the pre-pubescent corpse as heroine, model for all the protagonists of a literature at once juvenile and genteelly gothic.

Though the essential theme of the novel is, as we have come to see, love, it has never been forbidden in the spice of death; and in its beginnings, it presented both in one, though both in terms of a fully adult world. In the earliest bourgeois fiction, we remember, the reader was permitted to assist at the last moments of the betrayed woman, no more excluded from the deathbed than from the marriage bed or the couch of sexual betrayal. In the later, more genteel stages of the novel, however, when it was no longer considered permissible to witness female sexual immorality, the reader was banned from the bedrooms of mature women even at the moment of their deaths. He had to content himself with the spectacle of the immaculate child winning her father to God by her courage in the face of a premature end.

Little Eva is the classic case in America, melting the obdurate though kindly St. Clare from skepticism to faith. What an orgy of approved pathos such scenes provided in the hands of a master like Harriet Beecher Stowe. . . .

"Dear papa," said the child, with a last effort, throwing her arms about his neck. In a moment they dropped again; and, as St. Clare raised his head, he saw a spasm of mortal agony pass over the face—she struggled for breath, and threw up her little hands.

"O God, this is dreadful," he said, turning away in agony, and wringing Tom's hand. . . . "O, Tom, my boy, it is killing me!" . . .

The child lay panting on her pillows, as one exhausted—the large clear eyes rolled up and fixed. Ah, what said those eyes, that spoke so much of heaven? Earth was past, and earthly pain; but so solemn, so mysterious, was the triumphant brightness of that face, that it checked even the sobs of sorrow. . . .

The bed was draped in white; and there, beneath the drooping angel-figure, lay a little sleeping form—sleeping never to waken!

If there seems something grotesque in such a rigging of the scene, so naked a relish of the stiffening white body between the whiter sheets; if we find an especially queasy voyeurism in this insistence on entering the boudoirs of immature girls, it is perhaps the fault of our post-Freudian imaginations, incapable of responding sentimentally rather than analytically to such images. The bed we know is the place of deflowering as well as dying, and in the bridal bed, a young girl, still virgin, dies to be replaced by the woman, mourning forever the white thing she once was. At least, so an age of innocence dreamed the event; they did not have to *understand* what they dreamed. With no sense of indecorum, they penetrated, behind Mrs. Stowe, the bedroom of the Pure Young Thing and participated in the kill. (pp. 267-68)

It is the unendurable happy ending, as the white slip of a thing too good for this world prepares to leave it for the next, while readers and parents, lovers all, sob into their handkerchiefs. The Good Good Girl, blond, asexual goddess of nursery or orphanage or old plantation house ("Always dressed in white," Mrs. Stowe writes of Eva, "she seemed to move like a shadow through all sorts of places, without contracting spot or stain; and there was not a corner or nook . . . where those fairy footsteps had not glided, and that visionary golden head, with its deep blue eyes, fleeted along"), must die not only so we may weep—and tears are, for the sentimentalist, the true baptism of the heart—but also because there is nothing else for her to do. There lies before the Little Evas of the world no course of action which would not sully them; allowed to grow up, Little Eva could only become—since she is forbidden the nunnery by the Protestant ethos and the role of the old maid is in our culture hopelessly comic—wife, mother, or widow, tinged no matter how slightly with the stain of sexuality, *suffered* perhaps rather than sought, but, in any case, *there!* (p. 269)

Leslie A. Fiedler, "Good Good Girls and Good Bad Boys: 'Clarissa' as a Juvenile," in his *Love and Death in the American Novel,* revised edition, Stein and Day Publishers, 1966, pp. 259-90.

RICHARD YARBOROUGH

(essay date 1986)

[In the excerpt below, Yarborough examines Stowe's use of racial stereotypes in *Uncle Tom's Cabin.*]

Uncle Tom's Cabin was the epicenter of a massive cultural phenomenon, the tremors of which still affect the relationship between blacks and whites in the United States. Articulating most contemporaneous arguments regarding the Afro-American and endorsing a response to the race problem that has haunted black thinkers for over a century, Stowe's novel has had a particularly powerful artistic impact as well. As the black critic William Stanley Braithwaite observes, not only was *Uncle Tom's Cabin* "the first conspicuous example of the Negro as a subject for literary treatment," but it also "dominated in mood and attitude the American litera-

ture of a whole generation." In so doing, Stowe's work played a major role of establishing the level of discourse for the majority of fictional treatments of the Afro-American that were to follow—even for those produced by blacks themselves. This is not to underestimate the crucial prototypical role the slave narratives played in shaping the Afro-American fiction tradition, especially through their impact on white abolitionist writers (like Stowe), who, in turn, influenced black authors. A further important intergeneric connection can be discerned in the work of the ex-slaves William Wells Brown and Frederick Douglass, both of whom published narratives before turning to fiction. Finally, as Benjamin Quarles points out, "the vast audience that responded to [Stowe's] classic tale of Uncle Tom . . . had already been conditioned and prepared by the life stories of runaway slaves." Nonetheless, the lasting effect of Stowe's masterwork on popular American culture dwarfs that of the slave narratives. With its extraordinary synthesizing power, *Uncle Tom's Cabin* presented Afro-American characters, however derivative and distorted, who leaped with incredible speed to the status of literary paradigms and even cultural archetypes with which subsequent writers—black and white—have had to reckon. The grandeur of Leslie Fiedler's claim that "for better or worse, it was Mrs. Stowe who invented American Blacks for the imagination of the whole world" does not belie its essential truth.

Although Stowe unquestionably sympathized with the slaves, her commitment to challenging the claim of black inferiority was frequently undermined by her own endorsement of racial stereotypes. And it could hardly have been otherwise, for as Thomas Graham contends, "the Negro remained an enigma to her." Of necessity, Stowe falls back upon popular conceptions of the Afro-American in depicting many of her slave characters. As one result, the blacks she uses to supply much of the humor in *Uncle Tom's Cabin* owe a great deal to the darky figures who capered across minstrel stages and white imaginations in the antebellum years. The black pranksters Sam and Andy, for instance, provide a comic counterpoint to the melodramatic flight of Eliza and Harry from the slave trader Haley. And although the two slaves play a critical role in Eliza's escape by leading the white man astray, they ultimately seem little more than bumptious, giggling, outsized adolescents. Further, Stowe never attributes their tricksterlike manipulation of Haley to any real desire to help the fugitives to freedom. Rather, Sam and Andy realize that Mrs. Shelby does not want Eliza captured; eager to please their mistress, they are only too glad to oblige. Stowe's attitude toward these slaves is also revealed in Sam's remaining appearances, which are wholly comic. Primarily concerned with his own image, he is a pompous, philosophizing amateur politician, and his speeches are fraught with the tortured syntax and strained malapropisms that Stowe intends to be amusing.

Other frequent sources of humor for Stowe are the slave children, whom she evidently viewed as part of the quaint furnishings below the Mason-Dixon line. If we take *Uncle Tom's Cabin* literally, "little negroes, all rolled together in the corners" could be found in slaves' quarters, big-house kitchens, and barrooms throughout the South. Most closely resembling wild, boisterous puppies bent on driving the adults to distraction, these black children generally appear in tumbling heaps and bundles rather than as individuals. The only one whom Stowe seriously attempts to characterize is "poor, diabolic, excellent Topsy," as George Sand called her [see excerpt dated 1852]; consequently, this figure embodies in particular detail the traits the author felt to be endemic to the undomesticated African.

Stowe introduces Topsy as the stereotypical pickaninny, with teeth gleaming, hair in bristling braids, eyes round and sparkling. A quick-witted, hyperactive child of eight or nine, she acts entirely from impulse and perversely flouts the accepted rules of polite white society, particularly those championed by the chilly, puritanical New Englander, Miss Ophelia. Inured to whipping and recalcitrant in the extreme, Topsy claims no natural origin—or, to be more precise, she offers a now-famous explanation of her own conception in such outrageously "natural" terms that it approaches the atheistic absurd: "I spect I grow'd. Don't think nobody never made me." She also justifies her destructive prankishness with a despairing resignation that exasperates Ophelia no end: "Cause I's wicked,—I is. I's mighty wicked, any how. I can't help it." Despite her mistress's best efforts, Topsy's behavior remains quirkily schizoid. Assigned to clean Ophelia's room, she either does so flawlessly or else unleashes a "carnival of confusion"; she learns to read and write "as if by magic" but refuses to master sewing (Chap. 20).

Stowe also hints at an eerie, otherworldly side to the "goblin-like" Topsy. In one of the more memorable scenes, the child responds to her owner's whistle like a pet displaying a favorite trick:

The black, glassy eyes glittered with a kind of wicked drollery, and the thing struck up, in a clear shrill voice, an odd negro melody, to which she kept time with her hands and feet, spinning round, clapping her hands, knocking her knees together, in a wild, fantastic sort of time, and producing in her throat all those odd guttural sounds which distinguish the native music of her race; and finally, turning a summerset or two, and giving a prolonged closing note, as odd and unearthly as that of a steam-whistle, she came suddenly down on the carpet, and stood with her hands folded, and a most sanctimonious expression of meekness and solemnity over her face, only

broken by the cunning glances which she shot askance from the corners of her eyes.

Although this incredible passage incidentally reveals the author's rather odd and yet, for many whites of the time, entirely typical conception of Afro-American folk music and dance, of paramount importance is the emphasis Stowe places on the grotesque freakishness of Topsy's strange performance, for she identifies this darkly magical and faintly sinister quality of the "sooty gnome" with her unredeemed African nature. With her irrepressible penchant for "turning a summerset" and the mesmerizing power "her wild diablerie" maintains over Eva St. Clare and the other youngsters, Topsy is the imp child whose undisciplined devilish spirit must be controlled (Chap. 20).

Her scenes with Eva bring Topsy's allegedly innate African traits into sharpest relief. If Eva is the "fair, high-bred child, with her golden head, her deep eyes, her spiritual, noble brow, and prince-like movements," Topsy is her "black, keen, subtle, cringing, yet acute neighbor." Eva, "the Saxon," and Topsy, "the Afric," are both "representative of their races," and the moral struggle that ensues between them constitutes an important motif in *Uncle Tom's Cabin* (Chap. 20). On one side stands the precocious, cherubic Eva, whom Stowe describes [in *The Key to Uncle Tom's Cabin*] as "an impersonation in childish form of the love of Christ." On the other is Topsy, who embodies an innocent but still dangerous lack of self-control and restraint. And although fascinated by Topsy "as a dove is sometimes charmed by a glittering serpent" (the religious symbolism here is obvious), Eva holds the key to the black child's conversion as she tries to touch her "wild, rude heart" with "the first word of kindness" (Chap. 20). Initially, Topsy resists, linking her hopeless spiritual condition with her race: "Couldn't never be nothin' but a nigger, if I was ever so good. . . . If I could be skinned, and come white, I'd try then. . . . There can't nobody love niggers, and niggers can't do nothin'! *I* don't care." However, Eva's response—"O, Topsy, poor child, *I* love you!"—pierces her defenses. Prostrated by the gentle force of selfless love, Topsy breaks down, with Eva bending over her like "some bright angel stooping to reclaim a sinner" (Chap. 25). In Stowe's world, to be born black is to be born a pagan, but paradoxically close to a state of grace; once a character's heathen African nature is controlled, redemption becomes a possibility.

Stowe's depiction of Legree's henchmen, Sambo and Quimbo, reiterates this same formulation. Although easily the most immoral black characters in the novel, the two slaves here, Stowe hastens to point out, no real predisposition to cruelty. Their mocking of Uncle Tom and their participation in Legree's satanic, drunken revels result directly from their infamous master's example and instruction, for he "had trained them in savageness and brutality as systematically as he had his bull-dogs" (Chap. 32). In a subsequent discussion of African psychology [in *The Key to Uncle Tom's Cabin*], Stowe claims that blacks "are possessed of a nervous organisation peculiarly susceptible and impressible." Not only does this trait explain Sambo and Quimbo's degraded condition on the Legree plantation but, from a Christian perspective, it entails what we can term an infinite capacity for conversion. Like Topsy, Sambo and Quimbo simply need more positive influence in order to be saved. Thus, witnessing Tom's agony brings about an immediate change, and they shed tears of repentence and grief when exposed to the Holy Word. Because of the impressionablity and the innate fascination with things spiritual that allegedly typify the African race, Stowe's blacks, when apparently evil, are but misguided an always receptive to Christian rehabilitation.

Throughout *Uncle Tom's Cabin*, Stowe draws crucial distinction in personality and behavior between full-blood and mixed-blood blacks. In her portrayal of the former—Sam, Andy, Topsy, Sambo, and Quimbo—she emphasizes the racial gifts she saw as innately African. The traits of her mulatto figures, however, resemble those conventionally associated with whites. This is why, for example, Stowe stresses their physical attractiveness and why, in contrast to the dialect (or at least rough colloquialisms) of the full-blood blacks, the speech of the mulatto slaves is generally "correct." Nonetheless the dash of African blood ensures that many of these mixed-blood characters will never be more than poor approximations of genteel bourgeois whites. That is, when we laugh at the dandified, spoiled slave Adolph St. Clare as he tosses his head, fingers his perfumed hair, and waves his scented handerchief, we are laughing at a boy mimicking adult affectations. And in their obsession with showy displays of manner and finery, the servants Jane and Rosa are but two girls pretending to be grown ladies. In each case, the style is ill fitting and the "clothes" too large. The humor in these house slaves' futile attempt to be white gives way to pathos, however, when they are sold after their owner's death. Their helpless, hysterical reaction to the harsh realities of chattel enslavement pitifully dramatizes what Stowe contends is one of the greatest evils of the institution—the domestic insecurity of even the most pampered slaves. The dark-skinned St. Clare cook, Aunt Dinah, describes their true status with pithy directness: "Don't want none o' your light-colored balls . . . cuttin' round, makin' b'lieve you's white folks, Arter all, you's niggers, much as I am" (Chap. 18).

On the one hand, the tragic experiences of the two most important mixed-blood black characters, Eliza and George Harris, also derive from their status as relatively well-treated slaves who are suddenly confronted with unjust treatment. On the other hand, they

have precious little else in common with Adolph, Jane, and Rosa. In particular, Eliza and George rival any white in the novel in nobility of character and fineness of sensibility. That in a sense they *are* white suggests that they represent not only Stowe's attempt to have her target audience identify personally with the plight of the slaves but also her inability to view certain types of heroism in any but "white" terms.

A literate, polite Christian woman, the quadroon Eliza embodies the mid-nineteenth-century ideal of bourgeois femininity. In an attempt to counter the claim that female slaves lack maternal instincts, Stowe especially emphasizes the obsessive strength of Eliza's love for her son, Harry. Indeed, it is only this motherly devotion that leads to her frenzied, desperate flight from slavery, for her sheltered life and religious upbringing have taught her to accept her lot: "I always thought that I must obey my master and mistress," she says early in the novel, "or I couldn't be a Christian" (Chap. 3). Unfortunately, her maternal dedication and unshaken piety constitute virtually the entire range of her characterization; we see little real psychological depth or intellectual vigor.

In contrast, Eliza's husband, George, more fully engages Stowe's imagination, and his personality is rendered in greater detail as she dramatizes the fall into atheism that she feared would afflict the ill-treated, thoughtful slave. George's rational questioning of his condition marks the first stage in this process. Here he argues that by white society's own standards, he deserves freedom as much as, if not more than, his owner:

> My master! and who made him my master? That's what I think of—what right has he to me? I'm a man as much as he is. I'm a better man than he is. I know more about business than he does; I am a better manager than he is; I can read better than he can; I can write a better hand,—and I've learned it all myself, and no thanks to him,—I've learned it in spite of him; and now what right has he to make a drayhorse of me? (Chap. 3)

George soon asserts his independence without qualification: "I've said Mas'r for the last time to any man. *I'm free!*" (Chap. 11). This defiance, however, begins to undercut his belief in God. At one point, he confesses to his wife, "I an't a Christian like you, Eliza; my heart's full of bitterness; I can't trust in God. Why does he let things be so?" (Chap. 3). Later, in rejecting the hackneyed religious sentiments of a white acquaintance named Wilson whom he meets during his escape, George restates his doubts: "*Is* there a God to trust in? . . . O, I've seen things all my life that have made me feel that there can't be a God" (Chap. 11).

Stowe clearly appreciates George's position; nevertheless, she cannot let his corrosive anger and potentially violent self-assertiveness undercut her Christian conception of true heroism. Consequently, two chapters after his conversation with Wilson, he finds refuge in a utopian Quaker settlement, where a mixture of religious integrity, domestic security, and democratic egalitarianism quickly assuages his spiritual malaise:

> This, indeed, was a home,—*home,*— a word that George had never yet known a meaning for; and a belief in God, and trust in his providence, began to encircle his heart, as, with a golden cloud of protection and confidence, dark, misanthropic, pining atheistic doubts, and fierce despair, melted away before the light of a living Gospel. (Chap. 13)

Although still determined to fight for his own freedom and that of his wife, George now manifests a spirit softened, tranquilized by a reborn religious faith; he promises Eliza, "I'll try to act worthy of a free man. I'll try to feel like a Christian" (Chap. 17). His behavior in a heated battle with some slave hunters exemplifies this new attitude. After George shoots one of them, he, Eliza, and other escaping slaves help the wounded man to a Quaker household, where he is nursed back to physical and spiritual health.

Stowe's treatment of Harris reveals her deep reluctance to portray the pent-up rage of an intelligent, strong-willed male slave without marbling it with a Christian restraint that entails the eschewing of violence. No such qualification is necessary in the case of Uncle Tom, who stands in antithetical juxtaposition to the aggressive, embittered George. If Harris is the articulate mulatto, correct in speech, rational, and initially impatient with religion, Tom is the passive, full-blood black, simple in expression, solicitous of all around him, gentle, and rarely shaken in his Christian faith. In fact, about the only traits the two slaves share are a willingness to die for their beliefs and a disconcerting lack of a sense of humor. Otherwise, they inhabit different worlds, parallel dimensions that never intersect. A full-blood Clark Kent and a mulatto Superman, they are never on stage at the same time. One can imagine that, like matter and antimatter, if they were forced into contact, the result would be an explosion of immeasurable force that would leave only Tom, for he, not George, is Stowe's real hero. It is Tom, not George, who so quickly entered the stock of American cultural archetypes; it is Tom, to paraphrase Faulkner, who "endured."

We first hear of Uncle Tom when his master, Mr. Shelby, describes to a skeptical Haley how his most reliable slave elected not to escape while conducting business for him in Cincinnati. This steadfast refusal to violate a trust is one of Tom's most important traits. Whereas George rejects his master's attempt to control his life and runs away with a clear conscience, Tom cannot do so. Despite the urging of his wife after his sale, he still maintains, "Mas'r always found me on the spot—he always will. I never have broke trust, nor used my pass no ways contrary to my word, and I never will" (Chap. 5). In fact, Tom mentions that he wants to be free just three times in the novel. In the first case, Augustine St. Clare has already made plans to manumit him. Even then, after exclaiming that "bein' a *free man*" is "what I'm joyin' for," Tom vows that he will remain by his owner until "Mas'r St. Clare's a Christian"—an eventuality on which one would certainly not stake one's life (Chap. 28). During Tom's trials on the Legree plantation, the issue is raised again, this time by Cassy, who asks, "Tom, wouldn't you like your liberty?" He replies, "I shall have it, Misse, in God's time" (Chap. 38). The only occasion when he himself broaches the subject is after St. Clare's tragic death. With the utmost tact and humility, Tom approaches Ophelia and asks that she intervene for him with his master's widow, who feels no compunction whatsoever at reneging on her husband's promise to free him. Unfortunately, Stowe chooses not to present the scene in which Ophelia reports back to Tom, so we can only imagine the prayers he no doubt mutters under his breath when given the bad news.

Grounded in neither fear of recapture and subsequent punishment nor any explicit satisfaction with his enslaved condition, Tom's principled refusal to strike out aggressively for his freedom grows out of his unimpeachable personal integrity and his staunch faith in Providence. In her attempt to make Tom the ideal Christian, however, Stowe deprives him of most of his imperfect human nature; he becomes, as St. Clare observes, "a moral miracle" (Chap. 18). Not only does he exhort his fellow blacks to refrain from hating slave traders, but he also finds it in himself to bless "Mas'r George" after Shelby has sold him. Even the indulgent, resolutely cynical St. Clare is subject to Tom's tearful, teetotaling ministrations. Consequently, by the time he falls into Legree's clutches, Tom has become more of a saint than a man. His religious study having been "confined entirely to the New Testament," Tom approaches the Christlike in his passivity, piety, and resigned refusal to challenge the apparent will of God (Chap. 12). When he helps two old slave women, he does so in the spirit of Christian kindness, not from any sense of racial solidarity. And when he defies Legree, it is because the man is attacking his religion, not because the villain holds no rightful claim to him: "Mas'r Legree, as ye bought me," Tom pledges, "I'll be a true and faithful servant to ye. I'll give ye all the work of my hands, all my time, all my strength; but my soul I won't give up to mortal man. I will hold on to the Lord" (Chap. 36). Even his brief struggle with religious doubt and fear during his epic battle with Legree resembles Christ's momentary questioning of his fate shortly before his crucifixion more than it does Job's all-too-human response to his overwhelming misery.

Tom's relationship with Cassy, Legree's erstwhile mistress, best exemplifies his effect on other blacks. A proud, willful, mixed-blood woman who has been driven to infanticide by broken promises, sexual exploitation, and horrible suffering, Cassy resists her enslavement more fiercely and actively than any black character besides George Harris. It is Cassy who openly defies and steals money from Legree, and it is Cassy who plans her and Emmeline's elaborate escape. However, as he does with almost every lost soul he encounters, Tom soothes her intense bitterness and rights her unbalanced mind. In the face of Cassy's despair, Tom reminds her, "The Lord han't forgot us,—I'm sartin' o' that ar'. If we suffer with him, we shall also reign, Scripture says; but, if we deny Him, he also will deny us" (Chap. 34). Later, after refusing to help her murder Legree, Tom urges Cassy to give herself not to hatred and vengeance, but to love. Her furious contention that love for "*such* enemies . . . isn't in flesh and blood" receives a predictably earnest response from Tom: "No, Misse, it isn't . . . but *He* gives it to us, and that's the victory" (Chap. 38). At this point, Stowe apostrophizes the African race in the explicitly redemptive terms of sacrificial martyrdom: "And this, O Africa! latest called of nations,—called to the crown of thorns, the scourge, the bloody sweat, the cross of agony,—this is to be *thy* victory" (Chap. 38). An echo of Christ's final words, Tom's prayer just before his death completes the image: "Into thy hands I commend my spirit!" (Chap. 40). (pp. 46-84)

Richard Yarborough, "Strategies of Black Characterization in 'Uncle Tom's Cabin' and the Early Afro-American Novel," in *New Essays on Uncle Tom's Cabin,* edited by Eric J. Sundquist, Cambridge University Press, 1986, pp. 45-84.

SOURCES FOR FURTHER STUDY

Adams, John R. *Harriet Beecher Stowe.* New York: Twayne, 1963, 172 p.

Examines Stowe's literary technique "not only in *Uncle Tom's Cabin* but in her later, more representative and characteristic works."

———. "Structure and Theme in the Novels of Harriet Beecher Stowe." *American Transcendental Quarterly*, No. 24, Part 1 (Fall 1974): 50-5.

Analyzes recurring themes and structures in Stowe's body of work.

Brown, Gillian. "Domestic Politics in *Uncle Tom's Cabin*." In her *Domestic Individualism: Imagining Self in Nineteenth-Century America*, pp. 13-38. Berkeley: University of California Press, 1990.

Explores Stowe's depiction of nineteenth-century domestic life and property relations in *Uncle Tom's Cabin.*

Fields, Annie. *Life and Letters of Harriet Beecher Stowe.* Boston: Houghton, Mifflin, 1897, 406 p.

Influential biography of Stowe by her longtime friend, supplemented with Stowe's letters and correspondence.

Sundquist, Eric J., ed. *New Essays on 'Uncle Tom's Cabin.'* Cambridge: Cambridge University Press, 1986, 200 p.

Collection of essays on *Uncle Tom's Cabin,* focusing on themes such as Stowe's portrayal of blacks and women in the novel.

[Warren, Samuel]. *"Uncle Tom's Cabin." Blackwood's Edinburgh Magazine* LXXIV, No. CCCCLVI (October 1858): 393-423.

Discusses the literary and historical significance of *Uncle Tom's Cabin* and the phenomenal popularity of the novel in the first year of its release.

August Strindberg

1849-1912

(Full name Johan August Strindberg; also wrote under pseudonym Harved Ulf) Swedish dramatist, novelist, short story writer, poet, essayist, and journalist.

INTRODUCTION

Strindberg is considered one of the greatest dramatists in modern literature. He has been called the "father of expressionism," and his *Ett drömspel* (1907; *The Dream Play*, 1912) and the trilogy *Till Damaskus* (1898-1904; *To Damascus*, 1913) are recognized as forerunners of Surrealism and the theater of the absurd. The plays *Fadren* (1887; *The Father*, 1899) and *Fröken Julie* (1889; *Miss Julie*, 1912), reflect Strindberg's efforts to transcend naturalism by probing the psyche, focusing especially on the hidden roots of human conflicts. Although overshadowed by his dramatical works, Strindberg's novels, poems, and essays still attract considerable critical attention.

Strindberg was born in Stockholm; his mother was a former servant, and his father an impoverished aristocrat. An unhappy childhood, chronicled in his autobiography *Tjänstekvinnans son* (1886; *The Son of a Servant*, 1913), left a profound mark on Strindberg, whose life was filled with extreme mental anguish. Unable to settle into a conventional career, he led a rather chaotic life, managing, nevertheless, to devote considerable energy to literary work. The most significant writings of his early period are the satirical novel *Röda rummet* (1879; *The Red Room*, 1913), a social satire, and *Mäster Olof* (1881; *Master Olof*, 1915), a historical drama about the Swedish religious reformer Olaus Petri. Strindberg and his first wife, Siri von Essen, lived through financial and emotional difficulties, including his excruciating trial for blasphemy—provoked by the 1884 publication of his first short-story collection *Giftas* (1884-86; *Married*, 1913)—and exile during the period of 1883 to 1889. The marriage, which Strindberg bitterly described in *Le Plaidoyer d'un fou* (1895; *The Confession of a Fool*, 1912), an autobiographical work written in French, ended in 1891. Strindberg moved to Berlin in 1892, joining a group of European artists and writers, which included the Norwegian artist Edvard Munch and the Polish writer Stanislaw Przybyszewsky. Two years later, he settled in Paris, devoting his energy to alchemy and occult research. This period, which Strindberg himself called the "Inferno crisis" because it occurred while he was writing the novel *Inferno* (1897; *The Inferno,* 1912), was a time of isolation, doubt, painful psychological turmoil, serious mental instability, and literary sterility. Returning to Sweden toward the end of the 1890s, Strindberg settled in Stockholm in 1899. There he continued to write until his death in 1912.

The "Inferno crisis" had a profound effect on Strindberg's life and work. The feeling of isolation, despondency, and haunting doubt prompted him to embark on a spiritual quest, which included the study of various religious and mystical traditions, especially the ideas of the noted Swedish mystic visionary Emanuel Swedenborg. Strindberg's occult studies led him to the conclusion that human suffering is the result of sin, and the prerequisite for atonement and salvation. These meditations on human destiny formed the background of a series of chamber plays, written for the small *Intima* theater in Stockholm, which Strindberg managed with a young producer. The chamber plays culminated in the extraordinary *Spöksonaten* (1908; *The Ghost Sonata,* 1916), with its peculiar blend of occult, fantastic, and surreal elements.

Citing *The Father* and *Miss Julie* as examples of Strindberg's peculiar brand of psychological naturalism, critics have commented on the playwright's ability to concentrate on the "moment of struggle," the immediate conflict or crisis affecting his characters. Strindberg's deep concentration on the "moment" led him to eliminate any extraneous incidents or dialogue and thereby to significantly alter the traditional dramatic structure. But this formal sparseness, as critics contend, appears vastly compensated by the psychological intensity of his plays.

If conflict is the driving-force of Strindberg's mature plays, his principal theme, as exemplified by *The Father, Miss Julie,* and *Dödsdansen* (1905; *The Dance of Death,* 1912), is Friedrich Nietzsche's conception of life as a succession of contests between stronger and weaker wills. Strindberg applied this theory to his recurring motif of gender conflict, or battle between the sexes for intellectual and psychological supremacy. The playwright's female characters most often appear as diabolical usurpers of man's "naturally" dominant role, cruelly shattering his psyche and draining his intellect. According to critics, the alienated and abused male characters reflect the author's self-image as a perennial outcast and victim. However, as some commentators assert, Strindberg's attitude toward women was more ambivalent than purely negative: the ambivalence probably stemmed from the writer's acute awareness of the problems facing women in the patriarchal societies of nineteenth-century Europe.

The stylistic experiments of Strindberg's post-*Inferno* period proved a turning point in modern drama. From his studies, Strindberg concluded that earthly life is a hell which men and women are forced to endure, and that their experience of physical reality represents punishment for sins committed in a previous existence. *To Damascus, A Dream Play,* and *The Ghost Sonata* are based on this premise, presenting a fragmented and highly subjective view of reality. To translate his vision of the world into the language of drama, Strindberg employed dream symbolism, creating a suggestive realm of grotesque horror: individuals randomly appear and disappear; scenes and images change unexpectedly; and profound fears and ghastly fantasies easily materialize. *To Damascus* and *The Dream Play* prefigured the major dramatic movements of the twentieth century, exerting a powerful influence on dramatists such as Samuel Beckett, Eugene O'Neill, and Eugène Ionesco.

Because Strindberg was an intensely autobiographical and self-analytical writer, critics such as Desmond MacCarthy have dismissed his plays as "products of the unfortunate 'cathartic' type of creation, which purges no one but the creator." Most commentators, however, regard Strindberg as a major literary force. The general critical view of Strindberg is summed up by O'Neill's remark that Strindberg "was the precursor of all modernity in our present theatre."

(For further information about Strindberg's life and works, see *Contemporary Authors,* Vol. 104 and *Twentieth–Century Literary Criticism,* Vols. 1, 8, 21.)

CRITICAL COMMENTARY

EDWIN BJÖRKMAN
(essay date 1913)

[Björkman was a Swedish-American novelist and critic who introduced American readers to the works of major Scandinavian authors, including Strindberg, Bjørnstjerne Bjørnson, and Georg Brandes. In the following excerpt, he discusses Strindberg's principal works, emphasizing that Strindberg's writings, while seemingly autobiographical, should be understood as creations of a literary imagination.]

Regarding Strindberg primarily as an imaginatively creative writer, we find his career as such falling into three sharply defined periods. The first of these lasted from 1868 to 1885; the second, from 1886 to 1894; the third, from 1897 to his death. Between the second and the third periods occurred [an] interregnum of absolute unproductivity. . . . (p. 45)

For purposes of convenience, rather than with any claim at positive definition, those periods may be designated as: 1) the romantic; 2) the naturalistic; 3) the symbolistic. Of course, a tendency to naturalistic presentation of external facts characterized his work almost from the start, and it continued to assert itself even in the most mystical products of his final period. He was always a realist in the finest sense of that term—one insisting that art must cling closely to life as actually lived and stand firmly on this ground even when reaching most daringly into still unconquered realms of being. But on the other hand, there was always a touch of mysticism, of yearning idealism, of instinctive out-reaching for the life still to come, even in such characteristic works of the middle period as *The Father* and *Creditors.* It represented a strain of feeling and thought nearly inseparable from the Scandinavian temperament.

Of the first period, beginning with his initial gropings in the world of poetry, and coming to an end, in 1885, with the completion of the four short stories published collectively as *Real Utopias,* I have dared to speak as romantic chiefly because sentiment still holds almost equal sway with logic in the work belonging to it. (pp. 46-7)

The transition from the first to the second period caused no interruption in his creative activity. Evidence that some kind of border line was crossed about 1885 must be drawn from within the works then produced. But the moment we compare the preface of the first part of *Marriage,* dating from 1884, with that of the second part, written in 1886, we perceive that something of moment must have happened in the meantime. Of course, the real events took place in Strindberg's own mind. But the principal external facts connected with those inner changes were the confiscation of the first part of *Marriage* and the beginnings of his marital unhappiness. (pp. 49-50)

His altered attitude toward womanhood is the first thing that makes itself felt. . . . But back of it we suspect the presence of changes reaching much farther down into the writer's conception of life. The man who wrote the first part of *Marriage* and *Real Utopias* was, on the whole, well content with his world. The author of the second part of *Marriage* and of *The Father* strikes us, on the other hand, as a man doubting the very possibility of happiness as a human state.

I deem it highly regrettable that for many years hardly any works by Strindberg except those dating from his middle period became known in the English-speaking countries. For in many respects I cannot but think that period abnormal—representing a deviation from his true line of development. During those years between 1885 and 1894, the nature of Strindberg, which was no whit less capable of love and faith than of hatred and doubt, became sadly warped. All the world lay wrapt in grey mist. Woman, once angelic, turned into a devil incarnate. Life was seen as war to the hilt—and love was the worst form this war could assume.

To me it seems quite logical that this period, and no other, should see Strindberg turn from his former social outlook to a temporary acceptance of Nietzsche's ultra-individualistic superman theories. It is the works from this period that have brought him the name of a misogynist and the reputation of being too grim and gloomy for races which are essentially wholesome and optimistic in their tendencies. Yet the same period gave the world a series of exquisite pictures from life among the peasant-fishermen on those islands between Stockholm and "the edge of the sea" where Strindberg had previously sought and won the inspiration for his *Master Olof.* (pp. 51-2)

The play *Master Olof* was at first named *The Renegade,* and under this title I hope it will become known to the English-speaking world. To Strindberg himself it was largely what *The Pretenders* was to Ibsen—at once a questioning and a formulation of his own genius. The

Principal Works

Fritankaren [first publication] (drama) 1870

I Rom (drama) 1870

Röda rummet (novel) 1879
  [The Red Room, 1913]

Mäster Olof (drama) 1881
  [Master Olof, 1915]

Dikter på vers och prosa (poetry) 1883

Lycko-Pers resa (drama) 1883
  [Lucky Pehr, 1912; also published as Lucky Peter's Travels in Lucky Peter's Travels and Other Plays, 1930]

Giftas. 2 vols. (short stories) 1884-86
  [Married, 1913]

Sömngångarnätter på vakna dagar (poetry) 1884

Tjänstekvinnans son (novel) 1886
  [The Son of a Servant, 1913]

Fadren (drama) 1887
  [The Father, 1899]

Hemsöborna (novel) 1887
  [The People of Hemsö, 1959]

Fröken Julie (drama) 1889
  [Countess Julia, 1912; also published as Miss Julia in Plays by August Strindberg, second series, 1913; and Miss Julie in Miss Julie and Other Plays, 1918]

Den starkare (drama) 1889
  [The Stronger published in Plays by August Strindberg, second series, 1913]

Le Plaidoyer d'un fou (novel) 1895
  [The Confession of a Fool, 1912]

Inferno (novel) 1897
  [The Inferno, 1912]

Till Damaskus. 3 vols. [first publication] (drama) 1898-1904
  [To Damascus, 1913; also published as The Road to Damascus, 1939]

Folkungasagan (drama) 1899
  [The Saga of the Folkungs published in The Saga of the Folkungs. Engelbrekt, 1959]

Gustave Vasa (drama) 1899
  [Gustavus Vasa published in Plays by August Strindberg, fourth series, 1916]

Påsk (drama) 1901
  [Easter published in Easter, and Stories, 1912]

Dödsdansen, första delen (drama) 1905
  [The Dance of Death published in Plays by August Strindberg, first series, 1912]

Kamraterna [with Axel Lundegård] (drama) 1905
  [Comrades published in Plays, 1912]

En blå bok. 4 vols. (essays) 1907-12
  [Zones of the Spirit, 1913]

Ett Drömspel (drama) 1907
  [The Dream Play published in Plays by August Strindberg, first series, 1912]

Spöksonaten (drama) 1908
  [The Spook Sonata published in Plays by August Strindberg, fourth series, 1916; also published as The Ghost Sonata in Chamber Plays, 1962]

Stora landsvägen (drama) 1910
  [The Great Highway published in Modern Scandinavian Plays, 1954]

Plays by August Strindberg. 4 vols. (dramas) 1912-16

---

greater modernity of the Swedish work is shown by the fact that its principal hero, who is one of three central figures, fails equally to reach a triumph like that of [Oehlenschläger's] *King Håkon,* the man divinely commissioned, and to suffer a disaster like that of the self-doubting *Earl Skule.* Instead he lives on to complete his work—in compromise. To win his way, or rather a way for his mission, he has to sacrifice a part of his vision—and so he is denounced as a renegade by him who sees too far ahead and will sacrifice nothing. This is life, of course; and thus Strindberg may be said to have, for all time, given the true symbolization of the everlasting struggle between the genius and the mass on one side, and between true and false genius on the other.

The Red Room is a satirical novel, embodying the conflict between bohemianism and philistinism at Stockholm in the seventies, and written in a vein that shows a rare combination of youthful vigor and merci-less satire. But it gives also, as almost all of Strindberg's novels, a detailed study of social conditions in Sweden at that time. Hardly a phase of national existence is unrepresented, and each one of them is sketched in such manner that we also get an idea of the directional tendencies expressed through it. Strindberg's faculty for drawing lifelike pictures not only of individuals but of vast social groups and organisms is among the most striking of his gifts. And to the future historian his novels and autobiographical writings should prove exceedingly valuable. (pp. 54-6)

The first part of *Marriage* contains a dozen specimens of modern marital unions, presented in a far from unfriendly light. In the preface Strindberg laid out a programme concerning woman's position which vies in radicalism with that for which the women themselves are now fighting all over the world. Not only would he grant them the suffrage, but he insisted that normal social growth necessitated their having it. But in the second volume of stories issued under the same title, he made a frank attack on two principles generally accepted as essential to woman's complete emancipation, namely the right to hold property, and the right to work at anything for which they can qualify themselves. If their tendency be disregarded, the stories in both volumes will be found to possess high artistic value.

The Father was Strindberg's supreme effort to symbolize the life and death struggle between man and woman for such immortality as may be offered them by the child. The picture of that struggle is splendid but unfair. Man, as man, is given rational insight, while to woman is granted little more than low cunning. And as conscience is allied with reason, the victory falls to its unconscionable opponent. It may seem paradoxical to express a regret that the sex problem should enter at all into this play—a play designed wholly to exhaust that very problem. But there is a psychological side to the work that has nothing whatever to do with sex, and this side would hold our interest just as firmly if the conflict were raging between two men. The corrosive power of suggestion is here shown with diabolical skill. It is a duel of souls, with words for weapons, and by a seed of doubt sown in the right way at the right moment, one of those souls is shattered and scattered as fatally as a warship when its magazine explodes.

Miss Julie, perhaps the most widely known of Strindberg's works, was a frank experiment in new form. Not only are the stage arrangements unconventional, but intermissions have been dispensed with. Naturalism never came nearer to a conquest of the stage, and some of the innovations embodied in this drama are likely to form part of our future dramatic tradition. Again the plot seems to offer us nothing but a sex duel, with the man for winner. But back of Miss Julie and her valet-lover stand two contending strata of humanity—the so-called upper and lower classes. What Strindberg shows us is how a continued process of selective breeding may lead to over-refinement and a weakening of the vital instincts. The racial strain which has reached such a point can find salvation only in mixture with some strain less far removed from the general source of life. If class prejudices or other inhibitive tendencies prevent such a mixture, then the weakened strain will be sloughed off by the race, so that place will be made for other strains with unimpaired vitality and still dormant powers of refinement. (pp. 56-9)

It was during [his] middle period of embittered defiance that Strindberg first conceived the idea of a series of autobiographical novels, in which he would adhere closely to his own actual experience while the shock of such self-revelation was to be softened by a change of all proper names. The first volume of this se-ries, issued in 1886 under the title of *The Son of a Servant* gives a picture of child life that is full of startling revelations and exquisite interpretations. Strindberg himself has said somewhere that all fiction must be autobiographical in order to obtain full documentary validity. Even if we hold this assertion too sweeping, we must at least grant him to have proved that the most intimate personal experience may be turned into legitimate fiction.

While at all times, to use his own expression, Strindberg "had three strings to his lyre," he appeared during the third period primarily as a dramatist, and it was as such that he preferred to be considered. There is hardly one play from his final period that would not warrant special notice on some account or another. In the eyes of his countrymen, his dramatic presentations of Swedish history have tended to take precedence. And on their account some have dared to call him the Shakespeare of Sweden. But the historical plays of Strindberg are widely different in mettle from that displayed in the "histories" of Shakespeare. No matter how much we find to admire in the latter, they must be held melodramatic in form and rhetorical in expression. They are, in a word, artificial in their portrayal of the past. What Strindberg strove to do—and succeeded in doing, I think—was to reconstruct the everyday aspect of by-gone days. In order to bring the true inwardness as well as lifelike appearance of those days within the ken of our own, he put on the stage not imagined creatures of supernatural size, but plain-speaking men and women of our own kind. But back of these men and women we catch lurid glimpses of big social forces at work. In other words, his works are symbolical in the very best sense of this much misused term—symbolical in the same manner as man's own thinking. . . . (pp. 60-2)

But for the present his main dramatic contributions to universal literature during this final period must be sought among the plays of modern life, and particularly among those that derived from a frankly acknowledged Maeterlinckian impetus. It was the early Maeterlinck of the puppet plays that set Strindberg once more seeking for a new form. The immediate result of this search was the fairy play *Swanwhite,* a very charming but not convincingly original production. Had he stopped there, the charge of imitation sometimes heard might have had some warrant. But to speak of the author of *The Dream Play* or *Toward Damascus* as the imitator of anybody becomes palpably ridiculous the moment you read these works. In both—but especially in the former—he strove to reproduce the kaleidoscopic flexibility and whimsical logic of the dream. And in this way he succeeded as perhaps no one before him to press all life into the narrow confines of a play.

At one time he described *The Dream Play* as a "Buddhistic and proto-Christian drama." Thereby he indicated its underlying philosophy of enlightened resignation and of almost Tolstoyan passivity in the face of violence and injustice and wrong. But we must not be misled by this effort of the matured poet to grasp and vitalize an ideal foreign to his own temperament. "I am a soldier," says the hunter in *The Great Highway,* speaking as the *alter ego* of the author; "I am always fighting—fighting to preserve my personal independence." To me the most potent element in *The Dream Play,* the one most likely to germinate and survive not only as art but as philosophy, is its tolerant acceptance of every human aspect as an integral part of life. Its main shortcoming lies in a tendency to consider all such aspects as established for all future. Viewing life statically, however, and not kinetically—from the realist's viewpoint rather than from the idealist's—it will prove difficult to find an artistic symbolization of it more subtle or more convincing than that given us in *The Dream Play.*

Although the trilogy *Toward Damascus* is autobiographical in source as well as purpose—a sort of gigantic private reckoning worked out by one deeming himself too seriously tried by life—its appeal is nevertheless universal. We may forget the fate of him who projected those mighty dramatic cloud-shapes, and read out of them nothing but a masterly record of the stumbling progress made by a human soul in its search for harmonious correlation of its own conflicting elements—its desires and aspirations, its selfish and unselfish tendencies. In the third part we find Father Melchior calling out to the Strindbergian protagonist, here named The Strangers: "You began life by affirming everything; you continued it by denying everything. End it now with a coordination. Therefore, cease to be exclusive! Say not 'either—or,' but say instead 'both—and!' " Here we have Strindberg's onward march through forty years of thinking and working outlined in a couple of sentences—and we cannot fail to recognize its identity with the general course of human progress, which runs from blind belief through arrogant denial to a reasoned balancing of faith and doubt.

Close as the trilogy must have stood to what was Strindberg's innermost self, there is a professedly objective work that seems to have come still closer, though in a different manner—a work where Strindberg's artistic aloofness makes us almost forget that, in spite of it, he was still dealing with his own spiritual experiences, and with nothing else. This work, the double play named *The Dance of Death,* I am often inclined to count the crowning climax of his production, the work in which his always remarkable art reached its highest potency of perfection. It is as closely knit as a Greek drama or a play by Ibsen at his best. Only three characters figure in the first part, and five in the second. There are only two settings—one for each part. The dialogue has rarely, if ever, been surpassed for combined incisiveness and verisimilitude. Incident leads to incident with a fatality that vainly tries to mask its logic behind the leering face of chance. Some of the scenes are among the most tensely dramatic that may be found in modern literature, and yet the total impression is just what the author seems to have aimed at: a sense of the hopeless monotony underlying life's superficial disturbances.

A piece of the most delicate, and yet most deep-reaching symbolism (outwardly expressed by the round form of the room in which the action takes place) lies in the circular movement of the first part, whereby everything becomes reduced once more to the state of the opening scene. All the tumult of living is brought back to a pitiful striving at self-assertion on the part of the individual. Yet the suggestion is always present, that in all his seemingly futile striving the individual takes the place of a puppet in the hands of some higher power, working for great aims that he cannot perceive. Life and hell are rendered almost synonymous, but the Swedenborgian idea of hell as a state of mind is not for a moment left out of sight. The one possible agent of escape is the Hogarthian fiddler, always hovering on the horizon like a storm cloud before which all cower in panic. But when he comes at last and brings the dance to a close, he is seen to bring with him pardon and peace, mercy and harmony. One of the figures in the play, Curt, might be called the superman of Strindberg's final period: a touching incarnation of the struggle between reasoned humility and instinctive pride that was always raging in the author's own breast. But the most striking figure of all is that of the Captain, the embodiment of ruthless self-concern, to whom nevertheless is given the pronouncement of Strindberg's ultimate philosophical creed: "Wipe out and pass on!" (pp. 63-8)

Inferno [was] his most original effort at autobiographical fiction. . . . In 1903 he wrote another volume in the same series, *Alone,* which might be called the antithesis of his previous record of wandering through a self-made hell. It is a piece of pure poetry—the autumnal reverie of a man who, at last, has made his peace with the world and paid the price for it. And in this volume Strindberg's marvellous power of word-painting stands revealed in all its glory.

I cannot end this all too brief characterization of Strindberg's main works without calling attention to an additional and somewhat confusing aspect of his passion for self-revelation. Not satisfied with giving us a detailed story of his life and artistic development, he wrote also stories of the story, revelations of how previous revelations had come to be made. In a number of pamphlets, and particularly in those quaint collections of notes, sketches, aphorisms and speculations which he named "Blue Books" [*Zones of the Spirit*], material of this kind was piled up at a tremendous rate, until the image to be evoked became blurred by the superabundance of fact used to evoke it. I wonder, however, whether this condition may not alter as passing time places everything in proper perspective. For it would seem that concerning a mind so rich and so original, both in its coloring and in its tendencies, the amount of available data could hardly become too great. (pp. 70-2)

Edwin Björkman, "August Strindberg," in his *Voices of Tomorrow: Critical Studies of the New Spirit in Literature,* Mitchell Kennerley, 1913, pp. 11-120.

PÄR LAGERKVIST
(essay date 1966)

[Lagerkvist was a noted Swedish novelist, playwright, short story writer, and poet. In the following excerpt, he assesses Strindberg's contribution to modern drama.]

[Strindberg] has meant the renewal of the modern drama, and thereby also, the gradual renewal of the theatre. It is from him and through him that naturalism received the critical blow even though it is also Strindberg who gave naturalism its most intense dramatic works. If one wishes to understand the direction in which the modern theatre is actually striving and the line of development it will probably follow, it is certainly wise to turn to him first of all. (p. 24)

Strindberg's distinctly new creative work in the drama, where he is, more than in any other area, an *imaginative writer,* begins first after he had gone through the religious crisis out of which he emerges, on the whole, freer of alien influences, entirely absorbed in himself, enclosed in his own suffering and his own shattered, agonizing world. It is as if, confronted by the need of finding expression for these new, complex conditions of the soul where nothing is at rest, where all is unquiet, anguish, a never ceasing vacillation, where feeling is replaced by feeling, faith by doubt, when existence itself and the external world seemed to him to crumble, to dissolve; as if he then no longer found the old form sufficient, but had to press forward, seeking a new one in which all this could be reflected, one which was as restlessly changing and complex as the conditions of the soul which it should make intelligible. (pp. 24-5)

Hereafter, the drama—and the direct, intimate confession—is his true expression. And it is conceivable that it was to be the drama because it is in all respects, his most personal form, his finest tool.

Strindberg himself characterizes *Advent* as "a

mysterium." And not only here but also in *To Damascus* there is a mood of the Middle Ages, of Catholicism, and of severe and naïve religiosity which afterward always remains. I do not know if Strindberg specifically had the medieval drama in mind when he created this motif of the passion play to which he returns time and time again. But in the freedom with which the dramatic theme is handled, in the seeming looseness and the apparently fortuitous juxtaposition of the scenes which one feels in reading but which on the stage is not noticed, and in the immediacy anchness of the narration there is much of the medieval drama. But still, quite naturally, everything is entirely new. (pp. 25-6)

In regard to form, he succeeded completely for the first time in making a reality of all that he was profoundly seeking, in the chamber plays, in these extraordinary dramas which open a whole new world to our eyes, as rich in human experience as they are in poetry. (p. 26)

In the presence of these dramas no one can fail to see how insufficient the naturalistic form is and how narrow its limits. For no one can doubt that Strindberg, if he had been forced to develop the themes in *The Spook Sonata, The Pelican,* and *The Black Glove* in one fixed realistic plane, never could have wrung from them that fullness of moving humanity which has made them stand as the most profound and remarkable imaginative writing that he produced. Nor, can anyone doubt that it was just through the new mode of expression which he created that Strindberg was able to speak so directly and openly to us, to touch hidden strings in our consciousness which we perhaps had sensed but whose sound we had never before heard.

One may add that Strindberg is not a great dramatic writer because he found this new form.

But that this form allowed him to show the full magnitude of his greatness.

Strindberg's drama such as it gradually became signifies in all respects revolt and renewal. And one cannot imagine that it will have anything else but a revolutionary effect on modern drama because it so completely destroys the old foundations, creates new ones instead, and so clearly shows a way which leads forward.

Ibsen, who was long the modern writer *par préférence* because he exhaustively plodded through all of the social, sexual, and mental-hygienic ideas and ideals which happened to come up for discussion, merely weighs us down with his perfectly consummated and fixed form, impossible of further development; and besides, only fills, in an admirable way, an unoccupied place which otherwise would have been empty. Strindberg, on the other hand, opens a perspective forward which is stimulating and exciting and allows us a premonition of what lies deepest within us, not because he informs us about what we think or ought to think—for how often do we really share Strindberg's opinions?—but just because in him we find the very disquiet, uncertainty, and faltering pulse of our own day.

A new form has never been created more beautifully or more completely as a result of inner personal compulsion.

And yet, as the form finally appears to us, it is never purely and simply the fruit of personality; innumerable other factors have also had their influence: everything which lives and moves about the writer, all he has seen and experienced, all of the life and time which was granted to him. The *form* never becomes entirely his personal property, but that of his time and perhaps posterity's as well. (pp. 27-8)

[It] has been Strindberg's fate—and probably will continue to be for a long time yet—that he is valued first and foremost for his bad qualities, both as a writer and a man. All of his repellent and morbid features were seized upon; these have been regarded as the most interesting. For this best suited modern literature.

Perhaps, however, Strindberg can be viewed more reasonably without therefore losing any of his magnificence or interest. Perhaps one may love the beauty and the value in his work, and understand, but not love, its inferior qualities.

It would then be easier to see entirely without prejudice where he is greatest as an imaginative writer and where he falls short.

The sweeping renewal of the modern drama which Strindberg represents in his later development cannot be explained away. It is a revolt against the old, not a development from it. And it is this, his last achievement, that makes it impossible to circumvent him even if one has entirely different purposes and goals.

Ibsen can be circumvented like a milepost with a Roman numeral on it. But Strindberg is in the middle of the road and one is allowed to pass, only after one first understands him and what he actually signifies. (p. 29)

If the struggle for a new form does not also mean the struggle for a deeper personal view, then for heaven's sake it should be avoided. And if one does not need to understand Strindberg's importance one ought to leave him alone.

All I want to affirm is that Strindberg's newly created dramatic form, despite all its subjectivity, nonetheless corresponds to an artistic instinct in our age. (p. 30)

Foremost may be mentioned the intimate theatre which arose from the drama of Strindberg and whose founding Strindberg himself brought about through his remarkable preface to *Miss Julie.*

"First and last a small stage and a small auditorium" is the demand he makes. And afterward he always holds fast to it, throughout his entire development. His own theatre comes into existence chiefly to put this idea into practical effect. And here it acquires its most interesting form through the introduction of the so-called "drapery stage." This is the most extreme consequence, and it is better and more sensible than stopping halfway.

But whether this way is, on the whole, the right one is another question. Many of his plays—like much of naturalistic drama in general—could be played to advantage on such a stage. But many, and among them the most important ones, could only lose by it.

The fact cannot be avoided that a small stage implies, first and foremost, reduced possibilities. Such a stage is confined within a small space from beginning to end. When an effect built upon contrasts is necessary it is helpless and can do nothing. It has no possibility of expression through proportions, distance, and antitheses. (pp. 30-1)

The merit surely lies in the fact that in a time of confusion in such matters this theatre really implies a definite style. But in this there lurks a danger for the actor which weighs even heavier and which has already been felt—the danger that instead of enriching his acting skill and liberating his imagination, he is led to *stylize* his presentation, killing his individuality. Stylization is the antithesis of all art, and in our day it is the spectre which threatens everywhere. One need only think of a "stylized" landscape painting hung as a background to give "atmosphere"—as happened in Strindberg's theatre, and which he insisted upon in, to choose an example, the last scene of *The Spook Sonata*—in order to understand what the end would be.

On this point, and for that matter, in his whole attitude toward the theater, in his suspicion of it and his wish to see it changed quite simply into an awe-inspiring pulpit for the playwright, Strindberg is no more than the exponent of his own generation's taste and ought not to be regarded as anything else. It would be unfortunate if his instructions were taken *ad notam.* Unfortunate both for the effect of his own dramas and for later development. (pp. 31-2)

Pär Lagerkvist, "Modern Theatre: Points of View and Attack," in his *Modern Theatre: Seven Plays and an Essay,* translated by Thomas R. Buckman, University of Nebraska Press, 1966, pp. 1-38.

RICHARD GILMAN
(essay date 1969)

[Gilman is an American critic and educator. In the following excerpt, he contests the traditional view of Strindberg's early plays as examples of dramatic naturalism.]

In November of 1887, when Henrik Ibsen was at the height of his fame, he received a copy of August Strindberg's new play, *The Father.* A few days later he wrote to the Swedish bookseller who had sent it to him that although the younger dramatist's "experiences and observations in the area of life" with which the play was concerned were not the same as his own, he found it impossible to deny or to resist the author's "violent force" in his new work. (p. 199)

That Ibsen was well aware of the Swedish playwright's originality and power is clear. . . . (p. 200)

Ibsen is linked forever to something that wasn't synonymous with the well-made play but that had assimilated its technical means. Naturalism is one of the terms we use to see to it that art remains within the realm of "culture," that is to say within the domain of pedagogy. For Ibsen's contemporaries—Zola, for example, or, provisionally as we shall see, Strindberg—the word naturalism meant a number of things, but a shared meaning was that it marked out the field of an exploration that was at the same time a repudiation of unseriousness and artificiality in literature and drama, an assault on them for having taken their eyes off what existence was really like. It was a word to describe a procedure and a morale that were felt to be necessary in art at the time, and *as a word,* it is useful in the history of changing attitudes and ambiences in art. But it was never a thing, a substance, or even a specific style, in the same way that "absurd" art or expressionism are not actualities but signs, climates, and terms we use for the sake of historical order and the exigencies of textbooks. (p. 204)

This is essential to remember in the case of August Strindberg. For Strindberg, almost a generation younger than Ibsen, naturalism as I have been describing it was already the prevailing serious attitude toward literary art when he came to artistic maturity, and his first important plays were written in its atmosphere and with its élan. Yet Strindberg's dramatic imagination, like that of Ibsen, was too far-reaching and original to have been content with the operation of a literary mode that understood itself largely as a principle of earnestness, a repudiation of spectacle and arid fantasy

and a means of making the theater work for conscious, socially revelatory ends. Such things could not be much more than starting points, and in fact Strindberg early referred to himself as a *Nyanaturalist,* a "new" naturalist.

With less of a stake than Ibsen in maintaining a *plausible* theater, one in which a playwright worked to change things by indirection, withholdings and subtle departures, Strindberg was able to move more aggressively and quickly out of the well-madeness of naturalism as well as out of its area of social concerns, or at least socially oriented subject matter. For him, though he acknowledged Ibsen's contributions to the possibilities of a more open theater, the older writer remained essentially inside. Sharing in part what was then, as now, the reductive view of Ibsen, Strindberg saw his great fellow Scandinavian largely as an ideologue (on the wrong side of most issues; he thought *A Doll's House,* for example, was part of a feminist plot), a forensic dramatist and a man with whose spirit he felt no compelling impulse to link his own.

For all that his work plunged more deeply into psychic jungles than Ibsen's, was more "unconscious" and more taken up with extreme emotional states. Strindberg was a much more ready and voluble expositor of his own aesthetic ideas and attitudes. Ibsen's extreme reticence means that his imaginative starting points as well as his thinking about aesthetic problems have to be almost wholly inferred from the internal evidence of the plays, although there is some important help available from those scattered, lofty, understated pronouncements on process and those oblique essays in self-definition that we generally persist in ignoring: "I have been more the poet and less the social philosopher than people have generally been inclined to believe."

Strindberg has been more easily recognized as a poet, one reason being the closer coherence with our own concerns of his inquest into aberration and of his ambiguous lyricism. He was extraordinarily conscious and clear-sighted about his art, knowing at all times that he was making something new and that these new compositions whose music was one of implication, internal logic, protean change, intuition and epiphany were not going to be easily understood by the public and not easily shrugged off by other playwrights. Out of his letters, his obiter dicta and, most important of all, his prefaces to his own plays there takes shape a history of a revolution in imagination, one that amounted to nothing less than the overthrow of a sanctified way of organizing experience into the formal patterns of drama, at the same time as it was an opening out to new kinds of experience. (And it is this simultaneity, the response to the claims of new and not-yet-identified experience and the necessity to find means for its disposition as art, that we so often lose sight of because of our habit of thinking of art as the *record* of experience and not as its transformation.)

The history begins with Strindberg's first plays in the mood or genre of what we call naturalism. To this moment he is nearly everywhere taught as having composed two distinct and even inimical kinds of plays, two major kinds, that is, in addition to the historical pieces with which he filled out his dramatic *oeuvre*. "Naturalistic" and "symbolic": the two species go on bearing their names in the textbooks like identification plates outside the cages in a zoo, with nothing to connect them as the work of a single imagination except a theory of psychological change or else one of cultural inevitability.

Strindberg, according to the first of these notions, went from the naturalistic to the symbolic in his writing when his psyche had passed through some similar process, something that is usually described (although never explained) as his deepening emotional instability and near madness. What this ignores is that during the last years of his life Strindberg wrote a kind of play that cannot be labeled either naturalistic or symbolic, that even at his maddest he was never less than lucid about his aesthetic procedures, and that in any case the word "symbolic" tells us almost nothing about the nature of his art at any time. The bias here in favor of the "real" over the "symbolic" is, however, striking; even when the later, so-called symbolic plays are preferred to the earlier ones, as by some commentators they are, the choice is usually made on the grounds of a governing notion of art as a form of pathology—interesting, important, but aberrant for all that—and a particular feeling for Strindberg as both a conscious and unconscious explicator of pathology's ways.

A related approach is through history: Strindberg's symbolic plays are seen as reflections of the general cultural breakup and ferment, as icons of the new "dissociated" sensibility and the onrushing movement of all art into abstraction. What both these theories do of course is throw on to psychology or intellectual history the burden of finding out why his art was as it was and why it showed itself as it had to. (pp. 204-07)

When in his late thirties Strindberg wrote his first plays in the atmosphere of what we call naturalism—*The Father* and *Miss Julie*—he had behind him a body of traditional and *acceptable* work, plays on historical themes such as the established Swedish theater was easily able to assimilate. But during the years immediately preceding the writing of *The Father* in 1887, he had done scarcely any writing for the theater at all. The stage, he wrote, was "mere pose, superficiality and calculation," something "reprehensible" when compared to poetry or fiction, for example, fixed in conventions, impermeable to new consciousness, lacking almost all means for the expression of thought. During this period he wrote mostly autobiographical books and engaged heavily in psychological and sociological research, some of it eccentric but most of it of an uncommonly advanced and radical kind. It was a period, too, of marital discord and sexual turmoil of the kind he was to experience even more violently later on.

When he went back again to writing plays, it was evidently with a new morale and ambition. Having engaged in an exploration of his own being during the creation of the autobiographies, he was prepared now for an expansion of the self into drama, an investiture of its events and scenes with the actualities of his own experience and nature. It was something that among his contemporaries Ibsen alone, in his oblique and scarcely visible way (scarcely visible, at any rate, since *Brand*), had done. But to accomplish this, to put dramatic form to the uses of the self, meant having to apply pressure to the reigning notions of characters in drama. Inhabitants of a world outside the specificities and exigencies of personal being, archetypes and stock figures of a protected universe of publicly maintained artifice, bound to the expected gesture and the categorical utterance, dramatic characters stood against personality, against private vision and all visions of private actuality.

In the *Biographia Literaria* Coleridge had written: "There have been men in all ages who have been impelled as by an instinct to purpose their own nature as a problem, and who devote their attempts to its solution." Strindberg was such a man, and we mostly see his works as those kinds of attempts; what we don't so easily see is how the solution to himself lay in his being able to solve the problems of his art, to be able to create it.

In the preface of *Miss Julie* Strindberg composed a brilliant, elaborate justification for the dramatic practices of the play, for its aesthetic choices, and a manifesto for much future change on the stage. At the heart of his argument was the recognition of what "character" had come to mean on the stage and of how his own aesthetic urgencies could no longer be contained within that circumscribed meaning and use. . . . (pp. 208-09)

When we look at *Miss Julie* under the sign and governance of naturalism, it seems to be, like *The Father* before it, a work whose energies and apparatuses derive from life rather than from the stage, from an observed and inhabited world of social and psychic pathology into which acute insights have been made and a series of passionate incidents, a "plot," devised for their incarnation on the stage. A hard, violent, tightly constructed *equivalent* has been found for nature, in this case human nature in its extreme aspects of aggression, envy, fear, hatred, lust and so on. The naturalism of the play thus consists in its fidelity to these emotions as they show themselves in the world and not as abstract counters in a theatrical game, and the drama's revolutionary importance consists in its having gone beyond artifice and stock theatrical representation, in its having *told the truth.*

These are the assumptions on which the play is usually taught, and they are sophisticated assumptions for the most part. To hold them means, to begin with, to be open to the presence in art of emotion of a disturbing kind, not such an easy thing to be, and beyond that to be able to trace a kind of process, the aesthetic action itself, by which such emotion can make itself felt as significant. And yet the notion of equivalence—the idea that art making is the creation of counterparts to what exists already in other shapes—turns this way of contemplating plays and other works into a belief in art as surrogate history, as moral or social or psychological truth in a special form.

It leads finally, however much the pull of a sensuous appreciation holds out against it, to *Miss Julie's* being seen as a psychological or sociological document, or rather as both at once, its subject being changing class relations, the decadence of the Swedish aristocracy and the simultaneous rise of an aggressive, insensitive proletariat, along with the psychosexual manifestations and analogues of such a process. In the same way Chekhov's plays, so mysteriously and deceptively clear, full of arguments that make no points and of a reality that cannot have existed anywhere else, are nevertheless interpreted as "dramatized" accounts of the descent, through ennui, failure of nerve and irresistible

Lithograph of Strindberg by Edvard Munch, 1896.

social disqualification, of the Russian upper classes in the face of an ascending bourgeoisie.

The trouble with such interpretations (if it weren't trouble enough that for even their historical and sociological value to remain intact the most pointed and coerced analogies to our own experience have continually to be set out) is of course that they leave almost no space for the plays as art, which is to say for their existence as new, independent truths, new actualities. *Miss Julie* is indeed taken from "life," from experiences that have been gone through and not simply appropriated from the literary, the *invented,* past, and in its action a paradigm may indeed be traced for the new psychosocial actualities that have been the arena of those experiences. That, at the deepest level, was what naturalism was all about: a wheeling movement back to the sources in history of imagination, which had been feeding off itself, with more and more jejune results, for generations.

And yet that highest value of naturalism, that *truthfulness* (which art has again and again to recover), was something that had to be won aesthetically, achieved within the work and not simply applied there, as though through a transfer from one realm to another. Being so created, such truthfulness is no longer the equivalent or the recasting of data that has been obtained somewhere else, and it is no longer describable as a truth about "nature." Naturalism, like all such denotive terms, ceases to mean anything as soon as it is asked to account not for the starting point or the morale of a work of art but for the art itself.

Miss Julie is a social or psychological document only in so far as experiences have entered into it which it is possible to paraphrase into sociological or psychological information, such periphrasis being the responsibility of its perpetrator and not a true potentiality of the work. It is naturalistic only in so far as it begins with a repudiation of stage typologies and received artistic ideas, and as it wishes to be true, or rather—and most importantly—to *not be untrue* to what has been felt and observed. The poet is the man who sees, Ibsen had said, and Strindberg always had his eyes open. But what he saw was something more complex, fatal and unlocalized, above all more personal and unsystematic, than the changing class structure in Sweden or the armaments of a sexual combat, both of which served his purposes for the play as a kind of pretext, a necessary physical and histrionic ground. His preface tells us in part what he had *noticed:* how men and women have become "split" and "vacillating, a mixture of the old and new," how human souls are "fragments," "torn shreds . . . patched together."

To write a play is a problem in imagination, and just as Ibsen had had to struggle with the technical means available to him, to find means that would still be dramatic in a theater confined to only certain kinds of imaginative arrangements, so Strindberg had to devise a new kind of play, and not merely, as he remarked, "to create a new drama by pouring new ideas into the old forms." The play he needed to create was one that against all recent precedent would not simply incorporate what he had discovered, or *seen,* but would exist as the discovery itself.

The form he was seeking, in other words, was one in which fragmentation, gaps in connections, discontinuity, self-division and vacillation would be the content itself, the true subject of the play. This was to constitute the real revolution, the alteration in experience that now had its aesthetic form, which in turn provided a new experience. Men lived, Strindberg had seen, in a new atmosphere, a changed medium, and against this interrupted and discontinuous air they went on trying to bring about continuity and wholeness by fiat, by *previous* forms of the imagination, in so far as they tried to do the thing through art. Plays had been images of wholeness, whether they were farces, melodramas or "naturalistic" and sober dramas; their very forms were in opposition to the way life was being most crucially known and felt.

At the center of Strindberg's changed dramaturgy for *Miss Julie* is the remarkable compression he achieves in making the events of a single night issue in a tragic denouement. In this era of the theater such compression would have been employed only for the purposes of a swift unfolding of melodramatic or farcical events, as in the rapid, circumstantially linked, "outer-directed" plays of Scribe or Sardou. In *Miss Julie* it is the effect of a substantial cutting away of integumentary material, of all that explanation and exposition that had burdened the "serious" theater and made bourgeois tragedy, where it existed, into something very like a sermon on the logic and coherence of human life, no matter how disastrous the action being portrayed might be. The connections in this play are inward for the most part, unstated, carried by implication in the gestures and utterances of the two main characters, whose conversation is mainly a series of instigations to internal activity rather than an exchange of information, a species of repartee or a means of advancing the "action" of the drama. (pp. 211-15)

The play's action advances, as it were, by fits and starts, by reversals, leaps and regroupings, although the dominant motif and impetus remains the movement toward Miss Julie's final loss of self-esteem and subsequent (implied) suicide. Yet there is no single motive for her action: "Another thing that will offend simple souls is that the motivation of my play is not simple and that life is seen from more than one viewpoint . . . This multiplicity of motive is, I like to think, typical of our times. And if others have done this before me, then I congratulate myself in not being alone in my belief in these 'paradoxes' (the word always used to describe new discoveries)."

Yet Strindberg was almost wholly alone in this "paradox" when it came to the stage. The crucial thing to notice about Julie's suicide is that it is not brought about by anything inexorable in the working of the plot; it is not even, properly speaking, a denouement at all, not an inevitable outcome of a logic of cause and effect. Jean has seduced her, as the drama's central event, but even the fact that the news will become known to everyone is clearly no sufficient reason for killing herself, and Strindberg makes no pretense (a conventional playwright would have made a mainstay out of it) of its being so. Nor is her shame a sufficient reason either, even if such a thing could have been, as it is not, "dramatized," made into an active force, a motive.

Julie has killed herself, in rather the same way that Ibsen's Hedda Gabler did, because she cannot live (we do not die from our deaths, Charles Peguy wrote, but from our whole lives), and she has discovered this truth—or rather the play is the process of such discovery—through what she has been made to feel and think and say. She doesn't hang together, she lacks a principle of coherence, which is what self-esteem ultimately depends on; she is "split" and "vacillating." The "plot" is the story of her self-division, the image of it, not a vehicle in which she travels to her destruction. And the play in its entirety is the very form of such being, the new aesthetic environment for what has up to now been only intuition and feeling.

Julie of course is only half the play, one of its duelists, and in being absorbed in her fate we tend to lose sight of that of her adversary, the servant Jean. Nothing demonstrates better that Strindberg was not engaged in writing history than that the latter character also "loses," is made aware of his own unfreedom, his riven and incoherent self. He prods Julie to suicide but he cannot really live either, being on one level still bound to his subservience, fear and unaccountable guilt—his psychology—and, more deeply, to his invented and therefore sterile persona. They have fought each other to a standstill: "You take all my strength from me, you make me a coward," he tells her at the end.

In the most subtle fashion Strindberg has arranged one of his "dances of death," in which elements and faculties of the soul (for that is what these characters are beneath their provisional and tactical incarnations) move to administer death blows that have been conceived in a fatality known and lived through before this—the death of the consistency and harmony of the self—and that are now fictions, strokes of the imagination which has erected their new environment, so that they may be delivered from chaos, dispersion and the fate of being mere nameless impressions or, worse, data.

This new environment, a realm of existence for characters who had been dislodged from their habitual function in drama as *summary judgments* or as metonymic actions, had been built up by Strindberg at certain public costs and with some incompletions. As he had anticipated, people were disturbed and distracted by the absence of a single point of view, for this, like Ibsen's spiriting away of Nora at the end of *A Doll's House,* was more truly revolutionary than the violent moral vision that the play was in one of its appearances offering. They were disturbed, too, by the drama's elisions and ellipses, the way it moved to invisible promptings and arrived suddenly at its climaxes with only the faintest sound of theatrical machinery being heard.

Yet for the most part, again like Ibsen, Strindberg has remained within the largest conventions of the stage. His characters, although complex, unprogrammatic and uncoerced—souls now and not automata—were still recognizable, unified in their essential presence within the drama, possible to "identify" with, no matter how difficult that might be. His plot, though subterranean and unmechanical, still moved in a linear fashion, and his narrative could be repeated, which is to say paraphrased. Ten years later, after a series of further new-naturalist plays and an interval of silence during which for six years he lived in his "inferno," Strindberg wrote a play, *To Damascus,* that broke wholly through the bounds of drama as they had existed until then. (pp. 215-18)

Richard Gilman, "Ibsen and Strindberg," in his *The Confusion of Realms,* Random House, 1969, pp. 172-218.

V. S. PRITCHETT

(essay date 1973)

[Pritchett is a highly esteemed English novelist, short story writer, essayist, and critic. In the following excerpt from an essay originally published in the *New York Review of Books* in March, 1973, he praises the vitality of Strindberg's fiction.]

Among the Ancient Mariners who arrive to stop guests from getting into the wedding feasts of the European middle classes in [the last half of the nineteenth century], Strindberg had the most frenzied and unrelenting grip. The calms that lie between the bouts of paranoia are themselves dangerous. We can easily "place" the sexual guilt in, say, *The Kreutzer Sonata,* for Tolstoy has immensely wider interests. But except, apparently, in his historical novels (which few people outside Sweden have read), Strindberg's personal obsession rarely ceases. He is the perpetual autobiographer who has at

least three albatrosses—his three wives—hanging from his neck, and it is not long before he is telling us that the birds shot *him.* One of the surprising consolations of his life was that he liked going out into the country for a day's shooting, and it is a striking aspect of his lifelong paranoia in human relationships that he loved what he killed.

Strindberg's strange upbringing as the unwanted son of a successful businessman and a domestic servant, and as the victim of a stepmother; his poverty as a student; his quarrel with the Anabaptists and Pietists of a respectable society, who had him prosecuted for blasphemy because they hadn't the courage to bring him to court for his public campaign for sexual freedom; his flight from literature into experiments with sulphur that drifted into a half-insane obsession with something like alchemy; above all, his instability as a husband or lover—all these torments kept him at white heat. What astonishes is the lasting fertility—in his work—of these ingeniously exploited obsessions. I can think of no other writer with the possible exception of D. H. Lawrence who retold himself in so many impassioned ways.

One thought one had seen his case analyzed and dramatized for good in *The Father* where he is the sea captain, in fact the Ancient Mariner in person, who was driven mad by the cunning calculations of a respectable bourgeois wife—or in *Miss Julie.* Yet, in 1903, much later, the whole personal story is retold as a legend, folk tale or saga for children, in the droll story called **"Jubal the Selfless."** This tale appears to be serene, but its playfulness and resignation are deceptive. The title itself is misleading. Jubal's selflessness is not that of the saints. It is the selflessness of an opera singer who, in old age, realizes that his ego or will has been systematically destroyed by a conspiracy between his father, his mother, and his wife (an actress who uses him in order to supersede him in his career). When he looks into his mirror—this is typical of Strindberg's brilliant theatrical imagination—he sees he is a body without a face. It is only when he finds his lost mother and puts his head in her lap that he recovers his ego—and, needless to say, dies!

The fable is a characteristic experiment with Strindberg's own history and it contains a truth about him as an artist and a person: the history and character are *disponible.* He is a model for the early nineteenth-century concept of Genius: the genius is free and without character but compelled to seek martyrdom. This is a matter for Strindberg's biographers. The work is far more important. Reading any story, particularly in the first section of *Getting Married,* one sees the link between the short story writer and the dramatist. He is a master in the use of overstatement; and one knows at once he is attacking a sententious and cliché-ridden society by the abrupt use of the offhand, natural voice:

They had been married for ten years. Happily?
As happily as circumstances allowed.

(pp. 89-91)

This devilish, grinning abruptness gives his stories a swinging elation. In playwriting and story, the cutting from outside to inside the people has to be drastic and fast. There is no doubt of Strindberg's enormous talent; so that, in these stories, when he moves from one marriage to the next, one finds that as a realist with a message Strindberg is at ease in his mixture of the pugnacious, the pitying and the revealing.

[In the introduction to her 1972 translation of *Getting Married*] Mary Sandbach says that Strindberg's misogyny has been overstressed; that he is as much concerned with the false values of a powerful upper merchant class which produces the unbending man and the cunning, idle female. His attack on "Amazonian" women who wish to have careers or nondomestic interests is rooted in deep private jealousy of them—as in his first marriage—but he is talking of women who are "idle" only because they have a huge supply of working-class girls as servants.

The message in the first series of the stories is that men *and* women must be liberated. In the second series, the excellent little scenes of life in town and country, the delight in the sea journeys and outings which bring out his high quality as an imaginative writer give way to arid, harsher analysis and polemic. But in the first part of one tale, **"The Payment,"** one gets that compelling and shrewd power of social analysis which D. H. Lawrence was to take further. The story is a full statement of Strindberg's case: the stifling of the sexual instincts leads women to use sex as a weapon, so that the men become the slaves while the women grasp occupational power outside the home. It must be read in the context of nineteenth-century life, but it approaches the Lawrence of *St. Mawr*.

Helène, the young woman in the story, is the daughter of a general. In her home she sees the exaggerated artifices of respect paid to women and grows up to regard all males as inferiors. . . . One day she is out riding in the country alone—she in fact hates nature; it makes her "feel small"—and when she gets off her mare the animal bolts off to mate with a stallion before her eyes. She is shocked and disgusted. In the next phase she takes to the out-of-date library in her father's house and becomes infatuated with Mme de Staël's *Corinne*, and this leads her

. . . to live in an aristrocratic dream world in which souls live without bodies. . . . This brainfever, which is called romanticism, is the gospel of the rich.

After the horse-riding episode, the analysis of the mind of a frigid, proud and ambitious girl as it grows degenerates into an essay, but it is nevertheless very thorough and alive. . . . In the end Helène marries in order to trade on her scholarly husband's political reputation and get herself into public life: she is a recognizable high-bourgeois female type. (pp. 91-3)

Strindberg's story fails not because it is false—emancipated groups, classes or individuals are often likely to be tyrannical and reactionary when they get power, as every revolution has shown—but simply because in the later part of this story the artist has been swallowed up by the crude polemical journalist. He has turned from life to the case book. Trust the tale, not the case history.

The original artist in Strindberg survives in his imaginative autobiographies, in the powerful and superbly objective and moving account of his breakdown in *Inferno;* in certain plays, and in the best of these stories. In many of these, a curious festive junketing, a love of good food and drink, a feeling for the small joys of Swedish life, and the spirit of northern carnival, break through. In **"Needs Must,"** the story of a bachelor schoolmaster who runs into a midsummer outing in the country and is eventually converted to a marriage which is very happy—"no part of this story," says Strindberg drily—Strindberg suddenly flings himself into the jollities of the trippers. The schoolmaster listens to the accordion and "it was as if his soul were seated in a swing that had been set in motion by his eyes and ears." It is a story that contains one of his happiest "Bangs":

Then they began to play Forfeits, and they redeemed all their forfeits with kisses, real kisses bang on the mouth, so that he could hear the smack of them. And when the jolly bookkeeper had to "stand in the well" and was made to kiss the big oak tree, he did so with comical lunacy, putting his arm round the thick trunk and patting it as one does a girl when no one is looking, that they all laughed uncontrollably, for they all knew what you do, though no one would have wanted to be caught doing it.

If there is elation in the black Strindberg it springs like music out of his sunny spells. One is always compelled by something vibrant and vital in him. He is a bolting horse whatever direction he takes; and, as Mary Sandbach says, he brought new life to Swedish prose by his natural voice and his lively images. He was, as some have said, a cantankerous Pietist or Anabaptist turned inside out. His lasting contribution was his liberation of the language. He reader feels zest of that at once.

V. S. Pritchett, "August Strindberg: A Bolting Horse," in his *The Myth Makers: Literary Essays*, Random House, 1979, pp. 89-94.

RICHARD GILMAN

(essay date 1974)

[In the following excerpt, Gilman analyzes Strindberg's literary technique, commenting on the author's innovative and intriguing use of dreammaterial and unconscious forces.]

Although he was not to "solve" anything, least of all the enigma of his nature, August Strindberg fiercely proposed himself as dilemma and laboratory, making his life a succession of attempts—blind or lucid, apocalyptic or sly—to get hold of his own truth, which he regarded as extreme but still humanly representative, the way all writers in some fashion must. What he succeeded in doing—no writer has ever done it more violently—was to place his nature on exhibition, objectifying its contradictions, confusions, and ambivalences in the most amazingly varied forms. Yet we have to remember that Strindberg was an artist, a being for whom "nature," his own or any other, is as much an invention as a given fact.

Having multiple souls of his own, Strindberg sought alternately to give reign to one of them at the expense of the others, to fix them all in equilibrium, and to escape from all of them at the same time. Like most imaginative writers, he no doubt did this last thing best in his plays and fiction. (pp. 83-4)

He was immensely complex, and trickier than we think, a site of warring faculties and impulses but no simple victim of them; he was tragedian and clown, insurrectionary and quietist, obscurantist and seer. No playwright ever contained in his private and public experience so much of the raw material we think of as "dramatic" and none was ever so histrionic outside the work.

Few can have spread their intellectual and creative energies as widely. . . . But along with his plays (more than sixty of them) Strindberg wrote novels and short stories; poetry; sociological and literary essays; art criticism; historical works; seven books of autobiography; scientific, quasi-scientific, and alchemical studies; and even treatises in such far-flung areas as Scandinavian folklore and Sinology, besides all this being a brilliant, innovative painter. (pp. 84-5)

He considered *A Doll's House* a "scandalous" work and seems seriously to have believed that Ibsen was the ringleader of a feminist conspiracy, one of whose objectives was his own downfall. There is scarcely a significant play of Strindberg's, to say nothing of most of his other writings, that doesn't bristle at some point with sexual hostility or reveal a strange, mystical bitterness toward women.

Yet there is a whole other side to the matter. We know, for one thing, that Strindberg's anti-feminism was in no sense political, that it was accompanied by a conviction, for which he publicly fought, that women had been the victims of legal injustice; in that sense he was at least as much a believer in women's rights as Ibsen. (p. 86)

The connection of sex and writing, and the derogation of the latter as damaging fantasy, are recurrent motifs in Strindberg, indications, if we don't put too much on them, of how difficult he found it to keep separate what we ordinarily do so matter-of-factly; the carnal and the contemplative, daydreaming and formal imagination. In any case, *A Madman's Defense* had been written in a spirit of what he had convinced himself was scientific objectivity, though it was in fact as "literary" as anything he ever wrote. *The Father* appears to have emerged out of the same state of self-deception, although by now very much less complete.

The Father is enshrined now as Strindberg's first "naturalistic" play and, along with *Miss Julie,* the one he wrote soon after it, as one of the masterpieces of the genre. The vicissitudes of that genre come to our attention at this point. It is greatly significant that almost as soon as Strindberg had been identified as one of the leaders of naturalism he hastened to call himself a *nyanaturalist,* a "new" one. It was true that in their contemporary subjects and colloquial manner, their dealing with problematic immediate life, Strindberg's plays (and novels) of this period resembled those of the movement's acknowledged leaders, Zola and Hauptmann chiefly; but the differences were more important.

While the "old" naturalists were drawing upon sociological data and organizing their works according to principles of fidelity to social reality and repudiation of gross theatrical artifice, Strindberg, with a much more naturally histrionic sensibility and a greater access to unconscious and irrational sources, created plays of psychic and spiritual warfare which went far deeper dramatically, at the same time as they were more truly modern. For these reasons "naturalistic" is an inadequate and misleading term to describe his plays of contemporary life.

Above all, what distinguishes Strindberg's effort and achievement in *The Father*—and in *Miss Julie* even more—from those of the naturalists is the presence in them of self, personal existence. As different as their methods were from one another's, Strindberg and Ibsen share the honor of having brought drama back to individual being, to subjectivity and human specificity, after nearly two centuries during which the stage's uses had been almost wholly for the exhibition of archetypes. In these plays of Strindberg's experience is no longer codified, made into a system of emblematic gestures within a universe of accepted, unexamined meanings, but is allowed to issue forth in singular, unruly unexpectedness.

The Father can be said to be a domestic drama, but only in the sense that it takes place within a home and concerns family relationships. The first of Strindberg's plays of marital and sexual torment (its specific characters and setting will be used fifteen years later for his definitive work of this kind, *The Dance of Death*), it exhibits a ferocious struggle for power between a husband and wife, with their daughter as the prize. (pp. 90-1)

Yet the chasm isn't so neatly identified as being between husbands and wives, or even men and women. The wife's chief tactic is to plant doubt in the husband's mind as to whether or not he is actually the child's father. A theme rising directly from Strindberg's obsession with his own legitimacy, its presence in the play moves past that particularity to become a question—as it must have been for Strindberg all along—of what we might call the legitimacy of existence itself. For *The Father* gives off a sense of terror emanating from something wider and more mysterious than the details of the marital combat, from a region where the absence of any validation of our beings makes itself felt. . . . [The] Captain says of the struggle that "it's like fighting with air, a mock battle with blank cartridges. A real betrayal would have acted as a challenge. But now my thoughts dissolve, my brain grinds emptiness."

The speech reveals Strindberg's deepest anxiety, the metaphysical anguish that lay beneath the clinical facts of his psyche and was the true source of his creative power. For, as is true of the protagonist in this play, it was the opacity of the world, its infliction of a mysterious suffering having to do with the uncertainty of our identities, the divisions in our nature, that so affected him, alternately plunging him into acute depression, inspiring him to demented alchemical raids on existence's secrets, and rousing him to furious megalomanic rebellion. (p. 92)

This is not to say that *The Father* isn't "about" sexual and marital strife; Strindberg is not writing allegory. But it is about these things in much the same way *Hamlet* is about a familial and dynastic situation: these matters constitute the drama's occasion, its means of bodying forth something that will be palpable, actable, capable of being *seen*. Behind the details of event exists the play's true story, which is larger, less explicit, and more permanent than the physical life chosen for its exhibition. The invisible has always to be made known through the visible but is never conterminous with it, and the resulting gap between idea and incarnation is the theater's perennial problem. (pp. 93-4)

Strindberg wrote *Miss Julie* at great speed a year or so after finishing *The Father*. We cannot know the sources of what he had learned about dramaturgy in the interim, or what acts of criticism he might have performed on his previous work, but a leap had taken place. For all its "violent power" and original perception, *The Father* had been structurally and procedurally a rather conventional play, one that adhered fairly closely to theatrical traditions of orderly, accumulating plot and straightforward dialogue. With *Miss Julie* Strindberg's technical means expand, the body of the work becomes more supple and elusive, the dialogue gains a capacity for dangerous surprises, not in terms of its "content" but in the sense of being unpredictably organized, of not following the established theatrical grammar of progressive exchange and interchange. (p. 95)

[Strindberg] embraces the dilemma—the social and sexual antinomies—in a clasp of reconciliation, not factual or "real" but aesthetic. This is to say that while the sexes and the classes may war blindly in actuality and may do so forever, within the work of dramatic art they exist in interpenetration, necessary to each other, illuminating each other, arising as they do from the imagination, whose truths are indivisible.

Therefore, the first thing to see about *Miss Julie* is that the conventional description of it as a duel to the death between "objectively" irreconcilable opponents is false; the play's movement is instead that of a continual confrontation between aspects of the self. . . .

[For] all its accuracy as socio-sexual portraiture, its firm grasp of the observable phenomena of the life of the period, *Miss Julie* is not finally a psychological or sociological document, not a tragedy of contemporary misalliance or inequality. It is not a tale of the wreck of passions and aspirations but an anatomy of them. For all Strindberg's interest in his characters as representatives of determinable social and sexual realms, he is more interested in them as figures in an internal landscape of doubt, ambivalence, insurrection, and submission; his characters confront one another with a despairing sense of otherness, as agents of his own self-division. Such a concern is of a more durable order than that of the clinical gaze upon what is not the self. (pp. 100-01)

Whether they were farces, melodramas, or naturalistic and sober tales, plays for a long time had been images of wholeness, continuity, and coherence, stable little models for the reinforcement of the audience's illusory sense of their own world's fixity. *Miss Julie* establishes a counterworld of discontinuity, fragmentation, and contradiction, not simply as its theme but as its manner. This is the true purpose of the breaking up of the logical patterns of stage dialogue and the introduction into plot of a multiplicity of motives that Strindberg talked about. (p. 101)

Miss Julie was followed over the next three or four years by a number of plays more or less in its vein of *nyanaturalism,* among which perhaps the most durable are *Creditors* and *Playing with Fire.* But then in the early 1890's Strindberg entered on what he called his "inferno" period, a time when he suffered his nearest approach to actual madness. During these three or four years, most of which were spent in Paris, he engaged in attempts to make gold and in other alchemical research, underwent profound if rather cloudy religious and mystical experiences, and wrote only one work of permanent interest—a far-seeing essay in aesthetics called **"On the New Arts, or The Risk in Artistic Production"**—and nothing whatsoever for the theater. Then in 1897 he emerged with his creative faculties seemingly intact, the first product of this restoration being a new play, *To Damascus,* which was as radical in its relation to the body of existing drama as *Miss Julie* had been ten years before. (pp. 103-04)

On the most immediate level *To Damascus* is a product of the religious experiences Strindberg had had during the inferno period, two chief elements of which had been his excited discovery of his countryman Swedenborg and his intense interest in the Catholic Church. The title refers of course to the journey Saul was making when he underwent the mystical visitation that turned him into Paul. (p. 104)

How then can we account for its importance to modern drama? To begin with, the influence it exerted was actually part of a broader one emanating from an entire genre of Strindberg's late writing for the theater. *To Damascus* is the first of his "dream plays," of which the drama with that title, written in the same year as *To Damascus, Part III,* is the best known. From the works of this genre, which include, for all their special intentions, most of the later "chamber plays" and his last work for the stage, *The Great Highway,* arose a model of a new kind of dramatic procedure. It was not entirely without precedent, but it went beyond into a previously unoccupied imaginative zone. (pp. 105-06)

What was Strindberg actually proposing, or rather telling us he had in hand? The dream plays have sometimes been interpreted as plays written *as though they were dreams,* as though they had been authored by the unconscious storytelling mind. Yet what Strindberg says is that his play attempts to "reproduce the disconnected by apparently logical *form* of a dream," a very different matter. It is the logic of disconnection, a logic operating outside wakefulness, beyond ordinary processes of intellection, that is decisive here.

It was an internal principle of dramatic construction that had almost no direct antecedents in the theater, although models for it existed in recent poetry and certain types of new fiction. (p. 107)

The structures of the dream plays, while reasonable—logical—in themselves, were therefore not so by the criteria of accepted dramaturgy. Nothing was brought down with a louder crash than the Aristotelian unities of time and place, which had been broken before but not in such a thoroughgoing way. For time and space have disappeared as stable entities. (p. 108)

Along with this dreamlike procedure of having one place give way to another without narrative preparation, Strindberg goes immeasurably further in breaking up the unity and stability of characters than he had done in *Miss Julie.* There his characters had been internally divided, but now they separate out into other characters: the Lady has several guises, none of them adopted as a matter of narrative tactics—she is not impersonating someone else—but in the manner of that dream mechanism whereby a single being is afforded diverse shapes. (pp. 108-09)

Strindberg demonstrated how to borrow the methods of dreaming while keeping authority over their uses. The effect was to release new parts of the self into availability for artistic acts. In one of those apparent cultural coincidences that are really signs of a change in the universal air, Strindberg was finishing *To Damascus* and writing *A Dream Play* at the same time that Sigmund Freud was working on *The Interpretation of Dreams.* Freud always considered that book the keystone of psychoanalytic theory, since, as he said, to possess the secrets of dreaming was to be on "the royal road to the unconscious." And in the unconscious Freud first explored through the investigation of his own dreams he discovered the same things Strindberg had: that there are no "secrets" there, no "incongruities," "no scruples," and no negatives-everything is possible.

The access Strindberg's dramaturgy gave to the unconscious meant that irrational material could now be presented throughout a play, as part of its very texture, instead of being confined as it had been in the past to *irrational characters*—madmen, say, or persons temporarily crazed by passion. Above all, it could be presented without comment or apology; it would not have to undergo a later "correction" into rationality through denouements, happy or not, which emphasized conscious, normative values. It isn't hard to see how from this accession rose the possibility of the surreal and the absurd in the drama of our era. (p. 110)

Many years later, after there was no one left who could testify to what his presence had meant and he had been frozen into one of the narrow legends of modern literature, a countryman, the novelist Pär Lagerkvist, spoke of what had been done to him: "It has been Strindberg's fate, and probably will continue to be for a long time yet, that he is valued first and foremost for his bad qualities, both as a writer and a man. All of his repellent and morbid features were seized upon." Perhaps so; but there is a counterpressure to that fact, which comes from the continuing presence in living imaginations of the example he gave of creative unrestraint, visionary daring. (p. 115)

Richard Gilman, "Strindberg," in his *The Making of Modern Drama: A Study of Buchner, Ibsen, Strindberg, Chekhov, Pirandello, Brecht, Beckett, Handke,* Farrar, Straus, 1974, pp. 83-115.

SOURCES FOR FURTHER STUDY

Bradbrook, Muriel. "In Dreams Begin Responsibilities." In her *Women and Literature, 1779-1982: The Collected Papers of Muriel Bradbrook, Volume 2,* pp. 69-109. Totowa, N.J.: Barnes and Noble, 1982.

Examines Strindberg's dramatic treatment of women and marriage.

Brandell, Gunnar. *Strindberg in Inferno.* Translated by Barry Jacobs. Cambridge: Harvard University Press, 1974, 336 p.

Analysis of Strindberg's "Inferno crisis." Brandell discusses the causes of Strindberg's mental breakdown, the crisis itself, and the literary style that emerged as a result.

Carlson, Harry G. *Strindberg and the Poetry of Myth.* Berkeley: University of California Press, 1982, 240 p.

Identifies elements of traditional mythologies in Strindberg's major works.

Jarvi, Raymond. "Strindberg's *The Ghost Sonata* and Sonata Form." *Mosaic* V, No. 4 (Summer 1972): 69-84.

Analysis of the formal structure of *The Ghost Sonata.*

O'Neill, Eugene. "Strindberg and Our Theater." In *O'Neill and His Plays: Four Decades of Criticism,* edited by Oscar Cargill and others, pp. 108-09. New York: New York University Press, 1961.

Describes Strindberg as a seminal force in modern drama.

Valency, Maurice. "Strindberg." In his *The Flower and the Castle,* pp. 238-361. New York: Macmillan, 1961.

Thorough discussion of Strindberg's work and his influence on modern drama.

Jonathan Swift

1667-1745

(Also wrote under pseudonyms Isaac Bickerstaff and M. B. Drapier) Anglo-Irish satirist, essayist, poet, historian, and autobiographer.

INTRODUCTION

Swift is the foremost prose satirist in the English language and one of the greatest masters of that form in world literature. Throughout his career he utilized satire to examine both the achievements and shortcomings of individuals and society. His greatest satire, *Gulliver's Travels* (1726), is considered one of the most important works in the history of world literature. Alternately described as an attack on humanity and a clear-eyed assessment of human strengths and weaknesses, it is a complex study of human nature and of the moral, philosophical, political, and scientific thought of Swift's time that has resisted any definitive explication for nearly three centuries. In addition to his work as a satirist, Swift was also an accomplished minor poet, a master of political journalism, a prominent political figure, and one of the most distinguished leaders of the Anglican church in Ireland. For these reasons he is considered one of the representative men of his age, as well as one of the most important figures in the history of English literature.

Swift's parents settled in Ireland after the Restoration of King Charles II in 1660. The death of his father shortly before Swift's birth left Swift and his mother and sister dependent upon his father's family for support. Soon after her son was born Swift's mother returned to England, leaving him in the care of a nurse for three years, the first of several separations during Swift's childhood. Though emotionally insecure, the young Swift was financially well-provided for and well-educated in the best schools in Ireland. He was enrolled at Trinity College, Dublin, when, in 1689, a wave of civil unrest swept Ireland in the wake of the abdication of the Catholic King James II. Many Anglo-Irish fled Ireland at this time for the safety of England, and Swift was among them. In England he secured a position as secretary to Sir William Temple, a scholar and former member of Parliament who was engaged in writing his memoirs. Except for two trips to Ireland, Swift remained in Temple's employ and lived at his home, Moor Park, until Temple's death in 1699. During this period Swift came to intellectual maturity: he read widely, was introduced to many prominent individuals in Temple's circle, and determined upon a career in the Anglican church, an ambition thwarted by Temple's inaction in obtaining Swift a promised preferment in the church. Around this time he also met Esther Johnson, the stepdaughter of Temple's steward. "Stella," as Swift nicknamed her, became an intimate, lifelong friend and confidante to Swift. Despite rumors to the contrary, their relationship remained Platonic; Swift's correspondance with her was later collected in *The Journal to Stella* (1963).

Toward the end of this period, Swift wrote his first great satires, *A Tale of a Tub* and *The Battle of the Books,* both of which were completed by 1699 but were not published until 1704 under the title *A Tale of a Tub, Written for the Universal Improvement of Mankind, to which is Added an Account of a Battel between the Antient and Modern Books in St. James's Library.* Both works reflected his burgeoning religious, literary, and political beliefs, and both were concerned with highly topical matters. Within the framework of a history of the Christian church, *A Tale* satirized contemporary literary and scholarly pedants as well as the dissenters and Roman Catholics who opposed the Anglican church, an institution to whose defense Swift would devote a great deal of energy during his career. He firmly believed in the primacy of the Anglican church, and this, coupled with his office in the church, in part explains his zeal; however, his position was also grounded in his political beliefs. The Protestant control of England under Oliver Cromwell had resulted in an attempt by the government to impose the stringent, unpopular beliefs of Puritanism on the English populace. Swift detested such tyranny and sought throughout his career to prevent it through his writings. *The Battle of the Books* was written in defense of Temple. A controversial debate was being waged over the respective merits of ancient versus modern learning, with Temple supporting the position that the literature of the Greek and Roman civilizations was far superior to any modern creations. Swift addressed Temple's detractors with an allegorical satire that depicted the victory of those who supported the ancient texts. Although inspired by topical controversies, both *A Tale* and *The Battle* are brilliant satires with many universal implications regarding the nature and follies of aesthetics, religious belief, scholasticism, and education.

When Temple died in 1699 Swift was left without position or prospects. He returned to Ireland, where he occupied a series of church posts from 1699 to 1710. During this period he wrote much occasional prose and poetry, as well as an increasing number of satiric political essays on behalf of the ruling Whig party, whose policies limiting the power of the crown and increasing that of Parliament, as well as restricting Roman Catholic from political office, Swift staunchly endorsed. In these pamphlets Swift developed the device that marked much of his later satire: using a literary persona to express ironically absurd opinions. His political writing was extremely popular, but Swift began to harbor doubts about the Whigs, who were becoming increasingly tolerant of minority religious groups. When the Whig administration fell in 1709, Swift shifted his support to the Tory government, which, while supporting a strong crown unlike the Whigs, adamantly supported the Anglican Church. For the next five years, Swift served as the chief Tory political writer, editing the journal *The Examiner* and composing political pamphlets, poetry, and prose. Swift's change of party has led some critics to characterize him as a cynical opportunist, but others contend that his conversion reflected more of a change in the parties' philosophies than in Swift's own views; always one to place the interests of the church above party affiliation, he chose to serve the party that promoted those interests.

With the death of Queen Anne in 1714 and the accession of George I, the Tory party lost their power to the Whigs, and Swift returned to Ireland in 1714 to assume his role as dean of St. Patrick's Cathedral. Except for brief visits to London, Swift spent the rest of his life in Ireland. For the first five years after his return he refrained from political controversy; by 1720, however, he began to become politically active in the affairs of Ireland, producing a series of pamphlets attacking the economic dependence of Ireland upon England and criticizing the policies of Prime Minister Robert Walpole. The most important of Swift's Irish pamphlets are *The Drapier's Letters* and *A Modest Proposal. The Drapier's Letters,* a 1724 series of pamphlets written under the pseudonym of M. B. Drapier, a fictitious Irish tradesman, protested the attempt by the English government to supply Ireland with copper coins rather than gold or silver. The public outcry inspired by Swift's propaganda campaign forced Walpole to alter his decision. *The Drapier's Letters* are also historically important in that they united the Irish gentry in a common cause and made Swift a political hero and spokesman for Ireland. *A Modest Proposal* (1729) is a bitter satire inspired by the plight of the masses of impoverished Irish. In it, Swift ironically suggests that a growing population and widespread starvation could both be alleviated if the poor began eating their children. Considered one of the greatest satirical essays in world literature, Swift's piece attacks complacency in the face of misery and the coldly rational schemes of social planners who fail to perceive the pain resulting from their action or inaction.

Swift's greatest work of this period was *Gulliver's Travels* (published as *Travels into Several Remote Nations of the World, in Four Parts; by Lemuel Gulliver*), which depicts one man's journeys to several strange and unusual lands. Written over a period of several years, some scholars believe that the *Travels* had its origins during Swift's years as a Tory polemicist when he was part of a group of prominent Tory writers known as the Scriblerus Club. The group, which included Alexander Pope, John Gay, and John Arbuthnot, among others, collaborated on several satires, including *The Scriblerus Papers.* They also planned a satire called *The Memoirs of Martinus Scriblerus* which was to include several imaginary voyages. Many believe that *Gulliver's Travels* was inspired by this work. Although *Gulliver* was published anonymously, Swift's authorship was widely suspected. The book was an immediate success.

Swift remained active throughout the 1720s and 1730s as a political commentator, satirist, and, more importantly, as a poet. During this period he wrote much of his best poetry, including *Verses on the Death of Dr. Swift*. The last years of Swift's life, from approximately 1736 until his death, have been the subject of much legend and misinformation. During the eighteenth and nineteenth centuries, critics and biographers mistakenly concluded that Swift was insane during the years before his death. Throughout his life he had suffered from what is today known as Ménière's Syndrome, or labyrinthine vertigo, a disease of the inner ear that causes attacks of nausea, dizziness, temporary deafness, and extreme pain. He also suffered a paralytic stroke in 1740 that caused aphasia and loss of memory. Eventually, in 1742, he was declared incapable of caring for himself and placed in the custody of guardians. Biographers misconstrued the symptoms of conditions as indicative of insanity, an error which has been thoroughly discredited by modern biographers. Swift died in 1745 and was buried beside Esther Johnson in St. Patrick's Cathedral.

The philosophy underlying Swift's great satire stood in radical contrast to the prevailing intellectual opinion of his time. Beginning with the philosophical movement known as the Enlightenment, eighteenth-century thinkers espoused an increasing faith in the rationality of human beings and in the capacity of reason to improve and even perfect the human condition. Swift appears to have categorically rejected these views; educated in the seventeenth century, he held to that period's emphasis on the imperfection of human beings resulting from the Fall of Man. Although Swift believed humans capable of reason, he believed that they rarely exercised this capacity. Thus, while he endorsed some measures of social reform, he argued for their implementation through means which acknowledged a need to control human corruptibility. Swift's departure from the prevailing thought of his times earned him censure in his lifetime and for centuries afterwards by critics who accused him of misanthropy and portrayed him as a bitter individual who hated humanity and refused to acknowledge its positive qualities. However, his defenders, voicing the argument that has become prevalent in twentieth-century Swift criticism, argued that his acerbic prose merely expressed his pain at the disparity between the world as it was and the world as it should have been. By portraying people in shocking extremes of baseness and monstrosity, they argue, he argued for the better world implied in the works by its absence. For his part, Swift defended his view of humankind by writing: "I have ever hated all Nations, professions, and Communityes and all my love is toward individuals . . . I hate and detest that animal called man, although I hartily love John, Peter, Thomas and so forth."

By far the most discussed work by Swift has always been *Gulliver's Travels*: each of the four voyages has yielded a number of critical interpretations. The first voyage, for example, has been interpreted as an allegorical satire on the political events of the early eighteenth century, a commentary on the moral state of England, a general satire on the pettiness of human desires for wealth and power, and a depiction of the effects of unwarranted pride and self-aggrandizement. Throughout the voyages he attacked the baseness of human beings even as he suggested their greatest virtues; he attacked the folly of human learning and political systems as he implied the proper functions of art, science, and government. But most crucial to an understanding of *Gulliver's Travels* is an understanding of the fourth voyage, the voyage to the land of the Houyhnhnms (pronounced Hwin-ims), whose interpretation critic Merrel D. Clubb termed "the central problem of Swift criticism." Much of the controversy surrounds three possible interpretations of the Houyhnhnms, a species of intelligent horses, and the Yahoos, a race of ignorant, ape-like humans. One school of thought has traditionally viewed the Yahoos as the satiric representations of debased humanity, while discussing the Houyhnhnms as representatives of Swift's ideals of rationality and order. The two beings are thus interpreted as symbols of the dual nature of humanity, with Gulliver's misanthropy based on his perception of the flaws of human nature and the failure of humanity to develop its potential for reason, harmony, and order. Another position finds both the Houyhnhnms and Yahoos to be the subjects of satire, with the Yahoos representing the physical baseness of humans and the Houyhnhnms representing the fatuousness of utopian attempts to achieve a rationally ordered existence. Since the 1950s, however, a variety of critics have attributed a greater complexity of purpose to the fourth voyage. The Houyhnhnms and Yahoos are now most often discussed as both satiric objects and representatives of the duality of human nature. In particular, the Houyhnhnms are interpreted as symbols and examples for a human order that, although unattainable, deserves to remain an ideal, while the Yahoos are found to be representatives of the depths of humanity's potential fall if that ideal is abandoned.

The nature of Gulliver is another much debated element of the *Travels.* Early critics generally viewed him as the mouthpiece of Swift and accepted all that he said as the beliefs of the author. Modern critics, however, recognize him as a distinct character whom Swift uses to subtler purposes. The most significant contemporary debate is concerned with Swift's intentions regarding the creation of Gulliver—whether he is meant to be a consistently realized character, a reliable narrator, or a satiric object whose opinions are the object of Swift's ridicule. This debate over the nature of Gulliver is important because critics seek to determine whether Gulliver is intended to be a man with definite character traits who undergoes a transformation, or an allegorical representative of humanity. In general, Gulli-

ver is now considered a flexible persona manipulated by Swift to present a diversity of views or satirical situations and to indicate the complexity, and ultimate indefinability, of human nature.

The massive amount of contemporary criticism devoted to Swift reflects his continued importance; his work, particularly *Gulliver's Travels,* demonstrates the multiplicity of readings possible in a complex work of art. What has come to be of paramount importance is not any statement of ultimate meaning in the work of Swift, but its potential for raising questions in the mind of the contemporary reader. As Irvin Ehrenpreis has noted: "The problem of a moralist like Swift is less to redefine man in terms of new ideals than to knock down the fences around an accepted definition, compelling men both to measure themselves by this and to reexamine it."

(For further information about Swift's life and works, see *Dictionary of Literary Biography,* Vols. 39, 95, 101; *Literature Criticism from 1400 to 1800,* Vol. 1; and *Something about the Author,* Vol. 19.)

CRITICAL COMMENTARY

JONATHAN SWIFT

(letter date 1725)

[In the following two letters to British poet Alexander Pope, Swift epitomizes his opinions of mankind. These letters contain some of Swift's best-known comments on his own writing.]

I have employd my time (besides ditching) in finishing correcting, amending, and Transcribing my Travells, in four parts Compleat newly Augmented, and intended for the press when the world shall deserve them, or rather when a Printer shall be found brave enough to venture his Eares, I like your Schemes of our meeting after Distresses and dispertions but the chief end I propose to my self in all my labors is to vex the world rather then divert it, and if I could compass that designe without hurting my own person or Fortune I would be the most Indefatigable writer you have ever seen without reading. . . . I have ever hated all Nations professions and Communityes and all my love is towards individuals for instance I hate the tribe of Lawyers, but I love Councellor such a one, Judge such a one for so with Physicians (I will not Speak of my own Trade) Soldiers, English, Scotch, French; and the rest but principally I hate and detest that animal called man, although I hartily love John, Peter, Thomas and so forth.

This is the system upon which I have governed my self many years (but do not tell) and so I shall go on till I have done with them I have got Materials Towards a Treatis proving the falsity of that Definition *animal rationale* ["rational animal"]; and to show it should be only *rationis capax* ["capable of reason"]. Upon this great foundation of Misanthropy (though not Timons manner) The whole building of my Travells is erected: And I never will have peace of mind till all honest men are of my Opinion: by Consequence you are to embrace it immediately and procure that all who deserve my Esteem may do so too. The matter is so clear that it will admit little dispute. (pp. 102-03)

Drown the World, I am not content with despising it, but I would anger it if I could with safety. I wish there were an Hospital built for it's despisers, where one might act with safety and it need not be a large Building, only I would have it well endowed. . . . I desire you and all my Friends will take a special care that my Affection to the World may not be imputed to my Age, for I have Credible witnesses ready to depose that it hath never varyed from the Twenty First to the f—ty eighth year of my Life, (pray fill that Blank Charitably) I tell you after all that I do not hate Mankind, it is vous autres ["you others"] who hate them because you would have them reasonable Animals, and are Angry

Principal Works

*A Tale of a Tub, Written for the Universal Improvement of Mankind, to Which is Added an Account of a Battel between the Antient and Modern Books in St. James's Library (satire) 1704

Predictions for the Year 1708, Wherein the Month and Day of the Month Are Set Down, the Persons Named, and the Great Actions and Events of Next Year Particularly Related, as They Will Come to Pass. Written to Prevent the People of England from Being Further Impos'd on by Vulgar Almanack-Makers [as Isaac Bickerstaff] (satire) 1708

A Proposal for the Universal Use of Irish Manufacture, in Cloaths and Furniture of Houses etc., Utterly Rejecting and Renouncing Every Thing Wearable that Comes from England (essay) 1720

†A Letter to the Shop-Keepers, Tradesmen, Farmers, and Common People of Ireland, Concerning the Brass Half-Pence Coined by Mr. Woods, with a Design to Have Them Pass in This Kingdom [as M. B. Drapier] (essay) 1724

†A Letter to Mr. Harding the Printer, Upon Occasion of a Paragraph in His Newspaper of August 1st Relating to Mr. Wood's Half-Pence [as M. B. Drapier] (essay) 1724

†Some Observations upon a Paper Call'd The Report of the Committee of the Most Honourable the Privy-Council in England, Relating to Wood's Half-Pence [as M. B. Drapier] (essay) 1724

†A Letter to the Whole People of Ireland [as M. B. Drapier] (essay) 1724

†A Letter to the Right Honourable the Lord Viscount Molesworth [as M. B. Drapier] (essay) 1724

Travels into Several Remote Nations of the World, in Four Parts; By Lemuel Gulliver, First a Surgeon, and then a Captain of Several Ships (satire) 1726

A Modest Proposal for Preventing the Children of the Poor People from Being a Burthen to Their Parents, or the Country, and for Making Them Beneficial to the Publick (essay) 1729

The Lady's Dressing Room; To Which is Added a Poem on Cutting Down the Old Thorn at Market Hill (poetry) 1732

The Life and Genuine Character of Doctor Swift (poetry) 1733

Verses on the Death of Dr. Swift (poetry) 1739

Prose Works. 14 vols. (essays, satires, history, sermons, and autobiography) 1939-68

‡The Correspondence of Swift. 5 vols. (letters) 1963-65

The Complete Poems (poetry) 1983

*This work includes the satire A Discourse Concerning the Mechanical Operation of the Spirit.

†These works are collectively referred to as The Drapier's Letters.

‡This work includes The Journal to Stella.

---

for being disappointed. I have always rejected that Definition and made another of my own. (pp. 117-18)

Jonathan Swift, in letters to Alexander Pope on September 29, 1725 and November 26, 1725, in his *The Correspondence of Jonathan Swift: 1724-1731, Vol. III*, edited by Harold Williams, Oxford at the Clarendon Press, 1963, pp. 102-05, 116-19.

WILLIAM HAZLITT
(lecture date 1818)

[A dominant British critic of the first half of the nineteenth century, Hazlitt wrote what was later termed "impressionist" criticism, a deeply personal and subjective style that departed from eighteenth-century attempts at setting objective standards for criticism. In the following excerpt from an 1818 lecture, he praises Swift's sense of irony and derides those who would charge Swift with misanthropy.]

Swift's reputation as a poet has been in a manner obscured by the greater splendour, by the natural force and inventive genius of his prose writings; but if he had never written either the *Tale of a Tub* or *Gulliver's Travels*, his name merely as a poet would have come down to us, and have gone down to posterity with well-earned honours. His **"Imitations of Horace,"** and still more his [**"Verses on the Death of Dr. Swift"**], place him in the first rank of agreeable moralists in verse. There is not only a dry humour, an exquisite tone of irony, in these productions of his pen; but there is a touching, unpretending pathos, mixed up with the most whimsical and eccentric strokes of pleasantry and satire. His **"Description of the Morning"** in London, and [**"Description] of a City Shower,"** which were first published in the *Tatler,* are among the most delightful of the contents of that very delightful work. Swift shone as one of the most sensible of the poets; he is also distinguished as one of the most nonsensical of them. No man has written so many lackadaisical, slipshod, tedious, trifling, foolish, fantastical verses as he, which are so little an imputation on the wisdom of the writer; and which, in fact, only show his readiness to oblige others, and to forget himself. He has gone so far as to invent a new stanza of fourteen and sixteen syllable lines for Mary the cookmaid to vent her budget of nothings, and for Mrs. Harris to gossip with the deaf old housekeeper. Oh, when shall we have such another Rector of Laracor!—The *Tale of a Tub* is one of the most masterly compositions in the language, whether for thought, wit, or style. It is so capital and undeniable a proof of the author's talents, that Dr. Johnson, who did not like Swift, would not allow that he wrote it. . . . It is a pity the Doctor did not find out some graver author, for whom he felt a critical kindness, on whom to father this splendid but unacknowledged production. Dr. Johnson could not deny that *Gulliver's Travels* were his; he therefore disputed their merits, and said that after the first idea of them was conceived, they were easy to execute; all the rest followed mechanically. I do not know how that may be; but the mechanism employed is something very different from any that the author of *Rasselas* was in the habit of bringing to bear on such occasions. There is nothing more futile, as well as invidious, than this mode of criticizing a work of original genius. Its greatest merit is supposed to be in the invention; and you say, very wisely, that it is not *in the execution.* You might as well take away the merit of the invention of the telescope, by saying that, after its uses were explained and understood, any ordinary eyesight could look through it. Whether the excellence of *Gulliver's Travels* is in the conception or the execution, is of little consequence; the power is somewhere, and it is a power that has moved the world. The power is not that of big words and vaunting commonplaces. Swift left these to those who wanted them; and has done what his acuteness and intensity of mind alone could enable any one to conceive or to perform. His object was to strip empty pride and grandeur of the imposing air which external circumstances throw around them; and for this purpose he has cheated the imagination of the illusions which the prejudices of sense and of the world put upon it, by reducing everything to the abstract predicament of size. He enlarges or diminishes the scale, as he wishes to show the insignificance or the grossness of our overweening self-love. That he has done this with mathematical precision, with complete presence of mind and perfect keeping, in a manner that comes equally home to the understanding of the man and of the child, does not take away from the merit of the work or the genius of the author. He has taken a new view of human nature, such as a being of a higher sphere might take of it; he has torn the scales from off his moral vision; he has tried an experiment upon human life, and sifted its pretensions from the alloy of circumstances; he has measured it with a rule, has weighed it in a balance, and found it, for the most part, wanting and worthless—in substance and in show. Nothing solid, nothing valuable is left in his system but virtue and wisdom. What a libel is this upon mankind! What a convincing proof of misanthropy! What pre-sumption and what *malice prepense,* to show men what they are, and to teach them what they ought to be! What a mortifying stroke aimed at national glory, is that unlucky incident of Gulliver's wading across the channel and carrying off the whole fleet of Blefuscu! After that, we have only to consider which of the contending parties was in the right. What a shock to personal vanity is given in the account of Gulliver's name Glumdalclitch! Still, notwithstanding the disparagement to her personal charms, her good nature remains the same amiable quality as before. I cannot see the harm, the misanthropy, the immoral and degrading tendency of this. The moral lesson is as fine as the intellectual exhibition is amusing. It is an attempt to tear off the mask of imposture from the world; and nothing but imposture has a right to complain of it. It is, indeed, the way with our quacks in morality to preach up the dignity of human nature, to pamper pride and hypocrisy with the idle mockeries of the virtues they pretend to, and which they have not: but it was not Swift's way to cant morality, or anything else; nor did his genius prompt him to write unmeaning panegyrics on mankind!

I do not, therefore, agree with the estimate of Swift's moral or intellectual character, given by an eminent critic, who does not seem to have forgotten the party politics of Swift. I do not carry my political resentments so far back: I can at this time of day forgive Swift for having been a Tory. I feel little disturbance (whatever I might think of them) at his political sentiments, which died with him, considering how much else he has left behind him of a more solid and imperishable nature! If he had, indeed, (like some others) merely left behind him the lasting infamy of a destroyer of his country, or the shining example of an apostate from liberty, I might have thought the case altered.

The determination with which Swift persisted in a preconcerted theory, savoured of the morbid affection of which he died. There is nothing more likely to drive a man mad, than the being unable to get rid of the idea of the distinction between right and wrong, and an obstinate, constitutional preference of the true to the agreeable. Swift was not a Frenchman. In this respect he differed from Rabelais and Voltaire. They have been accounted the three greatest wits in modern times; but their wit was of a peculiar kind in each. They are little beholden to each other; there is some resemblance between Lord Peter in the *Tale of a Tub,* and Rabelais's Friar John; but in general they are all three authors of a substantive character in themselves. Swift's wit (particularly in his chief prose works) was serious, saturnine, and practical; Rabelais's was fantastical and joyous; Voltaire's was light, sportive, and verbal. Swift's wit was the wit of sense; Rabelais's, the wit of nonsense; Voltaire's, of indifference to both. The ludicrous in Swift arises out of his keen sense of impropriety, his soreness and impatience of the least absurdity. He separates, with a severe and caustic air, truth from falsehood, folly from wisdom, 'shows vice her own image, scorn her own feature'; and it is the force, the precision, and the honest abruptness with which the separation is made, that excites our surprise, our admiration, and laughter. He sets a mark of reprobation on that which offends good sense and good manners, which cannot be mistaken, and which holds it up to our ridicule and contempt ever after. . . . His better genius was his spleen. It was the biting acrimony of his temper that sharpened his other faculties. The truth of his perceptions produced the pointed coruscations of his wit; his playful irony was the result of inward bitterness of thought; his imagination was the product of the literal, dry, incorrigible tenaciousness of his understanding. He endeavoured to escape from the persecution of realities into the regions of fancy, and invented his Lilliputians and Brobdingnagians, Yahoos, and Houynhyms, as a diversion to the more painful knowledge of the world around him! *they* only made him laugh, while men and women made him angry. His feverish impatience made him view the infirmities of that great baby the world, with the same scrutinizing glance and jealous irritability that a parent regards the failings of its offspring; but, as Rousseau has well observed, parents have not on this account been supposed to have more affection for other people's children than their own. In other respects, and except from the sparkling effervescence of his gall, Swift's brain was as 'dry as the remainder biscuit after a voyage'. He hated absurdity. . . . (pp. 168-74)

William Hazlitt, "On Swift, Young, Gray, Collins, Etc.," in his *Lectures on the English Poets*, 1818. Reprint by Oxford University Press, London, 1924, pp. 160-89.

JOHN BROOKS MOORE

(essay date 1928)

[In the following excerpt, Moore takes exception with the view that Swift's characters are mere extensions of Swift's own personality, arguing that Lemuel Gulliver is a complex and distinct character in his own right.]

That Gulliver is not Swift himself in either intellect or disposition is abundantly certain. The Swift of 1726-27 (the period of *Gulliver's Travels*) was in his intellectual perceptions almost as keen as any recorded human being. With Gulliver, it is a very different matter: a good sound fellow enough, but slow to seize upon even an obvious new idea; far from brilliant. And Gulliver's disposition is equally remote from Swift's. Gulliver

possesses an easy good nature. He is ready of his sympathy and affection. He has a just sense of his own mediocrity (at least to begin with, he has!) and appears almost humbly unobtrusive in his ways. But in Gulliver lies that most precious capacity for acquiring knowledge: slowly, surely, he learns. Swift seems, on the other hand, to be afire with impatience that comes from too clear insight. While he was undoubtedly sympathetic, his sympathy was frequently obscured to the world by his so-called arrogance. (Can a man so genuinely superior as Swift was to his associates, in many ways, be justly called arrogant for realizing his superiority?) Swift was capable of devotion to individuals such as we look for in vain in Gulliver. Swift was profoundly humorous, while Gulliver, though he may be the cause that wit sparkles in other men, is hardly witty in himself. Scorn and rage at iniquity constitute the very temper of Swift. In Gulliver, these things are induced gradually, against the grain. Only that passion in readers for assuming the autobiographic can account for any confusion of Gulliver with Swift.

No more is Gulliver "the allegorical representative of man." He is not everyman, by any means, but as much an individual, almost, as Parson Adams or Squire Western (figures, both of them, somewhat typical and somewhat special). In certain ways, he surpasses the average man and, in certain other ways, he is peculiar or just different from the average without being superior or inferior. He is, to be sure, an example of a man getting knowledge or wisdom. But Swift is able for his purposes to create a human being much more perfectly appropriate and more real than a mere average or representative figure. So quietly natural is the process of creation in Swift's hands that it has scarcely been appreciated as a marvel of artistry. Gulliver is an entirely credible and probable person at the same time that he is precisely the person to enforce Swift's demonstration. Swift, obviously enough, desires to communicate his own thoughts and passions regarding human beings to the readers of his book. That is, in a general sense, one of the reasons for all efforts of an artistic sort. To infect others with his own ardent misanthropy, Swift could not have chosen a more effective human instrument than Lemuel Gulliver, it would seem.

Gulliver's individual traits stand forth sufficiently for anyone who seeks, in the two earlier voyages—that to Lilliput and that to Brobdingnag. (pp. 469-70)

Among the Lilliputians, Gulliver's character, both intellectual and moral, is thrown into relief. His natural inclinations emerge in spite of the astonishing circumstances, partly because of them. As always (or nearly always) he shows himself resourceful in ordinary and extraordinary physical emergencies. His bellowing and struggling very soon subside into meek-enough compliance and trust. "I thought it the most prudent method to lie still. . . . " Gulliver soon finds ways of getting along tolerably, be the people big, little, or equine. He is adaptable in the restricted sense of being able to endure all sorts of uncouth occurrences equally. This does not imply much plasticity on his part. Intellectually he is deliberate if not actually slow; for he fails to realize the implications for mankind in the absurdities of Lilliputian politics, wars, religion, education. It is only at the close of the conversations with the King of Brobdingnag that he gets an inkling of the significance to himself, to any Englishman, to any human being, of these adventures among the pygmies and the giants. He comes near to being a stolid Englishman. Not only is he intellectually deliberate; he is unsophisticated in many ways and capable only with considerable pains of sophistication. The whole book (all four voyages) might, not altogether inappropriately, be entitled *The Sophistication of Lemuel Gulliver.*

He is, congruously enough, decidedly good natured. He likes people—from six-inchers to sixty-footers. The Lilliputians who amused themselves by wantonly discharging arrows at Gulliver were treated by him with great gentleness. He is compact of various loyalties. Who is more enthusiastic about his "dear native land" than Gulliver? In his protracted account of England, her people and institutions, to the King of Brobdingnag, Gulliver is positively chauvinistic. . . . And for all the harsh criticism leveled at English institutions by the attentive King, Gulliver never admits that his own faith in her is at all seriously shaken. He is intellectually and temperamentally disinclined to alter his outlook upon human affairs and human beings; but we may probably assume that such downright condemnation of those beings and affairs as issued from the admired monarch's lips found subconscious lodgment in Gulliver's heart or brain. So his acquisition of wisdom may be supposed to have begun definitely in Brobdingnag; whereas his mature intellectual and temperamental stiffness had been proof against, what seems to most readers, the rather obvious exposure of the falseness of human affairs and human beings in Lilliput. (pp. 471-73)

Perhaps the honest optimism and good nature of the man emerge more distinctly in his relations with individuals in Lilliput and Brobdingnag. It is not in him to be mean or resentful either to creatures one-twelfth his size or to those twelve times his size. (p. 473)

Gulliver, our given quantity, turns out then, briefly, to be not an extraordinarily keen man in any way, not blessed (or cursed) with flashing and piercing insight. At the same time he is extraordinarily (though far from uniquely) endowed with a zest for experience, a curiosity to see and to know. He is, here, well above the average. In temperament, Gulliver is, again, not a mere typical man but a noticeably kindly, friendly, patriotic, perhaps even optimistic man. Sufficiently happy both in his family and in his profession, Gulliver is of a nature almost immune to meanness, selfishness, hatred, morbidity of any sort. If native land, wife, children, human race become dark and sinister and vile in his eyes, it will be (we must all admit) only for very potent, indubitable causes. His very predisposition is against misanthropy. But he has the capacity slowly and honestly to think. The human race may be conceived as individually pinning their faith to Gulliver, and reflecting, the while, "If Gulliver ever becomes a manhater that will be the perfect demonstration (for such of us as can think) that the race is hateful. Experiences that transform the good Gulliver into a misanthropist would much more surely transform us others should we pass through them." At least, Swift seems to calculate some such effect of Gulliver upon readers of the book.

Gulliver's Travels is in some sort the education of this man—his higher education, that is—and we see his so-to-speak Freshman and Sophomore experiences in Lilliput and Brobdingnag, bewildering experiences to him, with little seemingly vital result, but nevertheless an indispensable first tilling of the intellectual soil from which no genuine fruits are to be expected until later. This "later" means in Laputa and in Houyhnhnmsland. His final years may now be viewed, leading as they do to a sort of degree of ultimate understanding or sophistication. The goal of the book is not reached until the last page. To deal with it otherwise than as an organic unit is altogether to mutilate it.

In "Laputa" there are signs that the middle-aged, good-natured Gulliver is no longer impervious to the terrible suggestions and implications for him (and for any man!) of present events. He begins to apply what he observes to the case of human beings as such, wherever. (pp. 475-76)

That his disillusionment is well under way is indicated by certain reflections that we would never have heard upon the lips of that Gulliver who dealt so naïvely with the King and ministers of Lilliput. . . . In many instances, in the third voyage, it would not be difficult to maintain that, for the time, Swift speaks through the lips of Gulliver. That does not mean, of course, that Gulliver is a disguise for Swift but merely that Gulliver is attaining wisdom.

There is a late flare-up of Gulliver's native good nature, philanthropy, and idealism in his experience at Luggnagg, apropos of the Struldbrugs or the people who never die. Certain persons of quality in Luggnagg volunteer to expound and exhibit the Struldbrugs to Gulliver. The mere prospect moves him more profoundly than any danger or any marvel previously encountered in the travels. . . . Gulliver proceeds (for the last time in his life, we may be sure) to pour forth his most cherished aspirations, which are characteristically marked by great good will to man. It impresses as the final struggle of Gulliver's buoyant soul against the inevitable, imminent wisdom of misanthropy.

> . . . If it had been my good fortune to come into the world a Struldbrug, as soon as I could discover my own happiness by understanding the difference between life and death, I would first resolve by all arts and methods whatsoever to procure myself riches. . . . In the second place, I would from my earliest youth apply myself to the study of arts and sciences, by which I should arrive in time to excell all others in learning. Lastly, I would carefully record every action and event of consequence that happened in the public, . . . with my own observations on every point. . . . By all which acquirements, I should be a living treasury of knowledge and wisdom, and certainly become the oracle of the nation. . . .

Such words and ideas could flow only from a temperament sufficiently sanguine, a generous disposition. No sooner has Gulliver's nature thus expressed itself than he receives a chilling lesson. The inhabitants of Luggnagg are diverted at his ingenuousness. They inform him that an immortal (Struldbrug) becomes, *ipso facto*, a prey to "not only all the follies and infirmities of other old men, but many more which arose from the dreadful prospect of never dying." Furthermore, typical Struldbrugs are exhibited to Gulliver. The point for a Student of Gulliver's character and rôle to note here is the remarkable docility with which he learns the lesson in all its implications. He has surmounted that dulness which prevented him from appreciating the suggestions for human nature and human affairs at Lilliput and Brobdingnag. The seed of the idea sprouts promptly in the brain so long apparently sluggish or impenetrable. He admits a great loss of "appetite for perpetuity of life," and even entertains the project of transporting "a couple of Struldbrugs to my own country, to arm our people against the fear of death." Disillusioned as he is in many respects, Gulliver still is concerned to benefit people. His education is not finished; his pilgrimage as yet uncompleted.

In the light of the first three books of the *Travels*, it is not only necessary but natural to expect the fourth. The reader has been lured in the steps and into the thoughts of Gulliver by an unobtrusive and unwavering art not immeasurably less masterly though perhaps less lovely than the art of Milton in tracing the degeneration of Satan or that of Shakespeare in patiently following the gradual ruin of King Lear's body and mind.

Gulliver, after dwelling for a period among the admirable Houyhnhnms and observing with horror their filthy but thoroughly human slaves, the Yahoos, shows himself such an adept at receiving unfamiliar and uncongenial ideas that he may be pronounced educated or sophisticated more utterly than any other recorded man! For a measure of his growth in compre-

Esther Johnson, Swift's "Stella."

hension of things, it is convenient to contrast his account to his master, the Dapple Gray Houyhnhnm, of mankind (particularly Englishmen) with his account of the same species to the King of Brobdingnag. Every item in the account to the Dapple Gray is presented in a disagraceful light where each had been set forth with bellicose patriotism and philanthropism in the account at Brobdingnag. Our long and intimate acquaintance with Lemuel Gulliver in the earlier voyages has led us almost imperceptibly to cherish a not inconsiderable liking for him and (more significantly) to feel a measure of confidence in his good nature and his general capacity. The result is that we find ourselves inclined to accept his views. Shocking and ferocious as the attack on man may be in the "Voyage to the Houyhnhnms," we are conducted with singular gentleness, everything considered, by our friend Gulliver through all the desolation of humanity. We tend to believe him until the tale is done and we have had a chance to appreciate the indictment. Then comes the ferocious shock rather than in the reading.

Gulliver explains innocently his reason for the new attitude toward mankind:

> I must confess, the many virtues of those excellent quadrupeds [i.e., the Houyhnhnms] placed in opposite view to human corruptions, had so far opened my eyes and enlarged my understanding, that I

began to view the actions and passions of man in a very different light, and to think the honor of my own kind not worth managing [i.e., manipulating];. . . .

Gulliver's education is coming not only to flower but to fruit. He no longer considers ways of benefiting man as he had even so recently as during his visit to the Struldbrugs. The final revelation of wisdom has been apparently to refrain from human contact—a revelation convincing enough to transform a philanthropic Gulliver.

The full force of Gulliver's attainment of knowledge is not felt until he is forced back among men—an indubitable Yahoo. He is constrained to admit his Yahoo-nature humbly; to admit, also, that as a Yahoo he must depart the land of virtue forever. It is only when he finally reaches England and his wife and children that the realization comes of his utter disillusion, his complete wisdom! " . . . The sight of them filled me only with hatred, disgust and contempt. . . . " We know from our long intimacy with Gulliver that he is incapable of cruelty, hard-heartedness. We know he is not morbid or easily bored. He must have attained to whatever is the final attainment, extraordinary as the results of it may seem. . . . He has played out his rôle to perfection. Or possibly we might say that he has gone another pilgrim's progress, this time not to the Celestial City, but to a place equally difficult of human attainment if we may believe Swift—to Misanthropolis. And the pilgrimage is real to us in the reading (if not in the after-thought) because Gulliver is in disposition and in intellect so credible, probable, recognizable, and trustworthy. (pp. 476-80)

John Brooks Moore, "The Rôle of Gulliver," in *Modern Philology*, Vol. XXV, No. 4, May, 1928, pp. 469-80.

ARTHUR E. CASE

(essay date 1945)

[In the following excerpt, Case examines *Gulliver's Travels* as a satire of political and social institutions in eighteenth-century England.]

What, then, is the main design of *Gulliver's Travels*? It is customary to call the book a satire: it would be more accurate and more illuminating to call it a politico-sociological treatise much of which is couched in the medium of satire. Only secondarily and accidentally is it a book of travels. It belongs with the *Utopia*, the *New Atlantis, Candide,* and *Erewhon:* it succeeds in combining the depth of the two earlier tales with the narrative skill and human appeal of the two later. And it is perhaps

not surprising that many people in Swift's age, unaccustomed to so much brilliant embroidering of a serious philosophic theme, as well as unwilling to face the underlying indictment of European civilization, should have defended themselves, half unconsciously, by construing Gulliver as an amusing, imaginative romance marred by some regrettable misanthropic passages. (pp. 105-06)

The basis of Swift's political theory was contained in the principles of the old Whigs, of whom Sir William Temple was an eminent spokesman. Authority was held to reside in the whole of the body politic, though the administrative power, for practical reasons, had to be delegated to a small number of persons; perhaps, under certain circumstances, to one. The three estates of the realm—king, nobles, and commons—were of equal importance to the state, the king being charged with keeping the balance between the others. This form of government was frequently called the "gothic": it was assumed to be the natural, primitive government of the old English, and deviations from it were held to be corruptions. These deviations were always the result of an attempt by one of the estates to seize more than its share of the power for selfish reasons: if this attempt was successful it was inevitable that disturbances would result which would ultimately culminate in tyranny by one of the estates. This in turn would be done away with, after much suffering, and the old balance would be reestablished. It was the duty of intelligent men to preserve the balance as long as possible, and to restore it whenever it was destroyed.

The position of the church in such a state was, naturally, of great importance to Swift. He believed firmly in both the truth of the religion of which he was a priest and the propriety of its establishment as the state religion of England and Ireland. But he did not believe either that dissenters from the state church should be prevented from worshiping in accordance with their consciences, or that the church or its members should rebel against the constituted authority of the temporal government within the scope of its operations. His position was that of a moderate, reasonable Englishman who never found himself far out of agreement with the less extreme members of either party.

If the sincerity and depth of Swift's belief in these principles is once understood it is not difficult to explain what has sometimes been regarded as a turning of his political coat in or about the year 1710. Swift always insisted that he remained steadfast in his beliefs and that it was the parties that altered their creeds: history supports him in this. During his youth in Ireland the Tory party was associated with the theory of the divine right of the king over both church and state, and with the consequent threat of the reestablishment of Roman Catholicism. This seemed to Swift an instance of that tyranny which it was right for honest and intelligent men to destroy in order to restore the power to the whole rather than to a part of the state. Accordingly he subscribed to "revolution principles" (which, incidentally, he maintained even after his secession to the Tories, though many of his new associates publicly or privately repudiated them). But when the more radical Whigs began to urge the repeal of the sacramental test, in order that dissenters might hold places in the government, he became estranged from the party. Eventually he was convinced that the Tories, who upheld the test and resisted the tendency of the Whigs to weaken the power of the sovereign and place all authority in Parliament, were now the champions of sound governmental practice. (pp. 108-09)

At first sight it may seem odd that Swift, if he wrote *Gulliver's Travels* as a treatise on political theory, should have paid so little attention to ecclesiastical affairs. There are several possible explanations for his course. In the first place, both for his own sake and that of the church, the welfare of which was now one of his chief concerns, Swift probably had no intention of including in his satire anything which would give his enemies renewed grounds for accusing him of blasphemy, as they had done ever since the publication of *A Tale of a Tub*. Secondly, the introduction of religion into the *Travels* would have complicated an already complex design, and perhaps have focused more attention upon specific local questions than Swift would have wished in a book which he meant to apply to the world at large.

When the politico-sociological nature of the *Travels* is once clearly understood, the structure of the book, though complex, is easier to analyze. Each of the four voyages approaches the main problem in a different way. For the sake of variety there is an alternation between the negative and the positive statement of principles. The first and third voyages are chiefly attacks upon the evils of bad government, the second and fourth are expositions of good government. This accounts for both the dominant satiric tone of the voyages to Lilliput and Laputa, and the frequency in them of topical allusions. Over this fundamental design is super-imposed another. The first two voyages are carefully contrasted: the first, or negative one depicts a typical European government which has become more corrupt than the average, while the second, or positive one portrays a government better than the average. In neither case does Swift proceed to extremes: he seems to be trying to show the range within which, humanity being what it is, actual governments may be expected to move. Lilliput has some good features, Brobdingnag some bad. The reader gets the impression that while Swift the idealist would not be contented with Brobdingnag, Swift the realist would grudgingly accept it. It represents, perhaps, England as it could be made within his own lifetime if by some happy turn of the wheel the country might be put into the hands of himself and his friends. To reinforce this relationship between the voyages Swift not only employed the contrasting devices of pigmies and giants, but even constructed the two voyages, roughly, on the same pattern. (pp. 109-10)

If the design of the *Travels* were absolutely symmetrical, one might expect to find a connection between the last two voyages corresponding to that between the first two. This, however, is not the case. Having shown bad and good government as they actually exist, or might exist, Swift wished also to show ideally good government as he conceived it. Instead of presenting a contrasting ideally bad state in a separate voyage, he preferred to combine the two extremes in a single climactic book. This course not only made the contrast between the two ideals more vivid, but also made it possible for Swift's ideally good Houyhnhnms to understand the nature of evil, which would otherwise have been beyond their comprehension. The third voyage was therefore devoted to a second description of bad government *in esse*. It was not, however, an extension or repetition of the first voyage, but a complement to it. All of his life Swift blamed the misfortunes of mankind upon two causes, vice and folly, both of which were contrary to right reason, and either of which could destroy a state. In the first voyage he had emphasized the former cause: in the third voyage he concentrated upon the latter.

It is important to keep in mind the main purpose of this third voyage, which has universally been judged to be the least successful of the four, largely for lack of unity. It is impossible not to agree with the general verdict, but it is easy to overstate the degree of disorganization. Superficially the voyage seems to be divided into four sections, recounting the adventures in Laputa, in Balnibarbi, in Glubbdubdrib, and in Luggnagg. The first two sections are regarded as attacks upon science, the third as a criticism of history, and the fourth as a personal expression of Swift's fear of old age. In point of fact, the attacks upon science and history are subsidiary to a single main purpose—an attack upon folly in government, which, in Swift's view, was identical with theoretical innovation, as opposed to the following of old and tried methods, modified only by the adoption of such variations as have been proved successful in practice in other countries. Swift apparently felt that the Whigs had transferred to the scientists much of the encouragement which earlier administrations had given to men of letters, and he regarded this tendency as symptomatic of the inclination of the Whigs toward chimerical experimentation in all fields. (pp. 111-12)

In contrast with all this are the examples of good government in accordance with the tried, sound principles of ancient models, as described by the ghosts of Glubbdubdrib. The exemplar of "gothic" government in classical times is the Roman republic at its best. The great heroes are the two Brutuses and the younger Cato, and the Roman senate is described as "an Assembly of Heroes and Demy-Gods." Julius Caesar and the succeeding emperors are treated as tyrants, under whose rule corruption and luxury brought about the decay of all virtues. More than once modern European governments are likened to those of imperial Rome. . . . (p. 113)

The account of the struldbruggs near the end of the third voyage is the episode which, more than any other in the *Travels,* seems to be dissociated from the main scheme of the book. It is often spoken of a purely personal expression by Swift of his fear of senility. That this personal feeling intensified the author's emotions as he wrote the passage no one can doubt: nevertheless the incident is logically related to the purpose of the voyage. It will be remembered that Gulliver interrupts the Luggnaggian's first description of the struldbruggs with a rhapsody in which he allows his mind to speculate on the happiness which must be the lot of these immortal creatures and the benefits which their ever-increasing experience and wisdom must confer upon the rest of mankind. . . . The whole chapter is one more rebuke to human folly which, giving itself over to wishful thinking, conjures up imaginary and impossible ways of dealing with the ills of society, instead of recognizing the nature of mankind as it is and approaching human problems from a practical point of view.

Swift's decision to cast his treatise in the form of a narrative necessitated the creation of a protagonist. Gulliver is all too often identified with Swift himself. No single misinterpretation of Swift's intentions has done more to obscure the real purpose of *Gulliver's Travels.* Gulliver is not only a character distinct from his creater—he is not identifiable with any of the actual contemporaries whose vicissitudes sometimes, especially in the first voyage, serve as a basis for his adventures. His birth, training, and early activities are carefully calculated to make him the perfect observer of and commentator upon the civilizations with which he comes in contact. By birth he is the average middle-class Englishman, with an inclination toward the sea, and with a special aptitude for languages which is to stand him in good stead. His education is more rounded than that of most men of his day: upon a base of traditional classical training as prescribed in the universities is superimposed the scientific training of the physician. A naturally studious habit leads him to supplement this training with much reading: adventurousness, curiosity, a faculty for observation and analysis of human nature and customs, and, most important, a high regard for truth, complete the mental and moral equipment of the perfect travel author. (pp. 113-15)

The voyage to Brobdingnag brings about the first alteration in Gulliver's general complacency over European civilization. In the third chapter he is made to feel uneasy by the amused contempt of the King and the courtiers for his country and countrymen as he describes them. But it is in the famous sixth chapter that we find Gulliver really on the defensive for the first time. The grand climax of this chapter is, of course, the judgment of the King in response to Gulliver's long and careful account of Europe and its inhabitants. (p. 115)

In the third voyage Gulliver's emotions may be described as at a dead center. He appears to be cured of any extravagant admiration of European society: he has now become the detached and half-cynical commentator on human life from without. In this voyage alone he is an observer and not an actor. This is entirely appropriate to the development of his character, although it weakens the interest of the narrative and is, in fact, one of the most important reasons for the relative ineffectiveness of the voyage. Gulliver is coolly ironic in comparing Europe with Laputa, sometimes to the advantage of one, sometimes to that of the other, but in neither case with any show of partisanship. His comments upon his return to his country are the briefest and least emotional of the *Travels.* The opening paragraph of the last book speaks of his remaining at home "in a very happy condition" about four months, but this statement is for the purpose of providing a contrast with Gulliver's change of heart during the final voyage—a change of heart more significant and more carefully depicted than any that has gone before.

The changing attitude of Gulliver toward the yahoos and the Houyhnhnms is of the first importance in determining the significance of those two species and, in consequence, of the whole voyage—indeed, of the entire *Travels.* At the opening of the voyage Gulliver is a representative European, somewhat better, perhaps, than most of his class, but by no means a paragon, and certainly a man who has adjusted himself to a consciousness of the ordinary and even the extraordinary vices and follies of humanity. In this state he does not recognize that the yahoos have any likeness to man: they are, to him, "ugly Monsters," to be described as a traveler would describe any curious and loathesome beast he encountered in the course of his adventures. It is not until the Houyhnhnms place him beside a yahoo for purposes of comparison that he sees any resemblance between himself and these "abominable Animals," and then he emphasizes those physical aspects which the yahoos have in common with "savage Nations." At the same time he stresses the difference between the behavior of Europeans and that of yahoos, which is apparently something more repulsive than he has encountered in the whole breadth of his travels. . . . Gradually, in the course of the conversations with his master which occupy the fourth, fifth, sixth, and seventh chapters, Gulliver falls into the habit of referring to Europeans as yahoos, partly for convenience and partly because, as the perfection of the Houyhnhnms is borne in upon him and contrasted with the actions and thoughts of his countrymen, he becomes aware, little by little, of the discrepancy between ideal and actual man. (pp. 117-18)

The natural result of Gulliver's experiences among the Houyhnhnms, and of his mental development, is to be found in the last two chapters of the *Travels* and in the *Letter to Sympson.* The expressions about humanity which are found here are not those of Gulliver in his normal state of mind. Swift is employing a device which he has used once before, at the conclusion of the second voyage, when his hero returned from the earlier and less nearly perfect Utopia of Brobdingnag. Evidently Swift was fascinated by the idea of the difficulty of readjusting oneself to ordinary existence after a prolonged exposure to extraordinary conditions. (p. 119)

Swift shows us at the end of the fourth voyage his conception of the effects which would be produced in the mind of an intelligent man who spent a long period in the company of creatures who were perfect in every way. Such a man, Swift believed, would tend to exaggerate his own imperfections and those of the race to which he belonged, and would, in the end, find living with his former associates intolerable. Anything less than perfection would be abhorrent: degrees of imperfection would be imperceptible and irrelevant. The opinions concerning mankind which Gulliver gives vent to are his own, not those of his creator. To emphasize this, Swift provides Gulliver with an unusual rescuer from his last adventure—Captain Pedro de Mendez. The majority of the seamen in the *Travels* are a good sort, but Mendez is a paragon. His generosity, his acute perception of the state of Gulliver's mind, his unfailing kindliness in the face of repeated rebuffs, mark him as the finest of all the European characters in the book. Yet Gulliver, controlled by the exalted conception of virtue he has acquired from living with Houyhnhnms, and by his now fixed belief in the utter worthlessness of all yahoos, with whom he has come to group the human race, is unable to perceive even the most extraordinary goodness when it manifests itself in one of the hated species. (pp. 120-21)

Swift conceived himself as a positive moral and social reformer. From his earliest to his latest writings there is plentiful evidence of his conviction that he knew not only what was wrong with the world, but also the means by which the world could be brought nearer to perfection. Living as he did in an age which was habituated to a belief that the world tended to decline, whether from the Golden Age of classical mythology or from the Garden of Eden of Hebrew legend, it is not surprising that he proposed reforms which often (though by no means always) called for a return to a real or an imagined earlier practice that was nearer

to perfection. The range and the detailed practicality of his schemes may be studied in his pamphlets, from those which describe the ideal "gothic" form of government to those which recommend the licensing of beggars or the correction of the English language. In the *Travels,* as elsewhere, his advice is expressed sometimes directly, sometimes by inversion. . . . Only a dull intellect could fail to understand that a man who rails at filth advocates cleanliness. The Houyhnhnms and the yahoos represent the extremes between which human behavior may range. Swift certainly did not expect humanity to achieve the height or sink to the depth: he did feel that for the moment, at least, man's tendency was downward, and that strenuous efforts were needed if the trend was to be reversed. To this end he bent his efforts with increasing fervor. . . . What drove Swift to his occasional outbursts of fury was the consciousness of his own helplessness. In his youth his discontent had been due largely to the postponement of his entry into the world of affairs in a position suited to his capacity. During the few short years of the Oxford-Bolingbroke [Tory] administration he had employed all his energies in attempts to put into effect certain ideas with which he felt his powerful friends were in sympathy. Then had followed the blasting of his hopes by the triumph of the Whigs, and the gradually growing, bitter conviction that never again in his lifetime would he be in a position of political power. It is hardly to be wondered at that he sometimes allowed himself the relief of savage invective.

It is this savage invective that is responsible for the common belief that Swift was a misanthrope. Swift himself lent some color to this legend by his own statement in a letter [to Alexander Pope (see excerpt above, 1725)]. (pp. 123-25)

The words of this letter themselves show that Swift's "misanthropy" was something far different from the state of mind usually associated with the term. The actions of men in the mass infuriated Swift by their folly and criminality: for individuals he had boundless affection. If his letter had not thus made clear his real attitude toward mankind his whole biography would have done so. It is impossible to ignore the extent of Swift's practical charities, often contrived at the cost of great personal sacrifice to time and money. . . . It is impossible to forget the interest he displayed in the welfare of those who had been placed in his personal care, either as servant or as parishioners. . . . And above all it is impossible to shut one's eyes to Swift's need for human companionship and sympathy. This need Swift often tried to conceal, perhaps because of pride in a cherished self-sufficiency, but his constant seeking out of friends and his correspondence with those who were beyond his reach betray him. Conscience compelled him, as a self-appointed father to the world, to chasten his children, but he wanted their love as well as their obedience. And sometimes this craving for understanding and affection found expression—never more clearly than in the *Verses on the Death of Dr. Swift,* written some five years after *Gulliver's Travels* had fixed in the mind of many contemporaries the fiction of Swift, the enemy of mankind. It is an appeal that from a lesser man would have been pathetic: coming from a genius of the magnitude of Swift it lays bare a tragedy. (p. 126)

Arthur E. Case, "The Significance of 'Gulliver's Travels'," in his *Four Essays on "Gulliver's Travels",* Princeton University Press, 1945, pp. 97-126.

F. W. BATESON
(essay date 1950)

[In the following excerpt, Bateson praises Swift's poetry for its multiple levels of meaning and accessibility.]

It is time Swift's status as a poet was reconsidered. Although his verse is uneven and often slipshod, at his best he seems to me one of the great English poets. I prefer him to Pope. Pope is a superb *talker* in verse, endlessly vivacious and amusing, but it is difficult to take him or his opinions very seriously. . . . Swift, on the other hand, though he restricted himself to light verse, is fundamentally one of the world's most serious poets. Even his jokes have metaphysical implications. But to understand Swift he must be read in the social context of his own time. (p. 175)

The opening couplets [of **'Description of the Morning'**] are a straightforward parody of the heroic style. . . . But the parody is almost immediately abandoned for a catalogue of the activities of a Saturday morning (the traditional 'scrubbing day') in the West End of London. The clue to the poem's peculiar flavour . . . is the juxtaposition of what is morally neutral (the street cries, the charwoman, the boy searching the gutter), or at most venial behaviour (the careless apprentice, the loitering schoolboy), with real social evils (the sexual immorality and financial irresponsibility of the upper class, the appalling prison system). The implication is: 'This is life. Here you have a corner of London at the beginning of the daily round. You recognize the accuracy of the picture, don't you? A, B and C, men and women with immortal souls, are each carrying out in an almost instinctive way his or her particular function, side by side and yet completely independent of each other. But some of these functions, which we all take for granted, are criminal, aren't they? What

sort of a society is this in which you, gentle reader, are so deeply compromised?'

A paradox emerges. Like the Yahoos, these Londoners are human beings and yet they are *not* human beings. The dissociated individual, mechanically pursuing his own professional function, irrespective of its social consequences, and oblivious of the activities of his neighbours, possesses none of the qualities that constitute real humanity. (pp. 176-77)

The social order that Swift is attempting to discredit in this poem is the *laissez-faire* individualism of urban capitalism and the moral that he is enforcing is the Christian one that we are members of one another. 'Only connect.' But behind the ethical humanism, giving it depth and force, is something more primitive—the countryman's sense of fact. It is this conviction of actuality that makes the poem refreshing instead of depressing. Bad though the state of the towns may be there is no need to despair, Swift implies, as long as it is possible to face the facts of the situation. The amoral urban automata, once seen in their true light, *must* become objects of contempt. There is also an implicit contrast between the uncreative activities of London—even the coalman and the charwoman, whose professions might be thought useful, are only engaged in moving carbon from one place to another—and the rural partnership of man with nature. 'The difference is, that, instead of dirt and poison, we have rather chosen to fill our hives with honey and wax, thus furnishing mankind with the two noblest of things, which are sweetness and light.' The tonic quality of Swift's poem derives from the *sanity* of the underlying philosophy of life. Because he was insane when he died the nineteenth century dismissed everything that he wrote with which they did not agree as mad. To-day it is the Victorian division of labour and the Victorian piling up of *things* that seem mad. Swift's special distinction is that he exposed *laissez-faire* capitalism, and all that it stands for, while it was still no bigger than a cloud the size of a man's hand.

To some extent Swift's satiric effectiveness derives from the attitude he adopts towards his readers. This is different from either Dryden's or Pope's, or indeed any of his contemporaries. As James Sutherland has recently pointed out in [his *A Preface to Eighteenth-Century Poetry*] . . . , the reading public Swift was addressing was not *primarily* that of the upper classes of society:

It was his practice, we are told, to have two of his men-servants brought in to listen to his poems being read, 'which, if they did not comprehend, he would alter and amend, until they understood it perfectly well, and then would say, *This will do: for I write to the vulgar, more than to the learned.*' How well he succeeded may be seen on almost any page of his poetical works, where the idiomatic and familiar style carries his meaning easily and forcibly to the least learned reader. But here, as in some other matters, Swift was not wholly at one with his age.

Sutherland appears to impute *eccentricity* to Swift. In reality, in my opinion, he was not at one with his age only because he transcended it. The poems were, of course, read by the aristocracy. The parody in the opening lines of the **'Description of the Morning'** would only have been intelligible to the polite world. But Swift's uniqueness in his century lay in his ability to appeal to several social levels in one and the same work. It is this that sets him by Chaucer and Shakespeare.

Unlike Pope Swift's principal object as a satirist is not to get the reader 'on his side' against his enemies. . . . Swift's technique, on the contrary, is to insinuate himself into the enemy ranks disguised as a friend, and once he is there to spread all the alarm and despondency he can. 'I never wonder,' he wrote in *Thoughts on Various Subjects,* 'to see men wicked, but I often wonder to see them not ashamed.' It was above all a sense of shame that he tried to inculcate in the capitalists of the middle class. In *A Modest Proposal for Preventing the Children of Ireland from being a Burden to their Parents or Country* , perhaps the greatest of the prose ironies, the real object of Swift's attack is not, as is often asserted, the Irish policy of the Whig Government. The satire goes much deeper. It is an exposure of a whole social philosophy, of which the English economic discrimination against Ireland was only one instance. As in the **'Description of the Morning,'** which can be considered an early experiment in the *genre* perfected in *A Modest Proposal,* it is again competitive capitalism that Swift is trying to discredit, but the mode of insinuation is more carefully chosen. . . . [*A Modest Proposal*] talks the actual language of Cheapside and Threadneedle Street. It is to all appearances another essay in the 'political arithmetic' that was so popular in the City of London during the later seventeenth and early eighteenth centuries. The tone of voice, the method of argument, the statistical approach are exactly the kind of thing that the business world of the time had been accustomed to meet in the pamphlets of Sir William Petty, Charles Davenant and Daniel Defoe. Here was their old friend the Economic Man! The opening paragraphs have lulled any suspicions that Swift's authorship might have aroused, and the reader, who finds the Economic Man disposing of his surplus children to the butcher, is brought suddenly face to face with the contradiction between his own week-day and Sunday religions. It is the Augustan paradox, the familiar formula of the poetry of the squirearchy, but here it operates on a grander scale, charged with a higher intensity, than any of Swift's contemporaries were able to command. (pp. 177-80)

F. W. Bateson, "Swift's 'Description of the Morning'," in his

English Poetry: A Critical Introduction, Longmans, Green and Co., 1950, pp. 175-80.

JOHN M. BULLITT
(essay date 1953)

[In the following excerpt, Bullitt assesses the intent and discursive strategy of Swift's satirical prose.]

In its most serious function, satire is a mediator between two perceptions—the unillusioned perception of man as he actually is, and the ideal perception, or vision, of man as he ought to be. It is often argued, therefore, that satire can become a vital form of literature only when there is a fairly widespread agreement about what man ought to be. The satirist needs the conviction that fixed intellectual ideals or norms can give him, and the assurance that he will receive understanding from his readers. . . . But if satire is best able to develop from a basis of general agreement on intellectual and moral standards, it is not necessarily chained for that reason to passing conditions and values. The unillusioned perception of man as he actually is can go beyond the mere noting of abuses and customs that have only topical interest, and can expose weaknesses or vices that are a perennial danger. (p. 1)

[Swift's] satire is characterized by a penetrating if at times corrosive realism, and may therefore be described as a genuine exposure of things as they are and too often tend to be. As [Ricardo Quintana] has justly said, the theme of Swift's writing may be summed up in the injunction: "It is not as you think,—look!" This tendency of mind is the implicit premise shaping not only Swift's technical virtuosity but even more deeply his most fundamental attitudes, and it found its earliest and most explicit expression in *A Tale of a Tub.* In "A Digression Concerning Madness," Swift develops the central theme of all his satire—the idea that man's mind is contented only by the "*Superficies* of Things," and that happiness is "*a perpetual Possession of being well Deceived* . . . The Serene Peaceful State of being a Fool among Knaves." Swift's conception of reason, as opposed to the delusive imagination, was of an instrument "for cutting, and opening, and mangling, and piercing, offering to demonstrate" that only delusion could make man think the externals of life conform with its internal reality. . . . But Swift's realism, his vigorous, persistent, and at times almost tortured attempt to see things as they are, to "inspect beyond the Surface and the Rind of Things" even though the resulting wisdom proves to be a nut which "may cost you a Tooth, and pay you with nothing but a *Worm*"—this intense realism stands opposed to another quality with which it cannot be reconciled: his equally intense idealism. For to Swift, the discovery that "in most Corporeal Beings, which have fallen under my Cognizance, the *Outside* hath been infinitely preferable to the *In*," presented an unbridgeable disparity between the *real,* as he saw it rationally, and the *ideal,* as he desired it—and it is the horror of perceiving this continual disparity which informs the frightful understatement of his observation: "Last Week I saw a Woman *flay'd,* and you will hardly believe, how much it altered her Person for the worse." The essence of this idealism was the almost too earnest desire to make the inner reality resemble the more simple surface which the "imagination" presents. And from that very earnestness of desire, reality has appeared even more shrunk and deformed and horrible by contrast. This analytical and dissecting tendency of Swift's realism, combined with the poignant idealistic desire to rid life of the disparity between what actually "is" and what merely seems to be, provided the central impulse behind his satire.

It was impossible for Swift to perceive such a disparity between the real and the ideal without reacting strongly to it. . . .For Swift was incapable of a smug or carefree detour around the problem of evil and imperfection in the world—a detour summed up in the classic phrase of a blind optimism: "Whatever is, is right." To shatter this complacency, to make men share with him his own painfully acute awareness that what most often seems "right" in the world is merely the surface colouring of "Artificial *Mediums,* false Lights, refracted Angles, Varnish, and Tinsel"—in short, to force upon mankind his own realization that what truly "is" only *seems* "right" to minds content with being "well deceived," was the guiding intention of Swift's satire. Accordingly, we find in him an urgent need to speak out, an impelling drive to express his own dissatisfaction, because, as he wrote to Pope, "I never will have peace of mind till all honest men are of my opinion." (pp. 2-4)

A concise statement of the diverse possibilities of Swift's response is found in his belief that a reasonable man, when confronted with the disparity between pretended virtue and its concealed folly and viciousness, must be "tempted, according to the present turn of his humour, either to laugh, lament, or be angry; or, if he were sanguine enough, perhaps to dream of a remedy." The "turn" of Swift's humour led him to see life sometimes as a comedy, sometimes as a lamentable tragedy, often as a source of angry frustration—and most frequently and effectively, perhaps, in such satires as *A Modest Proposal* or *Gulliver's Travels,* Swift reacted in all ways at once. . . . But if Swift seldom found life to be wholly a laughing matter, only rarely did he permit himself to view it as wholly tragic: life to Swift became a comic tragedy. (pp. 5-6)

In addition to Swift's native exuberance and the comedy intrinsic to all affectation and pretense, two other aspects of his comic satire deserve mention, because they condition and modify his satiric techniques. In the first place, Swift shared with many of his contemporaries the conviction that laughter was generally a more forceful and effective instrument of moral reform than the serious discussion of good and evil. Accordingly, we find Swift defending comic satire for its *objective utility,* its usefulness as a stimulus to reform. . . . Another important element, which influenced Swift on a deeper and more personal level and which colored and modified the rest, is suggested by his observation . . . that comic satire, written without malice, affords the writer an innocent "personal satisfaction"; and Swift demands "whether I have not as good a title to laugh, as men have to be ridiculous, and to expose vice, as another hath to be vicious. If I ridicule the follies and corruptions of a court, a ministry, or a senate; are they not amply paid by pensions, titles, and power, *while I expect and desire no other reward, than that of laughing with a few friends in a corner.*" Now, the "personal satisfaction" Swift found in comic satire goes much deeper than he admits even in this passage. In fact, much of his seeming merriment and his habitual use of irony seem to have been the result of an almost compulsive desire to separate himself from the intensity of his own feelings, from a truly tragic involvement of his "moral sympathies" with the cruelty and folly and terror of life. . . . If comedy satisfied certain objective conditions for moral reform, it also had for Swift a *subjective utility* as well—a means of varying his angle of vision so that he would not care too much.

But, as he grew older, the "present turn" of Swift's "humour" seems to have concentrated increasingly upon the agony of life. A fundamental shift in focus has taken place between the acid but comic irony in *A Tale of a Tub,* where the motives of military conquerors are found to stem either from vapours or fistulas, and Gulliver's ironic and scarifying defense of modern warfare in "A Voyage to Brobdingnag." At the very heart of Swift's comic perception there is a tragic potentiality. For tragedy shares with comedy its concern with man's limitations, but differs from it, in one respect at least, in presenting these limitations as both disastrous and part of the ultimate configuration of life itself; tragedy, at its best and as distinct from mere pathos or melodrama, rests upon and implies a universal import in the structure of man's situation in the world. Now, Swift's comedy, as we have noted, is founded upon his perception of a disparity between reality and the ideal—a disparity of which mankind as a whole, he felt, was deceived into ignorance. Of all man's limitations, the one which most concerned Swift was man's self-deception, his wilful ignorance of his true worth. "There is a pedantry in manners, as in all arts and sciences; and sometimes in trades," Swift wrote; "Pedantry is properly the over-rating any kind of knowledge we pretend to." (If pedantry is the over-rating of knowledge, the ultimate stupidity of man is the over-rating of man's virtue). As Swift's reason increasingly universalized this tendency of mankind, finding it an apt description of a basic flaw not merely in particular persons but in human life itself, he approaches that generality of comment which gives tragedy its own unique dimension. Like the journey of Oedipus from ignorance to a tragic self-knowledge, so the rational journey of Gulliver was an experience which led him from the ignorant complacency of the typical Englishman towards an undeceived, though intensely bitter, knowledge of "reality." In this way, *Gulliver's Travels* can be said to assume a tragic significance. When Swift's eye was focused upon the absurdity of "man-deceived," he portrayed a comic affectation or self-delusion; but as he concentrated more upon the reality beneath, contrasting it with the surface deception, and as he attempted to shock men with graphic and concrete vividness into seeing how enormous was the disparity, what began in a comic spirit was liable to develop into a horror and disgust and loathing of life itself. (pp. 6-9)

Swift was deeply distrustful of life, and from an early age he often repeated the passage from Job, beginning: "Let the day perish wherein I was born, and the night in which it was said, There is a man child conceived." For Swift was unable through reason to justify God's ways to man, and he was forced to view God's purposes on earth as both inscrutable and terrible: "I hate life," he wrote after the death of Lady Ashburnham, "I hate life when I think it exposed to such accidents; and to see so many thousand wretches burdening the earth, while such as her die, makes me think God did never intend life for a blessing." This moving and utterly genuine distrust of life as being incompatible with man's rational sense of justice gives Swift's passage in his *Thoughts on Religion* a poignant despair:

> Although reason were intended by Providence to govern our passions, yet it seems that, in two points of the greatest moment to the being and continuance of the world, God hath intended our passions to prevail over reason. The first is, the propagation of our species, since no wise man ever married from the dictates of reason. The other is, the love of life, which, from the dictates of reason, every man would despise, and wish it at an end, or that it never had a beginning.
>
> (pp. 9-10)

If Swift, then, viewed man's life as a "ridiculous tragedy," comic or calamitous according to his point of view at the moment, his moral sensibilities were too intense to permit him the luxury of separating himself from it. Commentators on Swift have often noted that

the phrase on his epitaph, *saeva indignatio* ["savage indignation"], describes his most persistent reaction to the disparity he saw between the real world and his ideals. . . . Swift was evidently unique among misanthropes. For his professed hatred of mankind—which he disclaims in . . . [a letter to Alexander Pope (see excerpt dated 1725)]—springs from the despair of caring too much, and unlike other haters of man, Swift's love for individuals was not only strong but enduring. Because he valued so highly certain moral and rational qualities of which man is capable, he responded fervently to the rare individual who exemplified these qualities, and he recoiled with horror from the great bulk of human kind which does not attain that high standard. In other words, Swift's "misanthropy," as he called it, did not prevent him from treasuring human excellence when he found it, but the idealism upon which these affections were based made him perceive the gap between what man is and what man can be with an acute and pained exasperation. In the second place, and this is especially important as it pertains to his literary work, Swift was not, as he himself says, "content with despising" the world, and his desire to "anger it" reflects his strong urge, even in the midst of his hatred, to reform humanity. Although he was convinced that most men were not, by nature, reasonable animals, and were, therefore, . . . basically unchangeable, even his most bitter attacks assume some element of corrigibility in man. . . . As long as Swift could find vices and follies which were not ingrained in man by nature and which could therefore possibly be shamed out of existence, his satire had a place. At the same time, as his gloom deepened, his satiric intention tended more and more towards shaming men out of their vices not by *laughing at* but by*lashing* them. This tendency may be said to have reached its culmination in the fourth voyage of *Gulliver's Travels*. (pp. 12-14)

Although Swift's insight and temper transcended his own period, and although his most bitter criticism was often directed against ideas and beliefs which are commonly thought typical of the Age of Reason, his literary expression was markedly influenced by the very age he attacked. It is probable, as we have already noted, that some unanimity on moral standards, considered as both rational and permanent, is a necessary precondition for any great satiric effort. If indeed, these standards are broadly conceived and reflect a high idealism, almost every human action may be viewed as a departure from the established norm; and these departures constantly tempt and provoke a desire to criticize them. From this point of view, it may be questioned whether great satire can be written in a period of grave anxiety, such as the present day. Whether or not this argument is valid, a causal connection between the general acceptance of normative values and the satiric impulse seems to be almost inescapable in the late seventeenth and early eighteenth centuries—a period whose general intellectual character must, if we may judge from the quantity and quality of its satire, have been highly favorable to this genre. If one believes in an absolute standard that is fixed, ideal, and knowable through reason, then against the white light of that ideal the actual conduct of man will stand out dark by contrast. There is also a psychological effect subjoined to this. If too great an effort is made to see man as reasonable and just, and as part of a rational and fixed universal Nature, then man, as he is in actuality, as he is in the flesh, will appear to depart at every turn from the ideal, and he may even appear not merely defective but monstrous. And of course it is precisely this enormous discrepancy between the ideal and the actual which so strongly cuts into the intense idealism of Swift. (pp. 16-17)

If the impetus behind Swift's satire was his perception of the bestial depravity of mankind, and the inability of sheer reason to improve him, a similar though not identical skepticism and disillusionment dominated the satire of his contemporaries. Indeed, neoclassic satire may be said to have arisen from the ruins of a traditional basis for morality—from a sense of the failure of traditional institutions and beliefs to improve mankind. Certainly the new philosophy that "calls all in doubt," the philosophy of skeptical inquiry and scientific experiment, had corroded men's collective faith in the absolute certainty of final judgment. Not that all men, or even most men, had lost their religious scruples. But as the foundation of Christianity, the Bible, became, like other historical documents, the subject of experimental scrutiny, and as the system of heavenly rewards and punishments lost its concreteness and became increasingly abstract, speculative and even doubtful, many thinking men tended to pin their faith upon the rewards and punishments of this world—a faith founded on the belief in the capacity of reason to bring heaven down to earth. Whitehead has described this fundamental shift in values as being from a faith based on reason to a reason based on faith—a "faith in the order of nature." From this new optimism, engendered by the possibilities of reason and scientific inquiry, emerged a "Religion of Reason" as Newman later described it, "A religion of civilized times, of the cultivated intellect, of the philosopher, scholar and gentleman." In this atmosphere of intellectual rather than religious culture . . . conscience becomes "self-respect" and "sin is not an offence against God, but against human nature." Wrong-doing is punished in the individual by a sense of social degradation; vice becomes ugly and deformed and ridiculous; the religious sense of remorse is swallowed up in the social sense of shame.

Swift, needless to say, hardly pinned his faith to the view of human nature described by Newman and most familiarly associated with the Earl of Shaftesbury.

But it is equally evident that Swift joined other satirists in the belief that traditional religious, political, and rational standards had proved to be inadequate by themselves as means for the clarifying and improving of human morality. And if one result of the Religion of Reason was the moralist's appeal to man's shame, the result of Swift's skeptical antirationalism was a similar appeal to this social sense. (pp. 21-2)

A belief in the social utility of satire, then, is entirely consistent with Swift's own views of man. His delight and agreement with the maxims of Rochefoucauld—"who is my favorite, because I found my whole character in him"—testifies to his assumption that self-love is man's most basic motivating force. And the appeal of shame is, of course, directly to self-love, for, as Newman recognized, the eighteenth-century gentlemanly fear of shame was the fear of social censure—the humiliation of pride that comes from being laughed at by society. Swift's *A Project for the Advancement of Religion* is founded upon this same recognition. Here Swift proposes to equate piety and virtue with social and political success, thus making men's secular self-interest demand at least the pretense of morality. Here again Swift is affirming that most men are moved to action neither by a rational recognition of the good nor by religious fear of eternal punishment or hope for divine bliss; the single possible way of completing the process of leading men to correct their vices and follies is to relate such a correction to their own secular ambitions. But Swift seemed convinced that the *Project* was doomed to failure even before he wrote it, and the essay remains among his works merely as a piece of delightful and trenchant wishful thinking. For princes are neither virtuous nor strong enough to reward only piety and virtue with favors; it is the satirist who alone must take over the task of making men's vices socially disagreeable. (pp. 23-4)

It is doubtful whether any author in the history of English literature was more intent upon arousing the feelings of his readers than was Swift. Although he urged a style which was "like a Shrewsbury cake, short and sweet upon the palate," his intention was always to persuade with this unaffected style a highly directed emotional response; it was not only to portray the distance between appearance and reality, between reality and the ideal, but, by arousing laughter at the cosmic absurdity of this affectation, to make men ashamed of the disparity. Thus we see that one essential purpose of Swift's satiric technique is to stimulate an awakened and indeed a poetic awareness in the reader's mind—an awareness dulled by traditional and heavy-handed moralizing—of the vicious limitations of man. (p. 36)

If "the content of satire," as David Worcester sensibly remarked, "is criticism," the content of *effective* satire, of ridicule, was thought to be a derisive and laughing criticism. A direct attack upon an individual or institution creates an answerable argument, one that admits disagreement or defense; but ridicule, because it "drives out brangling and contention," also deprives the object of any effective vindication. Moreover, if ridicule is most effective in its impact on the person satirized, it is also most pleasing to the reader. For the reader—and Swift realistically and somewhat hopelessly recognized that few readers would include themselves among the objects of ridicule—is quickened to an awareness of the vicious disproportions of the world more by laughter than by solemn and direct moralizing. In this sense, then, if ridicule aims to deflate men's vanity by shaming their self-love, it also aims to excite the reader's interest by appealing to his own sense of superiority. Quite properly, then, Swift could claim for satire both *utile* and *dulce*. (p. 37)

John M. Bullitt, in his *Jonathan Swift and the Anatomy of Satire: A Study of Satiric Technique,* 1953. Reprint by Cambridge, Mass.: Harvard University Press, 1966, 214 p.

SOURCES FOR FURTHER STUDY

Donoghue, Denis. *Jonathan Swift: A Critical Introduction.* Cambridge: Cambridge University Press, 1969, 235 p.

>Survey of Swift's career that disputes several prevalent critical views of the author. Donoghue contends that Swift meant to portray the Houyhnhnms as an ideal race and that his vision was primarily negative; he also contends that critics read Swift on their own terms, finding irony where it was not intended.

Ehrenpreis, Irvin. *Swift: The Man, His Works, and the Age.* 3 vols. Cambridge: Harvard University Press, 1962-84.

>Definitive biography of Swift, including extensive analysis of his works.

Foster, Milton P., ed. *A Casebook on Gulliver among the Houyhnhnms.* New York: Thomas Y. Crowell Co., 1961, 319 p.

>Collection of essays on the fourth section of *Gulliver's Travels,* the interpretation of which is generally viewed as the most controversial aspect of Swift criticism.

Lee, Jae Num. *Swift and Scatological Satire.* Albequerque: University of New Mexico Press, 1971, 158 p.

>Discusses Swift's pervasive use of scatology to address moral and humanistic issues and to confront readers with their own animal nature.

Quintana, Ricardo. *Swift: An Introduction.* London: Oxford University Press, 1955, 204 p.

>Survey of the major elements of Swift's life, work, and thought by a scholarly authority on Swift.

Tuveson, Ernest, ed. *Swift: A Collection of Critical Essays.* Englewood Cliffs, N.J.: Prentice-Hall, Inc., 1964, 176 p.

>Collection of critical essays, including seminal work by F. R. Leavis (on Swift's negativity), John Traugott (on Swift and Utopian literature), and an introductory essay by Tuveson.

Algernon Swinburne

1837-1909

(Full name Algernon Charles Swinburne; also wrote under pseudonym Mrs. Horace Manners) English poet, dramatist, critic, essayist, and novelist.

INTRODUCTION

Swinburne is renowned as one of the most accomplished lyric poets of the Victorian era and as a preeminent symbol of rebellion against the conservative values of his time. The explicit and often pathological sexual themes of his most important collection of poetry, *Poems and Ballads* (1866), delighted some, shocked many, and became the dominant feature of Swinburne's image as both an artist and an individual. Nevertheless, critics have found that to focus exclusively on the sensational aspects of Swinburne's work is to miss the assertion, implicit in his poetry and explicit in his critical writings, that his primary preoccupation was the nature and creation of poetic beauty.

Born into a wealthy Northumbrian family, Swinburne was educated at Eton and at Balliol College, Oxford, but did not complete a degree. While at Oxford, he met the brothers William Michael and Dante Gabriel Rossetti, as well as other members of the Pre-Raphaelite circle, a group of artists and writers whose work emphasized medieval subjects, elaborate religious symbolism, and a sensual pictorialism, and who cultivated an aura of mystery and melancholy in their lives as well as in their works. In 1860 Swinburne published two verse dramas in the volume *The Queen-Mother and Rosamond*, which was largely ignored. He achieved his first literary success in 1865 with *Atalanta in Calydon*, which was written in the form of classical Greek tragedy. The following year the appearance of *Poems and Ballads* brought Swinburne instant notoriety. He became identified with the "indecent" themes and the precept of art for art's sake that characterized many of the poems in the volume. He subsequently wrote poetry of many different kinds, including the militantly republican *Song of Italy* (1867) and *Songs before Sunrise* (1871) in support of the *risorgimento*, the movement for Italian political unity, as well as nature poetry. Although individual volumes of Swinburne's poetry were occasionally well received, in general his popularity and critical reputation declined following the initial sensation of *Poems and Ballads.*

Swinburne's physical appearance, his personality, and the facts of his life have received much attention from biographers and from commentators exploring biographical bases of his works. He was small, frail, and plagued by numerous peculiarities of physique and temperament, including an overlarge head, nervous gestures, and seizures that may have been manifestations of a form of epilepsy. Throughout the 1860s and 1870s he drank excessively and was prone to accidents that often left him bruised, bloody, or unconscious. Until his forties he suffered intermittent physical collapses that necessitated removal to his parents' home while he recovered. In 1879, Swinburne's friend and literary agent, Theodore Watts-Dunton, intervened during a time when Swinburne was dangerously ill. Watts-Dunton isolated Swinburne at a suburban home in Putney and gradually weaned him from alcohol—and from many former companions and habits as well. Swinburne lived another thirty years with Watts-Dunton, whose role remains controversial. He denied Swinburne's friends access to him, controlled the poet's money, and restricted his activities. However, commentators agree that Swinburne's erratic conduct could have resulted in his death, and Watts-Dunton is generally credited with saving his life and encouraging him to continue writing into his old age. Swinburne died in 1909 at the age of seventy-two.

The most important and conspicuous quality of Swinburne's work is an intense lyricism. Even early critics, who often took exception to his subject matter, commended his intricately extended and evocative imagery, metrical virtuosity, rich use of assonance and alliteration, and bold, complex rhythms. At the same time, the strong rhythms of his poems and his characteristic use of alliteration were sometimes carried to extremes and rendered his work highly susceptible to parody. Critics note that his usually effective imagery is at times vague and imprecise, and his rhymes are sometimes facile and uninspired. After establishing residence in Putney, Swinburne largely abandoned the themes of pathological sexuality that had characterized much of his earlier poetry. Nature and landscape poetry began to predominate, as well as poems about children. Many commentators maintain that the poetry written during the years at Putney is inferior to Swinburne's earlier work, but others have identified individual poems of exceptional merit among his later works, citing in particular "By the North Sea," "Evening on the Broads," "A Nympholept," "The Lake of Gaube," and "Neap-Tide."

Throughout his career Swinburne also published literary criticism of great acuity. His familiarity with a wide range of world literatures contributed to a critical style rich in quotation, allusion, and comparison. He is particularly noted for discerning studies of Elizabethan dramatists and of many English and French poets and novelists. In response to criticism of his own works, Swinburne wrote essays, including *Notes on Poems and Reviews* (1866) and *Under the Microscope* (1872), that are celebrated for their wit and insight. Swinburne also published one novel, *Love's Cross-Currents* (1901), serially under a pseudonym, and left another, *Lesbia Brandon,* unfinished at his death. The first attracted little notice other than some speculation about its authorship. Some critics have theorized that *Lesbia Brandon* was intended as thinly disguised autobiography; however, its fragmentary form resists conclusive interpretation.

During Swinburne's lifetime, critics considered *Poems and Ballads* his finest as well as his most characteristic poetic achievement; subsequent poetry and work in other genres was often disregarded. Since the mid-twentieth century, however, commentators have been offering new assessments of Swinburne's entire career. Forgoing earlier dismissals of Swinburne's voluminous later writings and reexamining individual poems strictly on their own merit, critics have identified works of great power and beauty from all periods of his career.

(For further information about Swinburne's life and works, see *Contemporary Authors,* Vol. 105; *Dictionary of Literary Biography,* Vols. 35, 57; and *Twentieth-Century Literary Criticism,* Vols. 8, 36.)

CRITICAL COMMENTARY

ROBERT BUCHANAN

(essay date 1866)

[Buchanan, an English poet and novelist, is chiefly remembered as the author of critical attacks on Swinburne and Dante Gabriel Rossetti in which he castigated their "fleshly" themes. In the following excerpt from an 1866 essay, he condemns *Poems and Ballads* as ineffective, insincere, "prurient trash."]

Mr. Swinburne commenced his literary career with considerable brilliance. His *Atalanta in Calydon* evinced noticeable gifts of word-painting and of music; and his *Chastelard,* though written in monotone, contained several passages of dramatic force and power. In the latter work, however, there was too open a proclivity to that garish land beyond the region of pure thinking, whither so many inferior writers have been lured for their destruction. . . . The genuineness of the work as Art, we would suggest, can be the only absolute test of immorality in a story or poem. Truly sincere writing, no matter how forcible, seldom really offends us. When, however, we find a writer like the author of these *Poems and Ballads,* who is deliberately and impertinently insincere as an artist,—who has no splendid individual emotions to reveal and is unclean for the mere sake of uncleanness,—we may safely affirm, in the face of many pages of brilliant writing, that such a man is either no poet at all, or a poet degraded from his high estate, and utterly and miserably lost to the Muses. How old is this young gentleman, whose bosom, it appears, is a flaming fire, whose face is as the fiery foam of flowers, and whose words are as the honeyed kisses of the Shulamite? He is quite the Absalom of modern bards,—long-ringleted, flippant-lipped, down-cheeked, amorous-lidded. He seems, moreover, to have prematurely attained to the fate of his old prototype; for we now find him fixed very fast indeed up a tree, and it will be a miracle if one breath of poetic life remain in him when he is cut down. . . . Yet ere we go further, let us at once disappoint Mr. Swinburne, who would doubtless be charmed if we averred that his poems were capable of having an absolutely immoral influence. They are too juvenile and unreal for that. The strong pulse of true passion beats in no one of them. They are unclean, with little power; and mere uncleanness repulses. (pp. 30-1)

[All] the images are false and distracted,—mere dabs of colour distributed carelessly and without art. . . .

It would be idle to quote such prurient trash . . .—save for the purpose of observing that Mr. Swinburne's thought is on a fair level with his style of expression:—both are untrue, insincere, and therefore unpoetical. Absolute passion there is none; elaborate attempts at thick colouring supply the place of passion. Now, it may be fairly assumed that a writer so hopelessly blind to the simplest decencies of style, so regardless of the first principles of Art, can scarcely fail to offend if he attempt to discuss topics of importance to his fellow creatures, or deal with themes which demand the slightest exercise of thought properly so called. When, therefore, Mr. Swinburne touches on religious questions, he writes such verses as the subjoined which, though put into the mouth of a Roman, are purely personal, implying precisely the same conditions of thought as we find expressed in the lyrical poems elsewhere:—

> Wilt thou yet take all, Galilean? but these thou shalt not take,
> The laurel, the palms and the paean, the breasts of the nymphs in the brake; . . .
>
> (p. 32)

Here, as in the other poems, we find no token of sincerity. It is quite obvious that Mr. Swinburne has never thought at all on religious questions, but imagines that rank blasphemy will be esteemed very clever. He describes the Almighty as *throwing dice* with the Devil for the soul of Faustine. . . . (p. 33)

Gross insincerity in dealing with simple subjects, and rank raving on serious themes, make one suspicious of a writer's quality in all things; and a very little examination enables us to perceive that these poems are essentially imitative. Indeed, Mr. Swinburne's knack of parody is very remarkable, though it weighs heavily against his literary quality. Nothing could be cleverer than his imitation, here printed, of an old miracle–play; or than his numerous copies of the French lyric writers; or than his ingenious parrotings of the way of Mr. Browning. In no single instance does he free himself from the style of the copyist. His skill in transferring an old or modern master would be an enviable gift for any writer but one who hoped to prove himself a poet. Then again, though clever and whimsical to the last degree, he is satisfied with most simple effects. After a little while we find out there is a trick in his very

Principal Works

The Queen-Mother and Rosamond (dramas) 1860

Atalanta in Calydon (drama) [first publication] 1865

Chastelard (drama) [first publication] 1865

Poems and Ballads (poetry) 1866; also published as Laus Veneris, and Other Poems and Ballads, 1866

Notes on Poems and Reviews (criticism) 1866

A Song of Italy (poetry) 1867

William Blake (criticism) 1868

Songs before Sunrise (poetry) 1871

Under the Microscope (criticism) 1872

Bothwell (drama) [first publication] 1874

Essays and Studies (criticism) 1875

George Chapman (criticism) 1875

Songs of Two Nations (poetry) 1875

Erechtheus (drama) [first publication] 1876

Poems and Ballads: Second Series (poetry) 1878

A Study of Shakespeare (criticism) 1880

Mary Stuart (drama) [first publication] 1881

Tristram of Lyonesse, and Other Poems (poetry) 1882

A Study of Victor Hugo (criticism) 1886

Locrine (drama) [first publication] 1887

Poems and Ballads: Third Series (poetry) 1889

A Study of Ben Jonson (criticism) 1889

Studies in Prose and Poetry (criticism) 1894

The Tale of Balen (poetry) 1896

Rosamund, Queen of the Lombards (drama) [first publication] 1899

*Love's Cross-Currents (novel) 1901; also published as A Year's Letters, 1974

A Channel Passage, and Other Poems (poetry) 1904

Shakespeare (criticism) 1909

Contemporaries of Shakespeare (criticism) 1919

The Complete Works of Algernon Charles Swinburne. 20 vols. (poetry, dramas, novel, essays, criticism, and letters) 1925-27

Lesbia Brandon (unfinished novel) 1952

The Swinburne Letters. 6 vols. (letters) 1959-62

*This work was originally published as A Year's Letters in the journal Tatler in 1877.

---

versification, that it owes its music to the most extraordinary style of alliteration. . . . This kind of writing, abounding in adjectives chosen merely because they alliterate, soon cloys and sickens; directly we find out the trick our pleasure departs. We soon perceive also that Mr. Swinburne's pictures are bright and worthless. We detect no real taste for colour; the skies are all Prussian blue, the flesh-tints all vermilion, the sunlights all gamboge. The writer, who has no meditative faculty, evinces total ignorance of nature; his eye rolls like that of a drunkard, whose vision is clouded with fumes. (pp. 33-4)

Robert Buchanan, "Robert Buchanan in 'Athenaeum' 1866," in *Swinburne: The Critical Heritage,* edited by Clyde K. Hyder, Barnes & Noble, Inc., 1970, pp. 30-5.

ALGERNON CHARLES SWINBURNE

(essay date 1866)

[In the following excerpt, Swinburne responds to Buchanan's attack on *Poems and Ballads* (see above).]

Certain poems of mine, it appears, have been impugned by judges, with or without a name, as indecent or as blasphemous. To me, as I have intimated, their verdict is a matter of infinite indifference: it is of equally small moment to me whether in such eyes as theirs I appear moral or immoral, Christian or pagan. But, remembering that science must not scorn to investigate animalcules and infusoria, I am ready for once to play the anatomist.

With regard to any opinion implied or expressed throughout [*Poems and Ballads*], I desire that one thing should be remembered: the book is dramatic, many-faced, multifarious; and no utterance of enjoyment or despair, belief or unbelief, can properly be assumed as the assertion of its author's personal feeling or faith. Were each poem to be accepted as the deliberate outcome and result of the writer's conviction, not mine alone but most other men's verses would leave nothing behind them but a sense of cloudy chaos and suicidal contradiction. Byron and Shelley, speaking in their own persons, and with what sublime effect we know, openly and insultingly mocked and reviled what the English of their day held most sacred. I have not done this. I do not say that, if I chose, I would not do so to the best of my power; I do say that hitherto I have seen fit to do nothing of the kind.

It remains then to inquire what in that book can be reasonably offensive to the English reader. (p. 326)

I am informed, and have not cared to verify the assertion, that "Anactoria" has excited, among the chaste and candid critics of the day or hour or minute, a more vehement reprobation, a more virtuous horror, a more passionate appeal, than any other of my writing. Proud and glad as I must be of this distinction, I must yet, however reluctantly, inquire what merit or demerit has incurred such unexpected honour. I was not ambitious of it; I am not ashamed of it; but I am overcome by it. . . .

What my poem means, if any reader should want that explained, I am ready to explain, though perplexed by the hint that explanation may be required. What certain reviewers have imagined it to imply, I am incompetent to explain, and unwilling to imagine. I am evidently not virtuous enough to understand them. I thank Heaven that I am not. *Ma corruption rougirait de leur pudeur.* ['My depravity would blush at their modesty.'] (p. 327)

In this poem I have simply expressed, or tried to express, that violence of affection between one and another which hardens into rage and deepens into despair. The keynote which I have here touched was struck long since by Sappho. (p. 328)

[But] the descent is immeasurable from Sappho's verse to mine, or to any man's. I have striven to cast my spirit into the mould of hers, to express and represent not the poem but the poet. I did not think it requisite to disfigure the page with a footnote wherever I had fallen back upon the original text. Here and there, I need not say, I have rendered into English the very words of Sappho. I have tried also to work into words of my own some expression of their effect: to bear witness how, more than any other's, her verses strike and sting the memory in lonely places, or at sea, among all loftier sights and sounds—how they seem akin to fire and air, being themselves 'all air and fire'; other element there is none in them. As to the angry appeal against the supreme mystery of oppressive heaven, which I have ventured to put into her mouth at that point only where pleasure culminates in pain, affection in anger, and desire in despair—as to the 'blasphemies' against God or Gods of which here and elsewhere I stand accused—they are to be taken as the first outcome or outburst of foiled and fruitless passion recoiling on itself. After this, the spirit finds time to breathe and repose above all vexed senses of the weary body, all bitter labours of the revolted soul; the poet's pride of place is resumed, the lofty conscience of invincible immortality in the memories and the mouths of men. (pp. 329-30)

Next on the list of accusation stands the poem of "Dolores." The gist and bearing of this I should have thought evident enough, viewed by the light of others which precede and follow it. I have striven here to express that transient state of spirit through which a man may be supposed to pass, foiled in love and weary of loving, but not yet in sight of rest; seeking refuge in those 'violent delights' which 'have violent ends,' in

fierce and frank sensualities which at least profess to be no more than they are. This poem, like "Faustine," is so distinctly symbolic and fanciful that it cannot justly be amenable to judgment as a study in the school of realism. (pp. 330-31)

The insight into evil of chaste and critical pressmen, their sharp scent for possible or impossible impurities, their delicate ear for a sound or a whisper of wrong—all this knowledge 'is too wonderful and excellent for me; I cannot attain unto it.' . . . I have overlooked the evidence which every day makes clearer, that our time has room only for such as are content to write for children and girls. But this oversight is the sum of my offence.

It would seem indeed as though to publish a book were equivalent to thrusting it with violence into the hands of every mother and nurse in the kingdom as fit and necessary food for female infancy. Happily there is no fear that the supply of milk for babes will fall short of the demand for some time yet. There are moral milkmen enough, in all conscience, crying their ware about the streets and byways; fresh or stale, sour or sweet, the requisite fluid runs from a sufficiently copious issue. In due time, perhaps, the critical doctors may prescribe a stronger diet for their hypochondriac patient, the reading world; or the gigantic *malade imaginaire* called the public may rebel against the weekly draught or the daily drug of MM. Purgon and Diafoirus [in Molière's *Le malade imaginaire*]. We, meanwhile, who profess to deal neither in poison nor in pap, may not unwillingly stand aside. Let those read who will, and let those who will abstain from reading. *Caveat emptor.* No one wishes to force men's food down the throats of babes and sucklings. The verses last analysed were assuredly written with no moral or immoral design; but the upshot seems to me moral rather than immoral, if it must needs be one or the other, and if (which I cannot be sure of) I construe aright those somewhat misty and changeable terms. (pp. 332-33)

To all this, however, there is a grave side. The question at issue is wider than any between a single writer and his critics, or it might well be allowed to drop. It is this: whether or not the first and last requisite of art is to give no offence; whether or not all that cannot be lisped in the nursery or fingered in the schoolroom is therefore to be cast out of the library; whether or not the domestic circle is to be for all men and writers the outer limit and extreme horizon of their world of work. For to this we have come; and all students of art must face the matter as it stands. (p. 338)

Algernon Charles Swinburne, "Notes on Poems and Reviews," in his *Poems and Ballads* [*and*] *Atalanta in Calydon,* edited by Morse Peckham, The Bobbs-Merrill Company, Inc., 1970, pp. 325-41.

OSCAR WILDE

(essay date 1889)

[Wilde was one of the foremost figures of late nineteenth-century English literary Decadence. For his brilliantly mannered prose, poetry, and drama, as well as his flamboyant way of life, he is identified with the "art for art's sake" movement, which defied the contemporary trend that subordinated art to ethical instruction. In the following excerpt from an essay that first appeared in the *Pall Mall Gazette* in 1889, he notes Swinburne's sometimes overwhelming linguistic virtuosity and his mastery of the romantic ballad form.]

Mr. Swinburne once set his age on fire by a volume of very perfect and very poisonous poetry. Then he became revolutionary, and pantheistic, and cried out against those who sit in high places both in heaven and on earth. Then he invented Marie Stuart, and laid upon us the heavy burden of *Bothwell*. Then he retired to the nursery, and wrote poems about children of a somewhat over-subtle character. He is now extremely patriotic, and manages to combine with his patriotism a strong affection for the Tory party. He has always been a great poet. But he has his limitations, the chief of which is, curiously enough, an entire lack of any sense of limit. His song is nearly always too loud for his subject. His magnificent rhetoric, nowhere more significant than in the volume that now lies before us, conceals rather than reveals. It has been said of him, and with truth, that he is a master of language, but with still greater truth it may be said that Language is his master. Words seem to dominate him. Alliteration tyrannizes over him. Mere sound often becomes his lord. He is so eloquent that whatever he touches becomes unreal. (p. 146)

Verse of this kind may be justly praised for the sustained strength and vigour of its metrical scheme. Its purely technical excellence is extraordinary. But is it more than an oratorical *tour-de-force*? Does it really convey much? Does it charm? Could we return to it again and again with renewed pleasure? We think not. It seems to us empty.

Of course, we must not look to these poems for any revelation of human life. To be at one with the elements seems to be Mr. Swinburne's aim. He seeks to speak with the breath of wind and wave. The roar of the fire is ever in his ears. He puts his clarion to the lips of Spring and bids her blow, and the Earth wakes from her dreams and tells him her secret. He is the first lyric poet who has tried to make an absolute surrender of his own personality, and he has succeeded. We hear the song, but we never know the singer. We never even get near to him. Out of the thunder and splendour of words he himself says nothing. We have often had man's interpretation of Nature; now we have Nature's interpretation of man, and she has curiously little to say. Force and Freedom form her vague message. She deafens us with her clangours.

But Mr. Swinburne is not always riding the whirlwind, and calling out of the depths of the sea. Romantic ballads in Border dialect have not lost their fascination for him, and this last volume contains some very splendid examples of this curious artificial kind of poetry. The amount of pleasure one gets out of dialect is a matter entirely of temperament. To say "mither" instead of "mother" seems to many the acme of romance. There are others who are not quite as ready to believe in the pathos of provincialisms. There is, however, no doubt of Mr. Swinburne's mastery over the form, whether the form be quite legitimate or not. **"The Weary Wedding"** [in *Poems and Ballads: Third Series*] has the concentration and colour of a great drama, and the quaintness of its style lends it something of the power of a grotesque. The ballad of **"The Witch-Mother,"** a medieval Medea who slays her children because her lord is faithless, is worth reading on account of its horrible simplicity. . . . **"The Tyneside Widow,"** and **"A Reiver's Neck-verse,"** are all poems of fine imaginative power, and some of them are terrible in their fierce intensity of passion. There is no danger of English poetry narrowing itself to a form so limited as the romantic ballad in dialect. It is too vital a growth for that. So we may welcome Mr. Swinburne's masterly experiments with the hope that things which are inimitable will not be imitated. . . . Certainly "for song's sake" we should love Mr. Swinburne's work, cannot indeed help loving it, so marvellous a music-maker is he. But what of the soul? For the soul we must go elsewhere. (pp. 147-49)

Oscar Wilde, "Mr. Swinburne's Last Volume," in his *The Artist as Critic: Critical Writings of Oscar Wilde,* edited by Richard Ellmann, 1969. Reprint by Random House, 1970, pp. 146-49.

T. S. ELIOT

(essay date 1920)

[Eliot, an American-born poet and critic, is closely identified with many of the qualities denoted by the term Modernism: experimentation, formal complexity, artistic and intellectual eclecticism, and a classicist's view of the artist working at an emotional distance from his or her creation. He introduced a number of terms and concepts that strongly affected critical thought in his lifetime, among them the idea that poets must be conscious of the living tradition of literature if their work is to have artistic and spiritual validity. In the following excerpt, he assesses Swinburne's critical essays as essentially appreciative rather than judgmental and maintains that the salient characteristic of his poetry is its diffuseness.]

Three conclusions at least issue from the perusal of Swinburne's critical essays: Swinburne had mastered his material, was more inward with the Tudor-Stuart dramatists than any man of pure letters before or since; he is a more reliable guide to them than Hazlitt, Coleridge, or Lamb; and his perception of relative values is almost always correct. Against these merits we may oppose two objections: the style is the prose style of Swinburne, and the content is not, in an exact sense, criticism. The faults of style are, of course, personal; the tumultuous outcry of adjectives, the headstrong rush of undisciplined sentences, are the index to the impatience and perhaps laziness of a disorderly mind. But the style has one positive merit: it allows us to know that Swinburne was writing not to establish a critical reputation, not to instruct a docile public, but as a poet his notes upon poets whom he admired. And whatever our opinion of Swinburne's verse, the notes upon poets by a poet of Swinburne's dimensions must be read with attention and respect.

In saying that Swinburne's essays have the value of notes of an important poet upon important poets, we must place a check upon our expectancy. He read everything, and he read with the single interest in finding literature. (pp. 17-18)

With all his justness of judgment, however, Swinburne is an appreciator and not a critic. In the whole range of literature covered, Swinburne makes hardly more than two judgments which can be reversed or even questioned: one, that [John] Lyly is insignificant as a dramatist, and the other, that [James] Shirley was probably unaffected by [John] Webster. . . . Swinburne's judgment is generally sound, his taste sensitive and discriminating. And we cannot say that his thinking is faulty or perverse—up to the point at which it is thinking. But Swinburne stops thinking just at the moment when we are most zealous to go on. And this arrest, while it does not vitiate his work, makes it an introduction rather than a statement.

We are aware, after the *Contemporaries of Shakespeare* and the *Age of Shakespeare* and the books on Shakespeare and Jonson, that there is something unsatisfactory in the way in which Swinburne was interested in these people; we suspect that his interest was never articulately formulated in his mind or consciously directed to any purpose. As it is, there are to be no conclusions, except that Elizabethan literature is very great, and that you can have pleasure and even ecstasy

from it, because a sensitive poetic talent has had the experience. (pp. 19-21)

When it is a matter of pronouncing judgment between two poets, Swinburne is almost unerring. He is certainly right in putting Webster above [Cyril] Tourneur, Tourneur above [John] Ford, and Ford above Shirley. He weighs accurately the good and evil in [John] Fletcher: he perceives the essential theatricality, but his comparison of the *Faithful Shepherdess* with *Comus* is a judgment no word of which can be improved upon. . . . (pp. 21-2)

In the longest and most important essay in the *Contemporaries of Shakespeare,* the essay on [George] Chapman, there are many such sentences of sound judgment forcibly expressed. The essay is the best we have on that great poet. It communicates the sense of dignity and mass which we receive from Chapman. But it also illustrates Swinburne's infirmities. Swinburne was not tormented by the restless desire to penetrate to the heart and marrow of a poet, any more than he was tormented by the desire to render the finest shades of difference and resemblance between several poets. . . . Swinburne's essay would have been all the better if he had applied himself to the solution of problems like this. (pp. 22-3)

He did not apply himself to this sort of problem because this was not the sort of problem that interested him. The author of Swinburne's critical essays is also the author of Swinburne's verse: if you hold the opinion that Swinburne was a very great poet, you can hardly deny him the title of a great critic. There is the same curious mixture of qualities to produce Swinburne's own effect, resulting in the same blur, which only the vigour of the colours fixes. His great merit as a critic is really one which, like many signal virtues, can be stated so simply as to appear flat. It is that he was sufficiently interested in his subject-matter and knew quite enough about it; and this is a rare combination in English criticism. Our critics are often interested in extracting something from their subject which is not fairly in it. And it is because this elementary virtue is so rare that Swinburne must take a very respectable place as a critic. Critics are often interested—but not quite in the nominal subject, often in something a little beside the point; they are often learned—but not quite to the point either. (Swinburne knew some of the plays almost by heart.) (p. 24)

It is a question of some nicety to decide how much must be read of any particular poet. And it is not a question merely of the size of the poet. There are some poets whose every line has unique value. There are others who can be taken by a few poems universally agreed upon. There are others who need be read only in selections, but what selections are read will not very much matter. Of Swinburne, we should like to have the *Atalanta* entire, and a volume of selections which should certainly contain **"The Leper," "Laus Veneris"** and **"The Triumph of Time."** It ought to contain many more, but there is perhaps no other single poem which it would be an error to omit. A student of Swinburne will want to read one of the Stuart plays and dip into *Tristram of Lyonesse.* But almost no one, to-day, will wish to read the whole of Swinburne. It is not because Swinburne is voluminous; certain poets, equally voluminous, must be read entire. The necessity and the difficulty of a selection are due to the peculiar nature of Swinburne's contribution, which, it is hardly too much to say, is of a very different kind from that of any other poet of equal reputation. (p. 144)

We may take it as undisputed that Swinburne did make a contribution; that he did something that had not been done before, and that what he did will not turn out to be a fraud. And from that we may proceed to inquire what Swinburne's contribution was, and why, whatever critical solvents we employ to break down the structure of his verse, this contribution remains. The test is this: agreed that we do not (and I think that the present generation does not) greatly enjoy Swinburne, and agreed that (a more serious condemnation) at one period of our lives we did enjoy him and now no longer enjoy him, nevertheless, the words which we use to state our grounds of dislike or indifference cannot be applied to Swinburne as they can to bad poetry. The words of condemnation are words which express his qualities. You may say "diffuse." But the diffuseness is essential; had Swinburne practised greater concentration his verse would be, not better in the same kind, but a different thing. His diffuseness is one of his glories. That so little material as appears to be employed in **"The Triumph of Time"** should release such an amazing number of words, requires what there is no reason to call anything but genius. You could not condense **"The Triumph of Time."** You could only leave out. And this would destroy the poem; though no one stanza seems essential. Similarly, a considerable quantity—a volume of selections—is necessary to give the quality of Swinburne although there is perhaps no one poem essential in this selection. (p. 145)

If, then, we must be very careful in applying terms of censure, like "diffuse," we must be equally careful of praise. "The beauty of Swinburne's verse is the sound," people say, explaining, "he had little visual imagination." I am inclined to think that the word "beauty" is hardly to be used in connection with Swinburne's verse at all; but in any case the beauty or effect of sound is neither that of music nor that of poetry which can be set to music. There is no reason why verse intended to be sung should not present a sharp visual image or convey an important intellectual meaning, for it supplements the music by another means of affecting the feelings. What we get in Swinburne is an expression by sound, which could not possibly associate itself with music. For what he gives is not images and ideas and music, it is one thing with a curious mixture of suggestions of all three. . . . Now, in Swinburne the meaning and the sound are one thing. He is concerned with the meaning of the word in a peculiar way; he employs, or rather "works," the word's meaning. And this is connected with an interesting fact about his vocabulary: he uses the most general word, because his emotion is never particular, never in direct line of vision, never focused; it is emotion reinforced, not by intensification, but by expansion.

> There lived a singer in France of old
> By the tideless dolorous midland sea.
> In a land of sand and ruin and gold
> There shone one woman, and none but she.

You see that Provence is the merest point of diffusion here. Swinburne defines the place by the most general word, which has for him its own value. "Gold," "ruin," "dolorous": it is not merely the sound that he wants, but the vague associations of idea that the words give him. He has not his eye on a particular place. . . . It is, in fact, the word that gives him the thrill, not the object. When you take to pieces any verse of Swinburne, you find always that the object was not there—only the word. (pp. 146-48)

The world of Swinburne does not depend upon some other world which it simulates; it has the necessary completeness and self-sufficiency for justification and permanence. It is impersonal, and no one else could have made it. The deductions are true to the postulates. It is indestructible. None of the obvious complaints that were or might have been brought to bear upon the first *Poems and Ballads* holds good. The poetry is not morbid, it is not erotic, it is not destructive. These are adjectives which can be applied to the material, the human feelings, which in Swinburne's case do not exist. The morbidity is not of human feeling but of language. Language in a healthy state presents the object, is so close to the object that the two are identified.

They are identified in the verse of Swinburne solely because the object has ceased to exist, because the meaning is merely the hallucination of meaning, because language, uprooted, has adapted itself to an independent life of atmospheric nourishment. In Swinburne, for example, we see the word "weary" flourishing in this way independent of the particular and actual weariness of flesh or spirit. The bad poet dwells partly in a world of objects and partly in a world of words, and he never can get them to fit. Only a man of genius could dwell so exclusively and consistently among words as Swinburne. His language is not, like the language of bad poetry, dead. It is very much alive, with this singular life of its own. (pp. 149-50)

T. S. Eliot, "Imperfect Critics," and "Swinburne As Poet," in his *The Sacred Wood: Essays on Poetry and Criticism,* 1920. Reprint by Methuen & Co. Ltd., 1950, pp. 17-24, pp. 144-50.

JOHN D. ROSENBERG
(essay date 1968)

[Rosenberg is an American educator and critic who has written critical studies of John Ruskin and Alfred Tennyson and edited editions of Tennyson and Swinburne. In the following essay, he assesses various characteristics of Swinburne's poetry, commending in particular the author's skillful use of poetic language.]

Swinburne is a poet not of natural objects but of natural energies—of winds and surging waters. His scale is macrocosmic, his focus less upon the small celandine than upon the spines of mountains, less upon things seen than forces felt. At times he is nearly a blind poet, all tongue and ear and touch. His poetry moves away from the art of painting and toward the art of music; after reading Swinburne one retains not an image but a tonality and a rhythm.

Traditionally, the English poet has prided himself on particularity, which English criticism has exalted as the clearest sign of genius. Donne's "bracelet of bright haire about the bone" has dazzled the critics for half a century. The modern reader's very conception of poetry has been shaped by the practices of the Metaphysical poets and by Keats's dictum that the poet must have "distinctness for his luxury." We are at a loss in reading a poet who, like Swinburne, is diffuse not by default but by design.

From the perspective of Keats's principles, Gerard Manley Hopkins is in the main stream of nineteenth-century verse and Swinburne is the eccentric. For Hopkins' attempt to etch in words the dappled individuality of things was as much a cultural as a personal concern. Hopkins was simply an extreme exponent of the impulse to render with absolute accuracy the distinct profusion of nature itself. One recognizes the same impulse in the splendid exactitude of Tennyson's verse and Ruskin's prose, in the bright, crowded, microscopically accurate foliage of the Pre-Raphaelites, in Browning's eft, queer, creeping things, or, for that matter, in the solid clutter of any Victorian mantelpiece.

Memory betrays us into believing Swinburne to be far more ornate than he is. Dismissed as overlush and decadent, he is in point of diction the most *austere* of the greatly gifted poets of his century. Early in his career he evokes the heady, Pre-Raphaelite scent of oversweet violets, but in his greatest poetry Swinburne is more starkly monosyllabic than Wordsworth. The knight doomed to a sexually joyless service in **"Laus Veneris"** craves death in a stanza containing thirty-seven sparse words, all but four of them monosyllables:

Ah yet would God this flesh of mine might be
Where air might wash and long leaves cover me,
Where tides of grass break into foam of flowers,
Or where the wind's feet shine along the sea.

[In his introduction to *The Novels of Swinburne*] Edmund Wilson condemns Swinburne for his "generalizing visageless monosyllables"; I would praise him as the supreme master in English of the bleak beauty of little words.

Wilson has argued that Swinburne the poet is a nullity and that his true gifts lay with the novel, in which he escapes the monotonous vocabulary of his verse: "He can never surprise or delight by a colloquial turn of phrase, a sharply observed detail, a magical touch of color." This might be helpful if it were true, which it is not, or if it were reasonable to condemn Swinburne for not succeeding in what he did not attempt to do. If there are few sudden glories in his verse, they are suppressed in the interests of a more sustained harmony. Great art, he believed, does not vex or fret the beholder with "mere brilliance of point and sharpness of stroke, and such intemperate excellence as gives astonishment the precedence of admiration: such beauties as strike you and startle and go out" [Swinburne, **"Matthew Arnold's New Poems"**]. Hopkins pushes language as far as it can go toward pointedness and sharpness of stroke; Swinburne moves it with equal daring in the opposite direction, diffusing where Hopkins concentrates, generalizing where Hopkins specifies. Together, they are the linguistic bravos of Victorian verse.

By diffuseness, however, I mean something very different from vagueness. The vague poet cannot see or speak clearly—in short, is not a poet. Swinburne is often called vague, but no one who has read his best poetry closely could ever accuse him of imprecision or carelessness with words. T. S. Eliot did not look closely enough at a famous chorus of Swinburne and charged him with laxity:

Before the beginning of years
There came to the making of man
Time, with a gift of tears;
Grief, with a glass that ran. . . .

The verses appear to make a "tremendous statement, like statements made in our dreams," Eliot writes of this chorus from *Atalanta in Calydon;* "when we wake up we find that the 'glass that ran' would do better for time than for grief, and that the gift of tears would be as appropriately bestowed by grief as by time" ["Swinburne as Poet" in his *Selected Essays*].

The reversed verses that Eliot prefers—time with an hourglass, grief with tears—are trite, and Swinburne wisely avoided them. But he had more positive reasons for overturning our expectation, as immediately becomes clear if we complete Eliot's truncated quotation:

> . . . Grief, with a glass that ran;
> Pleasure, with pain for leaven;
> Summer, with flowers that fell;
> Remembrance fallen from heaven,
> And madness risen from hell;
> Strength without hands to smite;
> Love that endures for a breath:
> Night, the shadow of light,
> And life, the shadow of death.

The chorus, like the play it mirrors, is about the terrible ambiguity of the god's gifts to men. We are given the bittersweet gift of time, but it passes even as it is given, and hence our tears; yet the pangs of grief also fade with the hours, like the summer blossom. As we read the lines, we are half aware of the conventional imagery underlying them, our mind reacting as does our ear to a departure from regular rhythm, half hearing the normal beat and half hearing the eccentric.

Swinburne constantly breaks down our habitual word associations, but the rupture is so slight that we scarcely notice it. The kind of gentle dislocation that Eliot condemned in the chorus from *Atalanta* gives to Swinburne's poetry the quality of a prolonged, mildly mixed metaphor, a quality which Eliot himself brilliantly exploited in his own poetry. This sense of disorientation, together with Swinburne's insistent, mesmeric meters, induces a surrealist heightening of consciousness that we associate with dreaming and that Swinburne realized with beautiful daring in **"The Leper,"** a ballad about a necrophiliac monk who makes love to the remnants of his lady. Grotesquely explicit, the poem is also inexplicably lovely, like the disintegrating lady, "sweeter than all sweet." The word *sweet* floats like a perfume throughout **"The Leper."** It recurs most often at those moments when the sense of the poem is most repugnant, sweet sound and fetid sense miraculously counterpoised through thirty-five stanzas.

Swinburne's adjectives, as with *sweet* in **"The Leper,"** have a way of detaching themselves from the nouns they adjoin and modifying instead whole lines or stanzas. He deliberately suppresses the specifying, limiting function of the adjective in order to discharge its meaning through the total poem. The search for *le mot juste* ["the exact word"] is, in the young Swinburne at least, the search for *le ton juste* ["the exact tone"], for the word which will not stick like a burr in the consciousness but serve unnoticed as a supporting note in a chord of color. Hence the intentional blandness of his diction, and his overfondness for generalizing modifiers like *bright, sad, light, glad,* and *sweet.* Swinburne's earlier, Pre-Raphaelite imitations are especially rich in such diction and should be read as *études* in verbal coloration.

The opening lines of **"A Ballad of Life,"** the first of the *Poems and Ballads* of 1866, offer the reader a conditioning exercise in those lightly limiting adjectives and bland plural nouns that enable Swinburne to arrange words as if they were pigments, or notes in a scale. Pairs of *glads, sweets,* and *sads* resolve themselves into a single neutral chord, as muted as a flame rained upon:

> I found in dreams a place of wind and flowers,
> Full of *sweet* trees and colour of *glad* grass,
> In midst whereof there was
> A lady clothed like summer with *sweet* hours.
> Her beauty, fervent as a fiery moon,
> Made my blood burn and swoon
> Like a flame rained upon.
> Sorrow had filled her shaken eyelids' blue,
> And her mouth's *sad* red heavy rose all through
> Seemed *sad* with *glad* things gone.

In these flawless minor lyrics—**"A Ballad of Life," "Hermaphroditus," "A Match," "Before the Mirror," "The Roundel"**—language takes on a life independent of any ostensible subject. Words, severed from the soil of things, send out aerial roots of their own.

One seems to be overhearing an exquisitely beautiful voice singing at a distance; the melody carries, but the words come muffled, as if in a foreign tongue:

> If love were what the rose is,
> And I were like the leaf,
> Our lives would grow together
> In sad or singing weather,
> Blown fields or flowerful closes,
> Green pleasure or grey grief;
> If love were what the rose is,
> And I were like the leaf.
>
> • • • • •
>
> If you were queen of pleasure,
> And I were king of pain,
> We'd hunt down love together,
> Pluck out his flying-feather,
> And teach his feet a measure,
> And find his mouth a rein;
> If you were queen of pleasure,
> And I were king of pain.

> ("A Match")

Self-engendered, self-contained, the poem is inspired not by the emotion of love but by the emotion of poetry itself.

All that Swinburne learned in composing these exercises in verbal color he put to use in the much later and more ambitious *Tristram of Lyonesse.* The "Prelude" to *Tristram* usually makes its way into the anthologies, but the rest of the poem is virtually unread, although it is one of the great erotic poems in English. *Tristram* is undervalued largely because the wrong demands have been made upon it. As narrative or as a drama of action the poem inevitably disappoints, in precisely the ways that Wagner's *Tristan and Isolde* disappoints. In both of these essentially *lyrical* re-creations of the legend, action and characterization are wholly subordinate to the all-absorbing theme of love. Just as there are no independent arias in *Tristan,* so there are no striking images in Swinburne's *Tristram* that are not repeated as leitmotifs and thus reabsorbed into the enveloping texture of the verse. The Londoner who read Swinburne's poem upon its publication in 1882 and then, just one month later, heard the English première of Wagner's music drama might well have felt a certain *déjà entendu* [sense of something "already known"].

From its opening lines to its close, *Tristram of Lyonesse* is about four lips that "become one burning mouth." As so often in Swinburne, the "image" is more tactile than visual. It first appears when Tristram and Iseult drink the potion; it recurs in a series of variants, most notably in Tristram's praise of "the mute clear music of her amorous mouth," a line whose enunciation moves the mouth into the position of a kiss. The image closes the poem as Iseult bows her head over the dead Tristram, "And their four lips became one silent mouth."

Although love is doomed, bleak, sick and sterile in almost all of Swinburne's poetry, in *Tristram* one senses his unique exultation in portraying sex that is fulfilled, however fated. Perhaps it is *because* the lovers are so clearly foredoomed that he could write so richly of their fulfillment. In this central legend symbolizing the love-sickness of the Western world, Swinburne creates by far his healthiest love poetry:

> Only with stress of soft fierce hands she prest
> Between the throbbing blossoms of her breast
> His ardent face, and through his hair her breath
> Went quivering as when life is hard on death;
> And with strong trembling fingers she strained fast
> His head into her bosom; till at last,
> Satiate with sweetness of that burning bed,
> His eyes afire with tears, he raised his head
> And laughed into her lips; and all his heart
> Filled hers; then face from face fell, and apart
> Each hung on each with panting lips, and felt
> Sense into sense and spirit in spirit melt.

These lines occur in Canto II, "The Queen's Pleasance," the poem's great *Liebesnacht* in which rest at last gains mastery "in the lovely fight of love and sleep." All of nature is absorbed into the passion of love, until the perfumed air seems an extension of the lovers' breath, the soft grass an extension of their bodies. The erotic interpenetration of nature and man is one of the poem's pervasive motifs, most remarkably realized in lines from Canto I describing a spring sunrise and the parallel dawning of womanhood in Iseult. Images of light, heat, florescence and flame all fuse into a single Turnerian chord of color, as Iseult herself comes to full flower under the "august great blossom" of the sun:

>   . . . she felt
> Through her own soul the sovereign morning
>   melt,
> And all the sacred passion of the sun;
> And as the young clouds flamed and were undone
> About him coming, touched and burnt away
> In rosy ruin and yellow spoil of day,
> The sweet veil of her body and corporal sense
> Felt the dawn also cleave it, and incense
> With light from inward and with effluent heat
> The kindling soul through fleshly hands and feet.
> And as the august great blossom of the dawn
> Burst, and the full sun scarce from sea withdrawn
> Seemed on the fiery water a flower afloat,
> So as a fire the mighty morning smote
> Throughout her, and incensed with the influent
>   hour
> Her whole soul's one great mystical red flower
> Burst, and the bud of her sweet spirit broke
> Rose-fashion, and the strong spring at a stroke
> Thrilled, and was cloven, and from the full sheath
>   came
> The whole rose of the woman red as flame:
> And all her Mayday blood as from a swoon
> Flushed, and May rose up in her and was June.

Swinburne concluded *Tristram of Lyonesse* with a final verse paragraph that, to my knowledge, has no precedent in any version of the legend. King Mark builds the lovers a stone chapel at the sea's edge, and in their death the lovers undergo a second doom. For the waves shatter the chapel and the sea closes over their uncoffined bones. Fulfilled love in Swinburne pays the penalty of double death.

The association of love with death is the underlying theme of almost all of Swinburne's major poetry. He is of course best known for a variant on that theme—the pain implicit in all pleasure. Virtually incapable of using the word *pleasure* without its alliterative opposite, Swinburne is undeniably sadomasochistic, but this lurid aspect of his lyricism has obscured his true achievement. His greatest love poetry is addressed not to those literary ladies with sharp teeth—Dolores, Faustine, and the rest—but to his bitter, salt mother the sea, and to those bleakly beautiful, ravaged margins of earth that yield their substance to her.

Swinburne is the laureate of barrenness in all its forms. I find myself further from the essential matter of his poetry when I learn, as his critics stress of late, that he was fond of being whipped, than when I read his nobly sad letter congratulating Edmund Gosse on his marriage:

> I suppose it must be the best thing that can befall a
> man to win and keep the woman that he loves while
> yet young; at any rate I can congratulate my friend
> on his good hap without any too jealous after-

thought of the reverse experience which left my own young manhood "a barren stock." . . .

The signs of that "reverse experience" are everywhere in Swinburne's poetry. In the autobiographical **"Thalassius,"** for example, Swinburne tells of his painful encounter with the young god of Love. Terrifyingly transformed, Love "waxes immeasurable" and from his erected height says to the poet:

O fool, my name is sorrow;
Thou fool, my name is death.

Of course, Swinburne's trauma in love would not have so scarred him were it not for an antecedent disposition toward being bruised. His peculiar vulnerability and ambivalence to pain express themselves in the figure of the *femme fatale* who dominates all of his early writing. Although she is a familiar type in nineteenth-century literature, this "fair fearful Venus made of deadly foam" objectifies Swinburne's personal sense of the deathliness of desire and the desirability of death. The hero of *Chastelard,* for example, commits the curiously passive indiscretion of watching Mary Stuart disrobe, in order to compel her to behead him. In an ecstasy of self-prostration, Chastelard says to his Queen:

Stretch your throat that I may kiss all round
Where mine shall be cut through; suppose my
  mouth
The axe-edge to bite so sweet a throat in twain
With bitter iron, should not it turn soft
As lip is soft to lip?

Chastelard is too specialized in theme and derivative in style to engage the general reader, although as an exercise in unrelenting eroticism, this mid-Victorian *Salomé* retains the power to shock. In *Atalanta* Swinburne steps outside the torrid circle of his obsessions and creates a world as bright, virginal and swift as *Chastelard* is sick with too many roses. Yet he still manages to use the myth of the virgin huntress as a vehicle for his private sensibility. Atalanta is a *frigid* Venus who destroys her lover Meleager as mercilessly as Aphrodite destroys Hippolytus.

No tact is fine enough to discriminate among all the various shades in Swinburne's portrait of love. At times he takes a schoolboy's hot delight simply in handling the theme. At times he writes like a patrician revolutionary attacking sexual prudery as John Stuart Mill attacked intellectual conformity. Occasionally love serves him as an excuse for embroidering rhymes in which birds or flowers would do as well. But the theme can get out of hand, as in **"Anactoria,"** in which he writes with morbid power of the pleasures of inflicting pain:

I would find grievous ways to have thee slain,
Intense device, and superflux of pain;
Vex thee with amorous agonies, and shake

Swinburne in 1900, by R.P. Staples.

Life at thy lips, and leave it there to ache;
Strain out thy soul with pangs too soft to kill,
Intolerable interludes, and infinite ill;
Relapse and reluctation of the breath,
Dumb tunes and shuddering semitones of death.

• • • • •

Ah that my lips were tuneless lips, but pressed
To the bruised blossom of thy scourged white
  breast!
Ah that my mouth for Muses' milk were fed
On the sweet blood thy sweet small wounds had
  bled!
That with my tongue I felt them, and could taste
The faint flakes from thy bosom to thy waist!
That I could drink thy veins as wine, and eat
Thy breasts like honey! that from face to feet
Thy body were abolished and consumed,
And in my flesh thy very flesh entombed!

• • • • •

Would I not plague thee dying overmuch?
Would I not hurt thee perfectly? not touch
Thy pores of sense with torture, and make bright
Thine eyes with bloodlike tears and grievous light?
Strike pang from pang as note is struck from note,
Catch the sob's middle music in thy throat,
Take thy limbs living, and new-mould with these
A lyre of many faultless agonies?

The horror of the last couplet is heightened by its exquisite verbal wit, as faultless as Marvell's green thought in a green shade.

The passion in **"Anactoria"** goes well beyond Swinburne's desire throughout *Poems and Ballads* to *épater le bourgeois* ["shock the middle classes"]. Only in two or three prose passages of *Lesbia Brandon* does one sense the same overwhelming pressure toward personal release, the same breathing closeness of the author to his text. Elsewhere in *Poems and Ballads* Swinburne handles similar themes in cooler tones. Poems whose sadism and anti-theism aroused or shocked generations of readers seem today to veer away from blasphemy toward burlesque. Yet Swinburne's death occasioned a sermon by the Vice Dean of Canterbury Cathedral on the need of Christ's blood itself to wash away "the pollution which Swinburne's poetry introduced into English literature."

Instead of pollution, I find a certain innocence in Swinburne's perversity. As in his letters, with their Etonian slang and naughty allusions to the Divine Marquis, his eroticism is often more infantile than immoral. Perhaps critical judgment is so unsettled over Swinburne because he is at once a great poet of the solitude of loving and a precocious schoolboy making off-color rhymes. Nor does it simplify matters that he is possibly the most gifted parodist and mimic in English. Swinburne in jest often appears most in earnest, and his apparent earnestness is often a jest, as in his hymn to Notre Dame des Sept Douleurs:

> Could you hurt me, sweet lips, though I hurt you?
> Men touch them, and change in a trice
> The lilies and languors of virtue
> For the raptures and roses of vice;
> Those lie where thy foot on the floor is,
> These crown and caress thee and chain,
> O splendid and sterile Dolores,
> Our Lady of Pain.

• • • • •

> Thou wert fair in the fearless old fashion,
> And thy limbs are as melodies yet,
> And move to the music of passion
> With lithe and lascivious regret.
> What ailed us, O gods, to desert you
> For creeds that refuse and restrain?
> Come down and redeem us from virtue,
> Our Lady of Pain.

In this litany of a sadomasochist's lust, Dolores presides over the marriage of Pleasure and Pain in a ceremony that suggests a black mass. Beneath the deftly controlled surface, one recognizes several of the major themes of *Poems and Ballads:* the intricate connection of pleasure and pain; the dual desire to experience and inflict suffering; a will to fall prey to the destructive sexual force of woman, and the fear of so falling; a need for total self-abasement and a counterimpulse to rebel;

a deeply religious reverence before a mystery, and as profound a desire to blaspheme.

God is the supreme sadist in *Poems and Ballads.* Swinburne defies Him eloquently and delightedly: "Him would I reach, him smite, him desecrate," he writes in **"Anactoria"** of the God who grinds men in order to feed the mute, melancholy lust of heaven. At times Swinburne's poetry of pure defiance achieves a Job-like integrity; at times it suggests a schoolboy's provoking his headmaster to lay on the rod. This antitheist verse never succeeds as great poetry, although it is often great rhetoric, as in the **"Hymn to Proserpine,"** with its lament for the conquest of the pagan world by the pale Galilean.

Swinburne's rebellion against the tyrant God finds its complement in his worship of man. One recalls that this blasphemer of the pieties of his age once arrived at a dinner party bearing a footstool, so that he could pay proper homage to Robert Browning. In his verse, as in his life, Swinburne was both rigidly defiant and pliantly responsive, self-exultant and self-abasing, a rebel and a mimic. His long sequence of poems of praise begins with tributes to Walter Savage Landor and Victor Hugo in *Poems and Ballads* and ends, some fifty years later, with his humble effusions to the babies of Wimbledon Common.

Swinburne's second volume of poems, *Songs before Sunrise,* is in all apparent respects the opposite of *Poems and Ballads.* Erotic verses give way to marching songs in praise of Italian liberation. We leave the sultry atmosphere of the boudoir and breathe instead the bracing air of the *Risorgimento;* our Lady of Liberty displaces our Lady of Pain. Yet the two ladies inspire in Swinburne similar emotions of self-prostration and worship. In **"The Oblation,"** for example, he addresses Liberty as if she were a stern lover under whose feet he craves to be trampled:

> All things were nothing to give
> Once to have sense of you more,
> Touch you and taste of you sweet,
> Think you and breathe you and live,
> Swept of your wings as they soar,
> Trodden by chance of your feet.

The sincerity of Swinburne's attachment to the goddess of Liberty is unassailable, although he composed many of his odes to her while walking to a brothel where he paid to be flogged.

The fault with *Songs before Sunrise* and its companion volume, *Songs of Two Nations,* is not their covert pathology but their dullness. Dolores and Faustine at least could bite, but Lady Liberty merely bores. Perhaps the themes of sexual humiliation and theological defiance in *Poems and Ballads* are intrinsically richer than the parallel themes of hero-worship and political rebellion in *Songs before Sunrise.* At any rate, the abstract diction, the manic, trumpet-blast tone, the rhetorical straining—"O soul, O God, O glory of liberty"—soon exhaust the reader's capacity to respond.

With startling self-knowledge, Swinburne anticipated the cause of his relative failure in *Songs before Sunrise.* [The critic adds in a footnote that " 'Failure' is too harsh a term. There are at least a dozen distinguished poems in the volume, among them '**Super Flumina Babylonis,' 'Hertha,' 'Before a Crucifix,' 'Hymn of Man,' 'Genesis,' 'Christmas Antiphones,' 'Siena,' 'Cor Cordium,' 'Tiresias,' 'On the Downs,' 'Messidor,'** and '**Non dolet'.** But none of these reaches the standard set in *Poems and Ballads,* 1866, by '**Laus Veneris'** and '**The Triumph of Time'** and attained again in *Poems and Ballads,* 1878, by '**A Forsaken Garden'** and '**A Vision of Spring in Winter.'** I should add that other critics disagree with my tepid estimate of *Songs before Sunrise,* among them T. Earle Welby and Swinburne himself."] "There is I think room for a book of songs of the European revolution," he wrote to William Michael Rossetti on beginning the volume, "and if sung as thoroughly as Hugo or as Whitman would sing them, they ought to ring for some time to some distance of echo. The only fear is that one may be disabled by one's desire—made impotent by excess of strain." The love of liberty was one of the most abiding and intense emotions that Swinburne knew. His rhetorical excess in *Songs before Sunrise* marks his ineffectual effort to translate great conviction into great art.

All that is forced or febrile in *Songs before Sunrise* achieves quiet fulfillment in the *Poems and Ballads* of 1878. In the first series of *Poems and Ballads,* one felt the exuberance of genius discovering itself; in the second series the voice has achieved self-mastery and sings in chaste magnificence. The volume appeared during the grimmest period of Swinburne's life, when he lived alone in London in suicidal dissipation. One senses the solitude, but none of the squalor. In the splendid elegies to dead poets interspersed through *Poems and Ballads,* Swinburne seems to lay his own youth to rest and prepare to retire from the exercise of his highest powers. One year after the volume was published, he was removed from his rooms in Great James Street by his friend Theodore Watts-Dunton and taken to live at Putney. For thirty years their home at "No. 2, The Pines," served Swinburne as a kind of suburban sanitorium. "The Pines" became the tomb of a great poet and the birthplace of a distinguished man of letters who wrote on Shakespeare and Victor Hugo, Marlowe and Mary, Queen of Scots. One of the finest lyrics in *Poems and Ballads* is entitled "**A Vision of Spring in Winter**"; the volume itself is a pervision of Swinburne's long winter, seen from the last moment of his spring.

The leitmotif of *Poems and Ballads* is the triumph of time over love, over life, and over the generative powers of earth and man. These are Swinburne's essential themes, and *Poems and Ballads,* 1878, is remarkable only in that it plays upon them more persistently and with his subtlest music. The sadomasochistic verses of *Poems and Ballads,* First Series, are less the heart of Swinburne's poetic matter than a variation on this larger theme of the forces in nature that divide and destroy us. "**Laus Veneris,**" "**The Leper,**" and "**Anactoria**" are extreme cases of the classic Swinburne situation in which lovers are, so to speak, disjointed. Once in the First Series—in "**The Triumph of Time**"—and once in the Second Series—in "**A Forsaken Garden**"—all of these elements meet in perfect balance. They are Swinburne's archetypical lyrics, adjacent stanzas of a single, larger poem.

In both poems one feels the full force of loss, and the counterforce of its acceptance. This stoicism of the heart, which falls short of bitterness on the one hand, and the sentimentality of unresisted regret on the other, is the defining note of Swinburne's love poetry. It is struck in the opening stanza of "**The Triumph of Time,**" in which the propulsive rush of the meter paces time's triumph over the lovers, changing all things except the fact of their separation:

> Before our lives divide for ever,
> While time is with us and hands are free,
> (Time, swift to fasten and swift to sever
> Hand from hand, as we stand by the sea)
> I will say no word that a man might say
> Whose whole life's love goes down in a day;
> For this could never have been; and never
> Though the gods and the years relent, shall be.

I mentioned the lovers in "**The Triumph of Time,**" but, remarkably, there are scarcely any lovers in Swinburne's poetry. There is much passion but little conjunction; emotion is felt but not communicated and not returned. Swinburne has mistakenly acquired the reputation of an erotic poet; he is rather the poet of love's impossibility. Perhaps that is why, even in his most sensual verses, one feels a peculiar innocence, just as in his most moving love poetry one feels a profound barrenness:

> It will grow not again, this fruit of my heart,
> Smitten with sunbeams, ruined with rain.
> The singing seasons divide and depart,
> Winter and summer depart in twain.
> It will grow not again, it is ruined at root,
> The bloodlike blossom, the dull red fruit;
> Though the heart yet sickens, the lips yet smart,
> With sullen savour of poisonous pain.

All of Swinburne's finer love poetry is set by the sea—the cold, clean "mother-maid" who is more palpable than the evershadowy girl who refuses, or is unaware of, the poet's love. The return to the sea in "**The Triumph of Time**" occurs near the poem's end, in three stanzas more strange than Swinburne's critics have yet acknowledged:

> I will go back to the great sweet mother,
> Mother and lover of men, the sea.
> I will go down to her, I and none other,
> Close with her, kiss her and mix her with me;
> Cling to her, strive with her, hold her fast;
> O fair white mother, in days long past
> Born without sister, born without brother,
> Set free my soul as thy soul is free.
>
> O fair green-girdled mother of mine,
> Sea, that art clothed with the sun and the rain,
> Thy sweet hard kisses are strong like wine,
> Thy large embraces are keen like pain.
> Save me and hide me with all thy waves,
> Find me one grave of thy thousand graves,
> Those pure cold populous graves of thine
> Wrought without hand in a world without stain.
>
> I shall sleep, and move with the moving ships,
> Change as the winds change, veer in the tide;
> My lips will feast on the foam of thy lips,
> I shall rise with thy rising, with thee subside;
> Sleep, and now know if she be, if she were,
> Filled full with life to the eyes and hair,
> As a rose is fulfilled to the roseleaf tips
> With splendid summer and perfume and pride.

The lines are at once infantile—"save me and hide me"—and overwhelming. One recalls that Swinburne's earliest memory was of shrieking with delight as his father tossed him headfirst into the waves. Fifty years later he wrote to his sister of the ecstasy he felt in swimming off the Sussex Downs:

> I ran like a boy, tore off my clothes, and hurled myself into the water. And it was but for a few minutes—but I was in Heaven! The whole sea was literally golden as well as green—it was liquid and living sunlight in which one lived and moved and had one's being. And to feel that in deep water is to feel—as long as one is swimming out, if only a minute or two—as if one was in another world of life, and one far more glorious than even Dante ever dreamed of in his Paradise.

That paradise held many pleasures, among them the pleasure of death—that primordial return to "the great sweet mother," whose rocking rhythms Swinburne captures in lines that, like some fluid lullaby, mix the image of love-making with the image of drowning: "My lips will feast on the foam of thy lips, / I shall rise with thy rising, with thee subside." The passage is animistic in its primitiveness of emotion. The decadent, verbally sophisticated Swinburne was in another part of his being pre-civilized, a wind-worshiper and a sea-worshiper whose poetry springs from sources more antique than words.

In **"A Forsaken Garden,"** as in **"The Triumph of Time,"** this fusion of the artificial with the aboriginal achieves a fragile power. The setting is an eighteenth-century garden gone to seed and thorn. A faint, salt-sprayed scent of faded flowers and ghostly lovers hovers over the opening stanzas. It is springtime, but neither leaves nor loves will bloom again in this rocky wasteland poised over the sea. The actual garden that inspired the imagined garden of the poem was on the Isle of Wight, where Swinburne spent the springs of his childhood in a setting of near-tropical luxuriance. In late summer the Swinburnes drove north to the family seat at Capheaton, Northumberland, where the bare moors, gray seas, and autumnal summits must have seemed, to the young Swinburne, like winter suddenly overlaid upon spring. The two seasons became forever fixed in his mind in their sudden proximity and sharpness of contrast, so that he could scarcely feel the one without its opposite. The sea that rolls through the great closing stanzas of **"A Forsaken Garden"** is a chill, northern sea, a blast of death bringing a second ruin, as in *Tristram of Lyonesse,* to a rich but ravaged landscape:

> All are at one now, roses and lovers,
> Not known of the cliffs and the fields and the sea.
> Not a breath of the time that has been hovers
> In the air now soft with a summer to be.
> Not a breath shall there sweeten the seasons hereafter
> Of the flowers or the lovers that laugh now or weep,
> When as they that are free now of weeping and laughter
> We shall sleep.
>
> Here death may deal not again for ever;
> Here change may come not till all change end.
> From the graves they have made they shall rise up never,
> Who have left nought living to ravage and rend.
> Earth, stones, and thorns of the wild ground growing,
> While the sun and the rain live, these shall be;
> Till a last wind's breath upon all these blowing
> Roll the sea.
>
> Till the slow sea rise and the sheer cliff crumble,
> Till terrace and meadow the deep gulfs drink,
> Till the strength of the waves of the high tides humble
> The fields that lessen, the rocks that shrink,
> Here now in his triumph where all things falter,
> Stretched out on the spoils that his own hand spread,
> As a god self-slain on his own strange altar,
> Death lies dead.

As in all of his most powerful verse, Swinburne writes here not of time present, but of a time immemorially before time, or of the eternity that follows time. The steady pulse of the monosyllables, the starkness of the diction, the open generalized barrenness of the setting—"earth, stones, and thorns"—evoke some primordial drama of the elements, as though nature suddenly shed the coloration of millennia and resolved back into earth, water, fire, and wind. The lifeless landscape is charged with hidden life, only to make its final ravagement the more complete: the wind breathes, the rocks shrink, the sea rises, the gulfs drink, the fields are humbled. The wreck is so total that Death itself, with nothing mutable left to prey upon, lies dead. The personification ought to ring hollow—a poetical flourish in an elemental landscape. But this touch of artifice makes more awesome the larger, cosmic death that Swinburne heard blowing through nature like a low boneshaking rumble and that he here evokes in the form of the wind's last breath rolling sea over earth in the final Deluge.

One hears the same elemental music in **"At a Month's End,"** another lyric of doomed love in *Poems and Ballads,* Second Series. The lovers, no longer in love, stand by night at the sea's edge and watch the serried spears of the waves storm toward the shore:

Hardly we saw the high moon hanging,
Heard hardly through the windy night
Far waters ringing, low reefs clanging,
Under wan skies and waste white light.

With chafe and change of surges chiming,
The clashing channels rocked and rang
Large music, wave to wild wave timing,
And all the choral water sang.

The lapsed love plays itself out against a background of alliterative choiring of the elements. Drifting clouds, waves, gulls, wind, the earth's margins, these are the phenomena on which Swinburne's senses instinctually fix, the background of earth against which his people stand, dwarfed and apart:

Across, aslant, a scudding sea-mew
Swam, dipped, and dropped, and grazed the sea:
And one with me I could not dream you;
And one with you I could not be.

As the white wing the white wave's fringes
Touched and slid over and flashed past—
As a pale cloud a pale flame tinges
From the moon's lowest light and last—

As a star feels the sun and falters,
Touched to death by diviner eyes—
As on the old gods' untended altars
The old fire of withered worship dies—

• • • • •

So once with fiery breath and flying
Your winged heart touched mine and went,
And the swift spirits kissed, and sighing,
Sundered and smiled and were content.

The lovers in **"At a Month's End"** seem not only lost to each other but eclipsed by the larger motions of nature around them. Always in Swinburne the pure, fluid power of wind and sea sweeps everything before it, just as the cataclysmic rush of avalanche and inundation obliterates the paltry human figures in J. M. W. Turner's *Val d'Aosta.* Like Turner, too, Swinburne finds in the vast undifferentiated sea the visible emblem of his genius, with its exaltation of energy over form, infinite nuance over discrete detail. One stanza from **"At a Month's End"** might have come from Turner's own catalogue descriptions of his seascapes:

Faint lights fell this way, that way floated,
Quick sparks of sea-fire keen like eyes
From the rolled surf that flashed, and noted
Shores and faint cliffs and bays and skies.

One recognizes in both artists the same sophisticated virtuosity, alongside an enormous responsiveness to the aboriginal forces of nature. Swinburne's landscapes, like Turner's, abstract all the sharp, divisible aspects of nature into an elemental luminosity and motion, such as God might have beheld on completing the Creation:

. . . one clear hueless haze of glimmering hues
The sea's line and the land's line and the sky's.
                                              ("Thalassius")

"Indistinctness is my forte," Turner retorted to a patron who chided him for vagueness, a fault which modern critics still impute to Turner's early admirer, Swinburne. Both men practice a highly structured art that has nonetheless freed itself from the canons of conventional representation. No single word in a Swinburne poem quite corresponds to a given thing, just as no single dab of paint on a Turner canvas corresponds to a natural object; the correspondence is always between the total configuration of the poem or painting and the total configuration of nature. The adjective floating freely away from its substantive in a Swinburne poem is equivalent to the blob of pigment that is neither sea nor foam nor sky, but all of these, in a Turner painting. Such an art prizes color over outline, light over form, music over meaning. Its concern, as Swinburne wrote of poetry [in **"Notes on the Text of Shelley"**], but might as well have written of Impressionism in general, "is rather to render the effect of a thing than the thing itself." I had read the following lines from *Atalanta in Calydon* many times before they actually sprang into focus as a splendid rendering not of the thing itself, but of its effect upon the sun-dazed beholder. Althaea describes the bright blur of approaching hunters, as they ride between her and the slanted morning light:

. . . for sharp mixed shadow and wind
Blown up between the morning and the mist,
With steam of steeds and flash of bridle or wheel,

And fire, and parcels of the broken dawn,
And dust divided by hard light, and spears
That shine and shift as the edge of wild beasts' eyes,
Smite upon mine; so fiery their blind edge
Burns, and bright points break up and baffle day.

Swinburne's love of mixed effects gives to his descriptive verse much of its Turnerian quality. His poetry is charged with the tension of delicately poised opposites: shadows thinned by light, lights broken by shade, sunset passing into moonrise, sea merging with sky. He is obsessed by the moment when one thing shades off into its opposite, or when contraries fuse, as in **"Hermaphroditus,"** one of his earliest and finest poems. Yet apart from his profound esthetic affinity with Turner, there is the unique idiosyncrasy of Swinburne himself, who was equipped with superb senses, each of which must have transmitted a peculiar counterpoint. This basic, polarizing rhythm runs through his being and manifests itself in his compulsive use of alliterating antitheses in prose and verse. Much in Swinburne that has been criticized as mere mannerism—paradox, alliteration, elaborate antithesis—strikes me as deriving from his deepest impulses, although the question of "sincerity" is always vexing in his verse. In a sense, Swinburne *perceived* in paradoxes, and his recurrent synesthetic images express perfectly that passing of pain into pleasure, bitter into sweet, loathing into desire, which lay at the root of his profoundest experiences. He loves nature best in her moments of transition, as if drawn to dusk and dawn as the day's hermaphrodisms:

Over two shadowless waters, adrift as a pinnace in
    peril,
Hangs as in heavy suspense, charged with irresolute
    light,
Softly the soul of the sunset upholden awhile on the
    sterile
Waves and wastes of the land, half repossessed by
    the night.

                                    ("Evening on the Broads")

His imagery of these times of change is most mixed and rich, as when, in **"Evening on the Broads,"** he fuses touch, sound, and sight to describe twilight at sea as "a molten music of colour"; and in a line from **"Laus Veneris"** that is wisest not to gloss at all, the knight is maddened by erotic fumes rising from "the sea's panting mouth of *dry* desire."

At times Swinburne will elaborate a single antithesis into an entire poem. **"A Vision of Spring in Winter"** is a beautifully poised evocation of life arising from dormancy as the poet himself declines from spring toward winter; the countermovements of rebirth and loss are as delicately juxtaposed as the snowdrop set in the vanishing snow at the poems' opening. Muted antithesis is also at the heart of **"Ave atque Vale,"** an elegy to Baudelaire in which Swinburne un-

cannily evokes the mixed, sweetly-acrid scent of *Les Fleurs du Mal.* The elegiac convention of strewing flowers takes on sudden, sensuous reality as one *smells* the very leaves of Baudelaire's book, the paradoxical

Half-*faded fiery* blossoms, *pale* with *heat*
And full of *bitter* summer, but more *sweet*
To thee than on the gleanings of a northern
    shore . . .

The poem pays its subject the high tribute of perfect imitation. At its close we move away from the bitter-sweet scent of *Les Fleurs du Mal* to the chill smell of the earth that is to receive the poet's body. There is no "far-off divine event" to lighten grief, no advance to pastures new; only death, and this grim tribute of one great poet to another:

For thee, O now a silent soul, my brother,
Take at my hands this garland, and farewell.
Thin is the leaf, and chill the wintry smell,
And chill the solemn earth, a fatal mother,
With sadder than the Niobean womb,
And in the hollow of her breasts a tomb.
Content thee, howsoe'er, whose days are done;
There lies not any troublous thing before,
Nor sight nor sound to war against thee more,
For whom all winds are quiet as the sun,
All waters as the shore.

Only once again, in **Tristram of Lyonesse**, did Swinburne achieve the sustained excellence of **Poems and Ballads**, Second Series. He continued to publish volumes of verse into our own century, but for the most part the later poetry is a peculiarly vacant sort of versage that exists still-born in a world of its own. One thinks of Swinburne's increasing deafness at Putney, and somehow the poetry suggests a muted soliloquy. The saddest lines in all of Swinburne appear in **"A Midsummer Holiday"** (1884), dedicated to Watts-Dunton. The setting is indistinguishable from those great, bleak earlier lyrics of the sea's encroachments on the land; here, however, the sea has shrunk to a suburban pond reflecting the ghost of a dead poet:

Friend, the lonely land is bright for you and me
All its wild ways through: but this methinks is best,
Here to watch how kindly time and change agree
Where the small town smiles, a warm still sea-side
    nest.

Yet there are moments of astonishing strength in late Swinburne. Much of **"By the North Sea,"** more of the unknown **"Evening on the Broads,"** all of **"A Nympholept"** defeat one's impulse to impose a curve of growth, flowering, and decline upon the actual pattern of his creativity. Swinburne always wrote a good deal of dead and silly verse, rather more of both toward the end of his career. That his most lifeless poetry is in all formal respects—meter, diction, and subject—virtually indistinguishable from his greatest poetry is one of the mysteries of his art. His genius is extraordinary above all for its *intermittency;* the verse-making engine spins constantly for half a century, but the surges of engaged power are sudden and unpredictable. Tennyson called him "a reed through which all things blow into music." Sometimes the melody carries; often it does not. Swinburne had a curious passion for monotony, which was undoubtedly linked to his love of bleak, monochromatic effects. Out of this love came his most powerful poetry; out of it also came whole poems too like his own description of the Dunwich coast:

> Miles, and miles, and miles of desolation!
> Leagues on leagues on leagues without a change!
> **("By the North Sea")**

One's final reservation toward Swinburne has to do with a certain arrested development. Wordsworth's genius flowers, then endlessly wanes: *Tintern Abbey* un-

folds an organic evolution of growths, losses, and gains. Neither Swinburne nor his verse seems to undergo much change; a single note is struck early and held obsessively long. The reader wants a richer range of subject, more nuance of idea. Swinburne composes by compounding, not synthesizing. Too often, his method is merely quantitative: "I have added yet four more jets of boiling and gushing infamy to the perennial and poisonous fountain of Dolores." One wishes that his eccentric genius could have retained all its power while ridding itself of rigidity and repetitiveness. It did not, and the death of development in Swinburne may have been as large a loss to English poetry as the physical death of Keats. (pp. vii-xxxiv)

John D. Rosenberg, in an introduction to *Swinburne: Selected Poetry and Prose* by Algernon Swinburne, edited by John D. Rosenberg, The Modern Library, 1968, pp. vii-xxxiv.

SOURCES FOR FURTHER STUDY

Beetz, Kirk H. *Algernon Charles Swinburne: A Bibliography of Secondary Works, 1861-1980*. Metuchen, N. J.: Scarecrow Press, 1982, 227 p.

Chronologically arranged annotated bibliography of criticism.

Chew, Samuel C. *Swinburne*. Boston: Little, Brown, and Co., 1929, 335 p.

Critical study of Swinburne's prose and poetry.

Hyder, Clyde Kenneth. Introduction to *Swinburne Replies: Notes on Poems and Reviews, Under the Microscope, Dedicatory Epistle*, by Algernon Charles Swinburne, edited by Clyde Kenneth Hyder, pp. 1-14. Syracuse: Syracuse University Press, 1966.

Examines several critical esays in which Swinburne discusses his own poetry and addresses his critics.

Lafourcade, Georges. *Swinburne: A Literary Biography*. London: G. Bell and Sons, 1932, 314 p.

Concentrates on the circumstances surrounding the writing and publication of Swinburne's principal works.

Raymond, Meredith B. *Swinburne's Poetics: Theory and Practice*. The Hague: Mouton, 1971, 202 p.

Posits an aesthetic basis which applies to both Swinburne's poetry and criticism. Raymond analyzes Swinburne's critical style, then attempts to extract his theory of poetry from the "quasi-autobiographical" poems "Thalassius" and "On the Cliffs."

Thomas, Donald. *Swinburne: The Poet in His World*. New York: Oxford University Press, 1979, 256 p.

Anecdotal biography detailing Swinburne's relationships with those people who most affected his life and work: the Rossettis, Richard Burton, Richard Monckton Milnes, George Meredith, Adah Isaacs Menken, Benjamin Jowett, Giuseppe Mazzini, Mary Gordon, and Theodore Watts-Dunton.

Alfred, Lord Tennyson

1809-1892

English poet and dramatist.

INTRODUCTION

*T*ennyson is considered one of the greatest poets in the English language. He was immensely popular in his lifetime, especially in the years following the publication of his lengthy elegiac poem *In Memoriam* (1850). Epitomizing Tennyson's art and thought, this work was embraced by readers as a justification of their religious faith amid doubt caused by the scientific discoveries and speculations of the time. Queen Victoria declared that she valued it next to the Bible as a work of consolation, thus contributing to Tennyson's stature as the foremost poet of his generation and the poetic voice of Victorian England. While many critics have since found his poetry excessively emotive and moralistic, Tennyson is universally acclaimed as a lyricist of unsurpassed skill.

The fourth of twelve children, Tennyson was born in Somersby, Lincolnshire. His father was a rector who maintained his benefice grudgingly as a means of supporting himself and his family. The elder son of a wealthy landowner, he had obtained the rectory when his younger brother was designated as prospective heir to the family's estate. According to biographers, Tennyson's father responded to his virtual disinheritance by indulging in drugs and alcohol, creating an unpleasant domestic atmosphere often made worse by his violent temper. Each of his children suffered to some extent from drug addiction or mental illness, promoting the family's grim speculation on the "black blood" of the Tennysons, whose history of mental and physical debilities, epilepsy prominent among them, had become a distressing part of their family heritage. Biographers speculate that the general melancholy and morbidity expressed in much of Tennyson's verse is rooted in the unhappy environment at Somersby.

Tennyson's first volume of poetry, *Poems by Two Brothers*, included the work of his two elder brothers and was published in 1827. Later that year, Tennyson enrolled at Trinity College, Cambridge, where he won the chancellor's gold medal for his poem "Timbuctoo" in 1829. *Poems, Chiefly Lyrical,* published in 1830, was well received and marked the beginning of Tennyson's literary career; another collection, *Poems,* appeared in 1832 but was less favorably reviewed, many critics praising Tennyson's artistry but objecting to what they considered an absence of intellectual substance. This latter volume was published at the urging of Arthur Hallam, a brilliant Cambridge undergraduate who had become Tennyson's closest friend and was an ardent admirer of his poetry. Hallam's enthusiasm was welcomed by Tennyson, whose personal circumstances had led to a growing despondency: His father died in 1831, leaving Tennyson's family in debt and forcing his early departure from Trinity College; one of Tennyson's brothers suffered a mental breakdown and required institutionalization; and Tennyson himself was morbidly fearful of falling victim to epilepsy or madness. Hallam's untimely death in 1833, which prompted the series of elegies later comprising *In Memoriam,* contributed greatly to Tennyson's despair. In describing this period, he wrote: "I suffered what seemed to me to shatter all my life so that I desired to die rather than to live."

For nearly a decade after Hallam's death Tennyson published no further poetry. During this period he became engaged to Emily Sellwood, but financial difficulties and Tennyson's persistent anxiety over the condition of his health resulted in their separation. In 1842, yielding to a friend's insistence, Tennyson published his two-volume collection *Poems,* for which reviewers were virtually unanimous in expressing admiration. That same year, however, an unsuccessful financial venture cost Tennyson nearly everything he owned, causing him to succumb to a deep depression that required medical treatment. In 1845 he was granted a government pension in recognition of both his poetic achievement and his apparent need; contributing to his financial stability, the first edition of his narrative poem *The Princess: A Medley,* published in 1847, sold out within two months. Tennyson resumed his courtship of Sellwood in 1849, and they were married the following year.

The timely success of *In Memoriam,* published in 1850, ensured Tennyson's appointment as poet laureate succeeding William Wordsworth. *Idylls of the King* (1859), considered by Tennyson's contemporaries to be his masterpiece, and *Enoch Arden* (1864), which sold more than forty thousand copies upon publication, increased both his popularity and his wealth, and earned him the designation "the people's poet." Although the dramatic works written later in his career were largely unsuccessful, Tennyson completed several additional collections of poems in the last decade of his life, all of which were well received. In 1883 he accepted a peerage, the first poet to be so honored strictly on the basis of literary achievement. Tennyson died in 1892 and was interred in Westminister Abbey.

Tennyson's first two significant collections, *Poems, Chiefly Lyrical* and *Poems,* were considered by many critics to be of high poetic merit but devoid of meaning or purpose beyond their pure artistry. In a review of the latter collection, philosopher John Stuart Mill urged Tennyson to "cultivate . . . philosophy as well as poetry," expressing a sentiment not uncommon among Tennyson's early reviewers. The collection of *Poems* that appeared in 1842 included radically revised versions of his best poems from the earlier volumes, and addressed such themes as duty, self-discipline, and the complexities of religious faith, offering what critics considered to be a truer representation of human life than that of his early works. Such poems as "The Palace of Art," "St. Simeon Stylites," "The Two Voices," and "The Vision of Sin" reveal an attitude of moral determination that characterizes the collection as a whole, examining the conflict between indulgence and morality while expressing the need for social involvement. If "Recollections of the Arabian Nights," "The Hesperides," and others of Tennyson's earliest poems celebrate, as Jerome Buckley notes, "the flight into an exotic world of pure art," the *Poems* of 1842 demonstrate Tennyson's effort to face and not escape from the world. Nevertheless, Tennyson's attempts to confront important issues and ideas in his works have been regarded as largely unsuccessful. *The Princess* (1847), for example, which examined the education of women in Victorian England, was Tennyson's response to critics who urged him to address the major issues of his day. The focus of the poem, however, shifts from the establishment of women's colleges to a more general consideration of what Tennyson regarded as the unnatural attempt of men and women to assume identical roles in society. Many critics found Tennyson's treatment of the central question, women's education, to be shallow, and thus representative of what they considered the major weakness of his poetry. Summarizing this position, F. L. Lucas has written that Tennyson's detractors condemned him as "intellectually timid, a prophet of comfortable things, a priest without a real faith, a philosopher who could not reason, a political thinker who trimmed over the problems of poverty and turned the Woman's Question into a picnic." Nevertheless, *The Princess* was well received by the British public, to whom its idealism and celebration of domesticity greatly appealed.

Tennyson's next major work, *In Memoriam,* expressed his personal grief over Hallam's death while examining more generally the nature of death and bereavement in relation to contemporary scientific issues, especially those involving evolution and the geologic dating of the earth's history, which brought into question traditional religious beliefs. Largely regarded as an affirmation of faith, *In Memoriam* was especially valued for its reflections on overcoming loss. Comprising 132 sections written over the course of nearly two decades, the poem progresses from despair to joy and concludes with a marriage celebration, symbolically expressing Tennyson's faith in the moral evolution of humanity and reflecting the nineteenth-century ideal of social progress. The success of *In Memoriam* and his subsequent appointment as poet laureate assured Tennyson the opportunity to become the poetic voice of his generation, and in his ceremonial position he composed such poems as "Ode on the Death of the Duke of Wellington" and "The Charge of the Light Brigade," each of which is a celebration of heroism and public duty. *Maud, and Other Poems* (1855) was the first collection Tennyson published as laureate, but only his 1832 volume, *Poems,* elicited a more negative response. The title poem is a "monodrama" in which the changing consciousness of the narrator is traced through a series of tragedies that result in his insanity. Confined to an asylum, the protagonist is cured of his madness and asserts his love for humanity by serving his country in the Crimean War. George Eliot and William Gladstone denounced the poem as morbid and obscure, and were among many who disapproved of Tennyson's apparent glorification of war, which he depicted as an ennobling enterprise essential to the cleansing and regeneration of a morally corrupt society. *Maud* has since been reevaluated by critics who find it Tennyson's most stylistically inventive poem, praising its violent rhythms and passionate language. Modern critics largely agree with Christopher Ricks that *Maud* was for Tennyson an "exorcism"; as Ricks explains, "*Maud* was an intense and precarious attempt . . . to encompass the bitter experiences of four decades of a life in which many of the formative influences had also been deformative." Thus madness, suicide, familial conflict, shattered love, death and loss, and untempered mammonism, all central grievings in Tennyson's life, are attacked openly and passionately in *Maud,* with war cultivating the spirit of sacrifice and loyalty which Tennyson felt essential to avert the self-destruction of a selfishly materialistic society.

Tennyson's epic poem *Idylls of the King* followed the controversial *Maud* by examining the rise and fall of idealism in society. "I tried in my *Idylls,*" Tennyson wrote, "to teach men the need of an ideal." F. E. L. Priestley has observed that Tennyson used the "Arthurian cycle as a medium for discussion of problems which [were] both contemporary and perennial," and concludes that the *Idylls* "represent one of Tennyson's most earnest and important efforts to deal with the major problems of his time." Tennyson was concerned with what he considered to be a growing tendency to-

ward hedonism in society and an attendant rejection of spiritual values. *Idylls of the King* expresses his ideal of the British empire as an exemplar of moral and social order: the "Table Round / A glorious company" would "serve as a model for the mighty world." However, when individual acts of betrayal and corruption result from adultery committed by Arthur's wife and Lancelot, the ensuing disorder destroys the Round Table, symbolizing the effects of moral decay which were Tennyson's chief concern for the society of his day.

Tennyson completed a subsequent enlargement of *Idylls of the King* in 1874, and in the decade that followed he focused his efforts on the composition of historical dramas. *Queen Mary* (1875), his first published play, has been viewed by critics as characteristically indicative of the major flaws in Tennyson's dramatic works—resulting from his unfamiliarity with the limitations of theatrical production. Set changes were frequent and elaborate, and his meticulous adherence to detail lessened the play's dramatic impact. Moreover, Tennyson's verse was cumbersome and ineffective as dramatic dialogue, and *Queen Mary* was withdrawn after twenty-three performances. *Harold* (1876), completed the following year, was less complicated in its dramaturgy than its predecessor, but failed to find a producer during Tennyson's lifetime. While Tennyson completed five more plays, only *The Cup* (1884) and *Becket* (1884) enjoyed any success on stage, and neither, in Buckley's words, "seriously altered the course of the English theater."

Describing Tennyson's verse as "poised and stationary," Henry James presaged twentieth-century criticism when he stated in 1876 that "a man has always the qualities of his defects, and if Tennyson is . . . a static poet, he at least represents repose and stillness and the fixedness of things, with a splendour that no poet has surpassed." In 1937 Douglas Bush voiced the opinion of many of his contemporaries, writing that Tennyson was "an artist who had consummate powers of expression" but "not very much, except as an emotional poet, to say." Other critics contended that Tennyson's vision of a spiritually elevated world was betrayed by his concessions to a smug and materialistic Victorian ethic. Recent critics, however, have dismissed the generalization of their predecessors as part of a post-World War I reaction against the Victorian era and its supposed hypocrisy and narrow-mindedness, and Tennyson has once again come to be viewed, not as "the surface flatterer of his time," as T. S. Eliot described him, but as the embodiment of his age, a poet who reflected both the thoughts and feelings of his generation. The skill with which he did so has been the focus of a wealth of modern criticism, and much of the luster of Tennyson's early reputation has been restored, so that a present-day critic may well pose a question similar to that of Henry Van Dyke, who wrote shortly before Tennyson's death: "In the future, when men call the role of poets who have given splendour to the name of England, they will begin with Shakespeare and Milton—and who shall have the third place, if it be not Tennyson?"

(For further information about Tennyson's life and works, see *Dictionary of Literary Biography*, Vol. 32: *Victorian Poets Before 1850* and *Nineteenth-Century Literature Criticism*, Vol. 30.)

CRITICAL COMMENTARY

G. K. CHESTERTON
(essay date 1903)

[Regarded as one of England's premier men of letters during the first half of the twentieth century, Chesterton is best known today as a colorful bon vivant, a witty essayist, and creator of the Father Brown mysteries and the fantasy *The Man Who Was Thursday* (1908). Much of Chesterton's work reveals his childlike joie de vivre and reflects his pronounced Anglican and, later, Roman Catholic beliefs. His essays are characterized by their humor, frequent use of paradox, and chatty, rambling style. In the following excerpt, he defends Tennyson's poetry against charges that it is "commonplace."]

The attempts which have been made to discredit the poetical position of Tennyson are in the main dictated by an entire misunderstanding of the nature of poetry. When critics like Matthew Arnold, for example, suggest that his poetry is deficient in elaborate thought, they only prove, as Matthew Arnold proved, that they themselves could never be great poets. It is no valid accusation against a poet that the sentiment he expresses is commonplace. Poetry is always commonplace; it is vulgar in the noblest sense of that noble word. Unless a man can make the same kind of ringing appeal to absolute and admitted sentiments that is made by a popular orator, he has lost touch with emotional literature. Unless he is to some extent a demagogue, he cannot be a poet. A man who expresses in poetry new and strange and undiscovered emotions is not a poet; he is a brain specialist. Tennyson can never be discredited before any serious tribunal of criticism because the sentiments and thoughts to which he dedicates himself are those sentiments and thoughts which occur to anyone. These are the peculiar province of poetry; poetry, like religion, is always a democratic thing, even if it pretends the contrary. The faults of Tennyson, so far as they existed, were not half so much in the common character of his sentiments as in the arrogant perfection of his workmanship. He was not by any means so wrong in his faults as he was in his perfections.

Men are very much too ready to speak of men's work being ordinary, when we consider that, properly considered, every man is extraordinary. The average man is a tribal fable, like the Man Wolf or the Wise Man of the Stoics. In every man's heart there is a revolution; how much more in every poet's? The supreme business of criticism is to discover that part of a man's work which is his and to ignore that part which belongs to others. Why should any critic of poetry spend time and attention on that part of a man's work which is unpoetical? Why should any man be interested in aspects which are uninteresting? The business of a critic is to discover the importance of men and not their crimes. It is true that the Greek word critic carries with it the meaning of a judge, and up to this point of history judges have had to do with the valuation of men's sins, and not with the valuation of their virtues.

Tennyson's work, disencumbered of all that uninteresting accretion which he had inherited or copied, resolves itself, like that of any other man of genius, into those things which he really inaugurated. Underneath all his exterior of polished and polite rectitude there was in him a genuine fire of novelty; only that, like all the able men of his period, he disguised revolution under the name of evolution. He is only a very shallow critic who cannot see an eternal rebel in the heart of the Conservative.

Tennyson had certain absolutely personal ideas, as much his own as the ideas of Browning or Meredith, though they were fewer in number. One of these, for example, was the fact that he was the first of all poets (and perhaps the last) to attempt to treat poetically that vast and monstrous vision of fact which science had recently revealed to mankind. Scientific discoveries seem commonly fables as fantastic in the ears of poets as poems in the ears of men of science. The poet is always

Principal Works

Poems by Two Brothers [with Frederick and Charles Tennyson] (poetry) 1827

"Timbuctoo" (poem) 1829

Poems, Chiefly Lyrical (poetry) 1830

Poems (poetry) 1832

Poems. 2 vols. (poetry) 1842

The Princess: A Medley (poem) 1847

In Memoriam (poem) 1850

"Ode on the Death of the Duke of Wellington" (poem) 1852

Maud, and Other Poems (poetry) 1855

Idylls of the King (poetry) 1859; enlarged edition, 1874

Enoch Arden, Etc. (poetry) 1864

The Holy Grail, and Other Poems (poetry) 1869

Gareth and Lynette, Etc. (poetry) 1872

Queen Mary: A Drama (drama) 1875

Harold: A Drama (drama) 1876

Ballads and Other Poems (poetry) 1880

Becket (drama) 1884

The Cup and The Falcon (drama) 1884

Tiresias, and Other Poems (poetry) 1885

Locksley Hall Sixty Years After, Etc. (poetry) 1886

Demeter, and Other Poems (poetry) 1889

The Death of Oenone, Akbar's Dream, and Other Poems (poetry) 1892

The Foresters, Robin Hood and Maid Marian (drama) 1892

a Ptolemaist; for him the sun still rises and the earth stands still. Tennyson really worked the essence of modern science into his poetical constitution, so that its appalling birds and frightful flowers were really part of his literary imagery. To him blind and brutal monsters, the products of the wild babyhood of the Universe, were as the daisies and the nightingales were to Keats; he absolutely realised the great literary paradox mentioned in the Book of Job: "He saw Behemoth, and he played with him as with a bird."

Instances of this would not be difficult to find. But the tests of poetry are those instances in which this outrageous scientific phraseology becomes natural and unconscious. Tennyson wrote one of his own exquisite lyrics describing the exultation of a lover on the evening before his bridal day. This would be an occasion, if ever there was one, for falling back on those ancient and assured falsehoods of the doomed heaven and the flat earth in which generations of poets have made us feel at home. We can imagine the poet in such a lyric saluting the setting sun and prophesying the sun's resurrection. There is something extraordinarily typical of Tennyson's scientific faith in the fact that this, one of the most sentimental and elemental of his poems, opens with the two lines:

Move eastward, happy earth, and leave
Yon orange sunset waning slow.

Rivers had often been commanded to flow by poets, and flowers to blossom in their season, and both were doubtless grateful for the permission. But the terrestrial globe of science has only twice, so far as we know, been encouraged in poetry to continue its course, one instance being that of this poem, and the other the incomparable "Address to the Terrestrial Globe" in the "Bab Ballads."

There was, again, another poetic element entirely peculiar to Tennyson, which his critics have, in many cases, ridiculously confused with a fault. This was the fact that Tennyson stood alone among modern poets in the attempt to give a poetic character to the conception of Liberal Conservatism, of splendid compromise. The carping critics who have abused Tennyson for this do not see that it was far more daring and original for a poet to defend conventionality than to defend a cartload of revolutions. His really sound and essential conception of Liberty,

Turning to scorn with lips divine
The falsehood of extremes,

is as good a definition of Liberalism as has been uttered in poetry in the Liberal century. Moderation is *not* a compromise; moderation is a passion; the passion of great judges. That Tennyson felt that lyrical enthusiasm could be devoted to established customs, to indefensible and ineradicable national constitutions, to the dignity of time and the empire of unutterable common sense, all this did not make him a tamer poet, but an infinitely more original one. Any poetaster can describe a thunderstorm; it requires a poet to describe the ancient and quiet sky.

I cannot, indeed, fall in with Mr. Morton Luce in his somewhat frigid and patrician theory of poetry. "Dialect," he says, "mostly falls below the dignity of art." I cannot feel myself that art has any dignity higher than the in-dwelling and divine dignity of human nature. Great poets like Burns were far more undignified when they clothed their thoughts in what Mr. Morton Luce calls "the seemly raiment of cultured speech" than when they clothed them in the headlong and flexible patois in which they thought and prayed and quarrelled and made love. If Tennyson failed (which I do not admit) in such poems as **"The Northern Farmer,"** it was not because he used too much of the spirit of the dialect, but because he used too little.

Tennyson belonged undoubtedly to a period from which we are divided; the period in which men had queer ideas of the antagonism of science and religion;

the period in which the Missing Link was really missing. But his hold upon the old realities of existence never wavered; he was the apostle of the sanctity of laws, of the sanctity of customs; above all, like every poet, he was the apostle of the sanctity of words. (pp. 250-57)

G. K. Chesterton, "Tennyson," in his *Varied Types,* Dodd, Mead and Company, 1903, pp. 249-57.

JEROME HAMILTON BUCKLEY
(essay date 1960)

[Buckley is an American educator and critic who has written extensively on Victorian literature. In the following excerpt from a work that first appeared in 1960, he surveys Tennyson's dramas.]

Published in 1875, *Queen Mary* was developed not as a single dramatic structure but as a sprawling panorama, a pageant unfolded with a cinematic abundance and little regard for the limitations of the theater. The twenty-three separate scenes demanded frequent and often elaborate change of sets. The "Dramatis Personae" included forty-four characters drawn from all ranks of society and listed in addition a small army of nameless supernumeraries, "Lords and other Attendants, Members of the Privy Council, Members of Parliament, Two Gentlemen, Aldermen, Citizens, Peasants, Ushers, Messengers, Guards, Pages, Gospellers, Marshalmen, etc." Though the text and cast were severely cut for the production at the Lyceum in April 1876, in which Henry Irving appeared as King Philip, no editing could impose a real coherence upon the work. James's criticism of the printed play could have been applied with almost equal force to the acted version: *Queen Mary* in either form was but "a dramatized chronicle, . . . taking its material in pieces, as history hands them over, and working each one up into an independent scene—usually with great ability." The playwright, James complained, "has embroidered cunningly the groundwork offered him by Mr. Froude, but he has contributed no new material."

Tennyson indeed hewed so closely to the line of fact that he was not content to accept Froude's brilliant but biased interpretation as a full or adequate account of the sixteenth-century struggle. He carefully examined many primary and secondary sources, from Foxe's *Book of Martyrs* and the correspondence of Archbishop Parker down to the latest social and ecclesiastical histories of the period. Though his own loyalties were essentially Protestant, he tried to be scrupulously fair to the claims of Catholicism, for which his new friend W.

G. Ward had given him some real respect, and he strove in particular to do justice to the Queen herself, whom he felt Froude had misrepresented. If his scholarly caution, his reluctance to simplify by omission, needlessly complicated the action of his play, it nonetheless gave him a sharp sense of the instability, conflict, and confusion of Marian England. Whatever his inexperience and naïveté as dramatist, he succeeded admirably in suggesting the temper of an age. . . . (pp. 200-01)

Apart from its faithfulness as an historical record, which mitigates its power as a play, the strength of *Queen Mary* lies in its able characterizations. Each of the principal figures—except Philip of Spain, who in his ruthless self-sufficiency approaches caricature—emerges as a subtly rounded personality. Cranmer, in particular, is drawn in all the complexity of divided motives as politician and martyr, a man of courage, remorse, humility, and proud conviction. Cardinal Pole, driven to follow the courses of least resistance, is a convincing blend of sensitivity, fearfulness, and cruelty born of disappointment. And the princess Elizabeth, who hovers in the background as a symbol of ultimate social renewal, effectively combines sympathetic understanding with an imperious reserve willing to bide its time. But most impressive of all is the Queen herself, a real woman of tragic depth, far removed from the monster she had been in Victor Hugo's *Marie Tudor.* In the beginning Mary has the capacity to rise above the wrongs she has suffered, to forgive her enemies, even to practice a measure of tolerance so long as she may retain her religious faith. In the end she is destroyed by her unreasoning passion, her obsessive love for the loveless Philip. At first her desire is simply a yearning that troubles her private dreams; "It breaks my heart," says an attendant lady, "to hear her moan at night / As tho' the nightmare never left her bed." But ultimately her frustrations determine the violence she inflicts upon her whole realm. Abandoned by the Spaniard, she loses all purpose in living and with it all true title to sovereignty. As Lord Howard explains,

> Her life, since Philip left her, and she lost
> Her fierce desire of bearing him a child,
> Hath, like a brief and bitter winter's day,
> Gone narrowing down and darkening to a close.

Here the mood recalls that of the thwarted Guinevere or, more distantly, of the abandoned Oenone. Indeed, if Tennyson had paid less heed to the political background and given the character of his protagonist more centrality, he might have found for *Queen Mary* what the play most seriously lacks, a subject, such a theme as animates many of his more vital poems: the betrayal of the social conscience by a passionate self-interest.

Harold, published a year later, shows a considerable advance in structure. Each of its scenes—the number is reduced to eleven—develops a situation which contributes directly to the action of the play as a whole; and the key scene especially, in which Harold swears under duress to support the claim of William to the English throne, attains by skillful timing a high dramatic tension. Perhaps because he had fewer records to draw upon, Tennyson introduces many fewer characters than in *Queen Mary* and much less subsidiary historical detail. He focuses the interest of the drama where it should be, on the conduct of his hero. Unfortunately, however, Harold with all his strength, courage, and (except for the one false oath) truthfulness is too uncomplicated a person to command our sustained attention, and few of the others with whom he has to contend are drawn with enough color to assume a genuine life. The women who appear as rivals for Harold's love seem particularly factitious: Edith is a frail creature of sweet and ultimately maudlin sentiment, and Aldwyth is but a villainous schemer from popular melodrama. Far inferior in characterization to *Queen Mary,* this second chronicle could not expect even the brief *succès d'estime* in the theater which greeted the first. It awaited production on a public stage for over fifty years.

On a visit to Battle Abbey in 1876, Tennyson wrote a prefatory sonnet for *Harold* celebrating the field of Senlac "Where might made right eight hundred years ago." In effect the sonnet defines the theme of the play: the defeat of right by might, which may finally establish a new right but which first must demand the sacrifice of old values. Tennyson's ethical sympathies lie entirely with Harold, whose practical goodness resembles the intuitive religion of King Arthur and oddly prefigures the Victorian Broad-Church rejection of a rigid dogmatism:

> O God! I cannot help it, but at times
> They seem to me too narrow, all the faiths
> Of this grown world of ours, whose baby eye
> Saw them sufficient.

Harold instinctively resents the piety which drives Edward the Confessor, as it drove the seekers of the Holy Grail, to an ascetic withdrawal from social responsibility. Edward, who according to the "heretical" Archbishop Stigand has "A conscience for his own soul, not his realm," speaks with all the self-righteous unction of Tennyson's St. Simeon Stylites:

> I have lived a life of utter purity:
> I have builded the great church of Holy Peter:
> I have wrought miracles—to God the glory—
> And miracles will in my name be wrought
> Hereafter.—I have fought the fight and go—
> I see the flashing of the gates of pearl—
> And it is well with me, tho' some of you
> Have scorn'd me—ay—but after I am gone
> Woe, woe to England!

The woe in large part is of Edward's own making; for his indifference and indecision have irreparably weakened the English cause, and his approval—half envious and half fearful—of the disciplined Norman church has encouraged William to seek in the same assured and quite unEnglish orthodoxy spiritual sanction for his own quite secular designs. At the last Harold—without time enough to rally the England that Edward in his self-absorption has rebuked and neglected—must perish, resisting in vain an alien faith and a new order of despotic power.

The tension between might and right persists in *Becket,* which Tennyson had already begun before the publication of *Harold.* But now the wrong is mixed. Neither Becket himself nor Henry II, his antagonist, is blameless; both are betrayed by the external magnitude of office and the unconfessed falsity within, the personal desire for absolute dominion. Far from being a mere villain or even a ruthless self-seeker like the Conqueror, Henry is a genial and on the whole benevolent leader, eager for peace (on his own terms), filled with understanding of his subjects, often impulsive and hot-tempered, but relatively reasonable until pushed to the end of his patience by Becket's opposition to his authority and driven to sigh in exasperation, "Will no man free me from this pestilent priest?" Becket, on the other hand, is depicted as restless, ambitious, self-confident, able to inspire malice in his rivals and great affection in the common people, ready to give his all with intensity to his work whether as Chancellor at odds with the church or as Archbishop in conflict with the state. His sin, of which he never reaches full awareness, is pride of spirit, an arrogance commingling with his saintly strength of conviction. From the beginning of his tenure as primate he knows that he will resist rather than appease the king, who has hopefully elevated him:

> I served King Henry well as Chancellor;
> I am his no more, and I must serve the Church.
> This Canterbury is only less than Rome,
> And all my doubts I fling from me like dust,
> Winnow and scatter all scruples to the wind,
> And all the puissance of the warrior,
> And all the wisdom of the Chancellor,
> And all the heap'd experiences of life,
> I cast upon the side of Canterbury.

Before long he has exercised the power of anathema so freely that the ironic Walter Map, who serves briefly as Tennyson's chorus character, may warn him, "My lord, you have put so many of the King's household out of communion, that they begin to smile at it." Finally, as the death hour approaches, John of Salisbury, his most faithful confidant, must beg him to recognize the possible self-interest that may conceal itself in sanctified attitudes:

> And may there not be something
> Of this world's leaven in thee too, when crying
> On Holy Church to thunder out her rights
> And thine own wrong so pitilessly? Ah, Thomas,

The lightnings that we think are only Heaven's
Flash sometimes out of earth against the heav-
   ens. . . .
Thou hast waged God's war against the King; and
   yet
We are self-uncertain creatures, and we may,
Yea, even when we know not, mix our spites
And private hates with our defence of Heaven.

But Becket, committed wholly to the idea of self-sacrifice, declares himself as the agent of God's will quite "prepared to die" and refuses even to hear his friend's pointed reminder that "We are sinners all, / The best of all not all-prepared to die." Thus with magnificent consistency and fortitude, but without ever achieving complete self-confrontation, he faces the doom he has anticipated since he first considered the gravity of his new position: "I may come to martyrdom. / I am martyr in myself already."

As the murderers leave the fallen Becket, a "storm bursts" over the cathedral and "flashes of lightning" illumine the stage. Lest he be accused of forcing an effect, Tennyson explains in a footnote that the elements actually did so behave at the time of the assassination. Yet no appeal to fact can guarantee that a play will enjoy an independent life of its own. Once again Tennyson is embarrassed by the raw materials of history and too cautious to take imaginative liberties. J. R. Green, the medievalist whom he consulted about matters of historical detail, was grateful for the vivid portrayal of Henry and his court. But the succession of accurate tableaux does not achieve dramatic movement. Like *Queen Mary*, *Becket* is a loose chronicle with several striking characters and some ably framed separate scenes but no real coherence of total action. The subplot, which involves Henry's love for Rosamund de Clifford and the jealousy of his wife Eleanor, is intended to provide relief from the often rather arid debate between church and crown, but it succeeds only in proving a melodramatic distraction. Eleanor of Aquitaine is reduced to an enraged tigress. Rosamund, who appeared with some romantic grace in **"A Dream of Fair Women,"** is scarcely more credible than the sentimental Edith of *Harold.* And the encounter between the two, where Eleanor points a dagger at Rosamund's bosom and Becket steals up from behind just in time to wrench the weapon from her hand, may have had some parallel in fact but assuredly has no place in a serious work of art.

Rebuffed in his efforts to bring *Becket* to the stage, Tennyson published the play in 1884 with an apologetic dedication declaring that it was "not intended in its present form to meet the exigencies of our modern theatre." But he never abandoned hope that, properly edited, it might one day be produced; and in the last year of his life his confidence seemed after all well placed, for Irving after many delays finally agreed to reshape the piece as a personal vehicle. On February 6, 1893—exactly four months after Tennyson's death—*Becket* began its highly successful run of one hundred and twelve nights at the Lyceum with Irving as the Archbishop and Ellen Terry as Rosamund. Thereafter Irving repeatedly revived the role both in London and on tour, convinced, as he said, that "the play made me. It changed my whole view of life." Few later actors have shared Irving's enthusiasm, and *Becket* has more and more been relegated to the low dusty shelves where it awaits the very few readers of arm-chair literary drama. Since 1935, when it has been appraised at all, it has suffered by comparison with *Murder in the Cathedral,* to which it bears little resemblance. Less varied and precise in characterization than *Becket,* Eliot's play gains from its narrowed concentration on theme and its deft use of the anonymous interpretive Chorus of Women. Less dependent on fact, it attains far greater freedom of language, a poetry uninhibited by the standards of a documentary realism and at the same time closer than Tennyson's blank verse to the rhythms of real human speech. Whereas Eliot has attempted to create a new form suited to his own idiom, Tennyson sought to adapt his gifts of style and imagination to the demands of an outmoded convention, to the "exigencies" of a theatre that had not existed since the early seventeenth century. The difference in approach helps define Tennyson's major limitation as dramatist. (pp. 201-08)

Four new plays followed the composition of *Becket. . . .* (p. 208)

The slightest of the four is *The Falcon,* a one-act sentimental comedy, derived from Boccaccio's tale of the Count Federigo who, having squandered all his wealth but his falcon, does not hesitate to sacrifice even the cherished bird when he must extend the hospitality of his table to the Lady Giovanna. Tennyson thought his own version of the anecdote "stately and tender," and the play in fact enjoyed a limited success as part of a double bill at the St. James' Theatre in the winter of 1879-80. But, apart from its gentle irony, the piece has little dramatic substance. Though the exposition is adroit, the characters are flat and the happy denouement too easy and too rapid to be convincing. The dialogue in prose achieves some fluency and humor, but the verse spoken by the Count and the Lady is stilted in its old-world formality. Nowhere do we find the mark of Tennyson's peculiar strength, the power (as in the *Idylls,* for instance) to suffuse an old story with a freshly felt emotion.

Finished in 1881 but first produced in 1892 by Augustin Daly in New York, *The Foresters—Robin Hood and Maid Marian* proved more popular than its author had any right to expect. Particularly attractive to the American audience in a mood of genial Anglophilia was the lyric which opened the second act, "There is no land like England," the "National Song" (suppressed after publication in 1830), written, as Tennyson told Daly, "when I was nineteen." The bulk of the play might well have been the product of even earlier years, for the sentiment and derring-do are incredibly juvenile. The scene, for instance, in which Robin meets the disguised Marian, swears his love to her, and kneels as she shows him her sword, belongs only in the Neverneverland of Peter Pan. Robin's men dash to the rescue, and Much speaks:

> Our Robin beaten, pleading for his life!
> Seize on the knight! wrench his sword from him!
> > (*They all rush on Marian*)
> ROBIN (*springing up and waving his hand*)
> > Back!
> Back all of you! this is Maid Marian
> Flying from John—disguised.
> > MEN
> Maid Marian? she?
>
> > SCARLET
> Captain, we saw thee cowering to a knight
> And thought thou wert bewitch'd.
>
> > MARIAN
> > You dared to dream
> That our great Earl, the bravest English heart
> Since Hereward the Wake, would cower to any
> Of mortal build. Weak natures that impute
> Themselves to their unlikes, and their own want
> Of manhood to their leader!

The less "romantic" stretches of *The Foresters* are scarcely more adult. The good bad men of Sherwood, paragons all of virtue in revolt against tyranny, retain throughout a storybook naïveté; and their attempts at humor, largely in the form of shameless punning, read like boyish imitations of the bantering of Shakespeare's clowns. Tennyson was able to persuade himself that his subject matter had a certain historical gravity, for he claimed to have sketched in the play "the state of the people in another great transition period of the making of England, when the barons sided with the people and eventually won for them the Magna Charta." Such sober implications, however, are seldom apparent in the text; despite frequent hits at the villainy of Prince John, the manner of the whole is incompatible with cogent political commentary. Certainly no shadow of significance touches the Fairy Scene which Tennyson introduced at Irving's suggestion and in the stage copy transferred to the end of the third act—as his note tells us—"for the sake of modern dramatic effect." Sir Arthur Sullivan, who set all the songs to music, may have been largely responsible for making these facetious fairy rhymes the most warmly applauded lines of the play. If so, we can only wish that Gilbert had helped Tennyson furnish Sullivan a more rollicking libretto. For *The Foresters* is really a comic operetta which has failed to recognize its inherent burlesque.

Tennyson's two "tragedies," *The Cup* and *The Promise of May,* both of which were written and produced in the early eighties, at least give some scope to his more serious conviction. Suggested by W. E. H. Lecky's account of a story in Plutarch, *The Cup* concerns the revenge of a Galatian priestess, Camma, who, having seen her husband slain by the covetous Synorix, feigns love for the latter and so induces him to share with her a poisoned chalice. Lest he err in detail, Tennyson consulted the archaeologist Sir Charles Newton of the British Museum about the worship of Artemis in Galatia; but he felt freer than in the chronicle plays to mold his characters to his own purpose, and he strove to make Synorix a prototype, like his Tristram, of the sensualist who, denying the claims of a moral idealism, seeks fulfillment in selfish passion. But again he found the dramatic medium a distinct handicap. "The worst of writing for the stage," he complained, "is, you must keep some actor always in your mind." He had written *The Cup* expressly for Irving, and he could do little afterwards to change Irving's false interpretation of Synorix as "a villain, not an epicurean." Once in production, *The Cup* was Irving's own project. Irving devised the elaborate décor, the massive sculptured pillars, the antique lyres, and the sacred flames burning musky perfumes. He enlisted Ellen Terry for the role of Camma, and he helped select the hundred beautiful girls who served as vestal virgins, her attendants in the temple. The opening night, which attracted "a most distinguished audience—one of the richest in literature, art, science, and politics that has ever been seen at the Lyceum," seemed an aesthetic event of the first magnitude. We may guess the quality of the performance from a newspaper review which appeared the next morning:

> Not only do the grapes grow before us, and the myrtles blossom, the snow mountains change from silver-white at day to roseate hues at dawn; not only are the pagan ceremonies enacted before us with a reality and fidelity that almost baffle description, but in the midst of this scenic allurement glide the classical draperies and sea-green robes of Miss Ellen Terry, who is the exact representation of the period she enacts, while following her we find the eager glances of the fate-haunted Mr. Irving.

The two acts so heavily mounted must have seemed almost static in effect, but few in the audience left the theatre dissatisfied, for *The Corsican Brothers* by Dion Boucicault, which completed the Lyceum bill, supplied all the movement anyone could have asked. The materials from which Tennyson at another time might have made an effective classical idyl had been shaped by Irving into a lavish spectacle, and *The Cup* accordingly began its long successful run.

The Promise of May, on the other hand, fared ill from the beginning. Gladstone, who attended the

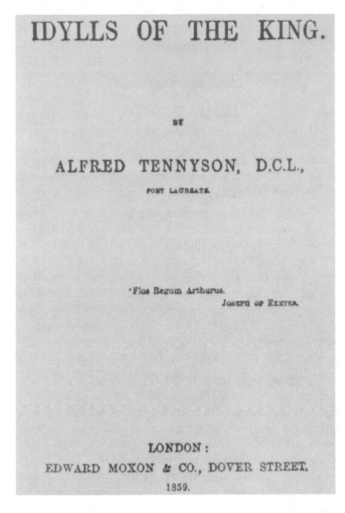

IDYLLS OF THE KING.

BY

ALFRED TENNYSON, D.C.L.,

POET LAUREATE.

'Flos Regum Arthurus.
JOSEPH OF EXETER.

LONDON:
EDWARD MOXON & CO., DOVER STREET.
1859.

Title page of the first of Tennyson's volumes based on the Arthurian legends.

opening at the Globe, thought it a good play but "above the comprehension of the vast mass of the people present." On the third or fourth night the Marquess of Queensberry, who felt that he saw its drift only too plainly, rose from his seat to denounce the piece as an "abominable caricature" of free thought and a gross insult to the British Secular Union, of which he was president. The ensuing commotion in the back rows was quelled just in time to avert a riot, but not soon enough to save the play's reputation. To no avail did Herman Vezin, the actor who filled the role of Edgar the tendentious rationalist, defend the tragedy in a letter to the press as a serious drama of ideas. "So also, in time," he concluded, "will plays presenting social and moral problems crowd out dramatic trivialities which amuse for an hour and are then forgotten. Mr. Tennyson . . . has inserted the thin edge of the wedge . . . in this, the boldest experiment in the modern drama." But, though the prediction was sound, the defense was not a happy one. The playwright was not Bernard Shaw; and the play, with its old-fashioned awkward plotting, stock

sentiment, and melodramatic gesture, did not bring new life to the English theatre.

Nevertheless, though hastily written and poorly edited for the stage, *The Promise of May* as the only one of the seven dramas with a contemporary setting does deal in ideas which Tennyson considered of immediate relevance to his own age. The story, to be sure, is contrived and improbable: Edgar, the city intellectual, seduces and abandons a naive country girl named Eva, then returns in disguise five years later and professes love for her sister Dora until the disgraced Eva reappears to expose, yet forgive with her dying breath, his perfidy. But Tennyson was far more interested in the motivations of Edgar than in the details of the action. Despite Queensberry's objection, Edgar is not a caricature of the honest "secularist," though his use or misuse of the secularist creed is plainly intended to suggest the necessity of a higher faith. He is not perhaps a "free-thinker" at all, but rather a sensualist who, having followed the courses of self-indulgence to the point of satiation, seeks to rationalize his conduct by the logic of various disturbing new philosophies. Toying with the proposition that man is but "an automatic series of sensations," he denies any possible responsibility for moral decision, yet claims for himself the right to cultivate pleasurable sensation and to ignore the painful experience of others. Like the hero of *Maud* before the coming of love, he argues from the analogy of nature that amoral self-development is the one law of an evolutionary world. When eager to free himself from the "entanglement" with Eva, he declares marriage "but an old tradition" and professes to find comfort in the belief that the immanent revolution, "the storm . . . hard at hand," will sweep away all established institutions. He looks to the day of liberation:

> And when the man,
> The child of evolution, flings aside
> His swaddling-bands the morals of the tribe,
> He, following his own instincts as his God,
> Will enter on the larger golden age,
> No pleasure then taboo'd; for when the tide
> Of full democracy has overwhelm'd
> This Old World, from that flood will rise the New.

But later when he begins to feel the power of a remorse which his hedonism cannot explain, he grows skeptical of his own too easy nonconformities. Perhaps because, as he admits ironically, he has now inherited his uncle's wealth, he denounces his erstwhile positions as "a Socialist, / A Communist, a Nihilist—what you will"; all these are now but

> Utopian idiotcies.
> They did not last three Junes. Such rampant weeds
> Strangle each other, die, and make the soil
> For Caesars, Cromwells, and Napoleons
> To root their power in.

But whatever their coloring, radical or reactionary, Edgar's speculations touch on many issues of real moment to Tennyson throughout his creative life, and Edgar himself is also, by endowment at least, an artist—"Born, happily, with some sense of art, to live / By brush and pencil." His intellectual crime lies not so much in the error of his opinions as in his proud aesthetic detachment from any consistent point of view. As the epigraph to the play labels him, he is "A surface man of theories, true to none." Like the Soul in **"The Palace of Art,"** he aspires to a godlike autonomy, an independence of all social and ethical ties; and, like the Soul's, his pride must be ultimately destroyed. Yet, since he appeals to modern knowledge to redeem him from traditional reverence, his sin is more than aesthetic; he is to the poet a symbol of the selfseeker who in a world of shifting values finally cannot believe even in the self. Because it says all this much too didactically and not just because it offended the "freethinkers," *The Promise of May* fails utterly as drama. Tennyson, however, concerned almost exclusively with his theme, refused to see the disastrous limitations of the play. He had tried, he said, to give the public "one leaf out of the great book of truth and nature"; and the public had rejected his effort. Bitterly disappointed, he wrote no more for the stage.

None of the plays seriously altered the course of the English theater. *Becket,* the most successful on the boards and perhaps the strongest of the seven, did little more than remind Irving and his fellow actors that there was still a place and even an audience for poetic drama. And *The Promise of May,* in most respects the weakest, demonstrated only that a playwright with ideas could stimulate controversy. But apart from their slight influence and despite their many defects, all remain a testimony to the remarkable, even if misdirected, energy that carried the aging poet into his last decade. Tennyson brought enthusiasm and resourcefulness to his dramatic experiment, and he gained from it both personal stimulus and new perspective on his work. Returning to his poetry, he found himself better able to objectify and so to release his emotion. More and more now he conceived of even the lyric as a dramatic utterance from a given situation. The dominant form of all his volumes from 1880 to the end is accordingly the monologue—the musing, the laughter, or the lament of an imagined character not to be directly identified with the author. "Under the mask of his Dramatis Persona" he could express at will the most intimate or the most alien feeling and yet maintain such detachment as would give the sentiment an independent life of its own. His experience as dramatist shows ultimately to best advantage in the vitality and abundance of his last poems. (pp. 208-15)

Jerome Hamilton Buckley, in his *Tennyson: The Growth of a Poet,* Cambridge, Mass.: Harvard University Press, 1961, 298 p.

JOHN D. JUMP
(essay date 1974)

[In the following excerpt, Jump provides a biographical background to Tennyson's works and surveys his major poetry.]

Dr George Clayton Tennyson, the Rector of Somersby in Lincolnshire, had entered holy orders against his inclination; he found his income insufficient to maintain his large family in what he considered decency; and he bitterly resented the preferment of his younger brother as their wealthy father's heir. Resentment unhinged his mind. He wrecked his health by taking to drink, and drinking tended to make him ungovernably violent. After years of misery, his wife had to insist upon a separation.

Alfred, born in 1809, the third of their children to survive infancy, grew up under the shadow of the family feud and in the gloomy presence of this learned and cultivated but unhappy and demented man. He evidently regarded his father with pity and fear, with anger and love, and at times with plain hostility. Trinity College, Cambridge, where he was admitted late in 1827, must have seemed to offer a haven from domestic storms. But Alfred was bored and lonely there until he met Arthur Henry Hallam in the spring of 1829. The two young men quickly became firm friends. Each could give the other support by his sympathetic understanding of the moods of despondency to which both were subject. They joined the 'Apostles', an informal debating society which included many of the ablest undergraduates among its members; and before the end of the year Hallam fell in love with Tennyson's sister Emily.

Hallam found satisfaction, and greatly assisted his friend, by acting as Tennyson's literary agent. He worked hard to get *Poems, Chiefly Lyrical* (1830) a favourable reception, and but for him Tennyson would not have brought out his second volume, *Poems,* as early as 1832. He praised Tennyson 'as promising fair to be the greatest poet of our generation, perhaps of our century'. Then, in the autumn of 1833, he died suddenly while touring in Austria with his father. Tennyson and his sister lost in Hallam a man whom both loved deeply and who fully returned the love of both. Tennyson's whole life seemed shattered; for a time he wished to die.

Not that Hallam's death was solely responsible for this wish. The circumstances of Tennyson's early life, and possibly hereditary factors, had predisposed

John Stuart Mill on Tennyson's poetics:

[Tennyson] possesses, in an eminent degree, the natural endowment of a poet—the poetic temperament. And it appears clearly, not only from a comparison of the [*Poems, Chiefly Lyrical* and *Poems*], but of different poems in the same volume, that, with him, the other element of poetic excellence—intellectual culture—is advancing both steadily and rapidly; that he is not destined, like so many others, to be remembered for what he might have done, rather than for what he did; that he will not remain a poet of mere temperament, but is ripening into a true artist. Mr. Tennyson may not be conscious of the wide difference in maturity of intellect, which is apparent in his various poems. Though he now writes from greater fulness and clearness of thought, it by no means follows that he has learnt to detect the absence of those qualities in some of his earlier effusions. Indeed, he himself, in one of the most beautiful poems of his first volume (though, as a work of art, very imperfect), the **'Ode to Memory,'** confesses a parental predilection for the 'first-born' of his genius. But to us it is evident, not only that his second volume differs from his first as early manhood from youth, but that the various poems in the first volume belong to different, and even distant stages of intellectual development;—distant, not perhaps in years—for a mind like Mr. Tennyson's advances rapidly—but corresponding to very different states of the intellectual powers, both in respect of their strength and of their proportions.

From the very first, like all writers of his natural gifts, he luxuriates in sensuous imagery; his nominal subject sometimes lies buried in a heap of it. From the first, too, we see his intellect, with every successive degree of strength, struggling upwards to shape this sensuous imagery to a spiritual meaning; to bring the materials which sense supplies, and fancy summons up, under the command of a central and controlling thought or feeling.

John Stuart Mill, in *The London Review*, July, 1835.

him to melancholia. Poems written before as well as after the autumn of 1833 express the desperate loneliness he was always prone to feel and the craving for oblivion to which it constantly led. Shortly before Hallam's death J. W. Croker had produced a brutally sarcastic review of *Poems* (1832; dated 1833), writing with the avowed intention of making another Keats of his victim. Hurt, despondent, and bereaved, Tennyson lapsed into the 'ten years' silence' which preceded the launching of his next collection, *Poems* (1842).

Early in this period, in 1834, he fell in love with Rosa Baring of Harrington Hall, near Somersby. Her wealth made her unattainable, and he soon came to see her as a rather commonplace young woman. But he was always to remember vividly the intensity of his brief, thwarted passion. In 1836 he fell in love with Emily Sellwood, a Lincolnshire solicitor's daughter, who was to become his wife after an engagement greatly prolonged and even interrupted by his lack of funds, by her family's anxiety about the mental health of the Tennysons generally, and by her own misgivings regarding his religious faith.

Poems (1842) comprised two volumes: the first contained selected poems, often much revised, from the earlier collections, the second a slightly greater amount of new verse. Both the public and the reviewers responded favourably. But, whereas Tennyson had written much during the greater part of the 'ten years' silence', he wrote little during the years immediately before and after the publication of *Poems* (1842), that broke it. Acute financial problems and the apparent loss of Emily were aggravating his recurrent fierce melancholia. Late in 1843 his friend Edward FitzGerald—subsequently to become famous for *The Rubáiyát of Omar Khayyám*—found him more hopeless than he had ever seen him; and in the following year Tennyson was receiving medical treatment. He continued to be a source of anxiety to his friends until after the publication of *The Princess* (1847).

From about that time, however, things took a turn for the better. Tennyson's financial position improved. A reading of *In Memoriam* in manuscript dispelled Emily's anxiety about his religious faith, and they married in the summer of 1850. Emily was to be a devoted and tireless wife, and their friends soon noted with pleasure the change in Alfred's health and spirits. For some years his reputation as a poet had been growing steadily, and towards the end of 1850 he succeeded William Wordsworth as Poet Laureate. (pp. vii-viii)

One after another [Tennyson's] books augmented his reputation. Admittedly, many reviewers complained that *Maud* (1855) was obscure and morbid. But the reading public did not lose interest, and the first four *Idylls of the King* (1859) and *Enoch Arden* (1864) raised his popularity to such a pitch that a writer in a weekly paper could think it likely that the age would become known as the age of Tennyson. (p. ix)

Even as brief a biographical summary as this can leave no one in doubt regarding certain sources of the melancholy which finds expression in one after another of Tennyson's poems. His deep love for his home must have made the distresses and frustrations of life at Somersby almost unbearable. They find an indirect outlet in his writing. He evokes an oppressive sense of decay in the **'Song'** beginning 'A spirit haunts the year's last hours'; he uses a beautifully particularized setting to compel his reader to share the loneliness and dejection of the abandoned woman in **'Mariana';** and in **'The Two Voices'** he confronts the case for escaping the weariness, the fever, and the fret of life by suicide.

The voice which tempts the speaker to this conclusion seems to come from within himself. It is a 'still small voice', which does not so much originate lines of argument as develop disconcertingly those which the speaker himself advances in trying to resist despair. It punctures his human pride by pointing out that there must be many creatures superior to man in a universe that is boundless; it undercuts his faith in progress by asking what is the significance of progress along a scale that is infinite; it derides his wish to leave an honourable name; and it seeks to allay the dread of something after death by persuading him that the dead are at peace. But the speaker needs to believe that death does not end all. Despite the voice's insistence upon the fact of pain, he wants 'More life, and fuller'; and he is strengthened in this desire by the sight of a happily united family walking to church. When the sceptical voice dies away, the second voice of the poem's title cheers the speaker by hinting at a 'hidden hope' of a divine love.

As this necessarily selective outline will have suggested, the argument of **'The Two Voices'** follows the vagaries of feeling rather than the routine of logic. The poem's rhyming triplets, which almost ask for a dubitative pause after each third line, serve well to record a process of anxious and tentative brooding. Admittedly, **'The Two Voices'** does not achieve the assured success of **'Mariana'** or the **'Song'**. It is awkward in some places, flat in others; and many twentieth-century readers have found its churchgoing family too good to be true. Nevertheless, it does honestly face the issues it raises, and it is frequently moving and memorable.

Since a draft of it existed three months before Tennyson learned of Hallam's death, the bereavement cannot have prompted the poem. Work on it continued for some time, however, so we may assume that grief at Hallam's death entered into **'The Two Voices'** as finally published. Tennyson himself declared that **'Ulysses'** was what he wrote under the immediate sense of the loss, with the feeling 'that all had gone by, but that still life must be fought out to the end'. The speaker in this dramatic monologue has resolved to embark upon a new, perilous, and possibly final voyage. Yet his mood is elegiac; a tone as of mournful acquiescence casts doubt on the strenuousness of his resolution. As a result, we imagine him less as striving, seeking, finding, and refusing to yield than as standing, in the words of a Victorian reviewer, 'for ever a listless and melancholy figure on the shore'. The ambiguity of the portrait springs from Tennyson's utter honesty. Life had indeed to be fought out to the end, but by one whom grief had immobilized and in whom early experience had implanted a longing for oblivion. **'Ulysses'** is one of the most complex and poignant of his shorter pieces.

Aldworth, Tennyson's home near Haslemere in Surrey.

The work that most readily brings Hallam to mind is *In Memoriam.* Critics have sometimes exaggerated the degree of unity that resulted when Tennyson arranged almost a gross of short lyrics to form this long philosophical poem. Admittedly it opens with the first crushing onset of grief, and it closes with the marriage of a sister of the poet. 'It was meant to be a kind of *Divina Commedia,* ending with happiness', stated Tennyson. Its three Christmas passages, implying a fictional span of almost exactly three years between the opening and the close, can be read as marking clear stages in the mourner's emotional and spiritual recovery: the first Christmas Eve falls 'sadly' (xxx), the second 'calmly' (lxxviii), and the third 'strangely' (cv). Lyrics marking other anniversaries serve this purpose, too. But when all has been said we must let Tennyson remind us that the lyrics 'were written at many different places, and as the phases of our intercourse came to my memory and suggested them. I did not write them with any view of weaving them into a whole, or for publication, until I found that I had written so many.'

This did not prevent him from distinguishing nine natural groups of lyrics in *In Memoriam* as finally shaped. A list of the nine, with some indication of their leading subjects or themes, will take us about as far as it seems reasonable to go in trying to see the poem as a strictly organized whole:

1 Grief at the news of Hallam's death overwhelms the mourner (i-viii).

2 In imagination, he follows the ship that is bringing home his friend's body for burial (ix-xx).

3 He recalls the four years of friendship he and the dead man had known (xxi-xxvii).

4 The pain of loss would be insupportable but for the hope of survival after death (xxviii-xlix).

5 Needing to believe in personal immortality and in the enduring value of human endeavour, the mourner longs for his friend to approach and sustain him (l-lviii).

6 His reliance upon Hallam's spirit continues despite the extent of their separation (lix-lxxi).

7 Though his grief is growing calmer, his dependence persists, and he still begs his friend's spirit to come to him. From about this point, springtime imagery tends to displace autumn and winter imagery. A fleeting mystical experience, recorded in xcv, forms the climax and turning-point of the poem (lxxii-xcviii).

8 The mourner's departure from the childhood home which Hallam had visited signalizes a fresh start (xcix-ciii).

9 The New Year hymn, cvi, further emphasizing this, leads to a series of affectionate and admiring recollections of his friend and to confident assertions of faith in the divine love (civ-cxxxi). This faith is the theme also of the prologue, which Tennyson wrote late but used to introduce the entire poem. A lyric on his sister's wedding forms the epilogue.

The need to believe in survival after death and in the enduring value of human endeavour had prevailed by the end of 'The Two Voices.' In the fifth group of lyrics composing *In Memoriam,* Tennyson reaffirms it in face of the appalling fact that not only individuals like Hallam but whole species of living creatures have been ruthlessly and arbitrarily swept away in the long course of time. The reaffirmation is cruelly difficult. What rôle can mind or spirit have had in the process traced by the geologists? Does not this process invite explanation in purely material or physical terms? Only 'faintly', in defiance of the evidence, can Tennyson 'trust the larger hope'. This, at all events, is as far as he can go in the first half of *In Memoriam.*

In the final group of lyrics he achieves a more confident assertion of faith. He rejects materialism as cripplingly reductive. Men cannot be satisfactorily explained as 'wholly brain' or mere 'cunning casts in clay'. Moreover, the evolutionary process moves towards the fulfilment of a providential plan; it is bringing into being 'a higher race', which was anticipated in Hallam. This providential plan implies a loving God. Experience of the kind recorded in xcv enables the poet to affirm his belief in the divine love. Simply and firmly, he can declare, 'I have felt.'

So the poem as a whole traces the gradual alleviation of the pain of bereavement and the eventual confirmation of an intuitive faith in the 'Strong Son of God, immortal Love'. But while we are actually reading it we pay less heed to these processes than to the particular phases of thought and feeling captured in the separate lyrics. Tennyson's stanza-form lends itself exactly to this presentation of a series of intellectual and emotional states, each one of which in turn appears to be almost immutable. The four lines composing the *In Memoriam* stanza are all iambic tetrameters. The second and third derive firmness and emphasis from their couplet rhyming. While the first and fourth, thanks to the rhymes which link them, seem to wrap around the couplet, their separation from each other weakens the conclusiveness of the fourth. The stanza turns on itself, encloses itself, pauses in earnest reflection, yet seems always to hint at resumption.

Tennyson's contemporaries had found much to admire in the short pieces published by 1842. Yet some even of the friendliest of them were not completely satisfied. They looked for something more strenuous and sustained. They wanted him to write a long poem, to handle an important contemporary subject, to show a deeper human sympathy, and to preach sound doctrine. Tennyson had responded with *The Princess* (1847), a fanciful contribution to the current discussion of women's education. Ironically, the poetic romance which forms the main part of this work has kept its appeal less well than have the exquisite and moving lyrics which are supposedly incidental to it. But with *In Memoriam* Tennyson solved his problem by shaping a long prophetic poem, as demanded by his critics, from the short personal lyrics that came more naturally to him.

Maud (1855) is another long poem made up of short lyrics. These purport to be the dramatic utterances of a young man whose distresses broadly resemble those of Tennyson himself: his father, wronged, resentful, and finally unbalanced, appears to have committed suicide; his mother has been lonely and unhappy; the wealth and social standing of Maud's family constitute as great a barrier to his union with her as those of Rosa Baring's family did to her union with Tennyson; bitter experience had made Tennyson quite as angrily aware of financial malpractices as his hero was to be; and when his hero expresses the grief of bereavement and the longing for reunion with a dead lover in the lyric beginning 'O that 'twere possible' (II.iv) he is elaborating lines that Tennyson had written immediately after Hallam's death. Was the happily married and successful Poet Laureate perhaps trying to come to terms through a fictional plot with the pains and grievances of his own earlier life?

He called the poem 'a little *Hamlet*'. Like the prince, its hero has been deprived of his inheritance by the man whom he holds responsible for his father's death. He sees this man as representative of a whole Mammon-worshipping age. Denouncing it in the manner of Thomas Carlyle or Charles Kingsley, he resolves to bury himself in himself (I.i).

He then sets eyes on this man's daughter, Maud, for the first time since childhood. He tries to dismiss her from his mind as 'Faultily faultless, icily regular, splendidly null' (I.ii). But he cannot forget her looks—though he thinks her proud—and he is captivated by her voice when she sings 'A passionate ballad gallant and gay, / A martial song like a trumpet's call' (I.v). Delighted when Maud shows him friendship, he nevertheless suspects 'some coquettish deceit' (I.vi).

Maud's brother, a selfish and arrogant young dandy with a genuine affection for his sister, is the principal obstacle to their developing relationship. Although their fathers have pledged long ago that the hero and Maud shall become man and wife, the brother wishes to marry her to the effete grandson of a wealthy, ruthless mine-owner.

But Maud and the hero draw together in love. Her acceptance of him is marked by the grave and beautiful lyric, 'I have led her home' (I.xviii). In this, a steady, assured, and customary iambic rhythm prevails for the first time at any length in a poem mainly characterized by hectic and throbbing anapaestic, or mixed anapaestic and iambic, patterns. The hero swears 'to bury / All this dead body of hate' (I.xix). The famous lyric in which he waits eagerly, impatiently, feverishly for her to leave the dance at the Hall, her home, and join him in the garden marks the climax of the poem (I.xxii).

The hero's fortunes now resemble Romeo's more closely than Hamlet's. Just as Romeo fights with Juliet's kinsman Tybalt and is banished, so the hero fights with Maud's brother and goes into exile. There are extenuating circumstances: the brother acts in defiance of the fathers' pledge and of the lovers' mutual affection; he calls the hero a liar and strikes him in the presence of his 'grinning' rival (II.i); and he receives his wound in a formal duel, after which he admits, 'The fault was mine' (II.i). Maud's death follows quickly on this calamity.

The hero retains two clear images of her. One shows her as she appeared when he was a happy accepted lover; the other shows her as she appeared when she uttered her 'passionate cry' (II.i) of grief at the bloodshed. This second image becomes the 'phantom' that haunts him in his exile and madness, a symbol of his guilt. His madness is powerfully rendered in a lyric,

II.v, which incorporates disordered reminiscences of all that has gone before.

Part III associates his recovery of his reason, and the final disappearance of the 'phantom', with his ceasing to bury himself in himself and instead devoting himself to a great cause. 'It is better to fight for the good than to rail at the ill' (III.vi).

This is on the whole the hero's version of what happens in *Maud*. Does the poem present any alternative version? A play allows different characters to take different views of what is going on—Lear's differs from Cordelia's, and hers from Goneril's and Regan's—but *Maud* is not a play. All the lyrics come from the hero's mouth. In such dramatic monologues as 'My Last Duchess', 'Andrea del Sarto', and 'The Bishop Orders his Tomb', Browning allows his characters to give their own accounts of things, but at the same time, by permitting a little over-insistence, for example, or by briefly releasing passions which the characters strive to repress, he implies alternative accounts which the reader may share with him. In this sense, Tennyson's lyrics are hardly dramatic at all. If we were to learn that the poem had not been written by Tennyson but by a young man who had himself loved Maud, shot and perhaps killed her brother, and enlisted in the army, we should find this only too easy to believe.

Does this matter? May we not read the poem as a series of lyrics expressing the changing moods of an isolated, unhappy, angry, neurotic young man; who is lifted out of his misery when he finds his love returned but is plunged into even deeper misery when circumstances lead him to wreck that love; and who emerges from his consequent madness only when he finds a great and noble cause which he can serve?

That 'great and noble cause' troubles many readers. They cannot view the Crimean War in that light. With the wisdom of hindsight, they can see that it was unnecessary; and they know that it was going to be mismanaged. But we can hardly blame the hero, or Tennyson, for not knowing all this at the time. What matters in the poem is that the hero is devoting himself to what he believes to be a struggle against falsehood and tyranny.

It is plausible enough, psychologically speaking, that he should be able to overcome his personal grief and guilt by achieving solidarity with others in such a movement. Moreover, he believes that the war will do for the nation something comparable with what he expects military service will do for himself. In the opening lyric and later he has castigated contemporary selfishness and greed. He has denounced the evils permitted or even encouraged by Victorian capitalism, and he has protested against the materialism of the age. He now trusts that the challenge of war will elicit in Englishmen a stronger sense of solidarity with, and of responsibility towards, one another and so lead them to eliminate these evils. Much of his criticism of the aggressive individualism of his time is justified; and both then and later men have urgently needed a strong sense of collective purpose. However, war seems an intolerably ruthless, destructive, and wasteful way of supplying this want, and one that can hardly supply it permanently.

Yet we scrutinize the poem in vain for any recognition by Tennyson that this is so. He is apparently content that the war should be fought to cure his hero's neurosis and to raise standards of behaviour in commerce and industry. In short, he seems to have surrendered his poem to his hero. Understandably, there were contemporaries who criticized Tennyson for identifying with his hero's bellicosity while sitting safely at home in the Isle of Wight.

Tennyson seems to identify not merely with his hero's bellicosity but with all his hero's changing and often passionate moods. As a result, *Maud* is not only a poem about a somewhat feverish hero; it is a somewhat feverish poem about such a hero. It is a skilfully planned series of personal lyrics written in an assumed character. This character is not dramatically projected. We are left to judge for ourselves the reliability of his testimony; we receive little or no guidance from the poem itself.

But his changing and often passionate moods are rendered with a marvellous intimacy and persuasiveness. *Maud* may hardly deserve the subtitle, *A Monodrama*. It is, however, a compelling, moving, exciting, lyrical sequence.

Tennyson cast several of his finest shorter poems in the form of dramatic monologues. In most of them, as in *Maud,* there is little point in trying to distinguish between what the character says and what the poem says. This is evidently the case with 'Ulysses'; and in 'Tithonus', also commenced shortly after Hallam's death, Tennyson places in a suitable speaker's mouth his own recognition that there are terms on which even immortality would become a curse and would produce a longing for extinction. 'Ulysses' and 'Tithonus' are two of the subtlest, richest, and most truly personal of his poems.

But they hardly aspire to be 'dramatic' in the sense in which 'St. Simeon Stylites' may be so described. In this, the speaker has sought salvation by mortifying the flesh. For thirty years he has confined himself to the top of a high pillar; he has grown emaciated, deformed, diseased; but he has, he hopes, acquired a degree of sanctity sufficient to qualify him to be a miraculous healer on earth and one of the blessed hereafter. Tennyson allows him to grow over-insistent in his pleading. Argumentatively, he asks Christ who, if not he, may be saved: 'Who may be made a saint, if

I fail here?' He boasts that 'no one, even among the saints, / May match his pains with mine'. Though he thanks God for 'His bounty' in making him an 'example to mankind, / Which few can reach to', his words inadvertently disclose his arrogant assumption that he has by his own effort 'reached' the state to which he is ostensibly thanking God for raising him.

By such touches, Tennyson makes his poem convey meanings which Simeon does not intend. As we read, we see Simeon both through his own eyes and through those of an independent observer. His monologue is dramatic in the sense in which one hesitates to apply the term to *Maud* or 'Ulysses' or 'Tithonus'. To say this is not to decry these three works and others like them; it is merely to define the kind of success characteristic of these more subjective monologues.

The grotesque traits in the portrait of Simeon may serve to remind us that Tennyson's writings exhibit a considerable variety both in content and in form. His melancholia and his efforts to dispel the fears it aroused, dominate most of the poems reviewed so far. *Maud* is not alone in bringing home to us how acute was his awareness of the subrational forces, both in the individual and in the world generally, that make for madness, violence, and destruction, and how earnestly he strove to understand and to manage these forces within his own life. The complement of this painful awareness is a craving for stability, security, and peace of mind. This can be expressed mawkishly, as in the evocation of 'settled bliss' at the end of 'The Miller's Daughter'. But it can equally be communicated with serene finality by the compellingly suggestive detail of a landscape, as when he speaks of the knolls 'where, couch'd at ease, / The white kine glimmer'd, and the trees / Laid their dark arms about the field' (*In Memoriam,* xcv) or of 'The pillar'd dusk of sounding sycamores' ('Audley Court').

His poetic renderings of natural phenomena are rarely less than brilliant. Patient and sensitive observation is served in them by his supreme skill in the handling of words, by what Walt Whitman called his 'finest verbalism'. During his later years, readers noted the conjunction of such verbalism with a gentle sadness and tenderness and spoke of him as the English Virgil. During his earlier years, its manifestation in such poems as 'Mariana', the 'Song' ('A spirit haunts the year's last hours'), 'The Lady of Shalott', and 'The Lotos-Eaters' led them to regard him as the successor to John Keats. His language in these is rich, deliberate, incantatory. 'The Lady of Shalott' shows how readily it can give access to that mediaeval dream-world which attracted so many nineteenth-century writers and painters.

Though Tennyson mediaevalizes in several early lyrical poems, his most distinguished achievement in that direction is an epic fragment, 'Morte d'Arthur'. In this, a poet who longed for settled ways comes to terms, through an Arthur who is dying, or passing to Avilion, with the irresistible and often violent processes of change. The fragment is haunting, poignant, and compelling.

Tennyson knew that many critics were currently demanding poems about contemporary life. So in self-defence he enclosed his fragment in what amounted to an apology, **'The Epic'.** Gradually conquering his timidity, he returned to the Arthurian material in middle age and eventually produced what many Victorians thought his masterpiece, *Idylls of the King.* Like *In Memoriam* and *Maud,* this is a long work built up from relatively short, separate items. Four of these appeared in 1859: **'Enid', 'Vivien', 'Elaine',** and **'Guinevere'.** Readers understandably saw them simply as four cabinet pictures related to the Arthurian legends. As picture followed picture during the next quarter-century, however, it became clear that there was what Tennyson called 'an allegorical or perhaps rather a parabolic drift' designed to unite them into a single whole. Thanks to this, the complete set of twelve *Idylls* offers an elaborate treatment of the struggle in human life between soul and sense.

The first of the *Idylls* as finally arranged, **'The Coming of Arthur',** opens the cycle with appropriate hints and ambiguities. **'Merlin and Vivien'** and **'The Holy Grail'** are among the most successful of those that follow. The finest of all is the last, **'The Passing of Arthur',** which incorporates **'Morte d'Arthur'** almost without alteration.

At the opposite extreme from the *Idylls,* with their collective aspiration to something like epic status, stand the songs and short lyrics in *The Princess.* These are among Tennyson's most delicate and evocative creations; here if anywhere, art aspires towards the condition of music. In particular, **'Tears, Idle Tears', 'Now Sleeps the Crimson Petal',** and **'Come Down, O Maid'** call both for high praise and for a confession that critical analysis cannot go very far towards explaining their charm. Equally fine achievements occur elsewhere. Many examples could be taken from *In Memoriam* and *Maud.* But two independent lyrics will suffice to complete this review: **'Break, Break, Break'** expresses with poignant indirectness the poet's desolation at Hallam's death; and **'Crossing the Bar'** sums up with simple dignity the outcome of a lifetime's brooding on faith and doubt.

Many of his shorter poems are neither songs nor song-like lyrics. **'To E. FitzGerald'** is an urbane and cordial Horatian ode; **'Northern Farmer—Old Style'** and **'Northern Farmer—New Style'** are humorous and racy dialect poems; the satirical impulse which contributes to them leads in **'A Character'** to a cool scrutiny of the victim's polished self-esteem; a similar satirical impulse enables the hero of *Maud* sharply to character-

ize his lover's overbearing brother (I.xiii); the vigorous rhetoric of **'The Charge of the Light Brigade'**, a poem on which Tennyson did not particularly pride himself, would shame most other Poets Laureate; and **'Vastness'** shows him late in his career resorting again to the denunciatory, prophetic tones already heard in **'Locksley Hall'** and in several sections of *Maud.*

But **'Vastness'** within itself exemplifies the variety of Tennyson's work. After a thirty-five-line Jeremiad, he breaks off, pauses, and quietly concludes, 'Peace, let it be! for I loved him, and love him for ever: the dead are not dead but alive.' Here, as in **'In the Valley of Cauteretz'**, the elderly poet can for the moment think of nothing but the greatly loved friend who died when they were both young and who has been present to him ever since. (pp. ix-xix)

John D. Jump, in an introduction to *Alfred Tennyson: In Memoriam, Maud, and Other Poems,* edited by John D. Jump, J. M. Dent & Sons Limited, 1974, pp. vii-xx.

HERBERT FOLTINEK
(essay date 1985-86)

[In the following excerpt, Foltinek examines "The Charge of the Light Brigade," focusing on Tennyson's treatment of societal constraints that impart a measure of inevitability to human existence.]

Tennyson's **'Charge of the Light Brigade'**, one of the most familiar poems in the language, has fared badly in English studies of a more recent date. Barred from most anthologies, it usually receives scant notice as a deplorable chauvinistic aberration which even the most sympathetic interpretation could not hope to ameliorate. Lord Tennyson himself, it is often pointed out, seems to have felt somewhat embarrassed about the composition on reflection. At one time he even thought of discarding it from the canon altogether. And yet he had taken considerable pride in the poem when it first appeared and is said to have been fond of reciting it in his old age. While this wavering attitude admits of various explanations, it might well indicate that the **'Charge'** cannot be all that easily dismissed as a collection of sabre-rattling sentiments. There is no denying that the apparent simplicity and rhetorical direction of the rousing ballad tend to favour such ready-made responses, yet these can hardly be reconciled with its highly elliptical texture from which further and even contradictory meanings may be deduced. The following . . . will elaborate this line of argument through a structural analysis that relates the poem to the historical context in which it originated, at the same time exploiting the vantage point of the twentieth-century reader, who is better equipped to assess the codes of war poetry than a Victorian literary audience. (p. 27)

Critics who dismiss the **'Charge'** as a piece of chauvinism often seem quite oblivious of the genesis of the work. There is no doubt that the news of the engagement in which British forces had conducted themselves with exemplary courage must have affected the author deeply. As Poet Laureate he might even have felt called upon to compose a tribute to the Queen's troops who had fought so bravely for a good cause. But this is the point where Tennyson's motivation becomes problematical. The operation had after all not ended in victory and the newspaper reports dwelt on the sheer lunacy of the instruction that had triggered off the carnage. Why should he then have chosen to commemorate a debacle which cast serious doubt on the competence of the British command, instead of celebrating a victorious operation? The often alleged inclination of the English to glory in defeat will hardly serve as a satisfactory explanation in this case. Conversely, it seems most probable that the author was initially moved to protest at the bungle, which in fact receives emphatic attention in the ballad. This view is fully supported by the circumstances of the composition. In the standard *Memoir* of 1897 Hallam Tennyson claims that the **'Charge'** was spontaneously written on 2 December 1854, "in a few minutes", after his father had been struck by the words "some one had blundered" in an article in *The Times* of November 13, where the "disaster" was treated at some length. There is probably no way of explaining how it came about that a newspaper more than two weeks old, referring to an event that had happened three weeks before the report should have excited the poet to such an extent. By that time Tennyson must have been sufficiently informed about the virtual loss of the Light Cavalry Brigade and could hardly have been impressed by yet another write-up of the affair unless it contained additional information or offered a new aspect that might put the incident in a different light. The first news had already reached England by the end of October. In the following weeks the British press had duly reported the debacle, commenting pointedly on the misleading order. We may then conclude that the inspiration for the poem came entirely from the emotive word "blunder", which must have made a great impact on Tennyson, so that he chose to employ it in a prominent position.

In fact, Hallam Tennyson was not quite accurate when he recorded the composition of the **'Charge'** years later. For one thing, the poet was not only indebted to an article in *The Times* of November 13, but also to an additional report in the following number, which may have reached him at the same time. More to the point, the article of November 13, to which Hallam Tennyson explicitly refers, actually used a slightly different phrase in discussing the event. It spoke in fact of "some hideous blunder" committed by the commanders, which Tennyson with or without thinking must have rephrased into the more colloquial and more dynamic "some one had blundered". In this way the key phrase of the poem came into existence. When Hallam Tennyson described its genesis he traced the sentence wrongly to *The Times,* but it had been of Tennyson's own making. One can see why the words should have imprinted themselves so emphatically on his mind. Apart from their ominous import, they already contain the brisk dactylictrochaic metre of the poem, which, as in many other cases, seems to have been rhythmically conceived by its author. At this point already Tennyson may have phonetically associated the word "blundered" with "hundred", thus attaining the first rhyme link of the composition.

Commentators have been at pains to point out that not "six hundred" but 673 cavalry were involved in the operation, as if excessive poetic licence had made the poet guilty of a false statement that required correction. Yet the two accounts in the newspaper had been quite inconsistent in this respect, as Tennyson himself indicated when he submitted the manuscript for publication. The first article had in fact mentioned seven hundred combatants, whereas the report in the following issue of *The Times* (14 November 1854), which the poet seems to have perused together with the first contribution, erroneously reduced the figure to 607. In addition, a nineteenth-century reader would have recalled the frequent appearance of the figure six hundred among the round numbers of the Old Testament. A few contemporary critics also complained about the impurity of the rhyme which connects the blunt "blundered" with the portentous "six hundred". The harshness may, however, have been intentional. The rough rhyme is indeed repeated in the following stanzas where "hundred" is linked with "wondered", "sundered" and "thundered", gaining additional emphasis in the process.

"Blundered", "wondered", "thundered"—we might go further and assume that the word had struck Tennyson so forcefully because it expressed the essence of the incident: hundreds of lives lost as the result of a flagrant mistake committed by somebody high up whose authority would never be called in doubt. Actually, the "hideous blunder" was made up of a series of failures, misunderstandings, and plain follies. But this is not how the common man judges the origin of a spoilt undertaking. An error of such magnitude will always be traced back to some anonymous offender, a privileged person no doubt, but one totally unqualified for the job. At the same time even a bungled order remains an imperative, as the soldier well knows, since the business of war requires absolute discipline, even against the individual's better knowledge. Thus an error may give rise to brave actions, though it will always remain a blunder which even the staunch self-sacrifice of the soldier could not ennoble into an act of fate. The role of fate, as Tennyson may have seen it, concerned only the suffering men, who rode to their doom in full awareness of the folly of the instruction. But could they really have known the scope of the mistake when the signal was given?

This raises the issue of the location of the conflict, which seems to have been quite ordinary and certainly lacking in sublime effects. Not a weird region circled by the "moaning sea" nor a picturesque gorge, but a wide stretch of undulating ground formed the setting of the encounter. Doubtless, Tennyson's imagination could have turned the scene into a doom-laden landscape, but he chose to reduce it to the bare outlines and the stylised lay-out that his account required. In the 'Charge' Tennyson entirely forgoes his inclination for evocative scene-painting. The actuality of scattered military postings across a hilly and broken country is transformed into the framing of a ritual. The flat sloping basin along which the cavalry advanced becomes a narrow corridor that might have been specifically constructed for the ordeal. Biblical images and traditional emblems evoke the obsessive dread of a confined passage surrounded by danger. The first article in *The Times* already employs the phrase "Valley of Death", which may have stimulated Tennyson's retentive and imaginative faculties. This is, then, a descent into infernal regions, the Pilgrim's Progress through the dark valley of the shadow of death past the mouth of hell. Though the military goal is still upheld, the mission proceeds as a veritable endurance test, a purgatory where only extreme fortitude can ensure survival. Passing through fire, braving death, the men are set to fulfil their task as if everything depended on their conduct. Only a schematised setting would have suited this allegorical rendering. What Tennyson wishes to convey is the essence of the action as he conceived it, not the incident itself, as it really happened. Hence the actual details of the environment had to be discarded.

For the same reason no individualisation of the riders is attempted. The six hundred know their predicament and move and suffer in one body. In the actual engagement the subsidiary units fared differently under their officers, some of whom proved excellent commanders. The retreat in particular seems to have comprised a variety of skirmishes and daring manoeuvres. Many of the men limped home on their own having lost their horses, others carried injured comrades to safety. Not so in the ballad, where the survivors return as they have advanced, as a collective, apparently even democratically constituted group. While no distinction is made between the officers and other ranks, the entire body of men are raised to a higher station as the "noble six hundred".

At the same time, the poem could not entirely omit the role of the commanders, as military actions are never collectively determined. The textual history of the composition is very revealing in this respect. The original printed version ascribes the imperative "Forward, the Light Brigade!" to Nolan, the unfortunate staff officer whose impetuosity seems to have largely contributed to the catastrophe—

'Take the guns,' Nolan said:
Into the valley of Death
Rode the six hundred. (1854. 11-14)

The 1855 reading in *Maud, and Other Poems*, which Tennyson soon discarded, cites one "captain" only, whereas the final text opts for an anonymous "he":

Half a league, half a league,
    Half a league onward,
All in the valley of Death
    Rode the six hundred.
'Forward, the Light Brigade!
Charge for the guns!' he said:
Into the valley of Death
    Rode the six hundred. (1-8)

A comparison of the extant variants as listed by Edward Shannon and Christopher Ricks supports the view that the author was deeply concerned about the ill-fated operation and was indeed searching for its cause. Doubtless he would have known that a mere captain could never have ordered the advance of a whole brigade. In fact Captain Nolan, who was killed in the fight, had only delivered the cryptic brief to Lord Lucan, adding that the troops should be set in motion forthwith. The decision to advance thus became Lucan's responsibility. The immediate order came, of course, from General Cardigan, who headed the charge so daringly and so obtusely. It seems as if the original wording sought to ascertain the false impulse of the action, tracing the initiative to a personage who was widely regarded as the scapegoat and whose name could be safely included. The 1855, altogether less outspoken version contained in *Maud, and Other Poems*, substitutes the entirely non-committal "captain", apparently still seeking to fix the blame of the debacle on a particular officer. But then the poet's attitude must have changed, possibly under the impact of the publicity which the poem had received in the meantime among the troops themselves. The later, less restrictive reading raises the issue to another level altogether. In its final form the poem is no longer trying to probe the circumstances of the mistake. What matters is solely the relationship between the men and the actuating authority, which is determined by mute obedience on their part.

It may have seemed unusual to Tennyson's contemporaries that a verse composition written in praise of the famous engagement should have omitted the name of Cardigan, who was shortly to receive a hero's welcome upon his return to England. To be sure, later readers of the final version might have associated the mysterious "he" of line 6 with him, as the ineffable speaker in **"The Lotos-Eaters'** is commonly identified as Ulysses—" 'Courage!' he said, and pointed toward the land". It is improbable, however, that such an understanding would have significantly modified the reception of the text. The ambiguity of the words contributes to the overall effect of the poem, which would be marred to some degree if a clear-cut attribution helped to decide the issue. The speaker of the ominous words is after all quite unimportant. Whoever tells the cavalry to advance is merely acting out an instrumental part soon to be relinquished. For he too shares their predicament, responding obediently to what he conceives to be a gross error. In the "Valley of Death" all the participants sink or rise to the same level. The aspect of leadership that figures so large in traditional tales of military exploits becomes irrelevant once the brigade has been set in motion. We are now in a position to consider the crucial lines of the poem within their specific context:

'Forward, the Light Brigade!'
Was there a man dismayed?
Not though the soldier knew
  Some one had blundered:
Their's not to make reply,
Their's not to reason why,
Their's but to do and die:
Into the valley of Death
Rode the six hundred. (9-17)

At first sight the second line of the second stanza might seem difficult if not impossible to accept. As a rhetorical question it may, however, hold more truth than the present-day reader can be expected to allow. After all, the soldiers of the Light Cavalry Brigade had been anxiously waiting for the signal to advance throughout the entire morning. In such a state every change of the current situation seems most welcome indeed. The excitement caused by the order, when it finally came, would have suspended the natural reaction of fear at least temporarily. As already noted, it seems unlikely that all and sundry could have immediately realised the lunacy of the operation. This is, however, a probability which Tennyson is not prepared to admit. Characteristically, he is emphatically speaking in the collective once more. "The soldier" who knew it all, represents a large body of troops, including high-ranking officers, who are thus reduced to the notions of the common man. For the common man may be expected to grasp the desperate situation intuitively and to foresee its outcome. A bungle has occurred for which he will have to pay, as is always the case. Unflinchingly he sets about his task:

neither pride
Nor hope rekindling at the end descried,
So much as gladness that some end might
be.

In this connection the function of the speaker in the **'Charge'** will have to be established. Tennyson obviously intended the verse to serve as a popular account in the tradition of the ballad. The metrical form and irregular stanzaic arrangement follow a somewhat different pattern; the brisk presentation, frequent use of repetition and simple diction, however, clearly point in this direction. The narrator or mediator is therefore best understood as a messenger who has weighty tidings to impart. Hence the abrupt delivery, hence the elliptical and yet heavily redundant style. In communicating the incident the speaker is acting out the part of the agents involved or alternatively commenting on past actions. The latter standpoint determines the final stanza: the ballad ends with a word of praise for the "six hundred" men who were killed or survived the charge. In the second stanza, however, the attitude expressed is that of the riders themselves. All of them, officers and privates, are aware that every command, even a blatantly erroneous one, is to be carried out, that orders are never to be debated, that men in action, whatever their place in the military or social hierarchy, cannot afford to reflect on the intelligence behind a line of conduct that is mapped out for them. "Obedience is the bond of rule."

"Their's not to reason why." Undoubtedly these lines speak primarily of military regulations, of the blind obedience of men in uniform throughout the ages, but the words have still wider implication. As mentioned above, Tennyson liked to declaim the poem and recordings of his delivery are extant. It is striking that he should have emphasised the word "knew" in reciting the lines under discussion, thus stressing the contradiction implied. For how could the truly obedient subordinate ever have surmised the event of a blunder if the most elementary mental process was expressly prohibited for him? Or is forbidden knowledge the cause of death, as suggested in the Biblical parable? It is unlikely that Tennyson was unaware of the subtle irony which his words convey. In fact, the inconsistency of the argument expresses the psychological dilemma of the situation quite adequately: we know only too well what we dare not think about.

In an earlier assessment of the **'Charge'**, Christopher Ricks has argued that the poem is indirectly concerned with the idea of suicide, which pervades Tennyson's early poetry, but can also be discovered in his later works. In armed combat self-extinction loses the stigma that traditionally attaches to it in Western society and is esteemed an honourable line of behaviour instead. There is little doubt that military actions have sometimes been prompted by an urge for annihilation. Seen from this angle, the enthusiastic self-sacrifice of soldiers, which was often observed in World War I, loses its heroic note but gains a profoundly human significance which would have appealed to Tennyson. It is important to note in this connection that his description deviates at one point from the steadfast regularity that otherwise characterises the advance. In the last stanza lavish praise is bestowed on the "wild charge" of the Light Brigade as if the poet had for once yielded to a secret conviction that the ride had a suicidal aspect—

> When can their glory fade?
> O the wild charge they made!
> All the world wondered.
> Honour the charge they made!
> Honour the Light Brigade,
> Noble six hundred! (50-55)

But the ballad is not merely an expression of suicidal determination. "Their's but to do and die." Inevitably the contemporary reader will be reminded of kamikaze missions, of guerilla assaults, and terrorist raids whose purpose is to inflict destruction on others through self-immolation. Would the Victorian Laureate have shuddered at the ferocities of a barbaric age that was still to come? The hero of *Maud,* a monodrama written shortly after the **'Charge'**, certainly approves of violent, self-destructive actions when they are inspired by genuine conviction:

> It is better to fight for the good than to rail at the ill;
> I have felt with my native land, I am one with my kind,
> I embrace the purpose of God, and the doom assigned.

The various analogies to which the text relates would suggest that the **'Charge'** comprises a still wider potential of meaning. Though the eventual clash between the British horsemen and their opponents undoubtedly forms the climax of the narrative discourse, the main theme of the poem is struck by a note of stoic endurance in the face of better knowledge:

> Not though the soldier knew
> Some one had blundered:

Even the suicide-motif arises from the argument advanced in the second stanza where the moment of awareness is expressly articulated. "Their's but to do and die": the steady progress of the collective body of troopers who pass lemming-like to their doom will raise associations that are more closely related to contemporary everyday life than to military engagement. The common man has become painfully aware of the infinite variety of administrative mishaps that devolve upon him in the shape of coercive patterns imposed from above. Legal restrictions, bureaucratic regulations, rigid codes of professional conduct, technocratic directions—the individual's existence is weighed down by constraints that we often know to be erroneous and yet are forced to comply with, since the rhythms of contemporary life depend on our enactment of predetermined roles. Moreover, the predicament requires distinctly more than sheeplike obedience. Fortitude and active dedication are called for if the rigorous discipline of the modern state is to be maintained. Advancing or retreating with the steady measure of a pendulum, men may at all times be forced into situations that could terminate in personal annihilation. It appears to be a peculiar feature of our seemingly unheroic age that self-destruction is silently condoned whenever unpremeditated complications occur. The phraseology which modern man applies to such cases amply indicates that the traditional ritualistic aspect has not entirely vanished. A high incidence of mortality is termed a "slaughter" or registered as the "death-toll", innovative projects are often held to involve considerable "sacrifice of life", and individual suffering may assume "tragic" dimensions when personal extinction has become inevitable. Modern society is still prepared to acknowledge the importance of unflinching loyalty on the part of the individual. Yet no purgatorial purification or spiritual reward, not even the certainty of lasting public esteem could still be attained through acts of selfless devotion, and this is precisely the point where the **'Charge of the Light Brigade'** falls short of illustrating the human condition in our time. Tennyson ended his poem on a note of praise promising everlasting glory for the victims of an administrative mess. He might have been profoundly perplexed to hear about a reading that revealed a subversive sub-text behind his patriotic war-song. And yet, as Robert Browning would have put it, "who can say?" (pp. 30-6)

Herbert Foltinek, " 'Their's Not to Reason Why': Alfred Lord Tennyson on the Human Condition," in *A Yearbook of Studies in English Language and Literature,* Vol. 80, 1985-86, pp. 27-38.

SOURCES FOR FURTHER STUDY

Beetz, Kirk H. *Tennyson: A Bibliography, 1827-1982.* Metuchen, N. J.: The Scarecrow Press, 1984, 528 p.

> Most comprehensive guide to secondary sources.

Jump, John D., ed. *Tennyson: The Critical Heritage.* London: Routledge & Kegan Paul Limited, 1967, 464 p.

> Presents thirty-five critical essays and reviews of Tennyson's works by his contemporaries.

Martin, Robert Bernard. *Tennyson: The Unquiet Heart.* Oxford: Clarendon Press, 1980, 643 p.

> Most comprehensive biography of Tennyson's life and career.

Ricks, Christopher, *Tennyson.* New York: The Macmillan Company, 1972, 349 p.

> Critical biography in which Ricks seeks to accomplish "three things: to create a sense of what Tennyson in his private life underwent and became; to make an independent exploration of his poetry, seeking to comprehend its special distinction and to establish distinctions; and to suggest some of the relationships between the life and the work."

Sinfield, Alan. *The Language of Tennyson's "In Memoriam,"* Oxford: Basil Blackwell, 1971, 223 p.

> Analysis of the diction, syntax, imagery, sound, and rhythm of *In Memoriam.* Sinfield's work has become a standard reference on Tennyson's artistry.

Tennyson, Hallam, Lord. *Alfred Lord Tennyson: A Memoir.* London: Macmillan and Co., 1897, 516 p.

> Memoir by Tennyson's son that includes correspondence to and from Tennyson.

William Makepeace Thackeray

1811-1863

(Also wrote under pseudonyms Michael Angelo Titmarsh, Samuel Titmarsh, George Savage Fitz-Boodle, Mr. Snob, Yellowplush, Ikey Solomons, The Fat Contributor, and Jeames de la Pluche, among others) English novelist, essayist, short story, fairy tale, sketch, and travel writer, poet, critic, and editor.

INTRODUCTION

Thackeray is best known for his satiric sketches and novels of upper- and middle-class English life and is credited with bringing a simpler style and greater realism to the English novel. *Vanity Fair: A Novel without a Hero* (1848), a panorama of early nineteenth-century English upper-middle class society, is generally regarded as Thackeray's masterpiece. This satiric novel comprises the most comprehensive treatment of the concerns central to all of Thackeray's works—the divisive effects of greed, class, and social ambition—and epitomizes the sardonic wit and apt character sketching for which he is esteemed. Although *Vanity Fair* has received more critical attention than any of his other works, many regard *The History of Henry Esmond, Esq., a Colonel in the Service of Her Majesty Q. Anne* (1852), a historical novel set in early eighteenth-century England, as his most well-planned and carefully executed work. Still others feel that his miscellaneous sketches and essays, particularly *The Yellowplush Correspondence* (1838) and the *Roundabout Papers* (1863), are the fullest expression of his genius.

Born in Calcutta, Thackeray was sent to England at the age of six following the death of his father. His mother, who remarried and remained in India, did not return to England for four years. During these years Thackeray attended several boarding schools where he was extremely unhappy. He later attended the prestigious Charterhouse School and then Trinity College, which he left before finishing his degree. After reading law for a short time he moved to Paris where he studied art. Although he eventually abandoned the idea of making his living as a painter, Thackeray continued to sketch and paint throughout his life and illustrated many of his own works. While studying in Paris he married a young Irishwoman named Isabella Shawe, and shortly after their marriage they returned to London where Thackeray began writing professionally, contributing to *Fraser's Magazine, The New Monthly Magazine,* and later to *Punch.* In 1839 the Thackerays' second daughter died in infancy, and the next year, shortly after the birth of their third daughter, Isabella went mad, never regaining her sanity. Because she outlived him, Thackeray was unable to remarry and was thus deprived of the family life he so desired.

During the years before the success of *Vanity Fair,* Thackeray wrote numerous reviews, essays, comic sketches, and burlesques under more than a dozen comic pseudonyms. Among the best-known of his early non-fiction is *The Yellowplush Correspondence,* a series of satiric sketches written in the guise of a cockney footman's memoirs. The most successful of the early burlesques is *Catherine* (1839-40), a parody of the crime story genre popular in Thackeray's day. This work is the strongest expression of Thackeray's contempt, discernible throughout his other works, for the prevalent literary convention of glorifying criminals. *The Luck of Barry Lyndon* (1844), his first lengthy novel, was strongly influenced by Henry Fielding's *Jonathan Wild* and demonstrates his keen interest in eighteenth-century literary forms. This work, which first revealed Thackeray's skill at depicting the language and manners of an earlier age, was also his first serious attack on social pretension. His increasing scorn for the shallow acquisitiveness of Victorian society is obvious in *The Book of Snobs* (1848), a collection of satiric character sketches which first appeared as *The Snobs of England, by One of Themselves* in *Punch.* This series denounces the snobbery and greed bred by the changes in social attitudes and relationships brought about by the Industrial Revolution and the resulting redistribution of wealth and power.

For *Vanity Fair,* his first signed work, Thackeray adopted the publication form of monthly periodical installments already made popular by Charles Dickens. This comprehensive satire of corruption in upper- and middle-class English society is set during the Waterloo crisis and revolves around the lives of two characters, the passive Amelia Sedley and the ambitious, conniving Becky Sharp. Thackeray's treatment of these characters has sparked endless debate, for although Becky is ostensibly the negative character, it is she who actively engages the reader's interest and sympathy, while Amelia, though good-hearted, appears in the final analysis to be dull and ineffectual. Becky Sharp is often praised, in fact, as one of the most memorable anti-heroines of the nineteenth century. The other major and minor characters are also noted for their lifelike complexity. The themes central to Thackeray's earlier writings are clarified and fully developed in *Vanity Fair,* in which he delivers his most scathing attack on the heartless pretension prevalent in nineteenth-century English life and concludes that self-interest is at the heart of human motivation. In addition, Thackeray first uses in *Vanity Fair* the narrative technique employed throughout his subsequent novels: the omniscient, didactic narrator who comments freely upon the motives and actions of the characters.

Finally successful and well-known, Thackeray went on to write *The History of Pendennis: His Fortunes and Misfortunes, His Friends and His Greatest Enemy* (1849-50), the first of three related novels based on his own experiences. *The History of Pendennis* chronicles the early life of Arthur Pendennis, who takes the role of the narrator in the sequels, which are titled *The Newcomes: Memoirs of a Most Respectable Family* (1854-55) and *The Adventures of Philip on His Way through the World* (1862). All three novels are set in contemporary London and are narrated in the manner, according to Thackeray, of "a sort of confidential talk." Although their narrative technique is often considered diffuse and overly didactic, these novels are praised for their convincing characterization and vivid depiction of Victorian society.

Henry Esmond is Thackeray's only novel completely written before publication and issued in book form without first being serialized. Critics often cite these circumstances when praising the novel's careful organization and elegant style. Set during the reign of Queen Anne, *Henry Esmond* is written in imitation of early eighteenth-century English prose. Although it offended some readers due to the incestuous overtones of Henry Esmond's marriage to Lady Castlewood, it is now regarded as one of the greatest nineteenth-century English historical novels. Its sequel, *The Virginians: A Tale of the Last Century* (1858-59), is generally considered to be inferior.

In 1859 Thackeray became the first editor of and chief contributor to *Cornhill Magazine.* During his last years he contributed numerous essays and several novels to the journal, including *The Adventures of Philip* and *Lovel the Widower* (1861). The essays collected in the *Roundabout Papers,* however, are probably the most highly valued of these contributions. In these nostalgic, rambling pieces Thackeray wistfully recounts his childhood experiences, travels, and his impressions of Victorian literature, politics, and social issues. He was in the midst of publishing *Denis Duval* in *Cornhill Magazine* when he died suddenly on Christmas Eve, 1863.

Criticism of Thackeray's works primarily revolves around several issues, including his narrative technique and his use of satiric irony. Many early critics were particularly disturbed by Thackeray's apparent cynicism; some, including novelist Anthony Trollope, chided him for dwelling too exclusively on the negative traits of humanity. Others claimed that his satiric depiction of self-interested rogues served a useful moral purpose and was sufficiently balanced with sensitivity and compassion. In contrast, his twentieth-century detractors have been far more critical of the sentimentality which often creeps into his works. Thackeray's omniscient narrative technique continues, however, to be the most controversial element in his fiction. While many claim that the authorial commentary is intrusive and interferes with dramatic unity, others believe that this method enhances Thackeray's work by creating a deliberate moral ambiguity that actively involves readers by forcing them to render their own judgments. Another area of interest for both critics and biographers is the possible autobiographical sources for Thackeray's works. Numerous studies have been published which examine the parallels between his private relationships and experiences and the characters and plots of his works. Critics often maintain that Thackeray's intense emotional involvement with characters based closely upon real-life models severely limited his artistic achievement.

During his life Thackeray's work was regarded as the great upper-class counterpart to Dickens's panorama of lower-class Victorian society; indeed, because of his precise rendering of character types and his acuity in describing the social mores of his time, some critics have contended that he is Dickens's superior as a historical chronicler. However, Thackeray's reputation declined at the turn of the century. Early twentieth-century critics often found his vision of society limited and his characterization impeded by his deference to Victorian conventions. More recently there has been a resurgence of interest in Thackeray and numerous studies have appeared which afford his works a more sympathetic treatment. Thus, although Thackeray is no longer widely ranked as an equal of Dickens, his works continue to inspire a diverse body of critical interpretation, and he is generally recognized as one of the major writers of the mid-Victorian era.

(For further information about Thackeray's life and works, see *Dictionary of Literary Biography*, Vols. 21, 55; *Nineteenth-Century Literature Criticism*, Vols. 5, 14, 22; and *Something About the Author*, Vol. 23. For related criticism, see the entry on the Victorian Novel in *Nineteenth-Century Literature Criticism*, Vol. 32.)

CRITICAL COMMENTARY

ANTHONY TROLLOPE

(essay date 1879)

[An English novelist and critic of the Victorian period, Trollope wrote *Thackeray* (1879), one of the first book-length critical studies of the author's career. In the following excerpt from that work, he praises Thackeray's lucid writing style while examining the novelist's view of human nature.]

[Regarding] the realism of Thackeray, I must rather appeal to my readers than attempt to prove it by quotation. Whoever it is that speaks in his pages, does it not seem that such a person would certainly have used such words on such an occasion? If there be need of examination to learn whether it be so or not, let the reader study all that falls from the mouth of Lady Castlewood through the novel called *Esmond,* or all that falls from the mouth of Beatrix. They are persons peculiarly situated,—noble women, but who have still lived much out of the world. The former is always conscious of a sorrow; the latter is always striving after an effect;—and both on this account are difficult of management. A period for the story has been chosen which is strange and unknown to us, and which has required a peculiar language. One would have said before hand that whatever might be the charms of the book, it would not be natu-

ral. And yet the ear is never wounded by a tone that is false. . . . Thackeray never disappoints. Whether it be a great duke, such as he who was to have married Beatrix, or a mean chaplain, such as Tusher, or Captain Steele the humorist, they talk,—not as they would have talked probably, of which I am no judge,—but as we feel that they might have talked. We find ourselves willing to take it as proved because it is there, which is the strongest possible evidence of the realistic capacity of the writer. (pp. 187-88)

[In another] division of pure fiction,—the burlesque, as it is commonly called, or the ludicrous,— Thackeray is quite as much at home as in the realistic, though, the vehicle being less powerful, he has achieved smaller results by it. Manifest as are the objects in his view when he wrote *The Hoggarty Diamond* or *The Legend of the Rhine,* they were less important and less evidently effected than those attempted by *Vanity Fair* and *Pendennis.* Captain Shindy, the Snob, does not tell us so plainly what is not a gentleman as does not tell us so plainly what is not a gentleman as does Colonel Newcome what is. Nevertheless the ludicrous has, with Thackeray, been very powerful, and very delightful. (p. 191)

No writer ever had a stronger proclivity towards

Principal Works

The Yellowplush Correspondence [as Yellowplush] (sketches) 1838

Catherine [as Ikey Solomons, Esq., Junior] (novel) 1839-40; published in journal Fraser's Magazine

The Luck of Barry Lyndon [as Fitz-Boodle] (novel) 1844; published in journal Fraser's Magazine; also published as The Luck of Barry Lyndon: A Romance of the Last Century, 1852

The Book of Snobs (sketches) 1848

Vanity Fair: A Novel without a Hero (novel) 1848

The History of Pendennis: His Fortunes and Misfortunes, His Friends and His Greatest Enemy. 2 vols. (novel) 1849-50

The History of Henry Esmond, Esq., a Colonel in the Service of Her Majesty Q. Anne (novel) 1852

The Newcomes: Memoirs of a Most Respectable Family. 2 vols. (novel) 1854-55

Miscellanies: Prose and Verse. 4 vols. (essays, sketches, short stories, and poetry) 1855-57

The Virginians: A Tale of the Last Century. 2 vols. (novel) 1858-59

Lovel the Widower (novel) 1861

The Adventures of Philip on His Way through the World (novel) 1862

Roundabout Papers (essays) 1863

Denis Duval (unfinished novel) 1864

The Complete Works of William Makepeace Thackeray. 30 vols. (novels, short stories, sketches, poetry, essays, travel sketches, letters, and lectures) 1904

The Letters and Private Papers of William Makepeace Thackeray. 4 vols. (letters and journals) 1945-46

parody than Thackeray; and we may, I think, confess that there is no form of literary drollery more dangerous. The parody will often mar the gem of which it coarsely reproduces the outward semblance. . . . But it must be acknowledged of Thackeray that, fond as he is of this branch of humour, he has done little or no injury by his parodies. They run over with fun, but are so contrived that they do not lessen the flavour of the original. . . . [He] has been grotesque without being severely critical, and has been very like, without making ugly or distasteful that which he has imitated. . . . The ludicrous alone is but poor fun; but when the ludicrous has a meaning, it can be very effective in the hands of such a master as this. (pp. 194-96)

Whatever Thackeray says, the reader cannot fail to understand; and whatever Thackeray attempts to communicate, he succeeds in conveying.

That he is grammatical I must leave to my readers' judgment, with a simple assertion in his favour. . . .

He quarrels with none of the laws [of grammar]. As the lady who is most attentive to conventional propriety may still have her own fashion of dress and her own mode of speech, so had Thackeray very manifestly his own style; but it is one the correctness of which has never been impugned. (pp. 199-200)

I am inclined to think that his most besetting sin in style,—the little earmark by which he is most conspicuous,—is a certain affected familiarity. He indulges too frequently in little confidences with individual readers, in which pretended allusions to himself are frequent. "What would you do? what would you say now, if you were in such a position?" he asks. . . . In the short contributions to periodicals on which he tried his 'prentice hand, such addresses and conversations were natural and efficacious; but in a larger work of fiction they cause an absence of that dignity to which even a novel may aspire. You feel that each morsel as you read it is a detached bit, and that it has all been written in detachments. The book is robbed of its integrity by a certain good-humoured geniality of language, which causes the reader to be almost too much at home with his author. There is a saying that familiarity breeds contempt, and I have been sometimes inclined to think that our author has sometimes failed to stand up for himself with sufficiency of "personal deportment."

In other respects Thackeray's style is excellent. . . . [The] reader always understands his words without an effort, and receives all that the author has to give. (p. 201)

Now let the reader ask himself what are the lessons which Thackeray has taught. Let him send his memory running back over all [his] characters . . . , and ask himself whether any girl has been taught to be immodest, or any man unmanly, by what Thackeray has written. A novelist has two modes of teaching,—by good example or bad. It is not to be supposed that because the person treated of be evil, therefore the precept will be evil. . . . [Thackeray's examples] have all been efficacious in their teaching on the side of modesty and manliness, truth and simplicity. (pp. 204-05)

There remains for us only this question,— whether the nature of Thackeray's works entitle him to be called a cynic. The word is one which is always used in a bad sense. . . . [They] who have called him a cynic have spoken of him merely as a writer,—and as writer he has certainly taken upon himself the special task of barking at the vices and follies of the world around him. Any satirist might in the same way be called a cynic in so far as his satire goes. . . . But that is not all that the word implies. It intends to go back beyond the work of the man, and to describe his heart. It says of any satirist so described that he has given himself up to satire, not because things have been evil, but because he himself has been evil. Hamlet is a satirist, whereas

Thersites is a cynic. If Thackeray be judged after this fashion, the word is as inappropriate to the writer as to the man.

But it has to be confessed that Thackeray did allow his intellect to be too thoroughly saturated with the aspect of the ill side of things. We can trace the operation of his mind from his earliest days, when he commenced his parodies at school; when he brought out *The Snob* at Cambridge, when he sent *Yellowplush* out upon the world as a satirist on the doings of gentlemen generally; when he wrote his *Catherine,* to show the vileness of the taste for what he would have called Newgate literature; and *The Hoggarty Diamond,* to attack bubble companies; and *Barry Lyndon,* to expose the pride which a rascal may take in his rascality. Becky Sharp, Major Pendennis, Beatrix, both as a young and as an old woman, were written with the same purpose. There is a touch of satire in every drawing that he made. A jeer is needed for something that is ridiculous, scorn has to be thrown on something that is vile. (pp. 206-08)

He was "crying his sermon," hoping, if it might be so, to do something towards lessening the evils he saw around him. We all preach our sermon, but not always with the same earnestness. He had become so urgent in the cause, so loud in his denunciations, that he did not stop often to speak of the good things around him. Now and again he paused and blessed amid the torrent of his anathemas. There are Dobbin, and Esmond, and Colonel Newcome. But his anathemas are the loudest. It has been so I think nearly always with the eloquent preachers. (p. 208)

Anthony Trollope, in his *Thackeray,* Gale Research Company, 1968, 216 p.

GEORGE SAINTSBURY

(essay date 1908)

[Saintsbury was one of the most influential British critics and literary historians of his day. In the following excerpt from an essay that first appeared in 1908, he offers a largely laudatory survey of Thackeray's fiction and essays.]

[In his early writings Thackeray] showed, almost from the first and in ever-increasing measure and with less alloy, qualities of the very rarest kind. The most unmistakable—or what ought to have been the most unmistakable—of these was the omnipresence of a peculiar humour, or wit and humour mingled, unlike that of any previous writer as a whole but bearing most resemblance to Fielding and Shakespeare—a humour casual,

unpremeditated, or at least never laboriously led up to, *parenthetic* as one may almost call it—rising, like bubbles in sparkling wine, independently of the substance of the narrative or discussion, but giving life to it. The second, more slowly developed, and perhaps hidden from careless or obtuse observers by the caricature and the dialect of such things as *The Yellowplush Papers,* was an especially remarkable command of character, sometimes revealed by only a very few strokes, but those of such a vivifying character as we must once more go to Shakespeare to equal. The third was a quite marvellous style. . . . [His style] may again owe something to Fielding, but it is in its essence almost wholly original. It is more like the result of thinking aloud than the style of any other writer. But it is also more than this. The writer thinks for himself *and* for 'the other fellow'—for an imaginary interlocutor who makes objections, spies the ludicrous side of what has been said, and so forth. Thus, the body of his critical and miscellaneous writings, and the framework of his novels, consists of a sort of fused dialogue or conversation, lighted up constantly by the humour and wit above mentioned, and vignetting the character-sketches, the descriptions, and the rest. This sort of thing could not be perfected at once, but it may be discovered in pieces which he wrote when he was not more than six-and-twenty, such as *The Professor.* (pp. 18-19)

[*Catherine*] is a very odd book—the oddest in all Thackeray's work, and the most difficult to 'place' satisfactorily. . . . For myself I prefer it to *Barry Lyndon,* though it is more immature. . . . It could hardly have been made more disgusting (in fact a good deal of repulsive detail was actually removed in the reprint) without becoming a mere study of horror and grime in itself and for its own sake. . . . On the other hand, if the object was what it holds itself out to be—the satire by parody of books like [Dickens's] *Jack Sheppard,* with something more than a glance backward at *Eugene Aram,* and something of a glance sideways at *Oliver Twist,* then one may question, first, whether it is not a little too disgusting as it is, and secondly, whether in any true sense it 'gets at' any of the originals. It is neither melodramatic enough, nor romantic enough, nor sentimental enough to do this: nor does it caricature any of these features sufficiently. On the other hand, as a piece of *Jonathan Wild* irony, though quite admirable in parts, it is not sustained enough: the author either cannot or will not keep on the grimace and gesture of the half-Mephistophelian, half-angelic mentor; and is constantly telling a plain tale, by no means disagreeable except for the unusual sordidness of the characters. . . . In short the author never knows quite what hare he is hunting: and the reader is perpetually puzzled and vexed at the way in which the dogs change scent and course. (pp. 51-3)

[Yet] *Catherine* is Thackeray's first considerable

and substantial *story*. Most of the things he had done in this kind had been slight sketches. . . . *Catherine* is a complete novel; there is beginning, middle, and end; not yet perfect but very well advanced character, sustained in different cases and personages throughout the book; good conversation and description; as well as no small manifestation of the author's peculiar fashion of showmanship; still more of his idiosyncrasy of style; and not a little of his predilection for a special subject and period—the manners, customs, speech, and folk of the eighteenth century. The opening chapters of *Catherine*, despite the company to which we are introduced, are absolutely of the best novel-romance kind. . . . There is a curious saturation with history and literature which betrays itself, not in digression or padding, but by constant allusion and suggestion; a light, current, apparently facile, sketching of scene and character which suddenly plunges (as a great phrase of Walt Whitman's has it) to 'the accepted hells beneath', but recovers itself at once and goes placidly on; above all, a shower of original and memorable phrases, never paraded, never dwelt upon too long, but more absolutely startling in its unique felicity than the most laboured conceits of mere phrasemongers.

It is of course true that before long, the want of thorough *digestion* in the scheme begins to betray itself; and the rather worse than picaresque degradation of the characters begins to be irksome. . . . Moreover, Thackeray has overloaded his story with incident in proportion to its length, and has made leaps and bounds of omission which, possible in a chronicle-drama, are dangerous in a novel. . . . [As] for 'Cat' herself, she is, like her history, that most dangerous thing, a failure of a masterpiece. And so it happens that though the excellences of the thing are plentifully provided up to the very close, ghastly as it is, the faulty disposition of these excellences and the company in which they find themselves make the book almost impossible to *enjoy*. (pp. 53-5)

[If *Hoggarty Diamond*] has less power than parts of *Catherine*, it is far less unequal; if it has not the wilder humour of *Yellowplush* and *Gahagan*, it tries more difficult strings and does not fail in the trial. And that extraordinary fullness and variety of living presentation which was to be—which was already—Thackeray's great and almost unique attribute appears here marvellously to those who have eyes. . . . The pathos of the whole need not annoy any sensible person: it is not dashed and brewed to mawkishness in the fashion of some writers, and it certainly sets off the comic and satiric parts legitimately enough. The richness and variety of these and of the characters that work them out are quite astonishing. . . . (pp. 67-8)

It may possibly be owing to natural perversity; but I confess that I like *Barry Lyndon* less than any other book of Thackeray's, less even than *Catherine*, which is much inferior in art, and very much less than *Philip*, which may be said to be inferior in art likewise. (p. 93)

Parts of [*Barry Lyndon*] are equal to almost anything that even he ever did. The opening Irish chapters are quite admirable; they show his marvellous powers of improving experience capitally. . . . Lady Lyndon's first husband and the elder Chevalier de Balibari—but especially the former—are creations of the author's best; no other living man could have drawn, with such few and such powerful strokes, a character, if only a minor character, so complete and so original as Sir Charles. Her Ladyship, though not quite so good as she would have been a few years later, is still excellent. Of the seasonings of eighteenth-century manners and so on the same may be said; while everywhere and all over the book there is abundance of the incomparable Thackerayan incident, situation, phrase, insinuation, suggestion, aside—as well as direct narrative and exposition. . . . [It] may be more than conceded—cheerfully and vigorously asserted—that the general style shows to the very full [an] advance in dignity, success without trick, flexibility, [and] general artistic achievement. . . . And yet—! To begin the devil's advocate part, Thackeray does not seem to me either to have conceived clearly, or to have maintained steadily, his own attitude towards the story. There can be no doubt—in fact it is agreed—that he took *Jonathan Wild* in no slavish sense as a model. But in doing this he hampered himself enormously by making it an autobiography. You *can* make a man represent himself as a scoundrel or a fool or both: . . . Thackeray himself has done it here with great success in parts. But it is a frightful strain: and it is a great question whether it can possibly be done on a very large scale without 'incompossibility'. . . . [Has] not Thackeray forgotten that he is Barry rather too often? . . . [Was] Mr. Barry Lyndon, either as Redmond Barry, as the Chevalier, or in his glory, exactly the person to moralize on the Seven Year's War, as he or his creator does Chapter IV? I have no objection to moralizing if 'de morals is goot'. Thackeray's sermons never bore me when they are his, or Mr. Pendennis's, or those of anybody *congruous*. But that Barry should preach me I own surprises me.

There is, moreover, another point in which the autobiographical scheme, not necessarily of course, but as a matter of fact and by likelihood beforehand, had hampered and clogged the narrative and exposition. We get too many things recounted and too few acted, with the effect of something like the *récits* in conventional French tragedy. (pp. 94-6)

In short, to make a clean breast of it, *Barry Lyndon* fails—to me—in interest. . . . (p. 96)

[The] advances and advantages in respect of all his former work are immense and unmistakable [in *Vanity Fair*]. In the first place he has at last given himself—or has been given—proper scope and scale. . . . As for construction, *Vanity Fair* is nearly the best of all its author's works—in fact it is almost the only one in which any attention is paid to construction at all. In scheme, as apart from details, it is difficult to remember any other author, except perhaps Defoe, who, having written so long and so much, suddenly made such a new and such an ambitious 'entry' in literary competition, and not merely in the particular department of novel-writing.

In that department, however, the novelty, if not so absolute as that of *Robinson Crusoe,* was of a higher strain. (pp. 165-66)

Only perhaps in his very earliest period and in his immature work is he guilty—if even there—of [the] 'lowest imitation',—[the] mere carrying off of whole figures from the pageant of life, and botching them into the tapestry of literature. That a very large number of his traits, incidents, individual details are taken from, or suggested by, actuality, there need be no doubt—it is in fact the secret and reason of his unsurpassed truth to life itself. But these things are all passed through the alembic or the loom of art—redistilled or rewoven into original and independent composition. . . . There are the books which depend for their interest on the fact that their characters *have been* live men and women; and those which depend for it on the fact that they *are* live men and women. Thackeray's books belong to the second.

Those other vivifying arts of his which have been many times sketched in general, appear to the full in *Vanity Fair.* Thackeray does not 'set' his scenes and situations with the minute touches of detail as to furniture and the like. . . . But he has a setting of his own which places things and persons quite firmly in the reader's conception: and he employs it here from the Academy for young ladies in Chiswick Mall to his final (or almost final) scenes at Pumpernickel. It is, however, perhaps not in actual description of any kind that his life-giving and individualizing touch most fully consists. It is in queer nondescript devices—though 'device' is a bad word for things that come so naturally—tricks of names, humorous or fantastic asides—indescribable confidences as it were between himself and his reader, which establish intimate relations. (pp. 171-72)

It is with these subtle condiments of humour and suggestion that the author seasons his whole book. Whether it has, or has not, 'the best story' as he himself thought, he was quite right as to the excellence of the title. In the steady maintenance of the point of view of that title—so admirably defined and described in the Preface—its greatest merit as a book, from the severe old critical standpoint, perhaps consists. Its greatest claim to admiration, with some at least, is in the lavish and masterly presentation of character—too uniformly sombre-tinted it may be, but faultlessly drawn—from the triumph of Becky downwards. But its greatest attraction of all is in the constant procession-pageant of scenes and incidents which serve to bring out these characters, and in the wonderful dexterity and variety of presentation and style . . . [The] Devil's Advocate may say, with some truth, that in the opening or ante-Waterloo part, which occupies half the book, the action somewhat drags, and that, though the Amelia and Becky stories are ingeniously enough intertwisted, the transitions from one to the other, and even some of the scenes themselves, do not 'go off trippingly' as Captain Clutterbuck says. Still, once more, the manner saves everything; and so it does in the latest division of the book which succeeds the discovery of Becky's misdoings.

But there is another part where, though the manner is more triumphant than ever, the matter partakes the triumph and is fully worthy of its less unequal partner. From the beginning of Chapter XLIV, when Sir Pitt *fils* comes to stay in Curzon Street, to the great catastrophe itself, the artist is thoroughly inspired, the rider has settled to the race, and is getting every possible effort out of the horse. Not merely is it all good, but there is in it that steady *crescendo* of expectation and satisfaction which only occurs at the supreme moments of life and of literature. The catastrophe itself is simply beyond praise—it is one of the greatest things in English: but it is perfectly led up to. For, as in other uncertain and accidental matrimonies, when matter and manner do go thoroughly together, then all is indeed well. In these hundred pages . . . there is not a line, not a phrase that is weak or wrong. There is nothing like them anywhere. . . . The variety, the intensity, the cool equal command, are not only unmatched, they are unmatchable in novel-literature: and the circumstances preclude their being matched in any other. . . . [The] manner plays up in unfailing provision of style and atmosphere, of satire, and pathos, and humour, and 'criticism of life'. (pp. 173-75)

[One] finds a curious unanimity among qualified and well-affected judges that *Pendennis* is, perhaps, the most *delightful* of Thackeray's novels. (p. 178)

The book is a long one, but from first to last it is prodigal of delights. . . . The remnant of self-distrust which threw the action of *Vanity Fair* back for half a generation has vanished entirely, and the society is practically contemporary. Almost every kind of life comes in, and the parts in these kinds are played by almost every sort of character. Much more trouble is taken with scene and setting. There is hardly anything in *Vanity Fair* (except the grim arch between the two staircases) which gives us the *décor* as a hundred things do in *Pendennis,* from Fairoaks and the country about it to Shepherd's Inn. If, as has been admitted, the texture of the story is very loose—if it is a chronicle-play rather than a drama of the Unities—there is the consolation (very much more than a compensation for some folk) that the scenes of which it is combined or strung together never flag or drag for one moment. (pp. 178-79)

Of scenes and incidents you may, they say, weary. I doubt it, but I think it possible. The play of character may become so familiar that the enjoyment of it is, at least, palled; but there is in *phrase*—in certain peculiar collocations of the written word—a charm like that of Cleopatra. It never wearies, because it is never quite the same. Imbedded as it is to a certain extent in its context, you may miss it wholly on one re-reading, and so it comes to you all the fresher at the next. Even if this does not happen, it has, if it is of the first water, a quality at once of the opal and of the diamond which is absolutely infinite and inexhaustible. (p. 186)

A greater novel than *Esmond* I do not know; and I do not know many greater books. It may be 'melancholy', and none the worse for that: it *is* 'grand'.

For though there may not be much humour of the potato throwing sort in *Esmond,* it will, perhaps, be found that in no book of Thackeray's, or of any one else's, is that deeper and higher humour which takes all life for its province—which is the humour of humanity—more absolutely pervading. And it may be found likewise, at least by some, that in no book is there to be found such a constant intertwist of the passion which, in all humanity's higher representatives, goes with humour hand in hand—a loving yet a mutually critical pair. Of the extraordinarily difficult form of autobiography I do not know such another masterly presentment. . . . The success is, in fact, the result of that curious 'doubleness'—amounting, in fact, here to something like *triplicity*—which distinguishes Thackeray's attitude and handling. Thus Henry Esmond, who is on the whole, I should say, the most like him of all his characters (though of course 'romanced' a little), is himself and 'the other fellow', and also, as it were, human criticism of both. At times we have a tolerably unsophisticated account of his actions, or it may be even his thoughts; at another his thoughts and actions as they present themselves, or might present themselves, to another mind: and yet at other times a reasoned view of them, as it were that of an impartial historian. The mixed form of narrative and mono-drama lends itself to this as nothing else could: and so does the author's well-known, much discussed, and sometimes heartily abused habit of *parabasis* or soliloquy to the audience. . . . But its efficacy in this peculiar kind of double or treble handling is almost indisputable, even by those who may dispute its legitimacy as a constantly applied method. (pp. 193-94)

If the champions of 'Unity' were wise, they would take *Esmond* as a battle-horse, for it is certain that, great as are its parts, the whole is greater than almost any one of them—which is certainly not the case with *Pendennis.* And it is further certain that, of these parts, the personages of the hero and the heroine stand out commandingly, which is certainly not the case with *Pendennis,* again. The unity, however, is of a peculiar kind, and differs from the ordinary non-classical 'Unity of Interest' which Thackeray almost invariably exhibits. It is rather a Unity of *Temper,* which is also present (as the all-pervading motto *Vanitas Vanitatum* almost necessitates) in all the books, but here reaches a transcendence not elsewhere attained. The brooding spirit of *Ecclesiastes* here covers, as it were, with the shadow of one of its wings, the joys and sorrows, the failures and successes of a private family and their friends, with the other fates of England and Europe; the fortunes of Marlborough and of Swift on their way from dictatorship, in each case, to dotage and death; the big wars and the notable literary triumphs as well as the hopeless passions or acquiescent losses. It is thus an instance—and the greatest of that revival of the historical novel which was taking place. . . . (p. 197)

[Nothing] has yet been said of one of the most salient characteristics of *Esmond.* . . . This is, of course, the attempt, certainly a very audacious one, at once to give the very form and pressure of the time of the story—sometimes in actual diction—and yet to suffuse it with a modern thought and colour which most certainly were *not* of the time. The boldness and the peril of this attempt are both quite indisputable. . . . (p. 198)

So far from there being anything illegitimate in this attempt to bring one period before the eyes of another in its habit as it lived, and speaking as it spoke, but to allow those eyes themselves to move as they move and see as they see—it is merely the triumph and the justification of the whole method of prose fiction in general, and of the historical novel in particular. . . . That a man should have the faculty of reproducing contemporary or general life is wonderful; that he should have the faculty of reproducing past life is wonderful still more. But that he should thus revive the past and preserve the present—command and provide at once theatre and company, audience and performance—this is the highest wizardry of all. And this, as it seems to me, is what Thackeray had attempted, and more, what he has done, in the *History of Henry Esmond.* (p. 200)

[With *The Newcomes,* once] more we have the abounding wealth and ease—the *copia*—of *Pendennis* without that certain disorderliness which has been admitted in the case of the elder masterpiece. . . . In a certain sense, too, the story is not merely more definite and coherent than that of *Pendennis,* but it is of a higher strain—the strands are not only more deftly twisted, but they are more various and of choicer quality. If there are no such unique presentations of special sides of life as those of the Oxbridge and Fleet Street parts of *Pendennis,* life itself at large is treated much more fully, freely, and variously. The higher society which had been partly anticipated in *Vanity Fair,* wholly so in *Esmond,* and slightly touched in *Pendennis,* is here grappled with and subdued to the purposes of art in the most fearless and triumphant fashion. It is infinitely more real in handling than Balzac's, and superior in artistic powers to any one else's attempts in the same kind. The mere variety, subordinated as it is to a fairly general scheme, is a wonderful thing, as is the way in which the great length of the book permits itself absolutely no *longueurs* of episode or padding. Above all, perhaps, there is no book in which Thackeray has attained to such a Shakespearian pitch of pure tragicomedy: that is to say, not tragedy with a happy ending, not comedy turned to tragic conclusions, but both blended and contrasted, grave and gay mixed, in the special English fashion of dramatic presentation. (pp. 209-10)

[Perhaps] in no book is Thackeray's peculiar fashion of 'address to the reader' more happily managed. The abundance of incident, character, and conversation possibly carries this off better than is the case in books where the story is less skilfully managed, or, at any rate, rather less abundantly provided. . . . [Here] its application is uninterruptedly felicitous, from the Fable before the beginning to the disposition of the characters after the end. (p. 220)

Many things in [*Philip*] are of his absolutely best: it has a sort of *bonus* of autobiographic interest—not intruded, but generously offered for those who like to take or leave—which is not equalled by any of the books except *Pendennis.* It is full of delightful scene, character, incident, talk. But still the warrior has gone into battle with his armour rather carelessly laced and braced; the builder has not looked in all cases to the tempering of his mortar. (p. 236)

The present writer is not ashamed to confess that he reads *Philip* as often as any of the books—that his objections as a critic do not interfere in the least with his enjoyment as a reader. But that is probably an unnatural state of things, begotten of long practice in separating personal likes from artistic appreciation. As a critic, though he certainly will not throw *Philip* to the wolves, he is bound to say that it is not the prettiest nor the best behaved of the children of its family. (p. 242)

Philip and Charlotte are quite real persons— . . . they exist, and behave themselves as they ought to do in accordance with the laws of their existence. But, in this one instance, Thackeray's experiments in the true realism may be thought to have brought him near that false realism of which we have since seen and are still seeing so much. It is true that, in the novel, to secure the highest artistic effect, and at the same time the greatest satisfaction to the reader, the characters must

be real, and their actions must be probable in themselves, or made so. But it is not true that this is sufficient. They must be made in some way or other *agreeable;* and if they are made disagreeable they will not and ought not to succeed. . . . Philip—Charlotte is rather null than anything else, she does not hinder, if she does not help—is not agreeable in any way. . . . [One] takes no interest in him; does not even passively enjoy his company; does not want to see him again. With the vast majority of Thackeray's characters you want to see them again very much. (pp. 242-43)

Thackeray is in this respect inferior to Shakespeare—that he either cannot, or does not choose to, leave his characters with the universal humanity which is of no special age at all; though he ransoms this to some extent by his unmatched faculty of giving them the character of their own age. . . . [With] his oddly mixed indifference to chronology and sense of actuality he has striven to give the newer *nuance* to Philip, to make him a young man not of the late 'thirties but of the early 'sixties. And I think the effect is rather one of 'confusion of kinds'. (p. 244)

Life and Abundance—these are the two things that are to be found in [Thackeray], to be found in him everywhere; and to be found out of him, in the same degree and to the same extent, nowhere, as I believe, in the English or in any novel. (p. 249)

[From Hunt, Lamb, and Hazlitt] came all the essayists and all the Essays of the English nineteenth century. Among these essayists I do not know a greater than Thackeray: among the collections of these essays I do not know one so great as the *Roundabout Papers.* (p. 255)

To me the *Roundabout Papers* are almost as much a whole, a microcosm, as many celebrated books of great writers composed nominally on a single theme: but of course they are individual wholes as well. And their individuality and, so to speak, 'promiscuousness' prevented that appearance of the desultory which, though it far exceeds the reality, is charged against his larger single works. (p. 256)

[Quick] changes and many-faceted presentations of thought had always been natural to Thackeray; and now at last he was at liberty to indulge them as he liked, and yet under the control of his own judgement. (pp. 256-57)

One very remarkable feature of this crop of the 'last of life for which the first was made' is to be found in the large number of passages which it contains directly consisting of, or indirectly conveying, literary criticism. . . . [In] earlier days this was Thackeray's very weakest point (except politics which here hardly figure at all); that, with occasional *aperçus* of surprising acuteness and truth, he was at the mercy of all sorts of gusts, not exactly of caprice, but of irrelevant and extraneous influence. Here the 'calmed and calming *mens adepta'* remedies all this in the most satisfactory fashion. (pp. 260-61)

[There] is perceptible, not a mere acceptance of what had previously been rejected or questioned, because the critic's powers of discrimination are blunted and his interests cloyed, but a true mellowing of perception and a determination to hold fast to that which is good. . . . You will not find Thackeray praising rubbish anywhere, and in these *Roundabouts* least of all. But you will find him no longer inclined to harp and carp on trifles; and not in the least ready to be blown away by some gust of doctrine (or ignorance) in regard of his subjects. In fact, these *Roundabout Papers* exhibit their author in a state only to be described by one of the stock adjectives of criticism, and one which has been even more abused than most of these hardly treated vocables. They are thoroughly *ripe*. . . . The abundance of matter and the perfection of handling match each other constantly: and over all and above all and through all there is perpetual suffusion of that unforced and inimitable style and phrase which makes subject almost indifferent and constitutes treatment of itself. Over all too there rules the true *Phantasus*—the principle of that part or side of the poetic quality which belongs equally to poetry and to prose, which Thackeray shows in both, and which goes hand in hand with his unerring truth to nature and reality. (pp. 262-63)

George Saintsbury, in his *A Consideration of Thackeray,* Oxford University Press, London, 1931, 273 p.

FRANK O'CONNOR
(essay date 1956)

[O'Connor was an Irish critic and short story writer whose criticism is characterized by an emphasis on the writer's creative process and the relationship between the artist and society. In the following excerpt, he discusses Thackeray's female protagonists in *Vanity Fair*.]

Vanity Fair is no mere random choice of a title; it expresses the whole meaning of the book. It is a wonderful novel, and a highly original one. Among English novels it comes closest to the Russian ideal of organic form, of a story that tells itself without recourse to invention by virtue of a certain unity of viewpoint and tone. The viewpoint, however, is an exceedingly disillusioned one. The mainspring of all human actions, if we are to believe the author, is self-interest. From the servant girl up to the Princess, the only motive to be distinguished is that of getting something for oneself. Intelligent people recognize this and act accordingly, and those who do not, behave as they do because their self-interest is of a different sort or because they are too stupid to do anything else. "To part with money is a sacrifice beyond almost all men endowed with a sense of order. There is scarcely any man alive who does not think himself meritorious for giving his neighbour five pounds. Thriftless gives, not from a beneficent pleasure in giving, but from a lazy delight in spending." Virtue, in Thackeray's eyes, is always weak or stupid. "She was a very good woman," he says of Lady Grizzel, "good to the poor, stupid, blameless, unsuspicious." If she had been an out-and-out criminal, he could not have blasted her more effectively.

This means that the contrast Thackeray sets up between instinct and judgment differs widely from that of all other novelists I know of. In Jane Austen the instinct represents the imaginative life, while the judgment represents morality. In Stendhal the instinct is also an aspect of the imagination, though the judgment usually represents irony. In Thackeray it would almost seem as if the instinct always represented some form of weakness, while the judgment represented selfishness. At any rate, it is he who links the two in describing Osborne's behavior after his son, George, is killed at Waterloo.

An illustration by Thackeray for *Vanity Fair.* Here, Amelia and her family encounter Becky at a London Fair.

Which of us is there can tell how much vanity lurks in our warmest regard for others and how selfish our love is? Old Osborne did not speculate much on the mingled nature of his feelings, and how his instinct and selfishness were combating together.

The thinking here is childish, as Thackeray's thinking so often is; it is the price one has to pay for so disillusioned a viewpoint; and, for what it is worth, the point he is making had been dealt with pretty effectively by Christ in the parable of the Good Samaritan. But it is clear from this, as from many other passages, that he regards instinct as weakness; selfishness, for all that he affects to denounce it, as strength. It was his preoccupation with selfishness which made him so much better a historian of his period than Dickens.

It is also characteristic of the novel that its real heroine, Becky Sharp, is an adventuress and the personification of human selfishness. She is also, by the same token, a prostitute and a murderess, though Thackeray deals gingerly with those aspects of her character while grumbling at the necessity for doing so. At the same time, what makes the book so remarkable is that, whether Thackeray likes it or not, he turns her into the heroine and even, in his shallow way, tries to defend her. "And who knows but Rebecca was right in her speculations, and that it was only a question of money and fortune which made the difference between her and an honest woman?"

Who *does* know? The answer quite obviously is "Thackeray and no one but Thackeray." The mere fact that the question can be asked at all shows that Becky Sharp is something more than a character in a novel. (pp. 115-17)

[Though] she is to a certain extent a character, she is also a point of view, and that point of view is very close to Thackeray's own, at least to that part of it which he would have attributed to his judgment. Becky lives by discovering the weak points of others and flattering their vanity or stimulating their lusts while herself remaining quite cold and, indeed, good-humored about it all. Becky is "bad," but she is also clever.

Now Amelia, her protagonist, is of course "good," but she is also intolerably stupid. And here we come to the most interesting point in Thackeray's moral dilemma. Amelia is also a mother in a sense in which Becky is not a mother at all. There was something about maternity that fascinated Thackeray, apparently because it broke down the crust of egotism and selfishness in a woman and left her vulnerable to circumstances. In an admirable passage of analysis, Lord David Cecil has pointed out the inconsistency of Becky Sharp's boxing her child's ears when she finds him listening to her singing, and argues quite correctly that "people of her temperament neglect their children, but their very selfishness makes them good-natured to them." At the

same time, this is not slipshod writing on Thackeray's part, as Cecil believes. It is quite deliberate and considered, and the same attitude is repeated again and again in the latter part of the book. Becky, as one of her lovers informs us, cannot like children "any more than the Devil can like holy water," and again and again we are told flatly that "gentle thoughts and simple pleasures were odious to Mrs. Becky; they discorded with her; she hated people for liking them; she spurned children and children-lovers." This is not carelessness, but a contradiction in Becky's character required by the fact that she is something other than a character, by the fact that she represents a point of view.

Becky is part of the antithesis that racks Thackeray more than any other novelist I know of. Every great writer, of course, has such antitheses; no matter how much of his material he draws from real life, his characters and situations necessarily form masses and contradict one another in ways that ultimately reveal the whole bent of his nature, but few writers are trying to balance such an unstable antithesis as Thackeray. Becky *cannot* like children because she is antithetical to Amelia, who can like nothing else. This was one of the ways his instinct operated, and if he had to have good women, he preferred them as mothers. When dealing with them he sometimes becomes unendurably mawkish, almost obscene.

As his eyes opened and his mind expanded, under the influence of the outward nature round about him, she taught the child, to the best of her humble power, to acknowledge the Maker of All; and every night and every morning he and she—(in that awful and touching communion which I think must bring a thrill to the heart of every man who witnesses or who remembers it)—the mother and the little boy—prayed to Our Father together, the mother pleading with all her gentle heart, the child lisping after her as she spoke. And each time they prayed God to bless dear papa, as if he were alive and in the room with them.

It is scarcely possible to believe that this was not written with the shadow of a sneer, and, indeed, . . . I wonder if Thackeray could ever be unselfconsciously emotional. But this was as earnest as he could be, because Amelia—as he, Mrs. Brookfield, and her husband all agreed—was inspired by Mrs. Brookfield. He had not concealed the Brookfield relationship from his mother, and she had done her best to console him. This is how he described her to Mrs. Brookfield at the time.

I look at her character and go down on my knees as it were with wonder and pity. It is Mater Dolorosa, with a heart bleeding with love. Is not that a pretty phrase? I wrote it yesterday in a book, whilst I was thinking about her—and have no shame somehow now in writing thus sentimentally to all the public; though there are very few people in the world to whom I would have the face to talk in this way tete-a-tete.

There is little question but that there was in Thackeray a childish strain that attracted him to women who resembled his mother, women who were soft, stupid, and indulgent. And there is no question but that the mature man in him was attracted to women of a very different type—cold, sensual, calculating women like Becky Sharp, Blanche Amory, and Beatrix Esmond. That is why *Vanity Fair* has the eternal appeal of its originality. It is the only novel written by a man of mature mind which makes a cold-hearted scheming adventuress into a heroine, and does it so successfully that, in spite of ourselves, we are charmed into accepting her point of view. (pp. 118-20)

Frank O'Connor [pseudonym of Michael O'Donovan], "Thackeray: 'Vanity Fair'," in his *The Mirror in the Roadway: A Study of the Modern Novel,* Alfred A. Knopf, 1956, pp. 111-24.

JULIET McMASTER

(essay date 1971)

[In the following excerpt, McMaster examines Thackeray's distinctive literary techniques, in particular his much-discussed use of authorial intrusion.]

Thackeray is a consummate artist very much in control of what he is doing, whose major novels are works of thematic coherence and aesthetic integrity; and . . . he is also a highly sophisticated ironist, exploiting to the full the potential of the various personae he adopts, and introducing ambiguity deliberately, to sharpen our moral perception and to evoke the complexity of experience itself. (p. vii)

Against the contention that Thackeray was a dilettante, too careless as an artist to mind whether his reader believed in the imaginative reality of his creation or not, I suggest that he was as conscious and painstaking in his art in his way, and as successful, as Keats or Sterne or James were in theirs, and that his commentary, his infamous 'lyric leak,' has its positive uses in involving the reader and so subtly increasing the 'sentiment of reality' of the novel. (p. viii)

[It] was Thackeray's achievement so to interweave his fiction with our lives that we draw on our memories of his novels almost as we draw on the material of our own past experience.

How is it done? To a large extent, I would suggest, by the presence of one character whom, if the reader has not been too much imbued with post-Jamesian criticism, he will perhaps have remembered and enjoyed as much as any of the others—Thackeray himself: or at least those facets of himself that he chooses to show us. And here we come, of course, as we were bound to, to the question of the authorial commentary. . . . Thackeray's novels are great works of art for various reasons, but not the least of them is the author's presence: they live because of his commentary, not in spite of it. Sounding through those great organisms, *Vanity Fair, Pendennis,* and *The Newcomes,* like the heartbeat in the body, is the unifying tone of the narrator, a regular and reassuring reminder of the life and harmony of the whole. For the life of the novels comes not just from the vitality of the characters and action depicted in them, but from the tone and reactions of the man who tells the story; and more—from the reader's own personal responses, elicited, though not determined, by his. (pp. 1-2)

[In] Thackeray's novels we have the sense that we are being told the story by a fellow human being: he is informative, though not usually analytical, about the characters and the context in which they act, and sympathetic in his relation of its relevance to his and our own lives, if often questionable in his preferences and values. (pp. 5-6)

In his fiction, of course, Thackeray was to make manifold use of this participation. His novels are certainly about Amelia, Becky, Arthur Pendennis, Clive Newcome, and the rest; but they are also *about,* and in no superficial way, our response to these characters and to the world they live in. His authorial presence is his strategy to elicit this response. And the moral experience of the novel is largely a matter of the reader's decision as to where he wants to place himself among the various attitudes dramatized for him in the author's commentary.

A standard objection to what has come to be known as 'authorial intrusion' is that it consists of *telling,* whereas it is the author's business to *show,* and the reader's to make up his own mind. To refute this charge one need only repeat that the commentator in Thackeray's novels is no ultimate authority. The commentary does not constitute the 'moral' of *Vanity Fair* or of any of the other novels, though it certainly is part of the moral experience of reading them. The reader has to be prepared to make his own independent judgments just as much in the passages of commentary as in the passages of direct scenic presentation, and frequently more so, because of the deceptive plausibility of the commentator's arguments. (pp. 8-9)

The passages of commentary are not directives on what to think. Each is at best only one way of looking at the matter; and the next may be a different way, or emphatically the wrong one. 'What Thackeray is saying' about the characters is to be found in the facts of the narrative, and only fragmentarily and often misleadingly in the commentary. The reaction of those readers of Thackeray who wish that he would stop *talk-ing* and get on with his subject is thus misguided, for the talk, with the attitudes expressed in it, is itself part of the subject. (p. 11)

In generalizing about the nature of the authorial presence in Thackeray's novels, one inevitably becomes involved in a series of qualifications; for it is a lambent light, playing on the fictional world sometimes brilliantly, but sometimes like an ultraviolet ray, invisible but still effective. None of the various names we use for this presence—Thackeray, the narrator, the persona, the implied author, the omniscient author—fully defines its nature, though they have their local applications. There are the various roles that the author chooses to play within the world of his characters. . . . [And the] range of interlocked roles extends continuously from the fiction to the history, from the imagined world to the actual world. Thackeray may infringe the rules of consistency, but in the process he can connect the novel's world with his reader's, and involve us personally in the lives of his characters.

In this context it is useful to examine the prologue to *Vanity Fair*, 'Before the Curtain.' Critics have traditionally denounced Thackeray's puppet metaphor as a derogation of the artist's duty to create life and to convince us of the imaginative reality of the world he presents. . . . Nevertheless, the prologue, far from being a piece of artistic irresponsibility, seems to me to be a study, as carefully wrought as one of Keats' odes, of the nature of the artist's relation to his artifice, and of both to the perceiver, the man to whom the artist's vision is to be communicated. (pp. 12-13)

It is in its way a kind of epitome of the whole novel: a concentrated statement of the content as well as the technique, proceeding not by descriptive analysis but, like a poem, by a series of images. (p. 13)

[Part] of Thackeray's achievement in 'Before the Curtain,' and in *Vanity Fair* as well [is] to see his own identity with the meanest figure of his creation. . . . This humility, as well as the god like confidence of the puppeteer, is embodied in *Vanity Fair* as in its prologue. (pp. 18-19)

It is a marvellous piece of work, that prologue—a kind of distilled essence of the novel, without being in any crude way an explanation or an apology or a synopsis. It not only gives a preview of the content of the novel . . . ; it gives also a foretaste of the method, offering a series of metaphors for that varying presence of the artist in his work, and preparing us for the tone and changing moods of the narrative and for the part that we, as spectators and evaluators, are to play ourselves.

So I do not defend Thackeray from the charge of exposing his own illusion. He certainly does assert his liberty to juggle with his characters, not just in calling

them puppets (which, by the way, is a matter of almost literal truth—the writer *is* the omnipotent being who proposes and disposes of his characters; Thackeray differs from other authors only in admitting it), but in various other ways in all his novels. For instance, in *The Virginians* he reassures us about the fate of Harry Warrington when he is knocked unconscious by telling us that he has no intention of squandering his hero so early in the novel . . . , and in *The Newcomes* confesses that it was a matter of expediency that he eliminated Lady Kew when he did. . . . (pp. 21-2)

It was part of both his moral and artistic purpose to force the reader, during the act of reading, to make comparisons from one world to the other, to bring to bear his knowledge of one on the evaluation of the other; in fact, to break down, or at least as far as possible to overlook, that barrier between illusion and reality. (p. 23)

[Thackeray] does not try for this kind of intensity. He persuades us to live not *through* his characters but, in our own identities, *with* them, and makes us feel that our lives unfold together. (p. 24)

Another means by which Thackeray cements the relationship between himself and the reader, which to so large an extent sustains his created illusion, is his use of burlesque. It is characteristic of the novelist who depends on irony and an intimate communication with his readers, like Fielding, Sterne, Jane Austen, and Thackeray, that parody is an initial creative impulse. (p. 29)

But for the most part Thackeray gave up direct parody in his novels for a light texture of burlesque supported by a sophisticated pattern of allusion, and frequent remarks on how 'I disdain, for the most part, the tricks and surprises of the novelist's art' . . . , and on his determination to write about men and women, not heroes and heroines, about the everyday occurrences of ordinary life, not the wild coincidences and providential resolutions of romance, and so on. His principle of realism, of course, prompted him in his reaction from romance, just as it has prompted similar remarks in most novelists who, as a matter of tradition, deny heroic status to their protagonists. . . . But Thackeray makes thematic use of his reaction. *Vanity Fair* deserves its subtitle of 'A Novel without a Hero,' because the specifically unheroic nature of man—and of woman too, for all the ironic claims for that title alternately for Amelia and Becky—is his subject. Literary, as well as social, pretension is to be Thackeray's satirical butt. It is to be the reader's business in *Vanity Fair*, as it is Catherine Morland's in [Jane Austen's] *Northanger Abbey*, to distinguish between the true and the false, both in life and in literature. . . . [Thackeray] allows the reader to retain his own location and his own identity, but makes him experience the novel's delusions and enlightenments for himself. (pp. 30-1)

[The] emphasis on the incongruity between romance and reality, or between the pose and the truth, is both subject and technique in *Vanity Fair.* Frequently the reader is ironically invited to see the sordid facts of the lustful and rapacious world through the rose-coloured spectacles of the novel of sentiment. (p. 32)

Because Thackeray speaks personally, the reader reacts personally, and is often provoked to take issue with the narrator on his judgments and allegiances among the characters. Such a reaction must be based on the supposition that somehow we know more of the characters and surrounding circumstances than he tells us—that is, that these are autonomous beings— people—whose faults and virtues may be speculated on, but not finally assessed. It is an unobtrusive process by which we are made to react in this way, for the comments to which we react are often diffused through the whole narrative, and take the form not only of passages of explicit evaluation but of brief interpolated phrases and adverbs, which may be from the narrator's personal viewpoint, or from that of some character in the action, or of some hypothetical reader. (p. 39)

The novelist can speak as the final authority on the actions and the motives of the characters he creates, whereas the raconteur who is telling us an anecdote of people he knows, and that we may know too, will frequently, as a matter of honesty or in deference to our feelings, admit to a limitation in his knowledge. Now Thackeray often makes such an admission: 'I think [Amelia] was more frightened than even the people most concerned,' he says, with an air of uncertainty. 'Perhaps [Becky] just looked first into the bouquet, to see whether there was a *billet-doux* hidden among the flowers.' The narrator's professed ignorance, not just on minor matters like these, but also in matters of substance, is one more of Thackeray's devices for endowing his narrative with something like the quality of life. We cannot know *all* about his characters, as we cannot know all about a person. Much of his writing seems to assume, and so helps us to assume, the existence of his literary creations outside the limits of his volume. And besides this, his professed uncertainty is an invitation for the reader's participation. (p. 42)

In declaring, as it were, open season on his characters by discussing them with us himself, he has given them the stature and ambiguity of real people. (p. 44)

And so, intricately, the reader is lured into the world of *Vanity Fair,* and made to recognize it as his world, and to think of the characters, to whom he has been introduced by his friend the author, and about whose domestic lives he has heard some piquante gossip, as his acquaintances. Such a proceeding may be a sort of heresy to the reader or the critic trained in the Jamesian scheme, who may exclaim angrily about 'aesthetic distance,' and the 'closed precinct' that a novel ought to be. But Thackeray simply does not believe in aesthetic distance, at least in any strict application of the phrase. For him a close and personal relation with the reader, albeit a varied one, and a confidential intercourse with him about his novel and his characters, and the rights and wrongs of their actions in a fallen world that author, reader, and characters equally inhabit, and the concerns they have in common—all this is the life blood of the illusion he creates. *Vanity Fair* is a great novel not in spite of that authorial presence but because of it, for it is what gives the novel its peculiar immediacy of appeal as well as its universality of application. (p. 48)

Qualification is necessary. Commentary, involving this rather dangerous process of breaking the illusion of reality, is not good in itself, but only when done well. . . . Thackeray himself, of course, was not always successful: *The Virginians* breaks down under the weight of the commentary, which there becomes turgid and lacks the sparkle and bite of the earlier novels. But he *could* do it well; and at its best it is not only entertaining and thematically relevant, but it works as a sort of magic to build a bridge between us and the characters, from the actual world around us to the imaginary world of Vanity Fair. (p. 49)

'First the world was made: then, as a matter of course, Snobs.' This is Thackeray's version of Genesis in *The Book of Snobs,* the work which established him as virtually the world authority on the subject. Through his career that initial vision of snobbery as the human condition expands into the greater concept of the world of Vanity Fair, and is carried on through the quest for the true gentleman in *Pendennis,* to the study of respectability in all its forms in *The Newcomes.* (p. 127)

Of course snobbery is not all that Thackeray's novels are about: they are far more than just lively studies of middle-class manners. His minutely realized social milieu is the context for individual dramas which have implications far beyond the business of mere status-seeking. But it is in this area, in his portrayal of the social universe, that much of the comedy and page-to-page vitality of his novels reside. . . . And though Thackeray's chosen setting is always that World, 'wherever there is a competition and a squeeze,' the effect is not repetitive, for he manages to make every snob also an individual. (pp. 127-28)

And, behind all his vivid dramatization of social climbing, inside all his incarnated snobs, there is a solid structure of ideas. Thackeray is a shrewd social commentator, even if, writing in the hungry forties, he did not choose manufacturers and factory operatives for his characters. (p. 128)

'It is among the RESPECTABLE classes of this vast and happy empire that the greatest profusion of Snobs is to be found' . . . , Thackeray declares. And so it is the vicissitudes of middle-class existence that he chronicles. He can range above and below this world that he knows so well, with some insight into the aristocracy. . . . But for the most part his lords are seen in relation not so much to each other as to the middle-class society which adulates them; and his lower orders are usually of the servant class. (pp. 128-29)

The middle-class world that Thackeray chose to write about is representative enough, we understand, of the rest of the world. He suggests the same struggles and status-seeking going on upwards in the higher levels of the aristocracy and downwards among the servants. (p. 129)

Thackeray was preoccupied with class as he saw the world around him was preoccupied with it. If a character's position on the social ladder does not always determine what he is, it is at least always relevant. Relations are constantly seen in terms of class gradations, so that even a short novel like *Lovel the Widower,* which has the old Cinderella plot of the low-born maid's marrying the master, becomes a little social history. (pp. 129-30)

A Snob is *'he who meanly admires mean things'* . . . : it is this inversion of values that Thackeray the social historian portrays, and Thackeray the satirist and moralist exposes. He depicts that elaborate confusion between status and function, between appearance and essence, with a show of being an impartial chronicler, often with the explicit assumption that these things are as they must and should be. But his irony is constantly implying the essential values that society has debased, and showing up the sham that has come to be accepted as the reality. (pp. 130-31)

There are various reasons why *The Newcomes* has always lagged so far behind *Vanity Fair* in popularity and critical attention. It is not as lively, the characters are less vividly animated, the incident and commentary are not as piquante. *Vanity Fair* contains more of the sparkling exaggerations of satire—showing, in effect, one Dobbin in a world of cheats and humbugs—and its satirical vision makes its theme more obvious, and more immediately interesting. The ratio of good to bad is perhaps more realistic in *The Newcomes,* which shows a number of characters who, if not good, are concerned with the problem of how to live according to conscience in a fallen world. But its scope is in certain ways the larger for this increased realism: its emotional appeal is greater, for ultimately we care less for the sirens and parasites like Becky and Amelia than for decent people like Clive, Ethel, and Colonel Newcome.

It is also slow to get going, and never achieves the pace of Thackeray's first novel. He takes his time to de-

scribe the various branches of the family, and to define the world in which Colonel Newcome is to grow old and his son is to grow up. Structurally, too, it does not hold together as tightly as *Vanity Fair.* With its vast number of characters, three of whom are rival claimants for the central position, and its spread of time and place, and its accumulation of detail, it is a novel that one easily gets lost in. . . . Nevertheless, it is not only endowed with life, but also thematically and artistically coherent, though its range and complexity tend to make its effect cumulative rather than immediate. (p. 153)

The Newcomes is the 'Memoirs of a Most Respectable Family,' and their claim to respectability rests as much on their money as on their solid Quaker background and their three generations of virtuous apprentices. And Thackeray's subject is that complex union of, or confusion between, financial and moral values, good and goods, which constitutes 'respectability.'

Money, as a determinant of respectability, is a central principle that holds together at once the Newcome family and the novel, permeating language and imagery and dominating character and action. . . . Through the novel people are judged by the size of their balance, relationships progress in terms of who opens and who closes how large an account, battles are fought in which the manoeuvres are transferring an account or bouncing a cheque.

As mercenary transactions dominate the action, so financial terminology pervades the language, giving a distinctive texture to the novel. Love, morality, art, and faith are all discussed in financial terms. (pp. 155-56)

The marriage market itself is of course a central image in the novel, and the repetition of the mercenary marriage and its outcome between various couples is a unifying structural principle. . . . According to the philosophy of Society, marriage 'is but a question of money on one side and the other.' . . . But those who hold this tenet, however substantial their actual bank balance, find through the course of the novel that there are multiple debts accruing in trust and affection. (p. 157)

It is part of the intricate structure of the novel that the great world which it depicts in such painstaking detail is reflected in miniature in numerous little microcosms through the book. Each little community or institution, each gathering of people, even a single object like the coconut tree, has the quality of being complete in itself, with its own centre of gravity and its own set of revolving satellites within the major system. (p. 162)

Learning how to live, at once with the world and with one's own consciousness, is one of the main subjects of the novel. This is the task before Ethel, who is a product of her environment and at the same time manages eventually to assert herself against it. 'You belong to your belongings, my dear,' Lady Kew tells her . . . ; but Ethel has to develop in moral consciousness to the point where her belongings belong to her. In the first part of the novel she is gaining money, prestige, or suitors; but by the end she has learned how to give them away.

Ethel Newcome is Thackeray's best heroine; indeed she compares favorably with any heroine of the nineteenth-century novel. Besides being both vivid and likable, she has a dynamism which most of Thackeray's major females lack: she learns about herself, and changes as a result of her knowledge. She has a full and complex moral life and development. She has Becky's strong character, without Becky's siren's tail. She is like Beatrix in many ways . . . but, where Beatrix is finally tainted by her ambition and selfishness, Ethel is redeemed, and convincingly so.

The Newcomes is slow to get going because Thackeray takes the necessary time to build up the world in which his individual dramas are to be enacted. The effect is the more powerful for being cumulative; and by the time Clive, Ethel, and the rest reach their moments of decision, we have a full awareness of the complex pressures to which they are subject. (pp. 163-64)

'To push on in the crowd, every male or female . . . must use his shoulders. If a better place than yours presents itself just beyond your neighbour, elbow him and take it.' . . . This is what *The Newcomes* is about, rather than how 'the fox is caught in his trap, the lamb is rescued from the wolf, and so forth.' In the Newcome world, your vices are your assets. . . .

The animal imagery that is a connecting motif of the novel works in two ways. Much of its connects with the moral fables of the opening and closing pages; the beasts with which the human characters are compared are anthropomorphic and humorous, and evoke a moral response. . . . [The] images present an ordered moral universe, in which behaviour can be classified as good or bad, wise or foolish.

But the animal imagery also suggests an amoral universe, and the topical view of nature as red in tooth and claw, a predatory struggle for survival. These animals—and birds and snakes predominate here—are drawn not from La Fontaine or the bestiaries but from natural history, and they are divided not into good and bad but into predators and victims. (p. 173)

And yet an exposition of *The Newcomes* suggesting that Thackeray presented English society as a savage and predatory struggle for survival needs some qualification. His faculty for seeing every side of a question prevented him from writing a *roman à thèse* in the manner of Zola and the naturalists. He is exposing the tendency of the middle classes to disguise their concern for making money as the concern for saving their souls, and to gush about romance while practising self-interest. But romance and the veneration for true goodness are not laughed out of court in the process. As Barnes Newcome represents the refined savagery of a greedily self-seeking society, so the artist J. J. Ridley stands for the truth of human ideals. He can conceive of beauty, love, and heroism in his imagination, and realize them in his art. . . . (p. 174)

[*The Newcomes*] is not just a sprawling narrative that contains some amusing characters and some graphic description of manners in mid-Victorian society. It is a carefully organized novel in which style and imagery, as well as character and action, contribute to a unifying theme, and in which the length is adapted to the complexity of the content. The action takes place, and the characters find their moral being, in a minutely realized milieu in which 'respectability' is the dominant operative standard. In relating his story in language that elevates 'fumbling in a greasy till' to heroism and reduces love and faith to mere commodities, Thackeray conveys society's confusion of values by stylistic means. And that counterpoint between style and matter does more than illuminate a contemporary vice; it reflects some of the contradictions of human existence. As the animal imagery suggests both the ordered moral universe of fable and the savage jungle of popular Darwinism, so the pattern of contrasts between illusion and reality, fantasy and hard fact, aspiration and achievement, conveys how far human practice falls short of human ideals. (p. 176)

Thackeray is, after all, an acknowledged master of the novel of manners, but his novels are also subtle and intense studies of human psychology. So far, I have considered his characters as animals in a social jungle, and as human beings for whom this society is a context for moral choice; but of course they exist at a level that is deeper than either of these, with motives that cannot be fully explained by social or moral aspirations, though they may be influenced by them.

It is curious to what an extent the active and often furious or agonized psychic life of Thackeray's characters has been overlooked. . . . There is a usual assumption, which is indeed part of the truth, that Thackeray depicts a superficial society, typified by superficial characters, tenth-rate people always trying to prove they are ninth-rate, uninterested in each other except as they are higher or lower in the pecking order, and operating according to a consistent if unpleasant rationale. (p. 177)

Extended analysis of a character or a relationship, of course, Thackeray does not give us. He does not enter the mind and describe its workings in detail in the manner of George Eliot, or chronicle the minute fluctuations of a relationship like James. What we know of his characters we must gather for the most part from speech and gesture, external manifestations. From these and from occasional supplementary comments the reader must do the work of the psychiatrist himself. But there is plenty of material to work on; for in the packed incident and among the crowds of characters there is always more going on than meets the eye. In an image or an apparently insignificant scene, in a word, a kiss, a blush, the reader has glimpses of depths of motive and ambivalence of emotion of which the characters themselves are often unaware.

The conflict of conscious and unconscious motivation is a strong force in all of Thackeray's work. This is why his characters so often escape close examination, for they themselves often rationalize in social terms the motives that have a deeper origin. (p. 178)

It is particularly the ambiguity in the relations between the generations that interests Thackeray. The love of two young people of marriageable age, which he is so ready to dismiss as just another instance of the same old inevitable attraction, becomes tense and absorbing when seen in relation to the love and demands of the parents' generation. Mothers and sons, daughters and fathers! (pp. 178-79)

The central emotional relationships in the novels repeatedly take the form of a triangle of which parent and child, either as lovers or as sexual rivals, are two of the corners. In a Victorian novel such a situation must necessarily be suggested rather than analysed in detail, but it was perennially interesting to Thackeray. (p. 180)

The mother-daughter-lover triangle is only one of the various possibilities of allegiances and rivalries between the generations that Thackeray explores. Such ambivalent relationships are not only the focus of emotional interest in the novels, but their recurrence and variation constitute a structural pattern which often has as much force as the formal plot. (p. 187)

In applying Freudian psychology to an interpretation of Thackeray's novels, there is a danger of being too solemn and so forgetting the air of amused ironic detachment that often plays about his depiction of these primal situations. And to reduce all his characters to Oedipuses and Electras is to rob them of both their humour and their individuality. Of course the novels are far from being just a set of textbook variations on [Freud's] *Totem and Taboo.* But, again, it is a question of emphasis. I assert only that Thackeray concerned himself, consciously and repeatedly, with that aspect of human relationships that Freud has best analysed, and this is one reason that his novels have subtlety and intensity. And not only subtlety and intensity, but humour too. (p. 221)

'If Fun is good, Truth is still better, and Love is best of all' . . . : it is Thackeray's familiar maxim. But a study of the triangle relationships between the gener-

ations involves yet another qualification to his moral of 'the vanity of success and of all but Love and Goodness'; for the more carefully we read the novels the more we can see that love is no more the *summum bonum* than is goodness. We are shown love that 'beareth all things, believeth all things, hopeth all things, endureth all things.' But we are also shown love that demands all things, grasps all things, and devours all things.

Indeed, in his best work Thackeray has in effect revised that scale of values he outlined in *The Book of Snobs.* Fun he never abandoned, though his fun is tinged with the sadness that made him think a 'jaundiced livery' best suited his part numbers, for all the jester's antics they contained. But love, and goodness too, he had examined so intently in all their operations in this fallen world of Vanity Fair that his reservations about them matched his veneration. It is truth, finally, that he values highest. . . . He will not shirk the disagreeable matter that he finds so intricately involved with the agreeable. For his vision is one that recognizes primarily the contradictions of existence. Whether we examine his personal standpoints, his social, moral, or psychological preoccupations, we find him showing how the quest for social eminence becomes snobbery, how the aspiration to sainthood becomes moral tyranny, how tenderness fosters aggression and an embrace turns into a stranglehold, and how truth itself includes a measure of illusion.

He will not let his reader shirk the business of assessment, either. We are to know the Beckys of this world for what they are; but his ironic stances, tempting us to align ourselves with the sentimental or the worldly-wise, undercut any glib judgments, for they make us know too the precarious moral bases from which we judge. (pp. 222-23)

His very technique of maintaining a confidential relation with his reader is determined by his desire to be honest, to look his audience straight in the eye, and so avoid as far as possible the posturing which he finds so easily to himself and to all who take it upon themselves to address a listening public. (p. 223)

In his major work at least, I believe Thackeray satisfies us, not only that he can tell the truth, but that the breadth of his vision, the truth he has to tell, is worth our listening to. His alternate poses as sentimental novel-reader, pillar of respectability, and detached cynic add up not to successive retreats but to a brave attempt to know all round a character or situation, from various viewpoints. The shifts of sympathy in which he involves us are not an evasion of judgment, but an inducement to us to judge responsibility. And his probing into the sensitive spot in the most hardened snob, and explorations of the ulterior motives and secret agonies that underlie the humdrum lives of ordinary individuals, are part of a deeply perceptive vision of humanity. His irony is a means of knowing. (p. 224)

Juliet McMaster, in her *Thackeray: The Major Novels,* University of Toronto Press, 1971, 230 p.

SOURCES FOR FURTHER STUDY

Ennis, Lambert. *Thackeray: The Sentimental Cynic.* Evanston, Ill.: Northwestern University Press, 1950, 233 p.

> Biography. Examines Thackeray's attitudes toward life and English society of his time as reflected in his works.

Harden, Edgar F. *The Emergence of Thackeray's Serial Fiction.* Athens: University of Georgia Press, 1979, 385 p.

> Discussion of the process by which Thackeray prepared his novels for serial publication in periodicals. Harden credits Thackeray with employing far more care and craft in his writing than some critics have acknowledged.

Olmstead, John Charles. *Thackeray and His Twentieth-Century Critics: An Annotated Bibliography, 1900-1975.* New York: Garland Publishing, 1977, 249 p.

> Expansive reference guide to Thackeray scholarship.

Ray, Gordon N. *The Buried Life: A Study of the Relation between Thackeray's Fiction and His Personal History.* London: Oxford University Press, 1952, 148 p.

> Examines the manner in which Thackeray drew on his personal life for character and incident in his novels.

——. *Thackeray: The Uses of Adversity, 1811-1846.* Vol. I; *Thackeray: The Age of Wisdom, 1846-1863.* Vol. II. New York: McGraw-Hill, 1955, 1958.

> The definitive biography.

Wheatley, James H. *Patterns in Thackeray's Fiction.* Cambridge, Mass., London: M.I.T. Press, 1969, 157 p.

> Examines the structure of Thackeray's fiction, with particular emphasis on the importance of parody in his novels.

Dylan Thomas

1914-1953

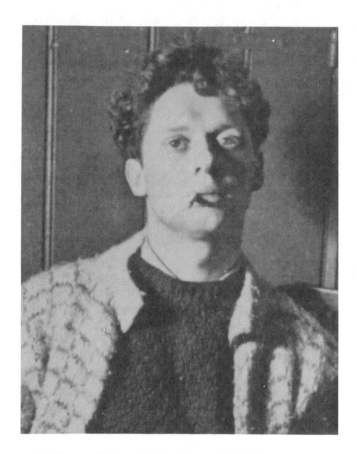

(Full name Dylan Marlais Thomas) Welsh poet, short story writer, dramatist, essayist, screenwriter, and novelist.

INTRODUCTION

*O*ne of the most renowned authors of the twentieth century, Thomas is as well known for his life of excess as for his iconoclastic, critically acclaimed writings. Viewing the act of writing as a process of self-discovery, he sought in both his poetry and his prose to explore the mysteries of his own existence and to communicate his discoveries, asserting: "I do not want to express only what other people have felt. I want to rip something away and show what they have never seen." Often focusing on such universal concerns as birth, death, love, and religion, Thomas's works remain distinctly personal through a blend of rich metaphorical language, sensuous imagery, and psychological detail.

Born in a suburb of the port of Swansea, on the southern coast of Wales, Thomas was the second child and only son of middle-class parents. His father, an English teacher who had a great love for literature, encouraged similar devotion in his son, even going so far as to read the works of Shakespeare aloud to the infant Thomas in his cradle. Such efforts were rewarded when Thomas began writing verses at an early age. He was an otherwise undistinguished student, however, and left school at sixteen to work for the *South Wales Daily Post* in Swansea.

Thomas continued to compose verse while working at the *Daily Post;* following his resignation from the paper early in 1933, poetry became his primary occupation. It was at this time that Thomas began to develop the serious drinking problem that plagued him throughout the remainder of his life and resulted in his death at the age of thirty-nine. His notebooks reveal that many of his most highly regarded poems were either written or drafted during this period and that he had also begun to experiment with short prose pieces. In May of 1933, his poem "And Death Shall Have No

Dominion" was published in the *New English Weekly*, marking the first appearance of his work in a London journal, and in December of the following year his first poetry collection, *18 Poems* (1934), was issued. Although this book attracted little attention, Thomas's second volume, *Twenty-five Poems* (1936), fared somewhat better, and as the decade progressed he gained increasing recognition for both his poetry and his prose.

In the summer of 1937, Thomas married Caitlin Macnamara, an aspiring dancer of Irish descent whose reputation for unconventional behavior rivaled Thomas's own. For the next twelve years the couple led a nomadic existence, staying with friends, relatives, and a series of benefactors. The stories later collected in *Portrait of the Artist as a Young Dog* (1940) were written primarily during their stay in the Welsh coastal village of Laugharne in late 1938 and early 1939. Too frail for active military service, Thomas wrote scripts for propaganda films during World War II, at which time he also began to participate in radio dramas and readings for the BBC. Thomas emerged from the war years a respected literary figure and popular performer; however, his gregarious social life and the excessive drinking it encouraged seriously interfered with his writing. Seeking an environment more conducive to poetic production, Thomas and Caitlin returned to Laugharne in 1949.

During the early 1950s, Thomas wrote several of his most poignant poems, including "Do Not Go Gentle into That Good Night" and "Lament." He also completed the radio drama *Under Milk Wood* (1954) and began work on an autobiographical novel, which was left unfinished at his death and published posthumously as *Adventures in the Skin Trade* (1955). Nevertheless, he feared that his creative powers were rapidly waning, and, partly in an attempt to avoid the pressures of writing, he embarked on a speaking tour of the United States in the spring of 1950. A highly charismatic speaker, Thomas charmed American audiences with his readings and shocked them with his often lascivious, irresponsible behavior. He returned to the United States three times in the next two years; during his final tour, in the fall of 1953, Thomas died from a massive overdose of alcohol.

The critical reception that greeted *18 Poems* was overwhelmingly positive; reviewers sensed in Thomas a highly unique yet traditional poetic voice. In many of these poems Thomas drew upon his childhood and adolescent experiences. Often described as incantatory, *18 Poems* records Thomas's experimentations with vibrant imagery and with sound as "verbal music." Thomas's brilliant debut—and subsequent brief career and life—would later prompt comparisons to the short, dazzling, and ultimately tragic career of American poet Hart Crane, who drowned himself in 1932. *Twenty-five*

Poems contains many of the same themes as his first work. William York Tindall referred to Thomas's first two books as the poet's "womb-tomb" period because of his penchant to focus on the polarity of birth and death. Critics also noted that Thomas frequently questions or comments upon religion, using images and terminology from Christian mythology, history, and doctrine. "And Death Shall Have No Dominion" was considered by many critics to be a breakthrough work in Thomas's career. In it, the poet addresses the Christian ideas of life and death, ultimately defying death and celebrating the possibility of eternal life. Another acclaimed poem, "Altarwise by Owl-light," is a sequence of ten sonnets discussing the crucifixion of Christ. Both poignant and comic, the sequence is generally regarded as one of Thomas's best works.

The Map of Love (1939), which also includes several short stories, indicates Thomas's use of surrealistic techniques. Throughout, the intrinsic world of the poet is contrasted with the exterior world of humanity. The outbreak of World War II and the subsequent plummeting economy hurt the volume's sales, and *The Map of Love* failed to achieve the popular and critical success of Thomas's previous works. However, with his next major book, *Deaths and Entrances* (1946), Thomas reached the pinnacle of his career. Critical reaction to the volume strongly confirmed his reputation as an important twentieth-century poet. In an initial review of *Deaths and Entrances* W. J. Turner asserted: "Dylan Thomas shows himself to be the authentic, magical thing, a true poet—original and traditional, imperfect but outstanding, with the unmistakable fire and power of genius. If anyone is looking for new contemporary poetry worthy of our great—and, I would add, world-supreme—English tradition, here it is." Less introspective than his earlier poetry, this volume centers more on nature and the shared anguish of humanity. Reviewers also noted that Thomas's religious attitude had evolved into one of positive acceptance, particularly in such acclaimed poems as "A Refusal to Mourn the Death, by Fire, of a Child in London" and "Vision and Prayer."

In "A Refusal to Mourn the Death, by Fire, of a Child in London," a sentimental, metaphysical elegy to suffering and war, the speaker will not mourn a child killed in an air raid because the death is too catastrophic for such conventional grief, and because the youth has been spared the disillusionment and corruption of adulthood. "Vision and Prayer" was hailed for its startling, mystic imagery. Emphasizing the passage of time through its hourglass shape, the poem celebrates Thomas's ultimate, triumphant acknowledgment of God's love. Edenic nature, Thomas's other dominant theme in *Deaths and Entrances,* is the subject of several pastoral poems, including "Poem in October" and "Fern Hill." Both works convey the beauty of the Welsh landscape and the simplicity and peace of childhood. Written while Thomas weathered the horrors of wartime London, these poems were considered to be particularly soothing, skillful evocations of a more harmonious age. Numerous critics contended that Thomas's finest poems were those of a gentle, romantic, and nostalgic nature. Karl Shapiro observed: "It is significant that his joyous poems, which are few, though among his best, are nearly always his simplest. Where the dominant theme of despair obtrudes, the language dives down into the depths; some of these complex poems are among the most rewarding, the richest in feeling, and the most difficult to hold to. But, beyond question, there are two minds working in Thomas, the joyous, naturally religious mind, and the disturbed, almost pathological mind of the cultural fugitive or clown." Thomas's pastoral concerns extended to his next work, *In Country Sleep* (1952), a collection of poems that received relatively little attention. In this volume, Thomas comes to terms with life while confronting the reality of his own death. Such poems as "In Country Heaven" and "Over St. John's Hill" exude beauty and confidence as the poet affirms the eternal cycle of life, death, and rebirth through rustic settings.

Thomas focused on writing prose and screenplays during the last years of his life. Previous to this period, his most important prose appeared in the semi-autobiographical short stories, *Portrait of the Artist as a Young Dog*, which stylistically and thematically bear comparison to Joyce's *Dubliners* and *Portrait of the Artist as a Young Man*. Both Joyce's and Thomas's works offer negative views of their respective backgrounds—Ireland and Wales—each depicting what "for artists," as Kenneth Seib observed, "is a world of death, sterility, and spiritual debasement." The most significant prose piece to issue from Thomas's later period is the "play for voices," *Under Milk Wood*. Again critics have noted similarities between Thomas and Joyce. In *Under Milk Wood* and *Ulysses*, each author captures the life of a whole society as it is reflected in a single day; for Joyce it is the urban life in Dublin, while for Thomas it is the Welsh village community of Llaregyub. David Holbrook, one of Thomas's harshest critics, considered *Under Milk Wood* unenlightening, unhumorous, and sexually perverse, reflecting an unfeeling and diseased view of life. Other critics, however, praised the work for its life-affirming, universal significance.

From the outset of Thomas's career there has been much critical disagreement as to his poetic stature and importance. Many commentators regard Thomas's work as being too narrow and unvarying; he essentially confines himself to the lyric expression of what Stephen Spender calls "certain primary, dithyrambic occasions," chiefly birth, love, and death. The influence of the seventeenth-century metaphysical poets is often cited in connection with Thomas's unorthodox religious imagery, while the influence of the Romantic poets is seen in his recurrent vision of a pristine beauty in childhood and nature. Though a poet of undetermined rank, Thomas set a new standard for many mid-twentieth-century poets through works that display his mastery of vivid imagery, involved word play, fractured syntax, and personal symbology.

(For further information about Thomas's life and works, see *Contemporary Authors*, Vols. 104, 120; *Dictionary of Literary Biography*, Vols. 13, 20; *Poetry Criticism*, Vol. 3; *Short Story Criticism*, Vol. 3; *Something about the Author*, Vol. 60; and *Twentieth-Century Literary Criticism*, Vols. 1, 8.)

CRITICAL COMMENTARY

D. S. SAVAGE
(essay date 1946)

[Savage is an English poet, literary scholar, and social reformer. In the following excerpt, he analyzes the artistic development in Thomas's first four volumes of poetry, noting the author's treatment of the mundane aspects of human experience.]

Dylan Thomas' status as a poet is now firmly established; informed opinion both in England and in America is unanimous in its agreement that his work is not only valid and important in its own right, but that, by inference, it provides a positive touchstone for current poetic practice and appreciation. We are fortunate indeed, in these days of deterioration, to possess such a touchstone. Dylan Thomas is a primary agent in keeping poetry alive among us, and through poetry, a proper sense of life, of values. Whatever may be said of Thomas' limitations must rest upon recognition of his superb qualities—a powerful and compelling imaginative vision held in delicate equipoise, matched by a subtle intelligence, wit and verbal sensitiveness and informed

Principal Works

18 Poems (poetry) 1934

Twenty-five Poems (poetry) 1936

The Map of Love (poetry and short stories) 1939

The World I Breathe (poetry and sketches) 1939

Portrait of the Artist as a Young Dog (short stories) 1940

New Poems (poetry) 1943

Deaths and Entrances (poetry) 1946

Twenty-six Poems (poetry) 1950

Collected Poems, 1934-1952 (poetry) 1952

In Country Sleep (poetry) 1952

The Doctor and the Devils (drama) 1953

Quite Early One Morning (sketches and essays) 1954

Under Milk Wood (drama) 1954

Adventures in the Skin Trade, and Other Stories (unfinished novel and short stories) 1955

A Prospect of the Sea, and Other Stories and Prose (short stories and sketches) 1955

Dylan Thomas: Letters to Vernon Watkins (letters) 1957

Selected Letters (letters) 1966

Poet in the Making: The Notebooks of Dylan Thomas (poetry, short stories, and sketches) 1967

Dylan Thomas: Early Prose Writings (short stories and essays) 1971

The Death of the King's Canary [with John Davenport] (novel) 1976

The Collected Stories (short stories) 1983

Dylan Thomas: The Collected Letters (letters) 1985

Dylan Thomas: Collected Poems, 1934-1953 (poetry) 1988

by passionate feeling. The recent publication . . . of Thomas' fourth volume of verse, *Deaths and Entrances,* provides the occasion for the following brief survey of his development up to the present.

To the question, what *sort* of a poet is Dylan Thomas, one can best reply that he is first of all a *maker,* that his poems must be apprehended as verbal structures before any attempt is made to torture a series of statements out of them. What Thomas—what any poet—says is precisely what is contained in the exact number and arrangement of words by which he says it. A clear understanding of this obvious truth will prevent a lot of idle talk about "obscurity." Having made this clear, it is possible to pass on to a further definition. Thomas is a poet to whom the overworked epithet "metaphysical" may without unfitness be applied. He is a poet preoccupied, not primarily with human experience as it is commonly apprehended, but with aspects

of that experience lifted out of their apparent context and seen in extra-mundane relationship to their absolute, vertical, determining conditions. Central to his work, therefore, is a proto-philosophical, impassioned *questioning* of the ultimates—origins and ends—of existence. The vision which results is not philosophical in the abstract sense, but concrete, imaginative, poetic. The poet is cerebrating, certainly, but in a primordial, mythologizing fashion, dealing, not impersonally with secondary counters of thought, but imaginatively with the primary data of his own particularized existence, in which he is emotionally involved. Therefore the deep seriousness of Thomas' central vision is accompanied by a corresponding intensity of emotion, expressed in the grand, sometimes majestic movement of his powerful and subtle rhythms.

In his poems we have no re-creation (as, *par excellence,* in the early Eliot) of a specific, localized social environment; no projection of separate human figures or dwelling upon particular experiences for their own sake. And this can only be for the reason that the vertical character of Thomas' vision tends to disrelate the components of immediate experiences in their field of local, temporal connectedness, where they are held together in a lateral sequence, in order to draw them into the instantaneous pattern of the poet's perception. His theme is thus that of the human condition itself; not, as I have said, the condition of man in his personal relationships or natural or social environment, nor even, as some have thought, his merely racial and biological origins and ends, but the essential or fundamental "existential" human state, which is also the cosmic state, the condition of being, itself. Taking his stand within concrete, particular existence, Thomas places birth and death at the poles of his vision. His viewpoint is at once individual and universal—"I" is also, and without transition, "man," and man is microcosmic. The individual birth, therefore, abuts immediately upon the cosmic genesis death, upon cosmic catastrophe. Seen thus absolutely, however, birth and death are instantaneous; time is, equally, timeless; so that human life is mortal and immortal, flesh has its ghostly counterpart; though the relationship of each to each is enigmatic. In fact, all Thomas' best poems are erected from the double vision which is the source of his understanding: their coherence and firm structure result from the "androgynous" mating, the counterpoising in equilibrium, of contraries. Add to all these briefly enumerated factors a quasi-mystical, cabalistic perception of the world itself as of a metaphorical nature, intimately related to the articulation of language, and you have a fairly complete picture of Thomas' mind and method of composition. This brief exposition is conveniently illustrated by a short and simple poem from his third book:

Twenty-four years remind the tears of my eyes.

(Bury the dead for fear that they walk to the
    grave in labor.)
In the groin of the natural doorway I crouched
    like a tailor
Sewing a shroud for a journey
By the light of the meat-eating sun.
Dressed to die, the sensual strut begun,
With my red veins full of money,
In the final direction of the elementary town
I advance for as long as forever is.
                                    (*The Map of Love*, 1939)

In what sense Thomas may legitimately be termed a religious poet is a question which has been too little considered. For Thomas makes central, and not merely peripheral, use of images and terminology drawn from Christian mythology, history and doctrine. And, of course, his perspectives are themselves those of religious insight. But he is a religious poet writing out of the indeterminate, subspiritual situation of a Hamlet. Accompanying Thomas' imaginative activity—the very activity of course which makes him so indubitably a poet—there is, one cannot fail to remark, a moral or spiritual passivity. In his poems there is no subjective activity beyond the agonized, suffering or exultant, but always passive, acceptance of that which is given by the inexorable nature of existence; the poet is the victim of his experience. . . . Thomas gains something poetically, perhaps, by his very inclusiveness, his undifferentiating, intoxicated embracing of life and death and the Yeats-like celebration of blind sexual vitality.

The knottiest problem for such a poet as Thomas is that of development. An intense imaginative activity accompanied by a psychological and moral passivity is bound eventually to result in a curbing of the growth to maturity and in consequent artistic repetitiveness and stultification. In this connection we may note the marked shift in emphasis from the earlier poems to the later. In the first, speculation and statement predominate:

In the beginning was the three-pointed star,
One smile of light across the empty face;
One bough of bone across the rooting air,
The substance forked that marrowed the first
    sun;
And, burning ciphers on the round of space,
Heaven and hell mixed as they spun.
                                    (*Eighteen Poems*, 1934)

Later there appears a more pronounced note of bewilderment and questioning:

Why east wind chills and south wind cools
Shall not be known till windwell dries
And west's no longer drowned
In winds that bring the fruit and rind
Of many a hundred falls;
Why silk is soft and the stone wounds
The child shall question all his days,

Why night-time rain and the breast's blood
Both quench his thirst he'll have a black reply.
                                    (*Twenty-five Poems*, 1936)

And this is succeeded, in the latest phase, by a positive, exulting note of acceptance and praise:

                            In
                        The spin
                        Of the sun
                    In the spuming
                Cyclone of his wing
            For I lost was who am
        Crying at the man drenched throne
        In the first fury of his stream
        And the lightnings of adoration
    Back to black silence melt and mourn
        For I was lost who have come
            To dumbfounding haven
                And the finding one
                And the high noon
                    Of his wound
                        Blinds my
                        Cry.
                                    (*Deaths and Entrances*, 1946)

This rapt and exalted note, in the latest volume, as it occurs in the celebration of birth, sexuality and death, predominates in the best and most sustained poems—**"Vision and Prayer," "Ballad of the Long-Legged Bait," "Ceremony after a Fire Raid," "Holy Spring"** and **"A Refusal to Mourn the Death, by Fire, of a Child in London."** It expresses, certainly, a development—but a development which takes the form of an accession of *intensity;* that is, it is an introversion and not an expansion. Simultaneously, in the same volume, however, there are unmistakable signs of an effort, prompted no doubt by the poet's recognition of the danger of repetitiveness, toward the lateral extension of scope. The poems are now for the first time entitled instead of numbered, and attached to specific, recognizable occasions. It is significant, then, that the best poems are still precisely those which directly celebrate birth and death: particular, localized births and deaths, indeed, but seen still in unavoidable relation to the absolute perspectives. Yet not all the poems in this latest collection achieve the same high level. **"Poem in October," "A Winter's Tale"** and **"Fern Hill"** are three of the poems which, as I have said, mark a new venturing toward the comprehension of specific lateral fields of experience. And in these poems, while the scope is indeed superficially extended, the result, removed from immediate relation to the birth-death polarity, is an unexpected diffusion and prolixity. One is led, furthermore, to wonder to what extent the too simple celebration of childhood, predominantly descriptive and correspondingly devoid of imaginative-metaphysical insight, in the last poem, is permissibly to be termed retrogressive; as indicating, that is, a deliberate avoidance of the complexities (which exist on the active level of moral choice and psychological discrimination) of adult, mature experience.

Faced with a poet of Dylan Thomas' ability, a fitting humility is called for in the critic. Thomas is still developing, and doubtless will do so in accordance with a true poet's fidelity to his own vision. Yet I cannot refrain from recording my strong feeling that authentic development for such a poet as Thomas lies not in a simple, lateral widening of scope, nor of course in a simple intensification of passionate feeling, but in something much more arduous, much more difficult, but also, ultimately, much more rewarding—in a spiritual, moral and intellectual movement toward the clarification and (perhaps, even,) systematization of the primary imaginative-poetical vision, involving struggle, discrimination, choice. This might well involve a bitter period of non-productivity, but if that were endured and overcome, we might yet find that we had in our midst a poet worthy to be classed with Dante, Shakespeare or Milton, and not merely with Hölderlin, Rimbaud or Hart Crane. (pp. 618, 620, 622)

D. S. Savage, "The Poetry of Dylan Thomas," in *The New Republic*, Vol. 114, No. 17, April 29, 1946, pp. 618, 620, 622.

STEPHEN SPENDER

(essay date 1952)

[Spender is most often associated with the young Oxford University poets who informally grouped themselves around W. H. Auden during the 1930s and who later became known as "The Auden Generation." In the following excerpt, he appraises Thomas as a romantic poet who emphasizes emotion over intellect in his works.]

Dylan Thomas represents a romantic revolt against [the] classicist tendency which has crystallised around the theological views of Eliot and Auden. It is a revolt against more than this, against the Oxford, Cambridge and Harvard intellectualism of much modern poetry in the English language; against the King's English of London and the South, which has become a correct idiom capable of refinements of beauty, but incapable of harsh effects, coarse texture and violent colours. The romantic tendency is to regard poetry as a self-sufficient kingdom of poetic ideas, owing no allegiance to any other system of thought, in which words become sensations and sensations words. For Keats his *Ode to Psyche* was a habitable bower in which the poet who had renounced everything except poetic experience could take up his residence.

The romantic characteristic of Dylan Thomas is that his poems contain the minimum material which can be translated into prose. He does not use words with the kind of precision to which Mr. Eliot has accustomed us—just as Keats did not use them with the precision of Pope—because they are not directed to any concept outside the poetry. They are related to one another within the poem, like the colours of a painting, by the exercise of that sensuous word-choosing faculty of his imagination which cares more for the feel of words than for their intellectual meanings. A powerful emotion—we may suppose—suggests to Dylan Thomas as an image or succession of images, and it is these which he puts down, without bringing forward into consciousness the ideas which are associated with such images. He suppresses the intellectual links between a chain of images, because they are non-sensuous.

The few critical comments which Dylan Thomas has made on his poetry show that he is perfectly aware of what he is up to. He is a highly intelligent man, determined to keep the intellect in its place. He is also the tough boy from Wales with the "gift of the gab" and a suspicion of London and all it stands for: a kind of literary Lloyd George breaking up an Asquithian conspiracy of writers from Oxford and Cambridge who ruled the roost when he came to town.

Dylan Thomas is frequently described as a "pure poet," but he is nothing so sophisticated, literary and (to use the word in a purely aesthetic sense) decadent. He is a romantic revolting against a thin contemporary classical tendency, and driven by a rhetorical urge. His poetry is not so much influenced by, as soaked in, childhood experiences of the Bible, and doubtless, also, Welsh bardic poetry. In his early poems there is much obscurely subjective material. As his detractors have pointed out, his metaphors are sometimes mixed and inexact; his images sometimes will not stand up to a severely "critical examination."

The weaker poems (mostly of what, at his present stage of development, must be called his "middle period") show that his poetry, unless it is galvanised into unity by some dramatically powerful situation, tends to fall apart into its separate components. It needs to be, in a quite obvious sense, inspired by a unifying vision, moment of self-realisation, great occasion, which organises the images around this centre. When this happens—as it does in the youthful poems inspired by a sense of adolescent wonder and the later ones which tend more and more to celebrate occasions—the writing becomes wonderfully coherent, and, if there are occasional obscurities, the poem as a whole is filled with joy and light.

The discipline in Thomas's best work has the quality which Goethe called "demonic." It is that of a very alive person able to relate his molten, turbulent ideas to certain primary, dithyrambic occasions. In poems like **"Ceremony After a Fire Raid"**, and **"Vision and Prayer"** Dylan Thomas has discovered not a subject-matter (that he has always had) but subjects which—after the impulse of the first juvenile poems—seemed rather lacking. This poetry is concentrated on the greater sensations of living: birth and death, vision and prayer, festive celebrations, like the two poems on his birthdays. In this poetry the reader feels very close to what Keats yearned for—a "life of sensations" without opinions and thoughts. (pp. 780-81)

Stephen Spender, "A Romantic in Revolt," in *The Spectator*, Vol. 189, No. 6493, December 5, 1952, pp. 780-81.

DAVID DAICHES

(essay date 1954)

[Daiches is a prominent English scholar and critic who has written extensively on English and American literature and is especially renowned for his studies of such writers as Robert Burns, Robert Louis Stevenson, and Virginia Woolf. In the excerpt below from an essay first published in *The English Journal* in 1954, he appraises what he considers the complex nature of Thomas's poetry.]

[Thomas's prologue to the collected edition of his poems] is a great hail to the natural world, and man as a part of it, and might be taken by the careless reader as an impressionist outpouring of celebratory exclamations:

Huloo, my prowed dove with a flute!
Ahoy, old, sea-legged fox,
Tom tit and Dai mouse!
My ark sings in the sun
At God speeded summer's end
And the flood flowers now.

Yet in fact this spontaneous-seeming poem is a cunningly contrived work in two movements of fifty-one lines each, with the second section rhyming backwards with the first—the first line rhyming with the last, the second with the second last, and so on, the only pair of adjacent lines which rhyme being the fifty-first and the fifty-second. Whether the ear catches this complicated cross rhyming or not, it is part of a cunning pattern of ebb and flow, of movement and counter-movement, which runs through the poem. This single piece of evidence is perhaps enough to prove that, for all the appearance of spontaneity and sometimes of free association that his poems present to some readers, Thomas was a remarkably conscientious craftsman for whom meaning was bound up with pattern and order. No modern poet in English has had a keener sense of

form or has handled stanzas and verse paragraphs—whether traditional or original—with more deliberate cunning. It is worth stressing this . . . because there are still some people who talk of Thomas as though he were a writer of an inspired mad rhetoric, of glorious, tumbling, swirling language which fell from his pen in magnificent disorder. He has been held up by some as the antithesis of Eliot and his school, renouncing the cerebral orderliness of the 1920s and the 1930s in favour of a new romanticism, an engaging irresponsibility. On the other hand there are those who discuss his poems as though they are merely texts for exposition, ignoring the rhyme scheme and the complicated verbal and visual patterning to concentrate solely on the intellectual implications of the images. The truth is that Thomas is neither a whirling romantic nor a metaphysical imagist, but a poet who uses pattern and metaphor in a complex craftsmanship in order to create a ritual of celebration. He sees life as a continuous process, sees the workings of biology as a magical transformation producing unity out of identity, identity out of unity, the generations linked with one another and man linked with nature. Again and again in his early poems he seeks to find a poetic ritual for the celebration of this identity. . . . (pp. 51-2)

He had no desire to be difficult or esoteric. He drew on the Bible and on universal folk themes rather than on obscure late classical writers or Jessie Weston's *From Ritual to Romance*. In **Under Milk Wood** he puts into simple yet powerful and cunning words a day in the life of a Welsh village, with each character rendered in terms of some particular human weakness or folly. Unlike Eliot, Thomas accepted man as he was: he had a relish for humanity. By the end of his life he had learned to be both poetically honest and poetically simple—a difficult combination, especially in our time. . . .

Was he a great poet? Against him it can be argued that his range was severely limited, that (in his earlier poems) he overdid a handful of images and phrases to the point almost of parodying himself, that many of his poems are clotted with an excess of parallel-seeking metaphors. I doubt if he wrote a dozen really first-rate poems; these would include, among those not hitherto mentioned here, **'In the White Giant's Thigh'** and **'In Country Sleep'**. In his favour it can be claimed that at his best he is magnificent, as well as original in tone and technique, and that he was growing in poetic stature to the last. Perhaps the question is, in the most literal sense, academic. It is enough that he wrote some poems that the world will not willingly let die. (pp. 60-1)

David Daiches, "The Poetry of Dylan Thomas," in his *Literary Essays*, Oliver & Boyd, 1956, pp. 50-61.

KARL SHAPIRO
(essay date 1955)

[Shapiro is an American poet and critic known for critical essays in which he attacks strict adherence to form and tradition in modern poetry. In the following excerpt from an essay that first appeared in *Poetry* in 1955, he discusses the dichotomous structure of Thomas's poetry.]

Thomas was the first modern romantic you could put your finger on, the first whose journeys and itineraries became part of his own mythology, the first who offered himself up as a public, not a private, sacrifice. Hence the piercing sacrificial note in his poetry, the uncontainable voice, the drifting, almost ectoplasmic character of the man, the desperate clinging to a few drifting spars of literary convention. Hence, too, the universal acclaim for his lyricism, and the mistaken desire to make him an heir to Bohemia or to the high Symbolist tradition.

Writers said of Thomas that he was the greatest lyricist of our time. The saying became a platitude. It was unquestionably true, but what did the word mean? It meant that, in contrast to the epic pretensions of many of the leading modern poets, he was the only one who could be called a singer. To call him the best lyric poet of our time was to pay him the highest, the only compliment. Nearly everyone paid him this splendid compliment and everyone knew its implications. Few realized, however, that this compliment marked a turning point in poetry. (p. 141)

Thomas is in somewhat the relation to modern poetry that Hopkins was to the Victorians—a lone wolf. Thomas resisted the literary traditionalism of the Eliot school; he wanted no part of it. Poetry to him was not a civilizing maneuver, a replanting of the gardens; it was a holocaust, a sowing of the wind. (p. 142)

Thomas' technique is deceptive. When you look at it casually you think it is nothing. The meter is banal. It is no better and no worse than that of dozens of other poets his age. There is no invention and a great deal of imitation. There is no theory. But despite his lack of originality, the impress of Thomas' idiom on present-day English poetry is incalculable. (p. 143)

It is hard to locate the distinctiveness of Thomas' idiom. There are a few tricks of word order, a way of using a sentence, a characteristic vocabulary, an obsessive repetition of phrase, and so on—things common to many lesser poets. Again, if we scrutinize his images and metaphors, which are much more impressive than

the things I have mentioned, we frequently find over-development, blowziness, and euphemism, on the one hand, and brilliant crystallization on the other. But no system, no poetic, no practice that adds up to anything you can hold on to. The more you examine him as a stylist the less you find.

What does this mean? It means that Thomas is a quite derivative, unoriginal, *unintellectual* poet, the entire force of whose personality and vitality is jammed into his few difficult half-intelligible poems. To talk about Thomas as a Symbolist is dishonest. Once in Hollywood Aldous Huxley introduced a Stravinsky composition based on a poem of Thomas'. Huxley quoted that line of Mallarmé's which says that poets purify the dialect of the tribe. This, said Huxley, was what Thomas did. Now anybody who has read Thomas knows that he did the exact opposite: Thomas did everything in his power to obscure the dialect of the tribe—whatever that high-and-mighty expression may mean. Thomas sometimes attempted to keep people from understanding his poems (which are frequently simple, once you know the dodges). He had a horror of simplicity—or what I consider to be a fear of it. He knew little except what a man knows who has lived about forty years, and there was little he wanted to know. There is a fatal pessimism in most of his poems, offset by a few bursts of joy and exuberance. The main symbol is masculine love, driven as hard as Freud drove it. In the background is God, hard to identify but always there, a kind of God who belongs to one's parents rather than to the children, who do not quite accept Him. (pp. 144-45)

Thomas, with no equipment for theorizing about the forms of nature, sought the "forms" that Hopkins did. The chief difference between the two poets in terms of their symbols is that Hopkins draws his symbology almost entirely from the God-symbol. God, in various attributes, is the chief process in Hopkins' view of the world. Sex is the chief process in Thomas' view of the world.

Thomas' idea of process is important. The term itself is rather mechanistic, as he uses it. He always takes the machine of energy rather than some abstraction, such as spirit or essence. Hence the concreteness of his words and images; obscurity occurs also because of the "process" of mixing the imagery of the subconscious with biological imagery, as in Hopkins. But there is also a deliberate attempt to involve the subconscious as the main process: Thomas' imagination, which is sometimes fantastic, works hard to dredge up the images of fantasy and dreams. Very often the process fails and we are left with heaps of grotesque images that add up to nothing. I would equate the process in Thomas' poetics with his rather startling views of the sexual process. Aside from those poems in which sex is simply sung, much as poets used to write what are called love poems, there are those poems in which sex is used as the instrument of belief and knowledge. Using the cliché of modern literature that everyone is sick and the whole world is a hospital, Thomas wants to imply that sex will make us (or usually just him) healthy and whole again. And there are suggestions of Druidism (perhaps) and primitive fertility rites, apparently still extant in Wales, all mixed up with Henry Miller, Freud, and American street slang. But sex kills also, as Thomas says a thousand times, and he is not sure of the patient's recovery. In place of love, about which Thomas is almost always profoundly bitter, there is sex, the instrument and the physical process of love. The activity of sex, Thomas hopes in his poems, will somehow lead to love in life and in the cosmos. As he grows older, love recedes and sex becomes a nightmare, a Black Mass.

Thomas moves between sexual revulsion and sexual ecstasy, between puritanism and mysticism, between formalistic ritual (this accounts for his lack of invention) and vagueness. . . . His dissatisfaction with his own lack of stability is reflected in his devices which tend to obscure even the simple poems; he leaves out all indications of explanation—quotation marks, punctuation, titles, connectives, whether logical or grammatical. In addition he uses every extreme device of ambiguity one can think of, from reversing the terms of a figure of speech to ellipsis to overelaboration of images. There is no poetic behind these practices—only catch-as-catch-can technique. One is always confused in Thomas by not knowing whether he is using the microscope or the telescope; he switches from one to the other with ease and without warning. It is significant that his joyous poems, which are few, though among his best, are nearly always his simplest. Where the dominant theme of despair obtrudes, the language dives down into the depths; some of these complex poems are among the most rewarding, the richest in feeling, and the most difficult to hold to. But, beyond question, there are two minds working in Thomas, the joyous, naturally religious mind, and the disturbed, almost pathological mind of the cultural fugitive or clown. On every level of Thomas' work one notices the lack of sophistication and the split in temperament. This is his strength as well as his weakness. But it is a grave weakness because it leaves him without defense, without a bridge between himself and the world.

Thomas begins in a blind alley with the obsessive statement that birth is the beginning of death, the basic poetic statement, but one which is meaningless unless the poet can build a world between. Thomas never really departs from this statement, and his obsession with sex is only the clinical restatement of the same theme. The idealization of love, the traditional solution with most poets, good and bad, is never arrived at in Thomas. He skips into the foreign land of love and skips out again. And he is too good a poet to fake love.

He doesn't feel it; he distrusts it; he doesn't believe it. He falls back on the love-process, the assault, the defeat, the shame, the despair. Over and over again he repeats the ritualistic formulas for love, always doubting its success. The process is despised because it doesn't really work. The brief introduction to the *Collected Poems* sounds a note of bravado which asserts that his poems "are written for the love of Man and in praise of God." One wishes they were; one is grateful for, and slightly surprised by, the acknowledgment to God and Man, for in the poems we find neither faith nor humanism. What we find is something that fits Thomas into the age: the satanism, the vomitous horror, the self-elected crucifixion of the artist. (pp. 147-49)

Karl Shapiro, "Dylan Thomas," in his *The Poetry Wreck: Selected Essays, 1950-70,* Random House, 1975, pp. 139-49.

HOWARD SERGEANT
(essay date 1962)

[Sergeant was an English poet and critic. In the following excerpt, he examines Thomas's religious poetry.]

From the time that his work began to appear in [the Welsh newspaper] *The Sunday Referee,* Thomas was preoccupied with spiritual values and the ultimates of existence, related through his peculiar, in some ways almost mystical, vision of sex, which he regarded as the unifying force of all creation:

And yellow was the multiplying sand,
Each golden grain spat life into its fellow. . . .

In the beginning was the mounting fire
That set alight the weathers from a spark,
A three-eyed, red-eyed spark, blunt as a flower;
Life rose and spouted from the rolling seas,
Burst in the roots, pumped from earth and rock
The secret oils that drive the grass.

Despite the legends of his outrageously bohemian mode of life, and the circumstances surrounding his death, Dylan Thomas was a naturally religious poet. With the Welsh Bethel as its probable source, his religious faith was so firmly implanted and so much a part of his poetic makeup that, unlike those who become Christians by deliberate choice, he was never at pains to declare it; or to attempt to define his beliefs in relation to experience. God, for him, was an established fact, and divine manifestations were to be celebrated rather than examined or questioned. Nevertheless, if he finally admitted, in the preface to his collected volume, that his poems were 'written for the love of Man and in praise of God', the religious element was somewhat obscured in his earliest poetry because he was so engrossed in sexual and prenatal experience, and because he seemed, in such poems as **"I have longed to move away"** to be denying the faith in which he had been brought up:

> I have longed to move away
> From the hissing of the spent lie. . . .

By 'the hissing of the spent lie', Thomas could be referring either to Christianity or to that stultification of spiritual life which institutionalised religion, with its empty platitudes and gestures, and church-attendance as a social habit, so often becomes. The latter construction is supported by the poet's use of the phrases 'from the repetition of salutes' (conventional expressions of fellowship) and 'half convention and half lie'. But even at this point of denial he hesitates in a state of uncertainty and, unable to suppress his religious instincts entirely, almost retracts the statement:

> I have longed to move away but am afraid;
> Some life, yet unspent, might explode
> Out of the old lie burning on the ground,
> And, crackling into the air, leave me half-blind.

Though his early poems were rich in Biblical symbols and allusions, they were used to express his own sexual interpretation of life and death. Yet at the centre of his vision was an awareness of the spiritual nature of man. It is interesting to trace the development of his religious outlook from 1934 when, in reply to a questionnaire, he wrote—'My poetry is, or should be, useful to me for one reason; it is the record of my individual struggle from darkness towards some measure of light'. In his second volume there are three *inclusions* which have special bearing on this particular aspect of his work, **"This bread I break," "And death shall have no dominion,"** and the sonnet sequence **"Altarwise by owl-light."** To take the last first, **"Altarwise by owl-light"** is a series of ten poems dealing with the crucifixion in Thomas's most complicated and obscure language, ranging from the near comic (though serious enough in its context) with its cowboy version of the Annunciation:

> And from the windy West came two-gunned Gabriel,

From Jesu's sleeve trumped up the king of spots,
The sheath-decked jacks, queen with a shuffled heart. . . .

to the poignant:

> This was the crucifixion on the mountain,
> Time's nerve in vinegar, the gallow grave
> As tarred with blood as the bright thorns I wept. . . .

Several critics have attempted to decipher the poem, but even when in possession of these elaborate keys, one is left floundering between the actual Biblical account and Thomas's idiosyncratic interpretation of the Scriptures, doctrinally confused as it is with its compressed imagery and sexual implications. But successful as poetry or not, the sequence does indicate the direction in which the poet was moving at the time he wrote it. In **"This bread I break"** Thomas gives a pantheistic emphasis to Christ's words at the Last Supper, on which both the Catholic Mass and the Noncomformist Sacrament of the Lord's Supper are founded:

> This bread I break was once the oat,
> This wine upon a foreign tree
> Plunged in its fruit;
> Man in the day or wind at night
> Laid the crops low, broke the grape's joy.

—and, engaged with his theme of the unity of all life, he comes close to a mystical view of the Catholic doctrine of Transubstantiation; though, if one is to judge by the sexual overtones of the third stanza, where the oat and grape are described as 'born of the sensual root and sap', this was obviously not his intention.

Of the poems in Thomas's second collection **"And death shall have no dominion"** is by far the most significant from a religious point of view, for three principal reasons—firstly, it marks a definite change of the poet's attitude towards death; secondly, it envisages human love as a dynamic force without limiting it to its sexual elements as do most of the earlier poems; and, finally, it celebrates what may reasonably be termed a Christian conception of life, death and resurrection, if not entirely an orthodox one in all its implications. (pp. 59-62)

Most critics of Thomas's work have observed that this poem is concerned with the continuity of life after death, and some have quoted Biblical texts referring to the Christian doctrine of the Resurrection, but few of them have given the poem really close attention (largely, I assume, because it is static and lacks poetic development). In *Vision and Rhetoric* Mr. G. S. Fraser describes it as 'a poem in which the poet faced by the harsh fact of death is not properly confronting it but cheering himself up'. No one, to my knowledge, has related it to the actual passage in the Bible from which the theme is derived, and as this text is the starting-point, so to

Thomas on the banks of Carmarthen Bay, Wales.

speak, and important to the understanding of the poem, perhaps we ought to have recourse to it:

> Now if we be dead with Christ, we believe that
> we shall also live with him:
> Knowing that Christ being raised from the dead
> dieth no more;
> Death hath no more dominion over him (Romans 6).

In the light of this passage it will be seen that the poem is . . . not an expression of some vaguely held belief in an after-life. . . . Such lines as:

> Though they go mad they shall be sane,

and

> Twisting on racks when sinews give way,
> Strapped to a wheel, yet they shall not
> break . . .

would surely have little significance in these days of brainwashing and concentration camps if all they were intended to mean was that at death man would merely achieve an impersonal state of oneness with nature. Least of all is the poem a poetic equivalent to the child

whistling in the dark to keep up his failing spirits, as Mr. Fraser would have it. On the contrary, it is a poem of affirmation and praise. Because the poet's faith in the Resurrection is so deeply rooted—that is, if I may be excused for putting it in a Christian terminology which Thomas would never have used himself, because he accepts the belief that Christ has triumphed over death—there is no problem of ideological development; it suffices for him to expatiate in his own individual way on the original statement that 'death hath no more dominion over him'. The unity to which he refers is already presented by the text—*Now if we be dead with Christ, we believe that we shall also live with him.* A new feeling of hope is reflected in the poem. To appreciate this change of tone we have only to compare the attitude expressed in **"And death shall have no dominion"** with that of the earlier poems in which death is portrayed as having almost absolute dominion over man, beginning at the very moment of birth—'and the womb / drives in a death as life leaks out'—and extending to all his activities, especially his sexual activities.

In his third book, *The Map of Love,* the poet acknowledges his state of conflict and admits that 'it is the sinners' dust-tongued bell claps me to churches', but, with one important exception, the poems in this collection are of a transitional character. The exception is **"After the Funeral,"** sub-titled "In Memory of Ann Jones." Previously, his poems dealing with birth and death, his favourite subjects, were strictly impersonalised. These were concerned with man in general on his journey from womb to grave—'In the groin of the natural doorway I crouched like a tailor / Sewing a shroud for the journey'—and failed to communicate any feeling for man in particular. In **"After the Funeral,"** however, we find not only that the new attitude to death and to human love is more positively presented, but that Thomas is concerned with a particular individual, the old aunt with whom he often stayed as a child, and all his natural affection, combined with respect and humility, is communicated to the reader:

> I know her scrubbed and sour humble hands
> Lie with religion in their cramp, her threadbare
> Whisper in a damp word, her wits drilled hol-
>   low,
> Her fist of a face died clenched on a round pain;
> And sculptured Ann is seventy years of stone.
> These cloud-sopped, marble hands, this monu-
>   mental
> Argument of the hewn voice, gesture and psalm,
> Storm me forever over her grave. . . .

This was quite unlike anything he had attempted before, and it seems to me that **"After the Funeral,"** with its intensely human sympathy, continues the line of development from **"And death shall have no dominion"** to the magnificent elegy **"A refusal to Mourn the Death, by Fire, of a Child in London"** in his next book, *Deaths and Entrances* (1946). The child concerned may be any child, for all the reader knows, yet the poignancy and solemn beauty of the poem seem to suggest that it is a particular child, and one for whom the whole intensity of the poet's experience is directed into the channels of majestic sorrow. It is almost a prayer in its effect, and Thomas's use of the phrase 'stations of the breath' carries with it the atmosphere of grief surrounding the Stations of the Cross. And the association here is singularly appropriate. No one could deny the religious depths of the final stanza:

> Deep with the first dead lies London's daughter,
> Robed in the long friends,
> The grains beyond age, the dark veins of her
>   mother,
> Secret by the unmourning water
> Of the riding Thames.
> After the first death, there is no other.

If the foregoing interpretation of **"And death shall have no dominion"** is correct, there can be no difficulty with the last line of the extract above—'After the first death, there is no other'—despite the apparent ambiguity. Thomas is back with Romans 6, the child '. . . being raised from the dead dieth no more. . . .'

Deaths and Entrances can hardly be said to reveal a new Thomas, since many of the features which make it so successful can be traced to his earlier poetry, but it does show that a new integrating force was at work, as if something which had previously been suppressed had suddenly thrust itself forth into the light and taken control. In his study of Dylan Thomas [*Dylan Thomas: 'Dog among the Fairies'*, 1956], Mr. Henry Treece has voiced the opinion that this phenomenon indicates that a change of heart had taken place. 'The poet', he says with reference to **"Vision and Prayer,"** 'has openly accepted God's love, and has rejoiced in his acceptance.' We do not know, and perhaps we shall never know, how much truth there is in this observation, but certainly such poems as **"This Side of Truth," "The Conversation of Prayer," "Holy Spring"** and **"There Was a Saviour"** provide evidence of a complete change of outlook. The most skeptical reader could not miss the Christian exaltation of **"Vision and Prayer,"** so reminiscent of Herbert in its hourglass form and of Thompson's "Hound of Heaven" in its mysticism:

> I turn the corner of prayer and burn
>   In a blessing of the sudden
>   Sun. In the name of the damned
>   I would turn back and run
>   To the hidden land
>   But the loud sun
>   Christens down
>   The sky.
>   I
>   Am found
>   O let him
>   Scald me and drown
>   Me in his world's wound
>   His lightning answers my
>   Cry. My voice burns in his hand.
>   Now I am lost in the blinding
> One. The sun roars at the prayer's end.

Thomas's antipathy towards dogma of any kind makes it extremely difficult to ascertain the real nature of the religious convictions he held towards the end of his life, or to identify them with orthodox Christian beliefs at more than a few isolated points. Even when he appeared to be on the verge of committing himself in his poetry there were inconsistencies and contradictions which can hardly be attributed to poetic license or a colourful imagination; for in his later poems Thomas paid more attention to craftsmanship than ever before, and although it might be a justifiable criticism of his early poetry to say that his words and images were not always used with precision, it would be quite inapplicable to his later work. Again and again he seemed to be saying something acceptable to a Christian frame of mind, only to give the poem a contradictory twist. (pp. 62-6)

Perhaps these ambiguities arose, not from any religious uncertainty or doubt, but out of the poet's method of composition; his manipulation of conflicting images set up in opposition to each other and his partiality for paradox. As the tension at the heart of Thomas's poetry was created by the resolution of such conflicts and paradoxes in the 'struggle from darkness to some measure of light', we can hardly quibble. There is, however, no ambiguity about the conclusion of the poem. Thomas seems to have had a premonition of his early death and referred to it increasingly towards the end of his life. In **"Poem on his birthday,"** one of the last poems he wrote, he counts his blessings:

> And this last blessing most,
>
> That the closer I move
> To death, one man through his sundered
> hulks,
> The louder the sun blooms
> And the tusked, ramshackling sea exults;
> And every wave of the way
> And gale I tackle, the whole world then,
> With more triumphant faith
> Than ever was since the world was said,
> Spins its morning of praise. . . . .
>
> . . . As I sail out to die.
>
> (pp. 66-7)

Howard Sergeant, "The Religious Development of Dylan Thomas," in *A Review of English Literature*, Vol. 3, No. 2, April, 1962, pp. 59-67.

DIANE ACKERMAN

(essay date 1987)

[Ackerman is an American poet, nonfiction writer, and dramatist. In the following excerpt, she comments on Thomas's frenzied use of metaphors and linguistics, asserting that "no poet gives a greater sense of the *feel of life*."]

It is unfortunate when a poet's personality, indeed his pageant of a private life, gets in the way of his poems, and perhaps even worse, thanks to the human love of spectacle, when his voice itself obtrudes. The trouble with Dylan Thomas is that he played up the bardic role for all it was worth, even to the extent of resorting to vocal melodrama as the redeemer of inferior poems (as well as the perfect embodiment of good ones). Trying to read him plain, on the page, gets one into the grandiosity that includes Yeats's cloak, the eyes Shelley saw

in nipples, and Byron's moonlit comminations among the ruins upon Sir Samuel Romilly. One has to try, though, and I've done so off and on out of a variety of motives: trying to hear the quieter and more straightforward poems without sideband splash from the turbulent, noisy ones; wondering how much genuine vision lay behind the mumbo jumbo and the sometimes frantic, Klein-bottled imager; trying to relate the knobbly concreteness of his poems about everyday surfaces to the omnipresent madman howling at the moon from the attic. After all, who hasn't puzzled about how to get from that aromatic, audible, by now rather hackneyed, Welsh Christmas to the visceral spirals of gristle, bone, hair, seaweed in his other poems? He doesn't shift from atom to star along logical lines of inference. It's almost an epistemological dyslexia. I think he wants to make the shift, but is kept from managing it by a specialized ignorance that restricts him to myth. I mean that you will find Adam or Gabriel in the way, the one with a rubber ball stolen from a toilet cistern, the other with a pair of six-shooters, and this gives even the best poems an air of facetious interpolation. Not that I assume certain things just can't be put into poems, or have poems made from them; or that the accumulated trivia in an idiosyncratic person's head cannot function as a lightning conductor for the gravest, the most inexplicable, and ravishing matters known. But it makes Thomas quirky when his rhythms announce something majestic in the offing. It makes him elliptical beyond most readers' willingness to make a leap of mind.

What he does provide, though, is a circular continuum in which things lose their identity in the identities of other things ("a rumpus of shapes") until the reader is haunted by an acute sense of how physical life is, and how freely things metamorphose one into another. No poet gives a greater sense of the *feel of life.* One thing in another's context works him into a frenzy of neighborly reverence, provoking metaphors that don't so much combine A and B as trail both A and B through the slush of other phenomena. I don't know when I last saw the word *nympholepsy* used, but I am going to use it now. It means, or meant, "a frenzy induced by having seen nymphs" and is no doubt common. It also means "an obsession for something unobtainable." Thomas gets into this state often enough for it to become a habit, and that other nymph-like sense of things—when the young of any insect undergoes metamorphosis—attracts him too because it suggests both the discrete entities in nature and the quickness of the life process itself. Thomas weds himself to as many forms of life as he can spot, in a frenzy that becomes an act of homage to Creation, and mainly to it in a state of chaos.

For Thomas, nature is a force field, an open-ended experiment. By garbling taxonomy and larding language with a free hand, he seems at times to reproduce in the linguistic medium itself the actual feel of life as it might come to a drunk, or a deer, or a devout astronomer freezing to death at his telescope aimed at the Virgo-Coma region of the galaxies. This primitive, atavistic mania is fairly uncommon, but the communication of it through language—the unlanguaged via language itself—is just about unique. Some readers will not want it, feeling that such poetry makes too many demands of their taxonomic sense, or that the whole idea is just a pretext for being obscure. Take this random sample:

> Because the pleasure-bird whistles after the hot
>   wires,
> Shall the blind horse sing sweeter?

Successive readings of, or guesses at, this can widen the couplet out until it becomes everything and nothing, not only an emblem of bird-song on telephone wires crammed with information a bird knows nothing about (any more than the horse in the field below which is blinkered like a resting falcon?), but also a dizzy meander among phenomena that don't belong together: wire of the canary's cage, wire in a jew's-harp, electricity flowing along a cable, nonsense through the mis-conductor of a bad syllogism (A bird cannot hear what's in the wires—the horse is minus a dimension too—so do both perform better for their being undistracted?). Admittedly these are not Thomas's most rewarding lines, but they share the speculative disruption of things that elsewhere raises itself to an exponential maximum equivalent to, at least, a vision of Rimbaud's. . . . (pp. 86-7)

Look now at one of the poems Thomas himself discussed: **"If my head hurt a hair's foot,"** a poem similar to the prenatal empathy of Louis MacNeice's "Prayer before Birth," or Beckett's *Texts for Nothing*, which tracks what seems to be the thirteen days between April 1st and Good Friday, April 13th, the day on which Beckett was born in 1906. The first stanza of Thomas's poem goes as follows:

> If my head hurt a hair's foot
> Pack back the downed bone. If the unpricked
>   ball of my breath
> Bump on a spout let the bubbles jump out.
> Sooner drop with the worm of the ropes round
>   my throat
> Than bully ill love in the clouted scene.

Histrionic delicacy is appropriate here. Perhaps we are not far from the day when instruments will give us an exact idea of how the fetus feels during labor (children have already been quizzed for their very first memories). The stanza teems with associations, most of which work into the poem and clarify it by multiplying its impact. The emergent head has hair of its own, so the care for hair is double. The idea of "down" works on several levels, from fleece to downward and as far

as fleece-clad bone, which includes skull too. There is no need to follow all the colliding implications of "unpricked ball," "Bump on a spout," and "bubbles"; enough to say we are in a realm of post-and pre-sexual Cartesian diving, with somewhere an unstated image of a child's balloon, which some readers will need more than others. As for "ropes" and "clouted," they are similarly ambivalent, the one oddly evocative of George Herbert's pulley, the other reminding us of an expression Thomas uses: *Don't cast a clout till May is out.* The whole stanza quivers with imminent energy, and what alliteration doesn't do to enact both stealth ("*h* ead *h* urt a *h* air's") and percussion ("*b* all of my *b* reath / *B* ump"), assonance delivers with its jarring, physical insistence. If sound alone can be eloquent, irrespective of what the words mean, the stanza is a bout of fragile whispers and implacable natural force, the point being (when you get into the conditionals the fetus utters) that the baby-to-be can do nothing about what's going on. Therefore the opening of the poem introduces us to an entire mood of helpless altruism, and this is moving: the speech of the infant-to-be reminds us that infants are so called because they cannot speak, never mind alliterate persuasively, and the result of that is a tuning-up of the reader's compassion. You *feel with* what hasn't been much represented in poetry, though grasses have sighed and stones have spoken.

Thomas's own comment on this unusual poem is full of his customary militant modesty.

> It is not a narrative, nor an argument, but a series of conflicting images which move through pity and violence to an unreconciled acceptance of suffering: the mother's *and* the child's. This poem has been called obscure. I refuse to believe that it is obscurer than pity, violence, or suffering. But being a poem, not a lifetime, it is more compressed.

It's a refreshing point of view. Who else has considered the obscurity of pity, violence, or suffering? *Are* they obscure? Their external configurations are not, but their roots—in the ancient areas of the brain, in body chemistry—are, and we might be grateful to a poet who tries to work such concepts into an almost tactile empathy. Notice that Thomas doesn't say the poem is *about* "pity, violence, or suffering"; he *equates* parts of the poem *with* these. The entire thing could have lapsed into foolish ventriloquism (chitchat during parturition), but it doesn't, partly because the sheer intensity of the images distracts us from the patent contraption of two speakers, partly because the poem exceeds his original intention and turns into an affirmation on a grander level than the immediate scenery implies. It's life addressing life about dangerous business. It's a racial impulse made vocal. And this is one of the ways in which Thomas, for all his skimpy knowledge of how nature works, waxes metaphysical; he makes the ineffable sayable, and he enacts a life process intricately through a whole register of discernible, almost palpable physical events. In other words, he creates more than most poets a physics to match his idea, so much so that in his best work (of which this poem is a sample) the mechanics of enunciation seem closer than we thought they could be to the behavior of the subject-matter cells.

Thomas achieves this startling effect in a variety of ways, willing to vary a sensation endlessly, to let it overlap with others. His handling of language implies a nod to denotation, an all-out welcome for connotation, a sign of his almost neurotic sensitivity to the flux that underlies our verbal concepts. He isn't often as prescient (accidentally so) as in "a nacreous sleep among soft particles and charms": particle physics had not evolved its fetchingly whimsical vocabulary when Thomas wrote this poem, but it's significant that, without knowing it, he had overreached into the terrain of the charm quark. That's a bonus over and above what the line tells about his attitude to phenomena. A Heisenberg couldn't be cagier about the very uncertainty of things, or a gypsy about the magic implied in "charms." And to say this is only to indicate in diffident fashion his uncanny openness to experience of all kinds, including the uncouth and the visceral, the electrostatic and the photosynthetical, the peptic and the congenital. He really does nibble the oat in the bread he breaks, intuit the monkey in the emergent baby, and, if you add myth to nature, the parting of the Red Sea in the breaking of the waters, the shroudmaker in the surgeon who sews after the Caesarian birth.

If we cast a wider net, assembling his least decipherable utterances ("Foster the light nor veil the man-shaped moon") and those of Thomas the clear-eyed reporter ("the mousing cat stepping shy, / The puffed birds hopping and hunting"), as well as Thomas the near-arguer who can sustain something like musical variations on one vivid concept ("The hand that signed the paper felled a city") alongside Thomas the celebrant of suburban Swansea, Thomas the interceptor of political ricochet ("Cry Eloi to the guns"), Thomas the lyrical birthday poet, and—we always run out of breath before he does!—we have a conspectus of the miscellaneous seer. I do not think it has been sufficiently recognized how ramshackle, how flea-market his fund of ideas was. He creates his ritual out of the most unceremonious attitude to things, and he extracts his scapegrace reverence from an almost grotesque jumble of schoolboy comics, dirty jokes, bible-pounding provincialism, beer-garden shibboleths, snippets of all kinds of superstitions, rumors and hokum and balderdash. He just about personifies the voracious Metaphysical sensibility of which Eliot wrote, the bizarre thing being that he was able to transform the Saturday-afternoon reputation of the planet—a couple of imposing-sounding tropics, its being called a "star," the Pyra-

mids, Jesus, Adam, radium, birth, death, masturbation—into something almost sacramental. Not neat. Not demure. Not explicit. Not argued or even structured. But bold, wild, and tenderly voluptuous.

This is not the place to rehearse the misdemeanors he has been charged with by exegetes straying off the reservation. Whether or not he commits pseudo-syntax is beside the point, which is much more complicated. Through his almost preternatural sensitivity to the interactions of juxtaposed words, he manages to write poems that feel indistinguishable from their subject matter, or (more alarming to a certain kind of reader) have no subject matter at all, but just *are,* transcribing nothing, modifying nothing, but (as if he had undertaken a dare) showing how far language can take us toward the nonverbal. This is why a case must be made for what are supposed his obscurest poems, which among other things provide feverish exercise, celebrate play and inventiveness and, above all, mimic the motion of life. Certain poems of his—**"The spire cranes"** and **"A Saint About to Fall,"** say—are as much exercises in calisthenics as they're anything else. It is no accident that he rarely uses the vocative: he doesn't feel apart enough from things or other people to muster the autonomies underlying a form of address; he is, in his invasive way, already at the heart of whatever he deals with. Listen to him in the act of turning into a bird, oddly graced with vocabulary:

> The spire cranes. Its statue is an aviary.
> From the stone nest it does not let the feathery
> Carved birds blunt their striking throats on the
>   salt gravel,
> Pierce the spilt sky with diving wing in weed and
>   heel
> An inch in froth. . . .

He grows more and more avian with each syllable. We have just witnessed a metamorphosis, although one not half so demanding as the almost sculptural rendering in **"A Saint About to Fall"** of the sensations attending moral and spiritual collapse:

> On the angelic etna of the last whirring feather-
>   lands,
> Wind-heeled foot in the hole of a fireball,
> Hymned his shrivelling flock,
> On the last rick's tip by spilled wine-wells. . . .

My point is that he doesn't intend such lines as these to correspond to anything else; they correspond only to themselves. Such language isn't referential, it's a sample of energy likely to sweep the reader along with it, even if "the angelic etna of the last whirring featherlands" never 'makes sense.' When Etna becomes 'etna' we are among the generic, but the specific connotation never gets lost, and it helps more than it hinders. Not one of his metaphors isn't a metaphor for the act of being metaphorical, which means that what often seems the superplus in his combinations—what doesn't need to be there—is present as a note to the activity itself, reminding us blatantly of what is going on, as when a clown falls once too often or a gymnast insists on virtuosity by doing something reckless. Not that we need to be warned: he overdoes things out of sheer natural abundance, in parallel with the Creation he hymns with ebullient lushness. What's abidingly uncommon about him is his untechnical command of what goes on in veins, capillaries, tissues, sinuses, and cells: the unseen physical, yet next door to the physical we see. In that sense he is the maestro of the fleshly neighborhood, the reluctant Canute of his own head's tides. He rides that rare, gorgeous flux like one appointed and sure of keeping his unique job. (pp. 88-92)

Diane Ackerman, "Among Soft Particles and Charms," in *Parnassus: Poetry in Review,* Vol. 14, No. 1, 1987, pp. 86-92.

SOURCES FOR FURTHER STUDY

Ackerman, John. *A Dylan Thomas Companion: Life, Poetry and Prose.* London: Macmillan, 1991, 309 p.

> Comprehensive study including biographical discussion as well as critical commentary on Thomas's poetry, prose, and dramatic works.

Brinnin, John Malcolm. *A Casebook on Dylan Thomas.* New York: Thomas Y. Crowell Co., 1960, 322 p.

> Collects reviews, essays, and appreciations by such noted critics as Elder Olson, Henry Treece, and Geoffrey Grigson, as well as a selection of Thomas's most noted poems.

FitzGibbon, Constantine. *The Life of Dylan Thomas.* Boston: Little, Brown and Co., 1965, 370 p.

> Authorized biography.

Kershner, R. B., Jr. *Dylan Thomas: The Poet and His Critics.* Chicago: American Library Association, 1976, 280 p.

> Designed to serve "as an introduction to the major areas of investigation for the reader whose interest in Thomas has no specific focus, and as a guide to more intensive studies . . . upon a single aspect of the poet's writings."

Olson, Elder. *The Poetry of Dylan Thomas.* Chicago: University of Chicago Press, 1954, 164 p.

> Important early study of Thomas's poetry with an extensive analysis of the "Alterwise by Owl light" sonnet sequence.

Tindall, William York. *A Reader's Guide to Dylan Thomas.* New York: Noonday Press, 1962, 305 p.

> Offers in-depth analyses of Thomas's poems. Tindall writes in the introduction that "this book is for holding in one hand while holding *The Collected Poems* in the other. In a word, this book in hand is a manual."

Henry David Thoreau

1817-1862

(Born David Henry Thoreau) American essayist, poet, and translator.

INTRODUCTION

*T*horeau is considered one of the key figures of the American Transcendental movement, and his *Walden; or, Life in the Woods* (1854), a record of two years that he spent living alone in the woods near Concord, Massachusetts, is viewed as one of the finest prose works in American literature. Part autobiography, part fiction, part social criticism, *Walden* is a highly individual work. In it Thoreau advocates a simple, self-sufficient way of life in order to free the individual from self-imposed social and financial obligations. He also pleads for a more intimate relationship between human beings and nature as an antidote to the deadening influence of an increasingly industrialized society. Thus, Thoreau's works embody the tenets of American Transcendentalism as articulated by Ralph Waldo Emerson and others. His aphoristic yet lyrical prose style and intense moral and political convictions have secured his place beside Emerson as the most representative and influential of the New England Transcendentalists. He is considered along with such figures as Emerson, Nathaniel Hawthorne, and Herman Melville as a major nineteenth-century American author.

Born in Concord, Massachusetts, Thoreau grew up in an atmosphere of genteel poverty. Although his father, a businessman with a history of failure, ultimately succeeded in pencil manufacturing, Thoreau's mother kept a boarding house to supplement the family's income. The only child in the family to receive a college education, Thoreau graduated in 1837 from Harvard, where he became interested in natural history, religious studies, the classics, and English, French, and German literature. Two important influences at Harvard were the famous naturalist Louis Agassiz and the rhetorics professor Edward Tyrel Channing. Following his commencement, Thoreau taught at the Concord Academy but was soon dismissed because of his opposition to corporal punishment. He and his brother John founded their own school in 1838 and became renowned for utilizing the progressive educational methods of the American Transcendentalist Amos Bronson Alcott. Yet Thoreau aspired to be a poet and when Emerson invited him in 1841 to live with him and his family in Concord, where he could write and earn his keep by acting as a general handyman, he accepted. The Concord community, already scandalized by Thoreau's unconventional way of life, ridiculed his lack of ambition and material success. However, Thoreau flourished with Emerson as his mentor. He kept an extensive journal and became an avid reader of Hindu scripture. He had ample time after his chores to write and think, and in Emerson's home he met many of the greatest figures of American Transcendentalism, including Sarah Margaret Fuller and George Ripley. Emerson and Fuller had recently founded a journal, the *Dial,* as the literary organ of the New England Transcendentalists, and there they published Thoreau's first efforts in prose and poetry. Thoreau also worked as an assistant on the *Dial* and regularly lectured at the Concord Lyceum during this period. He briefly lived in New York during 1843 and 1844 as a tutor to Emerson's brother's children. When he returned to Concord, he supported himself by working as a surveyor, managing his father's pencil factory, and securing odd jobs around town. But Thoreau and Emerson had grown distant due to differences of opinion and temperament and were no longer on close terms.

On July 4, 1845, Thoreau moved to Walden Pond, located on Emerson's property, where he remained for almost two years. Though he was actually near Concord and had many visitors daily, Thoreau was regarded as a hermit, mystic, and eccentric, an image that was enhanced by a night he spent in jail in Concord in 1846. Thoreau was incarcerated for refusing to pay taxes to the commonwealth of Massachusetts because of its endorsements of slavery and the Mexican War; Thoreau was morally opposed to both. He explored the individual's right to dissent from a government's policies in accordance with his or her own conscience in his later political essays, in which he also treated the issue of slavery. An active abolitionist in later years, Thoreau lectured widely and publically spoke against the Fugitive Slave Law of 1850. In keeping with his interest in naturalism, much of his writing and lecturing in the 1850s also concerned the conservation of natural resources. Thoreau had suffered from poor health most of his life and was stricken in 1860 with tuberculosis, from which he never recovered. Although he was considered cold, misanthropic, and disagreeable by some, he was much respected and admired by his circle of friends.

While some of Thoreau's poems, essays, and translations appeared in periodicals during his lifetime, most were not published until after his death. His two longer works, *A Week on the Concord and Merrimack Rivers* (1849) and *Walden,* both appeared during his lifetime. *A Week on the Concord and Merrimack Rivers,* a travel narrative interspersed with meditative essays, recounts a boating trip Thoreau took with his brother John in 1839. A leisurely, meandering book, it has been praised for its excellent nature descriptions, its joyous mood, and its union of the active and contemplative life. *Walden,* regarded by most critics as Thoreau's masterpiece, comprises a group of loosely connected essays which are organized in a seasonal sequence so that the narrative concludes in spring, a time of spiritual as well as natural rebirth. Thoreau telescoped his two years' experience at Walden Pond into the span of one year in order to fit his essays into his chosen time frame. Contemporary critics who had greeted *A Week on the Concord and Merrimack Rivers* with mixed reviews reacted to *Walden* with measured praise and also some cries of "humbug." Modern critics especially praise his playful, witty prose style in *Walden,* as well as the sense of humor manifested in his use of paradox, puns, and satire. Yet, whimsical and lyrical as Thoreau appears in *Walden,* he never loses sight of his philosophical intent—to insist on every person's right to independent thinking.

Thoreau's remaining writings can be generally divided into two groups—travel essays and political essays. *The Maine Woods* (1864), *Excursions* (1863), *Cape Cod* (1865), and the title piece of *A Yankee in Canada, with Anti-Slavery and Reform Papers* (1866), are travel narratives. They combine perceptive observations about flora and fauna with Thoreau's philosophical musings. The political essays—"Resistance to Civil Government," later published as "Civil Disobedience," "Slavery in Massachusetts," "A Plea for Captain John Brown," and "Life without Principle" are impassioned rhetorical statements of Thoreau's belief in individual choice and responsibility. Thoreau's poems, mostly celebrations of nature, are most often considered banal, whereas his prose is usually seen by critics to be especially poetic. His *Journal,* because of its completeness and intensity, is sometimes named as his greatest literary achievement.

Though Thoreau was not well known during his lifetime outside the circle of New England Transcendentalists, his reputation has gradually grown. Assessment of his literary merits was long hampered by James Russell Lowell's disparagement of his early work. An extremely influential critic, Lowell accused Thoreau of being an imitator of Emerson and attacked what he saw as his egocentrism and lack of humor. Robert Louis Stevenson deemed Thoreau a "prig," a "skulker," and an idler, but valued his "singularly eccentric and independent mind." Ironically, Emerson's funeral elegy on Thoreau served to reinforce the image of Thoreau as a cold, reclusive man. Thoreau's admirers, however, came to his defense: John Burroughs praised his dedication as a naturalist and Amos Bronson Alcott and Ellery Channing offered testimonials to his personal warmth and charm. There had been a Thoreau critical revival at the centenary of his birth, but Thoreau's critical reputation did not really blossom until the 1930s when the depressed American economy imposed a radically frugal, Thoreauvian lifestyle on many people, and when Thoreau's ideas about individual freedom and responsibility stood out in stark relief against the growing threat of fascism. In the 1940s, encouraged by F. O. Matthiessen's landmark study of sense imagery in *Walden*, scholars turned their attention to more particular matters of Thoreau's style and diction. Critics now almost universally admire Thoreau's prose style for its directness, pithiness, and variety. Though Lowell termed his poetry "worsification," modern critics praise Thoreau's vivid use of imagery and irregular rhythms and suggest that his poetry anticipated the experimental verse of the twentieth century. Many of the most recent studies of Thoreau, aided by closer examination of his journals and letters, are psychological in approach.

During the nineteenth century, Thoreau was generally considered an obscure, second-rate imitator of Emerson. Twentieth century critics, however, rank him as one of the greatest figures in American literature. "Civil Disobedience" has influenced such diverse writers and leaders as Leo Tolstoy, Martin Luther King, Jr., Jack Kerouac, Mohandas Gandhi, and Allen Ginsberg. *Walden*, the work of a man who spent almost his entire life in his native town of Concord, has been translated into virtually every modern language and is today known all over the world.

(For further information about Thoreau's life and works, see *Dictionary of Literary Biography*, Vol. 1: *The American Renaissance in New England; Concise Dictionary of American Literary Biography, 1640-1865;* and *Nineteenth-Century Literature Criticism*, Vols. 7, 21.)

CRITICAL COMMENTARY

RALPH WALDO EMERSON

(essay date 1862)

[Emerson was an American essayist and poet. As founder of the Transcendental Movement, he helped shape a distinctly American philosophy embracing optimism, individuality, and mysticism. In the following excerpt, originally unsigned, he provides a eulogistic tribute to Thoreau.]

[Thoreau] was equally interested in every natural fact. The depth of his perception found likeness of law throughout Nature, and I know not any genius who so swiftly inferred universal law from the single fact. He was no pedant of a department. His eye was open to beauty, and his ear to music. He found these, not in rare conditions, but wheresoever he went. He thought the best of music was in single strains; and he found poetic suggestion in the humming of the telegraph-wire.

His poetry might be bad or good; he no doubt wanted a lyric facility and technical skill; but he had the source of poetry in his spiritual perception. He was a good reader and critic, and his judgment on poetry was to the ground of it. He could not be deceived as to the presence or absence of the poetic element in any composition, and his thirst for this made him negligent and perhaps scornful of superficial graces. He would pass by many delicate rhythms, but he would have detected every live stanza or line in a volume, and knew very well where to find an equal poetic charm in prose. He was so enamored of the spiritual beauty that he held all actual written poems in very light esteem in the comparison. . . . His own verses are often rude and defective. The gold does not yet run pure, is drossy and crude. The thyme and marjoram are not yet honey. But if he want lyric fineness and technical merits, if he have not the poetic temperament, he never lacks the causal thought, showing that his genius was better than his talent. He knew the worth of the Imagination for the uplifting and consolation of human life, and liked to throw every thought into a symbol. The fact you tell is of no value, but only the impression. For this reason his presence was poetic, always piqued the curiosity to know more deeply the secrets of his mind. He had many reserves, an unwillingness to exhibit to profane eyes what was still sacred in his own, and knew well how to throw a poetic veil over his experience. (p. 246)

His riddles were worth the reading, and I confide, that, if at any time I do not understand the expression, it is yet just. Such was the wealth of his truth that it was not worth his while to use words in vain. His poem entitled **"Sympathy"** reveals the tenderness under that triple steel of stoicism, and the intellectual subtilty it

His virtues, of course, sometimes ran into extremes. It was easy to trace to the inexorable demand on all for exact truth that austerity which made this willing hermit more solitary even than he wished. Himself of a perfect probity, he required not less of others. . . .

The habit of a realist to find things the reverse of their appearance inclined him to put every statement in a paradox. A certain habit of antagonism defaced his earlier writings,—a trick of rhetoric not quite outgrown in his later, of substituting for the obvious word and thought its diametrical opposite. He praised wild mountains and winter forests for their domestic air, in snow and ice he would find sultriness, and commended the wilderness for resembling Rome and Paris. "It was so dry, that you might call it wet."

The tendency to magnify the moment, to read all the laws of Nature in the one object or one combination under your eye, is of course comic to those who do not share the philosopher's perception of identity. To him there was no such thing as size. The pond was a small ocean; the Atlantic, a large Walden Pond. He referred every minute fact to cosmical laws. Though he meant to be just, he seemed haunted by a certain chronic assumption that the science of the day pretended completeness, and he had just found out that the *savans* had neglected to discriminate a particular botanical variety, had failed to describe the seeds or count the sepals. (p. 247)

Had his genius been only contemplative, he had been fitted to his life, but with his energy and practical ability he seemed born for great enterprise and for command; and I so much regret the loss of his rare powers of action, that I cannot help counting it a fault in him that he had no ambition. Wanting this, instead of engineering for all America, he was the captain of a huckleberry-party. Pounding beans is good to the end of pounding empires one of these days; but if, at the end of years, it is still only beans! (p. 248)

The scale on which his studies proceeded was so large as to require longevity, and we were the less prepared for his sudden disappearance. The country knows not yet, or in the least part, how great a son it has lost. It seems an injury that he should leave in the midst his broken task, which none else can finish,—a kind of indignity to so noble a soul, that it should depart out of Nature before yet he has been really shown to his peers for what he is. But he, at least, is content. His soul was made for the noblest society; he had in a short life exhausted the capabilities of this world; wherever there is knowledge, wherever there is virtue, wherever there is beauty, he will find a home. (p. 249)

Ralph Waldo Emerson, in an originally unsigned essay titled "Thoreau," in *The Atlantic Monthly*, Vol. X, No. LVIII, August, 1862, pp. 239-49.

could animate. His classic poem on **"Smoke"** suggests Simonides, but is better than any poem of Simonides. His biography is in his verses. His habitual thought makes all his poetry a hymm to the Cause of causes, the Spirit which vivifies and controls his own.

> I hearing get, who had but ears,
> And sight, who had but eyes before;
> I moments live, who lived but years,
> And truth discern, who knew but learning's lore.

And still more in these religious lines:—

> Now chiefly is my natal hour,
> And only now my prime of life;
> I will not doubt the love untold,
> Which not my worth or want hath bought,
> Which wooed me young, and wooes me old,
> And to this evening hath me brought.

(pp. 246-47)

F. O. MATTHIESSEN
(essay date 1941)

[Matthiessen, a literary critic and historian, wrote groundbreaking studies of nineteenth-century American literature. Below, he discusses Thoreau's criticism of the materialism of his day, expanding on "The Service" as Thoreau's starting point for his interest in the use of rhythm and imagery.]

[Thoreau's] contribution to our social thought lies in his thoroughgoing criticism of the narrow materialism of his day. It is important to remember that when he objected to the division of labor, he was writing from an agrarian and craft economy where the forces of industrialism were still an encroaching minority. But his human values were so clear that they remain substantially unaltered by our changed conditions.

He objected to the division of labor since it divided the worker, not merely the work, reduced him from a man to an operative, and enriched the few at the expense of the many. As a critic of society he had the advantage of being close to its primary levels. The son of a man who had failed as a small merchant and had then set up as a pencil-maker, sign-painter, and jack-of-all-trades, Thoreau came about as close to the status of proletarian writer as was possible in his simple environment. (pp. 77-8)

The social standards that Thoreau knew and protested against were those dominated by New England mercantilism. He granted that the life of a civilized people is *an institution,* in which the life of the individual is to a great extent absorbed, in order to preserve and perfect that of the race.' But he insisted that it was essential to re-examine the terms under which that absorption was being made, to see whether the individual was not being ruthlessly sacrificed to the dictates of a mean-spirited commercialism. (pp. 78-9)

['The Service,' an essay by Thoreau which was rejected by *The Dial,*] is of cardinal value since it lets us follow the very process by which Thoreau found what he wanted to do with language. It has been suggested that the title, underscored by those of its first and last sections, 'Qualities of the Recruit' and 'Not how Many, but where the Enemy are,' was the product of Thoreau's private reaction to current discourses on pacifism. The repeated imagery of a crusade seems borrowed from Tasso's *Jerusalem Delivered,* which had been one of his favorites in college, and whose hero Godfrey is cited here. However, the campaign that Thoreau urges is quite other. The first section sounds the theme,

'For an impenetrable shield, stand inside yourself.' The final pages are a trumpet blast to rouse the soul hovering on the verge of life, to call man not to action against others, but to the realization of his submerged potentialities. All such passages are what Emerson found in Thoreau at this time, simply Emerson's own thoughts originally dressed. But the middle section, 'What Music shall we have?' hints, if somewhat obscurely, at Thoreau's special qualities, and at the way by which he was to arrive at them. One of its sentences, 'A man's life should be a stately march to unheard music,' may seem a vague enough acceptance of the romantic belief in such melodies. But it meant something compelling to Thoreau, since it became a recurrent image throughout his work. He varied it a decade later in his journal: 'It is not so much the music as the marching to the music that I feel.' He picked it up again in the conclusion to *Walden:* 'Let him step to the music which he hears, however measured or far away.' He obviously did not mean merely the disembodied harmony of thought, and it is worth trying to see upon what he grounded his image since it came to epitomize for him the relation between his life and his writing.

In 'The Service' Thoreau seems groping to convey his recognition, which was to grow increasingly acute, that a deep response to rhythm was his primary experience. He tried to develop it in this fashion: 'To the sensitive soul the Universe has her own fixed measure, which is its measure also, and as this, expressed in the regularity of its pulse, is inseparable from a healthy body, so is its healthiness dependent on the regularity of its rhythm.' The first statement is the usual transcendental doctrine of the merging of the individual with the Over-Soul; the remainder of the sentence, blurred as it is by its loose pronouns, still adumbrates what is going to be Thoreau's particular forte, his grasp of the close correspondence, the organic harmony between body and spirit. Emerson perceived this trenchantly when he said: 'The length of his walk uniformly made the length of his writing. If shut up in the house he did not write at all.' The context of the demand that Lowell mocked is nearly always forgotten: 'Give me a sentence which no intelligence can understand. There must be a kind of life and palpitation to it, and under its words a kind of blood must circulate forever.' Thoreau's first conviction about the artist was that his words should speak not to the mind alone but to the whole being. (pp. 83-5)

Thoreau's emergence from the cloud-land of 'The Service' onto similar solid earth was due in large part to his having clung fast to his perception that both language and rhythm have a physical basis. His theory of language, in so far as he recorded one, seems at first glance to approximate Emersons's. He held that the origin of words is in nature ('Is it not as language that all natural objects affect the poet?') and that they are symbols of the spiritual. He spoke of the difficulty in finding the word that will exactly name and so release the thing. But he had a more dogged respect for the thing than any of his companions, and limitless tenacity in waiting to find the word. (pp. 85-6)

Thus far nothing has really differentiated his position from what Emerson developed with much greater wealth of detail. But while discussing the primitive sense of words he made a remark that suggests what carried his practice such a considerable distance from his master's: 'We reason from our hands to our head.' Thoreau was not inclined to rate language as superior to other mediums of expression on the ground that it was produced solely by the mind and thence could share more directly in the ideal. On the contrary, he insisted upon its double parentage: 'A word which may be translated into every dialect, and suggests a truth to every mind, is the most perfect work of human art; and as it may be breathed and taken on our lips, and, as it were, become the product of our physical organs, as its sense is of our intellectual, it is the nearest to life itself.' (p. 87)

What separates Thoreau most from Emerson is his interest in the varied play of all of his senses, not merely of the eye, a rare enough attribute in New England and important to dwell on since it is the crucial factor in accounting for the greater density of Thoreau's style. You think first, to be sure, of his Indian accuracy of sight that could measure distances like the surveyor's instrument and tell time almost to the minute by the opening of the flowers. This alertness remained constant. . . . But usually he felt that sight alone was too remote for the kind of knowledge he wanted, that 'we do not learn with the eyes; they introduce us, and we learn after by converse with things.' He held that scent was 'a more primitive inquisition,' 'more oracular and trustworthy.' It showed what was concealed from the other senses: by it he detected earthiness. Taste meant less to him, though eating became a kind of sacrament and out in the berry field he could be thrilled to think that he owed a perception to this 'commonly gross sense,' that he had been inspired through the palate. (pp. 87-8)

He became ecstatic as he talked about touch: 'My body is all sentient. As I go here or there, I am tickled by this or that I come in contact with, as if I touched the wires of a battery.' He knew, like Anteus, that his strength derived from ever renewed contact with the earth. . . . But as his preoccupation in **'The Service'** has told us, he gave his most rapt attention to sounds. These alone among his sense impressions were to have a chapter devoted to them in *Walden.* He can hardly find enough verbs of action to describe what they do to him. They melt and flow, and he feels himself bathed in their surge. . . . The most exquisite flavor is not to be compared to the sweetness of the note of the wood

thrush. As he listens, it seems to take him out of himself: he leaves his body in a trance and has the freedom of all nature. After such an experience he can say, measuring his words, 'The contact of sound with a human ear whose hearing is pure and unimpaired is coincident with an ecstasy.' (pp. 88-9)

He was therefore intent to study the exact evidence of his senses, since he believed that only only through their concrete reports could he project his inner life. Sometimes he felt a danger involved in forming too exact habits of observation, for they could run to excess and yield him, instead of fresh knowledge, merely a flat repetition of what he already knew. His remedy for this was what he called a free 'sauntering of the eye.' The poetic knowledge he wanted would come only through something like Wordsworth's 'relaxed attention,' only if he was not a scientific naturalist, 'not prying, nor inquisitive, nor bent upon seeing things.' He described his desired attitude towards nature by calling it one of indirection, by repeating frequently that the most fruitful perception was 'with the unworn sides of your eye.' We remember Keats' delight in 'the sidelong glance,' and his feeling that his ripest intuitions came through indolence. Thus nonchalantly, almost unconsciously, Thoreau could catch the most familiar scene in new perspective, with possibilities hitherto untold to his direct scrutiny, and with a wholeness of impression that could give it composition in writing. (pp. 89-90)

[To] the end, even in his most sterile moods, he could respond to such never stale melodies as those of the wood thrush, though he could not recapture quite this earlier pitch: 'Where was that strain mixed into which this world was dropped but as a lump of sugar to sweeten the draught? I would be drunk, drunk, drunk, dead drunk to this world with it forever.'

In that moment Thoreau approached Keats, but, in the act of making the comparison, you recall that Thoreau's idea of luxury was to stand up to his chin in a retired swamp and be saturated with its summer juices. This man, who, unlike Whitman, hated to lie with the sun on his back, was constant in his dislike of sensuality. His desire was for 'no higher heaven than the pure senses can furnish, a *purely* sensuous life.' The double suggestion here of the need for clarified perception and of the vision into which it could lead him brings out the mystical element that always remained part of his experience. Yet even when he was swept beyond his moments of physical sensation he did not forget his debt to them. The triumphal strains to which he was set marching in **'The Service'** were not a nebulous fancy. They were the imaginative transformation of a rhythm he had actually heard and which he was trying to symbolize in words: 'In our lonely chambers at night we are thrilled by some far-off serenade within the mind, and seem to hear the clarion sound and clang of corselet and buckler from many a silent hamlet of the soul, though actually it may be but the rattling of some farmer's waggon rolling to market against the morrow.'

The checkrein of his senses was what held even such a passage from gliding away into a romantic reverie of escape. Their vigilance constituted his chief asset as an artist. It brought his pages out of the fog into the sunlight in which he wanted them to be read. (pp. 90-1)

In spite of his keenness in scrutinizing the reports of his senses, Thoreau remained wholly the child of his age in regarding the material world as a symbol of the spiritual. He who held that 'the poet writes the history of his body' declared in another mood that 'poetry is the mysticism of mankind.' He could even contradict his enunciation that it was not the subject but the roundness of treatment that mattered, by saying that 'a higher truth, though only dimly hinted at, thrills us more than a lower expressed.' He stated early and kept repeating that he was ever in pursuit of the ineffable: 'The other world is all my art; my pencils will draw no other; my jack-knife will cut nothing else; I do not use it as a means.'

Yet even in that affirmation of faith Thoreau does not disappear into the usual transcendental vapor. He gives us the sense that he is a man whose grip remains firm on this world as well, whose hand can manage both his knife and his pencil. In fact, Thoreau's success as an artist is exactly in proportion to such balance between means and end. On the occasions when he attempts a direct approach to his end, when, that is to say, he voices his bare thoughts, as in his pages on ideal friendship, his mind is revealed as much less capacious and less elastic than Emerson's. On the other hand, when he simply heaps up facts, as in the later volumes of his journal, he himself recognizes that facts so stated are parched, that they 'must be the vehicle of some humanity in order to interest us,' that they 'must be warm, moist, incarnated—have been breathed on at least. A man has not seen a thing who has not felt it.' This is to remark again that Thoreau was not specially equipped either for abstract theorizing or for strictly scientific observation. But when he could base theory on his own sturdy practice, as in **'Life Without Principle'** or **'Civil Disobedience,'** the impact of his humanity was dynamic. And when, as a writer, he could fuse his thought and his observation by means of a symbol, which was not just suggested but designed in sharp detail, he was able, in Coleridge's phrase, to 'elicit truth as at a flash.'

Thoreau's own description of his most fertile process, in the chapter **'What I lived for,'** is that 'we are able to apprehend at all what is sublime and noble only by the perpetual instilling and drenching of the reality that surrounds us.' The gerunds are characteristic, drawn from verbs of touch that penetrate to his inner being. They show the kind of fusion he could make by training into his writing the alertness of his senses. (pp. 93-4)

The rhythm [in the passage about the Concord fisherman in *A Week*] is a clear instance of what Thoreau meant by saying that it was not so much the music as the marching to the music that he felt. For here, as in many other typical passages, his eye is reinforced not by varied sounds so much as by impressions of movement and of muscular pressure. He catches the step of the fisher in unison with the sweep of his scythe, though the word 'undulatory' blends too with the flow of the river, merging the old man as closely as possible with the source of his former pleasures. In that fashion Thoreau projected his conception of the harmonious interaction between man and nature, without which he did not believe that man could be adequately described.

But the river in which so many things have gone down stream is also that of the fisherman's throat, of his drunken life, the disintegration of which Thoreau conveys entirely in concrete terms, each suggesting a significance beyond itself. The snake that the old man might encounter while mowing is likewise that of his temptation; and his own figure with its scythe calls up that of Time. The final metaphor may seem too literary, the romantic stock-in-trade. Along with Thoreau's fondness for his whimsical pun on 'fluid,' it may be the kind of thing Carlyle objected to when he called the *Week* 'too Jean Paulish.' However, 'the Great Mower' saves itself, at least to a degree that most of Richter's self-conscious fancies do not, by the fact that it has not been lugged in arbitrarily. It has grown integrally out of the context, and that lends some freshness to it.

The organic structure of Thoreau's symbols became more marked in *Walden,* as in the laconic: 'Having each some shingles of thought well dried, we sat and whittled them, trying our knives, and admiring the clear yellowish grain of the pumpkin pine.' The deft telescoping of sense impression and thought allows full play to both. We can share in the relish of what he has seen, since his delicate skill has evoked the very look of the wood at the moment of being cut into. But the desultory act of whittling becomes also the appropriate image for conversation between Alcott and Thoreau around the winter hearth in Thoreau's hut. The single sentence gives a condensed dramatic scene, the very way these two friends appeared while trying their minds on thoughts 'well dried' by use; and, in this case, Thoreau's double meaning is pungent, since it frees the air of the suspicion of solemnness that might be there without it. (pp. 94-5)

By [his] method of presenting an experience instead of stating an abstraction, Thoreau himself has elucidated both the meaning and the value of his long preoccupation with 'wholeness.' From the time he announced in **'The Service'** that 'the exploit of a brave life consists in its momentary completeness,' he continued to make brief definitions of that quality, and of how it might be gained. . . . The year after **'The Service'** he developed his sentence further: 'The best and bravest deed is that which the whole man—heart, lungs, hands, fingers, and toes—at any time prompts . . . This is the meaning of integrity; this is to be an integer, and not a fraction.' He subsequently shifted his symbols to correspond to his own mode of existence, and grouped them not around the warrior hero but around the scholar, who, if he is wise, 'will confine the observations of his mind as closely as possible to the experience or life of his senses. His thought must live with and be inspired with the life of the body . . . Dwell as near as possible to the channel in which your life flows.' In this respect more than in any other was the practice of Thoreau's scholar more thoroughgoing than Emerson's. (p. 96)

In desiring to push as near as possible to the boundaries between the visible and the invisible, to re-assert the primitive quality of wonder, Thoreau . . . approached Browne. . . . Attention to the objects around him, not intricate speculation, furnished him with his best analogies. . . . He was nearest the practice of the seventeenth-century poets when he insisted on the use of *all* materials that experience affords; but his experience was less complex if no less concentrated than Donne's. It approximated that of the explorers in its excited immediacy of discovery, though what he wanted to discover was himself. His ability to do whatever he did with his whole being was the product of an awakened scrutiny, not, as for them, an unconscious response of minds that had never conceived any arbitrary gap between thought and feeling and so reacted with equal directness to physical and spiritual adventures. So Thoreau's pages are inevitably more literary, a mixture of the cultivated and the wild. Indeed, one of his chief distinctions—and again he shares this with Browne—is the infusion of his reading into his perception. . . . (p. 117)

The structural wholeness of *Walden* makes it stand as the firmest product in our literature of . . . life-giving analogies between the processes of art and daily work. Moreover, Thoreau's very lack of invention brings him closer to the essential attributes of craftsmanship, if by that term we mean the strict, even spare, almost impersonal 'revelation of the object,' in contrast to the 'elaborated skill,' the combinations of more variegated resources that we describe as technique. (p. 173)

He had understood that in the act of expression a man's whole being, and his natural and social background as well, function organically together. He had mastered a definition of art akin to what Maritain has extracted from scholasticism: *Recta ratio factibilium,* the right ordering of the thing to be made, the right revelation of the material. (p. 175)

F. O. Matthiessen, in his *American Renaissance: Art and Expression in the Age of Emerson and Whitman,* Oxford University Press, 1941, 678 p.

JOSEPH WOOD KRUTCH
(essay date 1948)

[In the excerpt below from his *Henry David Thoreau,* Krutch discusses the philosophical convictions Thoreau expressed in *Walden.*]

A Week on the Concord and Merrimack Rivers had been the account of a vacation, which is to say of an interlude, a truancy, or an escape. *Walden* was an account of a way of life, even of a permanent way of life if one considers that what it describes is not merely a way of living by a pond but a general attitude capable of making life so simple that there is, as Thoreau put it, no need for the brow to sweat. The finder can be, as the seeker seldom is, gay; and *Walden* is, among many other things, a gay book. In the *Journal* Thoreau speaks often of joy and even of ecstasy. He may at most periods of his life have known a good deal of both, although it is also evident that he had moments, especially as he grew older, when the transcendental voices remained stubbornly silent and even nature awoke only feeble response. But neither joy nor ecstasy is the same as gaiety, and in *Walden* there is much that can hardly be called by any other name. He is gay when he describes the routine of daily living, gay when he reports his interviews with visitors human or animal, and gay when he flings into the face of his fellow citizens his account of their preposterous, self-imposed labors—Herculean in their magnitude, Sisyphean in their endless futility. And he is gayest of all, perhaps, when he goads them with some blasphemy, some gently insinuated renunciation of stern duty. (p. 105)

Walden is divided into eighteen chapters, each devoted to a topic. Some of them, like **"The Beanfield," "The Ponds," "Brute Neighbours,"** etc., are largely descriptive. Others, like **"Economy,"** which is the first, and **"Higher Laws,"** which is the eleventh, are expository or argumentative, and nowhere is there an orderly presentation of the thesis from first things to last. In other words the over-all shape of the book preserves the main outlines of the thing it professes to be: not an argument, but an account of the somewhat eccentric experiment concerning which Thoreau's neighbors had expressed a curiosity. The theses and the adjurations which actually constitute a considerable part of its bulk are, formally, to be considered as obiter dicta [incidental remarks or observations] or, at most, digressions, which the author permits himself in the course of his report on life at Walden. Actually, however, there are four related but distinct "matters" with which the book concerns itself, and they might be enumerated as follows: (1) The life of quiet desperation which most men lead. (2) The economic fallacy which is responsible for the situation in which they find themselves. (3) What the life close to nature is and what rewards it offers. (4) The "higher laws" which man begins, through some transcendental process, to perceive if he faithfully climbs the stepladder of nature whose first rung is "wildness," whose second is some such gentle and austere but not artificial life as Thoreau himself was leading, and whose third is the transcendental insight he only occasionally reached.

The elements of an inclusive system are present, scattered here and there through the logically (though not artistically) fragmentary discourse. Thoreau has, for instance, a theory of wages and costs ("the cost of a thing is the amount of what I will call life which is required to be exchanged for it, immediately or in the long run") and a somewhat Marxian—and Carlylesque—conception of production for use ("I cannot believe that our factory system is the best mode by which men get clothing . . . since, as far as I have heard or observed, the principal object is, not that mankind may be well and honestly clad, but, unquestionably, that the corporations may be enriched"). He has also, however, a theory of ultimate value which is metaphysical rather than economic. That theory of ultimate value, together with the distrust of mass action which goes with it, leads him away from any concern with social reforms other than those which every man can achieve for himself. It also leads him in the direction of a solitary life in nature to which he was temperamentally inclined and which can be justified on mystical grounds. It is a bridge across which he may go toward those ultimate ends the Transcendentalists and the wise Orientals are seeking.

The fact that he never attempts to schematize these various convictions has, moreover, the effect of making *Walden* more persuasive, or at least more difficult to controvert, than would otherwise be the case, because it makes it less easy for the reader to get hold of any link in a chain of reasoning which he is tempted to try to break. Thoreau does not so much argue that it is possible and desirable to live in a certain way as tell us how he lived and what rewards he discovered. He presents us, as it were, with a *fait accompli* [an accomplished and presumably irreversible thing], and, like Captain Shotover in Shaw's *Heartbreak House,* he will not abide our question. He discharges a shaft, and is gone again before we can object or challenge.

For all his seeming directness he is extremely difficult to corner. No writer was ever, at dangerous moments, more elusive, and no proponent of fundamental paradoxes ever more skillfully provided himself with

Walden pond, where Thoreau lived for two years.

avenues of escape. His residence at Walden is, when he wishes to make it so, an experiment whose results have universal significance; but it can, on convenient occasion, shrink to the status of a merely personal expedient. It is alternately, as a point is to be made or an objection to be met, a universal nostrum or the whim of an individual eccentric. . . . He did not come into the world, he had previously protested, to make it better; and yet, until you catch him at it, this is exactly what he is trying to do. When you do catch him at it, he retreats again into the extremest possible individualism. In some sense he is certainly suggesting that others imitate him; but he also protests that he would like to have as many different kinds of men in the world as possible. If you ask him what would happen if all tried to find a pond to live beside, he answers that he never suggested they should; that in fact he himself lived there for only two years; and that he left, perhaps, because he had some other lives to lead. (pp. 108-11)

In *A Week on the Concord and Merrimack Rivers* there is a minor element of burlesque. The setting sail is described in deliberately grandiose terms, as though the author had in mind at the moment the classical genre which Pope illustrated in *The Rape of the Lock.* An even fainter suggestion of the same thing is present in the scheme of *Walden*. Thoreau was not unaware of the comic element involved in a flight from civilization which took him only a mile from the edge of his native village, only one field away from the highroad, and only half a mile from his nearest neighbor. Indeed, as he himself tells us in the *Journal*, at least one reader thought the whole book a joke and relished the map of the pond as a caricature of the Coast Surveys. But Thoreau's jokes are almost always serious—*i.e.*, revelations of truths which are commonly overlooked, and that form of burlesque which consists in finding *multum in parvo* [much in little] is not for him merely burlesque. As he himself said, any place is as wild as the wildness one can bring to it, and Walden pond was a solitude for the simple reason that he could be alone there. (p. 116)

Different classes of readers inevitably find different portions of *Walden* the most meaningful. Comparatively few are, as Thoreau himself was, almost equally interested in the aspects of external nature, in mystical intimations, and in sociological deductions. But if one leaves aside the question which sections are the most engaging and the most valuable, there can be little doubt that the first chapter and the last are the most unforgettably vigorous pieces of writing, the most astonishing demonstrations of virtuosity. In the sections which lie between, Thoreau is often discursive, picturesque, and engaging, often humorous, persuasive, and charming; but he is also relaxed and almost conversational. It is chiefly in the first chapter and the last that he undertakes to hit hard and speak with the fiery earnestness of the man formally assuming the prophet's robe and determined that, willy-nilly, he will be heard.

Yet these two sections are too unlike in both substance and style to compete with one another or even to be compared. The first, called **"Economics,"** concerns itself with the most practical and homely aspects of his subject and hits hard with prose, earnestly describing the "penances" which drive men to quiet desperation and suggesting immediate, concrete remedies. The other is spoken from the tripod by a prophet whom the divine fumes have intoxicated and who, in his vision, sees things not quite utterable. Emerson would never have wished to be so down-to-earth as Thoreau was in the chapter on Economy; it is doubtful, on the other hand, if he ever succeeded in sustaining through an equal number of connected pages so original an Orphic strain as that which makes the chapter called merely **"Conclusion"** a succession of lightning flashes. (pp. 117-18)

Throughout whole paragraphs almost every sentence is a metaphor and the metaphors range all the way from those readily translatable into prose to those genuinely Orphic in their tantalizingly elusive implications. At the same time almost every sentence is illuminated by a grotesque humor which juxtaposes the homely to the ineffable, and is pointed by scorn for those who tamely prefer what is to what might be. Thoreau's mind seems to leap from subject to subject as though, in a moment of insight, truth had been revealed and the only danger was that no utterance could be found sufficiently elliptic to communicate it all before the moment passed. (pp. 118-19)

The brilliance of that final chapter is pyrotechnic in its effect, one seems to be present at the birth of a whole galaxy of dancing stars. How, the reader is likely to find himself asking, can any writer have been at any given time so sustainedly incandescent? And the answer—which is of course that Thoreau was not, and that perhaps no writer could be—is an answer which helps to explain why no other such masterpiece as *Walden* was ever to come from its author. The book as a whole was a crystallization and the last chapter was a mosaic of crystals. The moment of sustained and inclusive illumination never existed, and the Orphic profundities never fell as they seem to fall, one after another, from the lips of a prophet in the grip of a divine seizure. They had been written down as fragments, neither successive nor connected, and they were then, sometimes years later, carefully selected and carefully fitted together in such a way that what looks like explosive brilliance was actually the result of a patient craftsmanship carefully matching and arranging brilliants which had been hoarded one by one over the years. The reader of the *Journal* comes across them here and there, imbedded, often, in a matrix not in itself gleaming, and they leap out at his eye as they evidently leaped out at their author when he went searching through his own pages. In *Walden* we pass in a few minutes from the sentence about the wild goose who is more cosmopolite than we to the sentence about the necessity of speaking extravagantly. (pp. 119-20)

To the tidy mind of a technical philosopher, Thoreau's thought must seem hopelessly confused. Puritanism, New England Transcendentalism, and Hindu mysticism made some sort of peace with one another because all were to some degree dualistic, but they were also all at war with both an objective, quasi-scientific curiosity and a tendency to deduce from the results of that curiosity a religion of nature in which the worshiper is tempted on beyond good and evil as either can be defined in humanistic terms. But Thoreau was well served by this constant balancing of possibilities, by his very inability to hold firm to a doctrine. Because of the doubts, his relentless persistence in what appeared to outsiders a mere routine actually took on the character of a ceaseless quest, and the moments of empathy were all the more eagerly sought because Thoreau himself could never be sure what they meant. His "nature writings" have a quality which immediately distinguishes them not only from the almost trivial tranquillity of Gilbert White but also from a John Burroughs or a W. H. Hudson. To some readers, at least, they are more varied, and they have, besides, a certain tenseness, a certain excitement which is unique. Thoreau is an observer without the mere observer's coldness, and he is a lover of wisdom without the mere teacher's monotonous dogmatism. The quest remains exciting because he himself does not know what he is going to find. No doubt he was, as he himself insisted, a happy man; but he was not settled or certain. A hunger and a thirst are elements in his happiness and make it something other than mere content. And it is the hunger and thirst which are responsible for the excitement of his writing. (pp. 214-15)

Sometimes—more frequently perhaps than one would suspect if one did not take pains to note the occasions—Thoreau can employ an almost Gothically intricate ornamentation when he summons to his aid a splendor of bookish rhetoric obviously caught from Sir Thomas Browne; as, for example, in the passage that concludes the sixteenth chapter of *Walden,* or, to take a less hackneyed one, the paragraph from *A Week on the Concord and Merrimack Rivers* which begins, "It is remarkable that the dead lie everywhere under stones" and ends: "Fame itself is but an epitaph; as late, as false, as true. But they only are the true epitaphs which Old Mortality retouches." Perhaps the most remarkable thing about these bookish passages is the completeness with which they have been assimilated into the texture of a prose which is elsewhere so seemingly direct and simple. And that is, of course, an indication of the fact that Thoreau had, in his own consciousness, assimilated Concord into the universe so

that he not only said but felt that the local and the temporal were indistinguishably a part of the universal and the eternal. The grand style and the homely were not appropriate respectively to ancient and to contemporary, but indiscriminately to both; so that Therien, the woodchopper, could on occasion be seen as Homeric, and on other occasions Agamemnon could be treated like a Yankee.

These elaborately ornamented passages are, however, most likely to be reserved for Thoreau's more serenely elevated moments. For his hortatory and vituperative outbursts he is more likely to employ that strong, direct, hard-hitting, more austerely functional prose which, unjustly perhaps, we are more likely to think of as characteristic of him. (pp. 273-74)

"Powerful extravagance" would, indeed, serve as well as any mere pair of words could serve to describe the general effect of his most often remembered paragraphs, and the effect of power usually is produced by bold tropes which employ a reference to some familiar object or situation to drive home a point or make clear an attitude. Moreover, the individual sentences are frequently both deliberately extravagant in themselves and arranged, one after another, to create a mounting climax of what calmer writers would call overstatement. "I fear chiefly," he wrote in *Walden,* "lest my expression may not be *extra-vagant* enough," and it is clear that though extravagance was sometimes a rhetorical device, it was also, and perhaps more frequently, the inevitable result of his conviction that the truth about neither man's potentialities nor his failure to realize them could possibly be overstated. When he wrote to a friend the advice not to worry about his health because "you may be dead already," that was both a deliberately shocking statement and an expression of Thoreau's sincere conviction that most men were actually, in the realest possible sense, not alive.

These most often remembered passages of powerful extravagance are, it should be observed, usually argumentative or scornful. In intention they are almost always, directly or indirectly, didactic or hortatory. They are concerned with what Thoreau did not approve of rather than with what he did; with what he blamed others for "living for," not with what he lived for himself. And there is another whole body of writing markedly different in style and purpose which is considerably less well known—partly because readers have, on the whole, tended to understand and sympathize with his criticism of life as it is commonly lived rather more than they have with the positive aspects of his philosophy, partly because his protestant writing is more adequately represented outside the little-read *Journal* than the other kind is.

Probably he himself would have been distressed to think that he might be remembered chiefly as a satirist or a critic; as a man who had managed to convey only his dissatisfaction with the world and not the happiness which he believed to have been his. (pp. 275-76)

Certain of the intermediate chapters of *Walden* are devoted to the life he loved rather than the life he hated, and so too are a good many pages of *A Week on the Concord and Merrimack Rivers.* But much of the second is juvenile, and the *Walden* chapters do not seem to contain the best of his writing of the sort they attempt—perhaps because they actually do not, or perhaps only because their gentler tone cannot successfully compete for our attention against the powerful urgency of the sermonizing in the first chapter and the last. The posthumous *The Maine Woods* and *Cape Cod* are too nearly mere travel books, too deliberately directed at a relatively vulgar audience, to represent him at his best, though they contain some very fine passages; and so it is to the unquarried *Journal* itself that one must go for any adequate idea of the bulk or importance of a kind of writing which will contribute more to Thoreau's fame than it yet has, if it should ever be collected, as it easily might, into volumes selected to illustrate its own special intention and quality.

Much the largest part of the *Journal* is, it must be remembered, devoted not to Thoreau's criticism of his neighbors and their society but to a vast record of his intercourse with trees and flowers, with animals, wild and domestic, and with inanimate nature as well. The record of this intercourse varies in manner from the barest quasi-scientific, or sometimes merely perfunctory, jotting down of facts and observations to the most elaborately worked-up set pieces—many of which exhibit unmistakable evidence of having been carefully composed and suggest that they were probably several times rewritten. (pp. 277-78)

Most interesting, because most nearly unique, are those of the set pieces where the working up consists in a process for which dramatization rather than poetizing might be an appropriate word. Here the attempt is to keep the attention fixed on the object itself; to return again and again to its own various aspects rather than merely to use the object as something from which the mind can take off. It is not the meaning of the hieroglyph but the thing itself which the writer is trying to grasp and which he wishes the reader to grasp also, so that experience itself rather than any explanation or interpretation of it is what he is trying to communicate. (pp. 278-79)

The intermingling without incongruity of Thoreau's humor with his seriousness is a phenomenon essentially similar to the intermingling of his homely style with his bookishly elaborate one, and of his delight in simple physical things with his mystical exaltation. Indeed it might be maintained that to unite without incongruity things ordinarily thought of as incongruous *is* the phenomenon called Thoreau, whether one is thinking of a personality or of a body of literary

work. This is what constitutes his oneness, and the oneness of a man is the most important thing about him; is perhaps the man himself. (p. 286)

Joseph Wood Krutch, in his *Henry David Thoreau,* 1948. Reprint by William Morrow & Company, Inc., 1974, 298 p.

DON W. KLEINE
(essay date 1960)

[In the following essay, Kleine compares the precepts in "Civil Disobedience" with the ideas in *Walden,* concluding that "there is significant continuity between these two works."]

Thoreau's commentators in recent years have come to a juster sense of the multiplicity of their subject. Patently, the unity of this multiplicity in *Walden* and "Civil Disobedience" is to be found in these writings themselves; when suggesting the relationship of the earlier essay to *Walden,* modern scholars have for the most part quite properly stuck to their texts. But they have only suggested this connection, not spelled it out. Perhaps their omission is a natural one; the relationship seems obvious. Yet the link between the two is easy to acknowledge and then forget. It is a frequent strategy of Thoreau's critics to treat "Civil Disobedience" as a purely political manifestation of the Transcendental principles in *Walden.* Employed with discretion, this can be a useful tactic. But if it leads the cursory analyst to become fixated on his dichotomy of the two works at the expense of their much more important affinities it can hardly result in less than a distortion of Thoreau's thought.

The earlier essay, admittedly, might be said to declare the personal independence from communal obligation which would permit a Walden adventure. Yet this distinction is at best very limited. It refers to a difference of quantity rather than quality: *Walden* repeats that same manifesto, specifically with reference to the moral price we pay for tea, coffee, and meat:

> But the only true America is that country where you are at liberty to pursue such a mode of life as may enable you to do without these, and where the state does not endeavor to compel you to sustain the slavery and war and other superfluous expenses which directly or indirectly result from the use of such things.

Protest for Thoreau exists on the level of a self-liberated individual by definition opposed to a self-enslaved majority. The Walden "experiment" is, among other things, individual protest of quite the same order as the earlier refusal to pay the poll tax.

The results of the Walden sojourn were predetermined by the spirit in which it was undertaken. Thoreau already knew what were "the grossest groceries," for he had celebrated his awareness in **"Civil Disobedience"**:

> You must hire or squat somewhere, and raise but a small crop, and eat that soon. You must live within yourself, and depend upon yourself always tucked up and ready for a start, and not have many affairs.

Walden Pond was not an experiment at all, but—like the night in the Concord jail—protest magnified into gesture. Going to the woods, going to prison each make formal a withdrawal from the community which has been effected long before.

The target of both gestures is the same: bondage of man to the instruments of civilization, whether machines or institutions. *Walden* arraigns the varieties of such bondage—to houses, clothing, fire-engines, railroads, religions, tenderloin steaks, cablegrams and governments. **"Civil Disobedience"** specifically arraigns the last of these bondages,

> If one were to tell me that this was a bad government because it taxed certain foreign commodities brought to its ports, it is most probable that I should not make an ado about it, for I can do without them. All machines have their friction; and possibly this does enough good to counterbalance the evil. At any rate, it is a great evil to make a stir about it. But when the friction comes to have its machine, and oppression and robbery are organized, I say, let us not have such a machine any longer.

The bondage and not the machine rankles Thoreau (though sometimes he found it hard to tell them apart). In fact, a machine can act as a valuable stimulant, for an overbearing state offers welcome opportunity for wholesome exercise of the free man's freedom,

> I saw that the state was half-witted, that it was timid as a lone woman with her silver spoons, and that it did not know its friends from its foes, and I lost all my remaining respect for it, and pitied it.

Indeed, the very notion of civil *disobedience* has its comic application; to disobey the impotent blusterings of this "timid" half-wit exacts rather less than the highest heroism.

But most men *are* its victims. "It is, after all, with men and not with parchment that I quarrel." Thoreau's grudge is with his neighbors, rather than the intrinsically innocent devices to which they have heedlessly consigned the best of themselves,

> But it is not the less necessary for this; for the people must have some complicated machinery or other, and hear its din, to satisfy that idea of government which they have.

Once subject, most men cannot grope out of their "complicated machinery"; quiet desperation marks how they themselves have become machines,

> The mass of men serve the state thus, not as men mainly, but as machines, with their bodies. They are the standing army, and the militia, jailors, constables, posse comitatus, etc.

The Fugitive Slave Law is a burden upon men's consciences quite as much as the barns and savings banks of *Walden* are upon the time of men's lives. Men must become active masters of government, not its passive victims. The concept of redemption from passivity in self-directed activity is central to *Walden* too:

> Do not seek so anxiously to be developed, to subject yourself to many influences to be played on; it is all dissipation.

Thoreau seeks internal action in surface passivity. He calls for strenuous husbandry, but in the right vineyard. The unreasoned diligence of the tax-gatherer in **"Civil Disobedience,"** enforcing a law which violates even his own identity, the unthinking servitude of John Field in *Walden,* hammering tea, butter and beef from a barren farm, are the same spendthrift sloth. The central gestures of both works involve consumer resistance—a refusal to buy either protection from prison or material superfluities at the rate which the tax-gatherer and John Field are paying. And like a buyers' strike, Thoreau's is accomplished without external violence. He *permits* the state to imprison him; he shifts noiselessly to Walden Pond on the Fourth of July.

Both abdications *seem* quite personal affairs:

> My purpose in going to Walden Pond was not to live cheaply nor to live dearly there, but to transact some private business with the fewest obstacles.

Non-cooperation in **"Civil Disobedience,"** similarly, seems to owe more to personal ethical fastidiousness than to political zeal,

> It is not a man's duty, as a matter of course, to devote himself to the eradication of any, even the most enormous wrong; he may still properly have other concerns to engage him; but it is his duty, at least, to wash his hands of it, and, if he gives it no thought longer, not to give it practically his support.

But at the same time, Thoreau's consumer resistance is highly *public.* Iconoclastic refusal to buy becomes in both *Walden* and **"Civil Disobedience"** dramatized public self-exile.

We have been suggesting that *Walden* "contains" **"Civil Disobedience"**; of course we do not mean that **"Civil Disobedience"** contains *Walden.* Clearly, the Transcendental vision of the latter work rests partly on Thoreau's passionate apprehension of the life of the senses: man's animality—the submergence of unique identity in sensation—is quite as fundamental as his spiritual individuality. Admittedly the ironies of this dualism are not present in **"Civil Disobedience."** We do mean to suggest, however, that on another level Walden Woods, like Concord jail, is a conscious argumentative device. Intrinsic as Thoreau's representation of nature may be to his total literary achievement, it is accidental to his achievement as a philosophical polemicist. As polemics, the Walden venture becomes not so much a return to *nature* as a return to *premises.*

We have remarked that Thoreau, in going to Walden, is trying to *prove* something, not find something out. Literally, he seeks a warrant in physical nature for exactly the bed-rock self-reliance which is the philosophical basis of **"Civil Disobedience."** Thoreau, that is, goes to the woods for additional confirmation of the victory already symbolized by his night in jail. The lake, the trees, the sky approve his gesture; the rhythms of nature orchestrate Thoreau's studied pirouette, for the instinctive world is a condition of total thrift:

> We should be blessed if we lived in the present always, and took advantage of every accident that befell us, like the grass which confesses the influence of the slightest dew that falls on it; and did not spend our time in atoning for the neglect of past opportunities, which we call doing our duty.

There is no question of primitivism here; nature teaches the social man to cut his expenses within the framework of society,

> Let us spend one day as deliberately as nature, and not be thrown off the track by every nutshell and mosquito's wing that falls on the rails. Let us rise early and fast, or break fast, gently and without perturbation; let company come and let company go, let the bells ring and the children cry—determined to make a day of it.

Nature shows the individual that he must simplify his relationship to social instruments at whatever point these instruments threaten his personal identity. Nature shows the efficacy, in other words, of precisely the simplification of Thoreau's relationship to the state involved in his secession from it:

> The proper place today, the only place which Massachusetts has provided for her freer and less desponding spirits, is in her prisons, to be put out and locked out of the state by her own act, as they have already put themselves out by their principles.

If nature offers an object lesson in simplicity, Thoreau's own attitude toward nature at the Pond offers a similar object lesson. The disciplined hedonism of Thoreau's participation in cosmic thrift forestalls sentimentality in *Walden.* The rapport between man and beasts is terse but friendly. It sometimes leads to such a whimsy of social fraternity as, "I called to see" Mr. Gillian Baker's cat, but "she was gone a-hunting in the woods, as was her wont," or the account of the wayward dogs,

> He did not find his hounds that night, but the next day learned that they had crossed the river and put up at a farmhouse for the night, whence, having been well fed, they took their departure early in the morning.

Thoreau relates himself to other men with quite the same candor and reserve he does to animals. The colloquy with his barnburning jail mate significantly points this lesson of self-reliant thrift in personal relationships back to **"Civil Disobedience,"**

> He naturally wanted to know where I came from, and what had brought me there; and, when I had told him, I asked him in my turn how he came there, presuming him to be an honest man, of course; and, as the world goes, I believe he was.

Freedom, then, in both *Walden* and **"Civil Disobedience"** is a cheerful but inviolable solitude: "A man thinking or working is always alone, let him be where he will."

Such solitude is the sole basis of true sympathy between men. Thoreau's gregarious exile, therefore, is anti-social but not misanthropic. Lowell calls him a Stylite, and Thoreau's writings confess him exactly that: his cabin once housed thirty visitors. But if a moral of *Walden* is that hermitages do not make hermits, a moral of **"Civil Disobedience"** is just as surely that prisons do not make prisoners. Indeed, the prison cell in **"Civil Disobedience"** seems not the cell of a convict but of a hermit,

> The rooms were whitewashed once a month; and this one, at least, was the whitest, most simply furnished, and probably the neatest apartment in the town.

Yet like the cabin at Walden which it resembles, its austerity is deceptive. The Concord cell houses a recluse no more than the one in the woods, nor is its occupant less free. Society is a prison, for men, failing to simplify, are harshly shut from each other,

> I saw that, if there was a wall of stone between me and my townsmen, there was a still more difficult one to climb or break through before they could get to be as free as I was. I did not for a moment feel confined, and the walls seemed a great waste of stone and mortar. I felt as if I alone of all my townsmen had paid my tax.

Walden, like **"Civil Disobedience,"** declares the true nature of these barriers between men:

What sort of space is that which separates a man from his fellows and makes him solitary? I have found that no exertion of the legs can bring two minds much nearer to one another.

In a sense, then, Walden Pond and the Concord jail are the same place. Thrift has many guises; it is just as *natural* in a prison as in a wilderness,

Sell your clothes and keep your thoughts. God will see that you do not want society. If I were confined to a corner of a garret all my days, like a spider, the world would be just as large to me while I had my thoughts about me.

Anywhere will do for exploration of the self. Though thrift is the necessary concommitant of this exploration, place is irrelevant. It is not a journey in space, but a venture to the interior.

The Transcendentalist image of mental voyage thus figures prominently in both *Walden* and **"Civil Disobedience."** Thoreau's high celebration in *Walden* of this psychic adventure is well known:

What was the meaning of that South-Sea Exploring Expedition, with all its parade and expense, but an indirect recognition of the fact that there are continents and seas in the moral world to which every man is an isthmus or an inlet. . . .

Less well known is the fact that **"Civil Disobedience"** also celebrates such an adventure:

It was like traveling into a far country, such as I had never expected to behold, to lie there for one night. It seemed to me that I never had heard the town-clock strike before, nor the evening sounds of the village.

The perplexed townsmen who meet Thoreau after his release, having never traveled, are quite lost, dimly suspecting that the prisoner has somehow retrieved a prize from a distant place which, for all their "liberty," they were incomprehensibly denied:

My neighbors did not thus salute me, but first looked at me, and then at one another, as if I had returned from a long journey.

Thoreau wants external simplification, then, so that he can thrust into this deeper complexity of voyage. The alternative is simplification of *oneself,* being oneself a mere instrument; being, like the tax-gatherer, like John Field, a ship perpetually in drydock.

Walden encompasses **"Civil Disobedience."** There is nothing "in" the latter that is not in the former (indeed, much of the prison episode is bodily incorporated into *Walden*), though a great deal of *Walden* is not in the earlier essay. If either is "political" at all, *Walden* seems as much a political application of principles in **"Civil Disobedience"** as the other way around.

There is significant community between the two works for, despite incongruities and vagaries, Thoreau was all of a piece. What Joseph Wood Krutch in his *Thoreau* describes as "the balance and wholeness which Thoreau seems to achieve," is reflected in the unity of **"Civil Disobedience"** and *Walden.* There is a wholesome inevitability in the fact that by the time he stepped out of its jail, Thoreau, who traveled much in Concord, had gone a good part of the distance to *Walden.* (pp. 297-304)

Don W. Kleine, " 'Civil Disobedience': The Way to 'Walden'," in *Modern Language Notes,* Vol. LXXV, No. 4, April, 1960, pp. 297-304.

LEON EDEL
(essay date 1970)

[Edel is an American biographer and critic. In the following excerpt, he asserts that *Walden* offers an idealized version of the life its author lived on Walden Pond.]

Of the creative spirits that flourished in Concord, Massachusetts, during the middle of the nineteenth century, it might be said that Hawthorne loved men but felt estranged from them, Emerson loved ideas even more than men, and Thoreau loved himself. Less of an artist than Hawthorne, less of a thinker than Emerson, Thoreau made of his life a sylvan legend, that of man alone, in communion with nature. He was a strange presence in American letters—we have so few of them—an eccentric. The English tend to tolerate their eccentrics to the enrichment of their national life. In America, where democracy and conformity are often confused, the nonconforming Thoreau was frowned upon, and for good reason. He had a disagreeable and often bellicose nature. He lacked geniality. And then he had once set fire to the Concord woods—a curious episode, too lightly dismissed in the Thoreau biographies. He was, in the fullest sense of the word, a "curmudgeon," and literary history has never sufficiently studied the difficulties his neighbors had in adjusting themselves to certain of his childish ways. But in other ways he was a man of genius—even if it was a "crooked genius" as he himself acknowledged. (p. 5)

All of Thoreau's writings represent a continuous and carefully documented projection of the self. *Walden* announces itself autobiography—"I should not talk so much about myself if there were anybody else whom I knew as well." The book is an idealized and romantic account of Thoreau's sojourn in the woods. Even its beautiful digressions are a series of masks. In both of his works, *Walden* and *A Week on the Concord and Merrimack Rivers,* as in his miscellaneous essays, we find an ideal self rather than the Thoreau Concord knew. The artist in Thoreau improved on nature in the interest of defending himself against some of nature's more painful truths. (p. 6)

There is in all of Thoreau's writings an enforced calm; strange tensions run below the surface, deep obsessions. He is so preoccupied with self-assertion as to suggest that this was a profound necessity rather than an experience of serenity.

His struggle for identity gave him great powers of concentration and diligence. He was not a born writer, but he taught himself by imitation to carpenter solid verbal structures and give them rhythm and proportion. He went to school to Emerson, to Carlyle, to the Greeks, to the philosophers of India. He was first and foremost a reader of books—and only after them of nature. He read like a bee clinging to a flower, for all that he could extract from the printed page. He wrote poems, many of them banal; yet he poured a great deal of poetry into the more relaxed passages of his prose. This prose is seldom spontaneous; behind its emulation of the measure and moderation of the ancients one feels strain and subterranean violence. (pp. 8-9)

Walden is not a document, nor even the record of a calculated experiment. It is a work of art pretending to be a documentary. Thoreau talked as if he lived in the wilderness but he lived in the suburbs. He furnished his home with pieces retrieved from Concord attics. We have seen that he plastered and shingled the cabin when cold weather came. We know that he took his shoes to the Concord cobbler; that he baked bread using purchased rye and Indian meal; that he slept not in rough blankets but between sheets. He gave himself the creature comforts few Americans in the log cabins of the West could enjoy. . . . But the author of *Walden* discovered that his whim of living in the woods caught the fancy of audiences. Men and women were willing to listen to the fiction of his rude economy as if he were Robinson Crusoe [from the novel *Robinson Crusoe* by Daniel Defoe]. It is perhaps to Daniel Defoe that we may turn for a significant literary predecessor. The writer who had pretended he was keeping a journal of the plague year in London, long after the plague, who could invent a story of a man confronting the loneliness of life on a desert island, may be regarded as the forefather of Thoreau's book. The narrative of *Walden* is a composite of Thoreau's experiences in and around Concord. The little facts are so assembled as to constitute a lively fable. Thoreau blended his wide reading and his purposeful observations to the need of a thesis: and in his mind he had proved his "experiment" long before he began it. In the process of ordering, assembling, imagining, and interpreting, the artist often took possession of his data in a robust, humorous, whimsical, paradoxical, hammered style.

Walden has moments of exquisite beauty when the disciplined verbal power finds a tone and a mood expressing Thoreau's deepest artistry. . . . (pp. 29-30)

So too Thoreau can endow his narrative with the cadence of a child's storybook. . . . (p. 30)

Walden belongs with the literature of imaginary voyages which yet possess, within the imagined, a great reality of their own. It contains a rustic charm, a tender lyricism in the pages devoted to the seasons and to animal life around the pond and in the neighboring woods. (p. 31)

He is at his most imaginative—that is, his ear is perhaps truest to poetry—in the playful chapter in which he tells of his "brute neighbors" beginning with a sylvan dialogue between a Hermit and a Poet. One feels in the writing of these pages echoes of the playfulness of Carlyle; but in terms of posthumous influence this passage may have importance in its striking resemblance to the recurrent rhythms of James Joyce's *Finnegans Wake*. It was inevitable that Joyce, early in his "Anna Livia Plurabelle" section, should pun on "Concord and the Merrimake," for that chapter is compounded of river names and water imagery and associations. Thoreau's "Was that a farmer's noon horn which sounded from beyond the woods just now?" and Joyce's "Is that the Poolbeg flasher beyant, pharphar, or a fireboat coasting nyar the Kishna?" seem to have common stylistic origins and the entire Thoreauvian passage finds strong echoes—in an Irish accent—in passages in *Finnegans Wake*. Thoreau writes: "Hark! I hear a rustling of the leaves. Is it some ill-fed village hound yielding to the instinct of the chase? or the lost pig which is said to be in these woods, whose tracks I saw after the rain? It comes on apace; my sumachs and sweetbriers tremble." This has a singular rhythmic charm and one can find its parallel in Joyce. Did Thoreau and Joyce (who had much in common in their alienated temperaments) derive the rhythms and cadences from some common source? or did the Irish writer, in his exploration of rivers and water music, latch onto the peculiar Thoreauvian trouvaille of this chapter. In the strange world of letters in which songs sung in one country become new songs in another, the words of Thoreau by the Concord River have a powerful kinship with those of Joyce by the Liffey. (p. 33)

"Civil Disobedience" is an unusually cogent statement for Thoreau, who was a man of sentiment rather than of profound thought and who tended often to contradict himself. It remains a remarkable statement on behalf of individualism, as well as man's right to oppose and dissent. In the frame of Thoreau's life, however, it reveals the arbitrary nature of his philosophy. His defense of John Brown, with his espousal of violence in that instance, is hardly the voice of the same man. In both lectures, to be sure, Thoreau condemns government; but the preacher of nonviolence suddenly forgets his preachings. Brown had been wantonly destructive; he had staged a brutal massacre in Kansas and killed innocents. He was a man whose fanaticism might have made him in other circumstances a brutal Inquisitor. Thoreau's involvement in his cause has in it strong elements of hysteria. The passive countenance closes its eyes to truth; it sees only Brown's cause and Brown's hatred of authority. It does not see his cruelty or his counter-imposition of authority. The world has wisely chosen to remember **"Civil Disobedience"** rather than the three John Brown lectures—**"A Plea for Captain Brown," "The Last Days of John Brown,"** and **"After the Death of John Brown."** Whether the personal anarchism Thoreau preached is possible in every age remains to be seen. In his philosophy Thoreau saw only his own dissent; he seems not to have thought of the dangers of tyranny by a minority, as of a majority. (pp. 38-9)

[Thoreau's] journal was the mirror of his days; but it is not an autobiographical record in the usual sense. It is one of the more impersonal journals of literary history. Thoreau made it the account book of his days. There are notes on his readings, his observations of nature, his record of walks, scraps of talk, observations of neighbors; on occasion the journal becomes a log, a statistical record. . . . One finds in it much matter-of-factness and little feeling. "The poet must keep himself unstained and aloof," said Thoreau and his journal is distinctly "aloof." One discerns in it a continuing note of melancholy; there is little humor; the vein is always one of high seriousness. Mankind is regarded in the mass; the generalizations are large; there is not much leaning toward the precisions of science. Nor can one find any record of growth in these pages, some of them turgid and dull, others lucid and fascinating. From 1837 to 1861 we see the same man writing; he has learned little. If one notes a difference it is that he begins by being philosophical and in the end is more committed to observation.

The journal suggests that Thoreau was incapable of a large effort as a writer. He learned to be a master of the short, the familiar essay; he made it lively and humanized it with his whimsicalities. The method of the journal was carried over into his principal works, the journal providing the raw data, filed always for later use. . . . The assiduity with which he applied himself to his writing ultimately bore fruit. If Thoreau never forged a style and filled his work with the echoes of other styles, he nevertheless in the end learned his trade. Possessing no marked ego at the beginning of his adult life, he created a composite ego; and he learned to write by using a series of rhetorical tricks. (pp. 39-40)

Men will continue to discover these strange ambiguities in the author of *Walden*. If we are to dress a literary portrait of him, we must place him among those writers in whom the human will is organized to a fine pitch in the interest of mental and emotional survival. We must rank him with the "disinherited" and the alienated, with the writers who find themselves possessed of unconquerable demons and who then harness them in the service of self-preservation. Out of this quest sometimes mere eccentricity emerges; at other times art. There are distinct pathological traits in Thoreau, a constant sense—a few have discerned it—of inner disintegration which leads Thoreau in his *Walden* imagery to a terrible vision of human decay. One may venture a guess that this little observed Poesque streak in Thoreau testified to a crisis of identity so fundamental that Thoreau rescued himself only by an almost superhuman self-organization to keep himself, as it were, from falling apart. In doing this he clung obsessively to nature. A much deeper history of Thoreau's psyche may have to be written to explain his tenuous hold on existence in spite of the vigor of his outdoor life: his own quiet desperation, his endless need to keep a journal ("as if he had no moment to waste," said his friend Channing), and his early death of tuberculosis at forty-five in Concord during the spring of 1862. His works were the anchor of his days. He overcame dissolution during his abbreviated life by a constant struggle to assert himself in words. Some such strivings shaped his own recognition of his "crooked genius." (pp. 42-3)

Leon Edel, in his *Henry D. Thoreau*, University of Minnesota Press, Minneapolis, 1970, 47 p.

SOURCES FOR FURTHER STUDY

Canby, Henry Seidel. *Thoreau*. Boston: Houghton Mifflin Co., 1939, 508 p.

One of the first important critical biographies of Thoreau. Canby stresses Thoreau's importance as a creative thinker, social critic, and stylist. He also suggests, however, that Thoreau "was too maladjusted psychologically" to reach his full potential in any one area.

Cavell, Stanley. *The Senses of "Walden."* 1972. Reprint. San Francisco: North Point Press, 1981, 160 p.

An exploration of the philosophical bases of *Walden*. Cavell views Thoreau as a writer who wished to fulfill his prophetic calling, yet also felt the need to guard his words from his culture's "demented wish to damage and deny them."

Glick, Wendell, ed. *The Recognition of Henry David Thoreau: Selected Criticism Since 1848.* Ann Arbor: The University of Michigan Press, 1969, 381 p.

A collection of key critical essays on Thoreau's works, dating from 1848 to the late 1960s, that includes essays by James Russell Lowell, Robert Louis Stevenson, Mark Van Doren, Raymond Adams, and others.

Harding, Walter, and Meyer, Michael. *The New Thoreau Handbook.* New York: New York University Press, 1980, 238 p.

An overview of Thoreau's life and works. The authors include sections on Thoreau's sources, ideas, art, and reputation.

Porte, Joel. *Emerson and Thoreau: Transcendentalists in Conflict.* Middletown, Conn.: Wesleyan University Press, 1966, 226 p.

Explores the relationship between Emerson and Thoreau in terms of their attitudes toward nature, aesthetics, morality, and Transcendentalism. Porte concludes that for Thoreau "only the body exists," while for Emerson "only spirit exists."

Wolf, William J. *Thoreau: Mystic, Prophet, Ecologist.* Philadelphia: United Church Press, 1974, 218 p.

An interpretation of Thoreau's various guises in his writings. Wolf terms him "the theologian of creation, the apostle of wildness, and the prophet of social action."

J. R. R. Tolkien

1892-1973

(Full name John Ronald Reuel Tolkien) South African-born English novelist, essayist, short story writer, poet, translator, and editor.

INTRODUCTION

A leading philologist of his day, Tolkien was an Oxford University professor who, along with Oxford colleagues C. S. Lewis and Charles Williams, helped revive popular interest in the medieval romance and the fantastic tale. Tolkien is best known for his epic fantasy/romance trilogy of novels, *The Lord of the Rings* (1954-55). *The Lord of the Rings,* which is set in an enchanted world called Middle-earth, tells of a timeless struggle between the forces of good and evil, embodied in such magical beings as wizards, dwarves, elves, treelike beings called *ents,* orcs (goblins), trolls, and hobbits—the small, furry-footed creatures with human qualities that Tolkien introduced in the trilogy's prequel, *The Hobbit; or, There and Back Again* (1937). Beneath the charming, adventurous surface story of Middle-earth lies a sense of quiet anguish for a vanishing past and a precarious future. Tolkien gained a reputation during the 1960s and 1970s as a cult figure among youths disillusioned with war and the technological age; his continuing popularity evidences his ability to evoke the oppressive realities of modern life while drawing audiences into a fantasy world. Many critics claim that the success of Tolkien's trilogy has made possible the contemporary revival of "sword and sorcery" literature.

Tolkien was born the son of English-born parents in Bloemfontein, in the Orange Free State of South Africa, where his father worked as a bank manager. To escape the heat and dust of southern Africa and to better guard the delicate health of Ronald (as he was called), Tolkien's mother moved back to England with him and his younger brother when they were very young boys. Within a year of this move their father, Arthur Tolkien, died in Bloemfontein, and a few years later the boys' mother died as well. The boys lodged at several homes from 1905 until 1911, when Ronald entered Exeter College, Oxford. Tolkien received his B.A. from Oxford in 1915 and an M.A. in 1919. During the interim he married his longtime sweetheart, Edith Bratt, and served for a short time on the Western Front with the Lancashire Fusiliers. While in England recovering from "trench fever" in 1917, Tolkien began writing "The Book of Lost Tales," which eventually became *The Silmarillion* (1977) and laid the groundwork for his stories about Middle-earth. After the Armistice he returned to Oxford, where he joined the staff of the *Oxford English Dictionary* and began work as a freelance tutor. In 1920 he was appointed Reader in English Language at Leeds University, where he collaborated with E. V. Gordon on an acclaimed translation of *Sir Gawain and the Green Knight,* which was completed and published in 1925. (Some years later, Tolkien completed a second translation of this poem, which was published posthumously.) The following year, having returned to Oxford as Rawlinson and Bosworth Professor of Anglo-Saxon, Tolkien became friends with a fellow of Magdalen College, C. S. Lewis. They shared an intense enthusiasm for the myths, sagas, and languages of northern Europe; and to better enhance those interests, both attended meetings of "The Coalbiters," an Oxford club, founded by Tolkien, at which Icelandic sagas were read aloud.

During the rest of his years at Oxford—twenty as Rawlinson and Bosworth Professor of Anglo-Saxon, fourteen as Merton Professor of English Language and Literature—Tolkien published several esteemed short studies and translations. Notable among these are his essays "*Beowulf:* The Monsters and the Critics" (1936), "Chaucer as a Philologist: *The Reeve's Tale*" (1934), and "On Fairy-Stories" (1947); his scholarly edition of *Ancrene Wisse* (1962); and his translations of three medieval poems: "*Sir Gawain and the Green Knight,*" "*Pearl,*" and "*Sir Orfeo*" (1975). As a writer of imaginative literature, though, Tolkien is best known for *The Hobbit* and *The Lord of the Rings,* tales which were formed during his years attending meetings of "The Inklings," an informal gathering of like-minded friends and fellow dons, initiated after the demise of The Coalbiters. The Inklings, which was formed during the late 1930s and lasted until the late 1940s, was a weekly meeting held in Lewis's sitting-room at Magdalen, at which works-in-progress were read aloud and discussed and critiqued by the attendees, all interspersed with free-flowing conversation about literature and other topics. The nucleus of the group was Tolkien, Lewis, and Lewis's friend, novelist Charles Williams; other participants, who attended irregularly, included Lewis's brother Warren, Nevill Coghill, H. V. D. Dyson, Owen Barfield, and others. The common thread which bound them was that they were all adherents of Christianity and all had a love of story. Having heard Tolkien's first hobbit story read aloud at a meeting of

the Inklings, Lewis urged Tolkien to publish *The Hobbit,* which appeared in 1937. A major portion of *The Fellowship of the Ring* was also read to The Inklings before the group disbanded in the late 1940's.

Tolkien retired from his professorship in 1959. While the unauthorized publication of an American edition of *The Lord of the Rings* in 1965 angered him, it also made him a widely admired cult figure in the United States, especially among high school and college students. Uncomfortable with this status, he and his wife lived quietly in Bournemouth for several years, until Edith's death in 1971. In the remaining two years of his life, Tolkien returned to Oxford, where he was made an honorary fellow of Merton College and awarded a doctorate of letters. He was at the height of his fame as a scholarly and imaginative writer when he died in 1973, though critical study of his fiction continues and has increased in the years since.

A devout Roman Catholic throughout his life, Tolkien began creating his own languages and mythologies at an early age and later wrote Christian-inspired stories and poems to provide them with a narrative framework. Based on bedtime stories Tolkien had created for his children, *The Hobbit* concerns the reluctant efforts of a hobbit, Bilbo Baggins, to recover a treasure stolen by a dragon. During the course of his mission, the hobbit discovers a magical ring which, among other powers, can render its bearer invisible. The ability to disappear helps Bilbo fulfill his quest; however, the ring's less obvious faculties prompt the malevolent Sauron, Dark Lord of Mordor, to seek it. The hobbits' attempt to destroy the ring, thereby denying Sauron unlimited power, is the focal point of the *Lord of the Rings* trilogy, which consists of the novels *The Fellowship of the Ring* (1954), *The Two Towers* (1954), and *The Return of the King* (1955). In these books Tolkien rejects such traditional heroic attributes as strength and size, stressing instead the capacity of even the humblest creatures to prevail against evil.

The initial critical reception to *The Lord of the Rings* varied. While some reviewers expressed dissatisfaction with the story's great length and one-dimensional characters, the majority enjoyed Tolkien's enchanting descriptions and lively sense of adventure. Religious, Freudian, allegorical, and political interpretations of the trilogy soon appeared, but Tolkien generally rejected such explications. He maintained that *The Lord of the Rings* was conceived with "no allegorical intentions . . . , moral, religious, or political," but he also denied that the trilogy is a work of escapism: "Middle-earth is not an imaginary world. . . . The theatre of my tale is this earth, the one in which we now live." Tolkien contended that his story was "*fundamentally linguistic* in inspiration," a "religious and Catholic work" whose spiritual aspects were "absorbed into the story and symbolism." Tolkien concluded, "The stories were made . . . to provide a world for the languages rather than the reverse."

Throughout his career Tolkien composed histories, genealogies, maps, glossaries, poems, and songs to supplement his vision of Middle-earth. Among the many works published during his lifetime were a volume of poems, *The Adventures of Tom Bombadil and Other Verses from the Red Book* (1962), and a fantasy novel, *Smith of Wootton Major* (1967). Though many of his stories about Middle-earth remained incomplete at the time of Tolkien's death, his son, Christopher, rescued the manuscripts from his father's collections, edited them, and published them. One of these works, *The Silmarillion*, takes place before the time of *The Hobbit* and, in a heroic manner which recalls the Christian myths of Creation and the Fall, tells the tale of the first age of Holy Ones and their offspring. *Unfinished Tales of Numenor and Middle-earth* (1980) is a similar collection of incomplete stories and fragments written during World War I. *The Book of Lost Tales, Part I* (1984) and *The Book of Lost Tales, Part II* (1984) deal respectively with the beginnings of Middle-earth and the point at which humans enter the saga. In addition to these posthumous works, Christopher Tolkien also collected his father's correspondence to friends, family, and colleagues in *The Letters of J. R. R. Tolkien* (1981).

It is as a writer of timeless fantasy that Tolkien is most highly regarded today. From 1914 until his death in 1973, he drew on his familiarity with Northern and other ancient literatures and his own invented languages to create not just his own story, but his own world: Middle-earth, complete with its own history, myths, legends, epics, and heroes. "His life's work," Augustus M. Kolich has written, ". . . encompasses a reality that rivals Western man's own attempt at recording the composite, knowable history of his species. Not since Milton has any Englishman worked so successfully at creating a secondary world, derived from our own, yet complete in its own terms with encyclopedic mythology; an imagined world that includes a vast gallery of strange beings: hobbits, elves, dwarfs, orcs, and, finally, the men of Westernesse." His works—especially *The Lord of the Rings*—have pleased countless readers and fascinated critics who recognize their literary depth.

(For further information about Tolkien's life and works, see *Contemporary Authors*, Vols. 17-18; *Contemporary Authors Permanent Series*, Vol. 2; *Contemporary Literary Criticism*, Vols. 1, 2, 3, 8, 12, 38; *Dictionary of Literary Biography*, Vol. 15: *British Novelists, 1930-1959*; and *Something about the Author*, Vols. 2, 24, 32.)

CRITICAL COMMENTARY

CATHARINE R. STIMPSON

(essay date 1969)

[In the following excerpt, Stimpson discusses the moral code of Tolkien's works, criticizing the author's unambiguous portrayal of good and evil.]

Generously Tolkien wishes to preserve old myths and literary forms, magic swords and battle cries, for the hapless present. A kindly man, he also makes himself accessible to anyone without real knowledge of his sources and allusions. Ironically, many may safely wander through Tolkien in blissful, sleepy ignorance of all he so conscientiously is trying to transmit. It is also unfortunate for Tolkien that wonderful, but outworn, sources fail to ensure excellence. A writer's energy alone forges borrowed elements together to make his work transcend. James Joyce had such energy. Tolkien, despite erratic originality and perpetual persistence, does not. As a result, his earnest vision seems syncretic, his structure a collage, and his feeling antiquarian. Properly he praises the mythical mode of the

imagination: the ability to feel the prophetic meaning of material, including the supernatural. Yet Tolkien's exercise of the imagination has brought forth a hollow, inscribed monument, with many, many echoes. (p. 9)

Many find Tolkien's moral vision serious and impeccable. Surely men ought to be both courageous and charitable. Surely men ought not to be haughty and selfish. Of course, the good is creative. Of course, evil is corroding, then corrupting, and finally canceling. However, Tolkien seems rigid. He admits that men, elves, and dwarfs are a collection of good, bad, and indifferent beings, but he more consistently divides the ambiguous world into two unambiguous halves: good and evil, nice and nasty. Any writer has the right to dramatize, not to argue, his morality. However, Tolkien's dialogue, plot, and symbols are terribly simplistic. . . . Readily explicable, they also seem to conceal intellectual fuzziness and opaque axioms. Moreover, Tolkien gives way to a lust for miracles. Wizards, weapons, and thaumaturges, leaping in and out of the action at Tolkien's will, are as sophisticated as last-

Principal Works

A Middle English Vocabulary (glossary) 1922

Sir Gawain and the Green Knight [translator, with E. V. Gordon] (poetry) 1925

"Chaucer as a Philologist: The Reeve's Tale" (criticism) 1934; published in journal Transactions of the Philological Society

*"Beowulf: The Monsters and the Critics" (essay) 1936; published in journal Proceedings of the British Academy

The Hobbit; or, There and Back Again (novel) 1937

†"Leaf by Niggle" (short story) 1945; published in journal The Dublin Review

†"On Fairy-Stories" (essay) 1947; published in Essays Presented to Charles Williams

Farmer Giles of Ham (short story) 1949

‡The Fellowship of the Ring: Being the First Part of The Lord of the Rings (novel) 1954

‡The Two Towers: Being the Second Part of The Lord of the Rings (novel) 1954

‡The Return of the King: Being the Third Part of The Lord of the Rings (novel) 1955

The Adventures of Tom Bombadil and Other Verses from the Red Book (poetry) 1962

Tree and Leaf (short story and essay) 1964

The Road Goes Ever On: A Song Cycle (lyrics) 1967 [music composed by David Swann]

Smith of Wootton Major (novel) 1967

"Sir Gawain and the Green Knight," "Pearl," and "Sir Orfeo" [translator] (poetry) 1975

The Father Christmas Letters (novel) 1976

The Silmarillion (novel) 1977

Unfinished Tales of Numenor and Middle-earth (short stories) 1980

The Letters of J. R. R. Tolkien (letters) 1981

The Monsters and the Critics and Other Essays (essays) 1983

*This work was reprinted separately in 1958, and was later published in Tolkien's The Monsters and the Critics and Other Essays, 1983

†These works were collected and published in Tolkien's Tree and Leaf, 1964.

‡These three novels are known collectively as The Lord of the Rings.

---

minute cavalry charges in the more old-fashioned Westerns. (p. 18)

Tolkien generally ignores the rich medieval theme of the conflict between love and duty. Nor is it startling that the most delicate and tender feelings in Tolkien's writing exist between men, the members of holy fellowships and companies. Fathers and sons, or their surrogate figures, also receive attentive notice. When Tolkien does sidle up to genuine romantic love, sensuality, or sexuality, his style becomes coy and infantile, or else it burgeons into a mass of irrelevant, surface, descriptive detail. (pp. 19-20)

To give Tolkien the credit he deserves, his work is still incomplete. He has not yet published *The Silmarillion,* begun even before *The Hobbit.* . . . Perhaps *The Silmarillion* will strengthen Tolkien's moral vision and sense of emotional realities. (p. 20)

He writes, not for children, but for adults. He concentrates, not on character, but on narrative. (Tolkien never regrets his thin, neo-Aristotelian sacrifice of person to action. His own fiction, of course, suffers accordingly.) (pp. 22-3)

Tolkien vows that the purpose of his Perilous Realm is to amuse, to delight, to evoke emotion. Both he and his friends vow that he despises simple allegory, in which characters and plot signify one thing other than themselves. Bluntly, *The Lord of the Rings* is not

about the hydrogen bomb. Tolkien sets his readers free to find what they want and to take him as seriously as they need. Yet even genuine mythologies, which have the shape of art and the endless resonance of truth, embody themes. Tolkien's pastiche, wittingly or unwittingly, also makes explicit statements. Condemning selfishness and greed, it praises sacrifice and generosity. Ridiculing complacency, it magnifies sensitivity. Fearing evil, it exalts good. Most obviously, Tolkien, eloquently, rightly, lambasts power. . . . Yet his attack is oddly flawed. Both more and less than a symbol, the ring itself becomes a transferable band of active ill will. Tolkien's prose takes on a rollicking glee when the home team wins, surely an exercise of power. (p. 29)

In form and content [Tolkien's poetry] combines the lesser virtues of an Old Father Goose and a pale and chaste Algernon Charles Swinburne. Usually narratives, the poems are about courage and cowardice, friendship and isolation, conflict of obligations, and the supernatural and the natural. . . . The manipulation of the hackneyed symbols of cloud, mountain, tree, and star; plastic religiosity; and wistful romanticism are its most notable features. (p. 41)

Tolkien is bogus: bogus, prolix, and sentimental. His popularization of the past is a comic strip for grownups. *The Lord of the Rings* is almost as colorful and easy as *Captain Marvel.* That easiness is perhaps the source of Tolkien's appeal. His intellectual, emotional, and imaginative energies are timid and jejune. Yet to those who have puzzled over the ambiguous texts of twentieth-century literature in the classroom, he offers a digest of modern despair: *The Waste Land,* with notes, without tears. To those who pride themselves on cynicism, an adolescent failure, he spews forth a reductive, yet redemptive, allegory of the human urge to fail. For those who actually long for security, he previews a solid moral and emotional structure. His authoritarianism is small price for the comfort of the commands: Love thy Aragorn; fear the Nâzgul. . . . (p. 43)

Oddly, though Tolkien, Hermann Hesse, and William Golding are three very different writers, they have two suggestive common denominators. First, they caused student literary fads, which the adult world then acclaimed. Next, they offered the seductive charm of moral didacticism, cloaked in remote and exotic settings. (p. 44)

Tolkien ought to be what he wants to be. His audience is free to be what it wants to be. Yet readers might cultivate some critical awareness. If they do, they might find, not only midnight rides and unfurled banners, but weak prose and pernicious thought. They might begin by asking just one simple question. What does it mean that Tolkien so blandly, so complacently, so consistently, uses the symbol of light and of white to signify the good and the symbol of dark and of black to signify evil? He is, of course, following an enormously complex literary tradition. No arbitrary decision, but the physical heritage of Northern and Western Europe has shaped that tradition. . . . Like all alchemists, he appeals to us. His very ambition is attractive. Like all alchemists, he has his deceptive triumphs. But history has made alchemy remote. Science has fulfilled its more marvelous predictions. One might wish that history will make much of Tolkien remote. We need genuine myth and rich fantasy to minister to the profound needs he now is thought to gratify. (pp. 44-5)

Catharine R. Stimpson, in her *J. R. R. Tolkien,* Columbia University Press, 1969, 48 p.

GERALD MONSMAN

(essay date 1970)

[In the essay excerpted below, Monsman relates Tolkien's works to the Christian humanist tradition.]

J. R. R. Tolkien seems to [want] to make his art serve the cause of religion. . . . Forty years [after the *fin de siecle* decadents in England,] the tide had turned sufficiently for a group of new Christian humanists to emerge. Among scholars, the poets Eliot and Auden are possibly the best known of this group, though the reputations of C. S. Lewis, Charles Williams, and J. R. R. Tolkien are rising. Not until the latter part of the 1950's and the early 1960's did Tolkien's reputation as a creative writer (as distinct from that as an Anglo-Saxon scholar) become established. Yet it was in the latter part of the 1930's that his imaginative world and aesthetic theories took shape, just when the excitement of the new movement was running strongest. Tolkien's ideas are generally unfamiliar to scholars, but for the generation that has grown up on Eliot and Auden, a plunge into Tolkien is akin to the happy shock of recognition that would come if one found a new manuscript by a much loved and familiar author—the same ideas, but seen from a wholly fresh perspective. (p. 264)

Tolkien tells us that even as a child he had an almost compulsive desire to recreate Norse and Greek myths in his own words. Later his serious scholarly work convinced him that many of these legends were sketchy, had gaps, and (as in the poem of *Beowulf*) were weak in details though strong in structure. So Tolkien set out to improve on mythology by making it "credible." His name for his imaginary world of Middle-earth is, as he explained, "only an old-fashioned word for world," it being the *middangeard* of Anglo-Saxon myths. Tolkien has populated Middle-earth with men, hobbits, elves, trolls, Orcs, dwarves, Ents, and spirits drawn from European folklore, medieval literature, and his own imagination. (p. 265)

In Tolkien's imaginative world, all nature is animate, helping or hindering human (or nonhuman) will for good or ill. Eagles and birds can talk, forests crowd travelers with fell intent. . . . Only where evil dwells—in the dragon's mountain or in Mordor—is nature sterile, for evil is in its very being noncreative. Utilizing in *The Hobbit* a variation of the fisher-king legend, Tolkien describes the land of the King Under the Mountain as having a curse upon it—the dragon. Or to be more specific, the curse on the land is actually the "dragon sickness," the immoderate greed for material property. . . . As in T. S. Eliot's "Wasteland," so here in *The Hobbit* we have a story about the lifting of the curse from a stricken land and the new life which enters in. (pp. 268-69)

One might be tempted to say that because Tolkien's use of symbols is so complex he, like Joyce, is a Symbolist, his aim being to produce an epiphany through concentrated meditation on symbols which do not symbolize any exact thing, but rather are meant to produce such moments of insight. There is a similarity: the question of just precisely what Tolkien's ring symbolizes, for example, will always elude simple definition; indeed, to ask such a question at all betrays a certain naïveté. (pp. 271-72)

But Tolkien's Introduction, although warning us

against allegory, also puts us on our guard against seeing *The Lord of the Rings* as a Symbolist work. His emphasis upon "history, true or feigned," together with his insistence in *Beowulf* that myth must be incarnated in history, points towards an emphasis upon the temporal process which is alien to the thought of Symbolism. (p. 272)

Tolkien's affirmation of primary reality came at a crucial moment in the history of British culture. The industrial cities of Birmingham and Sheffield, which in the nineteenth century turned not only the face but also the soul of England black, gave way in the twentieth to a World War which completed the desacralization and fragmentation of natural and spiritual reality. The way of aestheticists and Symbolists was to flee to the subjectivity of a vision of beauty alien to this cultural wasteland. Unlike them, however, Tolkien, in company with the Christian humanists of his generation, chose to affirm the images of this world, seeing the rich thicket of nature as a potent reality in itself. As a Christian he could do little else, for the Incarnation had redeemed the temporal process, bestowing value on even the humblest objects. But although the original curse on the wasteland has already been lifted, the healing of the schism between fact and fantasy has not yet been wholly worked out in time. The quest, the web of story, will go on until all histories, true and feigned, will exist as an eternally complete whole. (p. 278)

Gerald Monsman, "The Imaginative World of J. R. R. Tolkien," in *South Atlantic Quarterly*, Vol. LXIX, No. 2, Spring, 1970, pp. 264-78.

GUNNAR URANG

(essay date 1971)

[Below, Urang discusses *The Lord of the Rings*, focusing on elements of myth, legend, history, and the Christian tradition.]

For J. R. R. Tolkien, fantasy is the art of creating an "other world." It is an "elvish craft," and the "secondary world" thus produced is a realm of enchantment. As a multitude of readers can now testify, to enter the "other world" called Middle-earth is to encounter both the strange and the familiar and, emanating from them, an extraordinary power.

To one reading *The Lord of the Rings* for the first time, that power may be felt simply as a *sense* of depths, of rich implications. But depth and richness, considered analytically, become levels or dimensions. . . . On reading Tolkien's work we find ourselves first in a dimension of *wonder,* the effect of authentic fantasy. On further reading we sense also a dimension of *import* or meaningfulness, the allegorical thrust of the fantasy. Finally, we may discover a dimension of incipient *belief,* a function of the "rhetoric" of this fiction, of what I have dared to call its "strategy." (p. 93)

In such a fairy-tale world [as Tolkien has created], actions beyond "nature" are taken for granted. The possibility of such supernatural action is conceived of because of the form of our active existence. We are aware of ourselves as active beings in interaction with an environment of other agents. We can vary the form or intensity of our activities; in other words, within our nature we are free. But that sense of freedom leads us to dream of passing through to supernatural deeds. When we attribute such action to trees and mountains and to more-than-human creatures, we have created the realm of faërie. (p. 95)

What lifts [*The Lord of the Rings*] above mere popular fantasy fiction, what elicits a response beyond simple excitement and closer to authentic wonder, is a certain tone and a certain aura of significance which are felt to surround the fantastic figures and their adventures. Professor Frye and his disciples have taught us to account for much of this sense of import by identifying such figures as archetypal and such stories as mythic. And it is clear that Tolkien does draw his material from sources close to their roots in ritual and myth.

One notices, for example, that many of the names for the Dwarves are taken from the *Eddas*. Tolkien's conception of the Elves, furthermore, is obviously close to that of the northern myths and legends; his are the Elves of Light, exceedingly fair, lovers of light, kindly disposed toward mankind. The story itself parallels in many ways Richard Wagner's *The Ring of the Nibelung* (Northrop Frye once described Tolkien's work as a "High Anglican version of Wagner's Ring-cycle").

We detect a more generalized archetypal resonance in certain images which take on a function reminiscent of motifs in primitive religions. Light at times is more than just the diffused glow that emanates from good or desirable things. It becomes the concentrated light, in a blaze or a shining surface, which communicates a sense of glory and splendor. (pp. 104-05)

Evil [in *The Lord of the Rings*] is presented . . . as a perversion of good. Often it is even a parody. . . . Evil represents, further, a privation of being. It is always the Dark *Shadow;* its blackness is the privation of light, its shadowiness the privation of substance. Its most fearful emissaries are the winged Nazgûl, wraiths whose black robes cover nothingness. Nevertheless, although it is not "real," evil is powerful. Its power lies in the evil will, and it is manifested in the several "falls" which are narrated or dramatized in *The Lord of the Rings* or in the appendixes. (p. 109)

"Inside" the tale, with Frodo or Sam, the reader feels their anxiety about the outcome, sees the signs, and hears the exhortations and reproofs. But from his higher point of vantage, "outside," he discerns heartening *patterns,* as well. Now, it must be understood at this point that the reader is to receive Tolkien's work imaginatively as a kind of analogy to history. The reference to "sources" such as the "Red Book of Westmarch" and the "Book of the Kings" of Gondor, the supplementary chronicles and genealogies in the various appendixes, and other comparable devices strengthen this impression. The patterning I have alluded to constitutes, then, something like a conceptual model for understanding history—not a philosophy, however, as it turns out, but a theology of history. (p. 113)

Biblical eschatology, first of all, is continuous with the doctrine of Providence; that is, faith in the ultimate divine control over the whole of history issues in hope also for the consummation of all things. Both beliefs presuppose, furthermore, certain notions about *time.* The fact that in *The Lord of the Rings* we hear of three "ages" makes it clear that time, in this analogical world, does not mean mere chronological succession or inevitable evolutionary progression. On the other hand, these "ages" are not "cycles," either. There is no mythological pattern of eternal recurrence; at the most there are typological patterns. For each age constitutes a kairos, a time of opportunity and fulfillment. It is a time-with-a content, sent for a purpose and demanding an appropriate response. Thus history as a whole is not an impersonal process but a matter involving personal will and freedom; and it consists of a continuum of "times," each with its own specific character and significance. (p. 116)

The Lord of the Rings, considered allegorically, speaks not only of the nature of the struggle against evil, the inescapability of involvement, the fact of freedom, the qualities of heroism, and the possibility for real loss. It also declares the viability of hope. It has a "happy ending." Frodo and Sam, their Quest achieved, wake in the sweet air of Ithilien. They see Gandalf again, and their other friends. They hear themselves acclaimed: "Long live the Halflings! Praise them with great praise!" They are seated in exaltation upon the throne of Aragorn. A minstrel of Gondor begins to sing the lay of Frodo and the Nine Fingers and the Ring of Doom. And then Sam, we are told, "laughed aloud for sheer delight, and he stood up and cried: 'O great glory and splendor! And all my wishes have come true!' And then he wept." This is the happy ending, indeed, what Tolkien has termed the *eucatastrophe.* And such a "sudden, joyous 'turn'" gives a fleeting glimpse of a joy which goes beyond the sense of wonder aroused by successful fantasy. It is analogous to the joy in the birth of Christ, which is the *eucatastrophe* of man's history, or in the resurrection, which is the *eucatastrophe* of the story

of the incarnation. "It may be," says Tolkien, "a far-off gleam or echo of *evangelium* in the real world." (p. 119)

The Lord of the Rings, although it contains no "God," no "Christ," and no "Christians," embodies much of Tolkien's "real religion" and is a profoundly Christian work. Tolkien requires no "God" in this story; it is enough that he suggests in it the kind of pattern in history which the Christian tradition has ascribed to the providence of God. Aragorn and Gandalf need not turn our thoughts specifically to the Christ of Christian faith; but they persuade us that if we are to have hope in our lives and in our history, it must be hope *for* the kind of power and authority revealed in Aragorn the king and *on the basis* of the kind of power revealed in Gandalf's "miracles" and in his return from the dead. Frodo is not a "Christian"; but what Frodo does and undergoes speaks to us of what a man's responsibility, according to the Christian faith, must always be—to renounce the kind of power which would enslave others and ourselves and to submit to that power which frees us to be all that we are capable of being. (pp. 121-22)

[If] the Christology implied in the figure of Gandalf is "classical," such a Christ liberates man by defeating death and the devil, he does not woo man's heart through moral goodness and suffering love. Man's moral agency, furthermore, tends to become moral passivity; the power is not within but without, and one submits rather than initiates. Hope arises not so much on the basis of certain qualities in a relationship as on the basis of arbitrary supernatural acts. Grace—to put it even more abstractly—is imaged not as persuasive personal relationship but as quasiphysical force, a concept which is always in danger of dissolving away the *moral* character of God. (p. 127)

[Instead of faultfinding, it] is better to recall and be grateful for what Tolkien *has* given us in *The Lord of the Rings.* He has taken us, first, into the enchanted world of Middle-earth and its inhabitants. That world lingers, as sights and sounds, in the memory. One remembers the radiance and the fresh, poignant colors of Lothlórien; the penetrating brown-and-green eyes of Treebeard; the Dead—"shapes of Men and of horses, and pale banners like shreds of cloud, and spears like winter-thickets on a misty night"—following Aragorn; and the snow-white hair, gleaming robes, and bright piercing eyes of the risen Gandalf. One continues to hear the muffled *doom, doom* of the mysterious drumbeats in Moria, the mad muttering of Gollum, the great horns of Rohan "wildly blowing," and "the sigh and murmur of the waves on the shores of Middle-earth" which Sam heard and which "sank deep into his heart." . . .

[What] Tolkien has created is not the rigid one-to-one allegory which this summary may suggest. It yields a much "freer" experience of meaning, not easily formulable propositions but haunting hints of significance. Meaning and belief are *included* in the reception of the vivid image which has been presented to the imagination. (p. 129)

Gunnar Urang, "J. R. R. Tolkien: Fantasy and the Phenomenology of Hope," in his *Shadows of Heaven: Religion and Fantasy in the Writing of C. S. Lewis, Charles Williams, and J. R. R. Tolkien,* Pilgrim Press, 1971, pp. 93-130.

ROBLEY EVANS

(essay date 1972)

[In the following excerpt, Evans examines *The Lord of the Rings*, emphasizing the work's themes of creative power and the heroic quest.]

Unlike writers of science fiction, Tolkien relies upon the literary traditions of the past as well as upon his imagination as sources for his fantasy. He does not wish to break with Western culture or with the Romantic tradition that knowledge gives us power to change the world for the better. The imagination has enriched us in the past; it can continue to do so, not by throwing out our inheritance but by building upon it, and especially upon its familiar and eternally meaningful myths, symbols and dreams. Furthermore, imagination is a power for good and for action in the real world, not just a tool for escaping reality. In Tolkien's understanding, the fantasist is a storyteller and historian who makes our past valuable by manifesting its power in the present. (p. 20)

Tolkien is a Renaissance man whose essentially Christian vision of the universe finds it ordered and purposive with places for all created beings whose relationships in the community of being provide their lives with moral and spiritual meaning. In this vision such ideas as individual responsibility, exercise of human will in choosing between good and evil, fellow-feeling for other creatures, have a positive function. And exactly because Tolkien can define the world as one organized by laws and purposes, he can show that action, too, is possible; men can choose to do good or evil and to make gestures which shape events and the lives of others, for better or worse. . . .

Tolkien's emphasis falls upon "function" in defining moral necessities. Furthermore, his vision includes the creative artist as a moral being who orders the world in his imaginative work and thereby expresses that Truth which lies at the source of lives and actions. In this sense the imagination takes on creative power and religious implications. . . . Words have power, and, finally, it is power with which Tolkien is concerned. He wishes to show how the imagination

gives man power over his life, a life in which he may fight evil and defend good. A life in which the past, history, may be used to change the future and so affect the course of Time. A life in which, as Tolkien writes, man may realize "imagined wonder." This is the value to us of Tolkien's fiction: it suggests how we may use our imaginative power, our ability to "make" fantasy, paradoxically in order to know truth. (pp. 23-4)

Tolkien distinguishes between two worlds: the Primary and the Secondary. The Primary World concerns the spatial and temporal existence we know through our senses, through the routines of living. . . . It is the universe of observed fact in which we are imprisoned without our consent. But the power of the imagination enables man to enter a Secondary World created by the storyteller or wordsmith. This world is free of the Primary World, even though it must draw much of its imagery from events in time and space. By creating this other existence, the artist becomes a "sub-creator." . . . [His] creation must seem consistent within itself. . . . Furthermore, such a world is implicit in the Primary World, and fulfills it, often provides it with meaning. . . .

Tolkien locates the sources for imagined reality in the feelings and wishes of human beings. He calls them "primal desires" that "lie near the heart of Faerie." Among these desires is the wish to "hold communion with other living things," that is, to talk with animals or trees. Another is the desire to live forever. These wishes are human and arise from man's life in the Primary World. And in this world man's wishes operate: an "essential power of Faerie," Tolkien tells us, is to make the visions of fantasy "immediately effective by the will." In this manner "natural objects" obtain their meaning, their "significance and glory" as a "gift" from man. Such opportunity may seem unimaginable to us if we are accustomed to see only "partial meanings" in experience, and to feel that effort in a meaningless universe is vain. But to say that man wishes to make his visions "effective" is to argue that he is active and constructive, that he has a will, and that he can shape his life according to his vision of the great truths which, Tolkien believes, exist for us. The invisible world, the Supernatural, is manifest through man, and in this view, he regains his significance in the world which much contemporary thought and writing seem to deny him. (pp. 27-8)

The making of words . . . , their "saying," provides an analogy for the way in which the imagination operates. Furthermore, they give man power over Nature because they express reality, the inner meaning of things and events. In this sense, the creation of fantasy, the world of Faerie, is not a flight from reality, an escape from the responsibility which power demands. It is an act which serves certain positive purposes in the Primary World. By making words, the sub-creator is in touch with the basic truths of life, and therefore presents us with a vision which is liberating at the same time that it explains and inspires.

Fantasy does not mean a dream world without roots in human reality, nor does "fairy story" mean a light tale involving small human figures with wings. Instead, Tolkien thinks of the Fairy-story or Fantasy as a high form of art, "the operative link between Imagination and the final result, Sub-creation." In fantasy, man finds equivalents for his primal desires and for his visions of reality in created beings, the images of his imagination. In this way fantasy is an equivalent of imagination in its suggestion of "freedom from the domination of observed 'fact', in short of the fantastic." (pp. 31-2)

[One] explanation for the appeal to many readers of *The Lord of the Rings* or any other fantasy is that it is essentially a religious experience to read such works. Faith in the imagined world is vital to fantasy, and to us. For it cannot exist if we do not believe in it, and if we cannot have faith in a meaningful world, then we must live in alienation and despair. Put another way, the task of the sub-creator is to create a world in which we can believe through his art. He must make a consistent, wonderful vision in which all that takes place there is "true," and we must be able to accept his vision as genuine. This gift which we as readers make to the artist if he paints or writes well is what Tolkien calls "Secondary Belief." The great fantasies are those in which the enchanter's art most successfully serves its purpose. . . .

In the first place, the realization of "imagined wonder" invites us to free ourselves from the Primary World through vision. We can become too accustomed to life; we tend to take for granted leaves on the trees, the color of the sky, the face of someone we love, worst of all, ourselves, prisoners in the world of habit which dulls and petrifies. With "creative fantasy" we can achieve what Tolkien calls "recovery". . . . (pp. 35-6)

By seeing things newly, by putting the familiar objects from the Primary World into unfamiliar stories and exotic contexts, we can re-experience the world outside ourselves, and with that sense of wonder which occurs when we find the world different from our expectations. In fantasy the life of the imagination and the life of the everyday world touch and illuminate each other. . . . [In] Tolkien's fantasies we find the unexpected in the expected: hobbits on their journeys encounter talking trees, for instance, altering their preconceived notions about trees. (pp. 37-8)

The wonder we feel at a Happy Ending is the manifestation of our delight in our freedom from observed fact and our discovery, necessarily to be repeated over and over, of our own recreation. But Tolkien suggests that the vision of this truth is more than a

wish: it is an act of freedom in itself which repeats in each man the truth of his own nature: not imprisoned and in despair, but immortal and joyous. Joy, for Tolkien, has finally a Christian character, for it is deliverance of the soul, that Joy known when the soul is reunited with God. Fantasy provides us with heroes like Frodo and heroines like Cinderella who achieve redemption, and therefore can promise this final joy to us. Tolkien's use of terms like "grace" and "deliverance" should suggest that for him fantasy is allegorical, taking its ultimate meaning from what he calls "the Christian Story." The truth "glimpsed" in a fairy-story is heavenly, that Joy which the Christian soul seeks to know as a Happy End. (p. 40)

Tolkien denies that he has written an allegory—that is, a fictional story with specific moral meaning connected to each character and event. But the general lines of allegory are everywhere evident in *The Lord of the Rings,* and a Christian reading of fantasy and man's history must ultimately be moral and hence allegorical. The fairy-story or fantasy is almost always based upon a struggle between good and evil. It tells of the recovery of man to spiritual health, in depicting a Happy Ending which prefigures the promised redemptive Happy Ending, the triumph of good over evil, of Christian theology. (pp. 41-2)

[We] can say that Tolkien is writing myth, not only in the sense of an imagined story, but in the sense of something larger. Myth also refers to a story of cosmic importance in which heroes defy the gods or perhaps act like gods; in any event myth suggests the presentation of the supernatural in our own world. Myths of gods and heroes give us images of archetypal human experience which have an imaginative and emotional effect upon us, and so convince us of their ultimate Truth. The most universal of these myths is that of the hero who sets off to gain knowledge for his people on a Quest. . . . [Myth] in its appeal, whether to primitive or sophisticated audiences, demands a religious response: we must *believe* in the quester and his search; we must have faith that he will succeed. Our emotional response to mythic journeys suggests that we can realize our own particular vision through such images. Thus myth or fantasy satisfies man's need to find more in life than that which he sees before him in the Primary World. (p. 43)

[In *The Lord of the Rings*], with the destruction of the One Ring, Sauron's world is destroyed. By extension, the Ring *is* the Dark Lord's power, even though, in another way, it is only the *symbol* of his power. In creative fantasy, the symbol and the "thing" are identified; the part of a thing stands for the whole. And so, just as Sauron attempted to reduce life to the simplistic level of his own being, the destruction of the Ring of Power reduces his empire to a voice wailing away on the wind. The simplicity of Tolkien's device is like the conclusion of fairy-stories. Tolkien is relying, as does the teller of fairy-stories, upon our faith, our "Secondary Belief," in this instant transformation of the world. And our faith is supported by the complex nature of the Quest seeking this end; by our faith in the characters who make this journey; by our confidence in the values of an imagined world beyond this real one. The Ring, paradoxically, is its own destruction, and that this is so is expressive of an ultimately *religious* vision of reality which has its source, finally, in Tolkien's confidence in words and their power. For, structurally, the Ring is also a "word," an image, a metaphor for its evil maker, and the creator of a successful Secondary World. (p. 56)

[It] must be emphasized that our response to *The Hobbit* or the Trilogy is not to words for themselves. We respond to the felt presence of the Secondary World they create. Our search for "moral and emotional Truth" is immediate; in Tolkien's writing we believe in the world he makes because he offers us an "escape" (in his sense) into imagination by making us "feel" the details of that world and know the characters and the landscape intimately. If we were set down by a broad, rather slowly moving, grey-green river flowing south toward a distant range of mountains, we would know without being told by any of the strange inhabitants along its banks that it was the Entwash, so successfully has Tolkien sketched in its nature and location with a few brief words. And behind those words, or images of the Entwash, lies the myth which gives them purpose in *The Lord of the Rings* and which they support and advertise, in turn. (p. 57)

[Myth] can take the place of religion in that it creates belief in the world's ultimate value. It may be for this reason that Tolkien's *Lord of the Rings* is read so widely today: the Secondary Belief which his creative ability inspires shares the organizational power of religious faith. And finally we must add that the great myths are communal in their meaning, believed in by a society, a community of like-minded beings who organize their lives around a common image. This aspect of myth must appeal to the members of contemporary society who feel alienated and alone in a culture seemingly without values upon which all its members can agree. And we find this element of myth reflected, in turn, in the myths or fantasies themselves. (pp. 59-60)

[The] principle mythic element to which all the others are related is the Heroic Journey or Quest. This central image in *The Hobbit* and *The Lord of the Rings* provides the moral and structural framework for both fantasies. More fully and complexly developed in the latter work, the Quest is a journey to the "center of life," to the interior of the world where the ultimate meaning of existence lies hidden from mortal men. In this sense, the journey the hero of a quest makes is from ignorance to understanding, or from imperfection to perfection, or from innocence to experience (or even from experience to innocence). It can be seen as a search, perhaps for an object precious to the society from which the searcher comes. Perhaps for the chance to destroy an evil enemy. Perhaps for enlightenment, that "regaining of a clear view," of which Tolkien speaks. But in any mythic Quest, the adventures the hero experiences quickly take on moral and spiritual significance: the Journey becomes a metaphor for man's inner life. (p. 63)

[He] is writing in a form which uses the historical past for richness and depth in the creation of the Secondary World. He is representing present actions, whether of hobbits or men, which have grown up out of the past, and are continually influenced by it, indeed, often repeat it. And finally, the literary forms Tolkien uses have come from the past of our civilization, for better or worse, and we need to know what he has done with them to create his own Secondary World and make us believe in it. How the imagination has achieved freedom in the past is important to those who wish to find it now. Tolkien is read, in part, because *The Lord of the Rings* argues that freedom can be found, not through rejection of power, but through acceptance of the challenge which it offers to the Primary World. (p. 90)

Man is constantly in the process of freeing himself from possessiveness. The regaining of "a clear view" of other beings "as things apart from ourselves" is never permanent, never final. . . . A halt at some point in the struggle would be impossible, for Tolkien's view of life is one of constant process and perception, and is therefore opposed to the purpose of the One Ring which is to "bind" life, enclose it within its circle forever. Consequently, the record of history, and the basic pattern of fantasy as Tolkien presents it, is a dialectic between the past and the imagination. The past has many weapons. It has time, which is gradually unrolling toward the end of the world and the death of civilization. Time repeats itself over and over so that men become accustomed to its possessive and destructive presence. The past contains acts of dead beings who at some time set in motion events or ideas affecting future generations. The past is not absurd, as the Existentialists maintain, beginning only a moment ago. It lives for all of us in the shapes our civilization takes now; in our ability to think about the present. . . .

But the imagination is a weapon too, and if rightly used, can counter and manipulate the past. The love of life which the imagination fosters; the respect for other living things, an imaginative act; the belief in ultimate good and the will to realize it—these are weapons in the inevitable conflict. . . . [The] imagination, which can show us the reality behind appearances, can also take time and the days and events of the past, and counter the threat to our freedom they portend. . . .

Man does not escape the demands of the past through fantasy. On the contrary, he chooses (or does not choose) to accept the responsibility of being free which his birth in time imposes on him, and to live or die as freely as he can. It is the congruence of history and imagination that makes *The Lord of the Rings* the effective work it is. (pp. 92-4)

Tolkien has taken archetypal images of trees and jewels, light and darkness, heroic warrior and malevolent enemy, and placed them in a time out of history when Nature was more than we know it to be now, when it glowed with light of the spirit, unfallen, heavenly. We thus have a "history" which is similar to that in our familiar catalogue of myths, and yet demands that our imagination and our sense of great deeds done in civilization's infant past award belief to this mythic history of Middle-earth, which is both like and unlike what we have always believed. (p. 97)

Evil is not, in Tolkien's reading, original with the creation of the world. But it must inevitably arise in a world where created beings are free to make choices, to exercise their free wills in a series of decisions which will either enlarge their imaginative life or narrow and pervert it. This is the ancient paradox of freedom, in that men (or in Tolkien's version, all created beings) must be free to choose the good on their own: they cannot be directed against their will. And so, of course, they may choose to do evil. . . . Those who choose to do evil, as we have said, keep cutting down their freedom until they can be said to have no will left for choosing. (pp. 152-53)

[The] wide-ranging selection of characters, representative of different races, of the past and the present, of different imaginative capacity and point of view is designed by Tolkien to show the wide variety of life in Middle-earth. Such variety must be respected, not reduced to conform to a dominant will. Furthermore, each race and each member of that race must assume the responsibility for the support of civilization in Middle-earth to the extent of his power. The figures like elves and dwarves drawn from the history of the Third Age, and figures like ents and hobbits imagined by Tolkien, cover the spectrum of imaginative life in the world and also make history meaningful by their participation in it. A struggle for power is inevitable, as time runs downward to its end, but individual beings participate in the decisions which direct the historical struggle this way or that. History is not just the inevitable working out of time in ways beyond the imagination's power. What we also see in this range of characters is a hierarchical ranking depending upon what they can do with the particular abilities at their disposal. And heroism is in turn a complex element in a world determined by choice. (pp. 163-64)

If we compare Tolkien to other contemporary writers, we see major differences. Unlike such writers

of fantasy as Kurt Vonnegut, Tolkien is never crudely satiric; gentleness and love pervade his work and soften the criticism of modern society implicit in it. Where other authors present a bleak picture of the wasteland in which the soul struggles to survive alone, Tolkien gives us the Fellowship of the Ring as a happier alternative, a small society of loving creatures who are not alone in the universe. Tolkien argues that there is much of value in Western culture which should be saved, which *will* be saved, by the imaginative beings who have power to believe in themselves. Tolkien is a conservative in this sense; for all the elements of the fantastic in his work, the preservation of traditional values is most important to him. The fantastic affirms those values rather than attempting to substitute something else for them. Tolkien's writing style, too, is not meant to surprise or shock us; it is always subordinate to the story being told. It is his retelling of our most deeply believed myths about ourselves that makes *The Lord of the Rings* so moving.

Tolkien is read because he tells a good story; his power to command Secondary Belief in his readers is real. History comes alive in the characters and events of *The Lord of the Rings* because Tolkien creates speeches and actions which have the "inner consistency of reality" and are not absolutely and destructively rooted in the "observed fact" of the Primary World. He has chosen to tell a story, rather than write a philosophic discourse, and this decision was important because a narrative presents "inner" reality in a way a discursive essay does not: imagined beings who take their life from the hands of their creator touch our emotions, our imaginations, our religious sense of wonder, in ways words addressed to the intellect alone cannot. . . .

Behind Tolkien's choice of form lies an assumption about the nature of man which shines through his work: that men can love, admire good deeds, can seek truth because it is good. They are not "bad"; they are imperceptive, they are weak insofar as excessive self-pride makes them misuse their particular powers; they are available, however, to correction, to change, to the Power, used only for good, of the Enchanter. Words and literary forms are not things apart from human beings. They come up from the body and the feelings attached to the Primary World, as they are, and they share in that reality. And much more. The "Joy" of which Tolkien writes in "On Fairy-Stories" is "heavenly" all right, but it underlies the events in *The Lord of the Rings,* too, in the "turn" of the happy ending, and in the life of the narration itself. (pp. 195-97)

[The] general respect for all created life in *The Lord of the Rings* speaks to those among us who fear the disappearance of redwoods and whales, mountain wilderness and hidden seashores to serve society's destructive needs. If we try to turn every mountain valley into a national park with camping areas, general stores and play grounds, we have remade it in our image, and so extended a step further "the drab blur of triteness or familiarity" which must ultimately threaten our own necessary sense of wonder at other forms of life. And under our heavy hand, such unique life can be extinguished. *Care for the world,* might be the theme of Tolkien's Trilogy. (pp. 198-99)

We should also remember that Frodo's self-sacrifice is not only for the defeat of evil; it is also for the good of society, for the whole Community of created beings. This suggests, in turn, that in the mind of the fantasist, society is worth saving. It is not a mechanical horror designed to grind the individual down. Instead, personal commitment—*service*—is honored by the citizens of Middle-earth. The individual finds a responsible place for himself in his society; those who live outside society are identified with tyranny and self-destruction. A major reason for Tolkien's popularity among students and the "rebellious young" may be his classic insistence that the individual finds true freedom in the service of good, and that good can be social, providing security and purpose for others without being destructive of singularity and wilfullness. (p. 201)

Robley Evans, in his *J. R. R. Tolkien,* Warner Paperback Library, 1972, 206 p.

A. N. WILSON

(essay date 1981)

[In the following review of *The Letters of J. R. R. Tolkien,* Wilson discusses Tolkien's imagination and religious faith as factors influencing his creation of *The Lord of the Rings.*]

J. R. R. Tolkien's genius was all of a piece. In his academic career and in his personal life and in his art, he was the same man. . . . Eminent scholars are, more often than not, bored with their subjects. And there is often so complete a division between the 'writing persona' and the 'real self' of an author that the task of biography becomes necessarily offensive. None of this applies to Tolkien. That is what gives his mythologies their power. Plenty of people have disliked them, or been jealous of their commercial success; but no one, with justice, could ever have thought them whimsical or posing. They sprang naturally out of his apprehension of the real world, as we can now perceive by reading this remarkable selection of letters [*The Letters of J. R. R. Tolkien*]. . . .

In many obvious senses [Tolkien] was not at home in the modern, materialist world. . . . [Not]

merely did he feel displaced in 'this polluted country of which a growing proportion of the inhabitants are maniacs'. In the human body itself, he felt a stranger. After an unpleasant session with a doctor in old age he wrote to his son, 'We (or at least I) know far too little about the complicated machine we inhabit'.

With good Augustinian, not to say Platonic, precedent, Tolkien's sense of the present world's futility, folly and unreality stemmed from his lively faith in a world beyond: and this other world was, primarily, the Heaven of conventional Catholicism. So, to his son Christopher, posted to South Africa during the war, he can write, 'Remember your guardian angel. . . . God is . . . behind us, supporting, nourishing us (as being creatures). The bright point of power where that lifeline, that spiritual umbilical cord touches: there is our Angel, facing two ways, to God behind us in the direction we cannot see, and to us'. . . .

When, years later, this umbilical cord was loosed and his correspondent lost a sense of this other world, it was an enormous grief to Tolkien: 'When I think of my mother's death . . . , I find it very hard and bitter when my children stray away from the Church'. In the same letter he writes, *'in hac urbe lux solemnis* has seemed to me steadily true'.

Yet its truth was best apprehended, in his distinctive imagination, when transformed into story and mythology. His love of language suggested much of the myth's substance. In the case of the 'ents', for example, the majestic walking trees of his story, 'as usually with me they grew rather out of their name than the other way about. I always felt that something ought to be done about the peculiar Anglo-Saxon word *ent* for a "giant" or a mighty person of long ago—to whom all old works are ascribed'. He was not content to leave the ents as they appear on the page of *Beowulf,* shadowy, unknown figures of an almost forgotten past. A natural story-teller, Tolkien invested them with shapes, voices and habits of his own creation. Many of his fellow-mediaevalists have found *The Lord of the Rings* perpetually irritating for this reason. Any student of Anglo-Saxon knows that an ent is not a walking tree: it is some sort of giant, perhaps a nickname for the Romans. But in the imaginations of the millions, in their Gandalf T-shirts, the ent has taken leave of its Anglo-Saxon origins and become something other. . . .

The objectors fail to recognise the wholeness of Tolkien's imaginative sweep. . . . [The tales] are an expression of his whole experience of life. This is what the *Letters* make so fascinatingly clear. At the beginning, in an undergraduate letter to his future wife, he reports that he has 'done some touches to my nonsense fairy language'; but the importance of this invented grammar had not yet dawned on him; he can still apologise for it as 'such a mad hobby'. . . . [By] the late 1930s, when Tolkien had returned to Oxford as

Rawlinson and Bosworth Professor, all the strands of his life had become enmeshed in their inevitable pattern: the love of philology; the sense of the Church as the one city in which *lux solemnis* shines on in a dark world; the zest for story-telling; the poignant and increasingly strong sense that 'Men are essentially mortal and must not try to become "immortal" in the Flesh'. Thus the divisions between his imagined world and the world of all of us grow shadowy. 'I am historically minded', he protests to one correspondent, 'Middle Earth is not an imaginary world . . . The theatre of my tale is this earth, the one in which we now live'. This is not whimsy. The letters reveal innumerable glimpses of how it was, in his own life, literally true. (p. 17)

These letters, then, are primarily interesting because they reveal more of the mind which created *Lord of the Rings*. There are extended epistles to admirers or publishers, giving commentary on the great tale and answering points of difficulty with donnish precision. (pp. 17-18)

But it must be stressed that these are very good letters in themselves, quite apart from their relevance to hobbit-lore. There are good gossipy vignettes of Oxford: C. S. Lewis downing three pints of beer before lunch and insisting that he was 'going short for Lent'. . . . There are letters which reveal Tolkien as a wise counsellor, a kind friend, an admirable father. The best, and most moving, are those written to his son Christopher during the war, sent out with installments of *Lord of the Rings* as the tale grew. In perhaps the most impressive of all, he recounts a sermon by Father Douglas Carter on the raising of Jairus's daughter. The sermon moved Tolkien so much because it captured what he called the *eucatastrophe* of that story: 'the sudden happy turn in a story which pierces you with a joy that brings tears'. (p. 18)

A. N. Wilson, "Beyond the Misty Mountains," in *The Spectator*, Vol. 247, No. 7992, September 12, 1981, pp. 17-18.

KATHARYN F. CRABBE

(essay date 1981)

[In the following excerpt, Crabbe analyzes *The Silmarillion*, focusing on the narrative structure, plot, themes, and symbols.]

The Silmarillion, Tolkien's posthumously published account of the First Age of the world, is the densest, the most difficult, and for the general reader the least attractive of all his works. As a backdrop to *The Lord of the Rings* and *The Hobbit*, *The Silmarillion* is perhaps the most essential of Tolkien's works; at the same time

it is the least able to stand alone as a unified vision. Although individual tales from this chronicle of the earliest age of Middle-earth may be exquisite, or majestic, or horrifying, *The Silmarillion* as a whole has neither unity of tone nor unity of style. In addition, the number of characters is simply staggering. So while *The Silmarillion* is Tolkien's most ambitious project, it is in many ways his most flawed performance. (p. 112)

Like the poem *Beowulf*, which Tolkien studied and loved, *The Silmarillion* is not really a narrative in the sense that it tells a story in a straightforward and sequential manner. Instead, the collection of tales with its cross-references, modifications, and contradictions is presented as a mythology which, having come from divers hands and divers places, cannot be expected to achieve any great degree of inner consistency. The pose of the narrator, then, as a translator or as an editor obviates criticism of the lack of unity in the work.

To say, however, that *The Silmarillion* lacks narrative unity is not to say that it lacks structure. Indeed, the work is highly structured, taking the form of a triptych, a three-paneled picture often used as an altarpiece. This structure seems to have been part of Tolkien's own plan for the work, for Christopher Tolkien notes in the Foreword that the first and third panels "are included according to my father's explicit intention."

The large central section, the *Quenta Silmarillion*, or "History of the Silmarils," is flanked on one side by the story of the creation in the *Ainulindalë* and the *Valaquenta*, and on the other by the story of the decline of the elves and the rise of men in the *Akallabêth* and *Of the Rings of Power and the Third Age*. As in an actual triptych, the central panel is the largest and carries the most meaning, but the two side panels provide a context for the central panel, give a perspective on it, and direct the eye toward it. . . . Thus by placement of the parts and by proportion, *The Silmarillion* is an account of the history of the elves of Middle-earth. It is, at the same time, a symbolic representation of the fall of man because it is in the nature of myths to link gods, demigods, and men.

In *The Silmarillion* the two most important influences in Tolkien's life came into direct opposition: his religion and his love for the ancient and heroic north. On the one hand, his philologist's mind told him that the mythology of the ancient Britons must be similar in most ways to other northern mythologies. On the other hand, as much as he loved those mythologies, and as much as he celebrated the heroes of the unbendable will, he was a Christian and thus could not rid his mind utterly of the notion that this life is but a prelude to another. *The Silmarillion* thus reflects a mythology that combines the values of the unconquerable will with the certainty that whatever the outcome of the temporal battle between good and evil, the last battle is yet to come. (pp. 113-15)

The first panel of the triptych, which depicts the creation of the universe, begins with the assumption of a single, ruling, creative force: "There was Eru, the One, who in Arda is called Illúvatar." In describing Eru and the creation, Tolkien uses the familiar notion of a world that is built to music and is, therefore, ideally "harmonious." He is quick to establish a tone which aspires to the heroic through the use of unusual words (Arda, Ilúvatar). . . . The combination of heroic tone and religious connotation identifies *The Silmarillion* as mythic. It also helps Tolkien to establish the ultimately hopeful nature of his work. Even in the first panel, as he raises the specter of the long trials that will comprise the central portion of the work, Tolkien evokes the splendor and the glory of the first conception of the world by the Ainur. . . . Tolkien immediately asserts without equivocation an eschatological vision of harmony: There will be an end to this world, and after that end perfection will once more be attained. But until that time, the music will be less than perfect. The vision of harmony after the end is one that Tolkien attributed to early Christians in Briton, and one that stands in dramatic contrast to the stark hopelessness of the more ancient northern mythologies. Thus, though he has created a mythology for England in *The Silmarillion,* he was providing it from the beginning with a Christian element. (pp. 115-16)

Like the *Ainulindalë,* the *Valaquenta* is at once foreboding and hopeful. As a narrative it is remarkably weak, for it simply focuses on each of the Valar in turn, describing their powers and their responsibilities. . . . It is a catalogue of characters, not a story. But though the *Valaquenta* tells no story, it heightens the sense of impending disaster at the same time as it encourages the careful reader to look ahead with hope. The sense of foreboding grows by virtue of the organization of the *Valaquenta.* Evil, introduced under the heading "Of the Enemies," is given the position of power: Morgoth and Sauron are introduced last, so that the section closes with an evocation of the darkness, suffering, and treachery they will visit upon Middle-earth. (p. 117)

As the overall structure of *The Silmarillion* is architecturally tidy, so is that of the central panel. The *Quenta Silmarillion* has twenty-four books; elves dominate the whole but are the exclusive subjects of the first half (men do not even appear until chapter 12). In the second half the *Quenta Silmarillion* develops the connection between elves and men and depicts the ultimate combining of the blood of the two kindreds in the greatest hero of the First Age, Eärendil the Mariner.

The *Quenta Silmarillion* is therefore not only the history of the Silmarils, but of the elves as well. (p. 118)

Although the title of *The Silmarillion* suggests

that the fate of the jewels draws the unnamed narrator to the tales of the elves, such does not actually seem to be the case, for many of the episodes have little direct connection with the jewels. Rather, the Silmarils are primarily important as the means by which elves and men become estranged from the Valar and thus from the One. The tales are unified not so much by the jewels as by the theme of the struggle against Morgoth, that personification of malice, greed, and destruction that is the evil side of the heroic life. . . . Thematically, *The Silmarillion* is first concerned with the undying, yet hopeless, struggle of man against evil and the inevitable decline of the children of the earth.

As long as the Eldar are content to accept the gifts of the Valar and Ilúvatar, they are innocent and protected. But in Fëanor comes the kind of knowledge that contributes both to the rise and to the decline of man. On the one hand, it makes men more nearly the equal of those beings they call gods; on the other, by destroying their innocence, it cuts them off from the protection they enjoyed in the unified world of the golden age. Fëanor's original name, *Curufinwë,* contains the root *skill* (curu); *Fëanor* itself means *spirit of fire.* From skill and spirit Fëanor brings to the Eldar, among other gifts, the letters "which the Eldar used ever after." Thus Fëanor, as *spirit of fire* is a culture hero like Prometheus. And as was true of Prometheus, his gift to his race is double-natured: It is an *ipso facto* blessing, but it is also the cause of great misery. . . . Fëanor's knowledge, like that of Prometheus, is gained at the cost of the happiness and peace of mind of the whole race.

Fëanor's rebellion and his transgression of the assumed law of Arda, obedience to one's betters, is an elvish fall from grace, analogous to the fall of Adam and Eve in the garden of Eden. When, like Adam and Eve, elves must leave the garden, a messenger appears at the very edge of the guarded realm to deliver "the Doom of the Noldor": "Tears unnumbered ye shall shed; and the Valar will fence Valinor against you, and shut you out, so that not even the echo of your lamentation shall pass over the mountains." (pp. 119-21)

Because of the pride and disobedience of the elves as symbolized in Fëanor, the world of the *Quenta Silmarillion* is a vale of tears. . . . [The] heroes of elves and men suffer physically and spiritually under the formidable assault of evil on Middle-earth. The recurrence of the torture of heroes in *The Silmarillion* points out the hopelessness of their earthly lives. (p. 121)

[Yet, for] all the suffering it recounts, the *Quenta Silmarillion* concludes with hope. After twenty-three chapters chronicling the failure of heroes to transcend the doom of the Noldor, the twenty-fourth, "Of the Voyage of Eärendil and the War of Wrath," tells of the forgiveness of the Valar and the return of divine mercy and pity to Middle-earth. Here Eärendil is a hero in the most mythic and the most religious sense: He is someone who saves us. In doing so, he not only secures the pardon of the Valar, he also succeeds in returning the elves to the west. Further, Morgoth is banished into the Void. Yet the world cannot be remade and the seeds of evil are still fertile even though Morgoth himself is destroyed. (p. 122)

The most important theme of the *Quenta Silmarillion* is the decline of mankind. The second most important is the union of opposites. As the tone is both foreboding and hopeful, as Eärendil is both man and elf, The Two Trees of Valinor also combine opposites. The Two Trees, the sources of the light of the Silmarils, are born from the green mound called Ezellohar, called forth by the song of Yavanna and the tears of Nienna. Yavanna is the giver of fruits, the lover of all things that grow. Nienna is the mourner: She mourns for the marring of the world by Morgoth and for those who wait in the halls of Mandos, i.e., those who are dead. From the moment of origin, then, the Two Trees and the light they literally shed on the ground of Valinor is made up of generation and decay, of growth and decline, of birth and death. (p. 123)

[The] Silmarils, like Christ, serve as a symbolic link between the spiritual and physical worlds, the realm of the Valar and the world of men and elves. Determined and self-sacrificing as he is, Eärendil cannot find the straight road to the west, the spiritual world, until he receives a Silmaril to light the way. It is the symbol of grace that allows men and elves to transcend the bounds of the mundane world. When the first Silmaril reaches its rest, bound to the brow of Eärendil, disposition of the two remaining Silmarils indicates the approaching equilibrium in *The Silmarillion*. . . . Fëanor's sons steal the gems only to find that they cannot bear to hold them. (pp. 124-25)

The third panel of the triptych, the *Akallabêth* or "Downfall of Númenor" and "Of the Rings of Power," provides a coda to the central panel, a recapitulation of the theme performed by different principals. Like the elves, the men of the three faithful houses are given a land of their own with every promise of a blissful life. But, like the elves, they come under the shadow—this time in the person of Sauron. The freedom, or *free-doom,* of the men of Númenor is reflected in the physical location of Númenor itself; it rises out of the sea between Middle-earth and Valinor, symbolizing their position midway between the totally spiritual and the totally physical. As was the case with both Morgoth and Fëanor, the desire to approach the godlike drives men toward evil. (pp. 125-26)

Like the two books that deal with the coming of the elves into the world, the books that tell of their parting are at once hopeful and filled with foreboding. The departure of the elves from Middle-earth is continually alluded to and used to evoke a state of loss. Without the presence of the elves, men are deprived of

"good counsel and wise lore" and fall into the "Darkness." The beauty of elvish voices and elvish arts is withdrawn from the world, as is the memory of a time without evil. In the Third Age, the image of what the world of the elves was is preserved only by the power of the elven rings. . . . When the destruction of the Ruling Ring ends the power of the three rings of the elves, the last traces of the Noldor pass out of the world.

At the same time, the destruction of the Ruling Ring achieves the final overthrow of Sauron. The greatest servant of evil is vanquished, and his final destruction marks a moment of rebirth as spring comes again to the earth. (pp. 126-27)

As the narrative quality of *The Silmarillion* resembles that of *Beowulf,* so does the strategy of the poet. Tolkien has created in *The Silmarillion* the illusion of surveying a past that reaches back to a long history of sorrow, one noble and fraught with great significance. The recurrent allusions to lost tales . . . serve to create a sense of a past that must have been truly heroic and noble to have given rise to so many heroic tales. The recurrent references to source poems also create the sense that the author is working in the context of a widely known and well-accepted body of literature—a living mythology. However, *The Silmarillion* as we have it is not the mythology itself, but a heroic, elegiac poem based on it. The poet's wide acquaintance with and knowledge of this heroic past allows him to see in the recurrent joyous creation and sorrowful destruction something of permanent value. He tells again the oldest of mythic tales, the unending struggle of good against evil; he depicts again the oldest of human tragedies, the inevitable death and destruction of man and all his works; and he balances the two possible responses to the inevitable end—the pagan and the Christian.

The pagan or pre-Christian eschatological view, as Tolkien explained in his essay on *Beowulf,* is based on "the creed of unyielding." In the northern mythologies, at least, the heroic assumption was that the destruction of man and his creations was inevitable. The creed of unyielding, then, holds that chaos will eventually triumph and that, for that reason, human life can be made meaningful only by opposing chaos with all one's strength and will until death inevitably comes. The heroic life may end, but the heroic will is indomitable. (pp. 129-30)

The concept of heroism in *The Silmarillion* is far more diffuse and ironic than in Tolkien's earlier works. In contrast with *The Lord of the Rings,* which provided heroes at every level of mimesis and at every level of society, *The Silmarillion* seems to lack even one unifying champion. Tolkien felt the lack of a single hero and at one time proposed to provide the needed continuity by framing the tales with a sea-farer to whom all the stories could be told. However, the sea-farer never materialized, and the continuity that does exist comes from the enemies, Morgoth and Sauron, rather than from the legions of elves and men who oppose or resist them. *The Silmarillion* shares this feature with another great collection of myths, the Bible, in which a succession of heroes of men all come to stand for one man who, in turn, stands for all men. This, then, is the key to the heroism of *The Silmarillion*: The heroes of the Valar, of the elves, and of men are all aspects of one man whose significance is universal, whose struggle is unending, and whose earthly fate is never in doubt. (p. 131)

The highest and only undefeated power of *The Silmarillion* is Eru, the one, also called Ilúvatar. It is he who creates the Valar and from whose thought they create Arda, "the Realm." It is also he who creates elves and men, and who decrees that the Valar are to be "chiefs" rather than "gods" to them. It is he alone who knows the fate of the world after the end of all the ages. Finally, it is he who knows and understands how the great design is unified, how everything has its origin in himself and contributes to his own greater glory.

In this conception of the One, Tolkien has clearly created a source of good like the Christian god and one which embodies the same paradoxes. For example, he is the source of all creation and yet is not responsible for the presence of evil. He knows what will occur (that is, he sees the whole "design") but he does not will it. . . . He is, in short, all powerful and all knowing, but also incomprehensible, and because he represents a heroism we cannot understand, much less hope to emulate, Ilúvatar is no more the hero of *The Silmarillion* than Jehovah is the hero of the Old Testament. For heroism as it is commonly understood, we must look to the lesser orders of beings.

Next in power below Ilúvatar are the Valar who, inspired by the thought of the One, create Arda. In them we see the first outlines of a comprehensible heroism in *The Silmarillion*, for the Valar are the first in Arda to oppose evil in the form of Morgoth. The heroism of the Valar is rooted in their determination to realize the visions that come to them from the One. Although they know that after the first assault on Arda by Morgoth they cannot achieve the perfection of the original vision, they persevere in their attempts to bring the world they have imagined into being. In doing so, they are creative, obedient to the will of Eru, and loving toward their fellow creatures. (pp. 131-32)

The relationship between the Valar and Ilúvatar is fundamentally Christian in nature because, although the Valar love the world they create and their creations for the world, they also understand that beyond the realm of the earthly is the realm of Ilúvatar, and that even the marring of Arda accrues to the glory of the One. To the elves, however, the world is a darker place than it seems to the Valar. Their characteristic attitude toward the world is more nearly pagan, marked by an unwavering will and a strict adherence to the law of loyalty to the lord that is the core of the heroic pagan code. . . .

Among the elves, the greatest protagonists are Fëanor, maker of the Silmarils, and Turgon, Lord of Gondolin. However, the tragedy of the elves is that, thanks to the oath of Fëanor and the ensuing doom of the Noldor, they have only heroes whose actions bring catastrophic results. Allegiance to the code of the will can not bring victory; it can only bring, at best, glorious defeat. (p. 134)

Fëanor shares with the Valar a desire to create, and as he is " . . . the most subtle in mind and most skilled in hand" of all the elves, he is so nearly godlike that his creations are nearly divine in their beauty. Unlike the Valar, however, Fëanor fails to respect the necessary freedom of all creations, including his own, and he fails to recognize or to accept responsibility for his fellow creatures. For example, the oath by which he binds his sons and followers to him effectively destroys the free will he should strive to enhance. In his desire to control others rather than to help them to be more fully themselves, he fails to be merciful or protective, or to discharge the responsibility of a leader. (p. 135)

Turgon, the second great hero of the Noldor, is one who swore Fëanor's oath and defied the Valar with him. Betrayed by Fëanor and left to brave the ice fields of the Helcaraxë, he turns away from the oath-keepers and, at the urging of Ulmo, Lord of Waters, builds a hidden city. The city of Gondolin . . . becomes the last refuge of the Noldor in Middle-earth, a city of bliss, beauty, and wisdom. But from the moment Turgon fails to repudiate the oath and his own will and make himself subject to the will of the Valar, the fall of Gondolin is foretold. That is, it too is part of the doom of the Noldor. The fall of the city is brought about by the same heroic flaw that drives Fëanor to his death: the overweening pride of the creator in his own creation. (pp. 135-36)

Among the race of men, heroes suffer less because they transgress the rules of obedience and responsibility than because they are victims of a world that fails to reward action with justice. For men, the world visits evil on the just and unjust alike. And as men are frailer, shorter-lived, and more limited in understanding than elves, they are even more susceptible to the evil of the world and less able to believe that a greater power loves and protects them than the elves. (p. 136)

Among the most celebrated creations of *The Silmarillion* are the texts of the tales that make up the work itself. Here, as in *The Lord of the Rings*, Tolkien creates a narrator who is styled as the translator and editor of old texts. His knowledge of Elvish mythology is wide and deep, and his delight in the Elvish languages is apparent in the attention he gives them in his appendices and glossaries.

Tolkien's fascination with languages is, by now, no surprise. What is surprising in this work is the difficulty that fascination creates for the reader. Of *The Lord of the Rings* one could say without hesitation that the language themes were beautifully integrated with other thematic concerns; in fact in that work the themes and the language are perfectly suited to one another. However, the success of Tolkien's uses of language in *The Silmarillion* is questionable. It can be argued, as Jane Nitzsche has done, that Tolkien's fascination with languages has made *The Silmarillion* nearly unreadable. . . . However, having acknowledged the limits of Tolkien's use of the language theme in *The Silmarillion,* one may go on to appreciate even a minor achievement. This "plethora of names" is not simply the self-indulgence of an aging writer; instead it is a major part of one of the most important themes of the work, the centrality of the creative impulse to human experience.

Thematically, the naming and renaming that is so prominent in these tales is a constant allusion to the principle that to use language, particularly to name, is to create. Impatience with *The Silmarillion* is often a result of expecting it to be something it is not: a well-plotted adventure story, say, like *The Hobbit* or *The Lord of the Rings.* But *The Silmarillion* is not basically a narrative; it backtracks, modifies, contradicts, and reconsiders far too often to be trying to tell a single story. Rather, its purpose is to tell *stories* and, in doing so, to evoke a feeling for a time, a culture, and a set of values. The issue is not what becomes of Fëanor, or even of Eärendil, but what becomes of people (good and bad) when pride and envy and blind fear conflict with humility and self-sacrifice. (pp. 140-41)

The Silmarillion, then, is the story of a world that is too dangerous and unforgiving to be comic; it is also the story of a world that is far too capricious, far too capable of rewarding even the good with ashes, to be really tragic. Instead, Tolkien here portrays a world that is ironic: Danger is everywhere, villains may be banished but not vanquished, the longed-for apple is rotten at the core. The inhabitants of this world live lives in which conventional notions of relations between actions and rewards are exploded. They live lives in which the odds against good winning over evil are almost absurdly high. However, caught in this trap between high odds and bad bets, Tolkien's heroes do the most heroic thing ironic heroes can do: They endure. (pp. 143-44)

Katharyn F. Crabbe, in her *J. R. R. Tolkien,* Frederick Ungar Publishing Co., 1981, 192 p.

SOURCES FOR FURTHER STUDY

Carpenter, Humphrey. *Tolkien: A Biography.* Boston: Houghton Mifflin, 1981, 464 p.

> The authorized biography. This work is illustrated and provides a complete biographical and critical survey, drawing upon letters written by Tolkien and his wife, Edith.

Glover, Willis B. "The Christian Character of Tolkien's Invented World." *Criticism* (Winter 1971): 39-54.

> Focuses on Christianity as a tradition influencing *The Lord of the Rings.*

Isaacs, Neil D. and Zimbardo, Rose A., eds. *Tolkien and the Critics.* Notre Dame: University of Notre Dame Press, 1968, 296 p.

> Includes critical essays discussing elements including plot, themes, structure, symbolism, and style in *The Lord of the Rings.*

Kopff, E. Christian. "Inventing Lost Worlds." *Chronicles of Culture* 9, No. 4 (April 1985): 6-8.

> Discusses Tolkien's approach to philology as revealed in *The Monsters and The Critics and Other Essays.*

Lewis, C. S. *"The Hobbit"* and "Tolkien's *The Lord of the Rings."* In his *On Stories and Other Essays on Literature,* edited by Walter Hooper, pp. 81-2, 83-90. New York: Harcourt, Brace, Jovanovich, 1982.

> Appreciative reviews of *The Hobbit* and the *Ring* trilogy. Of the former, Lewis wrote presciently: "Prediction is dangerous: but *The Hobbit* may well prove a classic."

Lobdell, Jared. *England and Always: Tolkien's World of the Rings.* Grand Rapids, Mich.: William B. Eerdmans Publishing Co., 1981, 94 p.

> Insightful criticism of Tolkien's trilogy and history of its composition.

Leo Tolstoy

1828-1910

(Full name Leo Nikolaevich Tolstoy. Also transliterated as Tolstoi and Tolstoj.) Russian novelist, dramatist, short story writer, essayist, and critic.

INTRODUCTION

Described by Fyodor Dostoyevsky as "a sublime artist," by Virginia Woolf as "the greatest of all novelists," and by Marcel Proust as "a serene god" in literature, Tolstoy was one of the most important figures in modern literary history. His *Voina i mir* (1869; *War and Peace*) and *Anna Karenina* (1877) are almost universally acclaimed as all-encompassing documents of human existence and supreme examples of the realistic novel. Commentary on these novels frequently mentions Tolstoy's feat of successfully animating his fiction with the immediacy and variousness of life. Particularly esteemed are his insightful examinations of psychology and society. Later in his career, Tolstoy was concerned primarily with religious and philosophical issues.

Tolstoy was born and lived throughout his life on his family estate near Moscow. After attending the University of Kazan, he returned to the estate and continued his education through personal study. He later served in the army in the Caucasus, at this time working on his first novel, *Detstvo* (1852; *Childhood*). This work gained notice in Russian literary circles, and elicited favorable reaction from Ivan Turgenev and Fyodor Dostoevsky. Short stories like "Nabey" ("A Raid") were the literary result of his experiences in the Caucasus, and his military service in the Crimean War is chronicled in his Sevastopol sketches. Subsequent short stories and short novels, including "Dva gusara" ("Two Hussars"), "Tri smerti" ("Three Deaths"), and *Kazaki* (1863; *The Cossacks*), reveal a more characteristic concern with issues of morality and the ideal of simple ways of life untainted by the complexity and temptations of society.

War and Peace has often been called the greatest novel ever written. A massive, multidimensional work extending over 1,500 pages and featuring more than 500 characters, the novel combines an epic depiction of the military struggle between Russia and Napoleonic France in the early decades of the nineteenth century, a chronicle of the interrelated histories of several families over the course of a generation, and Tolstoy's elaborate and controversial theory of history, set forth in disquisitions within the text and in a lengthy epilogue. Tracing the lives of his main characters from childhood and youth through maturity and death, Tolstoy portrayed with unparalleled fidelity the common events of everyday life, and his novel has been as highly acclaimed for the vividness and insight with which he depicted individual characters and scenes as for the grandeur of its conception.

While many critics have found fault with the way Tolstoy reconciled the diverse elements in *War and Peace,* most agree that his next work, *Anna Karenina,* displays a more purposeful structure. Tolstoy stated of *Anna Karenina,* ". . . I am very proud of its architecture—its vaults are joined so that one cannot even notice where the keystone is." In many ways, *Anna Karenina* is unique among Tolstoy's works. It has none of the self-assured moral didacticism of Tolstoy's later writings, and although it resembles *War and Peace* in its epic proportions, critics agree that *War and Peace* is essentially optimistic, while *Anna Karenina* is pervaded with a sense of tragedy. *Anna Karenina* also contains elements that critics now recognize as innovations foreshadowing the development of the twentieth-century psychological novel. Thematically, *Anna Karenina* parallels its heroine's moral and social conflicts with Constantine Levin's internal struggle to find meaning and guidance for his life. Levin's struggle is often said to be an embodiment of Tolstoy's own developing spiritual crisis.

In *Ispoved* (1882; *A Confession*) Tolstoy outlined a spiritual upheaval that caused him to question the basis of his existence. His attempt to resolve this crisis took the form of a radical Christianity whose doctrines ultimately included nonresistance to evil and total abstinence from sex. The artistic repercussions of his conversion are spelled out in *Chto takoe iskusstvo* (*What Is Art?*). The major concern of this essay is to distinguish bogus art, which he called an elitist celebration of aesthetics, from universal art, which successfully "infects" its recipient with the highest sentiment an artist can transmit—that of religious feeling. This conception of art led Tolstoy to dismiss most of history's greatest creators, including William Shakespeare and Richard Wagner, and to repudiate all of his own previous work save for two short stories. During this phase of his career Tolstoy began writing his many moral and theological tracts, for which he was eventually excommunicated. His pamphleteering on social, political, and economic subjects also resulted in the censorship of his work by the government.

While critics have traditionally granted Tolstoy's post-conversion writings a lesser stature than those of the earlier phase, many of these works have an artistic worth and interest in their own right. At this point in his career, Tolstoy was concerned with producing two types of fiction: simple tales written in a folk tradition for uneducated readers and more literary works focusing on his moral preoccupations of this period. The folktales, such as "Brazhe iepko, a bozhe krepko" ("Evil Allures but Good Endures"), were designed as examples of "universal art" and have often been praised for delivering their didactic point in an artful manner. Much the same estimation has been accorded Tolstoy's literary fiction of this time, including *Smert Ivana Ilyicha* (*The Death of Ivan Ilyich*) and *Kreitserova sonata* (*The Kreutzer Sonata*). If the moral stance of these fictional tracts on death and sex has been criticized as simplistic or severe, the two works have also been considered among the best examples of Tolstoy's art of storytelling. Of *The Kruetzer Sonata,* Anton Chekhov wrote: "You will hardly find anything as powerful in seriousness of conception and beauty of execution." However, Tolstoy's longest work of his post-conversion period and his last major novel, *Voskresenie* (*Resurrection*), is considered far less successful than the early masterpieces *War and Peace* and *Anna Karenina.* Although Tolstoy's genius for description and characterization are still evident in this work, the intrusion of social and moral issues is regarded as detrimental to the novel's artistic value. Among the later novels, *Khadzhi Murat* (*Hadji Murád*) is more often viewed as the work that shows the extent and endurance of Tolstoy's narrative power.

During his later period Tolstoy also produced a number of dramatic works in an attempt to express his post-conversion ideas in a genre outside fiction. Like many of his other works, these dramas are often highly regarded for their vivid and compelling sense of realism, and for the sincere and sometimes overwhelming urgency of the author's concerns. The chief work among these plays is *Vlast tmy* (*The Power of Darkness*). The somber action of the drama—adultery, murder, religious torment—culminates in the redeeming vision of Christian faith that was a spiritual focus of the elder Tolstoy. Bernard Shaw called *The Power of Darkness* "a true tragedy," while describing Tolstoy's other dramas as "terrible but essentially comedic" in their dissection of a subject through methods of satire and almost superhuman powers of analysis. In the social comedy *Plody prosvesh cheniya* (*The Fruits of Enlightenment*), the object of Tolstoy's criticism is aristocratic society, and in the unfinished drama *I svet vo tme svetit* (*The Light That Shines in Darkness*) it is the author's own life. The latter play is of particular interest for Tolstoy's view of his spiritual conversion and its effect on the people around him.

As a religious and ethical thinker Tolstoy has been criticized for the extremism, and sometimes the absurdity, of his ideas. However, he has also been admired for the gigantism of his ambition to discover absolute laws governing humanity's ethical and spiritual obligations amid the psychological and social complexities of the world. Whatever form Tolstoy's doctrines took, they were always founded on his expansive humanitarianism and based on one of the most intensive quests for wisdom in human history. Although Tolstoy ultimately believed that art should serve a religious and ethical code, he himself serves primarily as a model of the consummate artist, and his two greatest works exemplify the nature and traditions of the modern realistic novel.

(For further information about Tolstoy's life and works, see *Contemporary Authors*, Vols. 104, 123; *Short Story Criticism*, Vol. 9; and *Twentieth-Century Literary Criticism*, Vols. 4, 11, 17, 28, 43.)

CRITICAL COMMENTARY

PERCY LUBBOCK

(essay date 1921)

[Lubbock was an English critic. In the following excerpt, he examines the structure of *War and Peace*.]

Of *War and Peace* it has never been suggested, I suppose, that Tolstoy here produced a model of perfect form. It is a panoramic vision of people and places, a huge expanse in which armies are marshalled; can one expect of such a book that it should be neatly composed? It is crowded with life, at whatever point we face it; intensely vivid, inexhaustibly stirring, the broad impression is made by the big prodigality of Tolstoy's invention. If a novel could really be as large as life, Tolstoy could easily fill it; his great masterful reach never seems near its limit; he is always ready to annex another and yet another tract of life, he is only restrained by the mere necessity of bringing a novel somewhere to an end. And then, too, this mighty command of spaces and masses is only half his power. He spreads further than any one else, but he also touches the detail of the scene, the single episode, the fine shade of character, with exquisite lightness and precision. Nobody surpasses, in some ways nobody approaches, the easy authority with which he handles the matter immediately before him at the moment, a roomful of people, the brilliance of youth, spring sunshine in a forest, a boy on a horse; whatever his shifting panorama brings into view, he makes of it an image of beauty and truth that is final, complete, unqualified. Before the profusion of *War and Peace* the question of its general form is scarcely raised. It is enough that such a world should have been pictured; it is idle to look for proportion and design in a book that contains a world.

But for this very reason, that there is so much in the book to distract attention from its form, it is particularly interesting to ask how it is made. (pp. 26-8)

If the total effect of his book is inconclusive, it is all lucidity and shapeliness in its parts. There is no faltering in his hold upon character; he never loses his way among the scores of men and women in the book; and in all the endless series of scenes and events there is not one which betrays a hesitating intention. The story rolls on and on, and it is long before the reader can begin to question its direction. . . . What is the subject of *War and Peace*, what is the novel *about*? There is no very ready answer; but if we are to discover what is wrong with the form, this is the question to press.

What is the story? There is first of all a succession of phases in the lives of certain generations; youth that passes out into maturity, fortunes that meet and clash and re-form, hopes that flourish and wane and reappear in other lives, age that sinks and hands on the torch to youth again—such is the substance of the drama. The book, I take it, begins to grow out of the thought of the processional march of the generations, always changing, always renewed; its figures are sought and chosen for the clarity with which the drama is embodied in them. (pp. 28-9)

Youth and age, the flow and the ebb of the recurrent tide—this is the theme of Tolstoy's book. (p. 31)

Cutting across the big human motive I have indicated, there falls a second line of thought, and sometimes it is this, most clearly, that the author is following. Not the cycle of life everlasting, in which the rage of nations is an incident, a noise and an incursion from without—but the strife itself, the irrelevant uproar, becomes the motive of the fable. *War and Peace*, the drama of that ancient alternation, is now the subject out of which the form of the book is to grow. (pp. 31-2)

It is a mighty antinomy indeed, on a scale adapted to Tolstoy's giant imagination. With one hand he takes up the largest subject in the world, the story to which

Principal Works

Detstvo (novel) 1852

   [Childhood published in Childhood and Youth, 1862]

Otrochestvo (novel) 1854

   [Boyhood published in Childhood, Boyhood, Youth, 1886]

Sevastopolskiye rasskazy. 2 vols. (sketches) 1855-56

   [Sebastopol, 1887]

Yunost (novel) 1857

   [Youth published in Childhood and Youth, 1862]

Semeinoe schaste (novel) 1859

   [Family Happiness, 1888]

Kazaki (novel) 1863

   [The Cossacks, 1878]

Polikushka (novel) 1863

   [Polikouchka, 1888]

Voina i mir (novel) 1869

   [War and Peace, 1886]

Anna Karenina (novel) 1877

   [Anna Karenina, 1886]

Ispoved (essay) 1882

   [A Confession, 1885]

V chiom moya vera (essay) 1884

   [What I Believe, 1885]

Smert Ivana Ilyicha (novella) 1886

   [Iván Ilyitch published in Iván Ilyitch, and Other Stories, 1887; also published as The Death of Ivan Iliitch, 1888]

Vlast tmy (drama) 1888

   [The Dominion of Darkness, 1888; also published as The Power of Darkness in Plays, 1910]

Plody prosvesh cheniya (drama) 1889

   [The Fruits of Enlightenment, 1890]

Kreitserova sonata (novella) 1890

   [The Kreutzer Sonata, 1890]

Khozyain i rabotnik (novella) 1895

   [Master and Man, 1895]

Chto takoe iskusstvo (essay) 1898

   [What Is Art?, 1898]

Otetz sergii (novella) 1898

   [Father Sergius published in Father Sergius, and Other Stories and Plays, 1911]

The Novels and Other Works of Lyof N. Tolstoi. 22 vols. (novels, novellas, short stories, dramas, essays, and sketches) 1899-1902

Voskresenie (novel) 1899

   [Resurrection, 1899]

I svet vo tme svetit (unfinished drama) [first publication] 1911

   [The Light That Shines in Darkness, 1912]

Khadzhi Murat (novel) 1911

   [Hadji Murád published in Hadji Murád, and Other Stories, 1912]

Zhivoy trup (drama) 1911

   [The Living Corpse, 1912]

L. N. Tolstoi: polnoe sobranie proizvedenie. 90 vols. (novels, novellas, short stories, dramas, essays, and sketches) 1928-58

Tolstoy's Letters. 2 vols. (letters) 1978

---

all other human stories are subordinate; and not content with this, in the other hand he produces the drama of a great historic collision, for which a scene is set with no less prodigious a gesture. And there is not a sign in the book to show that he knew what he was doing; apparently he was quite unconscious that he was writing two novels at once. (p. 32)

The long, slow, steady sweep of the story—the *first* story, as I call it—setting through the personal lives of a few young people, bringing them together, separating them, dimming their freshness, carrying them away from hopeful adventure to their appointed condition, where their part is only to transmit the gift of youth to others and to drop back while the adventure is repeated—this motive, in which the book opens and closes and to which it constantly returns, is broken into by the famous scenes of battle (by some of them, to be accurate, not by all), with the reverberation of imperial destinies, out of which Tolstoy makes a saga of his country's tempestuous past. (p. 34)

It is now the war, with the generals and the potentates in the forefront, that is the matter of the story. Alexander and Kutusov, Napoleon and Murat, become the chief actors, and between them the play is acted out. In this story the loves and ambitions of the young generation, which have hitherto been central, are relegated to the fringe; there are wide tracts in which they do not appear at all. Again and again Tolstoy forgets them entirely; he has discovered a fresh idea for the unification of this second book, a theory drummed into the reader with merciless iteration, desolating many a weary page. The meaning of the book—and it is extraordinary how Tolstoy's artistic sense deserts him in expounding it—lies in the relation between the man of destiny and the forces that he dreams he is directing; it is a high theme, but Tolstoy cannot leave it to make its own effect. (p. 35)

[The] cycle of the war and the peace, as distinguished from the cycle of youth and age, is broken and fragmentary. (p. 36)

In *War and Peace,* as it seems to me, the story suffers twice over for the imperfection of the form. It is damaged, in the first place, by the importation of another and an irrelevant story—damaged because it so loses the sharp and clear relief that it would have if it stood alone. Whether the story was to be the drama of youth and age, or the drama of war and peace, in either case it would have been imcomparably more impressive if *all* the great wealth of the material had been used for its purpose, all brought into one design. And furthermore, in either case again, the story is incomplete; neither of them is finished, neither of them is given its full development, for all the size of the book. (pp. 40-1)

[The] broad lines of Tolstoy's book have always seemed uncertain and confused. Neither his subject nor his method were fixed for him as he wrote; he ranged around his mountain of material, attacking it now here and now there, never deciding in his mind to what end he had amassed it. None of his various schemes is thus completed, none of them gets the full advantage of the profusion of life which he commands. At any moment great masses of that life are being wasted, turned to no account; and the result is not merely negative, for at any moment the wasted life, the stuff that is not being used, is dividing and weakening the effect of the picture created out of the rest. That so much remains, in spite of everything, gives the measure of Tolstoy's genius; *that* becomes the more extraordinary as the chaotic plan of his book is explored. He could work with such lordly neglect of his subject and yet he could produce such a book—it is surely as much as to say that Tolstoy's is the supreme genius among novelists. (p. 58)

Percy Lubbock, in a chapter in his *The Craft of Fiction,* Jonathan Cape Ltd., 1921, pp. 26-58.

PRINCE D. S. MIRSKY
(essay date 1926)

[Mirsky was a Russian prince who fled his country after the Bolshevik Revolution and settled in London. While in England, he wrote two important histories of Russian literature, *Contemporary Russian Literature* (1926) and *A History of Russian Literature from Its Beginnings to 1900* (1927). In the following excerpt from a later printing of the former work, he provides a survey of Tolstoy's works after 1880.]

Tolstóy's writings after 1880 are divided by a deep cleft from all his earlier work. But they belong to the same man, and much of what appeared at first new and startling in the later Tolstóy existed in a less developed form in the early Tolstóy. From the very beginning we cannot fail to discern in him an obstinate search for a rational meaning to life; a confidence in the powers of common sense and his own reason; contempt for modern civilization with its "artificial" multiplication of needs; a deeply rooted irreverence for all the functions and conventions of State and Society; a sovereign disregard for accepted opinions and scientific and literary "good form"; and a pronounced tendency to teach. But what was disseminated and disconnected in his early writings was welded after his conversion into a solid consistent doctrine, dogmatically settled in every detail. (p. 294)

The teaching of Tolstóy is a rationalized "Christianity," stripped of all tradition and all positive mysticism. He rejected personal immortality and concentrated exclusively on the moral teaching of the Gospels. Of the moral teaching of Christ the words, "Resist not evil," were taken to be the principle out of which all the rest follows. He rejected the authority of the Church, which sanctioned the State, and he condemned the State, which sanctioned violence and compulsion. Both were immoral, like every form of organized compulsion. His condemnation of every form of compulsion authorizes us to classify Tolstóy's teaching, in its political aspect, as anarchism. (p. 295)

Tolstóy's conversion was, largely, the reaction of his fundamental rationalism against the irrationalism into which he had allowed himself to drift in the sixties and seventies. His metaphysics may be summed up as the identification of the principle of life with reason. . . . But for all its rationalism, Tolstóy's religion is in a sense mystical. . . . [In] all his more remarkable later works "conversion" is described as an essentially mystical experience. It is mystical in that it is personal and unique. It is the result of an intimate revelation, which may or may not be prepared by previous intellectual development, but is essentially, like every mystical experience, incommunicable. In Tolstóy's own case, as described in *A Confession,* it is led up to by his whole previous intellectual life. But all purely intellectual solutions to the essential question were unsatisfactory, and the final solution is represented as a series of mystical experiences, repeated flashes of inner light. The civilized man lives in a state of unquestioning sin. The questions of meaning and justification arise against his will—as the effect of fear of death—and the answer comes as a ray of inner light—the process described thus more than once by Tolstóy—in *A Confession,* in *The Death of Iván Ilyích,* in the *Memoirs of a Madman,* in *Master and Man.* The necessary consequence of this fact is that the truth cannot be preached, but may only be discovered for oneself. This is the doctrine of *A Con-*

fession, which does not attempt to demonstrate, but only to narrate and to "infect." (pp. 296-97)

The first of Tolstóy's works in which he preached his new teaching was *A Confession.* . . . *A Confession* is altogether on a higher level than the rest—it is one of the world's masterpieces. It is a work of art, and Tolstóy's biographer would give proof of too much simple-mindedness if he used it as biographical material in the strict sense of the word. (pp. 299-300)

Tolstóy's other moral and religious writings are not on a level with *A Confession,* though they are written in the same admirable Russian, sometimes with even greater elegance and precision. . . . *What Are We to Do?* is a kind of continuation of *A Confession,* but on a less mystical and more social plane. It is the story of Tolstóy's experience in the slums and night refuges of Moscow soon after his conversion. His religious views were systematized in a series of works, of which the first, *What I Believe,* was written in 1883-4. This was followed by a *Critique of Dogmatic Theology, The Kingdom of Heaven Is Within Us, An Exposition of the Gospels,* and *The Christian Doctrine. What I Believe* is the most comprehensive of his dogmatic writings. What he gave in *A Confession* in the form of a personal experience, in its process of becoming, is here crystallized and stabilized into a settled doctrine. *The Christian Doctrine.* . . is an exposition of the same doctrine in a still more logical and fixed form, after the manner of a catechism. It is a source of infinite pleasure to those who admire most in Tolstóy his lucidity and his skill at definition and precise statement. *The Exposition of the Gospels* has less of this quality and more of a very farfetched and not always bona fide interpretation. In *The Critique of Dogmatic Theology* he is a polemist well versed in all the little tricks of argumentative tactics, a cunning fencer, and consummate ironist. Ridicule and an appeal to common sense are his favorite polemical methods. "This is unintelligible nonsense," is his knock-out argument. His minor tracts are numerous and touch on a great variety of points of detail, or on topics of current interest. Such is *Why Do People Intoxicate Themselves?* denouncing drink and tobacco. Such is *I Cannot Be Silent,* a violent invective against the Russian government and the numerous executions during the suppression of the First Revolution.

The first stories he wrote after *A Confession* were a series of edifying short stories for the people. They were published in 1885 and the following years by the firm Posrédnik, founded for the special purpose of popularizing Tolstóy's teaching. They were written with regard to the existing conditions in Russia, that is, they were meant to satisfy the censor. Consequently they contain no violent and overt satire of the Church and State. The moral is always plainly present, often in the title—*Evil Allures, but Good Endures, God Sees the Truth but Waits*—but is not always peculiarly Tolstoy-

an. . . . One of the best is *Two Old Men,* the story of two peasants who set out on a pilgrimage to Jerusalem in fulfillment of a vow. (p. 304)

Later on, as his fame grew and he began to have a public all over the world, he wrote popular stories of a new kind, more universal and generalized. They approach still nearer to his ideal of being comprehensible to all men. Such are his adaptations from the French— *Francoise* (Maupassant's *La Vierge-des-Vents* pruned of realistic excrescences), *The Coffee-House of Surat,* and *Too Dear,* and his still later stories, *King Essarhadon, Work, Death, and Sickness,* and *Three Questions.* In these he approaches the style of the parable, which he had used with such powerful effect in *A Confession,* and of the oriental apologue.

The stories written with a view to the educated reader are different in manner: they are much longer, much fuller of detail, more "psychological," altogether nearer in style to his earlier work. There are problem stories, written not so much to teach as to communicate his own experience. They may be grouped into two categories, stories of conversion and stories on the sexual problem. The first group consists of [*The Memoirs of a Madman, The Death of Iván Ilyích,* and *Master and Man*]. . . . In all these stories the subject is the conversion of the dark and unregenerated educated or rich man before the face of death or madness. *The Memoirs of a Madman* is very much akin to *A Confession.* . . . In *The Death of Iván Ilyích* the hero is not a thinking and seeking man like Tolstóy of the *Confession* or like the madman. He is an ordinary, vulgar, average man of the educated classes, a judge (the class Tolstóy detested most of all). (pp. 304-05)

The "sexual" stories are [*The Kreutzer Sonata* and *The Devil*]. . . . The first, a study of jealousy and a diatribe against the sexual education of young men and women in modern society, is a powerful production but hardly a perfect work of art. It is not sufficiently concentrated; its preaching is not always artistically "necessary"; its manner strangely enough reminds one of the untidy and excited manner of Dostoyévsky. *The Devil* is more satisfactory. . . .

Of all Tolstóy's late narrative works, the one that attracted the greatest attention and became most widely known, and is consequently, more often than not, taken as typical of his last period, was *Resurrection.* . . . It is a novel in three parts—by far the longest of all his stories since 1880, almost comparable in length with *Anna Karénina* and *War and Peace.* This is the sole reason why it has usurped a principal position among his later work and is so often quoted by the side of the two earlier novels. It has often been used to prove that Tolstóy's genius declined after he became a preacher. If the imaginative work of his last thirty years is to stand or fall according to the merit of *Resurrection,* it will be in somewhat bad case, for it is quite obvious that *Resurrection* is very much inferior to *War and Peace* and *Anna Karénina.* But it is also much inferior to *Master and Man,* to *Hajjí Murád,* and to *The Living Corpse.* In spite of its size it is by no means the work into which Tolstóy put the most work and care. (pp. 306-07)

If in *Resurrection* Tolstóy is at his worst, in its twin novel he is at his best. *Hajjí Murád* was begun in 1896 and completed in 1904. It was published after his death. In it he tried to give a story that would answer to his ideal of "good universal," not religious, art. *Hajjí Murád* is a masterpiece of the highest order. (pp. 307-08)

Hajjí Murád, as well as *The Memoirs of a Madman* and *The Devil,* was published only in 1911, in the collected edition of Tolstóy's posthumous works. This collection also includes several plays and many other stories and fragments. One of these is *Father Sergius*. . ., the story of an aristocrat who became a monk and a hermit—a powerful study of spiritual pride and, once again, carnal desires. It is also an excellent example of Tolstóy's later rapid and "essential" narrative manner. Still better in this respect is *The False Coupon*. . ., the admirably constructed story of a succession of evils diverging from one initial evil action to converge by a contrasting succession of good actions towards the common salvation of all concerned. It is impossible to list all the numerous minor stories and fragments of these wonderful three volumes. But one at least must be mentioned: one of the shortest— *Alësha Gorshók.* . . . It is a masterpiece of rare perfection. It is the apotheosis of the "holy fool," who does not himself realize his goodness. (pp. 308-09)

Tolstóy's plays all belong to the period after 1880. He had not the essential qualities that go to the making of a dramatist, and the merits of his plays are not of the strictly dramatic order. (p. 309)

The dogmatic followers of Tolstóy were never numerous, but his reputation among people of all classes grew immensely. It spread all over the world, and by the last two decades of his life Tolstóy enjoyed a place in the world's esteem that had not been held by any man of letters since the death of Voltaire. (p. 311)

Prince D. S. Mirsky, "The End of a Great Age," in his *A History of Russian Literature Comprising "A History of Russian Literature" and "Contemporary Russian Literature,"* edited by Francis J. Whitfield, Alfred A. Knopf, 1949, pp. 291-332.

PRINCE D. S. MIRSKY
(essay date 1927)

[In the following excerpt from a 1949 printing of his 1927 study *A History of Russian Literature from Its Beginnings to 1900,* Mirsky provides a survey of Tolstoy's works before 1880.]

From the beginnings of his diary to the time he wrote *War and Peace,* writing was to Tolstóy above all a struggle to master reality, to found a method and a technique of reducing it to words. To this, from 1851, he added the problem of transforming notation of fact into literature. Tolstóy did not achieve it at a single stroke. His first attempt at imaginative writing, a fragment entitled *An Account of Yesterday,* is apparently the beginning of an account of an actual twenty-four hours spent by him, with no invention, nothing but notation. It was only to be fuller and less selective than the diaries and subordinated to a general design. In point of detail the *Account* is almost on a Proustian if not a Joycean scale. . . . For all his pioneering courage, Tolstóy did not have the audacity to continue in this line of extensive notation. It is almost a pity he did not. The sheer originality of *An Account of Yesterday* remains unsurpassed. If he had continued in that line, he would probably have met with less immediate recognition, but he might have ultimately produced an even more astounding body of work. In the light of *An Account of Yesterday, Childhood* seems almost a surrender to all the conventions of literature. Of all Tolstóy's writings it is the one where extraneous literary influences (Sterne, Rousseau, Töpfer) are most clearly apparent. But even now, in the light of *War and Peace, Childhood* retains its unique and unfading charm. It has already that wonderful poetry of reality which is attained without the slightest aid of poetical device, without the aid of language (the few sentimental, rhetorical passages rather tend to destroy it), by the sole help of the choice of significant psychological and real detail. (p. 254)

In all he wrote after *Childhood* and up to *War and Peace* he continued his forward movement, experimenting, forging his instrument, never condescending to sacrifice his interest in the process of production to the artistic effect of the finished product. This is apparent in the sequels of *Childhood—Boyhood*. . . and *Youth*. . . —when the poetic, evocative atmosphere of *Childhood* becomes thinner and thinner and the element of sheer untransformed analysis protrudes more and more. It is still more apparent in his stories of war and of the Caucasus: [*A Raid, Sevastópol in December,*

Sevastópol in May, Sevastópol in August, A Wood Felling]. . . . In them he set out to destroy the existing romantic conceptions of those two arch-romantic themes. To be understood in their genesis, these stories have to be felt against their background of romantic literature, against the romances of Bestúzhev and the Byronic poems of Púshkin and Lérmontov. (p. 255)

In the stories written in the second half of the fifties and early sixties Tolstóy's center of interest is shifted from analysis to morality. These stories—*The Memoirs of a Billiard Marker, Two Hussars, Albert, Lucerne, Three Deaths, Family Happiness, Polikushka,* and *Kholstomér, the Story of a Horse*—are frankly didactic and moralistic, much more so than any of the stories of his last, dogmatic period. The main moral of these stories is the fallacy of civilization and the inferiority of the civilized, conscious, sophisticated man, with his artificially multiplied needs, to natural man. On the whole they mark an advance neither, as the war stories did, in Tolstóy's method of annexing and digesting reality, nor in his skill in transferring the raw experience of life into art (as in *Childhood* and *War and Peace*). . . . *Lucerne,* for its earnest and bitter indignation against the selfishness of the rich (which, it is true,

he was inclined at that time to regard, semi-Slavophilwise, as a peculiarity of the materialistic civilization of the West), is particularly suggestive of the spirit of his later work. As a sermon in fiction it is certainly one of the most powerful things of its kind. The nearest approach to complete artistic success is *Two Hussars,* a charming story that betrays its purpose only in the excessively neat parallelism between the characters of the two Hussars, father and son. . . . Lastly, *Kholstomér, the Story of a Horse* is certainly one of the most characteristic and curious of all Tolstóy's writings. It is a satire upon civilized mankind from the point of view of a horse. (pp. 256-57)

Apart from the rest of his earliest work stands *The Cossacks.* . . . [It] is probably his masterpiece before *War and Peace.* . . . The main idea is the contrast of his sophisticated and self-conscious personality to the "natural men" that are the Cossacks. (p. 257)

Tolstóy's first literary work after his marriage was the (post-humously published) comedy *A Contaminated Family.* It shows already the conservative trend of his married mind. It is a satire of the nihilist, ending in the triumph of the meek, but fundamentally sensible,

Tolstoy with his wife, Sofia, in his study.

father over his rebellious children. It is a masterpiece of delicate character drawing and dialogue. It contains more genuine and good-humored humor than any other of his works. (p. 258)

War and Peace is, not only in size, but in perfection, the masterpiece of the early Tolstóy. It is also the most important work in the whole of Russian realistic fiction. If in the whole range of the European novel of the nineteenth century it has equals, it has no superiors, and the peculiarities of the modern, as opposed to the pre-nineteenth-century, novel are more clearly seen in it than in such rivals as *Madame Bovary* or *Le Rouge et le Noir*. It was an advanced pioneering work, a work that widened, as few novels have done, the province and the horizon of fiction. . . . In many respects *War and Peace* is a direct continuation of the preceding works of Tolstóy. The methods of analysis and of "making it strange" are the same, only carried to a greater perfection. . . . The glorification of "natural man," of Natásha and Nicholas Rostóv at the expense of the sophisticated Prince Andrew, and of the peasant Platón Karatáyev at the expense of all the civilized heroes, continues the line of thought of *Two Hussars* and of *The Cossacks*. The satirical representation of society and of diplomacy is completely in line with Tolstóy's disgust at European civilization. However, in other respects it is different from the earlier work. First of all it is more objective. . . . But the most wonderful difference of *War and Peace* from the earlier stories are the women, Princess Maria and especially Natásha. There can be no doubt that it was his increased knowledge of feminine nature, due to marriage, that enabled Tolstóy to annex this new province of psychological experience. The art of individualization also attains to unsurpassable perfection. . . . The roundness, the completeness, the liveness of the characters, even of the most episodic, are perfect and absolute. (pp. 258-59)

The transformation of reality into art is also more perfect in *War and Peace* than in anything that preceded it. It is almost complete. The novel is built along its own laws (Tolstóy has let escape him some interesting hints as to these laws) and contains few undigested bits of raw material. The narrative is a miracle. . . .

The philosophy of the novel is the glorification of nature and life at the expense of the sophistications of reason and civilization. It is the surrender of the rationalist Tolstóy to the irrational forces of existence. (p. 260)

There are two conceivable strictures on *War and Peace*, the figure of Karatáyev, and the theoretical chapters on history and warfare. Personally I do not admit the validity of the latter drawback. It is an essential of Tolstóy's art to be not only art, but knowledge. And to the vast canvas of the great novel the theoretical chapters add a perspective and an intellectual atmosphere one cannot wish away. I feel it more difficult to

put up with Karatáyev. In spite of his quintessential importance for the idea of the novel, he jars. He is not a human being among human beings, as the other two ideally natural characters, Natásha and Kutúzov, are. He is an abstraction, a myth, a being with different dimensions and laws from those of the rest of the novel. He does not fit in. (p. 261)

Anna Karénina is in all essentials a continuation of *War and Peace*. The methods of Tolstóy are the same in both, and the two novels are justly named together. What has been said of the personages of *War and Peace* may be repeated of those of *Anna Karénina*. . . . Perhaps there is even a greater variety and a more varied sympathy in the characters of *Anna Karénina*. . . . But Lévin is a much less happily transformed Tolstóy than are his emanations in *War and Peace*, Prince Andrew and Pierre. . . . Another difference between the two novels is that *Anna Karénina* contains no separate philosophical chapters, but a more obtrusive and insidious moral philosophy is diffused throughout the story. The philosophy is less irrational and optimistic, more puritan, and is everywhere felt as distinct from and alien to the main groundwork of the novel. The groundwork has the idyllic flavor of *War and Peace*. But in the philosophy of the novel there is an ominous suggestion of the approach of a more tragic God than the blind and good life-God of *War and Peace*. The tragic atmosphere thickens as the story advances towards the end. The romance of Anna and Vrónsky, who had transgressed the moral and social law, culminates in blood and horror to which there is no counterpart in the earlier novel. . . . He was never again to write a novel like these two. After finishing *Anna Karénina* he attempted to resume his work on Peter and the Decembrists, but it was soon forsaken, and instead, two years after the completion of his last idyl, he wrote *A Confession*.

Anna Karénina leads up to the moral and religious crisis that was so profoundly to revolutionize Tolstóy. Before he began it he had already begun to cast his eyes on new artistic methods—abandoning the psychological and analytical manner of superfluous detail and discovering a simpler narrative style that could be applied not only to the sophisticated and corrupt educated classes, but to the undeveloped mind of the people. The stories he wrote for the people in 1872 (*God Sees the Truth* and *The Captive in the Caucasus*, which by the way, is merely a translation into unromantic terms, a sort of parody, of the poem of Púshkin) already announce the popular tales of 1885-6. (pp. 261-63)

Prince D. S. Mirsky, "The Age of Realism: The Novelists (II)," in his *A History of Russian Literature Comprising "A History of Russian Literature" and "Contemporary Russian Literature,"* edited by Francis J. Whitfield, Alfred A. Knopf, 1949, pp. 245-90.

this, it should be added, is sought amid a setting of luxury. (pp. 298-99)

Next to Anna, the other most important character in this novel is Levin. It is striking to note in passing that these two do not meet until the latter portion of the narrative, but when they do, they immediately recognize each other's worth. Tolstoy's account of their meeting even suggests that, had they met under different circumstances, they could well have fallen in love.

Levin represents the landed nobility. In the city, he feels uncomfortable. He is often awkward, and is ill at ease even with intellectuals who are interested in the same problems as he is. . . . He needs to find a deeper meaning in life. Anna, in her way, seeks that deeper meaning in love. Levin, after a period of despair, discovers love. But unlike Anna's love, it is a spiritualized love, based on the example of Christ, and expressive of brotherhood for all men. In this respect Levin represents Tolstoy on the eve of the great religious change which occurred in the 1880's. He stands in contrapuntal relationship to Anna. Anna, as humanity, comes to a tragic end; Levin, the dissatisfied nobleman, grasps an image of humanity which permits him to go on living. In his period of despair he feared that he would destroy himself, and would not trust himself with a gun or a rope. Anna does destroy herself. When she can no longer love, she sees all of human life as motivated by hate.

These meanings can be brought out more clearly if *Anna Karenina* is related to *War and Peace*. Anna is a continuation of Natasha Rostov of the latter novel; she is like Natasha's older sister. In *War and Peace*, Natasha represents humanity, but as a girl becoming a woman. Natasha's motivations are similar to Anna's, and, like Anna's, different from those of most of the other aristocrats. Parallel to the similarity of Anna and Natasha, there is a correspondence between Pierre Bezuhov, the dissatisfied nobleman of *War and Peace*, and Levin. Neither of them can find occupation and meaning in life so long as they are motivated in terms of their class position and their social functions. They seek to discover humanity, and they find patriarchal peasants as models for this discovery. Unlike most of the other aristocrats in these novels, Pierre and Levin grow, develop in emotional depth. (pp. 301-02)

[The] conception of characters and events in *Anna Karenina* is based on the conception of history which Tolstoy formally stated at the end of *War and Peace*. The central problem treated is thus that of freedom, freedom and the self, or the personality. It is this same problem which concerns us at the present moment, in a further advanced period of our historical development; in fact, we can say we face this problem from the other side of progress. The satiety sometimes suggested when Anna and Vronsky are living in luxury has an almost contemporary ring. In like manner, many of the

---

JAMES T. FARRELL
(essay date 1946)

[Farrell, an American novelist, short story writer, and critic, is best known for his Studs Lonigan trilogy, a series of novels depicting the life of a lower middle-class man of Chicago. In the following excerpt from an essay written in 1946, he discusses theme and characterization in *Anna Karenina*.]

Among the works of nineteenth-century Russian literature, *Anna Karenina* is focal. No other Russian novel of the entire century so concentrates the so-called Russian problem, images and represents it so vividly, so directly, so immediately in terms of direct, vigorously drawn, and humanly credible characterizations. The fact that it is set in the time of most intense change in Russia is significant in understanding the novel. The intensity of the change, the transitional character of the times, the fact that Levin, the most intelligent character in *Anna Karenina,* realizes that everything is upside down and just taking shape—all this helps us to understand the richness, the all-sidedness, the significance of this work.

The character Anna Karenina is not merely the wife of a high bureaucrat who falls in love with a rich army officer, leaves husband and child for her paramour, and, driven to despair, commits suicide. Nor is her story a mere tale of adultery. More than this, the novel is a presentation of the author's vision of humanity. When we consider the richness of detail, the fullness in the presentation of all the problems of Russia in the very narrative, in the very characterizations, it should be clear that there is a central importance in the fact that Anna's name serves for the title. Anna is the most representative figure in this novel. She is symbolic. She is Tolstoy's image of humanity. With the exception of some of the peasants in these crowded pages, we can observe a striking difference in Anna's motivations, and in those of every other important character. Her motivations come from inside herself, and are not seriously influenced by her role, her function in society. She acts in accordance with her inner nature, and she wants, above all else, to love and to be loved. We know from Tolstoy's entire literary output that he considered the need to love and to be loved fundamental in the character of the natural man and woman. Anna is, then, the most natural member of the upper classes to be found in this work. Her actions are inspired by her emotions. . . . Her tragedy is that of humanity seeking to express the full nature of its need to love and to be loved in material, sensory, sexual relationships; and

emotions of the characters of this novel seem almost contemporary. Russia at the dawn of its capitalist development and America at the peak of its development seem to reveal many parallels. This gives to *Anna Karenina* a strong contemporary appeal. (pp. 303-04)

Anna Karenina establishes [Tolstoy's] view in terms of the living images of human beings. Tolstoy's alternative, the so-called doctrine of Tolstoyism based on nonresistance and individual moral self-regeneration, has not, however, been historically successful. When we read him, then, we must do so not for some rigid solution but for insight. *Anna Karenina* brings us face to face with a great mind, a great artist, and a work of artistic greatness which is one of the true masterpieces of world literature. (p. 304)

James T. Farrell, "An Introduction to 'Anna Karenina'," in his *Literature and Morality,* Vanguard Press, 1947, pp. 296-304.

GEORG LUKACS

(essay date 1950)

[A Hungarian literary critic and philosopher, Lukacs was a leading proponent of Marxist thought. In the following excerpt, he relates Tolstoy's brand of realism to the realistic tradition in the European novel.]

Tolstoy's oeuvre marks a step forward not only in Russian literature but in the literature of the world. This step forward was made, however, in rather peculiar circumstances. Although Tolstoy continued the great realistic traditions of the eighteenth and nineteenth centuries, the traditions of Fielding and Defoe, Balzac and Stendhal, he did so at a time when realism had already fallen into decay and the literary trends which were to sweep away realism had triumphed throughout Europe. Hence Tolstoy, in his literary work, had to swim against the current in world literature, and this current was the decline of realism.

But Tolstoy's position in world literature was unique for more reasons than this. It would be quite misleading to stress this divergence unduly and define Tolstoy's place in the literature of his age as though he had rejected all the literary trends and all the writers of his own time and had obstinately clung to the traditions of the great realists.

In the first place: what Tolstoy carried on was not the artistic and stylistic tradition bequeathed by the great realists. We do not wish to quote here Tolstoy's own judgments on the older and newer realists; these judgments are often contradictory and—like the judgments of most great writers—they vary a great deal according to the concrete requirements of each period of

their work. What never varied, however, was Tolstoy's healthy—and angry—contempt of the petty naturalism of his own contemporaries. (p. 129)

The older great realists had no demonstrable immediate influence on Tolstoy's style. The principles he followed in his realism objectively represent a continuation of the great realist school, but subjectively they grew out of the problems of his own time and out of his attitude to the great problem of his time, the relationship between exploiter and exploited in rural Russia. Of course the study of the old realists had a considerable influence on the development of Tolstoy's style, but it would be wrong to attempt to derive the Tolstoian style of realism in art and literature in a straight line from the old great realists.

Although Tolstoy continued and developed the traditions of the older realism, he always did so in his own original way and in accordance with the needs of the age, never as an epigone. He was always in step with his time, not only in content, in the characters and social problems he presented, but also in the artistic sense. Hence there are many common traits in his literary method and that of his European contemporaries. But it is interesting and important to note in connection with this community of method that artistic traits which in Europe were the symptoms of the decline of realism and contributed to the dissolution of such literary forms as the drama, the novel and the short story, regained their vitality and originality in Tolstoy's hands and served as the elements of a nascent new form which, continuing the traditions of the old great realism in a novel manner and in relation to new problems, rose to heights unsurpassed by the realist literature of any nation. (pp. 129-30)

Tolstoy himself was well aware that his great novels were genuine epics. But it was not only he himself who compared *War and Peace* with Homer—many known and unknown readers of the book had the same feeling. Of course the comparison with Homer, while it shows the profound impression made by the truly epic quality of this novel, is more an indication of the general trend of its style than an actual characteristic of the style itself. For in spite of its epic sweep, *War and Peace* is still from first to last a true novel, although of course, not a novel with the dramatic concentration found in Balzac. Its loose, spacious composition, the cheerful, comfortable, leisurely relationships between the characters, the calm and yet animated abundance of the epic episodes indispensable to the true storyteller—all these are related more to the great provincial idylls of the eighteenth-century English novel than to Balzac. (p. 149)

Tolstoy's great novels differ from those of his English predecessors in the specific nature of the social reality which they mirror and are superior to their English parallels in artistic richness and depth precisely because of this specific character of the reality presented. The world depicted by Tolstoy is a world much less *bourgeois* than the world of the eighteenth-century English novelists, but—especially in *Anna Karenina*—it is a world in which the process of capitalist development is more strongly apparent than in the English novels which nearly always depict only one particular phase of it. (pp. 149-50)

Tolstoy's literary career began and ended in a period of approaching revolutionary storms. Tolstoy is a *pre-revolutionary* writer. And precisely because the central problem in his works was the Russian peasant problem, the decisive turning-point in the history of western literature, i.e. the defeat of the 1848 revolutions, left no traces on them. In this connection it matters little how far Tolstoy himself, in the various phases of his development, was aware or unaware of this cardinal issue. What is important is that this issue is at the core of all his works, that everything he wrote revolves around this issue; it is only for this reason that he still remained a pre-revolutionary writer even after the disaster of the European revolutions of 1848.

But the village idylls of Tolstoy's great novels are always threatened idylls. In *War and Peace* the financial disaster of the Rostov family is enacted before our eyes as the typical disaster of the old-fashioned provincial nobility; the spiritual crises of Bezukhov and Bolkonski are reflections of the great current which broadened politically into the Decembrist rising. In *Anna Karenina* even darker clouds menace the village idyll and the enemy has already openly shown its capitalist countenance. Now it is no longer a question of financial disaster alone—here one can already feel the undertow of capitalism, against which Tolstoy makes so passionate a protest.

Constantine Levin, who really takes up the problems where Nikolai Rostov left them in *War and Peace*, can no longer solve them as simply and light-heartedly. He fights not only to recover his material prosperity as a landowner (without falling a victim to the capitalisation of the land) but has to carry on an incessant inner struggle, a struggle moving from crisis to crisis in trying to convince himself that his existence as landowner is justified and that he has the right to exploit his peasants. The incomparable epic greatness of Tolstoy's novels is based on the illusions which caused him to believe that this was not a tragic conflict out of which there was no way out for the honest representatives of the class, but a problem capable of solution.

In *Anna Karenina* these illusions were already shaken to a much greater extent than in *War and Peace*. This manifests itself among other things in the fact that the structure of *Anna Karenina* is much more 'European,' much more closely-knit and the unfolding of the story far less leisurely. The closer assimilation of the theme to those of the European novels of the nineteenth century is a further, even though external, indication of the approaching crisis; although the style of *Anna Karenina* still has the characteristics of Tolstoy's early period, certain traits of his later critical period are already showing themselves. *Anna Karenina* is far more novel-like than *War and Peace*.

In *The Kreutzer Sonata* Tolstoy takes another long step in the direction of the European novel. He creates for himself a great form of *novella* which resembles the perfected form produced by European realism and which is both broad and dramatically concentrated. He inclines more and more towards presenting the great catastrophes, the tragically-ending turning-points in human destinies by a detailed portrayal of all their manifold inner motives, i.e., in the most profound sense of the word, epically.

Thus Tolstoy approaches to some extent the form of composition used by Balzac. Not that Balzac had influenced his literary style; but the reality which they both experienced and the manner in which they experienced it drove both of them by an inner necessity to create such forms. *The Death of Ivan Ilyich* marks the culminating point of this later style of Tolstoy, but its effects can also be traced in his last great novel *Resurrection.* It is no accident that Tolstoy's dramatic works were also written in this period.

But the thematic assimilation to European literature does not mean artistic assimilation to the prevalent literary trends there, the very trends which broke up the artistic forms of the epic and the drama. On the contrary, to the end of his life Tolstoy remained, in all questions relating to art, a great realist of the old school, and a great creator of epic form. (pp. 150-51)

Georg Lukacs, "Tolstoy and the Development of Realism," in his *Studies in European Realism: A Sociological Survey of the Writings of Balzac, Stendhal, Zola, Tolstoy, Gorki and Others*, translated by Edith Bone, 1950. Reprint by Merlin Press, 1972, pp. 126-205.

ISAIAH BERLIN
(essay date 1953)

[Berlin is a Latvian-born English philosopher and critic. The following excerpt is taken from his influential essay *The Hedgehog and the Fox: An Essay on Tolstoy's View of History*. Here, he discusses a conflict in Tolstoy's works between his "instinctive judgment and theoretical conviction," maintaining that Tolstoy's ability to depict the diversity and multiplicity of life was unparalleled, but in direct opposition to his desire to propound a single and all-encompassing system of belief.]

There is a line among the fragments of the Greek poet Archilochus which says: "The fox knows many things, but the hedgehog knows one big thing'. (p. 7)

The first kind of intellectual and artistic personality belongs to the hedgehogs, the second to the foxes; and without insisting on a rigid classification, we may, without too much fear of contradiction, say that, in this sense, Dante belongs to the first category, Shakespeare to the second; Plato, Lucretius, Pascal, Hegel, Dostoevsky, Nietzsche, Ibsen, Proust are, in varying degrees, hedgehogs; Herodotus, Aristotle, Montaigne, Erasmus, Molière, Goethe, Pushkin, Balzac, Joyce are foxes. (p. 8)

[When] we come to Count Lev Nikolaevich Tolstoy, and ask this of him—ask whether he belongs to the first category or the second, whether he is a monist or a pluralist, whether his vision is of one or of many, whether he is of a single substance or compounded of heterogeneous elements, there is no clear or immediate answer. The question does not, somehow, seem wholly appropriate; it seems to breed more darkness than it dispels. Yet it is not lack of information that makes us pause: Tolstoy has told us more about himself and his views and attitudes than any other Russian, more, almost, than any other European writer; nor can his art be called obscure in any normal sense: his universe has no dark corners, his stories are luminous with the light of day; he has explained them and himself, and argued about them and the methods by which they are constructed, more articulately and with greater force and sanity and lucidity than any other writer. Is he a fox or a hedgehog? What are we to say? Why is the answer so curiously difficult to find? Does he resemble Shakespeare or Pushkin more than Dante or Dostoevsky? Or is he wholly unlike either, and is the question therefore unanswerable because it is absurd? What is the mysterious obstacle with which our inquiry seems faced? (pp. 10-11)

The hypothesis I wish to offer is that Tolstoy was by nature a fox, but believed in being a hedgehog; that his gifts and achievement are one thing, and his beliefs, and consequently his interpretation of his own achievement, another; and that consequently his ideals have led him, and those whom his genius for persuasion has taken in, into a systematic misinterpretation of what he and others were doing or should be doing. No one can complain that he has left his readers in any doubt as to what he taught about this topic: his views on this subject permeate all his discursive writings—diaries, recorded *obiter dicta,* autobiographical essays and stories, social and religious tracts, literary criticism, letters to private and public correspondents. But the conflict between what he was and what he believed emerges nowhere so clearly as in his view of history to which some of his most brilliant and most paradoxical pages are devoted. (pp. 11-12)

Those who have treated Tolstoy primarily as a novelist have at times looked upon the historical and philosophical passages scattered through *War and Peace* as so much perverse interruption of the narrative, as a regrettable liability to irrelevant digression characteristic of this great, but excessively opinionated, writer, a lop-sided, homemade metaphysic of small or no intrinsic interest, deeply inartistic and thoroughly foreign to the purpose and structure of the work of art as a whole. (pp. 12-13)

Tolstoy's central thesis—in some respects not unlike the theory of the inevitable 'self-deception' of the *bourgeoisie* held by his contemporary Karl Marx, save that what Marx reserves for a class, Tolstoy sees in almost all mankind—is that there is a natural law whereby the lives of human beings no less than those of nature are determined; but that men, unable to face this inexorable process, seek to represent it as a succession of free choices, to fix responsibility for what occurs upon persons endowed by them with heroic virtues or heroic vices, and called by them 'great men'. What are great men? They are ordinary human beings, who are ignorant and vain enough to accept responsibility for the life of society, individuals who would rather take the blame for all the cruelties, injustices, disasters justified in their name, than recognize their own insignificance and impotence in the cosmic flow which pursues its course irrespective of their wills and ideals. This is the central point of those passages (in which Tolstoy excelled) in which the actual course of events is described, side by side with the absurd, egocentric explanations which persons blown up with the sense of their own importance necessarily give to them; as well as of the wonderful descriptions of moments of illumination in which the truth about the human condition dawns upon those who have the humility to recognize their own unimportance and irrelevance. And this is the purpose, too, of those philosophical passages where, in language more ferocious than Spinoza's, but with intentions similar to his, the errors of the pseudo-sciences are exposed. (pp. 44-5)

In *War and Peace* Tolstoy treats facts cavalierly when it suits him, because he is above all obsessed by his thesis—the contrast between the universal and all-important but delusive experience of free will, the feeling of responsibility, the values of private life generally, on the one hand; and on the other, the reality of inexorable historical determinism, not, indeed, experienced directly, but known to be true on irrefutable theoretical grounds. This corresponds in its turn to a tormenting inner conflict, one of many, in Tolstoy himself, between the two systems of value, the public and the private. On the one hand, if those feelings and immediate experiences, upon which the ordinary values of private individuals and historians alike ultimately rest, are nothing but a vast illusion, this must, in the name of the truth, be ruthlessly demonstrated, and the values and the explanations which derive from the illusion exposed and discredited. And in a sense Tolstoy does try to do this, particularly when he is philosophizing, as in the great public scenes of the novel itself, the battle pieces, the descriptions of the movements of peoples, the metaphysical disquisitions. But, on the other hand, he also does the exact opposite of this when he contrasts with this panorama of public life the superior value of personal experience, the 'thoughts, knowledge, poetry, music, love, friendship, hates, passions' of which real life is compounded—when he contrasts the concrete and multi-coloured reality of individual lives with the pale abstractions of scientists or historians, particularly the latter, 'from Gibbon to Buckle', whom he denounces so harshly for mistaking their own empty categories for real facts. And yet the primacy of these private experiences and relationships and virtues presupposes that vision of life, with its sense of personal responsibility, and belief in freedom and possibility of spontaneous action, to which the best pages of *War and Peace* are devoted, and which is the very illusion to be exorcized, if the truth is to be faced.

This terrible dilemma is never finally resolved. Sometimes, as in the explanation of his intentions which he published before the final part of *War and Peace* had appeared, Tolstoy vacillates; the individual is 'in some sense' free when he alone is involved: thus, in raising his arm, he is free within physical limits. But once he is involved in relationships with others, he is no longer free, he is part of the inexorable stream. Freedom is real, but it is confined to trivial acts. At other times even this feeble ray of hope is extinguished: Tolstoy declares that he cannot admit even small exceptions to the universal law; causal determinism is either wholly pervasive or it is nothing, and chaos reigns. Men's acts may seem free of the social nexus, but they are not free, they cannot be free, they are part of it. Sci-

ence cannot destroy the consciousness of freedom, without which there is no morality and no art, but it can refute it. 'Power' and 'accident' are but names of ignorance of the causal chains, but the chains exist whether we feel them or not; fortunately we do not; for if we felt their weight, we could scarcely act at all; the loss of illusion would paralyse the life which is lived on the basis of our happy ignorance. But all is well; for we never shall discover all the causal chains that operate: the number of such causes is infinitely great, the causes themselves infinitely small; historians select an absurdly small portion of them and attribute everything to this arbitrarily chosen tiny section. How would an ideal historical science operate? By using a kind of calculus whereby this 'differential', the infinitesimals—the infinitely small human and non-human actions and events—would be integrated, and in this way the continuum of history would no longer be distorted by being broken up into arbitrary segments. Tolstoy expresses this notion of calculation by infinitesimals with great lucidity, and with his habitual simple, vivid, precise use of words. (pp. 47-50)

It is not a mystical or an intuitionist view of life. Our ignorance of how things happen is not due to some inherent inaccessibility of the first causes, only to their multiplicity, the smallness of the ultimate units, and our own inability to see and hear and remember and record and co-ordinate enough of the available material. Omniscience is in principle possible even to empirical beings, but, of course, in practice unattainable. This alone, and nothing deeper or more interesting, is the source of human megalomania, of all our absurd delusions. Since we are not, in fact, free, but could not live without the conviction that we are, what are we to do? Tolstoy arrives at no clear conclusion, only at the view, in some respect like Burke's, that it is better to realize that we understand what goes on as we do in fact understand it—much as spontaneous, normal, simple people, uncorrupted by theories, not blinded by the dust raised by the scientific authorities, do, in fact, understand life—than to seek to subvert such common-sense beliefs, which at least have the merit of having been tested by long experience, in favour of pseudo-sciences, which, being founded on absurdly inadequate data, are only a snare and a delusion. That is his case against all forms of optimistic rationalism, the natural sciences, liberal theories of progress, German military *expertise*, French sociology, confident social engineering of all kinds. And this is his reason for inventing a Kutuzov who followed his simple, Russian, untutored instinct, and despised or ignored the German, French, and Italian experts; and for raising him to the status of a national hero which he has, partly as a result of Tolstoy's portrait, retained ever since. (pp. 50-1)

If we may recall once again our division of artists into foxes and hedgehogs: Tolstoy perceived reality in its multiplicity, as a collection of separate entities round and into which he saw with a clarity and penetration scarcely ever equalled, but he believed only in one vast, unitary whole. No author who has ever lived has shown such powers of insight into the variety of life—the differences, the contrasts, the collisions of persons and things and situations, each apprehended in its absolute uniqueness and conveyed with a degree of directness and a precision of concrete imagery to be found in no other writer. No one has ever excelled Tolstoy in expressing the specific flavour, the exact quality of a feeling—the degree of its 'oscillation', the ebb and flow, the minute movements (which Turgenev mocked as a mere trick on his part)—the inner and outer texture and 'feel' of a look, a thought, a pang of sentiment, no less than that of the specific pattern of a situation, or an entire period, continuous segments of lives of individuals, families, communities, entire nations. The celebrated life-likeness of every object and every person in his world derives from this astonishing capacity of presenting every ingredient of it in its fullest individual essence, in all its many dimensions, as it were; never as a mere datum, however vivid, within some stream of consciousness, with blurred edges, an outline, a shadow, an impressionistic representation, nor yet calling for, and dependent on, some process of reasoning in the mind of the reader; but always as a solid object, seen simultaneously from near and far, in natural, unaltering daylight, from all possible angles of vision, set in an absolutely specific context in time and space—an event fully present to the senses or the imagination in all its facets, with every nuance sharply and firmly articulated.

Yet what he believed in was the opposite. He advocated a single embracing vision; he preached not variety but simplicity, not many levels of consciousness but reduction to some single level—in *War and Peace* to the standard of the good man, the single, spontaneous, open soul: as later to that of the peasants, or of a simple Christian ethic divorced from any complex theology or metaphysic, some simple, quasi-utilitarian criterion, whereby everything is interrelated directly, and all the items can be assessed in terms of one another by some simple measuring rod. Tolstoy's genius lies in a capacity for marvellously accurate reproduction of the irreproducible, the almost miraculous evocation of the full, untranslatable individuality of the individual, which induces in the reader an acute awareness of the presence of the object itself, and not of a mere description of it, employing for this purpose metaphors which fix the quality of a particular experience as such, and avoiding those general terms which relate it to similar instances by ignoring individual differences—'the oscillations of feeling'—in favour of what is common to them all. But then this same writer pleads for, indeed preaches with great fury, particularly in his last, religious phase, the exact opposite: the necessity of expelling everything that does not submit to some very general, very simple standard: say, what peasants like or dislike, or what the gospels declare to be good.

This violent contradiction between the data of experience from which he could not liberate himself, and which, of course, all his life he knew alone to be real, and his deeply metaphysical belief in the existence of a system to which they *must* belong, whether they appear to do so or not, this conflict between instinctive judgment and theoretical conviction—between his gifts and his opinions—mirrors the unresolved conflict between the reality of the moral life with its sense of responsibility, joys, sorrow, sense of guilt and sense of achievement—all of which is nevertheless illusion; and the laws which govern everything, although we cannot know more than a negligible portion of them—so that all scientists and historians who say that they do know them and are guided by them are lying and deceiving—but which nevertheless alone are real. Beside Tolstoy, Gogol and Dostoevsky, whose abnormality is so often contrasted with Tolstoy's 'sanity', are well-integrated personalities, with a coherent outlook and a single vision. Yet out of this violent conflict grew *War and Peace:* Its marvellous solidity should not blind us to the deep cleavage which yawns open whenever Tolstoy remembers, or rather reminds himself—fails to forget—what he is doing, and why. (pp. 62-6)

Isaiah Berlin, in his *The Hedgehog and the Fox: An Essay on Tolstoy's View of History,* Simon & Schuster, 1953, 86 p.

GEORGE STEINER
(essay date 1959)

[Steiner is a French-born American critic, poet, and fiction writer. In the following excerpt, he discusses the tension in Tolstoy's works between literary artistry and religious didacticism.]

The history of Tolstoy's mind and of the growth of Tolstoyan Christianity has often been misread. Tolstoy's condemnation of literature in the winter of 1879-80 was so emphatic that it suggested a radical dissociation between two eras in his life. Actually, most of the ideas and beliefs expounded by the later Tolstoy appear in his earliest writings and the live substance of his morality was plainly discernible during the years of apprenticeship. As [Léon] Shestov points out, in his essay on *Tolstoy and Nietzsche,* the remarkable fact is not the seeming contrast between the early and the late Tolstoy, but rather the unity and consequentiality of Tolstoyan thought.

But it would also be erroneous to distinguish three chapters in Tolstoy's life—a period of literary creation circumscribed on either hand by decades of philosophic and religious activity. In Tolstoy we cannot separate the two shaping powers; the moralist and the poet co-exist in anguished and creative proximity. Throughout his career, the religious and the artistic impulse grappled for supremacy. The struggle was particularly acute at the time when Tolstoy was in the midst of writing *Anna Karenina*. At one moment his capacious spirit inclined towards the life of the imagination; in another it yielded to what Ibsen called the "claims of the ideal." One has the impression that Tolstoy found tranquillity and equilibrium only through physical action and in the wild play of physical energy; through exhaustion of body he was able to silence momentarily the debate raging in his mind. (p. 242)

The perception of the specific and integral is the characteristic mark of Tolstoy's artistry, of his unrivalled concreteness. In his novels each piece of the world's furniture is distinctive and stands with individual solidity. But simultaneously Tolstoy was possessed by the hunger for final understanding, for the all-inclusive and justifying disclosure of the ways of God. It was this hunger which impelled him to his polemic and exegetic labours. . . .

[The] quest for unity, for the revelation of total meaning, underlies Tolstoy's art even where his sensuous perception is most enthralled by the boundless diversity of life. (p. 243)

It was Tolstoy's peculiar tragedy that he should have come to regard his poetic genius as corrupt and as an agent of betrayal. By virtue of their comprehensiveness and vitality, *War and Peace* and *Anna Karenina* had splintered yet further an image of reality in which Tolstoy was determined to discover a single meaning and a perfect coherence. They had opposed the disorder of beauty to his desperate search for the philosopher's stone. (p. 246)

Anyone familiar with Tolstoy's personal life and with the history of his mind will be sensible—perhaps too sensible—to the problematic and doctrinal implications inherent in everything he wrote. Perceived in their total context, the novels and tales play the part of poetic tropes and exploratory myths in an essentially moral and religious dialectic. They are stages of vision in the long pilgrimage. But if we set *Resurrection* to one side, it is clear that religious themes and acts of a religious character occupy a minor place in Tolstoyan fiction. Both *War and Peace* and *Anna Karenina* are images of the empiric world and chronicles of men's temporal works and days.

Even a momentary glance at Dostoevsky provides the contrasting note. In the novels of Dostoevsky, images and situations, the names of the characters and their habits of speech, the general terms of reference, and the qualities of action are prevailingly and dramatically religious. Dostoevsky portrayed men in crises of belief or denial, and often it is through denial that his characters bear witness most forcefully to the incursions of God. . . . The same cannot be asserted of Tolstoy. One may read *War and Peace* and *Anna Karenina* as the foremost of historical and social novels with only a vague awareness of their philosophic and religious tenor. (pp. 246-47)

Must we suppose that the conventional image of Tolstoy is, after all, accurate? Was there a decisive break (possibly in the period from 1874 to 1878) between the "pagan" creator of *War and Peace* and the Christian ascetic of *Resurrection* and the later years? I think not. Tolstoy's biography and the record he has left us of his spiritual life bear out the impression of an underlying unity. If we are right in supposing that *War and Peace* and *Anna Karenina* are nearer to Homer than to Flaubert, then the notion of paganism is not unexpected; indeed, it becomes a vital part of the metaphysics to which the analogies between Homer and Tolstoy refer us. There are in Tolstoyan Christianity, and particularly in Tolstoy's image of God, pagan elements; if the *Iliad* and *War and Peace* are comparable on formal grounds (as we have seen them to be), then their governing mythologies are comparable also. By keeping our attention responsive and uncommitted, we shall, I think, come to realize that Tolstoyan paganism and Tolstoyan Christianity were not diametrical opposites, but successive and interrelated acts in the drama of a single intelligence. *War and Peace, Anna Karenina,* and the tales of the early and middle years, sensuous, wondrously serene in their effect, were nevertheless forerunners and preparers of Tolstoy's sacrificial theology. They establish the world image which that theology will seek to interpret. Conversely, the doctrines of the later Tolstoy carry to the folly of conclusion premises laid down in the writings of his golden period. (pp. 247-48)

Much of the perfection of *Anna Karenina* lies in the fact that the poetic form resisted the demands of the didactic purpose; thus there is between them a constant equilibrium and harmonious tension. In the double plot the duality of Tolstoy's intent is both expressed and organized. The Pauline epigraph initiates and colours the story of Anna but does not utterly control it. Anna's tragic fate yields values and enrichments of sensibility that challenge the moral code which Tolstoy generally held and was seeking to dramatize. It is as if two deities had been invoked: an ancient, patriarchal God of vengeance and a God who sets nothing above the tragic candour of a bruised spirit. Or to put it otherwise: Tolstoy grew enamoured of his heroine, and through the liberality of his passion she achieved a rare freedom. Nearly alone among Tolstoyan characters, Anna appears to develop in directions which point away from the novelist's control and prescience. Thomas Mann was right in asserting that the commanding impulse behind *Anna Karenina* is moralistic; Tolstoy framed an indictment against a society which seized for its own upon a vengeance reserved to God. But for once, Tolstoy's own moral position was ambivalent; his condemnation of adultery was rather close to current social judgment. Like the other spectators at the opera—however mundane or acrimonious they may appear—Tolstoy could not help being shocked by Anna's behavior, by her tentative advances towards a freer code. And in his own perplexity—in the lack of a perfectly lucid case such as is argued in *Resurrection*—lay opportunities for narrative freedom and for the predominance of the poet. In *Anna Karenina* Tolstoy succumbed to his imagination rather than to his reason. . . . (p. 282)

After *Anna Karenina,* the moralistic and pedagogic strains in Tolstoy's inspiration, with their attendant techniques of rhetoric, became increasingly dominant. . . . Both *The Death of Ivan Ilych* and *The Kreutzer Sonata* are masterpieces, but masterpieces of a singular order. Their terrible intensity arises not out of a prevalence of imaginative vision but out of its narrowing; they possess, like the dwarf-figures in the paintings of Bosch, the violent energies of compression. *The Death of Ivan Ilych* is a counterpart to [Dostoevsky's] *Letters from the Underworld;* instead of descending into the dark places of the soul, it descends, with agonizing leisure and precision, into the dark places of the body. It is a poem—one of the most harrowing ever conceived—of the insurgent flesh, of the manner in which carnality, with its pains and corruptions, penetrates and dissolves the tenuous discipline of reason. *The Kreutzer Sonata* is, technically, less perfect because the elements of articulate morality have become too massive to be entirely absorbed into the narrative structure. The meaning is enforced upon us, with extraordinary eloquence; but it has not been given complete imaginative form. (p. 283)

It is difficult to think of *Resurrection* as a novel in the ordinary sense. . . . Tolstoy could not reconcile himself to the idea of fiction, particularly on a large scale. It was only when he saw in the work a chance to convey his religious and social program in an accessible and persuasive form that he could compel himself to the task. . . . It reflects these changes of mood and a puritanical conception of art. But there are wondrous pages in it, and moments in which Tolstoy gave rein to his unchanging powers. The account of the eastward transportation of the prisoners is handled with a breadth of design and aliveness which transcend any programmatic purpose. When Tolstoy opened his eyes on actual scenes and events, instead of keeping them fixed inward on the workings of his anger, his hand moved with matchless artistry.

This is no accident. In a full-length novel, even the late Tolstoy could allow himself a measure of freedom. Through the repeated exemplifications that a long novel makes possible, abstractions assume a colour of life. Ample flesh surrounds the bones of argument. In a short story, on the contrary, time and space are lacking. The elements of rhetoric cannot be absorbed into the fictional medium. Thus, the didactic motifs, the mythology of conduct in Tolstoy's late stories remain visible and oppressive. Through their sheer length, *War and Peace, Anna Karenina,* and *Resurrection* enable Tolstoy to approach that idea of unity which he pursued with such obstinate passion. (pp. 284-85)

George Steiner, in his *Tolstoy or Dostoevsky: An Essay in the Old Criticism,* Alfred A. Knopf, Inc., 1959, 354 p.

SOURCES FOR FURTHER STUDY

Bayley, John. *Tolstoy and the Novel.* New York: The Viking Press, 1966, 316 p.
> Examines Tolstoy's major fiction with respect to the traditions and devices of the nineteenth-century European novel, focusing primarily on *War and Peace.*

Christian, R. F. *Tolstoy: A Critical Introduction.* Cambridge: Cambridge University Press, 1969, 291 p.
> Chronicle of Tolstoy's literary career and descriptive survey of his works and their major themes, offering much relevant background information.

Jones, Malcolm, ed. *New Essays on Tolstoy.* Cambridge: Cambridge University Press, 1978, 253 p.
> Collection of essays by British scholars, including Henry Gifford, A. V. Knowles, W. Gareth Jones, E. B. Greenwood, and F. F. Seeley. The editor states that each essay "constitutes a reassessment of some aspect of Tolstoy's legacy to the modern reader. . . ."

Knowles, A. V., ed. *Tolstoy: The Critical Heritage.* London: Routledge & Kegan Paul, 1978, 457 p.
> Compendium of early criticism on Tolstoy's major works, especially useful for its translation of Russian critics.

Lavrin, Janko. *Tolstoy: An Approach.* New York: The Macmillan Co., 1946, 166 p.

Introduction to Tolstoy's fiction and philosophy.

Matlaw, Ralph E., ed. *Tolstoy: A Collection of Critical Essays.* Englewood Cliffs, NJ: Prentice-Hall, 1967, 178 p.

   Includes seminal essays by B. M. Eikhenbaum, George Lukacs, R. F. Christian, R. P. Blackmur, and Lev Shestov.

Anthony Trollope

1815-1882

English novelist, autobiographer, short story writer, dramatist, and essayist.

INTRODUCTION

*T*rollope was one of the most prolific English writers of the nineteenth century. Although most critics consider him a major Victorian novelist, the precise nature of his achievement has often proved elusive. In spite of conflicting interpretations, commentators tend to agree that his realistic characterizations form the basis of his importance and appeal, and they generally consider his finest efforts to be his two series of novels, each of which comprises six volumes. The Barsetshire series portrays middle-class life in an English cathedral town, while the Palliser series centers on a single character, Plantagenet Palliser, in the political milieu of London.

Born in London, Trollope was raised in poverty. His father failed at law and farming before going bankrupt, and his mother began what eventually became a lucrative writing career to support the family. Shy, awkward, and unkempt, Trollope was ridiculed by his wealthier classmates at Harrow and Winchester. At the age of nineteen he found work as a junior clerk at the Post Office and seven years later was transferred to Ireland. In 1859 he returned permanently to London, where he continued to work for the Post Office until 1867.

Trollope's move to Ireland inaugurated a period of change: for the first time in his life he was successful in work, love, friendship, and financial matters, and he began to write. His first novel, *The Macdermots of Ballycloran* (1847), received little critical attention, but recognition came with the publication of *The Warden* (1855), the first of the Barsetshire novels. *Barchester Towers* (1857), the second novel in the series, was a popular success, and many readers still regard it as the apogee of Trollope's achievement.

Framley Parsonage (1861), the fourth novel in the Barsetshire series, was Trollope's first work to appear in serial form, a method of magazine publication which promised a wide readership and greater critical response. The Barsetshire series elicited several comments which were repeated throughout Trollope's lifetime. Above all, critics warmed to his characters and praised both Trollope's lively, readable style and his humorous portrayal of everyday life. They also noted his fidelity to the English character, particularly in his portraits of young girls, although some critics noted that he overused the plot scheme of a heroine vacillating between two suitors. Trollope's early critics attributed a number of his faults, including careless construction, grammatical errors, and insubstantial story lines, to the fact that Trollope wrote quickly, and they blamed the exigencies of serial publication for his overly episodic and fragmentary plots. In addition, many commentators found Trollope's technique of allowing the narrator to constantly comment on the action and characters to be irrelevant and distracting. Still, the Barsetshire series contains Trollope's best-known and best-loved works, and many readers and critics consider these novels, particularly *Barchester Towers* and *The Last Chronicle of Barset* (1867), the standard against which all his other novels should be judged.

In the mid 1860s Trollope's focus shifted from the postal to the political world. In 1868, he unsuccessfully ran for a seat in Parliament; four years earlier he had written *Can You Forgive Her?* (1864), the first novel of the Palliser series. This series traces Plantagenet Palliser's evolution from the time of his marriage to Lady Glencora through the increasing political responsibilities that eventually lead to his position as prime minister of England. Despite their depiction of political activity, however, these novels resemble the Barsetshire series in their avoidance of political and social commentary in favor of perceptive character studies. Several characters reappear throughout the series, and critics praise their development from one novel to the next. In particular, critics repeatedly point to Plantagenet Palliser and Lady Glencora as Trollope's most intimate, subtle, and profound studies of character. Trollope concurred with this assessment of his work. In his *Autobiography* (1883), he wrote that of all his characters, he preferred the old duke of Omnium, Plantagenet Palliser, and Lady Glencora: "I look upon this string of characters . . . as the best work of my life. Taking him altogether, I think that Plantagenet Palliser stands more firmly on the ground than any other personage I have created." And yet the Palliser novels were not as well regarded by Trollope's contemporaries as the earlier Barsetshire series; readers apparently found the world of politics less familiar and pleasant than the provincial life of Barset.

The 1870s witnessed a decline in Trollope's popularity as his writing style and focus changed. Although they often include subjects similar to those in his earlier works, Trollope's later novels are more cynical and pessimistic in tone: *He Knew He Was Right* (1869) examines marriage and finds jealousy and corruption; *The Way We Live Now* (1875) studies society and uncovers financial and moral corruption. Critics objected to what they considered the sordid realism of these works, charging that Trollope ignored the novelist's responsibility of providing solutions to the social problems he depicted. In addition, because he was so prolific, Trollope was accused of commercialism.

Trollope's popularity and reputation, already failing at his death in 1882, deteriorated considerably following the posthumous publication of *An Autobiography*. The work's self-effacing tone reflects Trollope's modest opinion of his own talent and accomplishments. In *An Autobiography* Trollope described his rigidly-maintained writing schedule and his belief that writing was a craft, like shoemaking, that required perseverance and diligence for success. He denied that inspiration was necessary to literary work and claimed that his stories sprung from his pen without imaginative effort. Trollope's views on literature opposed the developing aesthetic theories of fin de siècle critics, who valued a carefully-honed work of literature. Trollope's discussion of his work methods provided ammunition for many of his detractors. They viewed his unrelenting schedules as proof that he had written too much and cited his comparison of novel-writing to shoemaking as proof that he was a simple craftsman.

Critics continue to dispute the nature of Trollope's achievement, and there is no general agreement on his rank among writers of fiction. Yet commentators universally applaud the quality of his characterizations and regard Mrs. Proudie and Reverend Crawley from the Barsetshire chronicles and Plantagenet Palliser and Lady Glencora from the Palliser series as great imaginative creations. Many believe that Trollope was able to paint characters of such consistency, veracity, and depth because of his profound insight into and sympathy for his creations. Trollope himself considered the ability to live with one's characters essential and defined the main work of the novelist as "the creation of human beings in whose existence one is forced to believe." Many critics would find in Trollope's statement an apt description of his finest achievement.

(For further information about Trollope's life and works, see *Dictionary of Literary Biography*, Vols. 21, 57 and *Nineteenth-Century Literature Criticism*, Vol. 6.)

CRITICAL COMMENTARY

LESLIE STEPHEN

(essay date 1901)

[Stephen, an English critic and essayist, was a major commentator on Victorian fiction. In the following excerpt from an essay that first appeared in *The National Review* (London) in 1901, he attempts to introduce Trollope to an unappreciative generation of readers.]

We can see plainly enough what we must renounce in order to enjoy Trollope. We must cease to bother ourselves about art. We must not ask for exquisite polish of style. We must be content with good homespun phrases which give up all their meaning on the first reading. We must not desire brilliant epigrams suggesting familiarity with aesthetic doctrines or theories of the universe. A brilliant modern novelist is not only clever, but writes for clever readers. He expects us to understand oblique references to esoteric theories, and to grasp a situation from a delicate hint. We are not to be bothered with matter-of-fact details, but to have facts sufficiently adumbrated to enable us to accept the aesthetic impression. Trollope writes like a thorough man of business or a lawyer stating a case. We must know exactly the birth, parentage, and circumstances of all the people concerned, and have a precise statement of what afterwards happens to everybody mentioned in the course of the story. We must not care for artistic unity. Trollope admits that he could never construct an intricate plot to be gradually unravelled. That, in fact, takes time and thought. He got hold of some leading incident, set his characters to work, and followed out any series of events which happened to be involved. . . . He simply looks on, and only takes care to make his report consistent and intelligible. To accept such writing in the corresponding spirit implies, no doubt, the confession that you are a bit of a Philistine, able to put up with the plainest of bread and butter and dispense with all the finer literary essences. I think, however, that at times one's state is the more gracious for accepting the position. There is something so friendly and simple and shrewd about one's temporary guide that one is the better for taking a stroll with him and listening to gossiping family stories, even though they be rather rambling and never scandalous. . . . Hawthorne said at an early period that Trollope's novels precisely suited his taste. . . . Trollope was delighted, as he well might be, with such praise from so different a writer, and declares that this passage defined the aim of his novels "with wonderful accuracy." They represent, that is, the average English society of the time more faithfully even than memoirs of real persons, because there is no motive for colouring the motives of an imaginary person. (pp. 178-80)

Trollope's best achievement, I take it, was the series of Barsetshire novels. They certainly passed at the time for a marvel of fidelity. Trollope tells us that he was often asked when he had lived in a cathedral close and become intimate with archdeacons; and had been able to answer that he had never lived in a close and had never spoken to an archdeacon. He had evolved the character, he declares, "out of his moral consciousness," and is pleasantly complacent over his creation. (p. 181)

The prosaic person, it must remember, has a faculty for ignoring all the elements of life and character which are not prosaic, and if Trollope's picture is accurate it is not exhaustive. The weakness comes from misapplying a good principle. Trollope made it a first principle to keep rigorously to the realities of life. He inferred that nothing strange or improbable should ever be admitted. . . . Trollope inclines to make everybody an average specimen, and in his desire to avoid exaggeration inevitably exaggerates the commonplaceness of life. He is afraid of admitting any one into his world who will startle us by exhibiting any strength of character. His lovers, for example, have to win the heroine by showing superiority to the worldly scruples of their relations. . . . [The] heroes have all the vigour taken out of them that they may not shock us by diverging from the most commonplace standard. When a hero does something energetic, gives a thrashing, for example, to the man who has jilted a girl, we are carefully informed that he does it in a blundering and unsatisfactory way.

By the excision of all that is energetic, or eccentric, or impulsive, or romantic, you do not really become more lifelike; you only limit yourself to the common and uninteresting. That misconception injures Trollope's work, and accounts, I suspect, for the decline of our interest. An artist who systematically excludes all lurid colours or strong lights shows a dingy, whity-brown universe, and is not therefore more true to nature. Barsetshire surely has its heroes and its villains, its tragedy and its force, as well as its archdeacons and young ladies bound hand and foot by the narrowest rules of contemporary propriety. Yet, after all, Trol-

Principal Works

The Macdermots of Ballycloran (novel) 1847

The Kellys and the O'Kellys; or, Landlords and Tenants (novel) 1848

*The Warden (novel) 1855

*Barchester Towers (novel) 1857

*Doctor Thorne (novel) 1858

The Three Clerks (novel) 1858

The Bertrams (novel) 1859

*Framley Parsonage (novel) 1861

Orley Farm (novel) 1862

†Can You Forgive Her? (novel) 1864

*The Small House at Allington (novel) 1864

The Belton Estate (novel) 1866

The Claverings (novel) 1867

*The Last Chronicle of Barset (novel) 1867

He Knew He Was Right (novel) 1869

†Phineas Finn, the Irish Member (novel) 1869

†The Eustace Diamonds (novel) 1873

†Phineas Redux (novel) 1874

The Way We Live Now (novel) 1875

†The Prime Minister (novel) 1876

The American Senator (novel) 1877

Is He Popinjoy? (novel) 1878

†The Duke's Children (novel) 1880

Ayala's Angel (novel) 1881

Dr. Wortle's School (novel) 1881

An Autobiography (autobiography) 1883

An Old Man's Love (unfinished novel) 1884

The Letters of Anthony Trollope (letters) 1951

*These works are collectively referred to as the Barsetshire series.

†These works are collectively referred to as the Palliser series.

lope's desire to be faithful had its good result in spite of this misconception. There are, in the first place, a good many commonplace people in the world; and, moreover, there were certain types into which he could throw himself with real vigour. He can appreciate energy when it does not take a strain of too obvious romance. His best novel, he thinks, and his readers must agree with him, was the *Last Chronicle of Barset.* The poor parson, Mr. Crawley, is at once the most lifelike and (in his sense) the most improbable of his characters. He is the embodiment of Trollope's own "doggedness." . . . [Mr. Crawley,] with his strange wrongheaded conscientiousness, his honourable independence, blended with bitter resentment against the more successful, and the strong domestic affections, which yet make him a despot in his family, is a real triumph of which more ambitious novelists might be proud. . . . [Mrs. Proudie] is one genuine type, albeit a very rare one, of the Englishwoman of the period, and Trollope draws her vigorously, because her qualities are only an excessive development of very commonplace failings. In such cases Trollope can deal with his characters vigorously and freely, and we do not feel that their vitality has been lowered from a mistaken desire to avoid a strain upon our powers of belief. He can really understand people on a certain plane of intelligence. His pompous officials at public offices, and dull members of Parliament, and here and there such disreputable persons as he ventures to sketch, as, for example, the shrewd contractor in *Dr. Thorne,* who is ruined by his love of gin, are solid and undeniable realities. We see the world as it was, only in a dark mirror which is incapable of reflecting the fairer shades of thought and custom.

Hawthorne's appreciation of Trollope's strain was perhaps due in part to his conviction that John Bull was a huge mass of solid flesh incapable of entering the more ethereal regions of subtle fancy of which he was himself a native. Trollope was to him a John Bull convicting himself out of his own mouth, and yet a good fellow in his place. When our posterity sits in judgment, it will discover, I hope, that the conventional John Bull is only an embodiment of one set of the national qualities, and by no means an exhaustive portrait of the original. But taking Trollope to represent the point of view from which there is a certain truthfulness in the picture—and no novelist can really do more than give one set of impressions—posterity may after all consider his novels as a very instructive document. . . . [Readers of the twenty-first century] will look back to the early days of Queen Victoria as a delightful time, when it was possible to take things quietly, and a good, sound, sensible optimism was the prevalent state of mind. How far the estimate would be true is another question; but Trollope, as representing such an epoch, will supply a soothing if rather mild stimulant for the imagination, and it will be admitted that if he was not among the highest intellects of his benighted time, he was as sturdy, wholesome, and kindly a human being as could be desired. (pp. 185-90)

Leslie Stephen, "Anthony Trollope," in his *Studies of a Biographer, Vol. IV,* G. P. Putnam's Sons, 1907, pp. 156-90.

GEORGE SAINTSBURY

(essay date 1920)

[Saintsbury was an English literary historian and critic. In the following excerpt, he asserts that Trollope occupies a permanent place among Victorian writers.]

The point at which decadence, real or alleged, begins [in Trollope's works], is perhaps itself a matter of some controversy. I have known some very good judges—though perhaps judges a little biassed by the fact of having begun with it—who see nothing decadent in *Phineas Finn*. I own that I see a sort of gap and drop between it and *The Last Chronicle*—which preceded it by not very many months—a gap and drop almost equal to a landslip—and that I do not think the higher level was ever recovered. It is true that Trollope did not now lose—that in fact he never lost—his remarkable faculty of telling a story. . . . [One of his latest], *Marion Fay*, is perhaps the weakest of all in this respect, though its predecessors by a year or two, *An Eye for an Eye, Cousin Henry*, and *Dr. Wortle's School*, are very far from strong. But a practised and judicial novel-critic will perceive in even the weakest of these something quite different from the case of the common circulating-library tale-teller who can't tell a tale. If you go back to *Is He Popenjoy?* [*sic*] or *John Caldigate* they will give you, though in changed degree, fresh evidence, and you may carry investigation further still through others including the 'Phineas-Eustace-Palliser' group itself, and, what is more, right back to weaklings of the greater period, always strengthening your provisional conclusion as you go. This conclusion will have been—at least if it agrees with the present critic's—that Trollope's novel-writing faculty, at its best of little below first-class quality, went through much the same vicissitudes as the mere physical faculties of other men, but that his economy or administration of it was peculiar and not always judicious. Before *The Warden*, and in that story and *The Three Clerks* to some extent, he did not know how to manage it at all, or how to direct it into his books. In *Dr. Thorne* he made a great advance. From *Barchester Towers* to *The Last Chronicle* he had it in fullest command and play in his greater books—*Barchester Towers* itself, *Framley Parsonage, Orley Farm* (not quite throughout), *The Small House, Can You Forgive Her?* and the [*Barsetshire Chronicle*]—less according to me in *The Bertrams, Castle Richmond*, and *The Claverings* (some good judges differ from me here but Trollope himself rather agreed), and least in the *Rachel Ray* group. (pp. 42-3)

Although Trollope has left a fair number of short stories he was not a good short-story-teller; and the slightly commercial view which he took of his art probably found support in a secret consciousness of this disability. The result was that he regularly made a short novel out of matter the substance of which was only enough for a short story; while the quality of it was not always suitable even for that. . . . Perhaps a born short-story-teller might have made short stories of *Rachel Ray, Miss Mackenzie,* and *The Belton Estate*. . . . But nobody could have made a good long or even short novel out of their material, nor out of that of *Sir Harry Hotspur* [or] *Lady Anna*. . . . The 'unekality' (as the elder Mr. Weller had it) of the spirit and the water in these compositions was too great. But the spirit itself remained. It gave itself in almost satisfactory quality in *Ayala's Angel* only a year or two before the close; and in the actual concluding pair—the finished *Mr. Scarborough's Family* and the unfinished, remarkable, and just at this time really valuable *Landleaguers*—It ought not to be missed by any intelligent reader. Indeed, in these two it is 'left to itself ' in an almost uncanny fashion, more particularly in *Mr. Scarborough's Family*. You don't care in the least for the clever heartless 'schemer' who gives it his name, or for the foolish *jeune premier*, or for the two sons (one a schemer like himself and the other a typical 'prodigal son') whom Mr. Scarborough plays off against each other, or for the heroine, or for anybody else. You don't very much want to know what is going to happen. And yet, if you have any sense of the particular art, you can't help feeling the skill with which the artist wheels you along till he feels inclined to turn you out of his barrow and then deposits you at his if not your destination. (pp. 44-5)

In respect, therefore, of the mere story, it may be possible to reply with some effect to the Devil's Advocate; in regard to all the weaker and not merely the later novels—let us for the moment pass from story to character. Here Trollope had always shown a curious inequality and uncertainty; an inequality and uncertainty which, let it be said at once, disqualifies him for the absolute front rank of novelists. Nothing distinguishes the members of this front rank so much as their unerring, or scarcely ever erring, grasp in creating and projecting personality. . . . But even in his early days Trollope had in this respect been unequal and uncertain. In almost all the books from the time when he made his mark with *The Warden* till *The Last Chronicle*, he maintains a high standard, though in *The Three Clerks* and *The Warden* itself he is by no means sure of hand. But in *Castle Richmond*, in *Miss Mackenzie*, in *Rachel Ray*, in *The Belton Estate*, all of them written before the Barsetshire series ceased, there is again a curious absence or at least relaxation of this grasp. Had Trollope's work ceased with *The Last Chronicle* there would have been a pretty opening for critics who like such things. In the cases where the command of character did not appear, was it real uncertainty of command or was it merely that the artist had not taken sufficient pains? (p. 45)

[There] were no doubt some minor reasons besides positive failure or exhaustion of power for the falling off. It may have been wise for Trollope to kill Mrs. Proudie (the death certainly produced some of his finest work) and even to turn off, almost entirely, the [*Barsetshire Chronicle*] tap of that fortunate county. But to some extent at the same time he drove himself out of Eden. The 'new faces, other ways' did not inspire him as the old ones did. It is very curious to see how, when he does allow himself and us renewal of old acquaintance, there is a momentary brightening up of the character-interest. (p. 46)

[There] is a cheerful theory that our faults always grow upon us, and Trollope had certain weaknesses which were likely to do so. One was, not coextensive with but a part result of, his fancy for dealing largely with love. In this fancy itself there was nothing reprehensible. Only very pretty or very ugly young ladies, very stupid or portentously clever young gentlemen disdain, or far more probably in two of the classes would pretend to disdain, love as motive. In fact a novel without love is, to adopt King Henry the Fifth's simile in less shocking fashion, 'like beef without mustard'. And Trollope had always recognized this truth: though even in his earlier days, as we may have to notice, his treatment of the subject was not impeccable. It grew much worse later. John Bold, Lucius Mason, and even Felix Graham, had been prigs; Mr. Slope was the modified villain for whose flogging at the gangway we cheerfully cheered; . . . Johnny Eames, though much the best of the lot as a lover, [was] not perfect. But they all (except the prigs) played their parts sympathetically enough (for it shows real sympathy in the villain to get himself flogged); and even the prigs were not quite despicable. Phineas Finn himself at the beginning of the decadence, and Lord Silverbridge in *The Duke's Children* near its end, are very despicable creatures indeed. Nothing short of kicking could fitly reward the Irishman for making Lady Laura Standish a confidante of his love (if you call it so) for Violet Effingham; kicking would perhaps be too much for Silverbridge's desertion of his first love—one of the most remarkable of Trollope's later characters—in favour of an American girl of whom we are told that she was pretty and rich, but who is not made actually attractive in any way whatever. Still, he deserves at least infinite contempt. On the other side of the account, it is undeniably true that women do manifest an inexplicable leaning towards 'bounders'. But, once more, the way in which *such* a bounder as Mr. Lopez in *The Prime Minister* made himself attractive to such a girl as Emily Wharton, and took in so acute a personage

as that Lady Glencora whom one hardly cares to call 'the Duchess', is never even suggested. Now these failures all show a lost command of character-touches. There is almost nothing so bad or so disagreeable that a novelist may not make his personages do it if he can fix our attention on the naturalness and necessity of their doing it. It is when this naturalness and necessity do not make themselves felt that criticisms of the kind just made are justified. (pp. 46-8)

The Way We Live Now, with some good things, is hardly one of the rare instances in which an author's attempt to 'bring himself up to date' has been successful: and if there were nothing else to say (something has been said) against *The Duke's Children,* it would weigh against it that Lady Glencora had to be killed to make it possible. Trollope was rather fond of this kind of murder. One cannot blame him for killing off John Bold between *The Warden* and *Barchester Towers,* for John had already been much luckier than he deserved, and his sole reason for existence had been to start the theme of *The Warden* itself. . . . But the butchery of Lady Glencora—even of the somewhat faded 'Duchess' of *The Prime Minister*—for no other reason than the same, is really sad; for she had been perhaps the most *delightful* of all his heroines.

If it has seemed to anybody that our revisiting of Trollope has hitherto been not very prolific of blessings on him, let the very last sentence of the last paragraph serve as a hinge for turning the table of judgement. If one deplores, almost resents, the death of Lady Glencora it is because one has recognized and rejoiced in the fact that she lived. And this is, for her creator, the highest possible praise in kind, though the question of degrees may remain. . . . For the present writer the ultimate questions have been [simple]. . . . Is the romance such that you see the perilous seas and ride the *barrière* as in your own person? Are the folk of the novel such that you have met or feel that you might have met them in your life or in theirs? If so the work passes; with what degree of merit is again a second question.

If there be any soundness in this view Trollope has 'passed' already. . . . The way of romance he does not take with any success, nor as a rule does he attempt it; still less that highest way of all where the adventurer tries and wins the combined event, romance *and* novel. . . . But the novel prize, if not in the highest possible degree, he takes. (pp. 50-2)

I do not think that he will, by the best judges, ever be thought worthy of the very highest place among novelists or among English novelists. He has something no doubt of the '*for* all time', but he is not exactly '*of* all time'. Or, to put the calculus the other way, he is by no means only '*for* an age'; but he is to a certain lowering though not disqualifying degree '*of* an age'. If you compare him with the really great novelists of his own century, all of whom were in actual drawing of breath his contemporaries, he cannot vie with Miss Austen in that quietly intense humanity which contends with and transcends a rather narrow scheme of manners and social habits; or with Scott in largeness of distinctly romantic conception. In absolute universality of 'this-worldliness' Thackeray towers above him; as in a certain fantastic command of not impossible other-worldliness does Dickens. But short of these four I do not know any nineteenth-century English novelist whose superiority to him in some ways—Kingsley's in romance; Charles Reade's in a certain strange infusion of positive genius; George Eliot's in appeal to the intelligentsia—is not compensated by their inferiority in turning out personages and fitting them with incidents of the kind indicated in the foregoing survey—the personages and incidents, that is to say, of actual contemporary life, touched, if not to supreme, at any rate to more than competent freedom from commonplaceness of the disqualifying kind in one way and from mere eccentricity in another. (pp. 64-5)

George Saintsbury, "Trollope Revisited," in Essays and Studies by Members of the English Association, Vol. VI, edited by A. C. Bradley, Oxford at the Clarendon Press, 1920, pp. 41-66.

MORRIS EDMUND SPEARE
(essay date 1924)

[In the following excerpt, Speare explores the Palliser novels and Ralph the Heir.]

[When] one surveys all that is to be found in Trollope's political novels, and seeks, so to speak, the common denominator of them, one is forced to the conclusion that Trollope's main interest, first and last, is to tell 'a rattling good story.' It was to weave a plot that would hold the reader's interest from first page to last, to infuse, wherever possible, a strong 'heart interest,' and to make all other things subordinate to that primary end. Long before he came to write his political novels Trollope had found his métier (which was to tell a straightforward English tale as Thackeray had told it), and he had found his audience, which was the world of average, normal human beings, less interested in psychological discernments and in the tracing of cause and effect than in the chronicles which dealt with broad surface values in human character and the portrayal of every-day domestic affections. Having therefore gained his reading public—a public which had learned to look for these definite things in him—Trollope, upon approaching the political genre of the novel, came to it with certain limitations already imposed upon him. The audience which had grown used to his 'style' necessarily sought only for those things which had interested them in his earlier novels and which they expected to find in these of the political genre as well. Had they missed here what they had learned to love in his other works . . . that reading public, always fickle, might easily have deserted him. Trollope, therefore, took no chances, but reproduced in this genre part of the world and much of the method which he had made popular in his earlier works. So, in [the] seven political novels we have again mainly the narrative writer, the clever draftsman filling his canvasses with English squires, country gentlemen, lords of the chase and the hunt, grand ladies of the drawing-rooms, fine gentlemen of the clubs. In all of these the social emotions are more significant than the play of intellectual wit and fancy, and in depicting the social emotions Trollope was a master. In the political milieu Trollope found another, a new, background as a source for story-telling, and he took seven distinct novels in which to exhaust the material of it. Upon characters which he knew well, and had drawn elsewhere with great success, he imposed a political emphasis, without forgetting to deal here, too, with the domestic and social emotions, and the 'heart interest' which had earned him in his own day a very wide reading public. That he was successful, in spite of the limitations under which he worked here, in making some definite contributions to the genre of the political novel . . . is evidence of his great resourcefulness as a writer, and of his fertility as a storyteller, as well as of his acquaintance with widely-varying types of human beings.

Since the method of one is the method of all, let us take for our fuller analysis the two Phineas novels, and here discover in what consisted Trollope's art as a political novelist. (pp. 192-93)

As a study of the character of a rising young politician battling his way to high office and to power Phineas is of course a complete failure. But then Trollope was not interested in delineating ambition in public office. If Phineas lacks any of that wit, culture, refinement, all those graces and the supreme idealism and the poetic quality which characterizes Disraeli's youth, and by force of which they often attain high place enough 'to move the world,' we must remember that Trollope's imagination is not Disraeli's. That this prosaic, homespun, altogether worldly youth finally succeeds in making Commoners sit in rapt attention while he rises to make his commonplace remarks, that lords of the Treasury confide their political philosophies to him, and a titled lady of a great family (having made an unfortunate marriage) acquires the bad habit of throwing her arms around his neck and burying her face upon his bosom for sympathy, are significant evidence that Trollope was less interested in drawing the character of a zealot touched by a great public cause, or a highly trained and highly spirited youth hungering to right great social or political injustices, than he was in setting forth a man made of common clay who was to be a focal point for as much as possible of domestic tragedy and romance, and one who would furnish 'copy' out of his political adventures for an absorbing tale. (p. 196)

If Trollope's knowledge of the intricacies of the political game is so imaginary, and his attachment to political convictions is so slight, as to make his primary political heroes altogether unconvincing (by which facts he stands at the very antipodes from Disraeli), we must, in his political novels, move away from the centre and seek for his contributions to the political *genre* in their 'outskirts' so to speak, upon the rim of the wheel which keeps the hub of it in motion. First in importance in the *Phineas* novels are the women. . . . [Lady Laura] is left by the author a pitifully broken wreck of her former high-minded self, without children or husband, a victim of her own ambition, suspicious, envious of others' good fortune,—a picture all the more pitiful to the reader who recalls her as the most high-minded, intelligent, perhaps the noblest woman character in all the political novels of Trollope, now completely fallen from her high estate. All this because she wished, in her own way, to be "politically powerful" and believed, after her father's

straightened circumstances, that she could best remain so through a marriage. (pp. 197-99)

[In] drawing rising statesmen Trollope is altogether unsuccessful. This is shown clearly enough in the portrait of Phineas, who, when all is said and done, appears to be a young politician running amuck in public affairs, and leaves the reader with the final impression that he was a better model for a Lothario than he was for a promising politician with the ambitions of a Younger Pitt. Certainly, it would be a sad day for England if men of his weak moral fibre and mental flabbiness became samples of 'an ambitious younger generation' struggling with public affairs. Trollope's portrait of Lady Glencora's husband who gives his name to *The Prime Minister* is not more successful. A slow, plodding, unimaginative and therefore peculiarly conscientious aristocrat, who was never as happy as when in *Phineas Redux* he spent his days and nights, while Chancellor of the Exchequer, in studying decimal coinage, shy, fretful, a man of stiff reserve so that he was too cold for friendship, uncommunicative, sensitive to the point of morbidity at the attack of a single public organ upon the acts of his Ministry, we can never understand how such a fearful specimen of a statesman could ever have been made the Head of a Coalition

Harting Grange, Trollope's country home in Sussex.

Ministry. . . . All of Trollope's principal politicians have this same unconvincingness and unreality. Let us name Gresham, Daubeny . . . , Bonteen the politician who is useful, dull, unscrupulous, well-acquainted with all the back-doors and by-paths of official life and therefore 'invaluable' to his party. There is the poor, blundering Lord Fawn who represents the lay-figure in English public life; Sir Orlando Drought, type of sublime mediocrity of talent and energy. . . . Measure all these various types by those created by Disraeli and you see the *pastiche* in them, the counterfeits of their make-up, and with what little insight into political psychology their author was endowed when he created them or imitated them from some living characters about whom he read in his contemporary press or whom he knew.

With his women Trollope stands on firmer ground: here he deals not with silhouettes and shadows but with the substance. The Duchess of Omnium acting the proud wife of a Prime Minister, stirred into great political ambitions of her own, a wealthy woman whose feelings and convictions only help to keep her straight rather than her scruples, is blazing her way in the London social season in order to advance her husband's greatness and popularity. . . . [She reminds the reader] of another lady who came down the river Cydnus on a barge whose poop was "beaten gold, purple the sails," and by her ambition for her husband and herself, of Lady Macbeth.

> I was made to marry, . . . before I was old enough to assert myself. . . . He's Prime Minister, which is a great thing, and I begin to find myself filled to the full with political ambition. I feel myself to be a Lady Macbeth, prepared for the murder of any Duncan or any Daubeny who may stand in my Lord's way.

(pp. 200-02)

It is easy enough to see that Trollope, who knew more about the domestic life of the English aristocracy than he did about the ways and means of the ruling classes at Downing Street and in the political clubs and committee rooms, had some definite convictions about the place of women in English public life. This he shows by both affirmative and negative methods. He shows it affirmatively in the fact that his two greatest 'political ladies,' Lady Laura and the Duchess of Omnium, when they once over-reach that natural measure of influence which the laws of Victorian propriety permitted them, become not helpers but meddlers, and their meddling is fraught with danger and even ruin for him whom they would aid. Negatively he proves that he had definite convictions by the fact that Madame Goesler, who afterwards becomes the wife of Phineas Finn (a rising young statesman in the last novel in which he appears before us in the Parliamentary Series) seems to be his picture of a model wife for a politician.

As Escott puts it in describing her, she "knows exactly when to help her husband by appearing in the foreground, and how to advance his interests by *unadvertised activity* behind the scenes." We see little of her maneuvering above board to give her husband place, but we remember, from her ingrained common sense and her practical measures taken in the *Phineas Redux* novel to save both the name and the life of her hero, . . . that in *her* Trollope paints the active woman with whom he had the greater sympathy. One of the most charming among the many women characters which Trollope knew so well how to draw, and which fill these novels, is Violet Effingham. (pp. 205-06)

It appears to me that as one looks later into the thoroughly happy home of this charming, keen-minded, altogether energetic matron, one finds in her the spokesman of Trollope's views upon woman's place in England. "I do not," she says in one place, "I do not think I shall marry Oswald. I shall knock under to Mr. Mill and go in for woman's rights, and look forward to stand for some female borough." But as a fact Mill's liberal views about Women's Rights was the very last thing that Violet ever thought of accepting. She wished rather to live a fuller life, a completer life, under the sure guidance of one whom she could trust, and whom therefore she could in turn help with her quick sympathies. When Lord Chiltern, as afterwards happens, turns out to be the man she hopes he might become, she appears to have found her complete happiness and the fulfillment of her desires. In the days of these novels, when Mill's theories of Feminism were beginning to startle some women, Trollope showed in these persons, for example, that a woman might live a broad and a full life under her husband's care, and so live it as to help him sanely and well. But her Liberty was to be guided according to him, we may be safe in saying, by an old-fashioned Puritan Principle: it was Liberty under the Law. If Trollope had some guiding conviction underlying his delineation of women who touched public life it seems to me that the conviction was embodied in some such Puritan ideal. To him Woman could be the greatest power in the affairs of England when she served a purpose, first, for which the Creator apparently chose her; to preside over the hearth and the home, and to make them the source of all that was true and of good report. . . . As soon as the woman began to have great public ambitions of her own, however, and began to over-reach herself by interfering with those things the intricacies of which she knew little or nothing, she became not a constructive force but a destructive influence. (p. 207)

[In] presenting his political figures one and all, Trollope never shows, in the political world at least, the interaction of character upon character; what help or injury there comes from one person upon another is always in material things. It is a misfortune that Trollope did not penetrate deep enough to paint these dramatic contrasts. . . . Trollope's political heroes are unconvincing *as* political characters: his prime minister, his Cabinet members, are men whose minds he shrewdly infers from their manners, and not because he knew them intimately; the slight reality they have for us is due to the fact that Trollope refrains from bringing them too close to the reader. Yet despite the fact that his political characters are unconvincing, there are still, in these novels, glimpses of profound knowledge of the parliamentary system of England. (p. 217)

Desirous first and always of picturing human nature as it shows itself in every-day, domestic surroundings, wishing to tell a good love-story in an easy, good-natured manner, he approaches his best characters (which are always the middle-class characters) with an observant, tolerant, and somewhat humorous outlook. Never offensive in his portraiture, with a comfortable interest in England and her sacred institutions, and the men who go up to make her laws in Parliament, he has no philosophy about public life, no ideas about what changes historical necessities call for, only opinions. . . . [Trollope was content] to *depict* his characters and his situations, to gratify his world of readers with the easily jogging narrative of sentiment to which they had already become accustomed in his earlier works. Dead earnestness and daring dreams of power in the mind of an aristocrat Trollope preferred to paint, or could paint merely, as the somewhat domestic and social manoeuvrings of the pale shades of the upper classes. The political life of England was never the integral part of Trollope's literary personality that it was of Disraeli's, to say the least. His political cabinets feed therefore always upon small talk and small ideas. His principal actors are somewhat mechanically-minded public leaders, when it is of them that he treats. Only when he steps down among the people that he knew most intimately, and whose daily fortunes, in their middle-class environment, he could easily follow, does he give us convincing situations and real flesh and blood. With the exception of the great ladies (whom he paints admirably, because he assumes them to be middle-class persons 'risen' to the level of 'high society,' but still with middle-class habits) his flesh-and-blood people are not the leaders in the fight, only the secondary characters. Trollope never took his politics more seriously than as a means of creating another background for the portrayal of human beings, for the telling of a good story, for the chance of reflecting more 'heart interest.' (pp. 218-19)

Morris Edmund Speare, "Anthony Trollope: The Victorian Realist in the Political Novel," in his *The Political Novel: Its Development in England and in America,* 1924. Reprint by Russell & Russell, 1966, pp. 185-220.

MICHAEL SADLEIR
(essay date 1945)

[Sadleir was an authority on Trollope's life and works. In the following excerpt, he defines Trollope's achievement and asserts that Trollope's greatness lies in his "profound understanding of ordinary life."]

The initial obstacle to a sober-minded definition of Trollope's novels is that they provide a sensual rather than an intellectual experience. A smell, a pain or a sound is not more difficult to describe than the effect—at once soothing and exciting—produced on the reader's mind by the leisurely, nonchalant commentaries on English social life which carry his name on their title-pages.

The phenomenon is partly explicable by the fact that a Trollope novel is of the very essence of fiction. At its best it represents a distillation of that element in story-telling on which all other elements depend, without which no blend—however skilful—of fact, incident, idea and description can be recognised for fiction at all—the element of characterisation.

There are novels more spiritual than his, more heroic and more beautiful; but there are none more faultless in this most delicate of all novel-writing problems. (p. 366)

[Power of characterisation] is the superlative quality of Trollope as a novelist. And as revealed by him, it is not a power of observation nor of imagination; not a power of knowledge nor of intuition; but a compound of all four, with a something added of the author's personality, giving to the whole a peculiar but elusive flavour.

For even granted characterisation, Trollope's quality remains intangible, baffles resolution. In theme familiar, in treatment undistinguished, his work is nevertheless potent in appeal, unrivalled in its power to hold the attention of readers of any kind and of any generation. And its elusiveness is the more extreme for being unexpected. It seems hardly fitting that a being, who in himself was so definite and so solid, who—like a solitary tower upon a hill—was visible for miles around in the wide landscape of Victorian England, should as a literary phenomenon be so difficult to seize and to describe; it is almost irritating that books in themselves so lustily prosaic should be so hard of definition.

There are, of course, certain qualities that Trollope as a novelist emphatically does not possess. He is no great philanthropist like Dickens; he has not Thackeray's pointed brilliance nor George Eliot's grave enthusiasm; he does not, like Meredith, paint a familiar scene in colours so vivid as to be of themselves a challenge. . . . Even in comparison with Jane Austen—the writer nearest to him as a novelist of manners—his curiosity seems suave rather than searching, his observation to have more of scope than of discrimination.

But not by elimination only can the quality of Trollope be appraised. He may be neither teacher nor word-painter, neither pantheist nor social reformer, but he is definitely something. What is he? Wherein lies that strange potency, which renders work so featureless, so sober and so undemonstrative an entertainment than which few are more enthralling?

It lies surely in his acceptance and his profound understanding of ordinary daily life. In the tale of English literature he is—to put the matter in a phrase—the supreme novelist of acquiescence. (pp. 366-67)

[Trollope] seeks for no doorway of escape. He is content with life, engrossed in it, never weary of its kaleidoscope of good and evil, of tears and laughter. Not only does he agree to the terms proposed by life, but he glories in them. And yet his work is born of a desire for beauty. He finds all of romance and courage and achievement within the unpretentious limits of the social existence of his day. He believes in individual capacity for perfection, but in terms of things as they are; his ideal of beauty and of proportion, whether in character or in happening, lies in the suave adjustment of personality to circumstance.

Trollope, then, is never a writer of revolt. But so complete is his acquiescence that he is not even a critical despot over the society of his imagination. Like a man in a crowded street who views his fellow-men, he is at once genially disposed but fundamentally detached. Also, to the point inevitable in detachment, he is cynical. He is without superiority; without presumption of omniscience. (pp. 367-68)

The long series of his books—so drab yet so mysteriously alive, so obvious yet so impossible of imitation—evade every criterion of what has become an academic judgment. They will stand no schooltests save those of the school of real life. They cannot but violate the modish canons of good fiction, as continually and as shamelessly as does life itself. Like life, they are diffuse, often tedious, seldom arrestingly unusual. Their monotony is the monotony of ordinary existence, which, although while actually passing it provides one small sensation after another, emerges in retrospect as a dull sequence of familiar things.

For in this queer sense of the absorbing interest of normal occupations lies the true realism of Trollope. He can reproduce the fascination of the successive happenings of the daily round, in the absence of which the human spirit would perish or go mad. Existence is made up of an infinite number of tiny fragments of excitement, interest and provocation, which carry men on from day to day, ever expectant, ever occupied. It is the second part of Trollope's claim to be a novelist that, by building up from just such multifarious trivialities the big absorptions which are his books, he gives the illusion that is of all illusions the most difficult to create—the illusion of ordinary life.

The art of Trollope, therefore, has two predominant qualities: power of characterisation and power of dramatisation of the undramatic. Within the limits of these rare capacities he designed and peopled a second England, virtually a replica of the London and counties of his day. But although in his imaginary England life seems (as indeed it is) utterly, almost exasperatingly, a series of unsensational sensations, a slow progression of meals and small ambitions, of love-making and disappointments, of sport and business, it would be an error to regard the Trollopian world as—other than superficially—without violent happenings. . . . It is one aspect of his amazing truth to life that he could contrive at the same time to be a novelist for the *jeune fille* and a most knowledgeable realist. For his books are lifelike in this also—that though compounded both of innocent and guilty, the guilt (as in life) is shrouded from the innocent, so that only such as know the signs of it may realise its presence or its nature.

This fact indicates those two of his personal qualities which most influence his handling of an imaginary social scene—his worldly proficiency and his good manners. There is nothing that he does not know; there is very little that, in his quiet skilful diction, he is not prepared to say. Socially speaking he is the wisest of English novelists; but because a large part of social wisdom is restraint, alike of gesture and of word, his books are restrained—not in incident or necessarily in emotion—but in expression. He writes adult books for adult people. But because he writes in terms of polite society, because he is in the truest sense a "man of the world," he is too civilised and too experienced to forget the social decencies for the sake of the social sins.

And not only had he a well-bred man's distaste for ugly realism; he was himself more interested in the deceptive calm of society's surface than in details of the hidden whirlpools beneath. . . . [The] clash between conventional poise and secret catastrophe, the delicate adjustment of repute and disrepute which kept the life of upper-class England outwardly serene for all its inward hazard, appealed to Trollope's sophisticated and rather cynical mind.

For in all things he was sophisticated and in social things more than a little cynical. . . . Contrast his books with those of the sensation-writers of his day or with those of novelists from a later generation who have been praised for their courageous realism. Trollope in geniality, in satire or in bitterness is calm; but to the others, in one way or another, existence is perpetually and disproportionately exciting. . . . To him everything is material for observation, nothing for declamation or for vanity. He approves virtue and deprecates vice, but he refuses to become excited either over ugliness or beauty. Like a connoisseur of wine he sips at this vintage and at that, selects to his taste and lays a cellar down. We, who inherit it, have but to drink at will, and in the novels that he left behind to savour the essence of life as once it was, as it still is, as in all likelihood it will remain. (pp. 369-73)

Michael Sadleir, in his *Trollope: A Commentary,* 1945. Reprint by Farrar, Straus and Giroux, 1947, 435 p.

JEROME THALE
(essay date 1960)

[In the excerpt below, Thale contends that Trollope's structural methods in his novels help reveal a broad and comprehensive vision of life.]

Trollope's novels have always had a reputation for being loose and rambling. *The Way We Live Now,* for example, has three or four major plot strands and three or four subplots—and even in this accounting there are a good many characters and situations left over. Trollope himself said that he was not very concerned with plot, and spoke of it [in *An Autobiography*] as "but the vehicle," "the most insignificant part of a tale." . . . In Trollope's time, when most readers accepted the novel as a picture of life, this was well enough. But we have come to expect more from the novel: discursiveness and inclusiveness no longer seem virtues in themselves, and the lack of structure has become a radical fault. There is surely no question that Trollope presents one of the fullest and most interesting pictures of nineteenth-century England, and if this is his only accomplishment it is a considerable one. But if we accept his novels primarily as documents, we may begin to wonder whether by our standards his works are really novels, whether we ought to hedge about his greatness. (p. 147)

In speaking of the Trollope novel I am referring not so much to the familiar shorter books like *The Warden* and *Barchester Towers,* but principally to the longer and (as most critics now seem to feel) major Trollope novels, such books as *The Way We Live Now, He Knew He was Right, The Last Chronicle of Barset,* and *The Duke's Children.* Let me take, as a representative example, *The Last Chronicle of Barset.* (p. 148)

[It is clear that *The Last Chronicle*] does not have a single unified plot line. Even the central action, that

about Mr. Crowley and the check, is not a dynamic one that springs from character and is resolved on the basis of change in it. It is largely mechanical and external. It is, to use Trollope's metaphor, the vehicle which allows for passengers and scenery, but whose destination is unimportant. It does not provide a vital organizing principle, an overall design to which parts are subordinated.

If the Trollope novel looks so centerless, if there is no single dramatic focus, if there are frequently four or five weakly related plots going at once, it is because plot, though present and not negligible, is not important. Or, to put it another way, time is not important. For what matters is not the succession of events but the accumulation of them, and the grouping of events and characters. A painting may be united through the repetition, echoing, contradiction, balancing, of such structural features as color, line, mass. In something of the same way, the Trollope novel depends upon parallels, contrasts, repetitions with slight variations. These things, which are present to some extent in any novel, become in Trollope the method of organization. In a Trollope novel, a large number of characters respond differently to the same situation, or do the same thing for different reasons. Half a dozen or a dozen people may fall in love and say "yes" or "no" in the same way but for different reasons, or in different ways but for the same reason. Thus the Trollope novel is the very opposite of the long comic strip, purely episodic; it is like a vast mural, one of those comprehensive images that cover walls, crammed with figures and united spatially.

If we examine the situations in *The Last Chronicle of Barset,* we discover that they are—to shift from a pictorial to a musical metaphor—variations on the basic motif of honesty. At the center of the novel is Mr. Crawley, a man of great pride and almost painful integrity. When his honesty is questioned because he cannot account for the stolen check, he himself does not know what to think. Pride in his obedience to authority makes him answer the Bishop's somewhat arbitrary summons to the palace. The same pride makes him refuse to be lectured at by the Bishop's wife. . . . At last pride and mistaken honesty compel him, against the advice of his friends, to submit his resignation. Only when the mystery is solved are his honesty, his sanity, and his reputation re-established.

After Mr. Crawley, the most important variation on the motif of honesty is the love affair of Grace Crawley and Major Grantly. The impediment of Mr. Crawley's troubles raises for them a different kind of question of honesty. Just as Mr. Crawley's difficulty begins with honesty about money and becomes one of honesty toward his position, theirs begins with honesty in their relations with each other and ends in questions of integrity to themselves. Though Grace loves the Major she does not feel that it is fair to let him commit himself while her family is in such difficulty; though she cannot accept his love, she will not deny that she loves him, for she must remain honest to herself. Major Grantly after some hesitation feels that fidelity to Grace and honesty to himself require that he should not let his love be deterred by Mr. Crawley's situation, and so he makes the declaration which is rebuffed. . . . Trollope presents the Major's honesty in a very complex and satisfying way—showing the Major as at once true to his love and disturbed at the thought of losing his money and position.

The problem of honesty to one's love and to one's self is paralleled and reversed with Lily Dale and John Eames. Their story, which is the main business of *The Small House at Allington,* is here re-used and continued in terms of the over-all motif of *The Last Chronicle.* Lily still loves the man who had jilted her. John

Eames, who has loved Lily for many years, resolves to press his suit again. If Johnny is persistent in being faithful to his love (even though it is becoming something of a joke), Lily is equally persistent in being faithful to her heart. Friends on both sides urge the match, the specter of old maidhood is facing Lily, and Johnny acquits himself manfully in extricating Crawley from his troubles. But Lily, though she acknowledges his merits, knows also that she does not love him, and so she will not marry him. (pp. 149-51)

An account of the large repetitions and variations on the main theme does not begin to indicate how thoroughly this method of repetition and variation pervades and organizes the novel, even in the presentation of subsidiary characters and situations. The novel opens, for example, with scenes in which we see the Walkers, the Grantlys, and the Crawleys at home, each discussing the incident of the check (and in each case we see how the wife—apparently under the control of a much stronger husband—manages him). The public response to Mr. Crawley's troubles is presented several times. The judgments come from a wide variety of characters and occur at various stages in the book; often of course they give us a double measure—of Mr. Crawley and of those who judge. . . .

The discussion of Mr. Crawley takes a formal and legal character when the magistrates meet. They do not want to bind Mr. Crawley over for trial, but the evidence seems against him, he offers no defense, and so they are compelled to bind him over. Later the Bishop appoints a clerical commission to investigate the matter, and a different set of judges examines the same material. The description of the meeting and the personalities is a miniature of the method of the novel, subtle and careful examination of the various possibilities for honesty and dishonesty. (p. 152)

In such situations as these, we see different people doing the same thing, being honest or dishonest but in different ways. In another type of situation a character repeats the same action—but under a different set of circumstances that gives us a different perspective on the action. When Mr. Crawley goes to the Bishop's he refuses to bend in the least to Mrs. Proudie and even to discuss the case with her. Our sympathies are all with him; he is being persecuted, and Mrs. Proudie is a meddlesome woman getting her comeuppance. But a few chapters later Mark Robarts goes to Mr. Crawley urging him to get legal help. Crawley refuses, and we are dismayed that he should so rudely reject the generous help of Robarts. If we reflect upon it, we realize that in spite of our different responses, Crawley's motive is essentially the same in both cases—stiff-necked pride, independence, assertion of his rights.

In its more complex uses, this method of repetition of an action under varying circumstances produces not simply a new perspective but a new meaning for the action. Sometimes the identical situation is repeated. John Eames proposes to Lily Dale at her home in Allington at about the same time that her old lover Crosbie writes that he still loves her; she decides against both of them. Later, on a visit to London, she comes to feel the attraction of a wider life and of marriage. John, in a wider circle himself, looks better to her, and she actually sees Crosbie. The earlier possibilities are repeated—John proposes again; Crosbie, who is more in love with her than ever, presents himself. With a larger and more direct experience, she comes to the same conclusion again—that she will not marry. Though she knows better what she is doing the second time, and her decision is more meaningful, the action is essentially the same. (pp. 153-54)

In all of these cases the method of variation is used for giving complexity of meaning to the main themes, for seeing actions and motives in many lights. Elsewhere in the novel, and often rather incidentally, Trollope uses the method not so much for moral perspective but as a compositional device for arranging characters and situations. Thus there are the two lawyers: one at the beginning, the other later in the book; one thinks Crawley guilty but is willing to stretch the law for him; the other is convinced of his innocence and also willing to stretch the law; one is sober and conservative, the other bustling and energetic; one a local man, the other from London. Each of the lawyers is basically honest (though in different ways), and each is willing to be a little dishonest (though again in different ways). (p. 154)

This same kind of structural principle that I have been describing in *The Last Chronicle of Barset* operates, as I have said, in most of the other large Trollope novels. It is by no means the most obvious or familiar structural principle in the English novel; whether it is the best of structural principles is unimportant. In Trollope's hands and in the hands of certain other novelists it is a way of examining a situation or problem with great breadth and complexity, of bringing a great deal of material into a vital relationship. It is a principle which makes the Trollope novel much more than a picture of life. The term panoramic suggests in a general way some of the features of this kind of novel. (pp. 154-55)

In trying to discern the structural principle which Trollope uses, I have not been trying to make his novels respectable by demonstrating that they have structure. . . . In *The Last Chronicle* structure is the means through which Trollope's wonderful disenchanted clarity of vision, his tolerance and accuracy, operate to produce a remarkably complex and balanced vision of human life. The end result of the massive examination in *The Last Chronicle* is to indicate how complex a thing honesty is, how much there is involved in being honest or dishonest, and indeed how complex a thing

human life is, viewed under this aspect. The method is static in the way that a mural is, taken in all at once, by a kind of exfoliation in which vision and technique are one. (p. 156)

Jerome Thale, "The Problem of Structure in Trollope," in *Nineteenth-Century Fiction*, Vol. 15, No. 2, September, 1960, pp. 147-57.

P. D. EDWARDS
(essay date 1977)

[In the following excerpt, Edwards asserts that there are "two streams running through Trollope's work": the stream of everyday life and the more sensational stream of, in Trollope's words, "great and glowing incidents."]

Though it has become fashionable to do so, . . . it is a mistake to regard Carlylean gloom, bitterness, and satirical rage, or a preoccupation with psychological abnormalities, as setting the dominant tone of Trollope's later work. Even in novels as satirical as *The Eustace Diamonds* and *The Way We Live Now,* a substratum of conservative decency persists; and it tends to come out on top in the end. But the tone of the novels is set above all by their comic energy and ingenuity, the excitement Trollope finds in the tortuosities of the human mind, the muted admiration that even the most antisocial deeds of his creatures appear to exact from him. Lizzie Eustace and Auguste Melmotte are great comic creations as well as social portents; and however degenerate the society that spawns and nourishes them, a good deal of its weakness for them, its subversive imaginative sympathy with them, clearly infects both Trollope himself and the reader. So that while, objectively, the world of the novels may often be ugly, vicious, even monstrous, their total effect is neither hysterical nor dispiriting.

Trollope, like James, takes the "great black things of life" for granted, neither wondering nor shuddering at them. He finds nothing unaccountable in monstrous evil any more than in simple goodness. Often it is only a slightly distorted version of the conventional modus vivendi of society in general, and the mental imbalance that produces it is scarcely distinguishable from what seems the normal state of mind. Almost invariably the people in his novels who do the most extraordinary things are in themselves quite ordinary. The sensational impact of their actions, such as it is, is only momentary. They look mysterious and shocking only from without, only because of the superficial contrast they offer to what we take for the normal, the ordinary. Once we look more closely we find their meaning, their moral logic easily comprehensible and quite commonplace. The novels are, in this sense, "at the same time realistic and sensational", as Trollope believed that a "good novel should be." . . . (pp. 168-69)

[*The Way We Live Now*] deals with the same phenomenon [as *The Eustace Diamonds*]: people's cynical admiration for successful dishonesty, their evasion of the tawdry moral realities underlying it for the sake of its surface glamour. But *The Way We Live Now*—Trollope's longest novel—examines the phenomenon both more widely and more deeply. *The Eustace Diamonds,* though it offers glimpses of other worlds, is essentially a satire on the haut monde of London, and for all its pungency it retains a buoyancy, a lightness of touch appropriate to the artificial pleasures of the idle rich. Lizzie Eustace, after all, entertains her world without greatly damaging its moral or material well-being; her career shows up society's existing corruption but hardly deepens or extends it. In *The Way We Live Now,* on the other hand, Melmotte is agent as well as creature of corruption. The infection that he carries is confined to no single social group or habitat but thrives in town and country and among rich and poor alike. It threatens both the prosperity and the moral order of society. *The Way We Live Now* comes closer than any of Trollope's other novels to admitting the possibility that all existing social institutions may be obsolete and doomed, no longer having any real moral and economic foundations.

Yet although so disillusioned in its vision of modern life, although picturing corruption as nearly all-pervasive, the novel is by no means embittered. Many of its scenes are highly comic, however sombre their implications, and the authorial tone is generally cool and urbane, with few outbursts of anger. (pp. 180-81)

[While] *The Way We Live Now* is perhaps more singlemindedly satirical than any of Trollope's other novels, its satire is seldom likely to seem exaggerated to a modern reader, and there is nothing in its picture of social evils as overcoloured as parts of *The Warden, The Bertrams,* and *Doctor Thorne.* Trollope, as usual, finds a few saving graces in nearly all his characters, even in Melmotte, the giant swindler who is the centre and prime exemplar of the commercial profligacy that permeates the whole world of the novel. The few characters who are shown as having no good in them at all—Miles Grendall and Sir Felix Carbury, for instance—are at worst only marginally more vicious than, say, an Undy Scott (in *The Three Clerks*) or a George Vavasor. And following Melmotte's death there is a general purgation of evil. (p. 182)

The moral norm of the novel's world is not represented by vicious unprincipled people like Melmotte, Sir Felix, and the Grendalls, any more than it is by inflexible goody-goodies like Roger and his rustic protégé, John Crumb. It is embodied, rather, in people like

the serviceable, shrewd, opportunistic Mr. Broune and the bishop of Elmham, the goodnatured, lazy, but essentially honest Paul Montague, Dolly Longestaffe, and Lord Nidderdale, and in Hetta Carbury, oldfashioned, decorous, and biddable in everything but her choice of lovers. . . . The moral of the novel, by no means a utopian or an ungenial one, is perhaps expressed in Lord Nidderdale's gentle lament for the lost "Paradise" of the Beargarden club, whose members have made it "too hot to hold [them]": "If one wants to keep oneself straight, one has to work hard at it, one way or the other. I suppose it all comes from the fall of Adam." . . . Virtue isn't altogether easy even for a Roger Carbury, and Trollope is as modest in his demand for it in *The Way We Live Now* as in most of his novels.

The tolerant restraint that marks his satire also extends to—indeed is inseparable from—his treatment of the more melodramatic parts of his story. None of his other novels containing a comparable amount of potentially sensational material is so unsensational in its total effect; in no others are crime, violence, and rebellious sexual passion more convincingly acclimatized to a generally low emotional temperature. How well the "two streams" of Trollope's fictional art consort in the novel can be seen in his presentation of four of the leading characters: Melmotte, Mrs. Hurtle, Sir Felix Carbury, and Georgiana Longestaffe.

All of these, it should be noted at the outset, derive from Victorian sensational archetypes: Melmotte from the criminal who hides his villainy behind a mask of respectability and his terrors behind a mask of prosperity; Mrs. Hurtle partly (like Melmotte) from the mysterious stranger, with foreign ways and a murky foreign past, and partly from the ageing and dangerously possessive "other woman"; Sir Felix from the dashing romantic villain who abducts heiresses and seduces country maidens; Georgiana from the young miss driven to rebellious violence by her isolation from the society of eligible men. Trollope, as we should expect, shows them all failing to meet the conventional romantic requirements of their situations, but supplying their world (and the reader) with welcome excitement in the process.

Melmotte is one of the most finely conceived and subtly drawn of all Trollope's characters. For most of the novel he remains a shadowy, half-legendary figure. His reputation for vast wealth invests him with mysterious power. What little we learn about his past and present activities is based on hearsay, and the facts emerge so slowly, so disjointedly that they hardly shake the popular illusion of him as a remote colossus. . . . The very vastness and diversity of [Melmotte's] affairs—which he cannot keep track of himself—defies public scrutiny. In the conventional imagination he becomes a figure of almost superhuman immanence and resource. . . . (pp. 182-85)

Until his decline begins, Melmotte is kept hardly less remote from the reader than from the general public. He is not discovered alone for any length of time until well into the second half of the novel, and we are seldom made aware, even for a moment, of what he really thinks when he is engaged in conversation. Even his own family judge him by his "moods" without inquiring into their possible causes. His legendary reputation dwarfs him and screens him from the rest of society; his true identity becomes hidden in the caricature created by his wealth and his secretiveness. (p. 185)

It is not till he has reached his peak of success, when he has begun to "despise mere lords, and to feel that he might almost domineer over a duke" . . . that Melmotte begins to betray himself. He becomes insufferably arrogant, having come, as we are told, "almost to believe in himself." . . . Yet for a long time people continue to tolerate him, and it is only gradually that we are made to see how weakly dependent he is on the illusion of power he has created, how hungry for recognition as a means not only of advancing his commercial success but also of shielding him from his own weakness. In his decline he sometimes looks stupid, irresolute, and vain. . . . But something of the magnitude of his reputation does carry over to the man himself. His consciousness of the greatness of his achievement in graduating from the gutter to the seats of the mighty is not entirely inflated. And he has at least an idea of how he should comport himself under the threat of destruction, at least a glimmering of the duty that his conception of his own "glory" imposes upon him. (pp. 185-86)

[Mrs. Hurtle] is in many ways complementary to Melmotte. Like him she is a foreigner whose past is shrouded in mystery and whom popular rumour credits with hidden, perhaps dangerous power. Gossip garbles and exaggerates her past deeds as it does Melmotte's. In the eyes of a tame, sensation-starved public her capacity for passion and violence becomes magnified in the same way as Melmotte's for conjuring up wealth. Like Melmotte she comes to see herself partly as the popular imagination sees her and to feel that she has a reputation to live up to. But she differs from him, and from nearly everyone in the novel, in that she eventually learns to recognize and accept her true nature, divests herself of the conventionally unconventional mask that she has worn as a defence against the world. (p. 189)

What makes her so impressive in the novel is not only the mystery, the unresolved contradictions, that surround her for so long, but also the force with which, despite her exoticism, she expresses feelings that nearly all women can share. Her power over Paul—such as it is—illustrates the power of illusion over the conventional mind as surely as does Melmotte's popular fame. But the sensational illusion of herself which she presents, half at the dictate of her unsavoury reputation, does correspond to something real in her own and in every woman's nature. Though not really the savage princess, the wildcat that she seems, she expresses in her atavistic pose a resentment against male domination that must have been shared by many women too proper to acknowledge it. (p. 191)

Mrs. Hurtle makes a sensational impact in the novel partly for the same reason as Lady Laura does in *Phineas Redux* and Lucinda in *The Eustace Diamonds*: because she is a woman of powerful but by no means ignoble passions in a world afraid of passion. In *The Way We Live Now* the only characters who express themselves with any real emotional conviction are Mrs. Hurtle, Roger Carbury, John Crumb, and, in his drunken and violent moments, Melmotte. (p. 192)

Sir Felix Carbury, the most despicable person in the novel, is in many respects a miniature Melmotte. He is, like Melmotte, a confidence trickster, but his victims are not greedy, gullible men of the world but romantic young women. The illusions they form about him enable him to exploit them, partly for mercenary reasons, partly to gratify his own vanity, just as Melmotte exploits his victims. To Sir Felix, as to Melmotte and the world at large, there is an excitement in the idea of dishonesty that makes it pleasurable in itself, regardless of rewards. But like Melmotte, only far more ignominiously, he fails to live up to his own idea of himself. The Beargarden club, where he plays cards and carries on what he calls the "game" of living, is to him what Abchurch Lane and the Stock Exchange are to Melmotte. He lives by gambling. . . . Like Melmotte, Sir Felix becomes reckless and finally disgraces himself under the influence of drink. (pp. 192-93)

The "great enterprise" of Sir Felix's life is to marry Melmotte's daughter Marie. But he displays none of the zeal one would expect from a gambler playing for such high stakes. The wooing is "weary work" and he gets through it only by studying his words and looks and "repeating them as a lesson." . . . But the heiress, a reader of romantic novels who has hitherto been starved of affection, unexpectedly conceives the idea that she is in love with him. In her eyes the romance of the affair is heightened by her father's opposition. But "romance" is not Sir Felix's "game" . . . , and he regards Melmotte's opposition as a fatal obstacle until Marie tells him of the fortune her father has made over to her as a precaution against bad times. She will share this with Sir Felix if he will elope with her. To his alarm she suddenly reveals a guile and resolution much superior to his own. . . .

Marie's mixture of moonstruck innocence, courage, and practical efficiency looks ahead to that of the typical Jamesian innocent: what she "knew" is no less surprising than what James's Maisie or even Maggie Verver "knew"; her corrupt knowledge makes her just as formidable and is just as hard to reconcile with her large residual innocence. She is one of Trollope's best ironical character studies. Like Dolly Longestaffe and Lord Nidderdale, she has the function in the novel of revealing the strength of innocence in a world where it is so little understood as to be credited with no judgment and no capacity for action at all. (p. 193)

If Sir Felix Carbury is Trollope's typically shabby version of the conventional romantic villain, Georgiana Longestaffe is his most notable satirical comment on another stock figure of sensational fiction: the female rebel. As such, she offers obvious parallels to both Mrs. Hurtle and Marie Melmotte. Her passions, like those of the French sisters in *He Knew He Was Right,* are in part a burlesque of those of more "serious" characters in the novel. But although essentially a comic character, she is presented a good deal more realistically than the French sisters had been—with much more restrained humour, and more concentration on what is socially typical, and socially portentous, in her character and situation. (p. 195)

Apart from a few of Mrs. Hurtle's outbursts, there is nothing in the novel to equal the violence of emotion, or at least of emotional language, aroused by Georgiana's engagement to Brehgert. Even Georgiana can justify herself only by blaming it on the sensational breakdown of the whole social order to which she had been accustomed. (p. 196)

Georgiana's escape from what all her friends regard as a tragic misalliance parallels the rescue of Ruby Ruggles from Sir Felix and of Paul Montague from Mrs. Hurtle. Though not an unambiguously happy ending, it at least represents a consolidation of English genteel values, and of the caste system upon which they are based, in the face of a threat from both within and without. Whether much remains in these values that is really worth preserving, the novel as a whole leaves in doubt, and it was presumably his feeling that this was so that caused Trollope to accuse himself of satirical exaggeration. But at less exalted levels of society—those of Paul and Hetta, John Crumb and Ruby, even Lady Carbury and Mr. Broune—the novel shows that some worthwhile values do persist, however precariously. (pp. 196-97)

P. D. Edwards, in his *Anthony Trollope: His Art and Scope,* 1977. Reprint by St. Martin's Press, 1978, 234 p.

SOURCES FOR FURTHER STUDY

Cockshut, A. O. J. *Anthony Trollope: A Critical Study.* New York: New York University Press, 1968, 256 p.

> Study of Trollope's novels after 1863, contending that each novel "reveals a futher stage in the steeping curve of the author's pessimism."

Hall, N. John, ed. *The Trollope Critics.* Totowa, N.J.: Barnes & Noble Books, 1981, 248 p.

> A collection of essays by many of the most important Trollope critics, from Henry James in 1883 through the commentators of the 1970s.

Halperin, John. *Trollope and Politics: A Study of the Pallisers and Others.* New York: Barnes & Noble, 1977, 318 p.

> A close study of Trollope's political novels.

McMaster, Juliet. *Trollope's Palliser Novels: Theme and Pattern.* New York: Oxford University Press, 1978, 242 p.

> Critical work debating assertions of earlier critics that Trollope's work has no underlying meaning or coherent structure.

Pollard, Arthur. *Anthony Trollope.* London: Routledge & Kegan Paul, 1978, 208 p.

> A laudatory survey of Trollope's work.

Pope Hennessy, James. *Anthony Trollope.* London: Jonathan Cape, 1971, 400 p.

> A detailed biography that provides commentary on Trollope's work and information about his critical reception.

Ivan Turgenev

1818-1883

(Full name Ivan Sergeyevich Turgenev. Also transliterated as Toorgenef, Tourghenief, Tourgeénief, Turgeneff, Turgenieff, and Turgéniew) Russian novelist, novella, short story, and sketch writer, dramatist, poet, and essayist.

INTRODUCTION

*T*he first Russian author to achieve widespread international fame, Turgenev was accounted his country's premier novelist by nineteenth-century Westerners and is today linked with Fyodor Dostoyevsky and Leo Tolstoy as one of the triumvirate of great Russian novelists of the nineteenth century. Turgenev's achievement is twofold. As a writer deeply concerned with the politics of his homeland, he gave to history vivid testimonials of the tumultuous political environment in Russia from the 1840s to the 1870s. Simultaneously, as a literary artist, he created works noted for their psychological truth, descriptive beauty, and haunting pathos.

Turgenev was born in the city of Orel into a family of wealthy gentry. His father, by all accounts a charming but ineffectual cavalry officer, paid little attention to Turgenev, whose childhood on the family estate of Spasskoye was dominated by his eccentric and capricious mother, Varvara Petrovna. Her treatment of her favorite son Ivan alternated between excessive affection and mental and physical cruelty; she ruled Spasskoye and its 5000 serfs with the same arbitrary power. Biographers have cited his mother's influence to explain much about the development of Turgenev's personality—particularly his horror of violence and hatred of injustice—and his fiction, populated as it is by strong women and well-meaning but weak-willed men. During Turgenev's early childhood, French was the primary language spoken in his household; though his mother later permitted the use of Russian, it is likely that Turgenev's first lessons in the vernacular came from the Spasskoye serfs. When Turgenev was nine, the family left the country for Moscow, where he attended boarding schools before entering Moscow University in 1833. At the university, he earned the nickname "the American" for his interest in the United

States and his democratic inclinations. In 1834, Turgenev transferred to the University of St. Petersburg. Upon graduation, he decided that the completion of his education required study abroad. In 1838, therefore, he went to Germany, enrolling at the University of Berlin. During the next several years he studied philosophy, never, however, finishing his degree. He returned to Russia in 1841, but for the rest of his life divided his time between his homeland and western Europe.

Although Turgenev had begun writing poetry as a student in St. Petersburg, publishing his first verses in 1838, biographers generally cite the narrative poem *Parasha,* published in 1843, as the beginning of his literary career. This work attracted little attention from his contemporaries, however, and more important for his subsequent life and literary development were the friendships he made in the mid-1840s, including those with Pauline Viardot and Vissarion Belinsky. Viardot was a successful opera singer and a married woman when Turgenev met her in 1843. The precise nature of their relationship is uncertain. While Turgenev's letters to her seem to indicate a grand passion, at least on his side, there is no evidence that the two were ever lovers. At any rate, their relationship endured for the rest of Turgenev's life; he frequently followed Viardot to wherever her career took her and was on excellent terms with her husband and the rest of her family. Belinsky, an extremely influential literary critic who believed that literature must both mirror life and promote social reform, was a political liberal and an ardent Westernizer who sought to bring Russia's culture and political system nearer to that of Europe. Belinsky was closely associated with the radical periodical *Sovremennik* (*The Contemporary*), edited by Nikolay Nekrasov, and it was in this journal that Turgenev published his first prose work, the short story "Khor i Kalinych" ("Khor and Kalinych"). Although Turgenev continued to write poetry and tried his hand at drama, he had found his niche and his audience in narrative prose. "Khor and Kalinych" was followed by a series of related pieces between the years 1847 and 1852, all first published in the *Contemporary* and later collected and published in book form in 1852 as *Zapiski okhotnika* (*A Sportsman's Sketches*). In these sketches, which range from brief slices of life to fully realized short stories, Turgenev adopted the persona of a hunter in the country, drawing on his experiences at Spasskoye and expressing his love for the land and people of rural Russia. Common to the sketches is the theme of the injustice of Russian serfdom. Because of this omnipresent concern, *A Sportsman's Sketches* is frequently compared to Harriet Beecher Stowe's contemporaneous anti-slavery novel *Uncle Tom's Cabin,* published in 1852. Unlike the American novel, however, Turgenev's work is understated, his moral message implied rather than overt. At their first publication, Turgenev's

stories were enormously popular with almost everyone but government officials. In fact, when Turgenev wrote an admiring obituary of Nikolay Gogol in 1852, he was arrested, ostensibly for excessive approval of a suspect writer but more likely because he was himself suspect as the author of *A Sportsman's Sketches.* After a month in jail, Turgenev was confined to Spasskoye, where he remained under house arrest for nearly two years. When the serfs were finally freed in 1861, there were many who credited *A Sportsman's Sketches* with having helped to effect their emancipation.

Turgenev's first novel, *Rudin,* which was published in 1856, introduced several character types and themes that appear in his subsequent fiction. The title character is a political idealist who combines a genius for words with an inability to act on them. Such "Russian Hamlets" recur frequently in Turgenev's work and were regarded by his contemporaries as insightful personifications of a national malaise of irresolution and indecision. Like Turgenev's later novels, *Rudin* is a love story. But while Nathalie, one of Turgenev's typically strong heroines, is willing to risk all for love, Rudin gives her up at the first sign of parental opposition: he is as ineffectual and passive in love as in politics, sounding early Turgenev's common themes of fatalism and frustration. *Rudin* was followed by *Dvoryanskoe gnezdo* (1859; *A House of Gentlefolk*), whose hero Lavretsky is as helpless to control destiny as Rudin. The heroine Liza shows her strength not in action but in renunciation, nobly retiring to a convent when Lavretsky's unfaithful wife, believed dead, reappears. Elena, the heroine of Turgenev's next novel, *Nakanune* (1860; *On the Eve*), possesses strength of a more active sort. Longing to dedicate her life to a worthwhile cause, Elena is confronted with a choice of suitors. Rejecting this novel's "Hamlet," she chooses Insarov, a man of resolution and action and, significantly, a Bulgarian rather than a Russian. Turgenev's contemporaries, attuned to the political significance of his characters, understood the novel to mean that Russia had not yet produced men of dedication and action, patriots willing, as are Insarov and Elena, to sacrifice themselves for the sake of a political ideal.

The Russia of the nineteenth century was indeed a divided and politically troubled country, unsure of its future political course. Tension existed not only between conservatives and liberals but also, in the latter camp, between the radicals, who called for immediate change and economic communism, and the moderates, who favored slow, peaceful reform and free enterprise. Turgenev managed to draw the enmity of nearly every Russian ideologue, from reactionary to revolutionary, with his next and most famous novel, *Ottsy i deti* (1862; *Fathers and Sons*). Bazarov, the protagonist of the book, is considered Turgenev's most successful and most ambiguous character (alternately attractive and repellent, he aroused ambivalent feelings even in his creator), as well as an intriguing portrayal of a political type just then coming into existence in Russia: the nihilist. While Turgenev did not invent the term nihilist, his depiction of Bazarov in *Fathers and Sons* brought it into general usage. Bazarov rejects every aspect of Russian political, social, and cultural life, believing in nothing but empirical science. As with all Turgenev's fiction, the plot is slight; most of the action consists of Bazarov's debates with his friend's uncle, Pavel, who symbolizes the older generation of Russian liberals. *Fathers and Sons* was denounced on every side: blasted by conservatives as a favorable portrayal of a dangerous radical, it was attacked by liberals as a damning caricature of radicalism.

Distressed by this unfavorable reaction, Turgenev spent more and more time abroad, and he counted among his friends some of the most illustrious authors of his era, including Gustave Flaubert, Henry James, Émile Zola, Guy de Maupassant, and George Sand. His absence from Russia left him vulnerable to charges, leveled at his subsequent novels, that he was out of touch and out of sympathy with his native land. Indeed, his next novel, *Dym* (1867; *Smoke*), was considered Turgenev's most bitter work, one that pilloried conservatives and liberals alike and that, in the disapproving eyes of many Russian commentators, depicted Russia's plight as a hopeless one. Pessimistic also is Turgenev's last novel, *Nov'* (1877; *Virgin Soil*), which deals with the inability of Nezhdanov, another ineffectual character, to put into practice his Populist principles by living and working with the common people. As a study of the Russian Populist movement of the 1870s, the book was considered inadequate by Russian readers. Following the publication of *Virgin Soil,* Turgenev, now virtually self-exiled from his homeland, no longer attempted to depict the Russian political scene. His remaining works—prose poems and stories—are described by critics as nostalgic, philosophical, and frequently pessimistic, and are often concerned with the occult. After a long and debilitating illness, Turgenev died in Bougival, near Paris, with Pauline Viardot at his side. His body was returned to Russia by train. There, notwithstanding the unfavorable reception of his later works and the efforts of the Russian government to restrict memorial congregations, Turgenev was widely mourned by his compatriots.

Because of the highly political content of most of Turgenev's works, the earliest Russian commentators tended to praise or disparage his writings along partisan lines. Similarly, foreign critics of the nineteenth century were interested in Turgenev's books for the light they shed on the volatile sociopolitical situation in Russia. Turgenev's novels and many of his novellas and short stories were quickly translated into French, German, and English. English and American readers considered Turgenev the most accessible Russian writer, and they—particularly American critics—took a lively, generally appreciative interest in his career beginning with the publication of *A Sportsman's Sketches.* Early Russian and English-language critics by no means neglected the aesthetic qualities of Turgenev's works, however, recognizing from the start that his fiction was more than simply the literal portrayal of the people and concerns of a particular country at a given historical moment.

Turgenev's literary reputation has remained generally stable over the years, with twentieth-century commentators echoing and amplifying the conclusions reached by their nineteenth-century counterparts. Critics agree that Turgenev's work is distinguished by solid literary craftsmanship, especially in the areas of description and characterization. Keenly observant, he infused his work with precise, realistic detail, bringing a natural scene or character into focus through the evocative power of his words. Given Turgenev's slight plots, interest in the novels centers largely on the characters. Readers note that his characters—recognized both as unique individuals and as representatives of universal human qualities—are drawn with a psychological penetration all the more effective for being suggested rather than overtly stated: the minds and personalities of his characters are revealed through their own words and actions, not through direct exposition by the narrator. Turgenev was particularly adept, critics contend, at portraying women in love and at creating an atmosphere of pathos but not sentimentality in his unhappy love stories. Fatalism and thwarted desires are hallmarks of the novelist's work: his characters are generally unable to control their destiny, either because of their own flaws or through the arbitrariness of fate. Scholars suggest that Turgenev's fiction reveals his own sense of the futility of life, but add that he tempered his essentially pessimistic outlook with an appreciation of life's beauty. As the author himself remarked, "Everything human is dear to me."

Turgenev is thus renowned for his dual role as social chronicler and literary artisan. In his stories and novels he described the political temper of a turbulent era, at the same time creating works of great literary merit. As Joseph Conrad wrote: "Turgenev's Russia is but a canvas on which the incomparable artist of humanity lays his colours and his forms in the great light and the free air of the world."

(For further information about Turgenev's life and works, see *Nineteenth-Century Literature Criticism,* Vol. 21 and *Short Story Criticism,* Vol. 7.)

CRITICAL COMMENTARY

EDWARD GARNETT
(essay date 1917)

[Garnett, an editor for several London publishing houses, discovered or greatly influenced the work of many important English writers, including Joseph Conrad, John Galsworthy, and D. H. Lawrence. He also published several volumes of criticism. In the following excerpt, he offers a chronological survey and appraisal of Turgenev's short stories.]

In addition to his six great novels Turgenev published, between 1846 and his death in 1883, about forty tales which reflect as intimately social atmospheres of the 'thirties, 'forties and 'fifties as do Tchehov's stories atmospheres of the 'eighties and 'nineties. Several of these tales, as *The Torrents of Spring*, are of considerable length, but their comparatively simple structure places them definitely in the class of the *conte*. While their form is generally free and straightforward, the narrative, put often in the mouth of a character who by his comments and asides exchanges at will his active rôle for that of a spectator, is capable of the most subtle modulations. An examination of the chronological order of the tales shows how very delicately Turgenev's art is poised between realism and romanticism. In his finest examples, such as **"The Brigadier"** and **"A Lear of the Steppes,"** the two elements fuse perfectly, like the meeting of wave and wind in sea foam. "Nature placed Turgenev between poetry and prose," says Henry James; and if one hazards a definition we should prefer to term Turgenev *a poetic realist.* (pp. 163-64)

[In 1846] appeared **"The Jew,"** a close study, based on a family anecdote, of Semitic double-dealing and family feeling; also **"Three Portraits,"** a more or less faithful ancestral chronicle. This latter tale, though the hero is of the proud, bad, "Satanic" order of the romantic school, is firmly objective, as is also **"Pyetushkov,"** whose lively, instinctive realism is so bold and intimate as to contradict the compliment that the French have paid themselves—that Turgenev ever had need to dress his art by the aid of French mirrors.

Although **"Pyetushkov"** shows us, by a certain open *naïveté* of style, that a youthful hand is at work, it is the hand of a young master carrying out Gogol's satiric realism with finer point, to find a perfect equilibrium free from bias or caricature. The essential strength of the realistic method is developed in **"Pyetushkov"** to its just limits, and note it is the Russian realism carrying the warmth of life into the written page, which

warmth the French so often lose in clarifying their impressions and crystallizing them in art. Observe how the reader is transported bodily into Pyetushkov's stuffy room, how the Major fairly boils out of the two pages he lives in, and how Onisim and Vassilissa and the aunt walk and chatter around the stupid Pyetushkov, and laugh at him behind his back in a manner that exhales the vulgar warmth of these people's lower-class world. One sees that the latter holds few secrets for Turgenev. . . . [In 1844] had appeared **"Andrei Kolosov,"** a sincere diagnosis of youth's sentimental expectations, raptures and remorse, in presence of the other sex, in this case a girl who is eager for a suitor. The sketch is characteristically Russian in its analytic honesty, but Turgenev's charm is here lessened by his overliteral exactitude. And passing to **"The Diary of a Superfluous Man,"** we must remark that this famous study of a type of a petty provincial Hamlet reveals a streak of suffused sentimentalism in Turgenev's nature, one which comes to the surface the more subjective is the handling of his theme, and the less his great technical skill in *modelling* his subject is called for. The last-named story belongs to a group with which we must place *Faust, Yakov Pasinkov, A Correspondence* and even the tender and charming *Acia,* all of which stories, though rich in emotional shades and in beautiful descriptions, are lacking in fine chiselling. The melancholy yearning of the heroes and heroines through failure or misunderstanding, though no doubt true to life, seems to-day too imbued with emotional hues of the Byronic romanticism of the period, and in this small group of stories Turgenev's art is seen definitely dated, even old-fashioned.

In **"The Country Inn,"** we are back on the firm ground of an objective study of village types, with clear, precise outlines, a detailed drawing from nature, strong yet subtle; as is also **"Mumu,"** one based on a household episode that passed before Turgenev's youthful eyes, in which the deaf-mute Gerassim, a house serf, is defrauded first of the girl he loves, and then of his little dog, Mumu, whom he is forced to drown, stifling his pent-up affection, at the caprice of his tyrannical old mistress. The story is a classic example of Turgenev's tender insight and beauty of feeling. As delicate, but more varied in execution is **"The Backwater,"** with its fresh, charming picture of youth's *insouciance* and readiness to take a wrong turning, a story which in its atmospheric freshness and emotional colouring may be compared with Tchehov's studies of

*Principal Works

Parasha (poetry) 1843

"Dnevnik lishnego cheloveka" (short story) 1850

   ["The Diary of a Superfluous Man" published in Mumu and The Diary of a Superfluous Man, 1884]

"Mumu" (short story) 1852; published in periodical Sovremennik

   ["Mumu" published in Mumu and The Diary of a Superfluous Man, 1884]

Zapiski okhotnika (sketches and short stories) 1852

   [Russian Life in the Interior; or, The Experiences of a Sportsman, 1855; also published as A Sportsman's Sketches in The Novels of Ivan Turgenev, 1895]

Rudin (novel) 1856; also published as Rudin [enlarged edition], 1860

   [Dimitri Roudine, 1873; also published as Rudin in The Novels of Ivan Turgenev, 1894]

Asya (novella) 1858

   [Annouchka, 1884; also published as Asya in The Novels and Stories of Iván Turgénieff, 1904]

Dvoryanskoe gnezdo (novel) 1859

   [Liza, 1869; also published as A House of Gentlefolk in The Novels of Ivan Turgenev, 1894, and A Nobleman's Nest in The Novels and Stories of Iván Turgénieff, 1903]

"Gamlet i Don Kikhot" (criticism) 1860; published in periodical Sovremennik

   ["Hamlet and Don Quixote" published in periodical Poet Lore, 1892]

Nakanune (novel) 1860

   [On the Eve, 1871]

Pervaya lyubov' (novella) 1860

   [First Love published in First Love, and Punin and Baburin, 1884]

Ottsy i deti (novel) 1862

[Fathers and Sons, 1867; also published as Fathers and Children in The Novels of Ivan Turgenev, 1899]

Dym (novel) 1867

   [Smoke, 1868]

"Stepnoi Korol' Lir" (short story) 1870

   ["A Lear of the Steppes" published in The Novels and Stories of Iván Turgénieff, 1903]

† Mesyats v derevne (drama) 1872

   [A Month in the Country published in The Plays of Ivan S. Turgenev, 1924]

Veshnie vody (novella) 1872

   [The Torrents of Spring published in The Novels of Ivan Turgenev, 1897]

Nov' (novel) 1877

   [Virgin Soil, 1877]

Stikhotvoreniya v proze (poetry) 1882

   [Poems in Prose, 1883; also published as Senilia, 1890]

Polnoe sobranie sochinenii. 10 vols. (novels, novellas, short stories, dramas, poetry, criticism, and letters) 1891

The Novels of Ivan Turgenev. 15 vols. (novels, novellas, short stories, and poetry) 1894-99

The Novels and Stories of Iván Turgénieff. 16 vols. (novels, novellas, and short stories) 1903-04

The Plays of Ivan S. Turgenev (dramas) 1924

Polnoe sobranie sochinenii i pisem. 28 vols. (novels, novellas, short stories, dramas, poetry, criticism, and letters) 1960-68

Turgenev's Letters (letters) 1983

*Most of Turgenev's works were originally published in periodicals.

†This work was written in 1850.

youth in *The Seagull,* a play in which the neurotic spiritual descendants of Marie and Nadejda, Veretieff and Steltchinsky, appear and pass into the shadows. This note of the fleetingness of youth and happiness reappears in **"A Tour of the Forest,"** where Turgenev's acute sense of man's ephemeral life in face of the eternity of nature finds full expression. The description, here, of the vast, gloomy, murmuring pine forest, with its cold, dim solitudes, is finely contrasted with the passing outlook of the peasants, Yegor, Kondrat, and the wild Efrem.

The rich colour and perfume of Turgenev's delineation of romantic passion are disclosed when we turn to *First Love,* which details the fervent adoration of Woldemar, a boy of sixteen, for the fascinating Zinaida, an exquisite creation, who, by her mutability and

caressing, mocking caprice keeps her bevy of eager suitors in suspense till at length she yields herself in her passion to Woldemar's father. . . . Here we tremble on the magic borderline between prose and poetry, and the fragrance of blossoming love instincts is felt pervading all the fluctuating impulses of grief, tenderness, pity and regret which combine in the tragic close. The profoundly haunting apostrophe to youth is indeed a pure lyric. Passing to **"Phantoms,"** . . . the truth of Turgenev's confession that spiritually and sensuously he was saturated with the love of woman and ever inspired by it, is confirmed. In his description of Alice, the winged phantom-woman, who gradually casts her spell over the sick hero, luring him to fly with her night after night over the vast expanse of earth, Turgenev has in a mysterious manner, all his own, concentrated the very essence of woman's possessive love. Alice's hungry yearning for self-completion, her pleading arts, her sad submissiveness, her rapture in her hesitating lover's embrace, are artistically a sublimation of all the impressions and instincts by which woman fascinates, and fulfils her purpose of creation. The projection of this shadowy woman's love-hunger on the mighty screen of the night earth, and the merging of her power in men's restless energies, felt and divined through the sweeping tides of nature's incalculable forces, is an inspiration which, in its lesser fashion, invites comparison with Shakespeare's creative vision of nature and the supernatural.

In his treatment of the supernatural Turgenev, however, sometimes missed his mark. **"The Dog"** is of a coarser and indeed of an ordinary texture. With the latter story may be classed **"The Dream,"** curiously Byronic in imagery and atmosphere, and artistically not convincing. Far more sincere, psychologically, is **"Clara Militch,"** a penetrating study of a passionate temperament, a story based on a tragedy of Parisian life. In our opinion **"The Song of Triumphant Love,"** though exquisite in its jewelled mediaeval details, has been overrated by the French, and Turgenev's genius is here seen contorted and cramped by the *genre.*

To return to the tales of the 'sixties. **"Lieutenant Yergunov's Story,"** though its strange atmosphere is cunningly painted, is not of the highest quality, comparing unfavourably with **"The Brigadier,"** the story of the ruined nobleman, Vassily Guskov, with its tender, sub-ironical studies of odd characters, Narkiz and Cucumber. **"The Brigadier"** has a peculiarly fascinating poignancy, and must be prized as one of the rarest of Turgenev's high achievements, even as the connoisseur prizes the original beauty of a fine Meryon etching. The tale is a microcosm of Turgenev's own nature; his love of Nature, his sympathy with all humble, ragged, eccentric, despised human creatures, his unfaltering, keen gaze into character, his perfect eye for relative values in life, all mingle in **"The Brigadier"** to create for us a sense of the vicissitudes of life, of how a generation of human seed springs and flourishes awhile on earth and soon withers away under the menacing gaze of the advancing years.

A complete contrast to **"The Brigadier"** is the sombre and savagely tragic piece of realism, **"An Unhappy Girl."** As a study of a coarse and rapacious nature the portrait of Mr. Ratsch, the Germanized Czech, is a revelation of the depths of human swinishness. Coarse malignancy is here "the power of darkness" which closes, as with a vice, round the figure of the proud, helpless, exquisite girl, Susanna. There is, alas, no exaggeration in this unrelenting, painful story. The scene of Susanna's playing of the Beethoven sonata (chapter xiii.) demonstrates how there can be no truce between a vile animal nature and pure and beautiful instincts, and a faint suggestion symbolic of the national "dark forces" at work in Russian history deepens the impression. The worldly power of greed, lust and envy, ravaging, whether in war or peace, which seize on the defenceless and innocent, as their prey, here triumphs over Susanna, the victim of Mr. Ratsch's violence. The last chapter, the banquet scene, satirizes "the dark forest" of the heart when greed and baseness find their allies in the inertness, sloth or indifference of the ordinary man.

"A Strange Story" has special psychological interest for the English mind in that it gives clues to some fundamental distinctions between the Russian and the Western soul. Sophie's words, "You spoke of the will—that's what must be broken," seems strange to English thought. To be lowly, to be suffering, despised, to *be* unworthy, this desire implies that the Slav character is apt to be lacking in *will,* that it finds it easier to resign itself than to make the effort to be triumphant or powerful. The Russian people's attitude, historically, may, indeed, be compared to a bowl which catches and sustains what life brings it; and the Western people's to a bowl inverted to ward off what fate drops from the impassive skies. The mental attitude of the Russian peasant indeed implies that in blood he is nearer akin to the Asiatics than the Russian ethnologists wish to allow. Certainly in the inner life, intellectually, morally and emotionally, the Russian is a half-way house between the Western and Eastern races, just as geographically he spreads over the two continents.

Brilliant also is **"Knock-Knock-Knock,"** a psychological study, of "a man fated," a Byronic type of hero, dear to the heart of the writers of the romantic period. Sub-Lieutenant Teglev, the melancholy, self-centered hero, whose prepossession of a tragic end nothing can shake, so that he ends by throwing himself into the arms of death, this portrait is most cunningly fortified by the wonderfully life-like atmosphere of the river-fog in which the suicide is consummated. Turgenev's range of mood is disclosed in **"Punin and Baburin,"** a leisurely reminiscence of his mother's household; but the delicious blending of irony and kindness in the treatment of both Punin and Baburin atones for the lengthy conclusion. . . . In considering **"A Lear of the Steppes,"** *The Torrents of Spring* and **"A Living Relic,"** we shall sum up here our brief survey of Turgenev's achievement in the field of the *conte.*

In *The Torrents of Spring* the charm, the grace, the power of Turgenev's vision are seen bathing his subject, revealing all its delicate lineaments in a light as fresh and tender as that of a day of April sunlight in Italy. *Torrents* of Spring, not Spring Floods, be it remarked, is the true significance of the Russian, telling of a moment of the year when all the forces of Nature are leaping forth impetuously, the mounting sap, the hill streams; the mating birds, the blood in the veins of youth. The opening perhaps is a little over-leisurely, this description of the Italian confectioner's family, and its fortunes in Frankfort, but how delightful is the contrast in racial spirit between the pedantic German shop-manager, Herr Klüber and Pantaleone, and the lovely Gemma. But the long opening prelude serves as a foil to heighten the significant story of the seduction of the youthful Sanin by Maria Nikolaevna, that clear-eyed "huntress of men"; one of the most triumphant feminine portraits in the whole range of fiction. The spectator feels that this woman in her ruthless charm is the incarnation of a cruel principle in Nature, while we watch her preparing to strike her talons into her fascinated, struggling prey. Her spirit's essence, in all its hard, merciless joy of conquest, is disclosed by Turgenev in his rapid, yet exhaustive glances at her disdainful treatment of her many lovers, and of her cynical log of a husband. The extraordinarily clear light in the narrative, that of spring mountain air, waxes stronger towards the climax, and the artistic effort of the whole is that of some exquisite Greek cameo, with figures of centaurs and fleeing nymphs and youthful shepherds; though the postscript indeed is an excrescence which detracts from the main impression of pure, classic outlines.

Not less perfect as art though far slighter in scope is the exquisite **"A Living Relic,"** one of the last of *A Sportsman's Sketches.* Along with the narrator we pass, in a step, from the clear sunlight and freshness of early morning, "when the larks' songs seemed steeped in dew," into the "little wattled shanty with its burden of a woman's suffering," poor Lukerya's, who lies, summer after summer, resigned to her living death. . . . (pp. 164-75)

Writers associated with the *Contemporary*. Seated from left to right are Iván Goncharóv, Turgenev, Aleksándr Druzhinin, and Aleksandr Ostróvsky; Leo Tolstoy and Dmítry Grigoróvich are standing.

Lukerya tells her story. How one night she could not sleep, and, thinking of her lover, rose to listen to a nightingale in the garden; how half-dreaming she fell from the top stairs—and now she lives on, a little shrivelled mummy. Something is broken inside her body, and the doctors all shake their heads over her case. Her lover, Polyakov, has married another girl, a good sweet woman. "He couldn't stay a bachelor all his life, and they have children."

And Lukerya? All is not blackness in her wasted life. She is grateful for people's kindness to her. . . . She can hear everything, see everything that comes near her shed—the nesting swallows, the bees, the doves cooing on the roof. Lying alone in the long hours she can smell every scent from the garden, the flowering buckwheat, the lime tree. The priest, the peasant girls, sometimes a pilgrim woman, come and talk to her, and a little girl, a pretty, fair little thing, waits on her. She has her religion, her strange dreams, and sometimes, in her poor, struggling little voice that wavers like a thread of smoke, she tries to sing, as of old. But she is waiting for merciful death—which now is nigh her.

Infinitely tender in the depth of understanding is this gem of art, and **"A Living Relic"** 's perfection is determined by Turgenev's scrutiny of the warp and woof of life, in which the impassive forces of Nature, indifferent alike to human pain or human happiness, pursue their implacable way, weaving unwittingly the mesh of joy, anguish, resignation, in the breast of all sentient creation. It is in the *spiritual perspective* of the picture, in the vision that sees the whole in the part, and the part in the whole, that Turgenev so far surpasses all his European rivals.

To those critics, Russian and English, who naïvely slur over the aesthetic qualities of a masterpiece, such as **"A Lear of the Steppes,"** or fail to recognize all that aesthetic perfection implies, we address these concluding remarks. **"A Lear of the Steppes"** is great in art, because it is a living organic whole, springing from the deep roots of life itself; and the innumerable works of art that are fabricated and pasted together from an ingenious plan—works that do not grow from the inevitability of things—appear at once insignificant or false in comparison.

In examining the art, the artist will note Turgenev's method of introducing his story. Harlov, the Lear of the story, is brought forward with such force on the threshold that all eyes resting on his figure cannot but follow his after-movements. And absolute conviction gained, all the artist's artful after-devices and subtle presentations and sidelights on the story are not apparent under the straightforward ease and the seeming carelessness with which the narrator describes his boyish memories. Then the inmates of Harlov's household, his two daughters, and a crowd of minor characters, are brought before us as persons in the tragedy, and we see that all these people are living each from the innate laws of his being, apparently independently of the author's scheme. This conviction, that the author has no prearranged plan, convinces us that in the story we are living a piece of life: here we are verily plunging into life itself.

And the story goes on flowing easily and naturally till the people of the neighbourhood, the peasants, the woods and fields around, are known by us as intimately as is any neighbourhood in life. Suddenly a break—the tragedy is upon us. Suddenly the terrific forces that underlie human life, even the meanest of human lives, burst on us astonished and breathless, precisely as a tragedy comes up to the surface and bursts on us in real life: everybody runs about dazed, annoyed, futile; we watch other people sustaining their own individuality inadequately in the face of the monstrous new events which go their fatal way logically, events which leave the people huddled and useless and gasping. And destruction having burst out of life, life slowly returns to its old grooves—with a difference to us, the difference in the relation of people one to another that a death or a tragedy always leaves to the survivors. Marvellous in its truth is Turgenev's analysis of the situation after Harlov's death, marvellous is the simple description of the neighbourhood's attitude to the Harlov family, and marvellous is the lifting of the scene on the after-life of Harlov's daughters. In the pages . . . on these women, Turgenev flashes into the reader's mind an extraordinary sense of the inevitability of these women's natures, of their innate growth fashioning their after-lives as logically as a beech puts out beech-leaves and an oak oak-leaves. Through Turgenev's single glimpse at their fortunes one knows the whole intervening fifteen years; he has carried us into a new world; yet it is the old world; one needs to know no more. It is life arbitrary but inevitable, life so clarified by art that it is absolutely interpreted; but life with all the sense of mystery that nature breathes around it in its ceaseless growth.

This sense of inevitability and of the mystery of life which Turgenev gives us in **"A Lear of the Steppes"** is the highest demand we can make from art. If we contrast with it two examples of Turgenev's more "romantic" manner, *Acia,* though it gives us a sense of mystery, is not inevitable: the end is *faked* to suit the artist's purpose, and thus, as in other ways, it is far inferior to **"Lear."** *Faust* has consummate charm in its strange atmosphere of the supernatural mingling with things earthly, but it is not, as is **"A Lear of the Steppes,"** life seen from the surface to the revealed depths; it is a revelation of the strange forces in life, presented beautifully; but it is rather an idea, a problem to be worked out by certain characters, than a piece of life inevitable and growing. When an artist creates in us the sense of inev-

itability, then his work is at its highest, and is obeying Nature's law of growth, unfolding from out itself as inevitably as a tree or a flower or a human being unfolds from out itself. Turgenev at his highest never quits Nature, yet he always uses the surface, and what is apparent, to disclose her most secret principles, her deepest potentialities, her inmost laws of being, and whatever he presents he presents clearly and simply. This combination of powers marks only the few supreme artists. Even great masters often fail in perfect *naturalness:* Tolstoy's *The Death of Ivan Ilytch,* for instance, one of the most powerful stories ever written, has too little of what is typical of the whole of life, too much that is strained towards the general purpose of the story, to be perfectly *natural.* Turgenev's special feat in fiction is that his characters reveal themselves by the most ordinary details of their everyday life; and while these details are always giving us the whole life of the people, and their inner life as well, the novel's significance is being built up simply out of these details, built up by the same process, in fact, as Nature creates for us a single strong impression out of a multitude of little details.

Again, Turgenev's power as a poet comes in, whenever he draws a commonplace figure, to make it bring with it a sense of the mystery of its existence. In *Lear* the steward Kvitsinsky plays a subsidiary part; he has apparently no significance in the story, and very little is told about him. But who does not perceive that Turgenev looks at and presents the figure of this man in a manner totally different from the way any clever novelist of the second rank would look at and use him? Kvitsinsky, in Turgenev's hands, is an individual with all the individual's mystery in his glance, his coming and going, his way of taking things; but he is a part of the household's breath, of its very existence; he breathes the atmosphere naturally and creates an atmosphere of his own.

It is, then, in his marvellous sense of the growth of life that Turgenev is superior to most of his rivals. Not only did he observe life minutely and comprehensively, but he reproduced it as a constantly growing phenomenon, growing naturally, not accidentally or arbitrarily. For example, in *A House of Gentlefolk,* take Lavretsky's and Liza's changes of mood when they are falling in love with one another; it is Nature herself in them changing very delicately and insensibly; we feel that the whole picture is alive, not an effect cut out from life, and cut off from it at the same time, like a bunch of cut flowers, an effect which many clever novelists often give us. And in **"Lear"** we feel that the life in Harlov's village is still going on, growing yonder, still growing with all its mysterious sameness and changes, when, in Turgenev's last words, "The storyteller ceased, and we talked a little longer, and then parted, each to his home." (pp. 176-83)

Edward Garnett, in his *Turgenev: A Study,* W. Collins Sons & Co., Ltd., 1917, 206 p.

PRINCE D. S. MIRSKY
(essay date 1927)

[Mirsky was a Russian prince who fled his country after the Bolshevik Revolution and settled in London. While in England, he wrote two important histories of Russian literature, *Contemporary Russian Literature*, published in 1926, and *A History of Russian Literature*, which appeared the following year. These works were later combined and portions were published in 1949 as *A History of Russian Literature*. In the following excerpt, first published in Mirsky's 1927 study, he traces Turgenev's career as a writer and assesses his place in Russian literature.]

Turgénev's first attempt at prose fiction was in the wake of Lérmontov, from whom he derived the romantic halo round his first Pechórin-like heroes (**"Andréy Kólosov," "The Duelist," "Three Portraits"**) and the method of the intensified anecdote (**"The Jew"**). In *A Sportsman's Sketches,* begun in 1847, he was to free himself from the romantic conventions of these early stories by abandoning all narrative skeleton and limiting himself to "slices of life." But even for some time after that date he remained unable in his more distinctly narrative work to hit on what was to become his true manner. Thus, for instance, **"Three Meetings"** is a story of pure atmosphere woven round a very slender theme, saturated in its descriptions of moonlit nights, with an excess of romantic and "poetical" poetry. **"The Diary of a Superfluous Man"** is reminiscent of Gógol and of the young Dostoyévsky, developing as it does the Dostoyevskian theme of humiliated human dignity and of morbid delight in humiliation, but aspiring to a Gógol-like and very un-Turgenevian verbal intensity. (The phrase "a superfluous man" had an extraordinary fortune and is still applied by literary and social historians to the type of ineffective idealist portrayed so often by Turgénev and his contemporaries.) At last **"Mumú,"** the well-known story of the deaf serf and his favorite dog, and of how his mistress ordered it to be destroyed, is a "philanthropic" story in the tradition of *The Greatcoat* and of *Poor Folk,* where an intense sensation of pity is arrived at by methods that strike the modern reader as illegitimate, working on the nerves rather than on the imagination.

A Sportsman's Sketches, on the other hand, written in 1847-51, belongs to the highest, most lasting, and least questionable achievement of Turgénev and of Russian realism. The book describes the casual and var-

ious meetings of the narrator during his wanderings with a gun and a dog in his native district of Bólkhov and in the surrounding country. The sketches are arranged in a random order and have no narrative skeleton, containing nothing but accounts of what the narrator saw and heard. Some of them are purely descriptive, of scenery or character; others consist of conversation, addressed to the narrator or overheard. At times there is a dramatic *motive,* but the development is only hinted at by the successive glimpses the narrator gets of his personages. This absolute matter-of-factness and studious avoidance of everything artificial and made-up were the most prominent characteristics of the book when it appeared—it was a new genre. The peasants are described from the outside, as seen (or overseen) by the narrator, not in their intimate, unoverlooked life. As I have said, they are drawn with obviously greater sympathy than the upper classes. The squires are represented as either vulgar, or cruel, or ineffective. In the peasants, Turgénev emphasized their humanity, their imaginativeness, their poetical and artistic giftedness, their sense of dignity, their intelligence. It was in this quiet and unobtrusive way that the book struck the readers with the injustice and ineptitude of serfdom. Now, when the issue of serfdom is a thing of the past, the *Sketches* seem once more as harmless and as innocent as a book can be, and it requires a certain degree of historical imagination to reconstruct the atmosphere in which they had the effect of a mild bombshell.

Judged as literature, the *Sketches* are frequently, if not always, above praise. In the representation of rural scenery and peasant character, Turgénev never surpassed such masterpieces as **"The Singers"** and **"Bézhin Meadow." "The Singer"** especially, even after *First Love* and *Fathers and Sons,* may claim to be his crowning achievement and the quintessence of all the most characteristic qualities of his art. It is the description of a singing-match at a village pub between the peasant Yáshka Túrok and a tradesman from Zhízdra. The story is representative of Turgénev's manner of painting his peasants; he does not one-sidedly idealize them; the impression produced by the match, with its revelation of the singers' high sense of artistic values, is qualified by the drunken orgy the artists lapse into after the match is over and the publican treats Yáshka to the fruit of his victory. **"The Singers"** may also be taken as giving Turgénev's prose at its highest and most characteristic. It is careful and in a sense artificial, but the impression of absolute ease and simplicity is exhaled from every word and turn of phrase. It is a carefully *selected* language, rich, but curiously avoiding words and phrases, crude or journalese, that might jar on the reader. The beauty of the landscape painting is due chiefly to the choice of exact and delicately suggestive and descriptive words. There is no ornamental imagery after the manner of Gógol, no rhetorical rhythm, no splendid cadences. But the sometime poet's and poets' disciple's hand is evident in the careful, varied, and unobtrusively perfect balance of the phrases.

The first thing Turgénev wrote after the *Sketches* and "Mumú" was "The Inn." Like "Mumú" it turns on the unjust and callous treatment of serfs by their masters, but the sentimental, "philanthropic" element is replaced for the first time in his work by the characteristic Turgenevian atmosphere of tragic necessity. "The Inn" was followed in 1853-61 by a succession of masterpieces. They were divided by the author himself into two categories: novels and *nouvelles* (in Russian, *romány* and *póvesti*). The difference between the two forms in the case of Turgénev is not so much one of size or scope as that the novels aim at social significance and at the statement of social problems, while the *nouvelles* are pure and simple stories of emotional incident, free from civic preoccupations. Each novel includes a narrative kernel similar in subject and bulk to that of a *nouvelle*, but it is expanded into an answer to some burning problem of the day. The novels of this period are *Rúdin, A Nest of Gentlefolk, On the Eve,* and *Fathers and Sons;* the *nouvelles, Two Friends, A Quiet Spot, Yákov Pásynkov, A Correspondence, Faust, Asya,* and *First Love.* It will be noticed that the civic novels belong chiefly to the age of reform (1856-61), while the purely private *nouvelles* predominate in the reactionary years that precede it. But even "on the eve" of the Emancipation, Turgénev could be sufficiently detached from civic issues to write the perfectly uncivic *First Love.*

The novels of Turgénev are, thus, those of his stories in which he, voluntarily, submitted to the obligation of writing works of social significance. This significance is arrived at in the first place by the nature of the characters, who are made to be representative of phases successively traversed by the Russian intellectual. Rúdin is the progressive idealist of the forties; Lavrétsky, the more Slavophil idealist of the same generation; Eléna, in *On the Eve,* personifies the vaguely generous and active fermentation of the generation immediately preceding the reforms; Bazárov, the militant materialism of the generation of 1860. Secondly, the social significance is served by the insertion of numerous *conversations* between the characters on topics of current interest (Slavophilism and Westernism, the ability of the educated Russian to act, the place in life of art and science, and so on). These conversations are what especially distinguished Turgénev's novels from his *nouvelles.* They have little relation to the action, and not always much more to the character of the representative hero. They were what the civic critics seized upon for comment, but they are certainly the least permanent and most dating part of the novels. There frequently occur characters who are introduced with no other motive but to do the talking, and whom one would have

rather wished away. But the central, representative characters—the heroes—are in most cases not only representative, but alive. Rúdin, the first in date, is one of the masterpieces of nineteenth-century character drawing. An eminent French novelist (who is old-fashioned enough still to prefer Turgénev to Tolstóy, Dostoyévsky, and Chékhov) has pointed out to me the wonderfully delicate mastery with which the impression produced by Rúdin on the other characters and on the reader is made gradually to change from the first appearance in the glamour of superiority to the bankruptcy of his pusillanimous breach with Natália, then to the gloomy glimpse of the undone and degenerate man, and to the redeeming flash of his heroic and ineffective death on the barricades of the faubourg St. Antoine. The French writer thought this delicate change of attitude unique in fiction. Had he known more Russian, he would have realized that Turgénev had merely been a highly intelligent and creative pupil of Púshkin's. Like Púshkin in *Evgény Onégin,* Turgénev does not analyze and dissect his heroes, as Tolstóy and Dostoyévsky would have done; he does not uncover their souls; he only conveys their atmosphere, partly by showing how they are reflected in others, partly by an exceedingly delicate and thinly woven aura of suggestive accompaniment—a method that at once betrays its origin in a *poetic* novel. Where Turgénev attempts to show us the *inner* life of his heroes by other methods, he always fails—the description of Eléna's feelings for Insárov in *On the Eve* is distinctly painful reading. Turgénev had to use all the power of self-criticism and self-restraint to avoid the pitfalls of false poetry and false beauty.

Still, the characters, constructed though they are by means of suggestion, not dissection, are the vivifying principle of Turgénev's stories. Like most Russian novelists he makes character predominate over plot, and it is the characters that we remember. The population of Turgénev's novels (apart from the peasant stories) may be classified under several heads. First comes the division into the Philistines and the elect. The Philistines are the direct descendants of Gógol's characters—heroes of *póshlost,* self-satisfied inferiority. Of course there is not a trace in them of Gógol's exuberant and grotesque caricature; the irony of Turgénev is fine, delicate, unobtrusive, hardly at all aided by any obvious comical devices. On the other side are the elect, the men and women with a sense of values, superior to those of vegetable enjoyment and social position. The men, again, are very different from the women. The fair sex comes out distinctly more advantageously from the hands of Turgénev. The strong, pure, passionate, and virtuous woman, opposed to the weak, potentially generous, but ineffective and ultimately shallow man, was introduced into literature by Púshkin, and recurs again and again in the work of the realists, but nowhere more insistently than in Turgénev's. His heroines are famous all the world over and have done much to spread a high reputation of Russian womanhood. Moral force and courage are the keynote to Turgénev's heroine—the power to sacrifice all wordly considerations to passion (Natália in *Rúdin*), or all happiness to duty (Líza in *A Nest of Gentlefolk*). But what goes home to the general reader in these women is not so much the height of their moral beauty as the extraordinary *poetical* beauty woven round them by the delicate and perfect art of their begetter. Turgénev reaches his highest perfection in this, his own and unique art, in two of the shorter stories, *A Quiet Spot* and *First Love.* In the first, the purely Turgenevian, tragic, poetic, and rural atmosphere reaches its maximum of concentration, and the richness of suggestion that conditions the characters surpasses all he ever wrote. It transcends mere fiction and rises into poetry, not by the beauty of the single words and parts, but by sheer force of suggestion and saturated significance. *First Love* stands somewhat apart from the rest of Turgénev's work. Its atmosphere is cooler and clearer, more reminiscent of the rarefied air of Lérmontov. The heroes—Zinaída and the narrator's father (who is traditionally supposed to portray the author's own father)—are more *animal* and vital than Turgénev usually allows his heroes to be. Their passions are tense and clear-cut, free from vagueness and idealistic haze, selfish, but with a selfishness that is redeemed by self-justifying vitality. Unique in the whole of his work, *First Love* is the least relaxing of Turgénev's stories. But, characteristically, the story is told from the point of view of the boy admirer of Zinaída and of his pangs of adolescent jealousy for his rival and father. (pp. 188-93)

The best of the novels and ultimately the most important of Turgénev's works is *Fathers and Sons,* one of the greatest novels of the nineteenth century. Here Turgénev triumphantly solved two tasks that he had been attempting to solve: to create a living masculine character not based on introspection, and to overcome the contradiction between the imaginative and the social theme. *Fathers and Sons* is Turgénev's only novel where the social problem is distilled without residue into art, and leaves no bits of undigested journalism sticking out. Here the delicate and poetic narrative art of Turgénev reaches its perfection, and Bazárov is the only one of Turgénev's men who is worthy to stand by the side of his women. But nowhere perhaps does the essential debility and feminineness of his genius come out more clearly than in this, the best of his novels. Bazárov is a strong man, but he is painted with admiration and wonder by one to whom a strong man is something abnormal. Turgénev is incapable of making his hero triumph, and to spare him the inadequate treatment that would have been his lot in the case of success, he lets him die, not from any natural develop-

ment of the nature of the subject, but by the blind decree of fate. For fate, blind chance, crass casualty, presides over Turgénev's universe as it does over Hardy's, but Turgénev's people submit to it with passive resignation. Even the heroic Bazárov dies as resigned as a flower in the field, with silent courage but without protest.

It would be wrong to affirm that after *Fathers and Sons* Turgénev's genius began to decline, but at any rate it ceased to grow. What was more important for his contemporaries, he lost touch with Russian life and thus ceased to count as a *contemporary* writer, though he remained a permanent classic. His attempts again to tackle the problems of the day in *Smoke* and in *Virgin Soil* only emphasized his loss of touch with the new age. *Smoke* is the worst-constructed of his novels: it contains a beautiful love story, which is interrupted and interlarded with conversations that have no relation to its characters and are just dialogued journalism on the thesis that all intellectual and educated Russia was nothing but smoke. *Virgin Soil* is a complete failure, and was immediately recognized as such. Though it contains much that is in the best manner of Turgénev (the characters of the bureaucratic-aristocratic Sipyágin family are among his best satirical drawings), the whole novel is disqualified by an entirely uninformed and necessarily false conception of what he was writing about. His presentation of the revolutionaries of the seventies is like an account of a foreign country by one who had never seen it.

But while Turgénev had lost the power of writing for the times, he had not lost the genius of creating those wonderful love stories which are his most personal contribution to the world's literature. Pruned of its conversations, *Smoke* is a beautiful *nouvelle,* comparable to the best he wrote in the fifties, and so is *The Torrents of Spring.* Both are on the same subject: a young man loves a pure and sweet young girl but forsakes her for a mature and lascivious woman of thirty, who is loved by many and for whom he is the plaything of a fleeting passion. The characters of Irína, the older woman in *Smoke,* and of Gemma, the Italian girl in *The Torrents of Spring,* are among the most beautiful in the whole of his gallery. *The Torrents of Spring* is given a retrospective setting, and in most of the other stories of this last period the scene is set in the old times of pre-Reform Russia. Some of these stories are purely objective little tragedies (one of the best is "**A Lear of the Steppes**"); others are non-narrative fragments from reminiscences, partly continuing the manner and theme of *A Sportsman's Sketches.* There are also the purely biographical reminiscences, including interesting accounts of the author's acquaintance with Púshkin and Belínsky and the remarkable account of "**The Execution of Troppmann,**" which in its fascinated objectivity is one of the most terrible descriptions ever made of an execution.

There had always been in Turgénev a poetic or romantic vein, as opposed to the prevailing realistic atmosphere of his principal work. His attitude to nature had always been lyrical, and he had always had a lurking desire to transcend the limits imposed on the Russian novelist by the dogma of realism. Not only did he begin his career as a lyrical poet and end it with his *Poems in Prose,* but even in his most realistic and civic novels the construction and atmosphere are mainly lyrical. *A Sportsman's Sketches* includes many purely lyrical pages of natural description, and to the period of his highest maturity belongs that remarkable piece **"A Tour in the Forest,"** where for the first time Turgénev's conception of indifferent and eternal nature opposed to transient man found expression in a sober and simple prose that attains poetry by the simplest means of unaided suggestion. His last period begins with the purely lyrical prose poem **"Enough"** and culminates in the *Poems in Prose.* At the same time the fantastic element asserts itself. In some stories (**"The Dog," "Knock! Knock! Knock!"** and **"The Story of Father Alexis"**) it appears only in the form of a suggestion of mysterious presences in an ordinary realistic setting. The most important of these stories is his last, **"Clara Mílich,"** written under the influence of spiritualistic readings and musings. It is as good as most of his stories of purely human love, but the mysterious element is somewhat difficult to appreciate quite whole-heartedly today. It has all the inevitable flatness of Victorian spiritualism. In a few stories Turgénev freed himself from the conventions of realistic form and wrote such things as the purely visionary **"Phantoms"** and **"The Song of Triumphant Love,"** written in the style of an Italian *novella* of the sixteenth century. There can be no greater contrast than between these and such stories of Dostoyévsky as *The Double* or *Mr. Prokhárchin.* Dostoyévsky, with the material of sordid reality, succeeds in building fabrics of weird fantasy. Turgénev, in spite of all the paraphernalia introduced, never succeeded in freeing himself from the second-rate atmosphere of the medium's consulting room. **"The Song of Triumphant Love"** shows up his limitation of another kind—the inadequacy of his language for treating subjects of insufficient reality. This limitation Turgénev shared with all his contemporaries (except Tolstóy and Leskóv). They did not have a sufficient feeling of words, of language as language (as Púshkin and Gógol had had), to make it serve them in unfamiliar fields. Words for them were only signs of familiar things and familiar feelings. Language had entered with them on a strictly limited engagement—it would serve only in so far as it had not to leave the everyday realities of the nineteenth century.

The same stylistic limitation is apparent in Turgé-

nev's last and most purely lyrical work, *Poems in Prose.* (Turgénev originally entitled them *Senilia;* the present title was given them with the author's silent approval by the editor of the *Messenger of Europe,* where they first appeared.) They are a series of short prose fragments, most of them gathered round some more or less narrative kernel. They are comparable in construction to the objectivated lyrics of the French Parnassians, who used visual symbols to express their subjective experience. Sometimes they verge on the fable and the apologue. In these "poems" is to be found the final and most hopeless expression of Turgénev's agnostic pessimism, of his awe of unresponsive nature and necessity, and of his pitying contempt for human futility. The best of the "poems" are those where these feelings are given an ironic garb. The more purely poetical ones have suffered from time, and date too distinctly from about 1880—a date that can hardly add beauty to anything connected with it. The one that closes the series, **"The Russian Language,"** has suffered particularly—not from time only, but from excessive handling. It displays in a condensed form all the weakness and ineffectiveness of Turgénev's style when it was divorced from concrete and familiar *things.* The art of eloquence had been lost.

Turgénev was the first Russian writer to charm the Western reader. There are still retarded Victorians who consider him the only Russian writer who is not disgusting. But for most lovers of Russian he has been replaced by spicier food. Turgénev was very nineteenth century, perhaps the most representative man of its latter part, whether in Russia or west of it. He was a Victorian, a man of compromise, more Victorian than any one of his Russian contemporaries. This made him so acceptable to Europe, and this has now made him lose so much of his reputation there. Turgénev struck the West at first as something new, something typically Russian. But it is hardly necessary to insist today on the fact that he is not in any sense representative of Russia as a whole. He was representative only of his class—the idealistically educated middle gentry, tending already to become a non-class intelligentsia—and of his generation, which failed to gain real touch with Russian realities, which failed to find itself a place in life and which, ineffective in the sphere of action, produced one of the most beautiful literary growths of the nineteenth century. In his day Turgénev was regarded as a leader of opinion on social problems; now this seems strange and unintelligible. Long since, the issues that he fought out have ceased to be of any actual interest. Unlike Tolstóy or Dostoyévsky, unlike Griboyédov, Púshkin, Lérmontov, and Gógol, unlike Chaadáyev, Grigóriev, and Herzen—Turgénev is no longer a teacher or even a ferment. His work has become pure art—and perhaps it has won more from this transformation than it has lost. It has taken a permanent place in the Russian tradition, a place that stands above the changes of taste or the revolutions of time. We do not seek for wisdom or guidance in it, but it is impossible to imagine a time when **"The Singers,"** *A Quiet Spot, First Love,* or *Fathers and Sons* will cease to be among the most cherished of joys to Russian readers. (pp. 194-98)

Prince D. S. Mirsky, "The Age of Realism: The Novelists (I)," in his *A History of Russian Literature Comprising "A History of Russian Literature" and "Contemporary Russian Literature,"* edited by Francis J. Whitfield, Alfred A. Knopf, 1949, pp. 169-204.

MARC SLONIM

(essay date 1950)

[Slonim was a Russian-born American critic who wrote extensively on Russian literature. Here, he seeks to illuminate Turgenev's philosophy of life and its effect on his writings.]

Turgenev called himself a Realist, and defined his artistic aim as the truthful and dispassionate portrayal of life. He often pointed out his own objectivity: being a Westernizer did not prevent him from presenting the Westernizer Panshin (in *A Nest of Gentlefolk*) unfavorably and making him come off second-best in the argument with the Slavophile Lavretsky; being an anti-Nihilist did not deter him from bringing out all the good points and even virtues of Bazarov; being an atheist did not affect his sympathetic comprehension of Liza's religious feelings.

Belinsky praised Turgenev's precise observation, his capacity for grasping the essence and the peculiarities of each character, and his superb artistry in revealing the causes and effects of human actions and in describing nature. Although he is justly considered one of the world's greatest storytellers, the story itself never attracted Turgenev: the plots of his novels and tales are so simple as to appear slight, and always hinge on the reversal of a love affair. The main thing for him is to show men and women, their relations and their emotions and ideas, without ever attempting a thorough psychological analysis—he always leaves such an analysis to the reader. The latter, however, it put on the right path by hints, allusions, and the mood created by landscapes and the rhythm of the language. The actual work of psychological penetration is done behind the scenes of the novel, by the highly intelligent author who allows only the ultimate results of his exploration to appear in his writings.

This method is responsible for the kind of psychological impressionism or imagism we always find in Turgenev's novels and stories. Turgenev has stated that he wrote not because certain incidents or adventures had occurred to him, but because he had in mind the representation of a certain person, whom he tried to conceive with factual and psychological completeness (he even wrote, for his own use, preliminary biographies of all his main characters). (p. 263)

This concreteness assumes the form of absolute compactness and economy of words. Turgenev's art is very different from Goncharov's factual thoroughness, Dostoevsky's metaphysical depth, or Tolstoy's universality. Turgenev limited himself in the scope and range of his writings, as well as in his ways of expression. His novels are short; the action unfolds without digressions or parallel plots and usually takes place in a brief span of time; the protagonists are reduced to a minimum: the author does not indulge in any analysis of their feelings or their behavior, always employing the method of indirect allusions and understatements.

When he wants to clarify a detail, however—to demonstrate Insarov's strength, for instance, or Bazarov's skeptical attitude toward accepted authorities— he does not beat around the bush but comes straight to the point. The dialogue—adroitly individualized and functional in psychological portrayal—also serves for the exposition of ideas. His protagonists not only talk, but also discuss facts and abstract concepts. Rudin and Lezhnev deliver long speeches on various subjects; Lavretsky and his friend Mikhalevich discuss the men and trends of the 'forties; Bazarov and Paul Kirsanov have arguments over love, science, and esthetics; Potughin and Litvinov exchange lengthy opinions on Europe and Russia's destinies. In general, Turgenev's heroes are defined more by what they say than by what they do.

It can be said of all his novels that they had the definite purpose of representing the aristocracy and the intelligentsia in their intellectual and social metamorphosis and that they form a gallery of Russian types as they actually existed between 1840 and 1870. His short stories, more concerned with the love episodes in the life of aristocrats, mostly Superfluous Men, are a sort of poetic accompaniment to the novels, although esthetically they are the best part of his literary bequest. But, if most of Turgenev's writings were social novels, what was their message? And, if there was none, what constituted their central theme, and what did they convey, and continue to convey, to their readers?

Turgenev did not see in life only material for his imagination. He looked for topics and people that corresponded to his personal inclinations. All the works of this objective realist were highly subjective and unraveled many inner conflicts that had tormented him since his early youth. He possessed a great gift for understanding contradictions, for picturing with an equal persuasiveness an idle aristocrat, a Nihilist, a dreamer, or a practical man. Was it objectivity or ambivalence?

It certainly could not be explained, as some critics have attempted to do, only by his insight and tolerance.

There was another reason for Turgenev's noncommittal attitude. A rational atheist, he did not believe in God and showed little enthusiasm for humanity. He kept to the middle of the road in politics, went along with the gradual reformers, was on friendly terms with radicals, but never committed himself to any definite group. In art he defended the objective representation of reality, praised harmony and balance as the main principles of an aimless estheticism, and took pride in the fact (contested by the critics) that his novels, both long and short, neither proved anything nor attempted to do so. He certainly appreciated freedom, human dignity, education, culture, and progress, but he never displayed any ardor in proclaiming those values.

As a matter of fact, there was very little positive affirmation in his work. The friends of his youth, such as Belinsky, Bakunin, and Herzen, had been enthusiastic about philosophy, anarchism, or Socialism; his contemporaries, such as Gogol, Dostoevsky, Tolstoy, struggled for religion, God, or morality but Turgenev did not identify himself with any doctrine or intense belief. Here, again, he kept to the middle of the road, like an intelligent onlooker who enjoys the show but will never take part in it as an actor. He lacked religiosity, which some people believe to be a Russian national trait, and was hardly interested in the quest of all-embracing, all-absorbing concepts or systems of ideas. (pp. 264-65)

Whoever will read several of Turgenev's novels and tales in succession will not fail to notice that they all have unhappy endings. Rudin, Insarov, Bazarov, Nezhdanov, Chertopkhanov, Pasynkov—all meet sudden and, for the most part, violent deaths. Liza dies for the world's sake; Lavretsky continues to vegetate in a sort of deadly atonement. All the love stories also end with failure or death (*Spring Freshets, First Love, Asya,* "Clara Milich", "Phantom", *Faust,* and so on). In general, in Turgenev's tales something always happens on the threshold of fulfilment: accidents or catastrophes meet his men and women at the very door of happiness.

This is not accidental. Turgenev, like his hero Litvinov in *Smoke,* felt the vanity of human illusions and the absurdity of life. The idea of eternity terrified him; he speaks of it time and again, like a man who has a long and involved account to settle with it. His *Senilia*—the most complete and frank expression of his true self—repeatedly deals with the fear of death. "**A Conversation,**" "**The Dog,**" "**The Hag,**" "**The End of The World,**" and a number of other poems in prose revolve around the one topic—the inevitability of annihilation. The mysterious female vampire Ellis in "**Phantoms**" (written in 1863) reflects his own qualms:

'Why do I shudder in such anguish at the mere thought of annihilation?' For merciless and aloof Nature the existence of man is no more important than that of a flea (**"Nature"**). From the summits of the Alps, for the Jungfrau and the Finsteraarhorn, centuries pass like seconds, and to them the humans in the valley look like ants who will disappear one day, leaving immaculate the white eternity of their snow (**"An Alpimalyan Dialogue"**). A blind woman of gigantic proportions pushes on a bony, stalwart female who holds the hand of a small, bright-eyed girl, the child struggles in vain, but is driven along—and these three figures are Fate, Force, and Freedom. Men are imprisoned within a circle of fatality—and there is nothing beyond its bounds except 'the clangorous barking from the thousand throats of death,' 'darkness, eternal darkness,' the interminable void of destruction. This fundamental pessimism overshadows not only the tales of Turgenev's old age but his earlier works, such as **"Andrei Kolossov,"** *Faust,* **"A Backwater," "Journey to Polessie,"**—all written in his thirties.

In one of his letters to Pauline Viardot he writes: 'I cannot stand the empty skies, but I adore life, its reality, its whims, its accidents, its rites, its swiftly passing beauty.' It was not an easy love. He fled from the 'empty skies' into the palpable reality of human affairs, he sought oblivion in the activity of others, in love and illusions. Eternity is madness, death is a nightmare, and Turgenev forgets them only when he meets some spontaneous manifestation of life, in beauty, action, or thought.

The charm of a momentary pleasure moves him to tears, for he always realizes how short and transitory it is bound to be. A green branch on a spring day fills him with tremulous delight: it is the very image of beauty, of the sweet joy of being. In his lecture, **"Hamlet and Don Quixote,"** he gave preference to the Knight of La Mancha, since the Spaniard's illusions overcame his fear of death; his love of action liberated him from the burden of reflection, which dissects and kills the spontaneity of existence.

As a friend and disciple of philosophers, Turgenev, of course, was much closer to the Prince of Denmark than to the ecstatic Spanish hidalgo. In picturing the superfluous men he was in part making self-portraits, particularly when he showed how the self-analysis and self-criticism of his heroes destroyed their ability for action. But he admired the Don Quixotes, and he also loved men like Bazarov, Solomin, and Insarov, who were the very antithesis of himself.

Another curious aspect is his interest in political and social struggles. He was always excited by men's most spectacular activity—that of social transformation—because he was a patriot and sincerely loved his country and also because in this activity he found another affirmation of life, another evidence of 'whims and accidents,' which helped him to forget 'the tooth-less Ancient.' He was not energetic or particularly active by nature, but the others' expenditure of energy gave him a sense of security and heartened him, in the way the love of other people inspired him with joy and admiration, not unmixed with melancholy. Beauty was another, though momentary, victory over annihilation; contemplation of it brought a rapture enhanced by the consciousness of its evanescence. His tears of ecstasy were mingled with tears of regret.

Well aware of his inner conflict, he dreamt of harmony and the simple, natural life. In *Faust,* and in the **"Journey to Polessie,"** he came to the conclusion that 'the quiet and slow animation, the unhurried restraint of sensations and impulses, the equilibrium of health in every individual being, are the prerequisites of happiness.' The only lasting happiness lies in the serenity of a somewhat monotonous existence based upon instinct and resignation. The same law applies to art: a good work of art must possess the same equilibrium, the same poise, even when dealing with anxiety or madness. He praised highly 'the tranquility in passion' of the great tragic actress Rachel, citing her as an example of the highest esthetic achievement.

Here again his duality was patent. Although he was denied the romantic vision of happiness, all his heroes aspire to its bliss. This aspiration is an irresistible human need, a manifestation of the life instinct—and it is doomed to failure and annihilation. With incomparable poetry he describes this wistful expectation of soul and flesh, this flowering of desire and love, this hope of triumphing over the ruthless domination of time. The best pages of Turgenev are devoted to this promise of happiness that reaches its height in the awakening of love and in the springtime of nature. In **"Three Encounters"** the image of the tense, almost painful, silence of a magnificent summer night filled with scents and susurrations and cravings, with the languor and yearnings of mind and body, with a strange sensation of happiness—a promise and a recollection—is one of the most lyrical passages in the European prose of the nineteenth century; and as a parallel to these pages, there are the chapters describing Liza's love for Lavretzky in *A Nest of Gentlefolk.*

Turgenev never pictured the fulfilment of love, the satisfaction of the senses and of the heart. For him the apex had been reached before—in the highest and most intense moment of a dream that can never come true. (pp. 266-68)

Certain severe critics contend that Turgenev's search for beauty often turned into prettiness, while his art became arty. It is true that his softness and gentleness have at times a cloying aftertaste. He makes life and nature appear rather tame, he avoids mentioning the seamy side of reality or plunging too deeply beneath its surface, for fear of encountering the monsters

of depravity, hatred, or abnormality. He takes great care not to pain or shock his readers, and his prose is decorous and seemly, suave and well-bred. His voice is never raised or altered; there are no surprises in his narrative, no breaks in his sentences. Whatever one may feel about this kind of literature, its craftsmanship is undeniable: Turgenev was an extraordinary artist.

This refined and intelligent writer whose irony—and there is far more irony in his works than is usually acknowledged—underscored his sadness, this accomplished stylist who believed that 'such a great, mighty, and free language' as Russian must have been given to a great people, this esthete who wrote social novels, this partrician who described the peasants, this democrat who sang requiems over the nobility, this realist who was so elegiac, this poet who was so precise, is one of the most beloved writers in Russia.

Widely read and enjoyed today, he will probably continue to be one of the most popular writers for many years to come—as long as his languor, his melancholic grief, combined with the exaltation in love and beauty, and his conception of art as an orderly arrangement of emotional values, still stir the poetic and esthetic senses of Russian readers. . . . (pp. 270-71)

Marc Slonim, "Turgenev," in his *The Epic of Russian Literature: From Its Origins through Tolstoy,* Oxford University Press, 1950, pp. 250-71.

AVRAHM YARMOLINSKY
(essay date 1959)

[Yarmolinsky was a Russian-born American translator, biographer, social historian, and critic who wrote extensively on Russian literature and edited numerous anthologies as well as works by Fyodor Dostoevsky, Anton Chekhov, and Alexander Pushkin. The following excerpt is from Yarmolinsky's frequently cited study of Turgenev. Here, he discusses *On the Eve*, Turgenev's essay "Hamlet and Don Quixote," and *Fathers and Sons*, focusing on the theme of the irresolute man versus the man of action.]

While the atmosphere of *Rudin* is one of futility and frustration, and nostalgia pervades *A Nest of Gentlefolk,* a buoyant spirit of expectancy and promise informs *On the Eve.* The action takes place in 1853, one of the last years of the reign of that iron autocrat, Nicholas I. It was a time of darkness, but the title is not alone in intimating that the darkness is soon to lift.

"My tale," said Turgenev, "is based on the idea that we must have *consciously* heroic natures in order to move forward." He was calling for tough-minded, dedicated individuals, devoted body and soul to a public cause. As he watched the social scene, sitting, not quite at ease, in his fauteuil, he looked in vain for such a man among his compatriots; the type had not yet emerged. Accordingly, he took for his protagonist a Bulgarian. This Insarov, a merchant's son, is an ardent patriot, preparing to take part in an insurrectionist movement against Turkey. The purpose to which he is vowed has the backing of the entire nation, which is ripe for revolt against the foreign tyranny. This gives him unfaltering firmness and strength. Turgenev, characteristically, has him carried off by consumption before he can strike a blow for the liberation of his people. Moreover, the author fails to interest the reader in this excellent and wooden creature. He is obviously contrived, a lay figure draped in the then fairly fashionable garments of militant nationalism.

Projected against a familiar Russian background, the story revolves less about Insarov's plotting than about his love affair with Yelena, the daughter of a family of Russian gentlefolk. It is she who is the central figure of the novel; to her it owes its force and meaning. Endowed with an intense, passionate nature and moved, in Turgenev's words, by "a vague, yet strong aspiration toward freedom," she is capable of making a brave choice and holding to it. She joins her lot to Insarov's without flinching from the hardships and dangers it involves. When, shortly after their marriage, he dies, she remains faithful to his memory by going on with the work to which he had been pledged. "Why return to Russia?" she asks in a farewell note to her mother. "What is there to do in Russia?" She deserts her country, this torpid land that can produce only self-centered dilettantes, well-meaning idealists capable of action, conscientious, cold-hearted officials.

The book is in a sense an impeachment of an age and a generation that have failed to breed a fit mate for such a woman. "There is no one as yet among us, there are no men, look where you will," soliloquizes Shubin, one of the heroine's unsuccessful suitors. He goes on to say that the country has brought forth only dark, grubbing souls, phrasemongers, self-consuming little Hamlets who keep feeling the pulse of their thoughts and sensations. "When will our time come? When will men be born among us?" he asks Uvar Ivanovich, another secondary figure, and that vast, gluttonous sphinx of a man replies: "Give us time. They will come." At the very end of the postscript to the novel, which deals with events separated from the main action by five years, Uvar Ivanovich, asked the same question in a letter, twiddles his fingers vaguely and fixes his enigmatic gaze on the distance. Was this intended to suggest that the author wondered whether in Russia, where the situation was a complex one and the foe not a foreign oppressor but an internal enemy, men of Insarov's kind

would arise? In any event, the skeptical note is too faint to mar the hopeful tone of the book. (pp. 171-72)

Simultaneously with *On the Eve* Turgenev published an essay of broad sweep, **"Hamlet and Don Quixote,"** which formulates a suggestive view of the patterns of personality. Mankind, he contends, can be divided into Hamlets and Don Quixotes, though in the fewest individuals is the type pure. The prince of Denmark is the skeptic, spoiled for action by too much thought, and wryly cherishing his own ego, for he finds nothing in the world he can cling to whole-heartedly. The knight of la Mancha embodies boundless faith in and selfless devotion to an ideal. He values life only as a means of assuring the triumph of truth and justice. A man of action, possessed of an indomitable will, his blind single-mindedness may make him ludicrous and is sure to make him great. The one is the complete ironist, the other the complete enthusiast. Don Quixote discovers, Hamlet elaborates. The former is belabored by the shepherds; the latter flagellates himself. The hidalgo is truly humble; Hamlet's self-abasement is mixed with a sense of superiority to others. Despising himself, he thrives on that contempt. The masses cannot look to him for leadership; they will see Don Quixote's failings as clearly as Sancho does, yet follow him through fire and water. The knight refuses to believe his eyes when Dulcinea appears to him in the guise of a slattern; Hamlet is cynical or rhetorical in his attitude toward Ophelia, being himself incapable of love. Don Quixote may fight windmills and mistakes a barber's tin basin for a magical golden helmet, but who knows exactly, asks the author, where reality ceases and fantasy begins? "It seems to me, therefore, that the principal thing is the sincerity and strength of our convictions; the result lies in the hands of the Fates . . . Our business is to arm ourselves and fight." If there are to be no more Don Quixotes, he concludes, "let the book of history be closed: there will be nothing in it worth reading." The death of either hero is moving, but Don Quixote's "unutterably" so. In his last moments the knight lays aside all his pride, declaring that, as in the old days, he is simply "Alonzo the Good." The essayist comments that "everything shall crumble to dust, but good deeds shall not vanish like smoke"; and he paraphrases the Apostle: "All things shall pass, love alone shall endure."

Turgenev, himself much the Hamlet, does not fail to sympathize with the Dane's predicament. He finds eternal values in the prince's nay-saying. The latter's skepticism is not to be mistaken for chilly indifference; he is as much an enemy of sham and other evils as his counterpart. Yet this essay, as, less explicitly, *On the Eve,* attests Turgenev's admiration for the knight errant, a type foreign to his own nature. (pp. 173-74)

In *Fathers and Children* the novelist put Bazarov through his paces by taking this brusque commoner on a visit to a house of gentlefolk; by leading him into arguments with his two middle-aged, cultivated hosts; by making him fall hopelessly in love with a beautiful lady, indolent and undersexed; by involving him in a stupid, almost comical duel with one of his hosts; by engaging him in talk with his earnest, apish, pliant disciple; by sending him home to see his pathetic old parents; by bringing upon him an untimely death, the result of an infection contracted at a rural post-mortem. (p. 196)

From the moment when we first see Bazarov taking his time about offering his bare red hand to his host, and turning down the collar of his nondescript coat to show his long, thin face, with its sandy side-whiskers and cool green eyes, to the moment, a few months later, when the dying atheist raises one eyelid in horror as the priest administers the last sacrament, we are in the presence of a figure that dwarfs all around him and carries the whole weight of the story. It is also a figure that shows the fullest measure of Turgenev's powers of characterization. He believed that a novelist must be "objective," concerned to represent the world about him rather than his response to it, that his art required an interest in and a cumulative knowledge of other people's lives, as well as an understanding of the forces that shaped them. Bazarov, the tough-minded, hard-fisted medic, with his brutal honesty, his faith in a crudely empirical science that he uses as a cudgel wherewith to hit out at the genteel culture he abominates, this professed "Nihilist," is an example of what the objective method can achieve. In some respects, he is perhaps fashioned after an image at the back of Turgenev's mind, the image of the man he admired and could not be. (pp. 196-97)

Turgenev's conscious attitude toward his protagonist was ambiguous. . . . Unquestionably the admiration the author felt for his hero went hand in hand with a desire to preserve the values that this iconoclast rejected. (pp. 198-99)

One of Bazarov's sentiments was undoubtedly shared by his creator—dislike of the nobility. Turgenev's treatment of it in this novel afforded him the satisfaction of the flagellant. . . . How well he knew these people—their good intentions, their feeble achievements, their tender sensibilities, so readily touched by a line of verse, a point of honor, enchanted memories of a dead love, the glow of a setting sun which makes the aspens look like pines! But the knowledge that made for contempt fed his sympathy, too, and Nikolay Kirsanov, at least, is a lovable fellow.

Throughout, his craftsmanship is at its best. Even the minor characters are deftly sketched in. The description of Bazarov's illness gave Chekhov, himself a physician, the sensation of having "caught the infection from him." Bathed in an atmosphere of tenderness and pathos, the passages about Bazarov's parents are among the most moving in literature. As he wrote the last lines, in which the old couple are shown visiting the grave of their only son, Turgenev had to turn away his head, so that his tears would not blot the manuscript, and even in such a dry-eyed age as ours, there must be readers who do not finish the paragraph without blinking.

True, the comings and goings crowded into the few weeks during which the action unfolds seem somewhat contrived. The structure of the novel lacks the formal beauty of *A Nest of Gentlefolk* and *On the Eve.* The touching passage at the close is flawed by the last few lines, with their suggestion of a half-hearted piety. These blemishes are negligible, however, in a work of such wide validity. *Fathers and Children* is a novel to which Turgenev gave his full powers: his intuitions, his insights, the fruit of his contacts with a variety of men and women, his reflections on experience, his sense of the pathos of the human condition. Rudin and Lavretzky can each be fully understood only in the context of his age and his country. Bazarov, while unmistakably Russian, is a universal and a profoundly attractive figure. (pp. 199-200)

[The] core of the novel is not so much the conflict of generations as the theme touched upon obliquely in *On The Eve:* revolution. The promise held out in the latter novel is to some degree fulfilled in *Fathers and Children.* . . .

"We mean to fight," Bazarov declares. But he has no more of a chance to carry out his intention than Insarov does. The author metes out a premature death to both. The Bulgarian's demise is wholly unmotivated; Bazarov, we are told, perishes because he was born too soon. One suspects, however, that this protagonist was killed off in obedience not solely to the logic of his situation but also to the law of the author's nature. Somehow he could not quite bring himself to grant his characters a sense of accomplishment which he himself seems never to have tasted fully. (p. 202)

Avrahm Yarmolinsky, in his *Turgenev: The Man, His Art, and His Age,* revised edition, 1959. Reprint by Octagon Books, 1977. 384 p.

SOURCES FOR FURTHER STUDY

Freeborn, Richard. *Turgenev: The Novelist's Novelist, A Study.* London: Oxford University Press, 1960, 201 p.

> Study which "sets out to illuminate the distinctive features of what is sometimes referred to as the 'Turgenevan novel' and to examine the development that it underwent at Turgenev's hands."

Magarshak, David. *Turgenev: A Life.* London: Faber and Faber, 1954, 328 p.

> Discusses Turgenev's works in the context of his life.

Matlaw, Ralph E., ed. *"Fathers and Sons" by Ivan Turgenev: The Author on the Novel, Contemporary Reactions, Essays in Criticism.* New York: W. W. Norton & Co., 1989, 345 p.

> Provides excerpts from Turgenev's correspondence defending his novel *Fathers and Sons* from its critics, essays by Turgenev's contemporaries who both justified and condemned the novel, introductory critical essays on the novel, and an English translation.

Pritchett, V. S. *The Gentle Barbarian: The Life and Work of Turgenev.* New York: Random House, 1977, 243 p.

> A biographical and literary study. Pritchett writes: "My chief concern has been to enlarge the understanding of [Turgenev's] superb short stories and novels and to explore the interplay of what is known about his life with his art. He was a deeply autobiographical writer."

Ripp, Victor. *Turgenev's Russia: From "Notes of a Hunter" to "Fathers and Sons".* Ithaca, N.Y.: Cornell University Press, 1980, 218 p.

> Examines Turgenev's novels and Russian culture by presenting discussions of several key cultural issues of Russian society including, among other topics, pedagogy, women's rights, and the debate surrounding the social consequences of the emancipation of the serfs, along with criticism of Turgenev's works.

Schapiro, Leonard. *Turgenev: His Life and Times.* New York: Random House, 1978, 382 p.

> Biography of Turgenev. Schapiro does not attempt to interpret the author but to portray "his thought, his actions, and his work, on the basis of the most reliable evidence available" and "then leave it to the reader to decide what kind of man he was."

Mark Twain

1835-1910

(Pseudonym of Samuel Langhorne Clemens; also wrote under pseudonyms Thomas Jefferson Snodgrass, Josh, Muggins, Soleather, Grumbler, and Sieur Louis de Conte) American novelist, short story writer, journalist, essayist, and dramatist.

INTRODUCTION

*T*wain is considered the father of modern American literature and is known in particular for his classic novel *The Adventures of Huckleberry Finn* (1884). Breaking with the genteel traditions of the nineteenth century, Twain developed a lively, vernacular narrative style which served as the vehicle for his satirical observations concerning human folly and social injustice and which, during his lifetime, led to widespread denunciation of his works as coarse and improper. Subsequently, however, Twain's works have come to be regarded as the first and finest literary expression of the American spirit of pragmatism, egalitarianism, and honesty. Ernest Hemingway wrote: "All modern American literature comes from one book by Mark Twain called *Huckleberry Finn*. . . . There was nothing before. There has been nothing as good since."

Clemens grew up in the Mississippi River town of Hannibal, Missouri, and he later noted that the river and the activities it supported provided some of the happiest moments of his childhood. At age twelve he quit school to become a printer's apprentice; by the time he was seventeen he was also writing stories and sketches for the newspapers he helped print. During the late 1850s Clemens piloted steamboats on the Mississippi, a job he held until the river was closed to commercial traffic during the Civil War. After brief service in the Confederate militia, he traveled west, working as a silver miner and reporter in Nevada and California. During this period Clemens began writing under the pseudonym Mark Twain, an expression used by riverboat crews to indicate that the water at a given spot was two fathoms deep and therefore easily navigable. In 1865 he published his first important sketch, "Jim Smiley and His Jumping Frog," in a New York periodical. The story was widely popular and was reprinted two years later in Twain's first book, *The Celebrated Jumping Frog of*

Calaveras County, and Other Sketches (1867), which appeared just as the author embarked on a cruise to Europe and the Middle East. The satirical letters Twain wrote to two American newspapers during this voyage proved immensely popular and were later collected as *The Innocents Abroad; or, The New Pilgrim's Progress* (1869). The success of this volume and Twain's growing reputation as a lecturer established him as the leading American humorist.

In 1874 Twain published his first novel, *The Gilded Age,* written in conjunction with Charles Dudley Warner. *The Adventures of Tom Sawyer,* a children's book chronicling the adventures of a mischievous boy in a Mississippi River town, appeared two years later to wide acclaim, and Twain immediately afterward began work on a sequel centering on Tom's friend Huckleberry Finn. According to Twain, Huck was inspired by the real-life Tom Blankenship, and Twain's description of Blankenship in his *Autobiography* could serve equally well for Huck: "He was ignorant, unwashed, insufficiently fed; but he had as good a heart as ever any boy had. His liberties were totally unrestricted. He was the only really independent person—boy or man—in the community." *Huckleberry Finn* records Huck's adventures as he accompanies Jim, an escaped slave, down the Mississippi in a quest for freedom. Amid abundant social satire provided by the various characters and situations Huck and Jim encounter, the narrative focuses on Huck's developing moral independence from the teachings of his society, and critics agree that *Huckleberry Finn* far surpasses *Tom Sawyer* in the depth of both its characterization and its themes. Although many of Twain's contemporaries objected to the novel's vernacular dialogue, coarse subject matter, and forthright social criticism, *Huckleberry Finn* was a great popular success.

During the late 1880s and 1890s, Twain suffered a series of major financial reverses, including the loss of hundreds of thousands of dollars invested in the development of the unsuccessful Paige typesetting machine, and many of his later works were written with the specific aim of making money. He also resumed lecturing to augment his earnings, and by 1900 he had repaid the vast bulk of his debts. As a result of the hardships of the 1890s and the personal tragedies of the early 1900s, which included the deaths of his wife and two of his three daughters, Twain's natural pessimism deepened into a fatalistic despair, and his work became more introspective and polemic. Critics have noted signs of this developing attitude in Twain's works as early as *A Connecticut Yankee in King Arthur's Court,* published in 1889, but note that its most overt expression is contained in the essay *What Is Man?* (1906), wherein humanity is depicted as inherently foolish and self-destructive. Twain died in 1910, and his *Autobiography* was posthumously published in 1924.

Scholars recognize in Twain a man divided in outlook between comic and tragic perceptions of existence. Throughout his career he looked back yearningly to the happy days of his youth on the shores of the Mississippi, finding in his memories spritual rejuvenation and inspiration. At the same time he was skeptical about the wisdom of humanity and the possibility of progress in human society. His longing for an idealized past as a haven from an increasingly hostile present is evident in most of his major works of fiction. However, Twain also believed that humanity had been given a chance to remedy its situation in the New World, where the foolish superstitions and false hierarchies of Western Europe could be replaced with egalitarianism and the true progress represented by improved living conditions. As a result, Twain's works offer a compelling vision of the American frontier. In *Huckleberry Finn,* for example, the frontier as exemplified by the Mississippi River allows Huck to escape the moral and social strictures of civilization and, confronted by the awesome power and beauty of nature, to develop an awareness of the importance of such simple values as courage, honesty, and common sense.

Twain remains one of the most widely read authors in American literature, and, from the prime of his career through the present, his work has remained an object of critical puzzlement and public controversy. While quick to praise his wit, inventiveness, and mastery of colloquial language, critics have not reached consensus on the serious elements of Twain's fiction. Scholars have noted that, although Twain addressed a number of political and philosophical topics, especially in his later work, he often appeared to support conflicting sides of the same issues. Twain's detractors, similarly, have censured—and often banned—his work for ideologically varied reasons, accusing it of profanity, misanthropy, and, more recently in the case of *Huckleberry Finn,* racism in its characterization of Jim. Perhaps the author anticipated the volatility of his body of work when, in the preface to *Huckleberry Finn,* he wrote: "[Persons] attempting to find a moral in it will be banished; persons attempting to find a plot in it will be shot." That Twain's *oeuvre* continues to provoke such interest and debate is testament to the enduring power of its satire and of its ideas.

(For further information on Twain's life and works, see *Concise Dictionary of American Literary Biography, 1865-1917; Contemporary Authors,* Vol. 104; *Dictionary of Literary Biography,* Vols. 11, 12, 13, 64, 74; *Short Story Criticism,* Vol. 6; *Twentieth-Century Literary Criticism,* Vols. 6, 12, 19, 36; and *Yesterday's Authors of Books for Children,* Vol. 2.)

CRITICAL COMMENTARY

WILLIAM DEAN HOWELLS
(essay date 1901)

[An important promoter of literary Realism, Howells was also one of Twain's closest friends. In the following excerpt from an essay that first appeared in *The North American Review* in 1901, he surveys Twain's career to the turn of the century.]

So far as I know, Mr. Clemens is the first writer to use in extended writing the fashion we all use in thinking, and to set down the thing that comes into his mind without fear or favor of the thing that went before or the thing that may be about to follow. . . . In other words, Mr. Clemens uses in work on the larger scale the method of the elder essayists, and you know no more where you are going to bring up in *The Innocents Abroad* or *Following the Equator* than in an essay of Montaigne. The end you arrive at is the end of the book, and you reach it amused but edified, and sorry for nothing but to be there. You have noted the author's thoughts, but not his order of thinking; he has not attempted to trace the threads of association between the things that have followed one another; his reason, not his logic, has convinced you, or, rather, it has persuaded you, for you have not been brought under conviction. . . . [What] finally remains with the reader, after all the joking and laughing, is not merely the feeling of having had a mighty good time, but the conviction that he has got the worth of his money. He has not gone through the six hundred pages of *The Innocents Abroad,* or *Following the Equator,* without having learned more of the world as the writer saw it than any but the rarest traveller is able to show for his travel; and possibly, with his average practical American public, which was his first tribunal, and must always be his court of final appeal, Mark Twain justified himself for being so delightful by being so instructive. If this bold notion is admissible, it seems the moment to say that no writer ever imparted information more inoffensively.

But his great charm is his absolute freedom in a region where most of us are fettered and shackled by immemorial convention. He saunters out into the trim world of letters, and lounges across its neatly kept paths, and walks about on the grass at will, in spite of all the signs that have been put up from the beginning of literature, warning people of dangers and penalties for the slightest trespass.

One of the characteristics I observe in him is his single-minded use of words, which he employs . . . to express the plain, straight meaning their common acceptance has given them with no regard to their structural significance or their philological implications. He writes English as if it were a primitive and not a derivative language, without Gothic or Latin or Greek behind it, or German and French beside it. The result is the English in which the most vital works of English literature are cast, rather than the English of Milton and Thackeray and Mr. Henry James. I do not say that the English of the authors last named is less than vital, but only that it is not the most vital. It is scholarly and conscious; it knows who its grandfather was; it has the refinement and subtlety of an old patriciate. You will not have with it the widest suggestion, the largest human feeling, or perhaps the loftiest reach of imagination, but you will have the keen joy that exquisite artistry in words can alone impart, and that you will not have in Mark Twain. What you will have in him is a style which is as personal, as biographical as the style of any one who has written, and expresses a civilization whose courage of the chances, the preferences, the duties, is not the measure of its essential modesty. It has a thing to say, and it says it in the word that may be the first or second or third choice, but will not be the instrument of the most fastidious ear, the most delicate and exacting sense, though it will be the word that surely and strongly conveys intention from the author's mind to the reader's. It is the Abraham Lincolnian word, not the Charles Sumnerian; it is American, Western.

Now that Mark Twain has become a fame so worldwide, we should be in some danger of forgetting, but for his help, how entirely American he is, and we have already forgotten, perhaps, how truly Western he is, though his work, from first to last, is always reminding us of the fact. But here I should like to distinguish. It is not alone in its generous humor, with more honest laughter in it than humor ever had in the world till now, that his work is so Western. Any one who has really known the West (and really to know it one must have lived it) is aware of the profoundly serious, the almost tragical strain which is the fundamental tone in the movement of such music as it has. Up to a certain point, in the presence of the mystery which we call life, it trusts and hopes and laughs; beyond that it doubts and fears, but it does not cry. It is more likely to laugh again, and in the work of Mark Twain there is little of the pathos which is supposed to be the ally of humor,

Principal Works

The Celebrated Jumping Frog of Calaveras County, and Other Sketches (sketches) 1867

The Innocents Abroad; or, The New Pilgrim's Progress (sketches) 1869

Roughing It (sketches) 1872

The Gilded Age [with Charles Dudley Warner] (novel) 1874

The Adventures of Tom Sawyer (novel) 1876

A Tramp Abroad (sketches) 1880

The Prince and the Pauper (novel) 1882

Life on the Mississippi (memoirs) 1883

The Adventures of Huckleberry Finn (novel) 1884

A Connecticut Yankee in King Arthur's Court (novel) 1889

The Tragedy of Pudd'nhead Wilson, and the Comedy Those Extraordinary Twins (novel and sketch) 1894

Personal Recollections of Joan of Arc [as Sieur Louis de Conte] (novel) 1896

The Man That Corrupted Hadleyburg, and Other Stories and Essays (short stories and essays) 1900

What Is Man? (essay) 1906

Extract from Captain Stormfield's Visit to Heaven (novella) 1909

The Mysterious Stranger (novel) 1916

Mark Twain's Autobiography (autobiography) 1924

erner, and the revolt against it is as constant in Mark Twain as the enmity to New England orthodoxy is in Doctor Holmes. But he does not take it with such serious resentment as Doctor Holmes is apt to take his inherited Puritanism, and it may be therefore that he is able to do it more perfect justice, and impart it more absolutely. At any rate, there are no more vital passages in his fiction than those which embody character as it is affected for good as well as evil by the severity of the local Sunday-schooling and church-going. (pp. 166-72)

We owe to *The Gilded Age* a type in Colonel Mulberry Sellers which is as likely to endure as any fictitious character of our time. It embodies the sort of Americanism which survived through the Civil War, and characterized in its boundlessly credulous, fearlessly adventurous, unconsciously burlesque excess the period of political and economic expansion which followed the war. Colonel Sellers was, in some rough sort, the American of that day, which already seems so remote, and is best imaginable through him. Yet the story itself was of the fortuitous structure of what may be called the autobiographical books, such as *The Innocents Abroad* and *Roughing It.* Its desultory and accidental character was heightened by the co-operation of Mr. Clemen's fellow-humorist, Charles Dudley Warner, and such coherence as it had was weakened by the diverse qualities of their minds and their irreconcilable ideals in literature. These never combined to a sole effect or to any variety of effects that left the reader very clear what the story was all about; and yet from the cloudy solution was precipitated at least one character which, as I have said, seems of as lasting substance and lasting significance as any which the American imagination has evolved from the American environment.

If Colonel Sellers is Mr. Clemens's supreme invention, as it seems to me, I think that his *Connecticut Yankee* is his highest achievement in the way of a greatly imagined and symmetrically developed romance. Of all the fanciful schemes in fiction, it pleases me most, and I give myself with absolute delight to its notion of a keen East Hartford Yankee finding himself, by a retroactionary spell, at the court of King Arthur of Britain, and becoming part of the sixth century with all the customs and ideas of the nineteenth in him and about him. (pp. 173-74)

[*Connecticut Yankee*] is a great fancy, transcending in aesthetic beauty the invention in *The Prince and the Pauper,* with all the delightful and affecting implications of that charming fable, and excelling the heart-rending story [*Personal Recollections of Joan of Arc*] in which Joan of Arc lives and prophesies and triumphs and suffers. She is, indeed, realized to the modern sense as few figures of the past have been realized in fiction; and is none the less of her time and of all time because her supposititious historian is so recurrently of ours. After Sellers, and Huck Finn, and Tom Sawyer, and the

little suffusion of apt tears from the smiling eyes. It is too sincere for that sort of play; and if after the doubting and the fearing it laughs again, it is with a suggestion of that resentment which youth feels when the disillusion from its trust and hope comes, and which is the grim second-mind of the West in the presence of the mystery. . . . Such, or somewhat like this, was the genesis and evolution of Mark Twain.

Missouri was Western, but it was also Southern, not only in the institution of slavery, to the custom and acceptance of which Mark Twain was born and bred without any applied doubt of its divinity, but in the peculiar social civilization of the older South from which his native State was settled. . . . No Northerner could have come so close to the heart of a Kentucky feud, and revealed it so perfectly, with the whimsicality playing through its carnage, or could have so brought us into the presence of the sardonic comi-tragedy of the squalid little river town where the store-keeping magnate shoots down his drunken tormentor in the arms of the drunkard's daughter, and then cows with bitter mockery the mob that comes to lynch him. The strict religiosity compatible in the Southwest with savage precepts of conduct is something that could make itself known in its amusing contrast only to the native Southwest-

Connecticut Yankee, she is the author's finest creation; and if he had succeeded in portraying no other woman-nature, he would have approved himself its fit interpreter in her. I do not think he succeeds so often with that nature as with the boy-nature or the man-nature, apparently because it does not interest him so much. He will not trouble himself to make women talk like women at all times; oftentimes they talk too much like him, though the simple, homely sort express themselves after their kind; and Mark Twain does not always write men's dialogue so well as he might. He is apt to burlesque the lighter colloquiality, and it is only in the more serious and most tragical junctures that his people utter themselves with veracious simplicity and dignity. That great, burly fancy of his is always tempting him to the exaggeration which is the condition of so much of his personal humor, but which when it invades the drama spoils the illusion. The illusion renews itself in the great moments, but I wish it could be kept intact in the small, and I blame him that he does not rule his fancy better. His imagination is always dramatic in its conceptions, but not always in its expressions; the talk of his people is often inadequate caricature in the ordinary exigencies, and his art contents itself with makeshift in the minor action. Even in *Huck Finn,* so admirably proportioned and honestly studied, you find a piece of lawless extravagance hurled in, like the episode of the two strolling actors in the flatboat; their broad burlesque is redeemed by their final tragedy—a prodigiously real and moving passage—but the friend of the book cannot help wishing the burlesque was not there. One laughs, and then despises one's self for laughing, and this is not what Mark Twain often makes you do. There are things in him that shock, and more things that we think shocking, but this may not be so much because of their nature as because of our want of naturalness; they wound our conventions rather than our convictions. (pp. 174-76)

Mark Twain was born to the common necessity of looking out for himself, and, while making himself practically of another order of things, he felt whatever was fine in the old and could regard whatever was ugly and absurd more tolerantly, more humorously than those who bequeathed him their enmity to it. Fortunately for him, and for us who were to enjoy his humor, he came to his intellectual consciousness in a world so large and free and safe that he could be fair to any wrong while seeing the right so unfailingly; and nothing is finer in him than his gentleness with the error which is simply passive and negative. He gets fun out of it, of course, but he deals almost tenderly with it, and hoards his violence for the superstitions and traditions which are arrogant and active. His pictures of that old river-town, Southwestern life, with its faded and tattered aristocratic ideals and its squalid democratic realities, are pathetic, while they are so unspar-

ingly true and so inapologetically and unaffectedly faithful. (p. 177)

He is deeply and essentially romantic in his literary conceptions, but when it comes to working them out he is helplessly literal and real; he is the impassioned lover, the helpless slave of the concrete. For this reason, for his wish, his necessity, first to ascertain his facts, his logic is as irresistible as his laugh.

All life seems, when he began to find it out, to have the look of a vast joke, whether the joke was on him or on his fellow-beings, or if it may be expressed without irreverence, on their common creator. But it was never wholly a joke, and it was not long before his literature began to own its pathos. The sense of this is not very apparent in *The Innocents Abroad,* but in *Roughing It* we began to be distinctly aware of it, and in the successive books it is constantly imminent, not as a clutch at the heartstrings, but as a demand of common justice, common sense, the feeling of proportion. It is not sympathy with the under dog merely as under dog that moves Mark Twain; for the under dog is sometimes rightfully under. But the probability is that it is wrongfully under, and has a claim to your inquiry into the case which you cannot ignore without atrocity. Mark Twain never ignores it. . . . He always gives his help, even when he seems to leave the pity to others, and it may be safely said that no writer has dealt with so many phases of life with more unfailing justice. . . . His indignation relieves itself as often as not in a laugh; injustice is the most ridiculous thing in the world, after all, and indignation with it feels its own absurdity. (pp. 179-180)

[The] earliest form of Mark Twain's work is characteristic of the greater part of it. The method used in *The Innocents Abroad* and in *Roughing It* is the method used in *Life on the Mississippi,* in *A Tramp Abroad,* and in *Following the Equator,* which constitute in bulk a good half of all his writings, as they express his dominant aesthetics. If he had written the fictions alone, we should have had to recognize a rare inventive talent, a great imagination and dramatic force; but I think it must be allowed that the personal books named overshadow the fictions. They have the qualities that give character to the fictions, and they have advantages that the fictions have not and that no fiction can have. In them, under cover of his pseudonym, we come directly into the presence of the author, which is what the reader is always longing and seeking to do; but unless the novelist is a conscienceless and tasteless recreant to the terms of his art, he cannot admit the reader to his intimacy. The personal books of Mark Twain have not only the charm of the essay's inconsequent and desultory method, in which invention, fact, reflection, and philosophy wander after one another in any following that happens, but they are of an immediate and most informal hospitality which admits you at once to the author's confidence, and makes you frankly welcome not only to his thought but to his way of thinking. (pp. 180-81)

In the case of the fictions, he conceives that his first affair is to tell a story, and a story when you are once launched upon it does not admit of deviation without some hurt to itself. In Mark Twain's novels, whether they are for boys or for men, the episodes are only those that illustrate the main narrative or relate to it, though he might have allowed himself somewhat larger latitude in the old-fashioned tradition which he has oftenest observed in them. When it comes to the critical writings, which again are personal, and which, whether they are criticisms of literature or of life, are always so striking, he is quite relentlessly logical and coherent. Here there is no lounging or sauntering, with entertaining or edifying digressions. The object is in view from the first, and the reasoning is straightforwardly to it throughout. . . . The facts are first ascertained with a conscience uncommon in critical writing of any kind, and then they are handled with vigor and precision till the polemic is over. It does not so much matter whether you agree with the critic or not; what you have to own is that here is a man of strong convictions, clear ideas, and ardent sentiments, based mainly upon common sense of extraordinary depth and breadth.

In fact, what finally appeals to you in Mark Twain, and what may hereafter be his peril with his readers, is his common sense. (pp. 181-82)

But it would be rather awful if the general recognition of his prophetic function should implicate the renunciation of the humor that has endeared him to mankind. . . . What we all should wish to do is to keep Mark Twain what he has always been: a comic force unique in the power of charming us out of our cares and troubles, united with as potent an ethic sense of duties, public and private, which no man denies in himself without being false to other men. I think we may hope for the best he can do to help us deserve our self-respect, without forming Mark Twain societies to read philanthropic meanings into his jokes, or studying the Jumping Frog as the allegory of an imperializing republic. I trust the time may be far distant when the Meditation at the Tomb of Adam shall be memorized and declaimed by ingenuous youth as a mystical appeal for human solidarity. (p. 185)

W. D. Howells, in his *My Mark Twain: Reminiscences and Criticisms,* Harper, 1910, 186 p.

H. L. MENCKEN
(essay date 1919)

[An American essayist and editor, Mencken is famous for scathingly satirical essays in which he ridiculed a number of American institutions that he saw as inspid and appealing to the lowest common denominator of the populace. In the following excerpt from a 1919 *Smart Set* essay, he assesses Twain's place in the body of American writing.]

The older I grow the more I am convinced that Mark was, by long odds, the largest figure that ever reared itself out of the flat, damp prairie of American literature. He was great absolutely, but one must consider him relatively to get at the measure of his true greatness. Put him beside Emerson, or Whitman, or Hawthorne, or even Poe; he was palpably the superior of all of them. (p. 183)

Mark was the first of our great national artists to be whole heartedly and enthusiastically American. He was the first to immerse himself willingly and with gusto in the infinitely picturesque and brilliant life of his time and country. He was the first to understand the common man of his race, and to interpret him fairly, honestly and accurately. He was the first to project brilliantly, for the information and entertainment of all the world, the American point of view, the American philosophy of life, the American character, the American soul. He would have been a great artist, I believe, even on the high-flung plane of Emerson or Hawthorne. He would have been *konzertmeister* even among the *umbilicarii.* But being what he was, his greatness was enormously augmented. He stands today at the head of the line. He is the one indubitable glory of American letters.

The bitter, of course, goes with the sweet. To be an American is, unquestionably, to be the noblest, the grandest, the proudest mammal that ever hoofed the verdure of God's green foot-stool. . . . But, as I have said, there is no perfection under heaven, and so even an American has his small blemishes, his scarcely discernible weaknesses, his minute traces of vice and depravity. Mark, alas, had them: he was as thoroughly American as a Knight of Pythias, a Wheeling stogie or Prohibition. . . . And what were these stigmata that betrayed him? In chief, they were two in number, and both lay at the very foundation of his character. On the one hand, there was his immovable moral certainty, his firm belief that he knew what was right from what was wrong, and that all who differed from him were, in some obscure way, men of an inferior and sinister order. And on the other hand, there was his profound intellectual timorousness, his abiding fear of his own ideas, his incurable cowardice in the face of public disapproval. These two characteristics colored his whole thinking; they showed themselves in his every attitude and gesture. They were the visible signs of his limitation as an Emersonian Man Thinking, and they were the bright symbols of his nationality. He was great in every way that an American could be great, but when he came to the border of his Americanism he came to the end of his greatness. (pp. 185-86)

With more courage, he would have gone a great deal further, and left a far deeper mark upon the intellectual history of his time. Not, perhaps, intrinsically as artist. He got as far in that direction as it is possible for a man of his training to go. *Huckleberry Finn* is a truly stupendous piece of work—perhaps the greatest novel ever written in English. And it would be difficult to surpass the sheer artistry of such things as *A Connecticut Yankee, Captain Stormfield, Joan of Arc* and parts of *A Tramp Abroad*. But there is more to the making of literature than the mere depiction of human beings at their obscene follies; there is also the play of ideas. Mark had ideas that were clear, that were vigorous, and that had an immediate appositeness. True enough, most of them were not quite original. As Prof. Schoenemann, of Harvard, has lately demonstrated, he got the notion of *The Mysterious Stranger* from Adolf Wilbrandt's *Der Meister von Palmyra;* much of *What Is Man?* you will find in the forgotten harangues of Ingersoll; in other directions he borrowed right and left. But it is only necessary to read either of the books I have just mentioned to see how thoroughly he recast everything he wrote; how brilliantly it came to be marked by the charm of his own personality; how he got his own peculiar and unmatchable eloquence into the merest statement of it. When, entering these regions of his true faith, he yielded to a puerile timidity—when he sacrificed his conscience and his self-respect to the idiotic popularity that so often more than half dishonored him—then he not only did a cruel disservice to his own permanent fame, but inflicted genuine damage upon the national literature. He was greater than all the others because he was more American, but in this one way, at least, he was less than them for the same reason. . . .

Well, there he stands—a bit concealed, a bit false, but still a colossus. As I said at the start, I am inclined year by year to rate his achievement higher. In such a work as *Huckleberry Finn* there is something that vastly transcends the merit of all ordinary books. It has a merit that is special and extraordinary; it lifts itself above all hollow standards and criteria; it seems greater every time I read it. The books that gave Mark his first celebrity do not hold up so well. **"The Jumping Frog"** still wrings snickers, but, after all, it is commonplace at bottom. . . . *The Innocents Abroad,* re-read today, is

largely tedious. Its humors are artificial; its audacities are stale; its eloquence belongs to the fancy journalism of a past generation. Even *Tom Sawyer* and *A Tramp Abroad* have long stretches of flatness. But in *Huckleberry Finn,* though he didn't know it at the time and never quite realized it, Mark found himself. There, working against the grain, heartily sick of the book before it was done, always putting it off until tomorrow, he hacked out a masterpiece that expands as year chases year. There, if I am not wrong, he produced the greatest work of the imagination that These States have yet seen. (pp. 188-89)

H. L. Mencken, "Final Estimate," in his *H. L. Mencken's "Smart Set" Criticism,* edited by William H. Nolte, Cornell University Press, 1968, pp. 182-89.

VAN WYCK BROOKS
(essay date 1933)

[In the following excerpt, Brooks discusses what he sees as a conflict in Twain between his private opinions and those he felt compelled to display to the public.]

At the circus, no doubt, you have watched some trained lion going through the sad motions of a career to which the tyrannical curiosity of men has constrained him. At times he seems to be playing his part with a certain zest; he has acquired a new set of superficial habits, and you would say that he finds them easy and pleasant. Under the surface, however, he remains the wild, exuberant creature of the jungle. (p. 219)

So it was with Mark Twain. . . . [He] conformed to a moral régime in which the profoundest of his instincts could not function: the artist had been submerged in the bourgeois gentleman, the man of business, the respectable Presbyterian citizen. To play his part, therefore, he had to depend upon the cues his wife and his friends gave him. Here we have the explanation of his statement: "Outside influences, outside circumstances, wind the man and regulate him. Left to himself, he wouldn't get regulated at all, and the sort of time he would keep would not be valuable." We can see from this how completely his conscious self had accepted the point of view of his trainers, how fully he had concurred in their desire to repress that unmanageable creative instinct of his, how ashamed, in short, he was of it. Nevertheless, that instinct, while repressed, continued to live and manifest itself just the same. . . . [In] the end, never having been able to develop, to express itself, to fulfill itself, to air itself in the sun and the wind of the world, it turned as it were black and malignant, like some monstrous, morbid inner growth, poisoning Mark Twain's whole spiritual system. (pp. 219-20)

[Is] it not plain that Mark Twain's books are shot through with all sorts of unconscious revelations of this internal conflict? According to the psychoanalysts, the dream is an expression of a suppressed wish. In dreams we do what our inner selves desire to do but have been prevented from doing either by the exigencies of our daily routine, or by the obstacles of convention, or by some other form of censorship which has been imposed upon us, or which we ourselves, actuated by some contrary desire, have willingly accepted. Many other dreams, however, are not so simple: they are often incoherent, nonsensical, absurd. In such cases it is because two opposed wishes, neither of which is fully satisfied, have met one another and resulted in a "compromise"—a compromise that is often as apparently chaotic as the collision of two railway trains running at full speed. These mechanisms, the mechanisms of the "wish-fulfillment" and the "wish-conflict," are evident, as Freud has shown, in many of the phenomena of everyday life. Whenever, for any reason, the censorship is relaxed and the censor is off guard, whenever we are day-dreaming and give way to our idle thoughts, then the unconscious bestirs itself and rises to the surface, gives utterance to those embarrassing slips of the tongue, those "tender playfulnesses," that express our covert intentions, slays our adversaries, sets our fancies wandering in pursuit of all the ideals and all the satisfactions upon which our customary life has stamped its veto. In Mark Twain's books, or rather in a certain group of them, his "fantasies," we can see this process at work. Certain significant obsessions reveal themselves there, certain fixed ideas; the same themes recur again and again. "I am writing from the grave," he notes in later life, regarding some manuscripts that are not to be published until after his death. "On these terms only can a man be approximately frank. He cannot be straitly and unqualifiedly frank either in the grave or out of it." When he wrote *Captain Stormfield's Visit to Heaven, Pudd'nhead Wilson, The American Claimant, Those Extraordinary Twins*, he was frank without knowing it. He, the unconscious artist, who, when he wrote his autobiography, found that he was unable to tell the truth about himself, has conducted us unawares in these writings into the penetralia of his soul.

Let us note, prefatorily, that in each case Mark Twain was peculiarly, for the time being, free of his censorship. That he wrote at least the first draft of *Captain Stormfield* in reckless disregard of it is proved by the fact that for forty years he did not dare to publish the book at all but kept it locked away in his safe. As for *The American Claimant, Pudd'nhead Wilson,* and

Twain's own copy of *The Adventures of Huckleberry Finn,* marked for oral delivery.

Those Extraordinary Twins, he wrote them at the time of the failure of the Paige Typesetting Machine. . . . [So] disturbed were his affairs, so disordered was everything, we are told, "that sometimes he felt himself as one walking amid unrealities." At such times, we know, the bars of the spirit fall down; people commit all sorts of aberrations, "go off the handle," as we say; the moral habits of a lifetime give way and man becomes more or less an irresponsible animal. In Mark Twain's case, at least, the result was a violent effort on the part of his suppressed self to assert its supremacy in a propitious moment when that other self, the business man, had proved abysmally weak. Is not that why these books that marked his return to literature appear to have the quality of nightmares? He has told us in the preface to *Those Extraordinary Twins* that the story had originally been a part of *Pudd'nhead Wilson;* he had seen a picture of an Italian monstrosity like the Siamese Twins and had meant to write an extravagant farce about it; but, he adds, "the story changed itself from a farce to a tragedy while I was going along with it—a most embarrassing circumstance." Eventually, he realized that it was "not one story but two stories tangled together" that he was trying to tell, so he removed the twins from *Pudd'nhead Wilson* and printed the two tales separately. That alone shows us the confusion of his mind, the confusion revealed further in *The American Claimant* and in *Pudd'nhead Wilson* as it stands. They are, I say, like nightmares, these books: full of passionate conviction that turns into a burlesque of itself, angry satire, hysterical humour. They are tripleheaded chimeras, in short, that leave the reader's mind in tumult and dismay. The censor has so far relaxed its hold that the unconscious has risen to the surface: the battle of the two Mark Twains takes place almost in the open, under our very eyes.

Glance now, among these dreams, at a simple example of "wish-fulfillment." When Captain Stormfield arrives in heaven, he is surprised to find that all sorts of people are esteemed among the celestials who have had no esteem at all on earth. Among them is Edward J. Billings of Tennessee. He was a poet during his lifetime, but the Tennessee village folk scoffed at him; they would have none of him, they made cruel sport of him. In heaven things are different; there the celestials recognize the divinity of his spirit, and in token of this Shakespeare and Homer walk backward before him.

Here, as we see, Mark Twain is unconsciously describing the actual fate of his own spirit and that ample other fate his spirit desires. It is the story of Cinderella, the despised step-sister who is vindicated by the prince's favour, rewritten in terms personal to the author. (pp. 228-32)

Observe, now, the deadly temperamental earnestness of **"The Man That Corrupted Hadleyburg,"** a story written late in life when Mark Twain's great fame and position enabled him to override the censorship and speak with more or less candour. "The temptation and the downfall of a whole town," says Mr. [Albert Bigelow] Paine, "was a colossal idea, a sardonic idea, and it is colossally and sardonically worked out. Human weakness and rotten moral force were never stripped so bare or so mercilessly jeered at in the marketplace. For once Mark Twain could hug himself with glee in derision of self-righteousness, knowing that the world would laugh with him, and that none would be so bold as to gainsay his mockery. Probably no one but Mark Twain ever conceived the idea of demoralizing a whole community—of making its 'nineteen leading citizens' ridiculous by leading them into a cheap, glittering temptation, and having them yield and openly perjure themselves at the very moment when their boasted incorruptibility was to amaze the world." It was the "leading citizens," the pillars of society with whom Mark Twain had himself been hobnobbing all those years, the very people in deference to whom he had suppressed his true desires, who admired him only for the success he had won in spite of what he was—it was these people, his friends, who had, in so actual a sense, imposed upon him, that he attacks in this terrible story of the passing stranger who took such a vitriolic joy in exposing their pretensions and their hypocrisy. "I passed through your town at a certain time, and received a deep offense which I had not earned. . . . I wanted to damage every man in the place, and every woman." Is not that the unmistakable voice of the misprized poet and philosopher in Mark Twain, the worm that has turned, the angel that has grown diabolic in a world that has refused to recognize its divinity?

Here, I say, in these two or three instances, we have the "wishfulfillment" in its clearest form. Elsewhere we find the wish, the desire of the suppressed poet for self-effectuation, expressing itself in many vague hopes and vague regrets. . . . [Consider] the unfinished tale of *The Mysterious Chamber,* "the story," as Mr. Paine describes it, "of a young lover who is accidentally locked behind a secret door in an old castle and cannot announce himself. He wanders at last down into subterranean passages beneath the castle, and he lives in this isolation for twenty years." There is something inescapably personal about that. As for the character of the Colonel Sellers of *The American Claimant*—so different from the Colonel Sellers of *The Gilded Age* who is supposed to be the same man and whom Mark Twain had drawn after one of his uncles—every one has noted that it is a burlesque upon his own preposterous business life. But is it not more than this? That rightful claimant to the great title of nobility, living in exile among those fantastic dreams of wealth that always deceive him—is he not the obscure projection of the lost heir in Mark Twain himself, inept in the business life he is living, incapable of substantiating his claim, and yet forever beguiled by the hope that some day he is going to win his true rank and live the life for which he was intended? (pp. 233-35)

Just before Mark Twain's death, he recalled, says Mr. Paine, "one of his old subjects, Dual Personality, and discussed various instances that flitted through his mind—Jekyll and Hyde phases in literature and fact." One of his old subjects, dual personality! Could he ever have been aware of the extent to which his writings revealed that conflict in himself ? Why was he so obsessed by journalistic facts like the Siamese Twins and the Tichborne case, with its theme of the lost heir and the usurper? Why is it that the idea of changelings in the cradle perpetually haunted his mind, as we can see from *Pudd'nhead Wilson* and *The Gilded Age* and the variation of it that constitutes *The Prince and the Pauper?* The prince who has submerged himself in the rôle of the beggar-boy—Mark Twain has drawn himself there, just as he has drawn himself in the *William Wilson* theme of **"The Facts Concerning the Recent Carnival of Crime in Connecticut,"** where he ends by dramatically slaying the conscience that torments him. And as for that pair of incompatibles bound together in one flesh—the Extraordinary Twins, the "good" boy who has followed the injunctions of his mother and the "bad" boy of whom society disapproves—how many

of Mark Twain's stories and anecdotes turn upon that same theme, that same juxtaposition!—does he not reveal there, in all its nakedness, the true history of his life?

We have observed that in Pudd'nhead's aphorisms Mark Twain was expressing his true opinions, the opinions of the cynic he had become owing to the suppression and the constant curdling as it were of the poet in him. . . . But he does so, we perceive, only by taking cover behind a device that enables him to save his face and make good his retreat. . . . As long as he never hit below the belt by speaking in his own person, in short, he was perfectly secure. And Mark Twain, the humorist, who held the public in the hollow of his hand, knew it.

It is only after some such explanation as this that we can understand the supremacy among all Mark Twain's writings of *Huckleberry Finn.* Through the character of Huck, that disreputable, illiterate little boy, as Mrs. Clemens no doubt thought him, he was licensed to let himself go. . . . That Mark Twain was almost, if not quite conscious of his opportunity we can see from his introductory note to the book: "Persons attempting to find a motive in this narrative will be prosecuted; persons attempting to find a moral in it will be banished; persons attempting to find a plot in it will be shot." He feels so secure of himself that he can actually challenge the censor to accuse him of having a motive. Huck's illiteracy, Huck's disreputableness and general outrageousness are so many shields behind which Mark Twain can let all the cats out of the bag with impunity. He must, I say, have had a certain sense of his unusual security when he wrote some of the more frankly satirical passages of the book, when he permitted Colonel Sherburn to taunt the mob, when he drew that picture of the audience who had been taken in by the Duke proceeding to sell the rest of their townspeople, when he made the King put up the notice, "Ladies and Children not Admitted," adding: "There, if that line don't fetch them, I don't know Arkansaw!" The withering contempt for humankind expressed in these episodes was of the sort that Mark Twain expressed more and more openly, as time went on, in his own person; but he was not indulging in that costly kind of cynicism in the days when he wrote *Huckleberry Finn.* He must, therefore, have appreciated the license that little vagabond, like the puppet in the lap of a ventriloquist, afforded him. . . . Mark Twain himself was free at last—that raft and that river to him were something more than mere material facts. His whole unconscious life, the pent-up river of his own soul, had burst its bonds and rushed forth, a joyous torrent! Do we need any other explanation of the abandon, the beauty, the eternal freshness of *Huckleberry Finn?* Perhaps we can say that a lifetime of moral slavery and repression was not too much to pay for it.

Certainly, if it flies like a gay, bright, shining arrow through the rather lukewarm atmosphere of American literature, it is because of the straining of the bow, the tautness of the string, that gave it its momentum. (pp. 236-40)

Van Wyck Brooks, in his *The Ordeal of Mark Twain,* revised edition, 1933. Reprint by AMS Press, 1977, 325 p.

CHADWICK HANSEN
(essay date 1963)

[In the following excerpt, Hansen examines the character of Jim in *The Adventures of Huckleberry Finn,* focusing on the way Twain used him to examine the position of blacks in pre-Civil War America.]

An understanding of Jim's character is by no means a simple matter; he is a highly complex and original creation, although he appears at first sight very simple. We meet him first as the butt of a practical joke played by Tom Sawyer, in Chapter II. While Jim is sleeping Tom takes three candles from the Widow's kitchen, leaving a five-cent piece on the table to pay for them. Then he slips Jim's hat off and hangs it on the limb of a tree over his head. Afterwards, Jim decides that his sleep was a trance induced by witches, who rode him all over the world and hung his hat on a limb "to show who done it," and he believes that the devil himself has left the five-cent piece. His version of the episode makes him a very important man in the Negro community. "Jim was most ruined, for a servant," says Huck, "because he got so stuck up on account of having seen the devil and been rode by witches."

The Jim of this first episode is a recognizable type-character, the comic stage Negro, a type who has trod the less reputable boards of the American theatre almost from its beginnings and who is still with us in the grade B movie and in certain television and radio programs. His essential quality in this particular case is that he feels no humiliation as a result of Tom's trick. His ignorance protects him from the mental pain of humiliation and enables him to turn the trick into a kind of triumph. If Jim had suffered as a result of the trick into a kind of triumph—a false triumph, to be sure, but still a triumph—we—the audience—would be inclined to feel pity for him. But since he does not suffer we are free to laugh at the incongruity between his account of the event and the reality. We are free to laugh at him, that is, because his ignorance is so sub-human that he cannot feel mental pain. (pp. 45-6)

Jim is still the stage Negro the next time we see him, when Huck asks Jim to have the hair-ball tell his fortune, but our attitude toward him is very much qualified, since in this episode Huck believes as firmly in Jim's magical powers as does Jim himself. In the first episode the audience was asked to think of itself as white men laughing at old Jim, the comical nigger. Here we are asked to think of ourselves as men, laughing at human ignorance and superstition. We could attribute Jim's ignorance to his color in the first episode; here we must attribute it to his humanity. Perhaps this is overstating the case, since the reader who does not wish to recognize the direction Twain is taking might feel that Huck himself is not fully human; he is only a child, and a White Trash child at that. It seems to me, however, that it requires considerable insensitivity to think of Huck as less than human, even at this early stage in the narrative, and in any case the direction of Twain's development of our attitude toward Jim is clear.

We see Jim next on Jackson's Island, where two episodes deserve particular notice. In the first of them Jim and Huck have been discussing "signs," and Jim predicts that he will be rich because he has hairy arms and a hairy breast. Then he gives us an account of his "specalat'n" in stock—livestock—and in a bank. The dialogue might have come from any minstrel show, and

Huckleberry Finn, by E.W. Kemble.

Jim has lost his money like any other stage Negro. But the conversation ends with Jim's reflection that "I's rich now, come to look at it. I owns mysef, en I's wuth eight hund'd dollars. I wisht I had de money, I wouldn' want no mo'." With this statement we move outside the world of low comedy, and Jim becomes something more than the ordinary stage Negro.

Twain has done enough by now to prepare us for the first of the tricks Huck plays on Jim. Huck kills a rattlesnake and curls it up on the foot of Jim's blankets. He expects, of course, that Jim will react like any other stage Negro. His eyes will bug out; his teeth will chatter; his knees will knock together; and Huck will have a good healthy laugh. But we are dealing now with someone who is more than a stereotype. "When Jim flung himself down on the blanket . . . the snake's mate was there, and bit him."

Huck is sorry and ashamed for what he has done. He throws the snakes away in the bushes, "for I warn't going to let Jim find out it was all my fault, not if I could help it." But he does *not* blame himself for failing to understand that Jim is a human being, who can be hurt if you play a stupid trick on him. There is something much simpler for which Huck can blame himself, and whenever he can, Huck will use Ockham's razor. "I made up my mind," he says, "I wouldn't ever take aholt of a snakeskin again with my hands, now that I see what had come of it." From this he proceeds to speculating on whether it isn't just as foolhardy to look at the new moon over your left shoulder.

Old Hank Bunker done it once, and bragged about it; and in less than two years he got drunk and fell off the shot tower and spread himself out so that he was just a kind of a layer, as you may say; and they slid him edgeways between two barn doors for a coffin, and buried him so, so they say, but I didn't see it. Pap told me. But anyway, it all come of looking at the moon that way, like a fool.

With the entrance of Hank Bunker we are back in the world of slapstick comedy, and we can recognize how very little Huck understands of what has happened. But the episode has, I think, made some impression. That snake-skin continues to haunt Huck's consciousness far down the river.

At the beginning of Chaper XIV we discover that Jim has a good deal of common sense, when he complains to Huck of how dangerous it is to go looking for the sort of adventures to be found on the *Walter Scott.* Huck has to admit that Jim is right. "He was most always right; he had an uncommon level head for a nigger." Having begun the chapter with Jim's "uncommon level head," Twain fills the rest of it with the dialogues on whether Solomon was wise and why a Frenchman doesn't talk like a man, which William Van O'Connor condemns as a cheap and inappropriate "minstrel show, end-men sort of humor."

Now there is a considerable distance between the world of the minstrel show and the world of William Van O'Connor, and most of that distance is, of course, to Mr. O'Connor's credit. But the distance is so great that it prevents him from seeing the ways in which these dialogues *are* appropriate. Jim is "down on Solomon" for threatening to cut a child in two, and this is plainly preparation for our later discovery that Jim cares very much for his own children, and blames himself for having been unintentionally cruel to his daughter.

The dialogue on why a Frenchman doesn't talk like a man is much more complicated. In order to understand it we must remember the conventions of the minstrel show, where Mr. Bones, although he seems at first sight to be abysmally ignorant in comparison to Mr. Interlocutor, is actually very clever and usually wins the arguments, just as Jim does. But what is important is not that Mr. Bones wins again; what is important is the terms in which the argument is won. Huck argues that since a cat and a cow "talk" differently, and since it is "natural and right" that they should do so, it is equally "natural and right" for a Frenchman to talk differently from an American. Huck's unstated assumption is that ethnic difference is founded in nature, and has, therefore, the same magnitude and necessity as difference in species. Jim immediately spots the fallacy. He agrees that there is a basic difference between a cat and a cow, which requires that they "talk" differently. But he asks:

"Is a Frenchman a man?"

"Yes," says Huck.

"*Well,* den! Dad blame it, why doan' he *talk* like a man? You answer me *dat!*"

Jim recognizes, and Huck does not, that all men share a common humanity. When we remember that this argument has been over differences in human language, when we remember that Twain boasted at the beginning of the book of accurately reproducing seven discrete dialects, and when we remember how thoroughly man is divided from man in the society of the Mississippi Valley, this little dialogue takes on an extraordinary richness of meaning.

But Huck's only conclusion is that "you can't learn a nigger to argue." He does not understand how he has been beaten, since, as Henry Nash Smith has clearly demonstrated, he is incapable of handling abstract ideas. But the careful reader will notice that while Huck is not capable of handling abstract ideas, Jim is. Chapter XIV is clearly minstrel show humor, and the Jim of this chapter is equally clearly Jim as Mr. Bones.

But within the framework of minstrel show dialogue Twain has created a cluster of meaning both significant and appropriate.

How much do we know about Jim at the end of Chapter XIV? We know that his character is partially a type-character, the comic stage Negro, but that it extends far beyond the limits of that type. We know that his superstitions are shared by some whites. We know that he is human enough to suffer physical pain. We know that he has a considerable amount of common sense, and that within the rather severe limits of his knowledge he is capable of handling abstract ideas. We know also that the ideas he expresses—that there is a kind of wealth in owning oneself, and that all men share a basic humanity—are most appropriate to his own situation.

Huck, of course, has learned much less than the reader. At the level of conscious thought, which is his weakest point, Huck has learned only that it is bad luck to handle a snake-skin, that Jim has "an uncommon level head for a nigger," and that in spite of his common sense "you can't learn a nigger to argue." But in Chapters XV and XVI Huck is placed in situations where he, as well as the reader, is forced to learn something new about Jim.

Chapter XV is devoted to the justly famous episode in which Huck is separated from Jim in a fog. He gets back to the raft while Jim is asleep, and convinces him that the whole experience was a dream, which Jim proceeds to "interpret." Then Huck points to the rubbish on the raft, evidence that the experience was real. He asks Jim what *it* means, and gets ready to laugh. But the laughter does not come. Instead, Jim tells him that "dat truck dah is *trash;* en trash is what people is dat puts dirt on de head er dey fren's en makes 'em ashamed." Not the least of Twain's achievements is his ability to give such dignity and force to Negro dialect (not that Negro dialect in itself is weak or undignified; but literary use of it has generally been both). The Jim of this episode, although he still speaks in the dialect of the stage Negro, is not the stage Negro, but man in the abstract, with all the dignity that belongs to that high concept, and he teaches Huck that it is painful, not funny, to play childish tricks on human dignity. Huck says,

> It was fifteen minutes before I could work myself up to go and humble myself to a nigger—but I done it, and I warn't ever sorry for it afterwards, neither. I didn't do him no more mean tricks, and I wouldn't done that one if I'd a knowed it would make him feel that way.

"If I'd a knowed." It is easy to penetrate Huck's feelings, but it is almost impossible to penetrate his mind. The idea that he hadn't really known Jim has penetrated, however, and it comes briefly to the surface of Huck's mind in Chapter XVI, when he wrestles for the first time with his "deformed conscience." Huck thinks,

> Here was this nigger which I had as good as helped to run away, coming right out flat-footed and saying he would steal his children—*children that belonged to a man I didn't even know;* a man that hadn't ever done me no harm. [my italics]

The ambiguity is evidence that Huck's mind has been touched at last. And when Jim calls him "de bes' fren' Jim's ever had" and "de on'y white genlman dat ever kep' his promise to ole Jim," Huck's reaction is "I just felt sick." Huck is not one to overstate his emotions; "sick" is as strong a term as he ever uses for them. He uses it here, and when he watches the Grangerford boys being butchered, and when the King and the Duke are ridden on a rail, and when he sees the farmers sitting with their guns in the Phelps' parlor. Jim's appeal to his friendship and his honor, coming immediately after he has betrayed Jim with a stupid trick and is about to betray him again, hits Huck very hard indeed. It makes it impossible for Huck to continue to be totally ignorant of who Jim is, and it makes it possible for him to win this first battle with his conscience.

There are four more passages which seem to me essential to an understanding of Twain's development of Jim's character. First, we have Jim laughing when Huck is washed overboard by a wave (Chapter XX). Huck was in no danger, so there is nothing vicious in Jim's laughter. All Huck can do is grumble that Jim "was the easiest nigger to laugh that ever was." The episode is one more illustration of Twain's fondness for playing brilliant variations on themes from folk humor. In this case he has simply and skilfully reversed the roles, making the white man rather than the Negro the butt of the humor.

Second, and more complex, is Jim's grief over his unintentional mistreatment of his four-year-old daughter (Chapter XXIV). He had told her to close the door, and when she didn't move, he struck her. Then he discovered that scarlet fever had left her deaf, and he tells Huck his reaction to this discovery:

> "Oh, Huck, I bust out a-cryin' en grab her up in my arms, en say, 'Oh, de po' little thing! de Lord God Amighty fogive po' ole Jim, kaze he never gwyne to fogive hisself as long's he live!' Oh, she was plumb deef en dumb, Huck, plumb deef en dumb—en I'd been a-treat'n her so!"

To understand what Twain is doing in this passage, we must remember that the popular culture of Twain's time was far more apt to sentimentalize family relationships than the popular culture of our own time. The sick or dying child; the old drunkard who deserves kindness because he is "somebody's grandpa"; mother;

the young girl with her child in her arms thrown out in the snow by the stern arm of father—these figures are, by and large, no longer with us. . . . [Since] that time the popular song has largely abandoned family sentimentality and devoted itself almost exclusively to the emotional spasms of the pubescent. It is easy for us to see how Twain is using popular culture when Huck describes Emmeline Grangerford's drawings and poetry, partly because the intention is so plainly satirical, and partly because Emmeline's emotions differ only in detail rather than in kind from those of the girls in present-day popular songs. But we must make a somewhat greater effort here.

Huck's reaction to Jim's feelings for his family is worth noticing. "I do believe he cared just as much for his people as white folks does for their'n," says Huck. "It don't seem natural, but I reckon it's so." "It don't seem natural." As on so many other occasions, Huck is more right than he knows, since, at the level we have been discussing, Jim's feelings are anything but "natural"; they are as conventional as they could possibly be. And yet they are convincing, primarily, I think, because they are given to us in Jim's language rather than in the "soul-butter" style which is used in "grieving" over two other children: William Dowling Botts, deceased, and Charles William Allbright, deceased (the latter is the baby in the barrel in the excised raftsman passage). Twain has produced here a variation on one of the tritest popular themes of his time, and has made it effective and genuine by giving it to Jim. He has achieved the unique distinction of producing the most magnificently written piece of *schmalz* in all American literature, and with it he has added one more dimension to Jim's character.

Third is a facet of Jim's character which is presented to us at many points, but is most completely described during Huck's second struggle with his conscience. This is the Jim who is kind and gentle, who stands Huck's watch on top of his own and always calls Huck "honey." This is Jim as Negro Mammy, and like several of the other faces of Jim it is a skilful variation on a type-character from folk and popular culture.

Fourth, and finally, we have the Jim who is capable of noble action, who sacrifices his freedom in order to save Tom's life. Like the Jim whom Huck tries to make a fool of on the raft, this Jim is man in the abstract, and in both cases he manages to assume this high role while remaining "nigger" Jim, the runaway slave. (pp. 47-55)

Jim is, in part, the comic stage Negro who can be made the butt of Tom's childish humor. But he is also a second Negro type, Mr. Bones, whose cleverness enables him to turn the joke back on the Interlocutor. He is also a third Negro type, the kindly old colored Mammy, the protector of the white child. He is a fourth type, the sentimental family man who weeps for the suffering of his own child. And he is a fifth type, man in the abstract—natural man, if you wish—with the reasoning power, the dignity, and the nobility that belong to that high abstraction. "Begin with an individual," said F. Scott Fitzgerald, "and before you know it you find that you have created a type; begin with a type, and you find that you have created—nothing." But what happens when you begin with *five* types?

Given Mark Twain's genius for piling theme-with-variations on top of theme-with-variations you arrive at a character who is relatively consistent, who manages to retain his identity through all of his varying roles. You arrive at a character who is human, unlike the type-characters of low comedy, since he can feel both mental and physical pain. You arrive at a character who is capable of a curious and highly original kind of development as he passes from the lower role to the next higher. But you do not, by any stretch of the imagination, arrive at a fully-rounded character.

It should be recognized that it is by no means easy to create a fully-rounded character for the fictional Negro. He is easily handled if you confine him to the limits of the low comedy type. And he is also easily handled if, like Harriet Beecher Stowe, you make him "the lowly," a person who is not a character in his own right but an object of the white man's character—more specifically, an object of the white man's Christian charity, a person whose chief non-minstrel characteristic is his desire for that freedom the author wishes to grant him. But if you try to make him more, he still tends to lapse into a type. Faulkner generally uses the name "Sambo" in speaking of the Negro in *Intruder in the Dust*, and even Dilsey, in *The Sound and the Fury*, is made generic by the characterization "they endured." The Negro's own attempt to discover his identity has been the central problem for the Negro author; it dominates the fiction of Richard Wright, and it is the central theme of Ralph Ellison's *Invisible Man*. But all of this is somewhat beside the point, because I do not believe that Jim's function in the novel requires that he be a fully-rounded character.

Before considering the question of Jim's function in the novel it is necessary to ask another question that has been asked many times before: why didn't Twain let Jim escape to the free states? He could have had him paddle across the river to the Illinois shore. He could have had him go up the Ohio river at Cairo. He could have sent him north when Huck found a canoe below the Grangerford plantation, just before the Duke and Dauphin came aboard. Since it was, after all, Mark Twain who made the book up, he could have sent Jim north at any point and in any manner he chose. And it would have been easy to start Jim north, since Jim's purpose is much more specific than Huck's. Huck is escaping from civilization, but the direction of that escape is, through most of the novel, a matter of supreme indifference to him. Jim is escaping from slavery in order to avoid being sold south, away from his family, and he intends to deliver his family from slavery as well. The fact of the matter is that it cost Twain a good deal of trouble, particularly at Cairo, to prevent Jim's more specific intention from dominating the novel. One can sense his relief once he gets Jim past Cairo and settled at the river's pace. And I don't think there can be any question here of Twain's not knowing what he was doing.

Huckleberry Finn is not primarily an anti-slavery novel, but certainly it is that in part, and it is my contention that letting Jim go north would spoil the anti-slavery theme and much more as well. Remember that Twain has given us, very early in the novel, a picture of the northern free Negro. In Pap's drunken tirade against the government we learn that the free Negro in Ohio is a college professor who talks all kinds of languages and knows everything, and the reader is being asked, of course, to contrast this to the situation of the Negro—and the white man—in a slave society. Now, with all due respect to Jim's virtues, including his mental ones, it must be recognized that Jim would tarnish this bright image the moment he set foot on Ohio soil. Jim is simply not college professor material.

Furthermore, how is Jim to accomplish his purpose? He intends to work and buy his family out of slavery, but he is an unskilled laborer, and he would have to save every penny for the rest of his life before he would have enough to buy one child. This could, I suppose, be made the theme of a very moving piece of fiction, but surely it is better suited to almost any other talent than Mark Twain's. Or suppose that Jim had taken the other alternative that has occurred to him, of getting an abolitionist to "steal" his family. Such a course would take us unavoidably into the realm of abolitionist ideas, and we have already seen that our narrator, Huck, is incapable of handling ideas. Twain could not report them to us without doing great violence to Huck's established character.

More important, this is a novel in which two innocents encounter every kind of viciousness and hypocrisy whenever they come in contact with society. If Twain had sent them north he would have had to face the issue of northern viciousness and hypocrisy, and surely this would have confused the anti-slavery theme. Whereas, by keeping them on the river he can admit through Colonel Sherburn that northerners have their own vices without in any way obscuring the reader's impressions of what was wrong with slave society.

Finally, and most important, this is not primarily an anti-slavery novel, nor even a novel in which two innocents encounter a corrupt society, although it is partly that. But first of all it is a novel about a boy escaping from civilization—from a civilization in which slavery is only the most conspicuous cruelty. Remem-

ber, however, that the escape is not complete. Twain referred to the book as a conflict between "a sound heart & a deformed conscience," and Huck's conscience still belongs to society. What is Jim's function in this novel? I think it is, quite simply, to be the white man's burden. I do not intend that phrase ironically. I mean that Jim's function is quite literally to be Huck's moral burden. Jim may, and does, disappear from Huck's view temporarily, but he always returns. And finally, by his constant presence, and his constant decency, and his constant humanity he forces Huck to do something more than drift with the river. He forces Huck to come to grips with that part of himself that belongs to society, forces him "to decide, forever, betwixt two things," forces him to decide to go to hell rather than betray his fellow human being. (pp. 55-8)

Chadwick Hansen, "The Character of Jim and the Ending of 'Huckleberry Finn'," in *The Massachusetts Review,* Vol. V, No. 1, Autumn, 1963, pp. 45-66.

ROBERT PENN WARREN

(essay date 1972)

[Celebrated equally for his contributions to American fiction and poetry, Warren was also an influential critic. In the following excerpt, he discusses *A Connecticut Yankee in King Arthur's Court* as a mirror of the social tensions of Twain's time and of the century that followed.]

In *The Prince and the Pauper,* a children's book laid in Tudor England, Mark Twain had . . . taken his first excursion into historical fiction. This work, which interrupted the composition of *Huckleberry Finn,* was nothing more than a piece of sentimental junk cynically devised to captivate his own children, clergymen of literary inclinations, nervous parents, and genteel reviewers, but it broke ground for *A Connecticut Yankee.* That work, however, was on the direct line of Mark Twain's inspiration; it was connected with the grinding issues of his nature, and it drew deeply on earlier work. Laid in the sixth century, in Arthurian England, it put the new American mind in contrast with feudal Europe, the remains of which the "Innocents" of the *Quaker City,* and their chronicler, had had to face on their tour. But *A Connecticut Yankee* also harks back to the contrast between the "feudal" South and the "modern" North that looms so large in *Life on the Mississippi;* it embodies not only the spirit of social criticism found in *Huckleberry Finn,* but something of Huck's pragmatic mind that always wanted to start things "fresh"; and in a paradoxical way, after it celebrates the new Yankee order of industry, big business, and finance capitalism, it also returns to the Edenic vision of Hannibal and the river found in *Tom Sawyer* and *Huckleberry Finn*.

Most deeply, however, *A Connecticut Yankee* draws on the social and personal contexts of the moment in which it was composed. At this time Mark Twain was totally bemused by one James W. Paige, the inventor of a typesetting machine which Twain was trying to organize a company to manufacture, and by which he dreamed of becoming a financial titan. Behind Hank Morgan, the Yankee, stands Paige. And, we may add, stands Twain himself, for if Hank (a superintendent in the Colt Arms Company) is an inventor (he claims that he can "invent, contrive, create" anything), he quickly becomes the "Boss"—a titan of business such as Twain dreamed of becoming.

The medieval values that Hank confronts were not confined to Arthurian Britain. For one thing, there was also present-day England, for whatever remnants had remained of an Anglophilia once cherished by Twain were now totally demolished by Matthew Arnold who, after a visit to America, had declared, in "Civilization in the United States," that the idea of "distinction" in this country could not survive the "glorification of 'the average man' and the addiction to the 'funny man.' " In his outraged patriotism and outraged *amour propre*, Twain, a "funny man," tended to merge the England of Arthur with that of Victoria.

In addition, the Romantic movement had discovered—or created—the Middle Ages, and made them current in nineteenth-century thought and art. (pp. 485-86)

This cult of medievalism had a strongly marked class element; usually it was cultivated by persons of aristocratic background or pretensions, often with an overlay of sentimental Catholicism. It was also associated with wealth, but with inherited wealth as contrasted with that, usually greater, of the new kind of capitalist; for inherited wealth, untainted by immediate contact with the crude world of business, was "genteel." It was only natural, then, that a poem like Sidney Lanier's "Symphony" and the early novels attacking business should use the aristocratic feudal virtues as the thongs with which to scourge the business man. So when Hank guns down Malory's knights in armor with his six-shooters, he is also gunning down Tennyson, Ruskin, Lowell, Lanier, *et al. A Connecticut Yankee* is, in fact, the first fictional glorification of the business man.

But Hank is arrayed not only against Sir Sagramar le Desirious and Alfred Lord Tennyson and their ilk, but also against the spectral legions of Lee, abetted by the ghost of Sir Walter Scott. (pp. 486-87)

If the anachronistically slaveholding society of Britain is an image of the Old South and if Hank's military masterpiece, the Battle of the Sand Belt, in which,

after the explosion of Hank's mines, the air is filled with the ghastly drizzle of the atomized remains of men and horses, is an image of the Civil War (the first "modern" war), then Hank's programs for Britain is a fable of the Reconstruction of the South and the pacification of that undeveloped country. Furthermore, in being a fable of that colonial project, this is also a fable of colonialism in general and of the great modern period of colonialism in particular, which was now well under way from the Ganges to the Congo; thus to Hank, Britain is simply something to develop in economic terms—with, of course, as a paternalistic benefit to the natives, the by-product of a rational modern society. In this context *A Connecticut Yankee* is to be set alongside Conrad's *Nostromo* and *The Heart of Darkness* and the works of Kipling.

There is, however, another and more inclusive context in which to regard it. More and more in our century we have seen a special variety of millenialism—the variety in which bliss (in the form of a "rational" society) is distributed at gunpoint or inculcated in concentration camps. So in this context, *A Connecticut Yankee* is to be set alongside historical accounts of Fascist Italy, Nazi Germany, or Communist Russia. This novel was prophetic. (pp. 487-88)

The body of the work has to do with Hank's operations from the moment when he decides that he is "just another Robinson Crusoe," and has to "invent, contrive, create, reorganize things." The narrative proceeds in a two-edged fashion: there is the satirical exposure of the inhuman and stultifying life in Arthur's kingdom, with the mission for modernization and humanitarian improvement, but there is also the development of Hank's scheme for his economic and political aggrandizement, his way of becoming the "Boss." By and large, it seems that the humanitarian and selfish interests coincide; what is good for Hank is good for the people of Britain, and this would imply a simple fable of progress, with the reading that techology in a laissez faire order automatically confers the good life on all. There is no hint, certainly, that Twain is writing in a period of titanic struggle between labor and capital, a struggle consequent upon the advent of big technology. In the new order in Britain there are no labor problems. The boys whom Hank had secretly recruited and instructed in technology are completely loyal to him, and as his Janissaries, will fight for him in the great Armageddon to come, enraptured by their own godlike proficiency; if they represent "labor" they have no parallel in the nineteenth-century America of the Homestead strike and the Haymarket riot.

In the fable there are, indeed, many lags and incoherences that, upon the slightest analysis, are visible. Twain had not systematically thought through the issues in his world, or his own attitudes, and he did not grasp, or did not wish to grasp, the implications of his own tale. During the course of composition he had written—in a letter of either cynical deception or confusion of mind—that he had no intention of degrading any of the "great and beautiful characters" found in Malory, and that Arthur would keep his "sweetness and purity," but this scarcely squares with the finished product. . . . And most telling of all, though *A Connecticut Yankee* was rapturously received, even by such discerning readers as Howells, as a great document of the democratic faith, and though Twain himself, sometimes at least, took it as such, Hank is not ethically superior to Jay Gould or Diamond Jim Brady in many of his manipulations. What Hank turns out to be is merely the "Boss," more of a boss than even Boss Tweed ever was, something like a cross between a Carnegie and a commissar.

There are various other logical confusions in *A Connecticut Yankee*, but one is fundamental. If the original idea of the book had been a celebration of nineteenth-century technology, something happened to that happy inspiration, and in the end progress appears a delusion, Hank's modernization winds up in a bloody farce, and Hank himself can think of the people whom he had undertaken to liberate as merely "human muck." In the end Hank hates life, and all he can do is to look nostalgically back on the beauty of pre-modern Britain as what he calls his "Lost World," and on the love of his lost wife Sandy, just as Twain could look back on his vision of boyhood Hannibal.

What emerges here is not only the deep tension in Twain, but that in the period. There was in America a tension concerning the Edenic vision, a tension between two aspects of it: some men had hoped to achieve it in a natural world—as had Jefferson—but some had hoped to achieve it by the conquest of nature. The tension, in its objective terms, was, then, between an agrarian and an industrial order; but in subjective terms the tension existed, too, and in a deep, complex way it conditioned the American sensibility from *Snow-Bound* through *A Connecticut Yankee* and Henry Adams' idea of the Virgin versus the dynamo, on through the poetry of T. S. Eliot and John Crowe Ransom, to the debased Rousseauism of a hippie commune.

The notion of the Edenic vision reminds us of *Huckleberry Finn,* for thematically *A Connecticut Yankee* is a development of that work—and the parallel in the very names of the heroes suggests the relation: *Huck/Hank.* Huck journeys through the barbarous South, Hank through barbarous Britain, both mythic journeys into a land where mania and brutality are masked by pretensions of chivalry, humanity, and Christianity. After each encounter with a shocking fact of the land-world, Huck returns to his private Eden on the river and in the end contemplates flight to an Edenic West. In other words, Huck belongs to the world of Jefferson's dream, in which man finds harmony with man in an overarching harmony of man in nature. Hank, however, is of sterner stuff. When he encounters a shocking fact he undertakes to change it—to conquer both nature and human nature in order to create a rational society.

Both Huck and Hank come to a desperate collision with reality, Huck on the Phelps farm and Hank at the Battle of the Sand Belt; but the end of the project of regeneration through technology and know-how is more blankly horrible than life on the Phelps farm, with not even a façade of humor but only the manic glee of the victors exalted by their expertise of destruction. The "human muck" has refused the rule of reason—and the prophet of reason has done little more than provide magnificently lethal instruments by which man may vent his mania.

When the book was finished, Twain wrote to Howells: "Well, my book is written—let it go. But if it were only to write over again there wouldn't be so many things left out. They burn in me. . . . They would require a library—and a pen warmed up in hell." But the pen had already been warmed enough to declare that dark forces were afoot in history and in the human soul to betray all aspiration, and with this we find, at the visceral level of fable, the same view of history later to be learnedly, abstractly, and pitilessly proclaimed by Henry Adams and dramatized in (to date) two world wars. (pp. 488-91)

Robert Penn Warren, "Mark Twain," in *The Southern Review,* Louisiana State University, Vol. VIII, No. 3, Summer, 1972, pp. 459-92.

SOURCES FOR FURTHER STUDY

Hill, Hamlin. *Mark Twain: God's Fool.* New York: Harper & Row, 1973, 308 p.

Detailed biography of the last decade of Twain's life, examining his growing bitterness and artistic difficulties.

Kaplan, Justin. *Mr. Clemens and Mark Twain: A Biography.* New York: Simon and Schuster, 1966, 424 p.

> Biography which examines conflicting elements in Twain's personality.

McMahan, Elizabeth. *Critical Approaches to Mark Twain's Short Stories.* Port Washington, N.Y.: National University Publications, Kennikat Press, 1981, 147 p.

> Collection of critical essays on Twain's short fiction, aimed at students and teachers of his work.

Paine, Albert Bigelow. *Mark Twain: A Biography; The Personal and Literary Life of Samuel Longhorne Clemens.* 4 vols. New York, London: Harper & Brothers Publishers, 1912.

> The authorized biography, which, although criticized by some scholars as biased and overly flattering to Twain, comprises the first extensive study based on Twain's papers.

Tenney, Thomas Asa. *Mark Twain: A Reference Guide.* Boston: G. K. Hall, 1977, 443 p.

> Annotated bibliography of Twain criticism. Annual supplements to the bibliography appear in the journal *American Literary Realism, 1870-1910.*

Wagenknecht, Edward. *Mark Twain: The Man and His Work.* 3rd rev. ed. Norman: University of Oklahoma Press, 1967, 302 p.

> An important biographical-critical study, which demonstrates extensive familiarity with pre-1960 Twain criticism and contains valuable footnotes and bibliographies.

Sigrid Undset

1882-1949

Norwegian novelist, short story writer, essayist, critic, biographer, poet, and dramatist.

INTRODUCTION

*U*ndset is a dominant figure among Scandinavian novelists and one of the foremost literary proponents of Christian ethics and philosophy. Her major works, the multi–volume *Kristin Lavransdatter* (1920–22) and the *Olav Aundunsson* series (1925–27; *The Master of Hestviken*), are skillfully rendered portrayals of medieval Norwegian life and have been praised as exemplary models of historical fiction, evidencing a detailed knowledge of and keen sympathy with their subject. On the strength of these works she was awarded the Nobel Prize in literature for 1928.

Born in Kalundborg, Denmark, Undset was the eldest of three daughters of Anna Charlotte Undset and the renowned Norwegian archeologist Ingvald Undset. Ingvald had come from Trondelag, an area of Norway accurately described in *Kristin Lavransdatter*. At the age of two, Undset moved with her family to the city of Christiania (now Oslo), where her father was associated with the archeological section of the University Museum. As Ingvald's health declined (he had caught malaria on an expedition to the Mediterranean), the family moved frequently, and Undset became intimately acquainted with many areas of the city of Oslo. As the daughter of an archeologist, she acquired an acute sense of history; the Undset home was filled with books, and the child was encouraged by her father to read extensively, especially works of history and Old Norse sagas. When Undset was eleven years old, her father died, and the family experienced genuine poverty.

At the age of fifteen, Undset chose to prepare for a secretarial career at the Christiania Commercial College. Her certificate from this school a year later helped her to obtain a position in the local office of the German Electric Company, where she worked for ten years. In her free time from her secretarial job, Undset turned her hand to writing. She submitted a historical novel to the Gyldendal publishing house in Copenhagen only to be told that she should turn to modern themes, which seemed more suited to her talents. Undset followed this advice, and her first contemporary social novel, *Fru Marta Oulie,* appeared in the fall of 1907. After the publication of three additional works of moderate success, Undset felt secure enough to quit her job for a full-time career as a writer. In 1909 she received a travel grant from the Norwegian government and went to Rome, where she met her future husband, the painter Anders Svarstad. Married in 1912, the couple lived first in London and later in Norway, where Undset continued to produce fiction, including *Kristin Lavransdatter.* After the births of three children, Svarstad and Undset eventually became estranged, and their marriage was annulled when she converted to the Catholic faith on All Saints' Day, November 24, 1924.

Remaining in Lillehammer, Norway, until 1940, Undset devoted herself both to her work and to her children. Maren Charlotte, who was born retarded, lived only to the age of twenty-three; Anders, Undset's eldest son, was killed in 1940 when German armies invaded Norway. With Hans, her only surviving child, Undset then made the long journey through Sweden to Russia, from there to Japan, and from there to San Francisco. During the war, she channeled her considerable energies into the war effort, giving lectures, writing propaganda, and calling attention to the plight of occupied Norway. In August, 1945, she returned to her homeland, and in 1947 King Haakon VII conferred upon her the Grand Cross of the Order of Saint Olav for service to her country. Undset died in Lillehammer on June 10, 1949.

Most of Undset's early writing was inspired by her knowledge of the working class of Oslo. *Fru Marta Oulie* is about infidelity in marriage. The novel, which is written in diary form, begins with the confession, "I have been unfaithful to my husband." Undset's only play, *In the Gray Light of Dawn,* is likewise concerned with adultery, and this theme is prominent in Undset's novels of the Middle Ages as well. Two collections of short stories, *Den lykkelige alder* (1908) and *Fattige skjebner* (1912), address problems of adolescence, motherhood, and spinsterhood in the lower economic classes of Norwegian urban society.

The novel *Jenny* (1912), which caused a sensation in Scandinavian feminist circles, is the story of a promising young artist who commits suicide. Jenny has, along the way, had an affair with her fiance's father, borne a child out of wedlock, suffered through the death of that child, and experienced frustration as a creative artist. Whether Jenny's suicide is caused by her failure as an artist or by her failure in erotic and maternal relationships remains a matter of dispute. The work is the most successful of all of Undset's social

novels with contemporary settings. Several later works also realistically treat problems of sexual fidelity and parenthood, stressing the importance of forgiveness and presenting the child as the element that can weld the most disparate parents together. Written towards the end of Undset's career, *Ida Elisabeth* (1932) presents a wife who sacrifices her personal happiness to remain faithful to her marriage vows, and *Den trofaste hustru* (1936; *The Faithful Wife*) records the disintegration of a childless marriage, though in the latter work a religious element, new to the social novels, is introduced. Through these novels Undset was placed squarely at the head of the women's movement in Scandinavia. An intelligent, creative working woman who also experienced marriage and motherhood, she could write eloquently of the problems that beset such women.

Showing a mastery of style lacking in the novels of contemporary life, *Kristin Lavransdatter* and *The Master of Hestviken,* also reveal the understanding of vanished cultures and love of the past instilled in Undset by her father. Her intimate knowledge of the laws, culture, and history of earlier ages had given her a sense of continuity and allowed her to meticulously recreate the details of medieval life.

Kristin Lavransdatter consists of three volumes, *Kransen* (*The Bridal Wreath*), *Husfrue* (*The Mistress of Husaby*), and *Korset* (*The Cross*), which chronicle the heroine Kristin's relationships with her father, her husband, and her seven sons. In the course of the trilogy Kristin learns to accept whatever destiny God inflicts on her. Here the work stresses the Medieval belief that the spiritual world has primacy over the material one, a belief with which Undset herself concurred but found lacking in most of her twentieth-century contemporaries.

Undset thoroughly researched the period of Norwegian history treated in her novel, although she deliberately chose for the setting an epoch for which sources are few. While some figures mentioned in the novel are historical (King Magnus, Erling Vidkunsson, Queen Ingibjrg), most of the characters are created; critics maintain that all are credible, and the unfolding of Undset's vast panorama is natural and effortless. The reader senses the religious nature of the fourteenth century but also the newness of Christianity. Superstition is rife, and some of the people revert to pagan sacrifice in desperation when the bubonic plague devastates the population. *Kristin Lavransdatter* contains realistic, graphic depiction of childbirth and death, of marriage and inheritance laws and customs, of religious practices, and of military and chivalrous codes of conduct. Most compelling, however, is Undset's recreation of the communal nature of life in the medieval period.

The Master of Hestviken, which stretches from

the second half of the thirteenth century to the early part of the fourteenth century, pivots around guilt and unconfessed sin. The novel's protagonist, Olav, kills a man and claims the man's son as his own. He is filled with remorse for the rest of his life, but finds himself unable to confess his crime. Margaret Mary Dunn, in her two *Scandinavian Studies* articles, contends that Olav eventually comes to realize that the greatest sin "is to despair of God's mercy." Chosen by God to bear much, the Job-like Olav thus becomes the man who "does full penance."

Whether they are set in modern times or in the Middle Ages, Undset's works explore both the importance of the family and the dangers inherent in selfish physical passion. Undset had an understanding of sensuality and a dislike of prudishness, but she also realized the risks to the psyche passion poses. As Carl F. Bayerschmidt explained, "Physical love has no rights of its own when it comes into conflict with moral and ethical laws. This is a thought which finds a constant echo in [Undset's] entire literary production." Although an emancipated woman herself, the novelist considered the natural desire of women to be for home and children and felt that a career should not be pursued instead of motherhood but only in addition to it. In her essay "Some Observations on the Emancipation of Women," the writer claimed that "the loneliest and most worn-out worker at a typewriter, in office, shop or factory, or at a sewing machine has the right to hope and wait and dream of a happiness as a lover and wife and mother."

Undset was alert to the problems of her society, and from her extensive reading and her familiarity with vanished cultures, she weighed the civilizations of the past against those of the present. She ultimately chose the medieval attitude that the individual is nothing more than a cog in a great wheel, a contributing member of clan, society, and humanity. Once Undset embraced this position, it followed naturally that she should become an articulate apologist for the Catholic church. She became the greatest moralist that the northern countries have ever produced. In accurately and forcefully evoking the medieval world, Undset sought to teach her contemporaries.

(For further information about Undset's life and works, see *Contemporary Authors*, Vols. 104, 129; *Major Twentieth–Century Writers;* and *Twentieth–Century Literary Criticism*, Vol. 3.)

CRITICAL COMMENTARY

HARRY SLOCHOWER

(essay date 1937)

[Slochower was an Austrian-born American educator and critic. In the following excerpt, he examines social and religious conflicts in *Kristin Lavransdatter*.]

Kristin Lavransdatter presents in a human and historic setting two forces at war: Pagan passion and Christian piety, embodied in the clash between Norse tradition and feudal Catholicism. In a wider sense, the story pictures the dissolution of medieval collectivism and the entry of Protestant individualism. Behind these historic currents lie fundamental conflicts between the call of the sea and attachment to the soil, between waywardness and stability. These are fought out by Kristin Lavransdatter, in her choice between surrender to a knightly, adventurous lover and marriage to a staid, conservative Northerner. It is a battle between her pagan blood and Gothic milieu. (pp. 26-7)

Kristin Lavransdatter is a profound rendering of basic human emotions. Although the novel is set in a definite period, it is not a historical novel, in the sense that the works of Scott and Tolstoy are. Undset has chosen a time when little of historic significance took place. . . . This choice of a period, in which historic happenings are unimportant, suggests the irrelevancy of the temporal factor, tends to indicate that the theme has universal and eternal import, that the issues presented are perennial.

The story of Kristin Lavransdatter is, in a sense, quite unexceptional. Joy and pain are caused by no untoward occurrences, but issue from the normal and necessary phenomena of life. The instability and hazard which operate in the life of this family, simply "happen" everywhere and always. So effective is Undset's underscoring of the inescapable difficulty of the human way, that the total impression created is of man placed in a great, wide expanse, in which unknown and treacherous winds blow, where tragic chance threatens, where nothing is certain except death, and individual frustration. The characters of this drama put up a kind of resistance; in the end, they turn, like frightened chil-

Principal Works

Fru Marta Oulie (novel) 1907

Den lykkelige alder (short stories) 1908

Fortaellingen om Viga-Ljot og Vigdis (novel) 1909
  [Gunnar's Daughter, 1936]

Jenny: Roman (novel) 1911
  [Jenny: A Novel, 1920]

Fattige skjaebner (short stories) 1912

Vaaren (novel) 1914

Splinten av troldspeilet (novellas, includes Fru Waage and Fru Hjelde) 1917
  [Images in a Mirror, translation of Fru Hjelde, 1938]

De kloge jomfruer (short stories) 1918

Kristin Lavransdatter: Kransen (novel) 1920
  *[Published in England as The Garland, 1922; published in the United States as The Bridal Wreath, 1923]

Kristin Lavransdatter: Husfrue (novel) 1922
  *[The Mistress of Husaby, 1925]

Kristin Lavransdatter: Korset (novel) 1922
  *[The Cross, 1927]

Olav Audunssón i Hestviken (novel) 1925
  [[Published in two sequential volumes: The Axe, 1928; The Snake Pit, 1929]

Olav Audunssón og hans bórn (novel) 1927

†[Published in two sequential volumes: In the Wilderness, 1929; The Son Avenger, 1930]

Gymnadenia (novel) 1929
  [The Wild Orchid, 1931]

Den braendende busk (novel) 1930
  [The Burning Bush, 1932]

Ida Elisabeth (novel) 1932
  [Ida Elisabeth, 1933]

Etapper: Ny raekke (essays) 1933
  [Stages on the Road, 1934]

Elleve aar (autobiography) 1934
  [The Longest Years, 1935]

Den trofaste hustru: Roman (novel) 1936
  [The Faithful Wife, 1937]

Madame Dorthea: Roman (novel) 1939
  [Madame Dorothea, 1940]

Tilbake til fremtiden (autobiography) 1943
  [Return to the Future, 1942]

*These novels were collected as Kristin Lavransdatter in 1929.

†These novels were collected as The Master of Hestviken in 1932.

---

dren, to run home and hide under the great white apron of their mother—the Catholic Church.

But Undset does not escape time. This is shown first by the conception of the position and the rôle of woman in *Kristin Lavransdatter.* Kristin becomes a strong woman; but she remains first and foremost a wife and a mother. Kristin's final insight that the highest self-development is impossible apart from acquiescence to one's social and religious tradition can be understood only in view of her particular milieu. Moreover, the central tragedy in the novel emerges from the transitional character of the period. The old paternal agrarianism is being challenged by a feudalism of absentee ownership and by a new economic aristocracy, the commercial bourgeoisie which arose toward the end of the thirteenth century. This new individualism of incipient Protestantism and commercialism, symbolized by Jofrid and her people, meets the old individualism of Nordic knighthood, represented by Erlend. Erlend dies, but Jofrid and Gaute go on. The existing order is shaken, the institution of the family tradition is no longer firm. Adultery and disobedience are widespread and frequent. Even Simon yielded somewhat to the new spirit when he allowed his betrothal to Kristin to be broken, and then he did something "unheard of in his kindred," wooed a widow independently of his

father's consent. Lavrans' household itself disintegrates.

Kristin Lavransdatter expresses the religious yearning for salvation through surrender. In a time when the pillars of society are crumbling, religion provides man with a feeling that he is not altogether helpless and alone. By portraying the futility of revolt, religion also helps for the "stabilization" of existing institutions. Individual revolt against social conventions is shown to result in dreadful consequences. "Disobedience," Kristin confesses at the end, "was the chief of my sins."

Undset's *Kristin Lavransdatter* is, despite its apparent medievalism, a characteristic modern expression. This appears both by implication and directly. Even though Undset argues for humility and resignation, her *art* reveals her attraction for the sinners. The presentation of young Kristin is more living than that of the older woman. Her drawing of Erlend excels that of Simon. Furthermore, while the novel purports to glorify religious piety, conformity to the godly way does *not* bring happiness to the characters. Lavrans and Simon suffer greatly, suffer more than the bohemian Erlend. Kristin's unhappiness actually *begins* with the assertion of her religious background and, what is even more significant, her very religious mood leads her to be *unjust* to Erlend. The religious attitude, instead of bringing peace and love, makes for turmoil and bitterness.

The novel pays tribute to the traditional family idea. But its overemphasis may mean that children will be ill prepared to cope with problems outside the home. In this sense, the Ragnfrids and the Lavranses as well as the Kristins are poor parents, precisely to the extent that they severely adhere to the family ideal. This absence of broader social interests also accounts for the total emptiness that enters, once the family group is broken up. After the death of Lavrans and of Erlend, their wives, Ragnifrid and Kristin, find nothing to live for. Thus, the very values championed in Undset's novel lead to frustration. It shows the irreligious consequences of religion, the disintegration of the individual members of a group through the narrowing circle of the family, the self-extinction that results from the quest for the Absolute. Kristin's last act is to "save" a dead body and the story of Kristin Lavransdatter "ends" in the Black Death.

There is another and direct aspect from which Undset's Catholic plea is modern. Protestantism was more akin to early capitalism, while Catholicism is nearer to the collectivism of developed capitalism. And divested of dogma and tie-up with business, Catholicism is close to the ideal communal spirit of socialism. As practiced by Lavrans and Kristin in her old age, Catholicism spells a sense of social responsibility for the downtrodden. . . . It should be further noted that socialist doctrine exposed only the bourgeois family as the bulwark of private property, which in turn became instrumental in the disintegration of home and family life. . . . Undset's conception of the family may be viewed as a symbolic representation of its break-up due to the modern chaos of capitalism, and her plea as compatible with and supporting the socialist conception. To be sure, in her novel, Undset presents an unreal dilemma in offering a choice between an extreme irresponsible, unconscionable individualism (Erlend) and a self-effacing collectivism (Kristin), between living for one's body and living to save dead bodies. (pp. 44-8)

[Reactionary] practices are not inherent, but extrinsic to the anti-commercial ethic of Undset's Catholicism. *Kristin Lavransdatter* ends with two men whose Christian names are almost identical, with Eilif, the priest and Ulf, the faithful servant. Both have been friends to men and servants of God. These two alone remain alive at the end, a symbolic union of matter and spirit, earthliness and godliness. Both are dear to the author. (pp. 48-9)

Harry Slochower, "Feudal Socialism: Sigrid Undset's 'Kristin Lavransdatter'," in his *Three Ways of Modern Man*, International Publishers, 1937, pp. 25-49.

ALRIK GUSTAFSON
(essay date 1940)

[Gustafson was an American authority on Scandinavian literature. In the excerpt below, he argues that the dominant theme in *Kristin Lavransdatter*, *The Master of Kestviken*, and other works is "a high morality: between the flesh and the spirit there exists a constant, intensive strife—and the spirit must eventually triumph over the flesh if man is to be good."]

Sigrid Undset is a moralist, first of all, though she is certainly not by temperament an ascetic. She has a profound, brooding awareness of the domination of the flesh in the average human life, the central place of passion in the average human destiny. To Sigrid Undset the immediate, as well as the ultimate truth about purely human life, is the central reality of sex; and in the recognition of this truth she is one with not a few of her contemporaries. Still she does not—as do some modern authors—accept the actual dominance of sex in human life as essentially a blessing, for which man must be grateful, or as a primarily constructive fact of human existence, upon which an adequate positive philosophy of life may be built. Though sex is to her of central importance, the free, natural functioning of sex is not looked upon by her as an unmixed blessing. It is, rather, simply a fundamental condition of human existence which has in it much of evil, simultaneously with some good—and man never attains the complete, the *good life* by means of it alone. Hers is, in the last analysis, a severe, a high morality: between the flesh and the spirit there exists a constant, intensive strife—and the spirit must eventually triumph over the flesh if man is to be good. This is the dominant theme of Sigrid Undset's two greatest works, the historical novels *Kristin Lavransdatter* . . . and *The Master of Hestviken* . . . , as well as her novels dealing with contemporary life which have appeared after *The Master of Hestviken;* and the theme is more or less explicit in the long series of early stories which came from her pen before the composition of *Kristin Lavransdatter*.

It is perhaps largely in consequence of such a rigid, uncompromising morality that the picture of the world which we come upon in the pages of Sigrid Undset is so heavy, so unyieldingly realistic, so essentially tragic in most of its immediate implications. (pp. 286-87)

We find in [her] early work much that is characteristic of Sigrid Undset at her greatest: a drab, severe, uncompromising realism, quite unafraid in its intensely honest depiction of those narrowly limited milieus in which her characters must live and move and have their being; a sombre, probing preoccupation with human character, for whom she reveals deep sympathies, and yet upon whom she does not hesitate to pass severe judgments; and a thoroughly unsentimental moral idealism, transforming itself by degrees—especially in the novels and short stories which come after *Jenny* . . .—into a morality increasingly affected by a profound religious instinct. All of this . . . moves again in *Kristin Lavransdatter* and *The Master of Hestviken.* In these two great historical novels, however, all of this is given a more magnificent perspective: it moves more freely, more easily, more naturally, yet without any loss of solidity, of mass, of honest, forthright realism; and it is conceived with a moral grandeur which is the mark of only the highest tragedy. But these are differences largely in degree, not in kind. (p. 299)

The bare outline of the story and the theme of *Fru Marta Oulie* [Sigrid Undset's first work] seems to suggest a very ordinary tale of modern married life enforcing a very trite and commonplace "moral." . . . [It] is not, however, quite as naïve in tone or ordinary in its manner of development as . . . its contents might suggest. . . . [In] one regard its steady, sober realism, its honest analysis of human passion, never led astray into hysterical sentimentalities or melodramatic poses—this little novel about domestic life has its own genuine fictional distinction. It is to be emphasized, moreover, that Sigrid Undset's "moralizing" in this novel is motivated neither by the repression complex of mere Puritanism nor by a timidly feminine escape psychology.

Neither in *Fru Marta Oulie* nor anywhere else in her work does Sigrid Undset seek to deny the central validity of love—even passionate love—in human life. In this respect, at least, she is sufficiently "modern." . . . Passion—Sigrid Undset insists already in her first novel—must not be denied; rather must it be subordinated to certain higher laws of being. These higher laws of being—so runs the reasoning in *Fru Marta Oulie*—have found expression in certain human institutions, particularly in the institution of the home. Later in Sigrid Undset's work we shall find her conservative moral instincts finding other than merely human authority for her conception of the sacred inviolability of the home. For the present she is satisfied with an idealism founded upon purely natural and human grounds. (pp. 302-03)

Den lykkelige Alder ("The Happy Age") [is] a volume taken up almost entirely by two short stories ["A Stranger" and "The Happy Age"] which are even more characteristic of Sigrid Undset's early years as an author than is *Fru Marta Oulie.* In a sense these stories remind one of her earlier novel; but on the whole they represent a distinct advance in narrative technique, being more vivid, more alive, and carrying their moral more naturally, less obtrusively. Both of these short stories deal with young women. . . . (p. 303)

The first of these two tales has a rather artificial plot, and it reflects at times a form of idealism that seems high-flown and forced; but the tale is saved from being a failure because of the intimately realistic study in milieu which it contains. The second—the tale which is concerned with Charlotte Hedel and Uni Hirsch— bears the stamp of living reality throughout; it remains to the present day one of Sigrid Undset's most consistently living fictional performances despite its short, concentrated *novella* form. Into the two young women's characters Sigrid Undset has poured a great deal of herself: she has not only *observed* such young women—in a sense she has *lived their lives.* She pours all of her sound, healthy natural instincts into Uni Hirsch, whose early dreams are not realized but who finally comes to find in her life certain solid human values of which her late adolescent world of romantic yearnings had never dreamed. Charlotte Hedel, on the other hand, is conceived largely in contrast to Uni Hirsch, especially toward the end of the story. She too has her dreams; but when they cannot be realized in the form which they had originally taken in her dreams she becomes a tragic victim of the eternal conflict between dream and reality. (pp. 303-04)

I cannot say that I share the almost unreserved admiration which Norwegian critics and literary historians have showered upon [*Jenny*], though it is doubtless to be ranked as the most *considerable* work of Sigrid Undset's before the publication of *Kristin Lavransdatter.* The novel employs somewhat improbable situations in order to prepare the reader for its final tragic action; it is not without episodes in a highly theatrical, even melodramatic manner; and its composition seems at times more wooden, more self-conscious than is usual even in Sigrid Undset's early work. . . . Despite these faults, however, the novel does somehow affect one: we do become intensely concerned about the destiny of Jenny—perhaps so much so that we are to an extent revolted (and *not* sentimentally) by the severe judgment which Sigrid Undset comes finally to pass upon her heroine. (pp. 305-06)

It is characteristic of Sigrid Undset that seventy pages . . . are devoted to a minute, circumstantial depiction of the horrors of the lonely, terror-filled period of [Jenny's] advanced pregnancy and childbirth and the violently tragic aftermath [of her suicide] in Rome. The novel reminds one of Guy de Maupassant's *Une Vie* in its brutal *lingering* over the sad details of the tragic dénouement. A normally precipitate tragic action is not permitted here. The reader must concentrate, with whatever patience he may have, upon a slow, steady *accumulation* of tragic detail: he must linger, all but sadistically, over the gradual stages in Jenny's final decay; he must finally come to see, always directly, never by subtle narrative implication, the "inevitability" of Jenny's tragic fate in the light of the severe ethical idealism of her earlier years. . . .

Sigrid Undset's heroines after Jenny, however, are almost without exception not tragic characters in this sense. Most of them ultimately learn to adjust themselves to life, though only after a more or less severe struggle. This is true of Rose Wegner in *Vaaren* ("Springtime" . . .), Sigrid Undset's most important work in the decade between *Jenny* and the publication of *Kristin Lavransdatter.* This is true also of most of the women characters in the two collections of short stories *Splinten av Troldspeilet* ("The Splinter of the Troll Mirror" . . .), and *De kloge Jomfruer* ("The Wise Virgins" . . .). And this is preeminently true of Kristin in *Kristin Lavransdatter.* . . . (p. 309)

It is to be noted that the moral emphasis in the stories which succeed *Jenny* becomes more pronounced with each new volume; and we find more and more that the prevailing moral emphasis in these stories becomes gradually invested with an increasingly significant religious element. In *The Wise Virgins* (the title itself is fraught with strong religious associations) the relation between religious faith and morality is clearly implied. The recurrent theme of this collection of stories is the necessity of a profound spiritual experience as the foundation for any sound, lasting love. (pp. 309-10)

Kristin Lavransdatter is certainly to be counted among the greatest historical novels of all time, and my feeling is that it ranks first among novels dealing with the Middle Ages. (p. 311)

[The] first thing that impresses us in *Kristin Lavransdatter* is the apparent *effortlessness* of the artistic performance, the seeming lack of any conscious narrative devices or tricks, the complete absence of *style* in the narrow literary sense of that word. It has been maintained by some critics, indeed, that Sigrid Undset is not an artist; and insofar as this means merely that she disdains the formal tricks of the conscious literary artist the judgment is true. She never resorts to artistic artifice; she does not pause to form her sentences with sedulous care, nor does she see any virtue in carefully turning her phrases, in searching intently for *le mot juste.* . . . Sigrid Undset's art—such as it is—simply *grows,* naturally, intensely, sometimes with strangely awkward pregnancy of utterance, out of the plentiful resources of a deeply sensitive, a profoundly serious genius. In consequence it has its faults: there are passages which might profit by greater concentration of phrasing; there are episodes which might move more swiftly, more decisively; there are details which at times might better be omitted. But by these we are only momentarily disturbed, if at all; for there is so much else in Sigrid Undset's pages to impress the reader—so much more to make him intensely conscious of the ex-

istence in *Kristin Lavransdatter* of a kind of truth in art that is more than art alone.

She has no "style," it is true—she merely *writes,* seemingly without especial care, without any particular form, yet under the marvelously sensitive intuitive guidance of an artistic spirit which has been gripped so deeply by her problem that she somehow finds the word that is appropriate, the image that is inevitable, the stylistic tempo and the narrative tone that fits the peculiar burden of her story. The secret of her art in *Kristin Lavransdatter* is to be found in the remarkable intensity, the brooding tenaciousness with which she comes to grips with her subject. (pp. 315-16)

The note is already struck in the forthright directness of the opening paragraphs in the novel; it accounts for much of the medieval idiom . . . which gives a natural color to the dialogue; it is characteristic of the incidental manner in which both historical background and natural background are employed throughout the novel; it is the secret of the leisurely tempo maintained in the novel's general narrative movement, and explains the apparently sudden intensification of this movement which we come upon in certain crucial scenes; and finally, it is present in Sigrid Undset's deliberately minute analysis of Kristin's character, and in the author's brooding awareness of the ethical values involved in Kristin's struggle with immediate circumstances and with her God. Some critics have insisted that there is nothing really natural in Sigrid Undset's almost morbid preoccupation with the general problem of evil; but this would be to insist upon a very limited conception of what constitutes "the natural." The most superficial analyses of Sigrid Undset's genius must admit that *to her,* at least, *the sombre is the natural*—to brood intently is to live deeply, strongly, completely. Though such a brooding preoccupation with the problem of evil might tend to lead other novelists to a spirit of complete disillusionment, to a sense of unrelieved, futile tragedy, even to a state of morbidity which would seem to be the opposite of the natural, it leads Sigrid Undset, in fact, to a grandeur of tragic moral conception which we have become accustomed to identify with great tragedy, with the tragic *katharsis* of the Aristotelian aesthetics. (pp. 316-17)

Sigrid Undset was guided by a marvelous artistic intuition when she placed the action of *Kristin Lavransdatter* in what one Norwegian critic has aptly called "an historical vacuum" . . . ; for our very lack of precise, detailed historical information on the period from 1320 to 1350 permits the imagination of the novelist to range freely, unobstructed by any of the rigidities of actual historical events. . . . The details of dress; foods and drink, and their preparation; household customs of all kinds; characteristic turns of speech; the manner of thinking and feeling in a still half-primitive Norwegian society;—these are the "historical materials" that are woven into the marvelously detailed and complex pattern of *Kristin Lavransdatter*. It is in this sense, primarily, that the novel is to be considered "historical." The reader is at no time particularly conscious of the actual historical precision with which Sigrid Undset handles her materials; for they are so subtly subordinated to the absorbing central motive of the novel—the story of Kristin—that they never call attention to themselves.

Natural background plays just as important a part in the novel as does historical background; but Sigrid Undset no more permits natural scene to dominate than she does the pageantry and intrigues incidental to historical episode or the numerous paraphernalia of medieval dress and custom and idiom. We are always subtly aware of the magnificent Norwegian landscape. . . . Yet natural background, impressive as it is . . . , is never described for its own sake; always it is introduced as an integral, and merely supporting, adjunct of the central action in the novel. (pp. 318-19)

She knew the Norwegian landscape with which she deals here into its minutest details. . . . Not only does she *see* these details; she *feels* their surfaces, their varied textures, with an acutely delicate and sensitive touch; she *hears* their faintest traces of sound with an ear that is marvelously alert; and, above all, she *smells* every pungent, acrid odor as well as every gentle fragrance given off by nature in her manifold sensory manifestations. And despite the careful, minutely realistic intimacy with which the reader becomes acquainted with the innumerable details of this natural background, Sigrid Undset can on occasion introduce a superb sweep, a magnificently broad perspective to her natural scene. (p. 320)

In its purely narrative movement the novel is slow, leisurely, unhurried, proceeding with a quietly deliberate solemnity, never impatient of detail, ever subtly alert to all those minute forms and phases of outward phenomena which register their impressions upon human character and human destiny. And yet this steady stateliness of general narrative movement gathers itself together at times, leaps into a blazing intensity of feeling or of action in certain individual episodes, only to recede again into its unhurried way—as unhurried as the ceaseless processes of nature and eternity and God. Suffusing it all there is a note of unutterable majesty, even of sublimity—the poignant sublimity with which a story of human fate can become invested when a profoundly unhurried artistry touches it and brings it into the delicately penetrating focus of an intensely serious creative imagination. In Sigrid Undset's work the majesty of nature combines subtly, as at times in life, with the majesty of a severely elevated moral consciousness; and her unhurried narrative movement is but the inevitable technical accompaniment of her sombre moral theme. Any other narrative tempo would be inconceivable in a story such as *Kristin Lavransdatter*.

Unhurried as the general narrative movement is, however, the story is never flat or insipid or tedious. . . . And Sigrid Undset shows herself master of a wide range of human emotions in her creation of the crucial episodes in her novel: they vary in their central motifs as well as in their use of detail, in their tempo as well as in their moods. (p. 324)

[In *Kristin Lavransdatter*] Ragnfrid's morbidly violent brooding over her secret sin—a brooding which amounted to a kind of self-immolation of the spirit—is typical of the central feminine characters almost everywhere in Sigrid Undset's novels. But in *Kristin Lavransdatter* this type of woman is developed with a relentlessly probing minuteness of psychological analysis nowhere else attained in these novels. Kristin herself is Sigrid Undset's greatest creation in this type of woman, though Kristin has her fictional prototypes in both Jenny Winge and Vigdis Gunnarsdatter. . . . Each of these women is violently intense in her inner idealisms, never capable of compromise, ever severe in judgement both upon herself and upon others. In *Jenny* this severity of judgment takes its toll primarily upon the heroine herself. In *Gunnar's Daughter* the heroine takes a fierce, thoroughly pagan vengeance upon the man who had wronged her, this despite the fact that she loved him. And in *Kristin Lavransdatter* both Kristin and Erlend must suffer because of Kristin's constant, brooding consciousness of a past sin, and her tendency, in weak moments, to hold Erlend responsible for all that had befallen her. In each case it is the heroine's inability to forget a wrong which accounts for her brooding, and for her distracted efforts to right in some way or other the wrong that had been done.

In *Kristin Lavransdatter* the type is much more convincing than in either of the earlier novels, perhaps largely because of Sigrid Undset's profoundly understanding ability to conceive of her central character over against a magnificently appropriate background—the complicated, restlessly paradoxical milieu of a relatively primitive society undergoing civilizing processes which as yet have only partially conquered the passionate brutality of an age which had but recently passed. (pp. 328-29)

Some critics have hailed the character of Kristin as Sigrid Undset's great triumph in the creation of the universal woman—a woman who, in her relation to her parents, her husband, and her children, as well as to the whole general world of moral and religious values, gives a profoundly moving expression to the noble urge supposed to exist in some form in all women of all times toward an ideal moral and religious order. In a sense, possibly, such a judgment is sound; and yet it is not the primary truth about Sigrid Undset's creation of Kristin—for Kristin Lavransdatter is, first of all, *a woman of medieval Norway.* Her unique temper, that which most immediately and most consistently attracts the discerning reader, is that she represents in her person a strong-willed, essentially pagan spirit being slowly broken—in a sense, perhaps, transformed—by the severe moral dogma of the medieval Church. In her we come to find perhaps the most profound delineation in world literature of the struggle between a Christian ethics and a pagan world.

It must be emphasized, then, that Sigrid Undset's analysis of Kristin's character is a triumph first of all in *historical* portraiture; only secondarily, if at all, is she to be considered representative of the purely hypothetical "universal woman" of which some critics have made so much. It is only if we look upon Kristin as a woman of medieval Norway that we can explain the fierce intensities of her moral brooding, the massively sombre coloring of her tragic earthly experience. (pp. 332-33)

[*The Master of Hestviken*] is even more heavy and sombre in tone and movement than is *Kristin Lavransdatter.* . . . [It] is definitely more unrelieved and dreary in its coloring, more stark in its general narrative outlines, and more relentlessly bleak in its portrayal of the inner moral struggle of its central character. (p. 346)

Only in the opening chapters is the reader given a glimpse of something fresh, buoyant, hopeful—this in the innocent youthful love of Olav and Ingunn. Brutally tragic forces lurk on every hand, however, and the charming young love idyll of Olav and Ingunn soon becomes a pathetic sacrifice to the darkling forces of violence and hatred which surround them. Before the end of *The Axe* . . . Olav has committed the sin of the flesh with Ingunn and has killed two men by violence; and yet he is a mere youth in these years, and by nature he is one who loves peace rather than violence. It is clear that the world of *The Master of Hestviken* is primarily a man's world, a world in which the moral struggle is bound to be very harsh in its outlines and in its inner complications—bleak and grim and starkly bare as a far northern landscape. (pp. 346-47)

That *Kristin Lavransdatter* is in the last analysis a greater novel than *The Master of Hestviken* must certainly be granted; but its relative greatness is hardly to be found in the fact that it is less gloomy, less essentially tragic in its final moral implications than is *The Master of Hestviken.* The latter novel is inferior to *Kristin Lavransdatter* for another reason.

The chief difficulty with *The Master of Hestviken* is that the religious dogma which determines its moralizing is entirely too obtrusive—never sufficiently subordinated to the narrative pattern of the novel. It must be admitted that *Kristin Lavransdatter* is almost equally full of long moralizing passages, which upon even cursory analysis are seen to contain formal Catholic dogma; but in *Kristin Lavransdatter* such dogma is

far more capably worked into the normal narrative processes, and so we find ourselves little disturbed by the dogmatic implications of the novel. In *The Master of Hestviken,* on the other hand, the free flow of narration is too often interrupted by the long moral homily, by a forced and definitely obtrusive religious dogma. In fact, Sigrid Undset is so intently concerned with purely dogmatic questions in this novel that she at times apparently introduces episodes merely for the purpose of providing a background or an occasion for the expression of a given dogma. (pp. 348-49)

In most respects, however, the story which is unfolded for us in *The Master of Hestviken* is quite convincing. The historical background, everywhere founded upon a minute knowledge of the times, is subordinated to the main narrative pattern with a rare intuitive power; the characters of Olav and Ingunn are revealed with that intimacy and penetration which one might expect from the author of *Kristin Lavransdatter;* the natural scene is marvelously alive and thoroughly congruous with the sombre moral theme; and the moral itself, though obtruding too obviously in certain episodes, is managed on the whole with a naturalness and power only exceeded by *Kristin Lavransdatter.* It might be added, in passing, that *The Master of Hestviken* has in it touches of humor too frequently lacking in *Kristin Lavransdatter,* though the latter novel is not entirely devoid of humor. The humor of *The Master of Hestviken* is distinctly broad, sometimes harsh and grim; but it serves admirably the twofold purpose of providing occasional bits of not unwelcome comic relief and of adding to our sense of historical illusion. (pp. 349-50)

Upon the completion of *The Master of Hestviken* Sigrid Undset returns again to the contemporary scene in a group of four novels. . . .

[*The Wild Orchid, The Burning Bush, Ida Elisabeth,* and *The Faithful Wife*] lack that sense of an immediate, pulsing physical life characteristic of her earlier, less ambitious tales dealing with contemporary life; and they fall far short of *Kristin Lavransdatter* and *The Master of Hestviken* in rich, intimate intensities of character portrayal. They deal, however, with their immediate contemporary problems in the spirit of straightforward, wholly unsentimental honesty that one has come with the years to associate with Sigrid Undset; and with all of their shortcomings as compared with Sigrid Undset's great historical novels, they are among the most important novels that have come out of Norway in the last ten years.

The chief fault of at least the first two of Sigrid Undset's late group of novels dealing with contemporary life is that they are too patently motivated by a particular religious dogma, that of the Roman Catholic Church. In the historical novels the central inclusion of religious dogma seems, on the whole, natural enough, these novels dealing with historical periods when "the Church" was coming increasingly to dominate human thought and human conduct in the North; though, as we have seen, a too intent preoccupation with dogmatic questions in *The Master of Hestviken* leads Sigrid Undset at times into serious artistic difficulties. In the later novels dealing with contemporary life, however, there seems to be far less necessity for a particular kind of religious emphasis; and it is obvious that Sigrid Undset's inclusion in these late novels of the materials of something just short of religious propaganda has resulted in a distinct falling off in the quality of these novels.

It must be said to Sigrid Undset's credit, however, that her propaganda is effective. . . . (pp. 354-55)

[Her charges] are in the last analysis to be considered only as particular phases of an aggressive frontal attack upon the whole structure of post-war materialism, whose characteristic doctrines, she insists, must be replaced by those of a dogmatic authoritarian Church if society is to survive. This becomes apparent in her late contemporary novels to anyone who reads with but ordinary discernment; and it becomes the central thesis of a series of critical essays [*Etapper: Ny raekke (Stages on the Road*)] which she has published in the two decades which followed upon the fearful cataclysm of the World War.

These essays [are] often penetrating analyses of post-war psychology and post-war politics. . . . They represent, as the titles hint, certain "stages"—or better, perhaps, "halting-places"—in Sigrid Undset's religious and intellectual development; and as such they are of first importance in any careful study of her general development as a thinker and as an artist. (pp. 356-57)

In these essays Sigrid Undset seems to have managed to shake off, at least for the moment, the narrower aspects of a purely Catholic dogma in the interests of a more inclusive, universal Christian view. In fact, she goes even farther at times, championing a kind of general religious view of life in broad opposition to certain tendencies in contemporary European national politics. (p. 357)

In her novels and essays are to be traced fairly clearly the successive steps in Sigrid Undset's religious growth. At first she developed a kind of moral idealism, which later became identified with a sort of ethical Christianity independent of church institutions or church dogma, and only finally, in the 1920's, took on a positive, specifically Catholic, form. (p. 359)

Sigrid Undset stands among the great novelists of all time. Among living novelists one is prone to rank her next to Thomas Mann. Among Scandinavian novelists she has no peer. Among women novelists she probably stands alone. (p. 360)

Alrik Gustafson, "Christian Ethics in a Pagan World: Sigrid

Undset," in his *Six Scandinavian Novelists,* 1940. Reprint by The University of Minnesota Press, 1967, pp. 286-361.

A. H. WINSNES
(essay date 1949)

[In the following excerpt from a work that first appeared in 1949, Winsnes discusses Undset as a Christian realist.]

[Sigrid Undset] does not experiment with new forms of literary expression, with a technique better fitted to grasp concrete realities, in the manner of a Virginia Woolf or a James Joyce. In this respect at least, she is old-fashioned. She carries on the tradition of the great realistic writers of the nineteenth century, Balzac, Dickens, Tolstoy, the style which began in Norway with Camilla Collett and achieved its triumph in Kristian Elster the elder, Alexander Kielland, Jonas Lie and Amalie Skram.

But she is bolder in her description of reality than were most of her great predecessors. The picture she gives of humanity, the passions, hate and love, betrayal and loyalty, the idyllic and the tragic, of the whole of life from the movement of the embryo in the womb to the withering of the body and death, from the smell of blood which a human child draws in as it comes into the world up to the highest forms of conscious existence—all this is presented by her without a trace of romantic idealisation or artificiality. Few writers have seen deeper into the unpleasantness of life, into mankind's destitution and wretchedness. (pp. 2-3)

Mrs Marta Oulie [(*Fru Marta Oulie*)] is written in the form of a diary, but it cannot be said to have a confessional character. An individual stamp is given to this remarkable first work . . . by the detached presentation, the cool objectivity, which nevertheless grips the reader. In the retrospective entries in this journal, almost in the same way as in the dialogue of a play by Ibsen, the curtains are drawn back to reveal the past and to enable us to follow step by step the belated self-realisation of the unfaithful wife. (p. 38)

The Happy Age [(*Den lykkelige alder*)] is the most sensitive piece of writing about girlhood that has ever appeared in Norwegian,—at the same time it is nearest to reality. These young women have a certain coolness and reserve, but these lie only on the surface, and are no more than the shield which covers the warmth imprisoned within. Casual love-affairs are not much heeded in the milieu of lodging-houses and rented rooms in which they live. But these girls are so constituted that they cannot regard them so lightly, whether their attitude is natural in them or depends on the inheritance they have brought with them from their homes. As Sigrid Undset writes of one of them, there is something in them which makes any stain show up clearly not only to others but, above all, to themselves. They are not prudish, but they live with the dream of something worthy of complete surrender, something which will demand their faith utterly and absolutely. (p. 43)

Jenny, like *Mrs Marta Oulie,* is also a kind of *roman expérimental.* Its tone is quite different, however, since in *Jenny* the author experiments with the possibilities lying within herself, and in making them actual she identifies herself with their extension into reality. In consequence, the novel has the character of a confession. Jenny belongs with the young women in *The Happy Age,* related not so much to Edele Hammer and Uni, both of whom succeed at last in making a compromise between their dreams and reality, as to Charlotte Hedels, who could find no object for her consuming longing and took her own life.

It is Charlotte's story which is told in new and profounder form in *Jenny,*—a love-story, sordid and unpleasant, but with a brilliance lent to it by Italy, Rome and the Campagna, by the life which blossoms in it, by the writer's joy in art and nature, and by the dream which comes true. (pp. 52-3)

There is not only the sheen of Italy over *Jenny;* one also finds occasionally a supernatural element. This is due to Jenny herself, for the foundation on which her character is built is her inherent religious nature. She is in fact intensely religious, longing to serve someone she sets higher than herself. But she does not believe in God. If she has faith in anything, it is in herself and her own strength. How far will that carry her?—that is the theme of the book. (p. 53)

Jenny is one of the most distinctive women characters in Norwegian literature. It would not seem out of the way to compare her to Ibsen's Nora and Gunnar Heiberg's Karen. . . . Jenny is no less exacting in her demands than Nora and Karen, but it is always on herself in the first place that those demands are made. It is not simply that she is more intelligent than they—there is in her a spiritual ferment, a more highly developed consciousness, with which Nora and Karen are unacquainted. (pp. 55-6)

The new elements in Sigrid Undset's writing in the years immediately following *Jenny* do not make themselves evident in any obvious or demonstrative fashion. The material in [*Poor Fortunes* (*Fattige skjaebner*), *Spring* (*Vaaren*), *The Splinter of the Magic Mirror* (*Splinten av troldspeilet*), and *The Wise Virgins* (*De kloge jomfruer*)] is on the whole the same as before—the reality of everyday life, with characters drawn chiefly from the middle-classes in Oslo. But to some extent, the attitude towards the material is different. The tone of personal confession, which often breaks through in her earliest writing, is now rarely heard, and when heard is damped down and restrained. The presentation of a story may now take on a retrospective character. On the whole, her material now seems to have been set at a greater distance. The intensity may be less, but not the fervour of her mind, not the sympathy and clearsightedness. There may be keen and clever satire, as in the descriptions of poor souls like Selma Brótter and Miss Smith Tellefsen, but there is satire too of the tenderest kind, where it trembles on the verge between tears and laughter, as in the masterly short story *Simonsen,* where the dissonances of life are resolved in a humour closely related to that of Dickens.

A love-story forms the theme of her great novel, *Spring,* as it does in other of her books. But the history of the child-love of Torkild Christiansen and Rose Wegener, their engagement and marriage, the collapse of that marriage and its resurrection, is related from a clearly conscious social point of view. *Spring* is essentially a social novel, and the story of Torkild and Rose and the people around them is used to throw light on a concrete social phenomenon—the home. All the characters are seen in relation to the homes from which they come, and they are explained, tried and judged, according to their ability to shoulder the responsibilities which the home, as the protocell of the life of society and of all higher culture, thrusts upon them. (pp. 67-8)

Closely related to *Spring* is *The Splinter of the Magic Mirror*. . . . It consists of two stories, one called *Mrs Hjelde,* the other *Harriet Waage,* though it is not by accident that the two are set side by side in the same volume. . . . The essential fact is that the two women, each in her own way and in quite sharp contrast to the other, are illustrations of the same case. Each of them has a splinter of the magic mirror in her eye—the mirror which, according to Hans Andersen, made people see everything crooked and distorted. (pp. 70-1)

The three stories in *The Wise Virgins* deal with characters from a more ordinary background. Here, as elsewhere, it is the common stuff of humanity that Sigrid Undset wishes to grasp, the instincts, needs and desires which may appear differently under different circumstances, but which remain essentially the same. The lives of the servant-girl, Helene Johansen, the dressmaker Fanny Erdahl, Klara in the factory and Emma in the milk-shop, are different in their externals from the lives of Mrs Hjelde and Mrs Waage. Nevertheless, where something primary like the sexual life is concerned, they belong to the same human family. Some women feel their sex as an impulse to live for someone else; others feel it as something which gives them the right to live on someone else. But splinters of the magic mirror have not perhaps reached so many of those who live in the milieu described in *The Wise Virgins.* All three stories are variations on the same theme of mother and child. The development of the theme in *Tjodolf* is masterly. The story of Helene Johansen's love for a little child she has taken to herself but must give up again, is one of Sigrid Undset's loveliest pieces on the theme of mother-love. It is built up with an eye to the effect of contrast, but there is nothing schematic or artificial about it. The opposition between the frivolous Fanny Erdahl, the real mother of the child, and the steadfast Helene, has the same solid basis in living reality as the opposition between Harriet Waage and Uni Hjelde in *The Splinter of the Magic Mirror,* or between the homes of Torkild Kristiansen and Rose Wegener in *Spring. Tjodolf* is more than a deeply moving and pathetic story: it bears the stamp of greatness, because in a flash it gives us insight into a mother's love, the love which in the psychic organism of this one human being is the very thread of life.

Some critics spoke scornfully of the moral messages in *Spring, The Splinter of the Magic Mirror* and *The Wise Virgins.* But this is not moralising literature—a better name for it would be literature about moral values and moral heroism. (pp. 73-4)

Sigrid Undset is in a special position. In none of

Portrait of Undset by A.C. Svarstad, Rome, 1911.

the other writers of the period do we find such a fundamental revolt against the materialist interpretation of life, with a criticism of contemporary culture so firmly based in point of principle and inspired by so clear a religious ideal. This applies both to her controversial and historical writing between the wars and to the novels of contemporary life which she also wrote in this period, particularly *The Wild Orchid* (*Gymnadenia*) and *The Burning Bush* (*Den broendende busk*). (p. 155)

She is no less a realist than before, and no less a realist than other contemporary Christian novelists, like François Mauriac and Georges Bernanos in France and Graham Greene and Evelyn Waugh in England. But, once again, she must be placed in a separate category. The psychological penetration of a writer like François Mauriac, for example, fastens above all on the evil in man and his wretchedness without grace. In this series of her modern novels, Sigrid Undset is chiefly occupied with man's inherent tendency towards truth and virtue. Sin and the sense of guilt, remorse and penitence, which were vital elements in the medieval novels, continue to play an important part, but another aspect also claims attention. In the medieval novels we meet the Augustinian type of Christianity. In the story of the conversion of Paul Selmer, in *The Wild Orchid* (*Gymnadenia*) and *The Burning Bush* (*Den broendende busk*), we find another type, which the French philosopher, Etienne Gilson, calls Thomist. (pp. 175-76)

These books contain some biting satire. It tends to be somewhat stylised when it is aimed at the Protestant clergy, especially the liberal theologians; but it is mercilessly accurate when it touches such things as the boom-mentality, baseness and superficiality, which prevailed amongst large social groups in Norway during the first World War. Equally sure and unsparing is her exposure of the self-satisfaction and fatuity of the un-Christian middle-class, or, as in *Ida Elisabeth,* her exposure of idealistic self-deception and the "nature-idyll".

The satire remains of minor significance, and here, as elsewhere, her greatness lies in her powers of self-identification with ordinary people. She had possessed that faculty from the beginning, but her ability to share in the life of others has perhaps never extended so far as in her portrayal of such "anonymous" characters as Lucy Sippen in *The Wild Orchid,* Ida Elisabeth in the novel which bears her name, and Nathalie in *The Faithful Wife* (*Den trofaste hustru*). This activity of her imagination has gained new strength from the Christian attitude, which conditioned the creation of these novels. (p. 176)

The novels, [*Ida Elisabeth* and *The Faithful Wife*] . . . , mark a new departure in Sigrid Undset's realistic treatment of modern life. In none of her other books is the everyday quality of both material and method so intimately connected with the whole idea of the novel and its artistic unity. Nevertheless,—or perhaps for this very reason—women characters like Ida Elisabeth or Nathalie in *The Faithful Wife* are endowed with monumental greatness. . . . Their greatness is revealed in their relationship to the common round of life. They neither flee from it nor are they swallowed up by it. They are loyal souls, and extract gold from the dross of everyday life. In a chaotic world, they stand for something stable; while the world totters on its supports, we find in them that which, in the final count, holds everything together. The art which portrays Ida Elisabeth and Nathalie is as far removed as can be from the art which idealises and embellishes, but in these characters we are given a glimpse of the eternally feminine, the prototype of womankind, in the Christian sense. (pp. 194-95)

Although the religious idea is the essential impulse in both these novels, it does not appear with such clarity and directness as in *The Wild Orchid* and *The Burning Bush*. Their construction depends on the opposition between those fundamentally different adjustments which a person can make to life—the natural on the one hand, the supernatural on the other—the antithesis, that is, between man's ineradicable need of the transcendental and that other view of life, which sees human beings as citizens only of this world. (p. 195)

In form *Ida Elisabeth* and *The Faithful Wife* are ordinary realistic novels of married life. The method is basically the same as in the experimental novel of the Zola school. But the Christian experimental novel certainly comes to very different conclusions from those of the naturalistic type. The Christian outlook counts on man's freedom. It is perhaps for that reason that the poetry does not fade away, and one feels it throughout as an undercurrent, a vital source, or as an effluence permeating the whole. Latent in these two novels is a hymn in praise of the ideals of virginity and Christian marriage and in honour of the traditional Christian institution of the family. (p. 204)

In Norwegian literature, *Eleven Years* [(*Elleve aar*)] is a unique volume of memoirs, recollections of past life which have their origin in a mental process of the kind described by Henri Bergson in *Matière et mémoire*. He calls it *mémoire pure*—memories which can well up when some chance sensation sets in motion a mental life which has, as it were, lain dormant. (p. 205)

With all its concrete objectivity and despite the absence of "the intoxicant of recollection", *Eleven Years* is none the less a work of the creative poetic imagination, and it is this which makes it such a remarkable study of child-psychology. An academic psychologist can observe and describe the same facts about a child, but only a writer has the power to fit them into a real and concrete whole, the complete context of which they form part, and then interpret them in rela-

tion to this totality. We see the child's world come into being: the intense egotism, contact with an outside world, dawning awareness of things and people and of an external will which interferes and against which revolt is made. We see the reactions, negative and positive, towards parents and towards reprimand and punishment; the world of religious ideas which is built up; the first acquaintance with sex; and the child's instinctive reaction against being prematurely snatched out of its feeling of security by adults. We see all the small events, in themselves insignificant, which can make a child intensely happy or intensely unhappy, the wounds which may never heal in a whole lifetime. And finally we see the home as a living organism, an integrating unit, where almost imperceptibly the child learns to understand what it is that gives substance to life. (p. 207)

[Sigrid Undset] sees isolated man's need for fellowship and his desperate attempts to find the communal solidarity, without which he cannot live. As no other contemporary writer, she has laid bare, in all its crying nakedness, the pseudo-liberalism of the nineteenth century and every form of irresponsible individualism. But she has been equally caustic and merciless in unmasking and branding the collective movements into which rootless modern man has flung himself in order to escape from his isolation. For this very reason, she is in a position to present the fellowship which does not engulf the individual but liberates him—Christian universalism. (p. 248)

In an age which was moving generally towards an anthropocentric philosophy of life, an age in which men were adopting the cult of self-worship, she declared the eternal message of religion—*Soli Deo Gloria*—and created one of the great monuments of our literature to stand high over the spiritual pilgrim-path of man. (p. 250)

A. H. Winsnes, in his *Sigrid Undset: A Study in Christian Realism*, translated by P. G. Foote, Sheed & Ward, 1953, 258 p.

JAMES WALTER McFARLANE
(essay date 1960)

[McFarlane is an English editor and critic. In the following excerpt, he argues that Undset's conversion to the Roman Catholic faith serves as "a kind of axis of symmetry" for her pre- and post-1924 works.]

It is the endless and seemingly effortless stream of realistic detail that is the first conspicuous quality of [Sigrid Undset's] work. At bottom, it is the realism of a diagnostic report, drafted in great elaboration with the earnest purpose of assisting the individual to a greater awareness of himself, the whole then powerfully enriched by the concentrate of years of minute observation and dedicated historical study. . . . Indeed the term 'realism', in its application to Sigrid Undset, is one of rich contradiction: the observed detail of her contemporary world, the grey and sombre setting for those characters whose longings are frustrated by routine work and financial cares, seems to possess all the poetic precision of an imaginative reconstruction; whilst the studied detail of the medieval works is shot through with all the vividness one might expect from an observer's report.

But all the apparently inexhaustible detail of 'landscape', of setting, of milieu, however integral it is to the purpose and direction of the novels, remains subsidiary to their moral purpose. It provides a background, it sets up a backcloth, it marks out an arena, against which and within which are performed a series of moralities. Each individual novel is disposed about a moral and religious axis in a fashion reminiscent of the way in which the whole corpus of Sigrid Undset's work is arranged about her year of decision—1924, the year of her conversion to the Roman Catholic faith. It is not merely that her decision was taken at very nearly the mid-point of her adult life; rather it is the astonishing way in which the one half of her work presents what is very nearly a mirror image of the other, with the fact of her conversion standing to the design of her life as a kind of axis of symmetry. Immediately to either side of it come the two first-magnitude, historical works, *Kristin Lavransdatter* . . . and *The Master of Hestviken*. . . . Flanking these are the two groups of 'contemporary' narrative works: the three novels and four volumes of short stories she published between 1907 and 1918; and the four, rather more confessionally inspired, modern novels that belong preponderantly to the 'thirties. And ultimately, providing yet further reinforcement for the idea of symmetry, one remarks the two other historical 'outriders', stationed thirty years apart and equidistant from her conversion, [*Gunnar's Daughter (Fortoellingen om Viga-Ljot og Vigdis)* and *Madame Dorthea*]. . . . (pp. 158-59)

The change [in Undset's work] from 'contemporary' to 'historical' [novels], the displacement of the action from the twentieth to the fourteenth century that came with *Kristin Lavransdatter* was essentially a technical change, on a par with the change in scale; . . . the characters in it, like those in her 'modern' works, are embodiments of a humanity and a human frailty that is timeless. The basic texture is the same; and if there seems at times a greater colourfulness in contrast to the earlier greyness, it is rather the lighting that has changed, and not the weave—like sackcloth illumined by stained glass. Some moments hint at the sagas, some of the linguistic elements of her style have a medieval-

ism that is occasionally just a little indiscreet. But the realism is that of an author quite evidently much more at home in the chronicle than in, say, the *Novelle.* Her realism exploits the arrangement of mass detail rather than the economical selection of significant, and regards elaborateness itself as something inherent in life which, if subject to too severe a selective process, inevitably suffers distortion. (p. 162)

The emphasis in the design of [*Kristin Lavransdatter*] rests on the relations between individuals rather than on the qualities of the individuals themselves; and there is built up a network of relationships in which Kristin herself is the central and co-ordinating element. In one respect the trilogy serves as a disquisition on woman's loyalties: on the one hand, those which her menfolk importunately claim, her father, her husband and her sons; and on the other, those absolute loyalties she owes to God. It traces the consequences which this multi-dimensional conflict of claims has upon her life, upon her standards of conduct, her sense of integrity and self-respect; it considers how these claims often merge with other factors, the calls of instinct and impulse and desire, the dictates of will and conscience. It examines the nature of the accessory phenomena of sin and guilt and remorse, making a boldly patterned design, in which the pieces belong together with all the digressionary consistency of an individual life. The progression of the narrative through childhood and early maturity to adulthood, parenthood and age has the rhythm of organic growth, in which each moment has a significance and each stage a meaningfulness quite apart from its relevance to the ultimate design of things. Sigrid Undset is not concerned merely to complete her narrative pattern, but is intent on examining her theme at each stage in its development, and on demonstrating the consequential changes that occur in the total design with the advent of each new motif. (pp. 164-65)

Sigrid Undset, like her heroines, betrays an interest in stability that is almost obsessive. (p. 165)

[The] defining characteristic of her early heroines was an unstable equilibrium as they crossed and recrossed the frontiers of respectability and disrepute, living between self-discipline and self-indulgence, between the observance of traditional decencies and the wilful pursuit of pleasure. Furthermore, it was the tampering with this situation that seems to make the later batch of 'contemporary' novels less of an artistic than a devotional expression. Sigrid Undset's conversion marked the completion of a process whereby her earlier scepticism of 'received' views found solace in the acceptance of dogma. . . . The artistic consequences were what D. H. Lawrence would not have hesitated to call 'immoral': 'Morality in the novel is the trembling instability of the balance. When the novelist puts his thumb in the scale, to pull down the balance to his own predilection, that is immorality.' (p. 168)

James Walter McFarlane, "Sigrid Undset," in his *Ibsen and the Temper of Norwegian Literature*, Oxford University Press, London, 1960, pp. 158-68.

KIRSTEN WISLØFF ANDRESEN
(essay date 1983)

[In the excerpt below, Andresen discusses Undset's presentation of women in her novels.]

Antifeminist! Reactionary! When words like these are used about a woman writer's opinions of women, we're astonished. What kind of woman would reject her own sex? Then, when we hear that the same writer believes women do not, in the least, take a backseat to men in ability and talent, but that women are capable of doing anything men can do just as well as men, we are again astonished. This is neither antifeminist nor reactionary. Quite the opposite. How is this dichotomy possible? Our curiousity is awakened, and it grows as we realize we are talking about a major author, one of the very few women to receive the Nobel Prize for Literature, the Norwegian Sigrid Undset. It is 100 years since Sigrid Undset's birth. Her memory, her books, are being reappraised, and this gives us a golden opportunity to examine what lies behind the conflicting viewpoints about her opinions of women. How did she really look upon woman's place in society?

In a memorial year we justifiably ask ourselves: do we remember this writer just for the memory, or do these books have something to give people in our modern and complicated world? Perhaps we become even more skeptical when we hear that Sigrid Undset received the Nobel Prize for Literature for historical romances set in the 1300's in Norway, 600 years back in time. What has this to do with us today?

The popularity and acknowledgement accorded the books about Kristin Lavransdatter in part speaks for itself. They are translated into innumerable languages, and they command interest the world over. This proves they are not just a limited description of Norwegian country life in the Middle Ages. These are books concerned with the "everyman" themes of life and death, of love and hate, doubts and beliefs and life's meaning in earthly and heavenly perspective. The descriptions are so alive and familiar that we recognize ourselves across the span of time. They are so earthy and realistic we feel as if we are facing a shared reality. The work about Kristin justly stands as a masterpiece. The searchlight which here examines the problems of life has such depth and universality that it is entirely relevant to modern life.

It is essential to establish that Sigrid Undset's purpose in utilizing an historical theme was precisely that of saying something general and timeless about human life. Her conviction was that although time changes, that which is innermost in the human does not change. Below the layers of actions, settings and customs belonging to each we will find an unchangeable core. Humans love and hate today as they did in the Middle Ages. They make mistakes, they hurt each other, they regret and they try to understand the meaning of life. Therefore Undset's characters have something in common regardless of whether she places them in the Middle Ages or in her own time. For this reason we remind ourselves that although it is for her historical works that Sigrid Undset is best known, nevertheless she is describing people from our own time in most of her books.

Sigrid Undset was particularly interested in women, and she gives realistic descriptions of countless different women, descriptions marked by great psychological insight and understanding. The women we meet through Undset are seldom soft and obedient. It is no exception when Kristin develops as strong and resourceful, while her husband, Erlend, despite his high position in society, shows a weaker and more tender nature. Nevertheless, the strong woman is not a fixed pattern in Sigrid Undset's books. She does not follow a formula for men and women. There are strong women and weak women, hard women and soft, those who cannot cope with life and knuckle under, and those who surmount their difficulties and live full, rich lives using the experiences only life can give. There are bitter women full of hate and revenge and women full of concern and thoughtfulness. As in life itself, Undset's books take in the whole spectrum of women—and of men. Throughout her fiction we find the same theme we find in Sigrid Undset's articles: woman is just as well endowed as man, she was not meant, by nature, to be a special carrier of 'soft' values. Differences of this sort are culturally and socially conditioned. There is not a trace of antifeminism. Even today this is a progressive view of women.

Attacks against Sigrid Undset's attitude toward women are directed at her having said that a woman can never achieve anything better than being a good mother nor anything worse than being a bad mother. A woman's most important contribution in life is precisely in being a mother. It is here that those who fight for women's rights prepare for battle today—exactly as they did in Sigrid Undset's own time. But let us pause before we speak out and try to take in *why* she expresses this viewpoint in light of her expressed belief in the equality of the sexes.

The point is not to downgrade women, nor is it

paying homage to the myth of the good, soft mother. Sigrid Undset believes that a woman has a natural feeling for her child, but she doesn't believe it necessarily breaks forth in a woman with the baby's birth. In certain instances it can be so repressed that it fails to perceptively manifest itself. She portrays women who set their newborn baby out to die. Here, too, maternal instinct has a latent dimension. This maternal instinct is, however, not identical with a vocation for mothering. As in all other human characteristics, the ability to mother is unequally distributed among women. When Sigrid Undset strongly emphasises woman's role as mother, it isn't something she justifies with feelings, but something which springs from her *social conscience.*

The industrial expansion was beginning to completely change society. Materially, conditions were becoming much better and people looked favorably upon the changes. But Sigrid Undset saw them as alarming. She was concerned that because of the human aspects in society there would be losses accompanying the development. Efficiency and success are the basic supports of this industrial culture. Professional success brings happiness. Profit is the key word in the motivation of this expansion. Sigrid Undset sees this culture as being the product of man's thinking and developed on man's premises. If we pay homage to the ideals built upon here, we lose important aspects of human ethics. When profit is most important will humane principles be sacrificed to calculation? Will it pay? This leads easily to people becoming pawns in other people's games. It is this commercialization of humans, the backside of the coin called progress, which bothers Sigrid Undset. It is an early criticism of the industrial society we see here, and it is in this context we must view Sigrid Undset's outlook on the meaning of the role of mother.

The women's movement fights to free women from traditional female roles: women should be equal with men in new social developments, they should be able to fulfil themselves professionally and not be fenced in or bound by man or child. But in the fight to free women from the home Sigrid Undset sees society getting tougher, and women adapting themselves in this manner to the industrial society. For everyone to be a wage earner does not mean women's emancipation. Sigrid Undset does not deny that some women—and men—develop themselves to capacity within their work. But she finds fallacious the statement that women can realize themselves at an assembly line in a factory. If women live by industrial society's values the loss will be in human terms, it will be a society where there is no room, or compassion, for groups that are not productive. Such a society will be poor in terms of human values. Children, who may feel like a hindrance today, are society's greatest richness because they represent the future. Child–raising is the most important assignment in society—much more important than what some men use to fill their lives. This is what the women's movement has forgotten. Instead of seeing their own worth, they have accepted the industrial society's values which are based on profit and production.

The mother's role, as Sigrid Undset sees it, has nothing to do with feelings or pampering. It is an occupation which completely demands each woman. It is a work demanding wiles and imagination, insight and understanding, consideration and care. It has such high priority that perhaps it can demand that one give up one's happiness. The goal is to shape adult, responsible people who can become the backbone of tomorrow's society. The importance of this cannot be minimized.

To give up one's own search for fulfilment to be a mother seems a hindrance to many. Sigrid Undset felt it was exactly the ability of people to set their own wishes aside in order to advance others that was the enduring strength in a society.

Today we might resist the idea Sigrid Undset had that children are a woman's task. She felt that because the woman nursed the baby this was a natural division of labor. But whatever our viewpoint on this question, we cannot avoid Sigrid Undset's warning about the development of society, which is central to her thinking. Perhaps we believe men should share in child-raising. Even so we must heed Sigrid Undset's emphasis on the importance of this work and her stress on the danger of being carried away by the industrial profit motive. Yes, perhaps her cautionary analysis is even more important now, when we see—more clearly than in her time—the weaknesses of the industrial society. We can see how intuitively Sigrid Undset foresaw the problems and that this insight clearly validates her writing and thinking for us today, 100 years after her birth. (pp. 12-15)

Kirsten Wisløff Andresen, "Woman's Place," in *Sigrid Undset,* edited by Carl Henrik Grøndahl, DYADE, 1983, pp. 12-15.

SOURCES FOR FURTHER STUDY

Bayerschmidt, Carl F. *Sigrid Undset.* New York: Twayne, 1970, 176 p.

> Concise critical biography.

Beach, Joseph Warren. "Variations: Sigrid Undset." In his *The Twentieth Century Novel: Studies in Technique,* pp. 263-72. New York: Appleton-Century-Crofts, 1932.

> Analyzes the narrative devices that structure the chapters in Undset's novels.

Brunsdale, Mitzi. *Sigrid Undset: Chronicler of Norway.* New York: St. Martin's Press, 1988, 160 p.

> Thematic survey of Undset's works.

Larsen, Hanna Astrup. "Sigrid Undset: Modern Works" and "Sigrid Undset: Medieval Works," in *The American-Scandinavian Review.* Vol. XVII, Nos. 6 & 7, June and July, 1929, pp. 344-52, 406-14.

> Compares Undset's novels set in Medieval Norway with those set in the present.

Vinde, Victor. *Sigrid Undset: A Nordic Moralist.* Seattle, Wa.: University of Washington Book Store, 1930, 37 p.

> Brief critical biography, focusing on Undset's moral themes.

Whitehouse, J. C. *Vertical Man: The Human Being in the Catholic Novels of Graham Greene, Sigrid Undset, and Georges Bernanos.* New York: Garland Publishers, 1990, 227 p.

> Discusses freedom, sexuality, religion, and morality in Undset's novels.

John Updike

1932-

(Full name John Hoyer Updike) American novelist, critic, short story writer, poet, essayist, and dramatist.

INTRODUCTION

A major contemporary American author, Updike is particularly noted for the subtle complexity of his fiction, verse, and criticism. His values derive from myth and Christianity and are evidenced in his work by his emphasis upon morality. Updike's major subject since the mid-1960s has been the domestic life of the American middle class and its attendant rituals: marriage, sex, and divorce. Against the mundane setting of American suburbia and in concurrence with his interpretation of the ideas of philosopher Søren Kierkegaard and theologian Karl Barth, Updike presents average people—usually men—searching for aesthetic or religious meaning in the secular awareness of their own mortality. Updike stated that his books center upon "insolvable dilemmas," and the dialectical tension in his work is often the result of the struggles of his characters to determine what is morally right in a constantly changing world.

In 1954, Updike graduated *summa cum laude* from Harvard University. He soon began contributing stories, poems, and criticism to *The New Yorker* and served as a reporter for the magazine's "Talk of the Town" column from 1955 to 1957. Although Updike left *The New Yorker* to pursue his literary career, he has regularly published fiction, verse, and criticism in the magazine; much of this work has been collected in numerous volumes. Updike's first major work, *The Carpentered Hen, and Other Tame Creatures* (1958), contains poems that whimsically attack such topics as modern values, sports, and journalism. Critics particularly praised "Ex-Basketball Player," discerning in Updike a talent for the exacting rhyme and meter associated with light verse. Reviewers warmly praised Updike's second volume of poetry, *Telephone Poles, and Other Poems* (1963), in which he blends wry wit with esoteric reflections. The title poem of *Midpoint, and*

Other Poems (1969) is considered Updike's most experimental work of verse. In this piece, he makes use of photographs and typography to reflect upon his life up to age thirty-five. Updike called "Midpoint" both "a joke on the antique genre of the long poem" and "an earnest meditation on the mysteries of the ego." *Tossing and Turning* (1977) secured Updike's reputation as a master of light verse. This volume examines such topics as suburbia, middle age, and the illusory nature of success. *Facing Nature* (1985) also elicited praise. The alternately humorous and serious reflections in this collection prompted comparison to the verse of W. H. Auden.

Updike's early short fiction, collected in *The Same Door* (1959), earned him a reputation as a leading practitioner of the short story form. Most of Updike's early stories are set in the fictional town of Olinger, which he modeled after his hometown of Shillington, Pennsylvania. Small-town concerns are the subject of Updike's second short story collection, *Pigeon Feathers* (1962), which addresses adolescent anxieties regarding love, marriage, and children. Further tales of small-town life are collected in *Olinger Stories* (1964). In the mid-1960s, the fictional Boston suburb of Tarbox largely replaced Olinger as Updike's setting, reflecting his actual move from New York City to Ipswich, Massachusetts. The stories set in Tarbox feature sophisticated, urbanized individuals whose marital problems and quests for identity mirror the social anxieties of their times. Tarbox is the setting of *Bech: A Book* (1970), in which Updike introduces his alter ego, Henry Bech. A Jewish bachelor and writer who fears the commitments of marriage and success, Bech aims in these stories to "confess sterility"—to demonstrate how authors betray their integrity for monetary or fashionable reasons. In *Bech Is Back* (1982), another collection of short stories, Bech concludes thirteen years of insecurity and writer's block by getting married and by writing an offensive, best-selling novel. Despite his success, however, his old fears return and his marriage ends in divorce. In *Too Far to Go: The Maples Stories* (1979), a husband and wife separate in mutual friendship. The moral of these stories, according to Updike, "is that all blessings are mixed." *Problems, and Other Stories* (1979) also centers on domestic conflicts. Updike received an O. Henry Award in 1966 for his story "The Bulgarian Poetess."

Updike's first novel, *The Poorhouse Fair* (1959), established his reputation as a major novelist. Set in Olinger, the book centers on the intense rivalries between elderly members of a poorhouse, who are permitted to stage an annual fair by a bureaucracy insensitive to their greater needs. Interpreted as an attack on behavioristic psychology and the welfare state, *The Poorhouse Fair* elicited a diverse critical response. D. J. Enright proclaimed it "a perfect little cameo of old age." Updike's second novel, *Rabbit, Run* (1960), is among his best-known and most widely analyzed works. This book explores the prolonged adolescence of an inarticulate working-class father and husband who misses the excitement of his high school years as a basketball star. Fearing responsibility, middle age, and an unhappy marriage, Harry "Rabbit" Angstrom seeks escape in an extramarital affair before realizing that "there can be achievement even in defeat." Updike wrote three sequels to *Rabbit, Run,* each reflecting a new decade in Rabbit's life. *Rabbit Redux* (1971) mirrors the unrest of the late 1960s, this time centering on the threat posed to Rabbit's marriage when he brings home a young drug addict and a black revolutionary. Critical reaction to the book was largely negative, but reviewers were nearly unanimous in their praise of *Rabbit Is Rich* (1981), for which Updike received the National Book Critics Circle Award, the American Book Award, and the Pulitzer Prize. A quiet tone of acceptance permeates this work, in which Rabbit, middle-aged and basically content with his marriage, must resolve his feelings regarding his daughter's death and his own mortality. The final book of the Rabbit tetralogy, *Rabbit at Rest* (1991), also won the Pulitzer Prize and the National Book Critics Circle Award. In this bleak novel, Rabbit, now 55 and grossly overweight, is forced to come out of retirement to work at the family Toyota dealership while his son Nelson, who formerly ran it, enters a drug rehabilitation program. Nelson's cocaine addiction has nearly brought personal and financial devastation to the Angstroms. Much of this work focuses on Rabbit's physical deterioration—his overeating, diminished libido, and two heart attacks, the last one of which kills him. Several critics have viewed Rabbit's fate as representative of the United States' decline. Thomas M. Disch observed: "Updike's Rabbit and the landscape he inhabits more closely resemble the world I've witnessed during the time span of the four novels—1959 through 1989—than any other work of American literature I know. And it does what art can in the way of redeeming the world it represents by valorizing its commonplaces."

Updike won the National Book Award for his third novel, *The Centaur* (1963). In this allegorical work, a rebellious son and his father are modeled after the mythological figures of Prometheus and Chiron. Like Prometheus, the legendary hero for whom the centaur Chiron sacrificed his immortality, the son learns to appreciate the value of his father's life only after the man has died. *Of the Farm* (1965), according to Updike, is "about moral readjustment" and "the consequences of a divorce." In this book, Updike focuses on a man who returns to his widowed mother's farmhouse with his new bride and stepson and soon realizes that his mother and his wife are equally demanding. Peter Buitenhuis called the novel "very clearly and very completely, a small masterpiece."

Beginning with *Couples* (1968), Tarbox replaces Olinger as the setting of Updike's novels. In this controversial work, Updike examines the sexual and spiritual quests of ten suburban couples. Religion and sexuality are again the focus of *A Month of Sundays* (1975), in which an adulterous preacher is unable to feel guilt even after he is cast out by his congregation. In *Marry Me: A Romance* (1976), two adulterers are caught in the ambiguous dilemma of wanting to marry but not wishing to hurt their respective families. *The Coup* (1978), a novel inspired by Updike's 1973 lectureship in Africa, represents a radical departure in his subject matter. Narrated by the black dictator of an emerging African nation, the book ridicules the idea of revolution as a vehicle for change as well as the attempts by superpowers to make third-world countries serve their economic interests.

Updike's recent novels have elicited mixed reviews. *The Witches of Eastwick* (1984) centers on three divorced women who acquire the powers of witches, casting evil spells and pursuing unhappily married men in their suburban community until the arrival of a demonic stranger throws them into competition. Greg Johnson summed up diverse critical interpretations of this work: "An allegory, a fable, a romance, a meditation on the nature of evil—*The Witches of Eastwick* is all of these, while remaining a high-spirited sexual comedy and a caricaturist's view of women's liberation." *Roger's Version* (1986) centers on a divinity school professor's dualistic feelings regarding a student's proposal to prove the existence of God by computer. This novel, which blends theology, eroticism, and science, is narrated by the ambiguous Roger, who claims to be the tale's villain. As its title indicates, Roger's version of the story is only one among many.

Updike's criticism, originally published in *The New Yorker,* appears with articles, anecdotes, and other pieces in four acclaimed collections: *Assorted Prose* (1965), *Picked-Up Pieces* (1975), the National Book Critics Circle Award-winning volume, *Hugging the Shore: Essays and Criticism* (1983), and *Odd Jobs: Essays and Criticism* (1991). Updike has also written a biographical drama, *Buchanan Dying* (1974), about James Buchanan, the fifteenth President of the United States. Several of Updike's novels and short stories have been adapted for film and television.

Critics rarely agree on the artistic value of Updike's works. Such literary figures as Norman Mailer and John W. Aldridge regard his style as superficial, masking a lack of statement or substance. Most critics, however, concede Updike's breadth of knowledge and mastery of presentation, and many consider him among America's most distinguished and erudite authors. John Cheever deemed Updike "the most brilliant and versatile writer of his generation."

(For further information about Updike's life and works, see *Concise Dictionary of American Literary Biography, 1968-1988; Contemporary Authors,* Vols. 1-4, rev. ed.; *Contemporary Authors Bibliographical Series,* Vol. 2; *Contemporary Authors New Revision Series,* Vols. 4, 33; *Contemporary Literary Criticism,* Vols. 1, 2, 3, 5, 7, 9, 13, 15, 23, 34, 43, 70; *Dictionary of Literary Biography,* Vols. 2, 5; *Dictionary of Literary Biography Documentary Series,* Vol. 3; *Dictionary of Literary Biography Yearbook: 1980, 1982;* and *Major 20th-Century Writers.*)

CRITICAL COMMENTARY

JOHN UPDIKE WITH CHARLES THOMAS SAMUELS
(interview date 1968)

[In the following excerpted interview, Updike discusses religious, mythical, stylistic, satirical, and psychological aspects of his work.]

[Samuels]: *In an interview you gave* Life *you expressed some regret at the "yes, but" attitude critics have taken toward it. Did the common complaint that you had ducked large subjects lead to the writing of* **Couples**?

[Updike]: No, I meant my *work* says "yes, but." Yes, in *Rabbit, Run,* to our inner urgent whispers, but—the social fabric collapses murderously. Yes, in *The Centaur,* to self-sacrifice and duty, but—what of a man's private agony and dwindling? No, in *The Poorhouse Fair,* to social homogenization and loss of faith, but—listen to the voices, the joy of persistent existence. No, in *Couples,* to a religious community founded on physical and psychical interpenetration, but—what else shall we do, as God destroys our churches? I cannot greatly care what critics say of my work; if it is good, it will come to the surface in a gener-

Principal Works

The Carpentered Hen, and Other Tame Creatures (poetry) 1958

The Poorhouse Fair (novel) 1959

The Same Door (short stories) 1959

Rabbit, Run (novel) 1960

Pigeon Feathers, and Other Stories (short stories) 1962

The Centaur (novel) 1963

Telephone Poles, and Other Poems (poetry) 1963

Olinger Stories: A Selection (short stories) 1964

Of the Farm (novel) 1965

Assorted Prose (criticism and essays) 1965

The Music School (short stories) 1966

Couples (novel) 1968

Midpoint, and Other Poems (poetry) 1969

Bech: A Book (short stories) 1970

Rabbit Redux (novel) 1971

Museums and Women, and Other Stories (short stories) 1972

Buchanan Dying (play) 1974

A Month of Sundays (novel) 1975

Picked-Up Pieces (criticism and essays) 1975

Marry Me: A Romance (novel) 1976

Tossing and Turning (poetry) 1977

The Coup (novel) 1978

Problems, and Other Stories (short stories) 1979

Too Far to Go: The Maples Stories (short stories) 1979

Rabbit Is Rich (novel) 1981

Bech Is Back (short stories) 1982

Hugging the Shore: Essays and Criticism 1983

The Witches of Eastwick (novel) 1984

Facing Nature: Poems 1985

Roger's Version (novel) 1986

Trust Me: Short Stories 1987

S. (novel) 1988

Self-Consciousness: Memoirs (autobiography) 1989

Rabbit at Rest (novel) 1991

Odd Jobs: Essays and Criticism 1991

---

ation or two and float, and if not, it will sink, having in the meantime provided me with a living, the opportunities of leisure, and a craftsman's intimate satisfactions. I wrote *Couples* because the rhythm of my life and my oeuvre demanded it, not to placate hallucinatory critical voices.

What do you mean by attributing the setting up of religious communities in **Couples** *to God's destruction of our churches?*

I guess the noun "God" reappears in two totally different senses, the god in the first instance being the god worshipped within this nice white church, the more or less watered down Puritan god; and then god in the second sense means ultimate power. I've never really understood theologies which would absolve God of earthquakes and typhoons, of children starving. A god who is not God the Creator is not very real to me, so that, yes, it certainly *is* God who throws the lightning bolt and this God is above the nice god, above the god we can worship and empathize with. I guess I'm saying there's a fierce God above the kind God and he's the one Piet believes in. At any rate, when the church is burned, Piet is relieved of morality, and can choose Foxy—or can accept the choice made for him by Foxy and Angela operating in unison—can move out of the paralysis of guilt into what after all is a kind of freedom. He divorces the supernatural to marry the natural. I wanted the loss of Angela to be felt as a real loss—Angela is nicer than Foxy—nevertheless it is Foxy that he most deeply wants, it is Foxy who in some obscure way was turned on the lathe for him. So that the book

does have a happy ending. There's also a way, though, I should say (speaking of "yes, but") in which, with the destruction of the church, with the removal of his guilt, he becomes insignificant. He becomes merely a name in the last paragraph: he becomes a satisfied person and in a sense dies. In other words, a person who has what he wants, a satisfied person, a content person, ceases to be a person. Unfallen Adam is an ape. Yes, I guess I do feel that. I feel that to be a person is to be in a situation of tension, is to be in a dialectical situation. A truly adjusted person is not a person at all—just an animal with clothes on or a statistic. So that it's a happy ending, with this "but" at the end. (pp. 100-02)

I'd like to move on to **The Centaur** *now. If I'm right in regarding it as formally uncharacteristic, I wonder why you prefer it to your other novels?*

Well, it seems in memory my gayest and truest book; I pick it up, and read a few pages, in which Caldwell is insisting on flattering a moth-eaten bum, who is really the god Dionysius, and I begin laughing.

What made you decide to employ a mythic parallel?

I was moved, first, by the Chiron variant of the Hercules myth—one of the few classic instances of self-sacrifice, and the name oddly close to Christ. The book began as an attempt to publicize this myth. The mythology operated in a number of ways: a correlative of the enlarging effect of Peter's nostalgia, a dramatization of Caldwell's sense of exclusion and mysteriousness around him, a counterpoint of ideality to the drab real level, an excuse for a number of jokes, a serious expression of my sensation that the people we meet are *guises,* do conceal something mythic, perhaps prototypes or longings in our minds. We love some women more than others by pre-determination, it seems to me.

Why haven't you done more work in this mode?

But I have worked elsewhere in a mythic mode. Apart from my short story about Tristan and Iseult, there is the St. Stephen story underlying *The Poorhouse Fair,* and Peter Rabbit under *Rabbit, Run.* Sometimes it is semi-conscious; for example, only lately do I see that Brewer, the city of brick painted the color of flowerpots, is the flowerpot that Mr. McGregor slips over Peter Rabbit. And in *Couples,* Piet is not only Hanema/Anima/Life, he is Lot, the man with two virgin daughters, who flees Sodom, and leaves his wife behind. (pp. 103-04)

What about violence? Many critics complain that this is absent from your work—reprehensibly, because it is so present in the world. Why is there so little in your pages?

There has been so little in my life. I have fought in no wars, and engaged in few fistfights. I do not think a man pacifist in his life should pretend to violence in fiction. . . . I feel a tenderness toward my characters that forbids making violent use of them. In general, the North American continent in this century has been a place where catastrophe has held off, and likewise the lives I have witnessed have staved off real death. All my novels end with a false death, partial death. If, as may be, the holocausts at the rim of possibility do soon visit us, I am confident my capacities for expression can rise, if I live, to the occasion. In the meantime let's all of us with some access to a printing press not abuse our privilege with fashionable fantasies. (p. 106)

I'd like to ask a question about **The Poorhouse Fair.** *Many people have been bothered in that book by Conner's foolishness. He seems a bit easy as the butt of satire. Do you think there is much justification in that charge?*

I'd have to reread the book to know. It could be that I was too little in sympathy with what I imagine him to be standing for. Of course a writer is in no position to alter a reader's reaction. Performance is all, and if I didn't really give you flesh and blood, then nothing I can say now will substitute. But it occurs to me that Conner was a preliminary study for Caldwell in *The Centaur:* the bulging upper lip and a certain Irishness, a certain tenacity, a certain—they're both poor disciplinarians, I notice in thinking about them. I wasn't satirical in my purpose. I may have been negative, but satire, no. I'm not conscious of any piece of fiction of mine which has even the slightest taint of satirical attempt. You can't be satirical at the expense of fictional characters, because they're your creatures. You must only love them, and I think that once I'd set Conner in motion I did to the best of my ability try to love him and let his mind and heart beat.

Isn't "The Doctor's Wife" an exception to your statement that you never satirize one of your characters?

You think I'm satirizing the doctor's wife? I'm *criticizing* the doctor's wife. Yes, I do feel that in some way she is a racist, but I'm not trying, I don't think I'm trying, to make her funny because she's a racist.

There's some satire in your poetry, isn't there? But I wonder why, with few exceptions, you only write light verse.

I began with light verse, a kind of cartooning in print, and except for one stretch of a few years, in which I wrote most of the serious poems in *Telephone Poles,* I feel uncertain away from rhyme to which something comic adheres. Bergson's mechanical encrusted upon the organic. But the light verse poems putting into rhyme and jaunty metrics some scientific discovery have a serious point—the universe science discloses to us is farcically unrelated to what our primitive senses report—and I have, when such poems go well, a pleasure and satisfaction not lower than in any other form of literary activity. (pp. 107-09)

In "The Sea's Green Sameness" you deny that characterization and psychology are primary goals of fiction. What do you think is more important?

I wrote "The Sea's Green Sameness" years ago and meant, I believe, that narratives should not be *primarily* packages for psychological insights, though they can contain them, like raisins in buns. But the substance is the dough, which feeds the story-telling appetite, the appetite for motion, for suspense, for resolution. The author's deepest pride, as I have experienced it, is not in his incidental wisdom but in his ability to keep an organized mass of images moving forward, to feel life engendering itself under his hands. But no doubt, fiction is also a mode of spying; we read it as we look in windows or listen to gossip, to learn what other people *do.* Insights of all kinds are welcome; but no wisdom will substitute for an instinct for action and pattern, and a perhaps savage wish to hold, through your voice, another soul in thrall.

In view of this and your delight in the "non-committal luminosity of fact," do you think you're much like the "nouvelle vague" novelists?

I used to. I wrote *The Poorhouse Fair* as an anti-novel, and have found Nathalie Sarraute's description of the modern novelistic predicament a helpful guide. I am attracted to the cool surface of some contemporary French novels, and, like them, do want to give inanimate or vegetable presences some kind of vote in the democracy of narrative. Basically, though, I describe things not because their muteness mocks our subjectivity but because they seem to be masks for God. And I should add that there is, in fiction, an image-making function, above image-retailing. To create a coarse universal figure like Tarzan is in some ways more of an accomplishment than the novels of Henry James.

As a technician, how unconventional would you say you were?

As unconventional as I need to be. An absolute freedom exists on the blank page, so let's use it. I have from the start been wary of the fake, the automatic. I tried not to force my sense of life as many-layered and ambiguous, while keeping in mind some sense of trans-action, of a bargain struck, between me and the ideal reader. Domestic fierceness within the middle class, sex and death as riddles for the thinking animal, social ex-istence as sacrifice, unexpected pleasures and rewards, corruption as a kind of evolution—these are some of the themes. I have tried to objectivity in the form of narrative. My work is meditation, not pontification, so that interviews like this one feel like a forcing of the growth, a posing. I think of my books not as sermons or directives in a war of ideas but as objects, with dif-ferent shapes and textures and the mysteriousness of anything that exists. My first thought about art, as a child, was that the artist brings something into the world that didn't exist before, and that he does it with-out destroying something else. A kind of refutation of the conservation of matter. That still seems to me its central magic, its core of joy. (pp. 116-17)

John Updike and Charles Thomas Samuels, in an interview in *The Paris Review*, Vol. 12, No. 45, Winter, 1968, pp. 85-117.

ALFRED KAZIN

(essay date 1973)

[A highly respected American literary critic, Kazin is best known for his essay collections *The Inmost Leaf* (1955), *Contemporaries* (1962), and *On Native Grounds* (1942). In the excerpt below, he assesses Updike's fiction through *Bech: A Book*, focusing on domestic and societal themes.]

Precocious, original, distinctly not a loner, a writer in the postwar suburban style who associated himself with families, townships, churches, citizens' commit-tees, Updike became a novelist of "society" in the Fif-ties, the age of postwar plenty and unchallenged do-mesticity for both sexes when many once-poor Ameri-cans, moving to the suburbs, felt they were at last com-ing into their reward. Domesticity is a dominant sub-ject of Updike's world—and so is the unavailing strug-gle against it, as in one of his best novels, *Rabbit, Run.* But there is in even the lucid emotions of *Rabbit, Run,* in the filial tenderness of *The Centaur,* a kind of bril-liant actionlessness, a wholly mental atmosphere. Up-dike, thanks not least to the marvelous movement within postwar society and its unprecedented inter-change of classes, backgrounds, social information, is an extremely adroit and knowledgeable observer of so-ciety and its customs. He likes to put Presidents into his work as a way of showing that President Buchanan (ancient history) and President Kennedy (the Sixties) are the real landmarks. But such historic moments just serve to date the personal mythology in his characters' minds; they are never forces. There is no struggle with American society; its character is fixed, though nothing else is.

Updike's characters represent many things to him; he glosses all his own novels. And because Updike fancies them as many-sided and intellectual designs, they are unusually distinct and memorable among characters in contemporary fiction. They always *mean.* Updike's fiction is distinguished by an unusually close interest in every character he writes about. But these characters who represent so much never struggle with anything except the reflections in their minds of a cir-cumscribing reality that seems unalterable. Updike is a novelist of society who sees society entirely as a fable. It stands still for him to paint its picture; *it* never starts anything. On the other hand, it is always there to say "American," now and in the future—Updike's first novel, *The Poorhouse Fair,* started with the future as tyranny, institutions that are there to say that institu-tions always take over.

The older American novelists of society were not this much used to it. Scott Fitzgerald, who loved its color, its prodigality, profoundly distrusted it and thought it would revenge itself on its critics. Updike, who persistently recalls Fitzgerald's ability to show so-ciety as a dream, has accommodated himself to its dom-inating possessiveness. Where there are no alternatives, even in one's memory, the proliferating surfaces en-courage myths, transferable symbols—a sense of situa-tion, not opposition. Updike is in the best sense of the word an intellectual novelist, a novelist of paradox, tension and complexity who as a college wit in the Fif-ties learned that we are all symbols and inhabit sym-bols. His easy mastery of social detail never includes any sense of American society as itself a peculiar insti-tution, itself the dynamo, the aggressor, the maker of other people's lives. Society is just a set of characteris-tics. Society—our present fate!—shows itself in mar-velously shifting mental colors and shapes. Brightness falls from the air, thanks to the God on whose absence we sharpen our minds. But Updike's own bright images of human perception fall along a horizontal line, meta-phors of observation that connect only with each other. The world is all metaphor. We are not sure *who* is think-ing these brilliant images in *Rabbit, Run.* Need Up-dike's fine mind be so much in evidence?

His day had been bothered by God: Ruth mocking, Eccles blinking—why did they teach you such things if no one believed them? It seems plain, standing here, that if there is this floor there is a ceiling, that the true space in which we live is upward space. Someone is dying. In this great stretch of bridge someone is dying. The thought comes from nowhere: simple percentages. Someone in some house along these streets, if not this minute then the next, dies; and in that suddenly stone chest the heart of this flat prostrate rose seems to him to be. He moves his eyes to find the spot; perhaps he can see a cancer-blackened soul of an old man mount through the blue like a monkey on a spring. . . .

Updike is indeed a great mental traveler through the many lands of American possibility. Though *The Poorhouse Fair, The Olinger Stories, The Centaur* and others of his best works deal with the southeastern-most corner of Pennsylvania he comes from, he no more judges the rest of America by it than puts America into it—as O'Hara put everything he knew into his corner of Pennsylvania. Updike has nothing of the primitive attachment to early beginnings that made a whole generation of American realists once describe the big city as a total dislodgement. As a believer in tradition rediscovered, he can weave a surpassingly tender novel about his father, *The Centaur,* into a set of mythological associations and identifications that in other hands would have academicized the novel to death. *The Centaur* is one of his best books. In *Rabbit, Run* he wrote the marriage novel of a period marked by an increasing disbelief in marriage as the foundation of everything. At the end of *Rabbit, Run* the oversize Harry Angstrom ran away from his mopey wife Janice, who while drunk had accidentally drowned their baby, and from the unfathomable insatiable domesticity of the "tranquilized fifties," as Robert Lowell calls them.

Rabbit Redux of course opens on the day in 1969 that saw the first manned American flight to the moon, "leaving the rest of us here." Harry was once too young and is now mysteriously too old. He is now a decaying man in an American city typically running down, is proud to support the Vietnam War when everybody else has seen through it, and in order to provide the reader with a glibly topical symposium, suddenly finds himself sharing his house with Jill, a wild young hippie runaway from her family, and her sometime lover and drug supply Skeeter, a young Black Vietnam veteran who has jumped bail. Yet even an inferior novel, *Couples,* the book of suburban marriage and its now conventional adulteries that shows Updike exercising his gifts and putting up his usual intellectual-religious scaffolding with somewhat too bountiful ease, is *not* a document, for Updike is happily a novelist excited by his characters. And in *Bech: A Book* Updike not only takes on the Jew, the Jewish novelist, a subject that has long fascinated and provoked him because "the Jewish novelist" is so much a fact of our times, so important a social category and rival, the most striking sudden success in a society of sudden successes—he even manages to show the comedy in Bech, a failure.

Everything seems possible to Updike; everything *has* been possible. He knows his way around, in every sense, without being superficial about it. His real subject—the dead hand of "society," the fixity of institutions—has gone hand in hand with the only vision of freedom as the *individual's* recognition of God. This is a period when, as Updike says, "God has killed the churches." There is no nemesis: just an empty space between those untouching circles, society and the individual. Updike has managed to be an intellectual without becoming abstract; in an era of boundless personal confusion, he has been a moralist without rejecting the mores. If poise is a gift, Updike is a genius. If to be "cool" is not just a social grace but awareness unlimited, Updike is the best of this cool world. All he lacks is that capacity for making you identify, for summoning up affection in the reader, which Salinger (now "poor Salinger") expressed when in *The Catcher in the Rye* he had Holden Caulfield reserve his praise for authors who make you want to call them up. (pp. 120-24)

Alfred Kazin, "Professional Observers: Cozzens to Updike," in his *Bright Book of Life: American Novelists & Storytellers from Hemingway to Mailer,* Atlantic-Little, Brown, 1973, pp. 95-124.

BERNARD A. SCHOPEN

(essay date 1978)

[In the excerpt below, Schopen analyzes the role of morality and faith in Updike's novels.]

The novels of John Updike have spawned a criticism rather remarkable in its contentiousness. His books have evoked critical outrage, bewilderment, condescension, commendation, and an enthusiasm approaching the fulsome. The same novel might be hailed as a major fictional achievement and dismissed as a self-indulgence or a failure. And evaluations of Updike's importance in the realm of contemporary American literature reflect a similar truculent diversity. However, a careful review of the commentary on Updike's work reveals that much of it is structured by assumptions that have little relevance to the themes, methods, and intentions of his fiction. This is especially true of those studies which discuss the relation of Updike's Christianity to the form and texture of his novels. While Updike has repeatedly expressed his views on religious and theological questions, his critics continue to interpret his work according to theories, religio-ethical systems, and ontologies he categorically rejects and his fiction does not embody. Updike's faith is Christian, but it is one to which many of the assumptions about the Christian perspective do not apply—especially those which link Christian faith with an absolute and divinely ordered morality. (p. 523)

Updike has often quoted approvingly Barth's remark that "one cannot speak of God by speaking of man in a loud voice." For both men the distinction between the divine and the human is absolute. God is Wholly Other. He is unreachable, unknowable. Thus the only religious—which is not to say theological—question is that of faith. But the existence of God, Barth and Updike jointly assert, cannot be proved. So the question becomes not, "Does God exist?" but rather, "Do I believe God exists?" To Updike, an affirmative answer to this question makes one a Christian: "I call myself a Christian by defining 'a Christian' as 'a person willing to profess the Apostles' Creed.'" And the Apostles' Creed is nothing more—and nothing less—than a statement of faith in the existence of God and the divinity of Christ. It requires only that one avow, "I believe."

Since Updike's Christianity is determined only by his profession of the Apostles' Creed, it contains no inherent moral system. Again his views are in accord with those of Karl Barth. (pp. 524-25)

For Updike . . . religious questions are those arising from the relationship between man and God. Moral questions are those which concern man's intercourse with his fellow man. The absolute qualitative difference between man and God, and consequently between ethics and faith, is the sine qua non of his theology. And there is no question that for Updike the problems of human morality are subordinate to that of faith. The problem of faith, though difficult, is simple and absolute; those of morality are relative, ambiguous, and "basically insoluble." Thus, insofar as it treats moral problems, Updike's fiction must be ambiguous and essentially static.

Updike has said that the central theme of each of his novels is "meant to be a moral dilemma," and that his books are intended as "moral debates with the reader." But to develop a moral theme in such a way that there is no resolution is to do something quite different from what the novel has traditionally attempted. All novelists deal with moral questions. Historically, however, the novelist has tried to resolve these problems, at least tentatively; he has tried to view the problems of human life from a moral perspective which indicates both their causes and possible solutions. Updike, however, believes that there are no solutions. And he specifically rejects the notion that literature should inculcate moral principles or precepts. On the other hand, many of his readers would agree with Wayne Booth's assertion that "an author has an obligation to be as clear about his moral position as possible." The work itself, this theory holds, must create a moral universe which clearly establishes principles upon which the actions of its characters can be judged. But Updike is up

to something else in his fiction. Since the theme of each novel is a moral dilemma, discriminations in the effects of human attitudes and behavior are essential to its development. Updike's focus on the complex implications of his characters' moral decisions is constant and sharp, so that the issues are always clear and the consequences of each decision fully developed. But while Updike's characters are quick to judge each other, their creator refuses either to bless or to condemn; and each novel clearly demonstrates that the specific moral problem it treats is irresolvable. The world Updike creates in his fiction is morally ambiguous. And it is so, in large part, because of the perpetual conflict between two antithetical forms of human morality.

Updike has suggested that the human conscience constantly suffers guilt for transgressing the laws of two different moralities. One is external, abstract, made up of biblical injunction, social and cultural mores, and all the precepts our civilization has established to enable men to live together in harmony. But "Another kind of morality is a sort of response to an inner imperative"; this subjective morality is less a system than a "feeling" or "sense" of the propriety of a given act. And while Updike believes that "Morality tries to keep us from pain," he admits that "I don't see either solution as being perfect."

In Updike's novels the dilemma created by this dual morality is often embodied in the women between whom the protagonists must choose. In *Rabbit, Run* Rabbit Angstrom vacillates between his wife and his mistress. The external and codified morality, of which Jack Eccles is the chief instrument, demands that Rabbit return to Janice; but Rabbit's inner apprehension of what is "right" for him directs him to Ruth. Similarly, Joey Robinson's dilemma is represented by his two wives, and also by Peggy and his mother. (pp. 525-27)

Many of Updike's readers find the moral ambiguity of his fictional world morally offensive. His refusal to establish a rigid and clearly discernible moral perspective from which his characters should be viewed often leads these readers to assert that Updike is unwilling or unable to deal with serious moral issues, that he has "nothing to say." The objective presentation of life's pervasive ambiguity also leads many of his sympathetic critics to misread him; they simply assume that Updike shares their own moral attitudes, or those associated with Christianity in general, and interpret his fiction accordingly. . . .

Much of the difficulty critics have with Updike's fiction stems from their unwillingness to acknowledge the validity of one or the other of the two moral imperatives Updike recognizes. To Updike, however, they are equally valid and equally imperfect. In his fiction they stand together as irreconcilable forces, distinct from and often irrelevant to the problem of faith. Thus they exist in ambiguity and tension, which are basic to the human condition as Updike understands it. It is this condition which is always the subject of his novels. (p. 527)

[His] more recent novels continue the patterns established in *Rabbit, Run.* Like it, they deal with the problem of faith and the difficulty of moral decisions; and they too dramatize a moral dilemma through the complexities of sexual love. But the key to understanding Updike's treatment of this aspect of his sexual themes is found not in his second novel but in his third. In the first chapter of *The Centaur,* when Venus attempts to seduce Chiron, the centaur hesitates, listening for the rumble of Zeus's thunder. Suddenly Venus disappears, for "Love has its own ethics, which the deliberating will irrevocably offend"; Caldwell/Chiron is left alone "with a painful, confused sense of having displeased, through ways he could not follow, the God who never rested from watching him." . . .

The "ethics" of love are of a piece with the "inner imperative" which Updike defends as a valid, if imperfect, form of morality. As such they will usually be in opposition to those ethical dicta by which society regulates the sexual impulse, and will demand behavior unsanctioned by that society—that is to say, adultery. However, while Rabbit Angstrom oscillated between these two ethics, the protagonists of Updike's later novels tend to hang suspended between them, to exist as best they can in an uneasy compromise with each. The inevitable result of this compromise is a constant sense of guilt and an overwhelming fear of decisive action.

This general inability to act is a primary brace in the psychological scaffolding Updike constructs around his lover/hero. Critics have made much of the "passivity" of his later protagonists, but the novels indicate that this is the result of something much more complex than moral indolence. These characters all become subject to so many conflicting moral demands, and are presented with so many insoluble problems, that they retreat into a sort of moral catatonia. (pp. 531-32)

There is an additional reason for the inertia of these characters: each experiences what is clearly an existential and religious crisis. More specifically, each has reached the halfway point in his life—precisely that position between birth and death which Updike described in a long poem. **"Midpoint"** is a poetic recapitulation of Updike's past for the purpose of determining the proper course for his future. And three of his protagonists confront the same situation. Joey Robinson and Piet Hanema are thirty-five, Harry Angstrom thirty-six—each at the midpoint of his allotted threescore and ten; and each must attempt to make some sense of his life, to understand himself and his relation to God and to his fellow man, and to defend himself—with faith and love—against the ominous possibility of eternal death. The specter of mortality haunts these novels

and their protagonists, who must leap again and again out of "total despair" to a faith assaulted on all sides by reason and doubt. And they must endure the distrust and recriminations of those characters who exist exclusively in the moral and merely human world. Invariably these characters are women.

Updike's remarks about the female characters in *Couples* apply to all the women in his later novels: "The women in that book are less sensitive perhaps to the oppressive quality of cosmic blackness, and it is the women who do almost all of the acting." (p. 533)

If Updike's protagonists are morally "paralysed," they are so in part because of their sensitivity to "the oppressive quality of cosmic blackness": obsessed by death, exhausted by their effort to believe, and convinced of the impossibility of sorting through the ramifications of each moral decision, they can merely wait, and hope, and suffer the guilt of the inactive even as they acknowledge that "all this decency and busyness, is nothing." Their women, unconcerned with the problems of death and faith, take control of love and life in the quotidian. (pp. 533-34)

Bernard A. Schopen, "Faith, Morality, and the Novels of John Updike," in *Twentieth Century Literature*, Vol. 24, No. 4, Winter, 1978, pp. 523-35.

VICTOR STRANDBERG
(essay date 1978)

[An American educator and critic, Strandberg is an authority on the religious and psychological elements of fiction. In the following excerpt, he examines the function of religious belief in Updike's novels.]

Back in the second decade of this century, Herman Hesse remarked that "Human life is reduced to real suffering, to hell, only when two ages, two cultures and religions overlap." . . . In the figure of John Updike, Hesse's crisis of culture attains what we might call a culminating expression. Unwilling to exorcise the dilemma by making a game of it, in the mode of black humor widely prevalent among his contemporaries, Updike has confronted the problem of belief as directly as did Tolstoy and Tennyson a century earlier, but with the added authority of a mind keenly aware of twentieth-century science and theology. . . . Moving out from an intensely imagined vision of death as its starting point, this search for a belief that might provide a stay against death comprises the "figure in the carpet" that Henry James spoke of, the master theme that, threading from book to book, gives design to Updike's work as a whole and marks him as one of the leading religious writers of his age.

"Our fundamental anxiety is that we do not exist—or will cease to exist." That statement from Updike's essay on Denis de Rougemont's writings (*Assorted Prose* . . .) compresses within its narrow pith the most recurrent nightmare in Updike's work. . . . The dread of Death stalks softly through all of Updike's books. . . . (pp. 157-58)

[For example,] *Couples* (1968) notably places its erotic episodes against a background saturated with news of expiring flesh: the slow death of Pope John, the mysterious sinking of the submarine *Thresher,* the death of the Kennedy infant, the Diem assassinations, the murder of the President himself, the killing of Lee Oswald (which the Hanemas watch on television), two planes crashing in Turkey, a great Alaskan earthquake. The fictional world of *Couples* can hardly compete with such real life extinctions, but it does offer the slow dying of John Ong by cancer in counterpoint with the insomniac dread visited upon Piet Hanema ever since his parents died in a crash. . . .

Beyond this prospect of personal extinction lies that ultimate formulation of doom from the science of Physics, the theory of Entropy, which foresees the whole universe eventually burning out into a final icy darkness. This idea horrifies a good many Updike people, a typical instance being the tortured insomniac at the end of *Pigeon Feathers* who wakes his wife at last to share his terror: "I told her of the centuries coming when our names would be forgotten, of the millennia when our nation would be a myth and our continent an ocean, of the aeons when our earth would be vanished and the stars themselves diffused into a uniform and irreversible tepidity." . . . Worst of all is the eternally "forgotten" state in the above passage, a final and total extinction of the self that has haunted George Caldwell in *The Centaur* ever since he witnessed his father's death, though Caldwell accepts both death and entropy cheerfully enough otherwise. (p. 159)

Updike might as well have been speaking of himself when he described Conrad Aiken's stories as projecting a world whose "horror is not Hitlerian but Einsteinian," concerned not with crime and war but with the "interstellar gulfs" and "central nihil" of "the cosmic vacuity." . . . All of Updike's major work to date may be seen as some kind of response to this trauma; his people variously resist death through Christian faith (John Hook in *The Poorhouse Fair*), through the way of Eros (the Rabbit books, *Couples*), through Agape (George Caldwell), through art (Bech, Peter Caldwell), and through the metaphysical intuition that Updike himself calls "duality" (*A Month of Sundays* and elsewhere). . . . *The Centaur,* which gathers them all in its purview, remains Updike's most satisfactory treatment of his grand obsession.

To deal with the threat of non-existence, Updike has resorted largely to the oldest modes of immortality known to man—God and sex, more or less in that order, but sometimes meshed in a dubious combination. To judge from the bulk of Updike's writing, we might well surmise that Freddy Thorne, the high priest of *Couples,* speaks for his author when he says, "In the western world, there are only two comical things; the Christian church and naked women. . . . Everything else tells us we're dead." (pp. 159-60)

Back in his earliest novel, *The Poorhouse Fair,* where a head-on debate between a Christian and an atheist comprises the intellectual center of the work, it is ominously the atheist whose argument carries the weightiest evidence. . . . Perhaps Updike's most harrowing—and most brilliantly written—plunge into the abyss of religious skepticism occurs in **"Lifeguard,"** whose divinity-student narrator skewers the whole line-up of Christian theologies like so much shish-ke-bob. (pp. 160-61)

When God goes, half-gods arrive; and in our post-Freudian age, what other god can stand before Eros, "the Genesis of All Things," as the Centaur teaches . . . , and the one surviving deity who delivers a kind of immortality people may yet live by. Perhaps it is natural that when faith fails, God and sex become blurred. . . . Some such subliminal transference seems to have worked itself out in Updike's fiction of the 1960's, whose tones have become steadily less Christian and more pagan, though without a clear victory on either side.

Updike's psychology of sex, as he himself has attested, owes a great deal to two books by Denis de Rougement, *Love in the Western World* and *Love Declared.* (p. 161)

Updike renders [the] connection between Eros, narcissism, and death metaphorically in his Erotic Epigram III . . . , which reads:

Hoping to fashion a mirror, the lover doth polish the face of his beloved until he produces a skull.

So Eros becomes another mask for death, after all, rather than death's adversary; and the servant of Eros becomes "Mr. Death," as Ruth calls Rabbit—that proud lover—at the end. Presumably, the very reason Rabbit insisted on having sex with Ruth without contraceptives was to loosen his seed against death, affirming his being in reproduction. . . . Yet the final effect of Rabbit's erotic adventures is to inflict death by water upon his new-born daughter, death by fire upon his girl friend (in *Rabbit Redux*), death by abortion upon his unborn descendant, and spiritual death upon both his wife and his concubine: "I'm dead to you, and this baby of yours is dead too. Now; get out." (p. 162)

Couples is Updike's ultimate statement on the

theme of Eros. Guided by Paul Tillich's headnote from *The Future of Religions* that our present world, like that of the Roman Empire, presents "a mood favorable for the resurgence of religion," we find in *Couples* just what that religion is likely to be: a worship of Eros complete with its high priest and prophet (Freddy Thorne), its sacrificial victims (Angela and Ken), and its lay communicants (the couples)—all under the purview of the town church with its "pricking steeple and flashing cock." . . .

In this book, Death is once again linked with Eros, in Foxy's abortion, for example. . . . More significant is the loss of personality, a kind of psychic death, that Eros exacts as its payment. Contrary to Freddy Thorne's sudden "vision" that "We're all put here to *humanize* each other," . . . Eros obviously dehumanizes his worshippers in this novel, not only—again—in victimizing the . . . "distressed and neglected children," but with respect to the lovers themselves: "Frank and Harold had become paralyzed by the habit of lust; she and Marcia, between blowups, were as guarded and considerate with one another as two defaced patients in an accident ward." . . . Those critics and readers who complained of the lack of character development

in *Couples*—the characters are mostly indistinguishable—have missed the point that it was meant that way. (p. 163)

Eros is in reality a living god of this world to whom all flesh must render service. And in that service may actually reside some measure of joy and hope and meaning, for here we encounter a strange paradox: the Christian hedonism of John Updike. He that lusteth after a woman in his heart hath defiled her already, according to Jesus Christ, but Updike's religious people seem marvelously at ease in their compliance with the laws of Eros. . . . Christ and Eros are not adversaries, he maintains, but collaborators, the asceticism of the Bible notwithstanding: "To desire a woman is to save her . . . Every seduction is a conversion." (p. 164)

The lifeguard's changing investment of belief, shifting from God to sex—that is, from a supernatural to a naturalistic mainstay against death—portends, I believe, a significant movement in Updike's larger career. . . . Certainly, his *Midpoint,* a collection of poems published in 1969 and narrated by Updike himself, would appear to verify a shift, though not a full

Dust jacket of Updike's 1982 novel *Bech is Back.*

break, away from Christianity towards hedonism in Updike's view of life. (pp. 164-65)

The "intelligent hedonism" of *Midpoint* and the "happy ending" of *Couples* . . . would appear to reflect an increasing commitment to the pleasure principle in Updike's thinking, as supernaturalism wanes and naturalism waxes. But Updike is nothing if he is not double-minded. *Rabbit Redux* (1971) gives us a revulsion against naturalism as powerful as T. S. Eliot's, where Eros is again the mad, cruel god, where all sexuality is joyless exploitation, and where drugs and the moon-landing (of 1969) prove empty substitutes for spiritual meaning. (pp. 165-66)

There is no subject, then, upon which Updike is so ambiguous in his judgments as the subject of Eros, doubtless because sex is so ambiguous a feature of actual life, almost evenly balanced between its pleasures and pains, its warmth and its cruelty, its powers to create and destroy. Looking at *The Centaur,* we find both attitudes locked in a typically dialectical configuration. (p. 166)

So the turn from Christ to Eros ends in paradox. On the one hand, in a time of failing belief Eros is at least one god that all men can believe in, one to whom bodies may be offered a living sacrifice and who may confer in return a provisional shelter against death and entropy and the protein acids ticking. On the other hand, the capture of civilization's inner citadel from its few rear-guard Christian defenders yields little joy to the army of neopagan victors, for the disappearance of Christianity in books like *Couples* and *Rabbit Redux* only displays the "central nihil" of the "cosmic vacuity" all the more intolerably. To find Updike's true refuge from death and its terrors we shall have to look to neither classical Eros nor orthodox Christian metaphysics but to a highly personal theology that sees Agape love and Erotic love as pointing toward "Duality," like two sides of a triangle or a Gothic arch whose base is Earth and whose tip pierces heaven. (p. 167)

The goodness Updike speaks of is what theologians call *agape,* that love which St. Paul placed at the top of his famous triad in I Corinthians 13; and though we see very little faith and not much hope in *The Centaur,* we do see an abundance of love in George Caldwell, love which in the Pauline phrases "suffreth long, and is kind . . . seeketh not her own, is not easily provoked, thinketh no evil." Moving through a world that otherwise seems a throwback to the pagan hedonism of pre-Christian antiquity, Caldwell anachronistically dispenses agape-love in all directions.

Here perhaps a few words from Updike's religious mentor, Karl Barth, will focus Caldwell's role more clearly: "In *agape*-love a man gives himself to the other with no expectation of a return, in a pure venture, even at the risk of ingratitude." (p. 168)

Love—as *agape*—is a mighty ethical force, but matters of even greater moment hang by this tale. Ultimately, love implies that the physical universe has a spiritual counterpart, that metaphysical dimension of reality whose existence has been so much in question, and whose power is the only final recourse against death and entropy. Updike's word that encompasses this metaphysical dimension is "duality." . . . (p. 169)

By setting off *The Centaur* against Updike's erotic novels—*Couples, A Month of Sundays,* and *Marry Me*—we may observe how the author designates Agape and Eros as the two alternative pathways that connect the dualistic realms of reality. The way of Agape is surer but much more difficult, of course—straight is the path and few there be who find it. None do find it after Caldwell, who was not the last Christian for Updike (for his lovers are all Christians too), but who was the last Christian capable of a life of *agape* love. The noble centaur's exit thus leaves Eros as the major vehicle of dual consciousness in our ongoing twilight era.

Here Denis de Rougemont's thought makes its greatest impact on Updike's writing, for de Rougemont's connection between Eros and Duality makes possible a molecular fusion between Updike's sexual and religious psychology. Beyond the pleasure principle, that is to say, the Unattainable Lady of Updike/de Rougemont, provides a stay against death by opening to her lover a secret corridor for periodic visitations into the next world. . . .

Just such a system of thought pervades Updike's latest novel, *Marry Me* (1976). (p. 170)

At the end of [this] book, Updike affirms de Rougemont's system one last time by bringing into his text that classic movie archetype of the unattainable lady, Marlene Dietrich, whose most famous film, *The Blue Angel,* bears a title that happens to suit Updike's purpose to perfection.

In the end, then, the idea that poor Sally is asked to serve, at the risk of being called a whore, is that of Jerry's immortality. . . . (p. 171)

In *Couples,* Updike sometimes verges upon making a stilted morality play with de Rougemont's system, with Piet's name meaning "Hanema/Anima/Life" . . . and with Piet's wife Angela taking the role of the Angel not possessable in this world. (p. 172)

The ambiguity of Updike's erotic love, a life force harboring brutality, selfishness and a "mask of Death" quality, renders agape-love that much more efficacious by comparison. (p. 173)

Critics like Leslie Fiedler and Norman Podhoretz have sometimes disparaged Updike's work, calling it poor, mindless, and irrelevant, but those of us who find *The Centaur* a brilliant, moving book will agree that in his portrayal of George Caldwell, Peter/Updike has netted a splendid catch indeed, worthy of its epic analogies. In this apostle of agape-love, Updike has presented what still remains his surest answer to the problems of nihilism and the changing of the gods. As a side effect, he has also insured that his own name, while civilization lasts, is not likely to be forgotten. (p. 175)

Victor Strandberg, "John Updike and the Changing of the Gods," in *Mosaic: A Journal for the Comparative Study of Literature and Ideas,* Vol. XII, No. 1, Fall, 1978, pp. 157-75.

SUZANNE HENNING UPHAUS
(essay date 1980)

[In the excerpt below, Uphaus delineates similarities between Updike's short stories and his novels.]

There are many similarities between Updike's short stories and his novels. . . . As in the novels, the short stories are often concerned with how the natural world (whether evidenced by pigeons or sexual encounters) relates to the supernatural. A frequent theme in both genres is the consideration of social and familial obligations as sacrifice, resulting in a diminishing of the protagonist's artistic or religious or sexual freedom. The nostalgia for the past, the tenuousness of middle-class institutions, particularly marriage and the family, the suspicion that Updike has always had for what seems, on the surface, to be heroic and unselfish action, all these are frequent themes in the short stories.

In the short stories Updike concentrates not as much on the event as upon the effect of outward events upon the protagonist. While the same may be said of the novels, Updike realizes that as a genre, novels demand more action simply to sustain their length. Because of their brevity, the short stories can sustain uninterrupted introspection, a spareness of overt action, in a way that novels cannot. Thus the genre of the short story allows Updike to present selected and detailed vignettes focused on the nuances of the protagonist's reaction to events.

For those readers used to dime-store thrillers, the plots in the short stories may seem bare: in one a man takes his daughter to a music lesson, in another a father tells his child a bedtime story, in many the temptations toward or suspicions of adultery are suffered but seldom confirmed. Moreover, within the brevity of the short story, Updike's remarkable style, unfailingly precise, often lyrical, occasionally ironic, becomes even more noticeable than in the novels.

Perhaps the most sustained stylistic achievement in any of the short stories comes in the frequently anthologized story **"Pigeon Feathers."** David is the young protagonist, an adolescent who has been plunged into religious doubt by his almost accidental reading of H. G. Wells's account of Jesus. Wells describes Jesus as "an obscure political agitator, a kind of hobo, in a minor colony of the Roman Empire," who "by an accident impossible to reconstruct . . . survived his own crucifixion and presumably died a few weeks later." Outraged by the sacrilege of this account, David's first reaction is astonishment that the man who had written such "blasphemy" had not been struck by lightning but had been allowed to continue writing, "to grow old, win honors, wear a hat, write books that, if true, collapsed everything into a jumble of horror."

In the weeks following, David's doubt and depression grow, as does his sense of alienation from his family and acquaintances. This sense of alienation is reinforced by the fact that David is an only child who has just moved, with his family, from town to farm. (These details correspond to events in Updike's own adolescence). The nature he contemplates in the loneliness of the farm reminds him of the persistence of death and decay in the natural cycle. In the darkness of the outhouse one night, David experiences a moment of consummate horror as he contemplates the possibility of his own death, without resurrection. He questions the minister during a church confirmation class but the other children laugh at his impertinence, and the clergyman, answering, reveals his own disbelief in the resurrection of each individual.

Weeks later, when David is asked by his mother to shoot the pigeons who are fouling furniture stored in the barn, he accepts the task with increasing eagerness. Since the universe has been revealed to him as possibly uncaring, there has developed a streak of meanness within David, a reflexive lack of caring. Into the darkness of the barn comes the destroyer, with his new gun, a fifteenth birthday present. The pigeons are his helpless victims.

In describing the pigeons, Updike's style becomes lyrical and precise. The sound of their cooing "flooded the vast interior with its throaty, bubbling outpour." David aims at a pigeon that is "preening and cooing in a throbbing, thrilled, tentative way" and shoots at its "tiny, jauntily cocked head." The bird, "pirouetting rapidly and nodding its head as if in frantic agreement," finally falls. As the cooing of the remaining pigeons becomes shriller, their "apprehensive tremolo made the whole volume of air seem liquid."

When David buries his victims, he notices, for the first time, the intricate individual design of each bird. The pattern of each feather is carefully and precisely colored. Each feather is trimmed to fulfill its purpose. One pigeon has plumage "slate shades of blue," another is "mottled all over in rhythms of lilac and gray." David becomes convinced that "the God who had lavished such craft upon these worthless birds would not destroy His whole Creation by refusing to let David live forever."

There is irony, of course, in this final statement of the story. David thinks that the birds are worthless, although they have shown so much to him. Moreover, in the self-centered manner of adolescents, he believes the universe has been created for his own pleasure, and that his death would imply its destruction; thus, David concludes he will "live forever."

In the lyrical description of the birds, Updike frequently uses words associated with the arts, with music, with dancing, and in the burial scene, with painting. Words like "tremolo" and "pirouetting" and the detailed description of the color and pattern of the feathers reinforce Updike's ultimate purpose, to suggest the existence of a design, and thus a Designer, in the natural world. While philosophical objections could be (and have been) made to the argument of design as proof of God's existence, the tone of gentle irony in the final paragraph assures us of Updike's control of his theme. As Robert Detweiler writes:

> The point is that Updike, through symbolic action and analogy, has written a moving religious narrative that does not presume to convince one of the objective truth of Christian faith, but that does testify to an individual's achievement of it.
>
> (pp. 121-24)

The short stories by Updike that are most familiar to readers of *The New Yorker* are the seventeen that trace the history and eventual dissolution of the marriage of Joan and Dick Maple. In 1979 these were collected into a volume entitled *Too Far To Go* and made into a television movie of the same title. The stories, written over a span of twenty-three years, follow the outward events of Updike's own first marriage: Dick Maple, like Updike, married in the early fifties when he was twenty-one; both couples had four children, separated after twenty-one years, and finally received one of the first no-fault divorces granted in the state of Massachusetts.

Most of the Maple stories are told from the point of view of Dick Maple who, like many of Updike's protagonists, suffers insomnia and frequent minor illnesses (a nervous stomach in Rome, a mysterious fever the day of a civil rights demonstration, innumerable colds). He recognizes that these are possibly psychosomatic, as his doctor suggests in the final story. These illnesses reflect Dick Maple's uneasy relationship with his own body; when it is not irritating him with illness, it plagues him with sexual hungers. His character reveals an uncomfortable conjunction of independence and insecurity, both aggravated not so much by his wife as by his married state.

In contrast, Joan Maple is revealed in these stories as being, for the most part, competent and conscientious. Dick finds her mysterious and distant, describing her as "solid but hidden," and finally, as "a secret woman he could never reach and had at last wearied of trying to reach." In the early stories she is clearly in control. In **"Wife-Wooing"** she refuses her husband's advances only to initiate sex with him the next night, when he is not expecting it. In the next story, **"Giving Blood,"** several years and one child later, she has convinced Richard, over his squeamish objections, to go to Boston with her to give blood for her cousin who is ill.

But in this story there is a new note of friction in the marriage. During the drive to Boston each accuses the other of flirting at a party the night before. Dick coolly accuses Joan of smugness and sexlessness. But joined by the strange sacrificial ceremony of giving blood, they make peace over the late breakfast in a restaurant, with Dick pretending that he is Joan's romantic suitor on a date until he finds his wallet empty and must take money from his wife.

Subsequent stories show them drawing further apart. They "had talked and thought about separation," but their "conversations, increasingly ambivalent and ruthless as accusation, retraction, blow and caress alternated and canceled, had the final effect of knitting them ever tighter together in a painful, helpless, degrading intimacy." One story centers on a mysterious telephone caller; each accuses the other that it must be his or her lover. In another, Dick warmly embraces a divorced woman whom he and Joan have been driving home from a party, and in another, he comes upon his wife and a mutual friend embracing in the kitchen of his house.

The accusations and suppositions, Dick's occasional attraction to his wife, and his frequent rejection of her continue through the stories. It is like an elaborate dance in which, pledged to keep each other as partners, the couple, perhaps because of this enforced commitment, draws farther and farther apart. The concentration in these stories is always on the couple; lovers remain shadowy background figures whose implied presence is incidental and not the cause of the distance between the couple.

It is ironic that this distance, rather than closeness, is the end result of so many, ultimately futile, conversations. The Maples talk endlessly over the years, but all these words fail to draw them closer. Thus, one of the effects of these stories is to demonstrate the limitations of words as a means of communication, as the writer depends on them to convey this message to the reader.

After twenty-one years of marriage, the Maples do decide to separate, and the story **"Separating"** records their painful breaking of the news to their children, now young adults and adolescents. Dick and Joan, concerned about the effect of the news they feel they must inflict upon the children, have waited months for the right moment. But, as [Robert Detweiler] puts it, "there turns out to be no proper moment for such a revelation." While the girls respond with a quiet stoicism, the younger son at first shouts at his parents accusingly, then jokes, and then dissolves in tears in a scene that rings painfully true. The older son seems to accept the separation with calm, yet as he kisses his father good night he moans in his ear the unanswerable question, "Why?"

Perhaps the Maples' closest moment is, ironically, in the courthouse right after their divorce is legalized. The final story of the volume, **"Here Come the Maples,"** links Richard's memories of his wedding with the formalities and red tape of getting a divorce. He must get a copy of their marriage license, and in doing so, Dick finds himself remembering, with increasing detail, his wedding day, the day they began what they are now about to end. When the Maples arrive in court they are as nervous as any young bride and groom, although their marriage is about to be dissolved, not solemnized. To the judge's questions Dick and Joan answer, "I do," echoing the marriage ceremony. As the ceremony ends, Dick turns to his former wife and kisses her, remembering to do what, twenty-two years before at their wedding ceremony, he had forgotten. (pp. 127-30)

In the Maple stories Updike has succeeded in being impartial and unblaming. It is always much easier to blame than to understand, and yet Updike has avoided this temptation. Out of his impartiality he has created a series of stories both poignant and sensitive. (p. 130)

Suzanne Henning Uphaus, in her *John Updike,* Frederick Ungar Publishing Co., 1980, 149 p.

FREDERICK R. KARL

(essay date 1983)

[Karl is an American critic who has written extensively on English literature and literary figures of the eighteenth, nineteenth, and twentieth centuries. He is particularly known for his studies of the life and works of Joseph Conrad. In the following excerpt, he chronicles Harry Angstrom's progress in the first three novels of the Rabbit tetralogy.]

In *Rabbit, Run* (1960), his second novel, Updike has written a moral fable for our times: about the self-absorption of a young man who lacks wit, charm, and intelligence. He does have consciousness, a sense of something missing, and a physical desire which transcends occasions. Harry Angstrom, or Rabbit, as a for-

mer star basketball player on his high school team, has conditioned himself to run. Those years in the limelight are his lost Eden. At the very beginning of the novel, he comes upon a group of boys playing a pickup game. Dressed in his business suit, now twenty-six, married, the father of a son, a demonstrator of vacuum cleaners in a local store, Rabbit is dying; but the game gives him vitality. "That his touch still lives in his hands elates him." When he's with his wife, Janice, who is also dying, he "tries to think of something pleasant. He imagines himself about to shoot a long one-hander; but he feels he's on a cliff, there is an abyss he will fall into when the ball leaves his hands." Rabbit runs to recapture the Eden of those days, and yet each move to discover it turns sour.

The novel is clearly a response to 1950s malaise, a political statement at the level of small-town life, with people gasping out their lives, a Sherwood Anderson scenario. *Rabbit, Run* overlaps with Malamud's *A New Life*, Roth's *Goodbye, Columbus*, Donleavy's *The Ginger Man*, some of Salinger's stories, Vonnegut's *Player Piano*, all of which have in common a character who has refused his role, or who is attempting to rediscover himself by running. Each novel is based on the feeling that to escape is to live, or try to live, whereas to remain placed is to accept death. Since the point is quintessential American and hardly original by the 1950s, the novels which focus there must themselves contain an original point. Malamud's is witty, full of the ironies of a Jew in the Northwest amidst Gentile enemies. Roth's titular story has the uneasiness of younger Jews located amidst the affluence and expectations of their elders. With this as pivot, he sees how "running" prevents suffocation, and he is quite prescient about the newer Jew of the 1960s, the Jewish activist and radical (American style). Vonnegut's protagonist must struggle for life against his organizational role in a machine-made world. For him, a farm is Eden.

Rabbit moves more constrainedly. The sole way he can replay those basketball games is in bed, apparently: orgasm itself, the warmth of flesh, and plenty of it. The most successful parts of the novel occur in Updike's descriptions of Rabbit's desire, his pleasure in the tactile sense of flesh. Whoever satisfies this aspect of Rabbit will hold him together; he moves from his wife to Ruth, a part-time prostitute, back to his wife, then to Ruth, each move creating chaos. His desertion of Janice leads to her excessive drinking and the death of their infant by drowning; he gets Ruth pregnant, and wants her to have the child but without marriage.

Updike is striving for a vision based on juxtapositions, some insight into Rabbit's need for freedom even as circumstances and the paltriness of his own desires draw him back. He is not a bad man; he is, however, hollow, and hollow in ways Updike does not recognize. The dread he runs from is undefined. While he has demands upon life which life cannot meet, he brings nothing to it. One could argue that Updike meant to present a cipher with a huge appetite—but then what is the point? Where does the author take his stand? Even emptiness must assume significance. Updike gives us no resting place; the tone of the novel is neutral. Rabbit does not seek our approval, and we should not disapprove. If neutrality is the aim—that is, we simply observe—then where do we locate ourselves morally? Rabbit is charmless, witless, a young man full of disaster, but even that on a small scale. Is he the archetypal American male?

As he tells Ruth, after one has been first-rate at something, the second-rate is a form of death. Yet he is himself a form of death and has not earned the right to express that. The problem, once again, lies here: Rabbit expresses feelings and ideas beyond him. The Reverend Eccles, who tries to help him and only creates muddles, says he can always redeem himself, that circumstance is not the master. But Rabbit understands only lust; like many other Updike protagonists, he is too shallow to investigate matters of will and chance. Such a passage as the following is far in excess of the character: "His [Rabbit's] life seems a sequence of grotesque poses assumed to no purpose, a magic dance empty of belief. *There is no God; Janice die* [in childbirth]: the two thoughts come at once, in one slow wave. He feels underwater, caught in chains of transparent slime, ghosts of the urgent ejaculations he has spat into the mild bodies of women." Not only is this excessive to what Rabbit can comprehend, it serves no function, for he cannot act upon what is, really, Updike's, not his, perception of events.

The language rings false: "ghosts of urgent ejaculations," "spat into the mild bodies," the water images. There is, throughout, an inappropriate adventurousness with language. For Janice, a real twit of a young woman, Rabbit's female equal, Updike uses a modified stream of consciousness, modeled apparently upon Joyce's Molly Bloom. And he repeats the method for Ruth, a woman of no interest, no charm, no qualities except the ability to draw breath and spread legs. (pp. 347-49)

Language regurgitates trivia. Rabbit sneaks into his house for his clothes, and every item he takes is listed. Boring food is described in detail. Yet trivia, unlike its use in Joyce or Oates, does not intensify into thematic importance or into stresses which highlight certain motifs. Experience itself is so trivialized that Rabbit's moments of glory—the remembered dream, intensity of orgasm, succumbing to abundant female fleshiness—are diminished. Running on the basketball court produced scores and winning games; running in society, as Rabbit learns, produces no results, merely a sequence of disasters.

This is a very significant American theme: fleeing

a static or enclosed life, a form of suffocation. From it derive all the elements novelists mock: gray-flannel-suited man, loveless marriage, importuning children, sexual frustration, boredom. The 1950s are located here. Rabbit foreshadows 1960s "opening up," the tryings-out which characterized the decade, even the solipsism and narcissism which demanded voices. One of the most effective episodes occurs when Rabbit sits with [his former teammate] Harrison in a run-down bar, and he recognizes that Ruth, *his* prostitute, has probably committed fellatio with Harrison. Rabbit then demands she do it with him, to humiliate her and let her know who is master. By degrading her—he has also spoken of his love for her—he will relieve the emptiness in himself; but the act proves disastrous for both. He gains no victory, only her humiliation; emptiness remains. He returns to his wife, only to desert her again, and that, in turn, leads to the drowning of the infant.

Rabbit Redux (1971), or restored, is Harry Angstrom's life ten years later, when he is thirty-six and the country, in 1969, is experiencing the moon shot, street riots, racial disturbances, and a general convulsion in morals. Rabbit is caught in the middle, back in Brewer, the small Pennsylvania town which is, apparently, a microcosm of America, just as Rabbit is a miniature of American life. Rabbit ten years later is a ranting, warmongering, frustrated individual coming into heaviness, gloom, and right-wing paranoia. Again, the strategical problem is that Rabbit's opinions, trials, erections, preference for large fleshy women have little significance.

Playing around Rabbit are the various phenomena of the sixties. Jill, a rich eighteen-year-old, has run (in a Porsche) from her Stonington, Connecticut, wealth to find new life among blacks, drugs, danger. She seeks new states of being by way of Zen, sex, which she does not appear to enjoy, and threatening associations. She also seeks humiliation. After Rabbit's wife leaves their home to live with Stavros, a Greek car salesman, Jill moves in with Rabbit and his son; later, the household is joined by Skeeter, a ghetto black.

A demonic element, Skeeter offers all the temptations which heighten life while destroying it: drugs, brutality, sex, and jive talk about race which finds Rabbit half sympathetic. The patter Updike has derived for Skeeter, however, lacks authenticity; Skeeter himself is simply words, failing to embody anything more than an idea. What makes this part of the novel so unconvincing, even embarrassing, is that Skeeter is what Flannery O'Connor called "an artificial nigger." He is the idea of a ghetto black, just as Jill is an artificial rebel. These two allegorical figures are set off against Rabbit, who is real, and styles clash. Talk, actions, responses are all efforts to mix what does not blend. Set into this is Rabbit's son, Nelson—in love with Jill, possibly even having sex with her, turned on by the excitement—but lacking resonance. The point of view is all Rabbit's, his ego, needs, solipsism.

Rabbit's basketball days are only a memory. Now heavy, he is short of breath, and only his hands are still graceful. He drinks after work, he sleeps around, he rants that the Vietnam War is necessary—if we must fight, we should fight *them there*—and yet he is attracted by the new. He is a mutant of sorts. He agrees to his wife's affair, is fascinated by Jill and sympathetic to Skeeter. But it is all in a frame of reference as a registering consciousness. Rabbit listens, responds, but cannot comprehend. The background is moon shot, moon walk, moon talk, but that, like everything else, passes him by. Updike has little sense of dread, personal disaster (beyond the grief of the moment), none of the intensity Joyce Carol Oates applies to a situation or character who is down.

Jill at one point conveys her Zen view, which is strikingly nineteenth-century, that the universe is a clean place once we can efface our own egos: " . . . all the animals and rocks and spiders and moon-rocks and stars and grains of sand absolutely doing their thing, unself-consciously." With Emersonian stress, she says "matter is the mirror of spirit." Man destroys the sense of things by thrusting ego and self into things. Rabbit is entranced by her talk, but it passes him by, for whatever did register could not matter. Jill is for him little more than a number of willing orifices, and it is fitting that while Rabbit is away playing with another woman, Jill is burned to death in his house, the fire set, apparently, by local people objecting to her and Skeeter. In the first novel, the infant is victim; here, Jill: one drowns, one burns, water and fire claiming the sacrifice. Janice and Rabbit reunite amidst the ruins.

Like Malamud with *The Tenant,* another effort to capture the "scene," Updike has little ear or sense of things when he moves from what he does know; and his use of Rabbit Angstrom as a registering consciousness in a long novel was an error. In another format, Skeeter's attempt to explain himself and blacks to a frustrated, conservative, even paranoiac white audience may have had significance; but Rabbit has so little of our faith that the stream of talk is only embarrassingly tedious. " 'Baboons, monkeys, apes: these hopeful sweet blacks trying to make men of themselves, thinking they'd been called to be men at last in these the Benighted States of Amurri-ka' "—so Skeeter goes on, mocking blacks who try to fit themselves into what whites want, only to be mocked in turn. Skeeter's barrage, which could have been meaningful if dramatized differently, if dramatized at all instead of sermonized, is verbal disaster.

With the publication of *Rabbit Is Rich* in 1981, it becomes clear that the three Rabbit novels should be read as a trilogy. A trilogy assumes that there is inter-woven material, that each novel is a slice of the pie, not the whole of it. If we view the books in this way, *Rabbit Redux*'s weaknesses can be partially papered over by the stronger novels on either side, and *Rabbit, Run* takes on a greater cultural urgency. If three, why not four? *Rabbit Is Rich* seems to foreshadow a fourth book, a kind of Brewer *Ring;* for Rabbit must begin to pay with his health for his excesses, and *that* is a subject. His heart will go bad, he will find himself losing his virility, he will be replaced, gradually, by his son, Nelson. Everything in *Rabbit Is Rich* suggests that Rabbit, now forty-six, has peaked, in an allegory of America itself in the later 1970s and early 1980s. What Rabbit represents as a piece of America is being transformed; and his own life, so much a microcosm of middle America, must undergo a similar transformation. It is a sign of Updike's achievement here that he has found, as Lewis did with Babbitt, a real voice for the country, or at least for the part of the society that would vote for Reagan and continue to support him.

Carter is President, the gas lines have lengthened, the Iranians have just taken their hostages, gold and silver are rising in price, inflation is rampant, and Rabbit is rich, the co-owner of a Toyota dealership in Brewer. He is now cozy with his wife, Janice, having accepted his fate after the disasters of *Rabbit Redux,* in which his affair with Jill ended with her fiery death and Janice had gone to live with Charlie Stavros, who now manages a division of the Toyota dealership. Rabbit is heavy, successful, a country club man, a golfer, faithful to Janice, but torn by doubts and intimations of mortality. The person who is the locus of his doubt is Nelson, his troubled son, who decides to return to Brewer after three years at Kent State University. Nelson returns with one young lady, Melanie, and then another appears, Pru, who is pregnant and whom he marries against his will. He, also, intends to get his start in the Toyota dealership, forcing Rabbit to acknowledge him. Although Rabbit fits well within his cozy life, he finds himself in a constant struggle with Nelson, who has Janice and her mother (the other co-owner of the dealership) on his side.

Nelson reminds Rabbit of all his own messes—in his disregard for property (he bangs up one car after another), in his moving from one girl to another, in making a marriage that seems doomed even before the ceremony. He is bitten by some disgruntlement which also gnawed at Rabbit and made him run. Unlike his father, Nelson has had no successes, only bad memories. He is a young man of the sixties, remembering the doomed Jill and Skeeter, the black revolutionary of *Rabbit Redux,* holding his father responsible for Jill's death. Skeeter, too, is now dead. The sixties have vanished. Nelson has nothing to hold on to but these recollections, since he senses intense hostility in his father and has nothing of his own to sustain him. Updike is very successful in making Nelson appear as unpleasant as he is supposed to be. Janice is sympathetic, but she is a heavy drinker, under the sexual sway of Rabbit, a woman seeking her own pleasures. Rabbit is still incapable of being a father, although he wants some closeness and pays heavily for Nelson's mistakes.

Rabbit Is Rich is the most effective of the three Rabbit books, the one with the most sustained tone. The now familiar characters have all reached a turning point, well illustrated in the book by the army of Toyotas, like gigantic ant colonies, which are overrunning America. American convertibles, cherished by Nelson, are now antiques, virtually fossils. The comfortable American car is a gas guzzler; the Toyota, while economical, has little inside space for large Americans, and yet Japanese cars are the cars of the present and future. They have made Rabbit rich. American cars, suitable as collectibles, are now a side item for him. The symbolism seems obvious, and yet Updike works it exceptionally well. He has always been compelling on cars as intimate cogs of American life, and even in a book as miscalculated as *The Centaur*, one recalls the aching grind of a car on a frozen night. Like Cheever with railroads, tracks, small-town stations, Updike shapes cars to the form of the American dream or nightmare. No passage in his other books matches the loving care with which he opens *Rabbit Is Rich:* the Toyota itself, Rabbit's showroom, the demonstration Rabbit gives to a young couple. The observable detail and intense attachment to the artifacts of decline compete favorably with a similar kind of thing we find in John O'Hara, Sinclair Lewis, Wright Morris. The passing of the American motorcar—that paradise lost—is, ironically, inversely related to Rabbit's growing girth.

Rabbit is, in many respects, an updated Babbitt. Updike does not work the town for its yokels and foibles, however, but uses a more modern post of observation to reach somewhat comparable conclusions. He is not a satirist, rather a historian of contemporary mores. Lewis put Babbitt into a context of social connections, so that he reflected Zenith and Zenith mirrored him. Updike, the heir of half a century of modernism, filters the town more restrictively through Rabbit, with occasional excursions into Nelson's consciousness. There is really a narrative dualism: the omniscient Updike, the Rabbit post of observation. The book's limitations are, in fact, directly associated with that intense, almost claustrophobic stress on Rabbit's consciousness.

The problem lies there: not in what Updike does, for he performs very well, but in what he does not do. Inevitably, with a character like Rabbit—and after three views of him, one thousand pages—his ordinariness transcends his performance. The accumulation of sexual thoughts and performances, the emphasis on women's bodies, their inner parts and protuberances, cannot hide the fact that sexual activity is being used

as a tease. Updike conveys delight in the female form, in the joys of heterosexual connection, in the varieties of sexual excitement a man and woman can conceive of—as experienced by the man. Even the return of Ruth—the part-time whore from *Rabbit Redux,* who bore Rabbit a daughter he has not seen—now fat and gray, brings back to him her heavy, sweet body. Rabbit not only performs well, he remembers well. All this is to be praised, since good sex has become a rare commodity in the American novel.

There is, however, a sameness to the performance, too many adolescent fantasies; the sex never achieves eroticism. Although Updike is aware of mortality—Rabbit comes close to heart attacks when he runs, and the birth of a granddaughter is, for him, a sign of his own imminent death—the indulgence of his body outpaces deeper thought. Rabbit's views are of little interest; his inner life, when not associated with sex or hostility to Nelson, is a waste land. Not even his dimmest ideas have content. Rabbit is something of a trap for Updike, as he must have recognized. For Updike had to exalt the ordinary without falling into the tedium that many naturalist novels repeat.

Part of the problem derives from the people around Rabbit; while he continues to perform, they more or less stand still or are frozen into roles. Janice remains a warm, trim body, full of alcohol and sexual desire, but little else. A cipher, she goes nowhere, except deeper into the marriage. Nelson's two girl friends are hardly defined; they are "the younger generation," symbols of what is growing up. The social set, in and around the local country club, cannot say anything that interests the reader; so that the latter, if male, must wait for the sexual action.

A vacation trip that three couples take late in the novel is predictable: it must lead to wife swapping. With his eye on the well-filled-out Cindy (she is only flesh, not life), Rabbit is more than willing to trade off Janice in order to get his hands and mouth on her opulence. But he ends up with slim, prim Thelma, who turns out to be sexual dynamite. What is disturbing is the predictability of the strategy; good sex is not being used as part of something else, but as a diversion, and yet Updike cannot maneuver into something significant because he has established such limited actors—whose movement is, indeed, best in bed, or thinking about the possibilities.

There is a hermetic quality to *Rabbit Is Rich* which derives not only from what is created but from what is omitted. For the ordinariness of ideas and conversation manifest in Brewer, in small-town Reagan territory, is a literary blind alley. Sinclair Lewis was able to sustain his vision of Zenith because, first, he got there before anyone else to establish the mode, and second, he saw George Babbitt as being slowly dehumanized by the rounds of clubs and meetings, the demands of business. Lewis was at ease with naturalism, and in its mechanisms he found images of Babbitt's decline even as he prospered. Updike is a less enthusiastic naturalist, and Rabbit remains on top. Decline will, of course, come, and there are, as we have seen, foreshadowings. But personal—as apart from social—decline is not a felt quality of the novel, and it does not work out in performance. Even the Oedipal struggle slips away, for Nelson runs off before Pru gives birth, and Rabbit is left as king of the hill.

He and Janice move into a new house, with money from the dealership and from his appreciated Krugerrands. In the new home, Rabbit rules the roost—more rooster than bunny—and even if Nelson does re-

turn eventually, even if he can learn to stop running, he will live not with Rabbit but with Janice's mother. Thus the potentially deadly struggle—deadly because Nelson flirts with death by car—is muted. Routine remains triumphant, and yet this evenness, this acceptance of values, this desire to keep the present going indefinitely—all of which are the novel's victories—are also the source of its limitations. Those intimations of mortality are little more than window dressing. (pp. 349-52)

Frederick R. Karl, "The 1960s: The (Wo)man Who Cried I Am," in his *American Fictions, 1940/1980: A Comprehensive History and Critical Evaluation,* Harper & Row, Publishers, 1983, pp. 276-383.

SOURCES FOR FURTHER STUDY

Detweiler, Robert. *John Updike.* New York: Twayne Publishers, 1984.
Well-regarded introduction to Updike's major works.

Greiner, Donald J. *The Other John Updike: Poems / Short Stories / Prose / Play.* Athens: Ohio University Press, 1981, 297 p.
First important study of Updike's non-novel writing.

———. *John Updike's Novels.* Athens: Ohio University Press, 1984.
In-depth exploration of Updike's novels through *Rabbit Is Rich.*

Hunt, George W. *John Updike and the Three Great Secret Things: Sex, Religion, and Art.* Grand Rapids, Mich.: William B. Eerdmans, 1980, 232 p.

Examines the importance of philosophers Søren Kierkegaard and Karl Barth to Updike's fiction.

Macnaughton, William R., ed. *Critical Essays on John Updike.* Boston: G. K. Hall and Co., 1982, 308 p.
Collection of reviews and essays on several aspects of Updike's work by some of his most noted commentators.

Modern Fiction Studies 37, No. 1 (Spring 1991): 5-156.
Special issue devoted to Updike. Contains essays on several facets of his novels, including the Rabbit tetralogy, *Roger's Version, The Coup,* and *Marry Me.*

Voltaire

1694-1778

(Born François Marie Arouet) French essayist, dramatist, poet, historian, critic, conte writer, and autobiographer.

INTRODUCTION

Voltaire was a principal figure of the French Enlightenment. He wrote dramas, poetry, history, occasional essays, literary criticism, political and social treatises, an autobiography, and contes—short tales of adventure. Among the latter, *Memnon: Histoire orientale* (1747), better known as *Zadig; ou, La destinée* (1749; *Zadig; or, The Book of Fate. An Oriental History*, 1749) and *Candide; ou, L'optimisme* (1759; *Candide*, 1759) are highly esteemed. He also composed analytical and philosophical works, notably *Letters concerning the English Nation* (1733; *Lettres philosophiques*, 1734) and *Dictionaire philosophique portatif* (1764; *Philosophical Dictionary*, 1765), and was an astonishingly versatile and prolific letter-writer. Throughout his long life, Voltaire was both lauded and despised. To the European literary world, he embodied the highest ideal of the Age of Reason: faith in humankind's ability to perfect itself. Yet he was feared and denigrated by victims of his biting wit. Today, Voltaire is recognized as a leading world philosopher, master essayist, and storyteller.

Voltaire was born François Marie Arouet in 1694, in or near Paris, the son of a prosperous solicitor. His mother, Marie Daumart, was from an upper middle-class family; she died when the boy was seven. Voltaire studied with the Jesuits at the Collège Louis-le-Grand from 1704 to 1711 and was, by all accounts, a brilliant and devoted student. He set out to make a name for himself as a professional writer, but his father, eager to crush his son's rising literary ambitions, sent him out of the country with the French ambassador. In Holland, Voltaire fell madly in love with Olympe de Noyer—nicknamed "Pimpette"—but the affair turned into a scandal and Voltaire was sent home. Back in Paris and miserable at the prospect of practicing law for the rest of his life, he wrote and circulated vitriolic verse attacks on the regent, Phillipe d'Orléans. These works deeply offended Phillipe and brought upon Voltaire state-mandated internal exile at the château of the duc de Sully. In 1717, having again incurred royal wrath, Voltaire was imprisoned for eleven months in the Bastille. Upon his release, his first drama, *Oedipe* (1719), enjoyed tremendous success. He next completed an epic about Henri IV, *La ligue; ou Henry le Grand* (1723; *La henriade,* 1728), infusing it with indictments of fanaticism and praise for religious toleration. These protests eventually led to an argument with the chevalier de Rohan, a member of one of the most powerful families of France, and resulted in Voltaire's arrest, imprisonment, and exile to England in 1726.

In England Voltaire found relative freedom in matters of conscience and religion. He met Jonathan Swift and Alexander Pope, found backing for a luxurious edition of *La henriade,* and began work on a highly sympathetic portrait of the English, *Letters concerning the English Nation.* Upon his return to France, he wrote drama upon drama, including the hugely successful *Zayre* (1732; *Zaire, Tragedy of Zara,* 1736) as well as his first historical work, *Histoire de Charles XII, Roi de Suède* (1731; *History of Charles XII, King of Sweden,* 1732). When *Letters philosophiques,* the French-language edition of *Letters concerning the English nation,* appeared in 1734, it was greeted with outrage and was ordered burned by censors who denounced the author's implied criticism of French institutions. Voltaire consequently exercised extreme caution in the voicing of his opinions for years thereafter.

While continuing to write successful dramas, notably the tragedies *Alzire; ou, Les Américains* (1736; *Alzire,* 1736), *Mahomet* (1742; *Mahomet the Impostor,* 1744), and *La mérope française* (1744; *Merope,* 1744), he began a love affair with the married Gabrielle Emile Le Tonnelier de Breteuil, Marquise du Châtelet. He also began a lively and intimate philosophical correspondence with the crown prince of Prussia. After the crown prince became Frederick II, King of Prussia, in 1740, he attempted to entice Voltaire to come live in Potsdam, but Madame du Châtelet strictly opposed such a move. Voltaire and madame were also briefly welcomed by Louis XV at Versailles, where the former was appointed king's historiographer and gentleman of the king's bedchamber until Voltaire and the marquise unleashed a series of highly critical remarks about court society. In 1747 Voltaire completed his first major conte, *Zadig,* and he and Madame du Châtelet returned to Lorraine, residing at the court of Stanislas, ex-king of Poland. When their romantic attachment abruptly dissolved, Voltaire accepted Frederick's invitation to live in Potsdam in 1750. The state of affairs between king and commoner was initially highly satisfactory for both, but in time they grew apart philosophically. Claiming poor health, Voltaire began his return to

France in 1752, only to be arrested in Frankfurt in 1753 and forced to surrender a volume of Frederick's poetry, earlier presented to him by the king himself.

Voltaire now found himself unwelcome in Paris and shunned at the great courts. Moreover, a stolen manuscript of his world history was published in a distorted and ludicrously adulterated version, causing the author much embarrassment. This incident prompted publication of an authorized text under the title *Essai sur l'histoire générale, et sur les moeurs et l'esprit des nations* (1756; *An Essay on Universal History, the Manners and Spirit of Nations,* 1759). With his new mistress, his niece Marie Louise Mignot Denis, Voltaire settled near Geneva on an estate he named "Les Délices." Henceforth, financially secure and relieved of the need to satisfy the whims of powerful acquaintances, he devoted himself to writing history and criticism. Above all, he championed the chief social issues of the age, religious and political toleration. In *Poème sur le désastre de Lisbonne* (1756), a strongly philosophical meditation upon the devastating 1755 Lisbon earthquake, he attempted to reconcile the disaster with the Leibnizian doctrine of Optimism, which held that this world is the best possible world, and with the idea of the existence of a benevolent providence. Three years later, in *Candide,* he again attacked Optimism. Meanwhile, to avoid possible interference with his work from the Protestant authorities of Geneva, he purchased two estates in France near the Swiss border, settling at Ferney. By about 1760 he had begun to attack organized religion, adopting the expression "Écrasez l'infâme"—"Crush the infamous"—as his personal motto. In numerous short, sarcastic works published anonymously or pseudonymously but unmistakably bearing his touch, he defended the Encyclopedists against charges of impiety, targeting conservative laymen and ecclesiastics alike. He also decried judicial malpractice and sought redress for victims of wrongful conviction. One such case, known as the Calas Affair, remains one of the most celebrated incidents of its kind. His best-known work of this period is his 1764 *Philosophical Dictionary,* which underwent extensive revisions and several title changes during the next decade or so. In 1778, at the age of eighty-four, Voltaire returned to Paris, where he was thunderously acclaimed at a performance of *Irène* (1778). He died soon after and was buried at the Abbey of Scellières. In 1791, his ashes were transferred to the Panthéon in Paris.

Voltaire was an extremely prolific author who wrote several acknowledged world masterpieces, including *Candide, Letters concerning the English Nation,* and the *Philosophical Dictionary.* Nevertheless, Voltaire is known more for the general tenets of his thought than for any particular text or group of works. Most commentators agree that this is because his motto, "Écrasez l'infâme," is mirrored to some degree in nearly everything he wrote, early or late, and helps to unify his literary canon under a general theme. Voltaire constantly fought prejudice and injustice. He embraced progress and liberty while denouncing what he perceived as wanton excesses of church and state. He tirelessly promoted freedom of speech and thought. He decried fanaticism and intolerance. In a way, critics have argued, he presaged in his writings a later fascination with the "common man." Sometimes militantly anticlerical, he was just as often determinedly eager to maintain at least the appearance of objectivity in his analyses of contemporary events. This is especially apparent in his historical works.

Critics concur that as a propagandist Voltaire was practically unrivaled in his day. In *Candide,* for example, he castigated Optimism with irony, tricking his readers into thinking about two of the most pressing intellectual issues of the age: God's role in world events and the apparent errors of metaphysics. By his own admission, he aimed thereby to improve the human lot. In religious matters, Voltaire was for most of his life a deist. He believed in God but abhorred false, "priestly" traditions. Above all, he faulted cultish closed-mindedness. These views are apparent in the contes, in the philosophical and topical works—even in the dramas. Critics are divided about the nature of Voltaire's most deeply held convictions, however. While it is clear that organized religion held no appeal for him, he nevertheless maintained a lifelong admiration of his Jesuit teachers. Equally, though he denounced Optimism as a doctrine, he apparently viewed the alleged "necessity" of despair with no less horror. In the end, scholars have noted, he probably saw life as a kind of insoluble mystery, fascinating to observe and quick to reward those who embrace it without prejudice.

Perhaps because of the enormity of his literary output and its tremendous variety, Voltaire has long defied capsule critical assessment. Most commentators, however, have freely acknowledged his unique place in eighteenth-century French literature. Wrote Gustave Lanson in his 1906 critical study of Voltaire: "We may consider Montesquieu, Rousseau, Buffon, and Diderot as greater geniuses, but Voltaire was, in the broadest sense, the most representative mind of his age, the one in whom the brilliance of eighteenth century French society was summed up most completely and brought to its most exquisite perfection. He embodied its good and bad features, its graces and blemishes, its breadth of view and its limitations, its impulses and enthusiasms as well as its hesitations and timidities." From earliest times, Voltaire was recognized as a genius who had something important to say. His topical essays were viewed as seminal analyses of pressing issues; his poems and plays were considered masterful examples of their respective genres; his epic *La henriade* was acclaimed as the French counterpart of *The Aeneid;* and his contes were enjoyed by casual reader and serious thinker alike. During the first third of the nineteenth century, however, Voltaire's reputation as the supreme dramatist and poet of his age was eclipsed somewhat, overshadowed by his elevation as one of the greatest thinkers of all time. Since then, critics have focused more on Voltaire's thought than on his technical skills as a writer. George Saintsbury, writing in 1911, assessed earlier criticism of Voltaire as decidedly partisan. "Most judgments of Voltaire," he claimed, "have been unduly coloured by sympathy with or dislike of what may be briefly called his polemical side. When sympathy and dislike are both discarded or allowed for, he remains one of the most astonishing, if not exactly one of the most admirable, figures of letters."

Today, Voltaire remains one of the chief figures of the French Enlightenment and an author of world importance. He played a major part in spreading the gospel of rational skepticism to the world, and he infused his message with pleas for religious and political toleration. His faith in humankind's ability to perfect itself was deep and abiding. A statement in his introduction to the seventh edition of the *Philosophical Dictionary* sums up much of his thinking: "Persons of every estate will find here something that will instruct, while it amuses, them. The book does not demand a continuous reading; but at whatever place you open it, you will find something to think about. Those books are most useful in which the readers do half the work themselves; they develop the thought whose germ has been presented to them; they correct what seems defective, and with their own reflections strengthen what appears weak."

(For further information about Voltaire's life and works, see *Literature Criticism from 1400 to 1800,* Vol. 14.)

CRITICAL COMMENTARY

GEORGE SAINTSBURY

(essay date 1911)

[Saintsbury was an English literary historian and critic. Hugely prolific, he composed histories of English and European literature as well as numerous critical works on individual authors, styles, and periods. In the following excerpt from a work first published in 1911, he considers the variety and intent of Voltaire's major writings.]

Vast and various as the work of Voltaire is, its vastness and variety are of the essence of its writer's peculiar quality. The divisions of it have long been recognized, and may be treated regularly.

The first of these divisions in order, not the least in bulk, and, though not the first in merit, inferior to none in the amount of congenial labour spent on it, is the *theatre*. Between fifty and sixty different pieces (including a few which exist only in fragments or sketches) are included in his writings, and they cover his literary life. It is at first sight remarkable that Voltaire, whose comic power was undoubtedly far in excess of his tragic, should have written many tragedies of no small excellence in their way, but only one fair second-class comedy, *Nanine.* His other efforts in this latter direction are either slight and almost insignificant in scope, or, as in the case of the somewhat famous *Écossaise,* deriving all their interest from being personal libels. His tragedies, on the other hand, are works of extraordinary merit in their own way. Although Voltaire had neither the perfect versification of Racine nor the noble poetry of Corneille, he surpassed the latter certainly, and the former in the opinion of some not incompetent judges, in playing the difficult and artificial game of the French tragedy. *Zaïre,* among those where love is admitted as a principal motive, and *Mérope,* among those where this motive is excluded and kept in subordination, yield to no plays of their class in such interest as is possible on the model, in stage effect and in uniform literary merit. Voltaire knew that the public opinion of his time reserved its highest prizes for a capable and successful dramatist, and he was determined to win those prizes. He therefore set all his wonderful cleverness to the task, going so far as to adopt a little even of that Romantic disobedience to the strict classical theory which he condemned, and no doubt sincerely, in Shakespeare.

As regards his *poems* proper, of which there are two long ones, the *Henriade* and the *Pucelle,* besides smaller pieces, of which a bare catalogue fills fourteen royal octavo columns, their value is very unequal. The *Henriade* has by universal consent been relegated to the position of a school reading book. Constructed and written in almost slavish imitation of Virgil, employing for medium a very unsuitable vehicle—the Alexandrine couplet (as reformed and rendered monotonous for dramatic purposes)—and animated neither by enthusiasm for the subject nor by real understanding thereof, it could not but be an unsatisfactory performance. The *Pucelle,* if morally inferior, is from a literary point of view of far more value. It is desultory to a degree; it is a base libel on religion and history; it differs from its model *Ariosto* in being, not, as *Ariosto* is, a mixture of romance and burlesque, but a sometimes tedious tissue of burlesque pure and simple; and it is exposed to the objection—often and justly urged—that much of its fun depends simply on the fact that there were and are many people who believe enough in Christianity to make its jokes give pain to them and to make their disgust as such jokes piquant to others. Nevertheless, with all the *Pucelle*'s faults, it is amusing. The minor poems are as much above the *Pucelle* as the *Pucelle* is above the *Henriade.* It is true that there is nothing, or hardly anything, that properly deserves the name of poetry in them—no passion, no sense of the beauty of nature, only a narrow "criticism of life," only a conventional and restricted choice of language, a cramped and monotonous prosody, and none of that indefinite suggestion which has been rightly said to be of the poetic essence. But there is immense wit, a wonderful command of such metre and language as the taste of the time allowed to the poet, occasionally a singular if somewhat artificial grace, and a curious felicity of diction and manner.

The third division of Voltaire's works in a rational order consists of his *prose romances* or *tales.* These productions—incomparably the most remarkable and most absolutely good fruit of his genius—were usually composed as pamphlets, with a purpose of polemic in religion, politics, or what not. Thus *Candide* attacks religious and philosophical optimism, *L'homme aux quarante écus* certain social and political ways of the time, *Zadig* and others the received forms of moral and metaphysical orthodoxy, while some are mere lampoons on the Bible, the unfailing source of Voltaire's wit. But (as always happens in the case of literary work where the form exactly suits the author's genius) the purpose in all the best of them disappears almost entirely. It is in

Principal Works

Oedipe (drama) 1719

La ligue; ou, Henry le Grand (poetry) 1723; also published as La henriade, 1728

[Henriade: An Epick Poem, 1732]

Histoire de Charles XII, Roi de Suède (history) 1731

[History of Charles XII, King of Sweden, 1732]

Zayre (drama) 1732; also published as Zaïre, 1736

[Tragedy of Zara, 1736]

Letters concerning the English Nation (prose) 1733; also published as Lettres écrites de Londres sur les Anglois et autres sujects, 1734; also published as Lettres philosophiques, 1734

Alzire; ou, Les Américains (drama) 1736

[Alzire, 1736]

Oeuvres de M. de Voltaire. 12 vols. (essays, dramas, philosophy, poetry, prose, history, and criticism) 1738-60

[The Works of Voltaire, 35 vols., 1761-69]

Mahomet (drama) 1742

[Mahomet the Impostor, 1744]

La mérope française, avec quelques petites pièces de littérature (drama and criticism) 1744

[Merope, 1744]

Memnon: Histoire orientale (prose) 1747; also published as Zadig; ou, La destinée, 1749

[Zadig; or, The Book of Fate. An Oriental History, 1749]

Le siècle de Louis XIV. 2 vols. (history) 1751

[The Age of Lewis XIV, 2 vols., 1752]

Le Micromégas de Mr. de Voltaire, avec une histoire des croisades & un nouveau plan de l'histoire de l'esprit humain (prose) 1752

[Micromegas: A Comic Romance, 1753]

L'orphelin de la Chine (drama) 1755

[The Orphans of China, 1756]

La pucelle d'Orléans (poetry) 1755; also published as La pucelle d'Orléans; ou, Jeanne d'Arc [complete edition], 1756

[La Pucelle, 1789]

Essai sur l'histoire générale, et sur les moeurs et l'esprit des nations, depuis Charlemagne jusqu'à nos jours. 7 vols. (prose) 1756

[An Essay on Universal History, the Manners and Spirit of Nations, from the Reign of Charlemaign to the Age of Lewis XIV, 4 vols., 1759]

Poèmes sur le désastre de Lisbonne et sur la loi naturelle (poetry) 1756

Candide; ou, L'optimisme, traduit de l'Allemand, de Mr. le Docteur Ralph (prose) 1759

[Candide; or, All for the Best, 1759]

Tancrède (drama) 1760

[Almida, 1771]

Le théâtre de M. de Voltaire. 5 vols. (dramas) 1762-63

Traité sur la tolérance (essay) 1763

[A Treatise on Religious Tolerance, Occasioned by the Execution of the Unfortunate Jean Calas, Unjustly Condemned and Broken on the Wheel at Toulouse, for the Supposed Murder of His Own Son, 1764]

Dictionnaire philosophique portatif (prose) 1764; revised editions, 1765, 1767; also published as La raison par alphabet [revised edition], 1769

[Philosophical Dictionary for the Pocket, 1765]

L'ingénu: Histoire véritable, tirée des manuscrits de Père Quesnel (prose) 1767

[The Pupil of Nature, 1771; also published as The Sincere Huron, 1786]

Irène (drama) 1778

Memoires de M. de Voltaire écrits par lui-même (autobiography) 1784

[Memoirs de M. de Voltaire Written by Himself, 1784]

these works more than in any others that the peculiar quality of Voltaire—ironic style without exaggeration—appears. That he learned it partly from Saint-Évremond, still more from Anthony Hamilton, partly even from his own enemy Le Sage, is perfectly true, but he gave it perfection and completion. If one especial peculiarity can be singled out, it is the extreme restraint and simplicity of the verbal treatment. Voltaire never dwells too long on his point, stays to laugh at what he has said, elucidates or comments on his own jokes, guffaws over them or exaggerates their form. The famous "pour encourager les autres" (that the shooting of Byng did "encourage the others" very much is not to the point) is a typical example, and indeed the whole of *Candide* shows the style at its perfection.

The fourth division of Voltaire's work, the *historical,* is the bulkiest of all except his correspondence, and some parts of it are or have been among the most read, but it is far from being even among the best. The small treatises on Charles XII. and Peter the Great are indeed models of clear narrative and ingenious if somewhat superficial grasp and arrangement. The so-called *Siècle de Louis XIV,* and *Siècle de Louis XV* (the latter inferior to the former but still valuable) contain a great miscellany of interesting matter, treated by a man of great acuteness and unsurpassed power of writing, who had also had access to much important private information. But even in these books defects are present, which appear much more strongly in the singular olla podrida entitled *Essai sur les moeurs,* in the *Annales de l'empire* and in the minor historical works. These defects are an almost total absence of any comprehension of what has since been called the philosophy of history, the constant presence of gross prejudice, frequent inaccuracy of detail, and, above all, a complete incapacity to look at anything except from the narrow standpoint of a half pessimist and half self-satisfied *philosophe* of the 18th century.

His work in *physics* concerns us less than any other here; it is, however, not inconsiderable in bulk, and is said by experts to give proof of aptitude.

To his own age Voltaire was pre-eminently a poet and a philosopher; the unkindness of succeeding ages has sometimes questioned whether he had any title to either name, and especially to the latter. His largest *philosophical* work, at least so called, is the curious medley entitled *Dictionaire philosophique,* which is compounded of the articles contributed by him to the great *Encyclopédie* and of several minor pieces. No one of Voltaire's works shows his anti-religious or at least anti-ecclesiastical animus more strongly. The various title-words of the several articles are often the merest stalking-horses, under cover of which to shoot at the Bible or the church, the target being now and then shifted to the political institutions of the writer's country, his personal foes, &c., and the whole being largely seasoned with that acute, rather superficial, commonsense, but also commonplace, ethical and social criticism which the 18th century called philosophy. The book ranks perhaps second only to the novels as showing the character, literary and personal, of Voltaire; and despite its form it is nearly as readable. The minor philosophical works are of no very different character. In the brief *Traité de métaphysique* the author makes his grand effort, but scarcely succeeds in doing more than show that he had no real conception of what metaphysic is.

In general *criticism* and *miscellaneous* writing Voltaire is not inferior to himself in any of his other functions. Almost all his more substantive works, whether in verse or prose, are preceded by prefaces of one sort or another, which are models of his own light pungent *causerie;* and in a vast variety of nondescript pamphlets and writings he shows himself a perfect journalist. In literary criticism pure and simple his principal work is the *Commentaire sur Corneille,* though he wrote a good deal more of the same kind—sometimes (as in his *Life* and notices of Molière) independently sometimes as part of his *Siècles.* Nowhere, perhaps, except when he is dealing with religion, are Voltaire's defects felt more than here. He was quite unacquainted with the history of his own language and literature, and more here than anywhere else he showed the extraordinarily limited and conventional spirit which accompanied the revolt of the French 18th century against limits and conventions in theological, ethical and political matters.

There remains only the huge division of his *correspondence,* which is constantly being augmented by fresh discoveries, and which, according to Georges Bengesco, has never been fully or correctly printed, even in some of the parts longest known. In this great mass Voltaire's personality is of course best shown, and perhaps his literary qualities not worst. His immense energy and versatility, his adroit and unhesitating flattery when he chose to flatter, his ruthless sarcasm when he chose to be sarcastic, his rather unscrupulous business faculty, his more than rather unscrupulous resolve to double and twist in any fashion so as to escape his enemies,—all these things appear throughout the whole mass of letters.

Most judgments of Voltaire have been unduly coloured by sympathy with or dislike of what may be briefly called his polemical side. When sympathy and dislike are both discarded or allowed for, he remains one of the most astonishing, if not exactly one of the most admirable, figures of letters. That he never, as Carlyle complains, gave utterance to one great thought is strictly true. That his characteristic is for the most part an almost superhuman cleverness rather than positive genius is also true. But that he was merely a mocker, which Carlyle and others have also said, is not strictly true or fair. In politics proper he seems indeed to have had few or no constructive ideas, and to have been entirely ignorant or quite reckless of the fact that his attacks were destroying a state of things for which as a whole he neither had nor apparently wished to have any substitute. In religion he protested stoutly, and no doubt sincerely, that his own attitude was not purely negative; but here also he seems to have failed altogether to distinguish between pruning and cutting down. Both here and elsewhere his great fault was an inveterate superficiality. But this superficiality was accompanied by such wonderful acuteness within a certain range, by such an absolutely unsurpassed literary aptitude and sense of style in all the lighter and some of the graver modes of literature, by such untiring energy and versatility in enterprise, that he has no parallel among ready writers anywhere. Not the most elaborate work of Voltaire is of much value for matter; but not the very slightest work of Voltaire is devoid of value in form. In literary craftsmanship, at once versatile and accomplished, he has no superior and scarcely a rival. (pp. 112-17)

George Saintsbury, in his *French Literature and Its Masters,* edited by Huntington Cairns, Alfred A. Knopf, 1946, pp. 94-118.

RICHARD ALDINGTON
(essay date 1925)

[Aldington was an English essayist, novelist, literary critic, and biographer. He is perhaps best known for his controversial biographies, including *Lawrence of Arabia: A Biographical Enquiry* (1955), in which he attacked Lawrence as an "impudent mythomaniac." In the following excerpt from his 1925 biography *Voltaire*, he surveys Voltaire's contes and philosophical pamphlets.]

Voltaire would have been astonished and grieved to learn that most of his readers in the twentieth century prefer *Candide* to *La henriade* and *Jeannot et Colin* to *Zaïre*. One can imagine the restless shade of Voltaire eagerly conferring with new literary arrivals in the Elysian Fields and wringing shadowy hands in anguish at the decline of "bon goût" in Europe. (Indeed, there would be some reason for this, but not in the way he would mean). The Voltaire we most admire is not the epic poet, the dramatist, the historian, but the charming poet of light verse, the witty correspondent and, above all, the brilliant satirist and prose stylist of the Romans and Mélanges. In the forty volume edition of Voltaire, the Romans and Mélanges fill eight volumes; and this is exactly four volumes too many. In spite of Voltaire's wit and artistry, his gift of variety in treating the same ideas and topics, many of these pamphlets are redundant and abound in vain repetitions. The explanation is that they were in most cases intended as nothing but journalism, as light skirmishes in the Philosopher's War, "philosophical" propaganda against l'infâme and the abuses of the French political system, a popularization of the *Encyclopédie* for the lower ranks of readers. And since Voltaire knew that truth for such people is that which they hear most often repeated, he indulged in repetition of his main points to an extent which is now tedious.

A reader who knows the Romans and other pamphlets only from modern selections, will no doubt feel inclined to protest against this view; let him read perseveringly through the whole eight volumes, and it will be surprising indeed if he does not agree. After the fourth volume (and, by the way, the four volumes of the *Dictionnaire philosophique* might be added to the eight mentioned above) a reader becomes more and more aware of the presence of certain Voltairean clichés. Finally, he gets to know what is coming in the pamphlet from reading only its opening paragraph. He grows weary of raillery at the absurdities, contradictions, and indecencies of the Bible—information chiefly derived from Bolingbroke, by the way. Directly this topic is broached, an experienced Voltairean reader knows that he will get the impostures of Moses, the immoral practices of the Patriarchs, the genealogy of the House of David with remarks on the private morals of this family, the indecent passages in Exodus, Genesis, and Ezechiel (particularly "Oohla and Oohlibah"), the singular commands of the Lord to Hosea. The Jesuits cannot be mentioned without a reference to Sanchez and his grotesque discussion of the relations between the Virgin Mary and the Holy Ghost. For the rest, the romans and pamphlets run upon the topics of the Inquisition, Jesuits, Jansenists and monks, bonzes, fakirs, mages, gymnosophists, the Sorbonne, the Papacy; Frederick, Catherine, Locke, Newton, the Encyclopédie, la saine philosophie, Deism, advantages of luxury, virtue of Chinese mandarins and North American Indians, fearful calamities, rapes, wars, shipwrecks, autos-da-fe, famines, earthquakes, mutilations, ghastly judicial executions, small-pox, venereal disease, petrified oysters on mountains, the Donation of Constantine, the constitution of England, the magnificence and brilliance of Paris, the trivial causes of wars, the example of Peter the Great, facile and faithless mistresses, imbecility and obstinacy of lawyers, indecency and peculation of monks, corruption of judges, superior antiquity and morality of the Far East, relative smallness of the Earth, insignificance of man, improbability of man's being immortal, rarity of human happiness, characteristics (usually arbitrary and inaccurate) of the nations of Europe; the frequency of human vanity, perfidy, cruelty, stupidity, persecution, sensuality, idleness, levity, inconsequence, drunkenness, heartlessness, calumny; and rare examples of "saine philosophie", hospitality, wisdom, tolerance, vegetarianism, contentment, righteousness, nobility of soul (usually among Turks, Chinese, brahmins, Indians, philosophers and agricultural small-holders).

This chaplet of clichés might be increased by a methodical compiler; however, the above list should be adequate for its purpose, which is to show that the romans and pamphlets repeat in popular form the notions and prejudices of the philosophe. But this repetition and a certain superficiality of thought do not destroy the art of Voltaire. He is usually praised as a satirist, and satire is indeed a true description of these innumerable pamphlets; but it is not a vituperative or gross satire. Sarcasm, raillery, irony, wit are the Voltairean weapons; he rarely breaks into serious denunciation and reproof, and still more rarely loses his temper, though when he does either, his satire loses its force and skill. The mood of Voltairean satire is complex, and is expressed metaphorically in the traditional Voltairean smile of Houdon's statue. That smile is malicious but humorous, sarcastic but not unkindly; it is that of a tolerant and witty man whose intelligence is prodigiously alert. And these are the qualities of Voltaire's prose satire. Human beings alternately aroused his pity and his mirth; their crimes and follies exasperated him, but he thought men could more easily be laughed and mocked than reproved and denounced out of them. At times the imbecilities of human conduct and of human systems left him aghast; but he took pity on us—poor ignorant creatures seduced by priests, crowned fools, stupid ideals, and mad prejudices—and laboured ceaselessly to enlighten us with the truths of "la saine philosophie", though with no great hope of permanently reforming us:

> Fools will be fools, say what we will,
> And rascals will be rascals still.

"In the name of common sense, act a little reasonably and learn to face facts" is the burden of these numberless diatribes. The personal attacks on his enemies are an invitation *urbi et orbi* not to take seriously the notions of people so unreasonable and foolish. But, on the whole, the Voltairean satire is an encouragement not to look at things and life too solemnly and lugubriously. Let us be reasonable, but let us make life endurable; we may not be immortal, the world may be and probably is a mass of ills, sufferings, and stupidities, but for God's sake let us crack a jest when we may. Let us, in fact, model ourselves upon the sage of Ferney; let us be active, industrious, sober, witty, ironic, philanthropic, Deistic, well-informed, and cheerful Rationalists; the deuce take the Pope and Rousseau, the Jesuits and the Jansenists, Leibnitz and Calvin, all the fanatics and the excessive, gloomy misanthropy and absurd optimism; let us mind our own business and cultivate our own gardens. Ituriel, the guardian genius of the earth, having received Babouc's report, "resolved to allow the world to go its way; for, said he, if all is not well, it is all tolerable." This is the "lesson" of many of these brilliant little pieces; it is madness to hope for the earthly paradise, fantastic to assert that all is well with the world, idiotic to be gloomy about it; make the best of what you have.

This Rationalist acceptation of the tolerability of life was quite common in the eighteenth century, at least among the upper classes. It is well put by Lord Chesterfield who in many respects was a living illustration of Voltaire's views and was in perfect sympathy with the Frenchman's philosophie.

> A wise man, without being a stoic, considers, in all misfortunes that befall him, their best as well as their worst side; and everything has a better and a worse side. . . . It is the rational philosophy taught me by experience and knowledge of the world, and which I have practised above thirty years. I always made the best of the best, and never made the bad worse by fretting; this enabled me to go through the various scenes of life, in which I have been an actor, with more pleasure and less pain than most people.

And again, in a letter to the Bishop of Waterfield, Chesterfield expresses an idea which is the very essence of Voltaire's rationalism:

> In the general course of things, there seems to be upon the whole a pretty equal distribution of physical good and evil, some extraordinary cases excepted; and even moral good and evil seem mixed to a certain degree, for one never sees anybody so perfectly good or so perfectly bad, as they might be.

Many instances of praise for these short pieces might be cited. One alone must suffice. Voltaire's "frère ennemi", the King of Prussia, who knew him so well, writes to him many years after the Frankfort episode: "You know I have always admired your writing and particularly those collections of short prose pieces called Mélanges." The wit, the gaiety, the diablerie, the clear sparkle, the absence of anything heavy or pedantic in these pamphlets, have kept them alive when Voltaire's more serious and ambitious works have fallen into disrepute. The romans especially are still regularly reprinted, and especially *Candide.* It is not unjust to say that thousands of readers know Voltaire only by that jeu d'esprit with which he amused himself in Switzerland. But others among the romans are equally brilliant and the wit of that brief satire on the nouveaux riches—*Jeannot et Colin*—is even more concentrated and amusingly malicious. The consummate art of these pieces has kept them young and fresh for a century and a half. It is not wholly a matter of wit and style, which are indeed almost imperishable when perfect, as with Voltaire they often were; but he possessed the art of telling a story—l'art de conter—in such a way that whatever he related became interesting and held the attention. We have testimony in abundance to Voltaire's charm of conversation and wonderful ability to retail anecdotes. The romans are simply wonderful examples of that charm and ability transferred to paper. The style is that of "polite conversation", chastened and polished without losing any of its familiarity and ease and without acquiring the least tinge of "literary" affectation and pedantry. The stories of his romans are told as lightly and without effort as he told a fable to young Florian. And just as Voltaire interested a child with the talking animals of a fable, so he interested the larger children of Europe with fanciful and fabulous tales in order to make them absorb his "lessons" while they scarcely knew they had done so. He smeared the rim of the cup with honey, as Tasso says, so that the reader, "deceived, drinks in the bitter juices and from his deceit gains life"—

> Succhi amari ingannato intanto ei beve,
> E dall' inganno suo vita riceve.

He drew on his extensive reading as well as on his experience of life for the machinery and setting of these tales; the old medieval French romances he pretended

---

The Gentleman's Magazine on Candide:

[Candide] is an attempt to ridicule the notion that 'all things are for the best,' by representing the calamities of life, artfully aggravated, in a strong light. . . .

To prove that the author of nature is not infinitely good, by proving that this is not the best possible system, it is necessary to know this and every other possible system perfectly in all their extent, relations, connections, and dependencies, which is impossible to man; but there are many arguments to prove that the author of nature is good, which lie within the compass of human knowledge, and as the only argument for the contrary lies confessedly beyond our knowledge, it may still be inferred, notwithstanding the mal-apert smartness of such witling-metaphysicians as M. *de Voltaire*, that whatever is, is right.

Voltaire seems indeed to have understood the opinion, which he has endeavoured to ridicule, and the arguments by which it is supported, in a very imperfect and confused manner; he has, in several places, confounded the scheme of the best with the scheme of *fitness*, & of *eternal relations of things*; & he has, like other ignorant persons, considered the appointments of providence as implying an absurd necessity, which, supposing poison to be offered a man to drink, would afford him this argument: It is now certain either that I shall die to night, or I shall not; if that I shall, I shall die, tho' I do not drink the poison; if that I shall not, I shall live, tho' I do drink it; so that my drinking, or not drinking the poison, is a matter of mere indifference, and can have no influence upon my life. Not considering, that the means and the end are inseparable, and that if it is certain that a man shall die by poison, it is also certain that he shall drink it.

From an anonymous review of Candide in *The Gentleman's Magazine and Historical Quarterly*, May, 1759.

---

to despise were levied upon, as well as many books of travel and imaginative literature, from Cyrano de Bergerac to the Arabian Nights, from Gulliver's Travels to Boccaccio. But Heaven forbid that anyone should laboriously seek for the "sources" of Voltaire's tales! The pure gold of the Romans is all Voltaire's own. . . . (pp. 213-20)

Candide appeared in 1759, under the pseudonym of *le Docteur Ralph;* but since the style and wit of every paragraph signed it "Voltaire", the precaution was wasted. All the world who read knew that only Voltaire could have written it. The object of attack was the optimistic philosophy of Leibnitz and the no less optimistic statement of Rousseau that "tout est bien." An ingenious modern critic has tried to show that some of the passages of Candide's adventures refer to the career of Baron Trenck, who was arbitrarily imprisoned by Frederick the Great; it is supposed that Voltaire knew of Trenck's sufferings and used *Candide* as a method of informing Frederick. However this may be, *Candide* is certainly one of the most entertaining prose satires ever penned. Its likeness to *Rasselas* is superficial; both Johnson and Voltaire show the misfortunes of man, but Johnson leads the reader to religion, Voltaire to rational acquiescence and a small garden. The manner of the two authors again is dissimilar; a squirrel and an elephant can both pick nuts, but the one does it nimbly and petulantly, the other with solemnity and ponderosity. *Candide* might by an extension of meaning be called "philosophical", because under its gay fiction and satire it combats two philosophical ideas; it attacks the theory of optimism formulated by Leibnitz, that God is the perfect monad, that He created a world to show His perfection, that He chose this out of the infinite number of worlds, that He was guided by the "principium melioris", and that therefore the universe is the "best possible"; and it attacks the optimism of Rousseau, who denied the doctrine of original sin and affirmed that man in a state of nature is wholly good, from which follows the abandonment of rational self-discipline and the paradoxical assertion of the aristocracy of the plebs. Both doctrines are obviously heavy with dangers to human society and both are repugnant and absurd to rational common-sense; their truth, if they be truths, is obviously mystic, and to Voltaire all mysticism was disgusting and barbarous. Vulnerable as Voltaire's Rationalism must be to a concerted metaphysical attack, it was good enough for most people, and he had the wit to bring the laughers over to his side. Nevertheless, the Rousseau paradox of the "domination of the proletariat" has survived Voltaire's "government by the enlightened" as a popular idea; no doubt because it flatters more people and is irrational—an additional proof of Voltaire's pessimistic attitude towards human nature.

The machinery of *Candide* is simple. An ingenuous youth called Candide grows up in the Westphalian home of the Baron Thunder-ten-Troncke, instructed in philosophy by Dr. Pangloss, who taught "metaphysico-theologo-cosmolonigologie", and proved that all is for the best in this best of all possible worlds. The adventures of Candide, which range from China to Peru, are one long and humorous contradiction of this assumption; they are also a contradiction of the natural goodness of man. Obviously, the art of the narrator lies in the fecundity of invention with which he devises new episodes, his skill in making each arise naturally from those before, and the indefinable gift of the raconteur which makes the incredible acceptable and compels interest. Voltaire's novels and tales are lively parables, not novels in our meaning of the word, and his characters . . . are allegorical, well-masked types or embodied opinions. But these parables of philosophie have many of the essential qualities of good fiction, and these types are so shrewdly observed and so skillfully portrayed that for all their abstraction and generalization they seem to live. What is true of *Candide* in this respect is true of most of them, though in the less successful romans (the *Lettres d'Amabed,* for instance) the device is too artificial.

In reading steadily through these romans, one is most delighted and entertained by the flashes of wit and satire; the stories themselves are often slight, but the satiric wit of situation and comment is incomparable. Candide thinks Pangloss "the greatest philosopher of the province and consequently of all mankind." He meets an eloquent anabaptist and ingenuously confesses that he had not heard the Pope was Antichrist: "The orator's wife put her head out of the window and, perceiving a man who doubted that the Pope was Antichrist poured on his head a full . . . O Heavens! to what excess are ladies carried by religious zeal!" "A lady of honour", says Cunegonde, "may be raped once, but her virtue is fortified by it." When Candide and Martin approach the coast of France, Candide asks what the country is like: "In some provinces half the inhabitants are mad, in others they are over cunning, elsewhere they think they are witty, and in all the principal occupation is making love, the second scandal, and the third talking nonsense." As a more extended example of Voltaire's "admirable fooling" in *Candide,* take this fragment of dialogue:

'Apropos,' said Candide, 'do you think the earth was originally a sea, as we are assured by that large book belonging to the captain?'

'I don't believe it in the least,' said Martin, 'any more than all the other whimsies we have been pestered with recently!'

'But to what end was this world formed?' said Candide.

'To infuriate us,' replied Martin.

'Are you not very surprised,' continued Candide, 'by the love those two girls of the country of the Oreillons had for those two monkeys, whose adventure I told you?'

'Not in the least,' said Martin, 'I see nothing strange in their passion; I have seen so many extraordinary things that nothing seems extraordinary to me.'

'Do you think,' said Candide, 'that men have always massacred each other as they do to-day? Have they always been liars, cheats, traitors, brigands, weak, flighty, cowardly, envious, gluttonous, drunken, grasping, ambitious, bloody, backbiting, debauched, fanatical, hypocritical, and silly?'

'Do you think,' said Martin, 'that sparrow-hawks have always eaten the pigeons they came across?'

'Yes, of course,' said Candide.

'Well,' said Martin, 'if sparrow-hawks have always possessed the same nature, why should you expect men to change theirs?'

'Oh!' said Candide, 'there is a great difference; free will . . . '

Arguing thus, they arrived at Bordeaux.

Amusing traits of this kind are scattered through all the romans. The *Vision de Babouc* is a fable to show the alternate good and evil of mankind and the world; Babouc is sent by the djinnee, Ituriel, to render an account of Persepolis, which needless to say is Paris. One day Barbouc is for destruction, the next for preservation, and so on alternately; finally he decides that there are "de très bonnes choses dans les abus" and, from his report, Ituriel decides to "let the world go on as it is, for if everything is not right, everything is tolerable." *Cosi-Sancta* is not a tale for puritans; it relates the misfortunes which occurred owing to the peevish chastity of a woman, and the good which resulted when her scruples dissolved. *Zadig* shows in a series of witty episodes the disadvantage of numerous estates of life and the misfortunes an honest man has to endure from the world; in short, the rarity and fragility of happiness. *Zadig* contains the famous verse which was sung every day to the conceited courtier by order of the king who wished to cure him of that vice:

Que son mérite est extrême!
Que de grâces! que de grandeur!
Ah! combine monseigneur
Doit être content de lui-même.

Memnon is a short but extremely clever satire on human prudence. Memnon one day "conceived the absurd project of being parfaitement sage". His fate in Voltaire's hands was assured; for apparently he was a disciple of Jean Jacques. *Bababec* is still shorter but even wittier; it is a satire on "fakirs" and hence upon those whom Voltaire chose to assimilate to fakirs:

Some walked on their hands; others swung on a loose cord; others always hobbled. Some wore chains; others a pack-saddle; some hid their heads under a bushel; *au demeurant les meilleurs gens du monde.*

Micromégas is a "philosophique" tale, inspired partly by Swift's Brobdingnagians and partly by Voltaire's astronomical studies. An inhabitant from Sirius and another from Saturn are dispatched to the world by Voltaire, in order to persuade us of our insignificance and the pettiness of our planet compared with the hugeness of inter-stellar space and the great suns of the universe.

To linger over these romans is to expose oneself to a "damnable iteration" of praise. Yet several others must be at least mentioned. There is *L'ingénu,* a kind of pendant to *Candide,* where a virtuous Huron is promenaded ruthlessly through the follies and ills of Europe; for a time the reader is anxiously asking himself whether Voltaire is not exposing for admiration one more specimen of the noble savage; but such is not the case, the Huron is an "honnête homme" and does not exhort us to return to caves and reindeer. *L'ingénu* is filled with amusing traits, like the famous: "l'abbé de Saint-Yves supposait qu'un homme qui n'était pas né en France n'avait pas le sens commun." *L'homme aux Quarante Ecus* is more nearly related to the political pamphlets and is one of the least interesting to us because it runs upon topics which have mostly lost all actuality. *La princesse de Babylon* forms another excuse for a vertiginously swift ramble through divers states of the world; the *Lettres d'Amabed* are a virulent satire on the Catholic missionaries in the East; *L'histoire de Jenni, Le taureau blanc, Aventure indienne, Les oreilles du Comte de Chesterfield* are all amusing for their wit and malice.

Turning from these gems of Voltairean art with their glitter and polish to the huge miscellany of pamphlets, one feels a sense of weariness, almost disgust, before the profuse repetitions of this abounding but limited mind. Take a few of them and the result is wholly pleasing; the Voltairean charm and wit achieve their effect, but after a time the mind is surfeited with raillery, disgusted with the diffusion and the repetition which are the inevitable mark of journalism. They are the relics of the campaigns of our Philosopher's War, and like all such relics look a little rusty and rather harmless when the war is over. They are ranged together helter-skelter like an unclassified museum of weapons, over-crowded and furnished with too many specimens of the same sort; any one taken separately will interest, in their disorderly bulk they weary and confuse the mind. In one of his pamphlets Voltaire described himself as a man who has spent his life "à sentir, à raisonner, et à plaisanter." The "sentir" might be disputed, but there can be no doubt about the "raisonner" and the "plaisanter"; the question is whether these functions may not eventually be abused. There is a quality in Voltairean raillery which is "agacant"—piquant but exasperating—as if he said, "Come, let us make fools of all who do not think as we think." The raillery of Voltaire must be intolerable to earnest-minded persons. Even to those who hope they take life more lightly this perpetual tittering becomes an irritation.

No doubt, the reason for this is that we weary of the same mood when it is prolonged beyond our appetite. It is amusing to spend an evening with an irrepressibly humorous man, but what a penance to be forced to live with him. Pass a few evenings over Voltaire's pamphlets, and you will be charmed and entertained; but read them solidly for a month, and you will be cloyed with raillery and you will turn for relief, as the age after Voltaire's turned, to poetry and sentiment and romance; you will understand then the immense vogue of Chateaubriand. In order to persuade men to live rationally, to abandon the dreams of mysticism, the "amour de l'impossible" which prevents us from being content with carnal and reasonable felicity; Voltaire concentrated the clear light of his intelligence upon the pettiness, the inconsistencies, the lamentable failures, the ignominies of mankind. His brilliant shafts flashed through the air and pierced unerringly all aspiring souls in their flight. He brings us back to the hard facts as pitilessly as the family solicitor, though with more wit. There is something almost gross in his utilitarianism, which sensitive minds feel instinctively as an affront. Not so Chateaubriand. Superbly disregarding the useful and the practical, he soars away into an empyrean of poetic sentiment. His works are a kind of Bible of Romanticism, devoted to the extirpation of the Voltairean spirit. Chateaubriand rehabilitated the picturesque, the mysterious, solitude and melancholy, the poetry of wild lonely places, of ruins and fallen grandeur, of fine sentiment and loyalty—all the ideas and ideals and sentiments which Voltaire had laughed away for half a century. The whole Romantic movement in France was in open hostility to Voltaire: the battle of Hernani was fought between the rear-guard of Voltaireans and the main body of Chateaubriand's pretorian legion. It was a Pyrrhic victory for the Romantics. Our world to-day is far more the world of Voltaire than of Chateaubriand. Vicisti, Ferniense!

The reaction of which Chateaubriand was the creator (or the mouthpiece) was a failure; as he lay dying, that dramatic genius which controlled his life wafted into his bedroom the clamour of the Revolution of 1848. Probably Chateaubriand joined battle with Voltaireanism on a false issue; at any rate, he failed. To us the important reflection is that the modern world of "Democracy and Progress" is to a large extent an awkward alliance of the ideology of Rousseau with the Rationalism and Utilitarianism of Voltaire and the Encyclopaedists. One must insist upon this, because few democratic politicians appear to be aware of their origins; and the political strife between left and right in commercial countries is often only the struggle between Rousseau's ideology and Voltaire's realism. The Church, which sits at the extreme right, is really hostile to both parties, but is fully aware of what she is contending with; moreover, the Church is more hostile to Rousseau then to Voltaire. I copy from to-day's *Times* a declaration of the Cardinal-Archbishop of Bordeaux: [8 October 1924]

> This programme [of the Government's] is none other than that of the "Social Contract" of Jean Jacques Rousseau, that well-known writer, who was born vicious and died insane, whose apothegms on the independence of man, individual or collective, who is subject neither to God nor morals, nor any principle whatsoever, have done more harm to France than the blasphemies of Voltaire and all the Encyclopaedists together.

I shall not pursue farther the polemics of the matter, but the Cardinal's heated words touch upon a problem which interests a student of Voltaire. To what extent do writers create public opinion and how far are they responsible for great mutations of the State? Was the French Revolution and all its tremendous consequences, which every one of us still undergoes, "created" by Rousseau, Voltaire, and the Encyclopaedists; or were they simply the mouthpieces which made audible and coherent a vast inchoate movement which would have been equally effective without them? Men "of the robe", whether authors or clergy, are inclined to overestimate the power of the spiritual leader; as the rest of mankind are apt to rate it too low. There is no possibility of estimating the extent of Voltaire's influence without an exhaustive examination of all kinds of documents by a body of scholars; and even then the results would be doubtful. Voltaire and Rousseau were only megaphones, if you like, but the advice they shouted gave direction to vast bodies of men wandering in perplexity or sunk in apathy. The rebellion against the Monarchy was an armed protest against misgovernment and despotism, such as the Fronde had been. The rebellion against the Church was the logical outcome of the Renaissance—the revival of pre-Christian Rationalism. The Reformation failed in France when Henri IV became a Catholic and ended the wars of the Ligue; the Fronde failed because it was merely a negative disturbance. But between 1789 and the flight to Varennes the French monarchy was faced with a Fronde backed by principles and a Ligue where the antagonists were not Huguenots and Catholics, but Rationalists and Christians. The combined attack was too powerful to be resisted; Monarchy and Church went down together. It seems to me that Voltaire and Rousseau, mutatis mutandis, stand in much the same relation to the French Revolution that Luther and Calvin do to the Reformation; some such movement was perhaps inevitable, given the circumstances, but these great minds set the mass in motion and gave it direction. (pp. 220-30)

[The] philosophie of Voltaire . . . was not philosophic speculation or a metaphysical system, but a practical Rationalism, addressing itself to ordinary common sense and proposing in truth only material ob-

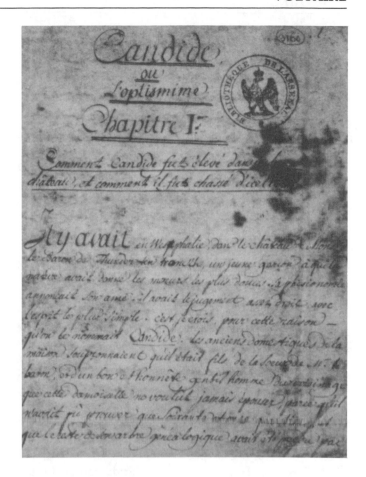

Opening page of the La Vallière manuscript of *Candide*.

jects as an aim in life. This Rationalist Materialism, with certain modifications, is the basis of the actions of most people in modern commercial democracies; it is the "philosophy" of the plain tired business man. The immense and indefatigable propaganda of the Ferney pamphlets undoubtedly contributed towards establishing that "philosophy" in France. Such a bombardment of the intelligence is probably unique in history. Think for a moment of the energy, the will-power, the perpetual mental tension, implied by that unremitting discharge of philosophical pamphlets. I have called them journalism and that is what they are—diluted and repetitive thought in a popular form; but Voltaire put something of his genius as well as his energy into every one of them. They are not the mechanical and conventional productions of a leader-writer; each had to contain a statement of a principle or principles of philosophie and each had to be entertaining. The eighteenth century public was pitiless, even to the Patriarch of Ferney; if he fell below his own standard they let him know it. All the resources of his wit and invention were drawn upon to the utmost to meet the situation, to continue the flow of propaganda in fresh and attractive ways. Hence the extraordinary variety of forms—sermons, dialogues, speeches, tales, allegories, letters, and a score of others—designed to pique the curiosity and satisfy the taste of innumerable readers. But the correctness and beauty of the prose, the eternal raillery are always there; necessarily, because they were Voltaire's manner and they were what principally charmed his readers.

The greater number of these pamphlets were directed against Christianity, the Roman Catholic Church, and the priests. They may be called blasphemies, if the reader chooses, but Voltaire was not the man to waste his time on mere senseless insults to a religion. Neither was he attacking only a corrupt clergy; for the Church possessed many worthy and good servants in the eighteenth century. For one libertin abbé there were fifty village priests of good morals. No, Voltaire was not merely blaspheming, not merely attacking the clergy; he wished to destroy belief in the divinity of Jesus Christ, the authority of the Old as well as of the New Testament, Protestantism as well as Catholicism. The attacks on the religious orders and the Church were political and a matter of economics; Voltaire wished to remove from the State the financial burden of a considerable non-productive population which controlled an immense income and paid taxes only as a "voluntary contribution". That end might have been attained without attacking Christianity. But why this perpetual disparagement of miracles, of the authenticity of the gospels? And why the attack on the Old Testament, which is not fundamental to the Church of Rome? Because, as a Deist and a Rationalist, Voltaire desired to overthrow all sects of Christianity, all revealed religion, especially the persecuting religions, Christianity and Mahommedanism. The purer Deism of Mahommedanism seemed to him preferable to the doctrine of the Trinity. He preferred Confucianism and the thought of a Marcus Aurelius to both. But, above all, the ideas of the incarnation of God in man profoundly repelled him and, whenever he dared touch upon it, he asserted that the belief was blasphemous. In the last analysis his view comes down to this: God exists, but remotely, intangibly, unknowably; the duty of men is to think and to act rationally. That is the substance of Voltaire's anti-religious pamphlets. (pp. 230-32)

Richard Aldington, in his *Voltaire,* George Routledge & Sons, Ltd., 1925, 278 p.

ANDRÉ MAUROIS

(essay date 1957)

[Maurois—born Emile Salomon Wilhelm Herzog—was a distinguished French biographer and literary critic. In the following essay, originally published in *Lecture mon doux plaisir* (1957), he explores the tone and tempo of Voltaire's philosophic fictions.]

Philosophical fiction is a difficult, because a hybrid, literary form. Since the author uses it for the purpose of espousing or attacking certain accepted ideas, it belongs to the class of essays or pamphlets. But because it narrates a sequence of imaginary events, it can also claim the title of fiction. It cannot, however, have either the seriousness of the essay or the credibility of the novel. Not that it even pretends to be credible. On the contrary, it deliberately stresses the fact that it is an exercise in intellectual ingenuity. Not Voltaire when he created *Candide,* nor Anatole France when he wrote *L'Île des Pingouins,* nor Wells when he invented *The Island of Dr Moreau* believed for a moment that the reader would mistake these fictions for reality. On the contrary, it was their considered intention to present these stories with a philosophical content as fantastic tales.

But why, it may be asked, should an author have recourse to this whimsical and indirect method of philosophizing? In order to enjoy greater freedom in expressing ideas which, in an essay, might seem to be subversive, shocking and unacceptable to the reader. The more he can be made to feel that he has been transported into a world where nonsense reigns supreme, the more reassured will he feel, and the reader to digest many surprising truths. Swift was able to say a number of disturbing things about human nature and the England of his own day, merely by pretending to describe a nation of midgets, a kingdom of giants, or a country in which horses ruled over human beings. Montesquieu was able, through the mouth of an imaginary Persian, to mock at customs for which his birth and position compelled him to make a show of respect.

The philosophical tale, or novel, will, therefore, be peculiarly well suited to a period in which ideas are changing more quickly than institutions and manners. Writers, tormented by the need they feel to say what they think, but hampered by the severity of police regulations, censorship or an Inquisition, will be tempted to take refuge in the absurd, and to make themselves invulnerable by making their books incredible. Such was the position in the France of the eighteenth century. To all appearances the monarchy was still powerful. It was the protector of religious and philosophic orthodoxy. Its judges administered the Law with a heavy hand. But, in fact, the writers and the members of the privileged classes had been won over to the new ideas, and were eager to air them. It was not altogether impossible for them to do so openly, as is proved by the publication of the *Dictionnaire philosophique,* the *Essai sur les moeurs* and the *Encyclopédie.* But there still remained a number of themes on which it was difficult to touch. There was, however, a good chance that, if treated as elements in a fictitious narrative, they could be brought to the notice of a more timorous and, therefore, a wider public, the more so since this type of reading matter was very much in the fashion. Ever since the publication of *The Arabian Nights* in Galland's translation (1704-1717) and of the *Lettres Persanes* (1721), the oriental mode had become the favoured and transparent mask of those who, in this way, could temper their audacities with prudence. Voltaire, more than anybody else, had recourse to it.

It is a matter for no little surprise that he should have adopted this lively and, in both senses of the word, free form at a comparatively advanced age. Apart from the *Adventures du Baron de Gangan* which never found its way into print, though its existence is proved by a series of letters exchanged between the author and the Crown-Prince of Prussia, Voltaire's first philosophic tale was *Le monde comme il va*, written in 1747. It was at this time that, as the result of an unfortunate episode, he, together with Mme du Châtelet, took refuge with the Duchesse du Maine at Sceaux. It was under her roof that *Babouc, Memnon, Scarmentado* and *Zadig* were composed. Voltaire wrote a chapter every day, which he showed to the Duchess in the evening. "Sometimes, after supper, he would read a tale or a short novel which he had written during the day for the express purpose of entertaining her. . . ."

These philosophic fictions, always contrived so as to illustrate some moral truth, were written in a gay and charming style, and the Duchesse du Maine took so great a delight in them that others soon expressed a wish to share her pleasure, with the result that Voltaire was compelled to read them aloud to a wider circle. This he did with the skill of a trained actor. The tales enjoyed a great success with his listeners, who begged that he would have them printed. For a long time he refused to do so, saying that such trivial works, designed for the amusement of a small and intimate circle, did not deserve to be perpetuated. Writers are bad judges of their own productions. At the age of eighteen Voltaire had believed that he would go down in literary history as a great tragic dramatist: at thirty, that he was destined to be a famous historian: at forty, an epic poet. He could not have foreseen, when he wrote *Zadig* in 1748, that it would still be regarded as entertaining reading, together with his other short tales, in 1958, whereas *La henriade, Zaïre, Mérope* and *Tancrède* would be condemned to an eternal sleep on library shelves.

In this matter Voltaire's contemporaries were no less wrong than he was. They attached but little importance to frivolous stories in which what struck them most forcibly were numerous allusions to the author's personal enemies. "It is easy to recognize Voltaire under the disguise of the sagacious Zadig. The calumnies and spite of courtiers . . . the disgrace of the hero are so many allegories to be interpreted easily enough. It is thus that he takes revenge upon his enemies . . ."

The abbé Boyer, who was the Dauphin's tutor and a powerful ecclesiastic, took in very bad part the attacks on one whose identity was but thinly concealed behind the anagram *Reyob*. "It would please me mightily if all this to-do about *Zadig* could be ended," wrote Mme du Châtelet, and it was not long before Voltaire disowned a book "which some there are who accuse of containing audacious attacks upon our holy religion". In point of fact the audacities of *Zadig* were pretty mild, and were limited to showing that men, at different times and in different places, have had different beliefs, though the solid basis of all religions is the same. Such a thesis was the most obvious common sense, but common sense was, at that time, most certainly not in general circulation.

Those who dared not attack Voltaire's theology accused him of plagiarism. That has always been an easy method of belittling a great writer. Everything has been said before—not excepting the statement that everything has been said before—and nothing is easier than to establish a connexion between passages in two different authors. Molière imitated Plautus who, in his turn, had imitated Menander who, no doubt, had imitated some earlier model unknown to us. Fréron (some twenty years later) charged Voltaire with having borrowed the best chapters of *Zadig* from sources "which that prize copyist took great pains to conceal". For instance, the brilliant *L'Ermite* chapter was borrowed from a poem by Parnell, and that entitled *Le Chien et le Cheval* (an anticipation of Sherlock Holmes) was lifted from *Le Voyage et les Adventures des Trois Princes de Serendip*. "Monsieur de Voltaire", wrote the treacherous Fréron, "reads often with intention, and much to his advantage, more especially in such books as he thinks have now been long forgotten. . . . From these obscure mines he brings a great many precious jewels to the surface."

Is that so terrible a crime? Must an author refuse to touch seams which have not been completely worked out? What honest critic has ever maintained that a writer can create *ex nihilo?* Neither Parnell's *The Hermit* nor *Le Voyage de Serendip* were original productions. "All these brief tales", says Gaston Paris, "were told long ago in many languages before being recast in that flexible and lively French which, today, gives them a seeming novelty . . . " The unique and brilliant character of Voltaire's *tales* lies not in originality of invention, but in that combination of diverse and seemingly contradictory qualities which are their author's own and unequalled contribution.

He had been educated by the Jesuits, and from them had learned intellectual discipline and elegance of style. During a temporary period of exile in England he had read Swift and studied his technique. "He is the English Rabelais," he had said of the author of Gulliver, "but without Rabelais' bombast." Under the influence of Swift he had developed a liking for strange fancies (whence *Micromégas* and *Babouc*), for travellers' tales which were no more than an excuse for satiric writing, and a literary variant of what we, today, should call a "poker face" which enabled him to give expression to the most monstrous propositions as though they were obvious and natural truths. Onto this living tree had been grafted the Galland of the *Arabian Nights.* "The combination of the classic French mind, with its love of proved statements, its lucid deduction of conclusions from strict logical premises, and the completely illogical view of life common in the fatalistic East, might have been expected to produce a new dimension: and this it did." The subject matter was provided by stories as old as the human race: the technique contained elements drawn from Swift, from Eastern story-telling and from Jesuit teaching: but it was the inimitable synthesis of all these influences that produced the tales which Voltaire continued to concoct over a long period of time.

It has already been pointed out that he began his experiments in this, for him, new literary form, in 1747, that is to say, when he was fifty-three. He wrote his masterpiece in that kind, *Candide,* when he was sixty-five; *L'ingénu,* which is another of his most successful products, when he was seventy-four, in the same year that saw the publication of *La princesse de Babylone;* and he was over eighty when he brought out such minor works as *L'histoire de Fenni, Le crocheteur borgne* and *Les oreilles du Comte de Chesterfield.* Hence, Paul Morand's generalization to the effect that French writers are never younger, never more free from constraint, than when they have passed their sixtieth birthday. By that time they have broken free from the romantic agonies of youth and turned their backs on that pursuit of honours which, in a country where literature plays a social rôle, absorbs too much of their energies during the years of maturity. Chateaubriand was never more "modern" than in his *Vie de Rancé,* and in the concluding sections of the *Mémoires d'Outre-Tombe.* Voltaire wrote his best book at sixty-five, and Anatole France his, *Les Dieux ont Soif,* at sixty-eight. The old writer, like the old actor, is a master of his craft. Youthfulness of style is no more than a matter of technique.

It has become customary to bring together under the blanket title of "Romans et Contes de Voltaire" a number of works greatly differing in kind and in value. Among them are such masterpieces as *Zadig, Candide* and *L'ingénu:* there are the relatively unimportant *princesse de Babylone* and *Le taureau blanc;* there are *Cosi-Sancta* and *Le crocheteur borgne* which are no more than short stories of ten pages or so, and genuine novels of a hundred; there are rough sketches of the general type of *Les voyages de Scarmentado,* which is really only a foretaste of *Candide; Les lettres d'Amabel* which belongs to the tradition of *Lettres Persanes,* and dialogues like *L'homme aux quarante ecus,* in which there is no fictional element at all, but only a discussion about political economy reminiscent of *Dialogues sur le Commerce des Blés,* by the abbé Galiani, or Voltaire's own *oreilles du Comte de Chesterfield* in which theology is argued instead of economics.

What have all these odds and ends of writing in common? First and foremost, the *tone* which, in Voltaire, is always mocking, mercurial and, at least apparently, superficial. There is not, in all these fictions, a single character who is treated with genuine seriousness. All are either embodiments of an idea or a doctrine (Pangloss stands for optimism, Martin for pessimism), or fairy-tale heroes from a lacquer screen or a piece of Chinese embroidery. They can be tortured or burned to death without the author or the reader feeling any real concern for them. Even the beautiful Saint-Yves, when dying of despair because she has sacrificed what she calls her honour in order to save her lover, can weep without bringing the slightest hint of moisture to the eyes of anybody else. The stories, catastrophic though they may be, are always dominated by the author's wit, and so rapid is their *tempo* that the reader is given no time in which to be deeply distressed. A *prestissimo* has no place in a Funeral March or a Requiem Mass, and the *prestissimo* or the *allegretto* are Voltaire's favourite "movements".

Puppets, variously labelled, jig to this devil's tattoo. Voltaire delighted in bringing on to his stage priests, to whom he gave the name of *magi;* judges, whom he called *mufti;* financiers, inquisitors, Jews, innocents and philosophers. Certain routine enemies reappear in all the tales, variously disguised. Of women he has no very high opinion. To judge from his treatment of them, their minds are exclusively occupied by the prospect of making love to handsome young men with good figures, though, being both venal and timid, they are prepared to hire their bodies to old inquisitors or soldiers if, by so doing, they can save their own lives or amass riches. They are inconstant, and will gladly cut off the nose of a husband fondly mourned in order to cure a new lover. For such conduct he does not blame them. "I have", says Scarmentado, "seen all that the world can offer of the beautiful, the good and the admirable, and am determined for the future to confine my attention to my household gods. I took me a wife in my own country: I was cuckolded, and concluded that my state was the pleasantest that life can give."

It is from the author's philosophy that these writings truly derive a unity. It has been described as "a chaos of lucid ideas", in short, incoherent. Faguet accused Voltaire of having considered everything, examined everything, and never gone deeply into anything. "Is he an optimist? Is he a pessimist? Does he believe in free-will or predestination? Does he believe in the immortality of the soul? Does he believe in God? Does he deny the validity of metaphysics? Is there something in him of the agnostic spirit, but only up to a certain point, in other words, is he really a metaphysician at heart? . . . I defy anybody to answer any of these questions with an unqualified yes or no."

All that is perfectly true. There is something of everything to be found in Voltaire, and also the opposite of everything. But the chaos is reduced to order as soon as one sees the apparent contradictions against the background of his times. In this case, as in that of most men, a personal philosophy was in a continuing state of evolution throughout his life. *La vision de Babouc* and *Zadig* were written when Fortune was smiling on him. He was enjoying the favour and protection of Mme de Pompadour, and, consequently, of a considerable section of the Court. All the kings of Europe were inviting him to visit them. Mme du Châtelet was attending to his sensual needs, giving him affection and assuring his independence. He had every reason, therefore, for finding life tolerable. That is why the conclusions reached in *Babouc* are, relatively speaking, lenient.

"Would you have me chastise Persepolis or destroy it?" the djinn Ituriel asks him. Babouc has an observant and impartial eye. He is present at a bloody battle, in which, on neither side, do the soldiers know why they are killing and getting killed, but that same battle is the occasion for innumerable acts of bravery and humanity. He enters Persepolis and finds there a dirty and ill-favoured people, temples where the dead are buried to an accompaniment of harsh, discordant voices, and women of the town on whose activities the magistrates turn an indulgent eye. But, as he continues his tour, he comes upon finer temples, a wise and polished people who are deeply attached to their king, an honest merchant. It is not long before he comes to like the city which is, at once, frivolous, scandalmongering, pleasant, beautiful and intelligent. When he reports his findings to Ituriel, the latter decides not even to try to correct its shortcomings, but "to let the world go its way, since though everything is far from well, everything is not too bad".

Zadig sounds a somewhat deeper note. In it Voltaire shows, by a series of ingenious parables, that it would be a rash man indeed who would maintain that the world is bad because it contains a certain number of evils. The future is hidden from us, and we cannot be sure that from these seeming errors of the Creator salvation may not come. "There is no evil", says the Angel to Zadig, "of which some goodness is not born." "But", asks Zadig, "what if everything were good and nothing evil?" "Then", says the angel Jesrad, "this world would be a different place: the interconnexion of events would belong to a different order of wisdom, and this different order, which would be perfect, could exist only in the eternal dwelling-place of the Supreme Being . . . "—a form of reasoning which is far from being irrefutable, since, if God is good, why did He not confine the world within the bounds of that eternal dwelling-place? If He is all-powerful, why did He not, in creating the world, keep it free from suffering?

Voltaire was far too intelligent not to have asked himself these questions, and, in *Micromégas*, he gives them a disillusioned answer. Micromégas is an inhabitant of Sirius who travels from planet to planet in the company of a dweller in Saturn. One day, the giant discovers the Earth and the almost invisible animalculae who live upon it. He is amazed to find that these tiny creatures can talk, and is outraged by their presumption. One of these midgets, wearing a doctor's cap, tells him that he knows the whole secret of existence, which, he says, is to be found in the *Summa* of St Thomas. "He looked the two celestial beings up and down, and informed them that their persons, their worlds, their suns and their stars had been created for the sole purpose of serving Man." Hearing this, Micromégas gives vent to Homeric laughter.

This laughter is Voltaire's own. So, human beings complain that the world is ill-made, do they? But ill-made for whom? For Man, who, in the immense design of the Universe is no more than an unimportant mould! The probability is that everything in this world which we think is botched or erroneous has its reasons at a totally different level of existence. The mould endures, no doubt, a small amount of suffering, but somewhere there are giants who, huge in stature as in mind, live in a state of semi-divinity. This is Voltaire's answer to the problem of evil. It is not very satisfactory because the mould need never have been created, and, in the eyes of God, it may well be that mere size is of no importance.

But *Micromégas* is still comparatively optimistic. Ridiculous though these human insects may be when they presume to speak of philosophy, they astonish the celestial visitors when they apply the principles of their science, and measure with accuracy the exact size of Micromégas, and the distance of Sirius from the Earth. That these all but invisible mites should have penetrated so deeply into the mysteries of the Universe in which they are themselves, perhaps, no more than accidents, was already causing no little wonder in Voltaire's time, and would still more surprise a Micromégas who should make a similar voyage of discovery in our own day. Pascal had already said as much, and so had Bacon. Men may be no more than mites, but mites who dominate the Universe by obeying its laws. Their absurdities are counter-balanced by their intelligence.

In *Micromégas* we have the second Voltaire of the "tales". The third is a far sadder figure, for he has come to understand that Man is not only absurd but also extremely wicked. By that time he had had his own personal misfortunes. Mme du Châtelet had deceived him with his best friend, and, got with child by Saint-Lambert, had died in labour. The Kings, whether of

France or Prussia, had treated him badly, and he found himself condemned to live in exile. True, it was a very comfortable exile. Neither Les Délices nor Ferney could be called unpleasing residences. But such happiness as he enjoyed there he owned to his own prudence, and not at all to his fellow men among whom he had met with such bitter persecution. But his worst sufferings resulted from public disasters. Too many wars, too much intolerance. Then, in 1755, to the cruelty of men was added the enmity of Nature. It was the year of the Lisbon earthquake which destroyed one of the finest cities in Europe. It had a profound effect upon him. No longer was it possible to maintain that everything is tolerable. The present, for him, was hideous.

One day, all will be well. That is our hope.
All is well now, that is an illusion.

One day all would be well, but only on condition that men set to work to transform society. In this poem we see the first sketch of a doctrine of progress and of the philosophy of *Candide.*

Candide was the outcome of Voltaire's own experiences and of the exasperation bred in him by the works of certain philosophers, such as Rousseau who had written: "If the Eternal Being has not done better, the reason is that he could not," or Leibnitz who laid it down that all was for the best in the best of all possible worlds. This generalization Voltaire put into the mouth of Pangloss, the teacher of optimism, and, to show how false it was, sent wandering about the world a simple-minded disciple of that same Pangloss, the young Candide, who saw at first hand armies, the Inquisition, murders, thievings and rapes, the Jesuits of Paraguay and conditions in France, England and Turkey. As a result of what he found in all these places, he came to the conclusion that everywhere and always Man is a very vicious animal. All the same, the last words of the book are: *Il faut cultiver notre jardin*—we must cultivate our garden—in other words, the world is mad and cruel: the earth trembles and the skies shoot lightning: kings engage in wars, and the churches tear one another to pieces. Let us limit our activities and try to do such humble work as many come our way, as best we can. That "scientific and bourgeois" conclusion was Voltaire's last world, as it was to be Goethe's. Everything is bad, but everything can be bettered. It sounds the prelude to our modern world, to the wisdom of the engineer, which may be far from complete, but is useful all the same. Voltaire, as Bainville said of him, "cleared the world of many illusions". On the ground thus swept and tidied it is possible to build anew.

Certain writers of our own day have discovered

that the world is absurd. But in *Candide* Voltaire said all that can be said on that subject, and he said it with wit and intelligence, which is a good deal better than merely growing irritable, and leaves to us that legacy of courage which we need for action.

Candide was the high-point of Voltaire's art. Of the tales that followed it, *L'ingénu* is the best. It still has the swiftness of the true Voltaire *tempo* and all his charm, but the themes round which it is constructed are of less importance than those of *Candide. L'histoire de Fenni* is a defence of Deism, "the sole brake on men who are so shrewd in the committing of secret crimes. . . . Yes, my friends, atheism and fanaticism are the two poles in a Universe of confusion and horror." *Les oreilles du Comte de Chesterfield* is a story which sets out to prove that fatality governs all things in this world. So, why reason and why worry? "Swallow hot drinks when you freeze, and cool drinks in the dog-days. Steer a middle course between the too much and the too little in all things. Digest, sleep and take your pleasure, all else is mockery." That is the conclusion of *Candide,* minus the poetry.

For the dominant quality of Voltaire's prose in his days of happiness is poetry. "There is", said Alain, "a prayer in every great work, even in Voltaire's tales." The poetry in all great writing is born, to a very large extent, of the fact that the madness of the universe is expressed by the disorder of ideas, but dominated by rhythm. In this, Shakespeare was a master with his witches' chants and his fairies' songs, so incoherent and so perfect. Voltaire's best work has the same two characteristics. Unforeseeable cascades of factual absurdities splash every page, yet the rapidity of the movement, the return at regular intervals of Martin's lamentations, of Candide's simplicities, of the misfortunes of Pangloss and of the Old Woman's stories, bring assurance to the mind of that tragic repose which only great poetry can give.

And so it is that Voltaire, who wanted to be a great poet in verse, and worked so hard at his tragedies and his epic, ended, though he did not know it, by finding pure poetry in his prose tales which he wrote for fun, and without, for a moment, thinking that they were important. Which proves, as he would have said, once again, that bad is good, good bad, and that fatality rules the world. (pp. 35-50)

André Maurois, "Voltaire: Novels and Tales," in his *The Art of Writing,* translated by Gerard Hopkins, The Bodley Head, 1960, pp. 35-50.

SOURCES FOR FURTHER STUDY

Besterman, Theodore. *Voltaire Essays, and Another.* London: Oxford University Press, 1962, 181 p.

> Besterman is the founder of the Institut et Musée Voltaire. This collection contains ten essays and lectures on Voltaire, including "Voltaire Judged by Flaubert," "Voltaire and the Lisbon Earthquake: or, The Death of Optimism," "Voltaire's Love Letters," and "The Terra-Cotta Statue of Voltaire Made by Houdon for Beaumarchais."

Bottiglia, William F., ed. *Voltaire: A Collection of Critical Essays.* Englewood Cliffs, N.J.: Prentice-Hall, Inc., 1968, 177 p.

> Collects essays on a variety of issues concerning Voltaire's life and writings. Of particular interest is Theodore Besterman's "The Real Voltaire through His Letters," a fourteen-part study of Voltaire's correspondence that focuses on the private side of Voltaire's life, "the real Voltaire."

Durant, Will, and Durant, Ariel. *The Age of Voltaire: A History of Civilization in Western Europe from 1715 to 1756, with Special Emphasis on the Conflict between Religion and Philosophy.* The Story of Civilization, Part IX. New York: Simon and Schuster, 1965, 898 p.

> Documentary history of intellectual life in Western Europe during the mid-eighteenth century, focusing on Voltaire's place in the "continuing conflict between religion and science-plus-philosophy."

Nablow, Ralph Arthur. *A Study of Voltaire's Lighter Verse.* Studies on Voltaire and the Eighteenth Century, edited by Theodore Besterman, Vol. CXXVI. Banbury, England: Voltaire Foundation, 1974, 320 p.

> Examines Voltaire's lighter poems—"the *contes en vers,* the *satires,* the *épîtres,* and the *pièces fugitives*"—from historical, analytical, and critical points of view.

Noyes, Alfred. *Voltaire.* New York: Sheed & Ward, 1936, 643 p.

> Comprehensive biography of Voltaire based on the author's extensive reading of primary and secondary sources.

Redman, Ben Ray. Introduction to *The Portable Voltaire,* by Voltaire, edited by Ben Ray Redman, pp. 1-47. New York: Viking Press, 1963.

> Surveys Voltaire's life and works, concentrating on the evolution of his literary interests and writing style.

Kurt Vonnegut, Jr.

1922-

American novelist, short story writer, dramatist, and essayist.

INTRODUCTION

Best known as the author of *Slaughterhouse-Five; or, The Children's Crusade: A Duty-Dance with Death* (1969), Vonnegut is acknowledged as a major voice in American literature and applauded for his pungent satirical depictions of modern society. Emphasizing the comic absurdity of the human condition, he frequently depicts characters who search for meaning and order in an inherently meaningless and disorderly universe, and he focuses in particular on the futility of warfare, the destructive power of technology, and the human potential for both irrationality and evil. He also mocks institutions such as government and religion, which, in his opinion, offer harmful, spurious dogma as remedies to such problems. Although his message is ultimately pessimistic, finding no remedy for the plight of humanity, Vonnegut approaches his subjects with humor and compassion; as a result, his works have been described by Richard Giannone as "comic masks covering the tragic farce that is our contemporary life."

Vonnegut was born in Indianapolis, Indiana, the son of a successful architect. After attending Cornell University, where he majored in chemistry and biology, he enlisted in the United States Army, serving in the Second World War and eventually being taken prisoner by the German Army. Following the war, Vonnegut studied anthropology at the University of Chicago and subsequently moved to Schenectady, New York, to work as a publicist for the General Electric Corporation. During this period, he also began submitting short stories to various journals, and in 1951 he resigned his position at General Electric to devote his time solely to writing.

Vonnegut published several novels throughout the 1950s and 1960s, beginning with *Player Piano* in 1952. However, his frequent use of elements of fantasy resulted in his classification as a writer of science fiction, a genre not widely accepted as "serious literature," and his work did not attract significant popular or critical interest until the mid-1960s, when increasing disillusionment with American society led to widespread admiration for his forthright, irreverent satires. His reputation was greatly enhanced in 1969 with the publication of *Slaughterhouse-Five,* a vehemently antiwar novel that appeared during the peak of protest against American involvement in Vietnam. During the 1970s and 1980s, Vonnegut continued to serve as an important commentator on American society, publishing a series of novels in which he focused on topics ranging from political corruption to environmental pollution. In recent years, Vonnegut has also become a prominent and vocal critic of censorship and militarism in the United States.

Although many critics attribute Vonnegut's classification as a science-fiction writer to a complete misunderstanding of his aims, the element of fantasy is nevertheless one of the most notable features of his early works. *Player Piano* depicts a fictional city called Ilium in which the people have relinquished control of their lives to a computer humorously named EPICAC, a substance that induces vomiting, while the *The Sirens of Titan* (1959) takes place on several different planets, including a thoroughly militarized Mars where the inhabitants are electronically controlled. The fantastic settings of these works serve primarily as a metaphor for modern society, which Vonnegut views as absurd to the point of being surreal, and as a backdrop for Vonnegut's central focus: the hapless human beings who inhabit these bizarre worlds who struggle with both their environments and themselves. For example, in *Player Piano,* the protagonist, Dr. Paul Proteus, rebels against the emotional vapidity of his society, wherein, freed from the need to perform any meaningful work, the citizens have lost their sense of dignity and purpose. Proteus joins a subversive organization devoted to toppling the computer-run government and participates in an abortive rebellion. Although he is imprisoned at the end of the novel, Vonnegut suggests that Proteus has triumphed in regaining his humanity.

Vonnegut once again focuses on the role of technology in human society in *Cat's Cradle* (1963), widely considered one of his best works. The novel recounts the discovery of a form of ice, called *ice-nine,* which is solid at a much lower temperature than normal ice and is capable of solidifying all water on Earth. *Ice-nine* serves as a symbol of the enormous destructive potential of technology, particularly when developed or used without regard for the welfare of humanity. In contrast to what he considers the harmful truths represented by scientific discoveries, Vonnegut presents a religion called Bokononism, based on the concept that there are no absolute truths, that human life is ultimately meaningless, and that the most helpful religion would therefore preach benign lies that encourage kindness, give humanity a sense of dignity, and allow people to view their absurd condition with humor. The motif of the cat's cradle, a children's game played by looping string about the hands in a complex pattern, is used by Vonnegut to demonstrate the harm caused by the erroneous paradigms presented by traditional religions: "No wonder kids grow up crazy. A cat's cradle is nothing but a bunch of X's between somebody's hands, and little kids look at all those X's . . . *no damn cat, and no damn cradle.*"

In *God Bless You, Mr. Rosewater; or, Pearls before Swine* (1965), Vonnegut presents one of his most endearing protagonists in the figure of Eliot Rosewater, a philanthropic but ineffectual man who attempts to use his inherited fortune for the betterment of humanity. Rosewater finds that his generosity, his genuine concern for human beings, and his attempts to establish loving relationships are viewed as madness in a society that values only money. The novel includes traditional religions in its denunciation of materialism and greed in the modern world, suggesting that the wealthy and powerful invented the concept of divine ordination to justify and maintain their exploitation of others.

Vonnegut described *Slaughterhouse-Five* as a novel he was compelled to write, since it is based on one of the most extraordinary and significant events of his life. During the time he was a prisoner of the German Army, Vonnegut witnessed the Allied bombing of Dresden, which destroyed the city and killed more than 135,000 people. One of the few to survive, Vonnegut was ordered by his captors to aid in the grisly task of digging bodies from the rubble and destroying them in huge bonfires. Although the attack claimed more lives than the bombing of Hiroshima and was directed at a target of no apparent military importance, it attracted little attention, and *Slaughterhouse-Five* is Vonnegut's attempt to both document and denounce this event. Like Vonnegut, the protagonist of *Slaughterhouse-Five,* named Billy Pilgrim, has been present at the bombing of Dresden and has been profoundly affected by the experience. His feelings manifest themselves in a spiritual malaise that culminates in a nervous breakdown. In addition, he suffers from a peculiar condition, that of being "unstuck in time," meaning that he randomly experiences events from his past, present, and future. The novel is therefore a complex, non-chronological narrative in which images of suffering and loss prevail. Charles B. Harris has noted: "Ultimately, [*Slaughterhouse-Five*] is less about Dresden than it is about the impact of Dresden on one man's sensibilities. More specifically, it is the story of Vonnegut's story of Dresden, how he came to write it and, implicitly, why he wrote it as he did."

In the works written after *Slaughterhouse-Five,*

Vonnegut often focuses on the problems of contemporary society in a direct manner. *Breakfast of Champions; or, Goodbye Blue Monday* (1973) and *Slapstick; or, Lonesome No More* (1976), for example, examine the widespread feelings of despair and loneliness that result from the loss of traditional culture in the United States; *Jailbird* (1979) recounts the story of a fictitious participant in the Watergate scandal of the Nixon administration, creating an indictment of the American political system; *Galapagos* (1985) predicts the dire consequences of environmental pollution; and *Hocus-Pocus; or, What's the Hurry, Son?* (1990) deals with the implications and aftermath of the war in Vietnam. Although many of these works are highly regarded, critics frequently argue that in his later works Vonnegut tends to reiterate themes presented more compellingly in earlier works. Many also suggest that Vonnegut's narrative style, which includes the frequent repetition of distinctive phrases, the use of colloquialisms, and a di-gressive manner, becomes formulaic in some of his later works.

Nevertheless, Vonnegut remains one of the most esteemed American satirists. Noted for their frank and insightful social criticism as well as their innovative style, his works present an idiosyncratic yet compelling vision of modern life.

(For further information about Vonnegut's life and works, see *Authors and Artists for Young Adults*, Vol. 6; *Concise Dictionary of American Literary Biography, 1968-1988; Contemporary Authors*, Vol. 3; *Contemporary Authors New Revision Series*, Vols. 1, 25; *Contemporary Literary Criticism*, Vols. 1, 2, 3, 4, 5, 8, 12, 22, 40, 60; *Dictionary of Literary Biography*, Vols. 2, 8; *Dictionary of Literary Biography Documentary Series*, Vol. 3; *Dictionary of Literary Biography Yearbook: 1980;* and *Major 20th-Century Writers*.)

CRITICAL COMMENTARY

TONY TANNER

(essay date 1971)

[Tanner is an English editor and critic whose works include critical studies of Joseph Conrad, Saul Bellow, and Thomas Pynchon. In the following excerpt, he surveys the range of moral issues explored in Vonnegut's novels.]

It is a growing awareness of the seriousness of Vonnegut's inquiries which has made people realize that he is not only the science fiction writer he first appeared to be.

His first novel, *Player Piano* (1952), was, to be sure, a fairly orthodox futuristic satire on the dire effects on human individuality of the fully mechanised society which technology could make possible. A piano player is a man consciously using a machine to produce aesthetically pleasing patterns of his own making. A player-piano is a machine which has been programmed to produce music on its own, thus making the human presence redundant. This undesirable inversion of the relationship between man and machine, suggested by the title, is at the heart of the novel. In this society of the future there is one part for the machines and the managers, and another part ('the Homestead') into which have been herded all the unnecessary people. Paul Proteus (whose initials suggest his relation to the theme of the title, and whose second name suggests a predisposition to change), is a top manager who believes in the system. But he starts to feel a 'nameless, aching need' which indicates a nascent dissatisfaction with the very social structures he has helped to erect. He realises that he is trapped in the system he serves. (pp. 181-82)

[*Player Piano* presents] a basic dilemma in Vonnegut's work. Both sides want to *use* the hero; both sides want to impose a particular role on him and make him into a special sort of messenger or conveyor of information; and as Paul discovers, between the two sides, 'there was no middle ground for him'. Paul is a typical American hero in wanting to find a place beyond all plots and systems, some private space, or 'border area'—a house by the side of the road of history and society. He would like not to be used, not to be part of someone else's plan. But the book shows this to be an impossible dream.

The Sirens of Titan (1959), Vonnegut's next novel, is also about people being used, this time on the sort of inter-galactic scale permissible in science fiction. . . . [Rumfoord] is a man who now exists as 'wave phenomena' as a result of having run his space ship into an 'uncharted chrono-synclastic infundibulum'. He is *'scattered far and wide, not just through space, but through time, too'*, and with his new-found power to arrange things to suit his patterns, free to handle time and space as he pleases and put people where he wants them, he is a suitably fantastic analogue of Vonnegut himself, who is doing just that in his book. But if Rumfoord is the user, he is also the used. (pp. 182-83)

It is man's status as agent-victim which preoccupies Vonnegut; once one of his characters comes to see this double aspect of human life and action he usually, like Malachi, becomes 'hopelessly engrossed in the intricate tactics of causing less rather than more pain'. (p. 183)

[A] possible attitude to the discovery of [the human] fate is implied in Beatrice Rumfoord's conclusion that " 'The worst thing that could possibly happen to anybody would be not to be used for anything by anybody.' " A corollary of this is Malachi's late decision that one purpose of human life " 'no matter who is controlling it, is to love whoever is around to be loved.' " This formulation, albeit very sympathetic, points to a detectable strain of sentimental sententiousness which recurs in Vonnegut's work. (p. 184)

With *Mother Night* (1961) we are back into the bleakest years of contemporary history. In this book . . . one may discern a shift in Vonnegut's style. There is less attempt at narrative fullness, and a greater use of short chapters which give the sense of the intermittencies and incompletenesses inevitable in any written version. The impression is of compressed selections suspended in an encompassing silence. . . . Howard Campbell is a quintessential Vonnegut hero: *the* agent-victim, the most uncertain and perhaps the most hapless of all Vonnegut's bemused messengers. (p. 185)

Campbell is a special 'agent'; but in Vonnegut's vision we are all agents, and the perception that we can never be sure of the full content and effect of what we communicate to the world, by word or deed, is at the moral centre of this novel. It also carries the implicit warning that our lies may be more influential than our truths, a consideration which writers in particular must ponder. (p. 186)

The book presents, almost in shorthand, a whole spectrum of fiction-making, from the vilest propaganda to the most idealistic art. There is no cynical attempt to identify these two extreme ends of the spectrum, but it is part of Vonnegut's meaning to suggest that the artist cannot rest in confidence as to the harmlessness of his inventions. . . . In one way it comes down to that suspicion of all communication which seems to go so deep in contemporary American fiction. As no one can be fully aware of the 'information' that goes out through him (just as you cannot control the information that is fed into you), the artist as a professional inventor and sender of messages must be very careful about what he puts out. He may think that, in [Sir Philip] Sidney's terms, he is delivering a golden world from our brazen one. But he might, all unawares, be contributing to the restoration of the ancient reign of Mother Night. (p. 188)

[Vonnegut] has seldom been more comically inventive [than he is in *Cat's Cradle,*] but then the whole novel is an exploration of the ambiguities of man's disposition to play and invent, and the various forms it may take. . . .

[Each character on the island of San Lorenzo] is following his dream, creating his fiction. And it is from this island that the process which will end the world is unwittingly launched. This may be Vonnegut's mordant way of predicting the possible final outcome of the human instinct to play. When this island of invention contains both [ice-nine], *and* representatives of the artistic and Utopian dreams which console and dignify the race, one can see that Vonnegut is pushing quite hard for a recognition of the deeply ambiguous creative/destructive aspects of the innate human instinct to play. (p. 189)

The title is explained in the book. Newt recalls that the one game his father played with him on the day the first atom bomb was exploded, was to make a cat's cradle and push it jeeringly into his face. On the island Newt makes a painting of the ancient game of cat's cradle, and adds " 'For maybe a hundred thousand years or more, grown-ups have been waving tangles of string in their children's faces.' " In Newt's view it is no wonder that children should grow up crazy, because when they look at the cross-crossed string, what do they see? *'No damn cat, and no damn cradle'*. A chapter in *Mother Night* is entitled 'No Dove, No Covenant'. It alludes to the same discovery which any child is likely to make; namely, that the religions or legends taught to him by adults are just fictions. There is no cat there; nor does God make a sign. On the other hand it is an axiom of Bokonism that man has to tell himself that he understands life even when he knows he doesn't. This is the justification for constructing fictions, for the necessity of art. It does, after all, take skill to weave the string, and something more again to imagine the cat. On the other hand one must confront the fact that the string *is* only string. The matter is summed up in what the narrator calls 'the cruel paradox of Bokonist thought, the heartbreaking necessity of lying about reality, and the heartbreaking impossibility of lying about it'. That, certainly, is what Vonnegut contrives to suggest in his own brilliant little fiction.

The distinctive tone of Vonnegut's work is very likeable and sympathetic; it obviously bespeaks a compassionate humane spirit. The economy and laconic wit prevent this from issuing in much overt sentimentality, though the tendency is there. However, at times it does seem as though he is using his fiction to issue short sermons on the state of contemporary America, or the world, and this can at times endanger the poise of his work. I think that some of the weaker aspects of his writing show up in *God Bless You, Mr. Rosewater* (1965), despite the wit and moral feeling with which the book is conceived and executed. (pp. 191-92)

[*Slaughterhouse-Five*] is a moving meditation on the relationship between history and dreaming cast in an appropriately factual/fictional mode. . . .

[Vonnegut] himself enters his own novel from time to time . . . and it becomes very difficult to hold the various fictional planes in perspective. . . . But the overall impression is that of a man who has brought the most graphic facts of his life to exist in the same medium with his more important fictions to see what each implies about the other. (p. 195)

[Although] one necessarily reads in sequence the many compressed fragments or messages which make up his novels, one nevertheless gets the impression of arrested moments suspended in time. In reading Billy Pilgrim's adventures we too become unstuck in time. As a result one is left with something approaching the impression of seeing all the marvellous and horrific moments, all at the same time. Vonnegut, the telephoner, has condensed and arranged his telegrams to good effect. He starts his account of the adventures of Pilgrim with the single word—'Listen'. This is to alert us. We are being messaged. (p. 197)

A motto which Billy brings from his life into his fantasy, or vice-versa, reads: 'God grant me the serenity to accept the things I cannot change, courage to change the things I can, and wisdom always to tell the difference'. In itself this is an open-ended programme. But immediately afterwards we read: 'Among the things Billy Pilgrim could not change were the past, the present, and the future'. Billy becomes completely quiescent, calmly accepting everything that happens as happening exactly as it ought to (including his own death). He abandons the worried ethical, tragical point of view of western man and adopts a serene conscienceless passivity. If anything, he views the world aesthetically: every moment is a marvellous moment, at times he beams at scenes in the war. Yet he does have breakdowns and is prone to fits of irrational weeping.

Here I think is the crucial moral issue in the book. Billy Pilgrim is a professional optometrist. He spends his life on earth prescribing corrective lenses for people suffering from defects of vision. It is entirely in keeping with his calling, then, when he has learned to see time in an entirely new Tralfamadorian way, that he should try to correct the whole erroneous Western view of time, and explain to everyone the meaninglessness of individual death. . . . The point for us to ponder is how are *we* to regard his new vision. According to the Tralfamadorians, ordinary human vision is something so narrow and restricted that, to convey to themselves what it must be like they have to imagine a creature with a metal sphere round his head who looks down a long thin pipe seeing only a tiny speck at the end. He cannot turn his head around and he is strapped to a flatcar on rails which goes in one direction. Billy Pilgrim's attempt to free people from that metal sphere, and his own widened and liberated vision, may thus seem entirely desirable. But is the cost in conscience and concern for the individual life equally desirable? (p. 198)

Perhaps the fact of the matter is that conscience simply cannot cope with events like the concentration camps and the Dresden air-raid, and the more general demonstration by the war of the utter valuelessness of human life. Even to try to begin to care adequately would lead to an instant and irrevocable collapse of consciousness. Billy Pilgrim, Everyman, needs his fantasies to offset such facts. (p. 199)

Billy's Tralfamadorian perspective is not unlike that described in Yeats's 'Lapis Lazuli'—'gaiety transfiguring all that dread'—and it has obvious aesthetic appeal and consolation. At the same time, his sense of the futility of trying to change anything, of regarding history as a great lump of intractable amber from which one can only escape into the fourth dimension of dream and fantasy, was the attitude held by Howard Campbell during the rise of Nazi Germany. Vonnegut has, I think, total sympathy with such quietistic impulses. At the same time his whole work suggests that if man doesn't do something about the conditions and quality of human life on Earth, no one and nothing else will. Fantasies of complete determinism, of being held helplessly in the amber of some eternally unexplained plot, justify complete passivity and a supine acceptance of the futility of all action. Given the overall impact of Vonnegut's work I think we are bound to feel that there is at least something equivocal about Billy's habit of fantasy, even if his attitude is the most sympathetic one in the book. At one point Vonnegut announces: 'There are almost no characters in this story, and almost no dramatic confrontations, because most of the people in it are so sick and so much the listless playthings of enormous forces'. It is certainly hard to celebrate the value of the individual self against the background of war, in which the nightmare of being the victim of uncontrollable forces comes compellingly true. In such conditions it is difficult to be much of a constructive 'agent', and Billy Pilgrim doubtless has to dream to survive.

At the end of the novel, spring has come to the ruins of Dresden, and when Billy is released from prison the trees are in leaf. He finds himself in a street which is deserted except for one wagon 'The wagon was green and coffin-shaped'. That composite image of generation and death summarises all there is actually to see in the external world, as far as Vonnegut is concerned. The rest is fantasy, cat's cradles, lies. In this masterly novel, Vonnegut has put together both his war novel and reminders of the fantasies which made up his previous novels. The facts which defy explanation are brought into the same frame with fictions beyond verification. The point at which fact and fiction intersect is Vonnegut himself, the experiencing dreaming man who wrote the book. He is a lying messenger of course, but he acts on the assumption that the telegrams must continue to be sent. Eliot Rosewater's cry to his psychiatrist, overheard by Billy Pilgrim, applies more particularly to the artist. 'I think you guys are going to have to come up with a lot of wonderful *new* lies, or people just aren't going to want to go on living.' Of course, they must also tell the truth, whatever that may be. Kafka's couriers could hardly be more confused. What Vonnegut has done, particularly in *Slaughterhouse-Five,* is to define with clarity and economy—and compassion—the nature and composition of that confusion. (pp. 200-01)

Tony Tanner, "The Uncertain Messenger: A Study of the Novels of Kurt Vonnegut, Jr." in his *City of Words: American Fiction 1950-1970,* Harper & Row, Publishers, 1971, pp. 181-201.

JEAN E. KENNARD
(essay date 1975)

[In the following excerpt, Kennard discusses Vonnegut's satirical techniques.]

[Almost] all the commentators on Vonnegut betray a certain uneasiness in talking about him as a satirist; he does not quite fit the mold. (p. 101)

Vonnegut's basic world view is Post-existential. He [rejects] all ethical absolutes. Vonnegut stresses the futility of man's search for meaning in a world where everything is "a nightmare of meaninglessness without end," where we are all the victims of a series of accidents, "trapped in the amber of this moment. . . . Because this moment simply is." In *Cat's Cradle* he shows how man's "nostalgia for unity," to use Camus' phrase, forces him to interpret mere chance as purposeful, leads him to create the meaning he wants to find and makes him believe in his own insubstantial structure, his own cat's cradle. Each of Vonnegut's novels shows us that there is no relation between human actions and the events that take place in human lives. All success—and, one supposes, failure—is the result of luck. . . . Man, like Billy Pilgrim in *Slaughterhouse-Five,* finds that among the things he cannot change are past, present and future. His actions serve no purpose he can hope to comprehend. Vonnegut also has his own version of [Jean-Paul] Sartre's theory of human identity. He talks about the desire of Being-For-Itself to become Being-In-Itself as the Universal Will to Become and claims that the moral of *Mother Night* is "We are what we pretend to be."

If Vonnegut denies the possibility of absolute values, then how can he be a satirist [since satire implies the existence of absolute values]? The answer is that he is not. He has the look of the satirist, but has no answer to give us. (pp. 102-03)

[He] employs the methods of satire as an attack upon satire itself, or rather upon the idea of a world in which the definite answers satire implies are possible. Vonnegut deliberately uses the expectations that satire arouses to tempt the reader into easy moral answers he subsequently undermines either by later attacking the acquired moral answer or by setting it in a Post-existential philosophic framework where no value is absolute. . . .

Vonnegut frustrates the reader's expectations in order to bring about in him an experience of the absurd. He allows the reader the temporary illusion that he has the answer and then disillusions him. This is not just a question, as perhaps it is in the case of such other pessimistic satirists as Swift or [Samuel] Johnson, of not believing man likely to adopt the alternative to the vices under attack. Vonnegut does not merely disbelieve that man will become benevolent, . . . but attacks the very idea of the workability of benevolence.

In his earlier novels, Vonnegut works chiefly against the expectations aroused by satire but more recently, particularly in his sixth novel, *Slaughterhouse-Five,* he has been making increasing use of those techniques of action, language, and characterization that work against the expectations of realism. (p. 103)

Vonnegut uses the form of the fable against the objectives of the fable. By suggesting, through obvious patterning of characters and contrasts between our own world and those of other planets, that he is arguing to a conclusion, he arouses our expectation for revelation. The pattern will work out; the final piece of the jigsaw puzzle will make the picture clear; the fable will reveal its moral. But Vonnegut's fables do not have morals, at least none which can stand as solutions to the Post-existential dilemma, just as his apparently satirical methods do not operate from any consistent ethical scheme. Again he is deliberately working to disillusion the reader. . . . [He] parodies himself; his novels gradually unmake themselves. . . .

[The central figure of *Player Piano,* Paul Proteus] feels "love—particularly for the little people, the common people, God bless them. All his life they had been hidden from him by the walls of his ivory tower. . . . This was *real,* this side of the river, and Paul loved these common people, and wanted to help, and let them know they were loved and understood, and he wanted them to love him too". . . .

If we accept, as most critics have, that this novel is a satire directed against technology, then the values expressed by Paul here are those Vonnegut expects us to accept also. But . . . a careful reader would surely have to be suspicious of the tone of this passage. Vonnegut is too conscious of language to use such phrases as "the common people," "the little people," "ivory tower" "this was real," without recognizing them as clichés. He is giving us an easy answer—charity, fellow feeling, remorse—to the problems of mechanization and inhumanity, and is indicating that the answer is simplistic by his use of clichés.

Nevertheless, it is easy to miss these early clues, and the novel does for a long time seem to be a satire. Vonnegut's targets are standard ones: daytime soap operas designed to keep everyone satisfied with the status quo; the big business aspects of college football now no longer related to academic life at all; ambitious wives who feign affection. Each of these targets is attacked through the usual satirical method of slightly exaggerating a situation already present to a lesser extent in our

society. Each of these targets also is an aspect of the apparently chief target of Vonnegut's novel, the mechanization of human lives. The great example of its opposite, human feeling and eccentricity, is Ed Finnerty, and Vonnegut sees to it that our sympathies lie with Finnerty and his friend Lasher throughout the novel. Who can resist the temptation to support man and human feeling against machines?

So far the novel is conventional. The methods are basically realistic, except for the use of a future world. Even the visitor from another country, the Shah of Bratpuhr, functions . . . as a naive observer, not as he would in later Vonnegut novels as a creature with more knowledge from a totally different world. (p. 104)

But *Player Piano* does not end conventionally. The values established by the satirical methods at the beginning of the novel are finally completely undercut. This is not to deny, of course, that Vonnegut prefers human warmth to mechanization; but he does not, in his novel, appear to see it as a viable situation. Those representatives of human feeling against mechanization, Finnerty and Lasher, treat Paul as an object. " 'You don't matter,' said Finnerty. 'You belong to History now' ". . . . They are prepared to kill him if it is necessary. (p. 106)

In *Player Piano* the easy answers of [Vonnegut's] initial satirical attacks are not refuted by placing them in a Post-existential framework and there are only the earliest hints of absurd techniques. But nevertheless Vonnegut does use here the basic method of all his novels; he tempts the reader into easy answers through satirical methods and later disillusions him.

The subject of man as machine is fare more imaginatively treated in Vonnegut's second novel, his first attempt at science fiction, *The Sirens of Titan.* In this novel Vonnegut takes the old sophomoric debate about first cause—if God created the world, then who created God—and gives it some new turns. He is concerned with the absurdity of man's "appetite for the absolute," with his inescapable tendency to attribute meaning to his existence on earth. (pp. 106-07)

Religious belief, says Vonnegut, is based on no evidence at all. Rumfoord believes he knows the meaning of certain earthlings' lives, since they are part of his plan to establish the Church of God the Utterly Indifferent on earth by leading an attack from Mars. Malachi Constant, later Unk, is used by Rumfoord. What Rumfoord doesn't know is that he is part of a more complicated plan, the ultimate aim of which is to transport a replacement part for a space ship stranded on Titan. So the meaning of human life is reduced to an absurdity. (p. 107)

If human life has a pattern, a scheme, it is not a merciful one. . . . If the plan of the universe is not merciful, suggests Vonnegut, it might just as well not

Major Media Adaptations: Motion Pictures

Happy Birthday, Wanda June, 1971. Columbia. Director: Mark Robson. Cast: Susannah York, Rod Steiger.

Slaughterhouse-Five, 1972. Universal. Director: George Roy Hill. Cast: Michael Saks, Valerie Perrine, Ron Liebman, Eugene Roche, Perry King.

Slapstick of Another Kind, 1984. S Paul Company [Adaption of *Slapstick; Or, Lonesome No More*] Cast: Jerry Lewis, Madeline Kahn, Marty Feldman, Pat Morita, Orson Welles.

have one. Our religious fantasies of all truth being revealed to us in another world might well turn out to be the truth revealed to us through the other worlds of Vonnegut's novel. At all events there is no possible way of our finding the truth. Each man is doomed to his own subjective version of it. . . .

All events come about through luck, though like Malachi Constant we choose to believe that "somebody up there" likes us. (p. 108)

The Sirens of Titan invites us to read it as a satire just as *Player Piano* does. The many early targets of the book—posted bulletins about someone's health that reveal nothing; man's need to feel superior to his fellows by remembering his own achievements—suggest a satire operating from some base of consistent values. A favorite target is one that epitomizes the theme of the book: man's belief in image without substance. . . .

The major satirical method is a traditional one, to be found in [Swift's] *Gulliver's Travels,* for example; Vonnegut ridicules the target by making the abstract concrete. Thus the support religion has historically given to big business in the U.S.A. becomes in the novel the literal making of money by using initials from the first sentence of the Bible; the handicaps of life become actual weights carried around by some people to make the race of life fair. (p. 109)

There are some positive images of human experience in this novel. . . . Beatrice, Malachi, and their son, Chrono, together on Titan towards the end of the novel, can be seen as an illustration of the truth that Constant believes he has found; that one of the purposes of human life is to love "whoever is around to be loved." In this novel Vonnegut, . . . does appear to see human emotion as a value, even if a relative one. . . . [But] Vonnegut's picture of Constant is of an old, lonely man accepting a comforting myth as the truth. Vonnegut, then, as in *Player Piano,* tempts the reader into accepting easy answers and then invalidates them. He also sets the assumed values in a Postexistential framework which makes them all relative. . . .

[In] Vonnegut's novels people are forced into new roles by others. The fact that people treat others as objects is illustrated by having the characters literally turn into machines—Malachi Constant becomes mechanized as Unk—much in the way Beckett's characters often do. In this way, of course, Vonnegut is working against the expectations of the reader for "human," rounded characters. He, then, undercuts his own method deliberately: Salo, a machine, is more humane than the earthlings. (p. 110)

The Sirens of Titan is the first Vonnegut novel to display an interest in the techniques of self-conscious art—in Vonnegut self-parody—that are so important in the later novels. His concern with the whole subject of the nature of fictional reality is revealed in the dedication: "All persons, places, and events in the book are real," reminding us of [Eugene] Ionesco's comment that fantasy is more real than realism. Throughout the novel Vonnegut draws our attention from what we are reading to the process of reading, by introducing other novels and stories which comment on the themes of his novel. (p. 112)

Superficially, at least, Vonnegut's third novel, *Mother Night,* is concerned with . . . the ways men use and destroy each other in the name of purpose. Given Vonnegut's concern with atrocities and his basic method of working against the expectations of the reader, it is not surprising that he should take as his subject the Nazis' treatment of the Jews. . . . [But in *Mother Night* an American is] about to be tried by Israel for broadcasting anti-Semitic speeches for Germany in World War II. As Campbell describes his postwar escape to New York and subsequent capture, the moral certainties become less clear. (pp. 112-13)

In *Mother Night* Vonnegut is primarily interested in two concepts. The first is the impossibility of absolute truth. We can only have absolute answers by blocking our minds to some obvious facts: "The dismaying thing about the classic totalitarian mind is that any given gear, though mutilated, will have at its circumference unbroken sequences of teeth that are immaculately maintained. . . . The missing teeth, of course, are simple, obvious truths". . . . All absolutes lead inevitably to tyranny. . . . There are no absolute reasons for action as Campbell discovers when he finds himself paralyzed, . . . because he has "absolutely no reason to move in any direction". (p. 113)

The second concept is Sartre's theory of human identity: "We are what we pretend to be." We cannot pretend to be evil, as Campbell does, and remain good secretly. We can choose our roles, but we are what we choose. Man, Vonnegut shows, has an infinite capacity for living in bad faith. Campbell can sustain a lovenest—a "nation of two"—while he helps destroy thousands. Stalin can love a romantic play about the Holy Grail and yet be Stalin. This play, one of Campbell's, functions as a comment on the novel itself for, in spite of its romantic treatment, its subject is the tyranny of Christianity, which, like the absolutes in *Mother Night,* has destroyed human lives.

The basic technique of *Mother Night* is that of *Player Piano:* to play against our preconceived attitudes and the expectations which the initial satirical attacks have aroused in us. . . . All absolutes, all preconceived notions, are undercut in this novel. The reader is left, as Campbell is, without any values to cling to. . . .

Cat's Cradle is perhaps Vonnegut's most successful novel. The use of the methods of satire to attack satire is at its sharpest; the techniques of science fiction are turned upon science itself. But the novel works primarily because of the quality of the two central images, ice-nine and cat's cradle, and because of a fundamental irony underlying Vonnegut's conception of the narrator. (p. 114)

[The] using of clichés in new ways, which Vonnegut has occasionally employed before, becomes a major technique in the novel. He takes this cliché, reverses the traditionally benign associations of it, and shows how our inheritance from the past is not necessarily benign at all. Evil, cold like ice, spreads like water and is inevitably passed, like the ice-nine, from one generation to the next. (pp. 114-15)

Throughout the early scenes of the novel there is much ironic juxtaposing of Christianity with inhuman technology. Christmas Eve is the night Angela Hoenikker divides up the ice-nine among the children. We are tempted into believing Vonnegut offers Christian compassion as the answer. Yet Christianity is associated with destruction too. . . . Perhaps, then, if capitalistic Christianity is no answer, communism is? Vonnegut undercuts that solution also. (p. 115)

There can be no absolute solution, of course, because there is no meaning to human existence. The second important image of the novel is the image of the child's game cat's cradle. . . . Cat's cradle is a structure without substance or the meaning ascribed to it. Cat's cradle is a concrete example of the religious and philosophic structures man seems driven to build to explain his existence.

The Post-existentialist world view of *Cat's Cradle* is that of *The Sirens of Titan.* Vonnegut has invented a religion called Bokononism, which most critics have described as Existentialism and take as Vonnegut's own philosophy. Certainly Bokononism recognizes that life has no purpose. . . . It is equally true that "Man got to tell himself he understand" . . . Bokonon recognizes that even his own cosmogony is a "pack of foma," all lies. Here, surely, is the point. . . . The narrator . . . calls himself a Bokononist, just as he used to call himself a Christian, and thus is in the ironic

position of believing in lies as his truth. Of course, Vonnegut claims, so are we all. (p. 116)

The action is full of [such] absurd coincidences as Jonah's chance meeting with Marvin Breed just after leaving his brother Asa, and the discovery of a pedestal on which his own name is engraved. There is little causal relation between the scenes; each is a short anecdote, often complete in itself. In many of these anecdotes action is exaggerated to the point of absurdity. . . . (p. 117)

[*Slaughterhouse-Five*] comes to terms with the question that has in one way or another been central to all his novels: What is the significance of human suffering? Is it possible for human beings to be other than cruel to one another in an Existentialist world. . . . For Vonnegut the firebombing of Dresden . . . is the ultimate symbol of purposeless human cruelty. . . . How, asks Vonnegut, can the knowledge of such suffering, the memory of it, be made bearable? Can anything make sense of it? (p. 122)

Vonnegut dramatizes for the reader that whatever scheme one may devise to handle the idea of death, nothing can minimize the fact of it. "So it goes" comes at us with increasing momentum. . . .

One of the effects of the "so it goes" on the reader is the effect produced by the disjunction of tone and subject. We expect death to be treated with more apparent concern. (p. 123)

Vonnegut constantly moves the reader between real life and fiction, mentioning the Kennedys, Martin Luther King, Harry Truman. . . . [There] are numerous references also to characters from his own earlier novels. . . . In this way he reminds us of the fictional nature of all experience. (p. 124)

More or less everything, he announces at the beginning of the novel, is true, not just metaphorically true, but actually true. Billy Pilgrim's attempt to come to terms with the horrors of Dresden is Vonnegut's own attempt. Billy Pilgrim creates an imaginary world, Tralfamadore; Vonnegut creates an imaginary world, *Slaughterhouse-Five.* In fiction, of course, as on Tralfamadore, all time is eternal, the past can be recaptured, the dead returned to life. Art is apparently a way of dealing with death, but the novelist of number is not Zeus and must ultimately fail. (pp. 124-25)

[For] all its Post-existential world view, [*Breakfast of Champions*] appears to argue that there are ways of living with the absurd dilemma: "It is hard to adapt to chaos, but it can be done". . . . [We] may be able to improve the human situation. (p. 125)

[This] is a world of interdependent people; we have the power to be each other's saviour rather than his slavemaster, but we are unaware of that fact, Vonnegut seems to be arguing.

The solution, apparently, is to set each other free. What is valuable . . . is the core of awareness in each one of us, an awareness which appears to be identical with Sartre's concept of Being-for-itself. . . . It is not enough to adopt the Kilgore Trout view, perhaps intended to represent Vonnegut's in his earlier novels, that everyone is a machine except oneself. (p. 126)

It seems to me, though, that Vonnegut, here as in all the other novels, undercuts this proposed solution which may remain an ideal but is seen in the novel as unworkable. Vonnegut decides to give Trout and all his other characters their freedom. . . . But Trout becomes once again Vonnegut's father, the man upon whom the character was modelled, and what he wants is not freedom but further control from his creator; "Here was what Kilgore Trout cried out to me in my father's voice: 'Make me young, make me young, make me young!' ". . . .

Has Vonnegut become an optimist? Hardly. Even if one does not read the ending of *Breakfast of Champions* as ironic, recognition of each other's value is not a solution to the Post-existential dilemma; it is at best . . . a way of making bearable the absurdity of the human condition. Vonnegut is ultimately a pessimist. (pp. 126-27)

Jean E. Kennard, "Kurt Vonnegut, Jr.: The Sirens of Satire," in her *Number and Nightmare: Forms of Fantasy in Contemporary Fiction*, Archon Books, 1975, pp. 101-28.

CHARLES B. HARRIS

(essay date 1976)

[Harris in an American educator and critic. In the following excerpt, he analyzes the narrative structure of *Slaughterhouse-Five*.]

Carefully read, Chapter One [of *Slaughterhouse-Five*] emerges as a functional and illuminating part of the novel as a whole. For the chapter contains passages that suggest three important facts crucial to a proper understanding of Vonnegut's novel: (1) the novel is less about Dresden than about the psychological impact of time, death, and uncertainty on its main character; (2) the novel's main character is not Billy Pilgrim, but Vonnegut; and (3) the novel is not a conventional anti-war novel at all, but an experimental novel of considerable complexity.

Billy Pilgrim, the putative protagonist of *Slaughterhouse-Five*, does not even appear in this chapter. Instead, the focus is on Vonnegut, the author-as-character. Emerging is a portrait of the artist as an aging man, "an old fart with his memories and his Pall Malls, with his sons full grown." He is a man of nostalgia who makes late-night drunken phone calls to almost-forgotten acquaintances, calls that seldom make connection. He reminisces about his days as a university student and police reporter in Chicago, as a public relations man in Schenectady, and as a soldier in Germany. The wartime memories, particularly as they concern the mass deaths at Dresden, especially haunt his reveries and of course form the basis of plot for the subsequent nine chapters.

Yet for one so apparently obsessed with the fleeting nature of time—he even quotes Horace to that effect—Vonnegut seems at times curiously vague and indefinite about time. He cannot remember the exact year he visited O'Hare and, upon returning to bed after a night of drinking and telephoning, cannot tell his wife, who "always has to know the time," what time it is. "Search me," he answers. His forgetfulness seems a shield, a defense against a medium that oppresses him. (pp. 228-29)

The Vonnegut of Chapter One appears simultaneously obsessed with and oppressed by time, the past, and death—particularly death. His preoccupation with death is reflected in the various figures he employs in Chapter One and throughout the novel. Among the most prominent of these is the flowing-frozen water metaphor. Vonnegut has used this motif before, especially in *Cat's Cradle*, when ice-nine, dropped accidentally into the ocean, ossifies everything liquid. But it recurs in a subtler though perhaps more pervasive way in *Slaughterhouse-Five*. Early in the novel, Vonnegut, on his way to visit Bernard V. O'Hare in Philadelphia, crosses the Delaware, then appropriates the river as a metaphor in his reflections upon the nature of time. "And I asked myself about the present: how wide it was, how deep it was, how much of it was mine to keep." Even before this association of time and the river, however, Vonnegut associates death with ice, frozen water. "Even if wars didn't keep coming like glaciers," he writes, "there would still be plain old death." Extending this metaphor throughout the novel, Vonnegut repeatedly portrays living humanity as water flowing, dead humanity as water frozen. "They were moving like water," he describes a procession of Allied POW's, " . . . and they flowed at last to a main highway on a valley's floor. Through the valley flowed a Mississippi of humiliated Americans." One of the POW's, a hobo, is dead, therefore "could not flow, could not plop. He wasn't liquid anymore." Later, Billy Pilgrim sees the dead hobo "frozen stiff in the weeds beside the track," his bare feet "blue and ivory," the color of ice. The phrase "blue and ivory" occurs seven times in *Slaughterhouse-Five*, twice to describe the frozen feet of corpses, five times to describe the feet of Billy Pilgrim, who, though still in the land of the flowing, is marked as mortal.

A similar figure applies to Vonnegut himself. Twice in Chapter One he refers to his breath as smelling of "mustard gas and roses." The phrase appears again in Chapter Four when Billy Pilgrim receives a misdialed phone call from a drunk whose breath, like the drunken "telephoner" of Chapter One, smells of mustard gas and roses. The full implication of the image becomes clear only on the next-to-the-last page of the novel. In the "corpse mines" of Dresden, as the dead bodies begin to rot and liquify, "the stink (is) like roses and mustard gas." Like Billy Pilgrim's "blue and ivory" feet, Vonnegut's breath marks him as mortal. This, the image suggests, is what time does to us all, not only when we lie dead like the Dresden corpses, but while we breathe. Life is a state of gradual but perpetual decay.

Time, then, is the enemy harrowing the brow of the first character we meet in the novel. It is important to recognize that the Vonnegut of Chapter One is, indeed, a *character* in *Slaughterhouse-Five.* Of course he is very much like Vonnegut the author, has had the same experiences, but he remains nonetheless the author-as-character. Moreover, he becomes the first-person narrator for the remainder of the novel, a fact obscured by the Billy Pilgrim plot, which is often read as the novel proper rather than the novel-within-the-novel-proper. Vonnegut-as-character introduces himself in Chapter One, informs us of his procedures in gathering materi-

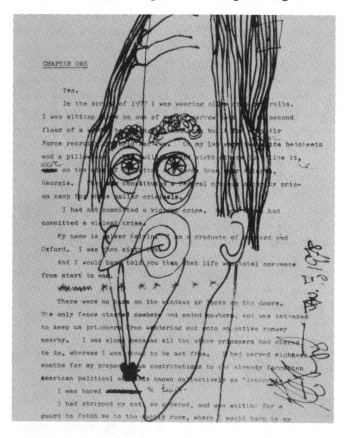

Manuscript page from a rejected draft of *Jailbird* (1979).

als for his novel, and confesses the difficulties he has had over the past twenty-three years in writing his story. Then, starting with Chapter Two, he begins narrating his novel, that is, the novel by the author-as-character *within* the novel by Vonnegut the author. (pp. 229-30)

It is not until the Tenth and final chapter that Vonnegut-as-character again "appears." He has not changed much since Chapter One. He again remembers conversations with O'Hare, he is still confused about time, placing the assassinations of Robert Kennedy and Martin Luther King only a month apart; and he still harbors thoughts of death. The most significant aspect of this chapter, however, is that in describing the Dresden "corpse mines" the narrator shifts for the first time in the novel to first person *plural:*

> Now Billy and the rest were being marched into the ruins by their guards. I was there. O'Hare was there. *We* had spent the past two nights in the blind innkeeper's stable. Authorities had found *us* there. They told *us* what to do. *We* were to borrow picks and shovels and crowbars and wheelbarrows from our neighbors. *We* were to march with these implements to such and such a place in the ruins, ready to go to work. (italics added)

The shift in number insists, however subtly, that the story just related is not merely Billy Pilgrim's story, but the *narrator's* as well. He, too, had suffered capture and malnutrition and the devastating firebombing. He, too, worked in the corpse mines and saw a friend shot for "plundering" a teapot from the ruins.

And so, we realize, did Vonnegut the author. Indeed, many autobiographical similarities linking Billy Pilgrim to his "creator," Vonnegut-as-character, extend even more to Vonnegut himself. Both Pilgrim and Vonnegut were born in 1922, had fathers who hunted, are tall; both were captured in Luxembourg during the Battle of the Bulge, were sent to Dresden, where they stayed in *Schlachthof-funf,* worked in a plant that manufactured malt-syrup for pregnant women; both survived the Dresden holocaust and helped dig up the corpses afterwards; both were discharged in 1945, returned to college, and were married soon afterwards. Billy thus becomes a dual persona, a mask not only for Vonnegut-as-character (who is already a mask of sorts for Vonnegut), but for Vonnegut the author as well. Vonnegut has thus removed himself at least twice from the painful Dresden experience. By including himself as a character in his own novel, he achieves the distance that must exist between author and first person narrator, no matter how autobiographically based that narrator is. The further inclusion of Billy Pilgrim as protagonist of the novel-within-the-novel removes Vonnegut yet another step from the scenes he is recreating.

Nowhere is this need for distance more evident

than when Vonnegut relates the actual firebombing itself. Since this scene constitutes the novel's *raison d'etre,* one might expect an extended and graphic presentation. The scene, however, is not only brief, but is couched in indirection, layered with multiple perspectives. At least one reviewer has criticized the scene's failure to describe more fully the Dresden catastrophe. But Vonnegut did not *see* the firebombing, he heard it, from within *Slaughterhouse-Five.* So does Billy Pilgrim.

> He was down in the meat locker on the night that Dresden was destroyed. There were sounds like giant footsteps above. Those were sticks of high explosive bombs. The giants walked and walked. . . . A guard would go to the head of the stairs every so often to see what it was like outside, then he would come down and whisper to the other guards. There was fire-storm out there. Dresden was one big flame. The one flame ate everything organic, everything that would burn.

Most significant about this scene is not its indirection, however, but the fact that it is a *remembered* scene. For the first time in the novel, Billy Pilgrim *remembers* a past event rather than time-travelling to it. Time-travel, it seems, would have made the event too immediate, too painful. Memory, on the other hand, supplies a twenty-year buffer. But if the firebombing, only indirectly witnessed, was distressing, the totally devastated city confronted the following day by the one-hundred prisoners and their four guards must have been almost overwhelming. To relate that scene Vonnegut-as-narrator requires even more distance than memory can provide. So the scene is revealed through a story Billy remembers having told Montana Wildhack on Tralfamadore. . . . Vonnegut-as-character removes himself as much as possible from the scene he narrates, cushioning it with multiple perspectives, constructing what is finally a story within a memory within a novel. (Vonnegut the author removes himself yet one step further, achieving a story within a memory within a novel within a novel.) Moreover, before relating this important scene, Vonnegut-as-narrator withdraws to the protective fantasy of Tralfamadore. Only from the perspective of that timeless planet can he at last come to artistic terms with a scene that has haunted him for twenty-three years.

The Tralfamadorian fantasy has generally been read as originating in Billy's consciousness. Much in the novel seems to support this reading. Once, after making love to Montana on Tralfamadore, Billy awakens in Ilium to discover he has had a wet dream. In Chapter Five, three different scenes—the zoo on Tralfamadore, the prison hospital in Germany, and the honeymoon apartment in Cape Ann, Massachusetts—are connected by Billy's urinating. Chapter Nine seems to provide much of the psychological source for Billy's

Tralfamadorian fantasy: he reads a Kilgore Trout novel about an earthling man and woman kidnapped by extraterrestrials and kept in a zoo on an alien planet, he sees an article in an "old girly magazine" speculating about the whereabouts of the missing Montana Wildhack, and he looks at pictures of Montana described as "grainy things, soot and chalk," a description repeated three pages later but applied to a photograph of Montana's mother kept in a locket around Montana's neck on Tralfamadore. The prayer inscribed on that locket hangs as well in a frame on the wall of Billy's optometry office in Ilium. In short, the entire Tralfamadorian adventure can be traced back to certain incidents in Billy's life as an earthling. That life, incidentally, has been a harsh one, involving a series of personal catastrophes that include the accidental death by gunshot of Billy's father, the bizarre death of his wife in an automobile wreck, his own injury in an airplane crash, a troubled childhood, a nervous breakdown, troublesome children, and of course the Dresden experience—a life sufficiently painful to motivate escape fantasies.

Despite the fact that such evidence provides an apparent psychological basis for the Tralfamadorian "fantasy," the narrator clearly implies that the Tralfamadorian experiences are real. Billy often "visits" that planet through time-travel, which, we are told, unlike fantasy, really happens. In Chapter Two, the narrator refers to Pilgrim's "delightful hallucination" about skating on a ballroom floor. "This wasn't time travel," Vonnegut explains. *"It had never happened, never would happen. It was the craziness of a dying young man with his shoes full of snow"* (italics mine). The narrator again distinguishes between time-travel and fantasy when he describes Valencia's daydream: "Valencia wasn't a time-traveller, but she did have a lively imagination. While Billy was making love to her, she imagined that she was a famous woman in history." According to the narrator, then, time-travel results from neither "craziness" nor vivid imagination.

Nor does it result from dreaming. Of the fifty-six scene shifts accomplished via time-travel, thirty-one occur while Billy sleeps. Yet Vonnegut clearly distinguishes between dreams and time-travel. After his plane crash, for example, an unconscious Billy dreams "millions of things," but only the "true things" are time-travel. Moreover, his dreams—unlike time-travel—do involve wish-fulfillment. Once, for instance, he dreams under morphine that he is a giraffe placidly munching sugar pears and fully accepted "as one of their own by the other giraffes"—"harmless creatures," like Billy Pilgrim, whose natural weapons, their horns, are "covered with velvet." The dream obviously fulfills the longings of a miserable misfit POW for peace and acceptance. Billy, in other words, along with other characters in the novel indulges in wish-fulfillment fantasy. But the Tralfamadorian episodes, insists the narrator, are not included in these fantasies. They constitute actual experience.

Thus Vonnegut seems to supply internal evidence for a psychological explanation of Tralfamadore while at the same time denying that evidence with a contradictory narrative statement. (pp. 231-35)

At its deeper levels of meaning *Slaughterhouse-Five* . . . posits an uncertain world and, as such, may be perceived as a metaphor for an indeterminate universe. But uncertainty in the novel also reflects the artistic problems of Vonnegut-as-character, specifically his attempts over the years to reconstruct and formulate accurately the Dresden experience. For twenty-three years, the narrator tells us, he had been attempting to write his "famous Dresden book." "I thought it would be easy for me to write about the destruction of Dresden, since all I would have to do would be to report what I had seen." But perception, Vonnegut learns, consists only partially of "seeing." Over the years Dresden does not remain a mere historical event, but becomes all the emotion and anguish associated in Vonnegut's mind with that event as well as the symbolic values the firebombing has come to accrue. Ultimately, Dresden represents for Vonnegut the inevitability and ubiquity of death. (pp. 235-36)

In its obvious subjectivity *Slaughterhouse-Five* implies what historical relativists such as Carl Becker insist upon, that history is written "in the service of Mr. Everyman's emotional needs" and that "every generation, our own included, will, must inevitably, understand the past and anticipate the future in the light of its own restricted experience." Ultimately, Vonnegut's "famous book about Dresden" is less about Dresden than it is about the impact of Dresden on one man's sensibilities. More specifically, it is the story of Vonnegut's story of Dresden, how he came to write it and, implicitly, why he wrote it as he did. Again, the historical relativists provide an analogy for coming to terms with the meaning of *Slaughterhouse-Five.* As Maurice Mandelbaum points out, "the relativist believes that to understand a history we must not only understand what is said in it but also *why* this is said." Similarly, the meaning of *Slaughterhouse-Five* rests not so much in its content, its plot, but in its form, in the very tactics Vonnegut employs in telling the story of his story. (p. 236)

Critics have explained the Tralfamadorian experience as Billy Pilgrim's fantasy because certain patterns seem to link that experience to Billy's life on earth. That is, they have viewed Tralfamadore through the perspective provided by Billy Pilgrim. Overlooked, however, is the fact that many of the incidents in the Billy Pilgrim plot also can be traced back to Chapter One and to the perspective provided by Vonnegut-as-character, who, after all, is the "creator" of the Billy

Pilgrim plot. Already mentioned are certain images— "mustard gas and roses," "blue and ivory," the flowing/frozen water motif—and the general concern with death and time, including Vonnegut's own experience of "time-travelling." But there are many others. Vonnegut's reference to The Children's Crusade, for example, is echoed by a British colonel in the German prison hospital. The Luftwaffe saber Billy takes as a souvenir of Dresden echoes the reference in Chapter One to Vonnegut's souvenir sabre. Like Billy Pilgrim, the Vonnegut of Chapter One has a favorite dog and listens to late-night radio talk shows. The woman reporter in Chapter One eats a Three-Musketeers candy bar, foreshadowing Valencia's eating one later in the novel as well as the name Weary applies to himself and the two scouts trapped behind enemy lines. The quotation from Horace is echoed two chapters later when Billy wonders, "Where have all the years gone?" And Gerhard Muller's paradoxical "if the accident will" adumbrates the Tralfamadorian dictum that everything happens because it is supposed to happen, that the universe contains neither accident nor free will, but simply *is.*

As such patterns recur throughout the novel they direct attention back to their referents in Chapter One, thereby suggesting that all patterns in *Slaughterhouse-Five* have their origin in that chapter and in the artistic consciousness introduced there. The very fact that *Slaughterhouse-Five* is so carefully patterned serves as reminder that the Billy Pilgrim plot is an aesthetic construct produced by an ordering imagination. This includes the Tralfamadorian episodes, which, while they are fantasies, are not the fantasies of Billy Pilgrim but of Vonnegut-as-character. Like "his" characters Eliot Rosewater and Billy Pilgrim, Vonnegut-as-character is reinventing his universe and turning to science fiction for ideas. One of these ideas is Tralfamadore.

On one level, Tralfamadore is a sexual fantasy, since Billy spends much of this time abed with the luscious Montana Wildhack. More important to the general wish-fulfillment nature of the Billy Pilgrim plot, however, is the Tralfamadorian conception of time. As stated earlier, time—since it leads inevitably to death— is the real enemy of Vonnegut-as-character. Death seems too real for Vonnegut to omit from his reinvented cosmos, but by reinventing the nature of time, Vonnegut deprives death of its sting. According to the Tralfamadorians time is not linear but *simultaneous.* Everything that has happened or will happen exists in a vast omnipresent eternal Now. (pp. 237-38)

The concept of simultaneous time not only informs the theme of Vonnegut's novel but determines its structure as well. "This is a novel," the title page proclaims, "somewhat in the telegraphic schizophrenic manner of tales of the planet Tralfamadore . . ." While on the flying saucer Billy sees a Tralfamadorian book, "laid out . . . in brief clumps of symbols separated by stars." Each clump describes a situation, but the books are not read clump-by-clump, but "all at once." Without beginning, middle, or end, without suspense, moral, or cause-and-effect relationship, the Tralfamadorian books reflect "the depths of many marvelous moments seen all at one time."

Originally, Vonnegut planned a conventional novel about Dresden. "As a trafficker in climaxes and thrills and characterization and wonderful dialogue and suspense and confrontations," he writes, "I had outlined the Dresden story many times." According to early plans, the novel's climax would be the death of Edgar Derby. But the very presence of a climax requires a complication that develops *through time* toward some resolution. And it is the very notion of linear time Vonnegut wishes to reject in his novel. Ultimately, he turns to a structure that is not linear but *spatial*. As Sharon Spencer points out, "the spatialization of time in the novel is the process of splintering the events that, in a traditional novel, would appear in a narrative sequence and of rearranging them so that past, present, and future actions are presented in reversed, or combined, patterns." Events so arranged become spatial since their "orientation to reality" is not *when* but "the place *where* they occur" in the novel. The primary effect achieved by spatialization, Spencer continues, is *simultaneity*, "the representation of two or more actions in different places occurring at the same moment in time." By reflecting structurally his thematic concern with simultaneity, Vonnegut achieves a novel in which form and content merge.

The novel denies linear time in other ways, too. One of these ways involves the manipulation of the novel's chronology. Specific references to relative time fill the novel. Yet any attempt to link these references into a logical time sequence proves futile. For example, we are told that Billy marries Valencia six months after his release from the veterans' hospital to which he had been committed in the spring of 1948. Since they honeymoon during Indian summer, the marriage must have occurred in the early fall of 1948. On that honeymoon, Robert Pilgrim is conceived, which, assuming a normal gestation period, would place his birth sometime in the summer of 1949. So far so good. But in Chapter Eight, Billy, after finally meeting Kilgore Trout, invites the writer to Billy and Valencia's *eighteenth* wedding anniversary party "two days hence." This event occurs in 1964, at least two years short of the eighteen years of marriage the party celebrates. Moreover, we are told that Robert is seventeen at this time. Yet if he was born in the summer of 1949 he could be no older than fifteen. (pp. 238-40)

The preponderance of such discrepancies—and many more could be cited—argues against dismissing them as careless errors. Indeed, they are perfectly consistent with the view of time that informs the novel's theme and structure. Chronological consistency would be paradoxically *inconsistent* with that theme and structure. Vonnegut ironically employs apparent contradiction to avoid actual contradiction. He does not merely deny the *relevance* of chronological order, as, say, Faulkner does through his temporal involutions in *The Sound and the Fury*; he denies its very *existence*. By making it impossible to link the novel's various dates into a coherent chronological sequence, Vonnegut effectively denies the pastness of Billy's past, the futureness of his future. Both past and future are now.

As Tony Tanner points out, "Pilgrim is not only slipping backwards and forwards in time; he is also astray in Vonnegut's own fiction." Every novel Vonnegut has written before *Slaughterhouse-Five* finds its way directly or indirectly into the Dresden novel. At least three characters—Eliot Rosewater and Kilgore Trout from *God Bless You, Mr. Rosewater,* and Howard Campbell, Jr. from *Mother Night*—as well as the Tralfamadorians, who first appear in *Sirens of Titan,* reappear in *Slaughterhouse-Five*. Each character therefore has a "past" supplied by the reader's memory of those previous fictions. Vonnegut, however, refuses to allow that past to remain fixed by changing the content of some of these previous novels. (p. 241)

Several possible explanations for these emendations exist. Such alterations deny metaphorically that the events alluded to remain preserved in permanent past and imbue them with the dynamic "live" quality of events in the process of occurring. Moreover, the appearance of uncertainty supplied by such apparent contradictions and inconsistencies contributes further to the novel as a metaphor of indeterminacy. But the most pertinent explanation seems a psychological one. We must remember that these "errors" occur in the novel-within-the-novel, hence are "made" by Vonnegut-as-character, the author of that novel-within-the-novel. Indeed, the entire novel represents the consciousness of Vonnegut-as-character in the same sense that *Moby Dick* represents the consciousness of its teller, Ishmael. The inconsistencies and errors therein should be attributed not to the carelessness of Vonnegut the author, but to the *psychology* of Vonnegut the character. They should be read as clues to the state-of-mind of Vonnegut the character, as reflections of his desires and fears. If the Vonnegut of the first and last chapters of *Slaughterhouse-Five* cannot keep his dates and other facts straight, it is because time, and the death time leads to, oppress him. The "novel" he narrates, the Billy Pilgrim plot, reflects (as it relieves) this oppression. Thus these very inconsistencies and errors—indeed, the entire mode of presentation in the novel—become the true locus of meaning in *Slaughterhouse-Five*. (pp. 242-43)

Somewhat in the tradition of Frost and Hemingway, Vonnegut conceals a complex texture beneath a deceptively simple surface. His use of contradiction and uncertainty as fictional devices alone represents a significant technical innovation. Vonnegut, we must come to understand, is a literary trickster, a Houdini of letters who escapes the straitjacket of intellectual conventions, swims deep beneath our frozen expectations, and, when he surfaces, comes up in several different places at the same time. But his literary sleight-of-hand is so skillful, so disarmingly simple, we often remain unaware a difficult trick has been performed. So we praise his themes while we ignore his artistry. (p. 243)

Charles B. Harris, "Time, Uncertainty, and Kurt Vonnegut, Jr.: A Reading of 'Slaughterhouse-Five'," in *The Centennial Review,* Vol. XX, No. 3, Summer, 1976, pp. 228-43.

C. BARRY CHABOT

(essay date 1981)

[In the following excerpt, Chabot examines Vonnegut's moral stance in *Slaughterhouse-Five.*]

There is a scene near the end of *Slaughterhouse-Five* which nicely captures Vonnegut's posture toward the world he would address. Having recently survived an airplane crash fatal to many acquaintances, including his father-in-law, and immediately thereafter suffering the accidental death of his wife, Billy Pilgrim journeys to New York City for the purpose of spreading the good news he has learned from the Tralfamadorians. While he has known this news for a considerable period, he had previously confined his missionary efforts to stray patients in need of comfort, such as a boy whose father had been killed in Vietnam. Now, however, the time is "ripe," and he comes to New York to address the populace at large. He checks into the Royalton Hotel and is assigned a room with a terrace overlooking Forty-fourth Street. As he prepares for his mission of mercy, he chances to look "down at all the people moving hither and yon. They were jerky little scissors. They were a lot of fun." The derision this passage directs against those whom Billy Pilgrim would succor compromises the comfort he would give, and this tangle of motives—concern and contempt—typifies not only Pilgrim's attitude toward his fellows, but Vonnegut's as well.

If the Tralfamadorian vision of things holds out for Pilgrim some relief from the harsh terms of his life, it must be recognized that to some extent Vonnegut himself concocted that vision in an attempt to come to terms with his experience of the bombing of Dresden and all that that experience had come to represent. The facts that they were both at Dresden, that both at least

give mouth service to the Tralfamadorian vision, that both seek some comfort from it, and that both broadcast it to their fellows bespeak the extent to which Pilgrim stands in for his author. We need not question either the genuineness of their distress at the lot and the conduct of man or their sincerity in addressing their audiences in suggesting that that vision is cruelly inadequate, that its comforts are the comforts of indifference, that it is the opiate of the terminally weary, the defeated. Its solace is purchased only at the cost of accommodating oneself to the things one would otherwise regret, thereby insuring that they will multiply. If *Slaughterhouse-Five* urges such attitudes on us, it nonetheless provides us with an opportunity to understand the impasse they represent and to locate the slippage which transforms indignation into indifference, concern into taut apathy.

Slaughterhouse-Five begins in pain and indignation. It is, we are told, Vonnegut's attempt to recount and come to terms with the trauma of witnessing the destruction of Dresden while a prisoner of war. He had initially assumed that it would be a comparatively simple undertaking, a recital of facts and observations. Of course he was mistaken; words came slowly, seemed inadequate to the task, and he did not finish the novel for twenty-three years. . . . What can one say about wanton destruction on this scale? Is it sufficient simply to tot up the loses, so many buildings, so many casualties, men, women and children?

As if the bombing of Dresden were not enough, during the course of the novel Vonnegut makes it emblematic of the destruction wrought by war generally. Thus he makes references to the concentration camps, the destruction of European Jewry, the bombing of Hiroshima, and behind them, as if to insist that such murderousness is no historical anomaly, to the children's crusades of another era. Beside these instances of mass slaughter, he sets references to smaller events, such as the executions of Private Slovik and Edgar Derby, which would seem comically disproportionate were their consequences not so dire. Corpses litter his pages. Since these deaths are all the fruits of man's own murderousness, they suggest that we are all secretly Roland Weary's and Paul Lazzaro's who derive some immense compensatory pleasure in the torture and destruction of our fellows. Of course this sense of man as casually destructive fully warrants Vonnegut's rage at such acts, and partially accounts for the particular acerbity of his depiction of the species as a whole.

However, deaths of another order are also recounted in *Slaughterhouse-Five.* The final chapter begins with these brief paragraphs:

Robert Kennedy, whose summer home is eight miles from the home I live in all year round, was shot two nights ago. He died last night. So it goes. Martin Luther King was shot a month ago. He died, too. So it goes.

And every day my Government gives me a count of corpses created by military science in Vietnam. So it goes.

My father died many years ago now—of natural causes. So it goes. He was a sweet man. He was a gun nut, too. He left me his guns. They rust.

While they extend the reign of murderousness both into the present and outside warfare, the first three paragraphs are nonetheless of a piece with the other incidents we have recounted: they offer further evidence of the murderousness of man. The final paragraph introduces another dimension; Vonnegut's father died of natural causes, not at the hands of others. However, the fact that it can be included as merely another item in this series, the fact that it too is punctuated by "So it goes," suggests that Vonnegut takes it to be loosely equivalent to the previous items in the series. This conflation of natural death with murders of various sorts is a consistent feature of *Slaughterhouse-Five.* Thus we are told early on in the novel that even were wars somehow eliminated (an unlikely eventuality, it is made clear), thus no longer being occasions for human misery and subsequent outrage, we would still be left with "plain old death." (pp. 45-7)

The extent to which death as such comes to replace human murderousness as the especial regret of *Slaughterhouse-Five* must qualify Vonnegut's rage at the latter. Even if men did not visit violence upon their fellows, they would still, one and all, be subject to the reign of "plain old death." If death itself is the outrage, then humans cannot be held accountable for it, since it is built into the very structure of things. While their actions might hurry it in any particular instance, human violence brings nothing to pass that would not occur in any event. Thus when Vonnegut broadens the scope of his complaint to include the mere fact of death—that is, when he equates gratuitous murder with passing away in one's sleep—he deprives himself of any reason for holding any special animus toward those who perpetrate the mass slaughters which so exercise him.

The novel actually carries this deflation one step further. Not only people die, but so do champagne, water, and the novel. The death of each is punctuated by "So it goes," thereby suggesting that they are all of a piece, roughly equivalent. Thus it is not just murder, not even the fact of human mortality, which outrages Vonnegut; it is rather the fact that all things in this universe apparently have some tropism toward death. Thus what began as an anguished outcry against particular atrocities becomes a lament at the manner in which the world happens to be put together. At this point one must ask if this does not trivialize the destruction of Dresden. Is there no difference among the items in this series: the bombing of Dresden, the assassinations of Kennedy and King, the executions of Slovik and Derby, the accidental death of Pilgrim's wife, and the deaths of champagne and water in a still glass? Are we to take each of them in the same way?

Vonnegut never lets us forget about death in *Slaughterhouse-Five.* The punctuation is insistent, relentless. By the time they have read any considerable portion of the novel, many readers find the reiterated phrase annoying, and I suspect that to some extent Vonnegut wants us to be annoyed. If the phrase "So it goes" insists that we attend to each and every death recounted in the novel, however, it also suggests a way to minimize its impact. We are told that the phrase, used by both Vonnegut and Pilgrim, originates with the Tralfamadorians, and if their version of things is accurate, death is not the terminal event we three-dimensional beings take it to be.

"The most important thing I learned on Tralfamadore," says Billy Pilgrim, "was that when a person dies he only *appears* to die." He continues:

He is still very much alive in the past, so it is very silly for people to cry at his funeral. All moments, past, present, and future, always have existed, always will exist. . . . When a Tralfamadorian sees a corpse, all he thinks is that the dead person is in bad condition in that particular moment, but that the same person is just fine in plenty of other moments. Now, when I myself hear that somebody is dead, I simply shrug and say what the Tralfamadorians say about dead people, which is "So it goes."

This obviously spatializes time, transforms moments into points on an eternal landscape. The future has already happened; it is just that those of us in three dimensions are ignorant of what is there. And if the future has already happened, if the next moment has already occurred someplace else, there can be no question of free will: our actions are thoroughly determined, our lives laid down like railroad tracks we simply travel along. Let us consider several consequences of this view.

First, if everything has already happened, from some perspective there can be no suspense. In other words, suspense is a function of our ignorance of an already existent future, not the result of the structure of a world whose figure remains to be made. This accounts for the structure of Tralfamadorian novels:

. . . the books were laid out . . . in brief clumps of symbols separated by stars. . . . [Each] clump of symbols is a brief, urgent message—describing a situation, a scene. We Tralfamadorians read them all at once, not one after the other. There isn't any particular relationship between all the messages, except that the author has chosen them carefully, so that, when seen all at once, they produce an image of life that is beautiful and surprising and deep. There is no beginning, no middle, no end, no suspense, no moral, no causes, no effects. What we love in our books are the depths of many marvelous moments seen all at one time.

The subtitle announces that *Slaughterhouse-Five* is something of a Tralfamadorian novel, and it surely meets many of the specifications. While we cannot read them at once, the novel is built up out of a series of brief fragments or episodes, which are in turn organized in such a manner that terms such as beginning, middle, and end do not capture its sequence. More substantially, Vonnegut deliberately undercuts the development of any suspense: the first chapter ends by providing the reader with the final words of the novel, and Edgar Derby is never mentioned without reference to the fact that he is to be executed for stealing a teapot, an event which is not finally narrated until the final pages of the novel. Each mention of Derby's fate serves as a reminder that his fate is already an accomplished fact.

Secondly, if there can be no question of human volition—if, as it were, determinism goes all the way down—people are relieved of all responsibility for their actions, for in such circumstances it cannot make sense to hold human agents accountable for their various doings. If Paul Lazzaro is craven and vicious, if he is to kill Billy Pilgrim, so be it. In this view he cannot be blamed; he is, like his victim, merely another bug caught in a particular piece of amber. He suffers his actions in the same manner that Billy Pilgrim does: he is, so to speak, simply a conduit for behavior that passes through him. Thus, in the Tralfamadorian view of things, guilt is a meaningless and empty notion; it can play no formative role in the conduct of human life. Moreover, not only are men absolved from the consequences of their actions, but they are relieved as well from the responsibility for acting at all; that is, this view thrusts an individual into a passive relationship to his own actions. A life is something to be suffered or endured, not something one makes. Thus, although he cannot know it until much later, the utter passivity of Billy Pilgrim throughout his life comes to seem prescient once he has been schooled on Tralfamadore.

Finally, since all moments, happy and painful alike, already exist, and since the Tralfamadorians have access to a fourth dimension, on the principle of making the best of what is allotted them the Tralfamadorians attend only to the happy moments. While telling Pilgrim about the wars which mark their history, a Tralfamadorian guide tells him that "There isn't anything we can do about them, so we simply don't look at them. We ignore them. We spend eternity looking at pleasant moments—like today at the zoo. Isn't this a nice moment." The guide goes on to urge that earthlings too conduct their lives on such a policy, and a passing remark in the first chapter suggests that Vonnegut has taken the advice—at least he will try to forget the pain he has lived through. Such a policy obviously removes the sting from disappointment and suffering; events which occasion them now take place behind one's back, without one ever submitting to their duration. With this move we are effectively immunized against death in any form.

Actually, this final piece of Tralfamadorian view of things introduces a telling inconsistency into the putative fabric of the novel. If all one's actions are as thoroughly determined as claimed, how is it that one can choose to "ignore the awful times, and concentrate on the good ones"? One could not. The only way this contradiction could be redeemed would be to grant the existence of psychic freedom in the midst of a physically determined universe. One can think what one will, but of course one's thought cannot alter the course of events, which will be what it must be. Thus psychic freedom has been purchased only at the cost of rendering thought impotent, of severing it completely from the events which otherwise compose one's life. This impotence in turn suggests another: for all that he would avail himself of this psychic freedom, Vonnegut seems unable to talk himself into complete accommodation to the ways of the world. (pp. 47-9)

Were he successful, Vonnegut would be impervious to the stresses of events and the claims of those about him. However, he would achieve this peace only at the cost of trivializing the very events that make it necessary. If the destruction of Dresden (or of Vietnam) is on a par with natural deaths, much less with that of water in a still glass, there is no reason to single it out for special lament or comment. On this view, in fact, there is not even any viable reason to prefer peace (nor any means to achieve it) over distress; one should be indifferent even as regards such temporary mental states. The truth is, of course, that Vonnegut cannot sustain such indifference: his mask of indifference is repeatedly broached by his irrepressible rage at the events he documents. (p. 50)

The residual anger testifies to the futility of Vonnegut's cultivation of indifference. It is futile on several scores. To the extent that social life provides the impetus, such quietism can only insure the triumph of all that one regrets, for it leaves the issue uncontested. Further, even were human events as impervious to concerted intervention as Vonnegut seems to think, it is not at all clear that the mere shrug of one's shoulders is thereby the sole or most appropriate response. Might one not still comfort the hapless in ways more substantial than simply suggesting that they ignore their distress and think instead of happier times? that they are, in a way, wrong to feel pained at all? The cultivation of indifference is also futile in the sense of being finally impossible. Despite the human capacity for self-deception, its project can never reach completion, if only because of the vigilance with which one must guard against the encroachment of what one would forget. In *Slaughterhouse-Five* Vonnegut's rage—however now wide of its mark, however displaced—constitutes the last remnant of his concern; if its presence marks a failure, it is a failure that saves the novel from being an inhuman exercise. (pp. 50-1)

C. Barry Chabot, " 'Slaughterhouse-Five' and the Comforts of Indifference," in *Essays in Literature,* Vol. VIII, No. 1, Spring, 1981, pp. 45-51.

SOURCES FOR FURTHER STUDY

Giannone, Richard. *Vonnegut: A Preface to His Novels.* National University Publications: Literary Criticism Series, edited by John E. Becker. Port Washington, N.Y.: Kennikat Press, 1977, 136 p.

> Critical study attempting to "put before the reader a systematic inquiry into the features of Vonnegut's novelistic art as it develops."

Goldsmith, David H. *Kurt Vonnegut: Fantasist of Fire and Ice.* Bowling Green, Ohio: Bowling Green University Popular Press, 1972, 44 p.

> Brief study containing chapters on "Vonnegut's Cosmos" and "Vonnegut's Technique."

Klinkowitz, Jerome. *Kurt Vonnegut.* Contemporary Writers, edited by Malcolm Bradbury and Christopher Bigsby. New York: Methuen, 1982, 96 p.

> Exploration of "Vonnegut's shift, both in form and reputation, from a genre writer to a modern experimentalist."

———, and Lawler, Donald L., eds. *Vonnegut in America: An Introduction to the Life and Work of Kurt Vonnegut.* New York: Delacorte, 1977, 304 p.

> Essay collection. Includes "Kurt Vonnegut as an American Dissident," by Donald M. Fiene; *"The Sirens of Titan:* Vonnegut's Metaphysical Shaggy Dog Story," by Lawler; and "A Note on Vonnegut in Europe," by Klinkowitz.

———, and Somer, John, eds. *The Vonnegut Statement: Original Essays on the Life and Work of Kurt Vonnegut, Jr.* New York: Delacorte, 1973, 286 p.

> Includes "Two or Three Things I Know about Kurt Vonnegut's Imagination," by Tom Hildebrand; "The Modes of Vonnegut's Fiction: Or, *Player Piano* Ousts *Mechanical Bride* and *The Sirens of Titan* Invade *The Gutenberg Galaxy,*" by James M. Mellard; and "Geodosic Vonnegut; Or, If Buckminster Fuller Wrote Novels," by Somer.

Lundquist, James. *Kurt Vonnegut.* Modern Literature Monographs, edited by Lina Mainiero. New York: Frederick Ungar Publishing, 1977, 124 p.

> Describes Vonnegut as "a Pinball Wizard of cosmic cool who, through the charm of his style and the subtle challenge of his ideas, encourages us to adopt his interplanetary midwestern viewpoint and to believe once again in such radically updated values as love, compassion, humility, and conscience."

Robert Penn Warren

1905-1989

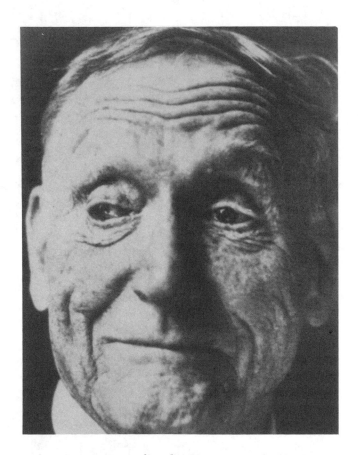

American poet, novelist, short story writer, biographer, editor, essayist, critic, dramatist, and author of children's books.

INTRODUCTION

Warren is one of the most distinguished figures in modern American literature. He received Pulitzer Prizes for both fiction and poetry, and in 1986, he was appointed by the Library of Congress as the first Poet Laureate of the United States. The tenor of Warren's writing conveys a passionate allegiance to his Southern heritage, and he often relied on dialect to render authentic characterizations and impart the local color of the rural South. While many of his works are based on actual regional incidents and legends, Warren focuses on the universal moral issues that engulf those events. Cleanth Brooks commented: "The poetry, the fiction, and even the critical essays of Robert Penn Warren form a highly unified and consistent body of work. But it would be impossible to reduce it, without distorting simplifications, to some thesis about human life. . . . In the best sense, it is inductive: it explores the human situation and tests against the fullness of human experience our various abstract statements about it."

Warren was born and raised in Guthrie, Kentucky. From an early age, he was instilled with an appreciation of his Southern agricultural heritage, and he attributed much of his knowledge and interest in history, poetry, and the oral tradition to his maternal grandfather, with whom he spent his childhood summers. In 1921, Warren enrolled at Vanderbilt University in Nashville, Tennessee, and studied under poet and critic John Crowe Ransom. At the invitation of Ransom, Warren became the youngest member of the Fugitives, a group of writers that also included Donald Davidson and Allen Tate. Between 1922 and 1925, these writers published the *Fugitive*, a literary journal containing poetry and criticism that upheld the values of Southern agrarian regionalism against the cultural influences of the North's industrial economy. Viewing the poet as an outcast and prophet, the Fugitives honored classical literature and metaphysical verse and espoused formal diction and meter in modern poetry. After receiving further education at several noted institutions, including Oxford University in England, Warren began teaching English at Louisiana State University. In 1935, with fellow faculty members Cleanth Brooks and Charles W. Pipkin, he co-founded the literary journal the *Southern Review,* an important literary magazine that served as an organ for the New Criticism. This approach to literature, which favored close textual analysis of a work, originated in part from discussions held by the Fugitives and the group that evolved from them, the Agrarians. Warren also collaborated with Brooks in writing the textbooks *Understanding Poetry* (1938) and *Understanding Fiction* (1943), influential works that introduced the New Criticism to several generations of teachers and students.

Warren's early poetry was heavily influenced by the Fugitives. The pieces collected in his first two volumes, *Thirty-Six Poems* (1935) and *Eleven Poems on the Same Theme* (1942), combine folk narratives of Warren's native Kentucky with the metaphysical verse championed by Ransom and Tate. He also makes use of sonnets, lullabies, and lyrics to examine the relationship between humanity and nature. According to James H. Justus, Warren "learned very early [from Ransom] not only the technical resources of strict forms but also the exciting modulations possible in poetic conventions. . . . From Tate, Warren observed how the dissociated modern sensibility, exploited so forcefully by Eliot and Pound, could be accommodated to the Southern temperament."

Selected Poems, 1923-1943 (1944) includes "The Ballad of Billie Potts," which is based on a Kentucky folk tale about a frontier innkeeper who makes his living by robbing and murdering travelers until he mistakenly kills his long-lost son. This work evidences Warren's evolving interest in narrative form and his preoccupation with original sin, which he details as an inevitable progression from innocence to knowledge and evil. In the extended poem *Brother to Dragons: A Tale in Verse and Voices* (1953; revised, 1979), Warren further addresses the nature of evil in this story of Lilburn Lewis, a nephew of Thomas Jefferson who murdered his slave for breaking a water pitcher that belonged to his deceased mother. *Promises: Poems, 1954-1956* (1957), for which Warren received his first Pulitzer Prize in poetry as well as the National Book Award, reveals a dramatic stylistic shift from narration to introspection. In contrast with the majority of verse written by the Fugitives, the poems in this volume are distinctly personal, and several are dedicated to Warren's children. Peter Stitt asserted: "[Before *Promises* Warren] was more a poet of despair and alienation than one of joy and union. . . . What we see in [*Promises*] is the poet questing to define, to understand, to apprehend, somehow to seize, the meaning of the joyous promise he senses."

Much of Warren's verse published during the 1960s and 1970s continued to express the importance of family and the need for self-examination. *You, Emperors, and Others: Poems, 1957-1960* (1960) offers a variety of styles, including narratives and parodies of nursery rhymes. *Incarnations: Poems, 1966-1968* (1968) is distinguished by Warren's experimentation with typographical arrangement and poetic diction. In the verse ballad *Audubon: A Vision* (1969), Warren chronicles the life of ornithologist and painter John James Audubon while celebrating the artist's ability to transform the brutality of nature into beauty through imagination. *Or Else: Poem/Poems, 1968-1974* (1974) features verse examining both the public and private life of its narrator, identified as "R.P.W." Warren received his second Pulitzer Prize in poetry for *Now and Then: Poems, 1976-1978* (1978). In this collection, he meditates on his life, beginning with his boyhood in rural Kentucky and progressing, in Warren's words, through "sixty years blown like a hurricane past." Warren's later verse is collected in *Being Here: Poetry, 1977-1980* (1980) and *Rumor Verified: Poems, 1979-1980* (1981) and is combined with earlier pieces in *New and Selected Poems, 1923-1985* (1985).

Warren published his first short story, "Prime Leaf," in 1930, his final year at Oxford. This piece initially appeared in Paul Rosenfeld's literary annual, the *American Caravan* and was later included in *The Circus in the Attic, and Other Stories* (1947). Set in Kentucky during the Black Patch Tobacco War of 1907, "Prime Leaf " examines a farmer's relationship with his son, focusing on events that test the two men's allegiances to their ideals and to each other. The action of the piece centers on the father's association with a group of tobacco farmers who have resorted to violence in their attempts to drive up tobacco prices. Angered by the group's brutality, the farmer severs his ties with them, an action which leads, following a series of confrontations with the group, to the murder of his son. As in many of his works, Warren employs an historical setting in "Prime Leaf," but he couches the story's episodes within the context of the emotional struggles and moral decisions faced by the father and his son. These types of filial confrontations are prominent throughout Warren's writings, and several critics consider "Prime Leaf " to be a preliminary treatment of the themes more extensively examined in his first novel, *Night Rider* (1939).

The novella *Blackberry Winter,* first published in 1946 and also collected in *The Circus in the Attic,* is Warren's most frequently anthologized story. This tale about the loss of innocence is related through the middle-aged narrator's recollections of an unseasonably cold June morning when he was nine years old after a violent storm had flooded the creek, damaging crops and leaving marks of destruction across the countryside. Throughout this story, Warren establishes a causal relationship between nature's sudden, devastating burst and a rash of unusual events in the community, as he recounts the startling images that the boy, Seth, sees. "Stringy and limp" bodies of drowned chicks, a crowd of people watching a dead cow float downstream, garbage strewn across the usually tidy lawn of Seth's friend Little Jeb, and a clash with a knife-wielding city tramp introduce Seth to a harsh reality that he had previously not known. Critical reaction to *Circus in the Attic, and Other Stories* has varied. While some commentators suggest that Warren's narrative art is better served by the more expansive format of the novel, others praise Warren for his precise and sensitive descriptions of both setting and character and consider several of his stories to be among the finest in the short story genre.

Warren is best known as the author of the novel *All the King's Men* (1946). This book offers a revealing examination of the complexities of political demagoguery in its portrayal of Willie Stark, an idealistic country lawyer who becomes corrupt after he is elected governor of an unnamed Southern state. Stark's rise and fall is documented by his cynical assistant, Jack Burden, whose moral beliefs are renewed following Stark's murder by a childhood friend. *All the King's Men* exemplifies Warren's fixation with original sin; in one passage, Stark articulates the state of humanity with his dictum: "Man is conceived in sin and born in corruption and he passeth from the stink of the didie to the stench of the shroud." At the time of its publication, this novel was regarded as a thinly-disguised biography of Huey "Kingfish" Long, the populist governor of Louisiana whose autocratic rule led to his assassination in 1935 and whose political machinations Warren observed during his tenure at Louisiana State University. Robert Gorham Davis called *All the King's Men* "brilliantly done, with magnificent brief set-pieces in which Robert Penn Warren writes prose equivalent to his poems in sound and rhythm and imagery." The winner of the Pulitzer Prize in fiction, *All the King's Men* was adapted into an Academy Award-winning motion picture in 1949 and has also been produced for the stage.

Many of Warren's other novels are based on specific events that took place in and around his native Kentucky. *At Heaven's Gate* (1943), Warren's second novel, was suggested by the career of Luke Lea, a Tennessee banker and politician whose unscrupulous activities and violent death generated scandal during the time that Warren attended Vanderbilt University. In *World Enough and Time* (1950), Warren offers an inter-pretation of an infamous homicide case that took place in antebellum Kentucky. From basic factual information, Warren creates a surrealistic tale centering on a young attorney who faces execution for the murder of a man who allegedly seduced his fiancée. *Band of Angels* (1955) addresses the nature of freedom and the search for identity. This work concerns a plantation owner's spoiled daughter who discovers her black ancestry and is sold into slavery following her father's death. While in bondage, the girl suffers many indignities before realizing her inner strength and resolve. *The Cave* (1959) derives from another incident that took place during Warren's undergraduate years involving a young explorer who died after being trapped inside a cave for eighteen days. Warren employs this tragedy as an allegory to comment on communal responsibility and moral knowledge. *Wilderness: A Tale of the Civil War* (1961) relates the adventures of a European Jew who emigrates to the United States to join the Union Army. Warren's next novel, *Flood: A Romance of Our Time* (1964), details the observations of a Hollywood scriptwriter who returns to his decaying Tennessee hometown to gather material for a film documenting the region's misfortunes. In *Meet Me in the Green Glen* (1971), an adulterous woman kills her husband and allows her lover to be sentenced to death for her crime. *A Place to Come To* (1977) dramatizes the efforts of Jed Tewksbury, a renowned classical scholar, to confront his squalid upbringing in order to live comfortably in the present. In his review of this book, Jonathan Yardley noted: "[Warren] is always straining to answer the big questions, to take on the great concerns of human existence."

Warren is also well known for his biographies of abolitionist John Brown and Jefferson Davis, the president of the Confederacy during the Civil War. His literary studies include *Modern Rhetoric* (1949; reprinted as *Fundamentals of Good Writing: A Handbook of Modern Rhetoric*) and *Democracy and Poetry* (1975). In addition, he has edited *Faulkner: A Collection of Critical Essays* (1966) and *Selected Poems of Herman Melville* (1971).

(For further information about Warren's life and works, see *Concise Dictionary of American Literary Biography, 1968-1988; Contemporary Authors*, Vols. 13-16, 129 [obituary]; *Contemporary Authors New Revision Series*, Vol. 10; *Contemporary Literary Criticism*, Vols. 1, 4, 6, 8, 10, 13, 18, 39, 53, 59; *Dictionary of Literary Biography*, Vols. 2, 48; *Dictionary of Literary Biography Yearbook: 1980 and 1989; Major 20th Century Writers; Something about the Author*, Vols. 46, 63; and *Short Story Criticism*, Vol. 4.)

CRITICAL COMMENTARY

DIANA TRILLING
(essay date 1946)

[In the following highly favorable review, Trilling describes *All the King's Men* as "a very remarkable piece of novel-writing."]

Robert Penn Warren's *All the King's Men* is not the first novel to draw its inspiration from the career of Huey Long. Some years ago there was John Dos Passos's *Number One,* which I have not read, and a few seasons ago there was Hamilton Basso's *Sun in Capricorn,* which, as I remember it, dealt rather freely with the actual biography of the Louisiana Kingfish. Mr. Warren would seem to stay closer to his original: he gives us a complete life-story, from the days when his Willie Stark was just an earnest, urgent, back-country farm boy to his early years in law practice and his first venture into politics, through his flashing rise to political power and the governorship, to finally, his assassination. I say "would seem" because, acquainted with only the broadest outlines of Long's life, I have no way of knowing how much of Mr. Warren's detail is a matter of record and how much supplied by the novelist's imagination. But since Mr. Warren offers his story wholly as fiction, the question of factual accuracy need not be raised.

And a very remarkable piece of novel-writing *All the King's Men* surely is. For sheer virtuosity, for the sustained drive of its prose, for the speed and evenness of its pacing, for its precision of language, its genius of colloquialism, I doubt indeed whether it can be matched in American fiction. Mr. Warren's method is the method of great photography, his poetry an overtone of photographic documentation. Perhaps one must imagine the camera of Walker Evans inching over mile after mile of the South, piling up its record of personal portraits and place portraits and portraits of things, catching fact after fact of the Southern heat and mystery, indolence and venality and despair, in order to begin to have a notion of what and how Mr. Warren sees.

Nor are its imposing gifts of composition the only recommendation of *All the King's Men.* There is also its largeness of intention. Mr. Warren's study of a political leader is intended to investigate the moral relativism inherent in the historical process. One might describe it as a fictional demonstration of Hegel's philosophy of history. For what Mr. Warren seems to be saying, with Hegel, is that spirit or goodness arises only out of the ruck of living and the clash of self-seeking wills. He is questioning the absolutes of good and evil which are so much the assumption of a large part our present-day political morality.

But all relativistic positions are peculiarly liable to misinterpretation, and the Hegelian relativism especially must be read very purely not to be translatable into a justification of means by their end, or not to be understood as the belief that good always, even often, has its source in evil. Yet here precisely is the inadequacy of *All the King's Men,* that it can give rise to just such misconceptions of what I am sure was its very much purer informing idea. It is in fact difficult *not* to infer from Mr. Warren's novel that a Willie Stark's absolute power is justified by such public benefactions as the fine hospital he builds, or that we are to welcome the Willie Stark type of political unpleasantness as a step in political progress.

In part, of course, this may be the inevitable result of translating the hero of history into a hero of fiction. For, concerned with the world historical figure, Hegel was concerned only with his historical or force aspect, not with his ethical aspect; but fiction always deals primarily with individual human beings, and only by suggestion with philosophical abstractions, and when Mr. Warren personifies his abstractions, as the novelist must, he in effect alters a way of viewing history into a system of personal morality from which, then, we evolve a system of political morality. Thus Willie Stark is not an evolutionary force, but first a person on whom his author exercises an ethical judgment; and if only because he is the hero of the novel, we must assume that this judgment is largely admiring or approving. The result is that it is the demagogue's usual dull ambivalence—half the obsession with power and half a soft generosity and idealism—that is made to stand for the dialectical struggle of good and evil in both individuals and society. . . .

All the King's Men is told through the point of view of a young newspaperman researcher attached to Stark—one of those prefabricated figures out of the city room whom Mr. Warren endows with a wonderful eye but with no equivalent gift of inward vision. . . . But although Jack Burden is so essentially shabby a person that he vulgarizes any thought he entertains or acts out, it is to him that Mr. Warren entrusts an idea of history that requires the nicest discriminations. It is Burden's

Principal Works

John Brown: The Making of a Martyr (biography) 1929

I'll Take My Stand: The South and the Agrarian Tradition [with others] (essays) 1930

Thirty-Six Poems (poetry) 1935

Night Rider (novel) 1939

Eleven Poems on the Same Theme (poetry) 1942

At Heaven's Gate (novel) 1943

Selected Poems: 1923-1942 (poetry) 1944

All the King's Men (novel) 1946

Blackberry Winter (novella) 1946

The Circus in the Attic, and Other Stories (short stories) 1947

World Enough and Time (novel) 1950

Brother to Dragons: A Tale in Verse and Voices (poetry) 1953; also published as Brother to Dragons: A Tale in Verse and Voices—A New Version [revised edition], 1979

Band of Angels (novel) 1955

Segregation: The Inner Conflict in the South (nonfiction) 1956

Promises: Poems, 1954-1956 (poetry) 1957

You, Emperors and Others: Poems, 1957-1960 (poetry) 1960

The Legacy of the Civil War: Meditations on the Centennial (nonfiction) 1961

Wilderness: A Tale of the Civil War (novel) 1961

Flood: A Romance of Our Time (novel) 1964

Who Speaks for the Negro? (essays) 1965

A Plea in Mitigation: Modern Poetry and the End of an Era (lecture) 1966

Selected Poems: New and Old, 1923-1966 (poetry) 1966

Incarnations: Poems, 1966-1968 (poetry) 1968

Audubon: A Vision (poetry) 1969

Homage to Theodore Dreiser (criticism) 1971

Meet Me in the Green Glen (novel) 1971

Or Else: Poems, 1968-1974 (poetry) 1974

Selected Poems, 1923-1975 (poetry) 1976

A Place to Come To (novel) 1977

Now and Then: Poems, 1976-1978 (poetry) 1978

Being Here: Poetry, 1977-1980 (poetry) 1980

Jefferson Davis Gets His Citizenship Back (essay) 1980

Rumor Verified: Poems, 1979-1980 (poetry) 1981

Chief Joseph of the Nez Perce (poetry) 1983

New and Selected Poems, 1923-1985 (poetry) 1985

New and Selected Essays (essays) 1989

---

morally ambiguous evaluation of Stark that we are forced to accept as Mr. Warren's.

And if the low quality of Burden's moral awareness is responsible for most of the ethical and political confusion of *All the King's Men,* so must it in some measure account, I think, for the failure of Mr. Warren's novel to achieve the artistic stature commensurate with the author's writing gifts. For one has the idea that were Mr. Warren's narrator to inhabit wider realms of thinking and feeling, he would not only alter our view of the book's central character but also give greater meaning to its subsidiary people, that he would raise all his associates out of the realm of the commonplace and raise their conflicts from melodrama to drama. Certainly the conception of almost all Mr. Warren's characters fails to match the energy of the prose in which they are delineated. While Mr. Warren's language draws upon every resource of actuality, his creation of people lacks all freshness of perception. It is the inner human mystery that Mr. Warren blinks as he pursues the mystery of the historical process.

Diana Trilling, "All the King's Men," in *The Nation,* New York, Vol. 163, No. 8, August, 1946, p. 220.

WALTER ALLEN
(essay date 1948)

[In the following excerpt, Allen praises *All the King's Men* as "a very formidable attempt at a novel on the grand scale."]

[*All the King's Men*] is a masterly rendering of life and government in a backward American state in which heat, dirt, squalor, illiteracy and the remains of a traditionally gracious way of life for the wealthy exist side by side. It is, as it were, the world of the decayed houses of Faulkner, of the moronic poor whites of Caldwell, set in their social and economic context.

But Mr. Warren is not content merely to tell the story of the rise and fall of Willy Stark; through his narrator, Jack Burden, he sets it in perspective. Burden will probably be something of a problem for the English reader. Stark's confidential secretary, he is a newspaperman talking with the tough cynicism that we expect of newspapermen in American fiction. So it comes as a shock to realise that Burden is much more than this, that he has been trained as an historian and a scholar and that almost by second nature he translates events during Stark's governorship into their historical analogies. And, as the book develops, Burden grows in importance, so that by the end it is his story rather than Stark's that Mr. Warren seems to be telling. Yet one is aware of no feeling of strain in Mr. Warren's handling of his parallel stories; they are indeed organically related; for the fall of Stark and his long consideration of the significance of the career of his former chief lead to Burden's redemption from what he calls the dream of the "great twitch," the principles of which are: "First, that you cannot lose what you have never had. Second, that you are never guilty of a crime which you did not commit." It is not until the end of the book that we realise that Burden's redemption, his discovery that "history is blind, but man is not," has been the outcome of events going far back into the past, that Mr. Warren has most cunningly been unwinding a plot of truly Ibsenite complexity. The occasional sentimentalities, the oversimplification of human relations into which Mr. Warren slips, are of the kind that seem inseparable from even the best contemporary American fiction. They do not prevent the book from being a very formidable attempt at a novel on the grand scale.

Walter Allen, in a review of "All the King's Men," in *The New Statesman & Nation*, Vol. XXXV, No. 900, June 5, 1948, p. 464.

MALCOLM O. SILLARS

(essay date 1957)

[In the following excerpt, Sillars explores populist elements in *All the King's Men*.]

All the king's men, and the king himself, can be clearly seen to represent the great American tradition of Populism that swept the poorer agricultural areas of the Middle West and the South in the late 1930's. It is surely far more than the narrow context of the life of Huey Long, as too many have mistakenly supposed. The spirit of Willie Stark has reared itself in many states and in many forms; in Bloody Bridles Waite of Colorado, Sockless Jerry Simpson of Kansas, William Jennings Bryan of Nebraska, Alfalfa Bill Murray of Oklahoma. Kissin' Jim Folsom of Alabama and many others. The political elements of *All the King's Men* are rooted in the past and yet are all, in one way or another, degenerative of the tradition they represent.

There are four such elements which should be isolated and their interrelationships known in order to see more clearly the novel's meaning. The hill people of the South represent a particular economic group who are now, as they were in the days of Willie Stark, and earlier in the days of Pitchfork Ben Tillman, set apart from the more aristocratic and proper conservative people of the flatlands. Willie Stark is an example of the leaders produced by the hills to do battle on their behalf. The political position of the aristocrats of the Delta illuminates Stark's rise and fall. Jack Burden is an aristocrat who loses, then finds himself in trying to bridge the gap between the hills and the Delta.

Essential to the understanding of Willie Stark is an understanding of the social construct which produced him. The hill people are a crucial phenomenon in the economic and social structure of middle-western and southern agricultural areas. The geographical dividing line between hills and black belt only serves to draw into sharper focus, in the South more than elsewhere, the economic battle. These hill people are holders of small plots of poor red farmland from which they eke out an existence with the assistance of amazing stubbornness, and an evangelical Protestant code of ethics. They see themselves as the chosen people who do battle with the more prosperous, and evil, Delta planters. They are fiercely individualistic.

They were less inclined to favor the Civil War because they had less interest in Negro slavery. They were more susceptible to Populism with its interest in freeing the small farmer from the control of the bankers, railroads, elevator operators and other more well to do elements of the society. . . . They supported the New Deal and in the election of 1948 they endorsed the Democratic party more than did the Delta, which found the politics of the New and Fair Deals threatening their power position by raising the standards of the Negroes and the rednecks of the hills.

The same Populist sentiment was strong in the Corn Belt and for similar reasons. In the South it was rocky red soil; in Kansas and Nebraska it was rainfall. In the late nineteenth century there was real correlation between the amount of rainfall and the intensity of Populist fervor in western Nebraska. *All the King's Men* is the product of a socio-economic vortex which reduced a proud people to desperate action.

The hill people have a concept of good and evil by which they see themselves as the chosen people who have had their birthright stolen. To the Populist, as to most liberals, good and evil are concentrated. One attribute is found in one group and one in another. Or, the individual is good and governments, or corporations or bankers or what have you, are evil. Thus, reasons the liberal, return the society to its natural owners and there will be peace in the land. (pp. 345-46)

One of the lessons to be learned from *All the King's Men* is that these conditions still exist and this latent evangelical liberalism is always present. In 1948 Henry Wallace (a curious combination of populist and aristocrat) tried to exploit this agrarian liberalism with his "Gideon's Army" and his promises to the "little people." His liberalism had lost its roots, however, and the stronger urban liberalism which dominated the Wallace campaign was not acceptable to rural people. Further, in 1948 Wallace had in Harry S. Truman, an opponent who better fit the picture of the hill people's leader. The conditions—economic, social and religious—which formed the amalgam producing Willie Stark are a significant part of American history. (p. 347)

Willie Stark, the leader produced by the conditions and prejudices of the hill people, is the second of the important social elements in Robert Penn Warren's novel, for while Willie Stark is an individual, he is also an institution. He has all the background and beliefs of the hill people mentioned earlier. As county treasurer he sacrifices his political life in a fight to see that the courthouse gang in Mason City does not make the new schoolhouse a political plum. His opponents tell the people that the company submitting the lowest bid would bring in Negroes from the lowlands and thus deprive the local people of jobs. Incidentally, they tell the people that the Negroes would be the semi-skilled workers and the hill people that were hired would be the common laborers. Essentially this is the point at which the hill people always break with the Negroes. They do not have as many to contend with as in the flat country and so do not fear their political power as the aristocrats do. But when the Negro threatens them economically, race becomes an issue. Willie fights but loses. Other real life Willie Starks are destroyed politically in just such a manner.

The fire escape of the schoolhouse, built of inferior materials, falls during a fire drill and three children are killed. Willie is thus made a political power. He had warned them about what the courthouse gang was trying to do and he was right. With this he advances to the second step in the rise of the redneck leader, what Professor V. O. Key calls the "friends and neighbors" politician. In the hills around Mason City he is a political power. His is the protest for the inarticulate people of the area.

His rise to statewide prominence comes when Willie again sacrifices himself politically. Convinced of his popularity he is induced to enter the race for Governor by Tiny Duffy, the perfect stereotype of the small-town political boss. During the campaign, Stark discovers that he has been nominated to take votes from MacMurfee, a candidate who is also popular in the hills. Willie goes to the political rally, rather symbolically pushes Tiny Duffy off the platform and reveals his part in the act. He tells the people to vote for MacMurfee and not for him. He tells them to sit in judgment on MacMurfee and remove him if he is wrong. MacMur-

fee wins the election. Willie, by this sacrifice, becomes a state-wide figure. He fits the standards of honesty that the hill people want and becomes their champion. He was duped as they had been, time and time again.

Probably of interest here is the change in the spoken rhetoric of Willie Stark. Previous to this time Stark talked about issues, about specific problems of taxes, education and roads. His speeches were clearly dull and unemotional. When he speaks at the rally he speaks to the emotional needs of the hill people. One might reflect that this was Willie's awakening, or rebirth if you will, to the realities of political power and the first step to his destruction. (pp. 347-48)

MacMurfee, of course, fails to live up to the promises of the election and the inevitable wave of the future sweeps Willie into the Governor's Mansion. But Willie is different from the rest. He cannot be bought by political machines. Instead he forms his own machine and like too few others who rose in a similar manner, he actually goes about attempting to solve the problems of the hill people. He builds highways, schools and hospitals. He raises the taxes of the rich (the lowland aristocrats) and defends the hill people in the courts.

The greatest fight is the one which Willie goes through in relating his past to the realities of politics. He finds out that there is both good and evil in all men. Byram B. White, as State Auditor, dips his hand into the till and Willie is shaken up. The little man from the hills is just as capable of evil as the folks of the lowlands. Not that putting one's hand into the till is so bad—for Willie had come now to realize that this is an essential part of the machinery of political power, but White does it behind Willie's back. In short, he is disloyal to the cause which Willie represents. And White's willingness to write an undated resignation deepens Stark's realization of his power over men. (p. 348)

Out of his experiences there grows the conclusion that life is not just a clash of good and evil but rather (returning selectively to his fundamentalist Sunday school) all evil. As Willie Stark puts it, "Man is conceived in sin and born in corruption and he passeth from the stink of the didie to the stench of the shroud."

This conviction influences Willie's concept of progress profoundly. His real concern is with the problem of producing that which is good. . . .

Indicative of his change in philosophy, there is a degeneration in Willie Stark's oral rhetoric. The genuine Populist cry for justice is dissipated into demagoguery. (p. 349)

There is further degeneration in Willie. It is exemplified by his infidelity to his wife, Lucy. Lucy, the prime mover in Willie's earlier high moral purpose, is relegated to the position of a publicity piece. She is used for the furtherance of the Governor's political ends. For sexual satisfaction Willie turns to a collection of women who are not the product of the hills. In short, Willie falls into the very pattern of life in his personal affairs which the hill people have hated (or perhaps envied) in the people of the lowlands—heavy drinking and infidelity. In the end it is Anne Stanton's brother Adam who kills Willie when he finds out that his sister had been Willie's mistress. Thus, Willie's failure to do the impossible and fulfill the picture which the redneck has of his leaders caused his downfall. (p. 350)

[In] death, Willie Stark returns to his roots. There is a solution to the evils of the society in which the hill people live and the solution is in the conquest of political power by an articulate spokesman who will act. Whether or not this belief is correct is not an issue. The real point is that the hopes and aspirations of these people are genuine and Willie's attempts to meet these needs are also genuine. It is in the red dirt and man's weaknesses that Willie's failures are rooted. The fallacy of Populism, and perhaps of all liberalism then, is the fallacy of not understanding nature.

The third social element in the novel is the aristocracy of the Delta. Like the geographical division between the hills and the plains, the aristocracy of the deep South is more clearly defined than in other sections of the country. On the plains of the deep South, the plantation owners have built a tradition of aristocratic conservatism. They use political power to protect a social system which is grounded in stability and respect for law. . . . But with all of their respectability they have almost always been lax in their willingness to help the poor farmers of the hills. They are the evil which the hill people see and react to. Because of the code and tradition of these people they do not understand Willie Stark. In *All the King's Men* Judge Irwin of Burden's Landing is the personification of this school of thought. Judge Irwin is the best of his tradition. He, unlike many of the more complacent men and women of the area, sees a need for social improvement. However, the judge is in a dilemma. The society which he represents will not allow change without the overt pressure of Willie Stark. Thus, there is no conservative way to solve problems, it seems. There is only Willie Stark's way and this is unacceptable to the judge.

Robert Penn Warren goes beyond this weakness, however, to show that even the people of the plain, when the hard crust of conservative respectability is removed, are not without corruption. Judge Irwin, while he was Attorney General, was involved in a kickback scheme which eventuated in the suicide of Mortimer L. Littlepaugh, Counsel for the American Electric Power Company. Governor Stanton had known of the action and shielded Irwin. The rectitude which is so lauded in the aristocracy is really only a façade. They are not above corruption when they find it necessary. This element dramatizes the sin of the aristocracy. Their real

sin is their failure to recognize and alleviate the economic conditions of the poorer people of the hills. Thus, in the South as well as elsewhere, the aristocracy has a respectable legal conservatism. They contribute greatly by giving powerful and intelligent leadership to the nation. But their conservatism is seldom respectable in dealing with the real socio-economic problems of the area and their legality is constructed to control such socio-economic improvement.

The fourth element in the novel is Jack Burden. From the standpoint of the political nature of the agrarian areas he is significant as a touchstone moving between the hills and the black belt. Jack Burden is a product of the aristocracy. His early association with Judge Irwin makes a great impression on him. His youth is spent with Anne and Adam Stanton. All the elements of his life are linked to the Delta, but his realization that there is something unsatisfactory in this self-satisfied existence sets him adrift. Given the chance to work for Willie Stark, he accepts and quickly falls in with all the activities which characterize Willie. His actions in working to find ammunition for Willie's plans eventually bring him to attack the very roots from which he sprang. Through his revelation of Judge Irwin's and Governor Stanton's actions he destroys the very people who had previously meant the most to him, Adam Stanton, Anne Stanton and Judge Irwin. Anne Stanton becomes Willie Stark's mistress, Adam Stanton kills Willie and is killed himself by Willie's bodyguard and Judge Irwin commits suicide.

Burden seems lost in his conviction that there is no code of ethics or morals but only the "big twitch." Although Willie feels that Jack is the only person who really knows him, Jack realizes that he does not understand Willie at all. Perhaps the products of the aristocracy can never really understand the hill people and their kind of leadership.

As the novel draws to a climax, Jack Burden looks through the cloud of action without purpose in which he has been existing and begins to see clearly. He does, in the end, bridge the gap. There can be, he seems to know, a connection between the hills and the Delta. There can be respect for law and at the same time socio-economic progress. As the novel ends he is telling the reader that he may get back into politics. If so, it will be to help Hugh Miller who resigned as Attorney General when Governor Stark refused to fire Byram B. White. Miller is the symbol of the very leadership which is necessary, a man of respectablity who wishes to use the law to help the people.

In surveying the rise and fall of a Populist politician and the people who support and oppose him, *All the King's Men* leaves the reader with the hope of Lucy Stark. Another Willie will come along and he will not fall into the snare of demagoguery, blackmail and thuggery. Contemporary politics would seem to show us that this is possible. George Norris in Nebraska and Bob La Follette in Wisconsin are clear examples of this tradition. And in the South, examples of respectable Populism like John Sparkman and Lister Hill of Alabama prove that agrarian democrats can be law abiding. Further, the enlightened conservatism of such men as Fulbright of Arkansas adds awareness to respectability. It is also true that shortsighted conservatism still exists in the agrarian areas in the personages of Thurmond, Byrnes, Byrd and the like. It is further true that Populism has gone sour of late not only in Huey Long and Theodore Bilbo but most recently in Joseph McCarthy of Wisconsin. But the gap can be bridged either by a Populist who climbs up or an aristocrat who bends down. This is the essential lesson of *All the King's Men* and perhaps of America. (pp. 351-53)

Malcolm O. Sillars, "Warren's 'All King's Men': A Study in Populism," in *American Quarterly*, Vol. IX, No. 3, Fall, 1957, pp. 345-53)

ROBERT PENN WARREN

(essay date 1963)

[In the following excerpt, Warren describes the evolution of *All the King's Men*.]

When I am asked how much *All the King's Men* owes to the actual politics of Louisiana in the '30's, I can only be sure that if I had never gone to live in Louisiana and if Huey Long had not existed, the novel would never have been written. But this is far from saying that my "state" in *All the King's Men* is Louisiana (or any of the other forty-nine stars in our flag), or that my Willie Stark is the late Senator. What Louisiana and Senator Long gave me was a line of thinking and feeling that did eventuate in the novel.

In the summer of 1934 I was offered a job—a much-needed job—as Assistant Professor at the Louisiana State University, in Baton Rouge. It was "Huey Long's University," and definitely on the make—with a sensational football team and with money to spend even for assistant professors at a time when assistant professors were being fired, not hired—as I knew all too well. It was Huey's University, but he, I was assured, would never mess with my classroom. That was to prove true; he was far too adept in the arts of power to care what an assistant professor might have to say. The only time that his presence was ever felt in my classroom was when, in my Shakespeare course, I gave my little annual lecture on the political background of *Julius Caesar;* and then, for the two weeks we spent on the play, backs grew straighter, eyes grew brighter, notes

were taken, and the girls stopped knitting in class, or repairing their faces.

In September 1934 I left Tennessee, where I had been living on a farm near Nashville, drove down across Mississippi, crossed the river by ferry . . . and was in North Louisiana. Along the way I picked up a hitchhiker—a country man, the kind you call a redneck or a wool-hat, aging, aimless, nondescript, beat up by life and hard times and bad luck. . . . He was, though at the moment I did not sense it, a mythological figure.

He was the god on the battlement, dimly perceived above the darkling tumult and the steaming carnage of the political struggle. He was a voice, a portent, and a natural force like the Mississippi River getting set to bust a levee. Long before the Fascist March on Rome, Norman Douglas, meditating on Naples, had predicted that the fetid slums of Europe would make possible the "inspired idiot." His predictive diagnosis of the origins of fascism—and of communism—may be incomplete, but it is certain that the rutted back roads and slab-side shacks that had spawned my nameless old hitchhiker, with the twine-tied paper parcel in his hand, had, by that fall of 1934, made possible the rise of "Huey." My nameless hitchhiker was, mythologically speaking, Long's *sine qua non.*

So it was appropriate that he should tell me the first episode of the many I had to hear of the myth that was "Huey." The roads, he said, was shore better now. A man could git to market, he said. A man could jist git up and git, if 'n a notion come on him. Did'n have to pay no toll at no toll bridge neither. Fer Huey was a free-bridge man. So he went on and told me how, standing on the river bank by a toll bridge (by what river and what bridge was never clear), Huey had made the president of the company that owned the bridge a good, fair cash offer, and the man laughed at him. But, the old hitchhiker said, Huey did'n do nothing but lean over and pick him up a chunk of rock and throwed it off a-ways, and asked did that president-feller see whar the rock hit. The feller said yeah, he seen. Wal, Huey said, the next thing you see is gonna be a big new free bridge right whar that rock hit, and you, you son-of-a-bitch, are goen bankrupt a-ready and doan even know it.

There were a thousand tales, over the years, and some of them were, no doubt, literally and factually true. But they were all true in the world of "Huey"— that world of myth, folklore, poetry, deprivation, rancor, and dimly envisaged hopes. That world had a strange, shifting, often ironical and sometimes irrelevant relation to the factual world of Senator Huey P. Long and his cold manipulation of the calculus of power. The two worlds, we may hazard, merged only at the moment when in September 1935, in the corridor of the Capitol, the little .32 slug bit meanly into the senatorial vitals.

There was another world—this a factual world—made possible by the factual Long, though not inhabited by him. It was a world that I, as an assistant professor, was to catch fleeting glimpses of, and ponder. It was the world of the parasites of power, a world that Long was, apparently, contemptuous of, but knew how to use, as he knew how to use other things of which he was, perhaps, contemptuous. This was a world of a sick yearning for elegance and the sight of one's name on the society page of a New Orleans paper; it was the world of the electric moon devised, it was alleged, to cast a romantic glow over the garden when the President of the University and his wife entertained their politicos and pseudo-socialites; it was a world of pretentiousness, of bloodcurdling struggles for academic preferment, of drool-jawed grab and arrogant criminality. (pp. 161-63)

For in Louisiana, in the 1930's, you felt somehow that you were living in the great world, or at least in a microcosm with all the forces and fatalities faithfully, if sometimes comically, drawn to scale. And the little Baton Rouge world of campus and Governor's Mansion and Capitol and the gold bathroom fixtures reported to be in the house of the University contractor was, once the weight of Long's contempt and political savvy had been removed by the bullet of the young Brutus in the Capitol, to plunge idiotically rampant to an end almost as dramatic as the scenes in the last bunkers of Berlin or at the filling station on the outskirts of Milan. (pp. 163-64)

But this is getting ahead of the story. Meanwhile, there was, besides the lurid worlds, the world of ordinary life to look at. There were the people who ran stores or sold insurance or had a farm and tried to survive and pay their debts. There were—visible even from the new concrete speedway that Huey had slashed through the cypress swamps toward New Orleans—the palmetto-leaf and sheet-iron hovels of the moss pickers, rising like some fungoid growth from a hummock under the great cypress knees, surrounded by scum-green water that never felt sunlight, back in that Freudianly contorted cypress bloom of cottonmouth moccasins big as the biceps of a prize-fighter, and owl calls, and the murderous metallic grind of insect life, and the smudge fire at the hovel door, that door being nothing but a hole in a hovel wall, with a piece of croker sack hung over it. There were, a few miles off at the University, your colleagues, some as torpid as a gorged alligator in the cold mud of January and some avid to lick the spit of an indifferent or corrupt administration, but many able and gifted and fired by a will to create, out of the seething stew and heaving magma, a distinguished university.

And there were, of course, the students, like students anywhere in the country in the big state universities, except for the extraordinary number of pretty girls and the preternatural blankness of the gladiators who were housed beneath the stadium to have their reflexes honed, their diet supervised, and—through the efforts of tutors—their heads crammed with just enough of whatever mash was required (I never found out) to get them past their minimal examinations. Among the students there sometimes appeared, too, that awkward boy from the depth of the 'Cajun country or from some scrabble-farm in North Louisiana, with burning ambition and frightening energy and a thirst for learning; and his presence there, you reminded yourself, with whatever complication of irony seemed necessary at the moment, was due to Huey, and to Huey alone. For the "better element" had done next to nothing in fifty years to get that boy out of the grim despair of his ignorance.

Yes, there was the world of the "good families," most of whom hated Huey Long—except, of course, for that percentage who, for one reason or another, had reached an accommodation. They hated him sometimes for good reasons and sometimes for bad, and sometimes for no reason at all, as a mere revulsion of taste; but they never seemed to reflect on what I took to be the obvious fact that if the government of the state had not previously been marked by various combinations of sloth, complacency, incompetence, corruption, and a profound lack of political imagination, there would never have been a Senator Huey P. Long, and my old hitchhiker by the roadside would, in September 1934, have had not tale to tell me.

Conversation in Louisiana always came back to the tales, to the myth, to politics; and to talk politics is to talk about power. So conversation turned, by implication at least, on the question of power and ethics, of power and justification, of means and ends, of "historical costs." The big words were not often used, certainly not by the tellers of tales, but the concepts lurked even behind the most ungrammatical folktale. The tales were shot through with philosophy.

The tales were shot through, too, with folk humor, and the ethical ambiguity of folk humor. And the tales, like the political conversations, were shot through, too, with violence—or rather, with hints of the possibility of violence. There was a hint of revolutionary desperation—often synthetically induced. In Louisiana, in '34 and '35, it took nothing to start a rumor of violence. (pp. 164-65)

Melodrama was the breath of life. There had been melodrama in the life I had known in Tennessee, but with a difference: in Tennessee the melodrama seemed to be different from the stuff of life, something superimposed upon life, but in Louisiana people lived melodrama, seemed to live, in fact, for it, for this strange combination of philosophy, humor, and violence. Life was a tale that you happened to be living—and that "Huey" happened to be living before your eyes. And all the while I was reading Elizabethan tragedy, Machiavelli, William James, and American history—and all that I was reading seemed to come alive, in shadowy distortions and sudden clarities, in what I saw around me.

How directly did I try to transpose into fiction Huey P. Long and the tone of that world? The question answers itself in a single fact. The first version of my story was a verse drama; and the actual writing began, in 1938, in the shade of an olive tree by a wheat field near Perugia. In other words, if you are sitting under an olive tree in Umbria and are writing a verse drama, the chances are that you are concerned more with the myth than with the fact, more with the symbolic than with the actual. And so it was. It could not, after all, have been otherwise, for in the strict, literal sense, I had no idea what the now deceased Huey P. Long had been. What I knew was the "Huey" of the myth, and that was what I had taken with me to Mussolini's Italy, where the bully boys wore black shirts and gave a funny salute.

I had no way of knowing what went on in the privacy of the heart of Senator Long. Now I could only hope, ambitiously, to know something of the heart of the Governor Talos of my play *Proud Flesh*. For Talos was the first avatar of my Willie Stark, and the fact that I drew that name from the "iron groom" who, in murderous blankness, serves Justice in Spenser's *Faerie Queene* should indicate something of the line of thought and feeling that led up to that version and persisted, with modulations, into the novel.

Talos was to become Stark, and *Proud Flesh* was to become *All the King's Men.* Many things, some merely technical, led to this transformation, but one may have some bearing on the question of the ratio of fact and fiction. In 1942 I left Louisiana for good, and when in 1943 I began the version that is more realistic, discursive, and documentary in method . . . than the play, I was doing so after I had definitely left Louisiana and the world in which the story had its roots. By now the literal, factual world was only a memory, and therefore was ready to be absorbed freely into the act of imagination. Even the old man by the roadside—the hitchhiker I had picked up on the way down to take my job—was ready to enter the story: he became, it would seem, the old hitchhiker whom Jack Burden picks up returning from Long Beach, California, the old man with the twitch in the face that gives Jack the idea for the Great Twitch. But my old hitchhiker had had no twitch in his face. Nor had I been Jack Burden.

I had not been Jack Burden except in so far as you have to try to "be" whatever you are trying to create. And in that sense I was also Adam Stanton, and Willie Stark, and Sadie Burke, and Sugar Boy, and all the rest.

And this brings me to my last notion. However important for my novel was the protracted dialectic between "Huey" on the one side, and me on the other, it was far less important, in the end, than that deeper and darker dialectic for which the images and actions of a novel are the only language. And however important was my acquaintance with Louisiana, that was far less important than my acquaintance with another country: for any novel, good or bad, must report, willy-nilly, the history, sociology, and politics of a country even more fantastic than was Louisiana under the consulship of Huey. (pp. 166-67)

Robert Penn Warren, " 'All the King's Men': The Matrix of Experience," in *The Yale Review,* Vol. LIII, No. 2, December, 1963, pp. 161-67.

SEAN WILENTZ

(essay date 1983)

[In the following excerpt, Wilentz reviews Warren's literary career, focusing on the author's *Chief Joseph of the Nez Perce.*]

As my grandfather said, there were only two benefits of modernity. One was fly screens, and the other was painless dentistry, and I think he was right.

—Robert Penn Warren

American historians have ceased to be poets; long ago, they broke W. H. Auden's commandment: Thou shalt not commit a social science! More irksome still, American poets have ceased to be historians. The great exception is Robert Penn Warren.

Warren has written 10 novels, 15 volumes of poetry, and nine nonfiction books; the antimodernist passion behind this prodigious output provokes ambivalence. On one side is Warren's shrewdness about the tricks of historical memory and his profound critique of capitalism's moral and material destructiveness; on the other, his utter condemnation of "modernity" mixed with a kind of grim fatalistic irony. It's a combination that can be pretty discouraging. But Warren has become a stronger poet as he's gotten older: now nearly 80, he can suffer contradictions in himself and the rest of the world, revise his opinions, and still look for truths. *Chief Joseph of the Nez Perce,* a vivid 64-page narrative, restates Warren's lifelong concerns with history, memory, and irony, and contains some of his biggest surprises yet.

Modern America, with its peculiar mixture of self-interest and squander, was born in 1877. In the South, a political deal removed the last federal troops, ended Reconstruction, killed the hopes of a generation of blacks, radicals, and reformers. In the North, labor disputes along the railways turned into the first mass strike in our history, a literal insurrection. (The troops called in to crush the strike included some of those taken from the South.) Meanwhile, in eastern Montana, the U.S. Army, under the command of General O. O. Howard (late head of the Freedmen's Bureau in the South), finally tracked down Chief Joseph and his band of Nez Perce. Warren has chosen his subject wisely; shifting the locale from his native South, he has found a web of historical circumstances well suited to his Jeffersonian instincts.

Joseph's was one of the saddest chapters in the brutal history of subjugation that had turned vicious with Jackson's persecution of the Cherokees and would end in 1890 with the Wounded Knee massacre. Breaking an 1855 treaty and an 1873 presidential agreement, the government ordered Joseph's band to the reservation. Joseph did not understand the settlers' eagerness: "For all things live, and live in their nature, / But what is the nature of gold?" The Nez Perce, unaccustomed to war, sent out a white flag, which was met by a bullet. . . .

For three months, Chief Joseph and his people evaded capture, in a masterpiece of maneuver. In September, ill, hungry, and outnumbered, they gave up. Joseph delivered his famous surrender, "I will fight no more forever." General Howard allowed a subordinate to set the terms, which turned out surprisingly generous—but the agreement proved unacceptable to military brass and was scrapped. The last of the Nez Perce left for the reservation. The man giving the orders was the Commanding General of the U.S. Army, William Tecumseh Sherman—whose name bore tribute to a slaughtered Indian warrior. In captivity, Joseph became something of an American hero, according to the fashion of the Gilded Age. . . .

Joseph died on the reservation in 1904—the death certificate said of a broken heart. He remained a fabled figure, but Warren sees through the accolades with a Southerner's knowledge of defeat and hypocrisy: "Great honor came, for it came to pass / That to praise the red man was the way / Best adapted to expunge all, all, in the mist / Of bloodless myth."

Thus far, the poem is classic Warren, in the Romantic style of his recent work but with a twist. The obliteration of a precapitalist agrarian order by the blue-bellies and the greedy, the treachery of the victor's myths, irony after irony in the legacy of the Civil War—all are classic Warren themes. The twist is in the subject. Maybe now that Warren is writing about the Indians and not the Confederacy, Yankee critics can better understand (without condoning) the conservative agrarian Warren of the '20s and '30s, and better appreciate the writer Warren has become. No apologist

for slavery or racism, he's more like a genuine but disillusioned upcountry Populist, saddened by America's course since the Civil War but tempered by 20th-century fears of unintended consequences and by a deep pessimism about the prospects for change.

Warren's big surprise comes when he tells of his pilgrimage to Joseph's monument at Snake Creek. He saw, as all tourists do, the plains' vastness, thought once again of the "squirming myriads" at his back:

> But suddenly knew that for those sound
> Of heart there is no ultimate
> Irony. There is only
> Process, which is one name for history. Often
> Pitiful. But sometimes, under
> The scrutinizing prism of Time;
> Triumphant.

In an instant the awesome ironies dissolve—the pessimistic, immobilizing ironies that spelled the end of an older idealism to Warren, as well as to a generation of fiercely modernist historians who came of age during the political traumas of the 1940s and '50s. To be sure, there is no absolute Good or Evil, even in this grotesque saga: Warren makes it clear that to imagine otherwise is as dangerous as it is foolhardy. But all does not end in ambiguity and irony, as one might expect from a Warren poem; the victory of what he calls modernity is not so overwhelming or one-sided that we are left only with grave laments and wry jokes about fly screens and laughing gas. In Joseph's story, and in the myriads of eternity, we can find the strivings and conflicts of the once-defeated, a living presence.

And, perhaps, we can find more, not all of it to our liking. Warren the antimodernist is still troublesome. The stubborn, truly traditionalist features of Warren's sensibility persist in *Chief Joseph,* his veneration of fatherly authority, his rage at modern life. Yet there is also much that inspires: apart from the poetic vindication of Joseph, there is Warren's vision of historical change—a vision not of some flight from "modernity," but of a retrieval of the more humane virtues of an earlier (and in some ways nobler) civilization, as part of a continuing development.

With this vision, and with the end of irony, it is possible to find some courage for the future. All master civilizations, all great empires have considered themselves the culmination of history, after which would come the barbaric deluge. Such claims by today's masters, East and West, are more persuasive and terrifying than any that have come before. But if history can be called process, if like Warren we can still see Chief Joseph in our own hearts and minds, then history may not be over after all.

Sean Wilentz, "The End of Irony," in *The Village Voice,* Vol. XXVIII, No. 40, October 4, 1983, p. 57.

HAROLD BLOOM

(essay date 1985)

[Bloom is an American literary critic and theorist. In the following excerpt from a review of Warren's *New and Selected Poems*, he examines Warren's evolution as a poet, praising the intensity and durability of his works.]

Robert Penn Warren, born April 24, 1905, in Guthrie, Kentucky, is at the age of eighty our most eminent man of letters. His position is the more remarkable for the extraordinary persistence with which he has made himself into a superb poet. A reader thinks of the handful of poets who wrote great poetry late in life: Browning, Hardy, Yeats, Stevens, Warren. Indeed, **"Myth of Mountain Sunrise,"** the final poem among the new work in [*New and Selected Poems: 1923-1985*], will remind some readers of Browning's marvelous "Prologue" to *Asolando,* written when the poet was seventy-seven. . . .

The epigraph to the new section of this [*New and Selected Poems*] is from Warren's favorite theologian, St. Augustine: "Will ye not now after that life is descended down to you, will not you ascend up to it and live?" One remembers another epigraph Warren took from the *Confessions,* for the book of poems *Being Here* (1980): "I thirst to know the power and nature of time." At eighty Warren now writes out of that knowledge, and his recent poems show him ascending up to living in the present, in the presence of time's cumulative power. Perhaps no single new poem here quite matches the extraordinary group of visions and meditations in his previous work that includes **"Red-Tail Hawk and Pyre of Youth," "Heart of Autumn," "Evening Hawk," "Birth of Love," "The Leaf," "Mortmain," "To a Little Girl, One Year Old, in a Ruined Fortress,"** and so many more. But the combined strength of the eighty-five pages of new poems that Warren aptly calls "Altitudes and Extensions" is remarkable, and extends the altitudes at which perhaps our last poet to attempt the ultimate questions of life and death continues to live and work. (p. 40)

Warren's poetry began in the modernist revival of the metaphysical poets, as a kind of blend of Eliot's *The Waste Land* with the gentler ironies of Warren's teacher at Vanderbilt, John Crowe Ransom. This phase of the poetry took Warren up to 1943, and then came to an impasse and, for a decade, an absolute stop. *At Heaven's Gate, All the King's Men,* and *World Enough and Time* belong to that decade of poetic silence, and perhaps the major sequence of his fiction usurped War-

ren's greater gift. But he was certainly unhappy in the later stages of his first marriage, which ended in divorce in 1950, and it cannot be accidental that his poetry fully resumed in the late summer of 1954, two years after his marriage to the writer Eleanor Clark.

The book-length poem, *Brother to Dragons* (1953, revised version 1979), formally began Warren's return to verse, and is undoubtedly a work of considerable dramatic power. I confess to admiring it only reluctantly and dubiously, ever since 1953, because its ideological ferocity is unsurpassed even elsewhere in Warren. This ferocity is manifested by its implicit assertion that Thomas Jefferson is somehow affected by the barbaric act of his nephews in butchering a black slave. Much improved in revision, it remains unnerving, particularly if the reader, like myself, longs to follow Emerson in forgiving himself, if not everything, then at least as much as possible. But Warren—unlike Emerson—does not wish us to cast out remorse. Like his then master, Eliot, though in a more secular way, Warren was by no means reluctant to remind us that we *are* original sin. *Brother to Dragons* is rendered no weaker by its extraordinary tendentiousness, but it is not necessarily persuasive, if you happen not to share its moral convictions.

Warren's shorter poems, his lyrics and meditations, evolve impressively through three subsequent volumes: *Promises* (1957), *You, Emperors and Others* (1960), and [*Selected Poems: New and Old, 1923-1966*] (1966), where the new work was grouped as "Tale of Time." I recall purchasing these volumes, reading them with grudging respect, and concluding that Warren was turning into a poet rather like Melville (whom he was to edit in a *Selected Poems of Herman Melville,* in 1971) or the younger Hardy. Warren's poems of 1934 through 1966 seemed interestingly ungainly in form, highly individual in genre and rhetoric, and not fundamentally a departure from Eliot's high modernist mode. A poetry of moral belief, with some of the same preoccupations as the *Four Quartets,* I would have judged it, rather dismissively, and not of overwhelming concern if a reader was devoted to Hart Crane and Wallace Stevens. Such a reader would also have preferred contemporary volumes like Elizabeth Bishop's *Questions of Travel* (1965) and John Ashbery's *Rivers and Mountains* (1966), which were in the poetic tradition of Crane and Stevens, of visionary skepticism rather than Eliot's poetry of belief in the "truth," whether moral or religious. I could not foresee the astonishing breakthrough that Warren, already past the age of sixty, was about to accomplish with *Incarnations* (1968) and *Audubon: A Vision* (1969).

Other critics of Warren's poetry see more continuity in its development than I do. But in 1968 I was a belated convert, transported against my will by reading *Incarnations,* and able at least to offer the testimony of a very reluctant believer in his poetic strength, a strength maintained by Warren throughout these nearly two decades since he began to write the poems of *Incarnations* in 1966.

Incarnations opens with a closely connected sequence of fifteen poems called "Island of Summer," which is the volume's glory. Unfortunately, Warren has included only five of these in his [*New and Selected Poems: 1923-1985*], but they are the best of a strong group, and I will discuss only those five here, since Warren subtly has created a new sequence or a condensed "Island of Summer." Like the original work, the sequence is a drama of poetic incarnation, or the death and rebirth of Warren as a poet. In what is now the opening meditation, **"Where the Slow Fig's Purple Sloth,"** Warren associates the fig with fallen human consciousness and so with an awareness of mortality:

> When you
> Split the fig, you will see
> Lifting from the coarse and purple
> seed, its
> Flesh like flame, purer
> Than blood.
>
> It fills
> The darkening room with light.

This hard, riddling style is now characteristic and has very little in common with the evocations of Eliot in his earlier verse. **"Riddle in the Garden"** even more oddly associates fruits, peach and plum, with negative human yearnings, suicidal and painful; with a horror of inwardness. A violent confrontation, **"The Red Mullet,"** juxtaposes the swimming poet and the great fish, eye to eye, in a scene where "vision is armor, he sees and does not / Forgive." In a subsequent vision of **"Masts at Dawn,"** the optical effect of how: "The masts go white slow, as light, like dew, from darkness / Condensed on them" leads to what in some other poet might be a moment of illumination, but here becomes a rather desperate self-admonition, less ironic than it sounds: "We must try / To love so well the world that we may believe, in the end, in God." This reversed Augustinianism is a prelude to a burst of Warren's poetic powers in the most ambitious poem he had yet written, **"The Leaf."**

When he was fifteen, Warren was blinded in one eye by a sharp stone playfully thrown by a younger brother, who did not see that Warren was lying down on the other side of a hedge. Only after graduating from Vanderbilt did Warren get around to having the ruined eye removed and replaced by a glass eye. Until then, the young poet suffered the constant fear of sympathetic blindness in his good eye. There may be some complex relations between that past fear and Warren's remarkable and most prevalent metaphor of redemption, which is to associate poetic vision both with a

hawk's vision and with a sunset hawk's flight. This metaphor has appeared with increasing frequency in Warren's poetry for more than half a century, and even invades the novels. (pp. 40-1)

"The Leaf " centers upon an image of redemption that of a hawk's flight, with the difference from earlier poems of Warren being in the nature of the redemption. Opening with the fig again, seen as an emblem of human mortality and guilt, and of "the flaming mullet" as an encounter in the depths, the poem proceeds to an episode of shamanistic force. . . .

Nothing in Warren's earlier poetry matches [the hawk episode of **"The Leaf "**] in dramatic intensity, or in the accents of inevitability, as the poetic character is reincarnated in him by his sacrificial self-offering "near the nesting place of the hawk." Much of the guilt and sorrow in Warren's earlier life come together here, with beautiful implicitness: the fear of blindness, the decade of poetic silence, the failure of the first marriage, and most mysteriously, a personal guilt at having become a poet. . . .

Warren's father died in 1955, at the age of eighty-six. Robert Franklin Warren, who wanted above everything else to be a poet, became a banker instead, solely to support not only his own children, but also a family of young children bequeathed to him by his own father, who had married again and then died. Reflecting upon all this, Warren has said: "It's as if I've stolen my father's life," somberly adding: "If he had had the opportunity I did, with his intelligence and energy, he'd have done a lot better than I did." This is probably part of the sorrow heard in: "I, / Of my father, have set the teeth on edge." From Warren's own account, one might think it the larger part of the sorrow, but imaginatively the heavier burden may have been his poetic inheritance, the influence of Eliot, which Warren here almost involuntarily disavows and overcomes. Eliot's "not the cicada" from *The Waste Land* becomes [in the next movement of **"The Leaf,"** which includes the line "My father's voice, in the moment when the cicada ceases, has called to me"] the moment when Eliot's presence in Warren's voices ceases, to be replaced by the poetic voice that Robert Franklin Warren had to abandon. The return of the father's voice becomes the blessing of Warren's new style, the gift given by Warren in his father's name. (p. 41)

From this poem on, Warren rarely falters, whether in *Audubon: A Vision* or in the half-dozen books of shorter poems (or new sections in selected volumes) that have followed. The achievement throughout these books necessarily is mixed, but there are several score of poems that manifest all the marks of permanence.

I want to look at just one of these poems, because it raises again, for me and for others, the ancient problem of poetry and belief. The poem is **"A Way to Love**

God" from "Can I See Arcturus From Where I Stand?," the section of new poems in [*Selected Poems, 1923-1975,* which] preceded the book under review. I quote only the poem's final vision, which is no grislier than the ones preceding it:

> But I had forgotten to mention an upland
> Of wind-tortured stone white in darkness, and tall,
>   but when
> No wind, mist gathers, and once on the Sarré at mid-
>   night,
> I watched the sheep huddling. Their eyes
> Stared into nothingness. In that mist-diffused light
>   their eyes
> Were stupid and round like the eyes of fat fish in
>   muddy water,
> Or of a scholar who has lost faith in his calling.
>
> Their jaws did not move. Shreds
> Of dry grass, gray in gray mist-light, hung
> From the side of a jaw, unmoving.
> You would think that nothing would ever again
>   happen.
>
> That may be a way to love God.

By loving God, Warren appears to mean loving what he calls "the truth," which is that all human beings are dreadfully involved in sin. This is an ancient and Augustinian polemic in all his work, poetry and prose, and does not pretend to settle what "truth" is, but rather asserts a necessarily personal conviction. Warren, despite the critical efforts of his more pious exegetes, is a skeptic and not a believer, but he is a Bible-soaked skeptic. His way of loving God is to forgive himself nothing, and to forgive God nothing.

The aesthetic consequences of this position, in the poetry written since 1966, seem to me wholly admirable, while the spiritual grimness involved remains a formidable challenge for many readers, myself among them. Missing from [*New and Selected Poems: 1923-1985*] is a notorious sequence, **"Homage to Emerson, On Night Flight to New York,"** to be found in the "Tale of Time" section of *Selected Poems: 1923-1975.*

I don't regret its deletion, but it has considerable value in clarifying Warren's lifeling distaste for Emerson. . . .

[The] entire poem vigorously thrashes Emerson for his supposedly deficient sense of fact. Accusing Emerson of an abstract heart is not original with Warren, but I wince properly at the effective anti-transcendentalism of: "At 38,000 feet Emerson / Is dead right." At ground level, I believe Emerson to be dead right also. "His Smile" [the first part of **"Homage to Emerson, On a Night Flight to New York"**] is a good polemic, and should be admired as such.

The vexed issue of poetry and belief arises rather when I reread a poem like **"A Way to Love God,"** which is an impressive nightmare from my perspective, but a truth from Warren's. A secularized conviction of sin, guilt, and error is an obsessive strand in Warren's work, and for him it helps to create a position that is more than rhetorical. However, the effect is only to increase the rich strangeness of his poetic strength, which is wholly different from that of the best living poets of my own generation: Ashbery, Merrill, Ammons, and others, and from their precursor, Stevens.

Ideological ferocity never abandons Warren, but he passionately dramatizes it, and he has developed an idiom for it that is now entirely his own. He would appear to be, as I have intimated elsewhere, a sunset hawk at the end of a great tradition. Because of our increasing skepticism, I doubt that we will ever again have a poet who can authentically take this heroic a stance. He has earned, many times over, his series of self-identifications with the flight of the hawk, or an aspect of the truth. The second new poem in [*New and Selected Poems: 1923-1985*], **"Mortal Limit,"** is a sonnet celebrating again his great image of the hawk. . . .

So long as he abides, there will be someone capable of asking that grand and unanswerable question: "Beyond what range will gold eyes see / New ranges rise to mark a last scrawl of light?" (p. 42)

Harold Bloom, "The Flight of the Hawk," in *The New York Review of Books,* Vol. XXXII, No. 9, May 30, 1985, pp. 40-2.

SOURCES FOR FURTHER STUDY

Bohner, Charles. *Robert Penn Warren.* Boston: Twayne Publishers, 1981, 176 p.

> Surveys Warren's life and works.

Chambers, Robert H., ed. *Twentieth Century Interpretations of "All the King's Men": A Collection of Critical Essays.* Englewood Cliffs, N.J.: Prentice-Hall, 1977, 161 p.

> Collects criticism on *All the King's Men.*

Clark, William Bedford. *The American Vision of Robert Penn Warren.* Lexington: University Press of Kentucky, 1991, 161 p.

> Examines Warren's treatment of American politics and social problems in his works.

Gray, Richard, ed. *Robert Penn Warren: A Collection of Critical Essays.* Englewood Cliffs, N.J.: Prentice-Hall, 1980, 206 p.

> Contains criticism and interpretation of Warren's works by a variety of commentators.

Graziano, Frank, ed. *Homage to Robert Penn Warren: A Collection of Critical Essays.* Durango, Colo.: Longbridge-Rhodes, 1981, 92 p.

> Essay collection. Includes bibliographies.

Ruppersburg, Hugh M. *Robert Penn Warren and the American Imagination.* Athens: University of Georgia Press, 1990, 202 p.

> Explores Warren's depiction of America in his works, focusing on myths and myth interpretation.

Evelyn Waugh

1903-1966

(Full name Evelyn Arthur St. John Waugh) English novelist, short story writer, travel writer, essayist, critic, biographer, journalist, and poet.

INTRODUCTION

During a career lasting four decades, Waugh was considered to be England's most prominent man of letters. He published highly regarded travel books, short stories, essays, and literary criticism. It is as a novelist, however, that Waugh is most remembered. Such early novels as *Decline and Fall,* (1928) *Vile Bodies* (1930) and *Black Mischief* (1932) established his literary reputation as a fine satirist, while such later works as *Brideshead Revisited* (1945) brought him popular acclaim from an international audience. He was "one of the most devastating and effective satirists in the history of English letters," Paul A. Doyle declared, "and one of its greatest stylists."

Waugh's father was an editor with the English publishing house of Chapman & Hall. His older brother, Alec, was a novelist and travel writer. Evelyn at first rebelled against the family's literary tradition: while attending Hertford College, Oxford, in the early 1920s, he was more interested in the decorative arts than in literature, and he designed stained glass windows. But he was forced to leave school because of his poor grades. Waugh attended an art school, then worked as a schoolmaster. After a teaching career ended (he was fired from three schools in two years), Waugh devoted himself to writing.

Decline and Fall, Waugh's first novel, written at the age of twenty-five, is a satiric work in which young Paul Pennyfeather is dismissed from Oxford and must make his own way in the world. Pennyfeather is a Candide-like innocent who passively watches the disturbing and corrupt events he finds himself in. The evil prosper, the good are punished, and no standards of behavior are operable. Pennyfeather lives in "a world as remote from moral considerations as a fairy story or a Marx Brothers film," Walter Allen wrote. Because of the scandalous nature of *Decline and Fall,* Waugh was forced by his publisher to remove certain scenes from the novel and to preface the book with a disclaimer. On a first reading, it may seem as if Waugh were "allowing all seven deadly sins to hold sway and was enjoying the triumph of evil and decadence . . . with the most carefree insouciance possible," as Doyle stated. But a more careful examination of the text, Doyle continued, showed that "underneath the surface of absurdity and seeming indifference, there lies a basic standard of decency and fair play against which human aberrations are sharply contrasted."

In his next novel, *Vile Bodies,* Waugh satirized his experiences at Oxford and the fast–paced, passionately decadent world of the "Bright Young Things" (the rich idle young of Britain). Because he has lost his belief in traditional values, Adam Symes innocently commits the most loathsome of crimes. The world he inhabits is unstable and in constant flux, symbolized in one scene in which a wild party is held in a dirigible. This instability is reflected in the narrative, which leaps randomly from scene to scene and has little coherent plot. *"Vile Bodies* is one of those rare novels, like *The Great Gatsby,* that seem to define and sum up a period. It can stand for one aspect of life in the England of the twenties," Allen believed. "It is a triumph of style and the comic spirit." *Black Mischief,* Waugh's third novel, is set in Africa and concerns the attempted modernization of the country of Azania. The Emperor Seth of Azania enlists the aid of the Englishman Basil Seal to bring his backward country into the twentieth century. But Seal's understanding of modern civilization is sadly shallow, and Seth's fervent efforts to follow Seal's guidelines result in tragedy for his people. Doyle called *Black Mischief* a "wild, rollicking comedy . . . with a more savage note of satire" than was found in Waugh's earlier books.

Waugh's early novels established his reputation as a satirist of the first order. But Edmund Wilson believed these books to be more than good satire, ranking them among the best novels written during the 1920s. Several critics saw the nihilistic chaos of Waugh's early novels as an attack on modern society and its lack of permanent values. Steven Marcus explained that in Waugh's early novels, he "was able to sustain a tone of bemused mournfulness over a society bent on smashing itself to pieces, while at the same time depicting the feckless innocence of both those who were most active in the smashing and those most hurt by it."

Waugh's disenchantment with modern society and the breakup of his first marriage contributed to his decision to convert to Roman Catholicism in 1930. As Doyle explained it, "he was searching for a focus of order and stability where marriage vows were taken seriously and moral values were constantly empha-

sized." Waugh's newfound religious purpose was first reflected in his novel *A Handful of Dust* (1934).

Largely autobiographical, the novel traces the collapse of Tony and Brenda Last's marriage after Brenda has an affair with John Beaver. Brenda's affair is encouraged by her sophisticated London friends. The novel ends in tragicomedy. A despairing Tony travels to the Brazilian jungle to forget his troubles but is taken prisoner by a Mr. Todd. Todd, a devotee of Charles Dickens, forces Tony into reading to him from Dickens' novels, presumably for the rest of his life.

A Handful of Dust is Waugh's statement on soulless contemporary society and a caution about the pitfalls of over-idealizing the past. The book is considered by many critics to be the best of his early work, and perhaps his writing as a whole. His characters believe in the Myth of Decline and, in order to escape this era's decadence, they seek meaning, beauty, and "rightness" in the past, a Golden Age which actually exists only in their minds. This preoccupation results, however, in the same neglect of responsibility, the same selfishness and insensitivity to immediate crises that these people condemn in others. Many critics believe that Waugh's characterizations become rounder and his satire more subtle in *A Handful of Dust.* Still others, however, see it as a satisfying continuation of the farcical treatment and the two-dimensional portrayals of the earlier works.

A Handful of Dust was strongly Catholic in tone, but it was not until *Brideshead Revisited: The Sacred and Profane Memories of Captain Charles Ryder* that Waugh wrote an overtly Catholic novel. The work chronicles twenty years in the lives of the Marchmains, a wealthy English Catholic family. It is narrated by Charles Ryder, who befriends Sebastian Marchmain while attending Oxford in the 1920s and is later engaged to Sebastian's sister, Julia. Sebastian is an alcoholic; Julia has her first marriage annulled; and their father, long separated from his wife, returns to the Church only on his deathbed. Despite their trials, the "Marchmain family, in their various fashions, all yield, ultimately, to the promptings of their faith and bear witness to its enduring virtue," Wilson noted. Upon witnessing Lord Marchmain's deathbed return to the Church, Charles, too, accepts Catholicism as his faith.

Because of its essentially Catholic message and its alleged idealizing of the English upper classes, *Brideshead Revisited* proved the most controversial of Waugh's novels. "Its sentimentality and its apparent obeisance to the old siren attractions of both the English gentry and the Church," L. E. Sissman wrote, "made [*Brideshead Revisited*] unswallowable to critics." Still, it was Waugh's most successful novel, becoming a best-seller in England and the United States and helping to make him internationally known. One reason for the book's success was the timing of its initial appearance. Written during the Second World War and published at the war's end, *Brideshead Revisited*, with its romantic evocation of upper class life in the 1920s, seemed exotic and sensuous to a war-weary audience accustomed to rationing. Much of the novel's success, however, lies in the power of its prose. A. C. Ward allowed that *Brideshead Revisited* "may well become [Waugh's] longest-remembered book, for its sense of period, the firmness of its character-drawing, and its convincing record of a Roman Catholic family." Called to Los Angeles by MGM to help adapt *Brideshead* for the screen, Waugh visited Forest Lawn cemetery in Santa Monica and was at once fascinated and appalled by its elaborate modern memorials. The visit resulted in a satire on the mortuary industry in California. *The Loved One* (1948) enjoyed great success in England and America, with critics praising it as a scathing satiric portrait.

In the trilogy composed of *Men at Arms* (1952), *Officers and Gentlemen* (1955), and *Unconditional Surrender* (1961)—later published in a single volume as *Sword of Honour* (1965)—Waugh wrote of another religious conversion, that of Guy Crouchback, who is transformed "from an unloving 'loner' to a man of compassion," as Doyle explained. Tracing Crouchback's military career during the Second World War, the trilogy combines Waugh's usual satire with an emotional depth not found in his previous works. The success of the trilogy moved Patrick O'Donovan to call it "the one genuine masterpiece to come out of the war." Evaluations of the *Sword of Honour* trilogy were sharply divided, with some reviewers generous in their appraisal while others disparaged Waugh's accomplishment.

Melvin Maddocks took exception to Waugh's disillusionment with the modern age, calling it "patently indefensible. . . . The real problem is that Mr. Waugh refuses to believe that human goodness can appear in more than one particular kind of period costume, and this narrows him inevitably, as an artist as well as a thinker." But other critics praised the trilogy as Waugh's greatest achievement.

Waugh's importance to modern English literature owes much to his style and craftsmanship. Earlier works were characterized by clever phrasing and broadly humorous plots, but in later works, he translated his observations into complex ironic structures, unifying content with form. Waugh also managed, for the most part, to maintain a balance between involvement and detachment toward his characters. Some critics contend that Waugh's books are timeless because their worlds transcend current history. Others, however, believe that his books will not endure because of his nostalgic preoccupations, the rigidity of his opinions and outlook, and the restricted range of his intellectual and political focus. The assessments of his writing skills are, nevertheless, virtually uniform in their recognition of his comic inventiveness, his highly individualistic style, his devotion to clarity and precision, and his ability to entertain.

(For further information about Waugh's life and works, see *Contemporary Authors*, Vols. 25-28, 85-88; *Contemporary Authors New Revision Series*, Vol. 22; *Contemporary Literary Criticism*, Vols. 1, 3, 8, 13, 19, 27, 44; and *Dictionary of Literary Biography*, Vol. 15: *British Novelists, 1930-1959*.)

CRITICAL COMMENTARY

EDMUND WILSON

(essay date 1950)

[In the following excerpt, Wilson praises the spontaneity of Waugh's early novels, noting that even though the author seems to get closer to "the conventions of ordinary fiction" with each work, he never truly reaches this stage.]

Nothing can taste staler today than some of the stuff that seemed to mean something [at the end of the twenties], that gave us twinges of bitter romance and thrills of vertiginous drinking. But *The Great Gatsby* and *The Sun Also Rises* hold up; and my feeling is that [Waugh's novels of the period] are the only things written in England that are comparable to Fitzgerald

and Hemingway. They are not so poetic; they are perhaps less intense; they belong to a more classical tradition. But I think that they are likely to last and that Waugh, in fact, is likely to figure as the only first-rate comic genius that has appeared in English since Bernard Shaw.

The great thing about *Decline and Fall,* written when the author was twenty-five, was its breathtaking spontaneity. The latter part of the book leans a little too heavily on Voltaire's *Candide,* but the early part, that hair-raising harlequinade in a brazenly bad boys' school, has an audacity that is altogether Waugh's and that was to prove the great principle of his art. This audacity is personified here by an hilarious

---

Principal Works

Decline and Fall (novel) 1928

Rossetti: His Life and Works (biography) 1928

Vile Bodies (novel) 1930

Black Mischief (novel) 1932

A Handful of Dust (novel) 1934

Scoop (novel) 1938

Put Out More Flags (novel) 1942

Brideshead Revisited: The Sacred and Profane Memories of Captain Charles Ryder (novel) 1945; revised edition, 1960

The Loved One: An Anglo-American Tragedy (novel) 1948

Helena (novel) 1950

*Men at Arms (novel) 1952

*Officers and Gentlemen (novel) 1955

*Unconditional Surrender (novel) 1961; also published as The End of the Battle, 1961

A Little Learning: An Autobiography, the Early Years (autobiography) 1964

The Diaries of Evelyn Waugh (diaries) 1976

The Letters of Evelyn Waugh (letters) 1980

*These works were published in a single volume as Sword of Honour in 1965.

---

character called Grimes. Though a schoolmaster and a "public-school man," Grimes is frankly and even exultantly everything that is most contrary to the British code of good behavior. . . . This audacity in Waugh's next book, *Vile Bodies,* is the property of the infantile young people who, at a time "in the near future, when existing social tendencies have become more marked," are shown drinking themselves into beggary, entangling themselves in absurd sexual relationships, and getting their heads cracked in motor accidents. The story has the same wild effect of reckless improvisation, which perfectly suits the spirit of the characters; but it is better sustained than *Decline and Fall,* and in one passage it sounds a motif which for the first time suggests a standard by which the behavior of these characters is judged: the picture of Anchorage House with its "grace and dignity and other-worldliness," and its memories of "people who had represented their country in foreign places and sent their sons to die for her in battle, people of decent and temperate life, uncultured, unaffected, unembarrassed, unassuming, unambitious people, of independent judgment and marked eccentricities."

In *Black Mischief* there is a more coherent story and a good deal of careful planning to bring off the surprises and shocks. . . . We note that with each succes-

sive book Evelyn Waugh is approaching closer to the conventions of ordinary fiction: with each one—and the process will continue—we are made to take the characters more seriously as recognizable human beings living in the world we know. Yet the author never reaches this norm: he keeps his grasp on the comic convention of which he is becoming a master—the convention which makes it possible for him to combine the outrageous with the plausible without offending our sense of truth. . . . There are two important points to be noted in connection with *Black Mischief.* The theme of the decline of society is here not presented merely in terms of night-club London: it is symbolized by the submergence of the white man in the black savagery he is trying to exploit. The theme of audacity is incarnated here, not in a Philbrick or a Grimes, but in a bad-egg aristocrat, who steals his mother's emeralds to run away from England, manipulates the politics of Azania by talking modern ideas to the native king and, forced at last to flee the jungle, eats his sweetheart unawares at a cannibal feast.

A Handful of Dust, which followed, is, it seems to me, the author's masterpiece. Here he has perfected his method to a point which must command the admiration of another writer even more perhaps than that of the ordinary non-literary reader—for the latter may be carried from scene to scene of the swift and smooth-running story without being aware of the skill with which the author creates by implication an atmosphere and a set of relations upon which almost any other novelist would spend pages of description and analysis. The title comes from T. S. Eliot's line, "I will show you fear in a handful of dust," but, except on the title page, the author nowhere mentions this fear. Yet he manages to convey from beginning to end, from the comfortable country house to the clearing in the Brazilian jungle, the impression of a terror, of a feeling that the bottom is just about to drop out of things, which is the whole motivation of the book but of which the characters are not shown to be conscious and upon which one cannot put one's finger in any specific passage. . . . The audacity here is the wife's: her behavior has no justification from any accepted point of view, whether conventional or romantic. Nor does the author help out with a word of explicit illumination. He has himself made of audacity a literary technique. He exemplifies, like so many of his characters, the great precept of Benjamin Jowett to young Englishmen just starting their careers: "Never apologize, never explain."

The next novel *Scoop* is not quite so good as the ones just before and just after it, but it has in it some wonderful things. . . . The story is simpler than usual, and it brings very clearly to light a lineup of opposing forces which has always lurked in Evelyn Waugh's fiction and which is now even beginning to give it a certain melodramatic force. He has come to see English life as a conflict between, on the one hand, the qualities of the English upper classes, whether arrogant, bold and outrageous or stubborn, unassuming and eccentric, and, on the other, the qualities of the climbers, the careerists and the commercial millionaires who dominate contemporary society. (pp. 140-44)

Put Out More Flags, written during and about the war, has an even more positive moral. Basil Seal, the aristocratic scoundrel who has already figured in *Black Mischief,* exploits the war to his own advantage by informing against his friends and shaking down his sister's county neighbors with threats of making them take in objectionable refugees, but finally he enlists in the Commandos, who give him for the first time a legitimate field for the exercise of his resourcefulness and nerve. Evelyn Waugh's other well-born wastrels are already in the "corps d'élite," somewhat sobered after years of "having fun." (pp. 144-45)

We see now that not only has the spirit of audacity migrated from the lower to the upper classes, but that the whole local emphasis has shifted. The hero of *Decline and Fall* was a poor student reading for the church, whose career at Oxford was wrecked by the brutality of a party of aristocratic drunks. . . . But it is now this young man, Percy Pastmaster, and Sir Alastair Digby-Vaine-Trumpington and the English county families generally who are the heroes of *Put Out More Flags.* Evelyn Waugh has completely come over to them, and the curious thing is that his snobbery carries us with it. In writing about Harold Nicolson, I remarked on his fatal inability to escape from the psychology of the governing class, which was imposed on him by birth and office. The case of Waugh is the opposite of this: he has evidently approached this class, like his first hero, from somewhere outside, and he has had to invent it for himself. The result is that everything is created in his work, nothing is taken for granted. The art of this last novel is marvellous. See the episode in which Basil Seal blackmails the young married woman: the attractiveness of the girl, which is to prompt him to try a conquest, and her softness, which will permit his success (Evelyn Waugh is perhaps the only male writer of his generation in England who is able to make his women attractive), are sketched in with a few physical details and a few brief passages of dialogue that produce an impression as clear and fresh as eighteenth-century painting.

Evelyn Waugh is today a declared Tory and a Roman Catholic convert; he believes in the permanence of the social classes and, presumably, in the permanence of evil. (pp. 144-46)

[But] his opinions do not damage his fiction. About this fiction there is nothing schematic and nothing doctrinaire; and, though the characters are often stock types—the silly ass, the vulgar parvenu, the old clubman, etc.—everything in it has grown out of expe-

rience and everything has emotional value. *Put Out More Flags* leaves you glowing over the products of public schools and country houses as examples of the English character; but it is not a piece of propaganda: it is the satisfying expression of an artist, whose personal pattern of feeling no formula will ever fit, whether political, social or moral. For the savagery he is afraid of is somehow the same thing as the audacity that so delights him. (p. 146)

Edmund Wilson, " 'Never Apologize, Never Explain': The Art of Evelyn Waugh," in his *Classics and Commercials: A Literary Chronicle of the Forties,* Farrar, Straus and Company, 1950, pp. 140-46.

EVELYN WAUGH AND JULIAN JEBB
(interview date 1962)

[In the following excerpt from a 1962 interview with Julian Jebb, Waugh discusses his novels *A Handful of Dust, Brideshead Revisited,* and *Men at Arms.*]

[Jebb]: *E. M. Forster has spoken of "flat characters and round characters"; if you recognize this distinction, would you agree that you created no "round" characters until* **A Handful of Dust?**

[Waugh]: All fictional characters are flat. A writer can give an illusion of depth by giving an apparently stereoscopic view of a character—seeing him from two vantage points; all a writer can do is give more or less information about a character, not information of a different order.

Then do you make no radical distinction between characters as differently conceived as Mr. Pendergast and Sebastian Flyte?

Yes, I do. There are the protagonists and there are characters who are furniture. One gives only one aspect of the furniture. Sebastian Flyte was a protagonist.

Would you say, then, that Charles Ryder was the character about whom you gave most information?

No, Guy Crouchback. [*A little restlessly*] But look, I think that your questions are dealing too much with the creation of character and not enough with the technique of writing. I regard writing not as investigation of character, but as an exercise in the use of language, and with this I am obsessed. I have no technical psychological interest. It is drama, speech, and events that interest me.

Does this mean that you continually refine and experiment?

Experiment? God forbid! Look at the results of experiment in the case of a writer like Joyce. He started off writing very well, then you can watch him going mad with vanity. He ends up a lunatic.

I gather from what you said earlier that you don't find the act of writing difficult.

I don't find it easy. You see, there are always words going round in my head; some people think in pictures, some in ideas. I think entirely in words. By the time I come to stick my pen in my inkpot these words have reached a stage of order which is fairly presentable.

Perhaps that explains why Gilbert Pinfold was haunted by voices—by disembodied words.

Yes, that's true—the word made manifest.

Can you say something about the direct influences on your style? Were any of the nineteenth-century writers an influence on you? Samuel Butler, for example?

They were the basis of my education, and as such of course I was affected by reading them. P. G. Wodehouse affected my style directly. Then there was a little book by E. M. Forster called *Pharos and Pharillon*— sketches of the history of Alexandria. I think that Hemingway made real discoveries about the use of language in his first novel, *The Sun Also Rises*. I admired the way he made drunk people talk.

What about Ronald Firbank?

I enjoyed him very much when I was young. I can't read him now.

Why?

I think there would be something wrong with an elderly man who could enjoy Firbank. (pp. 110-11)

It is evident that you reverence the authority of established institutions—the Catholic Church and the army. Would you agree that on one level both **Brideshead Revisited** *and the army trilogy were celebrations of this reverence?*

No, certainly not. I reverence the Catholic Church because it is true, not because it is established or an institution. *Men at Arms* was a kind of uncelebration, a history of Guy Crouchback's disillusion with the army. Guy has old-fashioned ideas of honor and illusions of chivalry; we see these being used up and destroyed by his encounters with the realities of army life.

Would you say that there was any direct moral to the army trilogy?

Yes, I imply that there is a moral purpose, a chance of salvation, in every human life. Do you know the old Protestant hymn which goes: "Once to every man and nation / Comes the moment to decide"? Guy is offered this chance by making himself responsible for the upbringing of Trimmer's child, to see that he is not brought up by his dissolute mother. He is essentially an unselfish character.

Can you say something about the conception of the trilogy. Did you carry out a plan which you had made at the start?

It changed a lot in the writing. Originally I had intended the second volume, *Officers and Gentlemen*, to be two volumes. Then I decided to lump them together and finish it off. There's a very bad transitional passage on board the troop ship. The third volume really arose from the fact that Ludovic needed explaining. As it turned out, each volume had a common form because there was an irrelevant ludicrous figure in each to make the running.

Even if, as you say, the whole conception of the trilogy was not clearly worked out before you started to write, were there not some things which you saw from the beginning?

Yes, both the sword in the Italian church and the sword of Stalingrad were, as you put it, there from the beginning.

Can you say something about the germination of **Brideshead Revisited?**

It is very much a child of its time. Had it not been written when it was, at a very bad time in the war when there was nothing to eat, it would have been a different book. The fact that it is rich in evocative description— in gluttonous writing—is a direct result of the privations and austerity of the times.

Have you found any professional criticism of your work illuminating or helpful? Edmund Wilson, for example?

Is he an American?

Yes.

I don't think what they have to say is of much interest, do you? (pp. 112-13)

Do you think it just to describe you as a reactionary?

An artist must be a reactionary. He has to stand out against the tenor of the age and not go flopping along; he must offer some little opposition. Even the great Victorian artists were all anti-Victorian, despite the pressures to conform.

But what about Dickens? Although he preached social reform he also sought a public image.

Oh, that's quite different. He liked adulation and he liked showing off. But he was still deeply antagonistic to Victorianism.

Is there any particular historical period, other than this one, in which you would like to have lived?

The seventeenth century. I think it was the time of the greatest drama and romance. I think I might have been happy in the thirteenth century, too.

Despite the great variety of the characters you have created in your novels, it is very noticeable that you have never given a sympathetic or even a full-scale portrait of a working-class character. Is there any reason for this?

I don't know them, and I'm not interested in them. No writer before the middle of the nineteenth century wrote about the working classes other than as grotesques or as pastoral decorations. Then when they were given the vote certain writers started to suck up to them.

What about Pistol . . . or much later, Moll Flanders and—

Ah, the criminal classes. That's rather different. They have always had a certain fascination.

May I ask you what you are writing at the moment?

An autobiography.

Will it be conventional in form?

Extremely.

Are there any books which you would like to have written and have found impossible?

I have done all I could. I have done my best. (pp. 113-14)

Evelyn Waugh and Julian Jebb, in an interview in *Writers at Work: The 'Paris Review' Interviews,* third series, edited by George Plimpton, The Viking Press, 1967, pp. 103-14.

STEPHEN JAY GREENBLATT
(essay date 1965)

[In the following excerpt, Greenblatt explores the central theme of Waugh's early novels: "the whole-sale demolition of the value structures of the past and the creation in their place of a vile and absurd habitation."]

Evelyn Waugh, like Charles Ryder [the narrator of *Brideshead Revisited*], is an architectural painter who sees, with anger, horror, and a kind of fascination, the destruction of old homes, the decay of institutions, the death of meaningful values. But Waugh refuses to create a merely sentimental picture of the achievements of the past at the moment of extinction; he insists, rather, upon recording in scrupulous detail the actual process of demolition. In Waugh's satiric vision, seeming trivial events—the breaking up of a manor house, the redecoration of an old room with chromium plating, a drunken brawl in an Oxford courtyard—are symbols of a massive, irreversible, and terrifying victory of barbarism and the powers of darkness over civilization and light. Waugh's early novels, especially *Decline and Fall, Vile Bodies, Black Mischief,* and *A Handful of Dust* are chronicles of that awful triumph. (p. 4)

The wholesale demolition of the value structures of the past and the creation in their place of a vile and absurd habitation is the central theme of Waugh's early novels. However, this theme does not always manifest itself in terms of a destroyed manor house. Man, in his fear and anxiety over the loss of values, unconsciously seeks dehumanization, but he may become a sort of animal as well as a machine. . . . [In Waugh's novels the] savage coexists perfectly with the streamlined man. . . . Against the technological skill of the ma-

chine and the voracity of the savage, culture, refinement, and tradition have little defense. The jungle is always threatening to overrun the city, the work crews are always tearing down a country estate, and hordes of howling aristocrats and gate-crashers are always sullying the sacred preserves of order and decency. (pp. 6-7)

Paul Pennyfeather, the young man so rudely thrust into the world [in *Decline and Fall*], is singularly unsuited for its trials, for Paul is a shadow-man, completely passive, completely innocent. One of Waugh's favorite satiric devices is suddenly to catapult a totally naïve individual into a grotesque and uncontrollable world, for, with this technique, he can expose both the corruption of society and the hopelessness of naïve goodness and simple-minded humanism. Since the essence of Waugh's criticism of Paul Pennyfeather's innocence is that it is too simple to cope with the complexities of the world, one cannot expect complex character delineation, and indeed Paul's flatness is very carefully and successfully pursued. "Paul Pennyfeather would never have made a hero," Waugh blandly observes in the middle of the novel, "and the only interest about him arises from the unusual series of events of which his shadow was witness." . . . (p. 8)

[The] laying of absurd religious doubt by equally absurd religious conviction, is the sort of hilarious and gruesome irony Waugh delights in. . . . [Gratuitous cruelty is] a quality of Waugh's work which many readers have found disturbing. The grotesque, the unreasonable, and the cruel are always asserting themselves in the satirist's world. . . . The amputation of Lord Tangent's gangrenous foot and his death, reported in widely separated and totally undramatic asides, are the source of great amusement in *Decline and Fall.* The deliberate accumulation of cruel details creates the atmosphere of [the novel's] world. . . . (p. 10)

[There is, however] a vital principle which has remained completely untouched by the change. This principle manifests itself in "the primitive promptings of humanity," epitomized by Captain Grimes. . . . Grimes is a powerful life-force existing outside the pale of conventional morality, and, audacious, elusive, outrageous, free, he represents the spirit of *Decline and Fall.* The growth of Waugh's pessimism is reflected in his treatment of Grimes spiritual heirs. Father Rothschild, S.J., in *Vile Bodies* and Krikor Youkoumian in *Black Mischief* are far less sympathetic, until, with Mrs. Beaver, in *A Handful of Dust,* the vital principle has become triumphant opportunism and moral blankness. (p. 11)

Decline and Fall was characterized by its wild audacity, but *Vile Bodies* is a comedy haunted by an inexplicable sadness. . . . One of the curious qualities of *Vile Bodies* is the reader's inability to discriminate between guilt and innocence. In *Decline and Fall* Paul

Pennyfeather was clearly an innocent suddenly thrown into a corrupt world, but the distinction is blurred in *Vile Bodies*. Adam sells his fiancée . . . and is an adulterer, but at the same time he exhibits an extraordinary naïveté and innocence, for he is conscious of breaking no moral norms.

Vile Bodies is an experimental novel. There is practically no plot and no continuity of narrative. The scenes shift wildly from the stormy English Channel to a party given for Mrs. Melrose Ape, the noted evangelist; from the intrigues of Father Rothschild, S.J., and the Prime Minister Walter Outrage to the small talk of two middle-class ladies on a train; from the drawing room of a huge mansion to the grease pit at the auto races. With this technique of disconnected and seemingly irrelevant scenes, Waugh is attempting to portray a world that is chaotic and out of joint. Readers have complained, with some justification, that the technique is all too successful, that the novel is disjointed and slights the affairs of Adam Fenwick-Symes and Nina Blount; but *Vile Bodies* is not a love story. Adam and Nina are significant only as representatives of the sickness of an entire generation, and their thwarted attempt to marry is meaningful and interesting only as a symbol of the frustrated search for values of all the Bright Young People. (pp. 12-14)

The fate of the old order with its decency, culture, and stability is represented by the fate of Anchorage House, the last survivor of the noble town houses of London. . . . A party at Anchorage House, "anchored" in custom and tradition, is juxtaposed with an orgy held by the Bright Young People in a dirigible, and the loss of the firm ground of the past is painfully obvious. (pp. 14-15)

Black Mischief is not a witty travelogue or, as some readers have felt, a vicious, racist attack on the African Negro. Rather, it treats precisely the themes of the earlier works—the shabbiness of Western culture, the decline and fall of institutions, the savagery underlying society.

Black Mischief chronicles the attempted modernization of a black nation by Seth, "Emperor of Azania, Chief of Chiefs of Sakuyu, Lord of Wanda and Tyrant of the Seas, Bachelor of the Arts of Oxford University." . . . As his title indicates, Seth's character is a paradoxical blend of savagery and civilization, the cannibal feast and the drawing room. He is unpredictable, cruel, naïve, insanely optimistic, lonely, terrified. . . . Seth's modernity . . . is not a meaningless label or a thin veneer of culture concealing the dominating violence of his black soul, for the meaning of *Black Mischief* is not the impossibility of civilizing the Negro. That the ideal of Progress in which Seth so fervently believes turns out to be a shabby concatenation of inane conventions is a condemnation far more of the cultivated Westerner than of the African. Seth serves

the artistic purpose of a Paul Pennyfeather: he is a naïve outsider who, in his contact with an alien society, is the means of satirizing that society. (pp. 16-17)

The abortive attempt to modernize Azania is not a statement of the African nation's inability to share in the glories of civilization but a sly and satiric examination of modernity itself. The struggle which Seth envisages as a mortal combat between barbarism and Progress is a miserable sham, for Western culture itself is no longer meaningful. Those Western ideas which might have given Seth's project real significance have been abandoned. . . . The inspiring motto "Through Sterility to Culture" is the banner not merely of the participants in the birth-control pageant but of the entire European civilization. Western culture is sterile, totally isolated from the realities of human life and incapable of making man's existence more pleasant.

Waugh uses Africa as a lens which renders grotesque and revealing images of English institutions and social classes. The Bright Young People and their silly parents, scheming politicians and unscrupulous soldiers of fortune, crude peers and nouveau riche socialites are all represented in the Azanian court. (pp. 18-19)

As *Decline and Fall* was signalized by its comic audacity and *Vile Bodies* by its comic sadness, *Black Mischief* is characterized by its comic cruelty. Recurring references, quite hilarious in their context, to starving children, executed men, and mutilated bodies constantly remind the reader that as Seth's blind infatuation with Western culture grows, the savagery underlying the calm surface of the superimposed civilization becomes increasingly agitated until it explodes. . . . (p. 20)

Waugh's delight in architectural images does not diminish in *Black Mischief*. The tough old Anglican Cathedral. . . , that impractical and "shocking ugly building," is marked for demolition by Seth and the Ministry of Modernization to make way for the Place Marie Stopes. But the Cathedral, despite its many years of disuse, has a remarkable solidity. . . . The attempt to replace the worship of God with the worship of Progress is even more obvious in the site of the Ministry of Modernization, which occupies what had formerly been the old Empress' oratory.

Seth's palace compound, like the concept of progress it embodies, is a haphazard conglomeration of strange structures, refuse, and, occasionally, the flyblown carcase of a donkey or camel. Modernity and barbarism are linked in the grand work-projects of leveling and draining which are pursued without any success by gangs of prisoners chained neck to neck. (pp. 20-1)

The sense of desolation and decay is best conveyed, however, by another structure—a wrecked automobile, lying in the middle of the Avenue of Progress, its tires devoured by white ants, its motor removed by pilfering, its rusting body reinforced by rags, tin, mud, and grass and used as a home by a native family. The rotting car appears throughout *Black Mischief* as an impediment which Seth tries in vain to remove, and, at the end of the novel, when the British and French hold Azania as a joint protectorate, it is still blocking traffic, unmoved by the entire force of the League of Nations.

Seth's deposition and murder seems to be the laying of the ghost of madness and instability. The protectorate, with its pukka sahibs, police stations, snobbery, European clubs, polished brass, and Gilbert and Sullivan, promises to be a grand step forward in the onward March of Progress, but, like the reign of Seth, it is a ridiculous sham. . . . The history of Azania, like the dance of the witch doctors and the life of the Bright Young People, is a savage, futile, comic circle.

In *A Handful of Dust* Waugh returns to England to tell a seemingly simple story of the failure of a marriage. . . . What might have been a rather dull "bedroom farce," however, is transformed by Waugh into a terrifying and bitter examination of humanism and modern society, which is the culmination of his art. (pp. 21-2)

By the accumulation of a great many seemingly irrelevant details, Waugh evokes a whole world, a philosophy, and a way of life as well as an architecture and a landscape. Hetton [Tony's country home] is a lovely, sentimental, idealized world of the past and of childhood, at once silly and charming, hopelessly naïve and endearing. Far in the past Hetton had been an abbey, but, as religion receded, it became "one of the notable houses of the country" . . . , and, finally, in the nineteenth century, at the height of the Gothic revival, this structure was totally demolished and the present house was built as a monument to Victorian aesthetics. If the true significance and beauty of Hetton had been destroyed in 1864 or earlier when it ceased to shelter pious monks, at least the glazed brick and encaustic tile of the present structure have a character and sentimental worth completely lacking in the cold, oversize boxes being constructed in London. In the twentieth century, however, the huge building, with battlements and towers, a huge clock with maddeningly loud chimes, lancet windows of armorial stained glass, pitch-pine minstrels' gallery, Gothic bedrooms, moldy tapestries, and a fireplace resembling a thirteenth-century tomb, is rather impractical, mildly uncomfortable, and completely unfashionable.

Like the house itself, Hetton's proprietor, Tony Last, is a simple-minded creature of the past who has never quite grown up. . . . (pp. 23-4)

The infidelity and the disintegration of the marriage are not analyzed in terms of the characters' deep, personal drives or romantic love or even blind lust. Brenda cherishes no illusions about her chosen lover. . . . There are no soul-searchings, no tortured moments of guilt, no remorseful thoughts of home and family. Brenda's choice of John Beaver is completely thoughtless and completely appropriate, for they inhabit a world and share a set of values about which Tony Last, content at Hetton, can know nothing.

The complete absence of any emotional life in the characters of Waugh's satires has irritated certain critics. . . . But one must not ask Evelyn Waugh or any satirist for a deep psychological examination of his characters, for this would be inimical to the satire itself. Satire, like comedy, is bound to be directed at the nonpersonal and mechanistic, for it sees man as an automaton, swept up in the mad conventions of society. . . . Satiric detachment can only be maintained when characters are soulless actors in a social drama, when the author treats his creations not as individuals with private lives but as symbols of societal forces. Any single character taken out of this context and forced to stand naked before the critic will naturally seem flat and unreal, but this individual emptiness is not a symptom of . . . Waugh's "brilliant faking." Rather it is the result of an attempt to portray characters who have lost their inner beings, their complexity, their moral and intellectual independence. The satirist's careful and quite conscious shrinking of his characters' personalities does not mean, however, that satire must deal with trivialities, for, seen in his proper ambient, Tony Last transcends a shallow characterization of a sap and becomes the complex symbol of a dying value system at once hopelessly naïve and deeply sympathetic, unable to cope with society and yet the last spark of human decency in a vile world.

Waugh's brilliance and the source of his bitter pessimism is his remarkable ability to sustain an ironic double vision, to laugh uproariously at his posing, lying, stupid, carnal, vicious, and unhappy characters at the same time that he is leading them on to damnation through those very qualities. The plot of *A Handful of Dust* is very much that of a typical bedroom farce—the stupid country squire with the beautiful wife is cuckolded by a young man from the city—and Waugh does not hesitate to employ all the stock devices of such comedy. The husband, now called "old boy" by his friends, is the only person in the world who does not know of his wife's affair. The clever wife treats her husband outrageously and then makes him feel guilty for being such a suspicious old fool. Assignations are kept right under the husband's nose, to the delight of all informed onlookers. Old maids and matronly ladies get immense vicarious pleasure from the affair, which they treat as a marvelous fairy story of an imprisoned princess rescued by a shining hero. But the unrestrained laughter with which the reader is conditioned to greet such situations is never wholly fulfilled, for the reader is aware of the double vision, of the bitterly ironic and unforgiving theme underlying the surface gaiety and flamboyance. (pp. 24-6)

Waugh's world is one in which the worst possible events implicit in any situation can and do happen, a world where the savagery underlying a seemingly innocent remark is always fully realized. . . . *A Handful of Dust* is a novel filled with improbable events and grotesque characters, but nothing ever happens for which the reader is not thoroughly prepared by Waugh. Even the fantastic ending in the jungles of Brazil is foreshadowed in the Vicar's Christmas sermon, and, though the reader may never consciously make the connection, the logic of the finale has been established. If we characterize Waugh's first three novels as comic audacity, comic sadness, and comic cruelty respectively, *A Handful of Dust* may be understood as comic bitterness, the comedy of rigidity and misunderstanding, the bitterness of betrayed ideals and fallen dreams. (p. 28)

In his reaction to [his] child's death, Tony reveals the terrible price he has paid for his simple-minded humanism, for he has lost the ability to assert his identity even in the moment of greatest suffering. In complete abnegation, Tony worries about everyone's feelings but his own. . . . Tony, ignorant [and] self-deceived, . . . is pitiable . . . , but he is certainly not a tragic or even a wholly sympathetic figure. By constantly denying his own feelings, he has gradually reduced himself to a cipher. The fantasy world into which he had retreated to avoid the mechanical, dehumanized society has, ironically, robbed him of his humanity. (pp. 28-9)

[The] total disintegration [of Tony's life] recalls the mad banquet of Trimalchio in the *Satyricon* and the "universal Darkness" in the *Dunciad;* it is the vision of hell which has tormented every great satirist and which underlies all of Waugh's early work. (p. 30)

Tony's distant ancestors might have sought a hardheaded, human solution to the problems of unidealized existence, but the family line has gone sour and Tony is heir to the rottenness, imbecility, and sham of his nineteenth-century forebears who tore down a noble house to build a pretentious and fraudulent structure in its place. Faced with the realities of human viciousness and supported by nothing but his useless humanism, Tony can only retreat into infantile fantasies. . . . The repeated juxtaposition of a scene in Brazil and a similar scene in London makes devastatingly clear Waugh's point that the foul, inhuman jungle in which Tony wanders feverishly is London transfigured. At the heart of darkness, the intricate and elaborate screen of lies with which modern man comforts himself is torn away, and the horror and savagery of society is laid bare. Here, in a world where the distinction between reality and nightmare has broken down, the inhabitants are avaricious, moronic, superstitious, insolent cannibals; reason can no longer control passion; nature is cruel and treacherous; exposed flesh is prey to the bloodsucking thirst of vampire bats and malarial mosquitoes.

Fever-ridden and raving, Tony at last grasps the whole of his life as a grotesque hallucination. In a remarkable and brilliant passage, all of the characters in the novel, ugly and distorted, dance around the sick man in a mad, fiendish circle. Rising from his hammock, Tony begins to plunge wildly through the jungle. . . . (p. 31)

[He reaches] a transfigured Hetton, but it is stripped of all the sentimental drivel. Instead of ceilings groined and painted in diapers of red and gold and supported by shafts of polished granite with carved capitals, there are palm thatch roofs and breast-high walls of mud and wattle; instead of a society of vicious sophisticates presided over by a cruel and unfaithful wife, there is a community of savages ruled by a cunning lunatic. . . . Tony Last, literally imprisoned now in a literal wasteland, has nothing left of his dream but a heap of broken images. The fulfillment of Tony's humanism, his selfless devotion, his abnegation is an endless self-sacrifice enforced by a madman in the midst of a jungle. There is no City. Mrs. Beaver has covered it with chromium plating and converted it into flats. (p. 32)

[Like Nina Blount in *Vile Bodies,* Waugh] regards what was once "a precious stone set in the silver sea" and is obsessed with an overwhelming sense of loss. His laughter at the masses of dirty, moronic, corrupt, and fornicating beings beneath him cannot conceal his bitter rage. For the glory, the beauty, the dignity, and the grace of England have been destroyed, and Waugh, like Nina, sees only straggling red suburb, nauseating filth, and appalling decay. (p. 33)

Stephen Greenblatt, "Evelyn Waugh," in his *Three Modern Satirists: Waugh, Orwell, and Huxley,* Yale University Press, 1965, pp. 1-34.

JAMES F. CARENS

(essay date 1966)

[In the following excerpt, Carens claims that *Brideshead Revisited* fails to "fulfill the promise of its brilliant opening" because Waugh subordinated satire to a sentimental evaluation of the 1920s and 1930s.]

Brideshead Revisited, less a satire than a romance,

marks the first accomplishment of the second stage of Evelyn Waugh's career. Though something of the old, hard brilliance remains, there is a new tone of lush nostalgia in this work, the first of Waugh's novels in which his Roman Catholicism is pervasive. Indeed, excepting *Helena*, it is Waugh's only novel to date in which a religious theme has been dominant; although Guy Crouchback is a Catholic and Roman Catholicism figures constantly in *Men at Arms, Officers and Gentlemen,* and *Unconditional Surrender,* the essential theme of these three volumes is the total collapse of civilized values which is the concomitant of war. In effect, in *Brideshead Revisited* Evelyn Waugh turned from the nihilistic rejection of his early satires to an affirmative commitment; to satisfy the other impulse of the artist-rebel, as Albert Camus has described him, Waugh affirmed a vision which he believed gave unity to life. *Brideshead Revisited* was his "attempt to trace the divine purpose in a pagan world."

Reviewing *Brideshead*, Edmund Wilson who had most highly praised the earlier satires, concluded that in this more normal world the novelist "no longer knows his way"; he found the novel to be "disastrous." By contrast, a reviewer for the *Catholic World* judged *Brideshead* "a work of art." (p. 98)

A novel which has provoked such diverse views deserves consideration. It may be an imperfect work; it can scarcely be a vapid one. Since the apologetic nature of the work is an issue, we should, before analyzing the effects of the subordination of satire to romance, determine whether Evelyn Waugh's vision has given life a form it does not have.

In honesty to the novel, we must note at once that if by "apology" we mean a systematic and reasoned defense of a theological system, then *Brideshead* is not an apology for anything. It is not a preachy book. To be sure, the Catholicism of the Flytes is sometimes discussed. But, if we turn to the longest discussion of a theological nature in the novel, one provoked by Bridey's insistence that his dying father must receive Extreme Unction, we find not didacticism but, instead, satire. The course of the conversation proves that most of the family are confused about the issue. (pp. 99-100)

Over this entire scene Waugh has cast his satirical irony; the scene exists for novelistic rather than dogmatic reasons, since it prepares for an important event in the action (Lord Marchmain's conversion), satirizes the varied and confused nature of religious faith among these people, and indicates a significant stage in the development of Ryder's character. Waugh must surely be absolved of apologetic didacticism.

Similarly, if by "apologetic novel" we mean one that crudely or even subtly simplifies experience and glosses over certain of life's complexities so as to flatter a fixed system of belief, then again *Brideshead* cannot

be classified as such a work. . . . Indeed, the author gives us no reason to believe that he is making a case for his Catholics qua Catholics, for the lives of the Marchmains and of Charles Ryder are not pretty ones, and their Catholicism is no easy consolation. Only Cordelia, the younger daughter, finds an honest contentment in faith. Her elder brother's religion is narrow adherence to system (which Waugh ridicules); and her mother's is resignation to suffering. The others—Lord Marchmain, Sebastian, Julia, and Ryder—know no rest.

Only if we choose to equate apologetics with the presentation of Catholics and Catholicism, through a "Catholic" vision of life, may we argue that the novel is an apology. (pp. 100-01)

If we grant that *Brideshead* is no mere work of apology, if we grant that its purpose is pre-eminently aesthetic rather than didactic, and if, as surely we must, we grant a writer the choice of a Catholic view of life, how do we account for the fact that *Brideshead* does not fulfill the promise of its brilliant satirical opening? I believe that Sean O'Faolain is illuminating on this point when he suggests that "the theme . . . is universally valid; the treatment is not." Perhaps an exploration of Waugh's "treatment," which depends upon the relation between his satire and his values, will pinpoint the reason for the failure.

Brideshead Revisited is elaborately architectonic, as are other later Waugh novels. Subtitled *The Sacred and Profane Memories of Captain Charles Ryder,* the novel begins in the profane modern world and ends in the sacristy of the chapel at Brideshead. In the prologue and the epilogue, which represent the present, we find the novel's most sustained satire. As the bitterly ironic prologue opens, Charles Ryder, a captain in the British Army during World War II, is shifted from one army camp to a second locale. Arriving at night, he does not discover until morning that his new headquarters are the baroque country seat of the Flytes. This discovery moves Charles in Book I to memories of his undergraduate days and of his warm friendship with Sebastian; and in Book II, wherein Sebastian, Lord Marchmain, and Julia are all drawn back to their faith by the urgency of God's will, to memories of his love affair with Lady Julia. Book I takes place in the middle twenties and Book II in the late thirties; the intervening years are sketched in so that continuity, in the chronological sense at least, is not impaired. In the epilogue, surrounded by the "sudden frost" of the modern age, Ryder enters the chapel at Brideshead, where he is revivified by the sight of a "small red light," the sacristy lamp, signifying to him the redemptive survival of faith in a pagan world. The prologue and the epilogue are something more than a mechanical use of the frame technique; they are not merely a device for setting off the memories, but a means of expressing Waugh's emotional attitude toward the past and his satirical view of the present.

Waugh's satirical-ironic projection of a sordid present against the rich traditions of the past is strikingly effective. The landscape of the prologue, bringing into relief the traditional values which Waugh associates with Brideshead, has symbolic force. (pp. 102-03)

For all these depressing satirical contrasts of the prologue and epilogue, however, and for all the pleasing parallels of several returns to faith, which we find in the body of the novel, the structure of *Brideshead* is not a success. A brief examination of the organization of the two major divisions may provide an explanation of this failure. Book I, composed of eight chapters, contains 201 pages; Book II, having five chapters, occupies 116 pages. So the first book of *Brideshead* is well over half again as long as the second book. . . . Is it possible that *Brideshead* has what Henry James called a "misplaced middle," that having extended himself in sentimentally recreating the glories of a vanished past and particularly of youth, Waugh then scanted what ought really to be the center of the novel, the religious conflict engendered by the love of Julia and Ryder? Perhaps Waugh himself answered this question when he revised *Brideshead* (1960), and divided the original two books into three, apparently in an attempt to emphasize Julia's role and to subordinate the Sebastian-Oxford part to the whole.

More disturbing even than the structural flaw of *Brideshead* is the novelist's tendency so to romanticize experience that his tone degenerates into sentimentality. Nowhere is this tendency more pronounced than in the Julia-Ryder love affair, a relationship which provokes one purple passage after another. (pp. 105-06)

The consequences of the subordination of satire to sentiment are particularly evident in the point of view—that of the first-person narrator, Charles Ryder—from which Waugh has chosen to present the novel. This fictional device, whatever its merits, has also its dangers. Not only has the first-person narrator contributed to the structural defect, but his presence has nearly banished from the novel the objective, ironic, satirical detachment which had hitherto distinguished Waugh's art. In *Brideshead*, Waugh is totally committed to his hero's, and his own, strengths—a love of the past, a sense of beauty, a moral awareness of the sterility of much contemporary life. But Waugh is also committed to Ryder's weaknesses—snobbery, smugness, narrowness of sympathy, and superficial idealizations. (pp. 106-07)

The terrible weaknesses of the Marchmain family are fully developed, but so many excuses are made for them (which is not done for the nonupper-class, minor characters, nearly all of whom are satirized), so extravagant are Ryder's claims for them, so romanticized is their class position, so much nostalgia is lavished on the life they were able to lead before the war, so many indications are given of their exclusive right to consideration, so much of Ryder's smugness and self-satisfaction permeates the whole, that the novel seems to accept Brideshead and everything it entails totally and at the expense of all other beings.

But the last words on *Brideshead* really belong to Evelyn Waugh. In the preface to the revised edition—itself a comment on the original—Waugh left no doubt at all as to his dissatisfaction with this work, which had damaged his reputation at the same time that it brought fame. He frankly admitted that its "rhetorical and ornamental language" had become "distasteful" to him. Indeed, in the very act of offering the revised novel to a new generation of readers, as "a souvenir of the Second War rather than of the twenties or of the thirties with which it ostensibly deals," he seemed to be unconvinced that he had greatly improved it. And, it must be said, the revised novel is not a success. Although Waugh did curb some of the excesses of the original, he did not obliterate its grosser qualities. (pp. 109-10)

James F. Carens, in his *The Satiric Art of Evelyn Waugh,* University of Washington Press, 1966, 195 p.

KATHARYN W. CRABBE

(essay date 1988)

[In the following excerpt, Crabbe explores the themes of spiritual sterility and the ineffectiveness of communication in *The Loved One*.]

In the three novels he wrote as the war wound down and the world settled into uneasy peace, Waugh came to grips with the theme at the center of his moral universe—the centrality of the Christian faith in the life of modern man. Although they are similar thematically, however, the novels are distinct from one another stylistically. *Brideshead Revisited* is a lush, romantic, melodramatic first-person narrative. *The Loved One* is a compact, terse satire on modern culture. And *Helena* is a historical novel based on the life of a saint. Despite the diversity of forms, these three novels represent the stage in Waugh's development in which he discovered a new voice and a new meaning in his vocation as a writer.

In *Brideshead Revisited* and *Helena,* Waugh moves away from the steadfastly external, Firbankian type of writer who wants to exploit the absurdities of surfaces, leaving the depths to his readers. Instead, he develops a greater sense of engagement with his characters, their feelings, and their motives. In *The Loved One* the style more nearly approximates his earlier allusive approach. But the books are linked by the centrality of the Christian experience.

As the styles differ, so do the rhetorical strategies employed. For example, in *Brideshead Revisited* and *Helena,* Waugh uses positive instruction by showing the Christian faith at work in the world and in the lives of his characters. In *The Loved One* he employs the satirist's strategy of negative instruction. The meaninglessness of the lives of the Southern Californians serves to illustrate the grotesquerie of a people who want the comforts of religious forms without having to be bothered to believe in them. (pp. 93-4)

When an invitation from MGM to adapt *Brideshead Revisited* for the screen resulted in a trip to Los Angeles for him and his wife, Waugh was as fascinated by the savagery of this new jungle as he had been by the Brazilian river valley of *A Handful of Dust.* He was particularly taken by the appalling commercializing of death and the accompanying euphemisms he discovered at Forest Lawn Cemetery. His gleeful disgust with the savage rites of the North Americans led to the masterful short novel *The Loved One.*

The Loved One was an instant success on both sides of the Atlantic. Cyril Connolly, introducing the novel to the readers of *Horizon,* wrote, "It is, in my opinion, one of the most perfect short novels of the last ten years and the most complete of Waugh's creations." The *New Republic,* agreed: "As a piece of writing it is nearly faultless; as satire it is an act of devastation, an angry, important, moral effort that does not fail." The *Times Literary Supplement* called it Waugh's "most mature and most awe-inspiring satire . . . a short piece of coruscating brilliance."

In a letter to Connolly preceding the publication of *The Loved One* in *Horizon,* Waugh wrote:

> The ideas I had in mind in writing were: 1st & quite predominantly overexcitement with the scene of Forest Lawn. 2nd the Anglo-American impasse—never the twain shall meet, 3rd there is no such thing as an American. They are all exiles, uprooted, transplanted & doomed to sterility. The ancestral gods they have abjured get them in the end. I tried to indicate this in Aimee's last hours. 4th the European raiders who come for the spoils & if they are lucky make for home with them. 5th Memento mori, old style, not specifically Californian.

The plot of *The Loved One* turns on the adventures of Dennis Barlow, an ex-airman and poet, who has left England for the milder climes of Hollywood and a term as a scriptwriter at the Megalopolitan film studios. Encouraged by Sir Francis Hinsley, an English man of letters who has been devoured by the studio system and rejected as a failure, Dennis leaves the movie business and, determined to return to poetry, takes a job at The Happier Hunting Ground, a pet cemetery, much to the distress of the English expatriates in the city.

When Sir Francis is fired by Megalopolitan Pictures and commits suicide, Dennis is commissioned by the English community to arrange a suitable funeral at Whispering Glades, where death is never mentioned and the dead are called "the loved ones." There, among debased traces of western culture, he finds Aimee Thanatogenos, and recognizes her as a true decadent, intrinsically different from the uniform, standard, hygienic, plastic, predictable American women around her.

Aimee, whose names mean "beloved bringer of death," is a cosmetician at Whispering Glades. She is in love with Mr. Joyboy, the chief embalmer. She is also "half in love with easeful death."

Poorly educated and impressionable, Aimee is much taken with the young English poet, Dennis, for his part, is intrigued by Whispering Glades and its decadent servant. Because she loves poetry but knows none of the classics, Dennis courts Aimee by sending her copies of some of the greatest lyrics in English, allowing her to assume that they are his own compositions.

When Aimee discovers that Dennis works at The Happier Hunting Ground (which desecrates the image of Whispering Glades by imitating it in some ways) and that he is not the author of the poems he has sent, she is furious and expresses her intention to break her engagement to Dennis and return to Mr. Joyboy. Dennis, however, refuses to release her from her vow of constancy, and the newspaper columnist who writes advice to the lovelorn loses patience and advises her to jump off a tall building. Instead, she commits suicide in Mr. Joyboy's embalming room.

Terrified that his career will be ruined by the scandal, Mr. Joyboy goes to Dennis for help. Dennis solves the problem by cremating his "Loved One" in the furnace of The Happier Hunting Ground. He departs for England, taking with him "a great, shapeless chunk of experience, the artist's load" and leaving for Mr. Joyboy a yearly postcard that reads, "Your little Aimee is wagging her tail in heaven tonight, thinking of you."

EVELYN WAUGH

Brideshead Revisited

Dust jacket of Waugh's 1945 novel, adapted in 1982 as an eleven-part series premiering on *Great Performances.*

Coming as it does after *Brideshead Revisited* and the explicit treatment in that novel of the tension between secular and religious values, *The Loved One* may at first appear to be among the most secular of Waugh's works. In fact, however, a religious enthusiasm informs the entire novel. It is the absence of a genuine religious impulse, the tendency to think of religion as a business rather than as an expression of the order of the world, that accounts for the spiritual sterility and, ultimately, the spiritual death characteristic of Waugh's fictional California.

Pagan religions abound in this version of the wasteland. Sir Francis searches Celtic mythology for the new incarnation of Juanita del Pablo; Aimee is a nautch girl (an Indian ceremonial dancer) and a vestal virgin at one time and a descendant of worshipers of ancient Greek gods at another. Of Orthodox Christianity, however, there is little. Of charity, the cutthroat world of Hollywood can offer even less. When Sir Francis can create a product that will sell, he is valuable. When he cannot, he is no longer considered to be human. The successful and the unsuccessful are of different orders of being. Of hope, there is less than charity, except in the basest sense. The city is a spiritual wasteland, from which not even death provides an escape. The recurrence of the suicide motif (Sir Francis and then Aimee) is ample illustration of the failure of the secular to provide hope. And in this culture, Christianity is represented only by nonsectarian clergymen who, like the modern churchmen of *Decline and Fall,* seem not to be required to believe anything. It is the absence of faith, of course, that accounts for the lack of hope and charity in this lost land between the mountains and the sea.

The theme of the exile is clearly central to *The Loved One.* For the English community, Hollywood is another scarcely civilized outpost of the empire, where preservation of the forms is essential. It is the attention to English conventions of dress and behavior that prevents them from "going native," that is, from picking up American habits and behaviors. They drink their whisky and soda, read *Horizon* (the magazine in which English readers first met this novel), and wear their old school ties. They even have a cricket club. But their treasured "Englishness" is strictly a matter of surfaces. In important matters, for example spiritual matters, they are as hopeless as the natives.

For Sir Francis Hinsley, the exile is threefold. He lives in a new and savage land, far from home; he has outlived the intellectual milieu in which he was comfortable, and he is a failure, which also sets him apart from the rest of the English community and, later, from all living souls. In fact, Sir Francis's plight illustrates the essential isolation of all the inhabitants of Hollywood.

As Waugh observed in his letter to Connolly, Americans too are all exiles. There is no such thing as a native Californian in the novel, although it is nonetheless possible to "go native." The sense of isolation Waugh wants to create is an integral part of the character of Aimee. Like so many Waugh characters, she is, for all practical purposes, an orphan. Her father, who "lost his money in religion," left her mother and the area. Aimee's mother then "went East to look for him . . . and died there." She explains her reason for moving to Whispering Glades by saying, "I was just glad to serve people that couldn't talk."

For Aimee, as later for Pinfold, the line dividing exile and withdrawal is faint. As a servant of death, she is set apart from the others, and she shares in the general American exile. But it is the secular nature of Whispering Glades that exacerbates her outsideness; if she were part of the sort of religious society for which Waugh longed, the sort that makes one part of "the communion of the saints," her sense of exile would be ameliorated. The essence of the California of *The Loved One,* however, is form over content, so she can have no sense of the traditions that could give meaning to her life or content to her empty forms. She is cut off from any system into which she can withdraw. For her there are no catacombs; when she rejects the world, nothing else remains.

Dennis, on the other hand, is only a physical exile. As an artist, he is in touch with the traditions of his literary world; similarly, as an explorer from the old world, he is aware of the traditions of civilization. His protection is his status as a traveler, a "frontiersman," a gatherer of material. Although he is in California, he never becomes a Californian; that is, he never adopts the attitudes and mentality that could mean he cannot go home. In this he differs from the English expatriates like Sir Francis Hinsley and Ambrose Abercrombie who have been so seduced by the spirit of Hollywood that they have "gone native" inwardly, though not, perhaps, outwardly.

Waugh also uses description of landscape, or at least certain epithets applied to landscape to enhance the sense of exile. When, in the opening paragraphs, we find "native huts," a "plot of weeds between the veranda and the dry water-hole," and a reference to Englishmen "exiled in the barbarous regions of the world," we anticipate a geographically isolated location for the tale. In fact, however, as the language suggests, the isolation is spiritual and psychological rather than physical. This conclusion is confirmed by the response Waugh attributes to Dennis when he finds himself in thrall to Whispering Glades: "In a zone of insecurity in the mind where none but the artist dare trespass, the tribes were mustering. Dennis, the frontier-man, could read the signs."

When the native huts are revealed to be bungalows and the dry waterhole a swimming pool, the reader recognizes that this is a world of spiritual and psychological isolation, rather than one of physical isolation. Other examples of Waugh's use of the physical to suggest the spiritual and psychological distances between people abound: Mr. Joyboy lives "a long way down Santa Monica Boulevard" in a housing development where many of the lots are vacant. The first poem Dennis reads in the novel is Tennyson's "Tithonus," which is about a beautiful young man who is cut off from humanity by being given eternal life but not eternal youth. The line Dennis takes as his mantra is "Here at the quiet limit of the world." Aimee lives in a "concrete cell which she called her apartment." And Dennis observes to Mr. Joyboy that "no one in Southern California . . . ever inquires what goes on beyond the mountains."

The generalization one can make about the Southern California of *The Loved One* is that everything is the opposite of what it seems. The civilization is so thoroughly debased that every value has been turned on its head. People talk, but "nothing they say is designed to be heard," as Sir Francis points out. Food is served, but it is not intended to be tasted—whether nutburgers ("It is not so much their nastiness as their total absence of taste that shocks one"), or Kaiser's Stoneless Peaches ("Dennis recalled that he had once tried to eat one of Mr. Kaiser's much-advertised products and had discovered a ball of damp, sweet cottonwool"). And Whispering Glades, through which humanity ought to pass on its way out of this world and in to the next, keeps its eye firmly fixed on the mundane and the transitory. Flowers, for example, are allowed in the cemetery because they are living and remind one of life, unless, of course, they are arranged in the shape of a cross. A cross is not allowed because it is not "natural" and because it reminds one of death.

The various zones of the park are committed to the pursuit of earthly delights: the Lover's Nest is characterized by "a very beautiful marble replica of Rodin's famous statue, the Kiss"; the Lake Isle, a favorite trysting place, is decorated with artificial bee hives (and artificial buzz); and the Lover's Nook features a Robert Burns poem that talks about love that lasts as long as life ("while the sands o life shall run") but omits the allusion to death with which the poem ends.

In the name of celebrating the "natural," the Dreamer and his staff perpetrate the most appalling assaults on the dead and on the survivors. In the interest of having the dead look "life-like," Mr. Joyboy arranges their features in one of several available "natural expressions." When he begins to court Aimee, he sends her corpse after corpse whose features have been manipulated into an absolutely inappropriate "Radiant Childhood smile." In addition, the unfortunate dead are painted for their appearance in the "Slumber Room" in colors that are obviously overdone but that theoretically will appear natural in the subdued light of the viewing room.

As Dennis discovers, however, the "natural" for which Whispering Glades strives is far more artificial and hence more disgusting than the bloody tooth and claw of authentic nature can be. When Aimee has finished with Sir Francis, Dennis looks at the body of his friend: "the face was entirely horrible; as ageless as a tortoise and as inhuman; a painted and smirking obscene travesty by comparison with which the devil-mask Dennis had found in the noose was a festive adornment."

Finally, the buildings of Whispering Glades illustrate the total confusion of the real and the artificial that reigns in this land. The University Church, for example, in which Sir Francis Hinsley's funeral service takes place, is identified in the recorded lecture not as the University Church but as the Church of St. Peter-without-the-walls. Not only does the Dreamer give the church one name and call it by another, but he willfully changes the meaning of the name by which it is called, so that "without-the-walls" (i.e., outside the walls) becomes *without walls* (i.e., having no walls). And that is not the end of the confusion. Having made the phrase mean "having no walls," he then gives the building walls "of glass and grade A steel." The chain of absurdity threatens to extend forever.

This confusion between what a thing is and what it is called is developed most delightfully in Waugh's treatment of the evolution of Juanita del Pablo. Originally called "Baby Aaronson," the woman is given a nose job and singing lessons and sent off to become another person. Sir Francis explains: "*I* named her. *I* made her an anti-Fascist refugee. *I* said she hated men because of her treatment by Franco's Moors."

The unnamed person originally called Baby Aaronson and then called Juanita del Pablo is about to be called by yet another name. Her case parallels the situation that occurred when Aimee's parents determined to change her name because of their disappointment with Aimee Semple McPherson's brand of religion: "Once you start changing a name, you see, there's no reason ever to stop. "Furthermore, Juanita's change of identity raises an interesting problem: If what a thing is changes when its name changes, can the thing be said to exist in any real way? The suggestion in Juanita's case is that she no longer exists; once the reality conferred upon her by language is removed, nothing remains.

The purpose of language in *The Loved One*, as the example of the various names of the University Church suggests, is not communication. In fact, a major theme is that the function of language is to avoid communication. Waugh is having so much fun developing devices by which his characters can fail to communicate, that

he can scarcely bear to represent a straightforward conversation. The theme of the debasing of language and its implications for human communication is first introduced in Hinsley's observation that the denizens of Hollywood "talk entirely for their own pleasure. Nothing they say is designed to be heard." Should anyone go so far as to listen, it is difficult to tell what he would make of what he would hear. Waugh presents characters whose language is intended to distort rather than to represent experience.

For example, when Ambrose Abercrombie appears at Hinsley's bungalow, he chides Sir Francis for dropping out of sight: "You shouldn't hide yourself away, Frank, you old hermit." Yet the narrator reveals that Sir Francis has been in exactly the same house for twenty years, and that Sir Ambrose, who has been ignoring his old friend, is clearly off the mark in this jovial accusation.

In just the same way, the operators of the two cemeteries in the novel deal in euphemisms to avoid the reality of their functions. Dennis is less apt at this game than the unnamed mortuary hostess of Whispering Glades, as his first professional conversation shows:

"Were you thinking of interment or incineration?"
"Pardon me?"
"Burned or buried?"

Such a clear translation of the jargon of the trade appears rarely if at all in the more-elevated society of Whispering Glades, although violent shifts in levels of diction are important in Waugh's arsenal of humorous techniques. Compare the performance of the mortuary hostess with Dennis's effort above: "Normal disposal is by inhumement, entombment, inurnment or immurement, but many people just lately prefer insarcophagusment." This is an absolutely brilliant sentence—look at the way the rhythm and sound of the words "inhumement, entombment, inurnment or immurement" ripple along musically to be set off by the jaw-breaking difficulty of "insarcophagusment." And look at the distance in intelligibility between the proffered "inhumement" and Dennis's translation, "We want my friend buried."

So safe are the employees of Whispering Glades with their language that obfuscates rather than clarifies, that any information that does not fit their rather arbitrary definition of reality is simply transformed into a satisfactory form. Thus it is that agnosticism becomes a religion when the mortuary hostess inquires about Hinsley's beliefs:

"Was your Loved One of any special religion?"
"An Agnostic."
"We have two non-sectarian churches in the Park and a number of non-sectarian pastors."

The exchange is similar when she asks about his race:

"I presume the Loved One was Caucasian?"

"No, why did you think that? He was purely English."

"English are purely Caucasian, Mr. Barlow. This is a restricted park."

In using language to make experience less rather than more immediate, Waugh's characters do precisely the opposite of what the artist does. The poems to which Dennis returns again and again and with which he courts Aimee are classics of English literature because they have spoken to generations of readers in ways that made experience more, not less, accessible. Response to these poems is the only thing Aimee and Dennis have in common. Yet Aimee's language is so limited (and because her language is limited, her thoughts are as well), that she can only describe some of the greatest love poems in the English language as "unethical." She simply has no other way to think about physical passion. "A rich glint of lunacy" is right.

In Mr. Slump, the Guru Brahmin, Aimee finds a counselor who fails to communicate as well. He will not, and sometimes cannot, read and understand, and his responses are a matter of empty forms embodied in someone else's style. Furthermore, Aimee's final telephone call to him illustrates the ubiquity of Hinsley's precept that "nothing they say is designed to be heard." When Slump puts the telephone receiver down on the bar and lets Aimee talk until she runs out of things to say, he is giving perfect form to Waugh's idea that everyone under the California sun is completely isolated.

The scene in which Mr. Slump puts the receiver down on the bar is, of course, a repetition of an earlier scene in which Dennis does the same thing to a hysterical caller to The Happier Hunting Ground. The repetition links Aimee's death with the death of the Sealyham terrier that introduces Dennis's profession, and the linkage is completed when Aimee finds her way to the same crematorium and burns as Dennis sits in the office and reads. The only difference is that this time he reads a novel instead of poetry.

On nearly every page there are additional examples of the use of language to disguise or deny experience. Mom's insults are "little jokes" and her rudeness is "treating you natural." People don't die, they "pass over." Embalmers and cosmeticians are "artists" and drunks are "Gurus." So the exile theme, begun by the geographical allusions that establish the inhabitants of Southern California as exiles, is picked up in the language theme that shows how they are cut off not only from the world but also from their own lives and experience. It's a sterile, deadly land.

In the hands of an artist, however, language makes experience more, not less, real. In this case, language makes the book and the experience one. Dennis leaves Los Angeles with "a great, shapeless chunk of experience, the artist's load; bearing it home to his ancient and comfortless shore." Of that experience he will make a work of art very like *The Loved One,* and language, carefully and precisely used, will be his medium. (pp. 106-17)

Katharyn W. Crabbe, in her *Evelyn Waugh,* Continuum, 1988, 188 p.

SOURCES FOR FURTHER STUDY

Carens, James F., ed. *Critical Essays on Evelyn Waugh.* Boston: G. K. Hall, 1987, 216 p.

 Collection of criticism on Waugh and his works.

Carpenter, Humphrey. *The Brideshead Generation: Evelyn Waugh and His Friends.* London: Weidenfeld and Nicolson, 1989, 523 p.

 Study of Waugh and his artistic contemporaries.

Davis, Robert M., ed. *A Bibliography of Evelyn Waugh.* Troy, N.Y.: Whitson, 1986, 500 p.

 Contains a listing of major criticism of Waugh's novels.

Gale, Iain. *Waugh's World.* London: Sidgwick and Jackson, 1990, 335 p.

 Critical discussion of Waugh's satirical art.

Littlewood, Ian. *The Writings of Evelyn Waugh.* Oxford: Blackwell, 1983, 241 p.

 Examination of Waugh's literary craftsmanship.

Sykes, Christopher. *Evelyn Waugh: A Biography.* Boston: Little, Brown, 1975, 462 p.

 Study of Waugh's life and writings.

John Webster

1580?-1634?

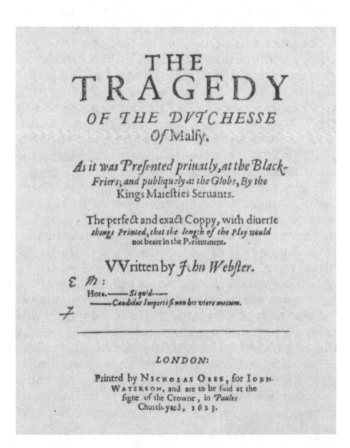

THE
TRAGEDY
OF THE DVTCHESSE
Of Malfy.

As it was Prefented privatly, at the Black-
Friers; and publiquely at the Globe, By the
Kings Maiefties Seruants.

The perfect and exact Coppy, with diuerfe
things Printed, that the length of the Play would
not beare in the Prefentment.

VVritten by John Webfter.

Hora.————Si quid——
————Candidus Imperti fi non his vtere mecum.

LONDON:

Printed by NICHOLAS OKES, for IOHN
WATERSON, and are to be fold at the
figne of the Crowne, in Paules
Church-yard, 1623.

English dramatist. No portrait of Webster is known to exist. The illustration above reproduces the title page of the first printing of *The Duchess of Malfi.*

INTRODUCTION

*C*ritics often rank Webster second only to William Shakespeare among Jacobean tragedians, and his two major works, *The White Devil* (1612) and *The Duchess of Malfi* (1614), are more frequently revived on stage than any plays of the period other than Shakespeare's. Webster's tragedies, while highly regarded as poetic drama by some commentators, have been attacked by others as being excessively grim and horrifying: his plays present a world in chaos, seemingly devoid of morality or any human feeling other than passionate sensuality. However, in performance Webster's highly charged verse often imbues his characters with a unique dignity and power.

Little is known about Webster's life. He was born around 1580 in London, the eldest son of a prosperous coachmaker and member of a prestigious guild, the Merchant Taylors' Company. Given his father's status, Webster was probably educated at the highly respected Merchant Taylors' School. Noting the prominence of legal concerns in Webster's dramas, scholars speculate that he may have also had some legal training. Records indicate that, like his father, Webster was a respected member of the community and upon the elder Webster's death assumed his membership in the Merchant Taylors' Company. Scholars usually date Webster's own death around 1634, the year that Thomas Heywood referred to him in the past tense in his *Hierarchie of the Blessed Angels.*

Webster's career in the theater began with collaborative work for Philip Henslowe, a man perhaps best known as the proprietor of London's Rose Theatre. Henslowe's *Diary,* which provides an invaluable view of English drama of the time, records in May 1602 that he paid Webster, Anthony Munday, Michael Drayton, Thomas Middleton, and Thomas Dekker for the now lost *Caesar's Fall, or The Two Shapes.* In October

1602, Henslowe paid Webster, Dekker, Heywood, Henry Chettle, and Wentworth Smith for a play called *Lady Jane.* This work no longer survives and is considered by scholars to be an early version of *Sir Thomas Wyat* (1602), a history play by various hands. Also in October, Webster and Heywood were advanced money for a play called *Christmas Comes But Once a Year.* Although he appears to have had no further connection with Henslowe, Webster continued to collaborate on dramatic works, and towards the end of 1604 he and Dekker wrote *Westward Ho,* a scandalous city comedy of middle-class London life. This satire spurred John Marston, George Chapman, and Ben Jonson to respond with the even more scandalous *Eastward Ho.* Dekker and Webster returned with *Northward Ho* in 1605, which many critics consider to be the better of the two Dekker-Webster comedies.

Webster's greatest accomplishments as a dramatist, *The White Devil* and *The Duchess of Malfi,* both reflect a sense of darkness encompassing human existence and a profound consciousness of evil and suffering in the world. Webster wrote during the Jacobean period, an age which began to question the preceding Elizabethan era's world-view, which was founded on the belief that all social, political, and even spiritual relations were defined in an unchanging hierarchy. The suggestion that chaos lies beyond such order—glimpsed in Elizabethan dramas such as Shakespeare's *King Lear*—became increasingly explicit in Jacobean drama. In particular, English society grew steadily more concerned over Machiavellian political theory derived from the writing of Niccolo Machiavelli, an Italian statesman who, in his 1513 work *The Prince,* described politics as an amoral and ruthless striving to acquire and maintain power. The spread of such ideas contributed to the deterioration of belief in traditional values and fostered a general fear of societal disarray, in which people would be left to drift aimlessly through an amoral world.

The influence of this pessimistic world-view is evident in Webster's first independent work, *The White Devil.* Based on Italian historical events, the tragedy relates a complex tale of love, murder, and revenge. It centers on the adulterous passion between the Duke of Brachiano and Vittoria Corombona, who together plot and direct the murders of their spouses. Brachiano's brothers-in-law instigate successful murder plots against the Duke and his mistress to avenge their sister's death. At the center of this corrupt world is Flamineo, Vittoria's brother and secretary to Brachiano. Completely amoral and unscrupulous, he willingly performs any service necessary to satisfy his employer's passions, including murder and procuring his sister for Brachiano. Flamineo also functions as a chorus figure in the play, cynically commenting on the action. Vittoria is a unique Jacobean heroine: although thoroughly corrupt, she is nonetheless sympathetic. Strong-willed and independent, she chooses to live in accordance with her own desires and eloquently acquits herself during the course of the play. As D. C. Gunby observed, "Vittoria is a white devil, but she is also a brilliant and resourceful woman, beautiful, courageous and highly intelligent, and we cannot help responding to her with some sympathy and warmth." While acknowledging the poignancy of Webster's portrayal of Vittoria, who struggles—albeit unsuccessfully—to control her own life, some critics maintain that the absence of any positive, truly moral figure makes the world presented in the play one of unrelieved bleakness.

Webster's next drama, *The Duchess of Malfi,* is widely acclaimed as his masterpiece. Algernon Charles Swinburne maintained that "this tragedy stands out among its compeers as one of the imperishable and ineradicable landmarks of literature," and many subsequent critics have echoed his opinion. Like *The White Devil, The Duchess of Malfi* is based on Italian history. The widowed Duchess, against the wishes of her brothers, secretly marries her servant Antonio. The brothers—the fanatical Ferdinand and the scheming Cardinal—plant a spy, Bosola, in their sister's household. A character similar to Flamineo in *The White Devil,* Bosola is even more complex, vacillating between delight and a sense of degradation in his sinister role. When Bosola uncovers the truth about the Duchess's marriage, her brothers ruthlessly harass her, drive her from her home, and eventually imprison her. In a famous scene she is tormented by madmen performing a stylized dance around her, and she is ultimately murdered. Critics have argued that Ferdinand's obsession with his sister is in part incestuous and that his descent into the madness of lycanthropy—the belief that he is a wolf—indicates that theatrically and spiritually he turns into a beast. Scholars agree that the Duchess herself is one of the greatest tragic heroines of the period. Her attitude of Christian resignation in the face of her brothers' vicious cruelty imbues her with a profound dignity, and the depiction of her murder is commonly judged one of the most moving scenes in all Jacobean drama.

Scholars note a significant decline in Webster's dramaturgy following the composition of *The Duchess of Malfi.* Most agree that his next play, the tragicomic *The Devil's Law-Case* (1619-22?), is the most difficult of Webster's works to assess. Its nearly incoherent plot involves a large number of shocking and absurd schemes, which preclude dramatic unity. It has only been performed once—in 1980—since Webster's time. Webster also contributed thirty-two character sketches to the sixth edition of Thomas Overbury's *New and Choice Characters, of Several Authors* (1615), and continued to collaborate on plays. *Appius and Virginia,* perhaps written with Heywood around

1634, is a Roman tragedy about the corrupt judge Appius who seeks to possess Virginia, the daughter of a famous general. Although admired by nineteenth-century critics for its classical simplicity of construction, this drama is not now highly regarded. Other plays attributed either wholly or partially to Webster include several lost works and *A Cure for a Cuckold* (1624-25?), which survives only in a carelessly printed edition.

From his own time to the present, some critics have praised the poetic brilliance of Webster's tragic vision, while others have scorned his plays as confused and excessively violent. To his peers, Webster was a slow, careful writer who "borrowed" lines from his fellow playwrights and used them to create powerful scenes. Although such borrowing was not uncommon during the Jacobean era, Webster utilized others' material to such a degree that he was satirized in Henry Fitzjeffrey's 1617 poem "Notes from Blackfriars." Calling the playwright "Crabbed Websterio," Fitzjeffrey jeered:

> Heer's not one word *cursively* I have *Writ*,
> But hee'l *Industriously* examine it.
> And it some 12. monthes hence (or there
>   *about*)
> Set in a shamefull sheete, my errors *out*.
> But what care I it will be so obscure,
> That none shall understand him (I am sure).

The great number of printings and revivals of Webster's plays during the seventeenth century attest to their continued popularity. In the eighteenth century, however, his reputation was eclipsed by a growing interest in Shakespeare. Increasingly, Webster was known only among bibliographers and scholars, who considered his plays scarcely more than period pieces, fine examples of the drama of the past but with little to offer contemporary audiences. In fact, his tragedies were performed only five times during the eighteenth century. In 1808 Charles Lamb renewed interest in Webster's plays with an enthusiastic appreciation of them in his *Specimens of English Dramatic Poets Who Lived about the Time of Shakespeare*. The noted critic William Hazlitt subsequently found that *The White Devil* and *The Duchess of Malfi* "come nearest to Shakespear of any thing we have upon record." The first collected edition of Webster's works appeared in 1830, and the first nineteenth-century production of *The Duchess of Malfi* took place twenty years later. Critics of the period were sharply divided on the merit of Webster's works, with one group agreeing with Hazlitt and celebrating the power of Webster's tragic vision, while the other attacked what they saw as absurd improbabilities, gross excesses, and episodic structures in the tragedies. William Archer, a member of the second group, argued that "Webster was not, in the special sense of the word, a great dramatist, but was a great poet who wrote haphazard dramatic or melodramatic romances for an eagerly receptive but semibarbarous public."

In the twentieth century, debate continues as to Webster's moral outlook; critics who see it as fundamentally negative outnumber those who assert that the plays reveal a profound belief that personal integrity can be maintained in a chaotic universe. Evaluations of Webster's artistry have revealed an intricate relationship between dramatic structure, characterization, and imagery in his plays. Examining Webster's use of language, Clifford Leech observed that "Webster excels in the sudden flash, in the intuitive but often unsustained perception. At times he startles us by what may be called the 'Shakespearian' use of the common word."

Both lauded and maligned for centuries, the dramatic art of John Webster remains difficult to assess. While undeniably horrifying, his depictions of people struggling to make sense of their lives in an apparently meaningless world possess a curiously modern sensibility. *The White Devil* and *The Duchess of Malfi* retain a vitality that continues to appeal to actors, audiences, and critics. That Webster's best works are still performed, read, and debated is perhaps the finest testament to his standing as a dramatist.

(For further information about Webster's life and works, see *Concise Dictionary of British Literary Biography*, Vol. 1; *Dictionary of Literary Biography*, Vol. 58: *Jacobean and Caroline Dramatists;* and *Drama Criticism*, Vol. 2.)

CRITICAL COMMENTARY

ROBERT ORNSTEIN

(essay date 1960)

[Ornstein is an American critic and scholar. In the following excerpt from his *The Moral Vision of Jacobean Tragedy,* he explores the morality of the major characters in *The Duchess of Malfi* and *The White Devil.*]

Although it is possible now to patronize the misguided William Archer, the specter of his criticism still hovers over Webster's plays. For however inadequate Archer's critical theories were, his attacks on the formlessness of Webster's tragedies contained an irreducible kernel of aesthetic truth. More sympathetic and judicious critics may not complain of Webster's "ramshackle looseness of structure," but they must agree with J. A. Symonds that

> we rise from the perusal of [Webster's] Italian trage-
> dies with a deep sense of the poet's power and per-
> sonality, an ineffaceable recollection of one or two
> resplendent scenes, and a clear conception of the
> leading characters. Meanwhile the outlines of the
> fable, the structure of the drama as a complete work
> of art, seem to elude our grasp. The persons, who
> have played their part upon the stage of our imagi-
> nation, stand apart from one another, like figures in
> a *tableau vivant.*

Of course the same observation has been made of other Elizabethan and Jacobean plays. As F. L. Lucas remarks, Shakespeare's contemporaries were not concerned with logical causality or consistency in plot. They worked in scenes and wrote for an audience that wanted "a succession of great moments"—"great situations ablaze with passion and poetry." Still we cannot say that the highest reach of Elizabethan dramatic art was a "succession of great moments" or that the architectural failings of Webster's tragedies are "conventional." All things considered, the plotting of *The White Devil* is not more episodic than the plotting of *King Lear;* it seems more episodic because *The White Devil* lacks the moral emphasis and focus which unifies the sprawling structure of Shakespeare's play. The relationship of form and vision is even more complex in *The Duchess of Malfi,* where Webster seems again and again to sacrifice dramatic structure to tragic idea. As we shall see, the Duchess must die "too soon," because her death is a touchstone as well as a turning point in the lives of the other characters.

Judging *The White Devil* to be Webster's finest achievement, Mr. Lucas explains the customary preference for *The Duchess of Malfi* as resulting from irrelevant moral considerations. Yet the "moral" preference for the *Duchess* may have its aesthetic basis. Undoubtedly *The White Devil* is a more brilliant and vigorous play; in contrast to the anticlimax of the *Duchess,* it rushes to a spectacular and supremely theatrical conclusion like a mighty river hurling itself over a fall. Still we ask from tragedy more than an unwearying display of human vitality or a thrilling clash of personalities. We expect a depth of vision that penetrates the surface violence or anarchy of life to illumine the underlying pattern and meaning of man's fate. Despite its errors and inconsistencies of plot, the *Duchess* is a greater play than *The White Devil* because it offers a more coherent and profound interpretation of experience. Its action has a rightness and inevitability that makes the unflagging energy of *The White Devil* seem, by comparison, artistically unpurposed.

Because Webster wrote the last Jacobean tragedies of heroic proportion, one is tempted to read a larger significance into the twilight and horror-ridden world of the *Duchess.* Here, one might say, is a vision of evil beyond which tragedy could not go and from which Webster and Jacobean drama as a whole retreated into tragicomedy. The truth, however, is that Webster's tragedies were not greatly admired or influential in their own time and were written after the vogue of tragicomedy had begun. Moreover the *Duchess* is not as flawed or illogical a play as critics have suggested; certainly it was not written by a playwright so unnerved by his nightmare intuition that he could not manage his plot. Take, for example, the notorious "absurdity" of Ferdinand's delayed revenge. In Act II, scene v, Ferdinand, maddened by news that his sister has had a "bastard" child, describes an insane plan of vengeance to the Cardinal. He promises to "sleep" until he knows his sister's lover and then leap to a furious revenge. Yet according to the conversation between Antonio and Delio in the next scene, the rash and hysterical Ferdinand "sleeps" several years and does not actually stir until his sister has had two more children. Then he confronts the Duchess *before* he knows who her lover is.

How ridiculous this all seems when we consider the plot in our studies. When the *Duchess* is staged, however, there is no impression of delay or absurd lag in action; immediately after Ferdinand announces his intended revenge (in II.v), he appears at the Duchess' court (in III.i) and begins the systematic torture of his sister. Thus time moves in the *Duchess,* as in some of Shakespeare's plays, at more than one rate; for Webster must, on the one hand, stress Ferdinand's irrational fury, and, on the other hand, emphasize the careless indifference of the Duchess and Antonio to their ignominious position. Webster achieves these cross-purposes by allowing the action to move forward uninterruptedly even as time is stretched out in the dialogue. The simultaneous rush and delay of Ferdinand's revenge is a remarkable bit of artistic legerdemain: the ear contradicts the eye but the mind is not insulted nor is integrity of character sacrificed. Thus what has been described as a symptom of weakening powers or carelessness might better be taken as evidence of Webster's grasp of his materials—of his bold willingness to be "inconsistent" in order to obtain the precise moral discriminations which are lacking in *The White Devil.*

To speak of the lack of moral discriminations in *The White Devil* is not to accuse Webster of the ethical confusion we find in *Bussy D'Ambois.* In Webster's tragedies there is no tampering with traditional values or

philosophical attempts to disguise vice as virtue. Murder is called murder; lechery is condemned as lechery. Webster's immoralists are warned that the wages of sin are death and when the moral reckoning falls due, they admit the justness of their fates. The dying Victoria announces:

O my greatest sinne lay in my blood.
Now my blood paies for't.

[V. vi. 240-41]

The dying Cardinal in the *Duchess* exclaims: "Oh Justice: / I suffer now, for what hath former bin." Similarly Ferdinand takes leave of life with a memorable moralistic epigram:

"Whether we fall by ambition, blood, or lust,
"Like Diamonds, we are cut with our owne dust.

[V. v. 91-92]

In both plays choric figures recite the final moral lesson. For Delio the bloody catastrophe of the *Duchess* proves that *"Integrity of life, is fames best friend."* Giovanni, scanning the holocaust of Lodovico's revenge, warns:

Let guilty men remember their blacke deedes,
Do leane on crutches, made of slender reedes.

[V. vi. 302-3]

Although these sententious aphorisms are not irrelevant to what preceded them, they seem a bit like annotations by another hand—Christian glosses, as it were, on a pagan epic of courage and consuming passion. They do not suddenly crystallize a moral judgment embodied in Webster's portrayal of character, nor do they capture the essential significance of the lives on which they comment so weightily. Just before she dies Vittoria exclaims:

O happy they that never saw the Court,
Nor ever knew great Man but by report.

[V. vi. 261-62]

This facile commonplace of the Elizabethan courtier would no doubt appear to advantage on Vittoria's tombstone, but like most tombstone verse it is dedicated to the living rather than the dead.

Unlike Shakespeare's Edmund, Webster's villains are not suddenly touched by moral feeling at their deaths. If they expire with sententious commonplaces on their lips it is because they are accustomed to playing the moral chorus at other men's tragedies. Francisco de Medicis, the master politician of *The White Devil,* is also the scourge of lechery and the defender of the sanctity of marriage. The Cardinal, Ferdinand, and Bosola are responsible for most of the ethical exhortation in the *Duchess.* In Shakespearean tragedy the hypocritical moralizing of Iago or Edmund emphasizes the deceptive surface of personality and the vulnerability of those who trust in human nature. The hypocritical moralizing in Webster's drama is more deeply subversive of ethical conviction because it is not intended to deceive. As there is no effective moral order to oppose them, Webster's immoralists can be frank in their duplicity. When Francisco and Brachiano or Vittoria and Monticelso confront one another with pious accusations and denials of guilt, their cards are on the table. They play with consummate skill the Machiavellian game of moral pretense that the world demands. They make the right gestures and speak the right words because while their society does not insist upon the reality of virtue, it insists upon the illusion. Not ready to take open vengeance on Vittoria, Francisco and Monticelso devise a trial in which they are both prosecutor and judge, and though it is nto a fair trial it has the form of legality, and the form suffices. Indeed, if Vittoria's defiance seems to nullify the charges hurled against her, it is not because she is more than innocent, but because innocence and guilt are not the primary issues in her arraignment.

There are few Jacobean tragedies in which innocence and guilt seem as irrelevant as in *The White Devil*. Despite the obliquity in *Bussy D'Ambois* there is a surge of moral passion that exceeds the demands of art and that overwhelms the conventionally contrived dramatic situations. In *The White Devil* the opposite seems true: the scorn and bitterness in its lines seem inadequate to the terror of the dramatic situations; even murders seem, to use Lodovico's phrase, no more than "flea-bytinges." Morally sensitive characters like Isabella and Marcello are weak and ineffectual, too easily silenced, murdered in dumb show or by a casual sword thrust. Those like Flamineo who effectively dissect the corruption of their world are part of that corruption and too perverse in their values to comprehend moral truths. Because their choric commentaries lack the moral accent of Vindice's speeches, we leave the play with the impression that the harshest reality of Flamineo's world is not the ruthless destruction of innocence but the ingratitude of princes and the venality of their underlings. In *King Lear* the perversion of the feudal bond of loyalty by servants like Oswald is a recurrent subject of moral commentary and a symbol of the annihilation of traditional moral and political values. But in *The White Devil* there are no faithful Kents to remind us that in the past servants did not always pander to their masters' wills. In the tragedies of Chapman, Jonson, and Tourneur, the decadence of the present scene is directly or indirectly contrasted with a previous norm of aristocratic values. But in *The White Devil* there is no suggestion that the courts of princes were once less corrupt or that the hunger for wealth, position, and sensual pleasure was not always the norm of human existence.

On the other hand, Webster does not deny the reality of virtue in *The White Devil*. He does not suggest that Isabella's devotion to Brachiano is sham or that Vittoria is the pattern of womanhood. Virtue does exist untainted and uncompromised, but it is impotent and ultimately meaningless—swept away into the same mist that enshrouds the fates of assassins and adulterers. The foolish, harmless Camillo exists only to be got rid of. The right-thinking Marcello is unable to break away from Brachiano's court and is killed as soon as he decides to oppose his brother. Isabella is effective only when she assumes Brachiano's guilt, and Cornelia, the moral chorus who prophesies retribution, lacks the strength to condemn Flamineo for the sin of Cain. Moreover while virtue is not an illusion, it breeds disastrous illusions about the meaning of marriage or the bonds of family love. It is defenseless against the violence that threatens it because it depends on words for protection against the passions of men who have contempt for words and who have no illusions about themselves or others.

One can understand why Webster's studies of sensual passion, his cynicism, and his taste for Italianate intrigue and horror have wed his tragedies to Tourneur's in the minds of critics and in the pages of anthologies. But we should not let a marriage of editorial convenience blind us to the profound differences between the two dramatists. In *The Revenger's Tragedy* and in *The Atheist's Tragedy*, reality is interpreted, as it were, through plot—through the concatenation of events that reveals an underlying moral purpose and order. In so far as he is capable, Tourneur delineates the nature of man's universe through the patterning of dramatic incidents. Webster, in contrast, seeks the meaning of existence in the supreme moments of agony and duress that lay bare the soul; the incidents of his plots serve primarily to bring his characters face to face with their mortal destinies. Like Tourneur he uses revenge as a motive to conclude his fable, but the routine appearances of the ghosts in *The White Devil* and the use of a minor figure (Lodovico) as the instrument of retribution suggest that his mind is engaged in other passions.

If Webster had a master in tragedy other than Shakespeare, it was Jonson, not Tourneur. Scornful of sham and pretense, Webster, like Jonson, seeks beneath moral illusion for the truths of experience that are scaled by hammer-blows of fate and refined in the incandescent crucible of violence. There is perhaps more of *Sejanus* in *The White Devil* than first meets the eye in Webster's imitations and in his prefatory lip service to Jonsonian classicism. In both tragedies virtue is unarmed; Machiavellian strength and cunning determine men's fates. In both tragedies the master politician achieves his Machiavellian goal and escapes the catastrophe that ensnares his henchmen. Like Jonson, Webster has no interest in philosophical issues or metaphysical ideals. There are occasional references in his plays to the philosophy of Padua and the atheism of antiquity, but they are incidental if not accidental. Like many of his comtemporaries he borrowed freely from Montaigne without being influenced by Montaigne's view of life. He was impressed by Montaigne's acute observations of detail and by the vividness of Florio's prose, not by the ironic attack on moral assumptions in the "Apologie." It is amusingly characteristic of Webster's "philosophical" attitudes that Hooker's metaphysical postulate, "Obedience of creatures to the Law of Nature is the stay of the whole world," is subordinated (in *The Devil's Law-Case*) to the cynical observation, several times repeated in Webster's drama, that nature is kind to bastard children.

I do not mean that Webster, like Fletcher, had no apparent intellectual interests and no genuine concern with ideas. His attitude towards philosophical questions suggests derision rather than neutrality. He presents in art the skeptical, pragmatic nominalism of the late Renaissance, the weariness with meaningless abstractions and endless debates over words. In his tragedies the Elizabethan faith in didacticism—in the moral power of words—is blown away by the first gust of violence. Humanistic learning is represented by a fool, a malcontent, and a madman. The stupid, impotent Camillo is the Aristotelian scholar of *The White Devil*. Bosola is spoken of as a "fantasticall" Paduan scholar,

> Like such, who studdy to know how many knots
> Was in *Hercules* club, of what colour *Achilles* beard was,
> Or whether *Hector* were not troubled with the toothach—
> He hath studdied himselfe halfe-bleare-ei'd, to know
> The true semitry of *Caesars* nose by a shooing-horne,
> And this he did
> To gaine the name of a speculative man.
> [III. iii. 50-57]

Even more fantastic is the Stoic "rationality" which enables an insane Ferdinand to place philosophy in perspective before he dies:

> . . . the paine's nothing: paine many times is taken away with the apprehension of greater, (as the tooth-ache with the sight of a Barbor, that comes to pull it out) there's Philosophy for you.
> [V. v. 78-80]

There is no reference in *The White Devil* to the rational cosmic order set forth by Renaissance philosophy. Perhaps men would like to believe that the institutions of religion, law, and family are expressions of universal decorum; but these institutions seem fragile defenses against the anarchy of human passion. Justice, as Lodovico points out, is indeed for the weak and the poor because the rich and the powerful escape judgment or bend the law to their purposes. Religion is the last refuge of whores and panders (witness Vittoria and Flamineo) and provides the sacrament and mask for Lodovico's vengeance. Before sexual and mercenary appetites and before the brutal coercions of wealth and place, traditional sanctities are meaningless: *brother, sister, husband, wife* become empty terms. Brachiano poisons his wife; Vittoria incites the murder of her husband. Flamineo panders his sister and kills his brother, and only Lodovico's intervention prevents Flamineo and Vittoria from destroying one another. When the customary ties of devotion slip, only the passions of lust and ambition bind men to each other and then only for self-gratification. Not surprisingly the great moments in *The White Devil* are those of individual assertion and defiance. At the trial Vittoria and Brachiano do not defy the world together nor do they defend their love against its judgment. Brachiano interrupts the proceedings momentarily to announce his personal defiance and then he leaves Vittoria to her fate. Vittoria will not admit that she loves Brachiano, although she is willing to confess that he attempted to seduce her. Brachiano is strangled while Vittoria waits in another room. She weeps at his death but when Flamineo threatens to kill her, all thought of her late husband vanishes as she concentrates on the immediate problem of survival. She dies in the company of Flamineo and Zanche, yet quite alone, like them unable to turn her thoughts outward from herself. "I doe not looke," says the dying Flamineo,

> Who went before, nor who shall follow mee;
> Noe, at my selfe I will begin and end.
> "While we looke up to heaven wee confound
> "Knowledge with knowledge. ô I am in a mist.
> [V. vi. 256-60]

One might say that the power of *The White Devil* is its dramatization of the *isolated* criminal will shattering moral restrictions. The opening scene introduces Lodovico, enraged by banishment, spurning the consolations of philosophy offered by Antonelli and Gasparo. They recall his riotous past and remind him of the crimes for which he has been justly sentenced. "Worse then these," Gasparo adds,

> You have acted certaine Murders here in Rome,
> Bloody and full of horror. Lod. 'Las they were flea-bytinges:
> Why tooke they not my head then? Gas. O my Lord
> The law doth somtimes mediate, thinkes it good
> Not ever to steepe violent sinnes in blood,
> This gentle pennance may both end your crimes,
> And in the example better these bad times.
> Lod. So—but I wonder then some great men scape
> This banishment, ther's *Paulo Giordano Orsini*,
> *The Duke of Brachiano*, now lives in Rome,
> And by close panderisme seekes to prostitute
> The honor of *Vittoria Corombona*,
> *Vittoria*, she that might have got my pardon
> For one kisse to the Duke. Anto. Have a full man within you,
> Wee see that Trees beare no such pleasant fruite
> There where they grew first, as where they are new

set.
Perfumes the more they are chaf'd the more they render
Their pleasing sents, and so affliction
Expresseth vertue, fully, whether trew,
Or ells adulterate. Lod. Leave your painted comforts,
Ile make Italian cut-works in their guts
If ever I returne.

[I. i. 31-52]

We cannot take Antonelli and Gasparo too seriously here, because they are Lodovico's henchmen, who are working to repeal his banishment and who later aid him in his bloody vengeance. Nevertheless they have a professed code of ethics. They try to placate their master with a pious phrase, a snatch of Boethius, an edifying simile from natural history. But he rips apart their cant with the logic of an experienced murderer who knows that dukes need not fear "gentle pennance." The other heroic figures in *The White Devil* are cut to Lodovico's measure. They listen impatiently to the voice of morality as one listens to the foolish babbling of a child; and when they answer, they silence it. When Isabella warns that Brachiano's adultery will anger heaven, he replies, "Let not thy Love / Make thee an unbeleever." When Cornelia protests against Flamineo's pandering, he answers, "Pray what meanes have you / To keepe me from the gallies, or the gallowes?" After Monticelso has expounded Vittoria's whoredom to the court at great length, she contemptuously replies:

These are but faigned shadowes of my evels.
Terrify babes, my Lord, with painted devils,
I am past such needlesse palsy—for your names,
Of Whoore and Murdresse they proceed from you,
As if a man should spit against the wind,
The filth returne's in's face.

[III. ii. 150-55]

Webster's villains are not gulled by words or placated by painted comforts. They know how to use pious phrases as well as how to accept them. Flamineo is a master of sanctimony; Brachiano announces at the trial that his interest in Vittoria is prompted by "charity. . . . To orphans and to widdows." It is also for charity's sake that Brachiano's murderers bar Vittoria from the room in which he is being strangled. And as Vittoria, Flamineo, and Zanche trade religious sentiments, we wonder if moral precept has any meaning at all.

In his "glorious villains" Webster creates heroic characters who escape the restrictive bonds and illusions of morality only to be swept to disaster by the irresistible tide of their desires. They are not slaves of passion in any ordinary sense, confused and blinded by uncontrollable appetites. In a strangely perverse way they know themselves better than do Cornelia and Isabella, but that self-knowledge is a tyranny as well as an emancipation. Because they see their goals so clearly they recognize no alternatives, and although they create the circumstances of their lives they never transcend them. Their existences are momentary, their reactions conditioned reflexes. Not burdened by sorrows or fears (except for temporary flashes of remorse) they respond vigorously to the stimuli of the immediate moment. But because they are completely absorbed in the tumultuous present they never see beyond it; they never lift their eyes to the larger horizons visible to Chapman's heroes. Those like Flamineo who understand the essential nature of their society are peculiarly unable to solve the problems of their own destinies. When at the threshold of death they gain a brief respite from the perpetual crisis of their lives, they glimpse only the pattern of their own fate, which becomes for them the eternal design of man's existence. They are all, like Brachiano, quite lost from the beginning despite the fierce energy that impels them onward. "Fate's a Spaniel," Flamineo decides at last,

Wee cannot beat it from us: what remaines now?
Let all that doe ill, take this precedent:
Man may his Fate foresee, but not prevent. [V. vi. 178-81]

In a sense the blind determinism of the emancipated will is the great unrecognized theme of *The White Devil*—the key to the otherwise incomprehensible futility of Flamineo's dramatic career. That there was joy in Flamineo's making we cannot doubt, for he is the most engaging and brilliant of Webster's villains: high-spirited, voluble, quick with scorn or admiration, so frank in his enjoyment of evil that we are perhaps a little ashamed of our uninspired virtue. Flamineo has, as Mr. Lucas observes, "more humour, a quicker wit, a deeper cynicism even than Iago." He has also more pride and candor. Unwilling to fawn or pretend virtue, he soothes his lacerated ego by parading his contempt for Brachiano. And yet his motives are contemptible beside the satanic hunger for destruction engendered by Iago's niggardly spite. Even the crude Machiavels of the Elizabethan stage had more grandiose ambitions for wealth, power, or bloodshed than Flamineo, who commits the basest crimes against his own blood to gain a paltry advancement. To secure himself against the gallows, he spends his life running the vile errands of men inferior to himself in mind and spirit. And even as his goal is incredibly mean his cynical "realism" is hopelessly naïve. Knowing from experience that those who serve "great men" will be discarded when they have served their purpose, he schemes feverishly to ensure the reward that will bring him Brachiano's security against the law. But his politic mind has no better answer to Marcello's challenge than a cowardly sword-thrust that binds him forever to Brachiano's "mercy." Only at his death does he realize that he engaged in a ludicrous attempt to avoid a self-imposed fatality, and then he sees the absurdity of all endeavor, not of his politic ambitions.

If Flamineo is a baffling character, it is not because Webster did not understand him, but because he suspected, even in *The White Devil,* that the Machiavellianism which seemed to release man's heroic potentialities was ultimately a negation rather than a fulfillment of life. Fearful of confounding knowledge with knowledge, Flamineo shuts his eyes to everything except the "necessity" which his own mind creates. Despite his intellect he pursues a base irrational goal, and like Webster's later Machiavels ends in a little point, a kind of nothing, playing desperate games with Vittoria before he is slaughtered, apparently without resistance, by his enemies.

I do not wish to deny the superb poetry and theatricality of Flamineo's death scene. For sheer dramatic impact it has no equal in Jacobean tragedy; yet it stuns the emotions without involving or moving them very deeply. It calls forth an instinctive gasp of pity and admiration for untamed, undaunted animals surrendering to the hunter's knife. We are not "engaged" in the fates of Flamineo and Vittoria because we do not share their

emotional responses, which are not only different in degree from normal feeling but different in kind as well. In the *Duchess* the strength and dignity of Webster's heroine are set off by contrast to Cariola and Bosola. In *The White Devil* there is no heightening contrast between Vittoria and her assassins or even between Vittoria and Zanche. It may be that instinctive fearlessness, however thrilling on the stage, does not lend itself to fine distinctions; one lioness at bay is like the next. In the very act of asserting their individuality Flamineo, Vittoria, Zanche, and Lodovico lose it: they imitate one another. Because Webster's dichotomies of strength and weakness are artistically and morally primitive, tragic heroine and whorish servant, noble aristocratic lady and silly cuckold exit alike into the mist.

Although Francisco's revenge imposes a conventional pattern on the final scenes of *The White Devil,* Lodovico's entrance is more of an interruption than a consummation of the drama of Vittoria's and Flamineo's lives. He wields a knife cunningly but his skill might have been spared, for Flamineo and Vittoria were already at each other's throats. In *Sejanus* the fall of the underling and the escape of the master politician are the final revelation of the amorality of politics. In *The White Devil* it does not seem to matter very much that Lodovico is apprehended while Francisco escapes, because both are no more than instruments of plot. It is only an accident of lust that makes Lodovico Brachiano's nemesis and only a chance insult that turns him against Flamineo. One misses in the denouement of *The White Devil* that sense of ironic inevitability which orders the sweepstake carnage of *The Revenger's Tragedy.* When the grand design of Webster's play should be finally elucidated, we see nothing more than a series of exterminations that temporarily rid Giovanni's court of vermin. (pp. 128-40)

Robert Ornstein, "John Webster," in his *The Moral Vision of Jacobean Tragedy,* The University of Wisconsin Press, 1960, pp. 128-50.

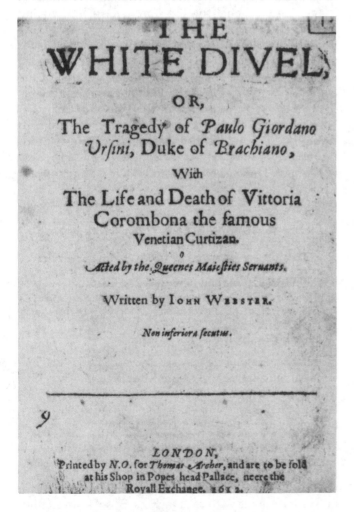

THE
WHITE DIVEL,
OR,
The Tragedy of *Paulo Giordano Urſini*, Duke of *Brachiano*,
With
The Life and Death of Vittoria Corombona the famous Venetian Curtizan.
o
Acted by the Queenes Maiesties Seruants.

Written by IOHN WEBSTER.

Non inferiora ſecutus.

9

LONDON,
Printed by N.O. for *Thomas Archer*, and are to be ſold at his Shop in Popes head Pallace, neere the Royall Exchange. 1612.

Title page of the first edition of *The White Devil.*

CLIFFORD LEECH
(essay date 1963)

[Leech was an English scholar who published numerous works on various dramatists, including John Ford, John Webster, William Shakespeare, Eugene O'Neill, and Christopher Marlowe. In the following excerpt, he traces aspects of Webster's construction of *The Duchess of Malfi,* focusing on structure, subplot, language, and inconsistencies.]

[In] contemplating our memories of *The Duchess of*

Malfi we are likely, I think, to have it promptly in our minds that this was a play written with deliberation. Webster, indeed, prided himself on his lack of fluency. In the address to the reader prefixed to the 1612 Quarto of *The White Devil* he retorted with some arrogance to those who had commented on his slowness:

> To those who report I was a long time in finishing this tragedy, I confess I do not write with a goose-quill, winged with two feathers, and if they will needs make it my fault, I must answer them with that of Euripides to Alcestides, a tragic writer: Alcestides objecting that Euripides had only in three days composed three verses, whereas himself had written three hundred: 'Thou tell'st truth,' (quoth he) 'but here's the difference,—thine shall only be read for three days, whereas mine shall continue three ages.'

Five years later a comic picture of Webster in the act of composition is given by Henry Fitzjeffrey of Lincoln's Inn:

> Was ever man so mangl'd with a *Poem?*
> See how he draws his mouth awry of late,
> How he scrubs: wrings his wrists: scratches his Pate.
> A *Midwife!* helpe! By his *Braines coitus,*
> *Some Centaure* strange; some huge *Bucephalus,*
> *Or Pallas* (sure) ingendred in his *Braine—*
> Strike, *Vulcan,* with thy hammer once againe.

Indeed, both in his use of words and in the management of the larger units of composition we can fairly easily come to realise how slow-moving and deliberate he was.

First, there is the matter of act-division. It is as well to remember that from the later years of the sixteenth century a division into five acts (with music in intervals between the acts) was normal for performances in private playhouses, that our knowledge is quite uncertain as to theatrical practice in the public playhouses around 1600, and that from about 1610 the five-act division (with intervals) seems to have generally established itself. A dramatist with a classical bent might plan his work in five units even if there were no act-break in performance, but he would obviously be encouraged to think in terms of five-unit composition if act-breaks were normal. And there is no doubt that Webster, both here and in *The White Devil,* divided his plot-material with care. This indeed will doubtless have been made apparent in the running commentary of the previous chapter. Act I, at Malfi, gives us the initial opposition between the Duchess and her brothers, Bosola's entry into employment both with the Duchess and with Ferdinand, and the wooing-scene. Enough time elapses between the first two acts for the Duchess to be brought to bed. Act II, first at Malfi, then at Rome, presents the circumstances of the child's birth and the sending of the news to the brothers. A longer time-lapse separates Act II from Act III, which begins with

Antonio's welcome of Delio to Malfi after he has been 'a stranger long'. In Act III, at Malfi, Rome, Loretto, we have Ferdinand's confrontation of the Duchess, Antonio's flight, the revealing of his identity to the brothers, the banishment from Ancona, the second flight of Antonio, the arrest of the Duchess. Act IV, wholly at Malfi, shows us the long torment of the Duchess and its effect on Ferdinand and Bosola. Act V, wholly at Milan, shows us the deaths of all the other major characters. Each act thus represents a separate phase in the story. Moreover, the emphasised time-lapses in Acts I-III make us see the action as slowly developing until the scene in the Duchess's bed-chamber in Act III: from that point there is no indication of a longer time-lapse than is required for a journey from Malfi to Milan. That scene thus becomes a ridge beyond which the descent is unchecked. (pp. 28-30)

The sub-plot of *The Duchess of Malfi* is slight and could easily have been omitted, as far as story-demands or the length of the play were concerned. Julia may make a silent entry in the first act. Apart from that we see her only three times: in II.iv visiting the Cardinal in Rome as his mistress, and receiving brusque addresses from Delio; in V.i obtaining an estate of Antonio's, begged on her behalf by the Cardinal; in V.ii wooing Bosola and dying as a consequence. The only justification for the introduction of her story is that Webster wanted to point a contrast, and suggest a resemblance, between her mode of sexual behaviour and that of the Duchess. In the previous chapter we have seen the resemblances as they emerge in the course of the play: both women are direct in their approach, both devise scenes with a hidden witness, both come to death through what they do. Yet the contrast is equally obvious. In II.iv Delio's approach to Julia is contemptuous:

> With good speed—I would wish you
> (At such time as you are non-resident
> With your husband) my mistress.
> (II.iv.72-4)

And before that she had to endure the Cardinal's observations on the malleability of women and on the thanks she owes him for his favour. In V.i Delio refers to her as 'such a creature' and the good Marquis of Pescara echoes him with 'strumpet'. For Bosola in V.ii she is 'this creature', while the Cardinal sees her as his 'lingering consumption' whom he would 'by any means . . . be quit of ': he is glad to poison her for secrecy's sake, as he thinks, using this as an excuse to free himself. Thus the general attitudes to Julia and the Duchess are polar opposites. We have seen how Antonio refers to his mistress's saintliness before her approach to him in Act I, and whatever his limitations he never slackens in his homage. Cariola, until her nerve fails, wants to die with the Duchess. Bosola admires her fortitude, and his reverent care for her dead body contrasts with the Cardinal's blunt directions for the removal of Julia's. The two women are opposed also in their respective constancy and promiscuousness, in the family relationship established at Malfi and the casualness of the Cardinal's protection. The introduction of Julia, and the fragments of action that involve her, thus help to govern the direction and degree of our sympathy in the play. At the same time we are made to see how fully involved in the world's deceit the Duchess and Antonio become through their secret marriage, and how erroneous it would be to regard the Duchess as outside their normal sphere of sexual passion. The Duchess approaches Antonio with immeasurably more dignity and grace than Julia has in approaching Bosola, but there is enough resemblance between the two actions of the play to keep strongly in our minds the force of the passion that urges the Duchess to speak.

Thus the sub-plot has been deliberately inserted, but we may feel some laboriousness in this. It is hardly convincing when the Cardinal reveals to Julia that he was a sharer in the Duchess's murder: he could easily enough have disposed of her without having that pretext to make her kiss the poisoned book. And Julia's wooing-scene with Bosola does not fit his general presentation very well. It introduces a diversion, for a few moments, in an act where he should be consistently a haunted and disappointed man. On the other hand, we need not object to the lightness of Julia's wooing-scene: it gives us the sense of improvisation and heedlessness that is right for the general atmosphere of Act V. Nevertheless, we are likely to conclude that Webster's deliberateness in the sub-plot has not brought him to the point of full assimilation. The planning obtrudes, and may suggest a here unfortunate influence from Fletcher, who loved the kind of comic parallelism that Julia's story offers.

Patterning is obvious too, but not obtrusive, in the disposal of the main characters in the play. On the one side the brothers, the Cardinal with his cold and casual lust, the Duke with his rage and maniacal laughter. In a sense they are church and state, but the Cardinal's investiture as a soldier blurs the distinction, putting a military dress on the church and emphasising the civil power that churchmen wield. The brothers differ in warmth of blood: they are equally ruthless, but one pays a greater price for villainy. If Webster has left obscure Ferdinand's motive in resenting his sister's remarriage (though perhaps it is not very obscure), he has been totally silent on the Cardinal's motive. We can simply assume that he did not want a male governor in Malfi who might exercise power independent of his. Against these two brothers we have the solitary figure of the Duchess. And we can see that the tragedy required Antonio to be kept in a subordinate position in the play. If the second husband of the Duchess had been a man of high natural authority, the battle would

have been more even. The tragic effect depends on the Duchess's physical weakness and her lack of a strong partner. Only in such lonely circumstances could she be reduced to the bereft condition which provides a human being with an occasion for ultimate authority. But in the brothers' campaign it is Ferdinand who acts: the Cardinal assents to everything, from distant Rome. Ferdinand, we are made to feel, has Rome behind him.

But Webster seems to have aimed at a special balance of relationship between Ferdinand and his sister. In the beginning of the play it is she who is active. Defying her brothers' injunction and her own given word, she marries Antonio. Despite the consequent scandal they live together, and Antonio publicly grows in favour and wealth. Even Ferdinand's presence in Malfi in Act III does not interrupt their course. When she knows he has discovered their marriage, she busily plans a future with Antonio and her children, remote from Malfi. But she makes the mistake of trusting Bosola. At that point the initiative passes to the long-sleeping Ferdinand. It is he who acts, through his agent Bosola, in the later scenes of Act III and the whole of Act IV. She becomes an emblem of suffering, a tragic figure with power only for the assertion of her own being ('I am Duchess of Malfi still') and for the dignified acceptance of death, with affection and passion still her own, almost with good humour, too, despite exhaustion. Then, when she is dead, it is Ferdinand's turn to know a suffering from which there is no escape in action. He can refuse Bosola his payment, he can mawl a stupid physician, he can stab his brother and Bosola, not knowing who they are. But these are minor and pointless things: from the moment when he looks on his sister's body and asks for her face to be covered, he is pursued by his own furies. He cannot respond to torment as the Duchess did. His caperings grow grotesque, as indeed the conduct of madness must be. Thus we have here a likeness and a contrast that we can compare with the relationship between Julia and the Duchess. Ferdinand and his sister alternate in action and suffering. Her action may be questionable, his is beyond question evil. Her suffering is noble, his is pitiful.

Between Ferdinand and the Duchess there stands Bosola, her servant as well as his, giving more loyalty to the one who pays best. Yet, linked in this way to both characters, he is also the link between them. It is he who sends messages from Malfi to Rome. It is he who arrests the Duchess and brings her to Ferdinand, now lord of her palace. It is he who represents Ferdinand in every moment of her torment except for the brief occasion when brother and sister meet in the dark. It is he who makes Ferdinand fix his eye on the dead body of his sister. In the last act it is he who unintentionally murders Antonio (with perhaps a deep irony, for, though he wished to save this man, he might resent his interloping position) and deliberately kills Ferdinand (the man whose death-pander he has been). The subtle handling of this figure of Bosola gives a special intricacy to the presentation of all four main characters in the play. (pp. 32-5)

But it is perhaps most of all in his language that Webster shows his habit of slow-moving deliberation. In 1907 Charles Crawford began the systematic study of Webster's borrowings from his reading, and his editors—M. W. Sampson, Mr. F. L. Lucas, Dr. J. R. Brown—have along with other commentators added to the record of these. Recently Professor R. W. Dent has devoted a large volume to the subject, using as a title-page motto Seneca's *'Quicquid bene dictum ab ullo, meum est'*. But the opening sentences of his introduction suggest he may have used the motto with some irony, for he expresses the view that his findings may bring aid and comfort to those who 'think Webster grossly overrated'. He adds: 'For the effectiveness of these tragedies [*The White Devil* and *The Duchess*], Webster was heavily indebted to his sources.' And so indeed he was, though debt is what a venturer must begin with. It appears established that this dramatist kept a note-book in which he entered any passage from his reading that won his special attention, perhaps with the notion that he might find it useful in his own writing. And certainly he goes beyond what we know of his contemporaries in taking over the very words of others. Shakespeare, it is true, might simply manipulate the words of North's Plutarch when he was using that book as a source for his Roman plays, but we are not here concerned with source-writings in the common sense of the term. In the tabulated list of Webster's imitations given as an appendix to Dr. Brown's edition of *The White Devil*, the two writers most frequently noted as borrowed from are Sir William Alexander and Montaigne: the plot of the tragedy came, of course, from elsewhere. In *The Duchess of Malfi* Webster has acquired a new main field for harvesting, Sidney's *Arcadia* (from which there is only one dubious echo in the earlier tragedy): though Sidney may have provided a hint for some incidents in the plot, it is as a word-quarry that the *Arcadia* proved most useful. But it will be as well to indicate the extent of the borrowing in a single passage. Here is the Duchess near the heart of her torment:

> I account this world a tedious theatre,
> For I do play a part in't 'gainst my will.

Bos. Come, be of comfort, I will save your life.

Duch. Indeed I have not leisure to tend so small a business.

Bos. Now, by my life, I pity you.

Duch. Thou art a fool then, To waste thy pity on a

thing so wretch'd As cannot pity itself:—I am full of daggers: Puff: let me blow these vipers from me.

Enter Servant.

What are you?

Serv. One that wishes you long life.

Duch. I would thou wert hang'd for the horrible curse Thou hast given me.

(IV.i.84-94)

And here are two relevant passages from the *Arcadia:*

> But she (as if he had spoken of a small matter, when he mencioned her life, to which she had not leisure to attend) desired him if he loved her, to shew it, in finding some way to save *Antiphilus.* For her, she found the world but a wearisom stage unto her, where she played a part against her will: and therefore besought him, not to cast his love in so unfruitfull a place, as could not love it selfe.
>
> (II.xxix)

> and he with an angry voice asked, Who was there? A poore Gentlewoman (answered the partie) that wish long life unto you. And I soone death to you (said he) for the horrible curse you have given me.
>
> (III.xxiii)

This at first sight is indeed startling, and on occasion Professor Dent can go further and show that Webster has, in taking over a passage, blunted and obscured it. Nevertheless, the formidable size of Professor Dent's volume may give a faulty impression. In some places he is noting the source of Webster's information, not his words, or he is offering (as he frankly indicates) commentary rather than evidence of borrowing, or he is drawing attention to a use of proverbial maxims that Webster shared with many of his contemporaries. This does not mean that we can disregard the evidence which has been accumulated over the past fifty years and has now reached an impressive bulk. As far as we can tell (for not all Elizabethan and Jacobean writers have been made subject to this kind of enquiry) Webster was unique among early seventeenth-century dramatists for the extent of his habit of adapting passages, presumably already in his note-book, for key-moments in his plays.

Nevertheless, it should be emphasised that this is a method of composition, not a cause for reproach. If a twentieth-century writer did it, he would be found out and rebuked, for we have developed a stronger sense of literary property than obtained in Webster's time. For him it was a way of working, just as the use of an existing plot was so common among the dramatists that we are puzzled and frustrated if we find a play with no recognisable source. What matters is what comes into being through the method: in this case *The Duchess of Malfi*. We could not ourselves fabricate this tragedy by putting together all the passages that Professor Dent and others have accumulated. It need not perhaps be further underlined that it is the result that matters. Nevertheless, we may note that in 1647 Robert Baron published a pastoral playlet called *Gripus and Hegio; or, The Passionate Lovers:* it contained a number of speeches taken almost verbatim from **The Duchess of Malfi,** but it is a poor play, deservedly forgotten. Baron could not make the use of Webster that Webster made of Sidney and Montaigne and others. Our interest in all this must primarily be in the further indication it gives of Webster's approach to his craft in his two major tragedies. He must often have spent some time searching his note-book for an appropriate phrase or idea. We have seen him blocking out his action and disposing his characters into an effective pattern: there he gave every sign of the slowness for which he was reproached, which he arrogantly admitted. The finding of words must have come with equal slowness to him. (pp. 40-3)

Deliberation is no safeguard against occasional inconsistency. Webster's total planning seems admirable, whatever the defects of the sub-plot and despite the grave difficulty of managing a fifth act without the Duchess. There seem, however, to be a few contradictions of detail in the writing. We have already noted the oddity of Delio's plan to establish Antonio's son 'In's mother's right', and this apparent forgetfulness of the Duchess's son by her first husband may appear too in Ferdinand's attempted exploration of his motives for opposing her remarriage. It is strange, also, that the horoscope of Antonio's eldest son should foretell 'a violent death' when this child is the family's one survivor at the end of the play. Other difficulties in the text may be more apparent than real. Antonio, characterising Bosola in the first scene, refers to his railing at vice only because he lacks the means to practise it, and then slightly later says:

> 'Tis great pity
> He should be thus neglected—I have heard
> He's very valiant: this foul melancholy
> Will poison all his goodness.
>
> (I.i.74-7)

But the paradox can be accepted: Bosola does rail because he is 'neglected', not because of a sincere hatred of evil; but, were he not neglected, he would be free of melancholy and might cultivate goodness and valour, not necessarily the vice he rails at. It is a complicated, and perhaps confusing, way of introducing a character who is to prove venal and a malcontent, with a love for manipulation and disguise, and a troubled inclination towards goodness. The interval of presumably two years (unless the second and third children were twins) between Acts II and III may be questioned as an improbably long time for Ferdinand to smother the rage that came on him at the birth of the first child. But, if Ferdinand's condition is what I think Webster makes

us recognise, we can see him as inhibited from all action at the end of Act II, as indeed he still is in Act III after his confrontation of his sister: only the flight to Ancona renders him truly awake and, with Bosola's help, free to kill. When in the scene with Ferdinand the Duchess declares 'My reputation is safe', she appears to contradict her previous admission that there is a scandalous report touching her honour. But her words in the bed-chamber scene may indicate only that her reputation can be made safe if the marriage becomes public. A vacillation in the attitude to the Duchess may appear to be induced in the play, as an offender, though a gracious one, in the earlier scenes, and as a great woman suffering in Act IV; but in this compound of attitudes I now think we have Webster's chief claim to major status in this play: the Duchess, along with Antonio, is involved in a corrupt society, is involved too in strong but normal sexual passion to a point where she acts without regard for her duty as a sovereign prince. But that brings her close to us, and we are never allowed in Act IV to forget that the one who suffers is of our kin.

The indubitable inconsistencies, then, are few and are certainly not noticeable in performance. We are likely to feel, both in the theatre and in later remembering and reading, that the play is a complex whole. The deliberateness of method and manner seems to have given us, almost throughout, writing at the level of a masterpiece. (pp. 48-9)

Clifford Leech, in his *Webster: The Duchess of Malfi,* Edward Arnold (Publishers) Ltd., 1963, 64 p.

IAN SCOTT-KILVERT
(essay date 1964)

[In the excerpt below, Scott-Kilvert provides background on Jacobean theatre and investigates Webster's use of language.]

The years of Webster's apprenticeship in the theatre coincided with a period of intense disillusion in the national life. The decline of landed wealth and the pursuit of money-making in its place, the downfall of the brilliant but erratic Earl of Essex, the death of Queen Elizabeth and the conspicuous absence of the magic of sovereignty in her successor, the disgrace and imprisonment of Raleigh, the series of conspiracies aimed at the throne and culminating in the Gunpowder Plot—these and many parallel events combined to produce a sense of the breakdown of established standards and beliefs, which was quickly reflected in the drama. Shakespeare and Chapman, survivors of the Elizabethan age, approach tragedy by way of the historical play, and we find them at all times keenly aware of the sanctity of kingship and the hierarchy of degree. Their protagonists are men and women of unquestioned authority, whose public life is brought to ruin by private weaknesses. The tragedy of Othello or of Antony lies not only in the hero's betrayal—real or imaginary—by his beloved, but in the collapse of his soldiership.

But with the younger generation of tragedians, Marston, Webster, Tourneur and Middleton, we feel at once the absence of this ideal order. The new playwrights are oppressed by an apparently irreconcilable conflict between the world of earthly experience and the world of the spirit:

> While we look up to heaven, we confound
> Knowledge with knowledge. O, I am in a mist!
> (*The White Devil*, V. vi.)

Humanity, they are compelled to recognize, is no better for its new-found knowledge, but rather more inhuman: indeed what marks out the tragedy of this period is the ingenuity and elaboration of the dramatists' conception of evil. The bond of nature is cracked, and the pragmatic creed of Machiavelli, with its assumption of the natural weakness and wickedness of men and its insistence upon *la verità effetuale della cosa,* has become the reality which forces itself upon the playwright's vision. Beyond this code of self-seeking, all is uncertainty, 'a mist' as Webster repeatedly describes it; the divine powers are indifferent, and the heavens high, far off and unsearchable.

By comparison with the Elizabethan approach, the new dramatic poetry is noticeably more sceptical, more sophisticated, more aware of inner contradictions. The very title, *The White Devil,* contains a multiplicity of meanings, which begin with the Elizabethan proverb, 'the white devil is worse than the black', and may be applied not only to Vittoria but to the hero, Bracchiano, and indeed to the society in which the play is set. The new poetry is also more condemnatory and satirical in tone, and in the case of Webster (though not of Marston and Tourneur, who caricature and distort to intensify the effect of their satire) it is more naturalistic in its handling of character and event. For Webster's audience *The White Devil* was a strikingly topical play: the actions which it depicts had taken place barely a quarter of a century before. And just as a subject which is remote in legend or history seems to emphasize the influence of fate upon the outcome, so the choice of a modern theme creates the opposite illusion: the more contemporary the characters, the greater their apparent freedom of action. Certainly by comparison with plays such as *Romeo and Juliet* or *Othello* the plots of Webster's tragedies owe very little to chance: at first glance his characters strike us as wilful to the last degree in courting their own downfall. Of course freedom and compulsion are necessarily the coordinates upon which all tragedy is plotted, and every dramatist of consequence

discovers as it were a new equation for the act of choice, which is the starting point for a tragic situation. But a closer study suggests that Webster differs from most of his contemporaries in choosing *not* to make this issue explicit. When Bosola exclaims

> We are merely the stars' tennis-balls, struck and bandied
> Which way please them.
> (*The Duchess of Malfi,* V. iv.)

we know that this is only a half-truth in the design of the tragedy, and in fact the continuous uncertainty as to whether fate or chance rules the world contributes powerfully to the horror which the play inspires in us.

What perhaps most astonishes the modern reader of Jacobean tragedy is the divergence between the avowed purpose of the dramatists and the actual effect of the drama, between the impression intended and the impression conveyed. Both the poets and the critics of the time were convinced that Renaissance tragedy was more improving than Greek. They found fault with the latter for its rebellious protest against divine providence, and praised the former for demonstrating, in Puttenham's phrase, 'the just punishment of God in revenge of a vicious and evil life'. Similarly the playwrights constantly defend the theatre against the attacks of the Puritans by stressing its reformative value. Yet in *The White Devil* it is perfectly clear that Webster's sympathies are strongly drawn towards the guilty lovers, while in *The Duchess of Malfi* the sufferings inflicted upon the heroine are out of all proportion to her offence. It was this discrepancy between the precept and the practice of Elizabethan and Jacobean tragedy which prompted Rymer's indignant question—which he might as well have applied to Webster's tragedies as to Othello—'If this be our end, what boots it to be virtuous?' Webster's sympathy, not only in his tragedies but also in his later plays, consistently goes out to what he calls "integrity of life', that is the determination to remain what you are, in the face of suffering, misfortune and death: admiration for this quality can scarcely be reconciled with conventional notions of good and evil. (pp. 13-16)

In the history of literature tragedy is generally regarded as an exceptionally stable form, which has somehow preserved throughout the centuries a recognizable resemblance to its Greek originals. But these resemblances are deceptive. Greek drama is essentially religious. Its primary concern is not to study the personality of the hero but to interpret the regulation of human affairs by the actions of the gods: its plots are drawn from a single body of mythology and its form is rigidly stylized. Elizabethan tragedy is essentially secular. The playwrights abandoned the scriptural or allegorical material which had supplied the themes of the mediaeval drama, and turned their attention instead to English and Roman histories or French and

Italian *novelle.* The mysteries which they explore are those

Of fate and chance and change in human life

and this change of direction has never been reversed. But if Elizabethan and modern tragedies share some resemblances in theme, they share very few in form or technique, and the reader will be led far astray if he expects the Elizabethan play to conform to the dramatic methods of Ibsen and his successors, themselves strongly influenced by the techniques of modern fiction.

The vital point to be grasped here—admirably developed by Miss M. C. Bradbrook in her *Themes and Conventions of Elizabethan Tragedy*—is that the Elizabethan playwright did not set out to devise a plot in the form of a logical or internally consistent narrative. The essential ingredients for his drama were striking episodes and memorable language. He could not, as his modern counterpart can, conceal his lack of poetic inspiration by attention to the details of construction. Yeats's criticism of the speech of modern dramatic characters is well-known: 'When they are deeply moved, they look silently into the fire-place', and he was referring to the modern playwright's assumption that he can achieve his emotional effect through the placing and sequence of events, rather than through the eloquence of his dialogue. To Elizabethan audiences eloquence was the very breath of drama, and they were interested above all in how a character spoke and acted in a moment of crisis rather than in how he arrived there. In this respect an Elizabethan tragedy is more like the score of an opera than the text of a novel. The elements of place and time, for example, are treated as freely and flexibly as possible. If they lend themselves to dramatic exploitation, well and good, but they possess few rights of their own. Much of the sustained effect of terror and anguish which is built up in the fourth act of *The Duchess of Malfi* depends on the vagueness of the location and the suspension of time during the Duchess's imprisonment.

This is not to say that the Elizabethans were incapable of the kind of mechanical dexterity which was so much admired by William Archer. Shakespeare achieves something of this cog-wheel effect in *Othello,* and Jonson in *Volpone,* while Beaumont and Fletcher were still more adroit in the plotting of their material. But most of the playwrights of the period were not thinking along the lines of the Aristotelian whole, and it would be difficult to select any play as a typical specimen of Elizabethan or Jacobean dramatic structure. Since the source material varied so widely, and since plays tended to be conceived as a series of striking situations, every major playwright developed a dramatic form of his own, the mould of which was shaped by the nature of his poetic gifts. At its best the imaginative

pressure and concentration of the language of Jacobean tragedy sweeps away the problems of dramatic illusion. The poets created a speech which could be simple or ceremonious by turns, and was at once direct in its elementary sense and rich in secondary meanings. In *The White Devil,* for example, Webster achieves one of the most powerful openings in the whole range of Jacobean drama. Lodovico's cry of 'Banish'd!' not only sums up the initial situation of the play and casts the shadow of the revenger over all that follows, but in a deeper sense it suggests the self-excommunication of this blood-crazed figure from the normal instincts of humanity. It is at once followed by other metaphors central to the play's meaning, such as those which hint at Vittoria's career—'Fortune's a right whore' and 'an idle meteor soon lost i'th'air'. The best of Webster's poetry, like that of Shakespeare, Tourneur, Middleton and other contemporaries, possesses this power of prefiguring the action by means of dramatic images which leap from the particular to the general and reveal the moral universe that surrounds the characters and the setting.

Webster is one of those rare dramatists who in his first independent play achieves at a single bound the height of his poetic powers. *The White Devil* offers us Jacobean verse in its full maturity: here Webster is exploiting after his own fashion many of the developments in style and versification which Shakespeare had first introduced into his great tragedies. The end-stopped blank verse pentameter has been completely remoulded, passages of any length are frequently enjambed, the rhythms of colloquial speech are counterpointed against the regular beat of the line, and the style and tone of the dialogue clearly reflects the demand for a greater naturalism in expression and performance. Like the best of his rivals in the theatre Webster quickly establishes a dramatic idiom which is unmistakably his own. Unlike his fellow satirists Marston and Tourneur, he shows himself sympathetic even to the most villainous of his characters and keenly aware of their individual and unpredictable qualities, and he shares something of Shakespeare's gift for coining images which can project a character within a single line of verse or prose.

The tone of his verse is at once witty, sardonic, allusive, full of nervous energy. His handling of metre is often as harsh and irregular as Donne's, and his frequent habit of introducing resolved feet reflects the complexity or deliberate outlandishness of his figures of speech:

Mark her, I prithee: she simpers like the suds
A collier hath been washed in . . .
                                        (*The White Devil,* V. iii.)

Elsewhere when he aims at a sententious effect he produces a *rallentando* through a sequence of heavily stressed monosyllables:

This busy trade of life appears most vain
Since rest breeds rest, where all seek pain by pain.
                                  (*The White Devil,* V. vi.)

If he lacks the architectonic sense, he comes nearest of all his contemporaries to Shakespeare in his power to produce striking yet subtle variations of mood, of strength and of pace within a scene. Some of his finest effects are achieved by sudden transformations of this kind, as in *The White Devil* with the entry of the boy Giovanni in mourning for his mother immediately after the passion and tumult of the court scene, or with Ferdinand's eavesdropping upon the careless jesting of the lovers in *The Duchess of Malfi.* While other dramatists employ song to great effect, Webster in *The White Devil* and *The Duchess of Malfi* without invoking the aid of music uses the dramatic lyric in a completely original fashion to introduce a different emotional dimension. Of Cornelia's lines:

Call for the Robin-red-breast and the wren,
Since o'er shady groves they hover,
And with leaves and flowers do cover
The friendless bodies of unburied men
                                  (*The White Devil,* V. iv.)

Lamb wrote:

I never saw anything like this dirge, except the ditty which reminds Ferdinand of his drowned father in *The Tempest.* As that is of the water, watery, so this is of the earth, earthy. Both have that intenseness of feeling which seems to resolve itself into the elements which it contemplates.

These achievements represent the peaks of Webster's art. On the other hand he is curiously unenterprising in his use of the soliloquy, which he normally employs merely to give notice of his characters' intentions rather than to explore their inmost qualities. And besides his didactic habit of rounding off an episode with a conventional platitude, he is apt to interrupt the progress of a scene with a tedious moral fable, thus destroying much of the tension which he has carefully built up.

This habit brings us to his borrowings from other authors. Commentators long ago remarked that his plays, especially *The White Devil* and *The Duchess of Malfi* contain many sentiments, images and even whole sentences which have been lifted from contemporary writers, in particular from Montaigne, Sidney, and the Scottish dramatist William Alexander. Of course originality was less highly prized in Webster's age than it is today. Quotation or adaptation from classical or foreign authors was regarded as a mark of erudition, and plagiarism was even to some extent encouraged by the educational system of the time which required students to keep a commonplace book. Mr. F. L. Lucas defends Webster's imitation and contends that he almost always transmuted what he borrowed into something

different and better. This is often the case, but it does not tell us the whole story. Certainly Webster excels in the final stroke, the expansion of some hitherto unremarked detail, which transforms a second hand perception into a touch of perfect aptness. He was not the kind of author who plagiarized in order to save himself mental effort. On the contrary he was an exceptionally laborious artist who took great pains to weave his borrowings into the texture and atmosphere of his plays. Nevertheless his borrowings so far exceeded the normal that they came to affect his methods of composition. If we analyse the sequence of his dialogue in passages where the borrowing can be traced, it becomes clear that his imagination was often prompted by what he had read rather than by his own invention. This habit of working from a commonplace book explains the peculiarly conceit-laden and disjointed style which Webster employs in a passage such as the following, which contains images drawn from three different authors:

Thou shalt lie in a bed stuffed with turtle-feathers, swoon in perfum'd linen like the fellow was smothered in roses. So perfect shall be thy happiness that as men at sea think land and trees and ships go that way they go, so both heaven and earth shall seem to go thy voyage. Shalt meet him, 'tis fixed with nails of diamonds to inevitable necessity.
                                  (*The White Devil,* I. ii.)

In the same way his longer verse passages do not flow as Shakespeare's do with an opulent succession of metaphors, in which each image springs naturally from its predecessor. Instead they often consist of a series of undeveloped metaphors or similes so loosely strung together that any one might be removed without damage to the rest, and the borrowing habit also seems to be responsible for the abrupt transitions of thought and feeling which so often occur in his verse. But when all this has been said, the fact that Webster's finest flights are often launched with the help of a borrowed idea does not diminish their effect. The study of his sources is valuable not in a derogatory sense, but because the identification of the original often helps to penetrate a meaning, clarify a dramatic effect, or define the qualities of a character which the commentators have missed.

Webster's use of figures of speech is closely related to his conception of tragedy, and his imagery throws much light upon the inner meaning of his plays. Both *The White Devil* and *The Duchess of Malfi,* for example, are pervaded by images of the fair show that masks inward corruption or poison, and the calm weather that hides an impending storm, and each of these sequences of metaphor is skilfully woven into the play so as to suggest the deceitfulness of fortune. The Elizabethan delight in the familiar objects and traditional beauties of the created world lies far behind him, and in his choice of metaphor and simile he deliberately singles out the curious, the grotesque and the sinister. His universe is a place of fear—it is noticeable that he is one of the few Elizabethans who does not celebrate the sublime and healing qualities of music. The birds which figure in his poetry are visualized in captivity or awaiting death, and when he describes the characteristics of plants or minerals it is the deformed and the deadly which fascinate him—witness his references to hemlock, mildew, poison, snakes and the mysterious properties of the mandrake. Often his visual symbols suggest a fearful immediacy, an icy touch, a suffocating embrace, a physical contact with the horrible. He strives to express and reconcile incongruity, above all that of the mortality of the graveyard and the sensuality of the living body. The symbolic act to which his imagination continually returns is that of tearing away the mask and uncovering the dreadful shape in the effort to resist the horror of death.

His poetry and prose follow two distinct styles of expression. The first is sophisticated, intellectually agile, staccato and restless in rhythm. In the second we find his imagination working at white heat, for he is a poet of brief and blinding insight rather than of steady illumination. This is the style which is reserved for the climaxes of his plays and which pervades his most highly wrought passages:

Your beauty! O, ten thousand curses on't
How long have I beheld the devil in crystal!
Thou hast led me, like an heathen sacrifice,
With music and with fatal yokes of flowers
To my eternal ruin. Woman to man
either a god or a wolf.

(*The White Devil,* IV. i.)

I am not mad yet, to my cause of sorrow:
The Heaven o'er my head seems made of molten brass,
The earth of flaming sulphur, yet I am not mad.
I am acquainted with sad misery
As the tanned galley-slave is with his oar;
Necessity makes me suffer constantly
And custom makes it easy.

(*The Duchess of Malfi,* IV. ii.)

At these moments Webster's language is unadorned. His vocabulary becomes predominantly Anglo-Saxon, enriched by the rare Latin word, his rhythm steady, his tone prophetic: his words seem to wield an absolute power, with which they suddenly gather together the thought and emotions of the whole play, state the tragic issue and create the moment of vision. (pp. 29-36)

Webster was . . . 'possessed' by the contrast between the wilful pretensions and desires of men and women and the reality which lies in wait for them. He does not follow Shakespeare's conception of tragedy as a fateful and exceptional conjunction of character and circumstance, whereby a man

Carrying, I say, the stamp of one defect . . .
His virtues else, be they as pure as grace . . .
Shall in the general censure take corruption
From that particular fault

(*Hamlet,* I.iv. 30-35)

for to Webster corruption is a matter of the general doom, not the particular fault. The world, as he sees it, is a pit of darkness through which men grope their way with a haunting sense of disaster, and the ordeal to which he submits his characters is not merely the end of life but a struggle against spiritual annihilation by the power of evil: it is noticeable that none of them, however intolerable the blows of fate, seeks refuge in suicide. The nature of this struggle is beset by a terror which is Webster's most original contribution to tragic art. At the end of a Shakespearean tragedy the forces of evil have spent themselves, the hero has in some measure learned wisdom. At the end of *The White Devil* death merely interrupts the worldly concerns of the protagonists, leaving them face to face with damnation. Only in *The Duchess of Malfi* do we receive a suggestion of a further vision, a hint that the spiritual chaos of the early seventeenth century is not eternity.

Webster is not an easy dramatist to appreciate, nor does he yield up his best at a first reading. His plots lack the unity and the impetus which are the reward of devotion to a single dominant theme. But judged by his individual scenes he remains, after Shakespeare, the most profound and theatrically accomplished tragedian of his age, who excels equally in the sudden *coup de théâtre* or in the gradual heightening of tension and the capacity to play upon the nerves of his audience. He surpasses Middleton and Ford in the imaginative depth and concentration of his poetry, and Chapman and Tourneur as a creator of living men and women and of roles which can still hold the stage. He succeeds better than any of his contemporaries in re-creating the colour and the spiritual climate of Renaissance Italy—in *The White Devil,* as Mr. Lucas says, we know at once that we have crossed the Alps. On the strength of his two great plays he stands in the history of English tragedy as second only to Shakespeare. (pp. 44-5)

Ian Scott-Kilvert, in his *John Webster,* Longmans, Green & Co., 1964, 51 p.

ELIZABETH M. BRENNAN
(essay date 1966)

[In the excerpt below, Brennan gives a brief appreciation of *The White Devil.*]

The dramatic form of [*The White Devil*] is that of a

tragedy of revenge for murder, a pattern dictated by the enormous success of Kyd's *The Spanish Tragedy,* probably written in the late 1580's, and other plays, including Shakespeare's *Hamlet,* which followed it. The incorporation of ghosts and scenes of real and feigned madness in the action and the use of disguise by Francisco and his accomplices in the pursuit of Brachiano and Vittora suggest the stock ingredients of the Elizabethan revenge plays of the late 1590's. The revenge plot is organized by Francisco de Medici, Duke of Florence and brother to Brachiano's murdered Duchess. His chief accomplice, Count Lodovico, bears a grudge against the state which banished him at the beginning of the play. A professed secret love of Isabella gives Lodovico a personal motive for avenging her death. In resolving his action according to the pattern of the tragedy of revenge for murder Webster was able to utilize the traditional moral implications of that pattern. Thus the murders of Brachiano, Flamineo and Vittoria satisfy human desires for revenge and, at the same time, represent divinely ordained punishment for evil lives. None the less, the instruments of this divine vengeance are themselves evil. They are therefore sentenced to punishment by the young Duke Giovanni, the fount of justice and rightful executor of God's vengeance in his own dukedom.

Francisco's plot provides a framework for a play which is chiefly concerned with Brachiano and Vittoria who, though indirectly responsible for evil and death, never stain their own hands with blood. Vittoria is a much more powerful figure than the Duke of Brachiano, yet Webster presents her almost impersonally. A mixture of sentiments—curses and considerations of religion—comes from her lips. Her interpretation on the stage must depend on the actress's performance. Vittoria could be characterized as an impudently immoral woman or as a girl bewildered at first by the force of her own beauty and its effect on a powerful Duke. She may be presented in a light which stresses her coldness, her ambition and her cruelty, or in one which gives prominence to her better qualities: her moments of consideration for her mother and her dying husband; her insistence on meting out justice to Flamineo, refusing to reward him for treachery and murder. An ideal performance might reconcile the conflicts of Vittoria's character by revealing her as a beautiful and lively woman, responsive to love and to goodness, but unable to resist the power of evil in the world around her. (pp. xviii-xix)

The White Devil is moving and disturbing, but it is difficult to act out to a coherent conclusion. The characters of Vittoria and her brother are complex, making considerable demands on the actors, and their most difficult scene—that of Flamineo's mock-death—comes so near the end of the play that faulty performances here can nullify the effect of its last moments. Despite some good examples of dramatic economy, despite the unifying force of Webster's thematic imagery, the construction of *The White Devil* remains episodic. The scene of the papal election provides colourful spectacle, but the amount of detail it includes is disproportionate to its relevance to the main plot. Brachiano and Vittoria are never seen alone together; rather they make a series of public appearances. Webster's great tragedies, like Shakespeare's, are rich in ideas as well as poetry. In Shakespeare's tragedies ideas and poetry are successfully fused with action; the plays communicate powerfully with a theatre audience. On the whole, *The White Devil* may offer as much to the reader as to the theatre-goer.

Though disappointed at his play's first reception in the theatre, Webster asserts, in his address to the reader, that he had 'willingly, and not ignorantly' chosen to disregard classical example. Praising the work of his contemporaries, he wishes that what he writes 'may be read by their light.' Perhaps he did not intend us to take the verb 'read' literally; but one of the most interesting features of Webster's writing—his extensive borrowing from a wide range of reading—encourages us to do so. A study of this borrowing does not reveal an unimaginative mind, but an original one engaged in an unique method of poetic and dramatic composition.

Originality is the most obvious quality of John Webster's drama. None the less, the major surviving plays—*The White Devil, The Duchess of Malfi* and *The Devil's Law Case*—are so few, and the flaws in their construction so manifest that many critics have felt, and some yielded to, the temptation to classify him as a minor dramatist. Yet no adverse criticism can explain away the peculiar power of Webster's work which distinguishes it from the achievements of his contemporaries. It is not just that his plays make us more aware of human misery than human happiness; it is, rather, that Webster had the courage to face the fact that, though happiness and hope exist, they are indeed often less real than misery and death. His work reveals not only his originality; it reveals his integrity, too. In recognizing this quality in John Webster's mind and art we find the reason for his stature as a dramatist expressed in his own words:

Integrity of life is fame's best friend,
Which nobly, beyond death, shall crown the end.

                              (pp. xxviii-xxix)

Elizabeth M. Brennan, in an introduction to *The White Devil* by John Webster, edited by Elizabeth M. Brennan, Ernest Benn Limited, 1966, pp. vii-xxxiv.

SOURCES FOR FURTHER STUDY

Boklund, Gunnar. *The Duchess of Malfi: Sources, Themes, Characters.* Cambridge, Mass.: Harvard University Press, 1962, 189 p.

> Discusses the historical background of the drama and traces the possible sources for Webster's version.

———. *The Sources of The White Devil.* Cambridge, Mass.: Harvard University Press, 1957, 226 p.

> Discusses the historical background of the drama and traces the possible sources for Webster's version, which, the critic maintains, presents "various degrees of evil at war."

Bradbrook, M. C. *John Webster: Citizen and Dramatist.* New York: Columbia University Press, 1980, 218 p.

> A useful study in two parts: the first provides a historical context for Webster, and the second offers a survey of his career as a dramatist.

Leech, Clifford. *John Webster: A Critical Study.* London: The Hogarth Press, 1951, 122 p.

> Seminal study of Webster's life and dramatic writings. Leech finds that the shorter speeches in Webster's works impress more than the longer passages, and that his plays excel in their flashes of brilliant verse.

Moore, Don D., ed. *Webster: The Critical Heritage.* London: Routledge & Kegan Paul, 1981, 161 p.

> Reprints important commentary on Webster to trace his critical reputation from the Jacobean era to the end of the nineteenth century. Includes remarks by Henry Fitzjeffrey, William Hazlitt, and William Archer.

Schuman, Samuel. *John Webster: A Reference Guide.* Boston: G. K. Hall, 1985, 280 p.

> Annotated bibliography of writings on the dramatist, covering the period from 1602 to the 1980s.

H. G. Wells

1866-1946

(Full name Herbert George Wells; also wrote under pseudonyms Sosthenes Smith, Walter Glockenhammer, and Reginald Bliss) English novelist, short story writer, historian, essayist, autobiographer, and critic.

INTRODUCTION

Wells is best known as one of the progenitors of modern science fiction. His pioneering works in this genre foretold such developments as chemical warfare, atomic weapons, and world wars. *The Time Machine* (1895), *The Island of Dr. Moreau* (1896), *The Invisible Man* (1897), and *The War of the Worlds* (1898) are classics that have profoundly influenced the course of twentieth-century science fiction. Although Wells's science fiction is informed by a pessimistic, apocalyptic vision, in speculative nonfiction works such as *The World Set Free* (1914), *The Outline of History* (1919-20), *The Shape of Things to Come* (1933), and *Guide to the New World* (1941) he developed an optimistic ideal of a utopian millennium. As a polemicist, Wells's advocacy of free love and socialism, as well as his attacks on what he considered the stifling moral constraints of Victorian society, contributed to the liberalization of modern Western culture.

Wells was born into a poor family in Bromley, Kent, a suburb of London. He sought to escape poverty, receiving an excellent education at London University and the Royal College of Science, where he studied zoology. One of his professors, the noted biologist T. H. Huxley, instilled in him the belief in social as well as biological evolution that Wells later cited as the single most influential aspect of his education. After graduating Wells wrote a biology textbook and began submitting fiction to various magazines. Following the great success of *The Time Machine*, Wells attained renown with what he termed "scientific romances." He wrote primarily science fiction until the turn of the century, when he began to write character and social-problem novels. Wells joined the socialist Fabian Society in 1903 but left after a long dispute with Bernard Shaw over some of the society's policies. Wells's socialist thought, combined with a belief in the perfectibility of humankind through evolution and scientific advances, is expressed in the serious, didactic fiction and speculative essays about the future that gradually succeeded his novel-writing during the first decade of the twentieth century. Prior to World War I, such works as *Anticipations of the Reaction of Mechanical and Scientific Progress upon Human Life and Thought* (1901), *A Modern Utopia* (1905), and *The New Machiavelli* (1911) established Wells as a leading proponent of socialism, world government, free thought, and free love, and as an enemy of the entrenched Edwardian establishment.

During the period of widespread disillusion that followed the First World War, Wells revised his essentially optimistic vision of the future. For example, his volume of essays *The War That Will End War* (1914), published shortly after the outbreak of World War I, inadvertently gave the world, through its title, a cynical catchphrase for obstinate naiveté in the face of widespread corruption. But throughout the 1920s and 1930s Wells wrote social and political criticism and prognostications about the future that were increasingly more pessimistic. His last book, *Mind at the End of Its Tether* (1945), predicts the destruction of civilization and the degeneration of humanity. Wells died in London in 1946.

Wells's critical and popular reputation rests primarily on his early works of science fiction. These works were enormously popular at the time they appeared; most are acknowledged classics of the genre which continue to be widely read and adapted into other media. Wells's science fiction was profoundly influenced by his adaptation of Huxley's philosophical interpretation of Darwinian evolutionary theory, contending that the course of life on earth, like that of any organism, follows a pattern of quickening, maturation, and decadence. Writing at a time when the notion was seriously advanced that "everything had been discovered"—that only refinements of existing scientific and technological advanced remained to be made—Huxley's "cosmic pessimism" was deeply disturbing, implying that humankind faced inevitable decline. Wells adopted this chilling notion in the stories and novels that he wrote in the 1890s, such as *The Time Machine, When the Sleeper Wakes* (1899), and *The First Men in the Moon* (1901). While Wells did not invent speculative fiction positing technological advances, his early science fiction pioneered the fiction exploration of such complex issues as the impact of technology on human affairs and the moral responsibility of scientists for the potentially harmful applications of their research and inventions. Wells's science fiction is also noted for its sophisticated satire of the author's own culture and times. Although Wells's character novels are considered lacking in psychological subtlety and do not possess the skilled construction of his science fiction novels, they are commended for the humor and sympathy that they display, and two of Wells's novels, *Kipps: The Story of a Simple Soul* (1905) and *The History of Mr. Polly* (1910), are considered among the finest English comic novels of all time. However, following the appearance of *The History of Mr. Polly,* he fully turned his imaginative powers to addressing social problems, publishing such novels as *Joan and Peter: The Story of an Education* (1918) and *The World of William Clissold* (1926), which proved overly didactic in tone and content. Of the social problem novels, only the early *Tono-Bungay* (1909) is universally praised. This ambitious portrayal of social and political decay is often considered Wells's finest novel.

Wells is regarded as one of the most prominent champions of the early twentieth-century spirit of British liberal optimism. His works are ranked with those of Bernard Shaw as exemplary of his era's exuberant sense of release from Victorian conventions and morals, and of unbridled confidence in the benefits that would derive from scientific progress. The continued popularity of his books, the tremendous body of criticism devoted to them, and the liberalizing effect that much of his work had on Western thought combine to make Wells a major figure of modern literature.

(For further information about Wells's life and works, see *Contemporary Authors,* Vols. 110, 121; *Dictionary of Literary Biography,* Vols. 34, 70; *Major Twentieth-Century Writers; Something about the Author,* Vol. 20; *Short Story Criticism,* Vol. 6; and *Twentieth-Century Literary Criticism,* Vols. 6, 12, 19.)

CRITICAL COMMENTARY

JOSEPH CONRAD
(letter date 1898)

[Conrad was an innovator of novel structure as well as one of the finest stylists of modern English literature. His novels are complex moral and psychological examinations of the ambiguities of good and evil. In the following excerpt from a letter to Wells, he commends the humanity and verisimilitude of *The Invisible Man*.]

[*The Invisible Man*] is uncommonly fine. One can always *see* a lot in your work—there is always a "beyond" to your books—but into this (with due regard to theme and length) you've managed to put an amazing quantity of effects. If it just misses being tremendous, it is because you didn't make it so—and if you didn't, there isn't a man in England who could. As to b— furriners they ain't in it at all.

I suppose you'll have the common decency to believe me when I tell you I am always powerfully impressed by your work. . . . And if you want to know what impresses me it is to see how you contrive to give over humanity into the clutches of the Impossible and yet manage to keep it down (or up) to its humanity, to its flesh, blood, sorrow, folly. *That* is the achievement! In this little book you do it with an appalling completeness. I'll not insist on the felicity of incident. This must be obvious even to yourself. Three of us have been reading the book . . . and we have been tracking with delight the cunning method of your logic. It is masterly—it is ironic—it is very relentless—and it is very true. We all three (the two others are no fools) place the *I.M.* above the *War of the Worlds*. Whether we are right—and if so why—I am not sure, and cannot tell. I fancy the book is more strictly human, and thus your diabolical psychology plants its points right into a man's bowels. To me the *W. of the W.* has less of that sinister air of truth that arrests the reader in reflexion at the turn of the page so often in the *I.M.* In reading this last, one is touched by the anguish of it as by something that any day may happen to oneself. It is a great triumph for you. (pp. 259-60)

Joseph Conrad, in a letter to H. G. Wells on December 4, 1898, in his *Joseph Conrad: Life and Letters, Vol. I* edited by G. Jean-Aubry, Doubleday, Page & Co., 1927, pp. 259-60.

JULES VERNE
(interview date 1904)

[Verne is acknowledged as one of the world's first and most imaginative modern science fiction writers. His works reflect nineteenth-century concerns with contemporary scientific innovation and its potential for human benefit or destruction. In the following excerpt from an interview with Gordon Jones, he commends the imaginative creativity with which Wells constructs his scientific fantasies and stresses the difference between Wells's style and his own.]

There is an author whose work has appealed to me very strongly from an imaginative stand-point, and whose books I have followed with considerable interest. I allude to Mr. H. G. Wells. Some of my friends have suggested to me that his work is on somewhat similar lines to my own, but here, I think, they err. I consider him, as a purely imaginative writer, to be deserving of very high praise, but our methods are entirely different. I have always made a point in my romances of basing my so-called inventions upon a groundwork of actual fact, and of using in their construction methods and materials which are not entirely without the pale of contemporary engineering skill and knowledge.

Take, for instance, the case of the 'Nautilus.' This, when carefully considered, is a submarine mechanism about which there is nothing wholly extraordinary, nor beyond the bounds of actual scientific knowledge. (pp. 669-70)

The creations of Mr. Wells, on the other hand, belong unreservedly to an age and degree of scientific knowledge far removed from the present, though I will not say entirely beyond the limits of the possible. Not only does he evolve his constructions entirely from the realm of imagination, but he also evolves the materials of which he builds them. See, for example, his story *The First Men in the Moon*. You will remember that here he introduces an entirely new anti-gravitational substance, to whose mode of preparation or actual chemical composition we are not given the slightest clue, nor does a reference to our present scientific knowledge en-

Principal Works

Text-Book of Biology (nonfiction) 1893

The Time Machine (novel) 1895

The Wonderful Visit (novel) 1895

The Island of Dr. Moreau (novel) 1896

The Wheels of Chance (novel) 1896

The Invisible Man (novel) 1897

The War of the Worlds (novel) 1898

*Tales of Space and Time (novellas and short stories) 1899

When the Sleeper Wakes: A Story of the Years to Come (novel) 1899; also published as The Sleeper Awakes [revised edition], 1910

Love and Mr. Lewisham (novel) 1900

Anticipations of the Reaction of Mechanical and Scientific Progress upon Human Life and Thought (essay) 1901

The First Men in the Moon (novel) 1901

Mankind in the Making (essays) 1903

The Food of the Gods, and How It Came to Earth (novel) 1904

Kipps: The Story of a Simple Soul (novel) 1905

A Modern Utopia (essay) 1905

The Future in America: A Search after Realities (essays) 1906

In the Days of the Comet (novel) 1906

New Worlds for Old (essay) 1908

The War in the Air and Particularly How Mr. Bert Smallways Fared While It Lasted (novel) 1908

Ann Veronica (novel) 1909

Tono-Bungay (novel) 1909

The History of Mr. Polly (novel) 1910

The Country of the Blind, and Other Stories (short stories) 1911

The New Machiavelli (novel) 1911

Marriage (novel) 1912

The War That Will End War (essays) 1914

The World Set Free (novel) 1914

The Research Magnificent (novel) 1915

Mr. Britling Sees It Through (novel) 1916

The Soul of a Bishop: A Novel (with Just a Little Love in It) about Conscience and Religion and the Real Troubles of Life (novel) 1917

Joan and Peter: The Story of an Education (novel) 1918

The Outline of History. 2 vols. (history) 1919-20

The World of William Clissold (novel) 1926

The Short Stories of H. G. Wells (short stories) 1927

The Open Conspiracy (essay) 1928

The Bulpington of Blup (novel) 1932

The Shape of Things to Come (essays) 1933

Experiment in Autobiography (autobiography) 1934

Guide to the New World (essay) 1941

Mind at the End of Its Tether (essay) 1945

*This collection contains the novella A Story of the Days to Come.

able us for a moment to predict a method by which such a result might be achieved. In *The War of the Worlds,* again, a work for which I confess I have a great admiration, one is left entirely in the dark as to what kind of creatures the Martians really are, or in what manner they produce the wonderful heat ray with which they work such terrible havoc on their assailants.

[In saying this], I am casting no disparagement on Mr. Wells' methods; on the contrary, I have the highest respect for his imaginative genius. I am merely contrasting our two styles and pointing out the fundamental difference which exists between them, and I wish you clearly to understand that I express no opinion on the superiority of either the one or the other. (p. 670)

Jules Verne, "Jules Verne at Home, in an interview with Gordon Jones," in *Temple Bar,* Vol. CXXIX, No. 523, June, 1904, pp. 664-71.

VIRGINIA WOOLF
(essay date 1919)

[Woolf was an English novelist, essayist, and critic. Like her contemporary James Joyce, with whom she is often compared, she employed the stream-of-consciousness technique in many of her fictional works. Her critical essays, which cover almost the entire range of English literature, contain some of her finest prose and are praised for their insight. In the following excerpt from an essay originally published in the *Times Literary Supplement* in 1919, Woolf charges Wells with materialism.]

[If] we speak of quarrelling with Mr. Wells, Mr. Bennett, and Mr. Galsworthy, it is partly that by the mere fact of their existence in the flesh their work has a living, breathing, everyday imperfection which bids us take what liberties with it we choose. But it is also true that, while we thank them for a thousand gifts, we reserve our unconditional gratitude for Mr. Hardy, for Mr. Conrad, and in much lesser degree for the Mr. Hudson of *The Purple Land, Green Mansions,* and *Far Away and Long Ago.* Mr. Wells, Mr. Bennett, and Mr. Galsworthy have excited so many hopes and disappointed them so persistently that our gratitude largely takes the form of thanking them for having shown us what they might have done but have not done; what we certainly could not do, but as certainly, perhaps, do not wish to do. No single phrase will sum up the charge or grievance which we have to bring against a mass of work so large in its volume and embodying so many qualities, both admirable and the reverse. If we tried to formulate our meaning in one word we should say that these three writers are materialists. It is because they are concerned not with the spirit but with the body that they have disappointed us, and left us with the feeling that the sooner English fiction turns its back upon them, as politely as may be, and marches, if only into the desert, the better for its soul. Naturally, no single word reaches the centre of three separate targets. In the case of Mr. Wells it falls notably wide of the mark. And yet even with him it indicates to our thinking the fatal alloy in his genius, the great clod of clay that has got itself mixed up with the purity of his inspiration. . . . It can scarcely be said of Mr. Wells that he is a materialist in the sense that he takes too much delight in the solidity of his fabric. His mind is too generous in its sympathies to allow him to spend much time in making things shipshape and substantial. He is a materialist from sheer goodness of heart, taking upon his shoulders the work that ought to have been discharged by Government officials, and in the plethora of his ideas and facts scarcely having leisure to realize, or forgetting to think important, the crudity and coarseness of his human beings. Yet what more damaging criticism can there be both of his earth and of his Heaven than that they are to be inhabited here and hereafter by his Joans and his Peters? Does not the inferiority of their natures tarnish whatever institutions and ideals may be provided for them by the generosity of their creator? (pp. 103-05)

Virginia Woolf, "Modern Fiction," in her *Collected Essays, Vol. II,* Harcourt Brace Jovanovich, 1967, pp. 103-10.

CHRISTOPHER ISHERWOOD

(essay date 1951)

[Isherwood, an English-born man of letters, is known for his largely autobiographical accounts of

pre-Nazi Berlin and for his detached, humorous observations on human nature and manners. In the excerpt below from an essay that first appeared in *Tomorrow* in 1951, he discusses Wells's creativity, pessimism, and spiritual beliefs.]

Wells felt that the novel in its traditional form was out of date. . . . Nevertheless, [he] was capable of fine writing, when he wasn't in too much of a hurry; and, throughout his career, he continued to produce novels.

As a matter of fact, Wells had all the gifts which go to make a 'traditional' novelist. He could create solid characters, write lively, naturalistic dialogue, and evoke the atmosphere of houses and places. His humour was Dickensian, lapsing sometimes into facetiousness but bold and warm at its best. These qualities are most apparent in *Kipps, Tono-Bungay* and *Mr Polly,* three books which drew largely upon the experience of Wells' own childhood and adolescence. Wells was always at his most vivid when he returned to that period; no doubt because he could look at it from a distance, objectively. He never gave himself time to do this in dealing with his later life. Everything had to be reported at once, as it happened—like the scribbling of a war correspondent in the midst of a still-smoking battlefield. There was no time to worry about form, or the technical problems of presentation; there was no question of excluding any portions of the given material because they didn't happen to 'fit'. Every bit of it had to go in.

The majority of Wells' realistic novels (I shall speak of his scientific fantasies later) deal with the impact upon their author of a person, or an idea, or a situation. The person is usually a woman, one of the many in Wells' life, very thinly disguised. The idea or the situation is presented subjectively, just as it struck Wells himself. This initial impact (the impact, for example, of World War I upon Wells in *Mr Britling Sees It Through*) is the author's point of departure into speculation and theorizing. 'What does it mean?' he asks himself aloud, 'what do I think about this?' (Wells isn't sure, because he is thinking even as he writes, thrashing the problem out before our eyes.) Along the lines of these speculations, which are like spacious corridors leading off in all directions, wander the minor characters. These are often brilliantly drawn, and their personal circumstances and doings engage our interest, even when they are somewhat irrelevant to the main theme. And then, beyond the open-ended, incomplete structure of the novel, we are aware of the surrounding contemporary world, with all the diversity of its business and its anxieties, ever present on the horizon of the author's consciousness.

It is a measure of Wells' genius that he was able to make these big untidy talkative books so alive and readable. From an artistic standpoint, most of them can only be described as failures; they simply don't 'compose'. But Wells achieved a larger kind of success; he showed how the tight classic form of the novel might be expanded to include a much wider area of reference. That he himself didn't know when to stop, that he expanded the novel until it burst, is not so important. You can't make experiments without explosions. He remains a great pioneer. (pp. 42-3)

Several of Wells' realistic novels were hugely popular, at the time of their publication, because of their topicality and the shock value of the problems they discussed. Today, his reputation is based chiefly upon the *Outline of History* and half a dozen of his scientific fantasies. Wells would not regret the survival of the *Outline;* it is a masterpiece. But he might well resent our preference for *The Time Machine, The Island of Dr Moreau, The Invisible Man, The War of the Worlds, The First Men in the Moon* and *The War in the Air.* No author cares to have his early works (these were all written before 1909) preferred to his later ones; Wells continued to write scientific fantasies throughout his life, but these, like the realistic novels, became increasingly discursive and were never very successful. Besides, he would probably complain that we have failed to understand the inner meaning of the stories themselves. We regard them as enjoyable thrillers—just as we regard *Gulliver's Travels* as a quaint book for children. (pp. 43-4)

When he looked into the future, Wells alternated between extremes of optimism and pessimism. The early scientific fantasies are deeply pessimistic; a fact which we usually overlook. There is the unutterable sadness of the Time Traveller's last glimpse of the dying world; the reversion of Moreau's fabricated humans into beasts; the wretched fate of the Invisible Man. Life and individual genius end in frustration and defeat. Nearly fifty years later, in his book *Mind at the End of Its Tether,* Wells repeated this message: 'The end of everything we call life is close at hand and cannot be evaded.' Yet his own character was essentially optimistic. A natural Utopian, he continued, despite many disappointments, to cling to his vision of a World State; he was still fighting for it in his old age, in the midst of World War II. (p. 44)

In his youth, Wells hated God and violently denied His existence; for 'God', in those days, was the God of the Big House, the feudal Overlord. But *Mr Britling,* shaken by the horror of the First World War, found that some Ultimate Reality was, after all, necessary to his peace of mind; so Wells rediscovered Him as 'the Captain of Mankind', a sort of supernatural President of the future World State. This God appears in two further novels, *The Soul of a Bishop* and *The Undying Fire;* but it is doubtful if Wells found Him either comforting or convincing. Indeed, He appears to be little more than a metaphor. His chief quality is negative; He is fundamentally opposed to His Church and to all organized Religion. He makes a last bow, in the guise of a weary and cynical old man, in *Joan and Peter,* telling the young hero that, if he doesn't like the world, he must change it himself.

Wells' 'theological excursion' was doomed to failure because he could never quite escape from the dualistic religious concepts of his upbringing: God high in Heaven and we, His servants, hopelessly far beneath. Such dualism is nauseating to any man of Wells' temperament because it immediately confronts him with his old enemy, established authority. Wells might try to persuade himself that "his" God was different, but he couldn't. The truth was that he didn't really want a Captain of Mankind any more than he had wanted a feudal Overlord. He wasn't a follower. Indeed, he had a horror of 'Great men'.

Nevertheless—and this is Wells' tragedy—he was always dimly but poignantly aware that something was lacking, some vital spark that would bring his New Utopia to life. Under the influence of Plato's *Republic,* which he had read as a schoolboy, he imagined an Order of Samurai—a group of dedicated and sternly disciplined young people who would give their lives to the work of building the society of the future. His writings on this subject actually inspired the formation of enthusiastic groups which looked to him for leadership. Wells, to his great mortification, was unable to offer them any; he couldn't devise a practical programme. 'Toward the end of his life he remarked on the fact that just about the time he made this unsuccessful attempt at practical construction, Lenin, "under the pressure of a more urgent reality", was quietly and steadily drawing up an "extraordinarily similar plan"—the Communist party organization.' But, even if a revolutionary situation had existed in England at that period, and even if Wells had been a born revolutionary leader, he and his Samurai would have found themselves, sooner or later, in trouble. For a dedicated group demands a faith; without one, it cannot continue to function. Lacking genuinely spiritual inspiration, it will turn to some substitute idolatry, such as nationalism or the cult of a leader; and so the movement defeats itself and the World State can never be founded, much less sustained.

Wells was always proclaiming his faith in the capacities of Man. Yet he refused to take account of Man's highest capacity—that of knowing and drawing strength from what is eternal within himself. Some inhibition or deeply-seated fear, it would seem, made Wells unable to accept the validity of the mystical experience, or to recognize its central importance in the scheme of human evolution. Why he couldn't bring himself to do this, despite all his urgent self-questionings, I don't know. (pp. 45-6)

Christopher Isherwood, "H. G. Wells," in his *Exhumations: Stories, Articles, Verses,* Methuen & Co. Ltd., 1966, pp. 38-46.

W. SOMERSET MAUGHAM

(essay date 1952)

[Maugham was an English dramatist, short story writer, and novelist. Best known for his autobiographical novel *Of Human Bondage*, he also achieved popular success with such plays as *Caesar's Wife*, *The Breadwinner*, and *Our Betters*. In the excerpt below from a work first published in 1952, he discusses the reasons for Wells's diminished popularity.]

[Wells] had no illusions about himself as an author. He always insisted that he made no pretension to be an artist. That was, indeed, something he despised rather than admired, and when he spoke of Henry James, an old friend, who claimed, as I have hinted, perhaps a little too often that he was an artist and nothing else, it was good-humouredly to ridicule him. "I'm not an author," H. G. would say, "I'm a publicist. My work is just high-class journalism." On one occasion, after he had been staying with me, he sent me a complete edition of his works and next time he came he saw them displayed in an imposing row on my shelves. They were well printed on good paper and handsomely bound in red. He ran his finger along them and with a cheerful grin said: "They're as dead as mutton, you know. They all dealt with matters of topical interest and now that the matters aren't topical any more they're unreadable." There is a good deal of truth in what he said. He had a fluent pen and too often it ran away with him. I have never seen any of his manuscripts, but I surmise that he wrote with facility and corrected little. He had a way of repeating in one sentence, but in other words, exactly what he said in the previous one. I suppose it was because he was so full of the idea he wanted to express that he was not satisfied to say it only once. It made him unnecessarily verbose.

H. G.'s theory of the short story was a sensible one. It enabled him to write a number that were very good and several that were masterly. His theory of the novel was different. His early novels, which he had written to earn a living, did not accord with it and he spoke of them slightingly. His notion was that the function of the novelist was to deal with the pressing problems of the day and to persuade the reader to adopt the views for the betterment of the world which he, H. G., held. He was fond of likening the novel to a woven tapestry of varied interest, and he would not accept my objection that after all a tapestry has unity. The artist who designed it has given it form, balance, coherence and arrangement. It is not a jumble of unrelated items.

His later novels, are, if not, as he said, unreadable, at least difficult to read with delight. You begin to read them with interest, but as you go on you find your interest dwindle and it is only by an effort of will that you continue to read. I think *Tono Bungay* is generally considered his best novel. It is written with his usual liveliness, though perhaps the style is better suited to a treatise than to a novel, and the characters are well presented. He has deliberately avoided the suspense which most novelists attempt to create and he tells you more or less early on what is going to happen. His theory of the novelist's function allows him to digress abundantly, which, if you are interested in the characters and their behaviour, can hardly fail to arouse in you some impatience. (pp. 222-24)

I think that is why his novels are less satisfactory than one would have liked them to be. The people he puts before you are not individuals, but lively and talkative marionettes whose function it is to express the ideas he was out to attack or to defend. They do not develop according to their dispositions, but change for the purposes of the theme. It is as though a tadpole did not become a frog, but a squirrel—because you had a cage that you wanted to pop him into. H. G. seems often to have grown tired of his characters before he was halfway through and then, frankly discarding any attempt at characterisation, he becomes an out-and-out pamphleteer. One curious thing that you can hardly help noticing if you have read most of H. G.'s novels is that he deals with very much the same people in book after book. He appears to have been content to use with little variation the few persons who had played an intimate part in his own life. He was always a little impatient with his heroines. He regarded his heroes with greater indulgence. He had of course put more of himself in them; most of them in fact are merely himself in a different guise. Trafford in *Marriage* is indeed the portrait of the man H. G. thought he was, added to the man he would have liked to be. (pp. 224-25)

"I've been saying the same things to people for the last thirty years," he said to me with exasperation, "and they won't listen." That was the trouble. He had said the same things too often. Many of his ideas were sensible, none of them was complicated; but, like Goethe, he thought that one must always repeat truth: *Man muss das Wahre immer wiederholen.* He was so constituted that never a doubt entered his mind that he was definitely possessed of *das Wahre*. Naturally people grew impatient when they were asked once more to listen to views they knew only too well. He had had an immense influence on a whole generation and had done a great deal to alter the climate of opinion. But he had had his say. He was mortified to find that people looked upon him as a has-been. They agreed with him or they

Major Media Adaptations: Motion Pictures and Radio

The First Men in the Moon, 1919. Gaumont. Director: J. L. V. Leigh. Cast: Lionel D'Arragan, Hector Abbas, Heather Thatcher.

Island of Lost Souls, 1932. Paramount. [Adaptation of *The Island of Dr. Moreau*] Director: Erle C. Kenton. Cast: Charles Laughton, Bela Lugosi, Richard Arlen.

The Invisible Man, 1933. Universal. Director: James Whale. Cast: Claude Rains, Gloria Stuart.

The Man Who Could Work Miracles, 1936. London Films. Director: Lothar Mendes. Cast: Roland Young, Ralph Richardson, George Zucco, George Sanders.

Things to Come, 1936. London Films. [Adaptation of *The Shape of Things to Come*] Director: William Cameron Menzies. Cast: Raymond Massey, Cedric Hardwicke, Ralph Richardson.

The War of the Worlds, 1938. Mercury Theater. [Radio broadcast] Director: Orson Welles.

The Passionate Friends, 1948. Rank. Director: David Lean. Cast: Claude Rains, Trevor Howard, Wilfred Hyde White, Ann Todd.

The War of the Worlds, 1952. Paramount. Director: George Pal. Cast: Gene Barry, Ann Robinson.

The Time Machine, 1960. MGM/Galaxy. Director: George Pal. Cast: Rod Taylor, Yvette Mimieux, Sebastian Cabot, Whit Bissell, Alan Young.

The First Men in the Moon, 1964. Columbia. Director: Nathan Juran. Cast: Lionel Jeffries, Edward Judd, Martha Hyer, Peter Finch. Special Effects: Ray Harryhausen.

Village of the Giants, 1965. Embassy. [Adaptation of *Food of the Gods*] Director: Bert I. Gordon. Cast: Beau Bridges, Ronnie Howard, Tisha Sterling.

Food of the Gods, 1976. American International Pictures. Director: Bert I. Gordon. Cast: Marjoe Gortner, Ida Lupino, Ralph Meeker.

The Island of Dr. Moreau, 1977. AIP/Cinema 77. Director: Don Taylor. Cast: Burt Lancaster, Michael York, Nigel Davenport, Barbara Carrera, Richard Basehart.

Phase IV, 1977. American International Pictures. [Adaptation of *Empire of the Ants*] Director: Bert I. Gordon. Cast: Joan Collins, Albert Salmi, Brooke Palance.

didn't. When they listened to him it was no longer with the old thrill of excitement, but with the indulgence you accord to an old man who has outlived his interest.

He died a disappointed man. (p. 228)

W. Somerset Maugham, "Some Novelists I Have Known," in his *The Vagrant Mood: Six Essays*, Doubleday, 1953, pp. 202–50.

MARK R. HILLEGAS

(essay date 1967)

[Hillegas is an American educator and critic who has written extensively on science fiction. In the following excerpt from his *The Future as Nightmare: H. G. Wells and the Anti-Utopians*, he defines the concept of "the Wellsian imagination" and discusses ways that Wells attacked complacency in his early science fiction.]

Wells turned naturally and easily to the writing of science fiction because he possessed what demands to be called "the Wellsian imagination." This Wellsian imagination is the key to his science fiction as well as to the nature of its impact, and I shall attempt to describe it briefly.

Wells is, of course, closely identified with a particular vision of a utopian World State, a vision which is important in explaining his relationship to the anti-utopians. . . . What I am dealing with now, however,

is a quality, a way of looking at things, which was first described at length by Van Wyck Brooks in 1915 [in his *The World of H. G. Wells*]. This quality, which must surely be a chief characteristic of the mind scientifically educated, is detachment. As Brooks remarked about Wells's fiction in general, and as we would say particularly about his scientific romances, future histories, and utopias, Wells saw men chemically and anatomically, the world astronomically. Brooks also put it another way: it is the distinction between the intellectual, who views life in terms of ideas, and the artist, who views life in terms of experience. Generally speaking, the intellectual dominated Wells's writings, though sometimes—most continuously in *Tono-Bungay, Kipps,* and *Mr. Polly*—the artist took over. But it must be emphasized that this distinction between "intellectual" and "artistic" refers to the angle at which reality is viewed, not to the quality of writing. Even at his most "intellectual," as in, say, *The Time Machine*, Wells was capable of vividness in both conception and expression. *The Time Machine,* though it differs greatly from ordinary fiction, has some right to the title of "art."

Surely the single most spectacular manifestation of this detached quality of the Wellsian imagination is its preoccupation with the future. This preoccupation, which is central to many of Wells's writings, is most enthusiastically explained in **"The Discovery of the Future,"** a lecture Wells delivered at the Royal Institution in January 1902, which was published in *Nature* the next month. In this lecture, Wells distinguished between two kinds of minds. The first, oriented to the past, regards the future "as sort of black nonexistence upon which the advancing present will presently write events." It is the legal mind, always referring to precedents. The second kind of mind, oriented to the future, is constructive, creative, organizing. "It sees the world as one great workshop, and the present is no more than material for the future, for the king that is yet destined to be." Finally, Wells predicted what might be accomplished if the future-oriented mind were given freedom to express itself:

> All this world is heavy with the promise of greater things, and a day will come, one day in the unending succession of days, when beings who are now latent in our thoughts and hidden in our loins, shall stand upon this earth as one stands upon a footstool and shall laugh and reach out their hands amidst the stars.

(In the context of that entire lecture, this passage is not, incidentally, the expression of simple optimism it can easily be taken to be.)

Along with the detached imagination and its preoccupation with the future go certain clearly defined and inevitable values and interests. Wells—not surprisingly for a former student and admirer of T. H. Huxley—was a supreme rationalist and believer in science and the scientific method, a Francis Bacon reborn. And so for Wells, as for one of his Utopians in *Men Like Gods,* there was no way out of the cages of life but by knowledge—knowledge of man himself and of man in relation to the things about him. Naturally the Wellsian imagination is drawn to certain characteristic subjects. It is fascinated by the revelations of man's place in time and space given to us by science, fascinated by the vistas of astronomy, particularly the death of the world and the vastness of interstellar space, fascinated by the vision of geological epochs, the evolution of life, and the early history of man vouchsafed by geology, paleontology, and archaeology.

The first, brilliant fruit of this Wellsian imagination were the scientific romances and stories written in the 1890's which led, in their turn, by a complicated process which also involved reaction against the Wellsian utopias, to the major anti-utopias of the twentieth century.

Ironically, Wells's early scientific romances and stories present a vision of man's nature, his place in the universe, and the power of science which is the complete antithesis of the vision that by the 1930's was commonly considered Wellsian. "Wellsian," it need hardly be said, came to connote a utopia filled with super-gadgets, mechanical wonders, run by an elite of scientists and engineers for the good of the people (the kind of thing the public saw in the tasteless movie made by Alexander Korda, *Things to Come*). The application of science had almost automatically brought this heaven on earth, which was inhabited by a finer race of human beings, who had inevitably evolved to their state of near perfection. Neither in spirit nor in detail are Wells's stories and romances at all similar to this commonly accepted notion of the Wellsian vision.

Odd as it may seem in view of the later widespread identification of Wells with scientific optimism, knowledgeable commentators have long been aware of the darkness which actually permeates much of the early science fiction—the stories and the great scientific romances like *The Time Machine, The Invisible Man, The Island of Dr. Moreau, The War of the Worlds,* and *The First Men in the Moon.* In the 1890's several reviewers, one of whom was W. T. Stead, were quick to note Wells's pessimism and "the gloomy horror of his vision." Certain later critics have been well aware that the Wells of the scientific romances is not "Wellsian." (pp. 13-17)

To understand the darkness and pessimism of the early stories and scientific romances, we must remember that they were written against the background of grave social injustice and economic distress, socialist agitation and labor unrest. Fifty years after Disraeli had written of the "two nations," England still consisted chiefly of the rich and the poor. At the bottom of the social heap were the exploited multitudes of the industrial proletariat, who, in spite of the fact that conditions had improved incredibly since the "Hungry Forties," still led horribly deformed and meaningless lives. Above them were the energetic and upward aspiring middle class, cramped by the conditions of their existence only at the bottom levels of the class. At the summit, the "unpremeditated, successful, aimless Plutocracy" led sterile lives of unproductive leisure. The middle and upper classes, who were seldom their brothers' keepers and usually ignored the inhabitants of the Abyss, managed, in the face of worsening conditions during these last years of the nineteenth century, to hold to their faith in "progress," managed to believe that things were somehow improving. In his scientific romances and stories written at this time, Wells set about vigorously to attack this late Victorian complacency, for in his opinion there was no greater enemy of progress than a belief in inevitable progress. He launched this attack, as I have pointed out elsewhere, from what is best described as the "cosmic pessimism" of T. H. Huxley. (p. 18)

In Huxley's philosophy of evolution there is an element of grave doubt about the outcome of the cosmic or evolutionary process—his "cosmic pessimism"—which was exactly suited to Wells's aesthetic and didactic purposes in the stories and scientific romances written in the 1890's. And it is this "cosmic pessimism" which inspired the details in the scientific romances (chiefly *The Time Machine, The Island of Dr. Moreau, When the Sleeper Wakes* and "**A Story of the Days To Come**," and *The First Men in the Moon*) that

---

Jorge Luis Borges on the artistry of Wells's novels:

Not only do [Wells's excellent first novels *The Island of Dr. Moreau* and *The Invisible Man*] tell an ingenious story; but they tell a story symbolic of processes that are somehow inherent in all human destinies. The harrassed invisible man who has to sleep as though his eyes were wide open because his eyelids do not exclude light is our solitude and our terror; the conventicle of seated monsters who mouth a servile creed in their night is the Vatican and is Lhasa. Work that endures is always capable of an infinite and plastic ambiguity; it is all things for all men, like the Apostle; it is a mirror that reflects the reader's own traits and it is also a map of the world. And it must be ambiguous in an evanescent and modest way, almost in spite of the author; he must appear to be ignorant of all symbolism. Wells displayed that lucid innocence in his first fantastic exercises, which are to me the most admirable part of his admirable work.

Those who say that art should not propagate doctrines usually refer to doctrines that are opposed to their own. Naturally this is not my own case; I gratefully profess almost all the doctrines of Wells, but I deplore his inserting them into his narratives. An heir of the British nominalists, Wells condemns our custom of speaking of the "tenacity of England" or the "intrigues of Prussia." The arguments against that harmful mythology seem to be irreproachable, but not the fact of interpolating them into the story of Mr. Parham's dream. As long as an author merely relates events or traces the slight deviations of a conscience, we can suppose him to be omniscient, we can confuse him with the universe or with God; but when he descends to the level of pure reason, we know he is fallible.

Jorge Luis Borges, in an essay in his *Other Inquisitions: 1937-1952.*

---

are repeated in the works by Forster, Zamyatin, Huxley, Orwell, and others and that make these romances by Wells something like the first modern anti-utopias.

By the 1880's Huxley had clearly formulated his idea that the evolutionary process will never lead to moral or social improvement, for cosmic nature is the "headquarters of the enemy of ethical nature" and the only chance for social and ethical progress is the "checking of the cosmic process at every step" and the substitution for it of the ethical. But, as Houston Peterson remarked [in his *Huxley, Prophet of Science*] Huxley had "no fantastic hopes" for the success of any such effort. The savagery in civilized men will not easily be eradicated because their cosmic nature is the outcome of millions of years of evolutionary training, while control of the cosmic process by manipulating the human organism is out of the question. Occasionally Huxley be-

came so pessimistic that he would almost have welcomed "some kindly comet" to sweep the whole affair away. (pp. 19-20)

The detached Wellsian imagination, obsessed by the Huxleyan cosmic pessimism, led Wells in the 1890's to produce two categories of attack on human complacency. The first and larger group contains stories chiefly of pure menace, and excellent fiction they are indeed, being among the very best things of this sort ever written. The second category, closely related to the first, consists of works anti-utopian in their assault on optimism.

The germ of the stories of menace, and probably of the one romance of the same type, is contained in an article Wells published in the *Pall Mall Gazette,* September 25, 1894, and entitled **"The Extinction of Man,"** an article which relates these stories and the romance to Wells's interest in the future. Wells began **"The Extinction of Man"** by questioning man's complacent assumption of his continued existence on this planet in the light of the evidence from geology: "in no case does the record of the fossils show a really dominant species succeeded by its own descendants." It is the familiar lesson of geology; again and again forms of life have risen to dominance, only to vanish away and be replaced by other forms:

What has usually happened in the past appears to be the emergence of some type of animal hitherto rare and unimportant, and the extinction, not simply of the previously ruling species, but of most of the forms that are at all closely related to it. Sometimes, indeed, as in the case of the extinct giants of South America, they vanished without any considerable rivals, victims of pestilence, famine, or, it may be, of that cumulative inefficiency that comes of a too undisputed life.

And so Wells came to caution his readers against the "too acceptable view of man's certain tenure of the earth for the next few million years or so." As possible threats, he cited, among others, the evolution of the ant and the cephalopod, thus foreshadowing two of his stories, **"The Empire of the Ants"** and **"The Sea Raiders."** (pp. 21-2)

And so Wells wrote numerous stories of menace. **"The Empire of the Ants"** (1905) describes a race of intelligent ants in the upper region of the Amazon who are beginning a march on civilization—"new competitors for the sovereignty of the globe." **"The Sea Raiders"** (1896) purports to be a "true account" of the attack on the coast of Devon and Cornwall of giant man-eating octopuses. **"The Flowering of the Strange Orchid"** (1894) deals with a man-eating plant; **"In the Avu Observatory"** (1894) with a giant and hostile bat; **"The Valley of the Spiders"** (1903) with a deadly floating spider. But the best of the stories is **"The Star"**

(1897), which deals, in remarkably solid, concrete detail, with the catastrophic approach to the earth of a large body of matter from the depths of space beyond the solar system.

Disaster also comes from outer space in the one scientific romance of pure menace type that Wells wrote and which is closely related to **"The Star"** and **"The Sea Raiders"**—the enormously effective *The War of the Worlds*. . . . In plot and fictional technique it bears some resemblance to Defoe's *A Journal of the Plague Year:* both novels are offered as eyewitness accounts of a great disaster which befalls mankind and particularly the inhabitants of London. In each case the disaster had a special topical interest at the time of publication: an outbreak of the plague in 1720 in Marseilles set Londoners to recalling the horror of 1665, while in the 1890's popular interest in Mars as the abode of life was, because of Schiaparelli's earlier discovery of the "canals," so intense that it at times amounted to a mania. At the same time this interest combines with a fascination for stories of an invasion of England which began, as I. F. Clarke has shown in *Voices Prophesying War,* with Sir George Chesney's "Battle of Dorking" (1872). (pp. 22-3)

Much more important for our purposes than the story of menace is the second category of Wellsian attack on human complacency, in which Huxleyan cosmic pessimism generates images and ideas central to the twentieth-century anti-utopian tradition. The major works in this "cosmic pessimism" category are *The Time Machine, The Island of Dr. Moreau, When the Sleeper Wakes,* **"A Story of the Days To Come,"** and *The First Men in the Moon.* (pp. 24-5)

[*The Time Machine* is] the first of Wells's scientific romances and perhaps the most nearly faultless example of the kind of fiction with which we are concerned. Its vitality and literary power are enormous, its credibility almost perfect, and, inspired by Huxleyan cosmic pessimism, it is rich in significant meanings. It is worth discussing its technique, not only to show how this kind of fiction works, but also to explain why *The Time Machine* had such an enormous impact on the twentieth century anti-utopia.

"For the writer of fantastic stories to help the reader to play the game properly," Wells wrote, "he must help him in every possible unobtrusive way to *domesticate* the impossible hypothesis. He must trick him into an unwary concession to some plausible assumption and get on with his story while the illusion holds." This is exactly Wells's technique in *The Time Machine.*

And so the story begins in the solid, upper-middle-class atmosphere of the Time Traveler's home, as he is expounding to his guests after dinner the mysteries of the geometry of Four Dimensions:

"I do not mean to ask you to accept anything without reasonable ground for it. You will soon admit as much as I need from you. You know of course that a mathematical line, a line of thickness *nil,* has no real existence. They taught you that? Neither has a mathematical plane. These things are mere abstractions."

"That is all right," said the Psychologist.

"Nor, having only length, breadth, and thickness, can a cube have a real existence."

"There I object," said Filby. "Of course a solid body may exist. All real things—"

"So most people think. But wait a moment. Can an *instantaneous* cube exist?" . . .

Before we know what has happened, we are tricked into the concession that Time could be another, a Fourth Dimension, along which one might travel as one does the other three dimensions. All we need is a vehicle.

And so Wells invented the Time Machine, thereby becoming the father of a new genre, the modern story of time travel. The invention was a major leap of the imagination, and it grew not only out of contemporary interest in the geometry of four dimensions but also the great vogue at the time for tales of the future. Such stories existed, of course, at least as early as Mercier's *L'An 2440* (1772), but their wide popularity began only with Edward Bellamy's *Looking Backward* (1888). In the late 1880's and early 1890's, dozens of these stories were written, and at least two besides *Looking Backward* are significant as literature: W. H. Hudson's *A Crystal Age* (1888) and William Morris's *News from Nowhere* (1891). *The Time Machine* is a natural evolution from all these stories and an improvement on them, for in each the visitor arrives in the future by means of such clumsy devices as dream, hypnosis, accident, or trance. Wells's machine is considerably more suitable, given the sophisticated requirements for plausibility of a new scientific and mechanical age. It may possibly have been suggested to him by the space vehicle of the cosmic voyage, obviously a related genre. (pp. 25-7)

It is impossible, really, to do justice to the perfection of Wells's effort to ease the reader into a willing suspension of disbelief in [the] first two framing chapters. All one can do is list some of the elements: the common-sense character of the narrator; the solid atmosphere of his home; the characterization of the guests to give them sufficient—but not too much—individuality for the purposes of the story; the skillful use of incidental details to create the air of reality. This same perfection continues in the next section, the journey through time to the year 802,701, and, indeed, throughout the rest of the romance.

In the description of the journey through time, Wells's powers of concretization, apparent throughout the story, are at their highest. The journey begins, as do most journeys into space in fiction and reality, with a shock at departure: "I drew a breath, set my teeth, gripped the starting lever with both hands, and went off with a thud." . . . The sensations of time travel are those of motion through space, and at first the Time Traveler finds them distinctly unpleasant. He has a feeling of helpless headlong motion and the horrible anticipation of an imminent collision. Later, the unpleasant nature of time travel begins to wear off and the Traveler experiences the kind of exhilaration felt by many voyagers through space in fiction from Domingo Gonsales and Cyrano de Bergerac to Elwin Ransom. Finally he watches awestruck the accelerated sequence of celestial phenomena. He sees the moon spinning swiftly through her quarters from new to full, the alternation of day and night merging into one continuous grayness, the sky taking on a wonderful deepness of blue, and the sun, like a streak of fire, burning a brilliant arch in space. As his velocity increases at a tremendous rate, he becomes apprehensive and decides to stop, and in his panic slows the machine down too suddenly. Traveler and machine go toppling over into the world of 802,701. Thunder rumbles and hail hisses around him as he sits on the grass of what seems to be a little garden.

This world, as we will see later, is central to the meaning of *The Time Machine.* Suffice it now to say that it is a disillusionment to the Traveler. Instead of a world far advanced beyond ours, he finds that in 802,701 mankind has evolved into two degenerate species: above ground, the Eloi, delicate little creatures with the intellect of a five-year-old; and below ground, the pale, ape-like Morlocks, who leave their subterranean world only at night. It is the sunset of mankind.

But at first glance, the earth in 802,701 seems to be a garden of Eden. Everywhere are beautiful flowers and fruit, and no hostile insects or animals—nature is seemingly in perfect subjugation to man. The weather is mild and warm, apparently because the earth is now closer to a sun into which have fallen one or more of the inner planets. Gone are the smaller houses and cottages of our time; instead our descendants live in magnificent, ornate palace-like buildings "dotted about among the variegated greenery." These are the buildings of utopia and the first manifestation of Wells's familiar preoccupation with housing and the physical features of the future.

But a second look reveals that it is only a ruined splendor. All human artifacts are slowly crumbling. Some of the buildings are already gone: "a great heap of granite, bound together by masses of aluminium, a vast labyrinth of precipitous walls and crumbled heaps, amidst which were thick heaps of very beautiful pago-da-like plants." And even the many still-standing buildings, in which the surface people live, are decaying. . . . (pp. 27-9)

Even more of a ruined splendor are the people the Time Traveler finds living in this great garden—the Eloi. Fragile little creatures perhaps four feet tall, they pass their time "in playing gently, in bathing in the river, in making love in a half-playful fashion, in eating fruit and sleeping." Human vigor and energy have passed into languor and decay.

In time the Traveler learns the purpose of the mysterious wells and towers scattered across the country: these structures are part of the ventilation system for a subterranean world, in which live the other degenerate descendants of men, the Morlocks. They are strange little beings whose pallid bodies are "just the half-bleached colour of the worms and things one sees preserved in spirit in a zoological museum." They are chinless, and in their faces are set "great lidless, pinkish grey eyes." At night they leave their subterranean world to hunt down Eloi for food.

Slowly the Time Traveler pieces together the history of mankind's horrible degeneration, a degeneration which has occurred because mankind, as T. H. Huxley feared, was ultimately unable to control the cosmic or evolutionary process. It is Huxley's cosmic pessimism which gives meaning and permanence to this first anti-utopia of the modern mechanical and scientific age. For all its exuberance and vitality of imagination, *The Time Machine* is a bleak and sober vision of man's place in the universe. By the year 800,000, the world, at least above ground, had become intelligent and co-operative, truly a modern utopia. Nature had been subjugated and man had readjusted the balance of animal and vegetable life to suit his needs. Disease, hardship, and poverty were eliminated. With the attainment of security and freedom from danger, man's restless energy turned to art, and for a time a great culture flourished. But it was a utopian age which could never last because the upperworlders ignored another of Huxley's warnings [from his "Evolution and Ethics"]: "If we may permit ourselves a larger hope of abatement of the essential evil of the world . . . I deem it an essential condition of the realization of that hope that we cast aside the notion that escape from pain and sorrow is the proper object of life." And so came languor and decay. The struggle to conquer nature had developed human intelligence, strength, and courage. But when the battle had been won, there was no force to select the most fit. In the new state of balance and security, intellectual and physical power were out of place. The weak were as well equipped as the strong, in fact even better equipped, for the strong were fretted by an energy for which there was no outlet. And so the inhabitants of the utopia above ground evolved to feeble prettiness, a process which constitutes one of the major criticisms in the twentieth century of the idea of utopia. The perfection and ease of utopia, say many of its critics—like Forster in "The Machine Stops"—can only lead to degeneration and decay.

But this was only half the explanation of the world of 802,701. The development of the Morlocks had followed a somewhat different course, and here the story becomes social criticism and very much a product of the 1890's, the years of increasing Socialist protest. The Eloi and Morlocks grew apart, just as earlier in the nineteenth century the widening of the social difference between capitalist and laborer had become more pronounced. As technology and industrialization progressed, factories went underground and with them their workers, who in time became adapted to the subterranean life and no longer came out into the light of day. . . . ([The] beginning of this process in the twenty-second century is later portrayed by Wells in the complementary stories, *When the Sleeper Wakes* and **"A Story of the Days To Come."**) Above ground the Haves pursued pleasure, comfort, and beauty; below ground the Have-Nots became continually adapted to the conditions of their labor. While the upper-worlders drifted to physical and mental ineffectiveness, the lower-worlders drifted to mere mechanical industry. However, since machines, no matter how perfect, require some intelligence to maintain, the Morlocks managed to retain some of their original intellectual strength, and, when the process of feeding the underworld became disrupted, the cosmic process reasserted itself and the Morlocks emerged to eat the Eloi. The world of 802,701 presents Huxley's trajectory of evolution some distance past the highest point, but still far from the end.

Escaping from the Morlocks, the Time Traveler pushes the levers in the wrong direction and rushes off into the even more distant future. The hand marking a thousand years sweeps by like the second hand on a watch, and he sees the earth nearing the end of the falling portion of Huxley's trajectory of evolution, thus bringing us to the idea which haunted Wells, Huxley, and others at the end of the nineteenth century—the death of our world. (pp. 29-32)

It is hard to exaggerate the significance of *The Time Machine.* Although Bellamy's *Looking Backward,* as Chad Walsh has said, inspired a great number of dystopias like Konrad Wilbrandt's *Mr. East's Experiences in Mr. Bellamy's World* and Richard C. Michaelis's *Looking Forward,* which show the evils of a socialist future, their impact was slight since all were trivial as works of art. In the 1880's or 1890's the only vivid pictures of the future—besides Wells's—were utopias or utopian romances: *Looking Backward, News from Nowhere,* and *A Crystal Age. The Time Machine* was thus the first well-executed, imaginatively coherent picture of a future worse than the present, a picture at the same time gen-

erally anti-utopian in its tendencies. Indeed, in imaginative qualities it excels later anti-utopias, such as even *We* and *Brave New World,* being both more successful in domesticating the incredible and more poetic in its conception. Its coherence and power explain why it not only contributed numerous details and images to twentieth-century anti-utopias but made available to the literary consciousness a new form (science fiction) and suggested one use for this form (the attack on utopias). (pp. 33-4)

Mark R. Hillegas, in his *The Future as Nightmare: H. G. Wells and the Anti-Utopians,* Oxford University Press, 1967, 200 p.

FRANK McCONNELL
(essay date 1981)

[McConnell is an American literary and film critic. In the following excerpt, he examines some major influences on and tendencies within Wells's science fiction.]

H. G. Wells has been called the father, the one authentic genius, even the Shakespeare of science fiction. All these judgments can be called into question. But even today, when science fiction is attracting more first-rate writers than ever and is taken more seriously by "official" literary critics than ever, the burden of proof is still on the person who wants to question such judgments, not the one who affirms them. Wells's first novel, *The Time Machine* . . . , was an immediate success. Between 1895 and 1914 he produced, among many other works, a series of "scientific romances" that, by the outbreak of the First World War, had helped to make him one of the best-selling and most controversial writers of his time. And the influence of those novels and stories on what came to be called "science fiction" continues to be nothing less than gigantic.

If science fiction is, as some defenders argue, mainly important as technological prophecy, Wells's record is impressive. *The Time Machine* can be read, as we shall see, as a prophecy of the effects of rampant industrialization on that class conflict which was already, in the nineteenth century, a social powder keg. Disraeli had warned—and Marx had demonstrated—that the industrialized state was in danger of becoming two nations, the rich and the poor; but the real horror, Wells warns, is that they might become two races, mutually uncomprehending and murderously divided. In *The War of the Worlds* . . . he hinted at, and in later stories fully anticipated, the disastrous innovations the discovery of flight could bring to the business of warfare. In *When the Sleeper Wakes* . . . he predicted a future society in which devices very like video cassettes have replaced printed books, and an ignorant populace is force-fed censored news through things he calls "Babble Machines." In **"The Land Ironclads"** . . . he predicted the use of armored tanks in war (he later got involved in a long and futile lawsuit, claiming royalties for the "invention" of the tank). Long before "ecology" became a fashionable phrase and concern, Wells was using it as one of the common concepts of his utopias. And in *The World Set Free* . . . perhaps his most celebrated anticipation—he invented the phrase "atomic bomb," and detailed with some accuracy the apocalyptic power of chain reaction weapons or, in his phrase, "continuing explosives."

But there are other ideas of science fiction beyond the weatherman's standard of accurate forecasting. Some very good science-fiction writers never do manage a prophecy that later history ratifies. And the rest, Wells included, guess wrong at least as often as they guess right. We can say that science fiction matters not just because of the occasional random prediction of technological innovation, but because it seriously examines the implications of scientific and technological development *as a whole* for our lives, and our sense of the nature and goals of our lives. "The history of science," write Robert Scholes and Eric S. Rabkin in their book, *Science Fiction,* "is also the history of humanity's changing attitudes toward space and time. It is the history of our growing understanding of the universe and the position of our species in that universe." Science fiction, then, like science itself, is a facet of the history of the human spirit. It is an authentic fiction for our time, whose visionary tales are not so much visions of "things to come" as versions of things as they are *right now,* though seen against the immense backdrops of geological time and sidereal space (which are, after all, the true stage on which the human drama is played).

This is a more or less sociological definition of the genre, and under its terms too, Wells is not only primary but preeminent. *The Island of Doctor Moreau* . . . and *The Invisible Man* . . . are versions, respectively horrible and tragicomic, of the conflict between knowledge and goodness, what less perceptive minds than Wells's have cheapened into the "mad scientist" theme. With penetrating insight into the problems besetting technology not only in his own time but in ours, Wells asks: though we demonstrably can do almost anything we want to do, may we do anything we want or is there still, in some deep sense, such a thing as Forbidden Knowledge? This is, of course, the theme of Mary Shelley's *Frankenstein* (1818), which also has claims to being the "first" novel of science fiction. But Wells's treatment, though no subtler or "greater" than Mary Shelley's, takes on an added force by being embedded in the giant fabric of his lifelong discussion of human science, human morality, and their conflict.

Once again in *The War of the Worlds* and *The First Men in the Moon* . . . he imagined extraterrestrial aliens who are not just the picturesque bug-eyed bogeymen of later science fiction at its simplest, but projections of the possible deformity of the human species if present trends toward bloodless intellectualism, the fissure of heart and head, were to continue. And beginning with *The Food of the Gods* . . . and *A Modern Utopia* . . . , and continuing nearly to the end of his life, he gave us a series of novels of more and more homiletic, more and more strenuous and urgent social analysis and prophecy whose explicit aim was to change the course of history, bringing human science into congruity with human moral development and thereby saving the world from a second, total, perhaps final world war.

These later utopias are not, by any means, his best books. Most of them are long out of print, and they are not often discussed in histories of science fiction. But that may be a mistake. Flawed though they are, they are flawed honorably. Wells's passion for social reform could overweigh his instincts as a storyteller; his desire to convince the reader could get in the way of his ability to keep the reader reading. But if all these later books in part (and some of them throughout) are musclebound, it is because they are strong. And if we wish to regard science fiction seriously as a sociological form, we have to remember that Wells, more than any other writer in the genre, tried to harness the powers of narrative to the great tasks of social change and man's salvation. (pp. 3-6)

Through a combination of historical moment and personal strategy, [Wells] transformed the scientific and social controversy of his time into an extended fable of apocalypse and terror that is sometimes grim and sometimes ennobling in its vision of the human condition, but always compelling and crafted with immense skill. And it is in terms of this artistry that he looms largest over the later development of science fiction. (pp. 6-7)

Nevertheless, there are some preliminary qualifications to be made about Wells and science fiction. The first, to which I have already alluded, is that Wells didn't really *write* "science fiction." The term was invented by Hugo Gernsback, who founded *Amazing Stories* in 1926. By that time Wells's output of "scientific romances" had dwindled to an occasional heavily sociological utopian novel every few years. (Of course, this was "dwindling" only for a man like Wells, who between 1895 and 1946 wrote an average of three books a year.)

This qualification is a version, perhaps, of the old cliché that Plato was no Platonist, Marx no Marxist. But it makes a difference. Because the form had not been named yet, it was freer to associate itself with the great mainstream tradition of storytelling. After Gernsback named science fiction, making it both a suburb and a ghetto of fiction itself, it would be many years before a writer in the field would unblushingly admit a sense of his own continuity with the works of Lucan, Rabelais, Swift, and Voltaire. Wells could, and often did, avow this debt.

The second qualification is implicit in the first. Those works of Wells that exercise the greatest influence on later science fiction were all written during the first twenty years of his fifty-year career as a writer and make up only a small percentage of his total output. (p. 7)

Wells, then, was the heir to not only the Victorian apotheosis of the Will, but its Darwinian negation. In his brief encounter with formal education, he studied at the newly formed Normal School of Science (now the Royal College of Science) under Thomas Henry Huxley, Darwin's defender and popularizer. It was an experience he never forgot. Those doubts, despairs, and depressions that the official, liberal myth of Victorianism had managed to suppress were openly admitted, in the wake of science after Darwin, to be the central and inescapable condition of human life. Defeat was man's fate, and, if he was strong enough to face it, man's supreme test. So that if Wells was a true Victorian in his faith in the power of Will, he was also a true Edwardian

in his open doubt about the final usefulness of that faith when weighed against the inexorable processes of uncaring nature. The narrator of *The Time Machine* says of the Time Traveller that he "thought but cheerlessly of the Advancement of Mankind, and saw in the growing pile of civilisation only a foolish heaping that must inevitably fall back upon and destroy its makers in the end." There speaks the evolutionary theorist, the connoisseur of futility. But, the narrator himself continues, "If that is so, it remains for us to live as though it were not so." And there speaks the romantic, the exponent of Will, the man who never stopped hoping that there might after all be some final appeal against entropy, against fate, against the Second Law of Thermodynamics.

Those two voices continue their debate in Wells's work to the very end of his life, and their uncertain contest is one of the great dramas of his writing. (pp. 10-11)

Think . . . of his projected epitaph; "God damn you all: I told you so." It is not just an epitaph, it is an open letter to the world. And what, after all, *did* he tell us? Well, just this: that the major disease of modern man is that his scientific and technological expertise has outstripped his moral and emotional development; that

Charles Laughton as Moreau in *Island of Lost Souls,* a 1932 film adaptation of Wells's *The Island of Dr. Moreau.*

the human race, thanks to its inherited prejudices and superstitions and its innate pigheadedness, is an endangered species; and that mankind must learn—*soon*—to establish a state of worldwide cooperation by burying its old hatreds and its ancient selfishness, or face extinction.

Today, these assertions are not shocking. They might appear in a presidential campaign speech or an address to the United Nations. (They would probably not be taken seriously, of course, but they have entered the realm of consoling pieties, buzzwords that do not raise eyebrows.) And even when Wells first uttered them, they were not being uttered for the first time. Wells was a brilliant man, but he was not an original thinker. His gift was for *imagining,* for realizing firmly, almost visually, the implications of his age's philosophy and science and for communicating those implications to his readers with the urgency of myth. The same may be said of Shakespeare.

If there was something permanently Victorian in Wells's optimism and permanently Edwardian in his qualifications of that optimism, there is nevertheless something distinctively modern about the whole man. (pp. 11-12)

Wells's major science fiction appeared between 1895 and the outbreak of World War I in 1914. It is . . . the Wells of these two decades . . . who seems, as years go by, to have the surest claim to permanence. But if the Wells of these years matters to us as much as he does, if he seems more and more one of us, it is because at the beginning of his career, he was so brilliantly and completely one of *them*—"they" being our ideological and spiritual ancestors around the turn of the century.

In the utopian novels he wrote after this period, he liked to refer to the origins of the modern era as the "Age of Confusion" (in *Men Like Gods*) or the "Age of Frustration" (in *The Shape of Things To Come*). And confusing, frustrating, upsetting the intellectual life of the years 1895-1914 certainly was. In an important study of *The Early H. G. Wells,* Bernard Bergonzi indicates the relationship between the scientific romances and that set of attitudes, emotions, and opinions tagged, by the people who held them, *fin de siècle.* (p. 32)

Wells caught this tone in his first scientific romances. *The Time Machine, When the Sleeper Wakes,* and *The First Men in the Moon* show us, through the eyes of eccentric, nervous, *fin de siècle* men, future human civilizations where technology has obliterated all struggle (for the rich at least), and yet where the beneficiaries of that gift have declined below the horizon of the really human. As Graham, the "sleeper" of *When the Sleeper Wakes,* dies he pronounces a single grim judgment on the men of the future struggling for their freedom: "Weak men." *The Island of Doctor Moreau, The*

Invisible Man, and *The War of the Worlds* show us not a future de-evolving toward weakness and mass suicide, but rather the explosion of the technological future *into* the present. The eruption of science's cold equations and bitter wisdom into the world of the everyday corrodes the comfortingly "normal" through the sheer power of its murderous efficiency. "Cities, nations, civilisations, progress—it's all over," shrieks the artilleryman to the narrator of *The War of the Worlds* as the Martians rampage toward London. "That game's up. We're beat."

In *The Food of the Gods, In the Days of the Comet,* and *The World Set Free,* Wells was to give these elementary situations a more positive, hopeful turn. And later still he was to make situations like these the vehicles for a full-scale attempt to save mankind from itself. But it is nevertheless true that his science fiction, always, remained an elaboration of one of these two central themes: a man of the present is cast or voyages into a possible future organization of mankind, or the future of mankind somehow invades or possesses—and tests—the resilience and vitality of men of the present. It is a sign of Wells's genius that these two archetypal situations are also, with very few exceptions, the two elementary forms of all science fiction written after him. It is also a sign of his genius that these archetypes are ones he inherited, and creatively transformed, from the anxious, self-doubting, apocalyptic *fin de siècle* world of his youth.

But Bergonzi's discussion of this end-of-the-century, end-of-the-world sensibility explains only part of the early Wells's science fiction. Queen Victoria died in 1901—she could hardly have chosen a more symbolic date—and was succeeded by her portly, self-indulgent, and (at least at first) liberal son, Edward VII. Wells himself described the transition from the late Victorian to the Edwardian spirit: "Queen Victoria was like a great paper-weight that for half a century sat upon men's minds, and when she was removed their ideas began to blow about all over the place haphazardly." Of course, there had been forward-looking, enthusiastic architects of social change before 1900, and there remained many celebrants of degeneration and decay after that date. But the total effect of the transition was largely of the sort Wells describes. William Bellamy, an important critic of Edwardian fiction, sees the transition as one from a culture-bound to a culture-free or "post-cultural" mental environment. While late Victorians had lived with the claustrophobic sense of a cultural inheritance too rich and too consolidated to allow for personal freedom, Edwardians—having survived the reign of the old Queen and lived past the magic year 1900—enjoyed a sense of new beginnings and of individual self-realization that often implied a possibility of personal fulfillment outside the conventional sanctions of society.

There is much justice in this description of the Edwardian mood, particularly since it allows us to see the close connection between the passions, enthusiasms, and warring ideologies of the Edwardian period and later twentieth-century movements of the same "post-cultural" sort. As Samuel Hynes observes in *The Edwardian Turn of Mind*, "virtually everything that is thought of as characteristically modern already existed in England by 1914: aircraft, radiotelegraphy, psychoanalysis, Post-Impressionism, motion picture palaces. . . . " The late Victorians, we can say, lived through and acted out all the modes of anxiety and despair that were to characterize the coming century; and the Edwardians—who were by and large the same people—felt and articulated that century's greatest expectations.

Here, too, Wells managed to be quintessentially a man of his time. . . . [His] personal revolution, his lifelong sexual adventurism, became full-fledged in the years just after the turn of the century. And parallel to this private transformation is a transformation in the tone of his speculative fiction. He begins to think not just in terms of the disasters awaiting technological man in his quest for survival, but of the chances available to him for transcendence, for final victory over the stern dictates of history and the struggle for existence. It is no accident then, following this argument, that to this period also belong the best of Wells's "realistic" novels: *Kipps* in 1905, *Tono-Bungay* and *Ann Veronica* in 1909, and *The History of Mr. Polly* in 1910. In these books he takes the common stuff of existence in an industrial society as his theme, without the apocalyptic trappings of voyages through time or invasions from beyond the atmosphere, and manages to demonstrate convincingly that the apocalyptic spirit, regardless of the trappings, is still there—that the life of the middle class in England is *already,* as he writes, moving toward a future which must be either radically liberating or radically destructive for the individual psyche.

His "realistic" novels of this period, in other words, should be read along with his more explicitly scientific romances, since they explore many of the same themes with only a slight change of tone. Stylistically, Wells was a shapeshifter. He seldom wrote the same sort of book twice, and if he did, the second one was usually a parody or inversion of the first. But ideologically, he was a remarkably consistent man. From his first books to his last, in despair or in optimism, his theme was obsessively that of middle-class man's chances for survival in a world which through the accumulated weight of technology and the inexorable pressures of evolutionary history threatens his life. If there is a single question to which all Wells's books are addressed, it might be phrased as this one: How shall Man live through his own coming of age? (pp. 33-5)

Wells's fiction, from its beginning, was also intimately related to the currents of social theory and reform which characterized the waning years of the century. (p. 43)

It has been a cliché for some time now to say that the nineteenth century "discovered" history as a science. And like many clichés, this one is fundamentally true. Historians of the late eighteenth and early nineteenth century, partly because of the upheavals in European society and culture taking place around them, began to regard the study of history as more than simply the preservation of the past or even the understanding of the present through the past. History, it came to be believed, might be approached with the same analytical rigor and, perhaps, predictive efficiency that had been so brilliantly employed in the physical sciences since Sir Isaac Newton. (p. 44)

[Wells] was by both class and temperament a revolutionary soul. He was also a true nineteenth-century ideologue, at least to the extent of insisting on "finished ideas" as the only possible basis for social action or social planning. But he was also—as Lenin is reported to have called him—a petty bourgeois. He mistrusted the brute force and inarticulate aspirations of the laboring class—that "mass man" whose existence Marx had discovered and whose destiny he had hymned as world dominion. He mistrusted the figure of the bombtoting, metaphysically inclined terrorist (or "anarchist" or "nihilist," to use the age's catchphrases), the man willing to commit the unspeakable for the sake of a theory. And, perhaps most of all, he mistrusted theory itself. A voracious assimilator of systems and abstractions, he was nevertheless skeptical of any system whose complexity appeared to overweigh its application to the observable and observed facts of the life around us. This pragmatism, or empiricism, has been often described as a particularly "English" as opposed to Continental trait of mind; or it may also be explained as the special genius for observation of the novelist, as opposed to the social scientist or philosopher. At any rate, it is one of the hallmarks of Wells's distinctive vision of social possibilities, and of the chance for utopia. From the beginning, he believed in the necessity and the reality of social change, or revolution. But to the end, he wanted his revolution to be both rational and sensible, both total and civilized.

It can be argued that Wells expressed his fears of revolutionaries most fully in his fiction of the 1890s, and his hopes for revolution most fully in his fiction of the Edwardian years and afterward. Just as the Eloi of *The Time Machine* are partly a vision of the aesthetes and decadents of the literary and artistic world, the cannibalistic Morlocks who prey upon the Eloi are a much more explicit projection of the proletariat, the "mass man" whose emergence Wells feared. His dislike and suspicion of the dedicated "scientific" anarchist are the basis of one of his early short stories, **"The Stolen Bacillus."** . . . And his suspicion of abstraction, of theory without humanity, may fairly be said to run through all his early fiction. Griffin, the antihero of *The Invisible Man,* and Dr. Moreau of *The Island of Doctor Moreau* are both ferociously intelligent men—the former a physicist, the latter a biologist—who erect upon their scientific discoveries plans for a new world empire, a new order of things, only to find their structures collapse on them in a suicidal rubble. In *The War of the Worlds* and *The First Men in the Moon* Wells shows us alternate societies—the octopuslike Martians and the insectlike Selenites—that have been built upon an absolutely efficient, rational collectivism, and which are equally anti-human (there is an important anticipation of both these books in his 1896 story, **"In the Abyss"**).

It is **"The Stolen Bacillus,"** though, that best catches his attitude toward social revolution. This very short story tells how a pale-faced anarchist steals a phial containing what he thinks is a deadly concentration of cholera bacteria. He intends to empty it into the London water system. But the phial breaks in the cab in which he is making his escape; undaunted, the anarchist greedily swallows the few drops of liquid in the bottom of the phial and charges off amidst the busy London crowds, himself now a living instrument of death and contagion, shouting "Vive l'Anarchie!" Only then do we learn that the phial did not really contain cholera bacteria, but rather a dose of a new compound whose only effect is to turn its recipient bright blue.

What began as a tale of terror ends as a joke: but a joke with a serious point. Men and women really did dread anarchy, and particularly the threat presented by the figure of the anarchist, that outwardly normal, rational man who might, unsuspected, be harboring thoughts and plans of the most unspeakable violence and hatred. If revolution, even in its maddest aspects, could now be "rational"—i.e., philosophically planned and supported—then it was, to all intents and purposes, invisible. Wells's invention of the Invisible Man had been an early, very resonant expression of this fear: the invisible minister of apocalypse, the hyperintelligent terrorist, part of whose terror is that you can't see him. Joseph Conrad, in his novel of 1907, *The Secret Agent,* and G. K. Chesterton in his novel of 1908, *The Man Who Was Thursday,* would both treat the theme of anarchy in ways perhaps suggested by *The Invisible Man:* in terms, that is, of its fundamentally frightening aspects of normality, its terrible quality of being unrecognizable until it is too late.

"The Stolen Bacillus" is a reassuring version of the same situation. The anarchist, for all his dedication and care, has made a stupid blunder; a blunder, moreover, that henceforth will render him immediately, unequivocally recognizable. He will be bright blue, an all too visible man.

We can see the difference between *The Invisible Man* and **"The Stolen Bacillus"** as part of the difference between the despairing and the optimistic halves of Wells's sensibility. But **"The Stolen Bacillus"** is also reassuring because it insists that anarchists and their like are not to be feared: their own excessive hatreds will lead them into comically excessive postures of impotent violence. But, the story insists, they will be led into these absurdities because of the workings of a slower, surer, and ultimately more total revolution, the revolution of scientific thought, which is changing the world daily by making the animosities and class hatreds of the past irrelevant. The scientist who prepares the "blue" solution does not know he is thwarting anarchy. But he is, and the single-minded blindness of his research is revealed to be also the wisdom of history (Hegelian theme), its comic judgment upon the impulse to mass murder.

Wells, then, heir to a century of metaphysical and social revolutionaries, was impelled to a version of revolution much quieter, much more explicitly middle class, than many which were abroad in his time. This can be thought of as a very *English* taste in revolution, though Wells was tumultuous enough in his personal life and far-ranging enough in his social vision to alienate or scandalize the more conservative of his revolutionary English friends. (pp. 47-9)

A number of his early critics were disturbed by the frequency and level of violence in Wells's scientific romances, and the incidence of violence has continued to be an easy cliché for critics discussing his work. And it is true that, especially from *The War of the Worlds* through the utopian visions of *The War in the Air, The World Set Free, Men Like Gods,* and *The Shape of Things To Come,* he imagined a period of chaos and apocalyptic warfare as the inevitable prelude to the establishment of a just state. Indeed, there was something in Wells that took a real delight in scenes of Old Testament-scale destruction and pillage. He wrote to a friend during the composition of *The War of the Worlds,* "I'm doing the dearest little serial for Pearson's new magazine, in which I completely wreck and sack Woking—killing my neighbours in painful and eccentric ways—then proceed via Kingston and Richmond to London, which I sack, selecting South Kensington for feats of peculiar atrocity." It is a lighthearted summary of the book's plot but also an accurate one, and the "feats of peculiar atrocity" Wells enjoyed imagining—or symbolically doing, as the letter makes plain—would characterize his fiction for the rest of his life. (p. 51)

It is important to understand the special quality of violence in Wells's prophecies. In book after book he describes a future that lurches toward a Golden Age across a no man's land of war, pestilence, and reversion to bestiality. But he insists that the ordeal by violence, though highly likely, is not necessary. Again and again in his utopias, there occur observations to the effect that if men had only understood themselves better, had only formed clear and useful concepts of their place in the universe, the Golden Age might have been reached without such an appalling waste of life. "If we had only *seen*": that is the sentiment whose melancholy harmony runs through all his future histories, and it is the central connection between his science fiction and his other writing, where he tried to *make* people see how the kingdom of man could be established without the spilling of blood. For all the violence of his imagination Wells differed from most social visionaries, from the author of the Book of Revelations down to and including Marx, in that he did not believe, or would not let himself believe, that the Golden Age had to be preceded by a Last War. But he feared it would be.

To comprehend the full complexity of his attitude, we must examine a third aspect of Wells's intellectual background, perhaps the most important one. As an heir to the problems and perils of the aesthetic tradition, and to the expectations and fears of nineteenth-century socialism, he would doubtless have written brilliant and successful books. But it is impossible to imagine the Wells we know without Science (the capital "S" put there by Wells's attitude toward it), and particularly without the awesome edifice of Darwinian evolutionary theory. (pp. 52-3)

From *The Time Machine* on, it was generally recognized that no writer had so completely or so perceptively taken Darwin to heart. Wells may not have been the first man to acknowledge the importance of Darwinian theory for the future of civilization and the business of fiction, but he was certainly the first to acknowledge and assimilate that theory, in all its corrosive effect upon ideas of what fiction was for and about. (p. 54)

Darwin's great defender T. H. Huxley—Wells's tutor in his first year at the Normal School of Science—examined the problem of the soul of man under evolutionary principles more explicitly. In 1893 Huxley delivered one of his most famous and most influential lectures, "Evolution and Ethics." It is probably the fullest statement of Darwinian principles as they affect moral and political concerns, and it is a very important anticipation of Wells's own thought on these matters—indeed, it is probably one of the chief influences. (p. 60)

Man's proper role, said Huxley, is not to imitate but to resist the cosmic process, to oppose, however unavailingly, the moral force of his tiny microcosm to the cruel exigencies of the cosmos at large. To say this is to argue that, in a universe governed by the Second Law of Thermodynamics, consciousness is the only power that resists the tendency of all things to spin their way down to the level of least energy. It is also to argue that the human enterprise—culture, art, intelligence—is both totally "artificial" and, in being totally artificial,

totally "natural." This is the crucial paradox on which Wells's science fiction—and, indeed, his lifework—is based. . . . (p. 63)

Frank McConnell, in his *The Science Fiction of H. G. Wells,* Oxford University Press, 1981, 235 p.]

ROBERT CROSSLEY
(essay date 1986)

[In the following excerpt from his critical biography of Wells, Crossley explicates Wells's short fiction, concluding that Wells's canon is "a testament to both the excellence and the pertinence of science fiction as a literary form."]

In his *Experiment in Autobiography,* Wells deprecates his "single sitting stories" as work "ground out" to subsidize his early career and, in their later reincarnations in anthologies, as unlooked-for insurance against his declining years. In fact, the short fiction includes many sophisticated and powerful tales and two imperfect though fascinating novellas. Apart from its usefulness in turning a quick profit, the short story form furnished Wells a playground of the mind, a small, enclosed space in which he could try out issues and techniques that might be more fully employed in the longer scientific romances. The title of his first volume of stories, *The Stolen Bacillus and Other Incidents,* accurately names the priority of most of the tales; they are basically reports of exhilarating or disturbing incidents, natural or preternatural, fantastic or technological shocks to the accepted norms and givens of daily life. But, as in the longer fictions, a Wellsian incident is seldom treated merely incidentally but as an occasion for speculation and critical inquiry.

Perhaps the kind of speculative story most often associated with Wells is the predictive tale like **"The Argonauts of the Air"** (1895), a forecast of the invention of flying machines—a theme whose implications never ceased to intrigue Wells. . . . Wells himself took a grim satisfaction in his prediction of tank warfare, a dozen years before its actual occurrence during the first World War, in **"The Land Ironclads"** (1903). Generally, though, despite their interest as illustrations of Wells's technological imagination, the predictive stories are not among his most accomplished fictions. The best of them may be **"Filmer"** (1901), the biography of the putative inventor of the first workable heavier-than-air flying machine. It focuses not on the fact of mechanical innovation but on its psychological implications for the inventor, who commits suicide on his day of glory. As a tale that speculates about "that recurring wonder of the littleness of the scientific man in the face of the greatness of his science," **"Filmer"** belongs in the company of those Wellsian fictions that ponder the insecurity of human intelligence and the tentativeness of civilization.

In one of his finest stories, **"The Star"** (1897), Wells takes the issue of the vulnerability of human civilization to an apocalyptic conclusion. In this panorama of disaster and panic occasioned by the approach of a huge comet to the earth, millions die, the climate grows hot, the planet's surface is remade by earthquakes and tidal waves, the lunar cycle is lengthened to eighty days, and the remnant of the human population migrates to the cool poles. The earth is barely rescued from annihilation by the interposition of the moon between the earth and the onrushing comet. The human species survives, but the tale offers neither reassurance nor the satisfaction of a minimally happy ending. The final paragraph takes us to Mars where astronomers—relatives, presumably, of the unsuccessful adventurers in *The War of the Worlds*—are observing through telescopes the spectacle of the collision of the comet and the moon and are preparing scientific papers on what they take to be the minor damage done to the earth. Wells's narrator then neatly upends homocentrist pretensions: "Which only shows how small the vastest human catastrophes may seem, at a distance of a few million miles."

Wells's perspectives on the contingency of civilization are not always extraterrestrial. **"In the Abyss"** (1896), a description of a primitive civilization at the bottom of the sea, is challenging and frightening in its suggestion that even on our own planet we may not be alone. Even a lightweight tale like **"The Stolen Bacillus"** (1894), in spite of its snickering treatment of both biological warfare and the tactics of modern terrorism, demonstrates the perverse human capacity to destroy its own culture. **"The Empire of the Ants"** (1905), a story with ideological links to *The First Men in the Moon,* ends with a vision of the gradual recolonizing of the earth by a remarkably clever and swiftly breeding strain of ants moving steadily through the Brazilian interior: "By 1920 they will be halfway down the Amazon. I fix 1950 or '60 at the latest for the discovery of Europe." Because we know what ensued from the "discovery" of the Americas by European conquistadors, the closing sentence is ominous. It puts human culture in its place—and that place is not at the center of creation.

Wells inquires more extensively and mythically into the nature of civilization in a pair of novellas published in 1897. **"A Story of the Stone Age"** and **"A Story of the Days to Come"** are picaresque fictions, anthologies of episodes from the lives of a paleolithic man and woman and of a couple from twenty-second-century London. The novellas are symmetrical in de-

sign and ideologically complementary: in each the protagonists are malcontents, exiled from the dominant culture, whether tribal or industrial; each is a story of fitness and survival; each portrays the hopeful genesis of a new stage in civilization that will replace and transcend a dying culture. Both stories depict individuals tensed against the societies that produced them and both offer a disquieting vision of the price in blood, anguish, and brutalizing labor that is paid for the achievements and adornments of civilization.

In the closing pages of **"Days to Come,"** Wells explicitly connects the story of Ugh-lomi and Eudena, exiles from the tribe of Uya, with the story of Denton and Elizabeth, economic and social rebels in futuristic London; the four misfits all occupy the same physical space, and Denton broods on the future, "trying in obedience to his instinct to find his place and proportion in the scheme" of human and cosmic history, while standing in the very spot that once was "the squatting-place of the children of Uya." To be civilized in the paleolithic age is nearly to die in the efforts to secure food, to tame a horse, to kill a grizzly bear; to be civilized in the future metropolis is to be born wealthy enough to live in elegant and extravagant indolence while others, unlucky enough to be born without money or to lose their money, labor at the production of luxuries they cannot enjoy. In the Stone Age, the price of civilization, though high in bodily harm, seems justified by the aspirations; in the days to come the price—psychological, spiritual, and physical—seems disproportionate to the purchase.

But Wells's point is not to suggest a mere linear devolution from stone-age vigor to post-modern decadence. The parallel design of the novellas emphasizes the *persistence* of certain human behaviors and cultural patterns. Human history is a story of continuities and recrudescences. Ugh-lomi establishes his independence by beating up his rival, Uya; Denton, thrust from a secure middle-class life into menial work in the Labour Company, quickly learns that in the twenty-second century "the fist ruled . . . even as it was in the beginning." Futuristic man discovers how much he remains stone-age man: "After all we are just poor animals, rising out of the brute." The poignancy of the mock-fairy-tale ending of **"The Stone Age"** lies in its placement of the provisional success of individual, heroic struggle within a larger, impersonal, Darwinian pattern of struggle: "Thereafter for many moons Ugh-lomi was master and had his will in peace. And on the fulness of time he was killed and eaten even as Uya had been slain." The same bitter contrast between individual suffering and social progress emerges when the future hero and heroine reflect on the misery of life in the Labour Company. Denton: "It will pass." Elizabeth: "We shall pass first."

Wells revisited his twenty-second century twice

in *When the Sleeper Wakes* and in **"A Dream of Armageddon"** (1901). The two novellas and the two later works represent a diffuse effort by Wells to work out a comprehensive explanation of human history, a myth which might explain why the distance between stone-age and future man is so slight and why civilization remains both the elusive goal and the nemesis of human activity. As in *The Time Machine,* the cosmos is indifferent to human effort, to the small risings and fallings and recoveries of the species. As Eudena listens rapt to Ugh-lomi narrate his gory murder of Uya, she is observed by silent, stellar witnesses—which also observe Denton and Elizabeth 50,000 fictional years later—which also observe the readers reading those fictions in "real" time. In their constancy and stability, those witnesses mock the splendor of Ugh-lomi and Eudena's small achievements and of ours: "It was a splendid time, and the stars that look down on us looked down on her, our ancestor—who has been dead now these fifty thousand years."

Both novellas suffer from failures in conception and execution. The language of **"The Stone Age"** is embarrassingly clumsy and stilted at times, while the plot of **"Days to Come"** dishonestly resolves Denton and Elizabeth's fall from social favor. Still, these short works are representative of Wells's ambivalence towards civilization in the great decade bounded by *The Time Machine* (1895) and *A Modern Utopia* (1905). **"A Story of the Days to Come"** is the richer of the two, its world exercised a greater hold on Wells's imagination, and along with *When the Sleeper Wakes* it has influenced the history of the modern urban dystopia. But in its awkward effort to create an anthropologically authentic portrait of prehistoric humanity, **"A Story of the Stone Age"** is one of Wells's most daring experiments and his most interesting failure. Despite their deficiencies, the two novellas document the Wellsian notions that human history is but a small part of planetary history and that the story of civilization is itself a short story.

Wells is renowned for perfecting a pseudo-documentary technique in his speculative fictions—what the narrator of the little-known romance *The Sea Lady* calls "the true affidavit style." But the mythic novellas are reminders of his imaginative versatility and the breadth of his range. **"The Stolen Body"** (1898), one of his several exercises in the tale of the preternatural, displays Wells at the height of his powers. A story of body snatchers from a parallel world who are loosed on the primary world by scientific dilettantes toying with mental telepathy, it provokes typical Wellsian questions: What are the consequences of aimless experimentation? In what respects is curiosity contaminated by failures of intelligence or foresight or moral sensibility? Are there limits beyond which human beings trespass only at the peril of life and sanity? Similar ques-

tions underlie the preternatural phenomena in stories like **"The Flowering of the Strange Orchid"** (1894), **"The Crystal Egg"** (1897), and **"The Door in the Wall"** (1906), the last of which is probably closer in spirit than anything Wells wrote to the luminous mysticism of George Macdonald's "The Golden Key" (1867) and *Lilith* (1895).

At the other end of Wells's spectrum are the comic stories concerning human manipulation of mysterious events or technological inventions for mundane ends. That group of tales includes **"The Purple Pileus"** (1896), **"The Man Who Could Work Miracles"** (1898), and **"The Truth About Pyecraft"** (1903). One of the funniest stories in this group, **"The New Accelerator"** (1901), is a prose cartoon about an unscrupulous professor who manufactures a kind of super-amphetamine that speeds up physical movement. Professor Gibberne combines the technical expertise of Cavor with the business sense of Bedford, and the gullible narrator is so impressed by the idea of a miracle drug that he is swept up unquestioningly into the "trip" Gibberne arranges for him. The drug allows the user to make mischief with impunity because he moves so quickly that his victims can't see him and, as he watches the rest of the world go by in slow motion, people appear as mechanisms and caricatures. The psychedelic vision afforded by the drug is inevitably inhumane. Promenaders look like dummies; a wink or a gesture becomes a grotesque thing; a suitor's innocent smile slows to a leer. For all its madcap charm, **"The New Accelerator"** is as pointed as any of Wells's soberer speculations. The professor and narrator plan to push the sale of the new drug as fast as possible despite any ethical reservations they might have about its use. The only problems they consider themselves competent to address are technical and marketing ones:

> Like all potent preparations it will be liable to abuse. We have, however, discussed this aspect of the question very thoroughly, and we have decided that this is purely a matter of medical jurisprudence and altogether outside our province. We shall manufacture and sell the Accelerator, and, as for the consequences—we shall see.

Several of the best stories are visionary in theme and method. In these tales the protagonists acquire, usually accidentally or involuntarily, some special angle or instrument of vision that enables them to see familiar reality freshly and unfamiliar reality with both wonder and terror. Often these tales are narrated not by the protagonist but by a skeptical rationalist, an outsider describing and assessing mysterious events to which he has been a (generally unwilling) witness. The narrator characteristically tells his story in a state of shell-shock, his comfortable and fundamental presuppositions about how reality works no longer secure.

In two of the visionary tales, **"The Remarkable Case of Davidson's Eyes"** (1895) and **"The Plattner Story"** (1896), the transformations of perception occur in laboratories, and the locale dramatizes the upsetting of scientific certitudes and mental habits by a sudden eruption of visionary experience. In Davidson's case a thunderstorm triggers a displacement of vision; while his body and other sensory experience remain rooted in England, visually he exists on a bleak Antarctic island. In **"The Plattner Story"** a green powder explodes in a school chemistry lab and causes the teacher to disappear for nine days. When Plattner abruptly returns as a literal nine-days' wonder, he tells of a numinous other world lit by a green sun, a limbo inhabited by souls who keep watch over the living in our world. Scientists eager to dismiss Plattner's story as hallucination are stymied by one incontrovertible fact: all his body organs and features have shifted position so that his anatomical structure is a mirror reversal of what it was before he disappeared. The investigators are mortified and disgruntled; although publicly skeptical about his claims, they are in fact embarrassed by the body that exists as a living refutation of scientific assurance and rational sufficiency.

Variants on the visionary mode can be found in **"Under the Knife"** (1896) in which the narrator, on a hospital operating table, inhales chloroform and goes on a mental journey whose satirical and spiritual texture recalls the conventions of medieval dream-visions. The narrator's dream of himself in the company of a host of "naked intelligences" moving through the cosmos may have given Olaf Stapledon the idea for the pilgrimage of disembodied minds in *Star Maker* (1937). In **"The Crystal Egg,"** another of Wells's Martian satires, a strange crystal allows an unhappy shopkeeper to escape the demands of his domestic life by providing a magic—or electronic—window on the arcadian world of Mars. (When the shopkeeper is startled by an immense pair of eyes peering at him from the other side of the crystal, the reader may be reminded of J. R. R. Tolkien's *palantir* in *The Lord of the Rings* in which the eye of Sauron appears to those seeking a glimpse of the land of Mordor.) Eventually the shopkeeper, a prototype of the television addict, abandons his work so that "he might comfort himself with what was fast becoming the most real thing in his existence." He is later found dead, clutching the crystal. An often anthologized visionary tale, **"The Country of the Blind"** (1904), is a parable about an El Dorado-like region in the Andes inhabited by blind people and accidentally discovered by a sighted man. While coldly refuting the proverb about the one-eyed man being king among the blind, the tale asserts the necessity of spiritual vision; blindness is treated not as a clinical phenomenon but as a metaphor for atrophied imagination and rigid dogmatism. (pp. 58-63)

The distinctively Wellsian quality of Wells's fantastic fiction may be studied in the two final stories to be considered here, both of which are fantastic parables rather than Tolkienian subcreations. In **"The Story of the Late Mr. Elvesham"** (1896), an old philosopher clings to life by spiking a liqueur with a magic powder which causes him to exchange bodies with the young materialist Mr. Eden. The premise is unblinkingly fantastic, but the heart of the story is the brilliant rendering of the duality of body and personality in the transformed victim. The account of Eden's gradual realization that he has awakened trapped inside the body of Elvesham, that he has in the space of a single night become wrinkled, toothless, thin-voiced, cold-footed, sniffling, bleary-eyed, bony-fingered, loose-skinned, wracked with cough, persistently and disablingly weary and slow while retaining all the desires and sensibilities and the lively consciousness of youth is one of the triumphs of Wells's imagination, the equal of some of the other great metamorphoses in the longer romances. Narrated by Eden "under restraint" in an effort to prove he is not crazy, the tale is closer than any of Wells's to Poe's monologues by demented narrators ("The Black Cat," "Berenice," "The Tell-Tale Heart"). But it is also a typical Wellsian assault on the modern confidence in the explicability of all phenomena and a portrait of a man imprisoned inside a miracle no one can credit. As Eden despairingly comes to see, the explanation of last resort—the explanation modern people apply to make otherwise intractable events tractable—is psychiatric. Unable to persuade anyone of his true identity, he is left with the choice of suicide or the asylum.

"The Man Who Could Work Miracles: A Pantoum in Prose" bypasses the horror of **"Elvesham"** and combines fantasy with whimsy in the adventures of the garrulous rationalist and materialist, Mr. Fotheringay, who finds himself in astonished possession of miraculous powers of mind over matter. The story follows the brief career of a man of slender intellect gifted with absolute power. Much of that career is devoted to puckish mischief-making, as when Fotheringay irritably tells a constable to go to Hades and immediately finds himself alone. But when he tries to alter nature, his power, neither harnessed by a modest sense of human limits nor wielded by a vigilant presence of mind, becomes cataclysmic. Under the influence of the revivalist Rev. Mr. Maydig, he attempts to duplicate Joshua's feat of making the sun stand still. Phrasing the command in colloquial English and with accurate scientific awareness of which heavenly body is moving, Fotheringay addresses the earth: "Jest stop rotating, will you?" But when the natural rhythms of the planet are interrupted, every person and thing on earth, in obedience to the laws of inertia, is whirled forward into annihilation. In the midst of chaos casually wrought,

Fotheringay conceives "a great disgust of miracles" and ends his career with two simultaneous and final wishes: to lose his thaumaturgical powers and to have everything revert to the way it was just before he discovered these powers. Thus the jinni is rebottled, the damage undone, and the story returned full circle (following the form of the "pantoum" of its subtitle) to its opening conversation. As a work of fantasy, this makes a thoroughly absorbing and satisfying retelling of the classic fairy tale of miraculous power, the story of Aladdin from the *Arabian Nights*. And (how Wells would have appreciated this unintended application of his tale!) later readers can hardly help but find in **"The Man Who Could Work Miracles"** a cautionary fable for the Nuclear Age.

While some of Wells's short fiction was written with the left hand while he worked on the longer romances, the two novellas and a dozen or more short stories belong to his major work. Readers have sometimes overlooked the stories because of the stature of the science-fiction novels and have assumed that the short fiction is inferior. But even many of the flawed tales help reveal the process of Wells's imagination. **"The Sea Raiders"** (1896), one of his lesser efforts, describes in a crisp you-are-there style the invasion of the English coast by deep-sea monsters; in both substance and method it is a dry run for *The War of the Worlds*. The failure of Fotheringay in handling absolute power is presented with the same mixture of fantasy and farce Wells perfected in the first half of *The Invisible Man*. He published **"The New Accelerator"** and *The First Men in the Moon* in the same year and they share issues, character types, and techniques; notably, the story anticipates the visual effects of the stop-action or slow-motion camera, as the lunar dawn in the longer work gives a foretaste of time-lapse photography.

But the greatest of Wells's stories do not have to be studied as tailpieces to the novels or patronized as the hackwork of a writer notorious for overproduction. Many can stand on their own as authentic achievements of Wells's resourceful imagination and technical ingenuity. In fact, **"A Story of the Days to Come"** is in many respects more convincing and coherent than its novelistic sequel, *When the Sleeper Wakes.* The issues of size and scale and of the management of technology Wells raises in **"Filmer"** are treated more diffusely and with less power in *The Food of the Gods. In the Days of the Comet* is a bloated version of **"The Star"** and of interest chiefly in those passages that imitate the panoramic techniques of the earlier story. And **"The Door in the Wall"** makes poignant and real the perilous lure of imagination treated so ludicrously in *The Sea Lady.*

Wells's self-criticism in the opening pages of his *Autobiography* is notable for its candor and scrupulousness: "It scarcely needs criticism to bring home to me that much of my work has been slovenly, haggard, and irritated, most of it hurried and inadequately revised." But the honest reader and critic will not simply take Wells at his word. His enduring work is the gift of a generous imagination, an exacting but evocative use of language, and passionate intellectual integrity. Wells's short stories and the great romances of 1895-1901 are a testament to both the excellence and the pertinence of science fiction as a literary form; they remain a repository of the exhilaration, reflection, and admonition that are the distinctive aesthetic and moral values of science fiction. (pp. 64-6)

Robert Crossley, in his *H. G. Wells,* Starmont House, Inc. 1986, 79 p.

SOURCES FOR FURTHER STUDY

Bergonzi, Bernard, ed. *H. G. Wells: A Collection of Critical Essays.* Englewood Cliffs, N.J.: Prentice-Hall, 1976, 182 p.

> Ten important essays on Wells and his work by such critics as Bergonzi, V. S. Pritchett, Anthony West, and Robert M. Philmus.

Brome, Vincent. *H. G. Wells: A Biography.* London: Longmans, Green and Co., 1952, 255 p.

> Offers interesting personal glimpses into Wells's life and includes many examples of the critical reception of his works.

Brooks, Van Wyck. *The World of H. G. Wells.* New York: Mitchell Kennerley, 1915, 189 p.

> Critical and biographical study focusing on the development of Wells's social and political thought.

Parrinder, Patrick, ed. *H. G. Wells: The Critical Heritage.* London: Routledge & Kegan Paul, 1972, 351 p.

> Collection of important reviews and studies of Wells's work.

Suvin, Darko, and Philmus, Robert M., eds. *H. G. Wells and Modern Science Fiction.* Lewisburg, Pa.: Bucknell University Press, 1977, 277 p.

> A collection of essays concerning Wells's influence on, and comparative stature within, modern science fiction. Included are essays on "The Garden in Wells's Early Science Fiction," by David Y. Hughes and "Evo-

lution as a Literary Theme in H. G. Wells's Science Fiction,'' by J. P. Vernier, as well as annotated listings of Wells's scientific writings.

West, Anthony. *H. G. Wells: Aspects of a Life.* London: Hutchinson, 1984, 405 p.

    Painstaking and unsparing biography by Wells's son with Rebecca West.

Eudora Welty

1909-

American novelist, short story writer, and essayist.

INTRODUCTION

Welty is considered one of the most important authors of the twentieth century. Although the majority of her stories are set in the American South and reflect the region's language and culture, critics agree that Welty's treatment of universal themes and her wide-ranging artistic influences clearly transcend regional boundaries. Welty is frequently linked with modernist authors such as James Joyce and Virginia Woolf, and some of her works, including the stories in her *The Golden Apples* (1949), are similar to theirs in the creation of a complex fictional world that is made comprehensible through a network of symbols and allusions, drawn primarily from classical mythology. The outstanding features of some of Welty's best-known work are her authentic replication of the Southern dialect, as in the story "Why I Live at the P.O.," and her skillful manipulation of realistic detail and elements of fantasy to create vivid character portrayals.

Born in Jackson, Mississippi at a time when that city had not yet lost its rural atmosphere, Welty grew up in the bucolic South she so often evokes in her stories. She attended the Mississippi State College for Women and the University of Wisconsin, where she majored in English Literature, then studied advertising at Columbia University; however, graduating at the height of the Great Depression, she was unable to find work in her chosen field. Returning to Jackson in 1931, Welty worked as a part-time journalist and copywriter and as a WPA photographer. The latter job took her on assignments throughout Mississippi, and she began using these experiences as material for short stories. In June, 1936, her story "Death of a Traveling Salesman" was accepted for publication in the journal *Manuscript,* and within two years her work had appeared in such prestigious publications as the *Atlantic* and the *Southern Review.* Critical response to Welty's first collection of stories, *A Curtain of Green* (1941), was highly favorable, with many commentators predicting that a first performance so impressive would no doubt lead to even greater achievements. Yet when *The Wide Net, and Other Stories* was published two years later, several critics, most notably Diana Trilling, deplored Welty's marked shift away from the colorful realism of her earlier stories toward a more impressionistic style, objecting in particular to her increased use of symbol and metaphor to convey themes. Other critics responded favorably, including Robert Penn Warren, who wrote that in Welty's work, "the items of fiction (scene, action, character, etc.) are presented not as document but as comment, not as a report but as a thing made, not as history but as idea."

As Welty continued to refine her vision her fictional techniques gained wider acceptance. Indeed, her most complex and highly symbolic collection of stories, *The Golden Apples,* won critical acclaim, and she received a number of prizes and awards throughout the following decade, including the William Dean Howells Medal of the Academy of Arts and Letters for her novella *The Ponder Heart* (1954). Occupied primarily with teaching, traveling, and lecturing between 1955 and 1970, Welty produced little fiction. Then, in the early 1970s, she published two novels, *Losing Battles* (1970), which received mixed reviews, and the more critically successful *The Optimist's Daughter* (1972), which won a Pulitzer Prize. Although Welty has published no new volumes of short stories since *The Bride of the Innisfallen* in 1955, the release of her *Collected Stories* in 1980 renewed interest in her short fiction and brought unanimous praise. In addition, the 1984 publication of Welty's *One Writer's Beginnings,* an autobiographical work chronicling her own artistic development, further illuminated her work and inspired critics to reinterpret many of her stories.

In his seminal 1944 essay on *The Wide Net, and Other Stories,* Robert Penn Warren located the essence of Welty's fictional technique in a phrase from her story "First Love": "Whatever happened, it happened in extraordinary times, in a season of dreams." It is, states Warren, "as though the author cannot be quite sure what did happen, cannot quite undertake to resolve the meaning of the recorded event, cannot, in fact, be too sure of recording all of the event." This tentative approach to narrative exposition points to Welty's primary goal in creating fiction, which is not simply to relate a series of events, but to convey a strong sense of her character's experience of that specific moment in time, always acknowledging the ambiguous nature of reality. In order to do so, she selects those details which can best vivify the narrative, frequently using metaphors and similes to communicate sensory impressions. The resulting stories are highly impressionistic. Welty typically uses traditional sym-

bols and mythical allusions in her work and, in the opinion of many, it is through linking the particular with the general and the mundane with the metaphysical that she attains her transcendent vision of human existence.

Welty's stories display a marked diversity in content, form, and mood. Many of her stories are light and humorous, while others deal with the tragic and the grotesque. Her humorous stories frequently rely upon the comic possibilities of language, as in both "Why I Live at the P.O." and *The Ponder Heart,* which exploit the humor in the speech patterns and colorful idiom of their southern narrators. In addition, Welty employs irony to comic effect, and many critics consider this aspect of her work one of its chief strengths. Opinions are divided, however, on the effectiveness of Welty's use of the grotesque. While Trilling and others find Welty's inclusion of such elements as the carnival exhibits in "Petrified Man" exploitative and superfluous, Eunice Glenn maintains that Welty created "scenes of horror" in order to "make everyday life appear as it often does, without the use of a magnifying glass, to the person with extraordinary acuteness of feeling."

Critics of Welty's work agree that these same literary techniques which produced her finest stories have also been the cause of her most outstanding failures, noting that she is at her best when objective observation and subjective revelation are kept in balance and that where the former is neglected, she is ineffective. They remark further, however, that such instances are comparatively rare in Welty's work. Many contemporary critics consider Welty's skillful use of language her single greatest achievement, citing in particular the poetic richness of her narratives and her acute sensitivity to the subtleties and peculiarities of human speech. Yet the majority of commentators concur with Glenn's assertion that "it is her profound search of human consciousness and her illumination of the underlying causes of the compulsions and fears of modern man that would seem to comprise the principal value of Miss Welty's work."

While critics do not concur on all aspects of Welty's fiction, the preeminence of her work remains unquestioned. Despite some early resistance to her style, Welty has garnered much critical and popular respect for both her humorous colloquial stories and her more experimental works. Although she is known chiefly as a southern writer, the transcendent humanity conveyed in her stories places her beyond regional classification, and she is widely regarded as one of the foremost fiction writers in America.

(For further information about Welty's life and works, see *Concise Dictionary of American Literary Biography, 1929-1941; Contemporary Authors,* Vols. 9-12; *Contemporary Authors Bibliographical Series,* Vol. 1; *Contemporary Literary Criticism,* Vols. 1, 2, 5,

14, 22, 33; *Dictionary of Literary Biography*, Vols. 2, 102; *Dictionary of Literary Biography Yearbook: 1987*; and *Short Story Criticism*, Vol. 1.)

CRITICAL COMMENTARY

KATHERINE ANNE PORTER
(essay date 1941)

[Porter was an American novelist, short fiction writer, and critic. The novellas *Noon Wine* (1937) and *Pale Horse, Pale Rider* (1939) are generally regarded as her best works and are viewed as near-perfect examples of the genre. Porter met and befriended Welty in 1938 and provided an introduction for *A Curtain of Green*, Welty's first short story collection. In the following excerpt from that essay, which is acknowledged as a critical touchstone of Welty's work, Porter briefly assesses Welty's talents.]

[The stories in *A Curtain of Green*] offer an extraordinary range of mood, pace, tone, and variety of material. The scene is limited to a town the author knows well; the farthest reaches of that scene never go beyond the boundaries of her own state, and many of the characters are of the sort that caused a Bostonian to remark that he would not care to meet them socially. Lily Daw is a half-witted girl in the grip of social forces represented by a group of earnest ladies bent on doing the best thing for her, no matter what the consequences. Keela, the Outcast Indian Maid, is a crippled little Negro who represents a type of man considered most unfortunate by W. B. Yeats: one whose experience was more important than he, and completely beyond his powers of absorption. But the really unfortunate man in this story is the ignorant young white boy, who had innocently assisted at a wrong done the little Negro, and for a most complex reason, finds that no reparation is possible, or even desirable to the victim. . . . The heroine of **"Why I Live at the P.O."** is a terrifying case of dementia praecox. In this first group—for the stories may be loosely classified on three separate levels—the spirit is satire and the key grim comedy. Of these, **"The Petrified Man"** offers a fine clinical study of vulgarity—vulgarity absolute, chemically pure, exposed mercilessly to its final subhuman depths. Dullness, bitterness, rancor, self-pity, baseness of all kinds, can be most interesting material for a story provided these are not also the main elements in the mind of the author. There is nothing in the least vulgar or frustrated in Miss Welty's mind. She has simply an eye and an ear sharp, shrewd, and true as a tuning fork. She has given to this little story all her wit and observation, her blistering

humor and her just cruelty; for she has none of that slack tolerance or sentimental tenderness toward symptomatic evils that amounts to criminal collusion between author and character. Her use of this material raises the quite awfully sordid little tale to a level above its natural habitat, and its realism seems almost to have the quality of caricature, as complete realism so often does. Yet, as painters of the grotesque make only detailed reports of actual living types observed more keenly than the average eye is capable of observing, so Miss Welty's little human monsters are not really caricatures at all, but individuals exactly and clearly presented: which is perhaps a case against realism, if we cared to go into it. She does better on another level—for the important reason that the themes are richer—in such beautiful stories as **"Death of a Traveling Salesman," "A Memory," "A Worn Path."** Let me admit a deeply personal preference for this particular kind of story, where external act and the internal voiceless life of the human imagination almost meet and mingle on the mysterious threshold between dream and waking, one reality refusing to admit or confirm the existence of the other, yet both conspiring toward the same end. This is not easy to accomplish, but it is always worth trying, and Miss Welty is so successful at it, it would seem her most familiar territory. There is no blurring at the edges, but evidences of an active and disciplined imagination working firmly in a strong line of continuity, the waking faculty of daylight reason recollecting and recording the crazy logic of the dream. There is in none of these stories any trace of autobiography in the prime sense, except as the author is omnipresent, and knows each character she writes about as only the artist knows the thing he has made, by first experiencing it in imagination. But perhaps in **"A Memory,"** one of the best stories, there might be something of early personal history in the story of the child on the beach, alienated from the world of adult knowledge by her state of childhood, who hoped to learn the secrets of life by looking at everything, squaring her hands before her eyes to bring the observed thing into a frame—the gesture of one born to select, to arrange, to bring apparently disparate elements into harmony within deliberately fixed boundaries. But the author is freed already in her youth from self-love, self-pity, self-preoccupation,

Principal Works

A Curtain of Green (short stories) 1941

The Robber Bridegroom (novella) 1942

The Wide Net, and Other Stories (short stories) 1943

Delta Wedding (novel) 1946

The Golden Apples (short stories) 1949

The Ponder Heart (novella) 1954

Selected Stories (short stories) 1954

The Bride of the Innisfallen (short stories) 1955

Thirteen Stories (short stories) 1965

Losing Battles (novel) 1970

The Optimist's Daughter (novel) 1972

The Eye of the Story (essays and reviews) 1978

The Collected Stories of Eudora Welty (short stories) 1980

One Writer's Beginnings (autobiography) 1984

that triple damnation of too many of the young and gifted, and has reached an admirable objectivity. In such stories as **"Old Mr. Marblehall," "Powerhouse," "The Hitch-Hikers,"** she combines an objective reporting with great perception of mental or emotional states, and in **"Clytie"** the very shape of madness takes place before your eyes in a straight account of actions and speech, the personal appearance and habits of dress of the main character and her family.

In all of these stories, varying as they do in excellence, I find nothing false or labored, no diffusion of interest, no wavering of mood—the approach is direct and simple in method, though the themes and moods are anything but simple, and there is even in the smallest story a sense of power in reserve which makes me believe firmly that, splendid beginning that this is, it is only the beginning. (pp. xix-xxiii)

Katherine Anne Porter, in an introduction to *A Curtain of Green and Other Stories* by Eudora Welty, Harcourt Brace Jovanovich, 1941, pp. xi-xxiii.

ROBERT PENN WARREN

(essay date 1944)

[Warren was an American poet, novelist, and short story writer. A native of Kentucky, he was strongly influenced by the South, often drawing inspiration from the land, the people, and the history of that region. In the following excerpt from an essay written in 1944, he refutes Diana Trilling's charges against

The Wide Net, and Other Stories, affirming the validity of Welty's literary techniques and defending her use of symbol and allegory to convey themes.]

If we put *The Wide Net,* Eudora Welty's second collection of stories, up against her first collection, *A Curtain of Green,* we can immediately observe a difference: the stories of *The Wide Net* represent a specializing, an intensifying, of one of the many strains which were present in *A Curtain of Green.* All of the stories in *A Curtain of Green* bear the impress of Miss Welty's individual talent, but there is a great variety among them in subject matter and method and, more particularly, mood. It is almost as if the author had gone at each story as a fresh start in the business of writing fiction, as if she had had to take a new angle each time out of a joy in the pure novelty of the perspective. (p. 156)

Behind the innocent delight of the craftsman, and of the admirer of the world, there was also a seriousness, a philosophical cast of mind, which gave coherence to the book, but on the surface there was the variety, the succession of surprises. In *The Wide Net* we do not find the surprises. The stories are more nearly cut to one pattern.

We do not find the surprises. Instead, on the first page, with the first sentence of the first story, **"First Love,"** we enter a special world: "Whatever happened, it happened in extraordinary times, in a season of dreams . . .". And that is the world in which we are going to live until we reach the last sentence of the last story. "Whatever happened," the first sentence begins, as though the author cannot be quite sure what did happen, cannot quite undertake to resolve the meaning of the recorded event, cannot, in fact, be too sure of recording all of the event. This is coyness, of course; or a way of warning the reader that he cannot expect quite the ordinary direct light on the event. For it is "a season of dreams"—and the faces and gestures and events often have something of the grave retardation, the gnomic intensity, the portentous suggestiveness of dreams. The logic of things here is not quite the logic by which we live, or think we live, our ordinary daylight lives. In **"The Wide Net,"** for example, the young husband, who thinks his wife has jumped into the river, goes out with a party of friends to dredge for the body, but the sad occasion turns into a saturnalian fish-fry which is interrupted when the great King of the Snakes raises his hoary head from the surface of the river. But usually, in *The Wide Net,* the wrenching of logic is not in terms of events themselves, though **"The Purple Hat"** is a fantasy, and **"Asphodel"** moves in the direction of fantasy. Usually the events as events might be given a perfectly realistic treatment (Dreiser could take the events of **"The Landing"** for a story). But in these cases where the events and their ordering are "natural" and not supernatural or fantastic, the stories themselves finally belong to the "season of dreams" because of the special tone and mood, the special perspective, the special sensibility with which they are rendered.

Some readers, in fact, who are quite aware of Miss Welty's gifts, have recently reported that they are disturbed by the recent development of her work. Diana Trilling, in her valuable and sobering comments on current fiction . . . , says that the author "has developed her technical virtuosity to the point where it outweighs the uses to which it is put, and her vision of horror to the point of nightmare." There are two ideas in this indictment, and let us take the first one first and come to the second much later. The indictment of the technique is developed along these lines: Miss Welty has made her style too fancy—decorative, "falsely poetic" and "untrue," "insincere," ("When an author says 'look at me' instead of 'look at it,' there is insincerity. . . . ") This insincerity springs from "the extreme infusion of subjectivism and private sensibility." But the subjectivism, Mrs. Trilling goes on to say, leads not only to insincerity and fine writing but to a betrayal of the story's obligation to narrative and rationality. Miss Welty's stories take off from a situation, but "the stories themselves stay with their narrative no more than a dance, say, stays with its argument." That is the summary of the indictment.

The indictment is, no doubt, well worth the close attention of Miss Welty's admirers. There is, in fact, a good deal of the falsely poetic in Miss Welty's present style, metaphors that simply pretend to an underlying logic, and metaphors (and descriptions) that, though good themselves, are irrelevant to the business in hand. And sometimes Miss Welty's refusal to play up the objective action—her attempt to define and refine the response rather than to present the stimulus—does result in a blurred effect. But the indictment treats primarily not of such failures to fulfill the object the artist has set herself but of the nature of that object. The critic denies, in effect, that Miss Welty's present kind of fiction is fiction at all: "It is a book of ballets, not of stories."

Now is it possible that the critic is arguing from some abstract definition of "story," some formalistic conception which does not accommodate the present exhibit, and is not concerning herself with the question of whether or not the present exhibit is doing the special job which it proposes for itself, and, finally, the job which we demand of all literature? Perhaps we should look at a new work first in terms of its effect and not in terms of a definition of type, because every new work is in some degree, however modest, wrenching our definition, straining its seams, driving us back from the formalistic definition to the principles on which the definition was based. Can we say this, therefore, of our expectation concerning a piece of literature, new or old: That it should intensify our awareness of the world (and of ourselves in relation to the world) in terms of

an idea, a "view." This leads us to what is perhaps the key statement by Diana Trilling concerning *The Wide Net:* she grants that the volume "has tremendous emotional impact, despite its obscurity." In other words, she says, unless I misinterpret her, that the book does intensify the reader's awareness—but *not* in terms of a presiding idea.

This has led me to reread Miss Welty's two volumes of stories in the attempt to discover the issues which are involved in the "season of dreams." To begin with, almost all of the stories deal with people who, in one way or another, are cut off, alienated, isolated from the world. There is the girl in **"Why I Live at the P.O."**—isolated from her family by her arrogance, meanness, and sense of persecution; the half-witted Lily Daw, who, despite the efforts of "good" ladies, wants to live like other people; the deaf-mutes of **"The Key,"** and the deaf-mute of **"First Love"**; the people of **"The Whistle"** and **"A Piece of News,"** who are physically isolated from the world and who make their pathetic efforts to re-establish something lost. . . . In some of the cases, the matter is more indirectly presented. For instance, in **"Keela, the Outcast Indian Maiden,"** we find, as in *The Ancient Mariner,* the story of a man who, having committed a crime, must try to re-establish his connection with humanity; or in the title story of *The Wide Net,* William Wallace, because he thinks his wife has drowned herself, is at the start of the story cut off from the world of natural joy in which he had lived.

We can observe that the nature of the isolation may be different from case to case, but the fact of isolation, whatever its nature, provides the basic situation of Miss Welty's fiction. The drama which develops from this basic situation is of either of two kinds: first, the attempt of the isolated person to escape into the world; or second, the discovery by the isolated person, or by the reader, of the nature of the predicament.

As an example of the first type, we can remember Clytie's obsessed inspection of faces [in **"Clytie"**] ("Was it possible to comprehend the eyes and the mouth of other people, which concealed she knew not what, and secretly asked for still another unknown thing?") and her attempt to escape, and to solve the mystery, when she lays her finger on the face of the terrified barber who has come to the ruinous old house to shave her father. Or there is Jennie, of **"At the Landing,"** or Livvie, or the man of **"Keela, the Outcast Indian Maiden."** As an example of the second type, there is the new awareness on the part of the salesman in **"The Hitch-Hikers,"** or the new awareness on the part of the other salesman in the back-country cabin.

Even in **"A Still Moment"** we have this pattern, though in triplicate. The evangelist Lorenzo, the outlaw Murrell, and the naturalist and artist Audubon stand for a still moment and watch a white heron feeding. Lorenzo sees a beauty greater than he can account for (he had earlier "accounted for" the beauty by thinking, "Praise God, His love has come visible"), and with the sweat of rapture pouring down from his forehead, shouts into the marshes, "Tempter!" He has not been able to escape from his own obsession, or in other words, to make his definition of the world accommodate the white heron and the "natural" rapture which takes him. Murrell, looking at the bird, sees "only whiteness ensconced in darkness," and thinks that "if it would look at him a dream penetration would fill and gratify his heart"—the heart which Audubon has already defined as belonging to the flinty darkness of a cave. Neither Lorenzo nor Murrell can "love" the bird, and so escape from their own curse as did, again, the Ancient Mariner. But there remains the case of Audubon himself, who does "love" the bird, who can innocently accept nature. There is, however, an irony here. To paint the bird he must "know" the bird as well as "love" it, he must know it feather by feather, he must have it in his hand. And so he must kill it. But having killed the bird, he knows that the best he can make of it now in a painting would be a dead thing, "never the essence, only a sum of parts," and that "it would always meet with a stranger's sight, and never be one with beauty in any other man's head in the world." Here, too, the fact of the isolation is realized: as artist and lover of nature he had aspired to a communication, a communion, with other men in terms of the bird, but now "he saw his long labor most revealingly at the point where it met its limit" and he is forced back upon himself.

"A Still Moment," however, may lead us beyond the discussion of the characteristic situation, drama, and realization in Miss Welty's stories. It may lead us to a theme which seems to underlie the stories. For convenience, though at the risk of incompleteness, or even distortion, we may call it Innocence and Experience. Let us take Audubon in relation to the heron. He loves the bird, innocently, in its fullness of being. But he must subject this love to knowledge; he must kill the bird if he is to commemorate its beauty, if he is to establish his communion with other men in terms of the bird's beauty. There is in the situation an irony of limit and contamination.

Let us look at this theme in relation to other stories. "A Memory," in *A Curtain of Green*, gives a simple example. Here we have a young girl lying on a beach and looking out at the scene through a frame made by her fingers, for the girl can say of herself, "To watch everything about me I regarded grimly and possessively as a need." (As does Audubon, in "A Still Moment.") And further: "It did not matter to me what I looked at; from any observation I would conclude that a secret of life had been nearly revealed to me. . . ." Now the girl is cherishing a secret love, a love for a boy

at school about whom she knows nothing, to whom she has never even spoken, but whose wrist her hand had once accidentally brushed. The secret love had made her watching of the world more austere, had sharpened her demand that the world conform to her own ideas, and had created a sense of fear. This fear had seemed to be realized one day when, in the middle of a class, the boy had a fit of nosebleed. But that is in the past. This morning she suddenly sees between the frame of her fingers a group of coarse, fat, stupid, and brutal people disporting themselves on the sand with a maniacal, aimless vigor which comes to climax when the fat woman, into the front of whose bathing suit the man had poured sand, bends over and pulls down the cloth so that the lumps of mashed and folded sand empty out. "I felt a peak of horror, as though her breasts themselves had turned to sand, as though they were of no importance at all and she did not care." Over against this defilement (a defilement which implies that the body, the breasts which turn to sand, has no meaning), there is the refuge of the dream, "the undefined austerity of my love."

"A Memory" presents the moment of the discovery of the two poles—the dream and the world; the idea and nature; innocence and experience; individuality and the anonymous, devouring life-flux; meaning and force; love and knowledge. It presents the contrast in terms of horror (as do "Petrified Man" and "Why I Live at the P.O." when taken in the context of Miss Welty's work) and with the issue left in suspension, but other stories present it with different emphases and tonalities. (pp. 157-63)

If this general line of interpretation is correct, we find that the stories represent variations on the same basic theme, on the contrasts already enumerated. It is not that there is a standard resolution for the contrasts which is repeated from story to story; rather, the contrasts, being basic, are not susceptible of a single standard resolution, and there is an implicit irony in Miss Welty's work. But if we once realize this, we can recognize that the contrasts are understood not in mechanical but in vital terms: the contrasts provide the terms of human effort, for the dream must be carried to, submitted to, the world, innocence to experience, love to knowledge, knowledge to fact, individuality to communion. What resolution is possible is, if I read the stories with understanding, in terms of the vital effort. The effort is a "mystery," because it is in terms of the effort, doomed to failure but essential, that the human manifests itself as human. Again and again, in different forms, we find what we find in Joel of "First Love": "Joel would never know now the true course, or the true outcome of any dream: this was all he felt. But he walked on, in the frozen path into the wilderness, on and on. He did not see how he could ever go back and still be the boot-boy at the Inn."

It is possible that, in trying to define the basic issue and theme of Miss Welty's stories, I have made them appear too systematic, too mechanical. I do not mean to imply that her stories should be read as allegories, with a neat point-to-point equating of image and idea. It is true that a few of her stories, such as **"The Wide Net,"** do approach the limit of allegory, but even in such cases we find rather than the system of allegory a tissue of symbols which emerge from, and disappear into, a world of scene and action which, once we discount the author's special perspective, is recognizable in realistic terms. The method is similar to the method of much modern poetry, and to that of much modern fiction and drama, but at the same time it is a method as old as fable, myth, and parable. It is a method by which the items of fiction (scene, action, character, etc.) are presented not as document but as comment, not as a report but as a thing made, not as history but as idea. Even in the most realistic and reportorial fiction, the social picture, the psychological analysis, and the pattern of action do not rest at the level of mere report; they finally operate as expressive symbols as well.

Fiction may be said to have two poles, history and idea, and the emphasis may be shifted very far in either direction. In the present collection the emphasis has been shifted very far in the direction of idea, but at the same time there remains a sense of the vividness of the actual world: the picnic of **"The Wide Net"** is a real picnic as well as a "journey," Cash of **"Livvie"** is a real field hand in his Easter clothes as well as a field god. In fact, it may be said that when the vividness of the actual world is best maintained, when we get the sense of one picture superimposed upon another, different and yet somehow the same, the stories are most successful.

The stories which fail are stories like **"The Purple Hat"** and **"Asphodel,"** in which the material seems to be manipulated in terms of an idea, in which the relation between the image and the vision has become mechanical, in which there is a strain, in which we do find the kind of hocus-pocus deplored by Diana Trilling.

And this brings us back to the criticism that the volume "has tremendous emotional impact, despite its obscurity," that the "fear" it engenders is "in inverse ratio to its rational content." Now it seems to me that this description does violence to my own experience of literature, that we do not get any considerable emotional impact unless we sense, at the same time, some principle of organization, some view, some meaning. This does not go to say that we have to give an abstract formulation to that principle or view or meaning before we can experience the impact of the work, but it does go to say that it is implicit in the work and is having its effect upon us in immediate aesthetic terms. Furthermore, in regard to the particular work in question, I do not feel that it is obscure. If anything, the dream-like effect in many of the stories seems to result from

the author's undertaking to squeeze meaning from the item which, in ordinary realistic fiction, would be passed over with a casual glance. Hence the portentousness, the retardation, the otherworldliness. For Miss Welty is like the girl in **"A Memory"**:

> . . . from any observation I would conclude that a secret of life had been nearly revealed to me, and from the smallest gesture of a stranger I would wrest what was to me a communication or a presentiment.

In many cases, as a matter of fact, Miss Welty has heavily editorialized her fiction. She wants us to get that smallest gesture, to participate in her vision of things as intensely meaningful. And so there is almost always a gloss to the fable.

One more word: It is quite possible that Miss Welty has pushed her method to its most extreme limit. It is also possible that the method, if pursued much farther, would lead to monotony and self-imitation and merely decorative elaboration. Perhaps we shall get a fuller drama when her vision is submitted more daringly to fact, when the definition is plunged into the devouring river. But meanwhile Miss Welty has given us stories of brilliance and intensity; and as for the future, Miss Welty is a writer of great resourcefulness, sensitivity, and intelligence, and can probably fend for herself. (pp. 166-69)

Robert Penn Warren, "Love and Separateness in Eudora Welty," in his *Selected Essays,* Random House, 1958, pp. 159-69.

EUDORA WELTY AND JAN NORDBY GRETLUND
(interview date 1980)

[In the following interview, which took place at Welty's home in Jackson, Mississippi, Welty discusses her novels, short fiction, and nonfiction, particularly addressing the complex relationship between her personal experiences and her works.]

I. PERSONAL, NOT AUTOBIOGRAPHICAL

[Gretlund]: *In an essay on Jane Austen, in 1969, you wrote that "the interesting situations of life can, and notably do, take place at home." Was your childhood home full of "interesting situations"?*

[Welty]: No, not especially. My family wasn't the usual kind in the South, because both my parents came from away. So there were no blood-kin—aunts, uncles, grandparents and so on. Different ones came from time to time, but in those days people couldn't lightly travel from Ohio and West Virginia to visit. So it was mostly our immediate family circle. Of course there were things going on. I had two younger brothers. But in the homes of my friends, who grew up with large families around them, that's where I got that insight—and when I went to my parents' homes, especially my mother's in West Virginia, where she had five brothers. But in the Jane Austen essay, I was writing a generalization of something I believe; I wasn't drawing it out of my own life in particular.

It's obvious from your fiction that you take great pleasure in oral narratives. Was there a tradition of story-telling in your family?

Yes, on my mother's side they were big story-tellers. When her brothers came here to visit, they would renew the stories of their youth, funny things that happened in West Virginia out in the country. They grew up on a farm. Every name they mentioned would bring out gales of laughter and reminiscences—and there would be songs: "Remember how we used to sing . . . ?" So they would all sing it.

In Delta Wedding, Laura says that Uncle George "evidently felt that old stories, family stories, Mississippi stories, were the same as very holy or very passionate, if stories could be those things." Can they?

To some people. Oh yes, sure. Laura is trying to comprehend that sort of thing. Family stories are where you get your first notions of profound feelings, mysterious feelings that you might not understand till you grow into them. But you know they exist and that they have power.

Some of Laurel McKelva's memories center on the library of her childhood home. Were the classics mentioned in The Optimist's Daughter (i.e., Tennyson, Dickens, and Gibbon) in your parents' library?

Yes, they were. Besides Mark Twain, Henry James, and Ring Lardner—he's a classic to me. My parents always had books, for which I am deeply grateful. I grew up in a family of readers. No book was prohibited to me. As far as Dickens goes, he meant a great deal to my mother. She had been given a set of Dickens as a little girl, as a reward for having her hair cut. She had chosen that over a pair of golden earrings to pierce her ears, in those days much favored by little girls, especially in Virginia and West Virginia. Her father was very poor, a country lawyer with a large family, but he ordered the books from Baltimore, and they came up the river packed in a barrel. She adored those books, so that later when she was married she brought them to Jackson. When our house caught on fire, she went back into the burning house, although she was on crutches at the time, and began throwing that set of Dickens out the window to save it.

You have said recently that parts of The Optimist's Daughter are "literal memory." To what extent are the West Virginia scenes literal memory?

The physical memory of how it looked—the

shoals, the mountains—and how it sounded; the memory of the entire setting.

You have mentioned that The Optimist's Daughter meant more to you personally than Losing Battles.

Yes, because of the strictly personal memories. The way my uncles looked coming home at night through the far-off fields, just white shirts showing down the mountain. And the sound of the horses. All the physical sensations were memories of about age three, when you really have very sharp sensory perceptions. I still recall this, and I just put it all in there.

You have often pointed out that you never write about people you know, about real people. And you take great pains to stress that Morgana and its inhabitants are fictitious. Miss Katherine Anne Porter (for one) has not accepted your disclaimer in The Golden Apples. Below it, in her copy of the book, Miss Porter has written: "All right honey, we shorely believes you!"

Well, this is the first time I heard about *that!* Of course, any character you write has bits and pieces of somebody; but they are really conceptions of the imagination, which are invented to carry out what I want to do in the story. Of course, I endow them with things I have observed, dreamed or understood, but no one represents a real person. I couldn't do it; it would defeat me in my fiction. I'm sure Katherine Anne was not being literal in the way you imagine. "Morgana" is a made-up name in the tradition of Delta names. I made it Morgana because of the Morgans that were there, although I made it Morgana first and *then* got the Morgans to name it from. I also like having the idea of *fata morgana,* to show that they were living absorbed in illusions. It all went of a piece like that.

If your fiction is not autobiographical, will you accept it if we call it very personal?

Oh yes, it is very personal; they aren't the same thing at all.

Do you feel that a critic has any right to be interested in your personal life?

It all depends on for what purpose. If it is about my work and if it bears on my work—but not just an idle question. It always reaches the point where people begin to ask you out of curiosity. That gets me edgy.

II. A SENSE OF PLACE

In 1951 you said that "in a story, character and place have almost equal, or even interchangeable, contributions to make." Do you still feel that this is true?

Now I wouldn't say "interchangeable"; but I think that place can be almost a character in a story. Place can have really important and even dramatic significance.

Obviously, Jackson, Mississippi is a place that's meant a great deal to you. Is that what is implied by the famous statement, supposedly first made to Miss Porter and later quoted by Flannery O'Connor, that you are usually "locally underfoot" in Jackson?

That is just an expression—it means I am always moving around here. "Underfoot" just means "present." It is just a localism, and it carries some tinge of being in the way.

I admire your house here in Jackson and also the Southern houses in your fiction. Do buildings like the Shellmound Mansion, the MacLain House, the Renfro Farmhouse, and the McKelva House have a special meaning for you?

They have a value in the work of fiction because they convey, I hope, the kind of person, the kind of background, the kind of economic background, to which they belong. It is just as evocative to a knowing reader as saying "they never went to school,". "they make so-and-so much a year," or "they are poor whites," or "they are ambitious people on the make." You can't make a mistake in something like that and write well. I think it is important, not strictly that you see the house in your mind's eye, but rather that you know these facts.

Mr. Walker Percy has written that "town and writer sustain each other in secret ways." Jackson, Mississippi, has obviously sustained you all your life; but is it necessarily "in secret ways"?

Eudora Welty as "Powerhouse"   John Sokol ©1986

EUDORA WELTY
EYE OF THE STORYTELLER

THE UNIVERSITY OF AKRON CELEBRATES
51 YEARS OF LITERARY POWER
A CONFERENCE SPONSORED BY BUCHTEL COLLEGE OF ARTS AND SCIENCES

AKRON, OHIO · SEPTEMBER 17th-19th, 1987

Poster for a national conference on the works of
Eudora Welty.

No. Unless he means that the ways are not very easy to communicate, and they probably have no bearing on what the writing is. The relationship exists, but it should be of no interest to the reader of a piece. I certainly agree that the ways are many and profound.

Do you feel that the essential part of what you say about your fellow Mississippians could have been said with equal validity about anybody else?

Think of it like this: What I was trying to say about Mississippi was like being drawn to a magnet of that one place—well, there's another magnet in the *next* place! I think the same kind of relationship exists, but the things related wouldn't be the same things. Mississippi and Alabama and maybe parts of Georgia would be sort of alike. Tennessee is very different. Louisiana is totally different. Virginia is different. They all have their own truths. I think the same relationship would exist, but not the same bindings would be there. Of course, this country, as you can see everywhere, is changing. Places are not as different as they were when I began writing.

Is it still possible here in Jackson to send your taproots down far enough to give you a sense of origin?

I don't know about the ones coming along now. But everybody I grew up with has that same feeling of roots. Children growing up now have lived in five or six houses by the time they are ten years old.

Does that make the children rootless and restless?

I suppose, and every place is getting to be somewhat alike. In the future, it's not going to be the same, but I think there will still be a deep sense of family to people who have grown up with that. I can't help but think that.

Judge McKelva is buried with a view to the new interstate highway under plastic poinsettias by Fay, his second wife. Is the portrait of Fay, "the little shallow vulgarian," a portrait of the future?

God, I hope not! But I did mean to suggest that she might have that element in her.

Fay does not seem to have a past.

And she doesn't miss it! She doesn't know what it is. I don't know if you happened to see the French reviews of *The Optimist's Daughter* when it came out in France? I am not a very good reader in French, but I did get the point—which was that the only sympathetic character in the book was Fay!

Are you fascinated by the Stovalls, Peacocks, Chisoms, Sistrunks, Reids, etc.?

Oh yes, I love them all!

Are you a little bit horrified also? It has been suggested that you're "looking down your nose" at these people.

Suggested by whom? That's absurd! I understand them very well indeed. I love them. I know just what's going on in their minds. I don't look down my nose at anyone among my characters. I wouldn't invent somebody in order to look down my nose at them. No, I see the absurd qualities in everybody, and it doesn't matter who they are. I saw the absurd qualities in Judge McKelva, who was of a different order. And in Edna Earle, who is sympathetically telling the story about all the people she herself looks down on.

Is Judge McKelva a "Compson"?

Oh yes.

Are the Stovalls "Snopeses" who are taking over the South?

Let's not be literal about things. People won't stand for being divided up like that. In the red clay hills, which is farther to the north and east of Yoknapatawpha, there is quite a different social structure. There is nobody else except what you'd call poor whites. Yoknapatawpha has an entire gamut running from Compson down to Snopes, with many in-between. So there is the friction of Snopeses trying to take other people's places. Nothing like that goes on in the red clay hills because nobody has anything. The only reason the Stovalls are different from the others is that they are just *meaner.* None of them has a dime.

You have said that in the early 60s there wasn't much difference between Compsons and Snopeses.

It was not I, but a friend who made the remark. That was when I was talking about my character in **"Where Is the Voice Coming From?"**—when someone told me that I had made my murderer a Snopes and he was a Compson. The remark meant that some of the people who are born so to speak in the Compson neighborhood or family had just as rotten ideas about race at that time as the Snopeses. People who could be racist could be in any part of society. It was meant only in that respect and only at that time, I think.

In her story "An Exile in the East," Flannery O'Connor called New York "no kind of place." You have called it a "no man's land," and you have said you can't write stories which take place in New York. Would it ruin your sense of place if you were to use a Northern setting?

All I meant was that you could not confine anything that you said if you wrote about New York. I love New York; that's why I wouldn't call it "a no man's land" except in the depiction of a character in a story. It was not out of my lack of affection. But as far as using it as material, I find even a town like Jackson too big for me to manage. I have to have a small enough stage, a small enough arena, to confine it and to be able to manipulate what I am doing.

You were in New York at the beginning of the 30s. It seems to have been a good time to be there.

It was indeed. It was a good time for me. It was my chance, the first I had ever had, to go to the theater, to the museums, to concerts, and I made use of every moment, let me tell you. I was taking a business course,

which meant I didn't have to study at all, so I went to the theater. In those days there were many theaters running, the way there are in London now. And you could go on the night you decided to go. Furthermore, you could get a ticket for $1.10 for the cheapest seat, at the cut-rate drugstore in Times Square. You could buy tickets for a show and rush straight over and see it. Also I didn't mind standing up for anything.

Everybody that was wonderful was then at their peak. People like Noel Coward, all the wonderful music hall stars—Beatrice Lillie, Bert Lahr, Fred Allen, both the Astaires, Jack Benny, Joe Cook, and Ed Wynn. Wonderful dramatic stars, even Nazimova! Katherine Cornell, the Lunts—if I sat down to it, I could make a list of everybody on God's earth that was playing. Martha Graham was dancing solo in a little cubby-hole somewhere. I would go and watch her dance. And Shan-Kar! Everybody was there. For somebody who had never, in a sustained manner, been to the theater or to the Metropolitan Museum, where I went every Sunday, it was just a cornucopia. We had a good group of people from Jackson there at Columbia to start with, so we had company for everything we wanted to do. We could set forth anywhere. We could go dancing in Harlem to Cab Calloway. We went a lot to Small's Paradise, a night-club in Harlem where all the great bands were playing then; whites were welcome as anybody else.

I was there at the opening of Mercury Theater, during the WPA days. I remember seeing the opening of the black *Macbeth,* which was put on in Harlem, directed by Orson Welles. The play's location was changed from Scotland to Jamaica. The witches were voodoo priestesses. The Queen wore crinolines, the banquet was outdoors under swinging paper lanterns, and the witches were playing the voodoo drums. Hecate was played by a black man dancing on a drum without any clothes on. After the opening night I believe he was made to wear something.

III. THE ACT OF WRITING

In a Paris Review interview (1972), you said that you do not think of yourself as writing out of any special tradition. Do you acknowledge a kinship with other Southern writers?

Oh yes, I feel that we are all like bathers in the same sea. We all understand and know what we are partaking of. But I think we're each going about it in our own way. So far as I know we haven't had any definite effect on each other's work. There could be many unconscious effects; I read all the time, I love to read, and I live in books a lot. But as far as the act of writing goes, I have never felt the touch of any other imagination on mine as I write. I think that must be true of all of us.

During a press conference at Oxford, Mississippi, in 1977, you were asked if you had been influenced by William Faulkner. You answered briefly, "Not any!" Is it as simple as that?

Of course not!

Are you simply fed up with the question?

I was sort of fed up with the question, and at a press conference how could I go into that? I think the answer is *no.* The answer is no, because I think what was meant by the question was whether or not he had helped me in specific and personal ways. It was a sort of arithmetical question. Just his existence and his works mean a great deal to me. Certainly they influenced me; they meant so much to me. He also in very specific ways taught me so much; how he had done things just dawned on me. I was telling you a while ago about houses. He showed me above all in his work how in Yoknapatawpha every single segment of society is represented by place and house and so on. He knew so *much* about all that. He wrote about a much vaster world than anything I ever contemplated for my own work, and he made all of that so visible and so exactly right. Every speech that comes out of a character's mouth *would* be made by a person in that situation, in that kind of family, at that time. He can't go wrong. He showed me the marvelous usage of dialogue and, well, of everything.

Have you consciously tried to avoid rewriting Faulkner?

No, I think that was what I was answering, too, when I said, "Not any!" It is not so self-conscious a process as that when you write. I think in the act of writing, "how I am going to handle something," and *not* "how would so-and-so have done it," or "I mustn't fall into this pitfall here." It is just trial and error on my own.

Two of your stories particularly remind readers of William Faulkner's work.

What are they?

"The Burning" *and* **"Clytie."**

As for **"The Burning,"** I think that is a bad story. I don't know why I tried to write anything historical. It is almost the only time I ever tried to write something historical. It is almost the only time I ever tried to write something which is not in our time and place. But I certainly never consciously thought—Heavens! I would hate to be assigned: "try to write something influenced by Faulkner." My pen would drop from my hand.

In retrospect, can you see why some critics would be tempted to see the Faulkner influence in those stories?

I think that my faults in **"The Burning"** were the kind of things they blamed Faulkner with. I think the story is too involved and curlicued around with things. I haven't gone back to read that story, but recently Shelby Foote, who is getting together an anthology of Civil War stories, wrote and said he wants to use **"The Burning."** I wrote back, "I hate for you to use it; I think

it is the worst story I ever wrote." He said, "I think it is a good story, and I'm a Civil War expert; you're not." I still didn't go back and read it, but I thanked him and told him to go ahead.

As far as **"Clytie"** goes, I am sure the answer is that there is "not any" Faulkner influence. I have seen here and there a family going to seed right in the public eye. These things exist in life; of course, Faulkner saw the same kind of thing in Oxford.

It has been taken as proof of the value you place on the concept of the family bond that Robbie Fairchild returns to the family in **Delta Wedding.** *Is this justified?*

Is proof needed? Without realizing it, I seem to have repeated a pattern like that in many stories. It is partly because for my point of view in that novel, I have to have an observer come in. In *Delta Wedding* it was the child; Robbie was another outsider. I think the Fairchilds would have accepted her as much as they could accept anyone. The same way that Gloria in *Losing Battles* and Fay in *The Optimist's Daughter* are different types of interlopers with different results.

You once said about a plot: "There has to be a story, to bear it." Did you worry about the plot when you wrote **Losing Battles?**

Yes, I did, because, owing to circumstances, I wrote it over an extra long period of time. So things had time to worry me at the intervals when I was not working. I had so much more than I needed, I could have said things in a hundred different ways. So the plot worried me in that respect, how best to show it.

I know you cut **Losing Battles** *substantially: Did you cut it enough?*

I think so. But I haven't read it again; I don't like to read my work over. I think there were complaints that it was too long. I am sure that disturbed some people. To me everything in there had its place, or I would have cut it. I can be very ruthless in cutting. I don't put in things because my loving hand wrote it. I felt they were there for a reason.

You have said that you feel more comfortable with the long short story. And you indicated that this is because you feel that less is resolved, more suggested, in a short story.

That's true, and yet in the short story you don't have the demands of a novel, where everything has to be accounted for. The short story can be suggestive for its own sake. You don't have to develop what you don't need. Whereas in the novel you have to carry everything through. Short-story writing is a freer, more imaginative way to work. Yet it is even tighter knit than a novel because it has to keep its sustained quality. You can't let it down in the middle. It has to be just right.

One of the differences between a short story and a novel is supposed to be that the characters in a short story are born "fully grown." Yet the characters in **Losing Battles** seem "fully grown" from the very beginning.

Some are and some aren't. You know, like the E. M. Forster classification, some are round and some are flat. The flat ones never change, and there are plenty of flat ones that don't ever change in *Losing Battles.* But all the main characters have many possibilities. There is a character like Aunt Beck, who is always gentle yet puts her foot in her mouth when she says things. The very time she wants to be the most tender, she says something that can really hurt, without knowing that she does it. There is Miss Lexie, who started out as a flat character. But all kinds of complications come in when we know about her life in nursing Miss Julia. All the torments she went through—I considered that *that* happens to her. I think Miss Julia is the factor that shows the depth of the others—the ones that were touched by her. And Judge Moody, who might have started as a flat character, is far from it. Everything is aroused in him by what happens. And Jack, who is not by any means just a straight hero-type, has deep feelings. He is deeper than Gloria, who claims to be the sensitive one. He feels where she can't. If she hadn't had that shallow streak, she would have done better by Miss Julia.

Yes, I feel that *Losing Battles* did give me room to develop the characters.

To what extent do you make conscious use of Greek and Roman mythology in your writing?

It is conscious, clearly. I've lived with mythology all my life. It is just as close to me as the landscape. It *naturally* occurs to me when I am writing fiction. It is not a far-out, reached-for something. I feel no sense of strain when I use mythology. Maybe I use too much of it; I don't know. I have grown up with legends and fairy tales and I've always loved them. I still like to read folk tales from all kinds of other lands.

Critics have been quick to refer to Frazer's Golden Bough *and Bulfinch's* Age of Fable *for many aspects of your fiction. Are the critics overdoing it?*

I have read the one-volume edition of *The Golden Bough,* but I didn't read that till I was out of college. But myths themselves I've read all my life. Many of my childhood books were of Greek and Roman myths, also Norse and Irish. The whole Andrew Lang series of fairy tales and fables, and *Aesop's Fables* were in my house.

Did you read Bulfinch's Age of Fable?

Never have read that one. I am interested in fables *as told.* I truly haven't read enough of the critics to make a sweeping statement. But I think that anyone who attributes my stories to myths very specifically and thoroughly is overshooting it. I would rather suggest things.

The ending of **The Golden Apples** *is a case in point. When Virgie is sitting alone on the Court House steps, she is joined*

by a black woman. One critic has seen the black woman as Minerva, the stealing servant, and Minerva, the goddess of wisdom.

Oh, that really drives me crazy. It makes me sort of frantic. The end of my book was the most natural thing in the world. It was just a drawing together of two people without a roof. The old black woman, who has nothing, and Virgie, who is bereft at that moment. Yet they both have something; one of them's got a chicken, and the other has got all these things in her mind. No! When I hear something like that, it drives me to the other extreme of saying something literal, like I have just said.

IV. THE WRITER'S BELIEFS

In an introduction to an interview with you, Ms. Alice Walker has maintained that "the past will always separate" the races. Do you believe this to be true?

I don't think so. I have black friends who agree with me that it isn't so. Recently I was at Yale with some humanities scholars, answering questions. The woman sitting next to me was black, and they were all talking about the problems of the 60s. Several of the scholars were from foreign countries, asking questions about the situation here, how strained it was. And the black woman said to me, "You know, during it all, when it was just at its worst back in the 60s, and I was a school teacher, my mother said to me, 'Why aren't you all upset about this?' And I was laughing. I said, 'I guess it is because I am a Southerner.'" Which I really loved. I, too, always knew we would understand each other; we always have in the past.

Your 1942 essay, **"Ida M'Toy,"** *is one of your great portraits of black women, but where is genuine black and white friendship in your fiction?*

I see it in a good many places. I meant to convey that Missouri, in *The Optimist's Daughter,* is a true friend of Laurel's. Missouri is her maid in the household, but they were also big friends and both of them knew it.

Does Missouri help Laurel much?

I think she does. When Judge McKelva's body is being carried out, it is Missouri that stands with Laurel and helps her. She helps her with the bird too, doesn't she? I mean, in these really wrenching experiences that Laurel is going through by herself, Missouri's instincts are perfect. She is always sensitive to what is going on. In *The Ponder Heart,* too, Narciss is the mainstay of the family.

In one of your manuscripts for **The Ponder Heart,** *you wrote: "I think they only asked [Miss Teacake] because she was somebody white, the rest of their testimony was black as midnight." Was this deleted for artistic or for political reasons?*

It isn't good writing. Nothing political had anything to do with the case. I am sure the reason I took that out was that it was out of character for Edna Earle to say that.

In the early 50s you showed great political interest in the career of Adlai Stevenson. Has there been anything in politics to be enthusiastic about since then?

Neither before nor since. He just really touched my mind and heart. I was so enchanted, to have a person like that wanting to be in public life. I happened to be in New York at the time he was running so that I got to hear him in person. I think a lot of people in this country felt the same way I did, wanting so much to help Stevenson be elected. When he didn't win, I lost interest again.

It has been claimed that you are indifferent to the larger social and political problems of your region. Is it true that you overlook the regional problems?

Whoever has claimed this, it isn't accurate at all. What is true is that I don't think of myself as a writer of fiction who seeks to make it a platform for my opinions. I am a very interested citizen and try to keep informed on everything and to vote. But I don't think fiction is the place to air those principles, except for the moral principles of right and wrong—and these I try to let characters show for themselves. I tried to put all this in a piece I wrote for *The Atlantic* [Oct., 1965] called **"Must the Novelist Crusade?"**

It is clear that the object of your fiction can't be social criticism, but can the novelist avoid crusading?

You can't avoid dealing with moral matters, because that's what life is about. But I think it is wrong when somebody like Steinbeck crusades in his fiction. That's why Steinbeck bores me so. The real crusader doesn't need to crusade; he writes about human beings in the sense Chekhov did. He tries to see a human being whole with all his wrong-headedness and all his right-headedness. To blind yourself to one thing for the sake of your prejudice is limiting. I think it is a mistake. There's so much room in the world for crusading, but it is for the editorial writer, the speech-maker, the politician, and the man in public life to do, not for the writer of fiction.

Yet readers of your well-known fiction find many topical elements. In **Losing Battles,** *for instance, you deal with electioneering, depletion of woods, bad teachers' training, and a poverty-stricken orphanage, just to mention some of the potentially political issues.*

These things are there. And there are people there who are living with all these handicaps and things that should be righted. *Losing Battles* was written about the 30s, when nobody had anything with which to do it. Injustice was staring everybody in the face—and they were living in spite of it and through it and with it. I am not saying that is a good way to be; I am saying it is a terrible way to be.

Welty at the age of twenty.

You do not seem to be interested in the concept of "sin" or in the idea of "evil." This is so uncommon in an American writer that perhaps it deserves a comment.

I am, though. *Not* in "sin"—not from a Roman Catholic point of view like Flannery O'Connor, because I am ignorant of that religion. But I do believe that there is "evil." I believe in the existence of "evil," or else your reaching for "good" could not mean anything. I do feel there is "evil" in the world and in people, very really and truly. I recognize its power and value. I do! I thought there was "evil" in Fay in *The Optimist's Daughter.* And there is "evil" in a society that does wrong things.

It seems that you think very little of organized religion.

I don't know where you got this opinion. I am not a frequent churchgoer, but I am a reverent person.

In your fiction you have always treated the prejudice between denominations with scornful humor.

Or amusement, I'd say. Up in the East, when Carter was running for President, everybody said, "How could a Baptist ever be President!" In the South, that is the structure of the society of a small town. It is in a churchy society that most Southerners are brought up, and it is what they mention in every other word in their conversation. In a small town like Banner, if the Baptists couldn't be against the Methodists, they'd have nothing to talk about. My amusement has nothing to do with reverence or with God, it is *society*, and I am writing about it in that aspect.

V. THE NON-FICTION

It is obvious that you don't like it when critics use novels as "fishponds" for their criticism. Isn't it surprising then that you yourself have written so much criticism?

Not especially, because I do think I write out of a fellow feeling for fiction writers. I'm really trying to get at what I think they were trying to do. I am not trying to take something there and put it here; I am trying to understand what *they* did. I like it when someone writes that way about me, which many critics do. On the whole I feel that I really do approach other fiction writers with the feeling of a fiction writer, instead of the feeling of a critic. I like to write about the processes of writing that I have discovered through my work, and what I think I have learned reading others.

In your new book of non-fiction, you chose not to include pieces like "The Abode of Summer" and your little essay on the nature of the fairy tale. Why did you leave them out?

Only because I thought they repeated material already in the collection. I took out the one on fairy tales because I had a piece called "Fairy Tale of the Natchez Trace." I cut a great number of things because I wanted to make a sort of balanced selection. I liked "The Abode of Summer," too, but I thought I had enough on Mississippi, such as "Notes on River Country," a more considered and longer piece. I chose among things of a kindred type and tried to take the one that I thought well-developed.

You have included most of your purely critical essays in the collection, such as "Place in Fiction," "Words into Fiction," and "The Short Story."

Yes, just about all of those, because they were considered essays on my part. I really worked on those; they were my long-time thoughts about fiction. Whereas a review is something done with a deadline. You do the best you can, but it is not something you've worked over for months.

There isn't anything by "Michael Ravenna," your World War II pseudonym, in your book of non-fiction.

No. I didn't save any of those reviews because they weren't worth saving. I don't even know what they were.

For how long did you write under a pseudonym?

This is to exaggerate my signing another name to an occasional book review. I didn't work at *The New York Times* very long, through a summer (1944). And I was writing reviews under my own name at the same time,

holding down a full-time job. So I didn't have too much time to be "Michael Ravenna."

Has your book-reviewing stolen time from the fiction you wanted to write?

I like reviewing books. I take my pick. I couldn't write about a book I really don't like, you know. It is a source of pleasure to write about books I do like, and I do that and other things to earn a little money on the side. That includes going around lecturing. I have had a year of that, which is unusual. I like it, but it takes a great amount of time and still more energy.

Are you working on any fiction at present?

That's what I'm waiting to do. I have just now finished writing a piece for Mr. Bruccoli. This was an "Afterword" on a novel called *The Great Big Doorstep* by E. P. O'Donnell from 1941. This is in the Lost American Fiction Series. I was asked if I had a nomination for such a series, and I nominated this book. I was thrilled when I was asked to write the "Afterword." (pp. 193-208)

Eudora Welty and Jan Nordby Gretlund, in an interview in *The Southern Humanities Review*, Vol. XIV, No. 3, Summer, 1980, pp. 193-208.

CAROL S. MANNING

(essay date 1985)

[In the following excerpt, Manning discusses the importance of the Southern oral tradition in the evolution of Welty's narrative voice.]

In "The Corner Store" (1975), an essay about her childhood, Eudora Welty remembers people she saw and adventures she had as she ran to and from the corner grocery on errands for her mother. Generalizing about this experience, she writes, "Setting out in this world, a child feels so indelible. He only comes to find out later that it's all the others along his way who are making themselves indelible to him." A sensitive comment on the forming of a child's consciousness, the remark also seems suggestive about the making of an artist. Surely Welty's own art has been influenced by all that she has met along her way. A keen observer and listener with a prodigious memory, she has a vast store of things seen and things heard on which she draws. She said as much in an interview when asked the source of the dialogue of her characters: "Once you have heard certain expressions, sentences, you almost never forget them. It's like sending a bucket down the well and it always comes up full. . . . And you listen for the right word, in the present. . . . [W]hat you overhear on a city bus is exactly what your character would say on the page you're writing." (p. 3)

But obviously ordinary life alone does not define her fiction, or the author would not have been called a romantic as well as a realist or have been said to write such varied fiction that it defies generalization. There is a second crucial influence on her fiction, one that might seem to run counter to the first. It is a love of stories and storytelling. (p. 4)

In the South that Welty knows, storytelling is a part of everyday life, and its subjects arise from the life of the community. Storytelling is not, however, mere imitation of life. Indeed, its major attraction might be the divergence of the story told *from* everyday life. Oral or written, storytelling appeals to and draws on the imagination. Whereas everyday life may seem dull and shapeless, storytelling brings structure to happenings ("you're following a story"), prunes away some things and emphasizes or exaggerates others to provide drama ("of a narrative and dramatic sturcture"), creates suspense and promises resolution ("[y]ou're listening for how something is going to come out"). In *One Writer's Beginnings,* Welty describes her childhood fascination with a neighbor's tale-telling: "What I loved about her stories was that everything happened in *scenes.* I might not catch on to the root of the trouble in all that happened, but my ear told me it was dramatic. Often she said, 'The crisis had come!' " (pp. 5-6)

Welty's early writing, represented in three books published in rapid succession—*A Curtain of Green, The Robber Bridegroom,* and *The Wide Net*—served her, it seems as an apprenticeship: an apprenticeship in the art of storytelling. In these works the young author introduced themes and tried out methods that she would expand, contract, refine, remold, or dispense with in the subsequent fiction. She seems to have been energetically learning her craft, stretching herself, experimenting. She varied technique and context in the seventeen stories of *A Curtain of Green,* so much so that, despite their Southern settings and their implications about place, no unifying vision emerges from the whole. The variety is such that, for Robert Penn Warren, "It is almost as if the author had gone at each story as a fresh start in the business of writing fiction," and for Robert Van Gelder, "[I]t is as though there were no brand of one mind upon the stories." Her next collection, *The Wide Net,* containing stories written within roughly a year's time, does give evidence of the "brand of one mind," but though seven of the eight stories are set along the Old Natchez Trace, the volume's unity does not derive from a shared image or theme related to a culture but, as critics regularly note, from a shared dreamlike quality. The legend and romance associated with the Natchez Trace and reflected in several of these stories seem to have inspired the author to experiment with various ways of evoking the suggestiveness of

dreams. *The Robber Bridegroom,* also set along the Old Natchez Trace, was a different experiment. Several times longer than any of the early stories, it is recognized as an exuberant mixture of motifs from fairy tales and American folklore, uniquely adapted to a Southern frontier setting. (pp. 6-7)

Evidently, in these early works Welty did not set out to mimic life—though that might be included, and certainly, as she has said, the story had to be "true to life"—but to tell a good story. In fact, some of the stories were inspired by stories she had heard others tell. Her very first published story, **"Death of a Traveling Salesman,"** had such an origin. A neighbor in Jackson, Mr. Johnson, told a tale about going to a farmer's house on business and being informed by the farmer's wife that her husband had " 'gone to borry some fire.' " That remark stuck with Welty: "I could not have made up 'He's gone to borry some fire,' but, beginner though I was as a writer, I think now I began truly, for *I knew that for a story when I heard it"* (emphasis added). Similarly, **"Keela, the Outcast Indian Maiden"** was inspired by a tale about a bizarre incident that someone told her. (p. 8)

Whereas early in her career the love of storytelling had led [Welty] to delight in the act itself of telling a story, eventually it would lead her to the oral culture of her region for subject and theme. For from *Delta Wedding* to *The Optimist's Daughter* (1972), Welty's portrayal of the family and community is, in large measure, a portrayal of a talkative, storytelling people. This development had been anticipated by a handful of early stories, stories such as **"Why I Live at the P.O.,"** **"Petrified Man,"** and **"Lilly Daw and the Three Ladies."** Welty has said that **"P.O.,"** a dramatic monologue narrated by a gregarious post mistress, "grew out of . . . a lifelong listening to talk on my block where I grew up as a child," and clearly **"Petrified Man,"** **"Lily Daw,"** *Delta Wedding,* and most of the subsequent fiction are also dependent on the author's lifelong interest in the South's oral tradition. (p. 18)

Given Welty's long fascination with family storytelling and Southern talk, it is not surprising that the oral culture should come to be represented prominently in her fiction. What may be surprising is not the frequency of her portrayal of the oral culture but the complexity and incisiveness of the resulting portrait. Despite her immersion in the oral culture, she is able to see it with objectivity. She exploits the realism and inherent comedy of ordinary speech, but not merely for the picturesqueness of such speech. She exposes the roles the oral tradition plays for the Southerner and hence its importance to the culture. She shows it to be ritual and mask, diversion, and sustainer of the past. It is at one and the same time a social art, entertaining the family and community, and a social menace, boring strangers and serving to villanize and to exclude persons deemed outsiders. Perhaps most crucially, through it the society makes heroes of ordinary men. In *Delta Wedding, The Golden Apples, The Ponder Heart, Losing Battles, The Optimist's Daughter,* and several separate stories, Welty characterizes, and undercuts, the Southerner's propensity for romanticizing. (pp. 19-20)

The oral tradition has shaped Welty's narrative voice extensively and deliciously. In the attitude she sometimes takes toward her characters, the way she describes their actions, the insight she brings to such descriptions, we can recognize a local tale-teller amusingly narrating a tale about a local event or a town character. In **"June Recital,"** the author smoothly and convincingly falls into the tone and style of oral narration when Old Man Moody and Mr. Fatty Bowles appear on the scene. In this story, which combines tragedy with comedy, the portrayal of Moody and Bowles provides a moment of bold comedy that relieves the tension created by the subtle portrayal of Miss Eckhart's unhappiness and isolation and that contrasts with the ironic but sympathetic portrayals of little Loch Morrison and his sister Cassie, through whose eyes much of the action is seen. As Miss Eckhart, now senile and more alone than ever, begins a fire in her former piano studio, town marshal Old Man Moody and Mr. Fatty Bowles arrive at the house on an errand. Peering through a porch window and discovering Miss Eckhart's arson, they turn brave crime-stoppers.

> They lifted the screen out, and Mr. Fatty accidentally stepped through it. They inched the sash up with a sound that made them draw high their muck-coated heels. They could go in now: they opened their mouths and guffawed silently. They were so used to showing off, they almost called up Morgana then and there.

> Mr. Fatty Bowles started to squeeze himself over the sill into the room, but Old Man Moody was ready for that, pulled him back by the suspenders, and went first. He leap-frogged it. Inside, they both let go a holler.

> "Look out! You're caught in the act!"

This portrayal of Old Man Moody and Mr. Fatty Bowles reveals Welty the storyteller at work—and play. The passage has all the marks of oral tale-telling. Its direct focus is actions; its sentence structure is simple; its language concrete, largely monosyllabic, and frequently colloquial; and its verbs in particular strong and colorful. Like many folk humor tales, it makes a recent happening seem absurd by reducing the people involved to stick figures or buffoons.

But the men look foolish not only because of their actions but especially because of the attitudes giving rise to the actions, which are the real point of the tale. Although young Loch Morrison observes the two men from his perch in a tree nearby, it is clearly not his view but Welty's—or a raconteur's—ironic view that is given, for it is an amused storyteller, not little Loch, who would be able to recognize, and likely to exaggerate, the men's feelings of self-importance: "They were so used to showing off, they almost called up Morgana then and there." Neither man wants the other to be more of a hero than is he, as is effectively intimated in the second paragraph quoted. Moreover, their yell " 'Look out! You're caught in the act!' " is a bit of swaggering, an excessive display of authority and courage, given that the villain is obviously weak and disoriented and the danger only the struggling flickerings of an unprofessionally set fire. And in the paragraph which follows those quoted, the storytelling voice is heard in simple diction and images which implicitly ridicule the men's grasping at the heroic and their attempt to prolong and intensify their little adventure. Rather than reporting flatly that the men ran around the table and into the parlor, Welty, the raconteur, adopts language appropriate to a description of the football players they might like to be: they "made a preliminary run around the table to warm up" and then "charged the parlor." Like explorers making their way through a dense jungle, they "trod down the barrier of sparky matting and stomped in"; heavyweights that they imagine themselves, "they boxed at the smoke" but only succeeded in hitting each other. Thus does the storyteller depict, and mock, the men's bravado. Yet while she reduces the men to buffoons for the sake of amusing her audience, they seem real nonetheless. They are local folk known to the tale-teller and to everyone else as "Old Man Moody" and "Mr. Fatty," and their desire to be heroic, to shine for a moment, is very human indeed.

The tone of delight which seems inherent in Welty's fiction and which we have observed previously has, then, still another chord. The characters' "tireless relish of life" is frequently enhanced by a tone suggesting the delight a small-town raconteur takes in regaling an audience with tales about local folk whom she expects the audience to recognize. This storyteller may embroider or color the facts and paint characters with irony, but she nonetheless views the characters with a mixture of love, penetrating insight, and tolerant amusement.

To return for a moment to the contrast between the early stories and the mature fiction, the elements of love and tolerant amusement are what are often missing in Welty's treatment of the early characters. Typically, the narrative voice of the early stories invites the reader to delight in the characters *as characters,* not as breathing, feeling, ordinary human beings. Does Old Mr. Marblehall of ["**Old Mr. Marblehall"**] really lead a secret double life with nearly identical wives and sons at opposite ends of the same town? Or does he only imagine that he does? But does the reader care whether he does or not, except as the ambiguity creates a literary puzzle to solve? In this story, in fact, Welty increases the reader's detachment from the main character by unsubtly employing an omniscient narrator or story-teller who, directly addressing her audience as "you," in effect invites the audience to join her in viewing Mr. Marblehall as a figure in a tale. Unlike the implicit ra-conteur of the Old Man Moody-Mr. Fatty Bowles pas-sage, who gives the impression of reporting (and mak-ing understandable) the actions of a couple of local fel-lows who are very much a part of a community, this omniscient storyteller seems to be pulling the strings of a puppet:

> Old Mr. Marblehall never did anything, never got married until he was sixty. You can see him out tak-ing a walk. Watch and you'll see how preciously old people come to think they are made. . . . They stand long on the corners but more impatiently than anyone, as if they expect traffic to take notice of them, rear up the horses and throw on the brakes, so they can get where they want to go. That's Mr. Marblehall. He has short white bangs, and a bit of

> snapdragon in his lapel. He walks with a big pol-ished stick, a present. . . . He has on his thick, beautiful, glowing coat—tweed, but he looks as gratified as an animal in its own tingling fur. You see, even in summer he wears it, because he is cold all the time.

> (pp. 23-5)

But though her stance as storyteller grows more subtle and tolerant as her vision matures, Welty is, early and late, a storyteller. She is also—but late more consistently than early—the poet and historian of a storytelling people . . . [She] has progressively painted a revealing picture of the Southern oral tradition ("a treasure I helped myself to") and the families and com-munities who share it. Writing in a conversational style born itself of the region's active oral tradition, Welty proves herself the oral culture's most discriminating admirer and its most incisive critic. (p. 25)

Carol S. Manning, in her *With Ears Opening Like Morning Glories: Eudora Welty and the Love of Storytelling,* Greenwood Press, 1985, 221 p.

SOURCES FOR FURTHER STUDY

Desmond, John F., ed. *A Still Moment: Essays on the Art of Eudora Welty.* Metuchen, N. J.: The Scarecrow Press, 1978, 142 p.

> Essay collection that explores the diversity of Welty's fiction.

Evans, Elizabeth. *Eudora Welty.* New York: Frederick Ungar Publishing Co., 1981, 172 p.

> Biographical and critical study. Evans notes that in Welty's works readers will find "fresh insights into the human condition presented in a style marked by clarity, sureness of image and dialogue, and richness in humor and technical skill."

Kreyling, Michael. *Eudora Welty's Achievement of Order.* Baton Rouge: Louisiana State University Press, 1980, 188 p.

> Comprehensive critical study of Welty's works.

MacKethan, Lucinda Hardwick. "To See Things in Their Time: The Act of Focusing in Eudora Welty's Fiction." In her *The Dream of Arcady: Place and Time in Southern Literature,* pp. 181-206. Baton Rouge: Louisiana State University Press, 1980.

> Addresses Welty's theory of the importance of setting as expressed in her longer works of fiction, noting that "for Miss Welty a sense of place is where art begins."

Prenshaw, Peggy Whitman, ed. *Eudora Welty: Critical Es-says.* Jackson: University of Mississippi Press, 1979, 444 p.

> Collection of essays by such prominent Welty scholars as Ruth Vande Kieft and Michael Kreyling.

Vande Kieft, Ruth M. *Eudora Welty.* Rev. ed. Boston: Twayne, 1987, 209 p.

> Influential study of Welty's life and works.

Edith Wharton

1862-1937

(Full name Edith Newbold Jones Wharton)
American short story writer, novelist, essayist,
and autobiographer.

INTRODUCTION

Wharton is best known as a novelist of manners whose fiction exposes the cruel excesses of aristocratic society in the United States at the beginning of the twentieth century. Her carefully crafted, psychologically complex novels, novellas, and short stories reflect concern for the status of women in society as well as for the moral decay she observed underlying the propriety of the upper classes. While her subject matter, tone, and style have often been compared with those of her friend and mentor Henry James, Wharton has achieved critical recognition as an original chronicler of the conflict between the inner self and social convention. Margaret B. McDowell observed: "[Wharton's] best work reveals her accomplished artistry, her grasp of social reality, her realization that manners are a key to the outer life of a society and the expression of an inner reality that escapes casual observation, her moral subtlety and incisiveness, and her unwavering insight into human nature."

Born into a wealthy New York family, Wharton was privately educated by governesses and tutors both at home and abroad. At an early age she displayed a marked interest in writing and literature, a pursuit her socially ambitious mother attempted to discourage. Nevertheless, Wharton finished her first novella at the age of fourteen and published a collection of verse two years later. From the perspective of an upper-class initiate, she observed the shift of power and wealth from the hands of New York's established gentry to the nouveau riche of the Industrial Revolution. Wharton considered the newly wealthy to be cultural philistines and drew upon their lives to create many of her best-remembered fictional characters and situations. In 1885 she married Edward Wharton. Becoming dissatisfied with society life and disillusioned with marriage, however, Wharton sought fulfillment in writing. Many of her stories and poems originally appeared in *Scribner's Magazine,* and both her first short story collection, *The Greater Inclination* (1899), and her novel *The House of Mirth* (1905) were well received by critics and readers. Suffering from ill health and forced to contend with her husband's growing mental instability, Wharton was granted a divorce in 1912. Soon after, she established residence in France. During World War I, Wharton organized relief efforts in France and cared for Belgian orphans, for which she earned the French Legion of Honor. While her war novella *The Marne* (1918), generated little positive critical interest, Wharton became the first female recipient of the Pulitzer Prize, for her novel *The Age of Innocence* in 1921. During the final years of her life, Wharton continued to write short stories and novels, many of which reflect her growing disillusionment with postwar America and the Jazz Age. Her final novel, *The Buccaneers,* remained unfinished when she died in St. Brice-sous-Forêt in 1937.

Wharton's fiction was especially effective at piercing the veil of moral respectability that sometimes masked a lack of integrity among the rich. In *House of Mirth,* for example, an intelligent and lovely girl must lose her status as a member of the leisure class if she is to avoid moral ruin. Lily Bart rebels against the standards of her social group enough to smoke, gamble, and be seen in public with married men; however, her sense of decency keeps her from marrying a wealthy but vulgar suitor merely to secure her fortunes. Her other opportunity consists of a young lawyer who makes fun of the "high society" his modest but adequate means entitle him to observe. When the first proposes, she turns him down; when the second proposes, it is too late—he finds the distraught Lily dead of an overdose of sleeping pills. Publication of this best seller in 1905 provoked much discussion in the United States, where it was hailed as one of the best novels the country had ever produced.

Wharton believed that good faith among the rich was not to be taken for granted, since it was grounded not in conformity to social standards but in an individual's commitment to respond to the needs of the less fortunate. She also understood that social pressure among the poor could be just as confining. In her novel *Ethan Frome* (1911), she shows how the title character suffers when he is caught between two women—his wife, Zeena, on whom he depends for economic survival, and his true love, a younger relative of his wife's who has come to the farm to help with the work. Ethan and his love see no way out except suicide, but their attempt fails, and they become invalids in the hands of Zeena. Edwin Bjoerkman has commented that Ethan lives "between those two spectres of his lost hopes: the woman he needed and the woman he loved. All other tragedies that I can think of seem mild and bearable beside this one." Though the novel is often re-

garded by reviewers as a departure from Wharton's usual subject matter, Bjoerkman suggested that, "after all, the tragedy unveiled to us is social rather than personal. . . . 'Ethan Frome' is to me above all else a judgment on that system which fails to redeem such villages as Mrs. Wharton's Starkfield. Those who dwell in our thousand and one Starkfields are [as] wrecked mariners, fallen into their hapless positions through no fault of their own. And though helpless now, they need by no means prove useless under different conditions."

Some critics felt that Wharton's portraits of men were unjustly negative. "Men especially have a hard time of it in Mrs. Wharton's novels," Irving Howe commented. He continued, "In their notorious vanity and faithlessness, they seldom 'come through'; they fail Mrs. Wharton's heroines less from bad faith than weak imagination, a laziness of spirit that keeps them from a true grasp of suffering; and in a number of her novels one finds a suppressed feminine bitterness, a profound impatience with the claims of the ruling sex." However, *New York Times Book Review* contributor Janet Malcolm, looking back on *The House of Mirth, The Reef* (1912), *The Custom of the Country* (1913), and *The Age of Innocence,* remarked that in Wharton's fiction, "the callousness and heartlessness by which this universe is ruled is the callousness and heartlessness of women. There are no bad men in Wharton's fiction. There are weak men and there are foolish men and there are vulgar New Rich men, but no man ever deliberately causes harm to another person; that role is exclusively reserved for women." While not accusing Wharton of misanthropy or misogyny, other critics have spoken of her pervasive pessimism. Howe related Wharton's "feminist resentment" to "a more radical and galling inequity at the heart of the human scheme. The inability of human beings to achieve self-sufficiency drives them to seek relationships with other people, and these relationships necessarily compromise their freedom by subjecting them to the pain of a desire either too great or too small. Things, in Mrs. Wharton's world, do not work out."

Other critics, however, stress the positive values that inform Wharton's novels. Howe pointed out, "In books like *The House of Mirth* and *The Age of Innocence* she could work on the assumption, so valuable to a writer who prizes economy of structure, that moral values can be tested in a novel by dramatizing the relationships between fixed social groups and mobile characters." The results of this testing were not always negative. Though far from idealistic, her novels argue the importance of living with a sense of duty to others. James W. Gargano explains in *American Literature,* "Faith, as Edith Wharton defines it, is no generalized and temperamental optimism; it is, instead, an almost mystical assurance that only moral action can save the ever-threatened community of human existence. Beset by dangers inherent in social arrangements, man clings to survival by the thread of his moral instincts; he is, at his best, motivated by what Mrs. Wharton calls, in *Sanctuary,* 'this passion of charity for the race.' In other words, goodness is useful, and men and women must, under pain of extinction, bequeath it to their children."

Wharton produced works that affirmed the need to conserve certain fundamental values that were quickly losing ground in the twentieth century. *The Valley of Decision* (1902), her first long novel, depicted the moral decline in Italy during the eighteenth century, and was deemed a successful work of history presented as exquisitely-crafted fiction. James W. Tuttleton explained that "she continually argued the necessity of the individual's commitment to the cultural tradition; . . . the catastrophe which ensues when social upheavals like revolution, anarchy, and war destroy the slowly and delicately spun web of that tradition; and the necessity of imaginatively preserving . . . the precious values of the past." By showing in her fiction what becomes of people when culture ceases to be a moral force, and by recording her memories of a time when it was, Wharton "hoped to revive the memory of a set of slowly evolved cultural values suddenly wiped out by a succession of destructive changes in American life beginning in the 1880's—including the rise of the industrial plutocracy ('the lords of Pittsburgh,' as she called them); massive immigration which totally altered the ethnic character of New York City; the First World War, the depression, and the New Deal; and the nationalistic hatreds, at the close of her life in 1937, building toward the Second World War." Wharton seems to have "felt that the universe—which for her is virtually to say, organised society—was profoundly inhospitable to human need and desire," Howe commented in *Encounter.* Q. D. Leavis wrote, "Mrs. Wharton, if unfortunate in her environment, had a strength of character that made her superior to it. She was a remarkable novelist if not a large-sized one, and while there are few great novelists there are not even so many remarkable ones that we can afford to let her be overlooked."

In addition to writing about the importance of values, Wharton validated them in her service to the less fortunate during and after the First World War. An energetic fund-raiser, she was aided by "Edith Wharton" committees in New York, Boston, Philadelphia, Washington, and Providence. With her financial support, an ambulance unit, a workroom for female garment workers, and a sanatorium for women and children with tuberculosis were established in France. She also raised money for American hostels for refugees and the Children of Flanders rescue committee. France recognized her philanthropy by awarding her the Cross of the Legion of Honor, and she was made Chevalier of the Order of Leopold in Belgium.

Books informed by her war experience, however, were not regarded as her best. Auchincloss explained that she saw the war "from a simple but consistent point of view: France, virtually singlehanded, was fighting the battle of civilization against the powers of darkness. It was the spirit that made men fight and die, but it has never, unfortunately, been the spirit of fiction. Reading *The Marne* . . . and *A Son at the Front* . . . today gives one the feeling of taking an old enlistment poster out of an attic trunk. . . . Mrs. Wharton knew that the war was terrible; she had visited hospitals and even the front itself. But the exhilaration of the noncombatant, no matter how dedicated and useful her services, has a shrill sound to postwar ears."

Written after the First World War, *The Age of Innocence,* another novel about Old New York society, again showcased passionate characters hemmed in by their desire to keep their membership in a dispassionate social group. Newland Archer is engaged to marry an acceptable and attractive girl, but falls in love with Ellen Olenska, a European divorcee. Olenska had married a Polish Count, a villain from whom she escaped with the eager aid of his secretary. Equally passionate but seeking to reestablish her honor in New York society (which is not sure she is acceptable), Olenska encourages Archer to keep his commitment. To make it easier for him, she returns to Europe. "Archer, with his insecurity, his sensitivity, and his passion has obeyed the moral imperatives of his class and time and has given up Ellen and love for the furtherance of the shallow-seeming aims, all amorphous as they are, of his [New York] world," observed Louis O. Coxe. Wharton allows Archer to confess that a life of duty has its rewards—and yet it is a lonely life, since the next generation, represented by Archer's son, enjoys freedom from social pressure and is unable to understand this kind of sacrifice, Coxe added. The novel was highly acclaimed as one of Wharton's best novels, and, according to *New York Times* writer W. L. Phelps, as "one of the best novels of the twentieth century"; it won the Pulitzer Prize in 1921.

Commenting on Wharton's place in literary history, Louise Bogan wrote, "Mrs. Wharton's work formed a bridge from the nineteenth-century novel to the magazine fiction of the present. . . . She contained in herself, as it were, the whole transitional period of American fiction, beginning in the bibelot and imported-European-culture era of the late nineties, and ending in the woman's-magazine dream of suburban smartness." Ten years before her death in 1937, Wharton was nominated to receive the Nobel Prize in recognition that she had become the most distinguished American writer of her generation. That she did not receive the award does not diminish either her achievement in letters or the high esteem granted to her by her contemporaries in both America and Europe. Percy Lubbock maintained in his *Portrait of Edith Wharton* in 1947, "The sagest and sternest of the craftsmen must admit that she meets them on their ground."

(For further information about Wharton's life and works, see *Concise Dictionary of American Literary Biography, 1865-1917; Contemporary Authors*, Vols. 104, 132; *Dictionary of Literary Biography*, Vols. 4, 9, 12, 78; *Short Story Criticism*, Vol. 6; and *Twentieth-Century Literary Criticism*, Vols. 3, 9, 27.)

CRITICAL COMMENTARY

KENNETH BERNARD
(essay date 1961)

[Bernard is an American dramatist, poet, short story writer, and critic. In the following excerpt, he analyzes imagery and symbolism in *Ethan Frome*.]

A common criticism of Edith Wharton's *Ethan Frome* is that it is too contrived. In the last analysis, the characters seem peculiarly unmotivated, put through their paces in a clever, but mechanical, way. Such an opinion can only be the result of a cursory reading. It is true that the book has a kind of stylistic and organizational brilliance. But it is not merely a display; it is invariably at the service of plot and character. The nature of her subject imposed certain difficulties on Wharton, particularly her characters' lack of articulation. How could she, without over-narrating, get a deep problem involving such characters when they do not speak enough to reveal that problem? Frome's character and his marital relationship are at the heart of the novel, but they are revealed only indirectly. Wharton solved her difficulty in a masterful way by her use of imagery and symbolism. It is in her use of imagery and symbolism that the depths of the story are to be found. Without an understanding of them, a reader *would* find the characters unmotivated and the tragedy contrived. For easy discussion, the imagery and symbolism may be divided into three parts: the compatibility of setting and character, the uses of light and dark, and the sexual symbolism. A survey of these three parts in the novel will, it is hoped, clarify the real story in *Ethan Frome* by adding a new dimension of meaning.

The beginning of this new dimension of meaning is the first mention of the New England village— Starkfield. On many levels the *locus* of the story is a stark field. The village lies under "a sky of iron," points of the dipper over it hang "like icicles," and Orion flashes "cold fires." The countryside is "gray and lonely." Each farmhouse is "mute and cold as a grave-stone." This characterization of Starkfield is consistent throughout the book. Frome, in all ways, fits into this setting. On several occasions his integration with it is described. The narrator, upon first seeing him, sees him as "bleak and unapproachable." Later he says of Frome, "He seemed a part of the mute melancholy landscape, an incarnation of its frozen woe, with all that was warm and sentient in him bound fast below the surface . . . he lived in a depth of moral isolation too remote for casual access." Frome, unhappily married to Zeena, and pining for her cousin Mattie, is indeed parallel to the Starkfield setting. Everything on the surface is hard and frozen. His feeling, his love, for Mattie cannot break loose, just as spring and summer are fast bound by winter's cold. Mattie, appropriately, has the effect of loosening the rigid physical and emotional landscape. At one point, when she speaks, "The iron heavens seemed to melt down sweetness." Again, she is "like the lightning of a fire on a cold hearth." Frome, however, who has suffered "the profound accumulated cold of many Starkfield winters," does not thaw easily. He remembers when his feelings were free, or, as he puts it, when he was once in Florida, climatically (and emotionally) the opposite of Starkfield: "Yes, I was down there once, and for a good while afterward I could call up the sight of it in winter. But now it's all snowed under." Finally there is Frome's inarticulateness. Not only are his feelings locked, frozen; his very speech is also, beyond the natural reticence of the local people. Neither he nor the landscape can express its warm and tender part. When Mattie once pleases him immensely, he gropes "for a dazzling phrase," but is able to utter only a "growl of rapture: 'Come along'." Later he is again thrilled by her: "Again he struggled for the all expressive word, and again, his arm in hers, found only a deep 'Come along'." He is truly a man of "dumb melancholy."

The separation of feeling from its expression, the idea of emotion being locked away, separated, or frozen, just as Starkfield is bound by ice and snow, is dem-

Principal Works

onstrated also by the Frome farm. The house seems to "shiver in the wind," has a "broken down gate," and has an "unusually forlorn and stunted look." More important, though, is the "L." Wharton gives a full description of the New England farm "L":

> that long deep-roofed adjunct usually built at right angles to the main house, and connecting it, by way of store-rooms and tool-house, with the wood-shed and cow-barn. Whether because of its symbolic sense, the image it presents of a life linked with the soil, and enclosing in itself the chief sources of warmth and nourishment, or whether merely because of the consolatory thought that it enables the dwellers in that harsh climate to get to their morning's work without facing the weather, it is certain that the "L" rather than the house itself seems to be the center, the actual hearth-stone of the New England farm.

Frome casually mentions to the narrator that he had had to take down the "L." Thus Frome's home is disjointed, separated from its vital functions, even as he is. The narrator, not unnaturally, sees in Frome's words about the "diminished dwelling the image of his own shrunken body." Just as Frome is emotionally trapped, just as Starkfield is frozen in the winter landscape, just as Frome's home is cut off from its vitals, so too is he cut off physically from his former strength, trapped in his crippled frame. Images of being caught, bound,

trapped are frequent. "He was a prisoner for life." "It seemed to Ethan that his heart was bound with cords which an unseen hand was tightening with every tick of the clock." "I'm tied hand and foot, Matt." Although Mattie is described with flight images like "the flit of a bird in branches," and birds making "short perpendicular flights," the last such image describing her is of her lashes beating like "netted butterflies," and her last "twittering" is her pitiful cry after the unsuccessful suicide attempt, when she is a broken, pain-racked body. Even Mattie, Frome's one hope of escape, is trapped. On top of this, Frome mentions that before the railroad came to a nearby town the road by his farm was a main route, implying that business was better: "We're kinder side-tracked here now." The farm, too, is separated from its former economic vitality. Thus the setting of the novel, the landscape and the farm, is parallel to Frome's condition and serves to illuminate it. But Wharton does not stop at this point.

There is hardly a page throughout the book that does not have some reference to light and dark. Wharton uses all of them with effect. The supreme light image is Mattie Silver, as her name implies. She is in contrast to everything in Starkfield; her feelings bubble near the surface. Frome, on the other hand, is all dark. He lives in the dark, especially emotionally. At the beginning of the novel, when he has come to meet Mattie, she is dancing gaily in a church filled with "broad bands of yellow light." Frome keeps "out of the range of the revealing rays from within." "Hugging the shadow," he stands in the "frosty darkness" and looks in. Later he catches up to her "in the black shade of the Varnum spruces," the spot from where they finally begin the attempted suicide that cripples them. He stands with her in "the gloom of the spruces," where it is "so dark . . . he could barely see the shape of her head," or walks with her "in silence through the blackness of the Hemlock-shaded lane." Blackness is his element. As they walk back to the farm he revels in their closeness. "It was during their night walks back to the farm that he felt most intensely the sweetness of this communion." Their love is a bloom of night. "He would have liked to stand there with her all night in the blackness." He does not see Mattie so much as sense her: " . . .he felt, in the darkness, that her face was lifted quickly to his." "They strained their eyes to each other through the icy darkness." Frome's favorite spot is a secluded place in the woods called Shadow Pond. On their last visit there "the darkness descended with them, dropping down like a black veil from the heavy hemlock boughs." Frome cannot seem to get out of the dark. And often, as in quotations above, the dark is pregnant with suggestions of death and cold. Frome's kitchen, on their return from the village, has "the deadly chill of a vault after the dry cold of night." As Ethan settles in his tomblike house, Mattie's effect on him dies away. He lies in bed and watches the light from her candle, which

> sending its small ray across the landing, drew a scarcely perceptible line of light under his door. He kept his eyes fixed on the light till it vanished. Then the room grew perfectly black, and not a sound was audible but Zeena's asthmatic breathing.

Without Mattie's "light" he is left with the ugly reality of his wife. In numerous small ways also Wharton makes the light and dark images work for her. When Mattie relieves Ethan's jealousy at one point, "The blackness lifted and light flooded Ethan's brain." When Mattie is told by Zeena she must go, and she repeats the words to Ethan, "The words went on sounding between them as though a torch of warning flew from hand to hand through a dark landscape." Before their suicide plunge, "The spruces swatched them in blackness and silence." A bitter argument between Ethan and Zeena is "as senseless and savage as a physical fight between two enemies in the darkness." After, Zeena's face "stood grimly out against the uncurtained pane, which had turned from grey to black." The cumulative effect of all these images is to tell us a great deal about Frome and his tortured psyche.

The most important thing the images of light and dark reveal about Frome is that he is a negative person. Frome is a heroic figure: nothing less than the entire landscape can suffice to describe him effectively; his agony is as broad and deep as that of the winter scene. But he is not tragic because he is a man of great potential subdued and trapped by forces beyond his capacity. His tragedy is entirely of his own making. He is weak. His character never changes. Both before and after the accident he is the same. Like his environment he has a kind of dumb endurance for harsh conditions. There are several indications of his weakness besides his identity with darkness. Frome married Zeena because she had nursed his mother through her final illness. He was twenty-one and she twenty-eight. He married her less because he loved her than because he needed a replacement for his mother. Certainly it is Zeena who cracks the whip in the household, and Ethan who jumps. What Zeena says, goes. Frome "had often thought since that it would not have happened if his mother had died in spring instead of winter . . . ." When he and Mattie are about to attempt suicide, Mattie sitting in front of Ethan on the sled, he asks her to change places with him. She asks why. Quite sincerely he answers, "Because I—because I want to feel you holding me." He wants to die being cuddled and comforted, leaving to Mattie the role of protecter and shelterer.

Throughout the book, Frome recognizes his futility and accepts it rather than trying to fight his way out of it. He does not ever realistically reach for a solution. His love inspires little more than dreams. He thinks of another man who left his wife for another woman and invests the event with fairy tale qualities: "They had a little girl with fair curls, who wore a gold locket and was dressed like a princess." Once he imagines Zeena might be dead: "What if tramps had been there—what if . . . ." When he spends his one night alone with Mattie, instead of thinking of a way to achieve permanence for their relationship he "set his imagination adrift on the fiction that they had always spent their evenings thus and would always go on doing so . . . ." Ironically, this is just about what he achieves by crippling instead of killing himself and Mattie. He did not, however, envision that Zeena would be a necessary part of the arrangement, as a nurse to Mattie.

The negation, the blackness, in his character is revealed also in his funereal satisfactions. When Mattie says she is not thinking of leaving because she has no place to go, "The answer sent a pang through him but the tone suffused him with joy." He rejoices in her helplessness; he is pained and thrilled at the same time because she has nowhere to go, because she too is trapped. Looking at the gravestones on his farm that have mocked him for years ("We never got away—how should you?"), he rejoices: " . . . all desire for change had vanished, and the sight of the little enclosure gave him a warm sense of continuance and stability."

"I guess we'll never let you go, Matt," he whispered, as though even the dead, lovers once, must conspire with him to keep her; and brushing by the graves, he thought: "We'll always go on living here together, and some day she'll lie there beside me."

The finest thought he can have is of the triangle going on forever, and then lying in the earth next to Mattie: "He was never so happy with her as when he abandoned himself to these dreams." Frome's aspirations do not finally go beyond darkness. His final acceptance of suicide is the culmination of his negative instincts: death is the blackest blackness.

Although the meaningful use of light and dark is pervasive in the book and is illuminating, it is the sexual symbolism that cuts deepest. The sexual symbolism is more dramatic than the two elements already discussed because it revolves around the key scenes in the book, Ethan and Mattie's night together and Zeena's return. It is also more significant because without an understanding of it the source of Zeena and Ethan's estrangement and antagonism remains unknown. After all, what *is* the deep gulf that lies between them? There is no explicit revelation in the book. In part, Wharton's use of symbolism to clarify the book's central problem is compatible with the inarticulateness of the characters. But perhaps also it represents a reticence or modesty of the author's. Ethan and Mattie's night together is ostensibly a mild affair. Wharton might well have revealed then the true relationship between Frome and his wife and demonstrated overtly Mattie and Ethan's transgression. But was it really necessary for her to do so? Even as it is, the evening progresses with the greatest of intensity. Every action, every word, even every silence quivers. It is because these apparently innocent actions and words exist in such intensity that they must be scrutinized. There are disproportions of feeling, particularly centering around the pickle dish, that are revealing. (pp. 178-82)

Barrenness, infertility, is at the heart of Frome's frozen woe. Not only is his farm crippled, and finally his body too; his sexuality is crippled also. Zeena, already hypochondriac when he married her, has had the effect of burying his manhood as deeply as everything else in him. In seven years of marriage there have been no children. Within a year of their marriage, Zeena developed her "sickliness." Medicine, sickness, and death are, in fact, rarely out of sight in the book. The farm itself, with its separation of its vital center, its regenerative center, suggests of course the sexual repression. The name Starkfield also connotes barrenness. However, Ethan and Zeena's sexual relationship is suggested most by the incident of the pickle dish, a dish which, unless understood, lies rather unaccountably at the very center of the book.

The red pickle dish is Zeena's most prized possession. She received it as a wedding gift. But she never uses it. Instead she keeps it on a shelf, hidden away. She takes it down only during spring cleaning, "and then I always lifted it with my own hands, so's 't shouldn't get broke." The dish has only ceremonial, not functional, use. The sexual connotations here are obvious. The fact that the wedding dish, which was meant to contain pickles, in fact never does, explains a lot of the heaviness of atmosphere, the chill, the frigidity. The most intense scenes of the book, the most revealing, center around this dish. For example, Zeena never does discover an affair in the making between Ethan and Mattie, nor does she ever say anything, except for one hint not followed up, that reveals such knowledge. Her only discovery (and it is *the* discovery of the book) is of her broken (and used) pickle dish. It is this which brings the only tears to her eyes in the entire book. When Zeena is gone for a day, Mattie, significantly, brings down and uses the pickle dish in serving Ethan supper. Only if the dish is properly understood can it be seen how her violation is a sacrilege, as Zeena's emotions amply testify. The dish is broken, and Ethan plans to glue it together. Of course the dish can never be the same. This kind of violation is irrevocable. Zeena does not discover that the dish is broken until she gets, again significantly, heartburn, the powders for which she keeps on the same private shelf as the pickle dish. The scene following is a symbolic recognition of the fact that Mattie has usurped her place, broken her marriage, and become one with Ethan, though in fact it was the cat (Zeena) who actually broke the dish. The fact that Zeena never truly filled her place, acted the role of wife, and is herself responsible for the failure of the marriage does not bother her. Ethan is hers, however ceremonially, and she resents what has happened. Her emotion transcends any literal meaning the dish may have, so much so that other implications of the dish force themselves on the reader. Speaking to Mattie, she says,

> " . . . you waited till my back was turned, and took the thing I set most store by of anything I've got, and wouldn't never use it, not even when the minister come to dinner, or Aunt Martha Pierce come over from Bettsbridge. . . . I tried to keep my things where you couldn't get at 'em—and now you've took from me the one I cared for most of all—" She broke off in a short spasm of sobs that passed and left her more than ever like the shape of a stone. . . . Gathering up the bits of broken glass she went out of the room as if she carried a dead body. . . .

The passage reveals most clearly the gulf between Ethan and Zeena. The body she carries out is the corpse of her marriage. The evening that Mattie and Ethan spend together, then, is not as innocent as it seems on the surface. That Mattie and Ethan's infidelity is so indirectly presented, whether because of Wharton's sense of propriety or her desire to maintain a minimum of direct statement, does not at all lessen the reality of that fact. If the overt act of infidelity is not present, the emotional and symbolic act is. The passage is full of passion; the moment, for example, when Frome kisses the edge of the piece of material Mattie is holding has climactic intensity.

The sterility of their marriage, Frome's emasculation, is represented elsewhere. For example, just before Zeena leaves for the overnight trip to a doctor, she finishes a bottle of medicine and pushes it to Mattie: "It ain't done me a speck of good, but I guess I might as well use it up. . . . If you can get the taste out it'll do for pickles." This is the only other mention of pickles in the book. Significantly, it is the last word in the chapter before the one devoted to Ethan and Mattie's night together. The action might be interpreted as follows: after Zeena has exhausted the possibilities of her medicine for her "trouble," she turns to sex—but she passes on that alternative to Mattie. Mattie may use the jar for pickles if she wishes. The action is a foreshadowing of Mattie's use of the pickle dish. In a sense, Zeena has urged her to that act, for she is abdicating the position of sexual initiative.

Again, in *Ethan Frome* each word counts. But there are some descriptions, obviously very particular, that do not fit in with any generalizations already presented. However, in the light of an understanding of the pickle dish incident, they are clarified. When Frome first points out his home, the narrator notes "the black wraith of a deciduous creeper" flapping on the porch. Deciduous means shedding leaves, or antlers, or horns, or teeth, at a particular season or stage of growth. Frome has indeed shed his manhood. Sexually he is in his winter season. Later, another vegetation is described on the porch: "A dead cucumber vine dangled from the porch like the crape streamer tied to the door for a death . . .". A cucumber is no more than a pickle. The pickle dish is not used; the cucumber vine is dead. That it should be connected with crape (black) and death is perfectly logical in the light of what has already been discussed about Frome. Frome's sexuality is dead. There is, of course, in all this the suggestion that Frome could revive if he could but reach spring, escape the winter of his soul. Mattie is his new season. At one point, where Mattie "shone" on him,

his soul swelled with pride as he saw how his tone subdued her. She did not even ask what he had done. Except when he was steering a big log down the mountain to his mill he had never known such a thrilling sense of mastery.

Mattie, as Zeena never does, makes Ethan feel the springs of his masculinity. But he never overcomes the ice of accumulated Starkfield winters. His final solution is to merge himself with winter forever.

Thus Ethan Frome, when he plunges towards what he considers certain death, is a failure but not a mystery. His behavior is not unmotivated; the tragedy is not contrived. The very heart of the novel is Frome's weakness of character, his negation of life. Behind that is his true, unfulfilled, relationship with Zeena. Wharton's economy of language in the novel is superb. There is hardly a word unnecessary to the total effect. Her final economy is the very brevity of the book. It fits the scene and character. There were depths to plumb; her people were not simple. To overcome the deficiencies of their natural reticence (and perhaps her own), to retain the strength of the severe and rugged setting, particularly the "outcropping granite," she resorted to a brilliant pattern of interlocking imagery and symbolism, three facets of which have been outlined here, to create a memorable work. The reader of *Ethan Frome,* then, need not find it merely a technically successful work, a virtuoso performance. With an understanding of the imagery and symbolism he can look into the heart of the book and see characters as full-bodied people in the grip of overwhelming emotional entanglements. He is also in a position to see the book's true dimensions as tragedy. (pp. 182-84)

Kenneth Bernard, "Imagery and Symbolism in 'Ethan Frome'," in *College English,* Vol. 23, No. 3, December, 1961, pp. 178-84.

PATRICIA R. PLANTE
(essay date 1963)

[In the following excerpt, Plante traces early critical reception of Wharton's stories and defends the author against literary detractors.]

Edith Wharton's chief concern in **"The Recovery"** as well as in other stories is a vivid presentation of the subject, and this she accomplishes with a high degree of competence. First, her short stories are never mere sketches or breathless summaries. For example, in the story under discussion, the subject of Keniston's original blindness and eventual enlightenment is analyzed in detail. Enough time is taken so that the reader can see him respond to Mrs. Davant and his other home town admirers, share his bewilderment when faced with the works of genius at the National Gallery in London and experience his failure when his paintings are exhibited in Paris. Second, her openings are not only effective and colorful, but contain the germ of the story about to be developed. **"The Recovery"** begins with the sentence, "To the visiting stranger Hillbridge's first question was, 'Have you seen Keniston's things?' " And finally, her skillful use of dialogue contributes greatly to the vividness of her presentation of a situation. It is used sparingly and discriminately, and only at moments of crisis in the tale. For example, in **"The Recovery"** it is used four times, and each time one of the most important phases of the situation is made clear. The first time dialogue is used, Mrs. Davant's uncritical and valueless opinion of Keniston's work is contrasted to his wife's perceptive and sensitive view of the same. The second time, Keniston's blind acceptance of Mrs. Davant's encouragement is made clear to Mrs. Keniston. The third time, Mrs. Keniston is given hints as to an approaching change in her husband's attitude, and the reader is prepared for the ending. And the last time, Keniston shares his artistic awakening with his joyful wife. Thus, the situation in Edith Wharton's **"The Recovery"** had been very clearly and vividly presented, but a doubt persisted in the critics' minds as to whether it had been worth presenting at all.

The Descent of Man and *The Hermit and the Wild Woman* fared about the same. There was no denying their brilliancy, their skill, their cleverness, but without explaining what they meant by "elemental art" reviewers shouted that these collections of short stories were without it—and seemingly, nothing could replace "it." Readers of the volume were also beginning to accuse Edith Wharton of monotony and coldness. One found no lifting from minor to major, no relieving touch of cheerfulness. Agnes Repplier wrote in *The Outlook* that the latter collection had the chill of winter in its pages and that it would best appeal to an impartial reader who was prepared to accept the ironies of life as a substitute for its illusions. *The Spectator* argued that the invariable recurrence of failure and disillusionment as leading motives made for both depression and monotony. *The Nation* repeated the charge in slightly different words and hoped that the uniformity of key was only coincidence.

What is most striking in these two volumes, other than the similarity of tone discernible in all the tales, is Edith Wharton's preoccupation with the irony of things—especially in connection with man's failures. The best example of this ironic spirit in dealing with the weaknesses of man is probably found in the story entitled **"The Other Two"** from the collection *The Descent of Man.* Again, the situation is all. Waythorn marries a beautiful woman who has had two previous husbands, Haskett and Varick. For personal and business reasons, the three men and Mrs. Waythorn are continuously brought together. At first, Waythorn's sense of decorum is offended, but gradually he comes to accept the fact that his wife's great talent for anticipating and fulfilling all of his domestic needs had had to be acquired at some school. "He even began to reckon up the advantages which accrued from it, to ask himself if it were not better to own a third of a wife who knew how to make a man happy than a whole one who had lacked opportunity to acquire the art." The

tale ends with all four parties involved happily taking tea together in the Waythorn parlor. Admittedly, Waythorn's concessions and his wife's pliability are not weaknesses which would suggest man's potential greatness. There is no hint of tragedy in Waythorn's final illumination concerning the disconcerting fact that his wife was "as easy as an old shoe—a shoe that too many feet had worn. Her elasticity was the result of tension in too many different directions."

If there is no tragedy in **"The Other Two,"** there is a great deal of humor which critics seemingly insisted on not discovering. Surely reviewers were right in drawing attention to Edith Wharton's vein of irony which ran through her tales, and they were also right in noticing that this ironic treatment of nearly all situations contributed to a nearly monotonous similarity of tone. However, when Agnes Repplier wrote in *The Outlook* that this irony is "remote from humor," one wonders whether Edith Wharton's spirit of fun was in reality too subtle or whether readers needed time to orient themselves to a writer whose humor was anything but obvious. At any rate, it seems fairly certain, in the light of her other works, that when Edith Wharton described the adaptability of a Mrs. Waythorn, who could diffuse about her a sense of ease and familiarity while offering her two former husbands and her present one a cup of tea, she was actually joining Waythorn himself who "took the third cup with a laugh." Edith Wharton's use of irony had always been the method best suited to both her purpose and talent in communicating humor. The ironic treatment of a situation always allowed her to juxtapose a character's view of himself and the circumstances in which he finds himself, with the author's own view of both revealed through description or dialogue. And this very juxtaposition is what makes for the Wharton variety of humor. For example, in **"The Other Two"** when Waythorn, watching his wife preparing his coffee, yields to feelings of possessorship, the author, through a sudden use of romantic phrases, makes it clear that poor Waythorn's feelings are quite unwarranted. "They were his, those white hands with their flitting motions, his the light haze of hair, the lips and eyes. . . ." At that very moment, Mrs. Waythorn pours cognac in the coffee. Unfortunately, Varick (husband number two), was the one who liked the combination of cognac and coffee. Waythorn utters an exclamation, and his thoughts of possessorship are given a violent jolt—much to the amusement of the reader.

It was generally agreed that the stories in Edith Wharton's next collection, *Tales of Men and Ghosts,* were of strangely unequal merit, but what is a bit disconcerting is that they were accused of two rather contradictory defects. On the one hand we read the by now familiar complaint that while maintaining a high literary standard as to form, diction, and structure, the author is too subtle and inconclusive and too deficient in action to please the average reader; and on the other, a new note was sounded when *The Nation* found the tales too patent and trumped up. For the first time, Edith Wharton was accused of writing magazine fiction. An announcement had been made the year before that she would come out with this collection in 1910, and some felt that here they were—skillfully turned out according to contract.

Only the rare and discriminating magazine fiction reader, it seems to me, would experience any satisfaction in reading *Tales of Men and Ghosts,* a collection of psychological studies of abnormal or supernatural episodes. By "ghosts" most readers would certainly expect something quite different from the clever suggestions of the preternatural happenings found in these pages. In **"His Father's Son,"** for example, a young man, at the height of his romantic folly, imagines that he is the illegitimate son of a very famous pianist; and discovers, to his chagrin, that he is truly the son of the man who brought him up—Mason Grew, inventor of a suspender buckle. The story involves very little action, and is told in a very unexciting way. The first half describes Mason Grew's background and relationship to his son; the second half records the conversation between the two wherein the son discovers his mistake. This type of subtle, mild satire against "Wertherian" excess is apt to cause but a ripple on the surface of the average imagination. And the ordinary reader is not apt to understand or sympathize with a Mason Grew whose unattractive person clothed a rare and sensitive nature.

Nor are the other stories in this collection made for popular wholesale acceptance. In **"The Daunt Diana"** a man impoverishes himself in order to own a beautiful statue of Diana and speaks of it almost in mystical terms: "I always cared—always worshipped—always wanted her. But she wasn't mine then, and I knew it, and she knew it. . . . and now at last we understand each other." In **"The Debt"** a protégé of a famous biologist repays the latter for all his guidance and encouragement by developing a scientific theory that destroys the older man's thesis. Again, these two understand each other, but it is to be doubted that the reader does—the reader of fiction who expects and welcomes patent, trumped-up tales. Those critics who claimed that such stories were the run-of-the-mill magazine type might have been forced to change their minds had they tried to find others to match them in subtlety and quiet thoughtfulness. (pp. 365-70)

[In *Xingu, and Other Stories*], Edith Wharton is decidedly the lady of various moods and the author of many talents. One need but look at the first and last tales—both of which attracted a good deal of comment—to get an insight into the amazing "grande dame's" power in handling the setting and characters of two nearly completely different worlds. The collection opens with **"Xingu,"** a story about society ladies and their literary pretensions. With the very first, and by now quite famous line, the author treats the reader to great satire: "Mrs. Ballinger is one of the ladies who pursue culture in bands, as though it were dangerous to meet alone." After reading this sentence, anyone who knows Edith Wharton is prepared for great fun, and all expectations are fulfilled on a grand scale. Mrs. Ballinger's Lunch Club, composed of herself and "other indomitable huntresses of erudition," is led from one literary *faux pas* to another until all the members very plausibly admit having read about and having practiced "Xingu." That "Xingu" is a river in Brazil is the story's well guarded secret, climactically revealed to the club and the reader at the same time. Edith Wharton's spirit of humor and masterful use of irony in such a scene as the visit of Osric Dane, the writer, foreshadow some of the great satirical theater and dinner scenes in *The Age of Innocence.*

In contrast to **"Xingu,"** the volume ends with a sombre novelette, **"Bunner Sisters"** filled with pathos. In portraying the emotionally starved lives of Ann Eliza and Evelina, who run a small shop in a shabby basement on a New York side street, Edith Wharton employs the grim simplicity of *Ethan Frome* without attaining its power. Ethan and Mattie's sufferings are every bit as painful as those of these two sisters, but one accepts them because they are made to bear a great theme. In this novelette, however, the pain inflicted on the protagonists seems meaningless, and the reader can only recoil at the sight of it. But having said this, there is no denying Edith Wharton's outstanding skill in recording manners. Hers is not merely the ability to picture the ways of her restricted world; for the back parlor of Ann Eliza and Evelina Bunner is as clearly *seen* as the Marvell's dining-room in *The Custom of the Country* or Pauline Manford's sitting room in her country home in *Twilight Sleep.* Indeed, Mr. Ramy's visits in that pathetic back parlor would be less painful to observe were Edith Wharton's description of them less sharp and vivid. As it is, one can but witness Evelina taking his thread-bare overcoat and shabby hat and laying them "on a chair with the gesture she imagined the lady with the puffed sleeves [a society lady] might make use of on similar occasions," and praise the author's power to select the very details which will render a passage unforgettable. Whether Edith Wharton etches the ladies of the Lunch Club looking up the word "Xingu" in the encyclopedia, or the Bunner sisters nervously attempting to entertain a guest, she is able to create a mood almost instantaneously through clever use of description.

A decade later, Wharton published her seventh collection of tales, entitled *Here and Beyond,* and the consensus at the time of its appearance seemed to be that although the six tales therein would add nothing to the author's reputation, they certainly would not detract from it. In fact, one of the sketches, **"Bewitched,"** was praised as very deft and as containing within its narrow field a great deal of tragic power. Its setting is the bare and bleak New England of *Ethan Frome* and *Summer,* but its plot contains "supernatural" elements not found in either of these novelettes. The noncommunicative Mrs. Rutledge requests the advice of her minister and of two other citizens on how to deal with an unusual family problem: her husband Saul is bewitched; he meets a dead former sweetheart in an old deserted house. Edith Wharton creates an atmosphere of mystery and witchcraft with such skill that the reader believes throughout the telling of the tale that the Deacon is right in claiming that an apparition is "sucking the life clean out of" Saul. The icy solitude, the tumble-down house of mystery, the spectral footsteps in the snow—all make for a most satisfying ghost story.

"The Seed of Faith," a story of religious fanaticism and martyrdom in a small Baptist mission under the blinding June sky of Africa, was also much admired. It is to the author's great credit to have been able to create the atmosphere of a small African town with every bit as much skill as she had that of a small New England one in **"Bewitched."** Edith Wharton may have been at her best when describing an aristocratic New York setting, but this volume should prove that she was not incapable of doing anything else. Admittedly, the collection was one which would appeal to those who had a penchant for their rather exotic and special qualities, and quite obviously, the old flame of conviction was probably burning less brightly; however, Edith Wharton's familiar grace of phrase, worldly wisdom, and urbane detachment were still happily present. Besides, the themes were made more poignant because the forms had an architectural quality for which contemporary magazine tales often substituted a flashy virtuosity. (pp. 371-73)

"After Holbein" really preserves in miniature all of Edith Wharton's finest gifts. This dreadful yet fascinating variation on the Dance of Death has as its protagonists Anson Warley and Evelina Jaspar, two old and ailing members of the high society set. In their senility and mental decay, the latter imagines that guests are coming to dine, and the other that he has been invited. And in one of the most macabre scenes in any short story, these two vestiges of the age of innocence entertain each other while observing all the minutiae of the accepted amenities. Death is actually calling each of them in the guise of the other, for what they prized most in life were shallow appearances—symbolized here by Mrs. Jaspar's and Warley's perfect dress even at the point of death. Warley appears in fastidious evening clothes, fur-lined overcoat, and thin evening watch in proper pocket, while Mrs. Jaspar is truly a "petrifying apparition" in purple wig, evening gown,

and weighty diamond necklaces. Coldness is not the basis of this caustic satire, but a realization that as a man lives, so he is apt to die. If the Jaspars and the Warleys have spent their days promoting vanity and superficiality, death-bed conversions are not to be expected. Those tempted to accuse Edith Wharton of blindness to the deficiencies of brownstone aristocracy, are amply refuted in **"After Holbein."** This is satire based on strong conviction, not on coldness or spleen. Edith Wharton's morality is based on taste, and Anson Warley and Evelina Jaspar's vanity is so grotesque that it violates all principles of taste—even if they did once serve ninety-five Perrier-Joust. (p. 375)

"Her Son" is certainly one of Edith Wharton's finest short stories. Like Henry James's tale, "Four Meetings," it is told from the point of view of the narrator who, at various intervals and in different countries, follows the adventures of an American woman deceived by conniving cosmopolitans. Mrs. Catherine Glenn, after the death of her husband, spends all her time and fortune looking for her illegitimate son, whom she has not seen since he was a baby, twenty-seven years ago. In Europe she meets Mr. and Mrs. Brown, who pass off a young man as Mrs. Glenn's son, Stephen. These three individuals proceed to ruin Mrs. Glenn financially, and in a malicious rage at her refusal to provide them with more money, Mrs. Brown tells her that Stephen is not her son. He is, in fact, Mrs. Brown's lover, who could conceive of no other means to support her and himself. Edith Wharton's contrast between the vulgar Browns with their incessant, arid talk and sophisticated Catherine Glenn with her desperate, fear-ridden meekness is excellent. The story's ending is probably one of the most skillful and compact in the canon of Wharton's tales. At the very moment when Mrs. Brown is convinced that she has dealt Mrs. Glenn the worst of blows by announcing that she and Stephen are lovers, the latter points to the speaker's disordered headgear and says, "My dear—your hat's crooked." For a moment the reader is bewildered, but he soon realizes that Mrs. Brown's blow never hit its intended mark. "A pitying fate had darkened Catherine Glenn's intelligence at the exact moment when to see clearly would have been the final anguish." Not only had Mrs. Glenn's intelligence mercifully clouded, but the shaft she had launched at her enemy had been in terms of her world—the world of good manners which placed such infinite importance on meticulously proper dress. A vulgar, conniving Mrs. Brown could be ruffled by such a remark, but she could never understand the depths of disapproval implied by it. Having uttered it, Mrs. Glenn could, indeed, lean back "with the satisfied sigh of a child." (pp. 376-77)

Whenever Edith Wharton is mentioned as a short story writer today, she is praised for her cool detachment, her fine finish, and her structural brilliance. She

with the roses, and was vexed at having spoken of them. He wanted
to say: "I called on your cousin yesterday," but hesitated. If
Madame Olenska had not spoken of his visit it might seem awkward
that he should. Yet not to do so gave the affair an air of mystery
that he disliked. To shake off the question he began to talk of
their own plans, their future, and Mrs.Welland's insistence on a
long engagement.

"If you call it long! Isabel Chivers and Reggie were
engaged for two years: Grace and Thorley for nearly a year and a
half. Why aren't we very well off as we are?"

It was the traditional maidenly ~~interrogation~~ *interrogation*, and he
felt ashamed of himself for finding it singularly childish. No
doubt she simply echoed what was said for her; but she was nearing
her twenty-second birthday, and he wondered at what age "nice"
women began to speak for themselves.

"Never, if we won't let them, I suppose," he mused, and
recalled his mad outburst to Mr.Sillerton Jackson: "Women ought to
be as free as we are —"

It would presently be his task to take the bandage from
this young woman's eyes, and bid her look forth on the world. But
how many generations of the women who had gone to her making had
descended bandaged to the family vault? He shivered a little,
remembering some of the new ideas in his scientific books, and the
much-cited instance of the Kentucky cave-fish, which had ceased to
develop eyes because they had no use for them. What if, when he
had bidden May Welland to open hers, they could only look out blankly at blankness?

"We might be much better off. We might be altogether
together — we might travel."

Her face lit up. That would be ~~lovely~~ *"lovely"*, she owned: she

Corrected typescript page of *The Age of Innocence,* Wharton's Pulitzer Prize-winning novel.

is even credited, along with Henry James, for having   contributed a great deal to the advancement of the form of the short story in this country. Yet these qualities are evidently not those by which modern readers are particularly moved, regardless of how much they admire them: there is no doubt whatever that Edith Wharton's popularity has declined and that many today would not question Robert Morss Lovett for calling her the last of the Victorians. It is difficult to state exactly to what depths her fame has plunged, for no graphs can be drawn where values are concerned. It is certainly significant, however, that her collections of short stories are now out of print and that editors such as Norman Foerster do not even mention her in their surveys. It is to be hoped that she will continue to be read by a discriminating audience because of her mastery of form and language and because of a few ideas which will always deserve universal attention: man's humanity or inhumanity to man, man's relation and responsibility to society, and the importance of such virtues as order, tradition, culture, and control. (p. 379)

Patricia R. Plante, "Edith Wharton as Short Story Writer," in *The Midwest Quarterly*, Vol. IV, No. 4, Summer, 1963, pp. 363-79.

GEOFFREY WALTON

(essay date 1971)

[In the following excerpt from his study *Edith Wharton: A Critical Interpretation*, Walton provides a survey of Wharton's career.]

Edith Wharton's first written effort, at the age of eleven, which began: " 'Oh, how do you do, Mrs. Brown?' said Mrs. Tompkins. 'If only I had known you were coming to call I should have tidied up the drawing-room' " shows that she was indeed almost predestined to become an interpreter of upper-class life, while her mother's crushing comment: " 'Drawing-rooms are always tidy' " forms an excellent indication of her need for observation and experience. She seems equally to have been predestined to become a follower of Henry James and one early novel is plainly derivative from his early work. When, after achieving celebrity with her collaborative book on *The Decoration of Houses* (with several drawing-rooms) and establishing herself as a novelist, she eventually became a close friend of the Master, she was, Percy Lubbock tells us, the only woman whom he regarded as an equal and they were "more and more never apart." He was critical of her and she of him, he wishing to "tether" her "to native pastures," she deploring the lack of local habitation for the characters in his later work. Both, however, laid great stress on organic unity and close writing in the novel. (p. 21)

The all-embracing theme of Edith Wharton's earlier work is the relationship, usually a hostile relationship, between the individual and society. . . . [She] came of a small and in many respects obsolescent community, but its basic ideals were taken over by the more grandiose and expansive commercial dynasties that succeeded it. Social ambitions soared and moral codes loosened, but merely doing as one liked was still inconceivable. . . . [Edith Wharton presents] a conflict between two distinct upper middle classes running through parts of *The House of Mirth* and, more obviously, with foreign noble allies on the wing, in *The Custom of the Country. Madame de Treymes* has a foreign setting and *The Reef* is mainly concerned with individual conflict against a Franco-American upper-class background. In *The Fruit of the Tree,* where part of the conflict is shifted down the social scale and becomes a phase in the class war, the main interest is again focused on individuals. In all these books the individual involves himself—or herself, for Edith Wharton was a great creator of heroines—in a prolonged and complicated struggle with the conventions of manners and morality, both public and private, which had been so long established among the upper classes of Western Europe and the eastern states of America before the First World War that they could be taken for granted as an unquestioned and unquestionable code of civilization. . . . In her very early historical novel, *The Valley of Decision,* Edith Wharton had carried the theme of individual rebellion back into Italy in the age of enlightened despotism. In the New England novels she shows us the plight of the individual, rather than his rebellion, within the equally distinct and stable lower social strata. Everywhere she shows a deep sense of the value of mutual understanding and toleration and also of the meaning and value of forms and decencies; her friend, the historian Gaillard Lapsley, once remarked that "she was possessed of a sense of compassion deeper and more authentic than [he had] ever seen in any human being."

In these earlier novels and stories she presents her chief characters against the background of a complex and changing, if still restricted, society, the whole studied with a depth of understanding that gives it the quality of a microcosm. This work has a richness and solidity that make it at least comparable to the early work of James. Physical detail and details of social custom are much more precisely and thoroughly presented than in his work, without losing their lasting and, as one says, universal appeal. The tremendous sense of the social hierarchy and of the meaning of class relationships, which one sees both in her novels and in her autobiography, reminds one not only of James but also of her other close friend and compatriot, Howard Sturgis. (pp. 22-4)

It seems to be a generally accepted opinion that

Edith Wharton's powers declined beyond recovery during the 1920s and that her later novels were fit for no better public than that of the women's magazines where they were serialized before publication in book form. There is some speculation as to whether the decline was not rather an enforced and deliberate effort to meet the taste of a public whose purveyors presumably paid handsomely for the prestige that her name must have given to their journals. . . . Her powers as a novelist did not collapse, though all her later work may not be of equal merit. She gives us in *A Backward Glance* an account of her artistic circumstances that seems in the main immediately acceptable, whatever objections may be raised against certain details in the book. *The Age of Innocence* was an escape into "childish memories of a long-vanished America." It is a *tour de force,* but should not be overrated to the detriment of all her later work. She finally attempted to put her war experience into serious artistic form in *A Son at the Front,* which she had brooded over for more than four years, but the result, despite certain powerful lines of irony, is heavily sentimental in outlook and crude in detailed treatment. After it she thought of ceasing to write; she felt, very much as E. M. Forster has told us he also felt, "incapable of transmuting the raw material of the after-war world into a work of art." Her attempt to do so in *The Mother's Recompense* justifies her fears. But in *Twilight Sleep* and *The Children* we find a revival of her old creative energy and narrative skill along with the play of irony, albeit of a rather less subtle kind, which is the distinguishing feature of her best work. As a writer Edith Wharton deals as surely and decisively with the world of Scott Fitzgerald as she did with him in person at the famous tea-party (or was it luncheon?) at the Pavillon Colombe. The fact that she based her accounts of New York on hearsay, which, as Percy Lubbock tells us, she received with fascinated disgust, makes them the more remarkable in their vitality.

Edith Wharton's main interest as a novelist remained social. The early work, as has been indicated, records the conflicts of the individual with the conventions and customs of a still strong and organized community; *The Custom of the Country* is the comedy of a pyrrhic victory by an individual. The novels from *Twilight Sleep* onwards deal with the helplessness of individuals—the plural is appropriate here—in a Society scattered without much differentiation on both sides of the Atlantic, where conflict that can lead to tragedy is no longer possible. Edith Wharton is very critical indeed of the world in which Gatsby flourished and Dick Diver disintegrated, quite as critical as she was of the pre-1914 millionaire world, but the problem is different. Now there are neither established forms of humbug nor established forms of goodness to which the humbug can cling. In *The Writing of Fiction* Edith Wharton says that a novelist's work should bear "a recognizable relation to a familiar social and moral standard." The standard, as she presents it in these books, has lost its group sanctions and become a matter of individual sincerity and generosity.

Mrs. Wharton reviewed her relationship to the prose fiction of her native land and replied to her critics, contemporary and future, in a fine article, **"The Great American Novel."** From this she went on, in *Hudson River Bracketed* and *The Gods Arrive,* to deal with the problem of the individual and society in an extreme form, namely that of the modern artist. Her last and unfinished novel, *The Buccaneers,* represents a significant new development. One senses that a vision of social reintegration would have emerged from the completed work. In fact Edith Wharton's work as a whole gives one a sense of continuous growth and inner development. A fine sensibility is responding imaginatively to changing circumstances. It is not however of the widest imaginative grasp and adaptability. It is decidedly a critical and a judging sensibility. Mrs. Wharton was also a pioneer realist who remembered that she had once been asked, " 'Have you ever known a respectable woman? If you have, in the name of decency write about her!' " and, though she satirized them severely, she did not flinch from the 1920s. She never saw much interest in "the man with the dinner-pail," as she described him. Her main achievement belongs to her "few yards of town-pavement"; but, as with James, how much takes place there! (pp. 25-7)

Geoffrey Walton, in his *Edith Wharton: A Critical Interpretation,* Fairleigh Dickinson University Press, 1971, 216 p.

RICHARD H. LAWSON

(essay date 1977)

[In the excerpt below, Lawson examines social criticism in Wharton's novels.]

Despite Wharton's professions of happiness in *A Backward Glance,* she was an unhappy human being. One even feels she was unhappy as a woman. Her society subjected women to special disadvantages; in this connection we think of the plight of Lily Bart. This society subjected a brilliant woman, like Wharton, to additional humiliation by simply not recognizing her brilliance or her literary accomplishment—those were things one did not talk about. Wharton was a feminist, however, only in a limited way. Social class was more important to her than sexual equality. She deplored the double standard as it applied to Lily Bart or Ellen Olenska; she defended it as it applied to Sophy Viner. Moreover, Wharton preferred to speak in fiction with a man's voice, to work from a fictional perspective which was male. That is, whenever she employed the device of the fictive narrator, that narrator was a male. And her narrators were in every way valid and convincing in their male perspectives.

On the whole Wharton did not deal kindly with the members of her own sex as they appeared in her fiction. Her special gifts as a writer of fiction were in the areas of plotting and style. She was not an innovator of novelistic form, but she did develop the possibilities of the traditional nineteenth-century novel as far as her virtuosity could take her, which in the cases of *The House of Mirth, Ethan Frome, The Custom of the Country,* and *The Age of Innocence* was very far indeed.

It has been frequently said that Wharton's novels consist of the trivial doings of trivial people. That is largely true. But her fictional people, with whom she was for the most part on remarkably close terms of acquaintance, were part of, acted in, and typified a society in crisis, about which there were things to be said. Wharton said them, and what she did not say she ironically implied.

There is a surge of interest in Wharton today, reflected in frequent reprinting of her works as well as in the publication of biography, interpretation, and criticism. It is a more substantial surge than that which often attends the rediscovery of a first-rate writer several decades after his or her death. The reason may lie in Wharton's particular appeal to a torn society, reflecting at once deep cynicism and muted, if occasionally effective, idealism.

It is not, however, as simple as our society being a mere copy, writ large, of Wharton's society. But we and Edith Wharton share the experience of living through a relatively rapid and perceptible social upheaval. Then, for example, materialism with its social reflections was coming in, and despite her very material comfort, she was materialism's sworn enemy. Now materialism is on the defensive; and we savor the accuracy, the bite, of Wharton's attack, perhaps admiring along the way, or perhaps not entirely grasping, her erudition. Then, there was social and sexual discrimination. There still is. Wharton supported the first, decried the second, as long as it did not impinge on the first. But she did decry, and that was something, then quite likely a lonelier role than now. Wharton had courage. We find that admirable. And if it was expressed, or implied, pointedly and with wit, we find it even more admirable. (pp. 97-9)

Richard H. Lawson, in a conclusion to his *Edith Wharton,* Frederick Ungar Publishing Co., Inc., 1977, pp. 95-9.

GORDON MILNE
(essay date 1977)

[In the excerpt below, Milne discusses Wharton's novels as portraits of old New York.]

A dominant theme in many of [Mrs. Wharton's] novels and stories is . . . the retreat of little old New York of the 1870s, the Knickerbocker aristocracy, marching backward when faced with the invasion of the plutocracy, the Astors and Vanderbilts, "the men who have risen," in the 1880s and 1890s. Mrs. Wharton knew well that the latter dynasty was to succeed, indeed, had succeeded, as symbolized in many cases by marriages uniting aristocrat and merchant. Her interest lay in contrasting the two social groups. Though her dislike of the arriviste—the Looty Arlingtons, the Indiana Frusks, the Undine Spraggs, even the Julius Beauforts, all those people from Pruneville, Nebraska—is more than apparent, and though her sympathy is drawn to the aristocrats proudly affirming their caste, she views the struggle between the two societies with detachment, not allowing her sympathies to warp her judgment. So, in *The Age of Innocence* . . . , the "first families" are shown wavering before the onslaught (the weeds pushing up between the ordered rows of social vegetables) of tasteless materialism, but deserving to be upset because their ostrichlike attitudes and dread of scandal indicate a declining culture. Similarly, in *The Buccaneers* . . . , Mrs. Wharton's last—and uncompleted—novel, the merchant class is conquering even the last stronghold of the aristocracy, England, a process that the author by no means wholly regrets, since the fresh charm of "the buccaneers," the invading American girls, counteracts the stodgy narrowness of the old society.

To explore this "old order changeth" theme, Mrs. Wharton makes full use of the novel of manners format. Her best-known novel, *The Age of Innocence,* may serve, initially, as our prototype, since it distinctly illustrates many characteristics of the genre. In the first place, the novel, from beginning to end, gives us a strong sense of contrasting social groups, the aristocrats and the plutocrats. (p. 118)

Endless examples, some positive, some negative, are proffered of the manners of the ruling—if threatened—class. Its members are wholeheartedly governed by "the thing," for example, the convention of arriving late at the opera. Such conventions, the reader is told, play as important a part in social circles as did the inscrutable totem terrors that had ruled the destinies of the forefathers of this society thousands of years ago. Life is molded by the conventions and the forms, with considerable deference paid to the arbiters of these. (pp. 118-19)

The Age of Innocence is given enormous sparkle by the tone of light irony maintained throughout the work. The narrator tempers her sympathy for her subject, the established rich, with a tart quality. Recoiling as she does from "society's" matriarchal aspect, its shrinking from responsibility, its dread of innovation, and its confining innocence and distrust of the creative intelligence, while at the same time approving of its *douceur de vivre,* she presents a frank, often satiric, occasionally nostalgic picture.

The setting of *The Age of Innocence* is vividly and quite extensively treated, as is apt to be the case in a novel of manners, in which the reader must see the people against the background that conditions them. Mrs. Wharton, herself very sensitive about both exterior and interior decoration, lovingly describes the houses in which her principals dwell. (pp. 120-21)

Mrs. Wharton's theme in *The Age of Innocence* is derived from an examination of the interrelationship among Countess Olenska, May Welland, and Newland Archer. In the novel she expounds, as she had before and would several times again, upon the cruelty of social convention and the tyranny of the "in" group. The social arbiters militate against the individual, forcing him to give up his happiness for the duty that they dictate, causing him to yield his ideals, which they regard as impractical in the social order. Here, Ellen Olenska and Newland Archer must sacrifice their ideal of love, since she is married (and subsequently, he) and the scandal of divorce is unthinkable. (p. 124)

The Age of Innocence, like the majority of Mrs. Wharton's novels, and, indeed, like the majority of novels of manners, is a well-constructed work of fiction, subscribing, one might readily say, to the author's dictum that "every great novel must first of all be based on a profound sense of moral values, and then constructed with a classical unity and economy of means." Mrs. Wharton places her "situation" before us, a conflict between group and individual standards, then develops it crisply. Beginning in a lively manner, offering "signposts" in the form of revelatory little scenes along the way, then mounting to a striking and ironic climax, she creates a focused yet naturally unfolded story. The narrative in *The Age of Innocence* falls into two segments: the events leading up to the setting of the marriage date, and those following, with the climax occurring when the marriage is saved at a threatening point later on. A quiet denouement ensues, the account of Archer's visit to Paris with his son thirty years after the novel's principal incidents, and his refusal at this time to see Madame Olenska. The "overness" of the affair is thus lightly accentuated. Throughout the novel, the affair, or "situation," remains central, and lying behind it the dissection of a certain social sphere.

Contributing to the sense of unity is the author's reliance on the restricted point of view as the means by which the story is told. Most of the action is channeled through Newland Archer, who appears in almost every scene and whose viewpoint on these scenes very much coincides with that of the reader. What the reader knows and thinks of Ellen Olenska, for example, is pretty much what Archer knows and thinks. The novel is given reality, intensity, *and* suspense by this device, with the question of the actual character and status of Ellen—and thus the larger question of whether society or the individual is "right"—remaining in doubt for a long time.

Mrs. Wharton tells her story in a style that is pungent, facile, and witty—again, one ventures to say, all but a requirement of this particular genre, which demands a sophisticated manner of writing in order to preserve its urbane air. The novel abounds, for one thing, in similes and metaphors, arresting in the satiric picture they conjure up. Thus, Mrs. Manson Mingott's appearance: "a flight of smooth double chins led down to the dizzy depths of a still-snowy bosom . . . with two tiny hands poised like gulls on the surface of the billows." (pp. 125-26)

The balanced sentences that predominate in the novel often contain flashing ironies (Mrs. Welland "signed a haggard welcome"; Mrs. van der Luyden shines on Ellen "with the dim benevolence which was her nearest approach to cordiality") and/or an epigrammatic cast ("our legislation favors divorce; our social customs do not"; "the worst of doing one's duty was that it apparently unfitted one for anything else"). The diction supports the syntax in conveying the book's ironic flavor, especially when Mrs. Wharton overstates (Mrs. Mingott's bedroom is on the ground floor "in *flagrant* violation of all the New York proprieties") in order to mock the social legalism of the Knickerbocker group, using the serious word for trivialities, or the one with moral overtones for conventions. Some of the proper names may symbolize ironically, too: Archer as the ineffectual bowman, Ellen a misplaced Helen, May as innocence, overlapped, here, with conformity. (pp. 127-28)

With its consistently ironic style, precisely delineated characters and settings, and carefully worked-out theme, *The Age of Innocence* qualifies as an excellent novel. More particularly, it qualifies as an excellent novel of manners, being devoted to so thorough a discussion of the mores of old New York. (p. 128)

The House of Mirth . . . offers an early example, the novel unfolding the tragedy of Lily Bart, a young lady brought up in "society," but lacking the necessary money to retain her place and therefore forced into the unenviable role of a social parasite. (pp. 132-33)

While unfolding Lily's conflict between the claims of "sense" and "spirit," the author lays out the social topography against which the conflict is posed, the settled aristocracy over here, the moving plutocracy over there. As a student of manners, Mrs. Wharton is able to "fix" both groups, the former, tepidly devoted to family, form, and culture, the latter, more concerned about the distribution of wealth and the social privileges resulting from it. Mrs. Wharton very effectively dramatizes the plutocracy's social-climbing adventure, outlining a "hundred shades of aspect and manner" as she describes how its representatives are engaged in determining their status in society. The climbing action of the plutocracy suggests society's pyramidal structure, and indeed *The House of Mirth* indicates several gradations. (p. 133)

The book's well-bred surface does not conceal its dark texture. The plight of its half-belonging, half-rebelling protagonist produces a somber reaction and reminds the reader that the novel of manners "can register both the surface of social life and the inner vibrations of spirit that surface reveals, suppresses and distorts." The subject of "civilization and its discontents"—to use Freud's phrase—does not promote levity.

Successor to *The House of Mirth, The Custom of the Country* . . . follows the former's lead in toning down the comic note as it deals with the standard Wharton topic of societal realignments. Shifting, in her choice of protagonists, from defender (Lily Bart) to invader (Undine Spragg), Mrs. Wharton grimly—almost too grimly—delineates the "climb" of Miss Spragg, all the way from Apex City to Paris. (p. 134)

The rampant state of the new materialism is mirrored in the meteoric rise of Undine Spragg. Very harshly Mrs. Wharton depicts her as amoral, unsentimental, conscienceless, and cheap, yet with society now constituted as it is, she can forge ahead unimpeded. Mrs. Wharton has concluded that the "custom of the country" decrees money to be the open sesame, with social convention now transmogrified into a superficial veneer of good manners, which hardly mask an essential vulgarity. The main characteristic of the social structure of the day, Mrs. Wharton implies, is instability, its hierarchy being rearranged on a simple pecuniary basis, thus leaving the field open to the social adventurer.

Inevitably disturbed by this phenomenon, Mrs. Wharton, in her subsequent fiction, looks to the ordered past and nostalgically—though the satiric edge is always there—summons up the pre-assault era. . . . [*Old New York*], a collection of novelettes (*False Dawn, The Old Maid, The Spark,* and *New Year's Day*), is devoted to picturing the 1840-1870 world of formidable brownstone mansions, academies of music, and "downtown"—the vaguely described place of business, where people, it would seem, seldom had to be. It is a world of sober precedence—the grandmother's carriage preceding the aunt's—of order and form, of leisure, and of a fair amount of taste. Houses are carefully appointed, clothes are carefully chosen, dinners are carefully given.

From the novelettes the reader learns of the self-assured nature of the New Yorkers, their clannishness, their adherence to custom (betrothals, weddings, and funerals all have their pattern—the mourning crape at a precise length—in this "most totem-ridden of communities"), their narrow point of view, and their esthetic limitations. However charming the surface, those polished manners, and tasteful ceremonies, the environment exudes an airless atmosphere. Delia Ralston in *The Old Maid* sees the walls of her own grave in her surroundings. Attitudes are reactionary, family pressure is too intense, the values are often distorted (if society would not condone drink and dishonesty, it did condone almost everything else, including the double standard of morality, hypocrisy, and snobbery), and the culture is decidedly barren. (pp. 135-36)

If perhaps more masked in *Old New York,* still the money motif is discernible, and the class barriers are demonstrably breaking down. Everyone; even the Wesson clan, now goes to the parties of the shoe-polish heiress Mrs. Struthers.

Mrs. Wharton continues her discussion of the amalgamation of the aristocracy with the plutocracy in *The Mother's Recompense,* where one sees the union accomplished under the heading of the "new tolerance." When Kate Clephane returns to America, after many years abroad, she is impressed by the sense of change in this essentially "manner-less-age." . . . It would appear that the merger of the old and new societies has cost each its true character and has introduced an inane composite face.

This somewhat petulant disdain for the "modern age" marred Mrs. Wharton's later novels (e.g., *Hudson River Bracketed* and *The Gods Arrive*), most critics agreeing that her treatment of the aristocracy's yielding to the predatory arrivistes grew into a sour caricature. But her last novel, the unfinished *The Buccaneers* . . . , proves a late-in-the-day exception. In this interesting and amusing tale, the Wharton touch returns, and a new-found sympathy with the parvenus considerably mitigates the caricature. Looking backward from the mid-thirties, the author regards the invasion of the "buccaneers" forty years earlier as perhaps a healthy movement, for, awkward, uncultured, and superficial though they were, still, they introduced new blood and vitality into both the effete New York society and into the English aristocracy as well. The charming invaders are now sanctioned by Mrs. Wharton, especially Nan St. George, a happy blend of the new world conjoined to a sensitive appreciation of the tradition and continuity of the old. (pp. 136-38)

Mrs. Wharton is most concerned with the marriage of Nan St. George to the Duke of Tintagel, a marriage that appears the best of all but which proves the least workable. Nan, far more sensitive than her fellow Americans and more in key with the British love of tradition—"At least life in England had a background"—is the most receptive to the English atmosphere, but her husband, if superficially typifying glorious old Albion, turns out to be an incredibly stuffy and empty individual, and their marriage is loveless and hollow. Nan *should* have married Guy Thwaite, one who is slightly less blue-blooded but infinitely more intelligent and worthy. Mrs. Wharton's working plan for the uncompleted portion of *The Buccaneers* reveals that Nan will run off with Thwaite to South Africa, thus utterly defying convention but very possibly achieving happiness. The novel would have become morally as well as socially radical! (p. 140)

The exploration in *The Buccaneers*—as in its predecessors—of the "art" of manners involved all the resources of Mrs. Wharton's formidable technique. *The Buccaneers* is as craftsmanlike a performance as *The Age of Innocence,* and the same might be said of *The House of Mirth,* of *Old New York,* and of most of her other work. (p. 142)

Gordon Milne, "Edith Wharton," in his *The Sense of Society: A History of the American Novel of Manners,* Fairleigh Dickinson University Press, 1977, pp. 116-49.

GORE VIDAL

(essay date 1978)

[Vidal is an American novelist, short story writer, dramatist, and essayist. He is particularly noted for his historical fiction and his iconoclastic criticism. Below, he takes issue with the common conception of Wharton as a stuffy *grande dame*, offering a short overview of her work and judging her, as an artist, to be the equal of Henry James.]

[To] my mind, Henry James and Edith Wharton are the two great American masters of the novel. Most of our celebrated writers have not been, properly speaking, novelists at all. . . . Mark Twain was a memoirist. William Dean Howells was indeed a true novelist but as Edith Wharton remarked (they were friendly acquaintances), Howells's "incurable moral timidity . . . again and again checked him on the verge of a masterpiece." She herself was never timid. Somehow in recent years a notion has got about that she was a stuffy grand old lady who wrote primly decorous novels about upper-class people of a sort that are no longer supposed to exist. She was indeed a grand lady, but she was not at all stuffy. Quite the contrary. She was witty. She was tough as nails. (p. viii)

Despite her reputation as being a stuffy *grande dame,* she had always been the most direct and masculine (old sense of the word, naturally) of writers; far more so than her somewhat fussy and hesitant friend Henry James. Spades got called spades in Edith Wharton's novels. As a result, she was always at war with "editorial timidity." Early on, she was told by one of the few good editors of the day that no American magazine would publish anything that might offend "a non-existent clergyman in the Mississippi valley; . . . [I] made up my mind from the first that I would never sacrifice my literary conscience to this ghostly censor." (p. xi)

The four stories that made up the volume *Old New York* together with *The Age of Innocence* can be read as a history of New York Society from the 1840s to the 1870s, all told from the vantage point of a brilliant middle-aged woman, looking back on a world that had already become as strange to her as that of the Pharaohs. . . .

[*Ethan Frome*] stands somewhat outside the canon of her work. For one thing, she herself is plainly outside the world that she is describing. Yet she is able to describe in a most convincing way a New England village filled with people of a sort that she could never have known well. The story is both readable and oddly remote. It could have been written by Daudet but not by her master Flaubert. Although she was very much under the influence of the French realists at the time, she does pay sly homage to Nathaniel Hawthorne, who had worked the same New England territory: a principal character in *Ethan Frome* is called Zenobia after the heroine of Hawthorne's *The Blithedale Romance.*

With the four New York stories and *The Age of Innocence* we are back in a world that she knew as intimately as Proust knew the Paris of much the same era. The stories begin. . . . But I am not going to say anything about them other than to note that they are precise and lucid, witty and passionate (there is no woman in American literature as fascinating as the doomed Madame Olenska). Not only does one live again in that lost world through Edith Wharton's art (and rather better to live in a far-off time through the medium of a great artist than to experience the real and probably awful age itself), but one is struck by the marvelous golden light that illuminates the world she reveals to us. How is this done? Through a total mastery of English. (p. xii)

In *The Age of Innocence* the language is unusually

beautiful. That is to say, the prose is simple, straight-forward, loved. When it comes to rounding off her great scene where Madame Olenska is decorously destroyed by the Old New Yorkers at a dinner, Edith Wharton writes with the graceful directness of the Recording Angel: "It was the old New York way of taking life 'without effusion of blood': the way of people who dreaded scandal more than disease, who placed decency above courage, and who considered that nothing was more ill-bred than 'scenes,' except the behavior of those who gave rise to them." . . .

Traditionally, Henry James has always been placed slightly higher up the slope of Parnassus than Edith Wharton. But now that the prejudice against the female writer is on the wane, they look to be exactly what they are: giants, equals, the tutelary and benign gods of our American literature. (p. xiii)

Gore Vidal, in an introduction to *The Edith Wharton Omnibus* by Edith Wharton, Charles Scribner's Sons, 1978, pp. vii-xiii.

SOURCES FOR FURTHER STUDY

Auchincloss, Louis. "Edith Wharton and Her New Yorks." *Partisan Review* XVIII, No. 4 (July-August 1951): 411-19.

Overview of Wharton's novels illustrating Wharton's love-hate relationship with American values.

Kronenberger, Louis. "Mrs. Wharton's Literary Museum." *The Atlantic Monthly* 222, No. 3 (September 1968): 98-100, 102.

Critical overview of many of Wharton's short stories and novels. Kronenberger concludes that Wharton was a stronger novelist than short story writer.

Lewis, R. W. B. "Introduction." In *The Collected Short Stories of Edith Wharton, Vol. 1,* by Edith Wharton, pp. vii-xxv. New York: Charles Scribner's Sons, 1968.

Examines a representative selection of Wharton's short stories, finding them reflective of the author's multifaceted personality.

McDowell, Margaret B. *Edith Wharton.* Boston: Twayne Publishers, 1976, 158 p.

Insightful biographical and critical overview.

Wilson, Edmund. "Justice to Edith Wharton." In his *The Wound and the Bow: Seven Studies in Literature,* pp. 159-73. New York: Farrar, Straus & Giroux, 1978.

Assesses the strengths and weaknesses of Wharton's novels.

Wolff, Cynthia Griffin. *A Feast of Words: The Triumph of Edith Wharton.* New York: Oxford University Press, 1977, 453 p.

Biography of Wharton that considers her major works reflective of her psychological development.

Phillis Wheatley

1753?-1784

(Full name Phillis Wheatley Peters) American poet.

INTRODUCTION

Wheatley was the first black person known to have published a volume of writings in North America. Historically significant in American letters, her *Poems on Various Subjects, Religious and Moral* (1773) was used as an exemplar of the power of education by proponents of the equalitarian and abolitionist movements who hailed the collection as a product of genius. Composed largely of neoclassical elegiac poetry that displays the controlled rhythms and rhyme patterns popularized by Alexander Pope, *Poems on Various Subjects* has been regarded as both brilliant and artistically inconsequential. Most modern assessments, however, recognize Wheatley's accomplishments as typical of the best poetry of her age.

Believed to have been born in West Africa (present-day Senegal and Gambia), Wheatley was purchased at a slave auction in 1761 by the wife of a wealthy Boston merchant who wanted a youthful personal maid to serve her in old age. Wheatley was about seven or eight years old when she arrived in America and appeared frail and sickly, though her gentle, demure manner was considered charming. Once in the Wheatley household, the child displayed a curiosity and aptitude for learning that led her owners to abandon plans to train her as a servant in favor of educating her through Bible study. Even they were shocked by her progress, however; within sixteen months Wheatley had mastered English and on her own had studied classical and contemporary poetry as well as French, Latin, and Greek literature. By her early teens, she had attained an education superior to that of most upper-class Bostonians. Her favor with her owners resulted in exceptional privileges for a slave, most notably a private room in their home furnished with a lamp and writing materials to be used should poetic inspiration come to her during the night. A major consequence of such favoritism, as numerous commentators have observed, was that Wheatley was forbidden to associate with other slaves.

Wheatley's first poem, "An Elegiac Poem, on the Death of That Celebrated Divine, and Eminent Servant of Jesus Christ, the Reverend and Learned George Whitefield," was published locally in 1770 as a broadside and a pamphlet; the poem was reprinted in newspapers throughout the American colonies and in England, gaining for Wheatley both national and international attention. On the advice of physicians, she sailed to England in 1773 with the Wheatleys' son Nathaniel to ease her asthma. She was astonished at her reception there: treated as a celebrity, she later recalled this visit as the high point of her life. Among the admirers she met was the ardent English abolitionist Selina Hastings, Countess of Huntington, who became her patron and secured publication of her collection *Poems on Various Subjects*. After being appointed an audience with King George III, Wheatley was forced to cancel the appearance when she was abruptly summoned to Boston to attend to her dying mistress. During the next few years the Wheatley family scattered throughout New England. Wheatley, having been freed three months before her mistress's death in March, 1774, attempted to publish another volume of verse, but her efforts were unsuccessful despite personal and public praise by such men as Voltaire, George Washington, and John Paul Jones. In 1778 Wheatley married John Peters, a free black man who worked as a lawyer and grocer, among other occupations, and was called "a remarkable specimen of his race, being a fluent writer, a ready speaker." However, financial difficulties led to Peters's incarceration in a Massachusetts debtor's prison, and his absence contributed to the death of their two infant children. Wheatley worked as a domestic in boardinghouses to support herself and a surviving infant. Untrained for menial labor and physically frail, she died in 1784, and her child, who died shortly afterward, was buried with her in an unmarked grave.

Wheatley was primarily an occasional poet who wrote elegies and honorific verse to commemorate the lives of friends and famous contemporaries as well as poems to celebrate important events, such as George Washington's appointment as commander in chief of the revolutionary forces ("To His Excellency General Washington"). Although these poems follow the then-widely imitated diction, meter, and rhyme patterns established by Alexander Pope and his school, Wheatley's strong technical skill sets her work apart from that of many of her contemporaries. Many critics consider Pope the primary influence on Wheatley and other minor poets of her era, and a number of scholars have provided detailed analyses of individual works to support the claim. Vernon Loggins has deemed Wheatley's verse as perhaps the best in her time, but agrees with J. Saunders Redding that her work unfortunately displays the genteel, artificial emotions characteristic of Pope's poetry as well. In addition to neoclassical influences, Christianity figures prominently in Wheatley's works; in "To Maecenas," "On Recollection," and other poems, Wheatley blends the two elements with what some critics consider Miltonic effect. Julian D. Mason and others have discussed this curious combination of neoclassicism and religion in terms of Wheatley's cultural environment.

Poems on Various Subjects was regarded as such an extraordinary accomplishment at the time of its initial publication that the first edition was prefaced with the signed testimony of such prominent Boston citizens as John Hancock, the Reverend Samuel Mather, and Thomas Hutchinson, governor of the Massachusetts Bay Colony, affirming its authenticity as the work of an African slave girl. Two early London reviews suggest the conflicting assessments that characterize evaluation of the whole body of Wheatley's poetry: a favorable review concludes that although the poems themselves "display no astonishing power of genius," they have special merit because of their singular creator, while a negative appraisal asserts that "most of those [black] people have a turn for imitation, though they have little or none for invention." However, another point of view gradually developed. In the mid-nineteenth century, Rufus Wilmot Griswold, noting the persistent partisanship of the two extremes, observed that *Poems on Various Subjects* is "quite equal to much of the contemporary verse that is admitted to be poetry by Phillis's severest judges," adding that "it would be difficult to find in the productions of American women . . . anything superior in sentiment, fancy, and distinction," a view with which other critics have concurred.

Modern African-American critics have scrutinized Wheatley's verse for evidence of racial pride or defiance of bondage. During the 1920s, when protest literature spawned by the Harlem Renaissance was at its height, James Weldon Johnson noted that while "To the University of Cambridge, in New England" and "An Address to the Earl of Dartmouth" make reference to Wheatley's capture and separation from her family, the poet betrays an "almost smug contentment at her own escape therefrom" which "cannot but strike the reader as rather unimpassioned." J. Saunders Redding wrote of the "negative, bloodless, unracial quality in Phillis Wheatley," about which Terence Collins has stated: "Wheatley's true legacy is the testimony her poetry gives to the insidious, self-destroying nature of even the most subtle, most gentle of racially oppressive conditions." Some critics have argued that Wheatley's subjects must be judged by examining the poetic models and social influences within her restricted sphere, noting the irony of her position as a pampered favorite of Boston's privileged class and of her enforced isolation from other slaves. Citing numerous self-references in Wheatley's works, Arthur P. Davis recognized race consciousness in them; he regarded Wheatley's praise of the black classical poet Terence along with Homer and Vergil in "To Maecenas" as one of the strongest examples. Sondra O'Neale has attributed conflicting views of Wheatley's race consciousness to an apparently intentional ambiguity and double meaning in the poetry in general and particularly in the religious verse, where Wheatley refers to her fellow slaves as "Ethiopians," a racial and biblical term used as a symbol of ancestral awareness and self-esteem. O'Neale has suggested that "through juxtaposition of . . . ancient concepts on the origin of race, Wheatley clearly implies that because Americans were ignoring Africa's status in biblical interpretations of 'chosen' nations, the slaves—denied knowledge of their inclusion in God's promises—were held in a psychological bondage even more demeaning than their physical enslavement."

Wheatley was a minor poet who followed the literary fashion of her age. Despite much supposition concerning her poetic gifts and potential under different circumstances, her poetry is considered a point of departure for the study of black literature in America. Many critics find in her verse poetry that excels that typical of her era, and instances of individuality which acquit her of the common charge of being a mere imitator. James Weldon Johnson has cautioned that "her work must not be judged by the work and standards of a later day, but by the work and standards of her own day and her own contemporaries. By this method of criticism [Wheatley] stands out as one of the important characters in the making of American literature, without any allowances for her sex or her antecedents."

(For further information about Wheatley's life and works, see *Black Literature Criticism; Concise Dictionary of American Literary Biography, 1640-1865; Dictionary of Literary Biography*, Vols. 31, 50; *Literature Criticism from 1400 to 1800*, Vol. 3; and *Poetry Criticism*, Vol. 3.)

CRITICAL COMMENTARY

JAMES WELDON JOHNSON
(essay date 1921)

[Johnson was a newspaper editor, lawyer, U.S. consul to Nicaragua and Venezuela, and a Broadway lyricist; his song "Lift Every Voice and Sing" has been adopted as the African-American national anthem. In addition, Johnson is known for the novel *The Autobiography of an Ex-Colored Man* (1912), which was originally published anonymously and later reissued under his name in 1927. In the following excerpt from his 1921 preface to *The Book of American Negro Poetry*, he provides a literary and historical overview of Wheatley's career.]

Phillis Wheatley has never been given her rightful place in American literature. By some sort of conspiracy she is kept out of most of the books, especially the text-books on literature used in the schools. Of course, she is not a *great* American poet—and in her day there were no great American poets—but she is an important American poet. Her importance, if for no other reason, rests on the fact that, save one, she is the first in order of time of all the women poets of America. And she is among the first of all American poets to issue a volume. (p. 23)

Anne Bradstreet preceded Phillis Wheatley by a little over one hundred and twenty years. She published her volume of poems, *The Tenth Muse,* in 1650. Let us strike a comparison between the two. Anne Bradstreet was a wealthy, cultivated Puritan girl, the daughter of Thomas Dudley, Governor of [Massachusetts] Bay Colony. Phillis, as we know, was a Negro slave girl born in Africa. Let us take them both at their best and in the same vein. The following stanza is from Anne's poem entitled "Contemplation":

While musing thus with contemplation fed,
And thousand fancies buzzing in my brain,
The sweet tongued Philomel percht o'er my head,
And chanted forth a most melodious strain,
Which rapt me so with wonder and delight,
I judged my hearing better than my sight,
And wisht me wings with her awhile to take my
   flight.

And the following is from Phillis' poem entitled **"Imagination":**

Imagination! who can sing thy force?
Or who describe the swiftness of thy course?
Soaring through air to find the bright abode.
Th' empyreal palace of the thundering God,
We on thy pinions can surpass the wind,
And leave the rolling universe behind.
From star to star the mental optics rove,
Measure the skies, and range the realms above;

Principal Works

An Elegiac Poem, on the Death of that Celebrated Divine, and Eminent Servant of Jesus Christ, the Reverend and Learned George Whitefield (poetry) 1770

Poems on Various Subjects, Religious and Moral. By Phillis Wheatley, Negro Servant to Mr. John Wheatley of Boston (poetry) 1773

An Elegy, Sacred to the Memory of that Great Divine, The Reverend and Learned Dr. Samuel Cooper (poetry) 1784

Liberty and Peace, A Poem (poetry) 1784

Letters of Phillis Wheatley, the Negro-Slave Poet of Boston (letters) 1864

Life and Works of Phillis Wheatley. Containing Her Complete Poetical Works, Numerous Letters and a Complete Biography of This Famous Poet of a Century and a Half Ago (poetry and letters) 1916

The Poems of Phillis Wheatley (poetry) 1966; revised edition, 1989

There in one view we grasp the mighty whole,
Or with new worlds amaze th' unbounded soul.

We do not think the black woman suffers much by comparison with the white. Thomas Jefferson said of Phillis: "Religion has produced a Phillis Wheatley, but it could not produce a poet; her poems are beneath contempt." It is quite likely that Jefferson's criticism was directed more against religion than against Phillis' poetry. (pp. 24-5)

It appears certain that Phillis was the first person to apply to George Washington the phrase, "First in peace." The phrase occurs in her poem ["**To His Excellency General George Washington"**], written in 1775. The encomium, "First in war, first in peace, first in the hearts of his countrymen," was originally used in the resolutions presented to Congress on the death of Washington, December, 1799.

Phillis Wheatley's poetry is the poetry of the Eighteenth Century. She wrote when Pope and Gray were supreme; it is easy to see that Pope was her model. Had she come under the influence of Wordsworth, Byron or Keats or Shelley, she would have done greater work. As it is, her work must not be judged by the work and standards of a later day, but by the work and standards of her own day and her own contemporaries. By this method of criticism she stands out as one of the important characters in the making of American literature, without any allowances for her sex or her antecedents.

According to *A Bibliographical Checklist of American Negro Poetry*, compiled by Mr. Arthur A. Schomburg, more than one hundred Negroes in the United States have published volumes of poetry ranging in size from pamphlets to books of from one hundred to three hundred pages. About thirty of these writers fill in the gap between Phillis Wheatley and Paul Laurence Dunbar. (pp. 25-6)

It is curious and interesting to trace the growth of individuality and race consciousness in this group of poets. . . . Only very seldom does Phillis Wheatley sound a native note. Four times in single lines she refers to herself as "Afric's muse." In a poem of admonition ["**To the University of Cambridge, in New England"**] she refers to herself as follows:

Ye blooming plants of human race divine,
An Ethiop tells you 'tis your greatest foe.

But one looks in vain for some outburst or even complaint against the bondage of her people, for some agonizing cry about her native land. In two poems she refers definitely to Africa as her home, but in each instance there seems to be under the sentiment of the lines a feeling of almost smug contentment at her own escape therefrom. . . . In the poem ["**To the Right Honorable William, Earl of Dartmouth"**], she speaks of freedom and makes a reference to the parents from whom she was taken as a child, a reference which cannot but strike the reader as rather unimpassioned. . . . (pp. 28-9)

The bulk of Phillis Wheatley's work consists of poems addressed to people of prominence. Her book was dedicated to the Countess of Huntington, at whose house she spent the greater part of her time while in England. On his repeal of the Stamp Act, she wrote a poem to King George III, whom she saw later; another poem she wrote to the Earl of Dartmouth, whom she knew. A number of her verses were addressed to other persons of distinction. Indeed, it is apparent that Phillis was far from being a democrat. She was far from being a democrat not only in her social ideas but also in her political ideas; unless a religious meaning is given to the closing lines of her ode to General Washington, she was a decided royalist:

A crown, a mansion, and a throne that shine
With gold unfading, Washington! be thine.

Nevertheless, she was an ardent patriot. Her ode to General Washington . . . , her spirited poem, **"On Major General Lee"** . . . , and her poem, **"Liberty and Peace,"** written in celebration of the close of the war, reveal not only strong patriotic feeling but an understanding of the issues at stake. (pp. 29-30)

What Phillis Wheatley failed to achieve is due in no small degree to her education and environment. Her mind was steeped in the classics; her verses are filled with classical and mythological allusions. She knew Ovid thoroughly and was familiar with other Latin authors. She must have known Alexander Pope by heart. And, too, she was reared and sheltered in a wealthy and cultured family,—a wealthy and cultured Boston family; she never had the opportunity to learn life; she never found out her own true relation to life and to her surroundings. And it should not be forgotten that she was only about thirty years old when she died. The impulsion or the compulsion that might have driven her genius off the worn paths, out on a journey of exploration, Phillis Wheatley never received. But, whatever her limitations, she merits more than America has accorded her. (p. 31)

James Weldon Johnson, "Preface to Original Edition," in *The Book of American Negro Poetry*, edited by James Weldon Johnson, revised edition, Harcourt Brace Jovanovich, Inc., 1931, pp. 9-48

VERNON LOGGINS

(essay date 1931)

[Loggins provides an overview of the styles and themes of Wheatley's works and appraises the poet's stature in American letters.]

The main body of Phillis Wheatley's verse belongs to that class of poetry which we call occasional. Eighteen out of her forty-six poems which are known to have come down to us are elegies. It has been said that she wrote them as consolatory poems at the request of friends. Five are on ministers, two on the wives of a lieutenant-governor and a celebrated physician, and the rest on unknown persons, including a number of children who died in infancy. The material is in each instance conventional, true to the traditions of the elegy in an elegy-making age, especially in Boston, where the writing of poems of condolence and epitaphs had been in great vogue since the days of Anne Bradstreet and Urian Oakes. The treatment is in accord with neoclassical standards. Whatever feeling there is, is impersonal and artificial; the method for achieving effect is mainly that of hyperbole; the ornamentation is elaborate and sumptious, with frequent invocations of the Muses, allusions to pagan gods and Biblical heroes, overuse of personification, and pompousness of diction. **"To the Rev. Mr. Pitkin on the Death of His Lady,"** which suggests the general mood of the elegies, opens in this strain—

Where Contemplation finds her sacred Spring;
Where heav'nly Music makes the Centre ring;
Where Virtue reigns unsullied, and divine,
Where Wisdom thron'd, and all the Graces shine;
There sits thy Spouse, amid the glitt'ring Throng;
There central Beauty feasts the ravish'd Tongue;

With recent Powers, with recent Glories crown'd,
The choirs angelic shout her welcome round.

Six of the poems were inspired by public events of importance, such as the repeal of the Stamp Act, the appointment of Washington as commander-in-chief of the Revolutionary forces, the betrayal of General Lee into the hands of the British, and the return of peace after the close of the Revolution; and a number are on minor happenings, such as the voyage of a friend to England, and the providential escape of an acquaintance from a hurricane at sea. These, like the elegies, are affected, written with an exaggerated dignity, with a straining attempt to force high eloquence.

But not all of Phillis Wheatley's poems are occasional. Following the New England custom of versifying selections from the Bible, begun back in the early days when the *Bay Psalm Book* was compiled, she worked out paraphrases of eight verses from the fifty-third chapter of Isaiah, and of the passage in the first book of Samuel which describes David's fight with Goliath. It is unnecessary to say that her neoclassical couplets deaden entirely the fire of Isaiah's rhapsody; she was so far away from the true Biblical ardor that she opened the paraphrase by invoking the "heav'nly muse." Her **"Goliath of Gath"** is more successful. In hearing the following lines one might feel that he is listening to the steady music of the opening of Pope's version of the *Iliad:*

Ye martial pow'rs, and all ye tuneful nine,
Inspire my song, and aid my high design.
The dreadful scenes and toils of war I write,
The ardent warriors, and the fields of fight:
You best remember, and you best can sing
The acts of heroes to the vocal string:
Resume the lays with which your sacred lyre,
Did then the poet and the sage inspire.

Also among her better achievements is the adaptation of that portion of the sixth book of Ovid's *Metamorphoses* which tells of Niobe's distress for her children. This classical paraphrase belongs to the small group of poems for which Phillis Wheatley did not look to her New England predecessors for models. Her pieces on abstractions, including **"Imagination," "Recollection,"** and **"Virtue,"** probably owe their subject matter to English rather than to American influences. And her companion hymns, **"Morning"** and **"Evening,"** place her among those eighteenth-century poets, numerous in England, who felt so greatly the splendors of Milton's "L'Allegro" and "Il Penseroso" that they attempted imitations.

What one most wishes Phillis Wheatley had done, she left undone: she wrote too rarely about herself. Her intimate personal interests were ignored. She composed verses on the deaths of those who meant little to her, but, so far as we know, she remained silent after the deaths of Mrs. Wheatley and Mrs. Lathrop and her own children. She dwelt at length on the common notions of her day regarding liberty, but she neglected almost entirely her own state of slavery and the miserable oppression of thousands of her race. In all of her writings she only once referred in strong terms to the wrongs of the Negro in America. The reference is in the poem addressed to the Earl of Dartmouth upon his appointment as George III's secretary for North America:

> Should you, my lord, while you peruse my song,
> Wonder from whence my love of *Freedom* sprung,
> Whence flow these wishes for the common good,
> By feeling hearts alone best understood,
> I, young in life, by seeming cruel fate
> Was snatch'd from *Afric's* fancy'd happy seat:
> What pangs excruciating must molest,
> What sorrows labour in my parent's breast?
> Steel'd was that soul and by no misery mov'd
> That from a father seiz'd his babe belov'd:
> Such, such my case. And can I then but pray
> Others may never feel tyrannic sway?

But with all of her outward neglect of self, Phillis Wheatley was too honest to veil her true personality in what she wrote. The sincerity of childhood and the delicacy of young womanhood, uniform in both the black race and the white, are constantly reflected, even when she is most artificial. Her gentle character, so often commented upon, lies revealed in every poem and letter.

But the dominant trait in the personality which her writings reveal is a capacity for intense religious faith. Without that faith she probably would never have written a line. She was not devout with the primitive adoration of a Jupiter Hammon, but with a belief balanced and controlled by Puritan training, such a belief as that of any other member of the Old South Church who might have seen worth in the emotionalism of George Whitefield. Every poem which was born in her mind, even the adaptation from Ovid, came forth filled with religious feeling. Her letters to Obour Tanner are to a great extent dissertations on the mercies and goodness of God. The one wholly subjective poem which came from her pen, **"On Being Brought from Africa,"** proves what religion was in her life.

> 'Twas mercy brought me from my *Pagan* land,
> Taught my benighted soul to understand
> That there's a God, that there's a *Saviour* too:
> Once I redemption neither sought nor knew.
> Some view our sable race with scornful eye,
> "Their colour is a diabolic die."
> Remember, *Christians, Negros* black as *Cain*,
> May be refin'd, and join th' angelic train.

It is interesting to speculate what her thinking might have been if it had not been nurtured by the Puritanism of eighteenth-century Boston and by the simple doctrines of the Countess of Huntingdon's circle. But speculate as we will, we cannot conceive of a philosophical system, whether based on the assumption that the savage is noble and superior or on any other assumption, which might have replaced her deep trust in the God of the Puritans.

That which is most important in a consideration of her work is her talent—a talent all the more difficult to explain because it is contradictory, in one respect spontaneous and intuitive, and in another respect rational and exceedingly self-conscious. Her success in absorbing the music of Alexander Pope, master of England's neoclassical verse-makers, gives her poems their highest claim to distinction; and it seems that she was not aware of what she was doing when she achieved that success. We are told that there were three books in the Wheatley library for which she had a particularly strong affection—the Bible, a collection of tales from classical mythology, and Pope's Homer. Her first publication, the elegy on Whitefield, shows that she was familiar with Gray. We know that after her visit to England she possessed a Milton, and that after 1774 she owned a collection of Shenstone's poems. There is reason to believe that she read every poem which she could find, whether in book, magazine, newspaper, or broadsheet. But it was Pope's translation of Homer which taught her most. We have already noticed, in the quotation from **"Goliath of Gath,"** how near she could come to her great master's idiom whenever her subject matter gave her the opportunity. In writing the following lines from **"Thoughts on His Excellency Major General Lee,"** she was probably thinking of the first book of *Paradise Lost,* but it is Pope's music which she reproduced:

> While thus he spake, the hero of renown
> Survey'd the boaster with a gloomy frown,
> And stern reply'd: "O arrogance of tongue!
> And wild ambition, ever prone to wrong!
> Believ'st thou chief, that armies such as thine
> Can stretch in dust that heaven-defended line?"

Even in her one poem in blank verse, **"To the University of Cambridge, in New-England,"** a quotation from which has been given, the line, with its strong rise, marked caesura, and hastened fall, is that of Pope. Indeed, reproduction of Pope's versification characterizes all of her poems with the exception of the few which she wrote in lyrical measures. She lived during the age when the poetical fashion in America was to imitate Pope; and while John Trumbull, Timothy Dwight, Joel Barlow, the Philip Freneau of the political satires, and numerous others among her contemporaries caught more of his general spirit, she perhaps excelled them all in reproducing his rhythms. Her power to attain this place of eminence must be pronounced as due to her instinct for hearing the music of words, an instinct which was possibly racial. As in Jupiter Hammon and many other Negro poets, in her the strange sense for imitating sound exercised itself of its own will. She never mentioned Pope, and only rarely touched upon themes such as he treated; but before she began writing, she had read his Homer with her deep-searching ear open for impressions which were to endure. (pp. 22-7)

Like all neoclassical poets, she borrowed images freely. One finds in her poems the favorite eighteenth-century *clichés*, such as *vaulted skies, roving fancy, crystal shower, feathered warbler, smiling fields, graceful tresses,* and *pensive bosoms.* One also finds an imagination imitating with a remarkable accuracy. The images indicated by italics in the following lines are the invention of a mind working with precision and with a clean recognition of nice artistic adjustment:

> All-conquering Death! by thy resistless pow'r,
> *Hope's tow'ring plumage falls to rise no more!*
>
> *We trace the pow'r of Death from tomb to tomb,*
> *And his are all the ages yet to come.*
>
> *The frozen deeps may break their iron bands,*
> *And bid their waters murmur o'er the sands.*
>
> Aeolus in his rapid chariot drove
> *In gloomy grandeur from the vault above:*
> *Furious he comes. His winged sons obey*
> *Their frantic sire, and madden all the sea.*
>
> He drops the bridle on his courser's mane,
> *Before his eyes in shadows swims the plain.*
>
> *Swift thro' his throat the feather'd mischief flies,*
> *Bereft of sense, he drops his head, and dies.*

Images of like character abound in Phillis Wheatley's poems. They are not direct copies, and they cannot be created by a mind that is not a master of itself. They prove as well as the smooth music in Phillis Wheatley's verse her genius at imitation. And it is not too much to presume that if she had been taught by a Wordsworth, who would have convinced her of the value of turning to her sincere religious self for her subjects and of using an idiom drawn out of her own personality, her work would stand on its own merits rather than on the fact that she, a Negro and a slave, produced it. If she had not fallen under the sway of the New England elegists and of Pope and his school, she might today be considered one of the ornaments in American literature as well as one of the most interesting curiosities. (pp. 28-9)

Vernon Loggins, "The Beginnings of Negro Authorship, 1760-1790," in his *The Negro Author: His Development in America to 1900,* 1931. Reprint by Kennikat Press, Inc., 1964, pp. 1-47.

J. SAUNDERS REDDING
(essay date 1939)

[Redding is a distinguished critic, historian, novelist, and autobiographer. His first book, *To Make a Poet Black* (1939), is a scholarly appraisal of African-American poetry that includes a historical overview as well as biographical information about individual poets. As one of the first anthologies of its type to be written by a black critic, this book is considered a landmark in criticism of African-American writers. In the following excerpt, Redding discusses the taming effect of Wheatley's upbringing upon her poetry.]

There is no question but that Miss Wheatley considered herself a Negro poet: the question is to what degree she felt the full significance of such a designation. Certainly she was not a *slave* poet in any sense in which the term can be applied to many who followed her. She stood far outside the institution that was responsible for her. As for the question of degree, though she refers to herself time and again as an "Ethiop," she seems to make such reference with a distinct sense of abnegation and self-pity. (pp. 8-9)

This attitude on the part of Miss Wheatley was the result of the training and conduct of her life. Treated as one of the Wheatley family on terms of almost perfect equality, petted and made much of, she was sagacious enough to see that this was due in part at least to her exotic character and sensitive enough to feel that her color was really a bar to a more desirable, if less flattering, attention. At best this life was not too dear to Phillis. She recounts the joys of the life to come in the strains of one who looks upon this life as though it were a strange and bitter preparation for an eternity of bliss. The Wheatleys had adopted her, but she had adopted their terrific New England conscience. Her conception of the after-life was different from that of most of the slaves as we find it expressed in songs and spirituals. No contemplation of physical luxuries of feastings, jeweled crowns, and snowy robes enticed her. Her heaven must be a place of the purest sublimation of spirit. Less than this would serve but to remind her of this dark bourne of flesh and blood.

But if the degree to which she felt herself a Negro poet was slight, the extent to which she was attached spiritually and emotionally to the slaves is even slighter. By 1761 slavery was an important almost daily topic. The Boston home of the Wheatleys, intelligent and alive as it was, could not have been deaf to the discussions of restricting the slave trade. . . . Not once, however, did she express in either word or action a thought on the enslavement of her race; not once did she utter a straightforward word for the freedom of the Negro. When she did speak of freedom in ["**To the Right Honorable William, Earl of Dartmouth**"], it was:

> Should you, my lord, while you peruse my song,
> Wonder from whence my love of freedom sprung,
> Whence flow these wishes for the common good,
> By feeling hearts alone best understood,
> I, young in life, by seeming cruel fate
> Was snatched from Afric's fancied happy seat.

"Seeming cruel" and "fancied happy" give her away as not believing either in the cruelty of the fate that had dragged thousands of her race into bondage in America nor in the happiness of their former freedom in Africa. How different the spirit of her work, and how unracial (not to say unnatural) are the stimuli that release her wan creative energies. How different are these from the work of George Horton who twenty-five years later could cry out with bitterness, without cavil or fear. . . . (pp. 9-11)

It is this negative, bloodless, unracial quality in Phillis Wheatley that makes her seem superficial, especially to members of her own race. Hers is a spirit-denying-the-flesh attitude that somehow cannot seem altogether real as the essential quality and core of one whose life should have made her sensitive to the very things she denies. In this sense none of her poetry is real. Compared to the Negro writers who followed her, Miss Wheatley's passions are tame, her skill the sedulous copy of established techniques, and her thoughts the hand-me-downs of her age. She is chilly. Part of her chill is due to the unmistakable influence of Pope's neoclassicism upon her. She followed the fashion in poetry. Overemphasis of religion was a common fault of the time. She indulged it in poetic epistles, eulogistic verse, verses written in praise of accomplishments. Her ready submission to established forms was a weakness of the period. First and last, she was the fragile product of three related forces—the age, the Wheatley household, and New England America. Her work lacks spontaneity because of the first, enthusiasm because of the second, and because of the third it lacks an unselfish purpose that drives to some ultimate goal of expression.

And yet she had poetic talent, was in fact a poet. No one who reads . . . **"Thoughts on the Works of Providence"** can deny it. . . . Judged in the light of the day in which she wrote, judged by that day's standards and accomplishments, she was an important poet. As a Negro poet she stands out remarkably, for her work lacks the characteristics of thought one would expect to find. (pp. 11-12)

J. Saunders Redding, "The Forerunners," in his *To Make a Poet Black*, 1939. Reprint by Cornell University Press, 1988, pp. 3-18.

ARTHUR P. DAVIS
(essay date 1953)

[Davis, an American author and scholar of black American literature, has contributed numerous articles, short stories, and book reviews to magazines, anthologies, and professional journals. He also coedited *The Negro Caravan* (1941) and *Cavalcade: Negro American Writers from 1760 to the Present* (1971). In the following excerpt, he counters arguments that Wheatley displayed no racial consciousness or personal sentiments in her poetry.]

The most frequently stated criticism of Phillis Wheatley is that she was too highly objective in her writing, that adhering too closely to the tenets of her neo-classic training and background, she failed to tell us enough about herself, her personal feelings and thoughts. This view has been expressed in varying forms by practically all of the scholars who have written concerning the fascinating little eighteenth-century poetess. (p. 191)

They all state or imply that Phillis Wheatley because of her identification with the literary viewpoint of her age simply did not write enough about slavery or herself. (p. 192)

[It] will be the purpose of this paper to show, through a reexamination of her poetry, that Phillis Wheatley does speak of her own problems more often than is commonly recognized.

The first thing that impresses the close reader of Miss Wheatley's verse is that in spite of the generally held contrary opinion she is definitely race conscious. Although she never belabors the issue, she keeps reminding the reader that she is not just a poet, but an "Afric" poet. Phillis Wheatley seems to realize full well the propaganda value of her race and condition, and she uses both to advantage. For example, in the poem **"To the University of Cambridge, in New England"** she admonishes the students to avoid sin, but she underscores this advice with the line: "An Ethiop tells you, 'tis your greatest foe." The admonition to shun sin certainly does not need the peculiar or special backing of an Ethiop to make it effective, but Phillis Wheatley has in mind the obvious contrast between her own disadvantage as a slave just recently brought from a pagan land and the silver-spoon opportunities of these Harvard young men. This sort of contrast is implied in much of her poetry. Using her race and her lowly position as a frame of reference, she points up the message currently given. We find the same approach in a poem addressed **"To His Honor the Lieutenant Governor on the Death of His Lady."** After describing the beauties of the late wife's heavenly existence, she says abruptly to the husband:

> Nor canst thou, Oliver, assent refuse
> To heav'nly tidings from the *Afric Muse.*

This racial underscoring also occurs in other ways. In the opening lines of **"On Recollection"** we find the racial tag:

> Mneme, begin. Inspire, ye sacred Nine,
> Your *ven'trous Afric,* in her great design.

There is no obvious reason for designating her race in an objective and abstract poem of this sort, but consciously or unconsciously Phillis Wheatley realizes the advantage of the race label and inserts it. She does the same thing in **"A Hymn to Humanity"** . . . when she asks the question: "Can *Afric's Muse* forgetful prove?" Her race awareness appears in yet another way in **"To Maecenas"**. . . . In this piece she mentions three great poets—Homer, Virgil, and Terence. The last-named is included for one reason only, he is an *Afric* genius; and as such she is proud of him, so proud in fact that she brackets him with two men who are not only infinitely superior to him in excellence but who write in a totally different field.

Far from being shy about her race and native land, Phillis Wheatley is sometimes capable of special pleading on that score. This is apparent in . . . lines from **"On the Death of the Reverend Mr. George Whitefield"**. . . . Phillis Wheatley gives one or two lines to each of the other groups listed . . . but four to "ye Africans." Unlike the men of this world Christ is "impartial" (she uses the word here and elsewhere in a strictly racial sense); he "longs" to help Africans because of their unhappy condition and will make them "sons, and kings, and priests to God." All through this passage there runs the obvious theme of escape through leveling which was Christianity's primary appeal to the slave. Phillis had experienced in her own life the power of Christianity to open doors before closed to her. Though still a slave she was a Christian "sister" even to her owners and a "saint" in the Boston of her day. It was the only way for Africans to enter into the "kingdom" both here and hereafter. Realizing this fully, she underscores the appeal.

Let us examine now the two best known racial passages in the Wheatley poems. The first of these is **"On Being Brought from Africa to America,"** the only poem in which she is totally subjective:

> 'Twas mercy brought me from my *pagan land,*
> Taught my benighted soul to understand
> That there's a God—that there's a Saviour too;

> Once I redemption neither sought nor knew.
> *Some view our sable race with scornful eye,*
> "Their color is a diabolic dye."
> *Remember, Christians, Negroes black as Cain*
> May be *refin'd,* and join th' *angelic train.*

"Refined" seems to be the key word here. It is one that she likes, and she uses it in emphatic positions in at least four other poems. As an African and a slave, Phillis Wheatley had felt the "scornful eye" all too often, but she knows that refinement furnished at least partial escape from that evil. And by refinement she had in mind not only Christian salvation but intellectual and cultural improvement as well. Her whole life was a serious and determined effort to acquire this sort of transforming refinement; and in the last two lines above—the lines with the imperative "remember"—she seems to be serving personal notice to the effect that she had achieved some measure of success on that score. There is a certain positiveness and assurance in these verses which impresses.

The second of these better known racial passages is that found in the verses **"To the Right Honorable William, Earl of Dartmouth."** It is Phillis Wheatley's strongest and most forthright utterance on slavery:

> Should you, my lord, while you peruse my song,
> Wonder from whence *my love of Freedom sprung,*
> Whence flow these wishes for the common good,
> By *feeling* hearts alone best understood,
> I, young in life, by *seeming cruel fate*
> Was snatched from *Afric's fancied happy seat;*
> What pangs excruciating must molest,
> What sorrows labor in my parent's breast! . . .
> Such, such my case. And can I then but pray
> Others may never *feel tyrannic sway?*

The above lines speak for themselves on the subject of freedom, but they take on added strength and significance when compared with the objective passages on the same theme in **"Liberty and Peace"** and **"His Excellency General Washington."** In the latter poems (q.v.) Freedom is a typical neo-classic abstraction; but the personal reference in this poem makes it as strong a protest against slavery as a slave could utter and expect to have his work published in a slave-holding community. Several critics, among them James Weldon Johnson [see excerpt dated 1921], have been irritated by the so-called smugness expressed in the phrases "seeming cruel fate" and "Afric's fancied happy seat." Phillis Wheatley also takes the same attitude towards her homeland in the verses **"To the University of Cambridge, in New-England,"** in which she refers to Africa as a "dark abode" and a "land of errors and Egyptian gloom." But to accuse her of smugness in this respect is to overlook the most important subjective element in these phrases. Phillis Wheatley is speaking here not as a native of Africa but as a Christian, and to the Christian Phillis, Africa or Asia or any other land which did not know and accept Christ could never be a truly "happy seat." In short she writes upon two levels. As a little African girl it was cruel to be snatched from her parents, but to find Christ as a result of this misfortune was more than ample compensation for this "seeming cruel fate." We must always bear in mind that Phillis Wheatley was deeply religious, and that her religion was inextricably tied up with practical everyday considerations such as acceptance in the best circles of her time. This talented little girl made the most of her Christianity, tying it in neatly with the added appeal that her racial and pagan background gave to it. This is not to say that she was opportunist or hypocritical. She was simply human and highly intelligent.

Another important subjective element in Phillis Wheatley's work is her concern with excellence as a poet. It is only fair to state here that many of the phrases she uses to characterize herself are the conventional ones typical of neo-classic writing; but there are others which seem to have unusual pertinence. For one thing, she is keenly aware of her own handicaps in the matter of education and status, referring to herself as a "groveling mind," "a languid muse in low degree," and "the last and meanest of the rhyming train." One notes that each of these phrases has a menial connotation. In spite of her position, however, she is convinced that "an intrinsic (natural) ardor" prompts her to write; she wishes to cultivate virtue to learn "a better strain, a nobler lay." . . . (pp. 192-95)

[Phrases] and passages of this sort may be conventional utterance, but in certain lines of the poem **"To Maecenas"** Phillis Wheatley seems to be voicing real disappointment at poetic failure. . . . Even after we discount the exaggeration and disparagement typical of such poems, we find that Phillis is saying in no uncertain words that she cannot expect to equal Terence as a poet because his position was "happier" than hers. Terence, who was also an African, had once been a slave but had gained his freedom presumably because of his excellence as a poet. At this time Phillis was still in bondage and as a result of her unhappy position and "grov'ling mind" the "faltering music" dies upon her tongue. One notes also that the poetess seems just a little piqued that the "partial" muses had allowed only one poet of "Afric's sable race" to achieve world fame. In short . . . [the] whole Terence passage is highly personal because of its racial and status comparisons. (p. 196)

And finally let us examine those few poems of Phillis Wheatley which touch on personal relationships. Our limited knowledge of the poet's life is a serious handicap in considering these pieces, but the verses say enough to show at least certain basic traits in the young lady. Strangely enough, . . . **"A Farewell to America,"** addressed to Mrs. Susannah Wheatley, the poet's mistress, seems the most stilted. Phillis was being sent to England for her health. The following lines are the only poetic reference to her mistress that we have:

> Susannah mourns, nor can I bear
>   To see the crystal shower,
> Or mark the tender falling tear
>   At sad departure's hour.
>
> Not unregarding can I see
>   Her soul with grief opprest;
> But let no sighs, no groans for me,
>   Steal from her pensive breast.

There is much more feeling in the **"Hymn to Humanity,"** addressed to one S. P. G., Esq.:

> For when they *pitying eye* did see
> The languid *muse in low degree;*
>   Then, *then at thy desire,*
> Descended the *celestial Nine;*
> O'er me methought they deigned to shine,
>   And deigned to string my lyre.
>
> Can *Afric's Muse* forgetful prove?
> *Or can such friendship fail to move*
>   *A tender human heart?*

We do not know who S. P. G. is, but it is obvious that he encouraged or helped Phillis in the writing of poetry. He is evidently an eminent person, and she is grateful that his "pitying eye" sought her out. There is a certain warmth in the last three lines entirely lacking in the lines to Mrs. Wheatley.

In the verses **"On the Death of the Reverend Dr. Sewall"** we find the strongest personal utterance in any of her poems. . . . It would be good to know just how Dr. Sewall helped Phillis, just how he urged her "mournful verse to close" (end?) Did he advise her to stop writing funeral elegies? We of course do not know, but we need no biographical help to get the full import of the last three lines above: In them the young poetess has dropped the objective tone habitually used in these elegies and speaks in the first person, straight from the heart.

One gets the impression from . . . [her] personal utterances that Phillis Wheatley was not so much the victim of her neo-classic training as of a congenital reserve. She seems to keep a perpetual guard on her emotions, holding them under rigid control. And when, as happens on occasion, she inadvertently lowers the guard in a brief personal passage, she seems immediately to regret it and then to run for shelter on the safe ground of religious generality. . . . It is this kind of guarded and grudging subjectivity which characterizes all of the personal passages in the poems of Phillis Wheatley.

In summary then, after a close reading of her poetry, one finds that Phillis Wheatley has written a few passages expressing stronger-than-customary personal feeling; that she does tell us some things concerning her ambitions and desires as a poet; and that above all else, she is definitely race conscious in her writings. These findings do not invalidate the opinions expressed by . . . [other critics], but they do tend to soften and tone down the charge of stern and unyielding objectivity which for too long has dominated all criticism of Phillis Wheatley. (pp. 196-98)

Arthur P. Davis, "Personal Elements in the Poetry of Phillis Wheatley," in *PHYLON: The Atlanta University Review of Race and Culture,* Vol. XIV, No. 2, second quarter (June), 1953, pp. 191-98.

ANGELENE JAMISON
(essay date 1974)

[In the following excerpt, Jamison charges that Wheatley's verse "is a product of a white mind, a mind that had been so engulfed in the education, religion, values, and the freedom of Whites that she expressed no strong sentiments for those who had been cast into the wretchedness of slavery by those she so often praised with her pen."]

Phillis Wheatley was a poet of the latter half of the eighteenth century who happened to be Black. Despite her position as a slave and despite the growing interest in the slave issue in Bostonian circles, of which she was a marginal part, she did not address herself in any significant degree to the plight of her people. She wrote to Whites, for Whites and generally in the Euro-American tradition at that time. That is, Phillis Wheatley was influenced by neo-classicism. And much of her poetry reflects various stylistic characteristics of Alexander Pope and his followers. **"On Being Brought from Africa to America," "Hymn to Evening,"** and many of her other poems reflect her ability to use effectively Pope's heroic couplet. (pp. 408-09)

Among the themes which permeate the poetry of Phillis Wheatley are Christian piety, morality, virtue, death, praises of classical heroes, and a celebration of abstractions such as the poems **"On Recollection"** and **"Imagination."** There are very few poems in which Phillis Wheatley points to her experiences as a Black and a slave. Her poetry embraces white attitudes and values, and it characterizes Phillis as a typical Euro-American poetess. She was detached from her people and her poetry could never be used as an expression of black thought. (p. 409)

Since Phillis Wheatley wrote primarily for the Whites and since we are concerned with re-examining her life and works in terms of their significance to us, it is important to analyze the image that those for whom she wrote had of her. Many were astonished at the poetry of Phillis Wheatley and showered her with praises because they had not expected such capabilities from an African. This kind of response was typical of those Whites who were willing to recognize the talents of Blacks. To them, Blacks who made contributions were always the exception and never the general rule regardless of the circumstances under which Blacks made their contribution.

[In his introduction to *The Poems of Phillis Wheatley*] Julian D. Mason, Jr., cites several examples of Whites who spoke favorably of Phillis Wheatley. Among them were William Joseph Snelling, a Boston writer, whose comments appeared in the May, 1834 edition of *The Christian Examiner,* and John Edward Bruce who discussed Phillis in his essay, "Negro Poets," in the March 6, 1897 edition of *The Literary Digest of New York.* Snelling

Facsimile of one of Wheatley's letters.

marveled at the level of intelligence reached by Phillis, but he felt that her poetry would receive lasting admiration from only those who were sympathetic towards Blacks. John Edward Bruce felt that she was an extraordinary young woman who did much to dispel the myth that Blacks were intellectually inferior.

Even though Snelling and Bruce made some positive comments about Phillis Wheatley, both were operating under the assumption that Blacks were inferior and incapable of intellectual pursuits. Neither saw her poetry as highly exceptional when compared to eighteenth century standards, but they were awed by the fact that here was a Black who could at least make attempts at expressing herself in poetry. And since Phillis' poetry was white-oriented, Snelling and Bruce seemed to have been convinced that she had intellectual potential.

Although Phillis Wheatley generally received some favorable comments from Whites during her life time and afterwards, there were also those Whites who harshly criticized her poetry purely on a racial basis. People like Thomas Jefferson were blinded by her color and their prejudices against Blacks. In his "Notes on Virginia," Thomas Jefferson said:

> Misery is often the parent of the most affecting touches in poetry. Among the Blacks is misery enough, God knows, but no poetry. . . . Religion, indeed has produced a Phillis Wheatley; but it could not produce a poet. The compositions published under her name are below the dignity of criticism.

Many of the other so-called critics who ridiculed the works of Phillis Wheatley fall into the category of white racists who refused to recognize any merits in the contributions of Blacks.

More important to us than the attitudes of Whites toward Phillis Wheatley are those of Blacks, and here the attitudes are just as diverse as those of Whites. Perhaps the first Black to pay tribute to Phillis Wheatley was Jupiter Hammon who wrote a poem to her in 1778 entitled "An Address to Miss Phillis Wheatly (sic), Ethiopian Poetess, in Boston who came from Africa at eight years of age, and soon became acquainted with the gospel of Jesus Christ." By referring to her in his title as an "Ethiopian Poetess," Hammon acknowledged her ancestry and her creative abilities. However, the main thrust of the poem to Phillis Wheatley is that she should be thankful to God for "bringing thee from the distant shore, / To learn his holy word." It is implicit in the poem that Jupiter Hammon was much more concerned with Phillis' salvation than he was with her poetry, and he wanted Phillis to give all praises to God for any gifts she might have had.

More recent black critics of Phillis Wheatley have been more concerned with examining her image as a Black rather than saving her soul. Several critics have pointed to her ability to write poetry but they have critically questioned her race consciousness. J. Saunders Redding, in his book, *To Make A Poet Black,* says " . . . the extent to which she was attached spiritually and emotionally to the slave is even slighter" than the extent she felt herself a Negro poet. He goes on to say that "she is chilly," and he holds Pope's neo-classicism responsible [see excerpt dated 1939]. Benjamin Brawley also points to Phillis Wheatley's lack of reference to race, but he seems to feel that she had no alternative but to model herself after writers with which she was familiar.

Statements like those of J. Saunders Redding and Benjamin Brawley have been compounded by more militant critics and readers of Phillis Wheatley. After reading various poems of Phillis Wheatley, the first comment of most students is that she was not Black enough and of course they are correct. But, we must move beyond that kind of statement into re-examining the poetry in light of the implications of her lack of race consciousness to the development of black thought.

Phillis Wheatley was a woman of African descent. However, when examining certain poems where she makes direct and indirect references to herself as an African, it is obvious that she lacked pride in her heritage. Her reference to herself as an Ethiopian gives no evidence that she had embraced the culture from which she was taken; rather it was a means of humbling herself. In her poem **"To The University of Cambridge in New England"** she requested that the students take advantage of all the opportunities presented to them and guard themselves against sin. In the concluding lines of the poem she pleaded:

> Ye blooming plants of human race divine
> An Ethiop tells you 'tis your greatest foe;
> Its transient sweetness turns to endless pain
> And in immense perdition sinks the soul.

Here she refers to the students, who were obviously white, as practically God-like, and she warns them against the pitfalls of evil. Her statement that "an Ethiop tells you . . . " reflects a lack of self-worth particularly within the context of the poem. If an Ethiop is aware of the danger of sin then certainly these "blooming plants of human race divine," those who belong to the best race, should also be aware. It would seem that Phillis, one who thought it necessary to warn these white students of the deadly potential of sin, would have included in her poem the greatest sin of slavery which had been committed upon her.

Her concept of herself as a poet was no better than her concept of herself as a Black. When writing poems to those for whom she had an extreme admiration, she felt it necessary to apologize for even attempting to address these Whites in poetic form. As a matter of fact, Phillis once implied in a response to the answer to a poem she had written to a gentleman in the Navy, that her poetry could never equal the poem she had received from him. In the same poem, after having placed herself in an inferior position, she states: "Then fix the humble Afric muse's seat / At British Homer's and Sir Isaac's feet." At this point, she is just humble and submissive enough to believe that the African muse belonged at the foot of the European.

Phillis Wheatley's self-image as it is reflected in her poetry is strongly related to her religious attitudes. The poem, **"On Being Brought from Africa to America,"** shows her gratitude for having been taken from what she perceived as a pagan land, brought to America and taught Christianity. Her lines, "Some view our sable race with scornful eye, / Their colour is a diabolic die," are indicative of some awareness of the existing attitudes of Whites toward Blacks. And in the last two lines of the poem, "Remember, *Christians, Negroes,* black as *Cain,* / May be refined and join th' Angelic train," she articulates that Blacks too have the opportunity to be saved. However, "Remember, *Christians, Negroes,* black as *Cain*" does not clarify whether she perceives Christians and / or Blacks can be black as Cain. The ambiguity indicates that possibly before Blacks can be equal to Christians, if ever, they must be refined. The lines also indicate Phillis Wheatley's acceptance of the curse of Cain and its racist implication.

To Phillis, God was an impartial and merciful Savior whose works deserved all praises from mankind. In the final lines of **"Thoughts on the Works of Providence,"** she muses, "To him, whose works array'd with mercy shine, / What songs should rise; how constant, how divine!" This God had been taught to Phillis Wheatley by Whites and her feelings towards Him enhanced her humbleness and submissiveness. Much of her poetry reflects the qualities she perceived as necessary in order to meet God's approval and, consequently, be received in heaven. Graciously and without question, Phillis Wheatley accepted the religion of the oppressor who had enslaved her. She never looked at her position as a slave as a contradiction to the goodness and graciousness of God.

Just as Phillis did not see a contradiction in the white man's concept of religion, neither did she see the contradiction in his concept of freedom. In no area does Phillis Wheatley's white orientation present itself more than in her poems dealing with freedom. In **"To His Excellency General Washington,"** after humbling herself and apologizing for what she perceived as possible inaccuracies in an introductory letter, Phillis Wheatley moves on to express her patriotism and her undying faith in the "honorable" General Washington. She praises his gallantry and sees him as "first in peace and honors," and "fam'd for thy valour, for their virtues more." (pp. 409-13)

In another poem, **"On Liberty and Peace,"** Phillis

Wheatley sees Columbia as being firmly protected by Heaven in the quest for freedom and peace. She sees Britian, in its effort to maintain control over the colonies, as a cruel and vicious menace, and she strongly supports other countries which come to the aid of the colonies in their fight for freedom. The blood that was shed in the war, the lives that were lost on both sides, the land that was destroyed were all necessary to Phillis because she felt heaven had ordained that Columbia be free, and as she points out "Freedom comes array'd with charms divine, / and in her Train Commerce and Plenty Shine." Throughout the poem, **"Liberty and Peace,"** she makes reference to the fact that some divine aid will always guide the path of Columbia, and that Columbia will be a model for peace.

> Where e'er Columbia spreads her swelling sails;
> To every Realm Shall peace her charms display,
> And Heavenly Freedom spread her golden ray.

Phillis saw the very country which enslaved her and other Blacks as one deserving some heavenly protection. How could she be so removed from the plight of her people and the attitudes towards her people as to glorify those who were responsible for that wretched condition of slavery? Did she feel that bringing peace to the colonies would bring peace and freedom to Blacks? It is clearly substantiated that she was brainwashed to the point of expressing totally the sentiments of Whites without giving any consideration to the fact that the white "heroes" of the American Revolution were concerned only about themselves. Blacks, to most of them, were a means of supplying labor and the questions of the freedom of Blacks had nothing to do with the freedom of Whites from the mother country.

Some readers of Phillis Wheatley might argue that her poem, **"To the Right Honourable William, Earl of Dartmouth, His Majesty's Principal Secretary of State of North America and C.,"** is a strong indication of her awareness of the position of Blacks in this country and her own plight particularly. From that poem, most refer to the following lines:

> Should you, my lord, while you peruse my song,
> Wonder from whence my love of freedom sprung,
> Whence flow these wishes for the common good,
> By feeling hearts alone best understood,
> I young in life, by seeming cruel fate
> Was snatch'd from Afric's fancy'd happy seat.
> What pangs excruciating must molest,
> What sorrows labour in my parents' breast?
> Steel's was that soul and by no misery mov'd
> That from a father seiz'd his babe belov'd:
> Such, such my case. And can I then but pray
> Others may never feel tyrannic sway?

In this stanza Phillis Wheatley seems to be trying to explain why she has concerned herself in her poetry with the freedom of the American colonies. Her reason which is weakly supported is that she was taken from her homeland, which she describes as "Afric's fancy'd happy seat." The implication here is that Africa may not have been as happy as imagined. Moreover, she talks about the pain and suffering endured by her parents but she never makes reference to having suffered herself. Slavery is not mentioned nor is it clearly implied. Also, as J. Saunders Reddings points out " 'seeming cruel' and 'fanc'd happy' give her away as not believing even in the cruelty of the fate that had dragged thousands of her race into bondage in America nor in the happiness of their former freedom in Africa."

In the last two lines of this stanza she is obviously talking about Whites when she says, " . . . and can I then but pray / others may never feel tyrannic sway," because Blacks already felt this tyranny.

Thus, Phillis Wheatley's poem to the Earl of Dartmouth provides no evidence of her Blackness nor does it show that her orientation was anything other than white. She was a poet who happened to be Black and it is a mistake to refer to her as a Black poet. However, it is much to the credit of black people that a slave girl was able to get a book of poems published at such an early age and during the seventeen hundreds. But in any literary analysis of the poetry of Phillis Wheatley from a Black perspective, we must accept the fact that her poetry is a product of a white mind, a mind that had been so engulfed in the education, religion, values, and the freedom of Whites that she expressed no strong sentiments for those who had been cast into the wretchedness of slavery by those she so often praised with her pen. Any student who is exposed to Phillis Wheatley must be able to recognize that her poetry expressed the sentiments of eighteenth century Whites because her mind was controlled by them, her actions were controlled by them, and consequently her pen. (pp. 413-15)

Angelene Jamison, "Analysis of Selected Poetry of Phillis Wheatley," in *The Journal of Negro Education,* Vol. XLIII, No. 3, Summer, 1974, pp. 408-16.

JULIAN D. MASON, JR.
(essay date 1989)

[Mason is an American poet, essayist, and educator whose works have appeared in numerous journals. In the following excerpt from the introduction to his revised edition of *The Poems of Phillis Wheatley*, he attempts a balanced analysis of the poet's strengths and limitations.]

Phillis Wheatley is important historically, and her works are of importance and interest in their own right, especially in the contexts of her time and place—though some of them easily transcend both. Phillis Wheatley, however, was not a great poet. She was not really a poet in the classical Greek sense of maker, seer, creator, nor were her concerns really much with Ralph Waldo Emerson's meter-making argument or Edgar Allan Poe's rhythmical creation of beauty. She had aspirations, but she also knew her shortcomings; and her concerns usually were not very august or pretentious. Her primary endeavor was to put into rhythmical, poetic forms thoughts that came to her or were brought to her attention by the crises and significant experiences of the people of Boston as they met life, death, and change, from day to day and year to year. Much of what she wrote of was not noted by the world outside of that place, though she occasionally did treat more general topics, particularly relating to the American Revolution, and did try for general pertinence while treating local particulars. While most successful writers strive for such pertinence, in her case it seems too often to have been a secondary goal that emerged most obviously when she revised a poem for a secondary audience, as in her revisions to make some of her Boston or American poems more acceptable, meaningful, or attractive to an English audience. Mostly, first of all she wrote for local audiences and local publication. When she occasionally did turn to more general emphases, she produced some of her best work, as in her hymns to morning and evening.

Nevertheless, on the basis of the poems that have survived her short career, she must be labeled as primarily an occasional poet, one interested in the clever crafting of verse. Such a craftsman is less concerned with selecting topics and creating patterns than with taking a given or obvious topic and fitting it skillfully to an already existing pattern. If she is a good craftsman, she is distinctive in her own right and possesses a gift that is worthy of the world's attention, if not its lasting praise. Such was Phillis Wheatley's gift and her concern, and she was a better craftsman of verse than most of the others attempting the same type of thing in America in the 1770s, a time and place that certainly produced more craftsmen than true poets. Her reward was in immediate praise—not that which echoes through the ages, but which appropriately sounds again from time to time.

Yet some of her poems reveal an exceptional being producing exceptional poetry. Most of her best work is in her nonoccasional poems, certainly in her more philosophic ones. In this regard it is interesting that various commentators have chosen different ones of her small body of poems to praise as the best, and almost all writers on this subject favor to some degree **"An Hymn to the Morning"** and **"An Hymn to the**

Evening." One would be amiss not to place in this company **"On Virtue"** and **"Goliath of Gath,"** and each reader might wish to include yet others; for in certain complete poems and in parts of others, Wheatley was able to surpass to a great degree what was at once both her great asset and her great liability—a favor for and a remarkable spontaneous ability to recreate the neoclassical poetic mode of Alexander Pope and his followers, in diction, meter, rhyme, and syntax. In such happy instances she avoided ordinary subject matter and clichés, using instead striking, appropriate poetic figures in pleasing form, which attracted both the mind and the ear. In these she was more than just an imitator, and she reflected a fortunate influence of the best neoclassicism. Unfortunately, she could not write this well consistently enough for such good poetry to dominate her work, leaving her to be known primarily as a prodigious imitator. For the same poet who wrote the exceptional poems mentioned above also wrote too many run-of-the-mill elegies.

Wheatley seems to have been fascinated with the device of invocation, and her mixing of Christian and classical in the many invocations in her poems (as well as in other parts of the poems) reflects the two greatest influences on her work, religion and neoclassicism. Indeed, this device and a few others remind one of Milton, though she certainly does not use them with his skill. For example, one can see the mixing of the Christian and the neoclassic in **"To Maecenas"** and **"On Recollection,"** and she apparently attempts the Miltonic device of vague exactness in measurement in **"Thoughts on the Works of Providence,"** when she says of the sun's distance from the earth, "Of miles twice forty millions is his height." Vernon Loggins has pointed to the influence of English writers on her poems dealing with imagination, recollection, and virtue and to the influence of Milton on her hymns to the morning and evening and her poem about General Lee. He also suggests the specific influence of Gray on her poem on Whitefield's death and of Addison and Watts on **"Ode to Neptune"** and **"Hymn to Humanity."**

The strongest influences on her work definitely were religion (including the Bible) and neoclassicism. Wheatley has been called a typical New Englander of the eighteenth century in her pious religious views, which seem to crop up everywhere. She is constantly aware of God, His Son, His beneficence, and His power; and she intends that her readers be aware of them too. Almost every poem produces a moral at some point, and the mood and message of her poem to the University of Cambridge sound as if it might have been issued from the pulpit. She had definite, if stereotyped, ideas that Heaven is a place of halos, angels, and reunion with God and His beloved; and she used these ideas with the same seriousness of purpose that surrounds her classical material. It is not at all strange that one

who attended Boston's Old South Meeting House should show such firm Christian convictions and concern with the soul, and these facets of her personality made it very appropriate for friends to turn to her for elegies. In this vein we should not overlook her embellishment of biblical accounts in her poems based on Isaiah and on the encounter of David and Goliath (following in an old New England tradition and beginning a long tradition of black writers' embellishing the Bible). In both of these poems she adds to the biblical narrative and couches it in the neoclassical form that was familiar to her from the poems she read most—iambic pentameter couplets, opening invocation of the muse, panoramic view, attempted elevation of language (especially in the august speeches of the characters), eye-catching details, and hyperbole.

It is clear that Wheatley read as much as possible. Her favorite volumes are reported to have been the Bible, a collection of tales from mythology, and Pope's Homer; and we also know that she read at least some of the Latin authors in the original. Although some of her subject matter can be traced to classical origins outside of Pope's translations and although it is difficult to pinpoint clearly indisputable instances of his influence on her, it still is held by most who study her poems that Pope's translation of Homer was the single most important influence on her work. To that view I too subscribe.

Certainly Pope's relatively fixed formulas for neoclassical poetic music found a ready response in this young African girl's natural imitative ability. However, I suspect that what led her back to Pope time and time again was really Homer's grand narrative, which had retained its greatness of concept even when encased in a neoclassic gait. Wheatley was content to take the form she found because she could use it with ease, but it seems that in choosing Snider, Niobe, David and Goliath, Lee, and Washington, she was also feeling the tug of Homer's heroes on her impressionable young mind. I believe it was the classical world which kindled her talent and interest, though she used the neoclassical approach because of its vogue, its availability to her, and her ability to employ it. Her best-treated subject matter tends to support this view. There has been conjecture about what the rising romanticism would have done to her work if she had lived either later or longer. One may with more pertinence wonder what her poems would have been like had she been immersed in Milton sooner, for what he had done seems to suit her basic interests more. Phillis Wheatley was not the wasp that Pope was, but tended to be more compatible with Milton's Christian classicism and its view of life. It is interesting to note that in a poem dated December 5, 1774, she acknowledges her proper place to be but at the feet of such men as Newton and Milton and reserves for

Milton, the grand creator—not for Pope, the translator—the title "British Homer."

On the other hand, even in the face of these facts and of the fact that her best poems seem to be those that depart most from neoclassical imitation, the strong influence of neoclassicism on her in her first, formative years as a poet may not have been a bad thing. It certainly gave her a respect for regularity (which even Wordsworth recognized as necessary), happened to be something she had a natural talent to reproduce (thus probably encouraging her in her own eyes and in the eyes of those who made Pope so popular), was readily available, and was usually not too deep philosophically. The pity is that events and her short career did not give her talent time enough to discover if it could broaden, mature, and diversify more.

The neoclassical influence also may have been responsible for the lack of much about Wheatley herself in her poems. She certainly leaves the reader of her poems only here and there aware of her being black and a slave. Saunders Redding has pointed out, "The Wheatleys had adopted her, but she had adopted their terrific New England conscience" [see excerpt dated 1939]. She was conscious of her color, but the degree to which she became a New Englander helped moderate this awareness during her most formative years. For her, Heaven was more to be desired than earthly toil, not so much for the physical rewards which many later slaves would emphasize, but rather for its spiritual rewards. Some seem to chide her for her apparent unconcern over slavery in a Boston where it was obviously much discussed, but it was probably better for her poetry that whatever feelings she had about this subject were sublimated in most of her poetry (it emerges more in her letters).

The few thoughts on Africa and slavery's effect on her that are included in her poems are interesting. Her individual situation did not equip her for abolitionism—indeed, her real and necessary poetic patron was the Wheatleys, particularly Susanna Wheatley. She came to America too young for that hard experience not to be modified by her being part of the Wheatley household. But she clearly was not entirely unmindful of blacks' delegated place in the popular mind of the time. She makes good use of this knowledge in her poems to the Earl of Dartmouth, to the University at Cambridge, and on Wooster's death, almost turning it to advantage to strengthen her points. She surely was aware that much of her own notoriety was the result of her work's being usually labeled as that of an African (and she is careful to so call herself in several poems and to entitle one poem **"To S. M., A Young African Painter, On Seeing His Works"**).

In her particular case, she seems to have viewed the captivity that brought her to Boston and to the Wheatleys as not entirely unfortunate. Her poem to Dartmouth speaks of "seeming cruel fate" which snatched her "from Afric's fancied happy seat," and she shows concern primarily for the sorrow of her parents. But she immediately makes it clear that she does not endorse slavers, slavery, or the usual results of slavery. Her poem **"On Being Brought from Africa to America"** sees the event as fortunate because it allowed her to be a Christian, and the poem almost sounds like the product of missionary propaganda (though she specifically refused to be a missionary to Africa). In this same vein she speaks to the students at the University at Cambridge of her not enjoying the advantages they have because of her having so recently come from a land of "errors" and "gloom," brought forth to safety by the "gracious hand" of God. However, in her poem dated December 5, 1774, to the "Gentleman in the Navy," she seems quite taken with western Africa as a place of peace, beauty, and plenty, but this may be simply a reaction to his poem to which this is a reply. At any rate, in **"To Maecenas"** she makes it clear that she thinks the muses ought to come to her aid and not give Terence alone claim to being an inspired African poet. (Of course, here is reflected the narrowness of her knowledge.) Incidentally, this also affords us one of the few instances when we learn anything of Phillis herself from her poems.

Although she did not write much of slavery, certain of her poems do reflect an awareness of current events affecting the society in which she lived. For example, see her poems to the king and to the Earl of Dartmouth and her poems on Snider, Lee, Wooster, and Washington and the poems **"Liberty and Peace"** and **"America."**

In her worst poems, Wheatley falls prey to the clichés of neoclassical poetic diction, to wrenched syntax, to trite devices, to runaway rhythm, and to an overemphasis on religion. These appear most frequently in her occasional verses. Over one-third of her extant poems are elegies. Loggins points out the long tradition of elegies in Boston and that hers too are impersonal and artificial in feeling, with much use of hyperbole, overuse of personification, and pompousness of ornamentation. Not only is neoclassical tradition to blame here, but also the fact that most of these were written for the occasion, to console loved ones and embellish the memory of the departed. Yet sometimes a genuine note of understanding and concern is found in her elegies, especially for persons who had played a part in her own life, at which times one feels even more the strain resulting from her poetic form. Sometimes her good product is found close by her poor one in the same poem. In **"To a Lady and Her Children, On the Death of Her Son and Their Brother,"** she speaks of the mother's realization of the death: "Th' unhappy mother sees the sanguine rill / Forget to flow, and nature's wheels stand still." However, later in the same poem we are rudely accosted by the cliché and the wrenched syntax of the following: "No more in briny show'rs, ye friends around, / Or bathe his clay, or waste them on the ground." In her better work, she is much more in control of the syntax and rhythm and employs them with unobjectionable diction and figures, if not always fresh or new ones. An example is found in **"Thoughts on the Works of Providence,"** in which she speaks of dawn and sunset: "Or when the morning glows with rosy charms, / Or the sun slumbers in the ocean's arms," and speaks of God "Which round the sun revolves this vast machine, / Though to his eye its mass a point appears," and of the moon, which "True to her course th' impetuous storm derides, / Triumphant o'er the winds, and surging tides." Or note the opening lines of **"An Hymn to the Evening"**: "Soon as the sun forsook the eastern main / The pealing thunder shook the heav'nly plain; / Majestic grandeur! From the zephyr's wing, / Exhales the incense of the blooming spring. / Soft purl the streams, the birds renew their notes, / And through the air their mingled music floats." These are not great lines, but they are good ones.

Of course, her favorite poetic form was the heroic couplet of English neoclassicism. All of her extant poems employ this form, with six exceptions. There are occasional interspersed three-line rhyme sequences, and **"An Answer to the Rebus"** departs from the heroic couplet in its last four lines to employ iambic tetrameter. She attempted her most complicated formal poetic pattern in **"An Hymn to Humanity,"** a poor poem; but her one use of ballad stanza was quite successful. However, she apparently found that the heroic couplet came easier, and she did not abandon it in her later poems.

Wheatley only occasionally used such devices as alliteration and onomatopoeia, and they were not significant in her poetic method. However, as with good neoclassicism, the caesura was important as she constantly attempted not just iambic pentameter couplets but the heroic couplet employed by Alexander Pope. Unfortunately, her work was subject to the uncertainties and irregularities of eighteenth-century English spelling and punctuation, and she was too dependent on elision for regulating her meter. She also rhymes in the eighteenth-century manner—for example, "join" with "divine." Nevertheless, the ear will not excuse her occasional lack of consistency in tense, especially noticeable in her poem on Goliath. If she were responsible for the order of the poems in the 1773 edition (which is somewhat chronological in relation to date of composition), we might note that the order is basically a good one. She seems to have preferred the medium-length poem of from forty to fifty lines, with the eight-line poems **"On Friendship"** and **"On Being Brought from Africa to America"** being her shortest and her two narrative poems on Goliath and on Niobe being her longest, each having 224 lines. Wheatley seldom employed her talents in narrative; but she was fairly good at it, sustaining the reader's interest with a good mixture of details, action, speech, and pacing.

For a good number of her poems we have variant versions (sometimes more than one) which show that she could improve the diction, poetic figures, syntax, rhythm, tone, rhyme, and general quality of her work through both changes and deletions, sometimes for different audiences. However, basically Wheatley was a spontaneous poet, not a laborious one. Therefore, the general regularity of her meter is striking.

Her poetic career began early in her life and was sporadic, brief, and in its later stages apparently difficult. Nevertheless, in the community where she lived, Wheatley practiced the art of poetry and was known there for that practice; and Boston in the years before and after the American Revolution was still the literary capital of America, as well qualified to produce, cultivate, encourage, and judge a poet as any community in the land. In part because she was young, in part because she was a female, and in part because she was black and nominally a slave, her work has too often been overpraised. On the other hand, she also has been too often dealt with unfairly or not at all because of this overpraising and the reasons for it. The proper position lies somewhere between these extremes, for her work definitely does have some literary merit, despite its obvious shortcomings. It becomes even more significant in any literary-historical or cultural consideration of it.

Her poems are certainly as good as or better than those of most of the poets usually included and afforded fair treatment in a discussion of American poetry before 1800, and this same evaluation holds true when she is compared with most of the minor English poets of the eighteenth century who wrote in the neoclassical tradition. Finding our early literary soil generally unfit for real poetry, Moses Coit Tyler in his *A History of American Literature, 1607-1765* and *The Literary History of the American Revolution* does, however, treat many "verse-writers," especially those of New England. In comparing his appraisals of these writers, as frank and blunt as the statements are, one still cannot help but conclude that his harsh treatment of Phillis Wheatley in the latter volume is unjust. For she certainly deserves as much praise, or as little blame (depending on whether one is measuring by a relative standard or by an absolute one, as Tyler was), as such early poets as Thomas Morton, Benjamin Tompson, Thomas Godfrey, Nathaniel Evans, Nathaniel Niles, Jonathan Odell, Joseph Stansbury, Michael Wigglesworth, Ebenezer Cook, Mather Byles, and perhaps Francis Hopkinson, John Trumbull, Timothy Dwight, Joel Barlow, and Anne Bradstreet (though Wheatley is not as sustained and consistent as these latter five, her best work certainly is worthy of inclusion with their best). There is no doubt whatever that she was the best black American author before

1800 and the best black American poet until Frances Ellen Watkins Harper in the middle of the nineteenth century.

As I have said, she was not a great poet; but in her way, in her time, and in her locale, she was a fairly good writer of poems generally in imitation of the neoclassical mode made popular by Alexander Pope. She deserves our consideration by either absolute or relative standards—and not just because of her youth, her sex, or her race. As Perry Miller and countless others have reminded us and shown us, it is indeed a mistake to think there is nothing worth reading in American literature before Washington Irving—and this applies to black authors as well, for there stands Phillis Wheatley of Boston, not one of the very best, but far from one of the worst of the many who, in spite of the struggles of establishment, felt the influence of the muses in colonial America. (pp. 13-22)

Julian D. Mason, Jr., in an introduction to *The Poems of Phillis Wheatley,* edited by Julian D. Mason, Jr., revised edition, The University of North Carolina Press, 1989, pp. 1-22.

SOURCES FOR FURTHER STUDY

Bell, Bernard W. "African-American Writers." In *American Literature: The Revolutionary Years, 1764-1789,* edited by Everett Emerson, pp. 171-93. Madison: The University of Wisconsin Press, 1977.

   Historical overview in which Bell attempts to delineate the social and political conditions that shaped Wheatley's life and works.

Odell, Margaretta Matilda. *Memoir and Poems of Phillis Wheatley: A Native African and a Slave.* Third Edition. Boston: Issac Knapp, 1838, 155 p.

   The earliest book-length study of Wheatley.

O'Neale, Sondra. "A Slave's Subtle War: Phillis Wheatley's Use of Biblical Myth and Symbol." *Early American Literature* XXI, No. 2 (Fall 1986): 144-65,

   Examines Wheatley's use of biblical parables and symbols to address her status as a slave.

Richmond, M. A. "The Critics." In his *Bid the Vassal Soar: Interpretive Essays on the Life and Poetry of Phillis Wheatley (ca. 1753-1784) and George Moses Horton (ca. 1797-1883),* pp. 53-66. Washington, D.C.: Howard University Press, 1974.

   Examines the style and vision of Wheatley's poetry and attacks the effect of slavery on the poet's artistic development.

Robinson, William H. *Phillis Wheatley in the Black American Beginnings.* Detroit: Broadside Press, 1975, 95 p.

   Assessment of Wheatley's verse in terms of race, politics, and religion. In discussing Wheatley's life and works, Robinson attempts to dispel long-standing critical arguments that her poetry falls short as literature and that she lacked self-awareness as an African-American woman.

———, ed. *Critical Essays on Phillis Wheatley.* Boston: G. K. Hall & Co., 1982, 236 p.

   Includes essays about Wheatley's life and career by such early and modern writers as Benjamin Franklin and Henry Louis Gates, Jr.

Walt Whitman

1819-1892

American poet, essayist, novelist, short story writer, journalist, and editor.

INTRODUCTION

Walt Whitman's *Leaves of Grass* is hailed as a masterpiece of American literature. Published in nine editions between 1855 and 1892, the collection pioneered a vision of humanity based on Whitman's radically egalitarian, democratic ideals and unveiled an ambitious poetic persona designed to serve as the embodiment of America. The poems of *Leaves of Grass* glorify America through evocations of its citizenry, landscape, and history as filtered through a prophetic and extremely sensual subjectivity—the "self" of the longest and most highly regarded poem, "Song of Myself." Eschewing conventional verse forms and diction, Whitman wrote in an unrestrained and idiosyncratic style that reflected the iconoclasm of his personal outlook. The influence of *Leaves of Grass* on American literature has been pronounced and lasting; as Roy Harvey Pearce has stated, "the history of American poetry could be written as the continuing discovery and rediscovery of Whitman, an on-going affirmation of his crucial relevance to the mission of the American poet."

The second of nine children, Whitman was born and educated on Long Island. At the age of eleven he left school to work as a clerk in a law office and then became a typesetter's apprentice. Later he taught school on Long Island and started his own newspaper, the *Long Islander.* He subsequently edited numerous papers for short periods, including the New York *Aurora* and the Brooklyn *Eagle.* During this time Whitman also published poems and short stories in various periodicals. Generally undistinguished, sentimental, and didactic, these early pieces are considered typical of the pious attitudes of the era. The verse, written in conventional rhyme and meter, gives no indication of the dynamic, free-flowing style Whitman later developed in *Leaves of Grass.* His first separately published work was a temperance novel titled *Franklin Evans; or, The Inebriate,* (1842). He later called it "damned rot," and claimed that it was written only as hackwork.

Whitman's sudden transformation from a conventional journalist into a radical poet remains unexplained, though commentators have suggested causes ranging from Ralph Waldo Emerson's 1842 lecture "The Poet"—in which Emerson called for an American poet to capture the spirit of the burgeoning republic— to the emotional freedom resulting from Whitman's discovery of his homosexuality. Whatever the motivation, critics note that from the publication of the first edition of *Leaves of Grass,* Whitman actively promoted himself as a representative of the common people. The first edition of *Leaves of Grass,* published when Whitman was thirty-five years old, contains twelve untitled poems and no indication of its author aside from the copyright notice, in which the holder is identified as "Walt Whitman, an American, one of the roughs, a kosmos," a phrase that is echoed in one of the poems. In a preface that has come to be regarded as one of literature's most influential expositions of artistic aims, Whitman outlined the methods and concerns of a new mode of poetry: "The art of art, the glory of expression and the sunshine of the light of letters is simplicity. Nothing is better than simplicity . . . nothing can make up for excess or for the lack of definiteness . . . [To] speak in literature with the perfect rectitude and insouciance of the movements of animals and the unimpeachableness of the sentiment of trees in the woods and grass by the roadside is the flawless triumph of art." In accordance with the preface, the poems in *Leaves of Grass* sharply break from the American verse tradition established by such poets as Henry Wadsworth Longfellow and William Cullen Bryant, employing unrhymed and unmetered lines, blending poetic and unpoetic speech, and addressing subjects that had been considered unfit for poetry, most conspicuously the body and human sexuality. Edgar Lee Masters recorded that America "was shocked to stupefaction" by the first poem of *Leaves of Grass,* to be called "Song of Myself" in later editions of the book. Although Whitman did attract a group of devoted disciples who viewed him as the prophet of American democracy, his contemporaries generally condemned *Leaves of Grass* as incoherent and vulgar; most of the favorable reviews were written by Whitman himself and published anonymously. Although Emerson congratulated Whitman on *Leaves of Grass* in a letter stating, "I greet you at the beginning of a great career," biographers note that he, too, disapproved of the sexually explicit passages in Whitman's work.

In the subsequent editions of *Leaves of Grass,* Whitman included new poems, revised and combined existing ones, added and altered titles, and shifted poems into thematic groupings. He once referred to the different editions of *Leaves of Grass* as "a succession of growths like the rings of trees." The poems Whitman incorporated into the 1856 edition include "Crossing Brooklyn Ferry," a poem described by Edwin Haviland Miller as "a hedonistic statement of faith" intended to quell desperation in the machine age. In the 1860 edition, Whitman added the sections "Enfans d'Adam"—later altered to its English equivalent, "Children of Adam"—and "Calamus." "Children of Adam" celebrates heterosexual relationships, or what Whitman called "amativeness," and includes "From Pent-up Aching Rivers," "I Sing the Body Electric," and "I Am He that Aches with Amorous Love." "Calamus" concerns itself with homosexual relationships, or "adhesiveness." In such poems as "Scented Herbage of My Breast" and "City of Orgies," Whitman articulated his dream of democracy founded on the existence of close bonds between men. "As I Ebb'd with the Ocean of Life," another important poem that was added to *Leaves of Grass* in 1860, is filled with anxiety about writing, death, and the "self," and as is characteristic of Whitman, the "self" becomes a metaphor for humanity as a whole. Often cited as one of his most moving poems, "As I Ebb'd with the Ocean of Life" has been read as a process of confronting fears and striving to transform them into hope.

During the American Civil War, Whitman tended wounded soldiers in army hospitals in Washington, D.C. while working as a copyist in the army paymaster's office. He described some of his wartime experiences in the collections *Drum-Taps* (1865) and *Sequel to Drum-Taps* (1865-66). The latter contains his eulogy for Abraham Lincoln, "When Lilacs Last in the Dooryard Bloom'd," which Whitman later incorporated into the "Memories of President Lincoln" section of *Leaves of Grass.* The poem is, as Betsy Erkkila described it in her *Whitman the Political Poet* (1989), "a kind of civil ritual" attempting to come to terms with the loss of the President on a collective level. Though another work occasioned by Lincoln's death, "O Captain! My Captain!", is Whitman's best-known poem, it is also the one he most regretted writing, as he felt it was too formally rigid and distant in emotion.

Following the war, he worked for the Department of the Interior until the secretary, James Harlan, discovered that Whitman was the author of *Leaves of Grass,* and dismissed him on grounds of immorality. He was immediately rehired as a clerk at the Justice Department and remained in this position until he suffered a paralytic stroke in 1873, two years after publishing his philosophical essay, *Democratic Vistas* (1871), and the fifth edition of *Leaves of Grass.* Although he lived nearly twenty more years and published four more editions of *Leaves of Grass,* Whitman produced little significant new work following his stroke. Primarily, he reworked and rearranged previous editions of *Leaves of Grass* and collected his early writings.

Despite the initial negative critical judgments of it, *Leaves of Grass* has come to be recognized as a remarkable accomplishment. Galway Kinnell has written about Whitman's "transformation, in the world of letters, from freak to master," theorizing that except for a few perceptive minds—Emerson and Henry David Thoreau in the nineteenth century, Carl Sandburg and Vachel Lindsay in the first half of the twentieth century—mainstream critics were generally too shocked or puzzled by *Leaves of Grass* to give it a fair and thoughtful reading. By the middle of the twentieth century, however, Whitman's poetry had gained wide acceptance, due in part to more open societal attitudes towards sex. It has been the task of critics to sort out the large quantity of myths generated by Whitman's detractors, his disciples, and the poet himself. In particular, critics have sought to explain the significance of sexual imagery in his poetry, and a major trend has been the application of psychoanalytic theory to his life and works. Textual analyses continue to reveal complexities and paradoxes in Whitman's work, and such investigations contribute to an evolving appreciation of his powers as a poet.

(For further information about Whitman's life and works, see *Concise Dictionary of American Literary Biography, 1640-1865; Dictionary of Literary Biography*, Vols. 3, 64; *Nineteenth-Century Literature Criticism*, Vols. 4, 31; *Poetry Criticism*, Vol. 3; and *Something about the Author*, Vol. 20.)

CRITICAL COMMENTARY

GEORGE SANTAYANA

(essay date 1900)

[Santayana was a Spanish-born philosopher, poet, novelist, and literary critic. In the following excerpt from his 1900 essay "The Poetry of Barbarism," he concedes that Whitman's poetry shows signs of genius but argues that the author failed in his mission to become a poet of the people.]

It was the singularity of [Whitman's] literary form—the challenge it threw to the conventions of verse and of language—that first gave Whitman notoriety: but this notoriety has become fame, because those incapacities and solecisms which glare at us from his pages are only the obverse of a profound inspiration and of a genuine courage. Even the idiosyncrasies of his style have a side which is not mere perversity or affectation; the order of his words, the procession of his images, reproduce the method of a rich, spontaneous, absolutely lazy fancy. In most poets such a natural order is modified by various governing motives—the thought, the metrical form, the echo of other poems in the memory. By Walt Whitman these conventional influences are resolutely banished. We find the swarms of men and objects rendered as they might strike the retina in a sort of waking dream. It is the most sincere possible confession of the lowest—I mean the most primitive—type of perception. All ancient poets are sophisticated in comparison and give proof of longer intellectual and moral training. Walt Whitman has gone back to the innocent style of Adam, when the animals filed before him one by one and he called each of them by its name.

In fact, the influences to which Walt Whitman was subject were as favourable as possible to the imaginary experiment of beginning the world over again. Liberalism and transcendentalism both harboured some illusions on that score; and they were in the air which our poet breathed. Moreover he breathed this air in America, where the newness of the material environment made it easier to ignore the fatal antiquity of human nature. When he afterward became aware that there was or had been a world with a history, he studied that world with curiosity and spoke of it not without a certain shrewdness. But he still regarded it as a foreign world and imagined, as not a few Americans have done, that his own world was a fresh creation, not amenable to the same laws as the old. The difference in the conditions blinded him, in his merely sensuous apprehension, to the identity of the principles.

His parents were farmers in central Long Island and his early years were spent in that district. The family seems to have been not too prosperous and somewhat nomadic; Whitman himself drifted through boyhood without much guidance. We find him now at school, now helping the labourers at the farms, now wandering along the beaches of Long Island, finally at Brooklyn working in an apparently desultory way as a printer and sometimes as a writer for a local newspaper. He must have read or heard something, at this early period, of the English classics; his style often betrays the deep effect made upon him by the grandiloquence of the Bible, of Shakespeare, and of Milton. But his chief interest, if we may trust his account, was already in his own sensations. The aspects of Nature, the forms and

Principal Works

Franklin Evans; or, The Inebriate (novel) 1842

Leaves of Grass (poetry) 1855, 1856, 1860-61, 1867, 1871, 1876, 1881-82, 1888, 1891-92

*Drum-Taps (poetry) 1865

*Sequel to Drum-Taps (poetry) 1865-66

Democratic Vistas (essay) 1871

*Passage to India (poetry) 1871

Specimen Days & Collect (essays and journals) 1882-83

*November Boughs (poetry) 1888

The Wound-Dresser; A Series of Letters Written from the Hospitals in Washington during the War of the Rebellion (letters) 1898

An American Primer (essays) 1904

The Half-Breed and Other Stories (short stories) 1927

The Correspondence of Walt Whitman. 6 vols. (letters) 1961-1977

*These works were incorporated in later editions of Leaves of Grass.

habits of animals, the sights of cities, the movement and talk of common people, were his constant delight. His mind was flooded with these images, keenly felt and afterward to be vividly rendered with bold strokes of realism and imagination.

Many poets have had this faculty to seize the elementary aspects of things, but none has had it so exclusively; with Whitman the surface is absolutely all and the underlying structure is without interest and almost without existence. He had had no education and his natural delight in imbibing sensations had not been trained to the uses of practical or theoretical intelligence. He basked in the sunshine of perception and wallowed in the stream of his own sensibility, as later at Camden in the shallows of his favourite brook. Even during the civil war, when he heard the drum-taps so clearly, he could only gaze at the picturesque and terrible aspects of the struggle, and linger among the wounded day after day with a canine devotion; he could not be aroused either to clear thought or to positive action. So also in his poems; a multiplicity of images pass before him and he yields himself to each in turn with absolute passivity. The world has no inside; it is a phantasmagoria of continuous visions, vivid, impressive, but monotonous and hard to distinguish in memory, like the waves of the sea or the decorations of some barbarous temple, sublime only by the infinite aggregation of parts.

This abundance of detail without organisation, this wealth of perception without intelligence and of imagination without taste, makes the singularity of Whitman's genius. Full of sympathy and receptivity, with a wonderful gift of graphic characterisation and an occasional rare grandeur of diction, he fills us with a sense of the individuality and the universality of what he describes—it is a drop in itself yet a drop in the ocean. The absence of any principle of selection or of a sustained style enables him to render aspects of things and of emotion which would have eluded a trained writer. He is, therefore, interesting even where he is grotesque or perverse. He has accomplished, by the sacrifice of almost every other good quality, something never so well done before. He has approached common life without bringing in his mind any higher standard by which to criticise it; he has seen it, not in contrast with an ideal, but as the expression of forces more indeterminate and elementary than itself; and the vulgar, in this cosmic setting, has appeared to him sublime.

There is clearly some analogy between a mass of images without structure and the notion of an absolute democracy. Whitman, inclined by his genius and habits to see life without relief or organisation, believed that his inclination in this respect corresponded with the spirit of his age and country, and that Nature and society, at least in the United States, were constituted after the fashion of his own mind. Being the poet of the average man, he wished all men to be specimens of that average, and being the poet of a fluid Nature, he believed that Nature was or should be a formless flux. This personal bias of Whitman's was further encouraged by the actual absence of distinction in his immediate environment. Surrounded by ugly things and common people, he felt himself happy, ecstatic, overflowing with a kind of patriarchal love. He accordingly came to think that there was a spirit of the New World which he embodied, and which was in complete opposition to that of the Old, and that a literature upon novel principles was needed to express and strengthen this American spirit.

Democracy was not to be merely a constitutional device for the better government of given nations, not merely a movement for the material improvement of the lot of the poorer classes. It was to be a social and a moral democracy and to involve an actual equality among all men. Whatever kept them apart and made it impossible for them to be messmates together was to be discarded. The literature of democracy was to ignore all extraordinary gifts of genius or virtue, all distinction drawn even from great passions or romantic adventures. In Whitman's works, in which this new literature is foreshadowed, there is accordingly not a single character nor a single story. His only hero is Myself, the "single separate person," endowed with the primary impulses, with health, and with sensitiveness to the elementary aspects of Nature. The perfect man of the future, the prolific begetter of other perfect men, is to work with his hands, chanting the poems of some future Walt, some ideally democratic bard. Women are to have as nearly as possible the same character as men: the emphasis is to pass from family life and local ties to the friendship of comrades and the general brotherhood of man. Men are to be vigorous, comfortable, sentimental, and irresponsible.

This dream is, of course, unrealised and unrealisable, in America as elsewhere. Undeniably there are in America many suggestions of such a society and such a national character. But the growing complexity and fixity of institutions necessarily tends to obscure these traits of a primitive and crude democracy. What Whitman seized upon as the promise of the future was in reality the survival of the past. He sings the song of pioneers, but it is in the nature of the pioneer that the greater his success the quicker must be his transformation into something different. When Whitman made the initial and amorphous phase of society his ideal, he became the prophet of a lost cause. That cause was lost, not merely when wealth and intelligence began to take shape in the American Commonwealth, but it was lost at the very foundation of the world, when those laws of evolution were established which Whitman, like Rousseau, failed to understand. If we may trust Mr. Herbert Spencer, these laws involve a passage from the homogeneous to the heterogeneous, and a constant progress at once in differentiation and in organisation—all, in a word, that Whitman systematically deprecated or ignored. He is surely not the spokesman of the tendencies of his country, although he describes some aspects of its past and present condition: nor does he appeal to those whom he describes, but rather to the *dilettanti* he despises. He is regarded as representative chiefly by foreigners, who look for some grotesque expression of the genius of so young and prodigious a people.

Whitman, it is true, loved and comprehended men; but this love and comprehension had the same limits as his love and comprehension of Nature. He observed truly and responded to his observation with genuine and pervasive emotion. A great gregariousness, an innocent tolerance of moral weakness, a genuine admiration for bodily health and strength, made him bubble over with affection for the generic human creature. Incapable of an ideal passion, he was full of the milk of human kindness. Yet, for all his acquaintance with the ways and thoughts of the common man of his choice, he did not truly understand him. For to understand people is to go much deeper than they go themselves; to penetrate to their characters and disentangle their inmost ideals. Whitman's insight into man did not go beyond a sensuous sympathy; it consisted in a vicarious satisfaction in their pleasures, and an instinctive love of their persons. It never approached a scientific or imaginative knowledge of their hearts.

Therefore Whitman failed radically in his dearest ambition: he can never be a poet of the people. For the people, like the early races whose poetry was ideal, are natural believers in perfection. They have no doubts about the absolute desirability of wealth and learning and power, none about the worth of pure goodness and pure love. Their chosen poets, if they have any, will be always those who have known how to paint these ideals in lively even if in gaudy colours. Nothing is farther from the common people than the corrupt desire to be primitive. They instinctively look toward a more exalted life, which they imagine to be full of distinction and pleasure, and the idea of that brighter existence fills them with hope or with envy or with humble admiration.

If the people are ever won over to hostility to such ideals, it is only because they are cheated by demagogues who tell them that if all the flowers of civilisation were destroyed its fruits would become more abundant. A greater share of happiness, people think, would fall to their lot could they destroy everything beyond their own possible possessions. But they are made thus envious and ignoble only by a deception: what they really desire is an ideal good for themselves which they are told they may secure by depriving others of their preëminence. Their hope is always to enjoy perfect satisfaction themselves; and therefore a poet who loves the picturesque aspects of labour and vagrancy will hardly be the poet of the poor. He may have described their figure and occupation, in neither of which they are much interested; he will not have read their souls. They will prefer to him any sentimental story-teller, any sensational dramatist, any moralising poet; for they are hero-worshippers by temperament, and are too wise or too unfortunate to be much enamoured of themselves or of the conditions of their existence.

Fortunately, the political theory that makes Whitman's principle of literary prophecy and criticism does not always inspire his chants, nor is it presented, even in his prose works, quite bare and unadorned. In *Democratic Vistas* we find it clothed with something of the same poetic passion and lighted up with the same flashes of intuition which we admire in the poems. Even there the temperament is finer than the ideas and the poet wiser than the thinker. His ultimate appeal is really to something more primitive and general than any social aspirations, to something more elementary than an ideal of any kind. He speaks to those minds and to those moods in which sensuality is touched with mysticism. When the intellect is in abeyance, when we would "turn and live with the animals, they are so placid and self-contained," when we are weary of conscience and of ambition, and would yield ourselves for a while to the dream of sense, Walt Whitman is a welcome companion. The images he arouses in us, fresh, full of light and health and of a kind of frankness and beauty, are prized all the more at such a time because they are not choice, but drawn perhaps from a hideous and sordid environment. For this circumstance makes them a better means of escape from convention and from that fatigue and despair which lurk not far beneath the surface of conventional life. In casting off with self-assurance and a sense of fresh vitality the distinctions of tradition and reason a man may feel, as he sinks back comfortably to a lower level of sense and instinct, that he is returning to Nature or escaping into the infinite. Mysticism makes us proud and happy to renounce the work of intelligence, both in thought and in life, and persuades us that we become divine by remaining imperfectly human. Walt Whitman gives a new expression to this ancient and multiform tendency. He feels his own cosmic justification and he would lend the sanction of his inspiration to all loafers and holiday-makers. He would be the congenial patron of farmers and factory hands in their crude pleasures and pieties, as Pan was the patron of the shepherds of Arcadia: for he is sure that in spite of his hairiness and animality, the gods will acknowledge him as one of themselves and smile upon him from the serenity of Olympus. (pp. 155-61)

George Santayana, "The Poetry of Barbarism," in his *Essays in Literary Criticism*, edited by Irving Singer, Charles Scribner's Sons, 1956, pp. 149-178.

MALCOLM COWLEY
(essay date 1946)

[Cowley was a prominent American literary critic. In the following essay, he speculates on Whitman's abrupt transformation from a minor journalist into a major poet with the publication of *Leaves of Grass*.]

There was a miracle in Whitman's life; we can find no other word for it. In his thirty-seventh year, the local politician and printer and failed editor suddenly became a world poet. No long apprenticeship; no process of growth that we can trace from year to year in his published work; not even much early promise: the poet materializes like a shape from the depths. In 1848, when we almost lose sight of him, Whitman is an editorial writer on salary, repeating day after day the opinions held in common by the younger Jacksonian Democrats, praising the people and attacking the corporations (but always within reasonable limits); stroking the American eagle's feathers and pulling the lion's tail. Hardly a word he publishes gives the impression that only Whitman could have written it. In 1855 he reveals a new character that seems to be his own creation. He

writes and prefaces and helps to print and distributes and, for good measure, anonymously reviews a first book of poems, not only different from any others known at the time, but also unlike everything the poet himself had written in former years (and only faintly foreshadowed by three of his experiments in free verse that the New York *Tribune* had printed in 1850 because it liked their political sentiments). It is a short book, this first edition of *Leaves of Grass;* it contains only twelve poems, including the **"Song of Myself "**; but they summarize or suggest all his later achievements; and for other poets they are better than those achievements, because in this first book Whitman was a great explorer, whereas later he was at best a methodical exploiter and at worst a mere expounder by rote of his own discoveries.

At some point during the seven "lost years," Whitman had begun to utilize resources deep in himself that might have remained buried. He had mastered what Emerson called the "secret which every intellectual man quickly learns"—but how few make use of it!—"that beyond the energy of his possessed and conscious intellect he is capable of a new energy (as of an intellect doubled on itself), by abandonment to the nature of things; that beside his privacy of power as an individual man, there is a great public power on which he can draw, by unlocking, at all risks, his human doors, and suffering the ethereal tides to roll and circulate through him; then he is caught up into the life of the Universe, his speech is thunder, his thought is law, and his words are universally intelligible as the plants and animals." Whitman himself found other words to describe what seems to have been essentially the same phenomenon. Long afterwards he told one of his disciples, Dr. Maurice Bucke: "*Leaves of Grass* was there, though unformed, all the time, in whatever answers as the laboratory of the mind. . . . The *Democratic Review* essays and tales," published before 1848, "came from the surface of the mind and had no connection with what lay below—a great deal of which, indeed, was below consciousness. At last the time came when the concealed growth had to come to light, and the first edition of *Leaves of Grass* was published."

Whitman in these remarks was simplifying a phenomenon by which, quite evidently, he continued to be puzzled until the end. The best efforts of his biographers will never fully explain it; and a critic can only point to certain events, or probable events, that must have contributed to his sudden discovery of his own talent. The trip to New Orleans in 1848 was certainly one of them. It lasted for only four months (and not for years, as Whitman later implied), but it was his first real glimpse of the American continent, and it gave him a stock of remembered sights and sounds and emotions over which his imagination would play for the rest of his life.

Whitman on *Leaves of Grass:*

My Book and I—what a period we have presumed to span! those thirty years from 1850 to '80—and America in them! Proud, proud indeed may we be, if we have cull'd enough of that period in its own spirit to worthily waft a few live breaths of it to the future!

Let me not dare, here or anywhere, for my own purposes, or any purposes, to attempt the definition of Poetry, nor answer the question what it is. Like Religion, Love, Nature, while those terms are indispensable, and we all give a sufficiently accurate meaning to them, in my opinion no definition that has ever been made sufficiently encloses the name Poetry; nor can any rule or convention ever so absolutely obtain but some great exception may arise and disregard and overturn it.

Whitman, in his "Backward Glance O'er Travel'd Roads" in the 1888 edition of *Leaves of Grass.*

A second event was connected with his interest in the pseudo-science of phrenology. The originators of this doctrine believed that the human character is determined by the development of separate facilities (of which there were twenty-six according to Gall, thirty-five according to Spurzheim, and forty-three according to the Fowler brothers in New York); that each of these faculties is localized in a definite portion of the brain; and that its strength or weakness can be ascertained from the contours of the skull. Whitman had the bumps on his head charted by L. N. Fowler in July, 1849, a year after his return from the South. In these phrenological readings of character, each of the faculties was rated on a numerical scale running from one to seven or eight. Five was good; six was the most desirable figure; seven and eight indicated that the quality was dangerously overdeveloped. Among the ratings that Whitman received for his mental faculties (and note their curious names, which reappeared in his poems), were Amativeness 6, Philoprogenitiveness 6, Adhesiveness 6, Inhabitiveness 6, Alimentiveness 6, Cautiousness 6, Self-esteem 6 to 7, Firmness 6 to 7, Benevolence 6 to 7, Sublimity 6 to 7, Ideality 5 to 6, Individuality 6 and Intuitiveness 6. It was, on the whole, a highly flattering report, and Whitman needed flattery in those days; for he hadn't made a success of his new daily, the Brooklyn *Freeman,* and no other position had been offered to its editor. Apparently the phrenological reading gave him some of the courage he needed to follow an untried course. Seven years later he had Fowler's chart of his skull reproduced in the second or 1856 edition of *Leaves of Grass.*

Another event that inspired him was his reading of Emerson's essays. Later Whitman tried to hide this indebtedness, asserting several times that he had seen nothing of Emerson's until after his own first edition had been published. But aside from the Emersonian ideas in the twelve early poems (especially the **"Song of Myself "**), there is, as evidence in the case, Whitman's prose introduction to the first edition, which is written in Emerson's style, with his characteristic rhythms, figures of speech and turns of phrase. As for the ideas Whitman expressed in that style, they are chiefly developments of what Emerson had said in "The Poet" (first of the *Essays: Second Series,* published in 1844), combined with other notions from Emerson's "Compensation." In "The Poet," Emerson had said:

> I look in vain for the poet whom I describe. . . . We have yet had no genius in America, with tyrannous eye, which knew the value of our incomparable materials, and saw, in the barbarism and materialism of the times, another carnival of the same gods whose picture he so much admires in Homer; then in the Middle Ages; then in Calvinism. . . . Our log-rolling, our stumps and their politics, our fisheries, our Negroes and Indians, our boasts and our repudiations, the wrath of rogues and the pusillanimity of honest men, the northern trade, the southern planting, the western clearing, Oregon and Texas, are yet unsung. Yet America is a poem in our eyes; its ample geography dazzles the imagination, and it will not wait long for meters.

> . . . Doubt not, O poet, but persist. Say "It is in me, and shall out." Stand there, balked and dumb, stuttering and stammering, hissed and hooted, stand and strive, until at last rage draws out of thee that *dream-power* which every night shows thee is thine own; a power transcending all limit and privacy, and by virtue of which a man is the conductor of the whole river of electricity.

Whitman, it is clear today, determined to be the poet whom Emerson pictured; he determined to be the genius in America who recognized the value of our incomparable materials, the Northern trade, the Southern planting and the Western clearing. "The United States themselves are the greatest poem," he wrote, he echoed in his 1855 introduction, conceived as if in answer to Emerson's summons. At first balked and dumb, then later hissed and hooted, he stood there until he had drawn from himself the power he felt in his dream.

There was, however, still another event that seems to have given Whitman a new conception of his mission as a poet: it was his reading of two novels by George Sand, *The Countess of Rudolstadt* and *The Journeyman Joiner.* Both books were written during their author's socialistic period, before the revolution of 1848, and both were translated into English by one of the New England Transcendentalists. *The Countess of Rudolstadt* was the sequel to *Consuelo,* which Whitman described as "the noblest work left by George Sand—the noblest in many respects, on its own field, in all literature." Apparently he gave *Consuelo* and its sequel to his mother when they first appeared in this country, in 1847; and after her death he kept the tattered volumes on his bedside table. It was in the epilogue to *The Countess of Rudolstadt* that Whitman discovered the figure of a wandering musician who might have been taken for a Bohemian peasant except for his fine white hands; who was not only a violinist but also a bard and a prophet, expounding the new religion of Humanity; and who, falling into a trance, recited "the most magnificent poem that can be conceived," before traveling onward along the open road. . . . *The Journeyman Joiner* was also listed by Whitman among his favorite books. It is the story—to quote from Esther Shephard, who discovered his debt to both novels—"of a beautiful, Christlike young carpenter, a proletary philosopher, who dresses in a mechanic's costume but is scrupulously clean and neat. He works at carpentering with his father, but patiently takes time off whenever he wants to in order to read, or give advice on art, or share a friend's affection."

Both books helped to fix the direction of Whitman's thinking; for they summarized the revolutionary ideas that prevailed in Europe before 1848. But the principal effect of these novels was on Whitman's picture of himself. After reading them, he slowly formed the project of becoming a wandering bard and prophet, like the musician in the epilogue to *The Countess of Rudolstadt*. He stopped writing for the magazines and, according to his brother George, he refused some editorial positions that were offered him; instead he worked as a carpenter with his father, like the hero of *The Journeyman Joiner* (and also like Jesus in his youth; for Whitman was planning to found a religion). About this time there is an apparent change in his personality. Whitman as a young editor had dressed correctly, even fashionably, had trimmed his beard, had carried a light cane, had been rather retiring in his manners, had been on good but not at all intimate terms with his neighbors and had shown his dislike for their children. Now suddenly he begins dressing like a Brooklyn mechanic, with his shirt open to reveal a red-flannel undershirt and part of a hairy chest, and with a big felt hat worn loosely over his tousled hair. He lets his beard grow shaggy, he makes his voice more assured and, as he wanders about the docks and ferries, he greets his friends with bear hugs and sometimes a kiss of comradeship. It is as if he has undertaken a double task: before creating his poems, he has to create the hypothetical author of the poems. And this author bears a new name: *Walter* Whitman, as he was always known to his family and till then had been called by his friends, now suddenly becomes:

Walt Whitman, a kosmos, of Manhattan the son,
Turbulent, fleshy, sensual, eating, drinking and
     breeding.

The world is his stage, and Whitman has assumed a role which he will continue to play for the rest of his life. Sometimes, in his letters, we can see him as in a dressing-room, arranging his features to make the role convincing. In 1868, for example, he sent his London publisher a long series of directions about how his portrait should be engraved from a photograph that he rather liked. "If a faithful presentation of that photograph can be given," he said, "it will satisfy me well—of course it should be reproduced with all its shaggy, dappled, rough-skinned character, and not attempted to be smoothed and prettified . . . let the costume be kept very simple and broad, and rather kept down too, little as there is of it—preserve the effect of the sweeping lines making all that fine free angle below the chin . . . It is perhaps worth your taking special pains about, both to achieve a successful picture and likeness, something characteristic, and as certain to be a marked help to your edition of the book." There is more in the same vein, and it makes us feel that Whitman was like an actor-manager, first having his portrait painted in costume, then hanging it in the lobby to sell more tickets.

He had more than the dash of charlatanism that, according to Baudelaire, adds a spice to genius. But he had also his own sort of honesty, and he tried to live his part as well as acting it. The new character he assumed was more, far more, than a pose adopted to mislead the public. Partly it was a side of his nature that had always existed, but had been suppressed by social conventions, by life with a big family of brothers and sisters and by the struggle to earn a living. Partly it represented a real change after 1850: the self-centered young man was turning outwards, was trying to people his loneliness with living comrades. Partly it was an attempt to compensate for the absence in himself of qualities he admired in others; for we know that Whitman at heart was anything but rough, virile, athletic, savage or luxuriant, to quote a few of his favorite adjectives. Partly his new personality was an ideal picture of himself that he tried to achieve in the flesh and came in time to approximate. You might call it a mask or, as Jung would say, a *persona* that soon had a life of its own, developing and changing with the years and almost superseding his other nature. At the end, one could hardly say that there was a "real" Whitman underneath the public figure; the man had become confused with his myth.

We might find it easier to picture the complexities of his character if we imagined that there were at least three Whitmans existing as separate persons. There was Whitman I, the printer and politician and editor, always described by his acquaintances as indolent, shy (except when making public speeches), awkward and rather conventional in his manners. He disappeared from public sight after 1850, yet he survived for thirty years or more in his intimate relations with his family. Then there was Whitman II, the *persona*, who characterized himself as "One of the roughs, large, proud, affectionate, eating, drinking and breeding, his costume manly and free, his face sunburnt and bearded, his posture strong and erect, his voice bringing hope and prophecy to the generous races of young and old." This second Whitman, ripening with age (and becoming a great deal more discreet after he moved to Washington and went to work for the government), at last emerged into the figure of the Good Gray Poet. He wrote poems too, as part of his role, but they were windy and uninspired. The real poet was still another person; let us call him Whitman III. He never appeared in public life; he was hardly more than a voice from the depths of the subconscious; but the voice was fresh, moving, candid; and it spoke in different words and in different tones not only from Whitman the editor but also from Whitman the self-styled bard of democracy. Whitman III was sometimes boastful but also tender and secret where Whitman II was bluff and lusty; he was feminine, maternal, rather than physically adventurous; at the same time he was a revolutionist by instinct where Whitman I was liberal and Whitman II merely sententious. He appeared from nowhere in 1855; he had little to say after 1860 and fell silent forever in 1873; yet during his short career he wrote (or dictated to other Whitmans) all the poems that gave *Leaves of Grass* its position in the literature of the world.

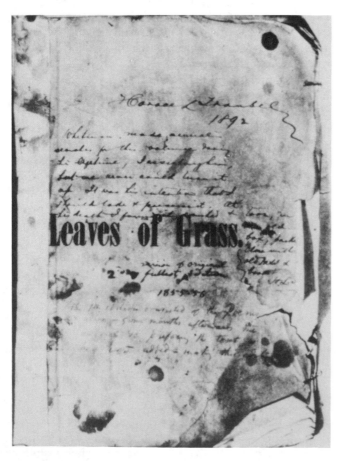

Whitman's annotated copy of *Leaves of Grass*.

But what explains the mystery of the poet's birth? There was an apparently very ordinary fellow named Walter Whitman, who wrote editorials and book reviews and moral doggerel; then there was an extraordinary showman named Walt Whitman who peddled his personality as if it were a patent medicine; but there was also for six years, and at intervals thereafter, a poet of genius known by the same name. How did he come to exist? Was it merely because Whitman the editor visited New Orleans, had a phrenological reading, was inspired by Emerson's doctrine of the representative individual, and tried to make himself over into a character by George Sand? Is there some other cause for what we must still regard as the Whitman miracle?

The only evidence that bears on this question consists of Whitman's early notebooks and the poems themselves, which are not often a trustworthy guide. Still, they return so often to one theme that its importance in his life seems fixed beyond dispute. Whitman had apparently been slow to develop emotionally as well as intellectually. The poems suggest that, at some moment during the seven shadowy years, he had his first fully satisfying sexual experience. It may have been as early as his trip to New Orleans in 1848, to judge by what he says in a frequently quoted poem, **"Once I Passed through a Populous City,"** which, incidentally, has more biographical value in the early draft discovered by Emory Holloway than it has in the altered and expurgated version that Whitman published. Or this Louisiana episode, if real, may have been merely an introduction to his new life, and the decisive experience may have come later, during his carpenter years in Brooklyn. Whenever it occurred, the experience was so intense that it became an almost religious ecstasy, a moment of vision that wholly transformed his world. Whitman describes such a moment in the fifth section of the **"Song of Myself":**

> Swiftly arose and spread around me the peace
>   and knowledge that pass all the argument of
>   the earth,
> And I know that the hand of God is the promise
>   of my own,
> And I know that the spirit of God is the brother
>   of my own,
> And that all the men ever born are also my
>   brothers, and the women my sisters and lovers,
> And that a kelson of the creation is love,
> And limitless are leaves stiff or drooping in the
>   fields,
> And brown ants in the little wells beneath them,
> And mossy scabs of the worm fence, heap'd
>   stones, elder, mullein and poke-weed.

After this experience, Whitman had to revise not only his philosophical picture of the world but also his personal and private picture of himself. "I am not what you supposed," he would say in one of his 1860 poems, "but far different." The discovery of his own sexual direction must have been a shock to him at first; but soon he determined to accept himself with all his vices and "smutch'd deeds," just as he accepted everything in an imperfect universe. He wrote: "I am myself just as much evil as good, and my nation is—and I say there is in fact no evil." All his nature being good, in the larger view, he felt that all of it should be voiced in the poems that he now determined to write.

At first his revelations concerning one aspect of his nature were made obliquely, in language that could be easily understood only by others of his own type. By 1860, however, when he was preparing the third edition of his poems, the impulse to reveal himself had become so strong that he was no longer willing to speak by indirection. "Come," he said, "I am determin'd to unbare this broad breast of mine, I have long enough stifled and choked." And in the first of his "Calamus" poems, written for that edition, he proclaimed his resolve "to sing no songs today but those of manly attachment":

> I proceed for all who are or have been young
>   men,
> To tell the secret of my nights and days,
> To celebrate the need of comrades.

There has been a long argument about the meaning of the "Calamus" poems, but it is or should be clear enough from the title under which they were published. Whitman is sometimes vague and a little hard to follow in his metaphysical symbols, but his sexual symbols are as simply conceived as an African statue of Potency or Fertility. The calamus root is one of these symbols, even though Whitman disguised the fact when writing to William Michael Rossetti, his English editor, who had asked him for an explanation. " 'Calamus' is a common word here," Whitman replied: "it is the very large and aromatic grass, or root, spears three feet high—often called 'sweet flag'—grows all over the Northern and Middle States—(see Webster's Large Dictionary—Calamus—definition 2).—The recherché or ethereal sense, as used in my book, probably arises from it, Calamus presenting the biggest and hardiest spears of grass, and from its fresh, a romantic, pungent bouquet." But if Rossetti had referred to Section 24 of the **"Song of Myself,"** he would have discovered what the poet really meant. In that section, Whitman exults in his own body and describes the various parts of it in metaphors drawn from the animal and vegetable world. The calamus plays its proper part in the description:

> Root of wash'd sweet-flag! timorous pond snipe!
>   nest of guarded duplicate eggs! it shall be you!

The sweet-flag or calamus root, the "growth by the margin of pond-waters," was simply Whitman's token or symbol for the male sexual organ. "This," he said in a poem, "O this shall henceforth be the token

of comrades, this calamus-root shall." The poems under this general title were poems of homosexual love, in its physical aspects and with its metaphysical lessons. They were "blades" or "spears" or "leaves" of the calamus, to use another of Whitman's favorite symbols; and, as he said in his letter to Rossetti, they were the biggest and hardiest of the grasses; in fact they were bigger and hardier than all the other leaves of grass. (pp. 385-88)

Malcolm Cowley, "Walt Whitman: The Miracle," in *The New Republic,* Vol. 114, No. 11, March 18, 1946, pp. 385-88.

GALWAY KINNELL
(essay date 1973)

[Kinnell is one of America's most renowned poets and the winner of both a Pulitzer Prize and an American Book Award for his *Selected Poems* (1982). In the following excerpt, he praises Whitman as a poet who strove to express basic truths about the self, the body, and the soul.]

Whitman knew that in its own time *Leaves of Grass* was a failure. But he belonged to that little era which had the dream of progress, and he could believe that one day the book would come into its glory. He tells poets to come:

> I myself write but one or two indicative words
>   for the future,
> I but advance a moment only to wheel and hurry
>   back in the darkness.
> I am a man who, sauntering along without fully
>   stopping, turns a casual look upon you and
>   then averts his face,
> Leaving it to you to prove and define it,
> Expecting the main things from you.

It has turned out as he hoped, but his transformation, in the world of letters, from freak to master, took a very long time. It took so long because, excepting Thoreau and Emerson, most American literati of the 19th century suffered from intense anglophilia and thought of Whitman as a queer cultist or a blethering yokel. In the 20th century this anglophilia has persisted among the New Critics and their poets. Furthermore, these critics, being true 20th century Americans—that is, of a technological cast of mind—took a very theoretical approach to poetry, and from their cerebral heights, they could only patronize this poet who lived on instinct.

A few American poets did feel attracted to Whitman—Vachel Lindsay and Carl Sandburg, and perhaps in a preverse, or reverse way, Robinson Jeffers too. But

---

Betsy Erkkila on "O Captain! My Captain!":

As it turned out, the American reading public liked Whitman best when he was being most traditional. "If Walt Whitman had written a volume of My Captains," wrote a contemporary reviewer, "instead of filling a scrapbasket with waste and calling it a book the world would be better off today and Walt Whitman would have some excuse for living." Recited by schoolchildren across the land, **"O Captain! My Captain!"** is both Whitman's most conventional poem and the only one to reach the masses of people he envisioned as the audience for his poems. The irony was not lost on Whitman: "I'm honest when I say, damn My Captain and all the My Captains in my book! . . . I'm almost sorry I ever wrote that poem . . . I say that if I'd written a whole volume of My Captains I'd deserve to be spanked and sent to bed with the world's compliments—which would be generous treatment, considering what a lame duck book such a book would have been!"

Betsy Erkkila, in her 1989 study
Whitman the Political Poet.

---

not until Hart Crane do we find an American poet who was drawn to Whitman's essential enterprise. In Crane's case, however, the temperamental differences were extreme, and also Crane was always being lectured on Whitman's faults by his literary friends, particularly Allen Tate. In the end Whitman's influence is barely visible in Crane's work; as far as I can see, except possibly in "The River" section of *The Bridge,* Crane was not even very deeply affected by that most affecting element, Whitman's musical line.

Great foreign poets, especially Lawrence and Neruda, absorbed Whitman's influence long before our own poets did, but for Pound, Eliot, Frost, and Williams, Whitman meant very little. Whitman's return to American poetry, if we can set a date, did not come until one hundred and one years after the appearance of *Leaves of Grass,* with the publication of Ginsberg's *Howl* in 1956. Other American poets were turning to Whitman about the same time, and some few, such as Tom McGrath and Robert Duncan, had begun as much as a decade earlier to retrieve Whitman's music. Only now is Whitman fully accepted as our greatest native master, the bearer of the American tradition.

In these notes I want to try to describe some of the attraction Walt Whitman holds for me—and I trust for others—to make out if I can one or two of his indicative words, to catch something of the casual gaze he turns towards us.

What first strikes me when I read Whitman is the music, what I can only call the mystic music, of his voice. There are debts to Shakespeare and the King James Bible, but Whitman was an original: no one be-

fore him had thrust his presence and actual voice so boldly onto the written page. The voice is unmistakably personal, and it is universal. It is outgoing and attaches itself to the things and creatures of the word; yet it speaks at the same time of a life far within. In this it resembles prayer. Its music is that which speech naturally seeks when given entirely to expressing inner burdens of feeling.

This music seems to flow from a source deeper even than its words. If you croon to a baby in iambs, the baby will laugh, for helpless creatures find control of nature amusing. A woman who has nursed many babies, however, croons to the infant in Whitmanesque lines, and the infant croons back also in Whitmanesque lines. They communicate perfectly, yet use no words, only that deep rhythm the words themselves will also have when their time comes. The rhythms of Whitman's line are not ornamental at all but an essential expressive element.

It is true that the nursery rhyme, which often uses countable meter, appeals to little children too, and not just because of its power to control nature. The iambic beat seems embedded in our language, and Whitman does not ignore it. His free verse speaks in iambs almost as much as do the more intense passages in Shakespeare's blank verse. Yet his iambic flow is never regular, never counted out, and connects seamlessly to surrounding passages that don't use iambs at all. D. H. Lawrence compares this music, which so profoundly affected him, to the flight of birds, now flapping, now flapping, now soaring, now gliding, as opposed to that of counted measures, which is like the plod of earthbound creatures.

Whimsical as it must strike a sensible person, I believe that long before Whitman came on the scene, ever since Milton in fact, poets writing in English unconsciously hungered for such a music as Whitman was to discover. It may have been heroic for the post-Miltonic poets, all of them brought up on the King James Bible and on Shakespeare, nevertheless to swear fealty to counted meter, in the faith that this was loyalty to poetry itself, but it is possible for me to imagine that more was lost than gained. In *Howl,* Ginsberg is an innovator; historically speaking, his revival of Whitman's line was long overdue, historically speaking, Whitman's discovery of his own line was overdue.

His music exerts a power on words. It draws from them both pre-historic and infantile resonances, these deepest sub-meanings, whereas most other 19th century poetry relies on overtones that are superficial and usually nostalgic. In Whitman's poetry, the words are spoken for the first time, while in Longfellow's or Tennyson's the great words appear to have already spent all their force: spent it already putting into the reader, in other poems, the emotions they try to elicit from him in these. Whitman knew that for the voice which loves it every word is virginal. There are "archaic" things, which may drag words along with them into the past, and there are archaic phrases, but very likely there is no such thing as an archaic word. (p. 9)

Whitman says that in *Leaves of Grass* his aim was to set forth "uncompromisingly, my own physical, emotional, moral, intellectual, and aesthetic personality . . . in a far more candid and comprehensible sense than any hitherto poem or book." He doesn't quite do that. It is impossible not to feel in this man who always proclaims his health, this good gray poet who writes constantly about himself yet about whom we know very little, something unavowed, a trouble, perhaps even a sickness, at least an intense loneliness and a more than ordinary fear of sex and dread of death

He protests too much, to begin with; no healthy person could generate that much energy merely to announce that he is healthy. Sometimes he almost suggests the nature of his troubles, the source of those wounds, still unhealed, which were inflicted on an exceptionally indulged child when it confronted the "reality principle," in this case an exceptionally puritan society.

He says, for instance:

I keep as delicate around the bowels as around
 the head and heart.
Copulation is no more rank to me than death is.

The explicit content is unexceptional. Yet something in the phrasing isn't quite right. The first line makes one think of people who, appalled by their own excrement, perform enemas on themselves daily. With the comparison in the second line, I can imagine Whitman trying it the other way around, "Death is no more rank to me than copulation is," before, still vaguely bothered, settling on the line as it is, even though its use, even in the negative, of "rank" to link fucking and death is still disquieting.

Whitman did not like us to see his troubled side. He wanted us to see him as he wished to be. His confessions of having experienced base emotions are concessions, claims to common humanity, which have a patronizing tone. His poems, therefore, rarely contain struggles of any kind. They begin in the same clarity in which they end. This is often their weakness; it is what spoils, for instance, **"When Lilacs Last in the Dooryard Bloomed,"** in which the grief is too thoroughly consoled before the first line is uttered. One of the exceptions is the curious **"This Compost,"** which begins with Whitman's telling us how frightened he is of the earth, since in it have been buried so many diseased carcasses.

Something startles me where I thought I was safest,
I withdraw from the still woods I loved,

I will not go now on the pastures to walk,
I will not strip the clothes from my body to meet my
 lover the sea,
I will not touch my flesh to the earth as to other flesh
 to renew me.

O how can it be that the ground itself does not sicken?
How can you be alive you growths of spring?
How can you furnish health you blood of herbs,
 roots, orchards, grain?
Are they not continually putting distemper'd
 corpses within you?
Is not every continent work'd over and over with the
 sour dead?

Where have you disposed of their carcasses?
Those drunkards and gluttons of so many genera-
 tions?
Where have you drawn off all the foul liquid and
 meat?
I do not see any of it upon you to-day, or perhaps
 I am deceiv'd.
I will run a furrow with my plough, I will press my
 spade through the sod and turn it up underneath,
I am sure I shall expose some of the foul meat.

At the end of the poem, of course, he comes around and blesses the earth, as healthy after all, but along the way he exhibits an ultra-fastidiousness which would strike me as hysterical if I were able to take it quite seriously.

Nevertheless, when Whitman does affirm his own health I believe him, even as I disbelieve him. The truth of prose is usually imponderable, for in prose to be persuaded one has to follow all the steps of its argument. Poetry verifies itself, telling us by the authenticity of its voice how true it is, in this respect resembling actual speech. I don't fully believe Thoreau, for example, when he says with just a touch of elegant cleverness, "we need pray for no higher heaven than the pure senses can furnish, a purely sensuous life . . . ," a skepticism which may have grounds, for Thoreau elsewhere remarks, this time in response to *Leaves of Grass:*

There are 2 or 3 pieces in the book which are disagreeable to say the least, simply sensual. He does not celebrate love at all. It is as if the beasts spoke. I think that men have not been ashamed of themselves without reason.

I am able to believe in Whitman's declarations of health because, being spoken in poetry, I hear the tone in which he speaks them, I listen carefully, I note the authentic music, the energy of the language, the hum, I could say of his valvèd voice. What he says is raised to the level of truth by the aliveness of his words. Is it absurd to say that even the passages that betray his sickness are convincing statements of health?

Leaves of Grass set out not only to rescue the

things and creatures of the world; it also tried, more seriously from Whitman's viewpoint, to redeem in the flesh this nineteenth century American puritan: to transform him from one who felt ill toward himself into one who exuberantly loved himself, to make him into "one of the roughs, a kosmos, disorderly, fleshy and sensual"—which, of course, in some way he must have been all along. The energy which made me feel his declarations of health to be false overflow; the surplus energy that remains in the poems gives them life; it is this surplus, this life, that convinces. I see the sickness; in the same moment I see the sickness healed. On Whitman's face, as it turns briefly towards us, there is both radiance and amazement: it is a face almost confident of its light and yet surprised by it, still trying to get used to this radiance that is all the more startling for coming from within, from an extremely unstable source. (pp. 10-11)

I know of only one account of Whitman written by someone who knew him both before and after the publication of *Leaves of Grass*. It describes a person rather different from the rapt and garrulous hero of the poems.

Walt Whitman had a small printing office and book store on Myrtle avenue, Brooklyn, where after his return from the South he started the *Freeman* newspaper, first as a weekly, then as a daily, and continued it a year or so. He always earned his own living. I thought him a very natural person. He wore plain, cheap clothes, which were always particularly clean. Everybody knew him; everyone, almost, liked him. We all of us [referring to the other members of his family—brothers, sisters, father and mother] long before he published *Leaves of Grass,* looked upon him as a man who was to make his mark in the world. He was always a good listener, the best I ever knew—of late years, I think, he talks somewhat more. In those early years (1849-54) he talked very little indeed. When he did talk his conversation was remarkably pointed, attractive, and clear. When *Leaves of Grass* first appeared I thought it a great book, but that the man was greater than the book. His singular coolness was an especial feature. I have never seen him excited in the least degree; never heard him swear but once. He was quite gray at thirty. He had a look of age in his youth, as he now has a look of youth in his age.

It is not surprising that Whitman was a listener. Ezra Pound's silence during his last years was perhaps his own tribute, paid too late (but paid), to that one law he had overlooked—that the mother of poetry is silence. Whitman gathered the world into his own silence. His poetry is his receptive consciousness turned inside out: the listener becomes the speaker, magnetism changes to radiance, the words glow with infra-reality.

I am fascinated by that observation about Whitman's changed appearance. "We poets in our youth begin in gladness, Whereof in the end come despondency and madness." The curse is often quoted. But to achieve his exemplary self-portrait—a self-portrait which would also portray everyone—Whitman had to lift the curse. He had to set against his despondency all his gratefulness, he had to clarify his madness, find in it possibilities of joyful health—and do this, moreover, as a work of supererogation: the surplus would be the poems. *He was quite gray at thirty. He had a look of age in his youth, as he now has a look of youth in his age.* If Whitman's poetry in some sense consists of wishes, it is useful for our faith in his enterprise to know that they came true in his own flesh.

Speaking in New York in the Spring of 1972, Pablo Neruda acknowledged Whitman to be his greatest master.

He said:

For my part, I, who am now nearing 70, discovered Walt Whitman when I was just 15, and I hold him to be my greatest creditor. I stand before you feeling that I bear with me always this great and wonderful debt which has helped me to exist.

I must start by acknowledging myself to be the humble servant of a poet who strode the earth with long, slow paces, pausing everywhere to love, to examine, to learn, to teach and to admire. The fact of the matter is that this great man, this lyric moralist, chose a hard path for himself: he was both a torrential and a didactic singer—qualities which appear opposed, seeming also more appropriate to a leader than a writer. But what really counts is that Walt Whitman was not afraid to teach—which means to learn at the hands of life and undertake the responsibility of passing on the lesson!

Whitman not only saved himself, not only resurrected himself in his body, but, being, as Neruda says, also a teacher, he bravely undertook that most difficult role, of being a model for others to do the same for themselves. He indicated to poets to come—and in fact to everyone—that one's poetry, and also one's life, is not to be a timid, well-made, presentable, outward construction. It is to be the consuming enterprise, leading if possible to intensified life, even to self-transfiguration. He indicated, too, that the great poem may or may not be set down on paper, but first it shall be written by the glory of this life in the flesh of a man or woman.

This is what you shall do: love the earth and sun and the animals, despise riches, give alms to everyone that asks, stand up for the stupid and crazy, devote your income and labor to others, hate tyrants, argue not concerning God, have patience and indulgence toward the people, take off your hat to nothing known or unknown or to any man or number of men, go freely with powerful uneducated persons and with the young and with the mothers of families, re-examine all you have been told at school or church or in any book, dismiss whatever insults your own soul . . . and your very flesh shall be a great poem and have the richest fluency not only in its words but in the silent lines of its lips and face and between the lashes of your eyes and in every motion and joint of your body.

(p. 11)

Galway Kinnell, "Whitman's Indicative Words," in *The American Poetry Review,* Vol. 2, No. 2, March-April, 1973, pp. 9-11.

HOWARD MOSS
(essay date 1981)

[Moss is an American poet, dramatist, and critic whose writings frequently appear in the *New Yorker.* In the following review of Justin Kaplan's *Walt Whitman: A Life* (cited in Sources for Further Study), he emphasizes Whitman's stature in American history.]

Certain writers belong not only to the history of literature but to History itself, and Whitman is one of them. He was crucially positioned: The American colonies declared their independence exactly forty-three years before his birth, in 1819, and the Revolution was still a vivid event in the minds of the adults around him. Psychically, his life stretched from the Revolution through the Civil War to the era of the robber barons. Truly an American poet of change, Whitman tends toward the heroic, the mythological. One of the great virtues of Justin Kaplan's *Walt Whitman: A Life* is its ability to rescue the man from the giant without diminishing his stature. Whitman was several men in one: Brahmin, bohemian, spokesman for a new democratic society, dandy, creator of an original kind of American poetry—a self-educated and self-intoxicated peasant of the ecstatic. Even the photographs in this volume—many of them unfamiliar—reinforce the kaleidoscopic sense of an ever-shifting personality. Mr. Kaplan, letting the various Whitmans speak, allowing for ambiguities, comes to no ringing conclusions.

A child of Long Island's "bare unfrequented shore," Whitman became, in time, a printer, newspaperman, teacher, and editor. He was the son of a dour housebuilder of English stock and a Quaker mother of Dutch descent, and his childhood was marred by instability. The record of insanity, intemperance, and failure in the Whitman family makes dismal reading. Living in the country provided no roots; the Whitmans moved from West Hills to Brooklyn and back. At the age of eleven, the poet stayed behind in Brooklyn, as a printer's apprentice, on his own. Mr. Kaplan estimates that by that time "Walt had lived in about a dozen different

houses." In Brooklyn and in Manhattan, "the blab of the pave" mingled with the "Howler and scooper of storms, capricious and dainty sea" to become strands in an original verbal amalgam that makes **"Song of Myself "**—the key poem of *Leaves of Grass"*—remarkable.

The first, 1855 edition of that book bore no author's name; an engraved daguerreotype of a gypsylike workman—one of Whitman's guises—adorned the frontispiece. Its poems untitled, the book opened with what is now **"Song of Myself."** In truth a song of everyone *but* myself—"Of every hue and caste am I, of every rank and religion"—it speaks for a consciousness beyond any individual ego: one made up of many. Whitman's ability to be androgynous and anonymous, his gifts of identification and sympathy are those of a great poet. They developed into an uneasy egotism later in life, as if the many characters of a literary work had filtered into the person who created them. Whitman's notion of himself *as* America, at first the mark of a passive generosity of spirit, grew overbearing, and narrowed into mere ambition. Empathy in the artist was reduced to role-playing in the man; the mythmaker and the self-server became interchangeable.

Whitman's homosexuality complicated his role as an American spokesman, just as his "mysticism" added an eerie note to his social views—those of a freethinker brought up on Quakerism, Carlyle, George Sand, and Margaret Fuller. Divorced from any traditional faith, his spiritual illuminations are closer to the sutras of the Oriental contemplative religions than to the visions of Christian saints. Denial and excoriation—the desert and the hair shirt—were alien to him. Divine irrationality—the kind we associate with Blake, Christopher Smart, and Rimbaud—is nearer the mark. These illuminations had to be accommodated to a nineteenth-century notion of progress. Queen Victoria and Whitman were born in the same year. Mr. Kaplan writes that "sex was a major disorder," and Whitman, the only writer of nineteenth-century America completely at odds with Puritanism, was—in his trust in an expansive commercialism, his "pursuit of health as the supreme good"—a true product of the Victorian age. No matter how original his thought, it wove in and out of commonly held beliefs. Phrenology, for instance, was accepted by the science of Whitman's time—Horace Mann, Henry Ward Beecher, Ralph Waldo Emerson, Edgar Allan Poe, and Daniel Webster all believed in it—and so was "animal magnetism." "I sing the body electric" was more a literal than a figurative reference. Life was seen as voltage and wattage. People were little wireless posts at the mercy of internal shocks and outgoing currents. Mr. Kaplan sums it up: "Whitman was a sort of storage battery or accumulator for charged particles of the contemporary."

In **"Song of Myself,"** we hear for the first time

Whitman's unique blend of Biblical cadence (particularly the Psalms), primitive chant, and the ongoing catalogue: devices eventually to be at the service of a cosmic universe made up of American particularities—a secular Bible of sorts, full of contradictions and oddities. No other major poem I know sets itself such contrary tasks: to reveal the oneness of things, to praise the freedom of the individual, to celebrate the multitude in song. The over-all title *Leaves of Grass* is brilliantly fitting: the mass individuated in the unique leaf, the leaf one with the general green. The musical side of the poem sprang from Whitman's love of voices. Aroused as a youth by fiery preachers and professional orators, he savored, as his taste matured, the delights of the theatre. Italian opera became a passion. The works and the singers opened up—were exemplars of—a whole hidden emotional life. Opera introduced Whitman to the fusion of sound and action, the projection of emotion through virtuosity. Thematic repetition in Whitman is conscious but has a characteristic sounding board. Many of the poems are best approached as long arias; even when Whitman is trying to transcribe the natural music of bird song, it has the calculated effect of a musical motif entering a score.

In 1848, Whitman, now editor of the Brooklyn *Eagle,* was fired after a political squabble with its owners. Invited to edit the New Orleans *Crescent,* he made with his brother Jeff a two-week journey south and west by train, stagecoach, and steamboat. Whitman's only reference points had been Long Island, Brooklyn, and Manhattan. Words had been his only form of travel. New Orleans, with its French and Spanish heritage, was sensuous and fruitful. "By the time he returned to Brooklyn," Mr. Kaplan writes, "he had travelled five thousand miles and seen democratic vistas of city and wilderness, river and lake, mountain and plain." The cosmic intentions of *Leaves of Grass* were accumulating a continental underpinning.

In his notebook, Whitman kept clarifying his thoughts, perfecting his design: "Make no quotations and no references to other writers. Take no illustration whatsoever from the ancients or classics. . . . Make no mention or allusion to them whatever, except as they relate . . . to American character or interests." Again, "[Make] the poems of emotions, as they pass or stay, the poems of freedom, and the exposé of personality— singing in high tones democracy and the New World of it through These States." The words after the dash are the kind of sentiments that put many readers off by their air of fake grandiosity. The grandeur was partly temperamental, partly defensive. Mr. Kaplan says, "There were hints that a less robust spirit had once prevailed, a spirit covert, hesitant, perturbed, lonely, and always unrequited. ('It is I you hold and who holds you,' he addressed his reader, becoming his own book, 'I spring from the pages into your arms.')" Whitman

was "cautious" and "artful," and told Edward Carpenter, one of his many English admirers, "I think there are truths which it is necessary to envelop or wrap up."

One of them was obvious—but to some not obvious enough. After the publication of the "Calamus" poems, Whitman found himself in a position for which he had no taste: that of an international advocate of homosexual love. John Addington Symonds was relentless in his pursuit of explications. What Symonds really wanted was for Whitman to declare himself. (There was a side to Whitman which Symonds could never have imagined. Referring to an essay by Symonds called "Democratic Art, with Special Reference to Walt Whitman," Whitman said, "I doubt whether he has gripped 'democratic art' by the nuts, or L[eaves] of G[rass] either.") A whole colony of English homosexuals trooped to Whitman's flag. His brother George could never understand why Oscar Wilde would travel all the way to Camden, hardly a pleasure spot, just to see "Walt." It was in a letter replying to Symonds that Whitman first mentioned his six illegitimate children. A "mulatto mistress" was a later embellishment. This story was taken seriously by scholars for years, even though no one ever came forward to claim the famous name and the possibly lucrative literary rights.

Whitman was attracted to ferry hands, drivers, and mechanics, enjoying their naturalness, their savvy, their lingo. Peter Doyle, a horsecar conductor whom he met in his Washington days, was the most satisfactory companion of his life. But even here he pressed too far:

Give up absolutely, & for good, from this present hour, this feverish, fluctuating, useless undignified pursuit of 16.4—too long (much too long) persevered in—so humiliating.

In Whitman's notebooks, 16 stands for "P" and 4 for "D"—the cryptography of a child. It becomes clear from Mr. Kaplan's book that Whitman's intense emotional affairs were all with men. Ellen O'Connor, the wife of Whitman's friend and critic William O'Connor, fell madly in love with him, and Anne Gilchrist, an English widow, wrote him passionate letters offering her hand in marriage. Whitman tried to put her off, to no avail. She came over and lived in America with her children for several years, only to return to England, in the end, disappointed. Not quite able to deny any form of idolatry, Whitman welcomed women cautiously, proffering them his person in place of his love. He became a familiar figure in the O'Connor household in Washington and in the Gilchrist ménage in Philadelphia. In fact, he liked nothing better than to "join" an already established domestic circle, adopting and being adopted by one family after another. In these establishments, he was the overgrown prodigal son come home to roost, or that friendly but remote familiar the genius uncle.

Leaves of Grass went through nine editions in Whitman's lifetime, its author striving in each successive recasting for the proper arrangement of the poems—readjusting sections and shifting sequences to accommodate additions to an ever-expanding work. It grew from the twelve poems of the 1855 edition to the more than three hundred and eighty poems of the so-called "Deathbed" edition, which bears Whitman's imprimatur. Lines and phrases were always being revised and stanzas tightened. As new poems were added, old ones were jettisoned to make room for them. Juvenile outpourings were discarded.

Leaves of Grass was full of prescriptions for the future. Emerson's clever description of it as "a singular blend of the Bhagvat Ghita and the New York Herald," meant as a put-down, would today be considered a compliment—but only because *Leaves of Grass* is already in place to show the way. Emerson's comment was a far cry from his first, spontaneous reaction to the poem, emblazoned forever in a famous letter: "I am not blind to the worth of the wonderful gift of *Leaves of Grass.* I find it the most extraordinary piece of wit and wisdom that America has yet contributed. . . . I find incomparable things said incomparably well. . . . I greet you at the beginning of a great career"—the most generous unsolicited response of one writer to another in the history of American letters. Without it, the poem, which had few takers, might have been lost forever. Whitman sent the letter to the New York *Tribune* and incorporated it into the second edition of *Leaves of Grass,* without permission from Emerson—two acts of insensitivity in Whitman's long career of self-advertisement. A poet, prophet, and public-relations man, he wrote three anonymous reviews of his own book, modestly characterizing it in one as "the most glorious of triumphs, in the known history of literature."

The true miracle of *Leaves of Grass* is that, for all its excesses, its extravagant claims, its endless catalogues, it is, at its very best, a poem of pure feeling—feeling that seeps through phrase after phrase, poem after poem. The transformation of its emotions into words on so vast a scale is astonishing. A long love affair with the future, broken in speech sometimes, eloquent beyond anything one remembers, remarkable in the minting of its language, it is a sad poem, a love poem to some "you" never found, some "you" not only personal, intimate, and sexual but connected with an epic largeness of democratic vistas, as if the poet were in love with Americans not yet born or always yet to come. No one, including Mr. Kaplan—and certainly not Whitman—has yet explained where it sprang from. Whitman encouraged the view of the "transformation miracle"—the "journalist-loafer" turned into the great poet and prophet, as if at the touch of a wand. His followers, sodden with worship, helped the idea along.

Actually, Whitman worked on it for years. It was *almost* a miracle—a flawed one, for there is always the problem in Whitman of the false prophecy, the naïve dream, the wished-for fulfillment seen as accomplished fact. *Leaves of Grass* did more than change opinions; it altered the intellectual climate of the world. (And the moral climate, too. "Free love?" Whitman once asked. "Is there any other kind?") Van Gogh, working on *The Starry Night* in Arles, was affected by it; Gerard Manley Hopkins took it to heart; LaForgue translated the "Children of Adam" poems; it was crucial to D. H. Lawrence and Hart Crane and García Lorca. People as wildly different as Thomas Eakins and Tennyson, Gertrude Stein and Henry James felt its impact. In our time, the Black Mountain School, the Beats, and the New York School of poets emerged from it.

When the Civil War started, *Leaves of Grass* had been through three editions. **"Out of the Cradle Endlessly Rocking,"** the "Children of Adam" poems, and the "Calamus" poems had all been added. Its message of brotherly love became literal. Just as one brother, Jeff, had been party to Whitman's expanding conception of America, it was concern for another, George, that led Whitman to the battlefields of the South. In a garbled casualty report, Whitman learned that George had been wounded. No news followed. Whitman left Washington for Virginia in search of him, found him, and saw at first hand what the war was really like. He dealt with it the only way he knew—as a healer. He returned to Washington to become a "wound-dresser" at Armory Square Hospital. Whitman came into the wards, according to Mr. Kaplan, like "a rich old sea captain, he was so red-faced and patriarchal-looking and big." He entertained the wounded, recited Shakespeare and Scott, told stories, wrote letters for the illiterate and the disabled, attended the feverish young, assisted at grisly amputations, and comforted the dying. The suffering was indescribable: "By the end of the war Whitman figured he had made over six hundred hospital visits and tours, often lasting several days and nights, and in some degree had ministered to nearly a hundred thousand of the sick and wounded of both sides." Yet there were compensations: the alleviation of pain; the sense of being part of a great design, of contributing. Paternal concern, brotherly companionship, mothering compassion were mixed up with emotions sometimes dangerously close to obsession. In the end, he was undone not only by the physical and mental suffering of the patients and the fatigue of the work but by his barely controllable feelings. Here is a letter from Whitman to Thomas P. Sawyer, one of the soldiers:

> Dear comrade, you must not forget me, for I never shall you. My love you have in life or death forever. I don't know how you feel about it, but it is the wish of my heart to have your friendship, and also that if you should come safe out of this war, we should

come together again in some place where we could make our living, and be true comrades and never be separated while life lasts. . . . My soul could never be entirely happy, even in the world to come without you, dear comrade. . . . Good bye, my darling comrade, my dear darling brother, for so I will call you, and wish you to call me the same.

Here is Sawyer's reply:

I fully reciprocate your friendship as expressed in your letter and it will afford me great pleasure to meet you after the war will have terminated or sooner if circumstances will permit.

The generalized "you," the beloved addressed in Whitman's poems, had, like a Platonic universal, an idealized counterpart in President Lincoln. As a poet of the body, Whitman believed "The scent of these armpits [is] aroma finer than prayer / This head more than churches, Bibles, and all the creeds;" but as a poet of the soul, having eschewed Christianity, he needed a god of his own. Mr. Kaplan writes that Lincoln became "his personal agent of redemption, a symbolic figure who transcended politics, leadership, and victory." His mother was the only other person in Whitman's life who had this idealized aura. The "Drum-Taps" poems came out of the war and were dutifully added to *Leaves of Grass.* Their price was high: "The perfect health Whitman was so proud of broke in the hospitals along with a delicate structure of denial and sublimation. Love became irreversibly linked with disease, mutilation, death, absence." In 1865, Lincoln was assassinated; in 1873, Whitman's mother died. Long before, he had written a line that now seemed perfectly appropriate: "Agonies are one of my changes of garments."

The year Whitman's mother died, he became partially paralyzed. Strokes were to cripple him the rest of his life. After living with the family of his brother George, in Camden, for several years, he bought a small house of his own. Some of Mr. Kaplan's most charming pages are devoted to Whitman's last years. Confined more or less to an upper front bedroom-workroom, he recovered, only to be laid back by another bout of illness. "It was not until old age that Whitman's presence and ambience became fully achieved"—Kaplan is using

John Burroughs, the naturalist, who knew Whitman for more than twenty years, as a source. "He created an overall impression of sunniness, equanimity, and contemplative leisure." Whitman, still fiddling with *Leaves of Grass,* stirred the mass of papers at his feet with his cane. Everything natural, found, or man-made was source material for the mesmeric catalogues of the poem. The house had the air of a ship's cabin—landlocked, and foundering in debris, in spite of the efforts of a sailor's widow who kept house for him. Whitman was a collector of people and things, but in both cases the choices had nothing to do with market values or current fashion. Like a bird building a nest, he knew exactly what was required (not much) for his comfort, and what he had to have (everything) for his poem. Whitman needed help to get around and always found it; he was surrounded by people who revered him to the point of idolatry. In 1893, he was finally laid to rest in the elaborate tomb in Harleigh Cemetery that had cost him more than the Camden house. By the time the reader comes to Whitman's death, he can almost take "My foothold is tenoned and mortised in granite / I laugh at what you call dissolution" as the literal truth.

Whitman's life is enigmatic not only by virtue of genius; it is steeped in the deliberately muddied waters of destroyed evidence and manipulated fact. Putting a coherent Whitman together is an exercise in conjecture; the more insistent the claim, the more suspicious its truth. Mr. Kaplan never insists; he merely presents. If he is sometimes long on Freud and short on philosophy, his is still the best all-around portrait we have of a man whose influence can only increase. Whitman bears a relation to Lincoln not unlike Shakespeare's to Elizabeth I and Michelangelo's to the Medici. In each instance, as the years pass the more obvious it becomes that the representative figure of the age, like a negative gradually developing in time, is not the ruler but the artist. (pp. 184-99)

Howard Moss, "A Candidate for the Future," in *The New Yorker,* Vol. LVII, No. 30, September 14, 1981, pp. 184, 190-94, 197-99.

SOURCES FOR FURTHER STUDY

Allen, Gay Wilson. *The Solitary Singer: A Critical Biography of Walt Whitman.* New York: New York University Press, 1967, 616 p.

Influential discussion of Whitman's life and works.

Black, Stephen A. *Whitman's Journey into Chaos: A Psychoanalytic Study of the Poetic Process.* Princeton, N.J.: Princeton University Press, 1975, 255 p.

Presents psychoanalytic criticism of *Leaves of Grass* as a model for studying poetry in general.

Hindus, Milton, ed. *"Leaves of Grass": One Hundred Years After.* Stanford: Stanford University Press, 1955, 144 p.

> Highly regarded selection of essays on *Leaves of Grass.*

Kaplan, Justin. *Walt Whitman: A Life.* New York: Simon and Schuster, 1980, 429 p.

> Critical biography of Whitman.

Miller, James E., Jr. *A Critical Guide to "Leaves of Grass."* Chicago: The University of Chicago Press, 1957, 268 p.

> A structural analysis of *Leaves of Grass.*

Woodress, James, ed. *Critical Essays on Walt Whitman.* Boston: G. K. Hall, 1983, 338 p.

> Anthology of important Whitman criticism, including assessments by William Dean Howells, William James, and Ezra Pound.

Oscar Wilde

1854-1900

Anglo-Irish dramatist, novelist, essayist, critic, poet, and short story writer.

INTRODUCTION

Wilde is best known as one of the foremost figures of late nineteenth-century literary Decadence and as a founder of the "art for art's sake" movement, which defied convention, subordinating ethical instruction to aesthetic value. This credo of aestheticism, however, indicates only one facet of a man notorious for resisting any public institution—artistic, social, political, or moral—that attempted to subjugate individual will and imagination. In contrast to the cult of nature purported by the Romantic poets, Wilde posed a cult of art in his critical essays and reviews; to socialism's cult of the masses, he proposed a cult of the individual; and in opposition to what he saw as the middle-class facade of false respectability, he encouraged a struggle to realize one's true nature.

Wilde was born and raised in Dublin, though unlike other expatriate Irish writers, he did not draw upon his homeland as a subject for his works. He began his advanced education at Dublin's Trinity College and concluded it with an outstanding academic career at Oxford. In college Wilde was influenced by the writings of Walter Pater, who in his *Studies in the History of the Renaissance* (1873) urged indulgence of the senses, a search for sustained intensity of experience, and stylistic perfectionism in art. Wilde adopted such aestheticism as a way of life, cultivating an extravagant persona that was burlesqued in the popular press and music-hall entertainments, copied by other youthful iconoclasts, and indulged by the avant-garde literary and artistic circles of London wherein Wilde was renowned for intelligence, wit, and charm.

Wilde published his first volume, *Poems,* in 1881. In 1884 he married Constance Lloyd, the daughter of a wealthy Dublin family, and thereafter promoted himself and his ideas with successful lecture tours of the United States, Canada, and Great Britain. In the late

1880s Wilde and his family settled in London, and he continued to crusade for aestheticism as a book reviewer and as the editor of the periodical *Lady's World,* whose name he immediately changed to *Woman's World.* Wilde's first collection of prose, *The Happy Prince, and Other Tales* (1888), displays his penchant for ornamentation and stylistic grace in his writings. *The Picture of Dorian Gray* (1891), Wilde's only novel, was published during a period of great creativity and productivity for Wilde that extended from 1888 to 1895. Most of his highly regarded critical essays, collected in *Intentions* (1891), as well as his best short fiction, gathered in *Lord Arthur Savile's Crime, and Other Stories* (1891) were published during this time. In addition, Wilde attained the greatest critical and popular success of his lifetime with the plays *Lady Windermere's Fan* (1892), *A Woman of No Importance* (1893), *An Ideal Husband* (1895), and *The Importance of Being Earnest* (1895). These stylized, well-made comedies of manners, sparkling with wit and abounding with quotable epigrams, are considered his crowning achievements.

During this period of creativity, Wilde met and became infatuated with Lord Alfred Douglas, son of the Marquess of Queensbury. His relationship with Douglas, the Marquess's violent disapproval of this relationship, and his own ill-advised legal action against the Marquess scandalized London. *The Importance of Being Earnest* was in production at the time of Wilde's 1895 trial on charges of "gross indecency between male persons." His conviction and subsequent imprisonment led to ignominy for Wilde and obscurity for his works. He continued to write during his two years in prison, producing the poems in *The Ballad of Reading Gaol, and Other Poems* (1898) and the essay *De Profundis* (1905). Upon his release, however, Wilde was generally either derided or ignored by literary and social circles. At the time of his death in 1900 the scandal associated with Wilde led most commentators to discuss him diffidently, if at all. While critical response no longer focuses so persistently on questions of morality, Wilde's life and personality still incite fascination. Biographical studies and biographically oriented criticism continue to dominate Wilde scholarship.

The appearance of the critical essays and dialogues in *Intentions* defined Wilde's artistic philosophy. "The Critic as Artist" develops its author's deeply held belief that originality of form is the only enduring quality in a work of art, a quality transcending its age. "The Decay of Lying" insists on the superiority of art to nature, and puts forth the paradox that "nature imitates art," using this thesis to work out an ingenious line of argument revealing insights into the relationship between natural and aesthetic worlds. "Pen Pencil and Poison" examines the relationship between art and morality, concluding that in fact there exists none. This theme receives fictional treatment in *The Picture of Dorian Gray.* While a number of critics have read the novel purely as a morality tale on the hazards of egoistical self-indulgence, others accept Wilde's viewpoint that the suffering and belated wisdom of the protagonist are incidental to the work's artistic form. Conceding what on his own terms was an artistic error, Wilde freely admitted that the book does indeed contain a moral, which he summed up with the simple remark: "All excess, as well as all renunciation, brings its own punishment."

In writing *The Ballad of Reading Gaol* and *De Profundis* Wilde attempted to derive personal and artistic meaning from misery and humiliation. The first work is recognized as Wilde's one great poetic achievement. The second, written in the form of a long letter to Douglas, is a document of self-examination. "I do not defend my conduct. I explain it," Wilde wrote to his future literary executor, Robert Ross, describing his motives for composing *De Profundis.* A number of critics have considered the motives behind this lengthy epistle self-serving and insincere, essentially another artistic pose whether intended or not. Others, however, find it a heroic composition which in the realm of emotion and psyche shares the same integrity that the author maintained in the realm of art.

Both Wilde's sincerity and integrity have long been issues in criticism of his works. His conception of artistic beauty was often considered a superficial taste for ornament, though for some time critics have acknowledged that this conception of beauty additionally demands, as Wilde's character Gilbert states, "thought and passion and spirituality." Commentators on Wilde have also come to stress the intellectual and humanist basis of his work. Traditionally, critical evaluation of Wilde has been complicated, primarily because his works have to compete for attention with his sensational life. Wilde himself regarded this complication as unnecessary, advising that "a critic should be taught to criticise a work of art without making reference to the personality of the author. This, in fact, is the beginning of criticism."

(For further information about Wilde's life and works, see *Contemporary Authors,* Vols. 104, 119; *Dictionary of Literary Biography,* Vols. 10, 19, 34, 57; *Something about the Author,* Vol. 24; and *Twentieth-Century Literary Criticism,* Vols. 1, 8, 23, 41.)

CRITICAL COMMENTARY

ARTHUR RANSOME
(essay date 1912)

[In the following excerpt, Ransome offers an overview of Wilde's poetry, essays, short stories, novels, and dramas.]

The most obvious quality of [the 1881 *Poems*], and that which is most easily and most often emphasized, is its richness in imitations. But there is more in it than that. It is full of variations on other men's music, but they are variations to which the personality of the virtuoso has given a certain uniformity. Wilde played the sedulous ape with sufficient self-consciousness and sufficient failure to show that he might himself be somebody. His emulative practice of his art asks for a closer consideration than that usually given to it. Let me borrow an admirable phrase from M. Remy de Gourmont, and say that a "dissociation of ideas" is necessary in thinking of imitation. To describe a young poet's work as derivative is not the same thing as to condemn it. All work is derivative more or less, and to pour indiscriminate contempt on Wilde's imitations because they are imitations, is to betray a lamentable ignorance of the history of poetry. There is no need too seriously to defend this early work. Wilde's reputation can stand without or even in spite of it. (p. 40)

Wilde's reputation as a poet does not rest on this first book, but on half a dozen poems that include '**The Harlot's House,' 'A Symphony in Yellow,' 'The Sphinx'** and '**The Ballad of Reading Gaol,'** and alone are worthy of a place beside his work in prose. (p. 51)

[*The Sphinx*] is work more personal to Wilde than anything in *Poems*. (p. 74)

The kinetic base, the obvious framework, of *The Sphinx* is an apostrophe addressed by a student to a Sphinx that lies in his room, perhaps a dream, perhaps a paperweight, an apostrophe that consists in the enumeration of her possible lovers, and the final selection of one of them as her supposed choice. It is a series rather than a whole, though an effect of form and cumulative weight is given to it by a carefully preserved monotony. In a firm, lava-like verse, the Sphinx's paramours are stiffened to a bas-relief. The water-horse, the griffon, the hawk-faced god, the mighty limbs of Ammon, are formed into a frieze of reverie; they do not collaborate in a picture, but are left behind as the dream goes on. It goes on, perhaps, just a little too long. So do some of the finest rituals; and *The Sphinx* is among the rare incantations in our language. It is a piece of black magic. (p. 75)

[Among the short stories, three] tales need detain no student of Wilde. '**The Canterville Ghost'** is just so boisterous as to miss its balance, but, because it is about Americans, is very popular in America. '**The Sphinx without a Secret'** betrays its secret in its title. '**The Model Millionaire'** is an empty little thing no better than the popular tales it tries to imitate. '**Lord Arthur Savile's Crime,'** however, is not only remarkable as an indication of what Wilde was to do both as a dramatist and as a storyteller, but is itself a delightful piece of buffoonery. Wilde is so serious. . . . The plot is no less moral than simple. Lord Arthur Savile learns from the palmist that at some period of his life it is decreed that he shall commit a murder. Unwilling to marry while a potential criminal, he sets about committing the murder at once, to get it over, and be able to marry with the easy conscience of one who knows that his duty has been satisfactorily performed. . . . Like much of Wilde's work, this story is very clever talk, an elaborated anecdote, told with flickering irony, a cigarette now and again lifted to the lips. But, already, a dramatist is learning to use this irony in dialogue, and a decorative artist is restraining his buoyant cleverness, to use it for more subtle purposes. There is a delicate description of dawn in Piccadilly, with the waggons on their way to Covent Garden, white-smocked carters, and a boy with primroses in a battered hat, riding a big grey horse—a promise of the fairy stories. (pp. 84-6)

In reading them, I cannot help feeling that Wilde wrote one of them as an experiment, to show, I suppose, that he could have been Hans Andersen if he had liked, and his wife importuned him to make a book of things so charming, so good, and so true. He made the book, and there is one beautiful thing in it, '**The Happy Prince,'** which was, I suspect, the first he wrote. The rest, except, perhaps, '**The Selfish Giant,'** a delightful essay in Christian legend, are tales whose morals are a little too obvious even for grown-up people. . . . There is a moral in '**The Happy Prince,'** but there is this difference between that story and the others, that it is quite clear that Wilde wanted to write it. It is Andersen, treated exactly as Wilde treated Milton in the volume of 1881, only with more assurance, and a greater certainty about his own contribution. We recognise Wilde by the decorative effects that are scattered throughout the book. He preferred a lyrical pattern to a prosaic per-

Principal Works

Poems (poetry) 1881

The Happy Prince, and Other Tales (short stories) 1888

A House of Pomegranates (short stories) 1891

Intentions (essays) 1891

Lord Arthur Savile's Crime, and Other Stories (short stories) 1891

The Picture of Dorian Gray (novel) 1891

Lady Windermere's Fan (drama) 1892

Salomé (drama) 1893

A Woman of No Importance (drama) 1893

An Ideal Husband (drama) 1895

The Importance of Being Earnest (drama) 1895

The Ballad of Reading Gaol, and Other Poems (poetry) 1898

*De Profundis (letter) 1905

Collected Works. 14 vols. (poetry, essays, short stories, novel, dramas, and criticism) 1908

The Letters of Oscar Wilde (letters) 1962

*This work was not published in its entirety until 1949.

spective, and, even more than his wit, his love of decoration is the distinguishing quality of his work. (pp. 87-8)

Wilde wrote, with the pen of Flaubert, stories that might have been imagined by Andersen, and sometimes one and sometimes the other touches his hand. It is not impossible that Baudelaire was also present. But all this does not much concern us, except that by subtraction we may come to what we seek, which is the personal, elusive, but unmistakable quality contributed by Wilde himself. (pp. 90-1)

Wilde, always perfectly self-conscious, was not unaware of this difference between his own writing and that of most of his contemporaries. When *Dorian Gray* was attacked for immorality, Wildle wrote, in a letter to a paper: "My story is an essay on decorative art. It reacts against the brutality of plain realism." *The Picture of Dorian Gray* was written for publication in a magazine. Seven chapters were added to it to make it long enough for publication as a novel. . . . The preface was written to answer assailants of the morality of the story in its first form, and included only when it was printed as a book. These circumstances partly explain the lack of proportion, and of cohesion, that mars, though it does not spoil, the first French novel to be written in the English language. England has a traditional novel-form with which even the greatest students of human comedy and tragedy square their work. In France there is no such tradition, with the result that the novel is a plastic form, moulded in the most various ways by the most various minds. (pp. 94-5)

There are a few strange books that share the magic of some names, like Cornelius Agrippa, Raymond Lully, and Paracelsus, names that possibly mean more to us before than after we have investigated the works and personalities that lie behind them. These books are mysterious and kept, like mysteries, for peculiar moods. They are not books for every day, nor even for every night. We keep them for rare moments, as we keep in a lacquer cabinet some crystal-shrined thread of subtle perfume, or some curious gem, to be a solace in a mood that does not often recur, or, perhaps, to be an instrument in its evocation. *Dorian Gray,* for all its faults, is such a book. It is unbalanced; and that is a fault. It is a mosaic hurriedly made by a man who reached out in all directions and took and used in his work whatever scrap of jasper, or porphyry or broken flint was put into his hand; and that is not a virtue. But in it there is an individual essence, a private perfume, a colour whose secret has been lost. There are moods whose consciousness that essence, perfume, colour, is needed to intensity. (p. 98)

[In *The Portrait of Mr. W. H.*] Wilde read something of himself into Shakespeare's sonnets, and, in reading, became fascinated by a theory that he was unable to prove. Where another man would, perhaps, have written a short, serious essay, and whistled his theory down the wind that carries the dead leaves of Shakespeare's commentators, Wilde tosses it as a belief between three brains, and allows it to unfold itself as the background to a story. The three brains are the narrator, Cyril Graham, and Erskine. Graham discovers the Mr. W. H. of the Sonnets in a boy-actor called Will Hughes, and by diligent examination of internal evidence, almost persuades Erskine to believe him. (p. 101)

It would be impossible to build an airier castle in Spain than this of the imaginary William Hughes; impossible, too, to build one so delightfully designed. The prose and the reasoning seem things of ivory, Indian-carved, through which the rarest wind of criticism may freely blow and carry delicate scents away without disturbing the yet more delicate fabric. Wilde assumes that Shakespeare addressed the sonnets to William Hughes, and, that assumption granted (though there is no William Hughes to be found), colours his theory with an abundance of persuasive touches, to strengthen what is, at first, only a courtesy belief. Though all his argument is special pleading, Wilde contrives to make you feel that counsel knows, though he cannot prove, that his client is in the right. The evidence is only for the jury. You are inclined to interrupt him with the exclamation that you are already convinced. But it is a pleasure to listen to him, so you let him go on. After all, "brute reason is quite unbearable. There is something unfair about its use. It is like hitting below the intellect." Wilde's *Portrait of Mr. W. H.* is more than a refutable theory, a charming piece of speculation. It is an illustration of the critic as artist, a foretaste of *Intentions.* It is better than 'The Truth of Masks,' as good as 'The Decay of Lying.' (pp. 102-03)

Unfamiliar truth was, at first, the most noticeable characteristic of Wilde's *Intentions,* but, though paradox may fade to commonplace, "age cannot wither nor custom stale" the fresh and debonair personality that keeps the book alive, tossing thoughts like roses, and playing with them in happiness of heart. (p. 105)

Wilde loved speech for its own sake, and nothing could be more characteristic of his gift than his choice [in *Intentions*] of that old and inexhaustible form that Plato, Lucian, Erasmus and Landor, to name only a few, have turned to such different purposes. Dialogue is at once personal and impersonal. "By its means he (the thinker) can both reveal and conceal himself, and give form to every fancy, and reality to every mood." . . . Nothing could better describe Wilde's own essays in dialogue.

The first of these essays is 'The Decay of Lying,' in which a young gentleman called Vivian reads aloud an article on that subject to a slightly older and rather incredulous young gentleman called Cyril. . . . [He] envisages the history of art as a long warfare between the simian instinct of imitation and the God-like instinct of self-expression. (pp. 106-07)

It is important to remember that throughout this dialogue, Wilde is speaking of pure art, a thing which possibly does not exist, and, recognising it as an ideal towards which all artists should aspire, is engaged in pointing out the more obvious means of falling short of it. He achieves a triumph, of a kind in which he delighted, by making people read of such a subject. Not wishing to be laughed at by the British intellect, and wishing to be listened to, he laughs at it instead, and, near the end of the dialogue, is so daring as to present it with a picture of what is occurring, confident that the individual will disclaim the general, and smile without annoyance at the caricature. (pp. 111-12)

'Pen, Pencil, and Poison,' the essay on [the murderer, forger, and author Thomas Griffiths] Wainewright, not in dialogue, has some of the hard angular outlines of the set article on book or public character. It fills these outlines, however, with picturesque detail and half-ironic speculation. It is impossible not to notice the resemblance between the subject of this essay and its author. It is difficult not to suspect that Wilde, in setting in clear perspective Wainewright's poisoning and writing, is estimating the possible power of crime to intensify a personality, was analysing himself, and expressing through a psychological account of another man the results of that analysis. Perhaps, in that essay we have less analysis than hypothesis. (pp. 112-13)

But the most striking and beautiful thing in *Intentions* is that dialogue between the two young men [Ernest and Gilbert in 'The Critic as Artist'] in a library whose windows look over the kaleidoscopic swirl of Piccadilly to the trees and lawns of the Green Park. (p. 114)

[Their] talk is far too good really to have been heard. They set their excellence as a barrier between themselves and life. Not for a moment will they forget that they are the creatures of art: not for a moment will they leave that calm air for the dust and turmoil of human argument. Wilde was never so sure of his art as in this dialogue, where Ernest, that ethereal Sancho Panza, and Gilbert, that rather languid Don Quixote, tilt for their hearer's joy. They share the power of visualization that made Wilde's own talk like a continuous fairy tale. They turn their ideas into a coloured pageantry, and all the gods of Greece and characters of art are ready to grace by their visible presence the exposition, whether of the ideas that are to be confuted or of those that are to take their place. "In the best days of art," says Ernest, "there were no art critics." . . . (pp. 116-17)

"But no," says Gilbert, "the Greeks were a nation of art critics." . . . And so the talk goes on. There is but one defect in this panoramic method of presenting ideas. Each time that Wilde empties, or seems to spill before us, his wonderful cornucopia of coloured imagery, he seems to build a wave that towers like the blue and silver billow of Hokusai's print. Now, surely, it will break, we say, and are tempted to echo Cyril in 'The Decay of Lying,' when, at the close of one of these miraculous paragraphs, he remarks, "I like that. I can see it. Is that the end?" Too many of Wilde's paragraphs are perorations. (pp. 117-18)

The fourth essay in the book ['The Truth of Masks'] is not on the high level of the others. It is more practical and less beautiful. . . . It is interesting, but less as a thing in itself than as an indication of the character of Wilde's knowledge of the theatre. (p. 129)

The character of Wilde's study of the theatre was shown in 'The Truth of Masks,' and in the dramatic criticism that he wrote in the years immediately following his marriage. It was a study of methods and concerned no less with stage-management than with the drama. Nearly thirty years ago he made a plea for beautiful scenery, and asked for that harmony between costumier and scene-painter that has been achieved in our day by Charles Ricketts and Cayley Robinson under the management of Mr. Herbert Trench. He remarked that painted doors were superior to real ones, and pointed out that properties which need light from more than one side destroy the illumination suggested by the scene-painter's shadings. From the first his dramatic criticism was written in the wings, not from the point of view of an audience careless of means, observant only of effects. *Vera* may have been dull, and *The Duchess of Padua* unplayable, but actors, at least, shall have no fault to find in the technique of *Lady Windermere's Fan.* That play seems to me to be no more than a conscious experiment in the use of the knowledge that Wilde had sedulously worked to obtain.

There was a continuity in Wilde's interest in the theatre wholly lacking in his passing fancies for narrative or essay-writing. . . . His most perfectly successful works, those which most exactly accomplish what they attempt, without sacrificing any part of themselves, are, perhaps, *The Importance of Being Earnest* and *Salomé.* Both these are plays. But neither of them seems to me so characteristic, so inclusive of Wilde as *Intentions, De Profundis, The Portrait of Mr. W. H.,* or even *The Picture of Dorian Gray.* His plays are wilfully limited, subordinated to an aim outside themselves, and, except in the two I have just mentioned, these limitations are not such as to justify themselves by giving freedom to the artist. Some limitations set an artist free for an achievement otherwise impossible. But the limitations of which I complain only made Wilde a little contemptuous of his work. They did not save his talent from preoccupations, but compelled it

Wilde with Lord Alfred Douglas in 1894.

to a labour in whose success alone he could take an interest.

It is impossible not to feel that Wilde was impatient of the methods and the meanings of his first three successful plays, like a juggler, conscious of being able to toss up six balls, who is admired for tossing three. These good women, these unselfish, pseudonymous mothers, these men of wit and fashion discomfited to make a British holiday; their temptations, their sacrifices, their defeats, are not taken from any drama played in Wilde's own mind. He saw them and their adventures quite impersonally; and no good art is impersonal. Salome kissing the pale lips of Iokanaan may once have moved him when he saw her behind the ghostly footlights of that secret theatre in which each man is his own dramatist, his own stage manager, and his own audience. But Lady Windermere did not return to her husband for Wilde's sake, and he did not feel that Sir Robert Chiltern's future mattered either way. He cared only that an audience he despised should be relieved at her return, and that to them the career of a politician should seem to be important. Not until the production of *The Importance of Being Earnest* did he share the pleasure of the pit. I know a travelling showman who makes "enjoy" an active verb, and speaks of "enjoying the poor folk" when, for coppers, he lets them ride on merry-go-rounds, and agitate themselves in swing-boats, which offer him no manner of amusement. In just this way Wilde "enjoyed" the London audiences with his early plays. He did not enjoy them himself. (pp. 132-36)

He consoled himself for his plots by taking extraordinary liberties with them, and amused himself with quips, bons-mots, epigrams and repartee that had really nothing to do with the business in hand. Most of his witty sayings would bear transplanting from one play to another, and it is necessary to consult the book if we would remember in whose mouth they were placed. This is a very different thing from the dialogue of Congreve on the one hand or of J. M. Synge on the other. The whole arrangement in conversation, as he might appropriately have called either *Lady Windermere's Fan, An Ideal Husband,* or *A Woman of No Importance,* was very much lighter than the story that served as its excuse and sometimes rudely interrupted it. It was so sparkling, good-humoured and novel that even the audience for whom he had constructed the story forgave him for putting a brake upon its speed with this quite separate verbal entertainment. (pp. 137-38)

It is not in the least surprising that *The Importance of Being Earnest,* the most trivial of the social plays, should be the only one of them that gives that peculiar exhilaration of spirit by which we recognise the beautiful. It is precisely because it is consistently trivial that it is not ugly. If only once it marred its triviality with a bruise of passion, its beauty would vanish with the blow. But it never contradicts itself, and it is worth noticing that its unity, its dovetailing of dialogue and plot, so that the one helps the other, is not achieved at the expense of the conversation, but at that of the mechanical contrivances for filling a theatre that Wilde had not at first felt sure of being able to do without. The dialogue has not been weighed to trudge with the plot; the plot has been lightened till it can fly with the wings of the dialogue. The two are become one, and the lambent laughter of this comedy is due to the radioactivity of the thing itself, and not to glow-worms incongruously stuck over its surface. (p. 139)

It is surprising to think that *Salomé* was not written with a view to production. (p. 144)

In writing *Salomé,* however, Wilde did not neglect the wonderful visual sense of the theatre that was, later, to suggest to him the appearance on the stage of Jack in mourning for his nonexistent brother. He was able to see the play from the point of view of the audience, and refused no means of intensifying its effect. . . . Control is never lost, and, when the play is done, when we return to it in our waking dreams, we return to that elevation only given by the beautiful, undisturbed by the vividness, the clearness with which we realise the motive of passion playing its part in that deeper motive of doom, that fills the room in which we read, or the theatre in which we listen, with the beating of the wings of the angel of death. (pp. 151-52)

In *De Profundis* Wilde wrote as harmoniously and freely as if his life were spent in conversation instead of in silence, in looking at books and pictures instead of in shredding oakum or in swinging the handle of a crank.

It is impossible too firmly to emphasize the division between the texture of the life in *De Profundis* and that of Wilde's life in prison, a division not only needing explanation but explicable in the light of later events. When he left prison he wrote *The Ballad of Reading Gaol.* Now that ballad would have been obscured or enriched by a silver cobweb of scarcely perceptible sensations if it had been written before or during his imprisonment. Wilde could not then have suffered some of the harsh and crude effects that are harmonious with its character and necessary to its success. The newly-learnt insensibility, that allowed him to use in the ballad emotions that once he would have carefully guarded himself from perceiving, had been taught in prison. In prison his nerves had been so jangled that they responded only to a violent agitation, so jarred that a delicate touch left them silent. But at the time of the writing of *De Profundis* these janglings and jarrings were too immediate to affect him. They disappeared like print held too close to the eye. He escaped from them as he wrote, for he wrote from memory. While the events were happening, had just happened, and

might happen again, that produced the insensibility without which he could not have secured the broad and violent effects of his later work, he returned, in writing, to an earlier life. When he took up his pen, it was as if none of these things were, unless as material for the use of an aloof and conscious artist. He was outside the prison as he wrote, and only saw as if in vision the tall man, with roughened hands, who had once been "King of life," and now was writing in a cell. (pp. 175-77)

What is remarkable in *The Ballad of Reading Gaol,* apart from its strength, or its violence of emotion, is a change in the quality of Wilde's language. A distinction between decoration and realism, though it immediately suggests itself, is too blunt to enable us to state clearly a change in Wilde's writing that it is impossible to overlook. (p. 183)

He could not, without doing violence to himself, have written *The Ballad of Reading Gaol* before his imprisonment.

Such an alteration in his attitude became apparent when he was released: not before. And he then proceeded to write a poem whose potentiality was not won at the expense of directness. The difference between the work he did before and after his release is the same, though not so exaggerated, as that between Mallarmé and the eighteenth-century poets. The later work falls midway between these two extremes. It is writing that depends, far more nearly than anything he had yet done, in verse, upon its actual statements. *The Ballad of Reading Gaol* is not more powerfully suggestive than *The Sphinx,* but what it says, its translatable element, is more important to its effect than the catalogue of the Sphinx's lovers. (p. 187)

Nowhere else in Wilde's work is there such a feeling of tense muscles, of difficult, because passionate, articulation. And this was the effect that he was willing to achieve. The blemishes on the poem, its moments of bad verse, its metaphors only half conceived (like the filling of an urn that has long been broken) scarcely mar the impression. It is felt that a relaxed watchfulness is due to the effort of reticence. I know of no other poem that so intensifies our horror of mortality. Beside it Wordsworth's sonnets on Capital Punishment debate with aloof, respectable philosophy the expediency of taking blood for blood, and suggest the palliatives with which a tender heart may sooth the pain of its acquiescence. Even Villon, who, like Wilde, had been in prison, and, unlike Wilde, had been himself under sentence of death, is infinitely less actual. . . . [Wilde] lives an hundred times life's last moments, and multiplies the agony of the man who dies in the hearts of all those others who feel with him how frail is their own perilous hold. (pp. 190-91)

Arthur Ransome, in his *Oscar Wilde: A Critical Study,* Martin Secker, 1912, 213 p.

OTTO REINERT

(essay date 1956)

[In the following excerpt, Reinert discusses Wilde's satiric targets and techniques in The Importance of Being Earnest.]

Almost everyone agrees that *The Importance of Being Earnest* is good fun, but few have tried to show that it is also a good play. To say that Wilde has written a brilliant farce is not to say why it seems both funnier and more significant than other superior farces, and to say that the farce satirizes Victorianism is not, at this late date, to tell us why it amuses at all. From some of the incidental comments once gets the impression that the play is untouchable, so exquisite that criticism would be fatal—stupid abuse of something bright and fragile. A few critics, who take their business more seriously, refuse even to be charmed. The play "never transcends . . . the incomplete or the trivial," Edouard Roditi writes in his generally perceptive book on Wilde [*Oscar Wilde,* 1947]: "Its tone is that of satire, but of a satire which, for lack of a moral point of view, has lost its sting and degenerated into the almost approving banter of a P. G. Wodehouse."

But only a curious form of critical blindness can dismiss *Earnest* as a trifle of dialogues. It merits attention both as satire and as drama. The farce is meaningful. Tone and plot have been successfully integrated, and the whole is more truly comic—because normative—than a well-made play to end all well-made plays, a vehicle for the utterance of witty nonsense. Awareness of its satirical strategy precludes the criticism that it is elusive of reasoned analysis for lack of any kind of rationale.

Wilde first employed a pattern of ironic inversion in *An Ideal Husband,* the play immediately preceding *Earnest.* Its hero, Lord Goring, is not the irresponsible dandy he seems to be, the surface frivolity is not the real man, and his flippant paradoxes emphasize the irony of his moral position relative to that of Lord Chiltern, the pretended pillar of society. (p. 14)

But though the brand of wit is similar in *Earnest,* such an attitude cannot be attributed to any one or several of the characters in the later play, simply because it has no hero (or heroine) in the sense in which Lord Goring is the hero of *An Ideal Husband.* The characters in *Earnest* never stop being flippant; their flippancy is their whole nature and not, like Lord Goring's, the mocking mask of enlightened irony in a pompous society. The only ironist in *Earnest* is Wilde himself, who

not only has abandoned the simple ethics of thesis melodrama but also has deliberately sacrificed the illusionistic conventions of naturalism in order to gain what Francis Fergusson calls (in *The Idea of a Theater*) . . . a "limited perspective, shared with the audience, as the basis of the fun," showing "human life *as* comic . . . because . . . consistent according to some narrowly defined, and hence unreal, basis."

That is why there is no reason to be embarrassed by the farce label. The play's merit is that it is *all* farce, capable of serving as a lucid image of the non-farcical reality that is kept strictly outside the play. Wilde has respected his paradoxes. He is no longer putting them to menial service as bright spots in sentimental thesis plays or as devices of crude melodramatic irony. *The Importance of Being Earnest* is one sustained metaphor, and esthetic detachment is the only mood in which it can be intelligently enjoyed. It insists on being acted straight, for if we should feel, even for a moment, that the characters are aware of what absurdities they are saying, the whole thing vanishes. Once object and image are confused there is a blurring of vision. No one in his right mind gets emotionally involved with the destinies of Algernon and Cecily, Gwendolen and Jack. But it is precisely their emotive neutrality as figures of farce that allows Wilde's characters to establish his "limited perspective": Wilde's basic formula for satire is their assumption of a code of behavior that represents the reality that Victorian convention pretends to ignore.

Algernon is explaining his reluctance to attend Lady Bracknell's dinner party:

> She will place me next Mary Farquhar, who always flirts with her own husband across the dinner table. That is not very pleasant. Indeed, it is not even decent . . . and that sort of thing is enormously on the increase. The amount of women in London who flirt with their own husbands is perfectly scandalous. It looks so bad. It is simply washing one's clean linen in public.

To say that Algernon's tone here is consciously flippant is to miss the joke altogether. The quip is not a quip; it means what it says. Algernon is indignant with a woman who spoils the fun of extramarital flirtation and who parades her virtue. He is shocked at convention. And his tone implies that he is elevating break of convention into a moral norm. He is not the first figure in English satire to do so; among his ancestors are Martin Scriblerus, other assumed identities in Pope and Swift (including Gulliver), and the apologist for Jonathan Wild. What they all have in common is that they derive their ideals for conduct from the actual practice of their societies, their standards are the standards of common corruption, they are literal-minded victims of their environments, realists with a vengeance.

Here is Algernon on conventional love institutions:

I really don't see anything romantic in proposing. It is very romantic to be in love. But there is nothing romantic about a definite proposal. Why, one may be accepted. One usually is, I believe. Then the excitement is all over.

(pp. 14-15)

The girls, too, implicitly accept this inverted code. In the proposal scene between Jack and Gwendolen the latter acts out reality: girls about to be proposed to quite realize the situation and are annoyed by their suitors' conventionally bungling approach. In the second act Gwendolen explains to Cecily that she always travels with her diary in order to "have something sensational to read in the train." One of Cecily's first speeches expresses her concern for "dear Uncle Jack" who is so "very serious" that "I think he cannot be quite well." When Algernon, at their first meeting, begs her not to think him wicked, she sternly replies:

If you are not, then you have certainly been deceiving us all in a very inexcusable manner. I hope you have not been leading a double life, pretending to be wicked and being really good all the time. That would be hypocrisy.

Paradoxical morality cannot be argued much further than this, and the speech upsets even Algernon. In context it cuts down to the very core of the problem of manners with which Wilde is concerned. It epitomizes the central irony of the play, for the Bunburying Algernon, in escaping the hypocrisy of convention, becomes a hypocrite himself by pretending to be somebody he is not. (Even Miss Prism participates. She is telling Cecily about her youthful novel: "The good ended happily, and the bad unhappily. That is what Fiction means.")

Only Jack and Lady Bracknell seem at first glance to be outside the pattern of inversion, expressing shock when confronted with the code of cynical realism. But their conventionality is not genuine. Jack is a confirmed Bunburyist long before Algernon explains the term to him, and Bunburyism is most simply defined as a means of escape from convention. He occasionally acts the role of naive elicitor of Algernon's discourses on Bunburyism and is not such a consistent theorist of the realist code, but his behavior is certainly not conventional.

One of Lady Bracknell's main plot functions is to be an obstacle to Jack's romance with Gwendolen, but a systematic analysis of her speeches will show, I think, that she has no illusions about the reality her professed convention is supposed to conceal: ". . . I do not approve of mercenary marriages. When I married Lord Bracknell I had no fortune of any kind." To her the speech is neither cynical nor funny. It represents that compromise between practical hardheadedness and conventional morality that she has worked out to her own satisfaction and behind which she has retired in dignified immunity. In other speeches she advocates Algernon's code with as much sanctimoniousness as he:

Well, I must say, Algernon, that I think it is high time that Mr. Bunbury made up his mind whether he was going to live or to die. This shilly-shallying with the question is absurd. Nor do I in any way approve of the modern sympathy with invalids. I consider it morbid.

She moralizes on behalf of people who take it for granted that illness in others is always faked and that consequently sympathy with invalids is faked also, a concession to an artificial and—literally—morbid code. The frivolous banter accomplishes something serious. It exposes the polite cynicism that negates all values save personal convenience and salon decorum. Life and death have become matters of *savoir-vivre*.

The following speech presents a somewhat more complex case, because Lady Bracknell is here simultaneously deferring to convention and exposing its sham:

French songs I cannot possibly allow. People always seem to think that they are improper, and either look shocked, which is vulgar, or laugh, which is worse. But German sounds a thoroughly respectable language, and indeed, I believe is so.

To laugh at presumably improper songs is to fly in the face of convention and break the delicate fabric of social decorum. But the opposite reaction is hardly less reprehensible. To register shock at indecency is indecently to call attention to something people realize the existence of but refuse to recognize. In her last sentence she quietly gives away the polite fiction that people in society know foreign languages.

When the pattern of inversion operates the characters either express or assume a morality that is deduced from the actual behavior of high society, though the existence of conventional morality is sometimes recognized as a fact to come to terms with. What the accumulation of paradox adds up to is an exposure both of hypocrisy and of the unnatural convention that necessitates hypocrisy. In elegant accents of pompous bigotry Wilde's puppets turn moral values upside down. "Good heavens," Algernon exclaims when Lane tells him that married households rarely serve first-rate champagne. "Is marriage so demoralizing as that?" We are made to share Wilde's view of the ludicrous and sinister realities behind the fashionable façade of an over-civilized society where nothing serious is considered serious and nothing trivial trivial.

But *Earnest* is, before anything else, a play, an imitation of *action*, and no discussion of tone apart from its dramatic setting can account for the extraordinary impact of the play as play. It is rather odd, therefore, to notice that even critics who have been aware of serious satiric implications in the dialogue have been prone to dismiss the plot as negligible, as, at best, "inspired nonsense." "The plot," writes Eric Bentley, in *The Playwright as Thinker* . . . "is one of those Gilbertian absurdities of lost infants and recovered brothers which can only be thought of to be laughed at," and he defines the function of "the ridiculous action" as constantly preventing the play from "breaking into bitter criticism." There is truth in that, but the action has another and far more important function as well: it informs the satiric dialogue with coherent meaning.

The action of *The Importance of Being Earnest* is about just that—the importance of being earnest. The title is as straight-forward a statement of theme as any literalist could ask for. Specifically, the play deals with the consequences of that way of not being earnest that Algernon calls Bunburying, and it is Bunburying that gives the plot moral significance. The key speech in the play is Algernon's little lecture to Jack:

> Well, one must be serious about something, if one wants to have any amusement in life. I happen to be serious about Bunburying. What on earth you are serious about I haven't got the remotest idea. About everything, I should fancy. You have an absolutely trivial nature.

Bunburying means to invent a fictitious character, who can serve as a pretext for escaping a frustrating social routine, regulated by a repressive convention. The pretended reason for getting away is perfectly respectable, even commendable, according to convention: to comfort a dying friend, to rescue a fallen brother. Thus defined, Bunburying is simply the mechanism that sets in motion the preposterously elaborate plot of mistaken identities. But the word has also a wider meaning. Significantly, Algernon *happens* to be serious about Bunburying—that is, it is not the subterfuge itself that is important, but the commitment to a course of action that will provide fun. The Bunburyist in the wider sense is serious about not being serious, and Bunburyism is the alternative to a convention that fails to reckon with the facts of human nature. It stands for behavior that will give experience the shading and perspective that convention denies it. To be serious about everything is to be serious about nothing; that is, to trifle. Algernon charges Jack (unfairly, as it happens) with a failure to discriminate among life values, to see that monotone of attitude blunts the spirit and deadens joy. And this is precisely Wilde's charge against Victorianism.

The Bunburyist lives in a world of irresponsibility, freed from the enslavement of a hypocritical convention. He enjoys himself. But life beyond hypocrisy is life in a dangerous climate of moral anarchy, and, like most states of revolt, Bunburyism is not ideal. The escape from convention is itself a flagrant instance of hypocrisy: pretense is the price the Bunburyist pays for freedom from the pretense of convention. In his title pun Wilde catches the moral failure of dandyism. Just as the conformist pretends to be, but is not, earnest, so Algernon and Jack pretend to be, but are not, Ernest.

What Wilde is saying, then, is that all normal Victorians who want to retain the respect of their conventional society are, perforce, Bunburyists, leading double lives, one respectable, one frivolous, neither earnest. Bunburyism, as Algernon confesses in the opening of the play, is the application of science to life, to the exclusion of sentiment. Sentiment properly belongs to art. The science is the science of having a good time. These are obviously false distinctions, and all that can be said for Bunburyism as a way of life is that it offers relief from a social round where, in Lady Bracknell's words, good behavior and well being "rarely go together," and where, according to Jack, "a high moral tone can hardly be said to conduce very much to either one's health or one's happiness." Bunburyism marks one of the extreme points in the swing of the pendulum, Victorianism the other.

Neither of the two Bunburyists is either earnest or Ernest—before the very end. [The critic adds in a footnote that: "It is the one flaw in a superbly constructed play that Algernon remains Algernon at the end and thus ineligible as a husband for Cecily. To say that she does not seem to mind at that point or that Dr. Chasuble is quite ready for the christening cannot conceal the flaw. It staggers the imagination to try to think of any way in which Wilde could have turned Algernon into a second Ernest, but, given the plot, he ought to have done so."] It is only [at the end that the two Bunburyists] become, and in more than a single sense, themselves. When the action begins they have already escaped the mortifying seriousness of convention, but it takes them three acts and the movement from town to country—the movement has symbolic relevance as a return to "naturalness"—to regain their balance and become earnest, that is, neither conventionally nor frivolously hypocritical. At the end of the play the respectable (though amorous) Miss Prism (her name suggests "prim prison") has been unmasked, the four young people are romantically engaged, Jack has discovered his Bunburying identity to be his true self, and Lady Bracknell must recognize the contemptible orphan of Act I, "born, or at any rate, bred in a handbag," as her own sister's son. The plot, as it were, makes a fool of respectability and proves the two Bunburyists "right" in their escapade. But it also repudiates Bunburyism. Algernon, who as a Bunburyist spoke cynically about proposals and matrimony in Act I, is happily proposing marriage to Cecily in Act II, and at the end

Major Media Adaptations: Motion Pictures

Salome, 1923. Nazimova Productions. [Silent] Director: Charles Bryant. Cast: Mitchell Lewis, Nigel de Brulier.

Lady Windermere's Fan, 1925. Warner. [Silent] Director: Ernst Lubitsch. Cast: Ronald Colman, May McAvoy, Irene Rich.

The Picture of Dorian Gray, 1945. MGM. Director: Albert Lewin. Cast: Hurd Hatfield, George Sanders, Angela Lansbury.

An Ideal Husband, 1947. British Lion. Director: Alexander Korda. Cast: Paulette Goddard, Hugh Williams, Michael Wilding.

The Fan, 1949. Twentieth-Century Fox. [Adaptation of *Lady Windermere's Fan*] Director: Otto Preminger. Cast: George Sanders, Madeleine Carroll, Jeanne Crain.

The Importance of Being Earnest, 1952. Universal. Director: Anthony Asquith. Cast: Michael Redgrave, Michael Denison, Edith Evans.

his initial false dichotomies between life and art, science and sentiment, have been resolved in romance. The radical remedy of Bunburying has effected a cure, the pendulum rests in the perpendicular, and we share Jack's final conviction of "the vital Importance of Being Earnest." The two adjectives have not been chosen lightly. (pp. 15-18)

Otto Reinert, "Satiric Strategy in 'The Importance of Being Earnest'," in *College English,* Vol. 18, No. 1, October, 1956, pp. 14-18.

PETER RABY

(essay date 1988)

[In the following excerpt, Raby examines the tension between life and art in *The Picture of Dorian Gray*.]

Wilde's novel *The Picture of Dorian Gray* originated as a story for *Lippincott's Magazine,* where it was published in the July number, 1890. In this form, it consisted of fourteen chapters, which represented a sustained effort of concentration for Wilde: 'I have just finished my first long story, and am tired out. I am afraid it is rather like my own life—all conversation and no action. I can't describe action: my people sit in chairs and chatter.' The disclaimer is not strictly accurate. Even in the original version the story contains three deaths, including a suicide and a murder. Nevertheless, the limited space given to action, together with Wilde's abrupt, idiosyn-

cratic handling of it, makes a noticeable feature of both versions, and raises questions as to the nature of the work, and how it was intended to be understood.

It was, inevitably, misunderstood, and Wilde turned his energies to constructing public replies to his critics, in particular those of the *St James's Gazette* and the *Scots Observer.* Wilde's first response included the declaration that he was 'quite incapable of understanding how any work of art can be criticised from a moral standpoint'. Such a statement, wholly to be expected from a writer such as Wilde, is none the less (and no doubt intentionally) ingenious, given the form and subject matter of the book. The central idea consists of a beautiful young man 'selling his soul in exchange for eternal youth'; the portrait, which is the physical representation of his soul, reflects Dorian Gray's sins; Dorian Gray himself confesses that he has been 'poisoned' by a book. It would be hard to avoid a certain amount of moral inference. Wilde admitted as much in a letter to the Editor of the *Daily Chronicle:* 'I felt that, from an aesthetic point of view, it would be difficult to keep the moral in its proper secondary place; and even now I do not feel quite sure that I have been able to do so. I think the moral too apparent.' Wilde continued by defining the moral element:

The real moral of the story is that all excess, as well as all renunciation, brings its punishment, and this moral is so far artistically and deliberately suppressed that it does not enunciate its law as a general principle, but realises itself purely in the lives of individuals, and so becomes simply a dramatic element in a work of art, and not the object of the work of art itself.

An excessively prominent moral element was one of the things Wilde hoped to correct in revising and expanding the *Lippincott's* version. His aim had been to keep the 'atmosphere of moral corruption' surrounding Dorian Gray 'vague and indeterminate and wonderful': 'Each man sees his own sin in Dorian Gray.' The indeterminate nature of Dorian's sins had already been assisted by J. M. Stoddart, the American publisher of *Lippincott's,* who had made numerous unauthorized deletions and substitutions. Wilde worked from the *Lippincott's* text, rather than from his original typescript, and only rarely reinstated his first version. One of his aims in the process of revision was to reduce the suggestions of homosexuality in the relationship between Basil Hallward and Dorian Gray, which he accomplished by stressing Dorian's importance for Hallward as artistic inspiration. At the same time, the inserted episodes such as Dorian's visit to the opium den in Chapter 16 have a greater specificity which runs counter to the claimed vagueness. In both versions the focus is not directed exclusively at either the aesthetic (Art) or the moral (Life), but at the tension between them.

The strength of *The Picture of Dorian Gray* derives primarily from the central and unifying idea of the picture itself. The artist Basil Hallward, obsessed and inspired by the youthful beauty of Dorian Gray, is about to complete his masterpiece, a full-length portrait. As Dorian poses, Lord Henry Wotton, the detached amoral observer, tempts him with words that stir him like music: 'Ah! realize your youth while you have it . . . Live the wonderful life that is in you! . . . Be always searching for new sensations.' Soon, the portrait is finished—'the finest portrait of modern times'—and when Dorian sees it, a look of joy comes into his eyes, 'as if he had recognised himself for the first time'. The sense of his own beauty comes on him like a revelation, and he expresses a fatal wish: 'If it were I who was to be always young, and the picture that was to grow old! . . . I would give my soul for that!'

The picture has become endued with terrible significance: Lord Henry offers to buy it at any price; to its creator Hallward, it represents his aesthetic ideal, though he secretly fears that it contains too much of himself; to Dorian, it reveals the transitory nature of his beauty so acutely that he is jealous of it, as though it had a life of its own. When Hallward takes up a palette knife to destroy the work which threatens to mar their relationships, Dorian tears the knife from his hand, crying out that it would be murder. The picture is preserved, and promised to Dorian. But the relationship between Dorian and Hallward has altered crucially. It is now Lord Henry who is to become Dorian's mentor.

This opening episode, contained in Chapters 1 and 2, establishes two patterns which are structurally important. The first involves the knife: Dorian tears the palette knife from Hallward's grasp, preventing a symbolic murder; he stabs Hallward to death in front of the portrait in Chapter 13; ultimately, he stabs the picture with the same knife—'As it had killed the painter, so it would kill the painter's work'—and his own body is discovered with a knife in the heart. The second pattern is concerned with the relationship between Dorian's actions and the picture's appearance, which serves as a record of his soul's progress. The picture, initially, functions as a perfect image of his beauty, a beauty of soul as well as of feature. When Dorian rejects his love Sybil Vane—a rejection caused by her failure in the art of acting—and so precipitates her suicide, the picture's expression changes: 'One would have said that there was a touch of cruelty in the mouth'; after Hallward's murder, a 'loathsome red dew' 'gleamed, wet and glistening, on one of the hands, as though the canvas had sweated blood'; when Dorian commits a good action, by sparing the innocent Hetty Merton, he hopes the portrait may reflect his new life, but is horrified to find no change, 'save that in the eyes there was a look of cunning, and in the mouth the curved wrinkle of the hypocrite'. Finally, at Dorian's death, the youth and

beauty which have been miraculously preserved in him are transferred back to the portrait, while he himself becomes 'withered, wrinkled, and loathsome of visage'.

Within the framework, and in addition to Dorian's relationships with Hallward and Lord Henry, who in places seem to function as good and evil angel to his Faustus, there are two major episodes. The first involves Dorian's passion for the actress Sibyl Vane. Sibyl, childlike and naive, acts 'all the great heroines of the world in one'; in a sordid little theatre, surrounded by third-rate players and grotesque scenery, she plays Juliet, Imogen, Rosalind, Ophelia, Desdemona. Dorian is entranced by her performance, and relates the nature of his happiness to Hallward and Lord Henry. (This act of confiding is frequently associated with danger in Wilde's writing, the process of convincing another leading to a failure of belief on the part of the speaker.) Sibyl was playing Rosalind, one of several glances at Gautier's Mademoiselle de Maupin, and a link also with Mr W. H. Significantly, Dorian defines Sibyl's qualities first in terms of art:

> She had never seemed to me more exquisite. She had all the delicate grace of that Tanagra figurine that you have in your studio, Basil. Her hair clustered round her face like dark leaves round a pale rose. As for her acting—well, you shall see her tonight. She is simply a born artist.

Next, he recounts the moment of ecstatic union:

> As we were sitting together, suddenly there came into her eyes a look that I had never seen there before. My lips moved towards her. We kissed each other. I can't describe to you what I felt at that moment. It seemed to me that all my life had been narrowed to one perfect point of rose-coloured joy.

It is noteworthy that Wilde presents this moment as reported rather than direct action, so that the emphasis is placed upon Dorian's attempt to define the experience. As though to justify himself, he proceeds to seek assurance:

> I have been right, Basil, haven't I, to take my love out of poetry, and to find my wife in Shakespeare's plays? Lips that Shakespeare taught to speak have whispered their secret in my ear. I have had the arms of Rosalind around me, and kissed Juliet on the mouth.

Hallward's response is tentative. Lord Henry, more deflationary, asks Dorian at what point he mentioned the word marriage. He proceeds to expand on the theme of Hedonism: 'When we are happy we are always good, but when we are good we are not always happy.' Ominously, Lord Henry drives away to the theatre with Dorian, leaving the painter, silent and preoccupied, to follow in a hansom. The revelation which Dorian has promised his friends does not materialise.

St. James's Gazette on ***The Picture of Dorian Gray:***

Not being curious in ordure, and not wishing to offend the nostrils of decent persons, we do not propose to analyse ***The Picture of Dorian Gray:*** that would be to advertise the developments of an esoteric prurience. . . .

The puzzle is that a young man of decent parts, who enjoyed (when he was at Oxford) the opportunity of associating with gentlemen, should put his name (such as it is) to so stupid and vulgar a piece of work. Let nobody read it in the hope of finding witty paradox or racy wickedness. The writer airs his cheap research among the garbage of the French *Décadents* like any drivelling pedant, and he bores you unmercifully with his prosy rigmaroles about the beauty of the Body and the corruption of the Soul. The grammar is better than Ouida's; the erudition equal; but in every other respect we prefer the talented lady who broke off with 'pious aposiopesis' when she touched upon 'the horrors which are described in the pages of Suetonius and Livy'—not to mention the yet worse infamies believed by many scholars to be accurately portrayed in the lost works of Plutarch, Venus, and Nicodemus, especially Nicodemus.

Let us take one peep at the young men in Mr. Oscar Wilde's story. Puppy No. 1 is the painter of the picture of Dorian Gray; Puppy No. 2 is the critic (a courtesy lord, skilled in all the knowledge of the Egyptians and aweary of all the sins and pleasures of London); Puppy No. 3 is the original, cultivated by Puppy No. 1 with a 'romantic friendship.' The Puppies fall a-talking: Puppy No. 1 about his Art, Puppy No. 2 about his sins and pleasures and the pleasures of sin, and Puppy No. 3 about himself—always about himself, and generally about his face, which is 'brainless and beautiful.' The Puppies appear to fill up the intervals of talk by plucking daisies and playing with them, and sometimes drinking 'something with strawberry in it.' The youngest Puppy is told that he is charming; but he mustn't sit in the sun for fear of spoiling his complexion. When he is rebuked for being a naughty, wilful boy, he makes a pretty *mouse*—this man of twenty!

"The Picture of Dorian Gray," in St. James's Gazette, 20 June 1890.

Sibyl Vane's beauty is as striking as ever, and when as Juliet she appears at her father Capulet's ball she is described in terms which seem to associate her with the perfected dancer, the human apotheosised in art, at once natural and artificial:

> Her body swayed as she danced, as a plant sways in the water. The curves of her throat were the curves of a white lily. Her hands seemed to be made of cool ivory.

But the revelation promised by her physical appearance proves misleading:

> The voice was exquisite, but from the point of view of tone it was absolutely false. It was wrong in colour. It took away all the life from the verse. It made the passion unreal.

the process of demythologising continues: 'The staginess of her acting was unbearable . . . Her gestures became absurdly artificial . . . ', until the final and laconic condemnation, 'It was simply bad art.'

The audience's reactions to the performance are interestingly differentiated. Wilde, somewhat unrealistically, makes even the 'common, uneducated audience of the pit and gallery' grow restless, and eventually tramp out. Hallward attempts to reassure Dorian by separating the girl from the actress, in one of those Wildean affirmations that carry scant conviction: 'Love is a more wonderful thing than Art.' Lord Henry delivers a dandiacal truth: 'It is not good for one's morals to see bad acting.' Dorian confesses that his heart is breaking. Backstage, after the performance, Sibyl is standing 'with a look of triumph on her face':

> When he entered, she looked at him, and an expression of infinite joy came over her. 'How badly I acted tonight, Dorian!' she cried.

Her explanation is the most significant speech Wilde gives to her. Before she meets Dorian, acting was the one reality of her life. She knew 'nothing but shadows', and thought them real. Dorian brought her 'something higher, something of which all art' was 'but a reflection'. She expected to be wonderful that night, found she could do nothing, and suddenly realised that it would be 'profanation' to 'play at being in love'.

However, just as Dorian's confession of love has stifled Sibyl's ability to act, so her withdrawal from art has killed Dorian's love: 'Without your art you are nothing.' He rejects her coldly, and tells her he can never see her again. Then, in a sequence closely modelled on Lord Arthur Savile's night-walking after Podgers's prophecy of murder, Dorian wanders through the dark London underworld before dawn breaks on a Covent Garden purified by pastoral overtones. It is on returning to his house that Dorian notices on his portrait lines of cruelty round the mouth. The next day he is full of remorse and resolves to make reparation to Sibyl:

> She could still be his wife. His unreal and selfish love would yield to some higher influence, would be transformed into some nobler passion, and the portrait that Basil Hallward had painted of him would be a guide to him through life, would be to him what

holiness is to some, and conscience to others, and the fear of God to us all.

As he finishes a passionate letter to Sibyl, imploring her forgiveness, Lord Henry arrives with the news of Sibyl's suicide, and consoles Dorian with the idea that her lonely death was simply an episode from art, 'a strange lurid fragment from some Jacobean tragedy': 'Mourn for Ophelia, if you like. Put ashes on your head because Cordelia was strangled . . . But don't waste your tears over Sibyl Vane. She was less real than they are.' Dorian thanks Lord Henry: 'You have explained me to myself.' An hour later 'and he was at the Opera, and Lord Henry was leaning over his chair'.

The Sibyl Vane relationship, which effectively occupies Chapters 4 to 9, forms the crucial action within the novel. It is the test which confirms Lord Henry's domination over Dorian: in terms of the choice with which Dorian is confronted, he instinctively chooses art rather than love, confirming in practice the poisonous theories which he first heard from Lord Henry in Basil Hallward's garden. Dorian's choice is analogous to Faustus's (and Faust's) first action of egotistical self-delight; and the Mephistophelean figure of Lord Henry is present to strengthen the protagonist's resolve. Dorian's action also prompts two self-destructive revelations. The first is that of Sibyl Vane herself, whose belief in art is destroyed by the declaration of Dorian's love, love which is itself presented as essentially ephemeral, an act of imagination, as suggested by her whimsical name for Dorian of 'Prince Charming'. The second comes from Basil Hallward, who calls on Dorian the day after Lord Henry's visit and is led into confessing his secret. Hallward defines the climactic moment when he drew Dorian not as Paris, Adonis, Antinous, but in his own dress and in his own time. Before, 'it had all been what art should be, unconscious, ideal, remote', but his wonderful portrait of Dorian in the method of realism would, he feared, reveal to others his idolatry. The inpenetration of personal feeling and the artistic process is presented as fatal. Dorian translated into art is lost to Basil Hallward; Sibyl Vane, translated out of art by Dorian, is lost to him. Wilde conveys vividly the extreme fragility and transitoriness of his images of perfection: the moment when the portrait is completed, which almost immediately informs Dorian of his mortality; the absorption of Sibyl Vane within her Shakespearean roles, which cannot be sustained within a context of reality. Against these exquisite but essentially tragic experiences Wilde sets the cool objectivity of Lord Henry, who remains a spectator, judging life by the standards of the connoisseur. For Dorian, once he has accepted as his mentor Lord Henry and his dictum—'to cure the soul by means of the senses, and the senses by means of the soul'—the portrait will become the living symbol of his Faustian choice:

Eternal youth, infinite passion, pleasures subtle and secret, wild joys and wilder sins—he was to have all these things. The portrait was to bear the burden of his shame: that was all.

The Sibyl Vane episode is handled more convincingly than the explanation of Basil Hallward's infatuation with Dorian, where Wilde seems, understandably, constrained by the need to suppress intimations of homosexuality. Absorption with the relationship between actress or dancer and her role is a prevalent theme in the nineteenth century, particularly since acting style became progressively more naturalistic. Wilde's choice of roles for Sibyl Vane—Juliet, Ophelia, Desdemona, Cordelia—recalls the Shakespearean characters in which Harriet Smithson appeared before Berlioz, who, like Dorian, imagined that by loving the transmitting actress he was somehow communing with Shakespeare himself. The descriptions of Sibyl as Rosalind owe something to *Mademoiselle de Maupin,* and perhaps to the open-air production of *As You Like It* produced by Lady Archibald Campbell and Godwin. There may also be an echo of Baudelaire's *La Fanfarlo,* in which the youthful Samuel Cramer, paying court to the actress in her boudoir, insists that she assume the makeup and costume of the stage role which she was portraying when he became infatuated with her, so recreating the artifice of the theatre within the context of reality.

For the extended version of **The Picture of Dorian Gray,** Wilde added a chapter (Chapter 5) which presents a number of difficulties. Its subject is Sibyl Vane and her family, her vulgarly melodramatic mother and her protective, morose brother James. The settings—their shabby lodging-house in Euston Road, the London streets, the park—have both a specificity and a shabby urban realism which contrast sharply with the decorated style which has dominated hitherto. This realism is continued in the descriptions of the tawdry theatre where Sibyl performs, and in Dorian's descent into the underworld in Chapter 16 (another addition to the original scheme). Chapter 5 is the only section in which Wilde focuses on a subject other than Dorian, who makes one brief appearance, driving past Sibyl and James as they sit in the park, but who is otherwise referred to only as Prince Charming. The change in focus is matched by an abrupt change in tone, or rather changes: the chapter contains the most uneven writing of the entire novel. In places, Wilde seems to be parodying the most banal examples of domestic melodrama:

Mrs Vane winced, and put her thin bismuth-whitened hands on her daughter's head. 'Happy!' she echoed, 'I am only happy, Sibyl, when I see you act. You must not think of anything but your acting. Mr Isaacs has been very good to us, and we owe him money.'

The girl looked up and pouted. 'Money, mother?' she cried. 'What does money matter? Love is more than money.'

Wilde signals awareness of the effect by imputing it to Mrs Vane:

Mrs Vane glanced at her, and with one of those false theatrical gestures that so often become a mode of second nature to a stage-player, clasped her in her arms . . . a young lad with rough brown hair came into the room . . . Mrs Vane fixed her eyes on him, and intensified her smile. She mentally elevated her son to the dignity of an audience. She felt sure that the *tableau* was interesting.

But in fact the melodramatic influence is pervasive, and even Sibyl's rebuke to James—'You are like one of the heroes of those silly melodramas mother used to be so fond of acting in'—does not justify or place securely the cumulative burden of derivative phrases. Wilde barely differentiates Sibyl's mode of expression from that of the rest of the family—or no more than the virtuous heroine is habitually differentiated from the rough-tongued, good-hearted brother or the vain mother. The plain and simple, unless within the artful context of a children's story, did not flow easily from Wilde. Wilde is, conceivably, presenting Sibyl's version of the romance as a fairy-tale—'Prince Charming rules life for us now'—and hence a counterpart to Dorian's equally transitory enchantment with the actress as Shakespearean heroine; but the narrative method is here too inconsistent to convey any clear structural purpose. The insertion forms a brief but disruptive interlude, compounded by its sequel, James Vane's attempted revenge and accidental death in Wilde's prefiguring of Isabel Colegate's *The Shooting Party*.

The second major episode in the novel concerns the 'poison' book, whose arrival is immediately preceded by the concealment of the picture in Dorian's former playroom. Returning to the library, Dorian finds two objects sent by Lord Henry: 'On a little table of dark perfumed wood thickly incrusted with nacre' was 'a book bound in yellow paper, the cover slightly torn and the edges soiled'; and, on the tea-tray, the *St James's Gazette*. In the newspaper paragraph Dorian reads of the ugly reality of Sibyl's death. Then, taking up the yellow book, he becomes absorbed:

It was the strangest book that he had ever read. It seemed to him that in exquisite raiment, and to the delicate sounds of flutes, the sins of the world were passing in dumb show before him. Things that he had dimly dreamed of were suddenly made real to him. Things of which he had never dreamed were gradually revealed.

In function, the book serves a similar purpose to that of Apuleius's *Metamorphoses* in *Marius the Epicurean*, and to Ronsard's works in Pater's unfinished novel *Gas-*

ton de Latour, which each exercised a powerful effect on the respective hero at a crucial stage of his development. (One might add the influence on Wilde himself of Pater's *The Renaissance*—'that book which has had such a strange influence over my life'.) For Dorian, however, the poison book is less a formative influence than a distraction once he has committed his self-defining act of objective cruelty towards Sibyl Vane, in something of the same way that the spectacle of the Seven Deadly Sins feeds Faustus's soul when he begins to waver. At the end of Chapter 11, Wilde summarises the novel's impact: 'Dorian Gray had been poisoned by a book. There were moments when he looked on evil simply as a mode through which he could realize his conception of the beautiful.' The book confirms Dorian in evil. The consequences of his cruelty towards Sibyl Vane have been unforeseen. He now embarks upon a course of life which consciously embraces sin.

In Wilde's typescript for *Lippincott's,* the novel is called '*Le Secret de Raoul* par Catulle Sarrazin' and it would seem that Wilde at one stage planned to create an imaginary book. In the event the poison novel bears, in spite of certain discrepancies, an unmistakable resemblance to Huysmans's *A rebours;* and Dorian shares a number of interests and enthusiasms with Huysmans's hero Des Esseintes. These interests are described by Wilde in an astonishing sequence of economical transcriptions, drawing on books he had recently reviewed, or on sources like the South Kensington Museum Handbooks for Precious Stones or Textile Fabrics. The descriptions are not particularly memorable, relying for effect on sheer cumulative weight of example, rather than on any sensory finesse in the language.

As to Dorian's sins, Wilde offers no detail. Here, indeed, as later in *De Profundis,* he appears obsessed by the word sin itself, as though its use was self-explanatory. Instead of the particularity of Huysmans—Des Esseintes's encounters with Miss Urania the American acrobat, or the ventriloquist enacting Flaubert's Chimera and Sphinx—Wilde offers only the disconcerting tone of popular fiction:

It was said that on one occasion, when he was brought into the smoking-room of the Churchill, the Duke of Berwick and another gentleman got up in a marked manner and went out. Curious stories became current about him after he had passed his twenty-fifth year. It was rumoured that he had been seen brawling with foreign sailors in a low den in the distant parts of Whitechapel, and that he consorted with thieves and coiners and knew the mysteries of their trade.

The style is reminiscent of the adventure fiction of John Buchan.

What holds the work together, here as throughout *The Picture of Dorian Gray,* is the sequence of passages which describe Dorian's relationship with his soul; the occasion when

> he himself would creep upstairs to the locked room, open the door with the key that never left him now, and stand, with a mirror, in front of the portrait that Basil Hallward had painted of him, looking at the evil and ageing face on the canvas, and now at the fair young face that laughed back at him from the polished glass. The very sharpness of the contrast used to quicken his sense of pleasure. He grew more and more enamoured of his own beauty, more and more interested in the corruption of his own soul. He would examine with minute care, and sometimes with a monstrous and terrible delight, the hideous lines that seared the wrinkling forehead or crawled around the heavy sensual mouth, wondering sometimes which were the more horrible, the signs of sin or the signs of age. He would place his white hands beside the coarse bloated hands of the picture, and smile. He mocked the misshapen body and the failing limbs.

This and similar passages convey a psychological conviction that validates Dorian's experiments in Hedonism, and precipitates the final crushing of conscience expressed through the murder of Basil Hallward, who calls, good angel-like, to ask Dorian if the terrible rumours he has heard about him are true. The two chapters which describe this episode, Chapters 12 and 13, contain the full range of Gothic effects: damp odour of mildewed candles, cold current of air, exclamations of horror, and finally the drip, drip of blood on threadbare carpet, and the secret press in the wainscotting. Here Wilde strikes one as being wholly in command of the idiom, using it consciously for precise effect. In the following chapter, he has Dorian stretch out on the sofa reading poems from Gautier's *Emaux et camées* while he awaits the arrival of his scientist friend Campbell, whom he blackmails into disposing of Hallward's body. The contrast between the two frames of reference, the decadent and the Gothic, seems appropriate both in literary and psychological terms:

> When he had stretched himself on the sofa, he looked at the title-page of the book. It was Gautier's *Emaux et camées,* Charpentier's Japanese-paper edition, with the Jacquemart etching. The binding was of citron-green leather, with a design of gilt trellis-work and dotted pomegranates. It had been given to him by Adrian Singleton. As he turned over the pages his eye fell on the poem about the hand of Lacenaire, the cold yellow hand 'du supplice encore mal lavée', with its downy red hairs and its 'doigts de faune'. He glanced at his own white taper fingers, shuddering slightly in spite of himself, and passed on . . .

Lacenaire, the murderer executed by guillotine, with his 'cold yellow hand', is juxtaposed with Dorian, who has committed a comparable crime, with his white taper fingers. But even when Lacenaire is transmuted into art, the trace of reality is too disturbing, and Dorian moves on to Gautier's exquisite lines upon Venice:

> Devant une façade rose,
> Sur le marbre d'un escalier.

Dorian's memories of Venice, however, are haunted by the recollection that Basil Hallward had been with him for part of the time; and even Gautier's evocation of the Sphinx cannot distract him from the terror of what he has done.

In the novel's original scheme, the horror of the disposal of Hallward's body, and the corresponding reaction registered by the picture, an image of 'loathsome red dew that gleamed, wet and glistening, on one of the hands, as though the canvas had sweated blood', leads swiftly on to the final episode, Dorian's attempt to commit a good action, his terrible discovery that he is incapable of change and the culminating act of destruction with the knife. While the *Lippincott* version is shocking in its abruptness, the four chapters which Wilde inserted here flesh out the course of Dorian's life, intensify our sense of his suffering and clarify the persona of Lord Henry. There are two London episodes, a society dinner party at Lady Narborough's and Dorian's visit to the London underworld of dockland opium dens; and two contrasting sequences at Dorian's country house, Selby Royal, one in the conservatory, a setting for elegant conversation, and the other in the pinewoods, where James Vane is accidentally shot. Throughout these scenes there is a recurrent motif of death. While Dorian receives repeated reassurances that he is safe, both from events and from Lord Henry, the sense that he is damned becomes increasingly insistent.

These chapters contain numerous echoes of Wilde's other work. Lady Narborough seems like a preliminary sketch for Lady Hunstanton, and several of Lord Henry's conversational flourishes will be given to Lord Illingworth in *A Woman of No Importance,* while Madame de Ferrol, *décolletée* in Vienna, presages Mrs Cheveley in *An Ideal Husband.* The rhythms, and indeed some of the content, of the dialogue between Lord Henry and the Duchess of Monmouth recur in Lord Illingworth's verbal fencing with Mrs Allonby. The descriptions of the London underworld reflect similar images in **'Lord Arthur Savile's Crime'** and **'The Harlot's House':**

> Most of the windows were dark, but now and then fantastic shadows were silhouetted against some lamp-lit blind. He watched them curiously. They moved like monstrous marionettes, and made gestures like live things.

Such echoes and repetitions might be taken sim-

ply as the consequence of hasty writing; more probably, they indicate Wilde's attempts to create a satisfactory unity out of the ideas, images and styles which
were his current concern. There are, too, passages
which have more resonance when read in conjunction
with *De Profundis,* and even *The Ballad of Reading
Gaol:*

> There are moments, psychologists tell us, when the
> passion for sin, or for what the world calls sin, so
> dominates a nature, that every fibre of the body, as
> every cell of the brain, seems to be instinct with
> fearful impulses. Men and women at such moments
> lose the freedom of their will. They move to their
> terrible end as automatons move. Choice is taken
> from them, and conscience is either killed, or, if it
> lives at all, lives but to give rebellion its fascination,
> and disobedience its charm. For all sins, as theolo-
> gians weary not of reminding us, are sins of disobe-
> dience. When that high spirit, that morning-star of
> evil, fell from heaven, it was as a rebel that he fell.
> Callous, concentrated on evil, with strained mind
> and soul hungry for rebellion, Dorian Gray hastened
> on, quickening his step as he went, but as he darted
> aside into a dim archway, that had served him often
> as a short cut to the ill-famed place where he was
> going, he felt himself suddenly seized from behind,
> and before he had time to defend himself he was
> thrust back against the wall, with a brutal hand
> round his throat.

In contexts such as this, Wilde gives indications that
the novel is a portrait of the artist; James Joyce detected
in it 'some wish to put himself before the world'.

If Wilde was intending to 'put himself before the
world', he contrived to do it in a complex, multiple
form. Pater, reviewing the novel, comments that Wilde
is 'impersonal: seems not to have identified himself
with any one of his characters.' Wilde himself wrote:
'Basil Hallward is what I think I am: Lord Henry what
the world thinks me: Dorian what I would like to
be—in other ages, perhaps.' In Wilde's myth, Basil Hallward is killed; Dorian, an image of perpetual youth, is
spiritually dead; and Lord Henry refuses to acknowledge the existence of the soul. Earlier on the night of
Dorian's death Lord Henry recounts to him how he
heard a London street-preacher yelling out, 'what does
it profit a man if he gain the whole world and lose—
how does the quotation run?—his own soul':

> 'I thought of telling the prophet that Art had a soul,
> but that man had not. I am afraid, however, he
> would not have understood me.'

> 'Don't, Harry. The soul is a terrible reality. It can be
> bought, and sold, and bartered away. It can be poi-
> soned, or made perfect. There is a soul in each one
> of us. I know it.'

> 'Do you feel quite sure of that, Dorian?'

> 'Quite sure.'

> 'Ah! then it must be an illusion. The things one feels
> absolutely certain about are never true. That is the
> fatality of Faith, and the lesson of Romance. How
> grave you are! Don't be so serious. What have you
> or I to do with the superstitions of our age? No: we
> have given up our belief in the soul. Play me some-
> thing. Play me a nocturne, Dorian, and, as you play,
> tell me, in a low voice, how you have kept your
> youth. You must have some secret. I am only ten
> years older than you are, and I am wrinkled, and
> worn, and yellow. You are really wonderful, Dorian.
> You have never looked more charming than you do
> to-night.'

The ageing Lord Henry, distancing death and divorce with Chopin nocturnes, curing the soul by means
of the sense, uses Dorian as the corner-stone of his philosophy, the perfect completed image:

> At present you are a perfect type. Don't make your-
> self incomplete. You are quite flawless now . . . I am
> so glad that you have never done anything, never
> carved a statue, or painted a picture, or produced
> anything outside of yourself ! Life has been your art.
> You have set yourself to music. Your days are your
> sonnets.

It is significant that Wilde places the emphasis
throughout the penultimate chapter on Lord Henry,
while Dorian is shown retreating more and more into
his renunciation of sin, and his resolution to be good.
Lord Henry's affirmations become increasingly declamatory as the scene reaches its close—'Art has no influence upon action. It annihilates the desire to act. It is
superbly sterile'—echoing the Preface which Wilde attached to the revised work. As Dorian leaves, he hesitates for a moment, 'as if he had something more to say.
Then he sighed and went out'. The work's final image,
the dead man 'withered, wrinkled, and loathsome of
visage', recognisable only by his rings, is set against the
previous chapter's farewell, and the plan to ride in the
park to see the lilacs. (pp. 67-80)

Peter Raby, in his *Oscar Wilde,* Cambridge University Press,
1988, 164 p.

SOURCES FOR FURTHER STUDY

Ellmann, Richard. *Oscar Wilde.* New York: Alfred A. Knopf, 1988, 680 p.

> Highly acclaimed biography.

——, ed. *Oscar Wilde: A Collection of Critical Essays.* Englewood Cliffs, N.J.: Prentice-Hall, 1969, 180 p.

> Critical essays and poetical tributes by W. B. Yeats, André Gide, Alfred Douglas, John Betjeman, Thomas Mann, and Jorge Luis Borges, among others.

Ericksen, Donald H. *Oscar Wilde.* Boston: Twayne Publishers, 1977, 175 p.

> Discusses sources, plot, characterization, language, and critical reception of Wilde's best-known works.

Mikhail, E. H. *Oscar Wilde: An Annotated Bibliography of Criticism.* Totowa, N.J.: Rowman and Littlefield, 1978, 249 p.

> Lists book and play reviews, earlier bibliographies of criticism, and whole and partial books of criticism on Wilde.

——, ed. *Oscar Wilde: Interviews and Recollections, Vol. I.* New York: Barnes & Noble, 1979, 255 p.

> Includes reminiscences of Wilde by friends, acquaintances, relatives, and professional associates.

Woodcock, George. *The Paradox of Oscar Wilde.* London, New York: T. V. Boardman & Co., 1949, 239 p.

> Devoted to resolving the contradictions of Wilde the man and the artist. Woodcock attempts an integrated view of Wilde as both serious thinker and superficial poseur and as Christian and pagan.

Thornton Wilder

1897-1975

American dramatist, novelist, and essayist.

INTRODUCTION

*T*he only author to receive Pulitzer Prizes for both drama and fiction, Wilder is best known for his award-winning plays *Our Town* (1938) and *The Skin of Our Teeth* (1942). The values Wilder promoted in his work—Christian morality, community, the family, appreciation of everyday pleasures—are traditional, yet his theatrical methods were highly unorthodox. Considered among the most innovative dramatists of the early twentieth century, he rejected naturalism in favor of techniques that frankly acknowledged the artifice of the theater and linked the lives of his characters with such universal themes as mortality and the existence of God. While critical assessments of Wilder's optimistic and life-affirming dramas have varied, *Our Town* endures as a widely performed American classic.

Wilder was born in Madison, Wisconsin, the surviving member of a pair of twin boys. In 1906, his father, Amos Parker Wilder, relocated the family to Hong Kong after accepting a post in the United States foreign service, the first of many such moves. As a result, Wilder obtained his early formal education from a variety of institutions that included German schools in Hong Kong and Shanghai, as well as the China Inland Mission School at Chefoo. In 1915, he graduated from high school in Berkeley, California, where he, with his mother and siblings, had ultimately settled while his father continued to work in the Far East. Wilder then entered Oberlin College at the insistence of his father, but after two years of study, the elder Wilder compelled him to withdraw and enter Yale. As a student, Wilder began writing short plays and essays for publication in the *Yale Literary Review,* and hoped, upon obtaining his degree, to pursue writing as a career. However, his father, concerned that his son maintain a stable income for the family, secured him a teaching position at Lawrenceville School, a select preparatory school for boys in Princeton, New Jersey.

During his early years at Lawrenceville, Wilder spent his summers chaperoning wealthy students on tours of Europe, an experience that inspired his first novel, *The Cabala*. Its publication in 1926 coincided with the first professional production of one of his plays, *The Trumpet Shall Sound*. A thinly disguised allegory concerning God's mercy toward humanity, the play focuses upon a master who forgives his servants after learning that they have deceived him. Considered significantly less accomplished than his later dramas, *The Trumpet Shall Sound* received little notice and closed promptly. Wilder continued writing, however, and in 1927 published his second novel, *The Bridge at San Luis Rey*. An extraordinary critical and popular success, this story of eighteenth-century Peru earned Wilder the Pulitzer Prize and afforded him the financial security to resign his position at Lawrenceville. He next published *The Angel That Troubled the Waters and Other Plays* (1928), a collection of extremely short scenes, many of which he wrote as a student at Oberlin College. These plays, which critics tend to regard as affected, have yet to be produced and are considered virtually impossible for the theater. For example, one stage direction reads: "Suddenly the thirty pieces of silver are cast upward from the revolted hand of Judas. They hurtle through the skies, flinging their enormous shadows across the stars, and continue falling forever through the vast funnel of space." Yet this blatant disregard for the limitations of the stage prefigures the innovative techniques of *Our Town* and *The Skin of Our Teeth*, which are considered among Wilder's major contributions to the theater.

When Wilder's next novel, *The Woman of Andros* (1930), appeared following the onset of the Great Depression, Michael Gold, a leader of the proletarian school of criticism, condemned its story of young love in ancient Greece as escapist and rebuked the author for not using his art to champion much needed social reform. Gold's scathing comments in part prompted Wilder to abandon historical settings and to focus upon elements of his own time and place. The plays collected in *The Long Christmas Dinner and Other Plays in One Act* (1931) reflect this shift while also revealing Wilder's growing interest in the experimental dramas of European playwrights such as Bertolt Brecht. Two plays of the collection, "Pullman Car Hiawatha" and "The Happy Journey to Trenton and Camden" integrate some of the original staging techniques that critics consider hallmarks of Wilder's work. Both plays feature a stage manager who speaks directly to the audience and who occasionally enters the drama as a minor character. Both are also devoid of scenery, using chairs as their only props. The title play, "The Long Christmas Dinner," prefigures the predominant theme

of *Our Town*—that life is a brief yet significant interlude before death—through its unusual presentation of a single holiday feast spanning ninety years. In the play, family members enter and exit through two doors representing birth and death while their time onstage represents their entire lives.

During the 1930s, Wilder gained entry into New York theatrical circles through his friendship with Alexander Woollcott, the influential critic for the *New York Times* to whom he dedicated *Our Town*, his first original Broadway offering. In *Our Town*, the central role belongs to the omniscient Stage Manager, who narrates the action, jokes with the audience, and, through his philosophizing, explicitly connects the people of the small New Hampshire town of Grover's Corners with the universe as a whole. As with Wilder's earlier dramas, *Our Town* features minimal props and scenery while the characters function as symbols rather than fully developed individuals. In the first two acts, entitled "Daily Life" and "Love and Marriage," he traces the prosaic existence of the Webbs and the Gibbses, two families who are united by the marriage of their children, George and Emily. In the final act, "Death," Emily, who has died giving birth, arrives at the town cemetery where other deceased members of the community sit quietly in chairs. Unlike the others, who have grown detached from earthly concerns, Emily longs to return to Grover's Corners, and so obtains the permission of the Stage Manager to relive her twelfth birthday. However, the experience becomes too painful when, knowing the future, she attempts to savor each trivial moment with her family but cannot because "it goes so fast. We barely have time to look at one another." Returning to the dead, Emily bids farewell to "new-ironed dresses and hot baths," before expressing the central moral of the play that human beings must "realize life while they live it."

While opening to an initially cool reception, *Our Town* eventually ran for 336 performances and earned Wilder his second Pulitzer Prize, thereby establishing his reputation as a major dramatist. Observers now consider it America's most produced play, and while some regard it as sentimental, most critics praise *Our Town* as a moving allegory that transcends the requirements of realistic theater. Rex Burbank asserted: "The artistic problem basic to *Our Town* is that of showing that the events of life are at once not all they could be because they are taken for granted—but are priceless. Wilder meets this problem by repeating the quotidian scenes and viewing them and the central actions of each act . . . from different perspectives of time and space and different metaphysical vantage points. By relating the ordinary events in the lives of these ordinary people to a metaphysical framework that broadens with each act, he is able to portray life as being at once significant and trivial, noble and absurd, miraculous and humdrum."

Wilder's reputation as a playwright also rests on two comedies, *The Matchmaker* (1955; originally performed as *The Merchant of Yonkers,* 1938) and *The Skin of Our Teeth.* A slightly revised version of his play *The Merchant of Yonkers: A Farce in Four Acts, The Matchmaker* is Wilder's most conventionally staged long play. It is based on nineteenth-century Viennese playwright Johann Nestroy's farce *Einen Jux will er sich machen,* which in turn was adapted from John Oxenford's English comedy *A Day Well Spent.* The title character of *The Matchmaker* is Dolly Levi, a vivacious, worldly-wise widow who attempts to dissuade an uncharitable merchant from opposing the marriage of his niece to an impoverished artist. In the course of her endeavor, she woos the merchant for herself and convinces him that his wealth should not be saved but spent for the good of all. Most consider this comedy a work of light entertainment that shares with Wilder's other writings a celebratory attitude towards life and adventure. However, others concur with David Castronovo's assessment that "for a play that has earned a reputation as a trivial farce, [*The Matchmaker*] offers a clever assessment of life in a competitive society. . . . Bubbling out of this farcical evening is a series of observations about isolation, neurotic self-involvement, and the waste of human potential." In 1964, Michael Stewart and Jerry Herman adapted *The Matchmaker* as their popular musical *Hello, Dolly!*

In *The Skin of Our Teeth,* a significantly more ambitious work than *The Matchmaker,* Wilder focuses upon the Antrobuses, a 1940s family from Excelsior, New Jersey, who symbolize humanity through the ages. Together they endure such cataclysmic events as the Ice Age and the Great Flood, as well as the malicious actions of son Henry, whose name was changed from Cain after the "accidental" death of his brother. The humor of *The Skin of Our Teeth* arises from the unexpected juxtaposition of events—for example the Great Flood interrupts a convention of mammals in Atlantic City—as well as from surprising staging techniques that emphasize theatricality. Actors step in and out of their roles to share their "true feelings" with the audience, and the "stage crew" rehearses to fill in for performers who have supposedly taken ill. Through the Antrobuses' struggle to overcome natural disasters and invent such civilizing tools as the wheel and the alphabet, Wilder underscores the ability of the human will to endure and ultimately flourish. While *The Skin of Our Teeth* earned Wilder his third Pulitzer Prize, the play was briefly the subject of controversy when Joseph Campbell and Henry M. Robinson, in a series of articles that appeared in the *Saturday Review,* accused Wilder of plagiarizing James Joyce's *Finnegans Wake.* Retrospective opinion vindicated Wilder's literary borrowing, yet critical reaction to *The Skin of Our Teeth* continues to vary. While some commentators regard the play as a disjointed farce directed toward "middlebrow" sensibilities, others consider it a thoughtful, inventive examination of human frailty.

Wilder's dramatic work following *The Skin of Our Teeth* consisted primarily of revivals, revisions, and productions in foreign countries, particularly Germany, where his work remains very popular. German theater groups produced his drama *The Alcestiad* (1955)—based upon Euripides' *Alcestis*—in its original form, then as an opera with libretto by Wilder. His one-act pieces "The Wreck of the 5:25" (1957)—which centers upon a commuter's attempted suicide—and "Bernice" (1957)—the story of an embezzler and his estranged daughter—both premiered in Germany, as did his satyr play *The Drunken Sisters* (1970). Wilder originally wrote "Bernice" as part of a proposed dramatic cycle entitled *The Seven Deadly Sins.* While he did not complete the series or its companion group *The Seven Ages of Man,* selections from both were performed in 1962, including "Someone from Assisi," "Infancy," and "Childhood." These plays, like many of Wilder's later theatrical offerings, elicited a generally unfavorable critical response. Although Wilder produced no further dramatic works, recognition for his achievements in the theater and other literary fields continued. In 1963, he received the United States Presidential Medal of Freedom and in 1965 was honored with the National Medal of Literature. He also garnered the National Book Award for his penultimate novel *The Eighth Day* (1967). Upon his death in 1975, Wilder was recognized as an accomplished dramatist and man of letters whose innovative works remain integral to discussions of the American theater.

(For further information about Wilder's life and works, see *Contemporary Authors,* Vols. 13-16, 61-64 [obituary]; *Contemporary Literary Criticism,* Vols. 1, 5, 6, 10, 15, 35; *Dictionary of Literary Biography,* Vols. 4, 7, 9; and *Drama Criticism,* Vol. 1.)

CRITICAL COMMENTARY

JOHN MASON BROWN
(essay date 1938)

[A highly respected drama critic and editor for the *Saturday Review* during the 1940s, Brown wrote several critical studies of the American theater. In the following assessment of *Our Town*, written in 1938 and later included in his *Dramatis Personae* (1963), he supports Wilder's rejection of contemporary political and social issues while lauding his portrayal of such fundamental human concerns as death, love, and the passage of time.]

No scenery is required for this play. Perhaps a few dusty flats may be seen leaning against the brick wall at the back of the stage. . . . The Stage Manager not only moves forward and withdraws the few properties that are required, but he reads from a typescript the lines of all the minor characters. He reads them clearly, but with little attempt at characterization, scarcely troubling himself to alter his voice, even when he responds in the person of a child or a woman. As the curtain rises the Stage Manager is leaning lazily against the proscenium pillar at the audience's left. He is smoking.

The chances are that if, during the course of one of those parlor games which offer to hostesses and guests alike an ideal retreat from bridge and conversation, some playgoers were asked to identify the play for which these stage directions were intended, they would not guess *Julius Caesar* at the Mercury. Yet they might be sufficiently foolhardy, in this season of sceneryless scripts, to pick upon Mr. Blitzstein's *The Cradle Will Rock* or Mr. Wilder's *Our Town.* If they choose *Our Town,* because the demand for a Stage Manager, leaning against the proscenium and smoking a pipe, brought the genial Frank Craven, [the originator of the role], to their minds, they would at least be "getting warm," as the gamesters have it. Still they would be very far from being "hot." Although Mr. Wilder is the author of these stage directions, *Our Town* is not the play for which they were intended. They were written for a charming one-act of his called **"The Happy Journey to Trenton and Camden"** which was copyrighted in 1931 and which can be found not only in a volume of his short plays called **"The Long Christmas Dinner"** but also in Professor Alexander Woolcott's first *Reader.*

I go back to Mr. Wilder's earlier usage of this frankly presentational form only because some theatregoers have been tempted to talk and write about *Our Town* as if it were a production which found Mr. Wilder and Mr. Harris trying to climb upon the Mercury's band wagon. It is important to note that when Mr. Wilder sent the script of **"The Happy Journey"** to Washington seven years ago, all he was attempting to copyright was the use to which he put this particular form in this particular script, and not the form itself. What really matters in all art is this very thing. Forms and subjects are comparatively few. Yet they can be made as various as are the talents of the many artists who have repossessed them.

Playgoers with short memories have found Benrimo's popularization of the conventions of the Chinese stage in *The Yellow Jacket* a convenient means of pigeonholing the outward form of *Our Town.* They might just as readily have recalled Quince, drawing up a bill of properties for *Pyramus and Thisbe,* "such as our play wants." Or the Chorus in *Henry V* asking the audience to let their "imaginary forces work." Or Mei Lan-fang. Or Ruth Draper and Cornelia Otis Skinner. Or the *Lutterworth Christmas Play.* Or the *Quem Quaeritis* trope. The form Mr. Wilder has used is as old as the theatre's ageless game of "let's pretend" and as new as the last time it has been employed effectively. The cooperation it asks an audience to contribute is at heart the very same cooperation which the most realistic and heavily documented productions invite playgoers to grant. The major difference is one of degree. Both types of production depend in the last analysis upon their audiences to supply that final belief which is the mandate under which all theatrical illusion operates. The form Mr. Wilder uses is franker, that is all. It does not attempt to hide the fact that it is make-believe. Instead it asks its audiences to do some of the work, to enter openly and gladly into the imaginative conspiracy known as the successful staging of a play.

What such a drama as Mr. Wilder's does, of course, is to strip theatrical illusion down to its essentials. Mr. Wilder has the best of good reasons for so doing. What he has done in *Our Town* is to strip life down to its essentials, too. There is nothing of the "stunt" about the old-new form he has employed. His form is the inevitable one his content demands. Indeed, so inevitable is it, and hence so right, that I, for one, must confess I lost all awareness of it merely as a form a few minutes after Mr. Craven had begun to set the stage by putting a few chairs in place. There have been those who have been bothered because the pantomime

Principal Works

The Cabala (novel) 1926

The Trumpet Shall Sound (drama) 1926

The Bridge of San Luis Rey (novel) 1927

The Angel That Troubled the Waters and Other Plays (drama) 1928

The Woman of Andros (novel) 1930

*The Long Christmas Dinner and Other Plays in One Act (drama) 1931

Heaven's My Destination (novel) 1934

Our Town (drama) 1938

The Merchant of Yonkers: A Farce in Four Acts (drama) 1938; revised as The Matchmaker, 1955

The Skin of Our Teeth (drama) 1942

Our Century (drama) 1947

The Ides of March (novel) 1948

The Alcestiad (drama) 1955; produced as A Life in the Sun 1955

"Bernice" (drama) 1957

"The Wreck of the 5:25" (drama) 1957

†Plays for Bleeker Street (drama) 1962

The Eighth Day (novel) 1967

The Drunken Sisters (drama) 1970

Theophilus North (novel) 1974

American Characteristics and Other Essays (nonfiction) 1979

*Contains "The Long Christmas Dinner," "Queens of France," "Pullman Car Hiawatha," "Love and How to Cure It," "Such Things Only Happen in Books," and "The Happy Journey to Trenton and Camden."

†Includes "Infancy," "Childhood," and "Someone from Assisi."

was not consistent, because real umbrellas were carried and no visible lawnmower was pushed, because naturalistic offstage sounds serve as echoes to the actions indicated on stage. I was not one of the bothered. I found myself surrendering, especially during the first two acts, to the spell of the beautiful and infinitely tender play Mr. Wilder has written.

John Anderson has likened *Our Town* to India's rope trick. He has pointed out it is the kind of play at which you either see the boy and the rope, or you don't. Although I refuse to admit there is anything of the fakir's touch in *Our Town,* I think I understand what Mr. Anderson means. Mr. Wilder's is, from the audience point of view, an exceptionally personal play. More than most plays, since by its sweet simplicity it seeks to get in contact with the inmost nerves of our living, it is the kind of drama which depends upon what we bring to it.

Mr. Wilder's play is concerned with the universal importance of those unimportant details which figure in the lives of men and women everywhere. His Grover's Corners is a New Hampshire town inhabited by decent New England people. The very averageness of these quiet, patient people is the point at which our lives and all living become a part of their experience. Yet Mr. Wilder's play involves more than a New England township. It burrows into the essence of the growing-up, the marrying, the living, and the dying of all of us who sit before it and are included by it. The task to which Mr. Wilder has set himself is one which Hardy had in mind in a far less human, more grandiose way, when he had the Chorus in *The Dynasts* say:

We'll close up Time, as a bird its van,
We'll traverse Space, as Spirits can,
Link pulses severed by leagues and years,
Bring cradles into touch with biers.

Mr. Wilder succeeds admirably in doing this. He shows us the simple pattern behind all simple living. He permits us to share in the inevitable anguishes and joys, the hopes and cruel separations to which men have been heir since the smoke puffed up the chimneys in Greece.

To my surprise I have encountered the complaint that Mr. Wilder's Grover's Corners is not like Middletown, U.S.A. It lacks brothels, race riots, huge factories, front-page scandals, social workers, union problems, lynchings, agitators, and strikes. The ears of its citizens are more familiar with the song of the robin than they are with the sirens of hurrying police cars. Its young people are stimulated to courtship by moonlight rather than by moonshine. They drink soda water instead of gin. Their rendezvous are held in drug stores rather than in night clubs. Their parents are hard-working people. They are quiet, self-respecting, God-fearing Yankees who get up early to do their day's work and meet their responsibilities and their losses without whining. The church organist may tipple, and thereby cause some gossip. But he is a neighbor, and the only good-neighbor policy they care about begins at home.

They do not murder or steal, borrow or beg, blackmail or oppress. Furthermore, they face the rushing years without complaints as comparatively happy mortals. Therefore to certain realists they seem unreal. "No historian," one critic has written "has ever claimed that a town like Mr. Wilder's was ever so idyllic as to be free from intolerance and injustice." Mr. Wilder does not make this claim himself. His small-town editor admits Grover's Corners is "little better behaved than most towns." Neither is Mr. Wilder working as the ordinary historian works. His interests are totally different interests.

He is not concerned with social trends, with economic conditions, with pivotal events, or glittering personalities. He sings not of arms and the man, but of those small events which loom so large in the daily lives of each of us, and which are usually unsung. His interest is the unexceptional, the average, the personal. His preoccupation is what lies beneath the surface and the routine of our lives, and is common to all our hearts and all our experience. It is not so much of the streets of a New England Town he writes as of the clean white spire which rises above them.

There are hundreds of fat books written each year on complicated subjects by authors who are not writers at all. But the ageless achievement of the true writers has always been to bring a new illumination to the simplest facts of life. That illumination has ever been a precious talent given only to a few. It is because Mr. Wilder brings this illumination to his picture of Grover's Corners that I admire *Our Town.* New Hampshire is the state which can claim Mr. Wilder's village, but his vision of it has been large enough to include all of us, no matter where we may come from, among its inhabitants. Personally, I should as soon think of condemning the Twenty-third Psalm because it lacks the factual observation of Sinclair Lewis and the social point of view of Granville Hicks as I would of accusing *Our Town* of being too unrealistically observed.

Anyone who hears only the milk bottles clink when early morning has come once again to Grover's Corners has not heard what Mr. Wilder wants them to hear. These milk bottles are merely the spokesmen of time, symbols for the bigness of little things. In terms of the Gibbses and the Webbs, Mr. Wilder gives the pattern of repetition of each small day's planning, each small life's fruition and decline. He makes us feel the swift passage of the years, our blindness in meeting their race, the sense that our lives go rushing past so quickly that we have scarcely time in which to hold our breaths.

Only once does he fail us seriously. This is in his scene in the bleak graveyard on the hill. Although he seeks there to create the image of the dead who have lost their interest in life, he has not been able to capture the true greatness of vision which finds them at last unfettered from the minutiae of existence. Both his phrasing and his thinking are inadequate here. He chills the living by removing his dead even from compassion.

Nonetheless Mr. Wilder's is a remarkable play, one of the sagest, warmest, and most deeply human scripts to have come out of our theatre. It is the kind of play which suspends us in time, making us weep for our own vanished youth at the same time we are sobbing for the short-lived pleasures and sufferings which we know await our children. Geographically *Our Town* can be found at an imaginary place known as "Grover's Corners, Sultan County, New Hampshire, United States of America, Continent of North America, Western Hemisphere, the Earth, the Solar System, the Uni-

verse, the Mind of God." Mr. Wilder's play is laid in no imaginary place. It becomes a reality in the human heart. (pp. 79-84)

John Mason Brown, "Wilder's 'Our Town'," in his *Dramatis Personae: A Retrospective Show,* The Viking Press, 1963, pp. 79-84.

MARY McCARTHY
(essay date 1938)

[An accomplished editor and novelist, McCarthy infused her critical work with the sophistication, wit, satire, and caustic frankness that characterizes much of her acclaimed fiction, including *The Company She Keeps* (1942) and *The Group* (1963). Her review of *Our Town*, written while she served as theater critic for the *Partisan Review*, praises Wilder's theatrical innovations and his lyric evocation of life's "tragic velocity." The debut production of *Our Town* opened in New York on 4 February 1938 and featured Frank Craven as the Stage Manager. It was performed 336 times in its initial run.]

Mr. Thornton Wilder's play, *Our Town,* at the Morosco, is the inverse of [Marc Blitztein's] *The Cradle Will Rock.* Both plays are done without settings or props; both employ a commentator who serves as intermediary between actors and audience; both deal with an American town. But while Mr. Blitzstein is a sort of public prosecutor of Steeltown of 1937, Mr. Frank Craven, stage manager and spokesman for Mr. Wilder, appears as a kind of indulgent defense attorney for a certain small New England town of thirty years ago. Mr. Blitzstein evokes an industrial town which is abstract and odious; Mr. Craven and Mr. Wilder, a home town which is concrete and dear. *Our Town,* like *Ah, Wilderness,* is an exercise in memory, but it differs from the O'Neill work in that it is not a play in the accepted sense of the term. It is essentially lyric, not dramatic. The tragic velocity of life, the elusive nature of experience, which can never be stopped or even truly felt at any given point, are the themes of the play—themes familiar enough in lyric poetry, but never met, except incidentally, in drama. Mr. Wilder, in attempting to give these themes theatrical form, was obliged, paradoxically, to abandon almost all the conventions of the theatre.

In the first place, he has dismissed scenery and props as irrelevant to, and, indeed, incongruous with his purpose. In the second place, he has invented the character of the stage manager, an affable, homespun conjuror who holds the power of life and death over the other characters, a local citizen who is in the town and outside of it at the same time. In the third place, he has taken what is accessory to the ordinary play, that is, exposition, and made it the main substance of his. The greater part of the first two acts is devoted to the imparting of information, to situating the town in time, space, politics, sociology, economics, and geology. But where in the conventional play, such pieces of information are insinuated into the plot or sugared over with stage business, and repartee, in Mr. Wilder's play they are communicated directly; they take the place of plot, stage business, and repartee. Mr. Craven himself tells the biographies of the townspeople; he calls in an expert from the state college to give a scientific picture of the town, and the editor of the local newspaper to describe its social conditions. The action which is intermittently progressing on the stage merely illustrates Mr. Craven's talk. Mr. Wilder's fourth innovation is the most striking. In order to dramatize his feelings about life he has literally raised the dead. At the opening of the third act a group of people are discovered sitting in rows on one side of the stage; some of the faces are familiar, some are new. They are speaking quite naturally and calmly, and it is not until one has listened to them for some minutes that one realizes that this is the cemetery and these are the dead. A young woman whom we have seen grow up and marry the boy next door has died in childbirth; a small shabby funeral procession is bringing her to join her relatives and neighbors. Only when she is actually buried does the play proper begin. She has not yet reached the serenity of the long dead, and she yearns to return to the world. With the permission of the stage manager and against the advice of the dead, she goes back—to a birthday of her childhood. Hardly a fraction of that day has passed, however, before she retreats gratefully to the cemetery, for she has perceived that the tragedy of life lies in the fragmentary and imperfect awareness of the living.

Mr. Wilder's play is, in a sense, a refutation of its own thesis. *Our Town* is purely and simply an act of awareness, a demonstration of the fact that in a work of art, at least, experience *can* be arrested, imprisoned, and preserved. The perspective of death, which Mr. Wilder has chosen, gives an extra poignancy and intensity to the small-town life whose essence he is trying so urgently to communicate. The little boy delivering papers, for example, becomes more touching, more meaningful and important, when Mr. Craven announces casually that he is going to be killed in the War. The boy's morning round, for the spectator, is transfigured into an absorbing ritual; the unconsciousness of the character has heightened the consciousness of the audience. The perspective is, to be sure, hazardous: it invites bathos and sententiousness. Yet Mr. Wilder has used it honorably. He forbids the spectator to dote on that town of the past. He is concerned only with saying: this is how it was, though then we did not know it. Once in a while, of course, his memory fails him, for young love was never so baldly and tritely

gauche as his scene in the soda fountain suggests. This is, however, a deficiency of imagination, not an error of taste; and except in the third act, where the dead give some rather imprecise and inapposite definitions of the nature of the afterlife, the play keeps its balance beautifully. In this feat of equilibrium Mr. Wilder has had the complete cooperation of Mr. Craven, the serene, inexorable matter-of-factness of whose performance acts as a discipline upon the audience. Mr. Craven makes one quite definitely homesick, but pulls one up sharp if one begins to blubber about it. (pp. 26-9)

Mary McCarthy, "Class Angles and a Wilder Classic," in her *Sights and Spectacles: 1937-1956.* Farrar, Straus and Cudahy, 1956, pp. 21-9.

ARTHUR MILLER
(essay date 1956)

[The author of *Death of a Salesman* (1949), *The Crucible* (1953), and numerous other dramatic works, Miller is ranked among the most important and influential American playwrights since World War II. In the following excerpt, he praises *Our Town* as a poetic work that effectively links daily life to "the generality of men which is our society and our world."]

We recognize now that a play can be poetic without verse, and it is in this middle area that the complexities of tracing the influence of the family and social elements upon the form [are] . . . more troublesome. *Our Town* by Thornton Wilder is such a play, and it is important not only for itself but because it is the progenitor of many other works.

This is a family play which deals with the traditional family figures, the father, mother, brother, sister. At the same time it uses this particular family as a prism through which is reflected the author's basic idea, his informing principle—which can be stated as the indestructibility, the everlastingness, of the family and the community, its rhythm of life, its rootedness in the essentially safe cosmos despite troubles, wracks, and seemingly disastrous, but essentially temporary, dislocations.

Technically it is not arbitrary in any detail. Instead of a family living room or a house, we are shown a bare stage on which actors set chairs, a table, a ladder to represent a staircase or an upper floor, and so on. A narrator is kept in the foreground as though to remind us that this is not so much "real life" as an abstraction of it—in other words, a stage. It is clearly a poetic rather than a realistic play. What makes it that? Well, let us first imagine what would make it more realistic.

Would a real set make it realistic? Not likely. A real set would only discomfit us by drawing attention to what would then appear to be a slightly unearthly quality about the characterizations. We should probably say, "People don't really act like that." In addition, the characterization of the whole town could not be accomplished with anything like its present vividness if the narrator were removed, as he would have to be from a realistic set, and if the entrances and exits of the environmental people, the townspeople, had to be justified with the usual motives and machinery of Realism.

The preoccupation of the entire play is quite what the title implies—the town, the society, and not primarily this particular family—and every stylistic means used is to the end that the family foreground be kept in its place, merely as a foreground for the larger context behind and around it. In my opinion, it is this larger context, the town and its enlarging, widening significance, that is the bridge to the poetic for this play. Cut out the town and you will cut out the poetry.

The play is worth examining further against the Ibsen form of Realism to which it is inevitably related if only in contrast. Unlike Ibsen, Wilder sees his characters in this play not primarily as personalities, as individuals, but as forces, and he individualizes them only enough to carry the freight, so to speak, of their roles as forces. I do not believe, for instance, that we can think of the brother in this play, or the sister or the mother, as having names other than Brother, Sister, Mother. They are not given that kind of particularity or interior life. They are characterized rather as social factors, in their roles of Brother, Sister, Mother, in *Our Town*. They are drawn, in other words, as forces to enliven and illuminate the author's symbolic vision and his theme, which is that of the family as a timeless, stable quantity which has not only survived all the turmoil of time but is, in addition, beyond the possibility of genuine destruction.

The play is important to any discussion of form because it has achieved a largeness of meaning and an abstraction of style that created that meaning, while at the same time it has moved its audiences subjectively—it has made them laugh and weep as abstract plays rarely if ever do. But it would seem to contradict my contention here. If it is true that the presentation of the family on the stage inevitably forces Realism upon the play, how did this family play manage to transcend Realism to achieve its symbolistic style?

Every form, every style, pays its price for its special advantages. The price paid by *Our Town* is psychological characterization forfeited in the cause of the symbol. I do not believe, as I have said, that the characters are identifiable in a psychological way, but only as figures in the family and social constellation, and this is not meant in criticism, but as a statement of the limits of this form. I would go further and say that it is not *necessary* for every kind of play to do every kind of thing. But if we are after ultimate reality we must make ultimate demands.

I think that had Wilder drawn his characters with a deeper configuration of detail and with a more remorseless quest for private motive and self-interest, for instance, the story as it stands now would have appeared oversentimental and even sweet. I think that if the play tested its own theme more remorselessly, the world it creates of a timeless family and a rhythm of existence beyond the disturbance of social wracks would not remain unshaken. The fact is that the juvenile delinquent is quite directly traced to the breakup of family life and, indeed, to the break in that ongoing, steady rhythm of community life which the play celebrates as indestructible.

I think, further, that the close contact which the play established with its audience was the result of its coincidence with the deep longing of the audience for such stability, a stability which in daylight out on the street does not truly exist. The great plays pursue the idea of loss and deprivation of an earlier state of bliss which the characters feel compelled to return to or to re-create. I think this play forgoes the loss and suffers thereby in its quest for reality, but that the audience supplies the sense of deprivation in its own life experience as it faces what in effect is an idyl of the past. To me, therefore, the play falls short of a form that will press into reality to the limits of reality, if only because it could not plumb the psychological interior lives of its characters and still keep its present form. It is a triumph in that it does open a way toward the dramatization of the larger truths of existence while using the common materials of life. It is a truly poetic play. (pp. 38-9)

Arthur Miller, "The Family in Modern Drama," in *The Atlantic Monthly*, Vol. 197, No. 4, April, 1956, pp. 35-41.

ROBERT W. CORRIGAN
(essay date 1961)

[In the following excerpt from an essay that first appeared in *Educational Theatre Journal* in 1961, Corrigan asserts that while Wilder presents an essentially tragic view of life in his works, he averts despair by espousing an "animal faith" in the world and the universe.]

Thornton Wilder . . . is thought of, together with O'Neill, Miller, and Williams, as one of our "Big Four," and yet his reputation is based on only three full-length plays and was made on one. . . . For some he is the great American satirist; for others he is a soft-hearted sentimentalist; and for still others he is our only "religious" dramatist. Furthermore. . . . Brecht, Ionesco, Duerrenmatt, and Frisch have all acknowledged their debt to this "great and fanatical experimenter." (p. 239)

Wilder has dealt boldly and affirmatively with the themes of Life, Love, and Earth. Each of his plays is a hymn in dramatic form affirming life. But the important question is: What is the nature of this affirmation? It is not, as some would have it, Christian. To begin with, Wilder has no belief—at least as expressed in his plays—in a religion that is revealed or historical. These are basic premises of Christianity. To be sure Wilder is deistic, but as almost all of his critics have pointed out, he is essentially a religious Platonist; and this position must ultimately reject the historic dimension as meaningful. (pp. 239-40)

Wilder is a humanist, an affirming humanist, a "yeasayer to life" as Bernard Hewitt calls him. When we examine the nature of Wilder's humanistic affirmation, what do we discover? His plays celebrate human love, the worth and dignity of man, the values of the ordinary, and the eternity of human values. From the little boy in Wilder's first play who says: "I am not afraid of life. I will astonish it!" to Dolly Levi and her cohorts in adventure in *The Matchmaker,* Wilder has always been on the side of life and life is seen to be most directly affirmed through love. Love, then, is his most persistent theme and it has been for him an inexhaustible subject. Of its worth he is convinced, but it is interesting to note that Wilder has never been able to make any commitments as to the reasons for its worth. Wilder can deal with life and love directly and concretely; but when he moves to the edges of life, the focus becomes less sharp. Certainly, Wilder deals with death—he is not afraid of it, but death in his plays is terminal. When Mrs. Soames says in Act Three of *Our Town:* "My, wasn't life awful—and wonderful," Wilder is reminding us that beauty is recognizable because of change and life is meaningful because of death. But as both John Mason Brown and Winfield Townley Scott have pointed out, Wilder never deals adequately with Death's own meaning. And as for what's beyond death? . . . Life is reality and eternity is the perfected essence of that reality to which we are too often blind and of which we can't stand too much.

It is this tendency, a tendency consistent with his Platonism, to reduce the dimension of eternity so that it can be encompassed by life itself, that has led me to believe, although he has written no tragedies, that Wilder has essentially a tragic rather than a Christian or even religious view of life. To be sure, Wilder has not created any Ahabs or Lears, but this is not because he lacks a tragic vision. He happens to believe, as did Maeterlinck, that there are times in each of our lives when we are conscious of moving into the boundary situations of the tragic realm, and that furthermore, life's tragedies can best be seen in the drama of the everyday, in life's smallest events. For this reason he does not dramatize great conflicts in order to capture the quintessence of tragedy. I think it is important to see the validity of this, although we must point out that while this approach is tragic it is not always dramatic. And this, I think, accounts for the fact Wilder's plays are usually referred to as "hymns", "odes," "songs," and so on, and most critics feel that there isn't much conflict in their plots. (pp. 240-42)

Over and over again in Wilder's work, the belief is stated directly and indirectly that "life is what you make of it." The fullest discussion of the idea is in his novel *The Ides of March,* where Caesar says: "Life has no meaning save that which we confer upon it." . . . [This] is really an existential position and . . . Wilder is very close to Sartre's "Man is condemned to be free."

In fact, upon reflection, we discover that in starting from "Life is what we make of it," Wilder is really in the mainstream of the modern drama beginning with Ibsen and Strindberg. And this is a dangerous position and usually in the drama has led to despair. The image of man in this drama is an image of collapse. . . . I think [Wilder] averts despair—and also tragedy, even though his view of life is essentially tragic—with a kind of Santayana-like belief in life. In fact, Wilder's Platonism can make sense only if it is seen as coming through Santayana. Wilder is, as probably most of us are, saved from despair and its paralyzing effects by what Santayana has called "animal faith." . . . [Our] animal faith, which bids us believe in the external world, is much stronger than all the logical arguments which tend to make life seem absurd. (pp. 242-43)

But although Wilder can assert meaning to life, the meaning is almost in the assertion itself and this is not a very comfortable position to be in. One gets the feeling that Wilder has to keep saying it to make sure that it is true. The danger of this position is that it lacks the necessary polarity and tension for full meaning. This in itself keeps Wilder from being a religious dramatist. In all great religious drama—the works of Sophocles, Calderón, *Everyman,* and in more recent times the later plays of Hofmannsthal, Eliot, and even Fry—there is the backdrop of religious belief which gives meaning to and informs the hero's "life is what you make of it." There is the greater stage . . . [and] the idea of man as a player on the world's stage becomes the very principle of the *mise-en-scène.* For God, the master, speaking from the top of the scaffold, actually orders the world to produce a play under his eyes, featuring man who is to act out his part on earth.

More important than the absence of a religious dimension to Wilder's work, however, are the many experiments he has made in theatrical technique to

---

Wilder on the purpose of *Our Town*:

Our Town is not offered as a picture of life in a New Hampshire village; or as a speculation about the conditions of life after death (that element I merely took from Dante's *Purgatory*). It is an attempt to find a value above all price for the smallest events in our daily life. I have made the claim as preposterous as possible, for I have set the village against the largest dimensions of time and place. The recurrent words in this play (few have noticed it) are "hundreds," "thousands," and "millions." Emily's joys and griefs, her algebra lessons and her birthday presents—what are they when we consider all the billions of girls who have lived, who are living, and who will live? Each individual's assertion to an absolute reality can only be inner, very inner. And here the method of staging finds its justification—in the first two acts there are at least a few chairs and tables; but when she revisits the earth and the kitchen to which she descended on her twelfth birthday, the very chairs and table are gone. Our claim, our hope, our despair are in the mind—not in things, not in "scenery." Molière said that for the theatre all he needed was a platform and a passion or two. The climax of this play needs only five square feet of boarding and the passion to know what life means to us.

Wilder, in a preface to his *Three Plays*, 1957.

---

compensate for this lack of an ultimate perspective. (pp. 243-44)

Wilder has not been interested in psychology and has never used psychological techniques to solve the "modernists'" problems in the theatre. This accounts, I think, for his great influence on the Continental avant-garde dramatists who are rebelling against our psychologically oriented theatre. Wilder sought to achieve the sense of an ultimate perspective by immaterializing the sense of dramatic place on stage. The bare stage of *Our Town* with its chairs, tables, and ladders, together with the Stage Manager's bald exposition, are all that he uses to create the town. The same is true of *The Skin of Our Teeth;* you never really know where the Antrobuses live, nor when. This is his second dominant technique; by destroying the illusion of time, Wilder achieves the effect of any time, all time, each time. But this is risky business, for without the backdrop of an ultimate perspective to inform a play's action, it can very easily become sentimental or satirical, or even pretentious. Wilder at his best keeps this from happening, but his only weapons are wit and irony. And a production which does not succeed in capturing these qualities (as, alas, most college and school productions do not) is bound to turn out pathetic and sentimental; when technique is used as a compensation for the ultimate perspective, the resultant work of art always lies precariously under a Damoclean sword.

It is important that we see the dangers in Wilder's methods, but that a tragic sense of life informs his plays is best illustrated by his sense of destiny. (p. 245)

What Wilder [says] is that human beings cannot stand to have a sense of destiny—the awareness that there is a continuity in all our acts, the awareness that every present moment comes from a past and is directed to a future. Only at moments, usually of emotional crisis, do we have this sense of destiny, this sense of awareness of the future. It is this sense of destiny that is the great human reality and the tragedy of life lies in our fragmentary and imperfect awareness of it. Wilder is aware, like Eliot, that "human kind cannot bear very much reality," but his plays fall short of tragedy because he takes the Platonic escape, he moves into a world that denies the reality and the nemesis of destiny. Nor does he have the solution of an Eliot. For in denying, finally, the reality of destiny he shuts out the possibility of ever providing the means to perfect our fragmentary and imperfect vision. He fails, to use Karl Jaspers' phrase, to go "Beyond Tragedy." That Wilder lacks this dimension is not to discredit him, however, for no other American dramatist more fully affirms that miracle of life which so much modern drama would deny. (p. 246)

Robert W. Corrigan, "Thornton Wilder and the Tragic Sense of Life," in his *The Theatre in Search of a Fix*, Delacorte Press, 1973, pp. 239-46.

MALCOLM GOLDSTEIN

(essay date 1965)

[In the following excerpt, Goldstein characterizes *The Skin of Our Teeth* as a highly successful comedy that combines elements of vaudeville with multilayered characterizations to convey the essential resiliency of the human race.]

The title itself [of *The Skin of Our Teeth*] announces the theme, which is that no matter how hard pressed or frightened, the human race has power to survive its great adventure in a world where physical nature and its own internal conflicts pose endless threats. Beneath this is the idea which forms the core of all Wilder's major works. As the action proceeds it becomes clear that the playwright holds man to be worth preserving for all his absurdity, and holds also that man's lot is worth the effort it costs him to sustain life, however great his misfortunes. For the purposes of this play, Wilder's vision of life is comic, and the action which supports the theme develops the comic possibilities of its disparate sources.

As he had done with *Our Town,* Wilder designed a presentational method which would permit the audience to be drawn toward the characters as individuals with private problems while recognizing that they also function in a broader sphere as the representatives of the entire race. This, however, is only part of a quite elaborate scheme. There is a deliberately old-fashioned, expressionistic vaudeville quality in much of the action which is reminiscent of John Howard Lawson's *Processional* of 1925 and similar plays by Lawson, Michael Gold, and John Dos Passos for the New Playwrights' Theatre of the late 1920's: plays which combine elements of the subliterary stage with the abstract characters of the contemporary expressionistic drama of Europe. It is this vaudevillesque aspect of *The Skin of Our Teeth* which led many reviewers to assert that Wilder had written his play under the influence of Ole Olsen and Chick Johnson's *Hellzapoppin,* a long-running extravaganza contrived from bits of burlesque and revue material, when in fact he had drawn nothing from it at all. On the other hand, George and Maggie Antrobus and their servant Sabina occasionally take part in low-comedy clowning of the vaudeville and Keystone Cops variety at the same time that they represent Adam, Eve, and Lillith and, as the name Antrobus indicates, All Mankind. Yet, because they stand for the entire race, they must have genuine human qualities as well. To stress the essentially human, Wilder frequently lets them drop their stage roles and appear as actors who have been engaged to appear in a play titled *The Skin of Our Teeth.* The development of characters on so many planes at once requires skill in balancing and adjusting dialogue in such a way as to avoid awkwardness in the transition from one level of personality to another. Present always is the danger of baffling the audience where the intention is to instruct. Wilder's success is evident in the intensity of feeling generated by the characters, which at the appropriate moments reaches the heights of *Our Town* without jarring against the comic elements. In observing that the audience sees double while watching the action, Wilder underestimated his achievement; the keenest members of the audience will see not merely two sorts of personality in each character, but three, four, or even five as the play unfolds.

Thus it is apparent that George Antrobus is Adam, since his family is the race itself. But he also is a burlesque comedian who greets his family with epithets bordering on the obscene, and in addition he is a go-getting American businessman, rejoicing in his invention of the wheel and the alphabet, having the time of his life at a convention (of mammals) in Atlantic City, planning impatiently to rebuild his home and his community after nature and warfare have demolished them. On the other hand, and more importantly, his inventions, his pride in the scholarly attainments, such as they are, of his children, and his overriding wish to preserve human knowledge and dignity in the face of disaster establish him as a figure representing the intellectual side of man's nature. Maggie, his wife, is Eve, the eternal homemaker and mother, cherishing even her wicked son Henry (who was called Cain before he killed his brother), looking after the well-being of the race, discovering that the tomato is edible. "If you want to know anything more about Mrs. Antrobus," her servant says, "just go and look at a tigress, and look hard." The home of the Antrobuses stands on Cedar Street in Excelsior, New Jersey, but like the Gibbs and Webb homes it stands at the same time in the center of creation, as the focal point of a struggling but venturesome race to sustain itself.

The sensual quality in mankind is presented by the servant Sabina, raped home like the Sabines and looking after man's desires, as opposed to Maggie, who looks after his needs. A new hat, a dish of ice cream, and a ticket to the movies are all that she requires for happiness, as Maggie remarks in a simplification of the sensual pleasures sought by humanity. By making her a comic figure, Wilder demonstrates his boundless tolerance of this element in human nature. She is potentially dangerous in one moment of the second act when she attempts to seduce Antrobus, but the scene passes too quickly to render her contemptible. Her anti-intellectualism is not confined to her roles as servant and temptress, but spills over into her personality as Miss Somerset, the hard-up actress who is taking the maid's part because no other is available. "I can't invent any words for this play," she says in desperation when Maggie fails to respond to the cue Sabina has fed her, "and I'm glad I can't. I hate this play and every word in it."

> As for me [she continues] I don't understand a single word of it, anyway,—all about the troubles the human race has gone through, there's a subject for you.
>
> Besides the author hasn't made up his silly mind as to whether we're all living back in caves or in New Jersey today, and that's the way it is all the way through.
>
> Oh—why can't we have plays like we used to have—*Peg o' My Heart,* and *Smilin' Thru,* and *The Bat,* good entertainment with a message you can take home with you?
>
> I took this hateful job because I had to. For two years I've sat up in my room living on a sandwich and a cup of tea a day, waiting for better times in the theater. And look at me now: I—I who've played *Rain* and the *Barretts of Wimpole Street* and *First Lady*—God in Heaven!

That she interrupts the action to make this complaint

is in keeping with her part, inasmuch as she moves the play in the direction of comedy and renders cherishable, as an aspect of humanity, the low-brow attitude which allows no time for presumably serious drama. If the plays she mentions have messages, so of course has *The Skin of Our Teeth,* and her deliberate stopping of the action underscores them.

Another of Sabina's functions is the enhancement of the mockery of domestic drama which enters the play in the first and last acts. As the curtain rises at the start, she is present with duster in hand, like the servant in a nineteenth-century play of middle-class household intrigue, to let the audience in on the manners and means of her employers. And as she cleans the room, the flats which form its walls flap, buckle, and fly out of sight in a merry parody of the box set, letting in a glimpse of the outside world. Typical of such a part is her fear that a dire accident has befallen her master, who has not yet come home across the Hudson River. Within moments, however, he makes his appearance, and the greater dimensions of the family as Adam and Eve and their household become evident.

With the interactions of these three characters and Henry, who as Cain represents the opposing self, Wilder spreads out his view of the human condition. As the various elements of the personality are frequently at war with one another within each human being, so do these characters quarrel and complain,

The original cast of *The Skin of Our Teeth.* Left to right: Tallulah Bankhead, Florence Eldridge, Frederic March, Frances Heflin, and Montgomery Clift.

only to discover that they cannot exist separately. To make the whole man, thought, love, and lust play parts, and troublesome as it is, the self-destructive impulse is always present. Wilder's thought is deistic, combining a belief that God made the world and left the running of it to man with a belief that human activity is psychologically determined. The play abounds in Biblical allusions and includes a re-enactment of Noah's flood, yet at no point makes the suggestion that the race has survived its catastrophes through divine intervention. It is only by chance and the playwright's careful calculation that a ship is present to save the Antrobuses from the flood, and that two of each kind of animal are also on hand, though the action which precedes the embarkation makes obvious references to the deadly sins.

Again as with *Our Town,* Wilder stresses those traits of personality which are especially appealing, thus cajoling us into accepting the characters as representatives of ourselves. Most serviceable for this purpose are the interruptions of the action, such as Sabina's quoted above. In the last act, which occurs after the conclusion of a horrendous war, Wilder finds two such opportunities. The first is a pause brought on by the sudden illness of actors engaged to play Spinoza, Plato, Aristotle, and the author of Genesis. They were to cross the stage at the end of the play, each bearing a sign for one of the hours of the night—"a poetic effect," as the company's stage manager calls it, borrowed from **"Pullman Car Hiawatha."** Since no other actors are available, the parts must be taken by the wardrobe mistress, a maid, the captain of the ushers, and Antrobus's dresser, all of whom are glad to serve. With this device Wilder implies that the writing of the great philosophers takes effect upon the members of the race even without their awareness of it. He assigns the Negro maid the task of articulating the idea, hinting all the while that a sense of racial inferiority slows down her words and renders them tentative or apologetic:

> Excuse me, I think it means—excuse me, Mr. Fitzpatrick . . . Mr. Fitzpatrick, you let my father come to a rehearsal; and my father's a Baptist minister, and he said that the author meant that—just like the hours and stars go by over our heads at night, in the same way the ideas and thoughts of the great men are in the air around us all the time and they're working on us, even when we don't know it.

The speech not only serves to express a concept of the intellectual life, but serves also, through its halting diction, to make an oblique plea for tolerance by warming us to the girl who speaks it.

Later, when the actor playing Henry comes close to strangling the actor playing his father, comes another passage pulsing with Wilder's humanitarian instinct. Here the younger actor attempts to show that his part in the play as the wartime enemy has elicited a harrowing response from his own, not his stage-character's, personality:

> HENRY: Nobody can say *must* to me. All my life everybody's been crossing me,—everybody, everything, all of you. I'm going to be free, even if I have to kill half the world for it. Right now, too. Let me get my hands on his throat. I'll show him. (*He advances toward* ANTROBUS. *Suddenly,* SABINA *jumps between them and calls out in her own person:*)

> SABINA: Stop! Stop! Don't play this scene. You know what happened last night. Stop the play. (*The men fall back, panting.* HENRY *covers his face with his hands.*) Last night you almost strangled him. You became a regular savage. Stop it!

> HENRY: It's true. I'm sorry. I don't know what comes over me. I have nothing against him personally. I respect him very much . . . I . . . I admire him. But something comes over me. It's like I become fifteen years old again. I . . . I . . . listen: my own father used to whip me and lock me up every Saturday night. I never had enough to eat. He never let me have enough money to buy decent clothes. I was ashamed to go downtown. I never could go to the dances. My father and my uncle put rules in the way of everything I wanted to do. They tried to prevent my living at all.—I'm sorry. I'm sorry.

> ANTROBUS (*Quickly*): No, go on. Finish what you were saying. Say it all.

> HENRY: In this scene it's as though I were back in High School again. It's like I had some big emptiness inside me,—the emptiness of being hated and blocked at every turn. And the emptiness fills up with the one thought that you have to strike and fight and kill. Listen, it's as though you have to kill somebody else so as not to end up killing yourself.

Henry is getting at the basis of man's antisocial drives, but at the same time that he reveals the seriousness of the matter he offers through his familiar, boyish imagery a plea for sympathetic understanding. At such moments of the play intellectual stimulus and emotional appeal are in precise balance.

These scenes occur shortly before the conclusion of action that spans the ages from the descent of the glaciers over North America to the end of the most grotesque war in history—presumably Wilder's image of the Second World War. Of the calamities which nearly put an end to the Antrobus family, each has a different cause. The great wall of ice which brings the coldest day of the year in the middle of August is malevolent nature, with which man must do battle constantly. The family conquers it with the warmth provided by coffee, group-singing, and a fire made of beds, tables, and the seats in the theater even as the ice pushes at the walls of their house in Excelsior. In other words, common sense and heartiness are sufficient for overcoming disasters in the natural world. The overwhelming flood of the second act is described as a storm, but is not altogether a natural phenomenon; apparently it is also a form of retributive justice handed down by an unnamed power. Wilder's unwillingness to identify the power as God obscures his message for part of the act, but ultimately he makes it clear that man is about to be punished for his sinfulness. All the family are sinners. We see Henry in ungovernable wrath picking a fight with a Negro and thus, it would seem, initiating race hatred. Mrs. Antrobus, filled with pride that her husband is the presiding officer at the convention of mammals, insults the man who ran against him for the position. Antrobus's sin is lust; he has succumbed to the effort of Sabina, now a beauty-contest winner named Miss Fairweather, to seduce him in a beach cabana. When the storm warnings have reached their peak, the Antrobuses and Sabina, who have recovered from their wickedness, board a ship which happens to be waiting off shore and take with them the two delegates to the convention of every species of animal.

The last act, which carries the play into the present, is a stronger expression of ideas. It begins, not with the outbreak of war, but, for the happy conclusion necessary for comedy and the furtherance of the theme of survival, with the coming of peace. The enemy posited in this act is not nature or original sin in any of its specific forms, but the self-destructive instinct within the human spirit, as represented by Henry—the deep-rooted, malign force that can measure its own growth only by killing. To contend successfully with this enemy is the gravest problem of all. Mankind can at best forge an uneasy truce with it by closely analyzing the phenomena which created it, as the actor taking the part of Henry attempts to do. When Henry is pacified for the time being by the sensual Sabina, it is possible to go on with the business of living, as though nothing worse could possibly happen. But Wilder is not so unastute as to wish to urge upon the audience the notion that evil is absolutely to be abolished with the end of the war, for the accumulated evidence of the millions of years of human life gives such a notion the lie. The ending, then, is only tentative. After a blackout the lights come up on Sabina in the Excelsior living room, her feather duster in her hand—precisely her stance at the beginning of the play.

At first thought it is astonishing that a play so full of stops, starts, tricks, and dodges should lay a strong grip upon the emotions. It is saved from archness by Wilder's humanity, which expresses itself in this play as in all the others through ordinary speech, though it does so in the midst of many-layered, allusive dialogue and commensurately complex action. In this respect the play bears a resemblance to the most stageworthy of the works of Bertolt Brecht, which despite the songs, lantern slides, and printed messages intended to hold the audience at a distance, are capable of arousing great feeling. Especially in the confrontations of the members of the Antrobus family with one another is the simplicity of speech effective. Families are families, even when the members are figures in an allegory, as Wilder had previously demonstrated in *Our Town*. Wilder's only defensive reply to his critics to date on any score has come as a response to complaints that *The Skin of Our Teeth* is "a bookish fantasia about history, full of rather bloodless school-masterish jokes." This he believes is not its usual effect, and for substantiation he cites productions in postwar Germany at which he witnessed gratifyingly warm reactions in the audience. It is not, however, a foolproof play. The production demands are very heavy, not only in comparison to *Our Town* but to the majority of twentieth-century plays, both as to stage equipment and acting skill. This limitation became apparent in the American production of 1955, when the play dwindled into dullness as a result of the inept performances of George Abbott as Mr. Antrobus and Mary Martin as Sabina. But, production difficulties notwithstanding, as the world spins from crisis to crisis, the play continues to live. It is certain to remain in the repertory of the intellectual theater. In 1964 plans were announced for a musical version, with Betty Comden and Adolph Green as librettists and Leonard Bernstein as composer.

The strongest complaints against *The Skin of Our Teeth* have risen, not in discussions of its theatrical viability, but in remarks on its sources. In December 1942 a thunderous controversy was initiated with two articles written for the *Saturday Review of Literature* by Henry Morton Robinson and Joseph Campbell, the young scholars then at work on the book ultimately to be published as *A Skeleton Key to Finnegans Wake*. Unable to discriminate between the legitimate assimilation of a source and downright theft, they accused Wilder of plagiarism and of the debasement of Joyce's work. Although they proceeded beyond reason in their charges, they were correct enough in pointing to the similarity of the play to the novel. It is evident in the structure itself, which like that of the novel is circular, repeating the lines of the opening at the close. It is evident also in the resemblance between the Antrobuses and the Earwickers of the *Wake*, and in the procedure of describing all history through the family's activity, the past mixed in with the present and the banal mixed in with the profound. One serious result of the controversy was the refusal of the members of the New York Drama Critics Circle to present their annual award to Wilder, despite the obvious superiority of his play to all others of the season. Partial compensation for this injustice came soon afterward with the bestowal of the Pulitzer Prize.

Although the charges of plagiarism still come up in introductions to the play for text anthologies and were renewed by Robinson as late as March 1957 in an article for *Esquire*, they are now largely, and properly, ignored. Equally unsound, and now dropped, is the charge that the play cheapens the novel. To reach the general audience, as opposed to the coterie audience of the academic theater, Wilder found it necessary to broaden the substance of the book in order to clarify it. Professorial adaptations of passages of the novel have come along in the years since, but they cannot survive outside the academic theater and even there make no great impact. Remaining silent through the heat of the controversy, Wilder appeared to be taking for granted that his public would recognize honest borrowing for what it was. At last in the preface to *Three Plays*, published in October 1957, he acknowledged his source: "The play is deeply indebted to James Joyce's *Finnegans Wake*. I should be very happy if, in the future, some author should feel similarly indebted to any work of mine. Literature has always more resembled a torch race than a furious dispute among heirs." Should Wilder make a practice of studying the writers of the so-called Theater of the Absurd, who rely on slapstick, allegory, and seeming non-sequiturs for their reports on the meaning of existence, he would see the debts mounting. (pp. 118-29)

Malcolm Goldstein, in his *The Art of Thornton Wilder*, University of Nebraska Press, 1965, 179 p.

HERMANN STRESAU

(essay date 1971)

[In the following excerpt, Stresau provides an overview of Wilder's achievements as a novelist and playwright.]

[Wilder's first novel, *The Cabala* (1926)] deals with a variety of plots, intrigues, and society gossip among a rather loosely joined group composed of wealthy, extremely conservative individuals—some of aristocratic backgrounds—living in modern Rome. Unable to adjust to modern political realities—the growing threat of fascism is mentioned occasionally—they cultivate ideas of a peculiarly retrogressive, highly reactionary utopia. (p. 14)

Wilder is obviously less interested in the history of the Cabala than in the character and fate of its individual members. Without exception they are cases of human existence on the borderline between reality and nonreality. Yet in the very marginal nature of their lives they reveal crises of the spirit that transcend the banal, the practical, and the purely factual. (pp. 14-15)

The novel actually consists of separate tales depicting the fate of each of these figures and their relationships to one another. There is a certain vacillation, a slight uncertainty in the grouping of motifs and in the entire subject matter. One incident appears as a harsh dissonance in the unity of the whole—and, strangely enough, it appears at the very beginning, before the individual stories. Blair and his friend visit a dying English poet, who begs the archaeologist to remind the painter who is nursing him that there must be no name on his grave. "Just write: 'Here lies one whose name was writ in water.' " This statement and the rest of the circumstances . . . all definitely point to the English poet John Keats. The episode has no sequel, it is never mentioned again. But since the first part of the narration—the more general introduction to the Cabala group—is written in an ironical key that subsequently gives place to a warmer note, it is not inconceivable that the plan of the whole was originally different and that the "Keats" episode had a somewhat different significance.

Superficially, the Keats figure serves as contrast: the poet is dying, but his short life was to have an immortal success. The Cabala circle as a whole, however, along with its individual members, seems condemned to hopeless failure. The Keats figure also represents a sacrifice, just as those Cabalists whose fate the narrator depicts are sacrifices. (pp. 15-16)

On a clear, starlit night, Virgil, the spirit of the West, the mediator between antiquity and Christianity, appears to the narrator aboard a ship returning to his American home. "Seek out some city that is young," he says. "The secret is to make a city, not to rest in it. When you have found one, drink in the illusion that she too is eternal." Rome, he continues, was great. He, Virgil, cannot enter Zion until he has forgotten Rome—but he cannot forget Rome. In the new world a new Rome awaits its greatness.

This is the underlying motif of *The Cabala*. As a young man, the narrator had a map of Rome hanging above his desk, and, longingly, he studied the plan of the Eternal City. Now, having come to the city, he recognizes instead "human ruins," and it is these he describes. And finally, he returns to the new world which, compared to Europe, is still "new." It is the Henry James theme of the relationship between America and the old world. The twilight of the gods has settled over the old world, but in it appears the image of Virgil, the great exemplar. It is as though this Roman could, to

some extent, invest the almost ridiculous inadequacies of the Cabalists with a humanity that lends warmth and beauty even to the decay. (p. 18)

[*The Bridge of San Luis Rey*] was extraordinary successful. Perhaps its success can be attributed to the unusual amalgamation of European classical elements with an American naturalness of form. Or perhaps it was the unusual subject matter. It was probably both and, not least, the mastery with which the various elements were woven together into a unity. (p. 20)

The reader may be struck by the fact that few of the characters have strong family ties. . . . This solitariness could, perhaps, have occurred as a theme only to a modern American. Again most of the characters live on the borderline between the real and the nonreal, though their cases, certainly, are not as extreme as those of *The Cabala*.

Whereas *Cabala* deals with very strange and even abstruse ideas, with women whose hysteria verges on psychosis, the characters of this novel are isolated, but comparatively normal, human beings. Their fate is not bound up with an ideology, but with something universally human—the inadequacy of striving. Wilder seems to imply that even the family offers no protection against this inadequacy. . . . (pp. 24-5)

From the point of view of the temporal life of man, there is a definitely pessimistic strain running through the novel. This is contrapuntally offset by a religiosity that is vague and casual and by an unsentimental, slightly ironical imperturbability in the storytelling. One reason for the success of the novel is the steady calm with which disturbing, even exciting events are related—events that show man's defenselessness, the suffocating meaninglessness of existence, the cold loneliness of the individual, and at the same time his deep longing for security, love, and meaningfulness.

In contrast to *The Cabala*, there is a more rigid form, a clearer composition, resulting from the greater aloofness of an omniscient narrator.

The reader is also likely to be impressed by descriptions of some very lovely moments. He is not offered many such pictures, but their very paucity makes them more telling. (pp. 25-6)

The brief description of the air, mountains, and stars seen from the pilgrimage town of Cluxambuqua evokes a vision of the awe-inspiring vastness of eternal and immovable nature in contrast to the pettiness of human destinies. (p. 26)

[With *The Woman of Andros*, Wilder] goes back to the late Hellenic age. The material is derived from *Andria*, a comedy of the Latin playwright Terence, who in turn based his work upon two comedies of the Greek dramatist and poet Menander. Thus, once again, the American utilized elements of European tradition, as he did in *The Cabala,* but this time he reached far back into ancient pagan civilization. (p. 36)

Terence's suspenseful but gay comedy has turned into a story weighted with human sorrow and suffering. Yet, in contrast to *The Bridge of San Luis Rey,* the burden of pessimism seems somewhat lightened by the entire atmosphere, by the restraint of the outward show of emotions, the tenderness of the young lovers, and the spirituality of the hetaera Chrysis.

The idea of inadequate family ties appears again in this novel. The relationship between Chrysis and her sister is contrasted with the bourgeois families of Simo and Chremes. Both women are defenseless against their fate, thrown back on their own resources.

The meaning of the story, however, is revealed above all in the figure of Chrysis. In the comedy of Terence she is a hetaera like any other of ancient Greece. Here she has become a highly differentiated figure of a woman who both intellectually and personally is far superior to her environment, even to Simo, whose social position is all but unattainable to her. (pp. 37-8)

Wilder seems to be concerned throughout his works with the question How does one live? This is especially so in *The Woman of Andros.* (p. 38)

The novel is epic in character simply because it takes place in a narrow and definitely circumscribed milieu, the island of Brynos. With deliberate yet spare realism the daily life of the island is described: the market, the palaestra, the harbor, the insignificant—and yet so significant—lives of human beings. The landscape seems to encompass more than an occasional vista. . . . The steep land, the occasional view of the sea at dusk, the shadowy profile of Andros on the horizon, the ships in the harbor, the comfortable busyness of the inhabitants, the heat of the day and the cool breeze at night—all give the work, slight as it is, an epic breadth and distinction, a definitiveness that things will always remain the same. Yet this vision is ever so slightly disturbed by the hint of an approaching, unknown change, by the possibility that one day things may be different. That is why the novel is introduced by a kind of description of the ancient world that is not usually encountered: the earth sighing as it turned in its course, the shadow of night creeping along the Mediterranean from an Asia left in darkness. (pp. 41-2)

The actual suspense of the novel lies in [the] contrast between local limitation and world scope. It is a dramatic suspense. This uniting of the epic and the dramatic is characteristic of *The Woman of Andros.* (p. 42)

In this work Wilder reached a high point in his artistic development. The composition, in the fusion of the epic and the dramatic, is almost faultless. *The Bridge of San Luis Rey,* in its subject matter alone, may have had a suspense that, in the story of *The Woman of Andros,* seems to be present only in two points: the

prologue and the epilogue. But this is only apparently so; the actual tension in *The Woman of Andros* lies in the almost greater meaninglessness of the individual lives it portrays. In the story of the five victims of the catastrophe the very scene of the action suggests hidden explosive forces within that remote, volcanically undermined country of the Inca civilization. In the present novel, the gentler and more delicate tension, softened by the idyllic setting, leads to a warmth that Wilder could scarcely have surpassed. (pp. 43-4)

In answer to the criticism of literary observers that he was apparently inclined to avoid the problems of present-day America, Wilder published the novel *Heaven's My Destination* (1935). With it he proved that he did not hesitate to set a novel in the twentieth century, even to set it in the immediate present, the period of the Great Depression. He showed himself quite capable of portraying an American similar to those who exist in the realistic literature of the United States. Even the numerous secondary figures of the story, in their conversations and views about life, behave like average Americans. (p. 50)

[*Heaven's My Destination*] could almost be considered a picaresque novel (in keeping with the chapter headings, which briefly summarize the contents) were it not for the ambivalent feelings that the hero arouses. This "saint" is by no means unlikable. Yet, in the long run, his extreme naïveté becomes repugnant or, at any rate, disagreeable. The child's doggerel verse from which the title is derived is actually meant to warn the reader not to take the hero too seriously. (pp. 51-2)

In comparison with the earlier works, this novel seems rather formless, almost improvised. There is, however, a certain rhythm: the hero's twofold breakdown—the first time in Kansas City after the episode in the brothel, the second time when he falls ill after attempting to lead a worldly life—divides the book into three parts. But having demonstrated the conflicts of the world on the basis of contemporary figures, Wilder put them aside and has not yet returned to them. (p. 54)

Wilder states in his Preface to *Three Plays* that he wrote *Our Town* in an effort to "find a value above all price for the smallest events of our daily life." He even tries to underline the minutiae that make up the lives of the two small-town families, the Gibbses and Webbs and their children, by contrasting them with the universality of the millions and millions of times that similar things have occurred. (p. 60)

It is the Stage Manager who gives the play its unique, almost improvised character and yet makes it appear as something "enduring." It is he who holds the threads in his hand, who knows everything and yet gives the characters the freedom to choose what they wish to do. He does not state the meaning—the meaning is implied in the interplay of characters. Here, too, there are no sentimental overtones. There is no intrusion of "actuality" until the third act. But again the meaning of life remains an open question; the Stage Manager's reply that the saints and poets may perhaps realize life to a certain extent is too vague to be more than a suggestion. Nevertheless, one feels a slight change here. The impression that the problem of life's meaning remains unanswered does not exclude a deeper impression that there is a meaning.

Whereas Wilder's novels (with the exception of *Heaven's My Destination*) owed so much to the spirit of Greece and Rome, with a Christian background, that superficially one might conclude they were written by a European, this is not true of the plays. These could have been written only by an American. In the drama, Wilder seems to have found his own form to express the ideas that basically mattered to him.

The Skin of Our Teeth, which appeared in 1942, seems to confirm this. The play has been criticized for being an historico-philosophical book drama containing a bloodless theory of history. From the formal point of view, *The Skin of Our Teeth* represents something positively revolutionary. But with it, Wilder—who raises such basic questions as: What shall we eat? What shall we drink?—was able to grasp the reality of the present. (pp. 61-2)

The setting is not quite as abstract as in *Our Town:* the house in which the Antrobus family lives at least has walls, though now and then they lean over or fly up into the loft. The play, however, might approximate a conventional stage setting were it not for the constant shifting of reality whose puzzling complexity—though it seems entirely "natural"—belies any such approximation. In fact, the levels of reality are shifted about to such an extent that it does not seem very important to distinguish between them. This, in addition to the fact that the cast of characters is almost twice as large, makes a strict absence of scenery not as necessary as in *Our Town.*

Again the fate of a family is portrayed. (It is interesting to note that Wilder the dramatist places the family at the center of the action—a position that Wilder the novelist avoids.) This is the story of Mr. and Mrs. Antrobus and their two children, Gladys and Henry. The family name and the content of the play suggest that this is basically a story of man (*Anthropos*) or of Adam and Eve and their son Cain, who killed his brother. (pp. 63-4)

Of all the trials that he must go through, the actual difficulty for Antrobus-Adam—and this is the point at which Wilder's play becomes relevant to the present—is the existence of his son Henry-Cain. He who as a boy slew his brother is now the "representative of strong, irreconcilable evil"; in other words, of individualism carried to extremes. (p. 66)

The Ides of March, despite its brevity, is in its internal dimensions perhaps one of the most exhaustive and significant descriptions of [the age of the Roman revolution]. . . . With *The Ides of March* Wilder, having already developed a revolutionary style in playwriting, became experimental with the novel form also. If the word "novel" is defined as something narrated, *The Ides of March* is not a novel: the narrative passages—Cleopatra's account of the garden party or Assinius Pollio's description of Clodia's dinner, recounted many years later from memory—are so isolated that they scarcely change the character of the whole. (pp. 74-5)

As Wilder points out, the book is not an historical reconstruction but rather a "fantasia on certain events and persons of the last days of the Roman republic." The author shifts a number of events and persons into a period in which they do not belong. . . . (pp. 75-6)

The characters seem altogether real, neither godlike nor legendary. They are the exponents of a worldly, very skeptical age marked by violence, civil wars, moral instability, and cynical nihilism. Caesar, the absolute monarch, plays the part of the reformer, a role that ultimately destroys him. Basically, this "novel" represents the struggle between the almost solitary ruler and his own age, or rather the human figures that personify that revolutionary age. The suspense, the excitement of the account, lies in the fact that even Caesar, with all his autonomous superiority and independence, is to a certain extent the product of his times. (pp. 76-7)

The Ides of March is an extraordinarily rich work. The abundance of life poured into this slight volume and the "truth" of the account are astonishing—an indication that mere accuracy does not determine the reality of truth; it resides in the self-contained cosmos of the work of art itself. And the central figure of this work of art, around which this cosmos revolves, is Caesar. The fact that this is Thornton Wilder's Caesar gives him, paradoxically, the appearance of objectivity, as though the historical Caesar could really have been like this. (p. 83)

Wilder does not answer nor does he presume to be capable of answering the question of how one lives with any ideological formula. And this is actually the point of departure, the motif of his art. One might be inclined to assume that Wilder had written *The Woman of Andros* for the sake of Chrysis's doctrine and her story of the hero, or *Our Town* for the sake of Emily's experience of life and death. But though we believe it possible to assert that Pamphilus's question How does one Live? is the guiding thought behind all Wilder's work, we must nevertheless keep in mind that his vital interest lay in the artistic shaping and grouping of the figures embodying that question.

When Wilder theorizes it is almost always about the problems of art. The purely conceptual problems that he expresses in his works are few compared to his images, and they leave no doubt of his artistic, rather than speculative, impulses. (pp. 94-5)

Although Wilder's themes were perhaps not conscious ideas, the speeches of the angel, of the Fates in "Nascuntur Poetae," and of the Grey Steward (Death) in "Mozart and the Grey Steward" are actually messages containing ideas, and what the angel says to the sufferer is reminiscent of the Cardinal's words in *The Cabala*: "Who has not suffered . . ."

The ideas expressed in these messages may sound alien in our modern world. This is a peculiarity of Wilder's work that must strike everyone who studies it: the modern industrial, technological world has no place in Wilder's writing. More specifically, it has no influence on the consciousness of Wilder's characters, or only a very general, indirect influence insofar as the question How does one live? has received special emphasis in the present age. (p. 96)

A motif that is mentioned again and again, especially in the early works, is the one of the dual reality, as Death expresses it in the Mozart play. This contrast is present in the world of Wilder's earliest fancies. A further motif was added; only the sufferer is destined to see the reality that lies behind or within actuality, and only he can give it perceptual form, for the sake of the millions who are unable to do so. (p. 98)

It is obvious that basically all these plays have a religious, more specifically, a Christian content. But Wilder does not commit himself. For him, even in the earliest works, religion is not a doctrine, not an "idea" or abstraction that, paradoxically linked with actual existence, burdens common sense with conflicting enigmas. One might almost say that religion for him is something perceptively tangible, though beyond the here and now. It is life that is accessible perhaps only to the imagination, but once revealed, it is seen to be meaningful and significant. (p. 99)

Other themes bound up with the "things that lie beyond the present" are the theme of permanence or eternity and that of limitless time and space. The latter determines the form of **"The Long Christmas Dinner,"** in which a family sits at an endless meal throughout generations. In **"Pullman Car Hiawatha,"** though the train is en route from New York to Chicago on a certain date, the human experiences that take place are seen as universal experiences.

These experiences beyond time and space, which are accessible only to the imagination but out of which human beings fashion their world, dominate Wilder's work. They can also lead to a certain buffoonery growing out of delusions, as in **"Queens of France."** Here several more or less respectable middle-class women of New Orleans are deluded by an uncanny, fraudulent lawyer into believing that they are legitimate heirs of the Bourbons and pretenders to the throne of France.

This delusion is treated as comedy in **"Queens of France,"** but for the characters in *The Cabala* the nonexistent dream world becomes tragic and destroys them. (pp. 99-100)

The theme of "things that lie beyond the present" is expanded and deepened by yet another element: the element of love. The characters in Wilder's early works, in *The Cabala, The Bridge of San Luis Rey,* and *The Woman of Andros,* live outside the family or in a family relationship of tension. Yet they are all directly or indirectly concerned with love, with a love that is unfulfilled in a worldly sense. (p. 101)

In his early works, up through *The Bridge of San Luis Rey,* Wilder draws a wide arc: from the hetaera Chrysis to the Christian Abbess Maria del Pilar, from priestlike Pamphilus to suicidal Esteban, from the mad sea captain Philocles in *The Woman of Andros* to Captain Alvarado in *The Bridge of San Luis Rey.* There is something extreme in the behavior of these people, a demand for the absolute. (pp. 101-02)

For those characters who long to live in "reality,"—a trait of self-destruction, or rather self-abnegation, drives them into the very heart of suffering, which is at the same time the core of the individual, the personality—of Alcestis or Pamphilus, for example. And at this point the theme passes over into the general; their suffering speaks for the millions who cannot give expression to their dull pain save in a cry of despair. (p. 102)

In all these works of Wilder, the religious question How does one live? is never formulated as a theory. If there is something absolute by which human beings can orient their lives, it is neither the state nor society nor the rationale of technology. All these authorities have their limits beyond which questions such as the relation of the individual to the universal become crucial.

We cannot ignore the theme of the future. Thornton Wilder's work, in an immaterial sense, contains the man of the twentieth century who, in the maelstrom of toppling orders, has frighteningly lost his orientation. Faced with the question of how to live, what is left for him but to trust, like Caesar, the promise that grows out of the unknowable? (p. 103)

Hermann Stresau, in his *Thornton Wilder,* translated by Frieda Schutze, Ungar, 1971, 130 p.

SOURCES FOR FURTHER STUDY

Burbank, Rex. *Thornton Wilder.* New York: Twayne Publishers, 1961, 156 p.

> Provides an overview of Wilder's life and works.

Castronovo, David. *Thornton Wilder.* New York: Ungar, 1986, 174 p.

> Critical survey of Wilder's career.

Goldstein, Malcolm. *The Art of Thornton Wilder.* Lincoln: The University of Nebraska Press, 1965, 179 p.

> Examines Wilder's novels and plays in chronological order and relates their themes to the ideas underlying his work as a whole.

Haberman, Donald. *Our Town: An American Play.* Boston: Twayne Publishers, 1989, 117 p.

> Offers a detailed analysis of *Our Town* and discusses the play's historical context, critical reception, and overall importance.

Harrison, Gilbert A. *The Enthusiast: A Life of Thornton Wilder.* New Haven: Ticknor and Fields, 1983, 403 p.

> Comprehensive biography of Wilder.

Williams, Mary Ellen. *A Vast Landscape: Time in the Novels of Thornton Wilder.* Pocatello, Idaho: Idaho State University Press, 1979, 120 p.

> Discusses Wilder's fluid concept of time as evidenced in such novels as *The Cabala, The Bridge of San Luis Rey,* and *The Ides of March.*

Tennessee Williams

1911-1983

(Born Thomas Lanier Williams) American dramatist, novelist, short story writer, poet, and screenwriter.

INTRODUCTION

Along with Arthur Miller, Williams is acknowledged as one of the two greatest American dramatists of the post-World War II era. His stature is based almost entirely upon works he completed during the first half of his career. He earned Pulitzer Prizes for *A Streetcar Named Desire* (1947) and *Cat on a Hot Tin Roof* (1955) and New York Drama Critics Circle Awards for *The Glass Menagerie* (1944), *Streetcar, Cat,* and *The Night of the Iguana* (1959). Williams's lyrical style and his thematic concerns are distinctive in American theater; his material came almost exclusively from his inner life and was little influenced by other dramatists or by contemporary events. One critic noted, "Williams has remained aloof from trends in American drama, continuing to create plays out of the same basic neurotic conflicts in his own personality."

Williams once told an interviewer, "My work is *emotionally* autobiographical. It has no relationship to the actual events of my life, but it reflects the emotional currents of my life." Critics have made much use of Williams's family background as a means of analyzing his plays. Williams's father, Cornelius, was a businessman from a prominent Tennessee family who traveled constantly and moved his family several times during the first decade of Williams's life. Cornelius was often abusive toward his son, calling him "Miss Nancy" because the child preferred books to sports. His mother, Edwina, was a southern belle and the daughter of a clergyman; she is frequently cited as the inspiration for the domineering and possessive mother figures in Williams's plays. Williams was very close to his older sister, Rose, who was institutionalized for schizophrenia for much of her life. The character of Laura in *The Glass Menagerie* is based upon this beloved sister. Williams began writing early in life, had his first works published in a magazine at the age of twelve, and by the time he was twenty, he had decided to become a dramatist. A lonely and sickly child, he sought an escape in writing and often endangered his already frail health by foregoing sleep in order to write. The derivation of the name Tennessee is uncertain: Williams claimed he adopted the name because his father's family was active in the making of the State of Tennessee; it is also said that he acquired the name, due to his southern accent, at the University of Iowa; others believe he changed his name in order to distinguish his early, admittedly puerile poetry from his later work; Signi L. Falk noted that Williams changed his name because he felt his given name sounded too formidable.

In 1944 Williams captured the public's attention with his first major play, *The Glass Menagerie.* Tom, the narrator of the play, dreams of being a writer and is said to represent Williams. Tom's sister, Laura, is crippled both physically and socially. His mother, Amanda, is a fading southern belle who lives in the past. The action of the play concerns Amanda persuading Tom to bring to the house a "gentleman caller," whom she hopes will marry Laura and provide for her future. Tom brings a man who is already engaged, upsetting his mother and causing Laura to retreat more deeply into her fantasy world of records and her glass animal collection. Tom then leaves his family, as his father had before him, to pursue his own destiny. The simplicity of *Menagerie*'s plot is counterbalanced by lyrical language and profuse symbolism, which some critics consider overwhelming. However, this emotionally compelling play was extremely popular, and Williams followed its formula in his later work. Laura is the typical Williams heroine in that she is too fragile to live in the real world. Laura's and Amanda's escapes from the world through fantasy and living in the past, respectively, foreshadow later plays where the characters escape through alcohol and sex.

Williams established an international reputation with *A Streetcar Named Desire,* which many critics consider his best work. The play begins with the arrival of Blanche DuBois at the home of her sister, Stella, and her brother-in-law, Stanley Kowalski, a lusty, crude, working-class man. Blanche has presided over the decay and loss of her family's estate and has witnessed the suicide of her young husband. She comes to Stella seeking comfort and security but clashes with Stanley. While Stella is in the hospital giving birth, Stanley rapes Blanche, causing her to lose what little is left of her sanity. At the end, Blanche is committed to a sanitarium. In *Streetcar,* Williams used Blanche and Stanley to illustrate dichotomies and conflicts, several of which recur in his plays: illusion vs. truth, weakness vs. strength, and the power of sexuality to both destroy and redeem. But he does not allow either character to become one-dimensional or to dominate the audience's sympathies. Stanley's brutishness is balanced by his love for Stella, his dislike of hypocrisy, and his justifiable anger at Blanche's mockery of him and her intrusion on his home. Blanche's hypocrisy—her pretentious refinement despite her promiscuity—is balanced by the ordeals she has endured and by her gentleness and capacity for love. Williams's skillful balancing of Stanley and Blanche, and the qualities each represents, has provided subject matter for many scholarly essays and has earned the admiration of critics.

Although none of Williams's later plays attained the universal critical and popular acclaim of *Streetcar* and *Menagerie,* several works from the 1940s and 1950s are considered significant achievements in American drama. In *Summer and Smoke* (1947), Williams continued his exploration of the tension between the spirit and the flesh begun in *Streetcar.* In *The Rose Tattoo* (1950), one of his most lighthearted plays, he celebrated the life-affirming power of sexuality. *Cat on a Hot Tin Roof,* which is set on a Mississippi delta plantation, revolves around lies and self-deception. This play involves some of Williams's most memorable characters: Brick, a homosexual, who drinks to forget his guilt over the death of a lover; Maggie, his wife, who struggles "like a cat on a hot tin roof" to save their marriage; and Big Daddy, whose impending death from cancer prompts his family to compete for the inheritance. *The Night of the Iguana,* which Williams said is about "how to get beyond despair and still live," was his last play to win a major prize and gain critical and popular favor.

Later in his career the "emotional currents" of Williams's life were at a low ebb. Such plays as *Suddenly Last Summer* (1958) and *Sweet Bird of Youth* (1956), which are filled with violence, grotesquerie, and black comedy, reflect Williams's traumatic emotional state at the time of their composition. In his *Memoirs* (1975), Williams referred to the 1960s as his "Stoned Age," and he explained in an interview that "after 1955, specifically after *Cat on a Hot Tin Roof* . . . I needed [drugs, caffeine, and alcohol] to give me the physical energy to work. . . . But I am a compulsive writer. I have tried to stop working and I am bored to death." Williams continued to produce plays until his death, but critical reception became increasingly negative. Much of Williams's later work consisted of rewriting his earlier plays and stories, and his new material showed little artistic development, according to critics. Gore Vidal said in 1976: "Tennessee is the sort of writer who does not develop; he simply continues. By the time he was an adolescent he had his themes. . . . I am not aware that any new information (or feeling?) has got through to him in the [past] twenty-eight years." It was not only a lack of new themes that caused critics to denounce Williams's later work, but the absence of freshness and dramatic soundness in his treatment of these themes. Gerald Weales, a noted

Williams scholar, voiced the critical consensus when he said: "Audiences have withdrawn from Williams—I suspect, not because his style has changed or his concerns altered, but because in his desperate need to cry out he has turned away from the sturdy dramatic containers which once gave the cry resonance and has settled for pale imitations of familiar stage images . . . and has substituted lyric argument for dramatic language."

Williams was subject to much negative and even hostile criticism during his lifetime. Many of the qualities for which he is faulted are praised in his other works. His lyricism and use of symbols are hallmarks of such plays as *Streetcar,* but in other plays critics accuse him of being overly sentimental or heavy-handed. Williams is lauded for his compassionate understanding of the spiritually downtrodden, but he has also been accused of crossing the line between sympathetic interest and perverse sensationalism. Although critics are nearly unanimous in expressing their disappointment and sadness that the mastery of Williams's early work was not continued in his later plays, they are quick to point out that Williams's contributions to American theater has been remarkable. This opinion was expressed in an editorial in *The Nation:* "The plays for which Williams will be remembered . . . are not the 'first act' of some mysteriously unfinished life in art— they *are* that life. They transformed the American stage, they purified our language, they changed the way we see ourselves. None of his later plays, however erratic they may have been, diminish that accomplishment by so much as a hair."

(For further information about Williams's life and works, see *Concise Dictionary of American Literary Biography, 1941-1968; Contemporary Authors,* Vol. 108; *Contemporary Authors New Revision Series,* Vols. 5-8; *Contemporary Literary Criticism,* Vols. 1, 2, 5, 7, 8, 11, 15, 19, 30, 39, 45; *Dictionary of Literary Biography,* Vol. 7: *Twentieth-Century American Dramatists; Dictionary of Literary Biography Documentary Series,* Vol. 4: *Tennessee Williams;* and *Dictionary of Literary Biography Yearbook: 1983.*)

CRITICAL COMMENTARY

BENJAMIN NELSON
(essay date 1961)

[In the following excerpt, Nelson evaluates Williams's plays, focusing on *The Glass Menagerie, A Streetcar Named Desire, Sweet Bird of Youth, Cat on a Hot Tin Roof,* and *Suddenly Last Summer.*]

In one of Tennessee Williams' early one-act plays, *The Lady of Larkspur Lotion,* an alcoholic writer, attempting to define his life by creating illusions, faces grim reality for a moment and asks an agonizing question:

Is there no mercy left in the world anymore? What has become of passion and understanding? Where have they all gone to? Where's God? Where's Christ?

This question reverberates throughout Williams' work; softly in *The Glass Menagerie,* with anguish in *A Streetcar Named Desire,* shrilly and hysterically in *Sweet Bird of Youth.* It is a question posed by Myra Torrance and Val Xavier in *Battle of Angels* and repeated twenty years later by the floundering Chance Wayne and Alexandra Del Lago of *Sweet Bird of Youth.* It is a question and a cry of the lonely, the frightened and the outcast and it illuminates the dominant theme in Williams' work: the loneliness of human existence.

It is a lonely idea, a lonely condition, so terrifying to think of that we usually don't. And so we talk to each other, write and wire each other, call each other . . . fight each other and even destroy each other because of this always somewhat thwarted effort to break through walls to each other. . . . Personal lyricism is the outcry of prisoner to prisoner from the cell in solitary where each is confined for the duration of his life.
[Williams, in a preface to *Cat on a Hot Tin Roof*]

The people with whom the playwright can most readily sympathize are the outcasts, those who by temperament or character or birth are anachronisms trapped in a world "lit by lightning." They are "the fugitive kind" whether they be Val Xavier, Laura Wingfield, Blanche DuBois or Kilroy and his plumed knight, and their great desire is to establish a meaningful relationship in a world which will not allow it. Many years ago, Williams wrote that his work dealt with the "destructive impact of society on the sensitive, nonconformist individual." The great difference between the *American Blues* plays and *Camino Real* or *Orpheus De-*

Principal Works

Cairo! Shanghai! Bombay! [with Bernice Dorothy Shapiro] (drama) 1935

Headlines (drama) 1936

The Magic Tower (drama) 1936

Candles to the Sun (drama) 1937

Fugitive Kind (drama) 1937

Battles of Angels (drama) 1940; also performed as Orpheus Descending, 1957

The Long Goodbye (drama) 1940

This Property Is Condemned (drama) 1942

The Gentleman Caller (screenplay) 1943

You Touched Me! [with Donald Windham] (drama) 1943

The Glass Menagerie (drama) 1944

The Purification (drama) 1944

Stairs to the Roof (drama) 1945

Moony's Kid Don't Cry (drama) 1946

The Last of My Solid Gold Watches (drama) 1947

Portrait of a Madonna (drama) 1947

A Streetcar Named Desire (drama) 1947

Summer and Smoke (drama) 1947; also performed as Eccentricities of a Nightingale, 1964

American Blues: Five Short Plays [first publication] (dramas) 1948

One Arm and Other Stories (short stories) 1948

The Roman Spring of Mrs. Stone (novel) 1950

The Rose Tattoo (drama) 1950

Camino Real (drama) 1953

Hard Candy: A Book of Stories (short stories) 1954

Cat on a Hot Tin Roof (drama) 1955

Something Unspoken (drama) 1955

Three Players of a Summer Game (drama) 1955

27 Wagons Full of Cotton (drama) 1955; also performed as All in One, 1955

Baby Doll (screenplay) 1956

In the Winter of Cities (poetry) 1956

Sweet Bird of Youth (drama) 1956

Period of Adjustment (drama) 1958

Suddenly Last Summer (drama) 1958

Talk to Me Like the Rain and Let Me Listen (drama) 1958

I Rise in Flame, Cried the Phoenix (drama) 1959

The Night of the Iguana (drama) 1959

Three Players of a Summer Game, and Other Stories (short stories) 1960

The Milk Train Doesn't Stop Here Anymore (drama) 1962

The Gnädiges Fräulein (drama) 1966; also performed as The Latter Days of a Celebrated Soubrette, 1974

The Knightly Quest: A Novella and Four Short Stories (novella and short stories) 1966

The Mutilated (drama) 1966

Androgyne, Mon Amour (poetry) 1967

The Two-Character Play (drama) 1967; also performed as Out Cry, 1971

The Seven Descents of Myrtle (drama) 1968; also performed as Kingdom of Earth, 1975

Dragon Country [first publication] (dramas) 1969

In the Bar of a Tokyo Hotel (drama) 1969

Confessional (drama) 1971; also performed as Small Craft Warnings, 1972

I Can't Imagine Tomorrow (drama) 1971

The Theatre of Tennessee Williams. 7 vols. (dramas) 1971-81

Eight Mortal Ladies Possessed: A Book of Stories (short stories) 1974

Memoirs (memoirs) 1975

Moise and the World of Reason (novel) 1975

The Red Devil Battery Sign (drama) 1976

This Is (An Entertainment) (drama) 1976

Vieux Carré (drama) 1977

Crève Coeur (drama) 1978; also performed as A Lovely Sunday for Crève Coeur, 1979

Tiger Tail (drama) 1978

Where I Live: Selected Essays (essays) 1978

Clothes for a Summer Hotel (drama) 1980

scending is that "society" has evolved into the universe.

The universe is the great antagonist in Tennessee Williams. It is as malignant as it is implacable. It has, through time, destroyed a way of life and a tradition that once meant civilization and has evolved a society that is grasping, repressive and destructive. Anything that was honorable is gone and the codes of the past have become anachronistic and ridiculous in the present. The standard bearers of this tradition are hopelessly inadequate in a world which calls for Jim O'Connor's "zzzzzzzzzp!" and yet if there is to be any meaning in life it will have to come, Williams is saying, from the

codes and tradition which his ragged cavaliers and tattered ladies are waving in the face of impending darkness.

This is the credo of the romantic, the cry of Don Quixote charging the windmills and Lord Byron making his final stand for Greek independence. But if Williams devoutly believes in the romantic revolt against the Philistines, he has no illusions about the triumph of this insurrection. While sympathizing with his romantics he is at the same time able to see and understand the futility of their quest. Williams is the romantic and the realist, and his best work is marked by this important juxtaposition of beliefs. Thus, in *The Glass*

Menagerie the author's sympathies for his ineffectual dreamers are tempered by his objective attitude toward them. While portraying their tragic attempts to establish contact with each other and with the world in which they live he is nevertheless able to see that they are doomed to failure because of their inability to do more than dream. Blanche DuBois also represents the honor, gentility and basic decency which is starkly contrasted against the world of Stanley Kowalski. Hers are the values which, untainted, should pervade our world, but they do not, and in seeking them in someone else she only hastens her final destruction. She refuses to give up her dream and her refusal is heroic, perhaps tragic. But in the end she is destroyed because she really has nothing but illusions and chimeras to throw in the face of the brute force of Kowalski's reality.

The Lauras, Amandas, Blanches and Kilroys possess the values which Williams feels endow life with whatever meaning and definition it has. But they lack the vitality, the strength and the force to preserve these values against a hostile universe. Their pathetic defiance is their gallantry; but their ineffectuality will never allow them to triumph. Only Benjamin Murphy and the cavaliers of *Camino Real* can claim any measure of victory, and only because in fantasy their creator could supply them with a new star and a Terra Incognita.

Marlon Brando and Jessica Tandy as Stanley Kowalski and Blanche DuBois in a Broadway production of *A Streetcar Named Desire.*

Tennessee Williams is the protagonist of the romantic quest, and yet it is precisely his inability to carry this quest through to fruition which gives his work its particular defining characteristic.

No one in Williams' universe can triumph because there is nothing to which the individual can appeal. The sins of the earth are its incompletions, Williams tells us; the universe is fragmented and man born into it is born into incompletion. Everything that governs human action emanates from this broken condition which is the root condition of the universe. Man's life is a constant attempt to compensate for this lack of wholeness which he feels in himself. In the work of Tennessee Williams, human action is defined by universal incompletion. Not only can the individual not appeal to forces beyond himself, but because his life is defined in terms of his universe and is thus marked by guilt and atonement, he cannot rely even upon personal responsibility. There is no sense of individual responsibility in this deterministic view of existence, and without this responsiblity no one can attain tragic fulfillment. If there is tragedy in Williams' work it is the tragedy of circumstance rather than character: Blanche trapped by her past and her dreams and fighting heroically for survival; Amanda struggling to hold a disintegrating family together; and Big Daddy Pollitt desperately attempting to save his son. With the exception of Big Daddy the characters are not large enough spiritually or morally to triumph even in their destruction. Their universe will not allow for tragic exaltation. Only Big Daddy possesses this possibility, but characteristically Williams is unable to sustain him.

If it is difficult for the artist to inspire tragedy in this closed and malignant universe, he can nonetheless create genuine beauty, and in his best plays, Williams accomplishes this with consummate skill. In depicting the stark and terrifying loneliness of individuals in their isolation, and their pathetic and often deeply moving attempts to communicate meaningfully to each other, he often attains heights of poetic beauty. The plight of the Wingfields, the destruction of Blance DuBois and the struggle of Margaret and Big Daddy for Brick Pollitt are presented with a compassion, perception and intensity which are characteristic of Williams' finest efforts. And in *Suddenly Last Summer,* which makes no attempt to transcend what Williams views as the human condition, the playwright has created a stunning work of art in which theme, imagery and presentation are almost flawlessly blended into a unified whole.

If we can claim as a function of art the objective formulation of thought, emotion and experience, the artist who performs this function, from whatever point of view, is fulfilling an artistic purpose by presenting us material for our particular response to experience. So far as Williams accomplishes this—and in *The Glass*

Menagerie, A Streetcar Named Desire, Cat On A Hot Tin Roof and *Suddenly Last Summer,* I believe he does—his work possesses genuine artistic validity. And in this context his drama

> may be violent, full of motion; yet it has that special kind of repose which allows contemplation and produces the climate in which tragic importance is a possible thing. . . .
>
> [Williams, in a preface to *The Rose Tattoo*]

It is when the drama of Tennessee Williams lacks the "repose which allows contemplation" that his violence and motion run amok and tip his plays from art into melodramatic artifice.

Williams is not a realist or a naturalist but his best works represent a tenuous but taut alliance between harsh realism and a poetic—even lyric—expressionism. We can see it in plays like *The Glass Menagerie* in Jim O'Connor's world and Laura Wingfield's world. Indeed the play is at once realistic and a protest against realism, a "slice of life" endowed with lyric beauty by its transformation into memory. *A Streetcar Named Desire* continually vacillates between the crash and clamor of Kowalski, the pungent sight, sound and smell of his world, and the mothlike quality of Blanche, the strains of the far-away Varsouviana and the thematic cry of street-vendor, *"Flores para los muertos." Cat On A Hot Tin Roof* again manifests this intense realism given expressionistic presentation. This alliance of the naturalistic and the expressionistic which John Gassner has termed "poetic naturalism," is the great source of Williams' strength. It also points to his major deficiency.

In his best plays Williams is able to maintain this uneasy alliance. He keeps the proper juxtaposition between the realistic and the expressionistic, the rational and the irrational, he does not allow his tendency toward the sensational to run unchecked. A vital tension is maintained through a discipline of thought and craft.

But Williams does not always maintain this control. Too often either the realistic or the expressionistic elements in his work dominate by sheer force of the author's indulgence, and the results are chaotic. This could be dismissed as youthful exuberance in a drama like *Battle of Angels,* but in plays like *Orpheus Descending* and *Sweet Bird of Youth,* written at the peak of the playwright's maturity, we must look for something more.

The tendency toward the violent and the sensational has been present in all of Williams' work. In his most effective plays it has been tempered by the author's objective admission of complexity in his situations. In some of his recent dramas this objective admission of complexity is noticeably absent. This is the result, I think, of a hardening philosophical commitment on the part of the playwright. If the human condition is marked by fragmentation, if life on earth holds no hope for any sort of redemption, if corruption is so inherent in the universe that time itself becomes the great enemy of man, for what can man hope? When Williams admits the complexity of his characters' plights and their efforts to give their lives definition, his plays have meaning for us whatever their points of view or visions of the universe. But when the artist distills the complexity out of his vision and views the earth as an unqualified evil and mortality as predestined to corruption, the situations and struggles of his characters begin to lose their dramatic as well as their moral validity. In *Camino Real* and particularly in *Orpheus Descending* and *Sweet Bird of Youth,* the playwright is moving away from complexity toward a terrifyingly simple view of life. The world is corrupt, the earth is the under-kingdom and the only salvation lies in withdrawal. Thus the longing of Kilroy for Terra Incognita, Val for the life of the legless bird and Chance Wayne for the sweet bird of youth all spell the same thing: detachment. As the universe becomes simplified the plights of individuals become simplified, and with this simplification the tendency toward sensationalism increases, as if the author feels he must compensate by effect what he has lost in subject matter. There are no Blanche DuBois and Big Daddy Pollitts and Amanda Wingfields; instead we are presented with gigantic figures representing purity on the one hand and corruption on the other. Involvement with the flesh spells ruin and salvation is achieved only in detachment, which after all is impossible, or in surrender to violent atonement. The author has unloosed the demons of his unconscious and rather than allowing us to reflect he insists we gorge ourselves. It is as if Williams were hypnotized by his creations, unable to control his material or objectify it for any sort of artistic contemplation. It is precisely this control which endows *Suddenly Last Summer* with artistic validity. And it is the lack of control which hurls *Orpheus Descending* and *Sweet Bird of Youth* into chaos. To the extent that these plays are battles of angels, clashes between light and darkness, subjective nightmares about purity and sin, they are meaningful possibly only to their creator. The ability to objectify what he is doing is absent. And without this ability, all the sound and the fury in the universe notwithstanding, art is impossible.

The question now for Tennessee Williams is what happens next? Has he come to the end of something and is he ready to set off in a new direction, or will he continue to explore his image of the universe which has hardened not only into a philosophical but an artistic commitment? His art is often so good that we find ourselves asking him for greater mastery, and deploring his loss of control. We tend to think less of what he has accomplished than what he could accomplish. We continually wonder if his art is great enough not only to sustain itself, but to develop further. And here, I suspect, we share an intriguing and perplexing question with the playwright. (pp. 287-94)

Benjamin Nelson, in his *Tennessee Williams: The Man and His Work,* Ivan Obolensky, Inc., 1961, 304 p.

R. H. GARDNER

(essay date 1965)

[In the following excerpt, Gardner examines *A Streetcar Named Desire* as the classic Williams play.]

The emotional quality of all Mr. Williams' serious work is essentially the same, and in theme, subject matter, and philosophy *A Streetcar Named Desire* is the classic Williams play. (p. 112)

Early in the proceedings Mr. Williams provides a clue to his intentions in his choice of names. He has a wonderful feeling for words and, like any poet, puts them to symbolic use. Belle Reve (beautiful dream), Elysian Fields (paradise), desire, cemetery, Blanche Du-Bois (white wood)—all combine to produce a double image of, on the one hand, a sublime purity too perfect to be real and, on the other, a reality (earthly passion, death) too harsh to tolerate that purity. The devastating impact of the latter upon the former is indeed the central theme that runs through most of Mr. Williams' work.

Stella is a standard sort of girl, healthy in both the animal passion she feels for her husband and pride in the baby she carries within her. Blanche, however, is a strangely delicate and defenseless creature. "You didn't know Blanche as a girl," Stella tells Stanley during one of their arguments on the subject. "Nobody, nobody, was tender and trusting as she was. But people like you abused her and forced her to change." As Blanche herself puts it, "I never was hard or self-sufficient enough. When people are soft—soft people have to shimmer and glow—they've got to put on soft colors, the colors of butterfly wings. . . . " And it is true that, though Blanche does not radiate the glow of physical health her sister does, she glows in a way that Stella doesn't. Behind all her transparent pretensions exists a genuine appreciation of beauty that Stella, being a normal, healthy girl, has never experienced.

Here we encounter another one of Mr. Williams' pet themes—the superiority of difference. "You know—you're—well—very different!" exclaims the gentleman caller to the crippled sister in *The Glass Menagerie.* "Surprisingly different from anyone else I know. . . . The different people are not like other people, but being different is nothing to be ashamed of. Be-

cause other people are not such wonderful people." There also appears to be something special about sick people. . . . [Maggie remarks] in *Cat on a Hot Tin Roof* about the charm of the sick and the defeated. Blanche, too, we now discover, thinks highly of the infirm. They have, she tells Mitch (the man she hopes to marry), "such deep, sincere attachments."

Mr. Williams' preoccupation with illness, disease, and death assumes at times the proportions of an obsession. . . . There is not a major Williams play in which the illness theme is not introduced in one way or another. No passage, however, can quite match Blanche's account of her last days at Belle Reve, before foreclosure set into motion the train of disastrous events culminating in her arrival in New Orleans.

> I, I, *I* took the blows in my face and my body! All of those deaths! The long parade to the graveyard! . . . You just came home in time for the funerals, Stella. And funerals are pretty compared to deaths. . . . You didn't dream, but I saw! *Saw! Saw!* And now you sit there telling me with your eyes that I let the place go! How in hell do you think all that sickness and dying was paid for? Death is expensive, Miss Stella! And old cousin Jessie's right after Margaret's, hers! Why the Grim Reaper had put up his tent on our doorstep! . . . Stella, Belle Reve was his headquarters!

We must bear in mind that Blanche herself is sick, afflicted with a psychic illness growing out of her inability—soft, glowing, beauty-haunted creature that she is—to face the harshness of human existence. The same is true, to a greater or less degree, of Brick in *Cat,* Alma in *Summer and Smoke,* Valentine in *Orpheus Descending,* Chance in *Sweet Bird of Youth,* and the Reverend Shannon in *The Night of the Iguana.* Their sickness is a symbol, a badge, a veritable *proof* of their vulnerability, their sensitivity, and, by extension of the same reasoning, their goodness. Good people cannot, in Williams' world, help but be sick, since goodness provides no defense against the brutal forces that cause sickness.

What, then, do we have in *Streetcar*? A central character whose gentleness and innate fineness of spirit do not equip her for a life in which brutality and death hold sway. Unable to bear the pressure, she has retreated to a world of fantasy and nightmare. But that is not all we have. There is another element, without which no Tennessee Williams play would be worthy of the name: sexual depravity. As a diversion from the grim life at Belle Reve, Blanche has taken up promiscuity on a grand scale. . . . She has chosen this road of sensuality, she explains, because of her feeling that the opposite of death (as suggested by the symbolism of the two streetcars) is desire.

Stella's husband, Stanley, loathes Blanche, not only because her pretensions to Old Southern refinement and strait-laced morality offend his earthy, Polish soul, but also because he recognizes in her genuine revulsion to his natural bestiality a threat to his relationship—founded upon that bestiality—with his wife. But there is another reason, too. Blanche, the embodiment of spiritual aspiration, is the exact antithesis of Stanley, the pure animal. Sensing this, he sets about deliberately to destroy her. The means by which he accomplishes his purpose are as systematic as they are heartless. First, he smashes the illusion of youthful innocence she has tried to create about herself. He does this by investigating her past and reporting it in flamboyant detail to Stella and Mitch, the latter of whom represents her last chance to escape into some semblance of domestic stability. Then, having deprived her of both mental (her illusions) and physical (Mitch) sanctuary, Stanley corners Blanche one night while his wife is in the hospital and rapes her. From this final horror, there is for her but one sanctuary—madness.

The play owes its distinctive power to the methodical, calculated manner in which Stanley goes about his task. Arousing revulsion in the spectator through the deliberate destruction of a helpless, suffering, or essentially innocent creature by a vicious force is Mr. Williams' specialty. In one way or another, he does it in most of his plays. (pp. 113-15)

And what is the fate of those unfortunate enough to have been born gentle and pure, with a hunger for beauty and an aching need for love? They naturally are the ones whose destiny it is to be eaten, to provide sport and sustenance for the vicious and greedy. But, before being devoured, they must first undergo a weakening ordeal, so that when the time comes they will be too helpless to put up a fight. This weakening process occurs through corruption—which, in the way it serves to debase the person in his own eyes, is somewhat Chekhovian. The difference is that, whereas Chekhov saw waste as the corrupting agent, for Williams it is sex.

It is indeed difficult to avoid the conclusion that Williams regards sex (because of its suggestion of use of one person by another) as a corrosive element of evil. It destroys, among other things, the purity of human relationships. (p. 118)

This unavoidably corrupting influence is the thing that seems to bother Mr. Williams the most—for, once corrupted, the pure do not simply join the ranks of the impure. They become, like the principals in *Sweet Bird of Youth,* something monstrous. Longing for their lost purity and loathing themselves for having lost it, they achieve satisfaction only by twisting the knife in the wound, weakening themselves through greater and greater excesses, seeking even more revolting forms of debauchery with which to punish themselves—until, drained of all goodness and flopping helplessly upon the exposed sands of the ultimate deg-

radation, they are pounced upon by the brutal forces of nature and devoured.

It is this portrayal of purity in terms of its opposite—moral putrescence—that gives Williams' work its unique flavor. Depravity alone would be intolerable; but, by contrasting depravity with the purity out of which it has sprung, he manages to give his characters the illusion of tragic stature—a trick comparable to, but not identical with, Shakespeare's projection of Antony's past strength into the play to contrast his present weakness. Williams' unerring ability to find a dramatic excuse for depicting degeneracy may, in view of the public's curiosity concerning such matters, be one of the reasons for his success at the boxoffice. (pp. 118-19)

[Shakespearean tragedy] arises from a contest in which two powerful adversaries fight to a climactic conclusion. Significance surrounds the struggle because of the hero's greatness and the fact that he has transgressed the natural, "good" order of the universe. His destruction at the end thus creates in us a sense of "rightness" at the same time that it saddens us with its example of waste. In any event, so great has the hero seemed—so huge in stature, so strong in character—that, when finally he is overcome, it is as if some immense edifice were toppling, shaking the earth with the force of its fall.

Williams' plays produce exactly the opposite impression. For, having equated goodness with weakness, strength with viciousness and universal order with evil, they convey no sense of "rightness" at the end. The destruction of the hero represents less a fall than an extermination. For one thing, there is no place for him to fall *to.* He has already sunk to the very bottom of the human barrel, where he lies, arms outflung, soft underbelly exposed, waiting for the heel of violence to squash him like a bug.

Rather than elevating, this experience is simply morbid—comparable in some respects to what the Romans must have felt while watching a decrepit Christian being eaten by a lion. The impact lies not in the power of the conflict but in the death shrieks of the victim. Much of Williams' dialogue, excellent thought it may be, is but a prolonged cry of agony.

The morbid impact of this experience is deepened as a result of Williams' willingness on occasion to exchange his role as a serious playwright creating a work of art for that of a small boy scribbling words on an outhouse wall. . . . Williams' smuttiness seems deliberate and, since it degrades the use of a fine talent, constitutes his most objectionable trait as a dramatist. A more crucial fault, of course, is his inability, despite his insistence upon their erstwhile goodness, to excite mature sympathy for his characters.

The closest we come to sympathy in a typical Williams play is the sickening kind of pity we might feel for a dumb animal caught in a trap and slowly tortured to death by forces beyond its comprehension; but this is overshadowed by our feeling of horror at the sheer brutality of the act. Thus, while eroticism, hate and low-grade pity are all involved, horror is the dominant emotion evoked by *Streetcar* and most Williams plays. And, since he offers no universal justification for the circumstances responsible for the horror, we perceive in them no larger meaning, no significant form, and, consequently, we experience no release at the end. Our spirits, instead of soaring, sag—oppressed by an insupportable weight of . . . horror.

We are thus forced to the conclusion that, though Tennessee Williams has a big talent, he does not write big drama. He is, in fact, the dramatic counterpart of Edgar Allan Poe—a dealer in horror. As such, he is, of course, magnificent. . . . Still, one cannot help regretting that his morbid outlook and fascination for the gutter prevent his putting his fertile imagination, poetic vision and superb sense of theater to better use. (pp. 120-21)

R. H. Gardner, "Streetcar to the Cemetery," in his *The Splintered Stage: The Decline of the American Theater*, The Macmillan Company, 1965, pp. 111-21.

S. ALAN CHESLER
(essay date 1977)

[In the following excerpt, Chesler assesses Williams's contribution to American theater.]

Critics agree that Tennessee Williams is one of the few outstanding playwrights in modern American theater history. Like his predecessor and compeer, Eugene O'Neill, who all but dominated the realm of American playwriting during the first thirty years of this century, Williams, along with Arthur Miller, has all but dominated the theater since World War II.

Williams has been an extremely prolific playwright. Bulk of output alone does not assure a dramatist a major position in theater history. Williams, however, has not only written a great number of plays; he has also enjoyed an extraordinary record of successful productions. Of the plays produced in New York, only his most recent were not successful. *Summer and Smoke, Camino Real,* and *Orpheus Descending* had also had less than successful runs when they opened on Broadway, but all three were later revived off Broadway where they were better received by critics and the public alike. Of the remaining ten plays, four won New York Drama Critics' Awards: *The Glass Menagerie, A Streetcar Named Desire, Cat on a Hot Tin Roof,* and

The Night of the Iguana; and two also won Pulitzer Prizes: *Streetcar* and *Cat.*

Critics note that Williams has been America's most popular modern dramatist. One reason for this enormous popularity has been the adaptation of many of his plays into motion pictures. Williams' concern with visual and auditory images has made his plays very suitable to cinematic adaptation. Twelve of his full-length plays have already been made into film: *The Glass Menagerie, A Streetcar Named Desire, The Rose Tattoo, Suddenly Last Summer, Summer and Smoke, Sweet Bird of Youth, Period of Adjustment, The Night of the Iguana, The Milk Train Doesn't Stop Here Anymore* and *The Seven Descents of Myrtle (Kingdom of Earth).*

Another reason for Williams' popularity is his plays' direct appeal to basic human emotions. This appeal results from both Williams' concentrated treatment of man's purely emotional response to his environment and the original, often symbolistic, means he employs to dramatize this concern. In communicating his conception of modern man's existential problems, Williams has utilized a wide range of theatrical and literary techniques which convey underlying human feelings that traditional, realistic drama could not present.

The majority of scholars agree that Williams' most significant contribution to the American theater has been this utilization of various theatrical techniques to universalize what on the surface seemed to be uniquely individual situations. By combining impressionistic and expressionistic staging devices with the naturalist's keen observations and the realist's objectivity in handling his materials, Williams has created a new poetic drama in the United States. From the opening of *The Glass Menagerie* in 1945 until the present, Williams has demonstrated his commitment to dramatic experimentation. His innovative "plastic theatre" has involved a more flexible and complete theatrical communication than is conveyed by dialogue alone. Williams has employed visual and auditory effects to previously unattempted extents by emphasizing color, music and scenic devices to increase the flexibility of the theater presentation of ideas and images, especially those representing human feelings.

The versatility of Williams' dramatic talents has been surpassed in America only by Eugene O'Neill. On merely the basis of having written his two greatest critical and popular successes, *The Glass Menagerie* and *A Streetcar Named Desire,* Williams must be considered an outstanding American playwright. Both plays have already established themselves as classics of the American theater. Remarkably, these two dramas, though produced only two years apart, show the wide range of Williams' extraordinary sense of the theater. At almost the same time in his career when he wrote *Menagerie,* a fragile mood piece loosely held together by various impressionistic and poetic techniques, Williams also created *Streetcar,* a tightly-knit naturalistic drama of brutal power and intensity. Whereas *Menagerie* is a series of almost actionless vignettes introduced, linked together, and commented upon by a narrator, *Streetcar* relies almost completely upon a naturalistic unfolding of plot line which develops more directly and more dynamically. But, despite their differences in form, the two plays have important similarities—which are characteristic of Williams' greatest gifts as a dramatist. In both works, Williams' characterization excels. He renders fascinating individuals who at the same time have abstract, representational values. Amanda Wingfield and Blanche DuBois are among the roles in American theater annals that entice, challenge, and satisfy our greatest actresses. Furthermore, although Williams does not directly comment on social problems in these dramas of personal struggles, the plays nonetheless reverberate with the economic, political, and social problems from which the personal conflicts emerge. The enduring appeal of *Menagerie* and *Streetcar* is largely derived from Williams' ability to base Amanda's and Blanche's conflicts in environments that are at the same time both specific and general.

Critics point out that when Williams was not in sufficient control of his craft, his attempts to broaden his plays' meanings resulted in stereotyped characterizations *(Camino Real, Sweet Bird of Youth, Orpheus Descending, The Rose Tattoo, The Seven Descents of Myrtle),* heavy-handed symbolism *(Summer and Smoke, Camino Real, Orpheus Descending, The Milk Train Doesn't Stop Here Anymore, Slapstick Tragedy, In the Bar of a Tokyo Hotel, Out Cry),* obtrusive moralizing *(Orpheus Descending, Camino Real, Sweet Bird of Youth, In the Bar of a Tokyo Hotel, Small Craft Warnings),* and unsuccessful experimentation *(Slapstick Tragedy, Small Craft Warnings, Out Cry).* But in his best plays, *Cat on a Hot Tin Roof, Suddenly Last Summer* and *The Night of the Iguana,* as well as *Menagerie* and *Streetcar,* his unique sense of the theater's enormous flexibility is usually combined with the necessary artistic control.

Another of Williams' dramatic gifts that critics praise is his command of dialogue. While functioning organically to further plot line, Williams' poetic dialogue fulfills esthetic purposes as well. In his finest dramas *(Menagerie, Streetcar, Cat, Suddenly,* and *Iguana),* the playwright's dialogue simultaneously serves the functions of plot progression, revelation of character, and thematic and symbolic patterns. Although they are functional, the lines of Williams' dialogue sound natural and appropriate to the characters who deliver them—a fact which testifies to the playwright's careful attention to nuances of speech.

Williams' attempts by means of symbolic and

nonrealistic dramatic techniques to shock people into recognition and understanding has often been mistakenly criticized by those critics who view his plays as traditional realistic dramas. However, the passing of time has already abated the shock value of Williams' sexual and violent symbolism so that during the past fifteen years several critics and scholars have begun to reassess with greater objectivity and insight such once shocking works as *Cat on a Hot Tin Roof* and *Suddenly Last Summer.*

Williams made another contribution to the American theater by dealing with subjects that had before his time been carefully avoided. Through his handling of sexuality and violence, Williams served as a harbinger for the new generation of playwrights who followed him—writers like William Inge, Edward Albee, Jack Richardson, and LeRoi Jones. The general favorable critical and popular reception of their bold treatment of sex and their hard-hitting dialogue is doubtlessly to some degree the result of Williams' having broken ground for them in these areas.

Critics agree that Williams' creation of a new poetic drama in the United States is the foundation upon which his permanent literary reputation is most likely to rest. Nevertheless, since Williams is still writing plays and since critics continue to revaluate his dramatic works, his position in American theater history will doubtlessly be modified with time. At present, the increasing respect accorded to *Cat on a Hot Tin Roof, The Night of the Iguana,* and *Suddenly Last Summer* during the past fifteen years, along with the fact that *The Glass Menagerie* and *A Streetcar Named Desire* have not diminished in stature during the twenty-five years since they were first produced, indicates that Williams, his failures notwithstanding, has already established himself not only as a crucial figure in the history of the American theater but also as a playwright of the first rank. (pp. 877-80)

S. Alan Chesler, "Tennessee Williams: Reassessment and Assessment," in *Tennessee Williams: A Tribute,* edited by Jac Tharpe, University Press of Mississippi, 1977, pp. 848-80.

FOSTER HIRSCH

(essay date 1979)

[In the following excerpt, Hirsch discusses the autobiographical nature of Williams's work.]

Nymphomania, promiscuity, rape, greed, alcoholism, impotence, homosexuality, profligacy, frigidity, crib fetishism, pedophilia, blowtorch killing, castration, dope addiction, venereal disease, cannibalism, mad-

Paul Newman and Elizabeth Taylor as Brick and Maggie in the film version of *Cat on a Hot Tin Roof.*

ness, panty fetishism, masturbation, coprophagy: gleefully listed by *Playboy,* these are the subjects that have preoccupied Tennessee Williams, our national poet of the perverse, "the man whom we pay to have our nightmares for us" [Tom Driver, in *The New Republic* (20 April 1959): 21]. Drawing on his own erotic fantasies, shocking and charming audiences with his hothouse visions of sex and violence, Tennessee Williams is a popular entertainer who is at the same time a serious artist.

With his poet's sense of rhythm and image, Williams embellishes his dramas with elaborate symbols. The glass menagerie, the streetcar named Desire, the rose tattoo, the *camino real,* the Venus fly trap in *Suddenly Last Summer,* the cavern in *Period of Adjustment,* the iguana in *The Night of the Iguana,* the clipped flowers in *In the Bar of a Tokyo Hotel,* are all bluntly insisted-upon signs and tokens of Williams's serious literary purpose. "My great bête noir as a writer," Williams has admitted, in the face of some hard criticism, "has been a tendency . . . to poeticize."

In his early and middle periods—his great creative

streak from *The Glass Menagerie* in 1945 to *The Night of the Iguana* in 1961—Williams was writing to reach a mass audience. "I feel it can dig what I have to say, perhaps better than a lot of intellectuals can . . . the bigger the audience, the better." Always wanting to please—"I have a great desire to *excite* people!"— Williams was at the same time anxious to write well, to deepen theme and characterization with a carefully worked out pattern of symbols. Williams has always tried to write emotionally complex plays in which he placed his characters within a cosmic frame. To that end, sex is never simply sex in a Williams drama: in *Suddenly Last Summer,* for instance, Sebastian Venable's sexual appetite symbolizes cosmic rapacity; his greed, his urge to devour, is but the echo of God's relation to man. In *A Streetcar Named Desire* Stanley Kowalski's seduction of Blanche Du Bois is not merely the victory of a hard-hat over a coy Southern belle, it is the representation of Williams's conviction that the meek shall *not* inherit the earth. The battle over the farm in *Kingdom of Earth* is not only a contest between two types of male sexuality, it is a symbolic struggle for possession of the South. Val Xavier, the hero of *Battle of Angels* and *Orpheus Descending,* is not simply a stud who infuriates a backwater Southern town, he is the savior who revitalizes every woman he meets. All of Williams's muscular heroes, in fact, from Val Xavier to Chance Wayne in *Sweet Bird of Youth* to Chris Flanders in *The Milk Train Doesn't Stop Here Any More,* are angels of mercy whose bodies are the instruments of resurrection and purification.

Although they often contain sensational elements, Williams's plays are as moralistic as they are literary. "Tom is not a dirty writer," his brother Dakin has insisted. "He is really turning out morality plays. . . . He is searching for pardon for the sinner in the mercy of an all-loving God." The plays are a series of moral allegories in which Williams, an entrenched puritan fascinated by his own and others' sinfulness, judges his characters. He is a moralist who exposes corruption: "I think that deliberate, conscienceless mendacity, the acceptance of falsehood and hypocrisy is the most dangerous of all sins. The moral contribution of my plays is that they uncover what I consider to be untrue." Williams's characters are thus examples of various roads to ruin and the consequences of sin. Since Williams has never shaken the notion that sex is at least partly sinful, all of his sexually troubled characters are held to a strict moral reckoning; and their unhappy histories are designed as warnings. Williams concocts exotic sexual fantasies, yet he hovers puritanically over the revels, seeing to it that the misbehaving characters are properly punished. Though Williams believes that sex is a form of grace, he also feels that sex is impure, and he often resolves his contradictory attitudes by contriving horrible destinies for his sexual athletes. Williams is a confused moralist, and his continuing battle with his puritanical impulses frequently complicates the dramas in interesting ways. The plays are filled with tantalizing ambiguities.

Williams creates driven characters who are unlike anyone most of us are ever likely to meet and yet they are almost all convincing and recognizable. Williams's special gift is exactly his ability to give universal dimension to his private fantasy figures. In his successful period, from 1945 to 1961, his plays appealed to millions, from matinee matrons to *The Partisan Review,* from adolescents to English professors. Different kinds of audiences were titillated, challenged, and absorbed by Williams's original vision. After enjoying long runs in New York, most of the plays had lengthy national tours before being made into popular movies. In his prime Tennessee Williams was an eminently commercial man of letters.

After *The Night of the Iguana,* though, the writer who converted private trauma into dramatic fireworks lost most of his audience. Williams's personal obsessions derailed him and the plays—from *The Milk Train Doesn't Stop Here* in 1963 to *Out Cry* in 1973—failed to communicate to most theatergoers. The pre-eminent popular playwright of the fifties became the coterie dramatist of the sixties and early seventies. Theatrical and engaging plays like *Cat on a Hot Tin Roof* and *Sweet Bird of Youth* gave way to small-scaled, experimental chamber plays like *Gnadiges Fraulein, In the Bar of a Tokyo Hotel, Small-Craft Warnings,* and *Out Cry.* Consumed by his own neuroses, Williams wrote these decidedly unpopular plays as forms of self-analysis, and the exorcism through his art was more important to him than the courting of public favor.

The details of Williams's fall are as well known as those of his spectacular rise. Like Ernest Hemingway, F. Scott Fitzgerald, Norman Mailer, and Truman Capote, Williams is a full-fledged literary celebrity, a household name whose erratic private life is as much the subject of the gossip column as the scholarly essay. Appearing on talk shows and interviewed by the press, Williams is as famous and as notorious as a misbehaving movie star. For the general public, as well as for the playwright himself, the plays and the life are intimately connected. The dramas, in fact, are written in such a way as to compel us to psychoanalyze their author. When *The Two-Character Play* (the original version of *Out Cry*) opened in London, a critic complained that only Williams's analyst would be able to understand it.

We "read" the man through his work, and the identification has been encouraged by Williams himself. Williams has conspired in the making of his own myth. "I suspect it has always been an instinctive thing with me, when being interviewed, to ham it up and be fairly outrageous in order to provide 'good copy.' The reason? A need to convince the world that I do indeed still exist and to make this fact a matter of public interest and amusement."

To many theatergoers, Williams is a contemporary embodiment of the pagan spirit; a sensualist and bohemian, he is considered in the popular mind to be the author of naughty plays and an ornament to café society. In an interview with Williams in *Esquire* [(September 1972): 108], Rex Reed provided a lush description of the playwright as an ultimate voluptuary and aesthete, living in a world that is a "gilt-edged invitation to decadence . . . with constantly recurring visions in a madhouse, laced with the beckoning insinuation of champagne and flaming foods, of Oriental rugs and dimly lit brothels, surrounded by exotic friends like Anaïs Nin and Anna Magnani. He has gathered his years slowly, savoring the lusty taste of living, taking swooning delight in extravaganzas of brocade, crepe suzettes, and a mild scent of orrisroot."

In addition to his bohemian style Williams's medical history has always been public information, and the author himself, in interviews, and later in his *Memoirs,* talks compulsively and with a sort of macabre glee, about his series of mental breakdowns, his problems with drugs and alcohol, his heart palpitations, his claustrophobia, his cataracts, his recurrent fears of imminent death, his intense depression over his sister's lobotomy, his suicidal mood after the death of Frank Merlo, the man with whom he had lived for fourteen years. At the lowest point in his personal and professional fortunes, in the late sixties, Williams's confinement to an institution received more attention than his plays.

"To tell the truth," Williams has said, "I'm just too damn self-centered. The problems of my private life occupy too much of my attention." Williams has called himself one of the world's "most egocentric" people; and for him, as for many of the characters in his later plays, life and art mingle incestuously. "At the age of fourteen I discovered writing as an escape from a world of reality in which I felt acutely uncomfortable. . . . [writing was] my place of retreat, my cave, my refuge." Williams even discontinued psychoanalysis because his doctor wanted him "to take a rest" from writing. "He'd shift my appointment hours to try to make it impossible for me to work. But if he said to come in at eight a.m., I'd get up at four and do my writing. I just couldn't face a day without work."

Dramatizing his own fears, his paranoia, his maladjustment to the "real world," his sexual conflicts, his intense guilt, Williams can write only about "things that concern me . . . I just have to identify with the character in some way, or the character is not real. I sometimes wish that my writing was less personal. In recent years I think my outlook became almost like a scream."

Trapped in his own "heart, body and brain, [which] are forged in a white-hot furnace for the purpose of conflict," Williams has been preoccupied in his plays with two consuming themes that are the dominant struggles in his own life: the conflict between the puritan and the cavalier, which absorbs him throughout his early and middle periods, and the artist's relation to art, which has detained him throughout the last decade. The body and the soul, life and art—these great dualities provide the conflicts in both the plays and the life of Tennessee Williams.

Williams inherits from his parents his continuing struggle between the flesh and the spirit. His mother is a rector's daughter descended from Quakers, and his father was a brawny manager of a shoe company who, says Mrs. Williams, "liked long poker games and drinking bouts . . . and would talk in a rough way in front of the children." Mr. Williams uprooted the family, and the move from a rural rectory in Mississippi to a grim city apartment in St. Louis represented for young Tom and his mother a rude cultural shock. Williams was always at war with his father, whose own virility was offended by his son's quiet manner and his interest in books. As Williams has often told interviewers, his father persistently called him sissy and "Miss Nancy." "When I was younger," Williams says, "I hated him with a passionate loathing. He was a big, powerful man, and he intimidated all of us. . . . My mother hated his guts too. She still does. She doesn't have a good word to say for him, and didn't even attend his funeral."

A father who strikes terror in the heart of his son ("he scared me all my life"), a mother who exemplified Southern gentility—here, in his unhappy family history, developed the conflict that appears in Williams's strongest plays. The real life models for hulking, threatening Stanley Kowalski and fluttery Blanche Du Bois were Mr. and Mrs. Williams.

Williams's family heritage is introduced in many of his major plays. Like the playwright himself, his characters are often caught between the world of the rectory and that of Moon Lake Casino, which is the symbol in the early plays of the fast party life to which Williams and characters like Alma Winemiller and Blanche Du Bois are both attracted and repelled. Williams has said that he identifies more with Alma, the divided heroine of *Summer and Smoke*, than with any of his other characters: "Alma is my favorite—because I came out so late and so did Alma, and she had the greatest struggle." Like Alma, Williams grew up in the

The cannibal scene from the 1959 film version of *Suddenly Last Summer*.

Major Media Adaptations: Motion Pictures and Television

The Glass Menagerie, 1950. Warner. Director: Irving Rapper. Cast: Gertrude Lawrence, Jane Wyman, Kirk Douglas, Arthur Kennedy.

A Streetcar Named Desire, 1951. Warner/Fox. Director: Elia Kazan. Cast: Vivien Leigh, Marlon Brando, Kim Hunter, Karl Malden.

The Rose Tattoo, 1955. Paramount. Director: Daniel Mann. Cast: Anna Magnani, Burt Lancaster, Marisa Pavan, Ben Cooper.

Baby Doll, 1956. Warner. [Adaptation of *27 Wagons Full of Cotton*] Director: Elia Kazan. Cast: Karl Malden, Eli Wallach, Carroll Baker, Mildred Dunnock, Lonny Chapman.

Cat on a Hot Tin Roof, 1958. MGM. Director: Richard Brooks. Cast: Paul Newman, Burl Ives, Elizabeth Taylor, Jack Carson, Judith Anderson.

Suddenly Last Summer, 1959. Columbia. Director: Joseph L. Mankiewicz. Cast: Elizabeth Taylor, Katharine Hepburn, Montgomery Clift, Albert Dekker, Mercedes McCambridge.

The Fugitive Kind, 1960. UA. [Adaptation of *Orpheus Descending*] Director: Sidney Lumet. Cast: Marlon Brando, Anna Magnani, Joanne Woodward, Victor Jory, Maureen Stapleton.

The Roman Spring of Mrs. Stone, 1961. Warner. Director: José Quintero. Cast: Vivien Leigh, Warren Beatty, Lotte Lenya, Jeremy Spenser, Coral Browne.

Summer and Smoke, 1961. Paramount. Director: Peter Glenville. Cast: Geraldine Page, Lawrence Harvey, Una Merkel, John McIntire, Pamela Tiffin, Rita Moreno.

Period of Adjustment, 1962. MGM. Director: George Roy Hill. Cast: Tony Franciosa, Jane Fonda, Jim Hutton, Lois Nettleton.

Sweet Bird of Youth, 1962. MGM. Director: Richard Brooks. Cast: Paul Newman, Geraldine Page, Ed Begley, Mildred Dunnock, Rip Torn, Shirley Knight.

The Night of the Iguana, 1964. MGM. Director: John Huston. Cast: Richard Burton, Deborah Kerr, Ava Gardner, Sue Lyon, Grayson Hall, Cyril Delevanti.

This Property Is Condemned, 1966. Paramount. Director: Sydney Pollack. Cast: Natalie Wood, Robert Redford, Mary Badham, Kate Reid, Charles Bronson, Jon Provost, John Harding.

Boom!, 1968. Universal. [Adaptation of *The Milk Train Doesn't Stop Here Anymore*] Director: Joseph Losey. Cast: Elizabeth Taylor, Richard Burton, Noel Coward, Michael Dunn, Joanna Shimkus.

The Glass Menagerie, 1973. ABC [Television]. Director: Anthony Harvey. Cast: Katharine Hepburn, Sam Watterston, Joanna Miles, Michael Moriarty.

Cat on a Hot Tin Roof, 1976. NBC [Television]. Director: Robert Moore. Cast: Laurence Olivier, Natalie Wood, Robert Wagner, Maureen Stapleton, Jack Hedley.

A Streetcar Named Desire, 1984. ABC [Television]. Director: John Erman. Cast: Ann-Margret, Treat Williams, Beverly D'Angelo, Randy Quaid.

Cat on a Hot Tin Roof, 1985. PBS [Television]. Director: Jack Hofsiss. Cast: Jessica Lange, Tommy Lee Jones, Rod Steiger.

The Glass Menagerie, 1987. Cineplex Odeon. Director: Paul Newman. Cast: Joanne Woodward, John Malkovich, Karen Allen, James Naughton.

---

rarefied atmosphere of a country rectory which both sheltered and stifled him; and like Alma, he left it for something racier—bohemian life in New Orleans. Williams, like the narrator in *The Glass Menagerie*, felt he had to leave his confining family home, but he was never able to escape his moralistic upbringing. Williams rebelled against the genteel tradition in which his mother raised him: "I try to outrage puritanism. I have an instinct to shock." But Williams is an uneasy rebel, since he feels that sex is sinful as well as liberating and since he alternately condemns and worships the life of the body. For Williams, as Marion magid has written, "normal adult sexuality" is a "catastrophe": "In the end, Williams's vision is revealed as a shocked outcry, a child's refusal to accept the fact of sex that, yes, grownups really do it."

Williams's discomfort with sex underlies most of the plays, and many of his characters are projections of varying parts of his own complicated sexuality. A character like Alma represents with almost diagrammatic simplicity Williams's own split between refinement and rapacity. A character like Serafina (in *The Rose Tattoo*) celebrates Williams's worship of sex, while a character like Blanche indicates his fear of it.

It was not until 1970 that Williams began to speak openly about his homosexuality, and it was not until his interview with *Playboy* in 1973 that he spoke about it without defensiveness. "Until I was twenty-eight, I was attracted to girls," Williams confided to *Playboy*,

but after that I fell in love with a man and felt it was better for me as a writer, for it meant *freedom*. . . . Women have always been my deepest emotional root; anyone who's read my writings knows that. But I've never had any feeling of sexual security—except with Frank Merlo, who served me as I had to be served . . . my first real encounter was in New Orleans at a New Year's Eve Party during World War Two. A very handsome paratrooper climbed up to my grilled veranda and said, "Come down to my place," and I did, and he said, "Would you like a sunlamp treatment?" and I said, "Fine," and I got under one and he proceeded to do me. That was my coming out and I enjoyed it.

In 1975 Williams published a novel, *Moise and the World of Reason,* and his *Memoirs,* in both of which he continues the sexual confessions begun in the now notorious *Playboy* interview. In the novel and particularly in *Memoirs,* Williams writes openly about homosexuality, in a way that he never felt free to in his great masked plays. The novel reads in fact like a dry run for the revelations in *Memoirs,* though the tone of *Moise* is darker than that of the autobiography, its treatment of sexuality less jubilant: its homosexual love story is an intimation of the expansive confessional mode that explodes full-force in *Memoirs.*

Moise and the World of Reason reads like a series of journal entries in which the author muses at random on art and sex, his twin preoccupations. The novel's compulsively voluble narrator clearly speaks to us in Williams's own palpitating voice, creating a portrait of the author as a sensual young man, "a distinguished failed writer" at thirty. Obsessed with his past, his sexual desires, and his rejection slips, the narrator uses his diary jottings as a defense against emptiness. His desk (as for Williams) is the center of his world; his writing imposes order and dignity on the experiences of a sometimes shabby life. Art heals, and the book records the process of the writer's salvation through the patterned arrangement of words on a page. Since it has no real story or tangible dramatic conflict, the novel is designed to show off its author's sensibility—Williams attempts to hold us with the fractured, fevered ruminations of a fictional character who nakedly enacts his own fears of artistic failure and isolation. On a long, dark night of the soul, after he has been abandoned at a party by his current lover, the narrator returns to his hovel to scribble and to reflect; and we are regaled with a free-form kaleidoscopic sampling of what is on his mind. Characters, anecdotes, images from Williams's own past compete for our attention. Williams is an exuberant, though inconsistent, master of ceremonies, and the quality of the remembered moments varies. Some are tantalizing, while others seem like pale carbon copies of past routines. A vivid caricature of a voracious woman called the Actress Invicta is presented in Williams's florid, Rabelaisian grand manner; but a scene between the narrator and his conservative Southern mother, who is shocked by her son's bohemian ways, is shrill and mechanical.

As always, Williams is a poet of sexual longing; and the most lyrical of the memories involve the writer and his first lover Lance, a black ice skater with an ideal physique and a generous, yielding spirit. Typically, Williams's attitude to sex is dense and contradictory as he sees it as both holy and infected, transcendent and tainted. Lance is a Williams stud like Stanley Kowalski and Chance Wayne who offers ecstatic release. Yet throughout these reminiscences sex is also sinister, as in the bizarre passage in which the young writer meets and feels threatened by a once-famous playwright who tries to entice him to go on a long journey. The crumbling playwright, so patently an embittered self-portrait, uses sex as magic but also as punishment. An experience that the narrator recalls from childhood also connects sex with doom. The remembered incident concerns the sudden appearance in the author's small Southern hometown of four elegant young men who lure boys into their car; to the narrator, the crusaders seem fatally corrupt, their compulsive, ritualistic cruising a prefiguring of early death.

Williams therefore remains a reluctant Dionysian, a guilt-ridden reveler; and for this Southern puritan, sex still sometimes promises catastrophe. But until this point in his writing, Williams had never before written so unguardedly about himself. The narrator is openly, at times even joyously, homosexual, so that sexual desire isn't disguised here as it was in the plays. Williams, however, is one of those writers for whom telling all may have a therapeutic effect on his spirit but a dampening result on his art. Written before gay liberation, his major plays required distance from and transformation of his actual experience, and Williams benefited, artistically, from the pressures imposed by social convention. (On one level *A Streetcar Named Desire* is a homosexual fantasy with Blanche as an effeminate male masked as a magnificently neurotic Southern belle; but American drama can be grateful that Williams didn't write Blanche as a man!) Except for *Memoirs, Moise and the World of Reason* is Williams's most open personal statement, and yet it has little of the surging erotic comedy or the dynamic tensions of the great partially closed plays.

Memoirs is Williams's ultimate coming out statement, and a vigorous reinforcement of the playwright's belief that the work and the life of a writer are inextricably bound. Like all of Williams's writing, these private revelations are obsessively concerned with sex, but here sexuality offers joy and refuge from isolation without the darker aspects of self-punishment and loss of self that often taint sex in the plays. Williams's relationships with men have caused him much pain, but in this wonderfully liberated and liberating book, Williams celebrates the pleasures of loving men. He writes about his homosexuality without apology. There is a serene self-acceptance evident here that represents a marked difference from the tortured, divided, sexually frustrated characters in many of his plays. He seems to have shed the puritanical values that have nagged him for most of his life: at long last, after years in the shadows of his grandfather's rectory, after years of analysis and conflict, Williams seems to be a free spirit, a true, guiltless voluptuary.

Because he wanted to get his plays produced,

Williams had to disguise the homosexual motifs that were given free rein in early stories like **"One Arm"** and **"Hard Candy."** Like Proust, Williams felt he had to transpose and readjust the sexual currents in order to reach a large audience. Because homosexuality was in the forties and fifties an unmentionable subject, Williams had to transfer to his often grasping, hot-blooded female characters his own intense attraction to men. What *Memoirs* makes clear is that, if social attitudes toward homosexuality had been different, his work would have been different, too. *Memoirs* doesn't change the plays, but it compels us to admit their masks and transpositions. Many critics have hinted at the homosexual aura of the plays, pointing out that it is almost always the men who are the sex objects, the sexual saviors and magicians. Now the atmosphere of critical innuendo, the veiled charges, can be dispelled, for Williams has given his critics enough frank details to liberate them as well as himself.

Williams takes evident delight in startling his readers, referring exhibitionistically to his mental and physical collapses. His section on his confinement in a violent ward of a mental institution is harrowing, though written with a kind of impish pride—Williams seems to take a perverse pleasure in recounting the sensational details of his incarceration, and the scenes in the hospital are shot through with flashes of grim comedy. Perhaps it is this sense of life's comedy that has saved Williams. *Memoirs* reveals his mordant sense of humor, his healing irony in the midst of pain, his great capacity for laughter. Williams's recent confessional writing, lively, direct, immediate, nevertheless misses the soaring, lyrical intensity of his best work. Yet an innocence emanates from these revved-up self-portraits; there is something, finally, unspoiled about Williams. As revealed in both the novel and *Memoirs,* his goal of unwavering dedication to his art and his ambition to be the best writer that he is capable of being, are altogether admirable. *Memoirs* shows enormous courage. It is a landmark in American letters that enriches our understanding of the work of a great playwright.

Williams didn't have to "come out," of course, for his audience to know the truth about his sexual preferences, since on one level, almost all the plays are homosexual fantasies. Williams's women desire spectacular males, and between the playwright and his ravenous females there is a deep emotional connection. In *Cat on a Hot Tin Roof,* Maggie pleads for Brick to go to bed with her; Alma has a schoolgirl's crush on the handsome doctor who lives next door; Blanche is both alarmed by and attracted to the sight of Stanley's rippling muscles; the women of a provincial Southern town pant after the sultry wanderer, Val Xavier, in *Battle of Angels.* In Williams's most exotic fantasy, *Suddenly Last Summer,* Sebastian Venable is eaten alive by a group of native boys; and in his most seemingly het-

erosexual play, *Period of Adjustment,* the army buddies are more comfortable with each other than with their shrill wives. The virile male, the peacock, the stud, is the central icon in play after play; he is the catalyst, the fought over, the scapegoat, the victim, the prize. Williams worships him, lusts after him, punishes him; the stud's sexuality is both reward and threat. The beautiful, muscled young man is the animate object that ignites the spinsters and the whores. In most of Williams's plays, the man rather than the woman is the desirable partner; and it is women who are sexually aggressive—the men don't have to be. No Williams play is written on the pattern of the traditional heterosexual chase.

The homosexual sensibility is always present, though it is almost never direct, since Williams writes about men with women rather than about men with men. Only in *Small-Craft Warnings* and *Vieux Carre* does Williams present an overtly homosexual relationship, and only in these plays do characters talk openly about the gay life. The homosexual impulse often masquerades as heterosexual courtship. Williams's women, however, must not be interpreted as drag queens. They "play" as women because Williams has transmuted private fantasy into art. There is no simple, easy equation between the playwright and his man-hungry women; rather, Williams has used his own deepest sexual impulses as the base on which to construct complex dramatic characters. His homosexuality necessarily colors the way he presents both his female and male characters; as he has often said, he identifies more with his women than with his men, but this does not mean that Williams's females are merely effeminate men in disguise, or that Williams is cheating by trying to pass off a character like Blanche as a woman. The millions of viewers and readers who have accepted Blanche as a woman have not been duped by a clever dramatist writing plays in code for a coterie audience; but there is much in Blanche's extravagantly stylized personality, in her flirtatiousness, her quivering sensitivity, her concern with surface, that is reflective of certain kinds of gay as well as "straight" female sensibilities. A character like Blanche, created by a homosexual, is a mixture of several different sexual currents. As either gay or straight, she is an outsider, like most of the playwright's characters, a reject from conventional society, and it is this sense of her absolute isolation that Williams creates so powerfully and that "mixed" audiences throughout the world have continued to respond to with great empathy. Though conceived by a writer who felt estranged and who suffered because he was homosexual, Williams's outcasts have significance for audiences beyond gay ghettoes. The universal resonance of his characters has of course been responsible for Williams's high literary reputation. And it is because he has always tried to reach "mixed" audiences that Williams has resisted writing specifically gay plays like *The Boys in the Band.* Except perhaps in *Cat on a Hot Tin Roof,* sexual masking in Williams is not then necessarily hypocritical, and it certainly does not diminish his creative strengths, no more than it does in Proust.

Williams does not write disguised gay liberation tracts that covertly exalt homosexual love. Plays like *Cat on a Hot Tin Roof* and *Period of Adjustment* present heterosexual relationships in an unattractive way, but this derision is never the central focus of Williams's work. The playwright may often exalt the male and humiliate the female, but he identifies always with his victims, and so his sympathy is reserved for his hounded, rejected, dishevelled women rather than his cool, self-absorbed Adonises, upon whom he inflicts appalling punishment: Chance Wayne in *Sweet Bird of Youth* is castrated; Val Xavier in *Battle of Angels* is lynched; Sebastian Venable in *Suddenly Last Summer* is cannibalized.

Ever present, homosexuality in Williams is almost always concealed. In that jittery mid-fifties play, *Cat on a Hot Tin Roof,* it is the disease that dare not speak its name, and it is equated with another dreadful affliction—cancer. When he touches on it directly, Williams frequently presents homosexuality in a grim context. The homosexual in *Small-Craft Warnings,* for instance, derides gay promiscuity; and since he has been corrupted and coarsened by gay experience, he has lost the ability to be surprised by life. In *Suddenly Last Summer* Williams treats gay cruising as the emblem of a rotting universe. Homosexuals in the plays are often stereotypes that confirm popular prejudice: gays in Williams are supremely sensitive artists; aesthetes who are too refined for the world as it is; sybarites compulsively addicted to sex. In *Cat on a Hot Tin Roof,* Brick's friend Skipper kills himself when he realizes that he is homosexual and Brick himself retreats to a kind of death-in-life.

Until *Memoirs,* it was only in Williams's novella, **"The Knightly Quest,"** that the overt homosexual was presented favorably. Gewinner Pierce is a romantic whose refinement is clearly superior to the bestial coupling of his gross heterosexual brother and his crass wife. Gewinner easily triumphs over brutish straights who inhabit a plastic countryside littered with hamburger joints. Together with two sympathetic women, Gewinner is transported in a spaceship to a better world than the rancid contemporary America he judges so harshly.

Williams has said recently that he never considered homosexuality a promising subject for a full-length play, and he has confined direct rather than masked or metaphoric treatments of the subject to short stories. In **"Desire and the Black Masseur"** a meek man meets his destiny being pummeled to death by a towering black masseur: the story is a fantasy con-

frontation between the ultimate masochist and the ultimate sadist. In **"One Arm"** the hustler protagonist services men rather than women. **"Mysteries of the Joy Rio"** and **"Hard Candy"** are two versions of the same subject, fleeting sex in the balcony of a fading movie palace. An old man finds pleasure with a series of compliant, anonymous, sometimes faceless young men and boys. The homosexual life patterns described in these stories are not presented from a liberated or crusading viewpoint. Sex in these explicit stories is dank and joyless, even if the stories end, curiously, with a kind of catharsis: unhappy sex is linked to death and a final mystical transfiguration. The characters are all sinners who are yet saved by compulsive, serial sex; impersonal sex leads to salvation, and the characters, who think of themselves as dirty and unworthy, are ultimately purified.

Mixing sex, death, and salvation in beguiling contradiction, Williams is something of a Southern Gothic version of Jean Genet. He is a guilty sex-singer, an unliberated bohemian, a hip puritan who nourishes his art with his own tangled sexual preoccupations. Much has been written about his indebtedness to D. H. Lawrence, and there are certainly connections to Genet in his plays, but Williams is the poet of his own private universe. Williams has claimed "an identification with Lawrence's view of life . . . a belief in the purity of the sensual life," but he is in fact a much more troubled sensualist than Lawrence. As Nancy Tischler has written, Williams is "not at home in the glorification of sex." Like many of his characters, the playwright wants to escape from the burdens of the flesh, and the horror that taunts him is that the flesh may be an inadequate means to deliverance and transcendence.

Lawrence, Genet, Strindberg, Lorca, Hart Crane, Chekhov, and Ibsen have been proposed at various times as principal influences on Williams. *Time* nominated Hawthorne, Poe, and Melville, "the triumvirate of American gloom and disquietude," as Williams's philosophical forebears: "With them, Williams shares transcendental yearnings, the sense of isolation and alienation, the Calvinist conscience, the Gothic settings and horror." But the only tangible influence on Williams's work has been the effects on him of his family, his friends, and his artistic and commercial fortunes: his warring parents; his genteel grandparents; his sister Rose, victim of a prefrontal lobotomy for which Williams feels partly responsible; his pliant lover of fourteen years, Frank Merlo; his identification with wounded people like Diana Barrymore and Carson McCullers and with exuberant voluptuaries like Anna Magnani; his breakdowns and confinements, his withdrawals and resurrections; his resounding critical and popular acceptance, his stunning critical and public rejection.

Williams does, however, belong to a tradition in American letters, that of Southern Gothic, and his settings, his themes, his use of language, share similarities with the work of writers like William Faulkner, Carson McCullers, Jane Bowles, Truman Capote, and Flannery O'Connor. Williams has described what are for him the characteristics that link these Southern writers:

> There is something in the region, something in the blood and culture, of the Southern state that has made [Southerners] the center of this Gothic school of writing. . . . What is this common link? a sense, an intuition, of an underlying dreadfulness in modern experience. . . . The true sense of dread is not a reaction to anything sensible or visible or even, strictly materially, *knowable.* But rather it's a kind of spiritual intuition of something almost too incredible and shocking to talk about, which underlies the whole so-called thing. It is the incommunicable something that we shall have to call *mystery* which is so inspiring of dread . . . that Sense of the Awful which is the desperate black root of nearly all significant modern art.

Like other writers of Southern Gothic, Williams is obsessed with the social outsider, the character who is unbalanced in extravagant and colorful ways. Edged with sexual hysteria, the work of the Gothic writers is intensely theatrical, lushly composed. Their work has a steamy texture, with language and characterization approaching ecstatic overstatement, even when, as in McCullers and O'Connor, there is a serious attempt to write in a cryptic and spare manner. Like other writers in this tradition Williams dramatizes Southern society and the history that hovers prominently behind it as, on the one hand, a malevolent, devouring force and, on the other, an intensely romantic, almost fantasy-like landscape, dotted with white-pillared plantations, weeping willows, and magnolia blossoms. In common with other Southern writers, Williams is absorbed by a romantic vision of the past—the Old South. In many of the plays (and most prominently in *A Streetcar Named Desire* and *The Glass Menagerie*) the characters cling to an idealized notion of plantation society. The picture of an elegant, enclosed society of fine gentlemen courting tremulous ladies in crinoline, while devoted family servants move discreetly in the background, comprises for many of Williams's characters an image of perfect social order. The decline of this rural ideal, as well as the characters' separation from their privileged Southern inheritance, is a measure of their fall from grace, their expulsion from Eden as conceived by the Southern imagination.

Williams's use of Southern history and Southern myth is thus highly sentimental and "aesthetic." In a recent study of the Southern "Renaissance," *The Literature of Memory: Modern Writers of the American South* [1977], Richard Gray evaluates Williams's treatment of Southern motifs as

decorative: it offers us a group of charming grotesques, preserved in amber. What is Southern about it, really, is not a certain quality of perception, a sense of engagement between past and present, the public and the private, myth and history: but a turn of phrase or personality, a use of the bizarre and sensational for their own sake, which has the net effect of creating distance. For regionalism is substituted a form of local color, and a very precious and slightly decadent form at that, in which the gap between drama and audience seems deliberately widened so that the latter can revel without compunction in a contemporary "Gothick" fantasy.

Even if, as Gray suggests, Williams's vision of the South is "decadent" and "reductive," the playwright is nonetheless a distinctly regional writer, and it is perhaps as a popularizer of Southern sensuality and gentility—Southern manners—that he is best known. A major influence on Williams as a creative artist has been precisely his attraction to Southern "style"—to that world of languor and refinement and sensual indulgence which for him are synonymous with the antebellum South. Brass beds, overhead fans, family mansions, suffocating heat, tropical plants—these aspects of the Southern scene permeate the plays, giving the dramas the exotic texture and lush sense of place for which they are famous.

Williams, then, is distinctly a regional writer, steeped in the Southern writer's absorption with the past. The workings of memory, and the collision between a dream of the past and the realities of an increasingly urbanized present provide inspiration for the plays as much as they do for the novels of Faulkner. Williams is writing in the tradition of the Southern "Renaissance," that explosion of literary genius in the twenties as a response to the World War and to the increasing separation of the South from its proudly remembered heritage; and in his tone and sensibility, in his lyricism and dependence on rhetoric, he has more in common with Faulkner and Thomas Wolfe, with Robert Penn Warren and Allen Tate and John Crowe Ransom, than with any tradition in American drama.

Williams, in fact, has exerted far more influence on American drama than he has absorbed from it. His dissection of sexual conflicts anticipated the greater sexual frankness in the plays as well as the films of the sixties and seventies. There is, however, no "school of Williams"—no major writer, or group of writers, has emerged who can claim Williams as a primary inspiration. Williams has remained aloof from trends in American drama, continuing to create plays out of the same basic neurotic conflicts in his own personality. Williams has continued, that is, to borrow from and to be influenced by his own work; as critics of the later plays have only too frequently observed, Williams, heedless of external influences, plagiarizes from himself. The later Williams is still nourished by the distinctive dramatic world created in the earliest plays. That world was so spectacularly scaled and intensely realized that Williams's persistent use of it has come to seem like self-parody. In a sense the playwright has been a victim of his own immediately recognizable style.

Tennessee Williams is a great American original whose work does not reflect his times in any direct way. His plays, though, contain social implications insofar as they are a barometer of what Americans will tolerate or respond to in the way of sexual fantasy and insofar as their acceptance by the public tells us something about the public: "A culture does not consistently pay the price of admission to witness a fable which does not ensnare some part of the truth about it," as Marion Magid noted. But Williams is not interested in being a recorder of public attitudes or social concerns; being among the most private and self-enclosed of famous authors, he writes in order to exorcise his own demons, and he is always triumphantly and inescapably himself. (pp. 3-17)

Foster Hirsch, in his *A Portrait of the Artist: The Plays of Tennessee Williams,* Kennikat Press, 1979, 121 p.

TENNESSEE WILLIAMS
(interview date 1981)

[The following interview with Williams was conducted by Dotson Rader in 1981. The interview began in Chicago, where Williams was working on the production of *A House Not Meant to Stand,* and was completed several weeks later in New York. Here, below, Williams comments about his writing, his goals as a writer, and his work habits. In a preface to the interview, Rader stated: "Williams very much dislikes talking about his work and the process through which he creates his art. But in New York, on that dreary, gray day, he was open to it and told me what he could about how he writes."]

THE GENESIS OF WRITING

I was a born writer, I think. Yes, I think that I was. At least when I had this curious disease affecting my heart at the age of eight. I was more or less bedridden for half a year. My mother exaggerated the cause. She said I swallowed my tonsils! Years later, when I had the *Time* cover story, and she was quoted, doctors looked it up and said, "A medical impossibility!"

But I do think there was a night when I nearly died, or possibly *did* die. I had a strange, mystical feeling as if I were seeing a golden light. Elizabeth Taylor had the same experience. But I survived that night. That was a turning point, and I gradually pulled out of it. But

I was never the same physically. It changed my entire personality. I'd been an aggressive tomboy until that illness. I used to beat up all the kids on the block. I used to confiscate their marbles, snatch them up!

Then that illness came upon me, and my personality changed. I became a shut-in. I think my mother encouraged me to be more of a shut-in than I needed to be. Anyway, I took to playing solitary games, amusing myself. I don't mean masturbation. I mean I began to live an intensely imaginative life. And it persisted that way. That's how I turned into a writer, I guess. By the age of twelve, I started writing. (pp. 147-48)

WHERE PLAYS COME FROM

The process by which the idea for a play comes to me has always been something I really couldn't pinpoint. A play just seems to materialize, like an apparition it gets clearer and clearer and clearer. It's very vague at first, as in the case of *Streetcar,* which came after *Menagerie.* I simply had the vision of a woman in her late youth. She was sitting in a chair all alone by a window with the moonlight streaming in on her desolate face, and she'd been stood up by the man she planned to marry.

I believe I was thinking of my sister because she was madly in love with some young man at the International Shoe Company who paid her court. He was extremely handsome, and she was profoundly in love with him. Whenever the phone would ring, she'd nearly faint. She'd think it was he calling for a date, you know? They saw each other every other night, and then one time he just didn't call anymore. That was when Rose first began to go into a mental decline. From that vision *Streetcar* evolved. I called it at the time, *Blanche's Chair in the Moon,* which is a very bad title. But it was from that image, you know, of a woman sitting by a window that *Streetcar* came to me.

Of course, the young man who courted my sister was nothing like Stanley. He was a young executive from an Ivy League school. He had every apparent advantage. It was during the Depression years, however, and he was extremely ambitious. My father had an executive position at the time with the shoe company, and the young man had thought perhaps a marriage to Rose would be to his advantage. Then, unfortunately, my father was involved in a terrible scandal and nearly lost his job. At any rate, he was no longer a candidate for the Board of Directors. He had his ear bit off in a poker fight! It had to be restored. They had to take cartilage from his ribs, and skin off his ass, and they reproduced something that looked like a small cauliflower attached to the side of his head! So any time anybody would get into the elevator with my father, he'd scowl, and people would start giggling. That was when the young man stopped calling on Rose. He knew the giggling had gone too far and gotten into the newspapers.

The idea for *The Glass Menagerie* came very slowly, much more slowly than *Streetcar* for example. I think I worked on *Menagerie* longer than any other play. I didn't think it'd ever be produced. I wasn't writing it for that purpose. I wrote it first as a short story called **"Portrait of a Girl in Glass,"** which is, I believe, one of my best stories. I guess *Menagerie* grew out of the intense emotions I felt seeing my sister's mind begin to go.

INFLUENCES

What writers influenced me as a young man? *Chekhov!*

As a dramatist? Chekhov!

As a story writer? Chekhov!

D. H. Lawrence, too, for his spirit, of course, for his understanding of sexuality, of life in general.

EFFECTS

When I write I don't aim to shock people, and I'm surprised when I do. But I don't think that anything that occurs in life should be omitted from art, though the artist should present it in a fashion that is artistic and not ugly.

I set out to tell the truth. And sometimes the *truth* is shocking. (pp. 152-53)

CHRISTIANITY

I was born a Catholic, really. I'm a Catholic by nature. My grandfather was an English Catholic (Anglican), very, very high church. He was higher church than the Pope. However, my "conversion" to the Catholic church was rather a joke because it occurred while I was taking Dr. Jacobson's miracle shots. I couldn't learn anything about the tenets of the Roman Catholic church, which are ridiculous anyway. I just loved the beauty of the ritual in the Mass. But Dakin found a Jesuit father who was very lovely and all, and he said, "Mr. Williams is not in a condition to learn anything. I'll give him extreme unction and just pronounce him a Catholic."

I was held up in the Roman Catholic church, with people supporting me on both sides, and I was declared a Catholic. What do you think of that? Does that make me a Catholic? No, I was whatever I was before.

And yet my work is full of Christian symbols. Deeply, deeply Christian. But it's the image of Christ, His beauty and purity, and His teachings, yes . . .but I've never subscribed to the idea that life as we know it, what we're living now, is resumed after our death. No. I think we're absorbed back into, what do they call it? The eternal flux? The eternal shit, that's what I was thinking.

POETRY

I'm a poet. And then I put the poetry in the drama.

I put it in short stories, and I put it in the plays. Poetry's poetry. It doesn't have to be called a poem, you know.

YOUNG WRITERS

If they're meant to be writers, they will write. There's nothing that can stop them. It may kill them. They may not be able to stand the terrible indignities, humiliations, privations, shocks that attend the life of an American writer. They may not. Yet they may have some sense of humor about it, and manage to survive.

WRITING

When I write, everything is visual, as brilliantly as if it were on a lit stage. And I talk out the lines as I write.

When I was in Rome, my landlady thought I was demented. She told Frank (Merlo), "Oh, Mr. Williams has lost his mind! He stalks about the room talking out loud!"

Frank said, "Oh, he's just writing." She didn't understand *that.*

REWRITING

In writing a play, I can get started on the wrong tangent, go off somewhere and then have to make great deletions and begin over, not *all* the way over, but just back to where I went off on that particular tangent. This is particularly true of the surrealist play that I'm currently writing. I'm dedicating it to the memory of Joe Orton. *The Everlasting Ticket* it's called. It's about the poet laureate of Three Mile Island. I'm in the third revision of *Ticket* at the moment.

I do an enormous amount of rewriting. And when I finally let a play go, when I know it's complete and as it should be, is when I see a production of it that satisfies me. Of course, even when *I'm* satisfied with a production, the critics are not, usually. In New York especially. The critics feel I'm basically anarchistic, and dangerous as a writer.

AUDIENCE

I don't have an audience in mind when I write. I'm writing mainly for myself. After a long devotion to playwriting I have a good inner ear. I know pretty well how a thing is going to sound on the stage, and how it will play. I write to satisfy this inner ear and its perceptions. That's the audience I write for. (pp. 155-57)

TITLES

Sometimes I'll come up with a title that doesn't sound good in itself, but it's the only title that really fits the meaning of the play. Like *A House Not Meant To Stand* isn't a beautiful title. But the house it refers to in the play is in a terrible state of disrepair, virtually leaking rain water everywhere. That house, and therefore the title, is a metaphor for society in our times. And, of course, the critics don't like that sort of thing, nor do they dare to openly approve of it. They know who butters their bread.

Some titles come from dialogue as I write a play, or from the setting itself. Some come from poetry I've read. When I need a title I'll usually reread the poetry of Hart Crane. I take a copy of Crane's work with me when I travel. A phrase will catch my eye and seem right for what I'm writing. But there's no system to it. Sometimes a line from the play will serve as its title. I often change titles a number of times until I find one that seems right.

There is a Catholic church in Key West named "Mary, Star of the Sea." That would make a lovely title for a play. (pp. 158-59)

HABITS OF WORK

In Key West I get up just before daybreak, as a rule. I like being completely alone in the house in the kitchen when I have my coffee and ruminate on what I'm going to work on. I usually have two or three pieces of work going at the same time, and then I decide which to work on that day.

I go to my studio. I usually have some wine there. And then I carefully go over what I wrote the day before. You see, baby, after a glass or two of wine I'm inclined to extravagance. I'm inclined to excesses because I drink while I'm writing, so I'll blue pencil a lot the next day. Then I sit down, and I begin to write.

My work is *emotionally* autobiographical. It has no relationship to the actual events of my life, but it reflects the emotional currents of my life. I try to work every day because you have no refuge but writing. When you're going through a period of unhappiness, a broken love affair, the death of someone you love, or some other disorder in your life, then you have no refuge but writing. However, when depression comes on of a near clinical nature, then you're paralyzed even at work. Immediately after the death of Frank Merlo, I was paralyzed, unable to write, and it wasn't until I began taking the speed shots that I came out of it. Then I was able to work like a demon. Could you live without writing, baby? I couldn't.

Because it's so important, if my work is interrupted I'm like a raging tiger. It angers me so. You see, I have to reach a high emotional pitch in order to work if the scene is dramatic.

I've heard that Norman Mailer has said that a playwright only writes in short bursts of inspiration while a novelist has to write six or seven hours a day. Bull! Now Mr. Mailer is more involved in the novel form, and I'm more involved in the play form. In the play form I work steadily and hard. If a play grips me I'll continue to work on it until I reach a point where I can no longer decide what to do with it. Then I'll discontinue work on it. (pp. 165-66)

HOMOSEXUALITY

I never found it necessary to deal with it in my work. It was never a preoccupation of mine, except in my intimate, private life. In my work, I've had a great affinity with the female psyche. Her personality, her emotions, what she suffers and feels. People who say I create transvestite women are full of shit. Frankly. Just vicious shit. Personally, I like women more than men. They respond to me more than men do, and they always have. The people who have loved me, the ratio of women to men is about five to one, I would say.

I know there's a right wing backlash against homosexuals. But at the age of seventy I no longer consider it a matter of primary concern. Not that I want anything bad to happen to other homosexuals. God knows, enough has.

I always thought homosexual writers were in the minority of writers. Nobody's yet made a correct census of the actual number of homosexuals in the population of America. And they never will be able to because there are still too many closets, some of them rather securely locked. And it's also still dangerous to be openly homosexual. (p. 167)

CURRENT WORK

I've been busy with the production of the new play, *A House Not Meant To Stand.* The production of a play is for me an event that eclipses everything else, even turning seventy. I love the Goodman Theater, and I'm going to work with them again. We're already making plans to move this play on to the main stage, and to do *Something Cloudy, Something Clear,* about the summer when I met Kip on the Cape, though I've added other characters besides Kip and me.

And I've got an important play, *In Masks Outrageous and Austere.* It's a line of Eleanor Wylie's from a poem by her. It goes like this: "In masks outrageous and austere / the years go by in single file; / Yet none has merited my fear, / and none has quite escaped my smile."

It happens to fit the play, which has a great deal of poetry in it and yet at the same time the situation is bizarre as hell. It's about the richest woman on earth. Babe Foxworth is her name. She doesn't know where she is. She's been abducted to Canada, on the east coast. But they don't know where they are. A village has been constructed like a movie set to deceive them. Everything is done to confine and deceive them while her husband is being investigated. Babe is really an admirable person, besides her hypersexuality, though that can be admirable. I think it is! It's a torture to her because she's married to a gay husband who's brought along his boyfriends. I think it's an extremely funny play.

ADVICE TO YOUNG PLAYWRIGHTS

What shouldn't you do if you're a young playwright? *Don't bore the audience!* I mean, even if you have to resort to totally arbitrary killing on stage, or pointless gunfire, at least it'll catch their attention and keep them awake. Just keep the thing going any way you can. (pp. 182-83)

Tennessee Williams, "The Art of Theatre V," in an interview with Dotson Rader in *The Paris Review,* Vol. 23, No. 81, Fall, 1981, pp. 145-85.

SOURCES FOR FURTHER STUDY

Bloom, Harold, ed. *Tennessee Williams: Modern Critical Views.* New York: Chelsea House Publishers, 1987, 168 p.

Collection of essays on Williams's plays.

Gunn, Drewey Wayne. *Tennessee Williams: A Bibliography.* Metuchen, N.J.: Scarecrow Press, 1980, 255 p.

Comprehensive primary and secondary bibliography of Williams.

Jennings, C. Robert. "*Playboy* Interview: Tennessee Williams." *Playboy* XX (April 1973): 69-84.

Well-known interview with Williams. The playwright discusses his homosexuality, his lover's death, and his ensuing nervous breakdown.

Spoto, Donald. *The Kindness of Strangers: The Life of Tennessee Williams.* Boston and Toronto: Little, Brown and Company, 1985, 409 p.

Biography of Williams. The critic introduces Williams thus: "His connections with his art, with his life, and with other people were both loving and selfish, involved and coolly detached, tender and brutal; in other words, he was a human being. The paradox resulted in a body of writing that often succeeded better than he did. His work is a series of variations on the great emotional cycles of his own tortured life."

Stanton, Stephen, ed. *Tennessee Williams: A Collection of Critical Essays.* Englewood Cliffs, N.J.: Prentice-Hall, 1977, 194 p.

Sixteen critical essays on Williams's work.

Williams, Dakin, and Mead, Shepherd. *Tennessee Williams: An Intimate Biography.* New York: Arbor House, 1983, 352 p.

Biography of Williams by his brother. Considered a companion to Williams's own *Memoirs.*

William Carlos Williams

1883-1963

American poet, novelist, critic, nonfiction writer, auto-biographer, and dramatist.

INTRODUCTION

Williams is regarded as an important and influential poet for his development of distinctly modern poetic forms, free from the influence of tradition. Experimenting with language and form, Williams concentrated on recreating American idioms in his verse, believing that language is a reflection of character. Williams stressed the importance of allowing a poem to take shape during the creative process and based his verse patterns on the natural pauses, cadences, and inflections of speech. Often praised for its vivid imagery, Williams's poetry focuses on objects rather than directly expressing sentiments or ideas. His famous dictum "No ideas but in things!" summarized his belief that the reader can understand and empathize with Williams's thoughts and feelings through the concrete descriptions in his poems. While Williams received only mild attention for much of his career, the publication of his five-volume epic *Paterson* (1946-58) secured his reputation as a major poet.

Williams was born in Rutherford, New Jersey, to middle-class parents who were lovers of literature and visual art, but he showed little interest in art as a child. After moving to Pennsylvania to attend medical school, however, Williams became enamored with poetry, and was for some time torn between his parents' wishes that he become a doctor and his own, less conventional aspirations. While in Pennsylvania, Williams befriended the poet Ezra Pound, a relationship that he later termed a watershed in his literary career: "Before meeting Pound," he said, "is like B.C. and A.D." Pound not only helped Williams develop his aesthetic of Imagism—a poetic approach that emphasized the concrete over abstractions—but also introduced him to a literary circle that included the flambouyant poet Hilda Doolittle (H. D.). By the time Williams completed his studies, he was committed to a writing career, yet he also entered medicine and maintained a private practice in Rutherford for over forty years. From his medical practice, Williams gained not only the financial freedom to write what he wished, but also, he later wrote, a rare and intimate insight into the lives of common people. His profession, he remarked, allowed him "to follow the poor defeated body into those gulfs and grottos . . . , to be present at deaths and births, at the tormented battles between daughter and diabolic mother."

Williams's immersion in and attachment to the lives of Rutherford's townsfolk was mirrored in the aesthetic principles he developed over the years; he consistently advocated and wrote literature that took its themes from ordinary life and its voice from the patterns of common speech. During much of his poetic career, however, these values ran counter to those of the critically-acclaimed poetry of the day—namely, the classicist, academic, and formal poetry exemplified by T. S. Eliot, Wallace Stevens, and Marianne Moore. During the '20s and '30s, Williams labored largely in obscurity; with the publication of the first *Paterson* volumes in the 1940s, however, Williams gained wider recognition, and the emerging Beat Generation poets of the 1950s venerated him for his rejection of formalism. His last book, *Pictures from Brueghel* (1962), won a Pulitzer Prize in 1963; shortly after receiving the honor, Williams died.

Formal in diction and conventional in versification, Williams's first volume of poetry, *Poems* (1909), is uncharacteristic of his later work; the author later described it as "obviously young, obviously bad." The volumes which followed, *The Tempers* (1913), *Al que quiere!* (1917), and *Kora in Hell: Improvisations* (1920), contain poems set in distinctly American surroundings and are characterized by precise imagery, spare language, and colloquial speech. *Spring and All* (1923) further exemplifies these qualities: it combines poetry and prose and vigorously defies the conventions of poetic structure. *Spring and All* contains the much anthologized pieces "The Red Wheelbarrow," a minimalist poem that reflects Williams's concentration on images, and "At the Ballgame," in which Williams draws material from a representative aspect of American life.

With the rise of the Objectivist movement in the 1930s, Williams's work gained wider recognition. Williams was a leading force in Objectivism, which expanded upon the Imagist concern with sight and sound by also emphasizing thought and feeling. Many of Williams's poems of this period celebrate life and are centered on the desirability of growth and change. Later in the decade, Williams began to develop a more dynamic form to accommodate his complex aims and ideas. The three-line form, or "triadic stanza," which dominates his later poems, makes its first appearance in *The Wedge* (1944), a volume infused with intense im-

agery reflecting the social conditions of the World War II era.

Many critics consider *Paterson* to be Williams's greatest achievement. In this work, Williams juxtaposes scenes, images, characters, and other aspects of modern life to form a portrait of both an American city—Paterson, New Jersey—and an artist—Noah Faitoute Paterson. Williams stated that "a man in himself is a city, beginning, seeking, achieving, and concluding life in ways which the various aspects of a city may embody." Williams employed both poetry and prose, drawing from such sources as letters, notes, and local histories to develop a work that would mirror the complexity of his subject. This montage structure is similar to techniques used by contemporary painters. Among the themes explored in *Paterson* are the relationship between the artist and society, loss of innocence, love, marriage, and the physical and intellectual desolation of modern life. While the first four books of *Paterson* are firmly rooted in the actual world, Book V centers on the imagination and is written in a more lyrical and meditative style. *Paterson* has been referred to as the crowning achievement of Williams's poetic career. Kenneth Rexroth called it "an extraordinary synthesis, a profoundly personal portrait of a man as the nexus of a community, which expands out from him and contracts into him like the ripples from a cast stone moving in both directions simultaneously." In his later poetry, Williams paid increasing attention to lyricism and to more personal concerns. The pieces in *The Desert Music and Other Poems* (1954), *Journey to Love* (1955), and *Pictures from Brueghel and Other Poems* evidence a more relaxed approach than those in previous volumes. The poem "Asphodel, That Greeny Flower" in *Journey to Love* is frequently cited as an example of his later, more emotionally urgent style. A long, meditative love poem addressed to William's wife, Flossie, "Asphedel, That Greeny Flower" was called "one of the most beautiful poems in the language," by W. H. Auden.

Like his better-known verse, Williams's novels and short stories usually revolve around the lives of ordinary people. *The Great American Novel* (1923), *A Voyage to Pagany* (1928), and *A Novelette* (1932) are written in an improvisational style that tests the limits of traditional fiction. In his best-known novels, collectively called *The Stetcher Trilogy—White Mule* (1937), *In the Money* (1940), and *The Build-Up* (1952)—Williams depicts the people and circumstances of his wife's youth to create a saga of an American family wracked by the desire for material success. The pieces in Williams's short fiction collections, *The Knife and Other Stories* (1932) and *Life on the Passaic River* (1938), dramatize the plight of the New Jersey poor. Neil Baldwin summarized Williams's fiction: "His poems show us Williams the pointillist. His novels and other short fiction show us the documentarian, engaged in the endless record of his life with others; the social being against an historic backdrop."

A poet who rebelled against formal structure and academicism in poetry at the same time that those qualities were evidenced in works by such writers as T. S. Eliot and Wallace Stevens, Williams spent much of his early career in relative obscurity, but he was firmly established as a major poet at the time of his death. Because of his experiments with language and form and his firm knowledge of contemporary trends in art and music as well as literature, Williams has been

linked with such movements as Modernism, Imagism, and Objectivism; he was also highly regarded by writers associated with the Beat movement. Williams's dedication to his craft and his independent and enthusiastic approach to life and literature have earned him an honored place in American letters.

(For further information about Williams's life and works, see *Contemporary Authors*, Vols. 89-92; *Contemporary Literary Criticism*, Vols. 1, 2, 5, 9, 13, 22, 42; and *Dictionary of Literary Biography*, Vols. 4, 16, 54, 86.)

CRITICAL COMMENTARY

RANDALL JARRELL

(essay date 1949)

[Jarrell was an American poet and critic. In the following excerpt, originally written as an introduction to Williams's *Selected Poems*, he discusses the emotional and empathetic qualities of the author's work.]

Anyone would apply to Williams—besides *outspoken, warmhearted,* and *generous*—such words as *fresh, sympathetic, enthusiastic, spontaneous, open, impulsive, emotional, observant, curious, rash, courageous, undignified, unaffected, humanitarian, experimental, empirical, liberal, secular, democratic.* Both what he keeps and what he rejects are unusual: how many of these words would fit the other good poets of the time? He was born younger than they, with more of the frontier about him, of the this-worldly optimism of the 18th century; one can imagine his reading *Rameau's Nephew* with delighted enthusiasm, but wading along in Karl Barth with a dour blank frown. (I don't mean altogether to dissociate myself from these responses.) And he is as Pelagian as an obstetrician should be: as he points to the poor red thing mewling behind plate-glass, he says with professional, observant disbelief: "You mean you think *that's* full of Original Sin?" He has the honesty that consists in writing down the way things seem to you yourself, not the way that they really must be, that they *are,* that everybody but a misguided idealist or shallow optimist or bourgeois sentimentalist *knows* they are. One has about him the amused, admiring, and affectionate certainty that one has about Whitman: *Why, he'd say anything*—creditable or discreditable, sayable or unsayable, so long as he believes it. (pp. 237-38)

Williams is one of those poets, like Hardy, whose bad or mediocre poems do repay reading and do add to

your respect for the poet. Williams' bad poems are usually rather winning machine-parts minus their machine, irrepressible exclamations about the weather of the world, interesting but more or less autonomous and irrelevant entries in a Lifetime Diary. But this is attractive; the usual bad poem in somebody's *Collected Works* is a learned, mannered, valued habit, a habit a little more careful than, and a little emptier than, brushing one's teeth.

The first thing one notices about Williams' poetry is how radically sensational and perceptual it is: "Say it! No ideas but in things." Williams shares with Marianne Moore and Wallace Stevens a feeling that almost nothing is more important, more of a true delight, than the way things look. Reading their poems is one long shudder of recognition; their reproduction of things, in its empirical gaiety, its clear abstract refinement of presentation, has something peculiarly and paradoxically American about it—English readers usually talk about their work as if it had been produced by three triangles fresh from Flatland. All three of these poets might have used, as an epigraph for their poetry, that beautiful saying that it is nicer to think than to do, to feel than to think, but nicest of all merely to look. Williams' poems, so far as their spirit is concerned, remind one of Marianne Moore's "It is not the plunder, / but 'accessibility to experience' "; so far as their letter is concerned, they carry scrawled all over them Stevens' "The greatest poverty is not to live / In a physical world"—and Stevens continues, quite as if he were Williams looking with wondering love at all the unlikely beauties of the poor:

One might have thought of sight, but who could think
   Of what it sees, for all the ill it sees.

Principal Works

Al Que Quiere! (poetry) 1913

Kora in Hell: Improvisations (poetry) 1920

The Great American Novel (novel) 1923

Spring and All (poetry) 1923

In the American Grain (essays) 1925

Collected Poems 1921-1932 (poetry) 1934

White Mule (novel) 1937

Life along the Passaic River (short stories) 1938

The Wedge (poetry) 1944

Paterson. 5 vols. (poetry) 1946-58

The Clouds (poetry) 1948

Selected Poems (poetry) 1949

Autobiography (autobiography) 1951

The Desert Music and Other Poems (poetry) 1954

Journey to Love (poetry) 1955

Pictures from Brueghel and Other Poems (poetry) 1962

Collected Poems. 2 vols. (poetry) 1988-89

All three poets did their first good work in an odd climate of poetic opinion. Its expectations of behavior were imagist (the poet was supposed to see everything, to feel a great deal, and to think and to do and to make hardly anything), its metrical demands were minimal, and its ideals of organization were mosaic. The subject of poetry had changed from the actions of men to the reactions of poets—*reactions* being defined in a way that left the poet almost without motor system or cerebral cortex. This easily led to a strange kind of abstraction: for what is more abstract than a fortuitous collocation of sensations? Stevens, with his passion for philosophy, order, and blank verse, was naturally least affected by the atmosphere of the time, in which he was at most a tourist; and Marianne Moore synthesized her own novel organization out of syllabic verse, extravagantly elaborated, half-visual patterns, and an extension of moral judgment, feeling, and generalization to the whole world of imagist perception. Williams found his own sort of imagism considerably harder to modify. He had a boyish delight and trust in Things: there is always on his lips the familiar, pragmatic, American *These are the facts*—for he is the most pragmatic of writers, and so American that the adjective itself seems inadequate . . . one exclaims in despair and delight: He is the America of poets. Few of his poems had that pure crystalline inconsequence that the imagist poem ideally has—the world and Williams himself kept breaking into them; and this was certainly their salvation.

Williams' poetry is more remarkable for its empathy, sympathy, its muscular and emotional identification with its subjects, than any modern poetry except

Rilke's. When you have read *Paterson* you know for the rest of your life what it is like to be a waterfall; and what other poet has turned so many of his readers into trees? Occasionally one realizes that this latest tree of Williams' is considerably more active than anybody else's grizzly bear; but usually the identification is so natural, the feel or rhythm of the poem so hypnotic, that the problem of belief never arises. Williams' knowledge of plants and animals, our brothers and sisters in the world, is surprising for its range and intensity; and he sets them down in the midst of the real weather of the world, so that the reader is full of an innocent lyric pleasure just in being out in the open, in feeling the wind tickling his skin. The poems are full of "Nature": Williams has reproduced with exact and loving fidelity both the illumination of the letter and the movement of the spirit. In these poems emotions, ideals, whole attitudes are implicit in a tone of voice, in the feel of his own overheard speech; or are expressed in terms of plants, animals, the landscape, the weather. You see from his instructions **"To a Solitary Disciple"** that it is what the landscape does—its analogical, anthropomorphized life—that matters to Williams; and it is only as the colors and surfaces reveal this that they are important.

At first people were introduced into the poems mainly as overheard or overlooked landscape; they spread. Williams has the knowledge of people one expects, and often does not get, from doctors; a knowledge one does not expect, and almost never gets, from contemporary poets. (For instance, what is probably the best poem by a living poet, *Four Quartets,* has only one real character, the poet, and a recurrent state of that character which we are assured is God; even the ghostly mentor encountered after the air-raid is half Eliot himself, a sort of Dostoievsky double.) One believes in and remembers the people in Williams' poems, though they usually remain behavioristic, sharply observed, sympathetic and empathetic sketches, and one cannot get from these sketches the knowledge of a character that one gets from some of Frost's early dramatic monologues and narratives, from a number of Hardy's poems, or from Williams' detailed and conclusive treatment of the most interesting character in the poems, himself. Some of the narrative and dramatic elements of his poetry seem to have drained off into his fiction. Williams' attitude toward his people is particularly admirable: he has neither that condescending, impatient, Pharisaical dismissal of the illiterate mass of mankind, nor that manufactured, mooing awe for an equally manufactured Little or Common Man, that disfigures so much contemporary writing. Williams loves, blames, and yells despairingly at the Little Men just as naturally and legitimately as Saint-Loup got angry at the servants: because he *feels,* not just says, that the differences between men are less important than their similarities—that he and you and I, together, are the Little Men.

Williams has a real and unusual dislike of, distrust in, Authority; and the Father-surrogate of the average work of art has been banished from his Eden. His ability to rest (or at least to thrash happily about) in contradictions, doubts, and general guesswork, without ever climbing aboard any of the monumental certainties that go perpetually by, perpetually on time—this ability may seem the opposite of Whitman's gift for boarding every certainty and riding off into ever infinite, but the spirit behind them is the same. Williams' range (it is roughly Paterson, that microcosm which he has half-discovered, half-invented) is narrower than Whitman's, and yet there too one is reminded of Whitman: Williams has much of the freeness of an earlier America, though it is a freedom haunted about by desperation and sorrow. The little motto one could invent for him—*In the suburbs, there one feels free*—is particularly ambiguous when one considers that those suburbs of his are overshadowed by, are a part of, the terrible industrial landscape of northeastern New Jersey. But the ambiguity is one that Williams himself not only understands but insists upon: if his poems are full of what is clear, delicate, and beautiful, they are also full of what is coarse, ugly, and horrible. There is no optimistic blindness in Williams, though there is a fresh gaiety, a stubborn or invincible joyousness. But when one thinks of the poems, of Williams himself, in the midst of these factories, dumps, subdivisions, express highways, patients, children, weeds, and wild-flowers of theirs—with the city of New York rising before them on the horizon, a pillar of smoke by day, a pillar of fire by night; when one thinks of this, one sees in an ironic light, the flat matter-of-fact light of the American landscape, James' remark that America "has no ruins." America is full of ruins, the ruins of hopes.

There are continually apparent in Williams that delicacy and subtlety which are sometimes so extraordinarily present, and sometimes so extraordinarily absent, in Whitman; and the hairraising originality of some of Whitman's language is another bond between the two—no other poet of Whitman's time could have written

The orchestra whirls me wider than Uranus flies,
It wrenches such ardors from me I did not know I possessed them,
It sails me, I dab with bare feet, they are lick'd by the indolent waves,
I am cut by bitter and angry hail, I lose my breath,
Steep'd amid honey'd morphine, my windpipe throttled in fakes of death,
At length let up again to feel the puzzle of puzzles . . .

I suppose that the third line and the *fakes of death* are the most extraordinary things in the passage; yet the whole seems more overwhelming than they. In spite of their faults—some of them obvious to, and some of them seductive to, the most foolish reader—poets like Whitman and Williams have about them something more valuable than any faultlessness: a wonderful largeness, a quantitative and qualitative generosity.

Williams' imagist-objectivist background and bias have helped his poems by their emphasis on truthfulness, exactness, concrete "presentation"; but they have harmed the poems by their underemphasis on organization, logic, narrative, generalization—and the poems are so short, often, that there isn't time for much. Some of the poems seem to say, "Truth is enough"—*truth* meaning *data brought back alive.* But truth isn't enough. Our crudest demand for excitement, for the "actions of men," for the "real story" of something "important," something strange—this demand is legitimate because it is the nature of the animal, man, to make it; and the demand can hardly be neglected so much as a great deal of the poetry of our time—of the good poetry of our time—has neglected it. The materials of Williams' unsuccessful poems have as much reality as the brick one stumbles over on the sidewalk; but how little has been done to them!—the poem is pieces or, worse still, a piece. But sometimes just enough, exactly as little as is necessary, has been done; and in these poems the Nature of the edge of the American city—the weeds, clouds, and children of vacant lots—and its reflection in the minds of its inhabitants, exist for good.

One accepts as a perfect criticism of his own insufficiently organized (*i.e.,* insufficiently living) poems Williams' own lines: "And we thought to escape rime / by imitation of the senseless / unarrangement of wild things—the stupidest rime of all"; and one realizes at the same time, with a sense of reassurance, that few people know better than Williams how sensible the arrangement of wild things often is. Williams' good poems are in perfect agreement with his own explanation of what a poem is:

A poem is a small (or large) machine made of words. When I say there's nothing sentimental about a poem I mean that there can be no part, as in any other machine, that is redundant . . . Its movement is intrinsic, undulant, a physical more than a literary character. Therefore each speech having its own character, the poetry it engenders will be peculiar to that speech also in its own intrinsic form. The effect is beauty, what in a single object resolves our complex feelings of propriety . . . When a man makes a poem, makes it, mind you, he takes words as he finds them interrelated about him and composes them—without distortion which would mar their exact significances—into an intense expression of his perceptions and ardors that they may constitute a revelation in the speech that he uses. It isn't what he *says* that counts as a work of art, it's what he makes, with such intensity of perception that it lives with an intrinsic movement of its own to verify its authenticity.

It is the opposition between the *without distortion* and the repeated *makes* of this passage that gives Williams' poetry the type of organization that it has.

One is rather embarrassed at the necessity of calling Williams original; it is like saying that a Cheshire Cat smiles. Originality is one of his major virtues and minor vices. One thinks about some of his best poems, *I've never read or imagined anything like this;* and one thinks about some of his worst, *I wish to God this were a little more like ordinary poetry.* He is even less logical than the average good poet—he is an intellectual in neither the good nor the bad sense of the word—but loves abstractions for their own sake, and makes accomplished, characteristic, inveterate use of them, exactly as if they were sensations or emotions; there is no "dissociation of sensibility" in Williams. Both generalizations and particulars are handled with freshness and humor and imagination, with a delicacy and fantasy that are especially charming in so vigorous, realistic, and colloquial a writer.

The mosaic organization characteristic of imagism or "objectivism" develops naturally into the musical, thematic organization of poems like *Paterson (Part I);* many of its structural devices are interestingly, if quite independently, close to those of *Four Quartets* and "Coriolan," though Eliot at the same time utilizes a good many of the traditional devices that Williams dislikes. A large-scale organization which is neither logical, dramatic, nor narrative is something that contemporary poetry has particularly desired; such an organization seems possible but improbable, does not exist at present, and is most nearly approached in *Four Quartets* and *Paterson (Part I).*

Williams' poems are full of imperatives, exclamations, trochees—the rhythms and dynamics of their speech are being insisted upon as they could not be in any prose. It is this insistence upon dynamics that is fundamental in Williams' reading of his own poems: the listener realizes with astonished joy that he is hearing a method of reading poetry that is both excellent—for these particular poems—and completely unlike anything he has ever heard before. About Williams' meters one remark might be enough, here: that no one has written more accomplished and successful free verse. It seems to me that ordinary accentual-syllabic verse, in general, has tremendous advantages over "free," accentual, or syllabic verse—in English, of course. But that these other kinds of verse, in some particular situations or with some particular materials, can work out better for some poets, is so plain that any assertion to the contrary seems obstinate dogmatism. We want to explain *why* Williams' free verse or Marianne Moore's syllabic verse is successful, not to make fools of ourselves by arguing that it isn't. The verse-form of one of their poems, as anyone can see, is essential to its success; and it is impossible to produce the same effect by treating their material in accentual-syllabic verse. Anyone can invent the genius who might have done the same thing even better in ordinary English verse, but he is the most fruitless of inventions.

Contemporary criticism has not done very well by Williams; most of the good critics of poetry have not written about him, and one or two of the best, when they did write, just twitched as if flies were crawling over them. Yvor Winters has been Williams' most valuable advocate, and has written extremely well about one side of Williams' poetry; but his praise has never had enough effect on the average reader, who felt that Williams came as part of the big economy-sized package that included Elizabeth Daryush, Jones Very, and Winters' six best students. The most important thing that criticism can do for a poet, while he is alive, is to establish that atmosphere of interested respect which gets his poems a reasonably careful reading; it is only in the last couple of years that any such atmosphere has been established for Williams.

Williams' most impressive single piece is certainly *Paterson (Part I):* a reader has to be determinedly insensitive to modern poetry not to see that it has an extraordinary range and reality, a clear rightness that sometimes approaches perfection. I imagine that almost any list of Williams' best poems would include the extremely moving, completely realized **"The Widow's Lament in Springtime"**; that terrible poem (XVIII in *Spring and All*) that begins, *The pure products of America / go crazy;* **"The Yachts,"** a poem that is a paradigm of all the unjust beauty, the necessary and unnecessary injustice of the world; **"These,"** a poem that is pure deprivation; **"Burning the Christmas Greens"**; the long poem (called **"Paterson: Episode 17"** in Williams' *Collected Poems*) that uses for a refrain the phrase *Beautiful Thing;* the unimaginable delicate **"To Waken an Old Lady"**; the poem that begins *By the road to the contagious hospital;* the beautiful **"A Unison,"** in which Nature is once again both ritual and myth; and, perhaps, **"The Sea-Elephant," "The Semblables,"** and **"The Injury."** And how many other poems there are that one never comes on without pleasure!

That Williams' poems are honest, exact, and original, that some of them are really *good* poems, seems to be obvious. But in concluding I had rather mention something even more obvious: their generosity and sympathy, their moral and human attractiveness. (pp. 238-49)

Randall Jarrell, "An Introduction to the Selected Poems of William Carlos Williams," in his *Poetry and the Age,* Alfred A. Knopf, Inc., 1953, pp. 237-49.

PAUL MARIANI
(essay date 1975)

[In the following excerpt, Mariani examines the themes and technical evolution of Williams's later poetry.]

Even before he finished the last part of *Paterson* as he had originally conceived it—with its four-part structure—Williams was already thinking of moving his poem into a fifth book. The evidence for such a rethinking of the quadernity of *Paterson* exists in the manuscripts for *Book IV*, for there Williams, writing for himself, considered extending the field of the poem to write about the river in a new dimension: the Passaic as archetype, as the River of Heaven. That view of his river, however, was in 1950 premature, for Williams still had to follow the Passaic out into the North Atlantic, where, dying, it would lose its linear identity in the sea of eternity, what Williams called the sea of blood. The processive mode of *Paterson I-IV* achieved, however, Williams returned to the untouched key: the dimension of timelessness, the world of the imagination, the apocalyptic moment, what he referred to as the eighth day of creation. (p. 305)

[The] apocalyptic mode is not really *new* for Williams in the sense that basically new strategies were developed for the late poems. Williams had tried on the approach to the apocalyptic moment any number of times; so, for example, he destroyed the entire world, imaginatively, at the beginning of *Spring and All* to begin all over again, in order that his few readers might see the world as new. And in *Paterson III,* the city is once again destroyed in the imagination by the successive inroads of wind, fire, and flood, necessary purgings before Dr. Paterson can discover the scarred beauty, the beautiful black Kora, in the living hell of the modern city. These repeated decreations are necessary, in terms of Williams' psychopoetics, in order to come at that beauty locked in the imagination. "To refine, to clarify, to intensify that eternal moment in which we alone live there is but a single force," Williams had insisted in *Spring and All.* That single force was the imagination and this was its book. But *Spring and All* was only *one* of its books or, better, perhaps, *all* of Williams' books are one book, and all are celebrations of the erotic/creative power of the imagination.

What *is* new about the late poems is Williams' more relaxed way of saying and with it a more explicit way of seeing the all-pervasive radiating pattern at the core of so much that Williams wrote. In fact, all of *Pat-*

terson and "Asphodel" and much else that Williams wrote, from *The Great American Novel* (which finds its organizing principle in the final image of the machine manufacturing shoddy products from cast-off materials, the whole crazy-quilt held together with a stitched-in design) to **"Old Doc Rivers"** (which constructs a cubist portrait of an old-time doctor from Paterson by juggling patches of secondhand conversations, often unreliable, with old hospital records), to *The Clouds* (which tries to come at Williams' sense of loss for his father by juxtaposing images of clouds with fragmentary scenes culled from his memory), in all of these works and in others Williams presents discrete objects moving "from frame to frame without perspective / touching each other on the canvas" to "make up the picture." In this quotation Williams is describing the technique of the master of the Unicorn tapestries, but it serves to describe perfectly his own characteristic method of presentation. (p. 306)

[What] marks poems like **"Asphodel"** and *Paterson V* as different from his earlier poetry is that Williams has come out on the other side of the apocalyptic moment. He stands, now, at a remove from the processive nature of the earlier poetry, in a world where linear time—the flow of the river—has given way to the figure of the poet standing above the river or on the shore: in either case, he is removed from the violent flux, from the frustrations of seeing the river only by fits and starts. Now the whole falls into a pattern: Paterson in *Book V* is seen now by Troilus/Williams from the Cloisters at Fort Tryon Park, the line of the river flowing quietly toward the sea, the city itself visible as a pattern of shades, a world chiming with the world of the Unicorn tapestries, the world of art which has survived. From this heavenly world, the old poet can allow himself more room for ruminations, for quiet meditation. It is a world which still contains many of the jagged patterns of Williams' own world of the early fifties: the Rosenberg trial, the cold war, Mexican prostitutes and G.I.s stationed in Texas, letters from old friends and young poets. But all of these are viewed with a detached philosophical air, as part of a pattern which are irradiated by the energy of the imagination. For it is Kora, who, revealed in the late work, glows at the center of the poetry, extending her light generously and tolerantly "in all directions equally." It is Kora again who like the Beautiful Thing of *Paterson III,* illuminates the poem, but it is a Kora apprehended now quite openly as icon, the source of permanent radiance: the fructifying image of the woman, the anima so many artists have celebrated in a gesture which Williams characterizes as a figure dancing satyrically, goat-footed, in measure before the female of the imagination. Now, in old age, Williams too kneels before the woman who remains herself frozen, a force as powerful and as liberating as Curie's radium, supplying light and warmth to all the surrounding details, tolerantly, democratically.

The icon presupposes a kind of paradise, or, conversely, most paradises are peopled at least at strategic points with figures approaching iconography. Dante for one felt this. It is no accident, then, that, as Williams moves into that geographical region of the imagination where the river of heaven flows, he will find other artists who have also celebrated the light. And there, in the place of the imagination expressly revealed, will be the sensuous virgin pursued by the one-horned beast, the unicorn/artist, himself become an icon in this garden of delights. Three points demand our attention, then: 1) the movement toward the garden of the imagination, where it is always spring; 2) the encounter with the beautiful thing, Kora, the sensuous virgin to whom the artist pays homage; 3) the figure of the artist, both the all-pervasive creator who contains within himself the garden and the virgin and also the willing victim, a figure moving through the tapestry, seeking his own murder and rebirth in the imagination. (pp. 307-08)

Williams discovered . . . that the old masters had their own way of transcending the idiocy of the single, fixed perspective. Like the cubists with their multiple perspectives, their discrete planes apprehended simultaneously, the old masters had also moved their subjects outside the fixed moment. They were able, therefore, to free themselves to present their figures in all of their particularity both within a specific moment and at the same time as universal types of patterns, moving frequently to the level of icon. This shift in perspective helps to explain the similarity (*and* difference) between the achievement, say, of a volume like *Spring and All,* and the later poems: the analogue, except in terms of scope, is between the cubist perspectives of a still life by Juan Gris and the multiple perspectives of the Unicorn tapestries centered around the central icons of the virgin and the unicorn. (p. 309)

In originally conceiving of *Paterson* in four parts, Williams had, as he pointed out, added Pan to the embrace of the Trinity, much as he felt Dante had unwittingly done in supplying a "fourth unrhymed factor, unobserved" to the very structure of the *Commedia.* (This factor appears if we note the creative dissonance developed by the unrhymed ending reappearing in any four lines after the initial four.) The world of *Paterson I-IV* is very much a world in flux, a world in violent, haphazard process, where objects washing up or crashing against the surfaces of the man/city Paterson are caught up into the pattern of the poem even as they create in turn the pattern itself. So such things as the chance appearance of a nurse who was discovered to have a case of *Salmonella montevideo,* written up into a case history in the *Journal of the American Medical Association* for July 29, 1948, or a letter from a young unknown poet from Paterson named Allen Ginsberg, or a hasty note

scribbled by Ezra Pound from St. Elizabeth's Hospital in Washington, letters from Marcia Nardi or Fred Miller or Josephine Herbst or Edward Dahlberg or Alva Turner find their way into the action painting of the poem. The lines too are jagged, hesitant, coiling back on themselves, for the most part purposely flat, only in "isolate flecks" rising to the level of a lyricism which seems without artificiality or undue self-consciousness, a language shaped from the mouths of Polish mothers, but heightened.

The first four books of *Paterson* are, really, in a sense, the creation of the first six days, a world caught up very much in the rapid confusion of its own linear, processive time, where the orphic poet like the carnival figure of Sam Patch must keep his difficult balance or be pulled under by the roar of the language at the brink of the descent into chaos every artist encounters in the genesis of creation. What Williams was looking for instead in a fifth book, after resting from his unfolding creation, was to see the river at the heart of his poem as the ourobouros, the serpent with its tail in its mouth, the eternal river, the river of heaven. This meant, of course, that time itself would have to change, and a new time meant a relatively new way of measuring, meant a more secure, a more relaxed way of saying. That was a question, primarily, of form, and the emphasis on the variable foot which the critics went after all through the fifties and sixties like hounds after an elusive hare was in large part a strategy of Williams' own devising. But it was an absolutely necessary strategy for him, because just here the real revolution in poetry would have to occur: here with the river, metaphor for the poetic line itself. (pp. 310-11)

It is she, Kora, around whom all of *Paterson V* radiates, and, in the tapestries, she appears again with the tamed unicorn amidst a world of flowers where Williams had always felt at home. In a sense, Marianne Moore's real toad in an imaginary garden finds its correlative here in Williams' icons of the virgin/whore situated among "the sweetsmelling primrose / growing close to the ground," "the slippered flowers / crimson and white, / balanced to hang on slender bracts," forget-me-nots, dandelions, love-in-a-mist, daffodils and gentians and daisies. We have seen this woman before: she is the woman in **"Asphodel"** caring for her flowers in winter, in hell's despite, another German Venus, his wife. Which, then, is the real, Williams' wife seen or his icon of his wife? And his wife seen now, at this moment, or his wife remembered, an icon released by the imagination from time, ageless, this woman containing all women? Rather, it is the anima, the idea of woman, with its tenuous balance between the woman as virgin and the woman as whore, the hag language whored and whored again but transformed by the poet-lover's desire into something virginal and new, the woman and the language translated to the eighth day of creation, assuming a new condition of dynamic permanence. In this garden, the broken, jagged random things of Williams' world are caught up in a pattern, a dance where the poem, like the tapestries themselves, can be possessed a thousand thousand times, and yet remain as fresh and as virginal as on the day they were conceived, like Venus, from the head of their creator.

The woman is of course all-pervasive in Williams' poems. What is different here in the long late poems is the more explicit use of Kora as the symbol, in fact, the central icon in his late poems. (p. 313)

Williams has made that consummate metapoem [*Paterson V*] far more explicit for several reasons, one comes to realize: first, because no critic, not even the most friendly and the most astute, had even begun to adequately sound the real complexities of the poem by 1956, ten years after *Paterson I* appeared. (Indeed an adequate critical vocabulary for the kind of thing Williams was doing was not even attempted by the critics and reviewers.) Secondly, Williams felt the need to praise his own tradition, his own pantheon of artists, to pay tribute to those others who had also helped to celebrate the light. Williams would show that, on the eighth day of creation, all of the disparate, jagged edges of *Paterson* could, as he has said in his introduction, multiply themselves and so reduce themselves to unity, to a dance around the core of the imagination.

In the dreamlike worlds of **"Asphodel"** and *Paterson V*, filled as they are with the radiant light of the imagination, all disparate images revolve around the virgin/whore, including the "male of it," the phallic artist who is both earthly Pan and Unicorn, that divine lover, who dances contrapuntally against his beloved. Williams, perhaps sensing that the old, crude fight against the clerks of the great tradition had been sufficiently won to let him relax, chooses now to celebrate a whole pantheon of old masters in **"Asphodel"** and again in *Paterson V*.

And if the presences of Bosch, Breughel, and the master of the Unicorn tapestries are the central presences in the three late long poems, still, there is room to celebrate a host of other artists who dance in attendance on the woman as well. We can do little more at this point than enumerate some of them: Toulouse-Lautrec, who painted the lovely prostitutes among whom he lived; Gauguin, celebrating his sorrowful reclining nude in *The Loss of Virginity*; the anonymous Inca sculptor who created the statuette of a woman at her bath 3000 years ago; the 6000-year-old cave paintings of bison; Cézanne for his patches of blue and blue; Daumier, Picasso, Juan Gris, Gertrude Stein, Kung; Albrecht Dürer for his Melancholy; Audubon, Ben Shahn, and Marsden Hartley.

We come, then, finally, to our third point: the figure of the artist himself, the male principle incessantly attracted to and moving toward the female of it: the anima. And here we are confronted with the comic and the grotesque: the figure of Sam Patch or the hydrocephalic dwarf or the Mexican peasant in Eisenstein's film, and, in the late poems, the portrait of the old man, all of these finding their resolution and comic apotheosis in the captive, one-horned unicorn, a figure, like the figure of the satyr erectus, of the artist's phallic imagination. There is, too, Breughel's self-portrait, as Williams thought, recreated in the first of Williams' own pictures taken from Breughel, and imitated in a cubist mode. . . . And, again, there is the head of the old smiling Dane, the Tollund Man, seen in a photograph; it is a portrait of a man, a sacrificial victim, strangled as part of some forgotten spring rite, the features marvelously preserved intact by the tanning effects of the bogs from which he had been exhumed after twenty centuries of strong silence, that 2000-year-old face frozen into something like a half-smile. That face chimes with Breughel's face as both chime with the strange, half-smiling face of Bosch peering out from his strange world where order has given way to an apocalyptic nightmare.

But the male remains the lesser figure of the two in Williams. As he told Theodore Roethke in early 1950, "All my life I have hated my face and wanted to smash it." . . . He was willing, however, to let the icon of the unicorn, the one-horned beast, stand. And he let it stand because it represented the necessary male complement to the female of it, the object desired, the beautiful thing: the language in its virginal state. No one but the virgin can tame the unicorn, the legend goes, and Williams had, like other artists before and after him, given himself up to that elusive beauty. Like Hart Crane in another mode, he had given himself up to be murdered, to offer himself not, as Pound had, to the pale presences of the past, androgenetically, but for the virgin, Kora. And yet, there was a way out, a hole at the bottom of the pit for the artist, in the timeless world of the imagination, the enchanted circle, the jeweled collar encircling the unicorn's neck. In the final tapestry of the series, the Unicorn kneels within the fence paling, (pomegranates bespeak fertility and the presence of Kora), at ease among the flowers here with him forever on the eight day of creation, a world evoked for Williams, from the imagination, the source from which even St. John must have created his own eighth day in his own time.

What was of central importance to Williams was not the artist, then, whose force is primarily directional and whose presence is in any event everywhere, but the icon which motivates the artist and urges him on: the icon of Kora, the image of the beloved. And this figure appears, of course, everywhere in Williams' writing, assuming many faces, yet always, finally one. Asked in his mid-seventies what it was that kept him writing,

Williams answered that it was all for the young woman whose eyes he had caught watching him from out in some audience as he read his poems. . . . With them Williams places his own icon of the lovely virgin. In that world of art, in that garden where spring is a condition of permanence, where the earthly garden chimes perfectly with the garden of paradise, the eye of the unicorn is still and still intent upon the woman. (pp. 315-17)

Paul Mariani, "The Eighth Day of Creation: William Carlos Williams' Late Poems," in *Twentieth Century Literature*, Vol. 21, No. 3, October, 1975, pp. 305-18.

LINDA W. WAGNER
(essay date 1980)

[In the following excerpt, Wagner discusses modes of speech in Williams's poems.]

For Williams, speech was identity. He had listened carefully through a lifetime to the diction and the inflection of his patients, his friends, his culture; he had used language signals as a means of making diagnoses; most important of all, he had based his own poetics on theories of speech rhythms. . . . (p. 115)

For the earnest young doctor of Rutherford, poetry was his most important activity. He was a pediatrician, yes; he loved being a pediatrician (and a general practitioner as well: sixty years ago a doctor was a doctor, no matter what his specialty); and his care for his patients surfaces often in both his fiction and his poems. But Williams knew, early, that he wanted a literary life. He worked as a physician so that he might write what he chose, free from any kind of financial or political pressure. From the beginning, in the early 1900s, he understood the trade-offs: he would have less time to write; he would need more physical stamina than people with only one occupation; he would probably demand more from his family. But Williams, with the help of his wife, the remarkable Flossie, was willing to live the kind of rushed existence that would be necessary, crowding two full lifetimes into one, juggling experience and meditation, learning from the first and then understanding through the second. (pp. 115-16)

Judging from his more than forty published books, from his position today as one of our most innovative and generous modern writers, we must conclude that Williams's sometimes frantic lifestyle did work successfully. . . . [It] may be that the combination of careers worked for him at least partly because it was in basic agreement with Williams's personal aesthetic position, even in the groping years when he scarcely had

one. Contact with people—happy people, troubled people, excited and nervous people—meant contact with language. Williams's most consistent principle in sixty years of writing was the use of natural speech rhythms, the line divided and spaced so as to suggest rhythmic breaks in the language as spoken. His hatred of prescribed forms like the sonnet and the influence of formal, British English stems from the same root: he considered such formality inimical to American English. . . . Williams chose to stay with what he was convinced *were* the true materials of his art—American people, American life—and create a poetics that could accommodate his multiple subjects. (p. 116)

Paterson is that remarkable mixture of poetry and prose, loose-lined poems cut by shorter-lined tercets, quasi-formal rhetoric, a section of verse play, and—superimposed—the montage of quotations from stodgy histories of Paterson, notes, and impassioned letters from other struggling writers. A hodgepodge, the American version of Pound's more famous "ragbag," *Paterson* grew from Williams's need to express his fascination with country/man/language; to put it all together instead of fragmenting it—this huge, stirring emotional nexus—so that it would fit into the tidy poems that he was then writing. (p. 117)

Amazing—Williams and the writing of this five-book poem. Completely abjuring any traditional form or genre, he began with what were for him central thematic issues—marriage and divorce, virtue, modern life, and man's search through it all for "a redeeming language." . . . [He] somehow wrestled from an already bewildering lifetime of experience (the quantity of materials he wanted to include is staggering in itself) a few characters, selected scenes, chary images to create the effective poem. But in the process of writing, he confronted again and again the problem of using real speech so that it was more than local color. There was a great difference between Williams's concept of "using" speech, of *finding* the character through his speech, and of just mixing in flavorful slang or idiom as relief in more formal poetic diction. Here is the most important difference, I believe, between Williams and poets like Vachel Lindsay, Sandburg, Cummings, the earlier Eliot, and even Whitman, who—for all his interest in the American character—always managed to write in the same heavily traditional vocabulary.

For Williams, any person's identity rested on his spoken language. Many of his short stories open with a character speaking; we hear the words with no introduction or setting given. . . . In *Paterson*, Williams continues this tactic of preserving natural speech. Whole pages from letters he had received appear unchanged in the poem; speech here, through arrangement, is raised to art. Earlier, in the Cotton Mather section of *In the American Grain*, Williams had used the same approach, by letting Mather's own language and phrasing "create" his personality. The device, for Williams, was not new. In his poetry, however, because of the intrinsic formal differences between poetry and prose, his reliance on this speech identity took on a new ramification. As he pointed out [in *I Wanted to Write a Poem*],

> The rhythmic unit usually came to me in a lyrical outburst. I wanted it to look that way on the page, I didn't go in for long lines because of my nervous nature. I couldn't. The rhythmic pace was the pace of speech, an excited pace because I was excited when I wrote.

Speech as the origin of form, of shape: set against T. S. Eliot's very moderate view of a poet's use of tradition, Williams explodes: "A false language. A true. A false language pouring—a language (misunderstood) pouring (misinterpreted) without dignity. . . . "

It is not that Williams opted entirely for innovation. Pound chanted "Make it new" for sixty years; Williams's parallel cry was "the American language." As Williams wrote, "Free verse was not the answer. From the beginning, I knew that the American language must shape the pattern." (pp. 118-19)

But Williams was looking for more than a technical ploy, and perhaps that is another reason his insistence on the use of the natural idiom is important. For he was throughout his life, even though he fought Wallace Stevens's designation, a great Romantic.

> All this—
>   was for you, old woman.
> I wanted to write a poem
> that you would understand. . . .

And he did. Williams really wanted to reach a public, a public at least partly comprised of actual people, and part of his anger with the academic establishment resulted from its ignoring him. (If no one anthologized his poems, how were the common readers to find them?) Williams wanted to reach people because he saw so many sterile, impoverished lives; poetry, art, beauty might somehow ease those terrors. . . . The theme occurs over and over in Williams's poems: he sees the poem as a way to self-knowledge, the poem as a means of reaching, of communicating, of—in simple—speaking. (pp. 120-21)

As poet or as doctor, Williams was fascinated with "the poem that each is trying actually to communicate to us." To his credit, he heard, unearthed, a good many of those inarticulate poems, and he made new shapes where none existed before, to embody the particular—and particularly American—beauties of his townspeople and their language. (pp. 121-22)

It could well be that in the future, Williams will be compared more often with those other great innovators of modern American literature—Stein, Hemingway, Dos Passos—than with his fellow "poets." And perhaps that will be just as well, for "speaking" in itself knows no *genre* distinctions. It is an act of voice—a human act—and its purpose is, and has always been, to reach. (p. 124)

Linda W. Wagner, "Speaking Straight Ahead . . . ," in her *American Modern: Essays in Fiction and Poetry,* Kennikat Press, 1980, pp. 115-24.

CHARLES DOYLE
(essay date 1982)

[In the following excerpt, Doyle surveys Williams's career, focusing on the author's artistic and intellectual development.]

For criticism, the important question is: what criteria are we to apply in judging Williams's poems? Many American poets, of the past two decades in particular, have signified their approval of his work either by imitating it or advancing it. Critical difficulty is encountered not so much in characterizing his discoveries concerning 'the poem' as in deciding which among his typical poems are successful, and good, poems, and why this is so.

At the beginning of his career, and by now the point has been made often enough, Williams's poems were highly literary, modelled on approved masters in the English tradition, both in diction and measure. When he broke away from this stale sense of poetry, it was first through the influence of Pound and Imagism. As he suggests in the Preface to *Kora in Hell,* Williams, at this period, escaped from a common mental attitude of the literary poet—considering, or thinking about, one thing in terms of another. Simile, analogy and metaphor he rejected as inappropriate to his sense of 'the poem', preferring to assert the necessity of keeping one's eye on the object. . . . Such insistence on the specific individuality of the object, as opposed to its likeness and relation to other objects, is distinctly American, as is the aim for 'vividness' rather than propriety.

Seeing clearly was, for him, the great virtue, as it was for his painter friends Demuth and Sheeler. Throughout Williams's career we encounter the isolation of the moment of clear perception or experience as if it were hard won from the ever-encroaching flux. In a constant state of alertness the artist makes his discoveries, but he is also active, and morally so, a selector, who 'must keep his eye without fault on those things he values, to which officials refuse to give the proper names.' . . . Genuine contact is made through concentration on the object with great intensity, to 'lift it' to the imagination. An object lifted to the imagination yields up its 'radiant gist'. Sometimes this is simply discovered, while at others (given that the field of energy does not stop at the skin or outer envelope of the human being), the process is completed by the poet by means of invention or structuring. In poems such as **"The Red Wheelbarrow,"** Williams draws our attention simultaneously to the world out there and to our relationship with it, which must be fresh, now. Here is one significance of his assertion that 'Nothing is good save the new,' . . . which is far from claiming that a thing is inevitably good *merely because* it is new.

'Nothing is good save the new' because what is important is here and now, our immediate experience. In the face of centuries of traditional poetic form, which had run into the nineteenth-century mire of 'moral homily' (seeing the poem as aiming for perfection in long-established verse-forms along with the expression of edifying or uplifting material), Williams had the insight to see that the significance of the poem is not in its subject-matter (which is nearly always 'phantasy' or 'dream'), but, as he asserts over and over again in many different ways, in its form. Given his deep convictions on the need for contact and that 'the

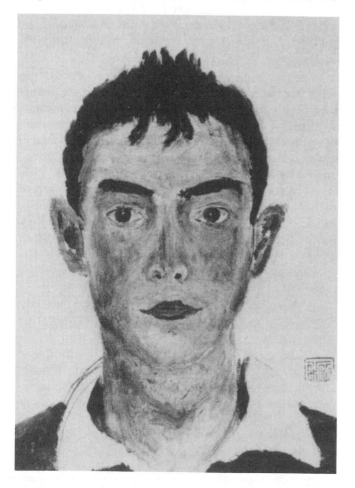

Self-portrait by Williams, 1914.

local is the only universal' it is natural that he should have rejected traditional forms and measure, since these are not local, nor have Americans direct access to their sources. Where to look, then, for new form?

Seen in this way, Williams's position is both perceptive and sensible. A poem is made with words and possesses whatever reality it may have through 'the shapes of men's lives in places'. What more natural than to use the language of those men? When, in his 1948 essay **"The Poem as a Field of Action,"** Williams, looking back, observed that 'Imagism was not structural: that was the reason for its disappearance,' . . . he meant that it did not derive purely from the speech-patterns of its day. Having recognized the vital link between poetry and speech, he then had to work for most of a lifetime before achieving a sound technical base (the variable foot), which could incorporate the American idiom on all occasions without strain. (pp. 169-70)

Only the tradition-bound will by now find it hard to accept Williams's innovations in the line. From *Al Que Quiere!* on, he largely escaped the tyranny of quantitative measure, employing instead a measure based on phrasing. A difficulty in making categorical assertions about Williams's measure (and therefore codifying it) is that his practice varies somewhat. Occasionally it is purely 'musical'. In this early, Imagist period it depended considerably on the syntax and phrasing of written statement. Very often, at its strongest throughout his career, it related to speech. Sometimes (as in **"Struggle of Wings,"** for example) it can be criticized as too long, or heavy; but even length is no sure criterion, as witness some writing in **"The Clouds."** . . . Generally, however, it can be said that the longer line is most successful when deployed to create a forward verbal flow. Much of the work in *Collected Later Poems* (**"The Mind's Games,"** for example, or **"Aigeltinger"**) is not easy to classify in terms of the line. Almost all of it is natural in flow, which saves it from the charge of being 'chopped-up prose', but a great deal of it is not far removed from prose. Sometimes (as in **"Aigeltinger"**) one suspects a deliberate tinkering with quantitative measure. Ultimately our bases for judging Williams's line must be broad ones: its energy in the specific instance, its 'naturalness' (which, almost inevitably, depends on the spoken word). (p. 171)

Traditional prosody is fixed, while for Williams measure in the poem is always relative. He never insisted on establishing a new set of rules, beyond observing the (for him) undeniable relationship between American measure and American speech. 'The only reality we can know is MEASURE,' . . . but different worlds call for different measures, each consonant with its own time and place. (p. 172)

Williams's basic short line was established in *Al Que Quiere!* Poem after poem in that volume, some quiet some less so, shows surprising tautness and strength of line. Much depends on the energy in the specific line, used with great range and subtlety:

> When I was younger
> it was plain to me
> I must make something of myself.
> Older now. . . .

Here, and in numerous other instances, the line disposition entirely suits the action of the poem (an obvious example here is the muting of line 4). Beyond this everything depends on the articulation of lines throughout. Hence, the poem is 'a field of action', and hence Williams's recognition of the rightness of Olson's theory of composition by field, rather than through accumulating well-turned lines.

Part of the outcome of this new sense of measure as 'relative' is a new respect for the individual word, accepting it freshly not as a label but as an alternative reality, an object in its own right. The word is a 'thing-in-itself', but it derives energy (usually in the form of 'meaning') through contact with other words. Much can be understood concerning Williams's use of the line if we recognize the range of his sentence structures. Vividness is gained very often by employment of the present tense, but he can (through syntactical arrangement) create a sense of immediacy without it. . . . Frequently Williams's poems begin with a question or an exclamation or exhortation, all indicating his eagerness, wonder, curiosity, and usually transmuting his excitement into the energy of the poem. Typically, throughout his career his language is simple and, despite subtle sentence variation, clearly and directly organized. In much of his verse of the late 1930s, early 1940s, which makes *Collected Later Poems* disappointing compared with *Collected Earlier Poems,* he allows himself discursive sentence structure, employing pause, parenthesis and qualification to a greater extent than he had earlier. Seen in the perspective of his whole development, it may be that much of the work of that period is preparatory for *Paterson,* an effort to extend his means deliberately in the direction of discursiveness, which bore fruit not so much in *Paterson* as in the assured, relaxed statement of many poems in *The Desert Music* and *Journey to Love.* Meantime, to the extent that he forgot Pound's dictum that the good writer 'uses the smallest possible number of words', Williams's work of that period lost distinction. (pp. 172-73)

Like Pound, Williams employs the technique of juxtaposition, but where Pound juxtaposes literary or cultural 'echoes' or apparent correspondences, Williams (until *Paterson*) tends to place together things-in-themselves. Even his juxtapositions in *Paterson* are treated so, not intended to suggest analogies, but to present the quality of American experience direct and without interference. Sometimes his juxtaposed objects possess 'one-thousandth part of a quality in common',

but often they deliberately (or carelessly) clash. Therefore, in some sense, juxtaposition is 'suggestive', but the reader is not necessarily led through a thought process, almost certainly to a flash of recognition which is an energy-discharge linking the juxtaposed items. Not that Williams is against activity of the intelligence. Traditional metaphor means the positive presence of the writer, in the text, directing his reader, contrary to Williams's belief that the artist should be 'remote from the field' and that art is created through 'concrete indirections.' . . . (p. 174)

Not the artist's autobiography, but the quality of his experience is important. To prevent his experience from being trammelled by convention it must be 'open' and not preconceived. A sense of form must be allied to a willingness to descend to the 'formless ground'. Williams's advice to 'write carelessly' is not really at odds with his insistence on accuracy of observation and rendering. What must be avoided is 'thought about' the object or experience, and (again from Williams's point of view) before *Paterson* evidence of deliberate thought in the *details* of a poem (like over-attention to 'subject-matter') would constitute a weakness in that poem. Perception and the imaginative disposition of perceptions, these are primary to the poem. Verbal and causal connectives, any verbal arrangement which is based on the structure of thought, these adulterate the poem, diminishing its purity and effectiveness. Apart from escaping the tyranny of quantitative measure, this must have been Williams's pre-eminent consideration in his search for, and development of, the variable foot.

All these criteria, and others, are positive and reasonable. Nothing can bridge the hiatus between Williams's intentions and those critics who cannot accept his major requirement—the rejection of quantitative measure for contemporary American poetry. However, almost everywhere the variable foot and composition by field have been accepted at least as legitimate, valuable extensions of the poetic means. Given this, Williams's own requirements for the poem offer adequate tools by which to assess his work, up to the mid-1940s.

Paterson poses fresh problems for the critic. What are to be his evaluative criteria for it? One is the valuable notion of the metamorphic poem implicit in the work, put forward by Sister M. Bernetta Quinn [in *The Metamorphic Tradition*]. Williams's own 'theory' of 'interpenetration' accords well with the metamorphic technique. His use of 'raw material' in the form of a variety of prose passages is of a piece both with his rejection of the 'anti-poetic' and his belief in the thing-in-itself.

To consider Williams's poetic development progressively is to wonder, at times, if he was sidetracked by Imagism and Objectivism. Although 'not structural', Imagism certainly persuaded him of the value of intense concentration upon the object. Objectivism may have intensified this in two ways: by emphasis on the removal of self from the poem and by (consequently) drawing the attention to the speech or music in which the objective experiences presented themselves. . . . (pp. 174-75)

Both Imagism and Objectivism are in the same theoretical line as Poe's insistence on the poem as a striving for a single effect. In its very name each of these 'movements' suggests a concentration on noun or thing as opposed to 'an easy lateral sliding' through a statement of abstractions easily divorced from reality. His insistence on the value of the thing-in-itself is important in Williams, but even more important is his sense of process. . . . Perhaps the crucial clue in the *Paterson* headnotes is 'by multiplication a reduction to one.' . . . Implying, as it does, movement, activity, this categorically shifts the emphasis of Williams's poem from thing to process, a passing through. His central means is in the metamorphoses of Paterson himself/itself. How are we to judge the value or success of this means? If the nature of Paterson, the man-city, becomes very clear at any one point in the poem, would not this be distracting? Would it not limit the range of possible response? Quest, perpetual change, fluidity, instability—these are characteristic of *Paterson,* giving it vitality. All objects in the poem are instantaneously there and are instantly gone. They are *here and now. Paterson I-IV* is a search for order. As originally conceived, the poem is search only, process only, and the failure of Paterson, the man-city, is comparable with that of, say, Père Sebastian Rasles in *In the American Grain,* a failure which has its own kind of success, in recognizing that *'La Vertue est toute dans l'effort'.* Notably, *Paterson V,* which concerns itself with the tapestry, the relationship of art to life and Williams's lifelong Kora-Venus preoccupation, has a greater immediate clarity, concentration upon the object, and a more obviously discursive point.

The earlier books of *Paterson* are sustained, paradoxically, as much by the fragments of 'experience' or 'thing' as they are by the necessarily fluid central metaphor. Curiously, metamorphosis *invites* discourse, while the 'gathering up' of its own weight has, at times, an effect opposite to the 'taking up of slack'. If one has any reservation about *Paterson V,* it is that the appeal to art, to imagination, is obvious rather than new, or penetrating, or decisive. Yet as a 'resolution', it confirms the tendency of Williams's whole career and is very much of a piece with all the work of his last phase.

Williams's late concentration on the imagination, his alignment of imagination and love, his self-searching, these are not narcissism. Rather his belief in the imagination is similar to his lifelong sense of the local. Emphasis is not on *his* locality, or imagination, because they are *his.* Imagination works from material in one's own experience (whoever one may happen to

be). That experience differs from one phase to another, so constant reference to it is simply carrying devotion to 'the new' to its ultimate conclusion.

From his Objectivist period onward all Williams's work implies a sense of the self other than the merely autobiographical or egotistical. In 1947 he observed: 'The objective in writing is to reveal. . . . The difference between the revealer and others is that he reveals HIMSELF, not you.' . . . Again, this stems from a realization that, just as the place a person can truly know is his own locality, so the only self he can truly know is his own. Avoidance of falsification, pretence, is at back of this and of the finally developed sense of imagination. In the long run, love is the important emotion in human experience. What keeps man alive (or kills him, for that matter) is his own imagination and how it relates to the world. Imagination has the power of transforming or maintaining the world, and is the chief metamorphic agent. . . . Williams's latest work is generally discursive in comparison with his pre-*Paterson* poems. Interestingly, this is due at least in part to his metrical experimentation. The stepping of the three-tiered line, which he had used first in 'The descent beckons' *(Paterson II),* has the effect of casting aside the static, fixed-object presentation of many earlier poems. To suggest that Williams was never discursive in his earlier work would be inaccurate. Even though expressed negatively ('No ideas but in things!'), Williams's awareness of the 'idea' in poetry is about as long as his career. His late development of 'the variable foot' allowed him to be discursive without abandoning the cadence and rapidity of natural speech. The order of speech, of prose statement, has replaced a repetitive, metronomic pattern, as the *expected* element in Williams's line. By and large, the line units are dictated by speech, but they have a flexibility and offer a range of possible discovery far exceeding those of traditional meter. Looking for criteria to judge 'the variable foot' we may suggest: (a) is it natural, true to speech? (b) are the variations vital and interesting? For Williams the anti-poetic would be aping of traditional literary forms or copying the speech and/or measure of others.

As an innovator, Williams shared many of his positions with Pound, but he may in the long run prove to be more influential. Pound to a much greater degree applied himself to, and found his material in, art and literature. Williams, likewise interested in simultaneity and interaction rather than causality, suggests his own far different sense of experience in chapter 54 of *The Autobiography.* He refers to the exciting secrets of the 'underground stream' of human experience itself, unselected. Attending closely to it, 'there is no better way to get an intimation of what is going on in the world.' . . . His whole objective, as it ultimately became clear to him, is to lift the 'inarticulate' up to imagination. A sense of the common people as prime source of life, shared in the early years with Eliot, seems never to have left Williams, despite a discouragement made plain at least as late as *Paterson II.*

A 'lifetime of careful listening' to the speech arising from his daily tasks and contacts, convinced him that poem and life, also, are one—and that each person is trying to communicate to the world the poem of himself. In many works, but particularly in *Kora in Hell, In the American Grain, Collected Earlier Poems, Paterson* and the late poems, he demonstrated the informing need for imagination, having realized early that 'The imagination transcends the thing itself.' . . . An explorer and discoverer, always conscious of the handful of men who had contributed positively to the shaping of the American spirit, he takes his place alongside them. (pp. 175-78)

Charles Doyle, in his *William Carlos Williams and the American Poem,* St. Martin's Press, 1982, 209 p.

MARVIN BELL

(essay date 1983)

[Bell is an American poet and critic. In the following excerpt, he considers the importance of the American idiom to Williams's poetry.]

William Carlos Williams is, arguably, our most American-American poet—as distinguished from such hybrids as Stevens (French-American), Eliot (British-American) and Pound (Italian-American). "Americanism," for Williams, meant that the circumstances of poetry are local, the tone of poetry is personal, the process of poetry is improvisational, and the subject of poetry is reality.

"Dedication for a Plot of Ground" is one of those one-of-a-kind poems, almost a "found" poem, a poem that is notable for its strategy and organization and one or two key "moves" amidst content that insists on its preeminence. I would understand if the reader were to think it artless. For its artistry resides, in large measure, in such seemingly unartistic "skills" and "talents" as personal energy, a belief that reality may be the content of a poem, feeling deeply without blurry eyes or fuzzy thoughts, and (above all!) strong values—local in origin, stated without irony.

Williams' writing stands in evidence against what most poetry is and even against what most people say *his* work is. Amidst the merely fanciful that dominates the poetry of any age, it stands out still for its sense of worthy content. By example, Williams' poems oppose the mind-set of literary convention in general, and the notion, in particular, that the naming of objects, the ac-

complishment of literary forms, or the geometrics of the imagination are the actual subjects of poetry. Their method tilts toward improvisation: an abandonment of the daily, reasonable and restrained self to force, need, momentum and invention. (p. 16)

Because of such ideas and methods, Williams is sometimes carried by his writing to a moment when words fail. That is, it takes him to the point where poems accomplish what is most rare and most worthy: they enlarge the silence. Hence, his work stands in forceful opposition to that poetry of any time which consists of lies, playful or weighty, which is based on theory, guesswork or manners, which is essentially entertainment, and which only fills up the silence. . . .

Williams' work is badly misunderstood—of course. From those poems of his we can only consider to have been finger exercises, many readers have decided that his is a poetry of cadence and object. Didn't he say, in *Book One* of *Paterson,* "Say it! No ideas but in things."? Yes, but by *Book Two,* he has already amended it to read: "No ideas but / in the facts"; and in *Book Five,* he writes: "You can learn from poems / that an empty head tapped on / sounds hollow / in any language!"; and one has only to read such poems as **"These"** and **"The Descent"** to see that he is a poet of intelligence and ideas. His poems, graphs of a mind, are as good as they are because his mind is as good as it is.

As for the "variable foot," the "triadic stanza" and the "American idiom"—these were all ways to beat the conventional poetic modes of his age and certain prevailing assumptions (still with us) about the nature of poetry. The foot, he said, not being fixed, must be variable. That was a way of using the vocabulary of the other guys to get away with something, since the foot, not being fixed, is not a foot. The triadic stanza—that was genius!—derives, I believe, from Williams' sense of his strength in writing—improvisation, taking the form of wildly various syntax—and his need to use the poetic line with and against whatever sentences energy, rapid association and "impure" diction might throw up. His genius lay in having sensed so definitely that prose can be poetry; that, indeed, it may be the prose of one's time that furnishes the language and strategies for what emerges later as the new poetry.

As for the American idiom, on the surface that means using the language as it is, where you live. Underneath, however, it signals a fundamental position on the nature of content. For if the common lingo is fit for poetry, so is the common man and woman. We are what we say. (pp. 16-17)

It is the actual, the thing or event which is its own best image and metaphor, which engages Williams. And so [in **"Dedication for a Plot of Ground"**] he begins to take stock of his grandmother's life. Just the *outer* events, you might notice. She was born, married, widowed, transported, remarried, and a second time widowed. She lost children, raised motherless grandchildren, and tended her lawn here for fifteen years.

Sure, when the facts by themselves begin to lose their distinction in the general welter of a life, he adds a little something to them: for example, "lived *hard* / for eight years in St. Thomas," or "*defended* herself," which are the additions of language; or "against flies, against girls / that came smelling about," which are the additions, also, of imagination; or "against the growing strength of the boys," which is the addition, *in addition,* of feeling and thought.

And so Williams arrives, by means of memory, association, momentum and improvisation, near to that silence where no more can be said because everything which needed to be said has been. What can he do, then, but return to the physical circumstances of the poem—the ground where somewhere she lies buried, the ground right here which still bears her life. He begins again from the plot of ground, and says what little is needed to conclude the story. When the end is in sight—*before,* that is, it has been stated—he merely interrupts the long litany of facts to say what he has thought all along: that this plot of ground is dedicated, not to a corpse, not to knowledge of death, not to fear, not to lush wonder or pained beseeching of the infinite, but to the *living presence* of one who lived, lived hard, and fought for her values. She was not just a carcass. Hence, if you can bring nothing but your carcass to this place (without bringing, say, intelligence, values and feelings), you might as well stay away. She was better than that.

It is worth noticing the free verse of this poem. Lines three, twenty and thirty-four end with the preposition "of," line seven with "with," lines thirty and thirty-five with "against." Line twenty-two is nothing more than the words "mothered them—they being." Stanza one is seven times as long as stanza two, and each stanza consists of only one sentence. Everyone knows why these things are unacceptable, right? What everyone knows, no one knows. Truisms are false. People are wrong. Williams is alive. If you can bring nothing to his work but your carcass, never mind. (pp. 18-19)

Marvin Bell, "Williams and 'Dedication . . . '," in *Field: Contemporary Poetry and Poetics,* No. 29, Fall, 1983, pp. 16-19.

SOURCES FOR FURTHER STUDY

Donoghue, Denis. "Williams, A Redeeming Language." In his *The Ordinary Universe,* pp. 180-93. New York: Macmillan, 1968.

> Discusses Williams's aesthetic emphasis on the physical world as being a particularly American one.

Fox, Hugh. "The Genuine Avant-Garde: William Carlos Williams' Credo." *Southwest Review* LIX, No. 3 (Summer 1974): 285-99.

> Rebuts the criticisms of such contemporaries of Williams's as Wallace Stevens, Hilda Doolittle, and Ezra Pound, who considered some of the poet's innovations ill-considered and inappropriate. Fox characterizes their attacks thus: "The pseudo-avant-garde, derivative, conventional, *déjà vu,* confronts the genuine avant-garde—the hitherto *undone*—and is confused."

Kallet, Marilyn. *Honest Simplicity in William Carlos Williams' "Asphodel, That Greeny Flower."* Baton Rouge: Louisiana State University Press, 1985, 163 p.

> Detailed explication of one of Williams's best-known poems.

O'Brien, Geoffrey. "William Carlos Williams and the Relativity of Theory." *VLS,* No. 40 (November 1985): 17, 21.

> Examines Williams's technical innovations and his difference with his Modernist poetic contemporaries in his emphasis on the concrete over the abstract.

Ostrom, Alan. *The Poetic World of William Carlos Williams.* Carbondale: Southern Illinois University Press, 1966, 178 p.

> Critical analysis of Williams's themes and body of work.

Whittemore, Reed. *William Carlos Williams, Poet from Jersey.* Boston: Houghton-Mifflin, 1975, 404 p.

> Biography of Williams.

Thomas Wolfe

1900-1938

(Full name Thomas Clayton Wolfe) American novelist, short story and novella writer, essayist, dramatist, and poet.

INTRODUCTION

Wolfe Is considered one of the foremost American novelists of the twentieth century. In his four major novels—*Look Homeward, Angel* (1929); *Of Time and the River* (1935); *The Web and the Rock* (1939); and *You Can't Go Home Again* (1940)—he took the facts of his own life and wove them into an epic celebration of the individual's search for spiritual fulfillment in America. Containing intense and lyrical portrayals of life in rural and urban America, Wolfe's novels are often compared to the poetry of Walt Whitman and are commonly perceived as forming a single *künstlerroman,* or body of work that evokes the spiritual isolation of an artist's progress toward personal and professional maturity.

Wolfe was born in Asheville, a city located in the mountains of North Carolina. His parents, who separated when Wolfe was a young boy, served as the models for some of his most intriguing characters. Extremely well-read in world literature and a bright student, Wolfe, at the age of sixteen, entered the University of North Carolina, where he developed an interest in drama. Upon graduation Wolfe continued his education at Harvard, where he wrote and produced plays as a member of George Pierce Baker's famous 47 Workshop. At Harvard Wolfe studied English under John Livingston Lowes, who propounded to his students that great literature is produced by the subconscious fusion of the author's literary influences, personal experiences, and imagination. After receiving a master's degree in 1922, Wolfe accepted a teaching post at New York University with the hope of having his plays accepted for production on Broadway. Unsuccessful in this endeavor and wearied by teaching, Wolfe resigned his position in 1925, determined to make writing his career. Shortly thereafter Wolfe met Aline Bernstein, a New York stage designer who became a central figure in Wolfe's life. During their five-year relationship, Bernstein provided Wolfe with the emotional and financial support that enabled him to write his first and, according to many critics, best novel, *Look Homeward, Angel.*

The acceptance of *Look Homeward, Angel* in 1928 by editor Maxwell E. Perkins of Charles Scribner's Sons initiated one of the most controversial editor-author relationships of the century. Confronted by the sprawling first-draft manuscript of Wolfe's novel, Perkins—who had worked for several years with such major American authors as F. Scott Fitzgerald and Ernest Hemingway—recognized Wolfe as a literary genius, but as a genius who lacked the editorial self-discipline necessary to shape his work into cohesive, publishable form. With Wolfe's reluctant cooperation, the manuscript of *Look Homeward, Angel* was extensively cut, and the resulting autobiographical novel was published in 1929 to popular and critical acclaim. In this work, Wolfe traced his own life story through the persona of Eugene Gant, a sensitive young man from the mountain city of Altamont. Like all of Wolfe's novels, *Look Homeward, Angel* possesses an epic quality—every thought, feeling, and action is depicted as monumental—and an all-encompassing empathy for humanity. Praising *Look Homeward, Angel* in his 1930 Nobel Prize acceptance speech, Sinclair Lewis recognized Wolfe as a significant new American author: "[*Look Homeward, Angel* can] be compared with the best in our literary production, a gargantuan creature with great gusto of life."

After several years of uncertainty, during which Wolfe was troubled by the emotional breakup of his relationship with Bernstein and moved to doubt his own abilities by a few unfavorable reviews of *Look Homeward, Angel,* Wolfe conceived of a multi-volume novel series titled "The October Fair," in which the story of Eugene and his family would continue. Wolfe's theme of the loneliness of the individual was expanded to include what he considered a universal quest: the search for a spiritual father, or "someone who can help you, save you, ease the burden for you." This theme, stemming from Wolfe's estrangement from his own father, surfaced in the turbulent, myth-ridden *Of Time and the River,* a massive novel that was culled by Perkins from several crates of manuscript composed and collected by the author during years of intense creative activity. *Of Time and the River* was greeted with mixed reviews upon its appearance in 1935. While many critics admired the sheer power of the novel, others had come to object to Wolfe's self-obsessed epic stance, the thinly disguised autobiographical cast of his novels, and the increasing intrusion of the author's voice in the narrative. One critical essay in particular, Bernard DeVoto's "Genius Is Not Enough," infuriated Wolfe, as the critic accused him of utter dependence upon Perkins and "the assembly line at Scribner's" to give form to his lengthy novels. Stung by such criticism and aware that relations with Perkins had grown increasingly strained, Wolfe left Scribner's in 1937, intent on proving to the critics that he was a self-sufficient artist. Working now with editor Edward C. Aswell of Harper and Brothers, Wolfe announced the abandonment of his autobiographical mode and set to work on an "objective" novel.

In 1938 Wolfe left New York, his home since the early 1920s, for a tour of the western United States. He left Aswell with a mass of manuscript consisting of all of his recent writings as well as portions deleted from his first two novels. While in the West, Wolfe contracted pneumonia, aggravating a long-dormant tubercular condition, and died shortly before his thirty-eighth birthday. After Wolfe's death his manuscript was honed by Aswell to form two complete novels and the fragment *The Hills Beyond.* Published in 1939 and 1940 respectively, *The Web and the Rock* and *You Can't Go Home Again* exhibit little evidence of Wolfe's promised progression to objectivity, although they do contain a powerful, more mature retelling of Wolfe's life story, with Eugene Gant now in the guise of George "Monk" Webber, and with Aline Bernstein appearing in the character of Esther Jack. In *The Web and the Rock* and *You Can't Go Home Again* Wolfe's artistic scope expanded from the individual's quest for fulfillment to include social concerns such as the ominous rise of the Nazis in Germany, an event witnessed by Wolfe while traveling in Europe during the 1930s.

Since his death, critics have debated Wolfe's merits as a novelist. While some scholars see in Wolfe's work the high-flown artiness of an eternal adolescent—one who continually, in his life and work, cast himself in the role of a tragic martyr to the cause of Art—others contend, as Wolfe himself had written of his father, that "though a man's work may be as full of flaws as a Swiss cheese it will somehow continue to endure if only it has fire." Most critics today concur with C. Hugh Holman, who wrote that "however flawed as novels and imperfect as art his books may be, Thomas Wolfe's works constitute a major and remarkably successful effort to write his autobiography as that of a representative American and to embody in the record of his time and deeds on this earth a vision of the nature and the hope of his democratic land." Emphasizing Wolfe's unique contribution to American literature, Maxwell E. Perkins asserted that Wolfe "knew to the uttermost meaning the literature of other lands and that they were not the literature of America. He knew that the light and color of America were different; that the smells and sounds, its people, and all the structure and dimensions of our continent were unlike anything before. It was with this that he was struggling, and it was that struggle alone that, in a large sense, governed all he did. How long his books may last as such, no one can say, but the trail he has blazed is now open forever."

(For further information about Wolfe's life and works, see *Concise Dictionary of American Literary Biography, 1929-1941; Contemporary Authors,* Vols. 104, 132; *Dictionary of Literary Biography,* Vols. 9, 102; *Dictionary of Literary Biography Documentary Series,* Vol. 2; *Major 20th-Century Writers;* and *Twentieth-Century Literary Criticism,* Vols. 4, 13, 29.)

CRITICAL COMMENTARY

JOHN CHAMBERLAIN
(essay date 1929)

[The following review of *Look Homeward, Angel* originally appeared in *The Bookman* in 1929.]

Among young American writers who have made impressive debuts in recent years, Thomas Wolfe is a distinct anomaly; he has not a nostalgic temperament. *Look Homeward, Angel* is not the book of a frayed spirit who is trying his level best to escape through elegiac writing; it is a rich, positive grappling with life, a remembrance of things past untinged by the shadow of regret, of one who has found his youthful experiences full of savor. No more sensuous (not to be construed as sensual) novel has been written in the United States. There is an easy, unforced strength to it that should be the despair of those beginners of the *New American Caravan* who have tossed overboard one genteel tradition only to fall into another. Inasmuch as it is not a novelist's novel, there will be quite intelligent devotees of fiction who will find its rough, fluid pattern too easy for their tastes. The answer to them would be that it is unfair to condemn a good chronicle novel simply because the chronicle, through over-emphasis, is now falling out of fashion.

For a good chronicle novel is precisely what *Look Homeward, Angel* is. The story is a familiar one: the life of a family set down as it progresses in time, with particular attention to one member who serves as a focal point. . . . Eugene Gant is born at the opening of the century, and his experiences have probably been matched by any number of our contemporaries. But Mr. Wolfe writes of Eugene's days with a difference. The sensitivity of the book is enormous, and it is not a sick sensitivity. There is either gusto or intensity to all of Eugene's activities. . . .

Mr. Wolfe's grasp of character is unhurried—a firm grasp in the old Thackeray sense. His people are

"flat"; they are tagged by their idiosyncrasies of speech and action. They do not change greatly . . . , but because they are the sort of people who are set in their ways (excepting Eugene) the imputation of flatness is no derogation. As for Mr. Wolfe's sheer dramatic power, we ask you to read the death of Ben and then compare it, as we did, with the death of Madame Bovary. Mr. Wolfe's scene is more intimate, it brings a sharper emotion of recognition to one who has been through such a ghastly ordeal. We do not say that it is greater artistically; we merely submit that it is substantially richer.

Look Homeward, Angel has its faults, but they are not those springing from a poverty of material. We might point out that a more logical effect would have been gained if Ben's adventure in the Greasy Spoon (which sets fineness against vulgarity in the manner of the Walpurgisnacht of *Ulysses*) had been left open somehow to the observation of Eugene, or if Gant's trip to California had been assimilated in some way to the narrative of Eugene's life. There are sentences that debouch here and there into meaningless rhetoric. But why seek flaws in the midst of abundance? Mr. Wolfe gives the impression of being inexhaustible, even though the book is largely autobiographical. His second novel will be his real test; for in it he will be forced to think more in terms of pattern and idea than he has in his first. But his observance is so inclusive, his antennae so sensitive to the world about him, that one can hardly regard *Look Homeward, Angel* as a flash in the pan. (pp. 344-46)

John Chamberlain, "Thomas Wolfe," in *The Idea of an American Novel,* edited by Louis D. Rubin, Jr. and John Rees Moore, Thomas Y. Crowell Company, 1961, pp. 344-46.

Principal Works

The Return of Buck Gavin: The Tragedy of a Mountain Outlaw (drama) 1919

Third Night (drama) 1919

The Mountains: A Play in One Act (drama) 1923

Welcome to Our City (drama) 1923

Look Homeward, Angel: A Story of the Buried Life (novel) 1929

From Death to Morning (short stories) 1935

Of Time and the River: A Legend of a Man's Hunger in His Youth (novel) 1935

The Story of a Novel (essay) 1936

The Face of a Nation (poetry) 1939

The Web and the Rock (novel) 1939

You Can't Go Home Again (novel) 1940

The Hills Beyond (short stories, drama, and unfinished novel) 1941

A Stone, a Leaf, a Door (poetry) 1945

Mannerhouse: A Play in a Prologue and Three Acts (drama) 1948

The Letters of Thomas Wolfe (letters) 1956

The Short Novels of Thomas Wolfe (novellas) 1961

The Autobiography of an American Novelist: The Story of a Novel (essays) 1983

Beyond Love and Loyalty: The Letters of Thomas Wolfe and Elizabeth Nowell (letters) 1983

My Other Loneliness: Letters of Thomas Wolfe and Aline Bernstein (letters) 1983

THOMAS LYLE COLLINS
(essay date 1942)

[In the excerpt below, Collins attempts to determine if Wolfe can be credited with writing a Great American Novel.]

[The] appearance of Thomas Wolfe may have been an event of the utmost significance in the history of American literature: certainly, at least, his power of description and narration is unexcelled in the entire range of our literature. There is even a possibility that future generations will come to regard him as the author of The Great American Novel which we have so long awaited. Let us then take this popular phrase, The Great American Novel, as a four-unit yardstick to measure him; for in these four words lie the four main problems which the modern critic encounters in the

novel. These four critical problems, in their respective order, are: *the problem of scope, the problem of greatness, the problem of significance,* and *the problem of form.* By this standard perhaps we may be able to decide how nearly Wolfe's novels approach the ideal of The Great American Novel. (p. 489)

The Problem of Greatness: True greatness, in the strictest sense of the word, always implies a certain transcendency, an ability to rise above the particular circumstance or experience to its more universal implications. This is precisely the quality which distinguishes Wolfe from his lesser contemporaries. This is precisely why the sentimental Mr. Steinbeck, although he is a more disciplined craftsman, is a less great novelist. Wolfe had a sort of super-vision which enabled him to see people in their several artistic dimensions. He found some people, such as the Simpsons, tremendously funny, and he shared with us his belly-laugh over them—but then he penetrated beyond the comic surface to the pathetic essence. He found the Pierces to be quite wonderful—for a while he thought he had discovered the "lane-end into heaven"—but then, rising above them, he saw beyond the cloud of glory which hid them and looked upon the weariness and decay which possessed them. He was completely taken in by the magic of Starwick's glamour, but he eventually saw through it. He was enraptured by Paris "sophistication", but he eventually saw through it. This is the key to Wolfe's genius, this ability to transcend his own experiences, and once having done so, to look back upon it all and write of it with power and clarity, flooding the scene with the rich light of his own personality. (pp. 495-96)

Wolfe's general theme is somewhat reminiscent of Wordsworth's *Odes on Intimations of Immortality* in that it is suggestive of the passage containing the lines "trailing clouds of glory do we come." On the title page of *Look Homeward, Angel,* Wolfe quotes this sentence from Tarr and McMurry—"At one time the earth was probably a white-hot sphere like the sun." Then the prefatory poem which follows explains in a measure both the quotation and the theme of the book. . . . (p. 496)

From this we may extract a brutally prosaic statement of Wolfe's theme: all through life we are searching for some sign—"a stone, a leaf, a door"—which will open up to us the universe of perfection and enchantment which we feel vaguely to have left behind us when we were born. The implication is that our souls have been torn from this enchanted heaven and imprisoned in corporeal frames here on earth. A spiritually necessary unity is wanting, for we are unable to communicate with our fellow-prisoners. Monads have no windows: "we seek the great forgotten language . . ."

Or: Wolfe notes a discrepancy between the ideal world and the real, the former figuratively represented by the sun, the latter by "this most weary unbright cinder", the earth.

Or: Wolfe believes, in a non-Christian sense, in Original Sin. We are born into the damnation of spiritual isolation, and must achieve grace by ending that isolation. (pp. 496-97)

At the heart of Wolfe's novels is an essential paradox which does not become apparent until Eugene's visit to England: it is that there is a door, there is a way to feel at home on the earth, there is a secret room—but though when you're outside you want in, when you're inside you want out! Tradition-less America is on the outside and wants in; traditional England is on the inside and wants out. (p. 497)

All his life Eugene had been seeking "an unfound door". The English had found a door; had they found *the* door? He found the answer when, upon his departure, Edith Coulson told him—

> We shall remember you . . . And I hope you think of us sometime—back here, buried, lost, in all the fog and rain and ruin of England. How good it must be to know that you are young in a very young country—where nothing that you did yesterday matters very much. How wonderful it must be to know that none of the failure of the past can pull you down—that there will always be another day for you—a new beginning. I wonder if you Americans will ever know how fortunate you are . . .

The answer is, then, that life without meaning is far better and more preferable than life with certainty and security, for the latter results in death-in-life, which Wolfe views with abhorrence in all his novels.

This paradox of man accounts for Eugene's fascination with Jewish people. Wolfe bestows upon them a symbolic rôle because they alone were at home on the earth without being enmeshed by it. They are not beset by death-in-life because their certainty is the true one—the certainty of Ecclesiastes, the certainty of pain and folly and useless endeavor. (pp. 497-98)

But the two principal symbols are love and death, for they are the only things that will end the spiritual isolation of the soul. In the great poem which prefaces *Of Time and the River,* these symbols are presented, symbols which are expanded throughout the novel. . . . (p. 498)

The other symbols now unfold to us with greater ease. Gant's father stands for his spiritual, certain past, a past to which he can never return for certainty. This symbol may have been derived from the Bloom-Dedalus relationship in James Joyce's *Ulysses,* particularly since Wolfe is self-admittedly indebted to Joyce. His brother Ben is the symbol for all men who cannot speak or give a sign of brotherhood. The Simpsons are the millions of lonely families in America "huddled below immense and timeless skies". In Starwick, Eu-

gene found the unfound door: Francis could order a spaghetti dinner and make it sound like a royal banquet—thus the great shock when Eugene's illusions about Starwick crumbled. Eugene's mad desire to read all the books ever written is due to his hunger to see out over the walls of his soul into the outside world. The trains rushing through America are symbols of America itself—violent, splendid, powerful, blindly rushing through the night. The night is also symbolic of America, and the lonely men who huddle about the streetlamps and in the lighted lunchrooms late at night take on a transcendent meaning.

It is this unity of the soul and the body of Wolfe's novels, this synthesis of the universal and the particular, which is the chief contributor to his greatness. The worlds of great artists are always complete. Homer's world was complete, as was Dante's, Shakespeare's, Goethe's. In other words, to put it crudely, they have an answer for everything. These artists, although they never lost sight of men, looked beyond and saw a vision of Man, eternal and immutable. Wolfe's *Weltanschauung* displays this same combination of completeness and accuracy, and therefore, in many ways, ranks him accordingly.

The Problem of Significance: The American reading public, made acutely self-critical by Mr. Mencken et al. during the Twenties, is very message-conscious in their reading of novels. What is the author's theme? What suggestion does he have to make in his novel for the political, economic, sociological, or cultural improvement of the nation? . . . I think this accounts in part, at least, for the hesitant reception of Wolfe's novels by the American critics. For Wolfe seemed much more concerned with his own personal problems than with the problems of America. This is why *You Can't Go Home Again* was greeted with such sighs of satisfaction, for at last Wolfe had become "significant".

I have already spoken of Wolfe's central theme of spiritual isolation. Its universal nature is apparent. Its particular application is that while it is true in varying degree for men of all time and place, it is most true for Americans of the present day. We *are* "like blind sucks and sea-valves and the eyeless crawls that grope along the forest of the sea's great floor . . . " Our poverty of tradition, our blind materialism, our barrenness of middle-class life could not be described better. One does not have to read *You Can't Go Home Again* to find "significance". There is significance a-plenty in Wolfe's first three novels if one will but read carefully some of the passages of "dark substance" therein.

And Wolfe for the most part avoids the sentimental fallacy of ascribing our evils to institutions. With a dim but perceptible certainty he sees that the fault lies not outside but inside, deep within the heart of man.

In *You Can't Go Home Again* this implied belief

becomes explicit. In his conclusion, called "Credo", he says "I think the enemy is single selfishness and compulsive greed." In the chapters called "Boom Town" and "The Company" he lashes out viciously at this single selfishness and compulsive greed. And in the chapter, "Piggy Logan's Circus", he achieves an effect of strange and gripping horror of a decadent aristocracy which will watch for hours the morbidly pointless antics of a giggling moron.

In regard to Wolfe's position in our national literature, I think it is safe to say that he stands, and will stand, very close to the top. For in his novels he caught that strange and unique combination of brilliant hope and black despair which is the quintessence of the American spirit.

The Problem of Form: The form of Wolfe's novels is enough to give any critic a nightmare. At first reading they seem to be little more than miscellaneous collections of autobiographical anecdotes and personal observations. But after complete reading and thoughtful contemplation, the nature of his literary form begins to emerge in one's mind.

First, however, a satisfactory definition of form must be found. (pp. 499-501)

Kenneth Burke has a practical and useful definition of form which will serve in this case. He says that "form is the creation of an appetite in the mind of the auditor, and the adequate satisfying of that appetite."

Applying this definition to Wolfe's works, I find three basic and interdependent forms. They are, in the order of excellence, the episode, the complete work, and the novel.

Sometimes these episodes, such as the one about the Simpsons, are very short. Sometimes, as in "The Child by Tiger" in *The Web and the Rock* and "The World That Jack Built" in *You Can't Go Home Again,* they are as long as a short novel. In the latter instance, they are subdivided into sub-episodes, and sub-sub-episodes, each one creating an appetite in the mind of the reader, and satisfying that appetite adequately; each one having a surprising singleness and intensity of effect. The sub-episodes which go to make up a complete episode do not always observe a time or place sequence; instead, Wolfe sketches in a detail here, makes a few strokes there, until finally the whole picture is completed. (pp. 501-02)

The second basic form, Wolfe's complete work of four novels, contains a spiritual evolution in which may be found the beginning of a conflict, the body of a conflict, and the resolution, elements of a form which should satisfy the most reactionary of critics. The beginning of the conflict is contained in *Look Homeward, Angel,* in which a boy of energy and ambition finds himself buried in a world of pettiness and animosity and meaninglessness, and determines to escape into the outside world, where he may seek glory and love and meaning. (p. 502)

Of Time and the River and *The Web and the Rock* constitute the body of the conflict. In the first he escapes into the world, and his interests and passions diverge in a thousand different directions in his Faustian search for glory and love and meaning. In the latter his passion strikes a lens and is focussed and concentrated in his love for Esther Jack. The lens is then shattered, and the last volume, *You Can't Go Home Again,* contains a desperate race between death and meaning. The last lines he wrote present his premonition of death and his triumphant reaffirmation of a spiritual idealism. . . . (p. 503)

The form of each novel, then, since it is so loose, is only important as a phase of Gant-Webber's spiritual evolution, and as a frame for Wolfe's episodic structure; it has no inherent and self-sufficient form to speak of. But Thomas Wolfe, genius that he was, had that inevitable instinct for form which served him twice where it failed him once.

The Problem of Scope: Wolfe wrote *great* American novels, he wrote great *American* novels, and, loosely speaking, he wrote great American *novels.* But he fails to measure up in the fourth respect: he did not write *the* great American novel. Contained in the phrase is the implication that the novel should summarize and epitomize the promise of America's becoming one of the great ages of man, just as Homer's *Iliad* epitomizes the heroic age of Greece, Dante's *Divine Comedy* the medieval age, and Shakespeare's plays the English Renaissance. This is virtually impossible. There are so many forces of disunity and skepticism present in present-day America that a novel, or even a series of novels, could not bring them all together into a coherent and comprehensible pattern. Homer and Shakespeare and Dante stand far above us because they stand at the peak of a high and mighty structure erected by men of great talent and culture, all working together. There was little in the modern world for Wolfe to stand on.

Also, Wolfe was not of the artistic temper to write such a work. The author of The Great American Novel must be dramatic and omnipresent; Thomas Wolfe was lyrical and unipresent. For him there was only one world and he was at the center of it.

But his third and gravest limitation was his genius: it was the tragic flaw, a flaw of which he was only too conscious. "Genius is not enough", sneers Mr. De Voto. On the contrary, the genius of Thomas Wolfe was too much. He was driven by a restlessness which kept him from achieving that cool perfection which often comes easy to lesser men. (pp. 503-04)

Thomas Lyle Collins, "Thomas Wolfe," in *The Sewanee Review,* Vol. L, No. 4, Fall, 1942, pp. 487-504.

PAMELA HANSFORD JOHNSON
(essay date 1948)

[Johnson's *Hungry Gulliver* (1948; later published as *The Art of Thomas Wolfe*, 1963) was the first book-length study of Wolfe's works. In the following excerpt from this study, Johnson provides an overview of Wolfe's accomplishments and suggests why his books appeal to the young.]

It is no accident that *Look Homeward, Angel* is the most clear-sighted of [Wolfe's] novels. Born into the lower middle-class life of a small mountain town, he pictured the familiar world with an objectivity altogether remarkable. The farther he journeyed from Asheville the more baffled he became, and the less sure of himself. When he left the mountains he discovered that he could not go home again, and for the rest of his life was haunted by the sense of being a wanderer and adrift. He was lost in the city and in the foreign lands; in 1929 the whole world of his most intimate experience came to an end, and he never came to terms with the new one. In his loneliness he was America herself, America of the nineteen-twenties: huge, young, aggressive, unfound, like an adolescent at a grownup party, and he looked with desire and awe upon the future. He managed to "greet the unseen with a cheer," proclaiming his certainties, thundering his reassurances; but he was never again as confident of himself as Eugene had been when he spoke with Ben's ghost beneath the stone angel. . . .

With all his gigantic faults, his prolixity, his ranting, his stupefying absurdities, Wolfe is incomparably the most significant figure in three decades of American literature. His egotism arises from a profound desire to analyse the nature of his own being, not from a passion to display himself to others. He is the egotist unconscious of an audience. . . . Wolfe is labouring upon a mental excavation that engages his entire attention; he would no sooner make a concession to an interruptor than a surgeon would break off in the middle of trepanning to look out of the window at a Salvation Army band. . . .

He never acquired "poise." His later work displays even more sharply than his earlier books the defiance that comes of being uncertain. His antagonism towards modern European culture sprang from worshipful envy of its long ancestry. By his references to "fancy" writing, he means the oversophisticated writing of the intellectual who believes fundamentally that his learning has made him superior to the common man; and this is a peculiarly European outlook. Wolfe felt that the foundations of an American literature were still being laid; and he therefore resented the writer whose ease arises out of a conviction that he is simply continuing, and adorning, a tradition. The youthfulness of his country weighed heavily upon Wolfe; he thought of America *culturally* as the brilliant but underprivileged board school boy matched against the university man of Europe—a boy who, because of his very disadvantages, must work twice as hard and succeed three times as brilliantly. . . .

He never acquired "professionalism." He never learned to trim his work, polish it, or play safe with it. . . . He wrote because he wished to communicate something that seemed to him inexpressibly urgent; nothing else mattered. This is why his books carry so powerful a sense of his personality; they are the most intimate writings, the most naked and the most trustful, of this generation. He set out in search of an impossible ideal—to communicate that which is incommunicable. He ended with a philosophy that is little more than a few vague conclusions and a few verifications. What he did achieve was a finished portrait of the artist as a young man, and within this man the portrait of a continent. "The whole thing's there—it really *is*." (pp. 154 57)

The most striking feature of the Gant-Webber novels is their youthfulness. They do, indeed, look outward upon the future as a boy looks out in fear and terrifying hope upon his manhood. Their sincerity is a boy's sincerity, and their confidence is that friendliness which is offered to all men only before experience has brought common sense and distrust, balance and corruption. . . .

When *Look Homeward, Angel,* was first published in England, it was the young people who greeted it with excitement and with that curious uprush of personal affection which upon rare occasion greets the author of a novel that has come upon certain hidden springs in the wilderness of the reader's desire. Young men and women between seventeen and twenty-three years of age felt that in some obscure way Wolfe was their spokesman; perhaps, after all, he had managed to send out some message from the incommunicable prison. His lyricism was the expression of their own longing to put into words the wonder and strangeness of coming out of childhood. The Laura James idyll which, to the mature critic, shows Wolfe at his weakest, to the adolescent represented love as he most deeply wished to find it. The boy who felt himself in any way restrained or subjected by his parents was moved by Eugene's protest to his family after the fight with Luke and Ben; this, thought the boy, is what *I* should like to have said, if only I could have found the words. The optimism towards the future, *despite the gain-saying of a dead man,* encouraged the young reader to feel himself Promethean, capable of defying not only those set in authority over him by reason of kinship, age and experience, but of defying also the supernatural authority—God and the voice of the Prophets. Wolfe gave to the young man a conviction that whatever might be the defeat of others, his own future would be straight and shining as the path of the sun across the sea.

He is American as Whitman was American, and like Whitman realises the *earliness* of the time at which he speaks. Although he cannot claim, as Whitman could, to be among the pioneers, he does believe himself in the company of those who follow after them to develop the ore and oil of a new continent. His tremendous pride, the pride that vented itself in hostility towards the friends of Esther Jack, towards the English, and towards the publishers "Rawng and Wright," is counteracted by an even greater joy in being young, in being uncertain, of sitting down with the primer and learning the world from the beginning as once he learned new languages. Alone among the writers of his generation he understands that the indigenous culture of his country today is as young as England's was when Chaucer struck open the great way of modern English letters, and that the spaces of her future are unbounded. (p. 164)

Pamela Hansford Johnson, in her *The Art of Thomas Wolfe,* Charles Scribner's Sons, 1963, 170 p.

LOUIS UNTERMEYER

(essay date 1955)

[Untermeyer was an American poet, editor, and critic. In the following excerpt, he surveys Wolfe's career.]

Thomas Wolfe was the epitome of gigantic need and illimitable excess, a symbol of the "enormous space and energy of American life," its rawness and richness, its frenetic successes and stupendous failures. The man who might have stood for the portrait of the magnified American hero—a shaggy black-haired, burning-eyed, six-foot-six Paul Bunyan, a craftsman who built everything on a monstrous scale—was vulnerable to the least murmur of criticism, tormented by the passing of time, and fearful of loneliness and the sense of being lost. Nothing ever conceived in America, except by Whitman, vibrated with so exuberant and desperate a craving for life—*all* of life, experienced simultaneously and on every level-as the four novels of the writer who died before he had lived thirty-eight years. (p. 726)

Writing came easily—often too easily—to Wolfe. Words flowed from him freely, inexhaustibly, furiously, as though they had been held back too long, sudden

freshets released and rushing uncontrollably out of orderly channels. At twenty the river which was to carry him in full flood was taking an uncertain course, but it was already beginning to rise. New plays were written, were praised, but were always rejected. Everyone was impressed with Wolfe's dramas, but no one wanted to produce them. (p. 727)

He had already begun to think of a kind of novel when he went abroad for a year. Forced to resume teaching, he returned, ran away again, and, in the fall of 1926, found himself in London. Alone, and in a foreign country, he began his book. Back in New York, after two and a half years more of teaching all day and writing all night, he finished it. "The book took hold of me and possessed me," he wrote in his revealing quasi-diary, *The Story of a Novel.* "In a way, I think it shaped itself. Like every young man, I was strongly under the influence of writers I admired. One of the chief writers at that time was Mr. James Joyce with his book *Ulysses.* The book that I was writing was much influenced, I believe, by his own book, and yet the powerful energy and fire of my own youth played over and, I think, possessed it all. Like Mr. Joyce, I wrote about things that I had known, the immediate life and experience that had been familiar to me in my childhood. Unlike Mr. Joyce, I had no literary experience. I had never had anything published before." . . . (pp. 727-28)

The work, finally called *Look Homeward, Angel,* was published a few days after his twenty-ninth birthday. Wolfe had worried that he had exposed himself—"the awful, utter nakedness of print, that thing which is for all of us so namelessly akin to shame came closer day by day"—and he was relieved when most of the critics hailed the book with surprised superlatives. He was, however, unprepared for the howls of outrage which arose from his home town. He was irrevocably hurt when he heard that the book had been denounced from the pulpits and reviled on street corners. (p. 728)

Six months after publication, his book went so well that he was able to resign from the faculty of New York University and, assisted by an award of a Guggenheim Fellowship, go abroad again. In Paris he felt a great wave of homesickness and, in "the almost intolerable effort of memory and desire," recreated and enlarged the entire progress of his life. The past came back to him "loaded with electricity, pregnant, crested, with a kind of hurricane violence." He says that the second book was not really written; it wrote him. It was to be called *The October Fair,* but the onrushing memories bore him along on a "torrential and ungovernable flood," and he decided on the inevitable title *Of Time and the River.* (p. 729)

He wanted to cram into it detail upon detail, to reproduce in its entirety "the full flood and fabric of a scene in life itself." There was always something more, he felt, that needed desperately to be said, something to be added to the thousands of pages in the packing case. . . . In March, 1935, after the author had worked on the continuation of his (or Eugene Gant's) story for almost six years, *Of Time and the River* appeared. (p. 730)

Although the next two novels continue the saga of the writer's life the four books are actually one book, one towering autobiography—Wolfe now calls his hero George Webber. . . . Except for the arbitrary distortions, Webber remains Gant and, with a somewhat toughened manner, Wolfe.

In *The Web and the Rock* and *You Can't Go Home Again,* both of which were published posthumously, the character of Gant-Webber-Wolfe changes only insofar as any man changes with age and experience. He is ambivalent, pitiful, perverse, sometimes even paranoiac, but always aware of his weaknesses; he analyzes his compulsive rages and ramping inconsistencies, balancing self-pity with self-mockery. Always he is something more than himself. He is (or meant to be) not only the ambivalent American artist but the symbol of America itself, intransigent and contradictory, looking to Europe for escape and inspiration and, at the same time, repudiating the past, denying any heritage but our own. . . . (p. 731)

Wolfe's faults are so obvious that it was all too easy for the critics to belabor them. The faults are part of his excess: the disorganized gusto, the fierce energy that will not be beaten into form, the confusion of philosophy and feeling, the contradiction between social consciousness and the failure to do anything about it. (p. 732)

It is not enough to say that Wolfe is great in spite of his faults; the exaggerations, the wild monologs, the overextended raptures must be accepted as integrated and inseparable parts of the man. The pared concision, the brusque epigram was not for him. Wolfe luxuriated in length; he had to have great expanses to stretch himself. . . . One must also grant Wolfe's inability to distinguish between eloquence and verbosity, letting rhetoric slide into rant; his personal and general jealousies; his mixed envy and hatred of the well-to-do sophisticates, especially the Jews, the intellectuals, "the liberated princelings"; his incredible total recall which, superficially like Proust's, was without Proust's magic power of revelation. Properly balanced, the defects are minor blemishes when weighed against Wolfe's major accomplishments: the inexhaustible vitality—only in Rabelais and Joyce is there a swifter spate of words, a more joyful use of speech—the exuberant optimism; the enigmatic but noble summaries, the salutations to his native soil, a country compounded of "nameless fear and of soaring conviction, of brutal, empty, naked, bleak, corrosive ugliness, and of beauty so lovely and so overwhelming that the tongue is stopped by it, and

the language for it has not yet been uttered." (pp. 732-33)

Wolfe tried too hard and stretched himself too far for perfection, but perfection was scarcely his aim. His furious desire to outreach time and space was bound to fail. But, as William Faulkner, Wolfe's fellow-Southerner and in many ways his opposite, contended, "Wolfe made the best failure because he had tried hardest to say the most . . . He was willing to throw away style, coherence, all the rules of preciseness, to try to put all the experience of the human heart on the head of a pin, as it were". (p. 733)

I'd rather be a poet than anything else in the world." [Wolfe once] cried. "God! What I wouldn't give to be one!" Two posthumous volumes—*The Face of a Nation,* a collection of poetical passages from his writings, and *A Stone, A Leaf, A Door,* segments of his prose rearranged as verse—prove that Wolfe not only wrote prose-poetry but that Wolfe was a poet who happened to use the medium of prose. He mistakenly thought that he was not a poet because he put the emphasis on conventional form and refused to believe that his sprawling lines could attain the art he most admired. Nevertheless, the beat of ecstatic life, the rise and fall of tidal emotions, and the restless flow of the river of time are held in Wolfe's rhythmical, strongly cadenced lines. In no prose and only in a small body of verse has there been expressed a greater sense of urgency, of unhappy adolescence and its insatiable desires, of loving kindness and unexpected cruelty, the wanderings of the human spirit. (p. 734)

Louis Untermeyer, "Thomas Wolfe (1900-1938)," in his *Makers of the Modern World: The Lives of Ninety-two Writers, Artsits, Scientists, Statesmen, Inventors, Philosophers, Composers, and Other Creators Who Formed the Pattern of Our Century,* Simon and Schuster, 1955, pp. 726-35.

LOUIS D. RUBIN, JR.

(essay date 1973)

[Rubin is an American critic and editor. In the following excerpt, he refutes accusations that Wolfe's works are stylistically unstructured and thematically immature.]

Encountering Wolfe, particularly if one is young and a would-be writer, has often turned out to be not merely an event; it is an emotional experience. There have been few American authors, I think, who have been capable of affording just this particular kind of intense experience. . . . What Wolfe did was not merely to dramatize the stories of his protagonists' lives; he also dramatized his desire to tell about those lives. . . . In a sense, all of Wolfe's novels are about the feelings of a young man who wants to write, and it is to this that so many of his readers have responded. (pp. 2-3)

[At the age of nineteen I first] read *Look Homeward, Angel,* and straightaway was transported into a realm of literary experience that I had not known could exist. No writer, as Thoreau once remarked of Whitman, can communicate a new experience to us; but what he can do is to make us recognize the importance of our own experience, so that we become aware, for the first time, of what it is that we feel and think and what it can mean for us. That is what Thomas Wolfe did for me. He described a young man whose sensuous apprehension of life was matched by his appetite for feeling. Not only did he render the concrete details of experience in brilliant specificity, but he responded to the details lavishly and lyrically. Everything he thought, observed, and did was suffused with feeling. For a young reader such as myself there could be an instantaneous and quite exhilarating identification, not only with the youthful protagonist Eugene Gant, but with the autobiographical author who was describing Eugene's experience with so much approval and pride. And it was on emotional response—not in its subtlety or discrimination, but in its intensity—that the highest premium was placed. (p. 3)

What Wolfe was saying was that feeling counted for everything and that if you could feel intensely enough about the things of your world, it was all the proof needed to know that you were virtuous.

It was the description, the concrete emotional evocation of the space and color and time of a young man's developing experience of himself and his world, that gave body to the Wolfe novels, anchored the rhetoric, and . . . ultimately helped to protect the art against the weakness of the rhetoric when, as sometimes in the early work and more frequently later, it tended to dissolve into empty assertion. (pp. 4-5)

Thomas Wolfe was brilliantly able, for readers such as . . . myself, to render the sense of being young. He did this in part with the rhetoric, to be sure—but most of all it was the world of experience that he opened up to vision. For a young man the world is apt to seem imminently there for the taking—and Thomas Wolfe portrayed it in glowing color and brilliant detail, shot full of emotional response. . . . Wolfe took the mundane, the ordinary, the humdrum and recreated them so sharply in language that you saw them for almost the first time. Or rather, he drew together and articulated the diffused and latent emotional impressions you had about something so that for the first time you recognized what you really saw and felt.

Wolfe's great subject, especially after *Look Homeward, Angel,* was America. He rendered in poetically, gave it a glamor and mystery, and made the

Wolfe in Berlin, 1936.

places you were living in, and just beginning to explore, seem full of promise and excitement. (pp. 6-7)

In *Look Homeward, Angel,* he sent Eugene Gant on a walk through downtown Altamont, and described dentist's offices, laundrywomen, undertaker's parlors, Y.M.C.A. secretaries, milliner's shops, and the like in a series of little vignettes of vivid color, and, concluded each with a quotation from a poem, as much as to say that in such mundane, everyday activities the same aesthetic response was appropriate as in the more literarily respectable objects depicted by the English poets. (p. 7)

No one could depict a train trip with more excitement than Wolfe. The poetry of motion was his forte; it was not merely a matter of making a trip in order to arrive at this destination or that, but the experience of going for its own sake that enthralled him, and he portrayed it in a way that caught the imagination. (p. 8)

Many of the most moving lyrical passages in Wolfe's work after *Look Homeward, Angel* involve . . . moments in which Eugene Gant, and less occasionally George Webber, look on people from a train window and recognize their kinship and their own loneliness. Such moments, however, are transitory; the human contact is limited to the momentary glimpse, whereupon the train moves on. (p. 9)

On the one hand there is, especially in *Look*

Homeward, Angel but often elsewhere as well, a portrayal of aspects of the American scene that are concrete, evocative, enormously affective. And there is also, in the work after the first novel, a deliberate and cumulative attempt to depict the idea of America itself—an attempt which, though involving much itemization and often long catalogs, is usually singularly impersonal in nature, in that the numerous specific items are chosen as typical examples rather than for themselves. The human contacts, in other words, are as viewed through a train window, and neither lasting nor individualized. Wolfe seeks to give them meaning through emotional rhetoric, the emotion belonging to his protagonist as he views them and to the novelist as he remembers viewing them. In page after page of *Of Time and the River* Eugene Gant is shown "experiencing" America, both while travelling across it and afterward through memory while in France. His longing for it while abroad is agonizing, his view of it as seen from train windows is full of love, compassion, desire. But when viewed in this way, as *America*, it consists entirely of lists, catalogs, assemblages of examples. It is, in other words, almost entirely quantitative, a collection of items, scenes, themes, names. There is little or no sorting out, no choosing of some of the items as more or less uniquely or typically American, more or less beautiful or meaningful, than others. And at the end what has been given is an abstraction, "America," along with a display of items that are proposed as typical examples of its makeup. (p. 10)

What the "America" episodes do is to dramatize both the Wolfean protagonist's and, importantly, the authorial personality's yearning for experience. The very fact that the emotional hunger is there in such abundance and that it cannot quite make contact with—or, to continue the metaphor, find adequate spiritual nourishment in—the substance at which it is being so urgently directed is itself a device for imaging the sense of loneliness and spiritual yearning that lies at the heart of the experience of reading the novels. And we go wrong, I think, if we refuse to accept that dimension and dismiss such a viewpoint as an example of the so-called "imitative fallacy." For the experience of fiction is a subtle and complex affair, and if we try to leave out the "rhetoric" of the art, the formal function of the presence of the storyteller in our reading of the story he is telling, we may impoverish our relationship with a work of fiction.

What I am getting at is that in his fiction, . . . Wolfe *dramatizes himself as author*, warts and all. Or more precisely, he dramatizes himself in the act of looking at himself. What is involved here is not just a biographical matter, a formal, literary relationship. Not only was Wolfe's protagonist a dramatized version of himself when a bit younger, but the rhetoric of the interpretative description serves to set up a myself-when-younger relationship between the storyteller and the protagonist. (pp. 10-11)

This dual identity as character and chronicler, enforced through rhetoric and attitude, is both the strength and the weakness of the Wolfe books. It enables Wolfe to bring to bear on his youthful protagonist's experience the impressive powers of his rhetoric. He can recognize, explore, and delineate the particularities of that experience. He can use the affective possibilities of rhetoric to intensify the meaning of the experience, and guide our response to it. He can, in other words, both show and persuade. Because the persuasion is coming from a formally established point of view, a recreating authorial personality, . . . it takes on an authority that would otherwise be lacking if it were merely arbitrary authorial embellishment. . . . (p. 12)

But just as surely, it can work that way only if we are willing to believe in the validity of both the youthful protagonist's experience and the recreating interpreter's delineation of its importance. If ever we feel that what the speaker tells us about the meaning of what happened is exaggerated, or confused, or actually inaccurate, and the whole relationship breaks down. For the rhetorical stance of this remembering sensibility has got to be plausible, too. When the author says that Eugene did or thought such and such, we accept that; but when he insists that what Eugene did or thought signifies this or that about human experience, and we believe that it doesn't so signify, he is in trouble; and when he tries to enforce his interpretation by cascades of affective rhetoric, what results is something very different from what he intends. Let me cite [an] example, from the material posthumously published as a novel, *The Web and the Rock*. [The passage contains the scene in which] Wolfe is describing young George Webber's feeling and behavior at a time when he had been quarreling with his mistress. His novel has been rejected, he is in bad shape emotionally, and sometimes, when he telephones his mistress' home to find her not in, he imagines that Esther is betraying him. (pp. 12-13)

[In this passage] there are two levels of experience. One is that of George Webber in love, as he suspects his mistress and suffers. However, by use of the conditional tense—George "*would* leave the phone to drain the bottle," and "*would* be hurled through tunnels"—the author makes it clear that the experience is one that happened to George on characteristic occasions, rather than just the time being described. Clearly, therefore, it is the authorial personality who is speaking to us, recapitulating and summarizing his protagonist's experience over a period of time. Now presumably what the author is doing is showing us how it was with young George Webber at a bad time. It is not that Esther Jack is really betraying George; rather, George, in his pain and torment, imagines that she is, and on such occasions goes off like a madman into the night to wander about the city in his anguish. Under such conditions, his behavior could hardly be termed inexplicable. Nor would it be improbable that at such a time, drunk, distraught, despondent, George might well envision the city through which he is wandering in just such [a hellish] fashion as described. But exactly who is it that sees the walk as a "prowl" along "a hundred streets," during which George looks "into a million livid faces seeing death in all of them"? To whom does "the ragged edge of Brooklyn" appear as "some hideous outpost," as "a wasteland horror of bare lots and rust and rubbish," and of "dismal little houses flung rawly down upon the barren earth"? Is it the distraught young protagonist or the supposedly more objective authorial personality who interprets what happened? The answer, syntactically and emotionally, is that both of them see and evaluate it that way. . . . [There] is thus little or no difference between the two perspectives. At such moments, all too frequent after *Look Homeward, Angel,* the reader is likely to refuse to accept the interpretation of George Webber's experience which the author is insisting upon. He can go along with the notion that young George Webber may have felt this way about the city at the time, and that George may indeed have imagined he was prowling a hundred streets and looking into a million livid faces, but when the story-teller, the remembering author who as interpreter and judge ought not still to feel betrayed and overcome with a sense of failure, also interprets and evaluates the experience in that fashion, without irony or humor or reservation of any sort, it is something else again. The sympathy and understanding the reader might have for the youthful George Webber at such times of torment is seriously undercut when he realizes that the author is in complete agreement with his protagonist, that he sees nothing excessive, nothing pathological, nothing childish or histrionic in George's attitude, but is recounting it with complete approval and endorsement.

The experience of Thomas Wolfe's fiction, therefore, involves two factors. One is the way in which the doings of the protagonists of the novels are described and communicated to us. The other is the way in which the authorial voice interprets and evaluates those doings. But these two factors cannot be separated from each other and considered in isolation. The impact of the first, as we have seen, is made possible in part by the second. (pp. 13-15)

[While] many readers will agree with the burden of De Voto's strictures, which is that *Of Time and the River* is an overwritten and unstructured book that would have profited greatly by a great deal more cutting and revising than the author was willing to give it, it should be recognized that De Voto's memorable assault fails to comprehend how the Wolfe novels actually work as fiction. De Voto's theory of fiction dismissed absolutely what we have seen is a necessary dimension to the art of fiction as practiced by Wolfe—that conscious presence of the authorial voice interpreting the doings of the protagonist. . . . De Voto said, "A novelist represents life. When he does anything else, no matter how beautiful or furious or ecstatic the way in which he does it, he is not writing fiction." . . . [But] part of the representing—in Aristotelian terms, the imitation—happens to be the act of giving order and meaning, and when Wolfe uses his authorial rhetoric to reinforce, interpret, comment upon his protagonist's actions and thoughts, we object not when the rhetoric as such shows up, but only as it fails to enhance our interpretation and evaluation of what the protagonist's life means. When it does fit the occasion, when what the authorial personality says about the protagonist seems believable and appropriate, then, far from being disconcerted by the presence of the rhetoric, we accept it and let it help us take part in the experience of the fiction. What I think De Voto really objected to was not the asserting, ranting, or detonating rhetoric of the novelist; it was the inappropriateness of such rhetoric as an accurate and believable interpretation of the experience being chronicled. . . . [The] more the author goes on . . . the less convincing he seems.

The intense experience that reading Wolfe can be for the young . . . is possible precisely because of the ability and the willingness of a certain kind of younger reader to accept, at face value and as a version of the truth, just the signification that the narrator is attaching to it. This reader identifies with the author. For him a rhetorical exercise such as that involving the spirit of America [represented by Eugene's train trip northward] isn't "placental" at all rather, it is an important part of the experience of reading *Of Time and the River,* because it pronounces the meaning and significance of the train trip and reinforces the feelings of the younger Eugene Gant who made the trip with the more "mature" rhetorical approval of the author telling about it. The book works by an alternation of viewpoint between the younger Eugene and his older writing self, in which the younger man acts and feels and thinks and then the older man not only expresses his approval but confirms the verdict in emotive rhetoric. The charm, for the younger reader, lies in the fact that although the older, commenting narrator is, by dint of his rhetorical skill and the obvious fact that he wrote the book, no mere youth first undergoing the experience, he nevertheless not only accepts and ratifies the younger viewpoint but extols it as being even more significant than the younger protagonist himself had realized. The verve, the self-importance, the romantic insistence upon uniqueness of sensibility, the essentially uncritical, quantitative hunger for sensation of the adolescent and postadolescent, free of qualification or ironic presentation by the older narrator, are enthusiastically received by many younger readers. (pp. 17-19)

The difficulty for the adult reader of the Wolfe novels, in particular after *Look Homeward, Angel,* is that not only does the autobiographical protagonist insist upon holding on to his immaturity, but the interpreting author equally insists upon the entire appropriateness of his doing so and upon the spiritual insensitivity of all who refuse to go along with him when he does it. Furthermore, the authorial commentator, for all his approval, appears to become increasingly apprehensive that others may not share his approbation, and his response is to double and treble his own rhetorical assertion of the rightness of Eugene's behavior, attempting to sweep away all possible objections, including perhaps his own, in a torrent of words. This is the material that De Voto calls placental. It is not that, so much as simply superfluous. (p. 21)

What we have in the Wolfe fiction, then, is the dramatized record of a talented and romantic young writer's encounter with the experience of being an artist in America, as it forced itself upon him. He described it happening, and he told us what he thought it meant. Especially after his first book, what he said it meant is often not what we think it really did mean, but there can be no mistaking the earnestness with which he presented his case or any questioning of the artistic honesty of the attempt. We may disagree with the interpretation, may feel sometimes that he is trying to justify what cannot and should not be justified, and sometimes even that he is using his rhetoric to persuade himself as well as the reader. But let this be said: he never spares himself, never hides behind cheap deceits or clever, modish poses. His aim, as Faulkner says, was to tell it all, and though by no means always sure of what it was he was telling, he did his best. This is why it seems to me that even *Of Time and the River,* for all its excess and its attitudinizing, comes out as a pretty good book. We may not like all of what we see in it, but there can be no doubt we have experienced something very formidable and very honest. What we have experienced is Thomas Wolfe trying to tell about himself as Eugene Gant; and I submit that this is worth having, and we should let no theory of the effaced narrator prevent us from recognizing that this is the formal experience of the encounter with *Of Time and the River.* What one may think about the experience may change a great deal over the decades, but there can be no doubt that the transaction is there to be read. . . . (pp. 24-5)

Louis D. Rubin, Jr., in an introduction to *Thomas Wolfe: A Collection of Critical Essays,* edited by Louis D. Rubin, Jr., Prentice-Hall, Inc., 1973, pp. 1-30.

C. HUGH HOLMAN
(essay date 1975)

[Holman was an American detective novelist and literary scholar. In the following excerpt, he discusses Wolfe's novels as epic works.]

To look at Wolfe's "book" as an attempt at an American epic helps us see what he is about and appreciate at least some of the causes for his successes and his failures. He felt a compulsive need to "sing America." As he expressed it in 1936: "I have at last discovered my own America. . . . And I shall wreak out my vision of this life, this way, this world and this America, to the top of my bent, to the height of my ability, but with an unswerving devotion, integrity and purity of purpose that shall not be menaced, altered or weakened by any one." In addition to this epic urge, the nature and content of his work was shaped by the quality of his personal experience, by the influence of John Livingston Lowes's theory of the imagination, and by the special way in which he wrote. Out of the interactions of these things with his powerful rhetoric and his dramatic talent came a body of writing which corresponds with remarkable accuracy to the special shapes and tensions of the American epic.

His brief life was successively pastoral, provincial, urban, national, and international; and it embraced a great range of experience. (pp. 161-62)

As he moved through these stages, Wolfe was formatively influenced in his concept of art and the artist by John Livingston Lowes's theories of the functioning of the creative imagination. He studied under Lowes while Lowes was writing his justly famous study of Coleridge, *The Road to Xanadu,* and heard Lowes read chapters of this new book to his classes. . . . Lowes's theory greatly encouraged Wolfe's innate epic impulse, for he believed that an artist stored experiences of all kinds—physical, emotional, intellectual, and vicarious—in his "deep well of unconscious cerebration," and that there, in the fullness of time, "the shaping power of the imagination" worked upon it to create an ordered cosmos out of this teeming and fecund chaos. Lowes said: "The imagination never operates in a vacuum. Its stuff is always fact of some order, somehow experienced; its product is that fact transmuted. I am not forgetting that facts may swamp imagination, and remain unassimilated and untransformed." At another place he said: "For the Road to Xanadu, as we have traced it, is the road of the human spirit, and the imagination voyaging through chaos and reducing it to clarity and order is the symbol of all the quests which lend glory to our dust. . . . For the work of the creators is the mastery and transmutation and re-ordering into shapes of beauty of the given universe within us and without us." Wolfe added to these ideas a conviction that *"conscious* interests and efforts at all times" are working in the making of art from the matter in the "deep well of unconscious cerebration." Thus Lowes's ideas, together with certain of his cadences and phrases, encouraged Wolfe's frantic attempt to "stock-pile" experience of all kinds, with the intention of later drawing consciously upon it for the materials of his art.

Out of his commitment to this view of the imagi-nation probably came at least the sanction if not the full impulse for Wolfe's effort to engulf all experi-ence. . . . Few writers have ever immersed themselves in the turbulent stream of experience more thoroughly than Wolfe; few writers have tried to touch more seg-ments of America and know them with greater sensory surety.

In addition to this passion for experience, Wolfe had too a sensibility and a memory unusual in their power to recall odors, sounds, colors, shapes, and the feel of things with great precision. When these quali-ties were combined with his hunger for experience, Wolfe possessed a subject matter appropriate to the ambition of an epic poet, and he could, with some justi-fication, feel that his experience approached that of ev-eryman-in-America's and was thus a subject adequate to describe the democratic protagonist.

Wolfe's method of working, too, yielded itself quite easily to the attempt at a modern epic. With a re-markable ear for speech and eye for physical detail and with an equally keen sense of character and of dramatic action, Wolfe as person encountered experiences which seem to have come to him in relatively short and self-contained units. Many of these units are self-sufficient short stories and short novels—both forms in which he did excellent work. It is when these short stories and short novels become the materials of the long narra-tives that they begin to lose much of their objectivity and dramatic intensity. Even in *Look Homeward, Angel,* frequently and accurately called his most uni-fied work, the individual episodes exist so indepen-dently that many can be extracted and published as self-contained units—short stories—without doing vi-olence to their fundamental meaning. The satiric por-trait of Professor Hatcher's playwriting course in *Of Time and the River* is a unified piece that is broken into four separate parts. The picture of Abraham Jones, a detailed character study in the same novel, is also frag-mented into three parts. The posthumously published novels were assembled by Edward Aswell and, there-fore, the unity or the fragmentary character of their ep-isodes cannot be directly attributed to Wolfe. However, some of their finest parts originally appeared as self-contained units in magazines; for example, "The Child by Tiger" in *The Web and the Rock,* "Boom Town," "The Party at Jack's," and " 'I Have a Thing to Tell You' " in *You Can't Go Home Again.*

Wolfe's method seemingly was to write these epi-sodes with much of the objectivity of an observer, and then later to fit them into the experience of the observ-er. Hence they play a part not unlike the long and var-ied vicarious experiences of Walt Whitman in *Song of Myself.* Such a method is not a very fruitful one for the novel, but for the epic it is reasonably workable. If we can consider the novel, at least in its "well-made" ex-amples, to be not unlike Aristotle's tragedy, we may use Aristotle to gain for the epic a liberty from these binding restrictions of plot, consistency, and causation to which the tragedy—and some forms of the novel—is subject. Indeed, although it is highly questionable that Wolfe ever sought or relied upon authority for his ar-tistic methods, Aristotle's discussion of the structure of the epic is almost a discussion of Wolfe's method in his "book." Aristotle says: "Epic poetry has, however, a great—a special—capacity for enlarging its dimen-sions." Distinguishing between a controlling action and episodes, he says: "Thus the story of the *Odyssey* can be stated briefly. A certain man is absent from home for many years; he is jealously watched by Poseidon and left desolate. Meanwhile his home is in a wretched plight—suitors are wasting his substance and plotting against his son. At length, tempest-tossed, he himself arrives; he makes certain persons acquainted with him; he attacks the suitors with his own hand and is himself preserved while he destroys them. This is the essence of the plot; the rest is episode." Indeed, Aristotle as-serts, "The epic imitation has less unity [than tragedy has] . . . the poem is composed out of several actions." Such a definition applied to Wolfe's "book" would find in its controlling action—that is, "the essence of its plot"—the experiences of Wolfe (under the guises of Eugene Gant and George Webber) as he moved from childhood and "the meadows of sensation" through adolescence to maturity in his search for identity as an American. The rest are "episodes," events which, how-ever real to those who participate in them, are signifi-cant in the making of this American primarily in what they teach him about the difficulty of being a demo-cratic man on this continent. The search aims at bring-ing him self-knowledge, but as he matures it aims in-creasingly at bringing him a definition of the represen-tative aspects of his national being. As his life was an outward movement, so are his books outward move-ments. From the absorption in the self, he moves to an absorption in society. The road from *Look Homeward, Angel* to *You Can't Go Home Again* is the trail of the epic impulse. From the baby's contemplation of its own toe, Wolfe moves to the serious portrayal of the social world, but always in terms of how that world registers on his own consciousness and becomes a part of his experience as a representative American.

Eugene Gant was a person of whom Wolfe could say that, as a boy, "He did not want to reform the world, or to make it a better place to live in." He came finally to see, even in those he loved "his vision of the grand America . . . the structure of that enchanted life of which every American has dreamed . . . a world distilled of our own blood and earth, and qualified by all our million lights and weathers, and we know that it will be noble, intolerably strange and lovely, when we find it." And before his career was to reach its untimely end, he was to be able to take his reader to the place "where the hackles of the Rocky Mountains blaze in the blank and naked radiance of the moon" and bid him "make your resting stool upon the highest peak." and from that vantage point survey the vast and lonely sweep of continent to east and west. And to find in a Negro boy in the Chicago slums, in a young baseball player in "the clay-baked outfields down in Georgia," and in an intense and studious Jewish boy in "the East-Side Ghetto of Manhattan" the essence of his native land and the symbols of its grand design and promise. Thus he can declare: "So, then, to every man his chance—to every man, regardless of his birth, his shining, golden opportunity—to every man the right to live, to work, to be himself, and to become whatever thing his manhood and his vision can combine to make him—this, seeker, is the promise of America."

However flawed as novels and imperfect as art his books may be, Thomas Wolfe's works constitute a major and remarkably successful effort to write his autobiography as that of a representative American and to embody in the record of his time and deeds on this earth a vision of the nature and the hope of his democratic land. (pp. 162-67)

C. Hugh Holman, "The Epic Impulse," in his *The Loneliness at the Core: Studies in Thomas Wolfe*, Louisiana State University Press, 1975, pp. 155-67.

JAMES BOYER

(essay date 1982)

[In the following excerpt from a 1982 lecture, Boyer surveys Wolfe's short stories, offering evidence that the later stories demonstrate a progressing artistic maturity.]

John Halberstadt's *Yale Review* article on Thomas Wolfe [Autumn, 1980] revived a criticism of Wolfe's work that has persisted ever since Bernard DeVoto wrote his scorching critical review of Wolfe's *Story of a Novel* in 1936. Not surprisingly, Halberstadt quotes a later DeVoto statement to establish a frame for his current argument: "You are manifestly and, if you will excuse me, absurdly wrong," DeVoto wrote to Struthers Bert in 1950, "when you say that I created 'the legend of the Wolfe who couldn't write without Papa Perkins.' It is no legend but a fact so widely established that I wonder you have missed it that at any rate he did not produce novels without Perkins' and later Ed Aswell's symbiotic editing." The gist of Halberstadt's charge in this recent article is that Aswell did indeed overedit the posthumous Wolfe novels, that in fact he went so far beyond the ordinary role of editor in order to create a structure in those books that while "the words . . . , most of them anyway—were written by Wolfe . . . , the books were made by Aswell. He was the dominant contributor to the books that bore Wolfe's name . . ."

It is not my purpose here to contend with Halberstadt; Richard Kennedy in *The Window of Memory* did a careful job of assessing what Aswell had done and why. Yet while Halberstadt's conclusions about Wolfe's work are overstated and extreme, it is true that those three posthumous novels contain an amalgam of Wolfe's early and late writing, making it difficult to assess his development as a writer through them. Thus even friendly critics tend to generalize about Wolfe and all of his work; Wolfe the eternal adolescent; Wolfe the giant of insatiable appetite; Wolfe the writer of formless autobiography.

It is possible to overcome some of this confusion on Wolfe's handling of formal matters, a confusion produced by the novels, if we turn to Wolfe's magazine stories, thirty-eight of which were published before his death in 1938. By examining this considerable body of work, we can see some important directions Wolfe's fiction was taking—specifically his increasing ability to control plot, character and conflict.

Objections, of course, can be raised here too. Elizabeth Nowell, Wolfe's agent for magazine publications, played a significant role in the production of Wolfe's short stories. . . . Nowell encouraged Wolfe's development in the form, but the significant changes in the products of the late period are clearly attributable to Wolfe himself.

One might also object, if we are making assertions about development, that while Wolfe revised stories before publication, he didn't write them in the order in which they were published. And this is true. But it is possible through information available in the Wisdom Collection at Harvard to date the writing of most stories, so that one can attribute particular characteristics in the writing to a particular time period in his career. It is these changing characteristics that I should like to consider in the following paper. What we shall find is that Wolfe was moving toward more conventional fiction, with plots more carefully organized, characters whose internal conflicts form the core of those plots, and imagery that supports and unifies.

In examining these magazine publications, it will be convenient to divide Wolfe's stories into three groups: those stories published between 1932-1934, most of them before Elizabeth Nowell became his agent; those published in 1935, many of which were republished with some alteration in *From Death to Morning;* and those published between 1936 and his death in 1938. Significant formal distinctions divide these three groups of stories.

One feature of the early stories, which begin to appear in *Scribner's Magazine* in 1932, is their length. Of the five published before 1934, only **"The Train and the City"** runs under 20,000 words. (It is about 10,000.) Wolfe had given up on writing drama in part because of the demands of that genre for concision; he was at this point unwilling to shorten works to make them more attractive to magazines. Indeed, after the middle period where many of the stories are quite short, he returns to fuller development in his best stories of the final period.

Some of the length of these early stories results from the use of long lyric passages elaborating major Wolfe themes—spring in the city, death as a brother, loneliness as a friend, America as a land of promise. While these passages contain some vivid images and personifications and employ a rhythmic, verse-like prose, they interrupt the narrative element of the story. Wolfe was reluctant to reduce them, since they were a distinctive feature of his style that brought praise from some critics. Only by the very end of 1934 does he begin to use such passages as separate magazine pieces or as carefully limited and balanced components, a practice he continues thereafter.

This early emphasis on theme and lyric refrain often results in a casual handling of the narrative element in the story. **"The Four Lost Men"** begins with a father, a son, and boarders on the porch of a boarding house in a small Southern town, discussing the beginning of World War I and earlier wars; but the setting and event are forgotten as the story moves to a lyrical vision of four lost Presidents and never returns to the porch and the people on it. In **"The Train and the City,"** the narrator's trip out from and back to the city, including the well-known passage where the two trains race, is overbalanced by paragraph after paragraph of lyric tribute to spring and to the American people. The only carefully controlled plots of the early period are found in **"The Sun and the Rain,"** where a simple chronology provides sufficient structure, and **"The Web of Earth,"** which is carefully wrought like the late stories but exceptional because of the controlling voice of the old woman who narrates.

Characters in these early stories tend to be static

rather than dynamic; often they represent something significant, but that something is a set idea little dependent on the action of the story. In the manner of Dickens, characters are identified by peculiar mannerisms rather than internal conflicts. What we remember about Bascom Hawke, in spite of a very long story that gives much of his life in summary, are his facial grimaces and "snuffling laugh"; his weakness and resignation, which in the end of the story are contrasted with the exuberance of the young narrator, come to the reader as a surprise. (pp. 31-4)

Short, then, on conventional plot structure and characters in conflict, many of these early stories are structured with simple contrast—hopeful youth and resigned age, or "wandering" and "earth again" or violent death and quiet death—rather than conflict. Elaboration in such stories is often accomplished through multiple illustration: all three of the 1933 stories (**"Death the Proud Brother," "The Train and the City,"** and **"No Door"**), as well as **"The Face of the War,"** written then but published later, are composed of a series of unrelated events, each illustrating the same themes.

Finally, many of these early stories have passages that mean little to the stories themselves but relate in some significant way to Wolfe's big books. Delia Hawke's interest in the burial of her husband's first wife is simply perplexing in **"Boomtown,"** as are the references to Esther Jack in **"Death the Proud Brother."** If one has read the novels, he recognizes the loss suffered when these episodes are removed from the larger context. By contrast the later stories often lose some of their meaning and effect when they are forced into the framework of the larger novel. Clearly, at this stage in his career, Wolfe had much to learn about story writing.

By the latter half of 1934, however, Wolfe was publishing stories very different from those described above, and the changes become more striking in 1935. Much of the change at this time results not from the writing process but from the selection process. Elizabeth Nowell, who had begun to work with Wolfe's fiction while part of Max Lieber's Agency in 1934, now opened her own agency, with Wolfe as her best-known client. During this period she played an increasingly important role in selecting suitable materials from the manuscripts and in suggesting ways to shorten them and strengthen them for use as stories. (pp. 34-5)

Even more consistently than in the earlier period, these 1935-36 stories are episodes cut from the larger work. Richard Kennedy calls them "captured fugitives," as indeed they are, many of them having come from the *Of Time and the River* manuscript. . . . Stories like **"Cottage by the Tracks"** or **"Bums at Sunset"** represent units complete in themselves which were to have functioned in the novel to illustrate various themes or facets of the national character. (pp. 35-6)

Of the twelve 1935 stories, most of which reappear in *From Death to Morning,* ten have fewer than 6,000 words. More than half of them present a single event. Emphasis consistently remains on the narrative element. This shift toward a simpler structure undoubtedly reflects Nowell's involvement in the selection. The result is this sequence of stories that make us aware of the diversity in Wolfe's work.

Contrasting with the prevailing serious, lyrical tone of the early stories, we find in these stories a great variety in tone. . . . Stories center on persons other than Eugene Gant—this is true, of course, of stories in the first period, too, but not so apparent in the novels. And we have some stories that demonstrate an increasing capacity in Wolfe, even when he is dealing with his Eugene-George protagonist, for getting outside himself. . . . (p. 36)

Along with varying tone, these stories present a great variety in dialogue. . . . Not only does he use these voices in dialogue; he uses them as narrators of episodes. (pp. 36-7)

Since the stories are short, character development is more limited than in the early period, but it is in some instances more interesting, too. . . . Some plots in these stories, too, show Wolfe's developing concern with structure. (p. 37)

But the finest examples of both plot and character development come a little later. (p. 38)

Wolfe had begun working on a new book, his *Vision of Spangler's Paul,* in March of 1936. . . . In a June 1936 letter to Heinz Ledig, his German editor, Wolfe explains his intentions: "The idea as I conceive it is the story of a good man abroad in the world—shall we say the naturally innocent man, the man who sets out in life with his own vision of what life is going to be like, what men and women are going to be like, what he is going to find, and then the story of what he really finds." Wolfe went on to cite *Don Quixote, Candide* and *Gulliver* as models for what he was attempting.

One notes, of course, that this frame is very flexible, allowing Wolfe to use any of his experiences, with the focus remaining on other people and events, the narrator serving simply as story teller and interpreter. Thus, though the 1937 stories are written as separate units and move in very different directions, Wolfe no doubt had a clear notion of how he would eventually incorporate all of them into the major work. Yet his impulse for writing them came from diverse sources rather than a single conception of the "big book," he spent considerable time with Elizabeth Nowell sharpening

and shortening them, and they are often more effective as separate units than as parts of the book. And a careful look at them reveals significant changes from the earlier stories in formal matters.

They are longer than the stories of the middle period; two of the best, **"I Have a Thing to Tell You"** and **"The Lost Boy,"** approach the length of **"Bascom Hawke."** But their content remains almost exclusively narrative. Gone are the long lyric passages of the earliest period and the visions of both earlier periods; gone are the expository passages on youth and exuberance.

Wolfe has become more careful, too, in use of images. Description effectively foreshadows and reinforces action or theme. The contrast of the dark forests of Germany, with "their legendary sense of magic and of time," and the shiny German tram, "perfect in its function," gives the first indication in **"I Have a Thing to Tell You"** of the two sides of the German character, its great heritage of art but its preoccupation with a dehumanizing scientific precision. . . . Not only descriptive detail but characters themselves are used to represent or reinforce theme. . . . It is not simply that Wolfe now sees persons, places or things as representational—he had always consciously done that—but he begins now to integrate them more carefully with action and theme to form a unified whole.

More important still, Wolfe is developing characters in conflict, characters who are trying to resolve something. All characters are functional, and the action of the stories brings both character and reader to a point of clarification. Prosser in **"Child by Tiger"** is a complex figure, his orderly exterior undercut by a smoldering anger over his blackness that erupts against everyone, black and white alike. . . . These characters, in their complexity and their reality, rank with the greatest of fictional creations.

The plots of these stories are generally simple, focusing on a few days in time, a crucial event, a single idea. **"I Have a Thing to Tell You"** takes place in one day, with only four important scenes, three of them on the train leaving Germany. (pp. 38-40)

Wolfe's reputation as a writer from whom a stream of undigested experience simply poured is undeserved. As the stories illustrate, his later writing shows genuine improvement in his craft—in dramatizing rather than telling, in careful plotting, in building characters with significant internal conflicts, and in using imagery to reinforce theme. (p. 41)

James Boyer, "The Development of Form in Thomas Wolfe's Short Fiction," in *Thomas Wolfe: A Harvard Perspective,* edited by Richard S. Kennedy, Croissant, 1983, pp. 31-42.

SOURCES FOR FURTHER STUDY

Field, Leslie, ed. *Thomas Wolfe: Three Decades of Criticism.* New York: New York University Press, 1968, 304 p.
> Collection of critical essays. Includes select bibliography of Wolfe criticism.

McElderry, B. R., Jr. *Thomas Wolfe.* New York: Twayne Publishers, 1964, 207 p.
> Biographical and critical appraisal of Wolfe's works with emphasis on his use of autobiographical material.

Phillipson, John S. *Thomas Wolfe: A Reference Guide.* Boston: G. K. Hall & Co., 1977, 218 p.
> Annotated bibliography of Wolfe criticism.

Rubin, Louis D., Jr., ed. *Thomas Wolfe: A Collection of Critical Essays.* Englewood Cliffs, N. J.: Prentice-Hall, 1973, 182 p.
> Examines the biographical, thematic, and stylistic elements of Wolfe's canon.

Turnbull, Andrew. *Thomas Wolfe.* New York: Charles Scribner's Sons, 1967, 374 p.
> Definitive biography.

Walser, Richard, ed. *The Enigma of Thomas Wolfe: Biographical and Critical Selections.* Cambridge: Harvard University Press, 1953, 313 p.
> Collection of essays on Wolfe's life and work, containing important commentary by his editors, Margaret Church, W. P. Albrecht, and others.

Virginia Woolf

1882-1941

(Born Adeline Virginia Stephen) English essayist, novelist, critic, short story writer, diarist, and biographer.

INTRODUCTION

Woolf is one of the most prominent literary figures of the twentieth century. Chiefly renowned as an innovative novelist, in particular for her contributions to the development of stream-of-consciousness narrative technique, she also wrote book reviews, biographical and autobiographical sketches, social and literary criticism, personal essays, and commemorative articles treating a wide range of topics. Concerned primarily with depicting the life of the mind, Woolf revolted against traditional narrative techniques and developed her own highly individualized style of novel-writing. Woolf's novels are noted for their subjective exploration of character and theme and their delicate poetic prose, while her essays are commended for their perceptive observations on nearly the entire range of English literature, as well as many social and political concerns of the early twentieth century.

Woolf was the daughter of the eminent literary critic and historian Sir Leslie Stephen and his second wife, Julia. While Woolf received no formal education, she was raised in a cultured and literary atmosphere, learning from her father's extensive library and from conversing with his friends, many of whom were prominent writers of the era. Her mother died in 1895, and, following the death of her father in 1904, Woolf settled in the Bloomsbury district of London with her sister, Vanessa, and her brothers Thoby and Adrian. Their house became a gathering-place where such friends as J. M. Keynes, Lytton Strachey, Roger Fry, and E. M. Forster congregated for lively discussions about philosophy, art, music, and literature. A complex network of friendships and love affairs developed, serving to increase the solidarity of what became known as the Bloomsbury Group. Here she met Leonard Woolf, the author, politician, and economist whom she married in 1912.

Woolf flourished in the unconventional atmosphere that she and her siblings had devised. The freedom afforded by the Bloomsbury milieu was conducive to her literary inclinations, and the need to earn money led her to begin submitting book reviews and essays to various publications. Her first published works—mainly literary reviews—began appearing anonymously in 1904 in the *Guardian,* a weekly newspaper for Anglo-Catholic clergy. Subsequently Woolf published reviews and essays in a number of other periodicals, including the *National Review, Cornhill,* and the *Times Literary Supplement.* Woolf 's letters and diaries reveal that her journalism occupied much of her time and thought between 1904 and 1909. By the latter year, however, she was becoming absorbed in work on her first novel, eventually published in 1915 as *The Voyage Out.* She attained great renown as a novelist and short story writer thereafter and continued to write and publish essays throughout her career.

Woolf 's fiction reveals an ongoing concern with subjective exploration of character and incident. Although *The Voyage Out* is rather conventional, its emphasis on character analysis rather than plot foreshadows Woolf 's later treatment of her characters' inner lives. In her third novel, *Jacob's Room* (1922), she attempted a wholly individual technique, minimizing external action and illuminating aspects of her characters' personalities through series of individual impressions revealed to the reader through interior monologue. *Mrs. Dalloway* (1925) represents Woolf 's first successful attempt to produce a novel in her own distinctive narrative style, rejecting the boundaries of traditional European narrative form, which she believed had become too artificial and restrictive for her increasingly poetic, impressionistic renderings of life. The novel marks the emergence of Woolf 's mature narrative voice, as well as the perfection of the experimental narrative technique employed tentatively in *Jacob's Room.* Encompassing one day in the life of an introspective, upper-class woman, *Mrs. Dalloway* is often discussed in terms of its affinities with James Joyce's similarly constructed *Ulysses* (1922). However, though both novels are written in stream-of-consciousness style, scholars stress that Woolf 's novel greatly differs from Joyce's not only in length, setting, and characterization, but, perhaps most importantly, in its development of Woolf 's lifelong aesthetic concern: the interrelationship of time, existence, and the human psyche. It is believed that by her treatment of these subjects in her strikingly individual prose style, Woolf composed one of the most subtly powerful and memorable English novels of the post-World War I era.

Regarded by many as Woolf 's finest achievement, her novel *To the Lighthouse* (1927) treats themes of marriage, time, and death. In a further development of her subjective mode, plot is completely abandoned, with unity and coherence provided instead by imagery, symbolism, and poetic elements. This technique reached its extreme in *The Waves* (1931). Here Woolf depicted the passage of time through the impressionistic interior monologues of six characters, and again attempted coherence through recurrent imagery and symbol. While critics praised the poetic prose of *The Waves,* many argued that Woolf 's method had become restrictive and artificial through a too-obvious imposition of pattern and significance upon her material. Woolf 's posthumously published novel *Between the Acts* (1941) combines prose, poetry, and dialogue, demonstrating Woolf 's continued desire to expand the scope of novel.

Woolf maintained that the purpose of writing an essay was to give pleasure to the reader, and she endeavored to do this with witty, supple prose, apt literary and cultural references, and a wide range of subjects. Aiming to identify closely with her audience, she adopted a persona she termed "the common reader": an intelligent, educated person with the will and inclination to be challenged by what he or she reads. While the majority of Woolf 's essays are devoted to literary matters, some of her most highly regarded nonfiction writings are topical and occasional essays treating such subjects as war and peace, feminism, life and death, sex and class issues, her own travels, and observations of the contemporary scene. She addressed social and feminist concerns in greatest depth in *A Room of One's Own* (1929) and *Three Guineas* (1938), discussing the cultural and economic pressures that hinder women's scholarly pursuits and exploring the underlying causes of war.

As a literary critic, Woolf undertook the appraisal of a wide range of authors. She reviewed and wrote extended critical commentary on her literary contemporaries, including Rupert Brooke, E. M. Forster, Henry James, Rudyard Kipling, and D. H. Lawrence; the great Victorian and Romantic poets and novelists; major figures of the eighteenth century and the Elizabethan age; and many lesser-known literary and historical personalities. Her literary criticism is largely appreciative and impressionistic, containing little that can be called objective or analytical. Woolf 's commentary on works by authors of the past usually includes a full consideration of the society in which the work originated, and critics have found these essays among her most effective. One of the best and most famous of her literary essays is *Mr. Bennett and Mrs. Brown* (1924), in which Modernist fiction—which Woolf 's own works exemplify—is contrasted with the Realist-Naturalist tradition represented by H. G. Wells, John Galsworthy, and Arnold Bennett. In addition to writing fiction and essays, Woolf was a prolific diarist and letter-writer. Because of her importance as an innovator in the modern novel form, and as a commentator on nearly the entire range of English literature and much European literature, Woolf's life and works have been the focus of extensive study.

(For further information about Woolf's life and works, see *Contemporary Authors*, Vols. 104, 130; *Dictionary of Literary Biography*, Vols. 36, 100; *Short Story Criticism*, Vol. 7; and *Twentieth-Century Literary Criticism*, Vols. 1, 5, 20, 43. For related criticism, see the entry on the Bloomsbury Group in *Twentieth Century Literary Criticism*, Vol. 34.)

CRITICAL COMMENTARY

E. M. FORSTER
(essay date 1915)

[Forster was a prominent English novelist, critic, and essayist whose works reflect his liberal humanism. In the following excerpt from an essay that first appeared in the *Daily News and Leader* in 1915, he favorably reviews *The Voyage Out*, noting that Woolf is deficient in character portrayal but excels in presenting action.]

[The] first comment to make on *The Voyage Out* is that it is absolutely unafraid, and that its courage springs, not from naiveté, but from education. . . . Here at last is a book which attains unity as surely as *Wuthering Heights,* though by a different path, a book which; while written by a woman and presumably from a woman's point of view, soars straight out of local questionings into the intellectual day. (pp. 52-3)

Mrs Woolf's success is more remarkable since there is one serious defect in her equipment; her chief characters are not vivid. There is nothing false in them, but when she ceases to touch them they cease, they do not stroll out of their sentences, and even develop a tendency to merge shadowlike. (p. 53)

[If] Mrs Woolf does not 'do' her four main characters very vividly, and is apt to let them all become clever together, and differ only by their opinions, then on what does her success depend? Some readers—those who demand the milk of human kindness, even in its tinned form—will say that she has not succeeded; but the bigness of her achievement should impress anyone weaned from baby food. She believes in adventure—here is the main point—believes in it passionately, and knows that it can only be undertaken alone. Human relations are no substitute for adventure, because when real they are uncomfortable, and when comfortable they must be unreal. It is for a voyage into solitude that man was created, and Rachel, Helen, Hewet, Hirst, all learn this lesson, which is exquisitely reinforced by the setting of tropical scenery—the soul, like the body, voyages at her own risk. . . . Mrs Woolf's vision may be inferior to Dostoieffsky's—but she sees as clearly as he where efficiency ends and creation begins, and even more clearly that our supreme choice lies not between body and soul, but between immobility and motion. In her pages, body v. soul—that dreary medieval tug-of-war—does not find any place. It is as if the rope has broken, leaving pagans sprawling on one side and clergymen on the other. . . . (pp. 53-4)

[A] word must be said about the comedy: the book is extremely amusing (p. 54)

The writer can sweep together masses of characters for our amusement, then sweep them away; her comedy does not counteract her tragedy and at the close enhances it, for we see that the Hotel and the Villa will soon be dancing and gossiping just as before, that existence will continue the same, exactly the same, for everyone, for everyone except the reader; he, more fortunate than the actors, is established in the possession of beauty. (p. 55)

E. M. Forster, in an excerpt in *Virginia Woolf: The Critical Heritage,* edited by Robin Majumdar and Allen McLaurin, Routledge & Kegan Paul, 1975, pp. 52-5.

CONRAD AIKEN
(essay date 1927-29)

[An American man of letters best known for his poetry, Aiken was deeply influenced by the psychological and literary theories of Sigmund Freud, Havelock Ellis, Edgar Allan Poe, and Henri Bergson. In reviews noted for their perceptiveness and barbed wit, he exercised his theory that "criticism is really a branch of psychology." In the following excerpt from an essay series that appeared in the *Dial* in 1927 and 1929, he assesses both traditional and innovative aspects of Woolf's fiction.]

Among contemporary writers of fiction, Mrs. Woolf is

Principal Works

The Voyage Out (novel) 1915

Kew Gardens (short stories) 1919

The Mark on the Wall (short stories) 1919

Night and Day (novel) 1919

Monday or Tuesday (short stories) 1921

Jacob's Room (novel) 1922

Mr. Bennett and Mrs. Brown (essay) 1924

The Common Reader (essays and criticism) 1925

Mrs. Dalloway (novel) 1925

To the Lighthouse (novel) 1927

Orlando (novel) 1928

A Room of One's Own (essay) 1929

The Waves (novel) 1931

The Common Reader: Second Series (essays and criticism) 1932; also published as The Second Common Reader, 1932

A Letter to a Young Poet (essay) 1932

Flush (biography) 1933

The Years (novel) 1937

Three Guineas (essay) 1938

Roger Fry: A Biography (biography) 1940

Between the Acts (novel) 1941

The Death of the Moth, and Other Essays (essays) 1942

The Haunted House, and Other Short Stories (short stories) 1943

The Moment, and Other Essays (essays) 1947

The Captain's Death Bed, and Other Essays (essays) 1950

A Writer's Diary: Being Extracts from the Diary of Virginia Woolf (diary) 1953

Hours in a Library (essays) 1957

Granite and Rainbow (essays) 1958

Contemporary Writers (criticism) 1965

Collected Essays. 4 vols. (essays, criticism, and journalism) 1966-67

The London Scene: Five Essays (essays) 1975

The Letters of Virginia Woolf. 6 vols. (letters) 1975-80

Moments of Being: Unpublished Autobiographical Writings (autobiographical essays) 1976; also published as Moments of Being, rev. ed., 1985

Books and Portraits (essays and criticism) 1977

The Diary of Virginia Woolf. 5 vols. (diaries) 1977-84

Virginia Woolf 's Reading Notebooks (notebooks) 1983

The Essays of Virginia Woolf. 3 vols. (essays) 1986-88

A Passionate Apprentice (journals) 1990

---

a curious and anomalous figure. In some respects, she is as "modern," as radical, as Mr. Joyce or Miss Richardson or M. Jules Romains; she is a highly self-conscious examiner of consciousness, a bold and original experimenter with the technique of novel-writing; but she is also, and just as strikingly, in other respects "old-fashioned." This anomaly does not defy analysis. The aroma of "old-fashionedness" that rises from these highly original and modern novels—from the pages of *Jacob's Room, Mrs. Dalloway,* and . . . from those of *To the Lighthouse*—is a quality of attitude; a quality, to use a word which is itself nowadays old-fashioned, but none the less fragrant, of spirit. For in this regard, Mrs. Woolf is no more modern than Jane Austen: she breathes the same air of gentility, of sequestration, of tradition; of life and people and things all brought, by the slow polish of centuries of tradition and use, to a pervasive refinement in which discrimination, on every conceivable plane, has become as instinctive and easy as the beat of a wing. Her people are "gentle" people; her houses are the houses of gentlefolk; and the consciousness that informs both is a consciousness of well-being and culture, of the richness and luster and dignity of tradition. . . . (p. 389)

But if, choosing such people and such a *mise en scène* for her material, Mrs. Woolf inevitably makes her

readers think of *Pride and Prejudice* and *Mansfield Park,* she compels us just as sharply, by her method of evoking them, to think of *Pilgrimage* and *Ulysses* and *The Death of a Nobody.* Mrs. Woolf is an excellent critic, an extremely conscious and brilliant craftsman in prose; she is intensely interested in the technique of fiction; and one has at times wondered, so vividly from her prose has arisen a kind of *self-consciousness* of adroitness, whether she might not lose her way and give us a mere series of virtuosities or *tours de force.* (p. 390)

[In *To the Lighthouse*] one's irritation is soon lost in the growing sense that Mrs. Woolf has at last found a complexity and force of theme which is commensurate with the elaborateness and self-consciousness of her technical "pattern." By degrees, one forgets the manner in the matter. One resists the manner, petulantly objects to it, in vain: the moment comes when at last one ceases to be aware of something persistently artificial in this highly feminine style, and finds oneself simply immersed in the vividness and actuality of this world of Mrs. Woolf 's—believing in it, in fact, with the utmost intensity, and feeling it with that completeness of surrender with which one feels the most moving of poetry. It is not easy to say whether this abdication of "distance" on the reader's part indicates that Mrs. Woolf has now achieved a depth of poetic understanding, a vitality, which was somehow just lacking in the earlier novels, or whether it merely indicates a final triumph of technique. . . . Certainly one feels everywhere in Mrs. Woolf's work this will to imagine, this canvassing of possibilities by a restless and searching and brilliant mind: one feels this mind at work, matching and selecting, rejecting this color and accepting that, saying, "It is this that the heroine would say, it is this that she would think"; and nevertheless Mrs. Woolf's step is so sure, her choice is so nearly invariably right, and her imagination, even if deliberately willed, is so imaginative, that in the end she makes a beautiful success of it. She makes her Mrs. Ramsay—by giving us her stream of consciousness—amazingly alive; and she supplements this just sufficiently, from *outside*, as it were, by giving us also, intermittently, the streams of consciousness of her husband, of her friend Lily Briscoe, of her children: so that we are documented, as to Mrs. Ramsey, from every quarter and arrive at a solid vision of her by a process of triangulation. The richness and copiousness and ease, with which this is done, are a delight. These people are astoundingly real: they belong to a special "class," as Mrs. Woolf's characters nearly always do, and exhale a Jane-Austenish aroma of smallness and lostness and incompleteness: but they are magnificently real. We live in that delicious house with them—we feel the minute textures of their lives with their own vivid senses—we imagine with their extraordinary imaginations, are self-conscious with their self-consciousness—and ultimately we know them as well, as terribly, as we know ourselves. (pp. 391-92)

The technical brilliance glows, melts, falls away; and there remains a poetic apprehension of life of extraordinary loveliness. Nothing happens, in this houseful of odd nice people, and yet all of life happens. The tragic futility, the absurdity, the pathetic beauty, of life—we experience all of this in our sharing of seven hours of Mrs. Ramsay's wasted or not wasted existence. We have seen, through her, the world. (p. 392)

● ● ● ● ●

That Mrs. Woolf is a highly ingenious writer has been made glitteringly obvious for us in *Mrs. Dalloway* and *To the Lighthouse:* which is not in the least to minimize the fact that those two novels also contained a great deal of beauty. That she is, and has perhaps always been, in danger of carrying ingenuity too far, is suggested, among other things, by her new novel, or "biography," *Orlando.* Whatever else one thinks about this book, one is bound to admit that it is exceedingly, not to say disconcertingly, clever. In England as well as in America it has set the critics by the ears. They have not known quite how to take it—whether to regard it as a biography, or a satire on biography; as a history, or as a satire on history; as a novel, or as an allegory. And it is at once clear, when one reads *Orlando,*

why this confusion should have arisen; for the tone of the book, from the very first pages, is a tone of mockery. (p. 392)

Mrs. Woolf apparently wants us to know that she does not herself take the thing with the least seriousness—that she is pulling legs, keeping her tongue in her cheek, and winking, now and then, a quite shameless and enormous wink. With all this, which she accomplishes with a skill positively equestrian, she is obliged, perforce, to fall into a style which one cannot help feeling is a little unfortunate. It is a style which makes fun of style: it is glibly rhetorical, glibly sententious, glibly poetic, glibly analytical, glibly austere, by turns—deliberately so; and, while this might be, and is, extraordinarily diverting for a chapter or two, or for something like the length of a short story, one finds it a little fatiguing in a full-length book. Of course, Mrs. Woolf's theme, with its smug annihilation of time, may be said to have demanded, if the whole question of credibility was to be begged, a tone quite frankly and elaborately artificial. Just the same, it is perhaps questionable whether she has not been *too* icily and wreathedly elaborate in this, and taken her *Orlando* in consequence a shade too far toward an arid and ingenuous convention. Granted that what she wanted to tell us was a fable, or allegory: that she wanted to trace the aesthetic evolution of a family (and by implication that of a country) over a period of three hundred years: and that she had hit upon the really first-rate idea of embodying this racial evolution in one undying person: need she quite so much have presumed on our incredulity? One suspects that in such a situation an ounce of ingenuousness might be worth ten times its weight in ingenuity; and that a little more of the direct and deep sincerity of the last few pages, which are really beautiful and really moving, might have made *Orlando* a minor masterpiece. (p. 393)

Conrad Aiken, "Virginia Woolf," in his *Collected Criticism,* Oxford University Press, Inc., 1968, pp. 389-94.

LOUIS KRONENBERGER
(essay date 1942)

[A drama critic for *Time* from 1938 to 1961, Kronenberger was a distinguished historian and literary critic. In the following essay, he discusses Woolf's literary criticism. This essay first appeared in the *Nation* in 1942.]

At the same moment we are given a posthumous book by Virginia Woolf [*The Death of the Moth, and Other Essays*] and two books about her. Of the two, [E. M.

Forster's *Virginia Woolf*], originally a Cambridge lecture, is the brief memoir of a friend, charming yet candid, full of sharp comments and animating touches, but too short to say all it might; [David Daiches's *Virginia Woolf*] is the interpretation of a critic, painstaking, sometimes penetrating, and too long for what there is to say. Virginia Woolf 's own book, like the two *Common Readers*, is made up mainly of critical essays, and coming when it does, perhaps serves to emphasize what Mr. Forster and Mr. Daiches tend to slight—the importance of Virginia Woolf 's criticism in the general body of her work. Mr. Forster gives but two or three sentences to her criticism, and Mr. Daiches a dozen of his 157 pages. The fact is easily explained: Virginia Woolf nowhere altered the face of criticism as she did the face of the novel, she extended no critical frontiers, she attracted no critical disciples. All the same, Mr. Forster's and Mr. Daiches's relative allotment of space may not be posterity's, for Mrs. Woolf forged her criticism into something quite as distinctive as her novels, and the best of it may well survive everything else she wrote except *To the Lighthouse* and *Mrs. Dalloway,* and may conceivably survive them.

Which is all the more interesting, seeing that, in addition to being no critical innovator, Virginia Woolf was in one sense really no critic. At least her real strength did not lie in any remarkable powers of mind, any systematic principles of criticism. In fifty pages of any first-rank critic we shall find more inseminating ideas than in all three volumes of Mrs. Woolf. Where we do find a purely critical perception, it is likely to seem neither new nor old, and we are likely to value it for its pertinence rather than its originality, or for the light it throws on Virginia Woolf. Thus she says of Euripides: "To understand him it is not so necessary to understand Greek as to understand poetry"; or of the Elizabethans: "The Elizabethans bore us because they suffocate our imaginations rather than set them to work"; or of Sterne: "Sterne, from fear of coarseness, is forced into indecency." These are things, we feel, that beyond any question Virginia Woolf discovered for herself, but we feel too that they say more succinctly what someone else has said first.

With rare exceptions ("**Modern Fiction,**" "**How It Strikes a Contemporary,**" *Mr. Bennett and Mrs. Brown*—all of them more or less critical defenses of her creative methods), Mrs. Woolf is hardly more a suggestive critic than she is a systematic one. She seldom reacts to literature in a purely critical way: to the writing of her own time she reacted as a writer; to the literature of the past she responded, for the most part, as a reader. She was in the one case more combative than critical, and in the other more appreciative. What seems best in her approach to the classics is a superb responsiveness: she had fine imagination and extraordinary sensibility; she was a born reader and could assimilate effortlessly, but she was also a very cultivated reader, and could correlate and compare.

Having both an esthetic and a historical sense, she was capable of really informed appreciation; but having an artistic gift also, she chose not merely to record an author's quality but to reproduce it in a form, a framework, of her own. What she distills is much less the meaning of a writer or a period than the temperament, the savor, the personality: she is a kind of highly skillful portrait-painter who catches the style of her model while imposing a style of her own. We shall not learn from her just what the Greeks or the Elizabethans, Montaigne or Chaucer, signify, but we do know how they look. She reveals them, with beautiful clarity, in a mirror: it is for others to peer down at them through a miscroscope. Accordingly her best work, most of which will be found in the first *Common Reader,* has about it a real charm of artistry. One reads it a little less for profit than for pleasure, for its freshness, its shapeliness, its sensitiveness, for its language, its wit, its sense of poetry. The poet in Virginia Woolf constantly pleads for a hearing in these essays, as in her novels it ultimately insists on being heard.

After the first *Common Reader* the language becomes a little too fine; the style, at moments, tends to inflate the contents. For, like too many other writers, Virginia Woolf began to evolve something approaching a formula; she lost the secret of her earlier distinction as soon as she discovered in what it lay. What had once been highly individual begins to seem, in *The Second Common Reader,* merely professional. There is less submerged poetry and more protruding rhetoric. The particular insights become fewer, the generalizations and analogies more frequent. Virginia Woolf is not so much writing about what she has read as reading something in order to write about it. A note even of cleverness has crept into it. On one page of an essay on Hazlitt a painfully smart sentence crops up, and on the next page a curiously flat one. There is something overwritten about the essay on Hardy. Mrs. Woolf still writes extremely well, but one feels that she has no desire to write differently. There is no sense here of trying to break the mold, to alter the pattern, as there always was in her fiction.

The Death of the Moth reveals a further decline, though some of it must be judged as early work and some as in not quite final form. But additional polish would hardly have given additional weight. Here, to be sure, are many things that give pleasure. Here is urbane and witty writing on urbane and witty writers— Gibbon, Walpole, Mme de Sévigné. Here are quick flashes of insight: Strachey, says Mrs. Woolf, succeeded with *Queen Victoria* because he respected biography as a craft, and failed at *Elizabeth and Essex* because he tried to make it into an art. "The phrase," she says of George Moore, "came before the emotion." Here are pointed, though sometimes rather shallow and even querulous, comments, as this one concerning modern poetry: "The poet is much less interested in what we have in common than in what he has apart." Here, indeed, is a good deal of the old skill. And yet there is far too much emptiness and inadequacy—nothing, for example, could be more disappointing than the essays on Henry James. Too many of these pieces are book reviews, lectures, *jeux d'esprit,* made-to-order things that disappoint even as they divert us. The style, moreover, is full of horrible Stracheyan flourishes.

> And then we turn to the book again, and to our amazement we find that the rocking-horse has left the ground; we are mounted on a winged steed; we are sweeping in wide circles through the air and below us Europe unfolds; the ages change and pass, a miracle has taken place.

Tradition, which hampered Virginia Woolf in fiction, greatly helped her in criticism, but only up to a certain point. She was at home in the past, and happy there; she accepted what the classics had to give without quarrel, sometimes without challenge; feasted off them, time and again envied the terms on which the old writers could write—with a sense of their age and their audience behind them. Aware—heavily aware, as a novelist—that all this had broken down in her own age of flux, she was possibly a little undiscerning and literary about the past, a little too fascinated with its décor and not quite enough concerned with its large outlines. For acute as her historical sense clearly was, it preeminently reflected the student of manners; she was most at home, after all, in the eighteenth century. What almost equally drew her to the past, however, were its echoing corridors, its grace of distance, its poetry. Both these interests reveal that intense literary feeling which was so distinctive and valuable a part of Virginia Woolf, and which she could embody in entirely consonant prose. This is what she could do best, and what she could do better than anyone else of her time. She will survive, not as a critic, but as a literary essayist recording the adventures of a soul among congenial masterpieces. For on the whole she did not approach—modern authors excepted—what she could not in some real sense enjoy. Her taste in the classics were surprisingly catholic, and her range, at first glance, seems amazingly broad. Yet the writers who are most downright, and masculine, and central in their approach to life—a Fielding or a Balzac—she for the most part left untouched. (They fathered, of course, the contemporary fiction that she most disliked.) Her own approach was at once more subterranean and aerial, and invincibly, almost defiantly, feminine. (pp. 244-49)

Louis Kronenberger, "Virginia Woolf as Critic," in his *The Republic of Letters: Essays on Various Writers,* Alfred A. Knopf, 1955, pp. 244-49.

MARK SCHORER
(essay date 1943)

[Schorer was an American critic and biographer who, in his essay "Technique as Discovery" (1948), argued that fiction deserves the same close attention to diction and metaphor that the New Critics had been applying to poetry. For Schorer, criticism must examine "achieved content," or form, as well as content. In the following review of *The Death of the Moth, and Other Essays,* he discusses the value of Woolf's criticism in providing insight into her fiction writing.]

Since Virginia Woolf's unhappy death—that great crime of our world, murderous in so many ways which still elude tribunal—a curious tendency to invert the relationship between her fiction and her literary criticism has asserted itself. Mr. David Daiches's handbook on the subject discussed her criticism with wholly disproportionate length and solemnity; Mr. William Plomer has said that she is more of a novelist in her criticism than in her novels, which, if it does not overestimate the criticism, at least denigrates the novels; still others have made the extreme judgment that she was first of all a critic, and then a critic writing fiction. [*The Death of the Moth, and Other Essays,* a] collection of short pieces posthumously prepared by her husband, substantiates, both in its examples and in its precepts, the older view, which is also the view of Mr. E. M. Forster's attractive essay: "It is as a novelist that she will be judged." What one means to say is only that her general essays, like her criticism, are finger exercises, drills—even when full-dress—for the novelist's sensibility, preliminary and exploratory essays wholly subordinate to the novels, and as such by her regarded.

The general essays—the first seven pieces in the book—are forms of reverie of the sort with which her novels abound; here she utilized the convenient amorphousness of the nineteenth-century familiar essay (even then an anomaly, now an anachronism) in order to manipulate images and other impressions which, when ordered within the frame of fiction, gave the old, outworn type a useful, original function. The essays on general literary subjects, like the famous *Mr. Bennett and Mrs. Brown,* are no less clearly related to the novels. The last seven selections in this book are of that order; and all are the means either of clarifying the novelist's own problems, intellectual and technical, or of justifying her conception of the function of the novelist, most particularly, of the woman novelist in an incompletely liberalized society, Virginia Woolf herself.

Her literary criticism—the twelve central selections—gives the argument its main support. "Say nothing about the learning and the industry, the devotion and the skill which have created these two huge volumes, and . . . record merely such fleeting thoughts as have formed in the mind," she writes of the Yale Edition of the Walpole-Cole correspondence; of Sara Coleridge's autobiography—"She said many things in those twenty-six pages, and Mr. Griggs has added others that tempt us to fill in the dots"; an imaginary letter to the antiquary, William Cole, opens imperiously: "In my opinion you are keeping something back"; and of the life of Gibbon she says, "But as we run over the familiar picture there is something that eludes us." These remarks reveal the active and aggressive temperament of the novelist, nothing of the critic. For the desire to comprehend experience directly (whether Walpole's or one's own) without intermediaries between the object and the sensibility; the desire to complete experience by giving it form, that is, to fill the dots of life, which is no less fragmentary than Sara Coleridge's slice of it; and finally, the desire to find a clue which will make experience cohere, to wring from life that "something" which it eternally keeps back, to seize at last upon that "something that eludes us"—all these are the motive of the novelist. And they have nothing to do with the critic, who is learned, who is concerned with the hard facts of literary discipline and technique rather than with the mysteries of experience, and who comes to literature with objective standards, not to life with a question.

Her literary criticism is subordinate to Mrs. Woolf 's fiction in still another way; illuminatingly, she writes: "For we are incapable of living wholly in the intense world of the imagination. The imagination is a faculty that soon tires and needs rest and refreshment. But for a tired imagination the proper food is not inferior poetry or minor fiction . . . but sober fact, that 'authentic information' from which . . . good biography is made." Hence her passion not only for biography but for history as well; her interest in correspondence, "the humane art"; the irrepressible impulse of her criticism to move from a text to the manners of the age which produced it, as from an author's work to his life. All this was the nourishment of her fiction, and the result provides an interesting paradox. For while Virginia Woolf, perhaps more than any writer of stature in the present century, insisted—and with her wonderful sensitivity, should have—upon seizing on life directly, and actually, in doing so, gave sensuosity a value which it had never had before in the English novel—in spite of all this, half the time she approached her material through literature, and in at least three ways. Her novels are crowded with literary echoes—that is to say, with borrowed modes of feeling—echoes which exasperated and finally alienated many readers. Most of her characters seem to be literary people, who approach

their experience with the benefit of Mrs. Woolf 's own exquisite sensibility and with the more dubious benefit of the artist's preconceptions and preoccupations generally. Finally, at least two of her books, *Orlando* and *Between the Acts,* derive their very structure from the history of English literature. What one reads is no less a portion of one's experience than any other activity; of present point is the fact that Virginia Woolf approached her reading, in her criticism, as she approached the whole of experience in her novels: with aggressive curiosity, a refined sensibility, but an exaggerated sense of the relevance of impression (which last Mr. Forster seems to regard as a property "essentially poetic," a gross error). What is lacking, finally, is the sense of value.

For what is that "something" which old William Cole held back? He may have been in love with a Miss Chester. And what is the "something that eludes us" in the life of Gibbon? Under the austerity and the learning, he was really—yes—lonely. Are these points worth making? All of us, in our time, have been in love with a Miss Chester and have lost her, and loneliness is the universal condition. This is a kind of sentimentality which overtakes even the most exquisite mind if it prefers to operate without objective values; and it was so that Virginia Woolf habitually wrote her criticism. The result is that it always tells us more about Virginia Woolf than about the text or the man in question; and it tells us important things about Virginia Woolf, the novelist.

In her novels as in her criticism she confused "value" with "theory," and that is a grave mistake. She finds the intellectual overtones in the novels of E. M. Forster a deficiency: "Exerting ourselves to find out the meaning, we step from the enchanted world of imagination, where our faculties work freely, to the twilight world of theory, where only our intellect functions dutifully." The artist must not "make his theories fit too tight to accommodate the formlessness of life," she wrote in *The Second Common Reader.* This is perfectly obvious, if they *are* theories; how but by values, however, can we "accommodate the formlessness of life" at all, how, that is, make the fragments of a world which our impressions give us cohere, how, indeed, come by that famous "something"? Mr. Forster makes a distinction in his little book which is interesting, if superficial: "There seem to be two sorts of life in fiction, life on the page and life eternal." The first, he says, Virginia Woolf had—her characters never seem unreal; the second she did not have—one does not remember them. Many people will not accept this judgment; and the critic cannot accept the distinction as final. It is again the question of the writer with objective values and the writer who declines them; and thus a novelist of relatively inferior equipment and trashy tastes, like Dickens, may succeed at precisely the point where Mrs. Woolf, with her remarkable equipment and impeccable tastes, fails. Another problem is involved. It was the great achievement of Proust and of James, for example, to derive philosophical weight from their impressions, and to give back to us whole and ordered worlds; it was the great achievement of Virginia Woolf, whose impressions did not transcend the value of psychology, to give back to us whole and ordered, if infinitely fragile worlds in at least three novels, including her last, *Between the Acts*. "The illusion is upon me," says Bernard at the end of *The Waves*, "that something adheres for a moment, has roundness, weight, depth, is completed." It is nothing short of extraordinary that, armed only with her sensibility and a zealous devotion to writing for the sake of writing (which Mr. Forster properly emphasizes), Virginia Woolf managed in at least three of her ten novels to put the illusion of completeness upon us. To observe that sensibility preening its feathers, as it were, has always been an excitement, in the present as in earlier volumes of non-fiction. And this book, as a matter of fact, would be invaluable to Mrs. Woolf 's admirers if only for one passage, an estimate of George Moore, which follows:

Not one of his novels is a masterpiece; they are silken tents which have no poles; but he has brought a new mind into the world; he has given us a new way of feeling and seeing; he has devised—very painfully, for he is above all things painstaking, eking out a delicate gift laboriously—a means of liquidating the capricious and volatile essence of himself . . . and that, whatever the degree, is triumph, achievement, immortality. If, further, we try to establish the degree we shall go on to say that no one so inveterately literary is among the great writers; literature has wound itself about him like a veil, forbidding him the free use of his limbs; the phrase comes to him before the emotion; but we must add that he is nevertheless a born writer, a man who detests meals, servants, ease, respectability or anything that gets between him and his art; who has kept his freedom when most of his contemporaries have long ago lost theirs; who is ashamed of nothing but of being ashamed; who says whatever he has it in his mind to say, and has taught himself an accent, a cadence, indeed a language, for saying it in which . . . will give him his place among the lesser immortals of our tongue.

A perhaps too reverent account of Moore; but was she, by that time, really thinking of Moore at all? One may say of Virginia Woolf, who was wonderful in more ways than she was vulnerable, that she had the power, and the poise, to compose so perfect an estimate of herself. Can one think of another who could, today? (pp. 377-81)

Mark Schorer, "Virginia Woolf," in *The Yale Review*, Vol. XXXII, No. 2, Winter, 1943, pp. 377-81.

DAVID CECIL
(essay date 1949)

[Cecil was an English educator, critic, and biographer. In the following excerpt, he discusses Woolf 's aestheticism as a salient characteristic of her writing.]

Through the eyes of one or more of her characters [Virginia Woolf] strove simply to record the actual process of living, to trace the confused succession of impression and thought and mood, as it drifted cloud-like across the clear mirror of consciousness. . . .

Instinctively she picks out for emphasis only those features of her subject which strike her as peculiarly significant. So that all the disordered matter of experience falls into a pattern imposed by the predominant motive force in her own inner life. This was her sensibility to the beautiful. Virginia Woolf was in the fullest, highest, extremest sense of the word, an aesthete. (p. 161)

The ugly and aesthetically insignificant she passes by; or admits only as they may serve as foil to the beauty that precedes and follows them. Thus she creates her perspective: thus she designs her pattern. (p. 162)

Aesthetic experiences are contemplative affairs. So also are the big moments in Virginia Woolf 's books. Action, event, play hardly any part in them at all. . . . She will take a chapter to describe a casual stroll in which a woman feels quickened to a deeper apprehension of experience: her death or marriage Virginia Woolf may pass over in a parenthesis. Indeed the title of her last book, *Between the Acts,* indicates her feeling that active drama supplies only a superficial view of life. The things that really matter happen "between the acts". (pp. 162-63)

Virginia Woolf 's characters are presented to us essentially as solitaries. Their inner life is what really matters about them. Even in company, they seem to be alone, absorbed in private unspoken trains of thought. Their relations to others are only valuable to them in so far as they feed and enrich their solitary experience, as they contribute to their moments of inner illumination and ecstasy. Not that their creator is only concerned to record moments of ecstasy. . . . When aesthetic receptiveness flags, when the imagination ceases to respond to the spectacle of the world, a terrifying sense of universal emptiness, a chill, as of spiritual death, assaults the spirit. Some of Virginia Woolf 's most memorable passages are concerned with describing this phenomenon. (p. 163)

Virginia Woolf's delight in beauty brings a correspondingly acute awareness of its frailty. Indeed, if her first impulse is to express life's loveliness, her second is to express its transience. . . . The fact of its fleetingness creates a sadness and bewilderment, a sense of unresolved discord at the very heart of her vision of experience. What is one to make of an existence in which what appears supremely significant and valuable is at the same time so ephemeral? (pp. 164-65)

Life, as shown in *Jacob's Room* and *Mrs. Dalloway,* is an insoluble mystery. But Virginia Woolf was too searching and too profound a spirit not to try and pierce deeper; and in her later works she seems to be feeling after some explanation for the enigma. There are hints that at moments she has attained to a vision of some ultimate principle of beauty, outside the flux of mortal things. (p. 165)

[At the end of *The Years*] in veiled, tentative fashion she suggests that there is a strain in the human spirit which is part of eternal reality, and which is inevitably unsatisfied as long as it is imprisoned in the wearisome condition of mortality: but which may, after it is freed from it, at last find fulfilment. (p. 166)

The end of life, so Virginia Woolf ponders, may be no blank, dark wall, but rather an opening into a region of light, where all is at last made clear. In *Between the Acts* she seems to be yet another step ahead nearer penetrating the mystery. (p. 167)

It is very unlike the vision presented by other novelists; and excludes some of the chief sources of their effects. There is no room for drama in it. Drama depends on the clash of character. . . . Imprisoned as they are, each in the solitary confinement of his own consciousness, the characters in Virginia Woolf's books never come into direct contact. Indeed, character, in the objective sense, hardly exists for her. Seen through the shifting haze of the observer's mood other people's individualities lose their clear-cut outline; while the observer's own self is dissolved into a succession of impressions.

Virginia Woolf's exclusive concentration on the aesthetic aspects of experience also prevents her from envisaging its moral aspects. People in her books are shown as happy and sad, beautiful and ugly but seldom as bad and good. Nor, in any consistent way, as loving or hating; the climate in which they live is cold and ethereal, the heart does not grow warm there for love or hate. . . . Even when Virginia Woolf describes a happy marriage like that of Mr. and Mrs. Ramsay in *To the Lighthouse,* she gets no further than indicating that at brief moments they felt an unusual harmony of soul one with the other. "We perish each alone," murmurs Mr. Ramsay to himself as he paces the beach. All Virginia Woolf's characters might have said the same thing. Not that she seems to regret it. On the

contrary . . . , solitude is for her the condition of the richest experience of which the human spirit is capable. (pp. 168-69)

A novel without drama, without moral values, and without character or strong personal emotion—it is a hard thing to write: and it cannot be said that Virginia Woolf is always successful. Sometimes she fails because she goes outside our own self-appointed limitations, because her plot entails her presenting aspects of life which her vision inevitably excludes. . . . [At] times she attempts, unsuccessfully, to draw characters in the objective external convention of the traditional novel. Hugh Whitbread and Sir William Bradshaw [of *Mrs. Dalloway*] are carefully observed portraits; but because their creator does not draw them from the inside they never come to life. They are meticulously dressed dummies, mere conventional types of snobbish worldling and hard, power-loving careerist. Moreover they are drawn in a spirit of moral indignation. This puts them out of focus with the rest of Virginia Woolf's picture. What basis is there for moral indignation in a world not concerned with moral values? (pp. 170-71)

Elsewhere she errs in the other direction. Her picture is so concerned with the inner life as to destroy our sense of the reality of the outer. This surely stops her most ambitious venture, *The Waves,* from making the impression at which it aims. . . . Indeed the balance between the internal world, which is her subject, and the external, to which she must convince us that it is in fact related, is extremely delicate. Only in *To the Lighthouse* does she succeed in preserving it throughout a whole book. Elsewhere, like so many English novelists, Virginia Woolf impresses by the heights to which she rises, rather than by the level of perfection she maintains.

But what heights they are! As might be expected, they are heights of beauty, they reveal her aesthetic sensibility. (p. 171)

But Virginia Woolfs aesthetic response is not confined to the accepted, recognised and official objects of beauty. Not only does she illuminate our appreciation of what we already think beautiful, she opens our eyes to new sources of delight. Far more successfully than any contemporary poet has she disengaged the aesthetic quality in the modern scene. In the first chapter of *Mrs. Dalloway* a summer morning in Bond Street, all buses and policemen and clamouring shoppers, is made to glow with the splendour of a picture by Vermeer. (p. 173)

These pictures are so fully visualised as to seem the work of a painter rather than a writer. A realistic painter too; here we come to the second outstanding quality in her sensibility. . . . [Always] she combines beauty with accuracy, and gets her effect, not by idealising and decorating it, but simply by isolating and indicating those aspects of her subject that appeal to the aesthetic sense. (pp. 173-74)

She is by far the most satisfying of aesthetes. . . . There is nothing languid or academic about her aestheticism. Casual and zestful, it is the expression of an intense vitality, at home in the bustle and clamour of the modern age. . . . As presented by her, the aesthetic life is as vigorous and satisfying as any other kind of life. And for us too, while we are reading her books: as long as their spell is on use we do not bother about the limitations of her vision. Indeed these limitations are seen to be a necessary condition of her success. In order to concentrate our eyes on the aesthetic aspects of experience, she has to exclude its other aspects. And they seem more beautiful for being thus isolated. Her coldness, her detachment from the hot earth, add to her vision a sea-fresh purity, a pearly gleam which set the spirit astir with a sort of delicate exhilaration. . . . How cleansing to be transported, if only for an hour, to a region where it is more important to be clever than to be good, and more important to be beautiful than to be either! (pp. 179-80)

David Cecil, "Virginia Woolf," in his *Poets and Story-Tellers: A Book of Critical Essays,* Constable & Company Ltd., 1949, pp. 160-80.

D. S. SAVAGE

(essay date 1950)

[Savage is an English poet, literary scholar, and social reformer. In the following excerpt, he charges that Woolf's works are ultimately unsatisfying because they depict a world in which disparate events are given no real differentiation and human life is accorded no special value.]

Among the women writers of our time there is none whose *prestige* stands higher than that of Virginia Woolf. It is because I believe this prestige to be unfounded that I am here proposing a drastic revaluation of her work.

The legend of Virginia Woolf as an 'artist' pure and simple, projecting, in an experiential vacuum, sensitive and delicate word-patterns devoid of all but the most essentially aesthetic content, is one which can have taken root only in a society in which there exists the most lamentable indifference both to life and art. The following passage from a review of a typically adulatory book about Virginia Woolf's novels is representative of the prevalent inert and thoughtless acceptance of this legend:

Of Mrs. Woolf's style this book does not directly treat, yet . . . here, if anywhere, the style *is* the writer . . . her best work is a sequence of illuminating moments woven into a complete design; and for that design her imagination used its own language— an impressionistic, highly charged, emotive prose that differs at times little, if at all, from poetry; its texture shot with grace, sensitivity, and subtle awareness. Over a human landscape of deliberately limited dimensions her delicate rhythms drift and play like soft clouds through which gleams the dappled sunlight of her pity and her humour, her sympathy for the sorrows and frustrations of her fellow men and women, and her ironic smile at their weaknesses and foibles. . . .

To the question, 'Yes—but what are Virginia Woolf's novels *about?* What view of life do they reflect? What particular insights do they display?' one receives no satisfactory answer.

That Virginia Woolf's novels are tenuous, amorphous and vague, that her prose expresses a state of sensitized generality, is true. Nevertheless, this condition has definite psychic roots, and in itself raises the question of value. . . . [Beneath] the imprecisions, vaguenesses and generalities of the particular work there is an underlying, basic preoccupation which gives rise to those qualities: that the merely aesthetic approach to her work begs the question, and that beneath the aesthetic surface there runs a theme of a totally non-aesthetic character. In bringing this theme to light, in revealing the unconscious psychological process which determines the aesthetic form of the work, my aim is to explode the theory of aestheticism, and to show that no artistic work can exist in independence of its maker's human preoccupations and beliefs. (pp. 70-1)

Virginia Woolf's work as a novelist falls roughly into three periods. There is the early period of conventional fictionalizing represented by her two first novels, *The Voyage Out* and *Night and Day.* There is the period of experiment marked by the discarding of those fictional properties which she was unable to utilize, and issuing in *Jacob's Room*—the first novel in what was to be recognized as her characteristic manner—and later, in an ascending scale, in *Mrs. Dalloway* and *To the Lighthouse.* And lastly, there is the descent into an increasingly despairing vacuousness and dissipation of perception through *The Waves, The Years,* and finally *Between the Acts,* marked by a disintegration of form expressing a surrender of all significance to the accidental process of time. (p. 71)

It is not until *Mrs. Dalloway* . . . that we reach a work in which it is possible to trace the drawing together in Virginia Woolf's mind of the impulsion towards belief [in the totality of life] on the one hand and on the other the inability to make any decisive movement of belief and thus to discriminate which led to the narrowing of vision to the elementary conditions of momentary experience. *Mrs. Dalloway* is curiously compounded of this dual movement of belief and unbelief.

In the early essay on **'Modern Fiction'**, Virginia Woolf charges the 'conventional' novelists whose manner she had attempted to follow, with writing of unimportant things, with spending their skill and industry on 'making the trivial and the transitory appear the true and the enduring'. 'For us at this moment,' she wrote, 'the form of fiction most in vogue more often misses than secures the thing we seek. Whether we call it life or spirit, truth or reality, this, the essential thing, has moved off.' What, then, is the enduring, the true, which it is the novelist's task to capture? She does not know; but she ventures to suppose that it may be found by a form of passive receptiveness to experience. 'Let us not take it for granted,' she wrote in that early essay, 'that life exists more fully in what is commonly thought big than in what is commonly thought small.' Unable to distinguish between this value and that she takes the barest unit of disparate experience and concentrates upon it, in the supposition or the hope that within that, if anywhere, must lie the secret of life's *indigenous* significance.

The inability to discriminate between levels of life, to make choices between 'good' and 'bad', 'right' and 'wrong', or 'desirable' and 'undesirable', besides thrusting the individual so affected back upon the naked and isolated moment of perception, places him furthermore in a position where, if any kind of positive 'significance' is to be attempted (and life can be endowed with significance only by an interior act of affirmation—of *belief*), then, inevitably, undifferentiated, elementary life has to be accepted unreservedly and in its totality. In *Mrs. Dalloway* we see not only the results of the period of experimental, impressionistic, *momentary* writing applied to the novel; we also see the attainment of a sustained, though of course ultimately spurious, 'significance' through the continuous act of complete and undiscriminating acceptance of every moment of undifferentiated existence, each separate atom of which is presumed to contain an equal fragment of *indigenous* meaning.

In *Mrs. Dalloway,* in fact, the specific absence of belief which is shown in the earlier novels is revealed in its reverse aspect. It takes on the appearance of belief—a positive acceptance and affirmation, not of any particular level of reality, but of *everything,* without discrimination: except, significantly enough, of that which would imply the possibility, or the need, of discrimination. 'One can only hope that they will have the same vision and the same power to believe, without which life would be so meaningless,' writes old Mrs. Hilbery, of Katharine and her fiancé in *Night and Day:* to be-

lieve, that is, not in any specific reality or value, but simply to believe, in everything, perhaps; in 'life'. And one can only take Clarissa Dalloway as exemplifying this 'belief '—a belief so total that it engulfs the whole of experience, and which on examination turns out to be a positive inversion of unbelief. Besides representing the combination of *happiness* and *belief,* Clarissa Dalloway is an incarnation of life itself, the stream and efflorescence of natural, material, feminine existence. A sentimental, worldly sort of average sensual woman, she is presented lyrically and quite uncritically through a rose-tinted haze, the trivialities of her pointless, sensational life inflated to universal proportions. (pp. 80-2)

The vague, fluid characters in this book—Clarissa herself, her whimsical, Puckish lover, Peter Walsh, and Septimus Warren Smith—are bathed in the tender warmth of their author's undiscriminating sympathy. It is interesting, that being so, to find that there are also portrayed two characters who are given at least potential definition by the decisiveness of their attitude to life, in which they stand in polar opposition to the indecisive fluidity of the other chief characters. And it is intriguing to watch the manner in which these two characters are pursued by their creator with a gratuitous vindictiveness which seems at first sight unaccountable.

To Clarissa Dalloway is opposed the maliciously-drawn minor figure of Miss Kilman, her daughter's teacher, who, she fears, is alienating the girl's affection from her. Between Mrs. Dalloway and Miss Kilman there is an unspoken but vibrant antagonism, which flashes out as Miss Kilman, leaving Mrs. Dalloway's house with the girl, encounters her employer on the landing. . . . Subsequently Miss Kilman is made to disgrace herself before Mrs. Dalloway's daughter, and is left, a pathetic figure, covered with humiliation.

Humiliation is the portion also of the other character who is so unsympathetic as to possess a definite, formulated attitude to life. Sir William Bradshaw, the nerve specialist who is called in to deal with the neurasthenic Septimus, is presented as a thick-skinned, domineering egotist, who applies to human beings a sovereign test of normality and sense of proportion. (pp. 84-5)

It would seem that just as Clarissa Dalloway and Septimus Warren Smith are linked in an unconscious psychic sympathy, representing as they do the human mind's state of fluid and unprincipled openness to the undifferentiated phenomena of elementary existence, so the decisive attitudes of Miss Kilman and Sir William Bradshaw converge—and converge upon that threatening imperative towards *conversion,* the imposition of a definite view of life upon the fluid, the indefinite, which is felt as inexpressibly menacing to everything that Clarissa Dalloway herself values and represents. Pondering on Miss Kilman, and the challenge she is seen to present to her own undiscriminating acceptance, Mrs. Dalloway asks herself:

> Why creeds and prayers and mackintoshes? when . . . that's the miracle, that's the mystery: that old lady, she meant, whom she could see going from chest of drawers to dressing-table. She could still see her. And the supreme mystery which Kilman might say she had solved, or Peter might say he had solved, but Clarissa didn't believe either of them had the ghost of an idea of solving, was simply this: here was one room; there another. Did religion solve that, or love?

Sir William Bradshaw, like Miss Kilman, is disgraced. When Septimus Warren Smith is in a condition of intense neurotic excitement, he insists upon entering his room, with the result that Septimus flings himself out of the window and is killed. Towards the end of the story, at Mrs. Dalloway's party, the climax of her day, she learns from Sir William Bradshaw, who is one of the guests, of the young man's death. . . .

> . . . But this young man who had killed himself—had he plunged holding his treasure? 'If it were now to die, 'twere now to be most happy,' she had said to herself once, coming down, in white. Or there were the poets and thinkers. Suppose he had had that passion, and had gone to Sir William Bradshaw, a great doctor, yet to her obscurely evil, without sex or lust, extremely polite to women, but capable of some indescribable outrage—forcing your soul, that was it—if this young man had gone to him, and Sir William had impressed him, like that, with his power, might he not then have said (indeed she felt it now), Life is made intolerable; they make life intolerable, men like that?

> Then (she had felt it only this morning) there was the terror; the overwhelming incapacity, one's parents giving it into one's hands, this life, to be lived to the end, to be walked with serenely; there was in the depths of her heart an awful fear. Even now, quite often if Richard had not been there reading the *Times,* so that she could crouch like a bird and gradually revive, send roaring up that immeasurable delight, rubbing stick to stick, one thing with another, she must have perished. She had escaped. But that young man had killed himself.

Such then is the psychological structure of *Mrs. Dalloway.* Although, as a novel, it represents the peak of Virginia Woolf's achievement, just as it marks the highest, most buoyant point on the graph of her emotional progression, it shows no authentic advance over her earlier works: no movement of the mind, that is, into new territory. Apparently, affirmative in mood, its innocency is in fact, retrogressive and corrupt. And its apparent affirmation of life is merely the reverse aspect of its rejection of that which alone could give life meaning and value: i.e., a positive, spiritual affirmation

which, facilitating the introduction of a principle of choice, of discrimination, would make life subject to differentiation and thus to the realization of meaning.

And yet, despite its at times cloying sentimentality, *Mrs. Dalloway* is perhaps Virginia Woolf's most satisfactory novel, for it has an organic structure which derives from the successful dramatic presentation of a view of life. It is in fact the only novel of Virginia Woolf's in which tension is achieved through the opposition of characters embodying contrary principles of conduct. The lack of such tension in the rest of her work results from the monistic conception of existence which sets all characters alike within the same undifferentiated flow of life, and makes inward and outward conflict alike inconceivable. (pp. 85-7)

D. S. Savage, "Virginia Woolf," in his *The Withered Branch: Six Studies in the Modern Novel,* Eyre & Spottiswoode, 1950, pp. 70-105.

LEON EDEL
(essay date 1961)

[An American critic and biographer, Edel is a highly acclaimed authority on the life and work of Henry James. In the following excerpt, he discusses Woolf's narrative techniques in her novel-writing, countering the contention that she was an innovator in the use of stream-of-consciousness narration.]

Virginia Woolf was not one of the architects of the stream-of-consciousness novel. She read Joyce, Proust, and Dorothy Richardson and absorbed their lesson. Her peculiar contribution to the novel of subjectivity lay in her awareness almost from the first that she could obtain given effects of experience by a constant search for the condition of poetry. The influence of James Joyce upon her is much more profound than is generally believed. Indeed, she herself was prompt to seize upon *Ulysses* as a transcendent work long before it was published and only a few chapters had been serialized. (p. 63)

Light, tone, colour play through her cadenced works in a constant search for mood and with no attempt to impart an individual character to the style of thought. There is no attempt at portrait painting; rather does she try to evoke a state of feeling by a kind of mental poesy. The same vein of poetry runs through all the minds she creates for us. It is as if she had created a single device or convention, to be applied universally, in the knowledge that the delicacy of her perception, the waves of feeling, will wash over her readers as she washes them over her characters.

This is alike her achievement and its fatal flaw. The bright flame-like vividness of her books creates beautiful illuminated surfaces. There is no tragic depth in them, only the pathos of things lost and outlived, the past irretrievable or retrieved as an ache in the present. And in this she has fused the example of Proust as of Joyce. I think of *Mrs. Dalloway* as a Joycean novel, diluted, and washed and done in beautiful water-colour; and *To the Lighthouse* is Proustian in its time-sense, but again the medium is a kind of water-colour of the emotions.

Like Proust and Joyce, Virginia Woolf clearly expressed her aesthetic of fiction. Once she had grasped the lesson of her two great predecessors, she seems to have known exactly how she would apply it. But her definition of fiction is more impressionistic than the carefully evolved analysis Proust made of his *métier*, or the Aquinian aesthetic of Joyce. She adds little to what has been said, and once we divest her ideas of the eloquence in which they are clothed, we find them rather thin and unoriginal. (p. 64)

Virginia Woolf tried to catch the shower of innumerable atoms, the vision of life, the iridescence, the luminous halo. It was her way of circumventing the clumsiness of words. . . . However much Mrs. Woolf might assert the need to record the shower of atoms "in the order in which they fall," she neither accepted that order, nor believed in describing their frequent incoherence. Her method was that of the lyric poet. She was interested in the sharpened image, the moment, the condensed experience. She saw the world around her as if it were a sharp knife cutting its way into her being.

From James Joyce, Virginia Woolf seems to have obtained a certain sense of *oneness* and the isolation that resides within it: from him she learned how to give meaning to the simultaneity of experience. London is to Mrs. Dalloway what Dublin is to Leopold Bloom. But her London is a large canvas background with light cleverly playing over it and, unlike Joyce, her people are distillations of mind and flesh. Clarissa Dalloway's day in London, also a day in June, as in *Ulysses,* begins at nine in the morning and finishes early the next morning. (Indeed, in most of Mrs. Woolf 's fiction, time is reduced to a few hours, so that even in *To the Lighthouse,* where a number of years are bridged in the middle passage, "Time Passes," it is but to link two single days at each end of that period.) (pp. 65-6)

[*Mrs. Dalloway's*] structure seems largely to be modelled on the multiple-scened chapter in *Ulysses* which is tied together by the progress of the vice-regal cavalcade through Dublin's streets. We are in many minds in the streets of London. But Mrs. Dalloway's mind, and that of Septimus Warren Smith, hold the centre of the book as did those of Bloom and Dedalus in *Ulysses.* The entire inwardness of the book, its limited time-scheme, the use of multiple views, so that we feel we have seen London through many eyes—and so are aware of it through many awarenesses—the glimpsing of certain characters and then the glimpse of them anew through the perceptions of the principal characters—all this becomes a subtle conversion to simpler ends of the Joycean complexities. But if Bloom and Dedalus are a father and son who meet for a brief moment at the end of a long day symbolically, as Odysseus met Telemachus after a lifetime of wanderings, Clarissa Dalloway and Septimus Smith seem to be two facets of the same personality—indeed, the projection by Virginia Woolf of two sides of herself. Mrs. Woolf 's diary shows that she conceived this novel as an attempt to show "the world seen by the sane and the insane side by side." (p. 66)

The whole of the novel conveys poignantly Virginia Woolf 's response to Joyce's success in reflecting how, in a big city, people's paths cross and dramas go on within range of dramas, and yet in spite of innumerable points of superficial contact and relation, each drama is isolated and each individual remains locked within walls of private experience. The book's brilliance, as writing and as poetry, lies in the skill with which Mrs. Woolf weaves from one mind into another. . . . This complex inner material could be rendered only by the use of brilliantly evocative prose-poetry. And this novel, like those which Virginia Woolf wrote after it, illustrates admirably the worth of the symbolist method in fiction. We have only to think of a Zola or a George Moore creating Clarissa after the manner of their naturalist doctrines to understand the difference. Clarissa would emerge as a commonplace woman, the façade described in detail, but no hint of the fascinating and troubled and mysterious personality behind her exterior. Mrs. Woolf extended with remarkable skill and literary virtuosity the creation of a novel that conveys inner experience. She was capable of finding the words that would show the world through her protagonists' minds: and she participated fully in the significant shift of emphasis, inaugurated by Henry James, from the outer social world—as explored by Balzac or the naturalists—to the sensibility with which that outer world is appreciated and felt.

If the general plan, the painting of the environment, is a scaling down of Joycean architectonics, the painting of the sensibility tends to be Proustian. And yet there is a significant difference. In Proust the odour of the lilacs is directly felt and explored with subtlety; his feelings well up out of the page and are carefully communicated. In Mrs. Woolf the odour bounces off the flowers and reaches the reader as a sharp, distinct but refracted sensation. One has indeed an effect of the bouncing-off of light and sound throughout the novel from people and objects and against the receiving mind. Proust touches experience directly. Mrs. Woolf 's method is refraction, through a kind of high, tense awareness. The poetry is there on every page and always a synthesis—a pulling together of objects and impressions. (pp. 67-8)

Leon Edel, "The Novel as Poem," in *Virginia Woolf: A Collection of Critical Essays,* edited by Claire Sprague, Prentice-Hall, Inc., 1971, pp. 63-9.

DAVID DAICHES
(essay date 1963)

[Daiches, a prominent English scholar and critic, is especially renowned for his insightful studies of Robert Burns, Robert Louis Stevenson, and Woolf. In the following excerpt from his *Virginia Woolf*, he assesses Woolf 's contribution to English literature.]

What . . . was Virginia Woolf 's contribution to English literature? It was a very real, if in some sense a limited, one. She developed a type of fiction in which sensitive personal reactions to experience can be objectified and patterned in a manner that is both intellectually exciting and aesthetically satisfying. It is a delicate art. The robustness that makes itself felt in her criticism and in *Orlando* is not to be discovered in her characteristic novels, whose function is to distil a significance out of the data discovered by a personal sensibility and, by projecting that significance dramatically through the minds of others, to maintain an unstable equilibrium between lyrical and narrative art. She achieved that with greatest success in *Mrs. Dalloway* and *To the Lighthouse.* In the earlier novels the scales come down too heavily on the side of narrative, with the result that the lyrical elements are not properly fitted in; while in *Between the Acts* the scales are weighted on the lyrical side and the narrative is never wholly justified. *The Waves* introduces a not quite successful device for carrying on a narrative by means of lyrical monologues, while in *The Years* the reader senses a virtuosity in excess of the novel's requirements. Only in the two middle novels is the precarious balance maintained throughout: only in these is she able to refine life sufficiently to make it fully adaptable to her characteristic treatment.

The Victorian novelist tended on the whole to produce a narrative art whose patterns were determined by a public sense of values. Virginia Woolf, on the other hand, sensitive to the decay of public values in her time, preferred the more exacting task of patterning events in terms of her personal vision, which meant that she had on her hands the additional technical job of discovering devices for convincing the reader, at least during his period of reading, of the significance and reality of this vision. The English novel in the eighteenth and nineteenth centuries was essentially a public instrument; antithetical to lyric poetry. Its function was to utilize the preconceptions of readers in the presentation of a patterned series of events. (Lyrical poetry ignores, as a rule, public preconceptions and endeavours to communicate violently and directly a personal awareness of the poet's.) That the distinction between these two forms of art should be deliberately broken down in the post-Victorian period was only natural, for the distinction between public and private truth in every field was becoming blurred. There were many ways of responding to this situation: that of Virginia Woolf produced a type of art which, at its best, possesses a subtle and fragile beauty that will outlast the more rough-hewn works of many of her contemporaries.

Into the influences that affected her method we need not enter. The important thing is not that Proust or Joyce or any other writer influenced her writing, but that she developed a view of her art which made her susceptible to that kind of influence. Influences are not accepted passively by writers; they are actively embraced, and only when they coincide with the attitude the writer has already come to have: the important thing for the critic is to understand that attitude and its meaning for the writer's art.

It is doubtful whether the work of Virginia Woolf has permanently expanded the art of fiction. Her techniques are not easily isolated or imitated. But an author's greatness is not measured by the extent to which he can be imitated. Virginia Woolf can afford to rest her claims on her novels, which show her to be one of the half-dozen novelists of the present century whom the world will not easily let die. There can be little question that she was the greatest woman novelist of her time, though she herself would have objected to the separation of her sex implied in such a judgment. (pp. 153-55)

David Daiches, in his *Virginia Woolf,* revised edition, New Directions, 1963, 169 p.

STELLA McNICHOL
(essay date 1990)

[In the following excerpt, McNichol asserts that an examination of the poetic rather than the psychological features of Woolf 's fiction results in a broader and more generally favorable assessment of the author's achievement as a novelist.]

Oscar Wilde's brilliant, if unfair, epigram at Browning's expense—'Meredith is a prose Browning, and so is Browning. He used poetry as a medium for writing in prose'—was a criticism both of the content and of the form of his poetry. To claim that Virginia Woolf is a poet who used prose fiction as her medium—the argument of the present study—is likewise to assert something both about the content and about the form of her novels. Often she has the cadences, sometimes even the rhymes, associated with lyric poetry:

So on a summer's day
the waves collect, overbalance, and fall;
collect and fall; . . .
. . .
that is all.

[*Mrs. Dalloway*]

Taking the term poetry in a more general sense, it can be shown that the imagery and the structure of her novels arise from a creative imagination that is profoundly poetic in nature. This is not, therefore, a stylistic study of the fiction of Virginia Woolf; or one which focuses narrowly on the lyric qualities of her writing. It does, however, focus on a specific poetic quality or aspect in each novel under discussion as a starting point for interpretation.

The first two chapters of this study indicate some of the ways in which poetic features intrude into the text of what is generally described as a traditional novel. In the case of *The Voyage Out,* for instance, occurrences and events as mundane as a dance and a picnic, ordinary episodes in the chronological sequence of events, take on a symbolic dimension which adds a further layer of meaning to that conveyed by the naturally unfolding plot. In *Night and Day* there is a move into fantasy as the central characters embark on a quest which takes them into a world of psychological confusion in which they learn to distinguish between dream and reality. The poetic aspect of this novel inheres mainly in its Shakespearean parallels. *Jacob's Room* is more experimental than the two novels that preceded it. It is Virginia Woolf's most theoretical work, yet even here meaning is conveyed poetically. First there is the dual movement of the novel whereby the optimistic thrust of the central character is undermined by the elegiac voice of the narrator, and second there is the way in which poetic connections are made between the episodes as images and motifs become interwoven into the fabric of meaning. These three novels contain writing of considerable sophistication and maturity.

The major fiction is approached in a more narrowly specific way: *Mrs. Dalloway* through its poetic rhythms, *To the Lighthouse* as a multi-perspectival exploration of a reality embodied in a single image, and *The Waves* as a playpoem. A new kind of poetry is to be found in the last novel.

The aspects of the poetic that constitute the different approaches to each novel in this study indicate something of the way in which Virginia Woolf altered her method as she developed from novel to novel, her method being dictated by different preoccupations.

The first novels are all about young people growing up in Edwardian England. The third of these moves further forward in time: Jacob Flanders dies in the Great War at the age of twenty-six. The second phase is that of the psychological novel. Virginia Woolf's most truly psychological novel is *Mrs. Dalloway.* It is significant that her Modernist manifesto, the essay 'Modern Fiction', was published in the same year. In this essay she expresses her commitment to an inward-looking fiction, recognizes the potential of the stream of consciousness technique (though she does not use that term), and sees that it is necessary to invent new narrative structures to reflect new insights into life. In her progression from *Mrs. Dalloway* to *The Waves* the emphasis of her concern shifts from the psychological to the mystical, the titles of the books reflecting that development: having explored and expressed psychological reality she moves beyond the human to the universal and cosmic reality that she from time to time glimpses as 'a fin in the waste of waters'. The novels of this period reflect the mood of England in the 1920s. The central characters are now middle-aged.

Virginia Woolf wrote two novels of the 1930s, *The Years,* a novel of realism, and the poetic novel *Between the Acts.* They reflect the mood of England in the decade that saw the Depression and the rise of Fascism, and that concluded with the outbreak of war. The bias of her late work is social and historical, and the central characters are elderly. Having plumbed the depths of the human psyche and explored the capacity of the individual to transcend time and the routine dailiness of life, Virginia Woolf turns outwards in her late fiction to consider his situation and significance in the continuum of history. *Between the Acts* has a time span (if one includes the pageant) of 500 years. The focus of this novel is on our consciousness of history whereby the self and history are interlocked in an evolving system. The self of the present assumes the past. (pp. xi–xiii)

[Considerations of Virginia Woolf as a psychological novelist] focus on the novels of her central period whereby the early novels are viewed dismissively as apprenticeship works, and those she wrote after *The Waves* as novels of decline. This view fails to do justice to her overall achievement as a novelist. In focusing on the poetic rather than the psychological features of her fiction it is possible in some measure to do justice to its greater range and variety. (p. xiii)

Stella McNichol, in her *Virginia Woolf and the Poetry of Fiction,* Routledge, 1990. 182 p.

SOURCES FOR FURTHER STUDY

Batchelor, John. *Virginia Woolf: The Major Novels.* Cambridge: Cambridge University Press, 1991, 157 p.

Critical examination of five of Woolf 's principal novels: *Jacob's Room, Mrs. Dalloway, To the Lighthouse, The Waves,* and *Between the Acts.* Separate chapters are devoted to her life and personality and to her narrative methods. Also includes a chronology and a selected secondary bibliography.

Dell, Quentin. *Virginia Woolf: A Biography.* New York: Harcourt Brace Jovanovich, 1972.

The standard biography, written by Woolf 's nephew and based largely on private family papers. Published in both one and two volumes, the one-volume edition cited retains a two-part structure, with separate paginations and indexes.

Bishop, Edward. *A Virginia Woolf Chronology.* London: Macmillan Press, 1989, 268 p.

Provides a chronological outline of Woolf 's life and career.

Gordon, Lyndall. *Virginia Woolf: A Writer's Life.* Oxford: Oxford University Press, 1984, 341 p.

Critical biography discussing Woolf 's works in relation to her life.

Kirkpatrick, Brownlee Jean, ed. *A Bibliography of Virginia Woolf.* Rev. ed. Oxford: Clarendon, 1980, 268 p.

The standard primary bibliography.

Majumdar, Robin, and McLaurin, Allen, eds. *Virginia Woolf: The Critical Heritage.* London: Routledge & Kegan Paul, 1975, 467 p.

Reprints and annotates important initial reviews of Woolf 's works, as well as some early critical essays. The editors supply a lengthy introduction surveying Woolf 's life and career and her critical reception.

William Wordsworth

1770-1850

English poet, critic, essayist, and dramatist.

INTRODUCTION

Wordsworth is considered the greatest and most influential English Romantic poet. For his innovative concept of nature, his earnest exploration of philosophical ideas, and his original poetic theories, critics regard Wordsworth as a key figure in English literature. Asserting in the Preface to his *Lyrical Ballads* (1798) that poetry should comprise "language really used by men," Wordsworth challenged the prevailing eighteenth-century notion of formal poetic diction and thereby profoundly affected the course of modern poetry. His major work, *The Prelude* (1850), a study of the role of the imagination and memory in the formation of poetic sensibility, is now viewed as one of the most seminal long poems of the nineteenth century. The freshness and emotional power of Wordsworth's poetry, the keen psychological depth of his characterizations, and the urgency of his social commentary make him one of the most important writers in English.

Wordsworth was born in Cockermouth, England, the second son of John and Anne Cookson Wordsworth. An attorney for a prominent local aristocrat, John Wordsworth provided a secure and comfortable living for his family. But with his wife's death in 1778, the family became dispersed: the boys were enrolled at a boarding school in Hawkeshead, and Wordsworth's sister, Dorothy, was sent to live with cousins in Halifax. In the rural surroundings of Hawkeshead, situated in the lush Lake District, Wordsworth early learned to love nature, including the pleasures of walking and outdoor play. He equally enjoyed his formal education, demonstrating a talent for writing poetry. The tranquility of his years at Hawkeshead was marred by the death of his father in 1783. Left homeless, the Wordsworth children spent their school vacations with various relatives, many of whom regarded them as nothing more than a financial burden. Biographers have pointed out that Wordsworth's frequently unhappy early life contrasts sharply with the idealized portrait of childhood he presented in his poetry.

Leaving his beloved Lake District in 1787, Wordsworth commenced study at St. John's College, Cambridge. His guardians hoped that he would choose the ministry, thus freeing them from their obligation to support him, yet Wordsworth scorned academics. The highlight of his college years, he later wrote, was a walking tour through France and Switzerland undertaken with his friend Robert Jones. Graduating in 1791, but restless and without definite career plans, Wordsworth lived for a short time in London and Wales and then traveled to France. The French Revolution was in its third year, and although he previously had shown little interest in politics, he quickly came to advocate the goals of the Revolution. Along with a heightened political consciousness, he experienced a passionate affair, the details of which were kept a family secret until the early twentieth century. During his stay in France he fell in love with a French woman, Annette Vallon, and in 1792 they had a child, Anne-Caroline. Too poor to marry and forced by the outbreak of civil war to flee France, Wordsworth reluctantly returned alone to England in 1793.

The next several years proved a time of great disequilibrium for the poet. England's official declaration of war on France a few months after his return precipitated Wordsworth's spiritual crisis. In addition to being apprehensive about the safety of Annette and Anne-Caroline, he felt deeply troubled by a perceived conflict between his patriotism and his sympathy with the French Revolution. Moreover, like many of his contemporaries, Wordsworth was shocked by the gradual degeneration of the idealistic spirit of the Revolution and by its aftermath, the Reign of Terror. For a time he sought consolation in the philanthropic doctrine of the English philosopher William Godwin, but he eventually became disenchanted with his emphasis on reason rather than emotion. However, Godwin, who had befriended the young Wordsworth, remained one of the most enduring influences on his thought. In addition to Godwin, several other events helped to raise Wordsworth's spirits in 1793. The first was the publication of his two volumes of poetry, *Descriptive Sketches* and *An Evening Walk.* Written in a conventional eighteenth-century style, the collections did not fare well critically. Later that year, his friend William Calvert invited Wordsworth to accompany him on a trip through the west of England. Shortly after returning, Wordsworth received a small legacy from a friend that enabled him to concentrate entirely on writing.

Following a brief sojourn in London, Wordsworth settled with his sister at Racedown in 1795. Living modestly but contentedly, he now spent much of his time reading contemporary European literature and writing verse. An immensely important contribution to Wordsworth's success was Dorothy's lifelong devotion: she encouraged his efforts at composition and looked after the details of their daily life. During the first year at Racedown, Wordsworth wrote *The Borderers,* a verse drama based on the ideas of Godwin and the German Sturm und Drang writers. The single most important event of his literary apprenticeship occurred in 1797 when he met the poet Samuel Taylor Coleridge. The two had corresponded for several years, and when Coleridge came to visit Wordsworth at Racedown, their rapport and mutual admiration were immediate. Many critics view their friendship as one of the most extraordinary in English literature. The Wordsworths soon moved to Nether Stowey in order to be near Coleridge. In the intellectually stimulating environment he and Coleridge created there, Wordsworth embarked on a period of remarkable creativity. Coleridge's influence on Wordsworth during this time was immense, and his astute critiques gave the young poet direction and fostered his artistic growth. Coleridge strove particularly to encourage Wordsworth's development as a visionary thinker capable of writing philosophical poetry. To that end, he introduced him to the writings of the philosopher David Hartley, whose theories had a profound effect on Wordsworth's poetry.

In 1798, the two friends collaborated on and anonymously published *Lyrical Ballads,* a collection of experimental poems. The majority of the pieces were written by Wordsworth, including the now-famous Preface, which was added to the 1800 edition of the poems. There, he emphasized the importance of an unadorned style; his distaste for the "gaudiness" of eighteenth-century poetic diction even led Wordsworth to make the revolutionary claim that there exists no "*essential* difference between the language of prose and metrical composition." Applying the principles he outlined in the Preface, Wordsworth concentrated in his poetry on subjects derived from "humble and rustic life." Writing in a deliberately simple and powerfully direct style, he depicted social outcasts, country folk, and the poor. Wordsworth's most striking contribution to the collection was "Lines Composed a Few Miles Above Tintern Abbey." One of his strongest poems, it explores the relationship between nature and immortality in the descriptive-meditative style most closely associated with Wordsworth.

The appearance of *Lyrical Ballads,* with its controversial technique and subject matter, firmly established Wordsworth in the public eye. With profits from the book, he, Coleridge, and Dorothy journeyed to Germany in 1798-99 to learn the language and attend university lectures. There Wordsworth composed the pieces that are collectively called the "Lucy" poems, as well as the first two books of *The Prelude.*

In 1802, Wordsworth married Mary Hutchinson. Realizing that Wordsworth now required a more steady source of income, Coleridge introduced him to Sir George Beaumont, a wealthy art patron who became Wordsworth's benefactor and friend. Beaumont facilitated the publication of the *Poems* of 1807; in that collection, Wordsworth once again displayed his extraordinary talent for nature description and infusing an element of mysticism into ordinary experience. Always fascinated by human psychology, he also stressed the influence of childhood experiences and memory on adult attitudes and actions, summarizing his view in the phrase "The Child is father of the Man." Critical reception of the *Poems* as a whole was mixed, but most reviewers singled out "Ode: Intimations of Immortality from Recollections of Early Childhood" as perhaps Wordsworth's greatest production.

The remaining years of Wordsworth's career are generally viewed as a decline from the revolutionary and experimental fervor of his youth. He condemned French imperialism in the period after the Revolution, and his nationalism became more pronounced. The pantheism of his early nature poetry, too, gave way to orthodox religious sentiment in the later works. When Wordsworth accepted a post as distributor of stamps for Westmorland county, a political appointment that ensured his continued prosperity, his transformation seemed complete. Such admirers as Percy Bysshe Shelley, who formerly had respected Wordsworth as a reformer of poetic diction, now regarded him with scorn and a sense of betrayal. Whether because of professional jealousy or because of alterations to his personality caused by prolonged drug use, Coleridge grew estranged from Wordsworth after 1810. Wordsworth continued to write in his later years, publishing, among other works, *The Excursion* (1814); the *Poems* of 1815, and three long narrative poems—*The White Doe of Rylstone* (1815), *Peter Bell* (1819), and *The Waggoner* (1819). Two additional works, *Yarrow Revisited and Other Poems* (1835) and *The Sonnets of William Wordsworth* (1838), received critical accolades upon their publication and evoked comparisons of Wordsworth's sonnets with those of William Shakespeare and John Milton. Having become a highly respected literary figure during the 1830s, Wordsworth was awarded honorary degrees from the University of Durham and Oxford University, and in 1843 he won the distinction of being named Poet Laureate. After receiving a government pension in 1842, he retired to Rydal. When he died in 1850, he was one of England's best-loved poets.

Wordsworth's greatest work, *The Prelude,* was published shortly after his death. Begun some fifty years earlier, the poem was completed in 1805 and then drastically revised over time. Greeted with uneven praise at its first appearance, the poem is now hailed as Wordsworth's greatest work. Critics laud *The Prelude*'s blending of autobiography, history, and epic, its theme of loss and gain, its mythologizing of childhood experience, and its affirmation of the value of the imagination.

Critics of Wordsworth's works have made his treatment of nature, his use of diction, and his critical theories the central focus of their studies. Early response to his poetry begins with Francis Jeffrey's concerted campaign to thwart Wordsworth's poetic career. His reviews of the works of the Lake poets— Wordsworth, Coleridge, and Robert Southey—and of Wordsworth's poetry in particular, were so vitriolic that they stalled public acceptance of the poet for some twenty years but brought many critics to his defense. To Jeffrey, Wordsworth's poetic innovations were in "open violation of the established laws of poetry," his compassionate depictions of social outcasts merely "splenetic and idle discontent with existing institutions in society." He described Wordsworth's stylistic simplicity as affectation and his focus on ordinary people and events as bathos. Despite Jeffrey's comments, Wordsworth's poetry eventually gained acceptance. By the 1830s, Wordsworth was England's preeminent poet.

Wordsworth's poetic theory has been an area of dispute among scholars ever since the publication of the 1800 edition of *Lyrical Ballads.* Although Jeffrey considered its Preface an anarchical manifesto, later critics have come to regard it as a milestone in nineteenth-century poetics and, according to Wordsworth scholar David Perkins, as "one of the finest critical achievements in English." Paradoxically, it was Coleridge who both clarified the merits of Wordsworth's poetic principles and, at the same time, most pointedly identified their defects. In writing about Wordsworth's theories in his *Biographia Literaria,* Coleridge praised his originality, "sane sentiments," and the "perfect appropriateness of the words to the meaning" in his works. Disagreeing with Wordsworth's preference for a poetic "language really used by men," Coleridge challenged his friend's assumption that humble diction and ordinary subjects were inherently superior to formal ones. He reasoned further that various poetic moods necessitate a wide range of styles and pointed out instances of elevated language in Wordsworth's own poetry. By doing so, Coleridge hoped to discourage Wordsworth from his "laborious minuteness" in describing rustic subjects and to encourage him instead to concentrate on meditative poetry. Such subsequent critics as Thomas De Quincey and George Saintsbury, like Coleridge, stated that Wordsworth fettered his genius by insisting on extreme simplicity of style. Wordsworth's views in the Preface were quite radical in their time, and twentieth-century critics, notably M. H. Abrams, have come to acknowledge the modernity of Wordsworth's theories; however, they also cite his debt to eighteenth-century thought. Early reviewers also objected to the didactic element they discerned in Wordsworth's poetry, particularly in his longer narrative works. But given his plea "to be considered as a teacher or as nothing," this tendency to instruct has been accepted as one of the hallmarks of Wordsworth's style.

Whether critics focus on the "simple" Wordsworth of the nature poems and the early lyrics, the "philosophical" Wordsworth of the meditative poetry, or the "innovative" Wordsworth of the *Lyrical Ballads*, they continue to be stimulated by the richness of Wordsworth's poetry. His wide-ranging intellect and originality in shaping a new poetic tradition have as-

sured him a central place in English literature, and his joyous celebration of the imagination has engaged the interest and admiration of each new generation of readers. The appeal of Wordsworth's poetry is perhaps best summarized in these lines from Matthew Arnold's memorial tribute:

> Others will strengthen us to bear—
> But who, ah who, will make us feel?

(For further information about Wordsworth's life and works, see *Dictionary of Literary Biography*, Vol. 93: *British Romantic Poets, 1789-1832* and *Nineteenth-Century Literature Criticism*, Vol. 12.)

CRITICAL COMMENTARY

FRANCIS JEFFREY

(essay date 1802)

[The founder and editor (1803-1829) of the *Edinburgh Review*, one of the most influential magazines in early nineteenth-century England, Jeffrey became famous for his unrelenting criticism of the Lake Poets (Samuel Taylor Coleridge, Robert Southey, and Wordsworth). Wordsworth's writings, in particular, became the central focus of Jeffrey's systematic and prolonged attack on modern poetry. Here, Jeffrey asserts that the use of simple diction as practiced by the modern poets is, in fact, an "affectation" that produces "meanness and insipidity" and ultimately debases poetry.]

[The modern poets] have, among them, unquestionably, a very considerable portion of poetical talent, and have, consequently, been enabled to seduce many into an admiration of the false taste (as it appears to us) in which most of these productions are composed. They constitute, at present, the most formidable conspiracy that has lately been formed against sound judgement in matters poetical; and are entitled to a larger share of our censorial notice, than could be spared for an individual delinquent. (p. 64)

Their most distinguishing symbol, is undoubtedly an affectation of great simplicity and familiarity of language. They disdain to make use of the common poetical phraseology, or to ennoble their diction by a selection of fine or dignified expressions. There would be too much *art* in this, for that great love of nature with which they are all of them inspired; and their sentiments, they are determined, shall be indebted, for their effect, to nothing but their intrinsic tenderness or elevation. There is something very noble and conscientious, we will confess, in this plan of composition; but

the misfortune is, that there are passages in all poems that can neither be pathetic nor sublime; and that, on these occasions, a neglect of the establishments of language is very apt to produce absolute meanness and insipidity. The language of passion, indeed, can scarcely be deficient in elevation; and when an author is wanting in that particular, he may commonly be presumed to have failed in the truth, as well as in the dignity of his expression. The case, however, is extremely different with the subordinate parts of a composition; with the narrative and description, that are necessary to preserve its connexion; and the explanation, that must frequently prepare us for the great scenes and splendid passages. In these, all the requisite ideas may be conveyed, with sufficient clearness, by the meanest and most negligent expressions; and, if magnificence or beauty is ever to be observed in them, it must have been introduced from some other motive than that of adapting the style to the subject. It is in such passages, accordingly, that we are most frequently offended with low and inelegant expressions; and that the language, which was intended to be simple, and natural, is found oftenest to degenerate into mere slovenliness and vulgarity. It is in vain, too, to expect that the meanness of those parts may be redeemed by the excellence of others. A poet, who aims at all sublimity or pathos, is like an actor in a high tragic character, and must sustain his dignity throughout, or become altogether ridiculous. We are apt enough to laugh at the mock-majesty of those whom we know to be but common mortals in private; and cannot permit Hamlet to make use of a single provincial intonation, although it should only be in his conversation with the gravediggers.

The followers of simplicity are, therefore, at all times in danger of occasional degradation; but the sim-

Principal Works

Descriptive Sketches (poetry) 1793

An Evening Walk: An Epistle in Verse (poetry) 1793

Lyrical Ballads, with a Few Other Poems [with Samuel Taylor Coleridge] (poetry) 1798; also published in revised form as Lyrical Ballads, with Other Poems, 1800, 1802, 1805

Poems (poetry) 1807

The Excursion, Being a Portion of The Recluse (poetry) 1814

Poems (poetry) 1815

The White Doe of Rylstone; or, The Fate of the Nortons (poetry) 1815

Peter Bell: A Tale in Verse (poetry) 1819

The Waggoner (poetry) 1819

The River Duddon: A Series of Sonnets, Vaudracour and Julia, and Other Poems (poetry) 1820

Ecclesiastical Sketches (poetry) 1822

Memorials of a Tour on the Continent, 1820 (poetry) 1822

Yarrow Revisited and Other Poems (poetry) 1835

The Sonnets of William Wordsworth (poetry) 1838

*Poems, Chiefly of Early and Late Years; Including The Borderers. 4 vols. (poetry and drama) 1842-54

†The Prelude, or Growth of a Poet's Mind: Autobiographical Poem (poetry) 1850

The Recluse (unfinished poem) 1888

The Letters of William and Dorothy Wordsworth. 6 vols. (letters) 1935-39; rev. ed., 1967-

Poetical Works of William Wordsworth. 5 vols. (poetry) 1940-49

The Prose Works of William Wordsworth (prose) 1974

The Cornell Wordsworth. 13 vols. to date. (poetry, prose, and drama) 1975-

*The Borderers was written in 1795.

†This work was written in 1799-1805.

---

plicity of this new school seems intended to ensure it. *Their* simplicity does not consist, by any means, in the rejection of glaring or superfluous ornament,—in the substitution of elegance to splendour,—or in that refinement of art which seeks concealment in its own perfection. It consists, on the contrary, in a very great degree, in the positive and *bona-fide* rejection of art altogether, and in the bold use of those rude and negligent expressions, which would be banished by a little discrimination. One of their own authors, indeed, has very ingenuously set forth, (in a kind of manifesto, that preceded one of their most flagrant acts of hostility [the *Lyrical Ballads*]), that it was their capital object 'to adapt to the uses of poetry, the ordinary language of conversation among the middling and lower orders of the people.' What advantages are to be gained by the success of this project we confess ourselves unable to conjecture. The language of the higher and more cultivated orders may fairly be presumed to be better than that of their inferiors: at any rate, it has all those associations in its favour, by means of which a style can ever appear beautiful or exalted, and is adapted to the purposes of poetry, by having been long consecrated to its use. The language of the vulgar, on the other hand, has all the opposite associations to contend with; and must seem unfit for poetry, (if there were no other reason), merely because it has scarcely ever been employed in it. A great genius may indeed overcome these disadvantages; but we scarcely conceive that he should court them. We may excuse a certain homeliness of language in the productions of a ploughman or a milkwoman; but we cannot bring ourselves to admire it in an author,

who has had occasion to indite odes to his college-bell, and inscribe hymns to the Penates.

But the mischief of this new system, is not confined to the depravation of language only; it extends to the sentiments and emotions, and leads to the debasement of all those feelings which poetry is designed to communicate. It is absurd to suppose, that an author should make use of the language of the vulgar, to express the sentiments of the refined. His professed object, in employing that language, is to bring his compositions nearer to the true standard of nature; and his intention to copy the sentiments of the lower orders, is implied in his resolution to make use of their style. Now, the different classes of society have each of them a distinct character, as well as a separate idiom; and the names of the various passions to which they are subject respectively, have a signification that varies essentially, according to the condition of the persons to whom they are applied. The love, or grief, or indignation of an enlightened and refined character, is not only expressed in a different language, but is in itself a different emotion from the love, or grief, or anger of a clown, a tradesman, or a market-wench. The things themselves are radically and obviously distinct; and the representation of them is calculated to convey a very different train of sympathies and sensations to the mind. The question, therefore, comes simply to be—Which of them is the most proper object for poetical imitation? It is needless for us to answer a question, which the practice of all the world has long ago decided irrevocably. The poor and vulgar may interest us, in poetry, by their *situation;* but never, we apprehend, by any sentiments that are peculiar to their condition, and still less by any language that is characteristic of it. The truth is, that it is impossible to copy their diction or their sentiments correctly, in a serious composition; and this, not merely because poverty makes men ridiculous, but because just taste and refined sentiment are rarely to be met with among the uncultivated part of mankind; and a language fitted for their expression, can still more rarely form any part of their 'ordinary conversations.' (pp. 64-7)

The qualities of style and imagery, however, form but a small part of the characteristics by which a literary faction is to be distinguished. The subject and object of their compositions, and the principles and opinions they are calculated to support, constitute a far more important criterion, and one to which it is usually altogether as easy to refer. Some poets are sufficiently described as the flatterers of greatness and power, and others as the champions of independence. One set of writers is known by its antipathy to decency and religion; another, by its methodistical cant and intolerance. Our new school of poetry has a moral character also; though it may not be possible, perhaps, to delineate it quite so concisely.

A splenetic and idle discontent with the existing institutions of society, seems to be at the bottom of all their serious and peculiar sentiments. Instead of contemplating the wonders and the pleasures which civilization has created for mankind, they are perpetually brooding over the disorders by which its progress has been attended. They are filled with horror and compassion at the sight of poor men spending their blood in the quarrels of princes, and brutifying their sublime capabilities in the drudgery of unremitting labour. For all sorts of vice and profligacy in the lower orders of society, they have the same virtuous horror, and the same tender compassion. While the existence of these of fences overpowers them with grief and confusion, they never permit themselves to feel the smallest indignation or dislike towards the offenders. The present vicious constitution of society alone is responsible for all these enormities: the poor sinners are but the helpless victims or instruments of its disorders, and could not possibly have avoided the errors into which they have been betrayed. Though they can bear with crimes, therefore, they cannot reconcile themselves to punishments; and have an unconquerable antipathy to prisons, gibbets, and houses of correction, as engines of oppression, and instruments of atrocious injustice. While the plea of moral necessity is thus artfully brought forward to convert all the excesses of the poor into innocent misfortunes, no sort of indulgence is shown to the offences of the powerful and rich. Their oppressions, and seductions, and debaucheries, are the theme of many an angry verse; and the indignation and abhorrence of the reader is relentlessly conjured up against

those perturbators of society, and scourges of mankind. (pp. 70-1)

Francis Jeffrey, in an originally unsigned essay titled "Southey's 'Thalaba'," in *The Edinburgh Review*, Vol. I, No. I, October, 1802, pp. 63-83.

WILLIAM WORDSWORTH
(essay date 1802)

[In the following excerpt from his preface to the 1802 edition of *Lyrical Ballads*, Wordsworth describes the nature of his poetic experiment, commenting on his controversial theory of diction and his perception of the role of the poet.]

What is a poet? To whom does he address himself? And what language is to be expected from him?—He is a man speaking to men: a man, it is true, endowed with more lively sensibility, more enthusiasm and tenderness, who has a greater knowledge of human nature, and a more comprehensive soul, than are supposed to be common among mankind; a man pleased with his own passions and volitions, and who rejoices more than other men in the spirit of life that is in him; delighting to contemplate similar volitions and passions as manifested in the goings-on of the Universe, and habitually impelled to create them where he does not find them. To these qualities he has added a disposition to be affected more than other men by absent things as if they were present; an ability of conjuring up in himself passions, which are indeed far from being the same as those produced by real events, yet (especially in those parts of the general sympathy which are pleasing and delightful) do more nearly resemble the passions produced by real events, than anything which, from the motions of their own minds merely, other men are accustomed to feel in themselves:—whence, and from practice, he has acquired a greater readiness and power in expressing what he thinks and feels, and especially those thoughts and feelings which, by his own choice, or from the structure of his own mind, arise in him without immediate external excitement. (p. 121)

What then does the Poet? He considers man and the objects that surround him as acting and re-acting upon each other, so as to produce an infinite complexity of pain and pleasure; he considers man in his own nature and in his ordinary life as contemplating this with a certain quantity of immediate knowledge, with certain convictions, intuitions, and deductions, which from habit acquire the quality of intuitions; he considers him as looking upon this complex scene of ideas and sensations, and finding every where objects that immediately excite in him sympathies which, from the necessities of his nature, are accompanied by an overbalance of enjoyment. (p. 123)

I have said that poetry is the spontaneous overflow of powerful feelings: it takes its origin from emotion recollected in tranquility: the emotion is contemplated till, by a species of reaction, the tranquility gradually disappears, and an emotion, kindred to that which was before the subject of contemplation, is gradually produced, and does itself actually exist in the mind. In this mood successful composition generally begins, and in a mood similar to this it is carried on; but the emotion, of whatever kind, and in whatever degree, from various causes, is qualified by various pleasures, so that in describing any passions whatsoever, which are voluntarily described, the mind will, upon the whole, be in a state of enjoyment. If Nature be thus cautious to preserve in a state of enjoyment a being so employed, the Poet ought to profit by the lesson held forth to him, and ought especially to take care, that, whatever passions he communicates to his Reader, those passions, if his Reader's mind be sound and vigorous, should always be accompanied with an overbalance of pleasure. (pp. 128-29)

William Wordsworth, in *Wordsworth's Preface to "Lyrical Ballads,"* edited by W. J. B. Owen, Rosenkilde and Bagger, 1957, pp. 111-33.

MATTHEW ARNOLD

(essay date 1879)

[A poet and literary critic, Arnold was one of the most influential authors of the later Victorian period. In the excerpt below, he acknowledges the uneven quality of Wordsworth's poetry but contends that, though not yet fully recognized as such, Wordsworth is the greatest English poet after William Shakespeare and John Milton.]

[Wordsworth] is not fully recognised at home; he is not recognised at all abroad. Yet I firmly believe that the poetical performance of Wordsworth is, after that of Shakespeare and Milton, of which all the world now recognises the worth, undoubtedly the most considerable in our language from the Elizabethan age to the present time. (p. 196)

This is a high claim to make for Wordsworth. But if it is a just claim . . . , Wordsworth will have his due. We shall recognise him in his place, as we recognise Shakespeare and Milton; and not only we ourselves shall recognise him, but he will be recognised by Europe also. Meanwhile, those who recognise him already may do well, perhaps, to ask themselves whether there are not in the case of Wordsworth certain special obsta-

cles which hinder or delay his due recognition by others, and whether these obstacles are not in some measure removable.

The *Excursion* and the *Prelude,* his poems of greatest bulk, are by no means Wordsworth's best work. His best work is in his shorter pieces, and many indeed are there of these which are of first-rate excellence. But in his seven volumes the pieces of high merit are mingled with a mass of pieces very inferior to them; so inferior to them that it seems wonderful how the same poet should have produced both. Shakspeare frequently has lines and passages in a strain quite false, and which are entirely unworthy of him. But one can imagine his smiling if one could meet him in the Elysian Fields and tell him so; smiling and replying that he knew it perfectly well himself, and what did it matter? But with Wordsworth the case is different. Work altogether inferior, work quite uninspired, flat and dull, is produced by him with evident unconsciousness of its defects, and he presents it to us with the same faith and seriousness as his best work. Now a drama or an epic fill the mind, and one does not look beyond them; but in a collection of short pieces the impression made by one piece requires to be continued and sustained by the piece following. In reading Wordsworth, the impression made by one of his fine pieces is constantly dulled and spoiled by a very inferior piece coming after it.

Wordsworth composed verses during a space of some sixty years; and it is not much of an exaggeration to say that within one single decade of those years, between 1798 and 1808, almost all his really first-rate work was produced. A mass of inferior work remains, work done before and after this golden prime, imbedding the first-rate work and clogging it, obstructing our approach to it, chilling the high-wrought mood with which we leave it. To be recognised far and wide as a great poet, to be possible and receivable as a classic, Wordsworth needs to be relieved of a great deal of the poetical baggage which now encumbers him. To administer this relief is indispensable, unless he is to continue to be a poet for the few only, a poet valued far below his real worth by the world. (p. 197)

[Wordsworth] deals with *life,* because he deals with that in which life really consists. This is what Voltaire means to praise in the English poets—this dealing with what is really life. But always it is the mark of the greatest poets that they deal with it; and to say that the English poets are remarkable for dealing with it, is only another way of saying, what is true, that in poetry the English genius has especially shown its power.

Wordsworth deals with it, and his greatness lies in his dealing with it so powerfully. (p. 200)

But we must be on our guard against the Wordsworthians, if we want to secure for Wordsworth his due rank as a poet. The Wordsworthians are apt to

---

Wordsworth on the poems in *Lyrical Ballads*:

The principal object . . . proposed in these Poems was to choose incidents and situations from common life, and to relate or describe them, throughout, as far as was possible in a selection of language really used by men, and, at the same time, to throw over them a certain colouring of imagination, whereby ordinary things should be presented to the mind in an unusual aspect; and, further, and above all, to make these incidents and situations interesting by tracing in them, truly though not ostentatiously, the primary laws of our nature: chiefly, as far as regards the manner in which we associate ideas in a state of excitement. Humble and rustic life was generally chosen, because, in that condition, the essential passions of the heart find a better soil in which they can attain their maturity, are less under restraint, and speak a plainer and more emphatic language; because in that condition of life our elementary feelings co-exist in a state of greater simplicity, and, consequently, may be more accurately contemplated, and more forcibly communicated; because the manners of rural life germinate from those elementary feelings, and, from the necessary character of rural occupations, are more easily comprehended, and are more durable; and,

lastly, because in that condition the passions of men are incorporated with the beautiful and permanent forms of nature. The language, too, of these men has been adopted (purified indeed from what appear to be its real defects, from all lasting and rational causes of dislike or disgust) because such men hourly communicate with the best objects from which the best part of language is originally derived; and because, from their rank in society and the sameness and narrow circle of their intercourse, being less under the influence of social vanity, they convey their feelings and notions in simple and unelaborated expressions. Accordingly, such a language, arising out of repeated experience and regular feelings, is a more permanent, and a far more philosophical language, than that which is frequently substituted for it by Poets, who think that they are conferring honour upon themselves and their art, in proportion as they separate themselves from the sympathies of men, and indulge in arbitrary and capricious habits of expression, in order to furnish food for fickle tastes, and fickle appetites, of their own creation.

Wordsworth, in the preface to the 1800 edition of *Lyrical Ballads*.

---

praise him for the wrong things, and to lay far too much stress upon what they call his philosophy. His poetry is the reality, his philosophy the illusion. Perhaps we shall one day learn to make this proposition more general, and to say: Poetry is the reality, philosophy the illusion. But in Wordsworth's case, at any rate, we cannot do him justice until we dismiss his philosophy.

The *Excursion* abounds with philosophy, and therefore the *Excursion* is to the Wordsworthian what it never can be to the disinterested lover of poetry—a satisfactory work. . . .

[However] true the doctrine may be, it has . . . none of the characters of *poetic* truth, the kind of truth which we require from a poet, and in which Wordsworth is really strong.

Even the "Intimations" of the famous Ode, those corner stones of the supposed philosophic system of Wordsworth—the idea of the high instincts and affections coming out in childhood, testifying of a divine home recently left, and fading away as our life proceeds—this idea, of undeniable beauty as a play of fancy, has itself not the character of poetic truth of the best kind; it has no real solidity. The instinct of delight in Nature and her beauty had no doubt extraordinary strength in Wordsworth himself as a child. But to say that universally this instinct is mighty in childhood, and tends to die away afterwards, is to say what is extremely doubtful. (p. 201)

And let us be on our guard, too, against the exhibitors and extollers of a "scientific system of thought" in Wordsworth's poetry. The poetry will never be seen

aright while they thus exhibit it. The cause of its greatness is simple and may be told quite simply. It is great because of the extraordinary power with which Wordsworth feels the joy offered to us in nature, the joy offered to us in the simple elementary affections and duties; and because of the extraordinary power with which, in case after case, he shows us this joy, and renders it so as to make us share it.

The source of joy from which he thus draws is the truest and most unfailing source of joy accessible to man. It is also accessible universally. Wordsworth brings us word, therefore, according to his own strong and characteristic line, he brings us word

Of joy in widest commonalty spread.

Here is an immense advantage for a poet. Wordsworth tells of what all seek, and tells of it at its truest and best source, and yet a source where all may go and draw for it.

Nevertheless we are not to suppose that everything is precious which Wordsworth, standing even at this perennial and beautiful source, may give us. Wordsworthians are apt to talk as if it must be. They will speak with the same reverence of **"The Sailor's Mother,"** for example, as of **"Lucy Gray."** They do their master harm by such lack of discrimination. **"Lucy Gray"** is a beautiful success; **"The Sailor's Mother"** is a failure. To give aright what he wishes to give, to interpret and render successfully, is not always within Wordsworth's own command. It is within no poet's command; here is the part of the Muse, the inspiration, the God, the "not ourselves." In Wordsworth's case, the accident, for so it may almost be called, of inspiration, is of peculiar importance. No poet, perhaps, is so evidently filled with a new and sacred energy when the inspiration is upon him; no poet, when it fails him, is so left "weak as is a breaking wave." . . . Wordsworth's poetry, when he is at his best, is inevitable, as inevitable as Nature herself. It might seem that Nature not only gave him the matter for his poem but wrote his poem for him. He has no style. He was too conversant with Milton not to catch at times his master's manner, and he has fine Miltonic lines; but he has no assured poetic style of his own, like Milton. When he seeks to have a style he falls into ponderosity and pomposity. (pp. 202-03)

Wordsworth owed much to Burns, and a style of perfect plainness, relying for effect solely on the weight and force of that which with entire fidelity it utters, Burns could show him.

> The poor inhabitant below
> Was quick to learn and wise to know,
> And keenly felt the friendly glow
> And softer flame;
> But thoughtless follies laid him low
> And stain'd his name.

Every one will be conscious of a likeness here to Wordsworth; and if Wordsworth did great things with this nobly plain manner, we must remember, what indeed he himself would always have been forward to acknowledge, that Burns used it before him.

Still Wordsworth's use of it has something unique and unmatchable. Nature herself seems, I say, to take the pen out of his hand, and to write for him with her own bare, sheer, penetrating power. This arises from two causes: from the profound sincereness with which Wordsworth feels his subject, and also from the profoundly sincere and natural character of his subject itself. He can and will treat such a subject with nothing but the most plain, first-hand, almost austere naturalness. His expression may often be called bald, as, for instance, in the poem of **"Resolution and Independence"**; but it is bald as the bare mountain tops are bald, with a baldness which is full of grandeur.

Wherever we meet with the successful balance, in Wordsworth, of profound truth of subject with profound truth of execution, he is unique. His best poems are those which most perfectly exhibit this balance. I have a warm admiration for **"Laodameia"** and for the great **"Ode"**; but if I am to tell the very truth, I find **"Laodameia"** not wholly free from something artificial, and the great **"Ode"** not wholly free from something declamatory. If I had to pick out the kind of poems which most perfectly show Wordsworth's unique power, I should rather choose poems such as **"Michael," "The Fountain," "The Highland Reaper."**

And poems with the peculiar and unique beauty which distinguishes these he produced in considerable number; besides very many other poems of which the worth, although not so rare as the worth of these, is still exceedingly high.

On the whole, then, . . . not only is Wordsworth eminent because of the goodness of his best work, but he is eminent, also, because of the great body of good work which he has left to us. (pp. 203-04)

I have spoken lightly of Wordsworthians; and if we are to get Wordsworth recognised by the public and by the world, we must recommend him not in the spirit of a clique, but in the spirit of disinterested lovers of poetry. . . . No Wordsworthian has a tenderer affection for this pure and sage master than I, or is less really offended by his defects. But Wordsworth is something more than the pure and sage master of a small band of devoted followers, and we ought not to rest satisfied until he is seen to be what he is. He is one of the very chief glories of English poetry; and by nothing is England so glorious as by her poetry. Let us lay aside every weight which hinders our getting him recognised as this, and let our one study be to bring to pass, as widely as possible and as truly as possible, his own word concerning his poems:—"They will cooperate with the benign tendencies in human nature and society, and will, in their degree, be efficacious in making men wiser, better, and happier." (p. 204)

Matthew Arnold, "Wordsworth," in *Macmillan's Magazine*, Vol. XL, No. 237, July, 1879, pp. 193-204.

F. R. LEAVIS

(essay date 1936)

[An influential English critic and teacher, Leavis articulated his views in lectures, critical works, and in *Scrutiny*, a quarterly he cofounded and edited from 1932 to 1953. In the following excerpt, he discusses Wordsworth's personal philosophy, attraction to naturalism, and "essential sanity and normality."]

Wordsworth's greatness and its nature seem to be, in a general way, pretty justly recognized in current acceptance, the established habit of many years. Clear critical recognition, however, explicit in critical statement, is another matter, and those who really read him to-day—who read him as they read contemporary literature—will agree that, in spite of the number of distinguished critics who have written on him, satisfactory statement is still something to be attempted. And to attempt it with any measure of success would be to revalue Wordsworth, to achieve a clearer insight and a fresh realization.

There is—a time-honoured critical blur or indecision—the question of Wordsworth's 'thought.' (p. 154)

Wordsworth's 'philosophy' certainly appears, as such, to invite discussion, and there is a general belief that we all know, or could know by re-reading *The Prelude,* what his doctrines concerning the growth of the mind and relation of Man to nature are. His philosophic verse has a convincingly expository tone and manner, and it is difficult not to believe, after reading, say, Book II of *The Prelude,* that one has been reading a paraphrasable argument—difficult not to believe, though the paraphrase, if resolutely attempted, would turn out to be impossible. Few readers, it would seem, have ever made the attempt, and, in fact, to make it resolutely is the real difficulty—if 'difficulty' can describe the effect of a subtle, pervasive and almost irresistible dissuasion from effort.

This, at any rate, describes fairly the working of Wordsworth's philosophic verse. His triumph is to command the kind of attention he requires and to permit no other. (pp. 155-56)

[Wordsworth's essential habit is to produce] the mood, feeling or experience and at the same time [to appear] to be giving an explanation of it. The expository effect sorts well with—blends into—the characteristic meditative gravity of the emotional presentment ('emotion recollected in tranquillity'), and in the key passages, where significance seems specially to reside, the convincing success of the poetry covers the argument: it is only by the most resolute and sustained effort (once it occurs to one that effort is needed) that one can pay to the argument, as such, the attention it appears to have invited and satisfied. (p. 159)

Even if there were not so much poetry to hold the mind in a subtly incompatible mode of attention, it would still be difficult to continue attending to the philosophic argument, because of the way in which the verse, evenly meditative in tone and movement, goes on and on, without dialectical suspense and crisis or rise and fall. By an innocently insidious trick Wordsworth, in this calm ruminative progression, will appear to be preoccupied with a scrupulous nicety of statement, with a judicial weighing of alternative possibilities, while actually making it more difficult to check the argument from which he will emerge, as it were inevitably, with a far from inevitable conclusion. (p. 162)

He had, if not a philosophy, a wisdom to communicate. . . . It may be said, fairly, that Wordsworth went on tinkering with *The Prelude* through his life instead of completing the great 'philosophic poem' [*The Recluse*] because, as he had in the end tacitly to recognize, his resources weren't adequate to the ambition—he very obviously hadn't enough material. But it must also be said that in letting the ambition lapse he was equally recognizing its superfluity: his real business was achieved. His wisdom is sufficiently presented in the body of his living work.

What he had for presentment was a type and a standard of human normality, a way of life; his preoccupation with sanity and spontaneity working at a level and in a spirit that it seems appropriate to call religious. His philosophizing (in the sense of the Hartleian studies and applications) had not the value he meant it to have; but it is an expression of his intense moral seriousness and a mode of the essential discipline of contemplation that gave consistency and stability to his experience. Wordsworth, we know, is the 'poet of Nature,' and the associations of the term 'Nature' here are unfortunate, suggesting as it does a vaguely pantheistic religion-substitute. . . . But Wordsworth himself, in the famous passage that, 'taken from the conclusion of the first book of *The Recluse,*' he offers 'as a kind of **"Prospectus"** of the design and scope of the whole Poem,' proposes something decidedly different when he stresses 'the Mind of Man' as

My haunt, and the main region of my song.

And Wordsworth here, as a matter of fact, is critically justified.

Creative power in him, as in most great poets, was accompanied by a high degree of critical consciousness in the use of it. His critical writings give a good view of his creative preoccupations. . . . (pp. 163-65)

Wordsworth's preoccupation was with a distinctively human naturalness, with sanity and spiritual health, and his interest in mountains was subsidiary. His mode of preoccupation, it is true, was that of a mind intent always upon ultimate sanctions, and upon the living connexions between man and the extrahuman universe. . . . (p. 165)

[One] of the most remarkable facts about Wordsworth's poetry is the virtual absence from it of . . . [erotic] associations and suggestions, and it is this absence that Shelley, when he calls Wordsworth 'cold,' is remarking upon. . . . (p. 168)

The absence no doubt constitutes a limitation, a restriction of interest; but it constitutes at the same time an aspect of Wordsworth's importance. (p. 169)

Spontaneity, . . . as Wordsworth seeks it, involves no cult of the instinctive and primitive at the expense of the rationalized and civilized; it is the spontaneity supervening upon complex development, a spontaneity engaging an advanced and delicate organization. He stands for a distinctly human naturalness; one, that is, consummating a discipline, moral and other. A poet who can bring home to us the possibility of such a naturalness should to-day be found important. In Wordsworth's poetry the possibility is offered us realized—realized in a mode central and compelling enough to enforce the bearing of poetry upon life, the significance of this poetry for actual living. The absence both of the specifically sexual in any recognizable form and of any sign of repression serves to emphasize this significance, the significance of this achieved natural-ness, spontaneous, and yet the expression of an order and the product of an emotional and moral training.

No one should, after what has been said, find it necessary to impute to the critic at this point, or to sup-pose him to be applauding in Wordsworth, a puritanic warp. Wordsworth was, on the showing of his poetry and everything else, normally and robustly human. The selectiveness and the habit of decorum involved in 'recollection in tranquillity' were normal and, in a wholly laudatory sense of the word, conventional; that is, so endorsed by common usage as to be natural. The poetic process engaged an organization that had, by his own account, been determined by an upbringing in a congenial social environment, with its wholesome sim-ple pieties and the traditional sanity of its moral cul-ture, which to him were nature. He may have been a 'Romantic,' but it would be misleading to think of him as an individualist. (pp. 170-71)

Wordsworth is often spoken of as a 'mystic,' and the current valuation would appear to rest his greatness largely upon the 'visionary moments' and 'spots of time.' Wordsworth himself undoubtedly valued the 'visionary' element in his experience very highly, and it is important to determine what significance he attri-butes to it. (p. 173)

If these 'moments' have any significance for the critic (whose business it is to define the significance of Wordsworth's poetry), it will be established, not by dwelling upon or in them, in the hope of exploring something that lies hidden in or behind their vague-ness, but by holding firmly on to that sober verse in which they are presented. (p. 174)

Wordsworth's roots were deep in the eighteenth century. To say this is to lay the stress again—where it ought to rest—on his essential sanity and normality.

But though he is so surely and centrally poised, the sureness had nothing of complacency about it. It rests consciously over unsounded depths and among mysteries, itself a mystery. This recognition has its value in the greater validity of the poise—in a kind of sanction resulting. So, too, Wordsworth's firm hold upon the world of common perception is the more no-table in one who knows of 'fallings from us, vanish-ings, blank misgivings' ('when the light of sense goes out'), and is capable of recording such moments as when

> I forgot,
> That I had bodily eyes, and what I saw
> Appear'd like something in myself, a

> dream,
> A prospect in my mind.

> (pp. 174-75)

[It] is now time to qualify the present account of [Wordsworth], as it stands now, by taking note of . . . [opposing criticism]. Does not, for instance, the formu-la, 'recollection in tranquillity,' apply to Wordsworth's poetry with a limiting effect that has as yet not been recognized? Is the tranquillity of this wisdom really at all close to any 'spontaneous overflow of powerful feel-ings'? Are the feelings, as recollected, so very powerful?

It has to be admitted that the present of this poet-ry is, for the most part, decidedly tranquil and that the emotion—anything in the nature of strong excitement or disturbance—seems to belong decidedly to the past. If, as might be said, the strength of the poetry is that it brings maturity and youth into relation, the weak-ness is that the experience from which it draws life is confined mainly to youth, and lies at a distance. What, an intelligent contemporary reader might have asked at the creative period, will happen as youth recedes? What did happen we know, in any case, and the fact of the decline may reasonably be held to have a bearing on the due estimate of Wordsworth's wisdom. (p. 176)

[The description of the Wanderer in *The Excur-sion*] is, fairly obviously, very much in the nature of an idealized self-portrait. If Wordsworth, even when well embarked on *The Excursion,* was not quite this, this clearly is what he would have liked to be. That he should have wished to be this is significant. That he should have needed to wish it is the great difference be-tween himself and the Wanderer. For Wordsworth's course had not been steady; he sought the Wanderer's 'equipoise' just because of the 'piteous revolutions' and the 'wild varieties of joy and grief ' that he had so dis-turbingly known. The Wanderer could not have writ-ten Wordsworth's poetry; it emerges out of Words-worth's urgent personal problem; it is the answer to the question: 'How, in a world that has shown itself to be like this, is it possible to go on living?'

Behind, then, the impersonality of Wordsworth's wisdom there is an immediately personal urgency. Im-pelling him back to childhood and youth—to their re-covery in a present of tranquil seclusion—there are the emotional storms and disasters of the intervening peri-od, and these are also implicitly remembered, if not 're-collected,' in the tranquillity of his best poetry. In so far as his eyes may fairly be said to 'avert their ken from half of human fate,' extremely painful awareness of this half is his excuse. For if his problem was personal, it was not selfishly so, not merely self-regarding; and it is also a general one: if (and how shall they not?) the sensitive and imaginative freely let their 'hearts lie open' to the suffering of the world, how are they to re-tain any health or faith for living? Conflicting duties seem to be imposed (for it is no mere blind instinct of self-preservation that is in question). Wordsworth is not one of the few great tragic artists, but probably not many readers will care to censure him for weakness or cowardice. His heart was far from 'unoccupied by sorrow of its own,' and his sense of responsibility for human distress and his generously active sympathies had involved him in emotional disasters that threatened his hold on life. A disciplined limiting of contemplation to the endurable, and, consequently, a withdrawal to a reassuring environment, became terrible necessities for him.

It is significant that (whatever reason Wordsworth may have had for putting it there) the story of Margaret should also, following, as it does, close upon the description of the Wanderer, appear in Book I of *The Excursion.* It seems to me the finest thing that Wordsworth wrote, and it is certainly the most disturbingly poignant. The poignancy assures us with great force that the Wanderer, for all his familiarity with the Preface to the *Lyrical Ballads,* is not Wordsworth—not, at any rate, the poet. . . . (pp. 178-79)

The difficulty does not merely appear in the poignancy of the poetry, which contrasts so with the surrounding verse; it gets its implicit comment in the by-play between Wordsworth and the Wanderer. At a painful point in the story 'the Wanderer paused' . . . . :

'Why should we thus, with an untoward mind,
And in the weakness of humanity,
From natural wisdom turn our hearts away;
To natural comfort shut our eyes and ears;
And, feeding on disquiet, thus disturb
The calm of nature with our restless thoughts?'

Wordsworth gladly acquiesced:

That simple tale
Passed from my mind like a forgotten
sound.

But it refused to be dismissed; it rose insistently up through the distracting idle talk:

In my own despite
I thought of that poor Woman as of one
Whom I had known and loved.

No doubt the particular memory of Annette asserts itself here, but that recognition (or guess) makes it all the more important to give due weight to the corrective hint thrown out by the Wanderer a little later:

''Tis a common tale,
An ordinary sorrow of man's life . . . '

—Wordsworth at this date cannot easily afford to suffer with those whom he sees suffer.

That is very apparent in the way 'that Woman's

sufferings' (which had 'seemed present') are, at the end of the story, distanced. (pp. 179-80)

[In **"Michael"** Wordsworth] has no need to withdraw his mind from the theme to a present 'image of tranquillity.' The things of which he speaks never 'seem present' in this story; they are seen always as belonging, in their moving dignity, to the past. 'Recollection' holds them at such a distance that serenity, for all the pathos, never falters; and an idealizing process, making subtle use of the mountain background, gives to 'human suffering' a reconciling grandeur. **"Michael,"** of course, is only one poem (and an exceptionally fine one), but the implied representative significance of this comparison with **"Margaret"** is justly implied. When in the characteristic good poetry of Wordsworth painful things are dealt with, we find them presented in modes, more and less subtle, that are fairly intimated by his own phrase (the context of which is very relevant):

Remov'd and to a distance that was fit.

In **"Michael"** Wordsworth is very much more like the Wanderer. What, the contemporary reader already invoked may be imagined as asking, will be the next phase in the development? What will happen as youth, where lie the emotional sources of his poetry—'the hiding-places of my power'—and young manhood, which, in the way suggested, provides the creative pressure and incitement, recede further and further into the past, and the 'equipoise' becomes a settled habit? (pp. 181-82)

The Wordsworth who in the **"Ode to Duty"** spoke of the 'genial sense of youth' as something he happily surrendered had seen the hiding-places of his power close. The 'equipoise' had lost its vitality; the exquisitely fine and sensitive organization of the poet no longer informed and controlled his pen. The energy of the new patriotic moral interests, far from bringing the poet new life, took the place of creative sensibility, and confirmed and ensured its loss.

In fact, the new power belongs, it might be said, not to the 'hiding-places'—it has no connexion with them—but to the public platform (a metaphor applying obviously to the patriotic development, with which, it should be noted, the religious is not accidentally associated): the public voice is a substitute for the inner voice, and engenders an insensitiveness to this—to its remembered (or, at least, to its recorded) burden and tone. For the sentiments and attitudes of the patriotic and Anglican Wordsworth do not come as the intimately and particularly realized experience of an unusually and finely conscious individual; they are external, general and conventional; their quality is that of the medium they are proffered in, which is insensitively Miltonic, a medium not felt into from within as something at the nerve-tips, but handled from outside. This is to question, not their sincerity, but their value and interest; their representativeness is not of the important kind. Their relation to poetry may be gathered from the process to which, at their dictation, Wordsworth subjected *The Prelude:* in the pursuit of formal orthodoxy he freely falsified and blunted the record of experience. (pp. 183-84)

F. R. Leavis, "Wordsworth," in his *Revaluation: Tradition & Development in English Poetry,* Chatto & Windus, 1936, pp. 154-202.

CARL WOODRING

(essay date 1965)

[In the following excerpt, Woodring portrays Wordsworth as a highly influential artist whose greatness lies in his simplicity, iconoclasm, and wide knowledge of meter and form.]

[Wordsworth] grew into the greatest English poet since Milton. Between 1789 and 1847, he had eight formative years, ten stupendous years, nine or ten important years, and thirty years of decent productivity and consolidation. His historical influence on language, ideas, and manners has been immense. Outside of literature, no English artist, whether painter, sculptor, musician, choreographer, or architect, has been more influential. Although he has been translated to little effect—little, that is, relative to a Dante, a Shakespeare, a Bunyan, or a Dostoevsky—his influence on the people who speak or read English has been sufficient to sway art and affairs universally. His indirect effect on Proust, for example, is similar to Rousseau's indirect effect on *him,* and a line of some rectitude could be drawn from Wordsworth through Thoreau to Gandhi.

What Coleridge admired as much as anything else in Wordsworth, and what we shall not do wrong to admire, was the application of a powerful intellect, combined with powerful emotions, toward the solution of the general but immediate problems of man. This application of power is notable even in the **"Memorials of a Tour in Italy, 1837,"** where strength of imagination has flagged. His was no metaphysical intellect, like Coleridge's; it was practical, like Swift's.

Most of all, Wordsworth turned the course of English poetry. As both the Preface and the "lyrical ballads" indicate, he sensed very early the importance of his leadership. Of more than one poem in the volume of 1798 it could be said that he did not invent the form but he invented the idea that it was art. This extension of boundaries has had limitless implications for the nineteenth and twentieth centuries. Alexander Calder was not the first to make a mobile, but he first con-

ceived, for our time, the idea that a continuously changing work could extend the plastic arts. Historical relativism in the judgment of works of art had been introduced in the eighteenth century, but no English artist before Wordsworth, in any medium, had anything like his effect in overthrowing the canons of taste by proclaiming the value of his own independent practice. For English-speaking peoples, only Beethoven had an equivalent effect, and there was no English musician worthy of the lesson. Giving to the word *experiment,* as applied to poetry, a meaning of something more permanent than an impromptu, *esquisse,* improvisation, or *commedia dell' arte all'improvviso,* Wordsworth pioneered in the movement of modern arts that has in fact given stature to improvisation as "something far more deeply interfused" than imitation of the masters.

Coleridge's ultimate commendation of Wordsworth may be put in the terms that a later poet and critic devised for a different purpose: In altering the whole existing order of the poetic past, Wordsworth restored poetry to the wholeness of its tradition after the dissociation of sensibility in Dryden and Pope and the Chinese wall of unfeeling language erected by Pope's followers. In Coleridge's view, Wordsworth brought thought and feeling together in the Elizabethan way after several generations had "thought and felt by fits, unbalanced." That he and Wordsworth disparaged Dryden and Pope unduly goes without saying.

When Coleridge makes a memorandum to write to the author of *The Recluse* "that he may insert something concerning *Ego,* its metaphysical Sublimity and intimte Synthesis with the principle of Co-adunation," we know that Colerdge recognizes Wordsworth's intellectual acumen, but we know also that Wordsworth would blur the edges of the idea and change the language drastically. Wordsworth's poetry is not ultimately simple, but its great historical influence has come from its relative simplicity of surface. In **"Lines Written in Early Spring,"** he presents a characteristic observation that the birds and flowers seem to enjoy the air they breathe:

> And I must think, do all I can,
> That there was pleasure there.

What other poet would have expressed the qualification in terms even as simple as, say, "try as hard as I may"? The phrase "do all I can" has the daring of a child, a Beethoven, or a Wordsworth.

With simplification as his guide, he made everything he assimilated into his own. Like T. S. Eliot, he put borrowed words to many uses, but he created enough memorable phrases of his own to prove his right even to "human form divine," which Blake also thought too universal for Milton to keep to himself.

Egotism aside, Wordsworth's virtues are those of

a prophet rather than of a polymath or a universal man. He is no Michelangelo, and no Goethe. Despite his kinship with Roman moralists, he is a poet of English solitude. Despite his wide knowledge of Italian poetry, he is less like Tasso or Ariosto than he is like Thomson and Beattie—except in the essential of genius. Despite his experiences near the heart of the French Revolution, he turns for guidance to Milton. He toured the Continent in search of images, but his skylarks are as English as his daisies. His view is not even as ample as the British Isles. He tried harder than the average Englishman, in the *Ecclesiastical Sonnets* and similar pieces, to remember the significance of Scotland, Wales, and Ireland for British institutions; but the confluence he honors is that of English throne, English Parliament, English Church, and English tongue.

Thomas Love Peacock was one of the first, but certainly not the last, to notice the absence from Wordsworth's poems of sexual passion. What is omitted from *The Prelude* is all that a diarist like Boswell would put into it. Love, and especially love for his wife, runs through the crevices of the later poetry, but the sexual images usually resemble the virginal dedication to poetry described in *The Prelude:*

> Gently did my soul
> Put off her veil, and, self-transmuted,
> stood
> Naked as in the presence of her
> God. . . .

Arnold's arithmetic was bad. Wordsworth averted his ken from no more than a third of human fate; but his "infernal brightness" told him never to linger over sex, squalor, or spasms of despair merely because the artist can claim a franchise to linger over what exists. Agreeing that an artist should express "all he sees," Wordsworth took the phrase qualitatively rather than quantitatively.

No feminist ever used as handbook *The White Doe of Rylstone.* Although Wordsworth spoke for nationalism, for the sanctity of childhood, and—before the Oxford Movement—for the doctrine of Incarnation above the doctrine of Atonement, it is hard, on our side of Baudelaire, Marx, and Nietzsche, to think of him as iconoclastic. Yet he was iconoclastic, as well as independent and stubborn. He opposed the whole modern megalomania of analysis and measurement. The discoveries of Freud and Einstein would not have shocked him. What he deplored in advance is not the discoveries but the amoral application of them. About amorality he was as stubborn as God.

His poetry has a remarkable range in matter, forms, and artistry. Precision and delicacy do not belong to the Wordsworth of conventional literary history. . . .

Yet William Wordsworth is also that master of brevity and condensation who wrote the Lucy poems, "**The Solitary Reaper,**" and a golden collection of such sonnets as those beginning "**The World Is Too Much with Us,**" "**Earth Has Not Anything to Show More Fair,**" "**Surprised by Joy,**" and "**I Thought of Thee, My Partner and My Guide.**" In my opinion, he earned the very highest rank among the precise artists who have—in Dr. Johnson's contemptuous phrase—carved heads on cherry stones.

Above all, it needs to be said that the many studies to date have left the mysteries of Wordsworth's performance far from exhausted.

All historical judgments are relative. But the absolute accomplishment endures, from his simple songs for thinking hearts to his explorations along the chasms and abysms of normal experience. Day in and day out, he proclaims in hammered verse the thrill of the ordinary. That, in our time, is a rarity indeed. (pp. 211-14)

Carl Woodring, in his *Wordsworth,* Houghton Mifflin Company, 1965, 227 p.

JUDITH W. PAGE
(essay date 1983)

[Here, Page explores the relationship between Wordsworth's lyrical poems and the traditional folk ballad, commenting on the poet's attempt to express complex sentiments through a simple style.]

By the time the first volume of *Lyrical Ballads* was published, both Wordsworth and Coleridge had already thought long and deeply about the renovation of English poetry. The plan that Wordsworth had in mind, and that Coleridge supported in lieu of his own career as an English poet, would involve major changes in the way people thought and felt. Wordsworth's program was one for *poetry*—not for the poet's progression through established genres or merely for the purification of language. In the minds of Wordsworth and Coleridge, the *Lyrical Ballads* marked only the beginning of an entire plan to change the course of English poetry, a program that would necessarily involve the poet, the poem, and the processes of thinking, composing, and reading. Because of the cultural and historical changes of the eighteenth century—the "accumulation of men in cities," the growth of "rapid communication," and the degeneration of poetry into sources of "outrageous stimulation"—Wordsworth felt the need for a program designed to awaken the minds of Englishmen from "a state of almost savage torpor."

In the *Lyrical Ballads* Wordsworth defies notions of propriety in order to jar his readers into thinking in fresh ways about passionate subjects and about literary decorum or its absence. Wordsworth presents his volume as a challenge to the mental and imaginative powers of his readers: to appreciate the poems, they must respond not only to the emotions dramatized but also to the ironies that arise from subtleties of style. If Blake's *Songs of Innocence and of Experience* had enjoyed a wider audience in the 1790s, perhaps Wordsworth's readers would have been more prepared for the 1798 volume. Both Blake and Wordsworth use simple forms but demand complex, sophisticated responses from readers.

We can best appreciate the sophistication of the *Lyrical Ballads* by viewing Wordsworth's experiment in the context of the folk ballad. The best-known collection of folk balladry in the late eighteenth century was Percy's *Reliques of Ancient English Poetry.* Despite Percy's "restorations" of decayed or otherwise fragmented manuscripts, many of the ballads are considered to be fairly authentic versions of oral tales. A reader of Percy's *Reliques* would be familiar with the basic formal characteristics of the genre: impersonal narration, formulaic diction, compression of events, stanzaic symmetry, parallelism, and repetition. Oral poetry requires these formal features of regularity in order for the listener to grasp the story. As C. S. Lewis explains in regard to the Homeric epic, "It is the prime necessity of oral poetry that the hearers should not be surprised too often or too much. The unexpected tires us: it also takes us longer to understand and enjoy than the expected."

This need for regularity often means that in the course of a recitation the balladeer will alter the natural stress patterns of words in order to maintain the metrical pattern as a constant. The folk ballad is therefore unlike written poetry, since in a written poem we assign an expressive meaning to the non-coincidence of linguistic stress and metrical patterning. Ballad rhythms have more kinship with the strong, insistent rhythms of nursery rhymes or chants than with the traditional literary verse designs. (pp. 293-95)

In ballads like the Matthew and Lucy poems Wordsworth plays off the generally easy stanzaic rhythms against more complex sentiments, so that the resulting incongruity widens the disjunction between the perspectives of youth and age, nature and human nature. These ballads, written or contemplated during the cold and alien winter of 1798-99 when Wordsworth was in Germany, represent a personal consciousness reflecting on past and present experiences. In order to capture the nuances of thought and shifts in emotion, Wordsworth uses specific kinds of stylistic variation or "foregrounding," even within the generally regular form of the ballad stanza.

As written texts, the *Lyrical Ballads* must depend on specific stylistic features designed to heighten or temper a reading. In contrast, when the folk ballad reaches print in a collection like Percy's *Reliques,* the stress patterns of words are often slanted in order to promote rhythmical regularity: the word "country," in the ballads, for instance, often falls in an unstressed-stressed position as "countrèe," with the accent mark signalling readers to invert the natural stress contours of the word. But a literary artist like Wordsworth must depend more on the element of surprise that arises from stylistic variation which occurs when language and meter do not coincide. As Wordsworth implies in the Preface, these impulses of surprise hold the reader's attention and make the reading more pleasurable, exciting, and challenging.

"The Two April Mornings" begins as a confidently merry ballad, with numerous words ("bright," "glittering," "blithe") linked by positive emotional associations and smooth assonance:

> We walked along, while bright and red
> Uprose the morning sun;
> And Matthew stopped, he looked, and said,
> "The will of God be done!"
>
> A village schoolmaster was he,
> With hair of glittering gray;
> As blithe a man as you could see
> On a spring holiday.
>
> And on that morning, through the grass,
> And by the streaming rills,
> We travelled merrily to pass
> A day among the hills.

The only real stylistic tension occurs in line 5, with "schoolmaster" placed in a stressed-unstressed-stressed position which causes a disruption of the jaunty rhythm. Perhaps the interrupted flow of the line is meant to anticipate our discovery of the incongruity and uneasiness of Matthew's life. When Matthew begins to speak, he explains to the narrator his sudden melancholy. The image of the cloud with a "long purple cleft" reminds Matthew of a day thirty years earlier, when

> With rod and line I sued the sport
> Which that sweet season gave,
> And, to the churchyard come, stopped short
> Beside my daughter's grave.

(29-32)

Line 31 makes a notable rhythmic change from the light, fairly regular lines: five successive strong stresses, a rare grouping in English verse—"churchyard come, stopped short"—halt the flow.

Matthew's painful recollection, in the form of an emphatic image, "Six feet in earth my Emma lay," comes as a surprise to the reader who had assumed "The Two April Mornings" would be a cheerful ballad. Yet another surprise occurs when Matthew relates that he had seen another "blooming Girl" but "did not wish her mine." By recognizing that no one can substitute for his dead child, Matthew rejects any easy consolation. The poem simply ends with the narrator's recollection that

> Matthew is in his grave, yet now,
> Methinks, I see him stand,
> As at that moment, with a bough
> Of wilding in his hand.
>
> (57-60)

Wordsworth frustrates the associations that we have with "lighter compositions," where "the ease and gracefulness with which the poet manages his numbers are themselves confessedly a principal source of gratification to the Reader." With rhymes such as "rills" and "hills," the gaiety of the form is like the surface that Matthew presents to the world. But the reader must see beneath the surface and between the lines in order to find, as the narrator presumably does, a sorrowful tale in the image of Matthew standing "at that moment" over his daughter's grave.

The temporal dimensions included in **"The Two April Mornings,"** time within time and memory within memory, imply the whole span of Matthew's life, as well as the narrator's development from merry youth to meditative poet. The poem begins with a past-tense narration. In the third stanza, a present-tense dialogue begins, but the discussion itself arises because Matthew remembers the earlier April morning. From stanzas 6-14 Matthew becomes the narrator of the ballad, and his recollection becomes the ballad tale. Within Matthew's narration, we learn that on the earlier morning Matthew's meditation by Emma's grave had brought back the memory of those "nine summers" of Emma's life. Since Matthew's memories on the present morning include his memories on the earlier one, he literally remembers himself remembering. With the final stanza we share the narrator's vision as he writes "now" of Matthew "at that moment." (pp. 300-02)

[The] sense of time and change in **"The Two April Mornings"** derives from the narrator's recollection of the personal history of a friend. Because Wordsworth is interested in the processes of development, he frames his ballad in a way that dramatizes the interplay between past recollections and present thoughts. The oral balladeer has a much more static sense of time: his shifts in perspective from one character or group to another do not allow for insight into individual development. (p. 302)

In [the] Matthew poems we have to read against the naive, youthful expectations established by the form in order to feel by contrast the impact of Matthew's sentiments. The incongruity between form and content helps to draw the contrast between the perspectives of innocence and experience and between conventional and unexpected sentiments, such as Matthew's mourning "less for what age takes away / Than what it leaves behind." Likewise, in the Lucy group the difficulty of the poems is actually intensified by the apparent easiness of the form.

In comparison to the technique of the other Lucy poems, **"Strange Fits of Passion"** relies on frequent rhythmical variation for its emotional impact. The emotional tension felt in **"Strange Fits"** stems from the speaker's unconscious association of Lucy with the sinking moon as he travels toward her cottage. Although the link between the moon and Lucy is never made explicitly, the progression and symmetry of each stanza after the second imply the parallel, as does the etymological link between Lucy and light:

> Strange fits of passion have I known:
> And I will dare tell,
> But in the Lover's ear alone,
> What once to me befell.
>
> When she I loved looked every day
> Fresh as a rose in June,
> I to her cottage bent my way
> Beneath an evening moon.
>
> Upon the moon I fixed my eye,
> All over the wide lea;
> With quickening pace my horse drew nigh
> Those paths so dear to me.
>
> And now we reached the orchard-plot;
> And as we climbed the hill,
> The sinking moon to Lucy's cot
> Came near, and nearer still.
>
> In one of those sweet dreams I slept,
> Kind Nature's gentlest boon!
> And all the while my eyes I kept
> On the descending moon.
>
> My horse moved on; hoof after hoof
> He raised, and never stopped:
> When down behind the cottage roof,
> At once the bright moon dropped.
>
> What fond and wayward thoughts will slide
> Into a lover's head!
> "O mercy!" to myself I cried,
> "If Lucy should be dead!"

From the beginning the moon encompasses all space, literally filling the lover's mind and environment: "Upon the moon I fixed my eye, / All over the wide lea." With the actual journey becoming metaphorical, the poem dramatizes the tension in the lover's mind between the image of inevitable loss, the sinking moon, and his desire for a living girl who is "Fresh as a rose in June." This traditional image represents the poet's yearning for a world in which lovers do remain as fresh as roses in June and bright moons do not sink.

The lover's uneasiness surfaces in the rhythmical patterning of line 11: "With quickening pace my horse drew nigh / Those paths so dear to me." While the first part of line 11 imitates the hurried pace through metrical regularity and elision ("quick'ning"), three successive strong stresses in the second half of the line ("horse drew nigh") slow it down. This tension may express the conflict between the association of Lucy with the "sinking Moon" (15), in which case the speaker would want to avoid facing death and loss, and the natural impulse to hurry to his lover's cottage. The tension only increases when the moon suddenly drops. The "At once," isolated at the beginning of line 24, marks the sudden flash in the speaker's mind, while the emphatic monosyllabic cluster "bright moon dropped" firmly implants the image in his memory. The last two lines, "O mercy!" to myself I cried, / "If Lucy should be dead!" are the spontaneous thoughts—grammatically incomplete because the speaker does not want to face the symbolic associations of the moon's disappearance.

Trying to regain the tranquillity lost in the tension of reliving the experience, the speaker as poet and lover had wanted to undercut his fear and ease the burden of memory by naming the utterance a "fond and wayward thought," a strange fit of passion. While writing the poem he has made conscious associations and now acts with the human impulse of denying the symbolic meaning. He tries to protect himself emotionally by saying, in effect, that Lucy will not die. The reader, the audience of lovers created by the poet-lover, is also left with a feeling of having had strange fits of passion. (pp. 303-05)

Despite Wordsworth's transformations of the folk ballad, the form has limited possibilities. As Wordsworth discovers in **"Tintern Abbey,"** one of the "other poems" included at the last minute in the 1798 volume, blank verse is a much more flexible medium for a meditative poet. Even in his earliest experiments with blank verse, Wordsworth expresses varied moods and captures nuances of thought and feeling. The relatively crude way in which a poem like **"The Idiot Boy"** or *Peter Bell* traces the fluxes and refluxes of the mind proves inadequate for the deeper meditations "On Man, Nature, and on Human Life" that Wordsworth was contemplating for the *Recluse* project. Sustained insights into the processes of the human mind in its various phases require a form more plastic than the stanzaic form used to illustrate the limited thoughts of Betty Foy or Peter Bell.

Ballads like the Lucy poems—ballads striving to become literary lyrics—also have limitations. Wordsworth learns from these poems ways in which the surface simplicity of a traditional form runs counter to an undercurrent of complex thought. This tension between surface and conception is characteristic of Wordsworth's best sonnets. But in the spring of 1802, when Wordsworth begins experimenting widely with forms of the lyric in addition to the sonnet, he discovers the potential of other combinations of mode and style. This discovery leads to such triumphs as the Chaucerian-Spenserian form of **"Resolution and Independence"** and the highly original variations of the **"Intimations"** Ode.

We must remember, too, that the *Lyrical Ballads* were designed not merely as stylistic exercises but were also experiments in literary taste. Assuming at least a limited success with a "fit audience" in 1798, Wordsworth begins to think more in terms of establishing a sense of decorum guided by traditional models and by insight into the psychological and expressive potential of different modes. This desire for a new decorum is reflected in the transformation of **"Michael"** from a crude ballad into a poem in which dignified blank verse elevates a simple rustic into a hero of biblical stature. For Wordsworth, the decorum of a particular mode, whether epic, ode, or pastoral, cannot be established a priori: it must be affirmed and reaffirmed with each production.

Wordsworth's program to change the structure of English poetry made all-encompassing demands on poet and reader. Such a program resulted from the conviction, shared by Wordsworth, Coleridge, and Blake in the 1790s, that poetry could reform the world by awakening the mind. Coleridge left the task to Wordsworth, who gave it up and became hardened by the time he wrote the 1815 Preface; but Blake went on in the face of neglect and disappointment. And yet, despite what Wordsworth saw as neglect of *his* genius, the plan begun with the *Lyrical Ballads* did change English poetry by laying the foundations for more flexible notions of decorum, for innovative approaches to poetic language and rhythm, and for a revaluation of the reader's role in the entire enterprise. (pp. 309-10)

Judith W. Page, "Style and Rhetorical Intention in Wordsworth's 'Lyrical Ballads'," in *Philological Quarterly,* Vol. 62, No. 3, Summer, 1983, pp. 293-313.

SOURCES FOR FURTHER STUDY

Abrams, M. H., ed. *Wordsworth: A Collection of Critical Essays.* Englewood Cliffs, N. J.: Prentice-Hall, 1972, 214 p.

> Collection of essays on Wordsworth's style, the early poems, *The Prelude,* and the later poems. Represented are such critics as David Ferry, Stephen Maxfield Parrish, Paul de Man, and John Jones.

Cowell, Raymond, ed. *Critics on Wordsworth.* Readings in Literary Criticism, no. 12. London: George Allen and Unwin, 1973, 114 p.

> Selection of Wordsworth criticism from the nineteenth and twentieth centuries. Included are pieces by such commentators as Henry Crabb Robinson, Thomas Love Peacock, William Minto, Salvador de Madariaga, and Albert S. Gérard.

Davis, Jack, ed. *Discussions of William Wordsworth.* Discussions of Literature. Boston: D. C. Heath, 1964, 178 p.

> Important collection of critical essays, including pieces by Coleridge, M. H. Abrams, F. R. Leavis, and Paul Goodman.

Jones, Alun R., and Tydeman, William, eds. *Wordsworth: "Lyrical Ballads," A Casebook.* Casebook Series, edited by A. E. Dyson. London: Macmillan, 1972, 253 p.

> Comprises key nineteenth- and twentieth-century essays on the *Lyrical Ballads,* a critical bibliography, and tables of contents from the 1798 and the 1800 editions of the work.

Logan, James V. *Wordsworthian Criticism: A Guide and Bibliography.* Columbus: Ohio State University Press, 1961, 316 p.

> Guide to Wordsworth criticism, arranged by date and topic. Each chapter discusses a segment of Wordsworth criticism, ranging from the early periodical reviews to 1944.

Moorman, Mary. *William Wordsworth, A Biography: The Early Years, 1770-1803.* Rev. ed. Oxford: Clarendon Press, 1965, 632 p.; and *William Wordsworth, A Biography: The Later Years, 1803-1850.* Rev. ed. Oxford: Clarendon Press, 1966, 632 p.

> Two-part study that is considered the standard modern biography of Wordsworth.

Richard Wright

1908-1960

American novelist, autobiographer, short story writer, nonfiction writer, essayist, scriptwriter, dramatist, poet, and editor.

INTRODUCTION

A seminal figure in black literature, Wright has been called one of the most powerful and influential writers of twentieth-century America. He was one of the first writers to portray—often in graphic, brutal accounts—the dehumanizing effects of racism on blacks. His stories usually center on alienated and impoverished black men who, denied freedom and personal identity, lash out against society. Scholars have hailed *Native Son* (1940) and *Black Boy: A Record of Childhood and Youth* (1945) as Wright's most accomplished works. Critic Irving Howe declared: "The day *Native Son* appeared, American culture was changed forever." Of *Black Boy*, another reviewer simply announced: "[This] is a masterpiece." Although some critics fault the works as too violent and unabashedly propagandistic, such prominent writers as James Baldwin and Ralph Ellison consider them essential works of black literature. "Wright's stories of helpless or long-suffering blacks victimized by societal and individual white brutality mark the beginning of a new era in black fiction," William Peden observed, "and even his least important pieces contain unforgettable scenes and characters that burn their way into the reader's consciousness."

Wright's childhood was harsh and filled with fear. He was born on a plantation near Natchez, Mississippi, in 1908. His mother was a former schoolteacher and his father a sharecropper who drank heavily. When Wright was six years old, his father abandoned the family, forcing his mother to work as a cook for a white family. Life in the South was difficult, and Wright and his younger brother Leon frequently went without food. In his autobiography, *Black Boy*, Wright recalled a familiar childhood event: "I would feel hunger nudging my ribs, twisting my empty guts until they ached. I would grow dizzy and my vision would dim." Wright's first indelible encounter with racial hatred and violence occurred during the family's brief stay with an uncle, who was murdered by a group of white men trying to seize his property. Fearing for their own lives, the Wrights fled to West Helena, Arkansas; young Wright was about eight or nine years old. They eventually returned to Mississippi, but Wright went to live with his grandmother when his mother became ill. Grandmother Wilson was a religious Seventh-Day Adventist, and she forced Wright to pray and attend church so that his soul might be saved. While under the pretense of praying in his room, he wrote his first story when he was twelve or thirteen years old. Later, in *Black Boy,* he described the excitement and pride he felt: "There was no plot, no action, nothing save atmosphere and longing and death. But I had never in my life done anything like it; I had made something, no matter how bad it was; and it was mine. . . . "

Wright was largely self-educated. His formal schooling, frequently interrupted as he moved from town to town, ended when he was seventeen. Thereafter, he read widely, beginning with H. L. Mencken, whose books he obtained from a "whites only" public library by forging a note: "Dear Madam: Will you please let this niggor boy have some books by H. L. Mencken?" Wright was strongly affected by Mencken, whose trenchant language and outspoken critical opinions awakened him to the possibility of social protest through writing. He also read the fiction of Fyodor Dostoyevsky, Sinclair Lewis, Sherwood Anderson, and Theodore Dreiser. In 1927 Wright left the South for Chicago. He worked at various menial jobs, all the while reading and writing extensively. During the Depression he joined the WPA Writers' Project and became active in the Communist Party, contributing articles, poems, and short stories to various communist newspapers. Several years later, however, Wright found himself repelled by the narrowness and rigidity of his fellow communists, whose minds he found "sealed against new ideas, new facts, new feelings, new attitudes, new hints at ways to live. They denounced books they could never understand, and doctrines they could not pronounce." In 1944, after witnessing the trial of a party member for ideological "deviationism," Wright resigned from the party.

Until 1938, Wright's work appeared only in left-wing publications such as *New Masses* and *Left Front.* In that year, *Story* magazine offered a $500 prize for the best book-length manuscript by a writer connected with the Federal Writers' Project. Wright's collection of four long stories inspired by the life of a black communist he had known in Chicago won the contest and was published as *Uncle Tom's Children: Four Novellas* (1938). Malcolm Cowley found the book "heartening, as evidence of a vigorous new talent, and terrifying as the expression of a racial hatred that has never ceased to grow and gets no chance to die." All of the stories (a fifth, "Bright and Morning Star," was added to subsequent editions) deal with the oppression of black people in the South, of the violence of whites against blacks, and the violence to which the black characters are driven by their victimization. Some critics found the stories in *Uncle Tom's Children* too melodramatic and marred by the infusion of Communist ideology. But Houston A. Baker, in his *Black Literature in America,* wrote: "Wright showed a mastery of style and a dramatic sense far superior to that of most of his black contemporaries and predecessors and on a par with that of his most talented white contemporaries. The violence and the terrible effects of prejudice are perhaps nowhere more skillfully set forth."

Although *Uncle Tom's Children* was well received, Wright was dissatisfied with the public's response. He realized, he wrote later, "that I had written a book which even bankers' daughters could read and weep over and feel good. I swore to myself that if I ever wrote another book, no one would weep over it; that it would be so hard and deep that they would have to face it without the consolation of tears." The book he wrote next was *Native Son,* the story of Bigger Thomas, a young black man in Chicago who accidentally murders a white woman and is condemned to death. To depict the dehumanization of blacks in the "hard and deep" manner he wished, Wright avoided making his protagonist a sympathetic character. As reviewer Margaret Marshall wrote in the *Nation:* "Mr. Wright has chosen for his 'hero,' not a sophisticated Negro who at least understands his predicament and can adapt himself to it, but a 'bad nigger,' a 'black ape,' who is only dimly aware of his extra-human status and therefore completely at the mercy of the impulses it generates. . . . Mr. Wright has laid bare, with a ruthlessness that spares neither race, the lower depths of the human and social relationship of blacks and whites. . . . It is not pleasant to feel at the end that one is an accessory to the crimes of Bigger Thomas; but that feeling is impressive evidence of the power of Mr. Wright's indictment with its cutting and accurate title of 'Native Son.' "

Bigger Thomas is a young, petty thief who is hired as a chauffeur by a rich white man. He drives his employer's daughter, Mary, to a political lecture. He meets Mary's friend Jan, a white communist who insists on treating Bigger as an equal. But Bigger interprets Jan's "kindness" as mockery: "Were they making fun of him? What was it that they wanted? . . . He was very conscious of his black skin and there was in him a prodding conviction that Jan and men like him had made it so that he would be conscious of that black skin. Did not white people despise black skin? Then why was Jan doing this?" Bigger drives Mary and Jan, at their insistence, to Ernie's Kitchen Shack, "one of those places where colored people eat." At the restaurant, Mary gets drunk; Bigger takes her home and carries her to her room. When Mary's blind mother enters the bedroom, Bigger accidentally smothers Mary while trying to keep her from revealing his presence. He burns Mary's body in a furnace, then conceives a scheme to extort money from her parents by pretending to have kidnapped her. When Mary's charred bones are discovered, Bigger kills his girlfriend, Bessie, who was his accomplice in the kidnap plot. He is captured by the police and, despite an eloquent defense by his communist lawyer, convicted and condemned. The lawyer argues that Bigger cannot be held responsible for his crimes, that the greater guilt lies with the society that would not accept him as a full human being and so drove him to his brutal acts. Bigger feels that he has at last found a measure of freedom in the act of murder: for the first time in his life, he feels truly alive and unafraid.

James Baldwin, who began his writing career as Wright's protégé, called *Native Son* "the most powerful and celebrated statement we have yet had of what it means to be a Negro in America." But he also criticized Wright for stereotyping Bigger Thomas and for failing to convey a sense of "group reality" in *Native Son:* "Bigger has no discernible relationship to himself, to his own life, to his own people, nor to any other people. . . . It is remarkable that, though we follow him step by step from the tenement room to the death cells, we know as little about him when this journey is ended as we did when it began. . . . What is missing in this situation and in the representation of his psychology . . . is any revelatory apprehension of Bigger as one of the Negro's realities or as one of the Negro's roles. This failure is part of the . . . failure to convey any sense of Negro life as a continuing and complex group reality." Darryl Pinckney, in the *Village Voice,* argued otherwise: "*Native Son* is unmatched in its power. The rage, the human misery, seizes the mind and there is no relief. It is not true, as Baldwin claims, that Bigger Thomas, the doomed, frustrated black boy, is just another stereotype. . . . Baldwin criticizes Wright for not giving us black life, black community, the sense of shared experience. . . . It is wrong to read this novel as a matter of group reality, a matter of race. Bigger had no real relations with other blacks. Everyone was an enemy. . . . [Wright] claimed he valued the 'state of abandonment, aloneness.' In this he was, finally, a true product of Western culture. . . . In *Native Son* he gave us a lasting record of the howl of modern man."

As popular and acclaimed as *Native Son* is, it is *Black Boy* that has garnered critics' highest praise. *Black Boy* has been called a masterpiece. A work structured in many ways like a novel, the book recounts Wright's experiences as a youth in the South. "In scene after scene," noted Morris Dickstein in *Gates of Eden,* "Wright represents his younger self as a rebellious misfit. . . . He makes an intense effort of self-restraint, but try as he will there is always a provocative hint of pride and self-respect, a touch of the uppity nigger about him. A latecomer to the white world, he is unable to quite master the shuffling, degraded, but apparently contented manner that will tell whites he not only knows his place but loves it." Ralph Ellison described *Black Boy* thus: "Imagine Bigger Thomas projecting his own life in lucid prose, guided, say, by the insights of Marx and Freud, and you have an idea of this autobiography." In this work, Wright attacks both white oppression and the predatory nature of members of his own race. He rebukes his strict religious upbringing and reprimands blacks for their servile response to racial subjugation. While some reviewers contended that *Black Boy* offered a bleak, one-sided view of black life in the South, Raymond Kennedy argued otherwise: "This, with few exceptions, is precisely how race relations are in the Southern States: clean-cut black and white. The Negroes must either surrender and allow themselves to be spiritually stunted and deformed, or they must get out of the South."

After the commercial success of *Native Son* and *Black Boy,* Wright moved with his second wife and daughter to Paris, France, in 1947. Here, he found refuge from the racial tensions of the United States and became friends with several noted intellectuals, including Simone de Beauvoir, Jean-Paul Sartre, and Albert Camus. Wright's literary output during this period, including the novels *The Outsider* (1953), *Savage Holiday* (1954), and *The Long Dream* (1958), is generally considered inferior to his earlier achievements. Many critics attribute Wright's creative decline to his newfound interest in existentialism, which they believe stripped his work of its urgency and power. Gloria Bramwell declared: "Wright, an emotional writer, could paint a stunning picture of the Negro's plight but when he attempted to intellectualize it he embraced it from the wrong angle, from the inside out rather than in terms of his own characters." *The Outsider,* the first novel Wright produced after leaving the United States, is one of the first existentialist novels written by an American author. Avoiding racial issues in this work, Wright recounted the story of a man who joins the Communist Party and kills several of its members in his search for identity and meaning. Critics generally dismiss *The Outsider* as an ambitious but unsuccessful work. Wright's next novel, *Savage Holiday,* is a psychological thriller about a white insurance salesman who becomes a symbol for modern alienated humanity. Few critics reviewed this book, and those who did deemed it Wright's least effective work. Wright followed *Savage Holiday* with *The Long Dream,* a novel that returns to his early thematic concerns. Set in Mississippi, this work depicts the psychological growth of Fishbelly, a middle-class black youth who must come to terms with his father's amoral business practices and the racial conflicts ravaging the South.

After serving a prison sentence for a crime he did not commit, Fishbelly leaves for France, fleeing the violence and oppression of his past. Like Wright's other expatriate novels, *The Long Dream* received unfavorable notices from reviewers, many of whom argued that Wright had lost touch with the black American experience. *Eight Men* (1961), a posthumously published collection of short stories, contains "The Man Who Lived Underground," which is often regarded as Wright's most important fictional work of the 1950s. Reminiscent of Dostoyevsky's *Notes from the Underground*, this story concerns a black man who attempts to escape punishment for a crime of which he is innocent by hiding in the city sewer system.

In addition to his novels and short stories, Wright produced several nonfiction works: *12 Million Black Voices: A Folk History of the Negro in the United States* (1941), a textual and photographic history of racial prejudice in the United States; *Black Power: A Record of Reactions in a Land of Pathos* (1954), a work that recalls Wright's visit to Takoradi, a British colony in Africa where a black man had been appointed prime minister; and *The Color Curtain: A Report on the Bandung Conference* (1956), Wright's reflections on a conference held in Indonesia by the free nations of the Third World. *Pagan Spain* (1957) recounts Wright's bitterness over the poverty and corruption he observed while traveling in Spain, and *White Man, Listen!* (1957) contains four lectures by Wright on race relations. Wright died in Paris at the age of fifty-two on November 28, 1960.

Wright's reputation ebbed during the 1950s as younger black writers such as James Baldwin and Ralph Ellison gained in popularity. But in the 1960s, with the growth of the militant black consciousness movement, there was a resurgence of interest in Wright's work. Wright's place in American literature remains controversial: some contend that his writing is of sociological and historical, rather than literary, interest. In the judgment of many critics, however, Wright remains the most influential black protest writer in America. According to Ellison, Wright "converted the American Negro impulse toward self-annihilation and 'going-underground' into a will to confront the world, to evaluate his experience honestly and throw his findings unashamedly into the guilty conscience of America."

(For further information about Wright's life and works, see *Black Literature Criticism; Black Writers; Contemporary Authors*, Vol. 108; *Contemporary Literary Criticism*, Vols. 1, 3, 4, 9, 14, 21, 48; *Dictionary of Literary Biography Documentary Series*, Vol. 2; and *Short Story Criticism*, Vol. 2.)

CRITICAL COMMENTARY

RICHARD WRIGHT

(letter date 1938)

[The following letter was written by Wright in 1938 to his literary agent, Paul Revere Reynolds, in New York City. Here, Wright discusses contract negotiations for *Native Son*.]

My dear Mr. Reynolds:

A faulty phone connection no doubt made it difficult for us to hear each other Saturday, so I'm sketching the facts about the novel in a letter.

As I said, the first draft of the book is done, amounting to now some 576 pages. When it is finished, it will be somewhat less. I took this first draft to Mr. Whit Burnett of Story Press (you remember that my book is being printed under the double imprint of Harper' and Story Press?). Mr. Burnett read it and passed it on to Harper's. When I submitted the script I told them that it was not finished. My main object in letting them see it in its present condition was to ask for an advance. Both Story Press and Harper's seem to like the book, and Mr. Edward Aswell, the editor at Harper's said that he would be willing to sign a contract for it. As for an advance, he suggested $250 and asked me if I thought that ample. I did not give him any definite answer, but told him I would let you talk to him about it.

I have reason to believe that they like what I'm doing, so I think that perhaps a little more than $250 can be gotten. If, however, they balk, I'm willing to take whatever you can get as an advance from them.

I have found no satisfactory title for the book as yet. The title at present is *Native Son*, I'm going to try to find a more colorful one before the book is published. Meanwhile, Story Press will try to find an appropriate one also.

I shall keep in mind the idea of making at least

Principal Works

Uncle Tom's Children: Four Novellas (short stories) 1938; also published as Uncle Tom's Children: Five Long Stories [enlarged edition], 1940

*Native Son (novel) 1940

"How Bigger Was Born" (essay) 1940; published in periodical The Saturday Review of Literature

12 Million Black Voices: A Folk History of the Negro in the United States (nonfiction) 1941

Black Boy: A Record of Childhood and Youth (autobiography) 1945

The Outsider (novel) 1953

Black Power: A Record of Reactions in a Land of Pathos (nonfiction) 1954

Savage Holiday (novel) 1954

The Color Curtain: A Report on the Bandung Conference (nonfiction) 1956

Pagan Spain (nonfiction) 1957

White Man, Listen! (lectures) 1957

The Long Dream (novel) 1958

†Eight Men (short stories) 1961

Lawd Today (novel) 1963

Daddy Goodness [with Louis Sapin] (drama) 1968

American Hunger (autobiography) 1977

The Richard Wright Reader (essays, novel excerpts, letters, and poetry) 1978

‡Richard Wright: Works. 2 vols. [edited by Arnold Rampersad] (novels, essays, and autobiography) 1991

*This work was adapted for the stage in 1941 and made into a movie in 1951, with Wright in the role of Bigger Thomas, and again in 1986.

†This work contains "The Man Who Lived Underground," Wright's most acclaimed short story.

‡Vols. 55 and 56 of "Library of America." Includes restored texts of Native Son, Lawd Today, and The Outsider, incorporating passages deleted or altered at time of first publication.

---

three copies of the book, so that you may have one to send to the movie people and to England.

Mr. Aswell wants the book for spring publication. I'm going to try as hard as possible to have it ready by then. He understands, however, that if I cannot have it ready by spring, I'll have it ready for early fall.

I hope that this is enough information for you in your dealings with Harper's. If not, if you drop me a line at the above address, I shall be more than glad to come in and discuss it further.

> Sincerely yours,
> Richard Wright

Richard Wright, in a letter to Paul Revere Reynolds on October 23, 1938, in *Dictionary of Literary Biography Documentary Series, Vol. 2,* edited by Margaret A. Van Antwerp, Gale Research Company, 1982, p. 401.

RICHARD WRIGHT

(essay date 1940)

[The following excerpt is from an essay that originally appeared in *The Saturday Review of Literature* in 1940. Here, Wright reveals his inspiration for Bigger Thomas and discusses his initial reluctance and fear in publishing *Native Son.*]

I am not so pretentious as to imagine that it is possible for me to account completely for my own book, *Native Son.* But I am going to try to account for as much of it as I can, the sources of it, the material that went into it, and my own years' long changing attitude toward that material. (p. vii)

The birth of Bigger Thomas goes back to my childhood, and there was not just one Bigger, but many of them, more than I could count and more than you suspect. But let me start with the first Bigger, whom I shall call Bigger No. 1.

When I was a bareheaded, barefoot kid in Jackson, Mississippi, there was a boy who terrorized me and all of the boys I played with. If we were playing games, he would saunter up and snatch from us our balls, bats, spinning tops, and marbles. We would stand around pouting, sniffling, trying to keep back our tears, begging for our playthings. But Bigger would refuse. We never demanded that he give them back; we were afraid, and Bigger was bad. We had seen him clout boys when he was angry and we did not want to run that risk. We never recovered our toys unless we flattered him and made him feel that he was superior to us. Then, perhaps, if he felt like it, he condescended, threw them at us and then gave each of us a swift kick in the bargain, just to make us feel his utter contempt.

That was the way Bigger No. 1 lived. His life was a continuous challenge to others. At all times he *took* his way, right or wrong, and those who contradicted him had him to fight. And never was he happier than when he had someone cornered and at his mercy; it seemed that the deepest meaning of his squalid life was in him at such times.

I don't know what the fate of Bigger No. 1 was. . . . But I suspect that his end was violent. Anyway, he left a marked impression upon me; maybe it was because I longed secretly to be like him and was afraid. I don't know.

If I had known only one Bigger I would not have written *Native Son*. Let me call the next one Bigger No. 2; he was about seventeen and tougher than the first Bigger. Since I, too, had grown older, I was a little less afraid of him. And the hardness of this Bigger No. 2 was not directed toward me or the other Negroes, but toward the whites who ruled the South. He bought clothes and food on credit and would not pay for them. He lived in the dingy shacks of the white landlords and refused to pay rent. Of course, he had no money, but neither did we. We did without the necessities of life and starved ourselves, but he never would. When we asked him why he acted as he did, he would tell us (as though we were little children in a kindergarten) that the white folks had everything and he had nothing. Further, he would tell us that we were fools not to get

Dust jacket of Wright's non-fiction work, a "folk history of Negro Americans."

what we wanted while we were alive in this world. We would listen and silently agree. We longed to believe and act as he did, but we were afraid. . . . Bigger No. 2 wanted to live and he did; he was in prison the last time I heard from him.

There was Bigger No. 3, whom the white folks called a "bad nigger." He carried his life in his hands in a literal fashion. I once worked as a ticket-taker in a Negro movie house . . . and many times Bigger No. 3 came to the door and gave my arm a hard pinch and walked into the theater. Resentfully and silently, I'd nurse my bruised arm. Presently, the proprietor would come over and ask how things were going. I'd point into the darkened theater and say: "Bigger's in there." "Did he pay?" the proprietor would ask. "No, sir," I'd answer. The proprietor would pull down the corners of his lips and speak through his teeth: "We'll kill that goddamn nigger one of these days." And the episode would end right there. But later on Bigger No. 3 was killed during the days of Prohibition: while delivering liquor to a customer he was shot through the back by a white cop.

And then there was Bigger No. 4, whose only law was death. The Jim Crow laws of the South were not for him. But as he laughed and cursed and broke them, he knew that some day he'd have to pay for his freedom. His rebellious spirit made him violate all the taboos and consequently he always oscillated between moods of intense elation and depression. . . . He had no job, for he regarded digging ditches for fifty cents a day as slavery. "I can't live on that," he would say. Ofttimes I'd find him reading a book; he would stop and in a joking, wistful, and cynical manner ape the antics of the white folks. Generally, he'd end his mimicry in a depressed state and say: "The white folks won't let us do nothing." Bigger No. 4 was sent to the asylum for the insane.

Then there was Bigger No. 5, who always rode the Jim Crow streetcars without paying and sat wherever he pleased. I remember one morning his getting into a streetcar . . . and sitting in the white section. The conductor went to him and said: "Come on, nigger. Move over where you belong. Can't you read?" Bigger answered: "Naw, I can't read." The conductor flared up: "Get out of that seat!" Bigger took out his knife, opened it, held it nonchalantly in his hand, and replied: "Make me." The conductor turned red, blinked, clenched his fists, and walked away, stammering: "The goddamn scum of the earth!" A small angry conference of white men took place in the front of the car and the Negroes sitting in the Jim Crow section overheard: "That's that Bigger Thomas nigger and you'd better leave 'im alone." The Negroes experienced an intense flash of pride and the streetcar moved on its journey without incident. I don't know what happened to Bigger No. 5. But I can guess.

The Bigger Thomases were the only Negroes I know of who consistently violated the Jim Crow laws of the South and got away with it, at least for a sweet brief spell. Eventually, the whites who restricted their lives made them pay a terrible price. They were shot, hanged, maimed, lynched, and generally hounded until they were either dead or their spirits broken. (pp. viii-xi)

[Why] did Bigger revolt? No explanation based upon a hard and fast rule of conduct can be given. But there were always two factors psychologically dominant in his personality. First, through some quirk of circumstance, he had become estranged from the religion and the folk culture of his race. Second, he was trying to react to and answer the call of the dominant civilization whose glitter came to him through the newspapers, magazines, radios, movies, and the mere imposing sight and sound of daily American life. In many respects his emergence as a distinct type was inevitable.

As I grew older, I became familiar with the Bigger Thomas conditioning and its numerous shadings no matter where I saw it in Negro life. It was not, as I have already said, as blatant or extreme as in the originals; but it was there, nevertheless, like an undeveloped negative.

Sometimes, in areas far removed from Mississippi, I'd hear a Negro say: "I wish I didn't have to live this way. I feel like I want to burst." Then the anger would pass; he would go back to his job and try to eke out a few pennies to support his wife and children.

Sometimes I'd hear a Negro say: "God, I wish I had a flag and a country of my own." But that mood would soon vanish and he would go his way placidly enough.

Sometimes I'd hear a Negro ex-soldier say: "What in hell did I fight in the war for? They segregated me even when I was offering my life for my country." But he, too, like the others, would soon forget, would become caught up in the tense grind of struggling for bread. (pp. xiii-xiv)

It was not until I went to live in Chicago that I first thought seriously of writing of Bigger Thomas. Two items of my experience combined to make me aware of Bigger as a meaningful and prophetic symbol. First, being free of the daily pressure of the Dixie environment, I was able to come into possession of my own feelings. Second, my contact with the labor movement and its ideology made me see Bigger clearly and feel what he meant.

I made the discovery that Bigger Thomas was not black all the time; he was white, too, and there were literally millions of him, everywhere. The extension of my sense of the personality of Bigger was the pivot of my life; it altered the complexion of my existence. I became conscious, at first dimly, and then later on with increasing clarity and conviction, of a vast, muddied pool of human life in America. It was as though I had put on a pair of spectacles whose power was that of an x-ray enabling me to see deeper into the lives of men. Whenever I picked up a newspaper, I'd no longer feel that I was reading of the doings of whites alone (Negroes are rarely mentioned in the press unless they've committed some crime!), but of a complex struggle for life going on in my country, a struggle in which I was involved. I sensed, too, that the Southern scheme of oppression was but an appendage of a far vaster and in many respects more ruthless and impersonal commodity-profit machine. (pp. xiv-xv)

As my mind extended in this general and abstract manner, it was fed with even more vivid and concrete examples of the lives of Bigger Thomas. The urban environment of Chicago, affording a more stimulating life, made the Negro Bigger Thomases react more violently than even in the South. More than ever I began to see and understand the environmental factors which made for this extreme conduct. It was not that Chicago segregated Negroes more than the South, but that Chicago had more to offer, that Chicago's physical aspect—noisy, crowded, filled with the sense of power and fulfillment—did so much more to dazzle the mind with a taunting sense of possible achievement that the segregation it did impose brought forth from Bigger a reaction more obstreperous than in the South. (p. xv)

There is in me a memory of reading an interesting pamphlet telling of the friendship of Gorky and Lenin in exile. The booklet told of how Lenin and Gorky were walking down a London street. Lenin turned to Gorky and, pointing, said: "Here is *their* Big Ben." "There is *their* Westminister Abbey." "There is *their* library." And at once, while reading that passage, my mind stopped, teased, challenged with the effort to remember, to associate widely disparate but meaningful experiences in my life. For a moment nothing would come, but I remained convinced that I had heard the meaning of those words sometime, somewhere before. Then, with a sudden glow of satisfaction of having gained a little more knowledge about the world in which I lived, I'd end up by saying: "That's Bigger. That's the Bigger Thomas reaction."

In both instances the deep sense of exclusion was identical. The feeling of looking at things with a painful and unwarrantable nakedness was an experience, I learned, that transcended national and racial boundaries. It was this intolerable sense of feeling and understanding so much, and yet living on a plane of social reality where the look of a world which one did not make or own struck one with a blinding objectivity and tangibility, that made me grasp the revolutionary impulse in my life and the lives of those about me and far away.

I remember reading a passage in a book dealing with old Russia which said: "We must be ready to make endless sacrifices if we are to be able to overthrow the Czar." And again I'd say to myself: "I've heard that somewhere, sometime before." And again I'd hear Bigger Thomas, far away and long ago, telling some white man who was trying to impose upon him: "I'll kill you and go to hell and pay for it." While living in America I heard from far away Russia the bitter accents of tragic calculation of how much human life and suffering it would cost a man to live as a man in a world that denied him the right to live with dignity. Actions and feelings of men ten thousand miles from home helped me to understand the moods and impulses of those walking the streets of Chicago and Dixie.

I am not saying that I heard any talk of revolution in the South when I was a kid there. But I did hear the lispings, the whispers, the mutters which some day, under one stimulus or another, will surely grow into open revolt unless the conditions which produce Bigger Thomases are changed. (pp. xvii-xviii)

All Bigger Thomases, white and black, felt tense, afraid, nervous, hysterical, and restless. From far away Nazi Germany and old Russia had come to me items of knowledge that told me that certain modern experiences were creating types of personalities whose existence ignored racial and national lines of demarcation, that these personalities carried with them a more universal drama-element than anything I'd ever encountered before; that these personalities were mainly imposed upon men and women living in a world whose fundamental assumptions could no longer be taken for granted: a world ridden with national and class strife; a world whose metaphysical meanings had vanished; a world in which God no longer existed as a daily focal point of men's lives; a world in which men could no longer retain their faith in an ultimate hereafter. It was a highly geared world whose nature was conflict and action, a world whose limited area and vision imperiously urged men to satisfy their organisms, a world that existed on a plane of animal sensation alone. (p. xix)

From these items I drew my first political conclusions about Bigger: I felt that Bigger, an American product, a native son of this land, carried within him the potentialities of either Communism or Fascism. I don't mean to say that the Negro boy I depicted in *Native Son* is either a Communist or a Fascist. He is not either. But he is product of a dislocated society; he is a dispossessed and disinherited man; he is all of this, and he lives amid the greatest possible plenty on earth and he is looking and feeling for a way out. Whether he'll follow some gaudy, hysterical leader who'll promise rashly to fill the void in him, or whether he'll come to an understanding with the millions of his kindred fellow workers under tradeunion or revolutionary guidance depends upon the future drift of events in America. But, granting the emotional state, the tensity, the fear, the hate, the impatience, the sense of exclu-

sion, the ache for violent action, the emotional and cultural hunger, Bigger Thomas, conditioned as his organism is, will not become an ardent, or even a lukewarm, supporter of the *status quo.*

The difference between Bigger's tensity and the German variety is that Bigger's, due to America's educational restrictions on the bulk of her Negro population, is in a nascent state, not yet articulate. And the difference between Bigger's longing for self-identification and the Russian principle of self-determination is that Bigger's, due to the effects of American oppression, which has not allowed for the forming of deep ideas of solidarity among Negroes, is still in a state of individual anger and hatred. Here, I felt, was *drama!* Who will be the first to touch off these Bigger Thomases in America, white and black?

For a long time I toyed with the idea of writing a novel in which a Negro Bigger Thomas would loom as a symbolic figure of American life, a figure who would hold within him the prophecy of our future. I felt strongly that he held within him, in a measure which perhaps no other contemporary type did, the outlines of action and feeling which we would encounter on a vast scale in the days to come. Just as one sees when one walks into a medical research laboratory jars of alcohol containing abnormally large or distorted portions of the human body, just so did I see and feel that the conditions of life under which Negroes are forced to live in America contain the embryonic emotional prefigurations of how a large part of the body politic would react under stress. (pp. xx-xxi)

But several things militated against my starting to work. Like Bigger himself, I felt a mental censor—product of the fears which a Negro feels from living in America—standing over me, draped in white, warning me not to write. This censor's warnings were translated into my own thought processes thus: "What will white people think if I draw the pictures of such a Negro boy? Will they not at once say: 'See, didn't we tell you all along that niggers are like that? Now, look, one of their own kind has come along and drawn the picture for us!'" I felt that if I drew the picture of Bigger truthfully, there would be many reactionary whites who would try to make of him something I did not intend. And yet, and this was what made it difficult, I knew that I could not write of Bigger convincingly if I did not depict him as he *was:* that is, resentful toward whites, sullen, angry, ignorant, emotionally unstable, depressed and unaccountably elated at times, and unable even, because of his own lack of inner organization which American oppression has fostered in him, to unite with the members of his own race. And would not whites misread Bigger and, doubting his authenticity, say: "This man is preaching hate against the whole white race"?

The more I thought of it the more I became convinced that if I did not write of Bigger as I saw and felt him, if I did not try to make him a living personality and at the same time a symbol of all the larger things I felt and saw in him, I'd be reacting as Bigger himself reacted: that is, I'd be acting out of *fear* if I let what I thought whites would say constrict and paralyze me. (pp. xxi-xxii)

Another thought kept me from writing. What would my own white and black comrades in the Communist party say? This thought was the most bewildering of all. . . . How could I create such complex and wide schemes of associational thought and feeling, such filigreed webs of dreams and politics, without being mistaken for a "smuggler of reaction," "an ideological confusionist," or "an individualistic and dangerous element"? Though my heart is with the collectivist and proletarian ideal, I solved this problem by assuring myself that honest politics and honest feeling in imaginative representation ought to be able to meet on common healthy ground without fear, suspicion, and quarreling. Further, and more importantly, I steeled myself by coming to the conclusion that whether politicians accepted or rejected Bigger did not really matter; my task, as I felt it, was to free myself of this burden of impressions and feelings, recast them into the image of Bigger and make him *true*. (p. xxii)

There was another constricting thought that kept me from work. It deals with my own race. . . . I knew from long and painful experience that the Negro middle and professional classes were the people of my own race who were more than others ashamed of Bigger and what he meant. Having narrowly escaped the Bigger Thomas reaction pattern themselves—indeed, still retaining traces of it within the confines of their own timid personalities—they would not relish being publicly reminded of the lowly, shameful depths of life above which they enjoyed their bourgeois lives. Never did they want people, especially *white* people, to think that their lives were so much touched by anything so dark and brutal as Bigger. (pp. xxii-xxiii)

But Bigger won over all these claims; he won because I felt that I was hunting on the trail of more exciting and thrilling game. What Bigger meant had claimed me because I felt with all of my being that he was more important than what any person, white or black, would say or try to make of him, more important than any political analysis designed to explain or deny him, more important, even, than my own sense of fear, shame, and diffidence. (p. xxiii)

I don't know if *Native Son* is a good book or a bad book. And I don't know if the book I'm working on now will be a good book or a bad book. And I really don't care. The mere writing of it will be more fun and a deeper satisfaction than any praise or blame from anybody.

I feel that I'm lucky to be alive to write novels

today, when the whole world is caught in the pangs of war and change. Early American writers, Henry James and Nathaniel Hawthorne, complained bitterly about the bleakness and flatness of the American scene. But I think that if they were alive, they'd feel at home in modern America. True, we have no great church in America; our national traditions are still of such a sort that we are not wont to brag of them; and we have no army that's above the level of mercenary fighters; we have no group acceptable to the whole of our country upholding certain humane values; we have no rich symbols, no colorful rituals. We have only a money-grubbing, industrial civilization. But we do have in the Negro the embodiment of a past tragic enough to appease the spiritual hunger of even a James; and we have in the oppression of the Negro a shadow athwart our national life dense and heavy enough to satisfy even the gloomy broodings of a Hawthorne. And if Poe were alive, he would not have to invent horror; horror would invent him. (p. xxxiv)

Richard Wright, "How 'Bigger' Was Born," in his *Native Sons,* Harper and Row, Publishers, 1966, pp. vii-xxiv.

RONALD SANDERS
(essay date 1968)

[In the following excerpt, Sanders evaluates Wright's novels.]

[In] *Native Son* Wright almost succeeds in achieving the imaginative liberation he sought by writing it. The book eventually runs aground in the author's own intellectuality, a quality which, for the novel's sake, he had succeeded in suppressing both too well and not well enough.

The first two-thirds of *Native Son* constitute one of the most exciting stretches of melodrama in American literature. (p. 33)

From [the moment of Mary Dalton's death] until Bigger's capture by the police on a snow-covered tenement rooftop some two hundred pages later the novel is pure movement, the kind of overwhelming narrative torrent that Wright had already made into a trademark in a story like **"Down By the Riverside."** In *Native Son* this narrative flow serves the additional function of showing what has happened to Bigger's existence. Every one of his acts now, in contrast with the torpor that had prevailed in the descriptions of his life prior to the murder of Mary Dalton, is swift, vigorous and meaningful, another element in a headlong process of self-definition.

Wright spares no horror in this unfolding of the

hidden meaning of his protagonist's existence; Bigger's ultimate and most completely unforgivable act of violent self-assertion is his murder of his mistress Bessie, with whom he has shared his secret and whose life has therefore become intolerable to him. According to Constance Webb, Wright wanted to include this episode in the novel so that there would be no mistaking Bigger's stark responsibility for his acts, no catering to the sensibilities of bankers' daughters. In retrospect, it seems also to be another of the novel's prophetic glimpses of the ghetto revolt of the sixties, ultimately turning against itself and burning down homes with black women and children inside. This, then, is the culminating act of Bigger's self-emancipating revolt, his one unequivocally wilful act of annihilation—performed upon a poor black working-girl. Did Wright mean for the irony to read this way? Is it an intended qualification to his vision of a black revolutionary apocalypse, or an inadvertent prophecy? Miss Webb does not tell us, but this much must be said: if this is ultimately the outcome of Bigger's revolt, then it is not so likely to disturb the sensibilities of bankers' daughters after all.

The last third of the novel, dealing with Bigger's imprisonment and trial, is Wright's final bout with the Communist worldview, and the narrative moves slowly and indecisively again. . . . He seems to want to

Wright (left) with his younger brother, Leon, in Arkansas, 1916.

give what he can back to the Communists after the heresy he has committed in the first two-thirds of the book; it is only they, for example, who show compassion and some understanding towards Bigger, and he is deeply appreciative of this despite his refusal to be categorized by them as a mere phenomenon of the oppressed part of mankind. . . . The old lawyer Max tries to defend Bigger from the death sentence in a long courtroom summation indicting society's injustices. Max is even able to see, beneath the blanket of Communist myth, the more unruly revolutionary force that Bigger represents. . . . But ultimately it is Max who comes forth, not only in the courtroom but within Wright's internal moral dialectic, as the last defender of the old vision of a coalition of the oppressed. . . . (pp. 34-5)

The spirit of Max, partly consumed in a European nostalgia shared by every American Jewish intellectual, was never completely exorcised by Wright. He had absorbed this nostalgia as part of his education, and his vision of black revolt was as blurred by it as his pursuit of the vision was spurred by a passion to shake it off. This is the meaning of Bigger's final but somehow inconclusive show of defiance before Max in his death cell, ending with "a faint, wry, bitter smile" through the bars as the lawyer walks down the corridor. Here is the way Wright's revolt ends, not with a bang but a smirk. . . .

In his search after a certain notion of the primitive, Wright had come dangerously close to creating a character who was a mere vehicle for ideas. Bigger still works despite the ambiguity, but Wright's growing preoccupation with the metaphysics of blackness turned many of the characters he subsequently created into hardly more than metaphors. . . . ["**The Man Who Lived Underground**"] is an interesting attempt to use blackness as a metaphor for the condition known in Jewish literature as that of "one who sees but is not seen"; but the idea—originally inspired by a reading of Dostoyevsky—is more appealing than the realization is unsuccessful. . . . (p. 36)

[*Black Boy*] is his masterpiece, and yet it would seem, from Miss Webb's narrative, that it was written almost inadvertently, after Wright's agent surprised him by suggesting that he try an autobiography. Persuaded to drop the mantle of a writer of fiction for a moment (although he uses the techniques of the novel here most effectively), Wright has recourse in this book to "telling it like it is" without drawing upon his arsenal of symbolism and melodramatic plot-making. A simple and powerful account of his boyhood and young manhood in the South, it is his one book-length narrative that does not border on solipsism but contains a whole array of real characterizations. Even the whites that appear, almost all of them as persecutors, are more real and hence human than such caricatures as Dalton or the private detective in *Native Son.* Focusing more resolutely on real experience than he had ever done before, Wright had lighted upon conventions that were, for the first time, entirely his own. Evoking, as Ellison says, "the paradoxical, almost surreal image of a black boy singing [the blues] lustily as he probes his own grievous wound" [see excerpt dated 1945], the book suggests possibilities for a whole genre of Negro writing, signs of which we are now beginning to see today.

But in Wright's own life and work, *Black Boy* proved to be the swan song of his struggle to achieve his own identity as a writer and a man in America. In the latter half of 1946 he visited France as the guest of its government, and in the summer of the following year he brought his wife and five-year-old daughter to Paris to settle there for good. . . . By merely trading in the lilt with which he once had sung the blues, Wright became eligible to put on the French-made mantle of Negritude, whose graceful and classic lines obscured the homely contours of Mississippi and Chicago. In other words, his color became in France what he had always sought to make it: a kind of metaphor.

This transmutation is reflected in Wright's next book, *The Outsider.* . . . It is a novel laden with language and concepts borrowed from French existentialism. . . . Cross Damon, a new variant of Bigger Thomas perceived through the French philosophical sensibility, commits a series of murders that read like ritual metaphors for the series of rejections Wright had made in his own life. . . . In the end it is not the law but the Communists who destroy him, shooting him down in the street.

The thrust of Wright's work had now brought him to a point of extreme alienation. His next novel, *Savage Holiday* . . . is a suspense thriller about a retired white insurance executive who, stepping out of the shower to pick up his newspaper in the hallway one Sunday morning, finds himself trapped there naked when his door accidentally slams shut. Caught naked in the hallway—this is what had become of Wright's creative metaphor, of his very inner identity!

During the next few years, Wright made strenuous efforts to recover roots for a theme that had now become, in literary terms, a mere abstraction. . . . [*Pagan Spain*] was a recapitulation of his old quest for a primitive reality behind the mask of Communist myth. Pagan Spain, whose border with France marks "the termination of Europe and the beginning of Africa," was the dark truth that had reposed beneath the right-left conventions of the Spanish Civil War era. So also, at the Bandung Conference, did Wright perceive an underlying reality—formed out of race and religion—that was "beyond left and right." He was thus moving in the direction of what was in fact another left-wing myth—that of the Third World—

which was being generated in France during this period. It was a possible outcome of the logic of his own development: in a sense, Bigger Thomas could be viewed retrospectively as a representative of Frantz Fanon's theories about the self-realization of the colonized through violent revolt. But this, in the end, would tend to make Bigger as much a creature of Jean-Paul Sartre's universe as the lawyer Max had wanted to make him of the universe of American Communism in the nineteen-thirties.

Wright did not seem content with this resolution, either; he had been very keenly aware, for example, of the gulf between himself and the black man of Africa during his trip there. The short time that now remained of his life was filled with what seems to have been a frantic struggle to recover his themes, as he thrashed about through possibilities both old and new. He tried writing again about the Negro in the American South, but the resulting novel, *The Long Dream,* published in 1958, was severely criticized for its manifest remoteness from reality; it was far more popular in France than in the United States. His short stories, mere fanciful creations, were better because they were able to bear up somehow under the weight of being intellectual constructs. A story published in 1957, **"Big Black Good Man,"** suggests the possibility that the course of Wright's sensibility was seeking to come full circle. . . . Does the similarity of name to those of Big Boy and Bigger suggest what Wright was trying to do? It is one of his few stories displaying some of the sunniness and humor for which he was apparently well known in person. Was he making his peace at last, and if so, where was it to take him? No one will ever know, for he was dead three years later, in the fall of 1960. (pp. 36-9)

Ronald Sanders, "Richard Wright and the Sixties," in *Midstream,* Vol. XIV, No. 7, August-September, 1968, pp. 28-40.

EDWARD MARGOLIES
(essay date 1969)

[In the following excerpt from his *The Art of Richard Wright,* Margolies discusses Wright's development as a writer, focusing on the thematic progression of Wright's fiction.]

Wright at his best was master of a taut psychological suspense narrative. Even more important, however, are the ways Wright wove his themes of human fear, alienation, guilt, and dread into the overall texture of his work. Some critics may still today stubbornly cling to the notion that Wright was nothing more than a proletarian writer, but it was to these themes that a postwar generation of French writers responded, and not to Wright's Communism—and it is to these themes that future critics must turn primarily if they wish to re-evaluate Wright's work. (p. 3)

Wright not only wrote well but also he paved the way for a new and vigorous generation of Negro authors to deal with subjects that had hitherto been regarded as taboo. [His] portraits of oppressed Negroes have made a deep impression on readers the world over. (p. 4)

Wright's existentialism, as it was to be called by a later generation of French authors, was not an intellectually "learned" process (although he had been reading Dostoevsky and Kierkegaard in the thirties) but rather the lived experiences of his growing years. The alienation, the dread, the fear, and the view that one must construct oneself out of the chaos of existence—all elements of his fiction—were for him means of survival. There were, of course, externals he grasped for as well. (p. 6)

In general, Wright's nonfiction takes one of two directions. The first concerns itself with the devastating emotional impact of centuries of exploitation on its individual victims. The second is the overall cultural characteristics of oppressed peoples. The first is largely psychological; the second socio-anthropological. Obviously no such absolute division obtains since it is impossible to discuss one without making reference to the other, but for purposes of analysis it may be said that Wright lays greater or lesser stress on one or the other of these issues in each of his works of nonfiction. *Black Boy* (1945), Wright's autobiography of his Southern years, serves perhaps as the best point of reference from which to make an examination of his ideas, since, as we have seen, Wright generalizes from his own experiences certain conclusions about the problems of minorities everywhere. (p. 15)

Possibly the problems presented by *Black Boy* are insoluble since the environment in which *Black Boy* operates is so alien to the average reader that it is almost essential for Wright to hammer home in little digressive essays the mores of the caste system so that *Black Boy*'s psychology and behavior may be better understood. As a result, its authority as autobiography is reduced—Wright frequently appears to stand aside and analyze himself rather than allow the reader to make inferences about his character and emotions from his actions—and its strength as sociology seems somewhat adulterated by the incursions of the narrative. Yet, despite these failures—or possibly because of them—the impact of the book is considerable and this perhaps is Wright's artistic triumph. (p. 16)

Wright's theme is freedom and he skillfully arranges and selects his scenes in such a way that he is constantly made to appear the innocent victim of the tyranny of his family or the outrages of the white community. Nowhere in the book are Wright's actions and thoughts reprehensible. The characteristics he attributes to himself are in marked contrast to those of other characters in the book. He is "realistic," "creative," "passionate," "courageous," and maladjusted because he refuses to conform. Insofar as the reader identifies Wright's cause with the cause of Negro freedom, it is because Wright is a Negro—but a careful reading of the book indicates that Wright expressly divorces himself from other Negroes. Indeed rarely in the book does Wright reveal concern for Negroes as a group. Hence Wright traps the reader in a stereotyped response—the same stereotyped response that Wright is fighting throughout the book: that is, that all Negroes are alike and react alike. (p. 18)

[It] is in [*Uncle Tom's Children*] that the reader may find the theme, the structure, the plot, and the ideational content of all his later fictional work. Although Wright, when he wrote these stories, was a convinced Communist, it is revealing how related they are to the later phases of intellectual and political development. Here, for example, one finds Wright's incipient Negro nationalism as each of his protagonists rises to strike out violently at white oppressors who would deny him his humanity. More significantly his Negro characters imagine whites as "blurs," "bogs," "mountains," "fire," "ice," and "marble." In none of these stories do his heroes act out of a sense of consciously arrived at ideology (most of them, as a matter of fact, are ignorant of Marxism), but rather out of an innate, repressed longing for freedom—or sometimes merely as an instinctive means of self-survival. Often the act of violence carries along with it a sudden revelatory sense of self-awareness—an immediate knowledge that the world in which the protagonist dwells is chaotic, meaningless, purposeless, and that he, as a Negro, is "outside" this world and must therefore discover his own life by his lonely individual thoughts and acts. We find thus in these first short stories a kind of black nationalism wedded to what has been called Wright's existentialism—the principal characteristics of Wright's last phase of political and philosophical thinking.

Paradoxically, Wright's Marxism seldom intrudes in an explicit didactic sense. . . . To be sure, Communists are viewed in a kindly light in the last two of Wright's stories, but they are only remotely instrumental in effecting his heroes' discovery of themselves and their world. Oddly enough, in three of the stories (**"Down by the Riverside," "Fire and Cloud,"** and **"Bright and Morning Star"**), Wright's simple Negro peasants arrive at their sense of self-realization by applying basic Christian principles to the situations in which they find themselves. In only one (**"Bright and Morning Star"**), does a character convert to Communism—and then only when she discovers Communism is the modern translation of the primitive Christian values she has always lived. There is a constant identification in these stories with the fleeing Hebrew children of the Old Testament and the persecuted Christ—and mood, atmosphere, and settings abound in biblical nuances. Wright's characters die like martyrs, stoic and unyielding, in their new-found truth about themselves and their vision of a freer, fuller world for their posterity. . . . The spare, stark accounts of actions and their resolution are reminiscent in their simplicity and their cadences of Biblical narrations. The floods, the songs, the sermons, the hymns reinforce the Biblical analogies and serve, ironically, to highlight the uselessness and inadequacy of Christianity as a means of coping with the depression-ridden, racist South. Even the reverse imagery of white-evil, black-good is suggestive in its simple organization of the forces which divide the world in Old Testament accounts of the Hebrews' struggle for survival. (pp. 57-9)

There is a thematic progression in these stories, each of which deals with the Negro's struggle for survival and freedom. In the first story ["**Big Boy Leaves Home**"] flight is described—and here Wright is at his artistic best, fashioning his taut, spare prose to the movements and thoughts of the fugitive. (p. 61)

Although "**Big Boy**" is a relatively long story, the rhythm of events is swift, and the time consumed from beginning to end is less than twenty-four hours. The prose is correspondingly fashioned to meet the pace of the plot. The story is divided into five parts, each of which constitutes a critical episode in Big Boy's progress from idyll, through violence, to misery, terror, and escape. As the tension mounts, Wright employs more and more of a terse and taut declaratory prose, fraught with overtones and meanings unspoken—reminiscent vaguely of the early [Ernest] Hemingway. (pp. 62-3)

"**Down by the Riverside**," the next story in the collection, is not nearly so successful. If flight (as represented by "**Big Boy Leaves Home**") is one aspect of the Negro's struggle for survival in the South, Christian humility, forbearance, courage, and stoic endurance are the themes of Wright's second piece. But here the plot becomes too contrived; coincidence is piled upon coincidence, and the inevitability of his protagonist's doom does not ring quite as true. (p. 63)

Yet, there is a certain epic quality to the piece—man steadily pursuing his course against a malevolent nature, only to be cut down later by the ingratitude of his fellow men—that is suggestive of [Mark] Twain or [William] Faulkner. And Mann's long-suffering perseverance and stubborn will to survive endow him with a rare mythic Biblical quality. Wright even structures his story like a Biblical chronicle, in five brief episodes, each displaying in its way Mann's humble courage against his fate. But if Mann's simple Christian virtues

failed to save him, it was in part because the ground had not yet been laid on which these virtues might flourish. The recognition that the bourgeois ethic is incapable of providing men with the possibility of fulfilling themselves is an element of Wright's next story ["**Long Black Song**"]. (p. 65)

The success of the story, perhaps Wright's best, lies in the successful integration of plot, imagery, and character which echo the tragic theme of Silas's doomed awareness of himself and the inadequacy of the bourgeois values by which he has been attempting to live. Silas's recognition is his death knell, but he achieves a dignity in death that he had never known in life. (pp. 65-6)

It is Sarah, though, who is the most memorable portrayal in the story. The narrative unfolds from her point of view—and she becomes, at the end, a kind of deep mother earth character, registering her primal instincts and reactions to the violence and senselessness she sees all about her. But for all that, she remains beautifully human—her speech patterns and thoughts responding to an inner rhythm, somehow out of touch with the foolish strivings of men, yet caught up in her own melancholy memories and desires. . . . Wright conveys her mood and memories and vagaries of character in sensuous color imagery—while certain cadences suggest perhaps Gertrude Stein whom Wright regarded as one of his chief influences. (pp. 66-7)

Sarah is Wright's most lyrical achievement, and Silas, her husband, Wright's most convincing figure of redemption. (p. 67)

Wright's militant Negroes, despite their protestations to the contrary, often sound more like black nationalists than Communist internationalists. It was perhaps this facet of Wright's work, in addition to the obvious, extreme, and frequent isolated individualism of his heroes that [began] to disturb Communist Party officials. Yet regardless of whether Wright had been at heart a Communist, an outsider, or a nationalist when he wrote these pieces, there can be little doubt that they draw a good deal of their dramatic strength from the black and white world Wright saw. There is little the reader can do but sympathize with Wright's Negroes and loathe and despise the whites. There are no shadings, ambiguities, few psychological complexities. But there are of course the weaknesses of the stories as well.

How then account for their overall success? First of all, they *are* stories. Wright is a story teller and his plots are replete with conflict, incident, and suspense. Secondly, Wright is a stylist. He has an unerring "feel" for dialogue, his narrations are controlled in terse, tense rhythms, and he manages to communicate mood, atmosphere, and character in finely worked passages of lyric intensity. But above all they are stories whose sweep and magnitude are suffused with their author's impassioned convictions about the dignity of man, and a profound pity for the degraded, the poor and oppressed who, in the face of casual brutality, cling obstinately to their humanity. (pp. 72-3)

Unlike the pieces in *Uncle Tom's Children,* [the stories in the posthumously published *Eight Men*] are not arranged along any progressively thematic lines; instead the order in which they are assembled indicates that Wright was more concerned with showing a variety of styles, settings and points of view. To be sure, they all deal in one way or another with Negro oppression, but they do not point, as Wright's previous collection of stories did, to any specific social conclusion. (p. 73)

The only significant work of fiction Wright produced in the decade of the forties was his long story, **"The Man Who Lived Underground."** (p. 76)

Here Wright is at his storytelling best, dealing with subject matter he handles best—the terrified fugitive in flight from his pursuers. Like Wright's other fugitives, Fred Daniels exercises a kind of instinct for survival that he perhaps never knew he possessed. But what makes him different from the others is that he is not merely a victim of a racist society, but that he has become by the very nature of his experiences a symbol of all men in that society—the pursuers and the pursued. For what the underground man has learned in his sewer is that all men carry about in their hearts an underground man who determines their behavior and attitudes in the aboveground world. The underground man is the essential nature of all men—and is composed of dread, terror, and guilt. Here then lies the essential difference between Wright's Communist and post-Communist period. Heretofore dread, terror, and guilt had been the lot of the Negro in a world that had thrust upon him the role of a despised inferior. Now they are the attributes of all mankind. (pp. 78-9)

Fred Daniels is then Everyman, and his story is very nearly a perfect modern allegory. The Negro who lives in the underground of the city amidst its sewage and slime is not unlike the creature who dwells amidst the sewage of the human heart. And Fred Daniels knows that all of the ways men attempt to persuade themselves that their lives are meaningful and rational are delusions. . . . But paradoxically despite Fred's new found knowledge of the savagery of the human heart and the meaninglessness of the aboveground world, he recognizes its instinctive appeal as well, and he must absurdly rise to the surface once more. (pp. 79-80)

The dread, the terror, the guilt, the nausea had always been basic thematic elements in Wright's fiction—and now in **"The Man Who Lived Underground,"** they are made the explicit components of the human personality. Like Wright's heroes, the charac-

ters of existentialist authors move about in a world devoid of principles, God, and purpose—and suffer horror at their awesome godlike powers as they create their own personalities and values out of the chaos of existence. But in some respects Wright's heroes are different. They are alienated often enough not from any intellectually reasoned position (at this stage in Wright's career), but by chance happenings in their lives or an accident of birth—race, for example. (In Fred Daniels' case, for instance, he is a Negro who quite by chance happened to be near the scene of a crime.) They arrive then accidentally at their insights, and as a result of having discovered themselves outside the rules of conventional social behavior recognize that they are free to shape (and are therefore responsible for) their own lives. But this is not primarily why they suffer guilt. Wright seems to prefer a Freudian explanation; guilt is instinctively connected with the trauma of birth. Hence, for Wright, a man's freedom is circumscribed by his very humanity. In ways he cannot possibly control, his nature or "essence" precedes his existence. But however different the routes French existentialist authors and Wright may have taken, they meet on common ground in regard to their thrilled horror at man's rootlessness—at the heroism of his absurd striving.

"The Man Who Lived Underground" undoubtedly owes something in the way of plot and theme to [Victor Hugo's] *Les Miserables,* and to what Camus called the "Dostoevskian experience of the condemned man"—but, above all, Fred Daniels' adventures suggest something of Wright's own emotions after ten years in the Communist underground. The air of bitterness, the almost strident militancy are gone—momentarily at least—and in their place a compassion and despair—compassion for man trapped in his underground nature and despair that he will ever be able to set himself free. (pp. 80-1)

The fifties saw Wright experimenting with new subject matter and new forms. Problems of race remain the central issue, but are now dealt with from changing perspectives. For the first time there are two stories with non-American settings, and race neurosis is treated more as the white man's dilemma than as the black man's burden. This shift in emphasis from black to white is accompanied by corresponding shifts in social viewpoint. Racial antagonisms do not appear to be immediately—or for that matter remotely—traceable to compelling class interests. It is clear that Wright was trying to broaden the range and scope of his fiction—that he was trying to move away somewhat from the psyche of the oppressed Negro peasant or proletariat toward characters of varying social and ethnic backgrounds. The three novels Wright produced in this ten year period bear out this conclusion. In the first, *The Outsider* (1953), he wrote of his hero that though a Negro "he could have been of any race." *Savage Holi-*

day, written the following year, contains no Negro characters and deals with the misfortunes of a white, "respectable" middle-aged retired insurance executive. *The Long Dream* (1957) is written from the point of view of an adolescent, middle-class Negro boy. Wright was apparently reaching for a universality he felt he had not yet achieved—but his craft was not quite equal to the tasks he had set for himself. Too often, as before, his whites appear as stereotypes, and his Negroes are a bit too noble or innocent. In the 1930's Wright's social vision lent his stories an air of conviction, a momentum all their own; in the 1950's Wright's quieter catholicity, his wider intellectuality, perhaps removed his stories from this kind of cumulative dread tension, the sense of urgency, that made his earlier works so immediately gripping.

Nonetheless it cannot be said that Wright's new stories do not possess their own narrative qualities. . . . What these stories sorely lack are the charged, vibrant rhythms and vivid lyric imagery that so rounded out character and theme in his earlier works. Perhaps Wright wanted to pare his prose down to what he regarded as bare essentials—just as he may have fancied his idol, Gertrude Stein, had done. Whatever the reasons, the results are only occasionally successful. (pp. 82-3)

Native Son possesses many of the characteristic failings of proletarian literature. First, the novel is transparently propagandistic—arguing for a humane, socialist society where such crimes as Bigger committed could not conceivably take place. Secondly, Wright builds up rather extensive documentation to prove that Bigger's actions, behavior, values, attitudes, and fate have already been determined by his status and place in American life. Bigger's immediate Negro environment is depicted as being unrelentingly bleak and vacuous—while the white world that stands just beyond his reach remains cruelly indifferent or hostile to his needs. Thirdly, with the possible exception of Bigger, none of the characters is portrayed in any depth—and most of them are depicted as representative "types" of the social class to which they belong. Fourthly, despite his brutally conditioned psychology, there are moments in the novel when Bigger, like the heroes of other proletarian fiction, appears to be on the verge of responding to the stereotyped Communist version of black and white workers marching together in the sunlight of fraternal friendship. Finally, Wright succumbs too often to the occupational disease of proletarian authors by hammering home sociological points in didactic expository prose when they could just as clearly be understood in terms of the organic development of the novel.

Yet if *Native Son* may be said to illustrate some of the more flagrant conventions of proletarian fiction, there are aspects of this novel that reveal Wright ex-

ploring problems of character portrayal, prose style, and theme. . . . [There] is first of all the sympathetic presentation of perhaps one of the most disagreeable characters in fiction. That Wright had to a large degree achieved this may be attested to as much by the loud protests of his critics as by the plaudits of his admirers. Second, although *Native Son* makes its obvious sociological points, one should bear in mind that for well over two thirds of the novel Wright dwells on the peculiar states of mind of his protagonist, Bigger, which exist somehow outside the realm of social classes or racial issues. . . . Hence if categorizing terms are to be used, *Native Son* is as much a psychological novel as it is sociological, with Wright dwelling on various intensities of shame, fear, and hate. . . . To require of his readers that they identify themselves with the violent emotions and behavior of an illiterate Negro boy is no mean feat—but Wright's success goes beyond the shock of reader recognition with its subsequent implications of shared guilt and social responsibility. A re-reading of Wright's novel some twenty-five odd years after its publication suggests that Wright was probing larger issues than racial injustice and social inequality. He was asking questions regarding the ultimate nature of man. What indeed are man's responsibilities in a world devoid of meaning and purpose? . . . The contradiction is never resolved, and it is precisely for this reason that the novel fails to fulfill itself. For the plot, the structure, even the portrayal of Bigger himself are often at odds with Wright's official determinism—but when on occasion the novel transcends its Marxist and proletarian limitations the reading becomes magnificent. (pp. 104-07)

The entire action described in Book I totals fewer than seventy-seven pages. Bigger's character and circumstances are related in a few quick almost impressionistic episodes—but the real plot movement does not actually commence until Bigger confronts the Daltons. Yet Wright has forecast Bigger's doom from the very start. Bigger knows deep in his heart that he is destined to bear endless days of dreary poverty, abject humiliation, and tormenting frustration, for this is what being a Negro means. Yet should he admit these things to himself, he may well commit an act of unconscionable violence. . . . Hence, Bigger's principal fear is self-knowledge—and this, of course, is the theme and title of Book I. The other kinds of fear that constitute Bigger's life are by-products of this basic error. (pp. 108-09)

[Bigger opts for] the identity of a murderer. In an absurd, hostile world that denies his humanity and dichotomizes his personality, Bigger has made a choice that has integrated his being; "never had he felt [such] a sense of wholeness." Ironically, Bigger has assumed the definition the white world has thrust upon the Negro in order to justify his oppression. If the Negro is a beast at heart who must be caged in order to protect the purity of the white race, Bigger will gladly accept the definition. It is at least an identity—preferable to that of someone obsequious, passive, and happily acquiescent to his exploitation. Bigger's choices are moral and metaphysical—not political or racial. He might have chosen love or submission, instead he has elected violence and death as a sign of his being, and by rebelling against established authority—despite the impossibility of success—he acquires a measure of freedom. None of the above is intended to deny that oppressive environmental factors do not limit the modes of Bigger's actions; nonetheless, environment by itself does not explain Bigger. (pp. 110-11)

The chief philosophical weakness of *Native Son* is not that Bigger does not surrender his freedom to Max's determinism, or that Bigger's Zarathustrian principles do not jibe with Max's socialist visions; it is that Wright himself does not seem to be able to make up his mind. There is an inconsistency of tone in the novel—particularly in Book III, "Fate," where the reader feels that Wright, although intellectually committed to Max's views, is more emotionally akin to Bigger's. Somehow Bigger's impassioned hatred comes across more vividly than Max's eloquent reasoning. (p. 113)

The failures of *Native Son* do not then reside in the proletarian or naturalistic framework in which Wright chose to compose his novel. Any great artist can after all transcend the limitations of form—if he so wishes. In any event if Wright had stuck closer to an organic naturalistic development, his novel might have achieved more consistent artistic results. The basic problems of *Native Son* lie elsewhere. There is an inconsistency of ideologies, an irresolution of philosophical attitudes which prevent Bigger and the other characters from developing properly, which adulterate the structure of the novel, and which occasionally cloud up an otherwise lucid prose style. There are three kinds of revolutionism in *Native Son*—and none of them altogether engages the reader as representing Wright's point of view. Max's Communism is of course what Wright presumes his novel is expressing—yet this kind of revolutionism is, . . . more imposed from without than an integral element of Bigger's being. . . .

A second kind of revolutionism is of a Negro nationalist variety—and this is far more in keeping with Bigger's character. (p. 115)

But Bigger's nationalism, whatever its components, is nothing compared to what Camus has subsequently described as metaphysical revolution. "Human rebellion ends in metaphysical revolution," Camus writes in *The Rebel*—and it is in the role of the metaphysical revolutionary that Bigger looms most significantly for modern readers. The metaphysical revolutionary challenges the very conditions of being—the needless suffering, the absurd contrast between his inborn sense of justice and the amorality and injustice of the external world. He tries to bring the external world more in accord with his sense of justice, but if this fails he will attempt to match in himself the injustice or chaos of the external world. (p. 116)

Bigger's crimes then signify something beyond their therapeutic value. In a world without God, without rules, without order, purpose, or meaning, each man becomes his own god and creates his own world in order to exist. Bigger acts violently in order to exist and it is perhaps this fact, rather than his continued undying hatred of whites, that so terrifies Max at the close of the novel. It is possible that Max senses that as a Communist he too has worked hard to dispense with the old social order—but the metaphysical vacuum that has been created does not necessarily lead men like Bigger to Communism, but may just as easily lead to the most murderous kind of nihilism. (pp. 116-17)

James Baldwin writing of *Native Son* says every Negro carries about within him a Bigger Thomas—but that the characterization by itself is unfair in that there are complexities, depths to the Negro psychology and life that Wright has left unexplored. To depict Bigger exclusively in terms of unsullied rage and hatred is to do the Negro a disservice. In Baldwin's view Bigger is a "monster." This, of course, is precisely the point Wright wishes to make—and herein lies its most terrible truth for the reader. Wright is obviously not describing the "representative" Negro—although he makes clear that what has happened to Bigger can more easily befall Negroes than whites. He is describing a person so alienated from traditional values, restraints, and civilized modes of behavior, that he feels free to construct his own ethics—that for him an act of murder is an act of creation. . . . But do such "monsters" as Baldwin calls them exist? Our tabloids could not exist without them. But even supposing they do not commit murder, their sense of isolation and alienation is growing in the face of an increasingly impersonal, industrialized mass society. And in mass, the isolated, the alienated, are capable of consent or indifference to nuclear holocaust or extermination camps. It is perhaps in this respect that *Native Son* is so much more disturbing a novel today than when it was first published. It is not that Bigger Thomas is so different from us; it is that he is so much like us. (pp. 119-20)

Edward Margolies, in his *The Art of Richard Wright,* Southern Illinois University Press, 1969, 180 p.

SOURCES FOR FURTHER STUDY

Blau, Eleanor. "The Works of Richard Wright, This Time Published as Written." *The New York Times* (28 August 1991): B1, B2.

> Discusses the discovery of hitherto overlooked galleys of original passages that were deleted from *Native Son, Lawd Today,* and *The Outsider* at time of first publication. Restored texts of these and other works appear in *Richard Wright: Works* (1991), edited by Arnold Rampersad and published as Vols. 55 and 56 of "Library of America."

Bloom, Harold, ed. *Modern Critical Views: Richard Wright.* New York: Chelsea House Publishers, 1987, 246 p.

> Ten critical essays on various aspects of Wright's writing, including works by Edward Margolies, Michel Fabre, and Houston A. Baker, Jr.

Brignano, Russell Carl. *Richard Wright: An Introduction to the Man and His Works.* Pittsburgh: University of Pittsburgh Press, 1970, 202 p.

> Biographical and critical study that examines the ideological bases of Wright's works.

Hakutani, Yoshinobu, ed. *Critical Essays on Richard Wright.* Boston: G. K. Hall & Co., 1982, 305 p.

> Anthology of criticism of Wright's work. Contributors include Irving Howe, Lewis Leary, Michel Fabre, and Ralph Ellison.

Negro Digest XVIII, No. 2 (December 1968).

> Issue devoted to Wright that includes articles on his work, life, and influence on black literature.

Ray, David, and Farnsworth, Robert M., eds. *Richard Wright: Impressions and Perspectives.* Ann Arbor: University of Michigan Press, 1973, 207 p.

> Collection of essays, letters, and miscellaneous observations about Wright and his works. The pieces are arranged chronologically according to the periods of Wright's career and includes several articles on Wright's early years in Memphis and Chicago.

William Butler Yeats

1865-1939

Irish poet, dramatist, essayist, critic, short story writer, and autobiographer.

INTRODUCTION

Yeats is considered one of the greatest poets in the English language. Although his interest in Irish politics and his visionary approach to poetry often confounded his contemporaries and set him at odds with the intellectual trends of his time, Yeats's poetic achievement stands at the center of modern literature. Devoted to the cause of Irish nationalism, he played an important part in the Celtic Revival Movement and founded an Irish literary theater, the Abbey, with the help of Lady Augusta Gregory and J. M. Synge. Yeats also promoted the literary heritage of Ireland through his use of material from ancient Irish sagas in his poems, dramas, and short stories. Desiring to recapture the Ireland of heroic times, he believed that only by "expressing primary truths in ways appropriate to this country" could artists hope to restore to modern Ireland the cultural unity that he felt was needed to bring an end to his country's internal division and suffering. In addition to the myths and history of Ireland, magic and occult theory were also important elements in Yeats's work. Yeats viewed the poet as kindred to the magician and the alchemist, and he was deeply interested in spiritualism, theosophy, and occult systems. Many of the images found in his poetry are derived from Rosicrucianism and his own occult researches as described in the prose work *A Vision* (1925).

Yeats was born in Dublin. His father, J. B. (Jack) Yeats, was the son of a once-affluent family whom Oscar Wilde's father, Sir William Wilde, described as "the cleverest, most spirited people I ever met." For as long as he lived, Jack Yeats, a painter, exercised an important influence on his son's thoughts about art. Yeats's mother, Susan Pollexfen, was the daughter of a successful merchant from Sligo in western Ireland. Many of the Pollexfens were intense, eccentric people interested in faeries and astrology. From his mother Yeats inherited a love of Ireland, particularly the region surrounding Sligo, and an interest in folklore.

Yeats received no formal education until he was eleven years old, when he began attending the Godolphin Grammar School in Hammersmith, England. He continued his education in Ireland at the Erasmus Smith High School in Dublin. Generally, he was a disappointing student—erratic in his studies, prone to daydreaming, shy, and poor at sports. In 1884, Yeats enrolled in the Metropolitan School of Art in Dublin, where he met the poet George Russell. Russell shared Yeats's enthusiasm for dreams and visions, and together they founded the Dublin Hermetic Society for the purposes of conducting magical experiments and promoting their belief that "whatever the great poets had affirmed in their finest moments was the nearest we could come to an authoritative religion and that their mythology and their spirits of water and wind were but literal truth." This collaboration marked the beginning for Yeats of a lifelong interest in occult studies, the extent of which was only revealed by the examination of his unpublished notebooks after his death. Following his experience with the Hermetic Society, Yeats joined the Rosicrucians, the Theosophical Society, and MacGregor Mathers's Order of the Golden Dawn. He frequently consulted spiritualists and engaged in the ritual conjuring of Irish gods. Yeats found occult research a rich source of images for his poetry, and traces of his esoteric interests appear everywhere in his poems. "The Rose upon the Rood of Time," for example, takes its central symbol from Rosicrucianism, and "All Soul's Night" describes a scrying, or divination, ceremony.

In 1885, Yeats met the Irish nationalist John O'Leary, who was instrumental in arranging for the publication of Yeats's first poems in *The Dublin University Review* and in directing Yeats's attention to native Irish sources for subject matter. Under the influence of O'Leary, Yeats took up the cause of Gaelic writers at a time when much native Irish literature was in danger of being lost as the result of England's attempts to anglicize Ireland through a ban on the Gaelic language. O'Leary's ardent nationalism and resolute opposition to violence also impressed Yeats and were instrumental in shaping political views that he held for the rest of his life. On January 30th, 1889, he met the actress Maud Gonne, an agitator for the nationalist cause whose great beauty and reckless destructiveness in pursuit of her political goals both intrigued and dismayed him. He began accompanying her to political rallies, and though he often disagreed with her extremist tactics, he shared her desire to see Ireland freed from English domination. During this period he wrote the drama *Cathleen ni Houlihan* (1902) for Gonne, and she was featured in the title role in its initial production. Yeats considered the play, which is about a noblewoman who sells her soul to the devil in order to save starving peasants, as appropriately symbolic of the activities to which Gonne had dedicated her life. Although Gonne's repeated refusals to marry Yeats brought him great personal unhappiness, their relationship endured through many estrangements, including her brief marriage to Major John MacBride, and nearly all of the love poetry that Yeats wrote during his career is addressed to her. In his verses she is associated with Helen of Troy, whose capriciousness led to the destruction of a civilization. To Yeats she represented an ideal, and throughout his life he found the tension between them, as well as their friendship, a source of poetic inspiration.

It was not until 1917, when he was fifty-two years old, that Yeats married. On their honeymoon his young wife, Georgiana Hyde-Lees, discovered that she had mediumistic abilities and through the technique of automatic writing could receive communication from a supernatural realm. Her efforts over many months produced the notes and materials on which Yeats based the text of *A Vision*—his explanation of historical cycles and a theory of human personality based on the phases of the moon. Late in his life, when decades of struggle by the Irish nationalists had finally culminated in the passage of the Home Rule Bill, Yeats became a senator for the Irish Free State. He left the senate in 1928 because of failing health, intending to devote his remaining years to poetry. He died in 1939.

In his earliest poetic works, such as *Mosada* (1886), Yeats took his symbols from Greek mythology; however, after meeting John O'Leary, he turned instead to Irish mythology as a source for his images. The long narrative poem, "The Wanderings of Oisin" was the first he based on the legend of an Irish hero. Recognizing that faerie songs were less suited to the tragic themes that preoccupied him than were more realistic narratives, he began, with the poems of *In the Seven Woods* (1903), to write verses describing actual events in his personal life or in the history of Ireland. One of his most famous lyrics, "Easter 1916," about a rebel uprising that resulted in the martyrdom of all who participated, belongs to this latter group. In his maturity, Yeats wrote little narrative poetry. Instead he adopted the dramatic lyric as his most characteristic form of expression. Influenced by Ezra Pound, he simplified his diction and modified his syntax to more closely reflect the constructions of common speech, and in works such as *Responsibilities, and Other Poems* (1914), *The Wild Swans at Coole* (1917), and *Michael Robartes and the Dancer* (1920) his verses began to take on the rhetorical, occasionally haughty tone that readers today identify as characteristically Yeatsian.

Yeats considered his dramas an aspect of his plan to revitalize Irish culture. He wanted to create dramas that were symbolic and austere—a reflection not of life, but of "the deeps of the mind." However, the form that such dramas should take and the manner in which they should be staged eluded him for many years. In his early works, such as *The Shadowy Waters* (1900) and *The Land of Heart's Desire* (1894), he found that conventional stage techniques and realistic characters were not suited to the poetic portrayal of spiritual truths and psychological realities. It was not until Pound introduced him to the ancient Nō plays of Japan that he found a form he felt was suited to the heroic and tragic subjects that he wished to depict. In *Four Plays for Dancers* (1921) as well as in subsequent works such as *Purgatory* (1938), Yeats experimented with techniques borrowed from the Nō, such as ritualized, symbolic action and the use of masks. These plays contain some of his most highly regarded verse, and critics now believe that Yeats's approach to drama in many ways anticipated later developments in modern theater.

Yeats's most important prose writings are his *Autobiographies* (1926) and *The Celtic Twilight* (1893). A source of controversy among critics, Yeats's *Autobiographies* provides a sensitive, if sometimes ironic, view of his age while revealing little about his own life and thoughts. Nonetheless, these memoirs are a valuable source of information about Yeats's views on art and his theories of personality. In *The Celtic Twilight,* his collection of Irish folktales, Yeats endeavored to record the folk legends of Irish peasants in a simple and dignified manner, rather than in the patronizing and comic way such materials were often treated by English writers. Yeats not only wished to preserve these legends, he also wanted to make them more widely available to the Irish people, who had lost touch with ancient Irish traditions. He sought in this way to promote the "unity of culture" that he believed could only be achieved in modern Ireland through an increased awareness of Ireland's heroic past.

Yeats was awarded the Nobel Prize in literature in 1923. However, for many years his intent interest in subjects that others labelled archaic delayed his recognition among his peers. At the time of his death in 1939, Yeats's views on poetry were regarded as eccentric by students and critics alike. This attitude held sway in spite of critical awareness of the beauty and technical proficiency of his verse. Yeats had long opposed the notion that literature should serve society. As a youthful critic he had refused to praise the poor lyrics of the "Young Ireland" poets merely because they were effective as nationalist propaganda. In maturity, he found that despite his success, his continuing conviction that poetry should express the spiritual life of the individual estranged him from those who believed that a modern poet must take as his themes social alienation and the barrenness of materialist culture. As Kathleen Raine wrote of him: "Against a rising tide of realism, political verse and University wit, Yeats upheld the innocent and the beautiful, the traditional and the noble," and in consequence of his disregard for the concerns of the modern world, was often misunderstood. As critics became disenchanted with modern poetic trends, Yeats's Romantic dedication to the laws of the imagination and art for art's sake became more acceptable. Indeed, critics today are less concerned with the validity of Yeats's occult and visionary theories than with their symbolic value as expressions of timeless ideals.

(For further information about Yeats's life and works, see *Contemporary Authors*, Vols. 104, 127; *Dictionary of Literary Biography*, Vols. 10, 19, 98; *Major Twentieth-Century Writers;* and *Twentieth-Century Literary Criticism*, Vols. 1, 11, 18, 31.)

CRITICAL COMMENTARY

SEÁN O'FAOLÁIN
(essay date 1935)

[One of the greatest Irish short story writers of the twentieth century, O'Faoláin has also earned a wide reputation as a novelist, biographer, dramatist, editor, and critic. In the following excerpt, he discusses Yeats's poetic self-image and examines the evolution of his presentation of conflict.]

The statues of Mausolus and Artemesia at the British Museum, private, half-animal, half-divine. . . . became images of an unpremeditated joyous energy that neither I nor any man, racked of doubt and enquiry, can achieve, and that yet, if once achieved, might seem to men and women of Connemara or Galway, their very soul.

In *Four Years.*
We were the last romantics, chose for theme
Traditional sanctity and loveliness.
Whatever written in what poet's name
The book of the people. . . .
But all is changed, that high horse riderless. . . .
    In *The Winding Stair, and Other Poems.*

That conflict and that desire is all over Yeats from

Principal Works

Mosada (poetry) 1886

The Wanderings of Oişin, and Other Poems (poetry) 1889

The Countess Cathleen, and Various Legends and Lyrics (poetry) 1892

The Celtic Twilight (folklore) 1893

The Land of Heart's Desire (drama) 1894

Collected Poems (poetry) 1895

The Secret Rose (short stories) 1897

The Wind among the Reeds (poetry) 1899

The Shadowy Waters (drama) 1900

Cathleen ni Houlihan [with Lady Gregory] (drama) 1902

In the Seven Woods (poetry) 1903

The King's Threshold [with Lady Gregory] (drama) 1903

On Baile's Strand (drama) 1904

Stories of Red Hanrahan (short stories) 1904

The Golden Helmet (drama) 1908

The Green Helmet, and Other Poems (poetry) 1910

Responsibilities, and Other Poems (poetry) 1914

At the Hawk's Well (drama) 1916

The Wild Swans at Coole (poetry) 1917

Per Amica Silentia Lunae (essay) 1918

The Player Queen (drama) 1919

Michael Robartes and the Dancer (poetry) 1920

Four Plays for Dancers [first publication] (dramas) 1921

Later Poems (poetry) 1922

The Cat and the Moon, and Certain Poems (poetry) 1924

A Vision (essay) 1925; also published as A Vision [enlarged edition], 1937

*Autobiographies (memoir) 1926; also published as The

Autobiography of William Butler Yeats [enlarged edition], 1938

The Tower (poetry) 1928

The Winding Stair (poetry) 1929

The Dreaming of the Bones (drama) 1931

Words for Music Perhaps, and Other Poems (poetry) 1932

The Collected Poems of W. B. Yeats (poetry) 1933

The Collected Plays of W. B. Yeats (dramas) 1934; also published as The Collected Plays of W. B. Yeats [enlarged edition], 1952.

The King of the Great Clock Tower (poetry) 1934

Wheels and Butterflies (drama) 1934

A Full Moon in March (poetry and dramas) 1935

The Herne's Egg (drama) 1938

New Poems (poetry) 1938

Purgatory (drama) 1938

Last Poems and Two Plays (poetry and dramas) 1939

On the Boiler (essays and poems) 1939

Last Poems and Plays (poetry and dramas) 1940

The Death of Cuchulain (drama) 1949

The Letters of W. B. Yeats (letters) 1954

W. B. Yeats: Essays and Introductions (essays) 1961

The Poems: A New Edition (poetry) 1983

*This work includes the memoirs Reveries over Childhood and Youth and The Trembling of the Veil. The enlarged edition of 1938 also includes the memoirs Dramatis Personae, Estrangement, The Death of Synge, and The Bounty of Sweden.

---

his childhood on. It is part of him, as it was part of his father John Yeats, before him—a desire for "the abounding glittering jet," and a conflict with everything that in disintegrating the soul—character, intellect, speculation—prevents spontaneous and instinctive vision.

"It is always to the Condition of Fire where emotion is not brought to any sudden stop, where there is neither wall nor gate, that we would rise," he said in *Per Amica Silentia Lunae,* and we remember that Luna means to him the occult way to all generation, as on his ring the butterfly contrasts with the hawk which is the straight road of logic for which he has small liking. But then he goes on:—

> When I remember that Shelley calls our minds "mirrors of the fire for which all thirst," I cannot but ask the question, as all have asked, "What or who has cracked the mirror." I begin to study the only self

that I know, myself, and to wind the thread upon the perne again.

He wishes the condition of fire, and he begins therefore to speculate on himself !

So, from the beginning to the end he winds and unwinds his thread, out and in, from his isolated self—"for triumph can but mar our solitude"—out to the triumph of the world, and back from all human preoccupations, even the preoccupations of sexual desire or patriotic avocations, into his own bowel. "Innocence!" he seems to cry. "Where shall I find innocence again? Hero and saint and fool have had it. But not I—The Janus poet—caught between two shapes of myself."

For Yeats has never been content to be a merely lyric poet; he has been trying always to purify himself, as a saint might, to reach that condition of fire in which the Holy Ghost would light upon him and he speaks in divers tongues the wonders of God. For no other reason, I feel, was he so much attracted by Shelley, as a young man, than because he felt that the Intellectual Beauty contained all beauty; to the hocus-pocus of Blavatsky, but because he felt her spirits, allied to the faery world of Sligo would link him with the Great Memory that contains all truth; to Blake but because his Divine Passion kills the reason and generates the imagination which is the "first emanation of divinity"; to Symbolism, but because it "entangles a part of the Divine essence." So his loyalties are the passionate man, the imaginative man, the man fused into an unity with himself and with Being by a traditional faith or a mood or an ecstacy, until his characteristics fall away and his naked personality becomes more symbol than man, an Alastor, an Axel, a Manfred, an Ahasuerus, "half-animal, half-divine."

It is a romantic's desire, a Celt's reaching out for the Star of Indefinite Desire. And in a world which had long since broken down into fragments from a condition of common faith and hopes still existed, to a dream of creating a new Prometheus Unbound, with Columcille or Patrick for Prometheus, and Croagh Patrick or Ben Bulben for the Caucasus. Then at last life might become whole again and he, as part of that wholeness, see "artist and poet, craftsman and day-labourer" accept a common design.

Life, and particularly life in so poor a country as Ireland, had other ambitions, however, and yet she seduced him from his heights. He came, sadly, though I think, prematurely, to confess his folly. "That a modern nation can return to Unity of Culture is false; though it may be we can achieve it for some small circle of men and women and these leave it till the moon bring round its century." He left his plays and his committees—"a curse on plays"—that had kept him busy from 1902 to 1912, and he returned to a deeper and more persistent study of this matter of Unity of Being. But he who had betrayed the Intellectual Beauty and the Divine Passion, spent nearly fifteen years in cleansing himself for readmission to the temple. *The Wild Swans at Coole* is the mark of his return to the fold, and no study of the essential Yeats but must begin at that date, or somewhat before, for the reasons implicit in what I have said about these secret and deepest desires of his heart.

One may attempt to trace this in his poetry, keeping to his poems alone; but sooner or later one comes on this internal conflict, and is obliged to declare that though much of it is more personal to the man than to the poet, it is, from 1900 on, more and more essential to him *as artist.*

What had been his course before, roughly, 1912, as seen in his verse? He had begun in the Ivory Tower, and his genius made of it *The Wanderings of Oisin.* But he needed more than that, and needed to enlarge his personal world to do more than that. He was interested

in the occult from, at least, '85, in Blake and Symbolism from '90—though he did not meet Verlaine until '94, and Symons probably not until about '96; but symbolism was at its height, in any case, from 1890 to, say, 1910. Had it not been for Ireland he might have petered out (or come sooner up against himself) with the petering out of the shallow inspiration of the Yellow Book period, or the exhaustion of the symbolist impulse. *The Wind among the Reeds* marks, in fact, the last wine he sucked from the symbolist flagons, and he had exhausted even Ireland—in so far as it meant only the Celtic Twilight kind of thing—by 1900. Then he got new lease of life from Ireland, and was vitalized by Synge and the theatre, so that we find him by 1903 saying that he is trying to put a "less dream-burdened will" into his work, and by 1906, driving out of his cocoon of self, delighting in "the whole man, blood, intellect and imagination running together." It was as if his will then said to him: "Well, are you always going to be just a lovely lyric poet? Finding stimulus here, there and everywhere, from Florence Farr and the psaltery, or theosophical maunderings about the Infinite, or spooks in Soho? When are you going to make something out of your own guts?"

He did not need to reply. He was come, by the very act of leaving his own self behind, into this conflict of which I have spoken; found his naked personal self engaged in a war with his anti-self. He had gone too far. Bitterly he reveals it in *The Green Helmet,* a slim volume that is all he can show of verse for the six years before 1910, where he rails at all that has been distracting him, the day's war, plays, management of men; he is still railing in *Responsibilities* four years later, at the nationalists, the realists, the haters, the miserly Paudeens, the men who damned the *Playboy,* and who would not help Hugh Lane, and who not only embittered him and wasted his time, but stole him from the Eternal Beauty. He is eager, it is clear, to fly back to the Ivory Tower. But there is the crux; other selves have been born within him in the meantime, shell within shell, and whether he knew it or not that twin and triplet birth was to bring him his finest verse of all. For, after all, conflict *is* "spontaneous energy," and breeds without thought. (pp. 680-83)

So he wrote in 1916:

I would be ignorant as the dawn,
That has looked down
On that old queen measuring a town
With the pin of a brooch,
Or on the withered men that saw
From their pedantic Babylon
The careless planets in their courses,
The stars fade out where the moon comes,
And took their tablets and did sums;
I would be ignorant as the dawn
That merely stood, rocking the glittering coach

Above the cloudy shoulders of the horses;
I would be—for no knowledge is worth a straw—
Ignorant and wanton as the dawn.

It is an Elegy for Innocence, and it goes rightly with **"Lines Written in Dejection,"** where, under the symbolism of sun and moon—the moon being the obscure and shadowy cave of generation—he sighs that being come to fifty years he must endure the timid sun—the timid, objective, unmysterious sun.

I do not see that it matters if Yeats really does not wish to be ignorant as the dawn, or if he knows well that his complex and arrogant and coloured nature could never conceivably have any bridge across to these who are really ignorant and innocent and simple and spontaneous. Indeed, if one even said, "It is all a great pose," I do not see that that matters a pin. . . . Something had been felt by him, even if felt no more deeply than a great actor feels a part, and it had helped him, so feeling, to dramatize himself out of the Anima Mundi into a symbol.

Thereby, then, so curiously, by 1919, comes the finest of Yeats' verse. See a poem like **"Ego Dominus Tuus,"** in *The Wild Swans at Coole,* too long to quote, or the magnificent:

There is a queen in China or maybe it's in Spain,
And birthdays and holidays such praises can be
    heard
Of her unblemished lineaments, a whiteness with
    no stain
That she might be that sprightly girl trodden by a
    bird;
And there's a score of duchesses, surpassing woman
    kind,
Or who have found a painter to make them so for
    pay
And smooth out every blemish with the elegance of
    his mind;
I knew a phoenix in my youth, so let them have their
    day. . . .

That is the poetry of a personality self-dramatized with arrogance, moving towards the creation of a new Beatrice. Again and again he beats out that deeper and more vibrant note of a Narcissus-Faustus:—

Never until this night have I been stirred.
The elaborate starlight throws a reflection
On the dark stream,
Till all the eddies gleam,
And thereupon there comes a scream,
From terrified invisible beast or bird:
Image of poignant recollection.

Or it is heard again in:

Turning and turning in the widening gyre
The falcon cannot hear the falconer;
Things fall apart; the centre cannot hold;
Mere anarchy is loosed upon the world,
The blood-dimmed tide is loosed and everywhere

The ceremony of innocence is drowned;
The best lack all conviction, while the worst
Are full of passionate intensity. . . .

Or in that lovely, lovely poem, **"A Prayer for My Daughter"**. . . . (pp. 684-85)

After that comes *The Tower* and *The Winding Stair,* where his verse becomes so powerful and so evocative and so tragic that one who did not know the sequence of his work, or the sequence of his life, or have the key to his internal conflict, could never have thought it possible for the rather feminine poet of *The Wanderings of Oisin,* to write:—

It is time that I wrote my will;
I choose upstanding men
That climb the streams until
The fountain leap, and at dawn
Drop their cast at the side
Of dripping stone: I declare
They shall inherit my pride
The pride of people that were
Bound neither to Cause nor to State
Neither to slaves that were spat on,
Nor to the tyrants that spat,
The people of Burke and of Grattan,
That gave, though free to refuse—
Pride, like that of the morn,
When the headlong light is lose,
Or that of the fabulous horn,
Or that of the sudden shower
When all the streams are dry,
Or that of the hour
When the swan must fix his eye
Upon a fading gleam,
Float out upon a long
Last reach of glittering stream
And there sing his last song.
And I declare my faith:
I mock Plotinus' thought
And cry in Plato's teeth,
Death and life were not
Till man made up the whole,
Made lock stock and barrel
Out of his bitter soul,
Aye, sun, moon, and star, all,
And further add to that
That, being dead, we rise
Dream and so create
Translunar Paradise. . . .

I wish I could quote it all, but the quality of it is apparent, and it is a quality of poetry that is clearly driven up out of a man preoccupied with self, yet rising out of the bonds of self. He has not unified himself, he never could have unified himself, but he has not corroded within himself as all men do who vainly eat their own hearts, feed on and feed their own dreams.

I am a young man, and my generation in Ireland sometimes finds it hard to make a bridge across to the generation of Yeats. We find a lack of wisdom in it, of humanity, and of sincerity. We feel we are of the age of steel and that these last romantics are of the age of gold, to use his imagery again. Though what one really means by "lack of sincerity" is, no doubt, that our values differ, and our insistence on intellectual sincerity and his insistence on emotional sincerity must both of them be tested by time; since there is, no doubt, in both, equal room for self-deceit.

That preoccupation of Yeats with his own conflicts is, I think, dangerous and seductive, and I feel that wherever, in that poetry of conflict, one is aware, not of the conflict, but of Yeats, as in a drama one might suddenly become aware not of the theme but the author, his poetry is at its weakest. Graceless though it be, I close with a poem of that sort, a section in a long poem called **"Vacillation,"** beginning:—

"Between   extremities   man   runs   his   course. . . . " it says:—

> Must we part, Von Huegel, though much alike, for we
> Accept the miracles of the saints and honour sanctity?
> The body of Saint Teresa lies undecayed in the tomb,
> Bathed in miraculous oil, sweet odours from it come,
> Healing from its lettered slab. Those self-same hands perchance
> Eternalised the body of a modern saint that once
> Had scooped out Pharoh's mummy. I—though heart might find relief
> Did I become a Christian man and choose for my belief
> What seems most welcome in the tomb—play a predestined part,
> Homer is my example and his unchristened heart.
> The lion and the honeycomb, what has Scripture said?
> So get you gone, Von Huegel, though with blessings on your head.

Conflict on conflict! Yeats was born in 1865, seventy years ago this month, and has been wavering ever since, between that romanticism and this realism, between that traditionalism and this revolt, that prettiness and this ugliness, that loyalty to the *moi* and this loyalty to the *nous* that inwardness and this outwardness, that picturesque Ireland and this raw Ireland, that kind of truth and this. "We were the last romantics" . . .

> But all is changed, that high horse riderless,
> Though mounted in the saddle Homer rode
> Where the swan drifts upon the darkening flood.

He has lived long enough to see a world go and a world come, and he is so vigorous and so alive and so emotionally intact that he cannot deny the validity of either of them. Which may explain why neither generation trusts him, and each claims him, and both give

him the fullness of their admiration for the loveliness he has taken—I might even say, robbed without payment from each time. (pp. 686-88)

Seán O'Faoláin, "W. B. Yeats," in *The English Review,* Vol. LX, No. 6, June, 1935, pp. 680-88.

W. H. AUDEN
(essay date 1940)

[Often considered the poetic successor of W. B. Yeats and T. S. Eliot, Auden is also highly regarded for his literary criticism. In the following excerpt he praises Yeats as a great lyric poet.]

"Everything he wrote was read," Yeats said in one of his last poems, and, indeed, he was unusually fortunate, for few poets have so managed to complete their career without suffering any reverses of reputation, at least with the young, and still fewer have written their most widely-acclaimed work in the second half of their life. The universal admiration which his later poems have commanded is all the more surprising when one remembers how antaganostic were both his general opinions and his conception of his art to those current in recent literary movements. . . . I find it encouraging that, despite this, Yeats was recognized as a great poet, for it indicates that readers are less bigoted, less insistant upon the identity of the poet's beliefs with their own, and, when they can find some that is not completely trivial in subject, more appreciative of poetry that sounds well, that *sings,* than they sometimes appear.

The first thing that strikes one about Yeats is that he really enjoyed writing poetry. Some moderns make one feel that they regard it merely as a necessary means to some other end, the communication of ideas, mystical experience, self-analysis, castigation of abuses or what-have-you, and that the medium in which they work, the sounds and patterns of words, irrespective of the subject, give them little or no pleasure. Yeats, on the other hand, was always more concerned with whether or not a phrase sounded effective, than with the truth of its idea or the honesty of its emotion.

Both attitudes, the Puritanical and the Esthetic, have their dangers. The first, in forgetting that poetry is an *art,* i.e., artificial, a *factible* not an *agibile,* may defeat its own purpose by producing drab stuff which is so harsh to the ear and lacking in pattern, that no one can take any pleasure in reading it; the second, by ignoring the fact that the artist is a human being with a moral responsibility to be honest, humble, and self-critical, may leave the poet too easily content with ideas which he finds poetically useful and effective. Not bothering to reexamine them, to throw out the false elements and develop the rest further, he is prevented from reaching his full potential poetic stature, and remains playing variations on the old tune which has served him so well in the past.

It cannot be said that Yeats completely escaped this second temptation. There are, particularly in [*Last Poems*], more frequent echoes from his own previous work, both in phrasing and rhythm, than there ought to be, and, though every short poem, no doubt, expresses an attitude which in so far as it is one out of many possible moods may be called a pose, its singularity should not obtrude, and on occasion Yeats indulges in an embarrassing insistence upon an old man's virility, which some one who was more self-critical, not as a poet, but as a man, would have avoided.

Further, his utter lack of effort to relate his esthetic Weltanschauung with that of science, a hostile neglect which was due, in part at least, to the age in which he was born when science was avidly mechanistic, was perhaps the reason why he never succeeded in writing a long poem. . . .

Much of his best work. . . . is concerned with the relation of Life and Art. In this relation he had, like Thomas Mann and Valéry, a profound sense of what Kierkegaard called the Dialectic, but his vision of other kinds of relations was two-dimensional. Hence his onesided determinist and "musical" view of history, and the lack of drama which not all his theater can conceal. I cannot but feel, for instance, that the two plays in this volume are worthless.

Yet how little we care. For it is the lyrics we read. In lyric writing what matters more than anything else, more than subject-matter or wisdom, is diction, and of diction, "simple, sensuous and passionate," Yeats is a consummate master.

W. H. Auden, "Yeats: Master of Diction," in *The Saturday Review of Literature*, Vol. XXII, No. 7, June 8, 1940, p. 14.

LEONARD E. NATHAN
(essay date 1965)

[In the following excerpt from his conclusion to *The Tragic Drama of William Butler Yeats*, Nathan assesses the degree to which Yeats realized his dramatic aims.]

Yeats, in one of his last critical pronouncements, speaks of a perpetual war "where opposites die each other's life, live each other's death." This is no less than the war of "spiritual with natural order," the subject of *The Secret Rose* nearly forty years earlier—the war at the heart of human experience and therefore, so Yeats believed, the most serious subject for the drama. On the strength of that belief, he labored, often in bitterly discouraging circumstances, to find a dramatic form that would suit a living stage. The intensity of Yeats's desire to find a suitable embodiment for this chosen subject can be measured by his ruthless self-criticism; he was, both as poet and playwright, a constant and careful reviser. From the beginning he got little enough help from the English theatre where the only war was between the proponents of a dying traditional drama and the advocates of the realistic problem play. In this situation the temptation for a literary man, with an inclination for playwriting, would be closet drama or, perhaps, dramatic monologue. But Yeats wanted to write plays for a living theatre, "character in action," not "action in character"; the result was years of experiment that began in the shadowy precincts of Pre-Raphaelite moodiness and ended in the lucid depths of the individual mind, scene of a relentless but sometimes ennobling conflict between spirit and nature. (pp. 251-52)

[The] last period in the long search contains the best plays because in them Yeats had for the first time satisfied his own dramatic requirements. When the supernatural order appeared on stage in *The Only Jealousy of Emer* it could not by any rationalization be passed off as a symbol for psychological or sociological realities; the supernatural, in the last plays, is the supernatural or the spiritual reality either in the self or beyond it, no more and no less. This achievement cannot be claimed for the earlier plays.

It is perhaps indicative of their failure to offer a serious presentation of the supernatural that *The Land of Heart's Desire, The Countess Cathleen,* and even *On Baile's Strand* are so easily accepted into the traditional repertory. If *Purgatory* is also accepted, I think that must be laid to the fact that the play looks a little like *Waiting for Godot,* that is, seems to fit into the new fashion.

The question then is this: Do the last plays, understood as serious embodiments of spiritual reality, have any place in the tradition of plays that deserve a stage, or are they brilliant closet dramas at best, despite Yeats's intention? One easy answer is to "interpret" these plays in some way so that they do become psychological after all. Another such answer, a better one, is to invoke the "willing suspension of disbelief," to say, in substance, that in their own terms the plays are valid, as *The Divine Comedy* is valid for non-Catholics or unmedieval Catholics.

The first answer will not do; the second is somewhat evasive and fails to do justice to . . . Yeats's philosophical seriousness as a playwright. For Yeats demands belief, if not in his system, then in the reality the system names and orders. Just how much belief he demanded is indicated by the requirements for staging his dance plays: better than fair actors, unremitting adherence to the convention, and an audience that comes with no expectation of daily reality or some noble form of it. Yeats saw to it, in short, that his last words in the drama would not be easily domesticated to the modern stage. And naturally enough the reaction from those not willing to make concessions to so stubborn an eccentric has been indifference, baffled irritation, or patronizing dismissal. It is one thing to admit the "theatre of the absurd" into the repertory; it is quite another to admit what looks very odd but lays claim to being just the opposite. Yeats is perhaps *too* clear to misinterpret on this score. So he can be safely left to the bravery of college theatres which may not be quite so devoted to fashion and so much the victims of box office. Or the plays can be studied in class as literature, an adjunct to the poems but less important than some of the secondary texts used.

Yeats understood the consequences of his position but was willing to take the risks. He never expected, at least in our era, that he would be regarded as another in a long line of tragic playwrights of the western tradition and that his last plays would be familiar to a wide audience, so perhaps any justification of these plays as part of the great tradition is beside the point. In *On the Boiler* he sums up his awareness with a fine clarity:

> The theatre has not . . . gone my way or in any way I wanted it to go, and often looking back I have wondered if I did right in giving so much of my life to the expression of other men's genius. According to the Indians a man may do much good yet lose his own soul. Then I say to myself, I have had greater luck than any other modern English-speaking dramatist; I have aimed at tragic ecstasy and here and there in my own work and in the work of my friends I have seen it greatly played. What does it matter that it belongs to a dead art and to a time when a man spoke out of an experience and a culture that were not of his time alone, but held his time, as it were, at arms length, that he might be a spectator of the ages.

Yet I think there is reason to regard the best of the last plays as fit for the modern stage, even if one grants their obvious and demanding limitations. *Purgatory* and *The Only Jealousy of Emer* are moving works not because they fit neatly into categories like the psychological or social that give moderns a way of interpreting even the strangest kinds of art but because they treat man's fate with the ruthless honesty and convincing dignity open to the tragic dramatist, more especially open, if history is any proof at all, to the tragic dramatist who is also a great poet. Nor are the honesty and dignity alien to moderns. Yeats's last plays restate, in a new way, the traditional position of tragedy: man, di-

vided and complex, vulnerable both to the world and to himself, is forced to make choices that give him his destiny. Built into this very situation is the possibility—almost probability—that he will bring down suffering on his head and injure others in the process. The total reality of his condition compels him to make his choice; this reality involves a mystery that goes beyond the "natural" or the social, and one cannot account for this mystery by reducing it to psychological, sociological, or historical categories. It is a vital, sometimes terrible presence that man recognizes in moments when his passions seem to break out of the circle of the human. Call the presence anything you like, Apollo or daemon, it is a fact of experience and, in the drama, a fact that inspires belief. The hero is a man who draws this presence to him; it arouses him, by its opposition, to great passion and to action that leads to calamity and suffering in which he discovers his destiny and the wonder of his humanness. In this discovery there can be something like joy, or at least that high, resonant calm in which the whole being accepts what must be and finds its part in the nature of things. If, as in *Purgatory,* the passion falls back on itself without achieving the calm of acceptance, at least the audience has been in the presence of an intensity that is a revelation of one great human possibility.

> O bitter reward
> Of many a tragic tomb!
> And we though astonished are dumb
> Or give but a sigh and a word,
> A passing word.

Leonard E. Nathan, in his *The Tragic Drama of William Butler Yeats: Figures in a Dance,* Columbia University Press, 1965, 307 p.

CAIRNS CRAIG
(essay date 1982)

[In the following excerpt, Craig examines several of Yeats's poems written before 1925, the year Yeats began revising his early poetry. Craig traces the reappearance of images from these early poems in "Sailing to Byzantium," which he considers one of Yeats's greatest poems.]

It is the contradictory pulls of the romantic desire to transcend time and the associationist dependence on time that forms the basis of much of Yeats's early poetry. Yeats, of course, named himself among the 'last romantics', and his early poetry is often dismissed as a poetry of romantic longing and escape which fails to connect with the real world. Within that poetry, however, there is a rarely acknowledged degree of self-awareness that is the result, I would suggest, of the conflict between competing conceptions of the powers and purposes of art. The poem as a whole may represent an escape from the modern world—in that it deals with Irish mythic subjects in an archaic manner—but because Yeats's conception of such subjects was that they formed the end point of the memory invoked by modern art, the poems often turn back upon the reader to comment on their own status and to comment on the aesthetic experience of which they are a part. They are, despite their apparent naivete, 'self-conscious'.

Probably the finest of the very early poems is **'The Madness of King Goll'.** Yeats presents us with the story of an ancient Irish king, Goll, whose success as a king has been to establish peace and prosperity among his people, a success which perhaps involves a denial of those heroic values which he would wish to live by and for which he is interesting to readers of Yeats's poem. . . . 'Tumult' was a word Yeats often used to describe ancient art . . . and Goll's success in driving 'tumult and war away', banishing the need for the heroic, mirrors nineteenth-century society's destruction of the 'world of selfless passion in which heroic deeds are possible and heroic poetry credible'. Called again to battle against invaders, however, Goll does not recover his heroic stature, but undergoes a revelation that destroys his own ability to live the heroic life. . . . The moment of interaction between the eternal—'keen stars'—and the temporal—'keen eyes of men'—is a source of revelation used regularly by Shelley and a part of Yeats's romantic inheritance. The visionary who has been vouchsafed a sudden insight into the eternal beauty that occasionally visits itself upon the temporal world is cast out of human society in search of apocalyptic fulfilment of his vision. Like Shelley's Alastor, Goll becomes a wanderer, and even Yeats's imagery is an echo of Shelley's, for it is by the mirroring of eyes that Shelley often symbolises union between different ontological dimensions of existence: 'yellow flowers / For ever gaze on their own drooping eyes, / Reflected in the crystal calm'. But in Yeats's mirroring in **'King Goll'** there is no revelation of spiritual compatibility between mind and eternity: the stars mirror the eyes of men in battle, their exaltation the lust for destruction. Goll is not led to a transcendental consciousness of time resolved into the eternal, but is trapped in an awareness of endless, and endlessly destructive time. The poem's refrain, with its emphasis on decay never resolved by death—'the leaves a-flutter round me, the beech leaves old'—posits a world of time forever in motion and decaying and yet without end. Time itself is equal with eternity in that it never passes away. Nature, so often the instantiation of the spirit of eternity for the romantics, is here an image only of unending process, an eternity not of salvation but of destruction. Yeats's choice of 'a-flutter' to describe the

leaves, its archaism balancing verbal and adjectival against each other, creates the sense of motion and stasis conjoined, as the reiterated refrain balances the sense of temporal process which it describes ('old') against the stasis which its repetition enacts. No apocalypse will save the world of time from its own unceasing, endless change, a condition which Goll mirrors in his endless 'wandering' . . . (pp. 78-80)

In Goll's endless wandering, however, we can see an image not only of an eternity of time within which mankind is trapped, but an image of the poem's own conception of the nature of art. Goll's moment of insight comes from 'a whirling and a wandering fire' and passes on into further wandering, just as the associational process reaches through a train of images to some overwhelmingly powerful image that will set the mind wandering again from 'idea to idea, emotion to emotion'. The endless movement of associations around the stasis of the work of art is almost figured in the endless flutter of the beech leaves, as though the refrain mirrors the process by which we experience and give significance to Yeats's image. Goll's exclusion from eternity is identical with the poem's inability to lead our minds to anything but further experiences of temporal process. Such mirroring between Yeats's story and the reader's experience might seem fanciful were it not for the fact that the poem's final stanza presents us with Goll mimicking Yeats's own art, for he finds 'this old tympan' and begins to sing:

I sang how, when day's toil is done,
Orchil shakes out her long dark hair
That hides away the dying sun
And sheds faint odours through the air:
When my hand passed from wire to wire
It quenched with sound like falling dew,
The whirling and the wandering fire;
But lift a mournful ulalu,
For the kind wires are torn and still,
And I must wander wood and hill.

The 'dying sun' operates here on two different levels, one faithful to Goll's sense of the world and one that refers back upon ours. For Goll it is a metaphor for sunset, or an animistic conception of daily recreation of the universe; for us, 'dying sun' all too accurately describes the realities of our universe as revealed by science. Goll's song of Orchil does the same for him as Yeats's poem is doing for its readership; both hide away the dying sun behind figures who inhabit an apparently timeless realm. For us, however, the timeless figure of Goll re-enacts within his own realm of existence the dilemmas from which we sought escape in art, and reveals the extent to which art itself is no pathway to some ultimate transcendence of our human condition. Art, in its associational recall of the past, has its power only by its recall of a tumultuous past. . . . It is therefore trapped in an endless process of time, and neither heroic action nor visionary insight will release it into a different ontological status.

The failure of heroism and of visionary insight to offer a romantic access to the Infinite dominates Yeats's early poems: the heroes are never satisfied by their great actions, the visionaries never consoled by their insights. Both are haunted by the sense of time as endless series, denying any value to individual action, and by an eternity which is merely an infinite repetition of the events of time. Thus in **'Fergus and the Druid'** . . . , Fergus the warrior king seeks the 'dreaming wisdom' of the Druid, and to gain it has given up his kingship and become, like Goll, a wanderer. . . . Fergus is . . . given by Yeats a consciousness of what he will become as a part of Yeats's poem and our own memory 'another's dream'. His heroism may give eternity of a kind to his name, but it cannot save him; neither, however, can the wisdom of the Druid, for instead of offering a romantic access to the eternal, what the Druid reveals is a world of boundless repetition of the experience of time, a knowledge which is endless memory rather than the transcendence of a world of time and the need for memory that Fergus sought. . . . (pp. 80-1)

What Yeats is presenting in both Fergus and Goll are images of the tensions within his own art. The romantic artist who is the inheritor of the powers of the

The actress Maud Gonne was the object of much of Yeats's love poetry.

magus and the druid would like to offer his art as an entry into eternity, as an escape from time, but the art itself denies any such release, and can lead to no ultimate revelation of what is permanent in the world. Associational process, the continual generation of a train of images moving outwards and away from the work of art itself, is mirrored in Goll surrounded by the endlessly ancient and fluttering leaves, is mirrored in Fergus's discovery of the chain of images of which his being is a part. The romantic demand that art, through the spiritual power of the imagination, should save us from the world of time is undone by the knowledge that art works only through memory and is devoted to the endless recall of the events of time. The characters of the poems act out the failure of the romantic desire, ironically commenting on what we have sought from the poem. The conditions from which we have sought to escape are repeated in the world we escape into, and the tension between our desire for transcendence through art and the real nature of what we can be offered by art is perhaps summed up in an image from another early poem, **'The Indian to His Love'**:

A parrot sways upon a tree
Raging at his own image in the enamelled sea. . . .

The parrot rages at the more perfect life in the 'enamelled sea', but his image there is only a repetition of the condition in which he already exists.

My point in drawing attention to these early poems is not merely to suggest that some of Yeats's early work is more complex than usually taken to be: the conflict which they reveal between the sense of art as a transcendence of time and of an associationist art's necessary complicity with time was to be a pervasive theme of Yeats's poetry. And the technique of playing off the real nature of the reading experience . . . against the apparent stasis of the poem and the possible unchanging reality to which it testifies was one which he was to exploit with ever-increasing subtlety. In 1925 Yeats began a revision of the whole body of his early poetry, and the images and tensions in the three poems I have mentioned seeped into one of his greatest poems. **'Sailing to Byzantium'**, written in the following year. The first stanza recapitulates the sense of a world of endless change in which Goll finds himself, process become eternal in its negation of any other dimension of existence. . . . (pp. 82-3)

The second stanza of **'Sailing to Byzantium'** offers us Yeats—'A tattered coat upon a stick'—in the same guise as the Druid whose knowledge could be of no comfort to Fergus. . . . Knowledge such as the Druid's cuts him off from the pleasures of active life; cut off from the pleasures of active life, Yeats sets off after knowledge as compensation for what time has taken from him. But his journey to Byzantium is paradoxical, poised between real and hypothetical as was the journey of the lovers in **'The Indian to His Love.'** . . . (pp. 83-4)

The echoes between early and late poems continue in the imagery of 'song': In **'King Goll'** the mad song allows the goddess to be called up who 'hides away the dying day'; in **'Sailing to Byzantium'** the sages are called from the work of art just as the goddess was called from eternity, but are called to be singing masters. . . . Goll's song puts him in touch with eternity through artifice; the song in **'Sailing to Byzantium'** conceals death by incorporating the speaker into artifice. The origins of the golden bird that Yeats decides to take as his form in the afterlife may be in Hans Andersen's clockwork nightingale and Keats's 'immortal bird', but it also takes us back to the parrot, for while in the early poem the bird rages at its aesthetic mirror image, enamelled by the sea, in the later poem the poet crosses into the world of art to become an 'enamelled' golden bird. In **'The Indian to His Love'** the voyage of escape to the island turns back upon itself, for the lovers' conversation is of what they have left behind, of 'how far away are the unquiet lands', and in exactly parallel fashion **'Sailing to Byzantium'** turns back upon itself, as the artificial bird, released from time and change, sings of 'what is past, or passing, or to come'. That turning back to the world which one has desired to escape has, since its first publication, always presented problems to Yeats's critics. Why should the achievement of an eternal stasis in a perfect world be qualified by a return to time in the bird's song? The comparison with the early poems allows us to see, I think, that this is not just an accidental or contradictory element in Yeats's writing of this particular poem, but an essential part of his view of art. The contradictions from which one seeks an escape through art always repeat themselves within the world of art, and **'Sailing to Byzantium'** is no exception. And that internal movement of the poem is related to the formal tension between its apparent stasis—a 'monument of unageing intellect'—and the temporal process of association upon which it depends for its full experience. If the work of art succeeded in defying time it would destroy its own essential power, which comes from the trains of thought it generates in time, from what 'is past, or passing, or to come'. The bird's singing does not mean that it has the gift of prophecy (Yeats cancelled 'future' from the drafts), but that it sings what is always to come, and what dominates the rest of the volume *The Tower*, to which it is the introduction—death and loss and destruction. As a part of a remembered tradition, however, it also introduces what is to be placed against those eternal enemies—the powers of memory.

The problems which **'Sailing to Byzantium'** has posed revolve largely around the fact that Byzantium is supposed to be Yeats's ideal city of the imagination—or 'Condition of Fire', as Harold Bloom calls it [in his

Yeats, 1970]; it is supposed to be a symbol of the symbolising faculty's ability to carry us into a spiritual eternity. But the desire for such transcendence is set within a concept of art based on invoking into the matrix of the reader's experience a succession of images from the past, and in reading it we are driven necessarily, therefore, to defy the fixity to which the poetic persona aspires. **'Sailing to Byzantium'** is not a failed poem of the 'Condition of Fire' or of the romantic imagination, as Bloom, for instance would have us believe, but a poem ironically commenting upon the ways in which poets will create heavens from their art in spite of that art's real nature. Just as the early poem **'The Indian upon God'** presents us with a peacock who imagines God 'a monstrous peacock,' . . . so the poetic persona in **'Sailing to Byzantium'** invents a heaven which the poem itself undercuts as it forces him to turn back to the world of time. And that turning back is something that we, too, are forced to experience as we read the final lines. . . . Where is the golden bird, so much the subject of critical debate? To know the form the speaker will take we have to return to the 'birds in the trees / Those dying generations' of stanza one: we have to make a journey back in memory to the world of time, or, if we are lucky, back in memory to previous descriptions of such artifacts. It is not the golden bird that figures for us Yeats's conception of art, defying time in the perfection of its beauty, but the whole dialectic of the poem. Yeats's art is a combining of the flux of time, to which the art of music is the appropriate correlative, and the sculpted stasis of the monumental image: the time transcending images of the poem recall a world of time in our associations and it is through those associations that the images gain their power and significance. It is the song of the dying generations *and* the fixity of the artistic form together that are the basis of Yeats's concept of art; it is the forward movement of the poem, a song in time, towards an image that is apparently beyond time, as though sculpted, but releasing the reader's mind into an associative reverie that will carry him far into the past, that constitutes the essential structure of Yeats's poetic. And within such a poetic the associations with which we enclose the poem may, from the point in time when the poem was written, be in the future: thus can it sing what is yet 'to come'. (pp. 85-7)

Cairns Craig, "Yeats: The Art of Memory," in his *Yeats, Eliot, Pound and the Politics of Poetry: Richest to the Richest,* University of Pittsburgh Press, 1982, pp. 72-111.

Yeats on magic:

I believe in the practice and philosophy of what we have agreed to call magic, in what I must call the evocation of spirits, though I do not know what they are, in the power of creating magical illusions, in the visions of truth in the depths of the mind when the eyes are closed; and I believe in three doctrines, which have, as I think, been handed down from early times, and been the foundations of nearly all magical practices. These doctrines are:—

(1) That the borders of our mind are ever shifting, and that many minds can flow into one another, as it were, and create or reveal a single mind, a single energy.

(2) That the borders of our memories are as shifting, and that our memories are a part of one great memory, the memory of Nature herself.

(3) That this great mind and great memory can be evoked by symbols.

I often think I would put this belief in magic from me if I could, for I have come to see or to imagine, in men and women, in houses, in handicrafts, in nearly all sights and sounds, a certain evil, a certain ugliness, that comes from the slow perishing through the centuries of a quality of mind that made this belief and its evidences common over the world.

Yeats, in his 1901 essay "Magic" published in *Essays and Introductions* (1961).

is what the sense of being at the end of a tradition amounts to—you can have no such energy of purpose. [The best modern English poets]—Hardy, Thomas and Gurney—consider that they are at the end of the line. Their sense of the past includes a sense of its absolute uncoupling from the future. Whether they are correct is not my concern. Their conviction is. Their best poetry comes out of a last, desperate, deeply rooted wish to testify to the worth of what they are convinced is about to disappear. It is possible to say that there is nothing new in this, that it is in fact a strategy that had been employed by poets so otherwise different from each other as Pope and Wordsworth. But the difference is this: that none of these later poets has any sense of a fit audience, be it ever so few, to whom they can address their work, so that their producing poetry of worth is a triumph against the odds which they feel to be stacked against them. Pope had his circle, Wordsworth had his. But Hardy, Thomas and Gurney feel themselves to be living out on the end of an event. You may, if you like, argue that their sense of an ending is properly to be seen in terms of the end of particular class formations or of the role of the déraciné poet in an increasingly complex society; or you may say that all three of them are victims of the historical process which they lack the terms (or will) to understand. There is truth in all these contentions. But the fact remains that whatever the cause or the explanation, you come face to face with the inescapable truth that the best English poets [of the period] cannot feel themselves responsible to the kinds of large social issues that engage Yeats. (pp. 114-15)

JOHN LUCAS
(essay date 1986)

[Lucas is an English poet and critic who writes primarily on nineteenth- and twentieth-century fiction. In the following excerpt, he examines Yeats's attitudes toward twentieth-century Ireland as manifested in his poetry and prose.]

[Yeats] is radically different from nearly all English poets of the twentieth century, simply because they lack his complex sense of responsibility. You cannot hope to be fully responsible to your art unless you know—or at least take into consideration—what art is for. For Yeats, poetry serves the profoundly critical and creative purpose of being both for and about a nation's culture. It is an intervention in the history of that culture, meant to contribute to it in crucial ways, to testify to its vitality, to modify the stance of others, to engage in what is seen as a living process. But if you live at what you conceive to be the end of a culture—and that

It is this ability to intervene in current, critical issues which makes Yeats's poetry so different from and more valuable than contemporary English poetry. To say this is by no means to endorse all his positions. In what follows I shall offer reservations against some of his stances and I am even more critical of others. But this is possible—even necessary—just because Yeats's poetry occupies public space, as it were. This means that although much of it springs from deeply held or long-pondered convictions, it can come into being as a way of writing to the moment: it is occasional in the sense that a particular event requires Yeats to comment, and the comment is tested by and puts to the test the values, certainties, commitments, that he has fashioned out of his developing sense of responsibilities. Given this it is inevitable that Yeats is vulnerable to the charge of "getting it wrong" or of "misunderstanding"; or of an improper certainty. But this is what being his kind of poet necessarily entails. Yeats both takes away from poetry its Arnoldian "infallibility" and at the same time gives it a centrality which Arnold's way of thinking about the poet and poetry could never achieve. These comments bear particularly on the poems I am here considering.

According to [Elizabeth Cullingford in her study *Yeats, Ireland and Fascism*, 1981], Yeats thought that "the great man is genuinely the servant of his people, although he alone determines the form his service will take. For Nietzsche the 'noble' man has rights but no obligations: for Yeats rights entail duties." Perhaps, but what I find in **"To a Wealthy Man"** is a rancorous contempt, even hatred, that cannot be fully explained or justified by the events of 1912/13. The events become somehow displaced by Yeats's determination to compare Lane with great Italian Renaissance princes:

> What cared Duke Ercole, that bid
> His mummers to the market-place,
> What th'onion-sellers thought or did
> So that his Plautus set the pace
> For the Italian comedies?
> And Guidobaldo, when he made
> That grammar school of courtesies
> Where wit and beauty learned their trade
> Upon Urbino's windy hill,
> Had sent no runners to and fro
> That he might learn the shepherds' will.

It would be absurd to deny the panache of these lines. If you except Tennyson's lovely, late poem to Edward FitzGerald you have to go back to Marvell before you will find the tetrameter better handled. Yet this panache comes near to, and occasionally topples into, posture. It is the posture of a snobbish ranter. "Onion-sellers," "shepherds"; aren't they the equivalent of that peasantry which Yeats is usually so keen to invoke as integral to his dream of an Ireland united in politics as well as culture?

There is an analogous problem about **"September 1913."** Here, Yeats's contempt for the prudential values of those who oppose him—Murphy and his ilk—leads him to contrast contemporary Ireland with a past rich with heroes whose "wasteful virtues" brought each of them a martyr's death.

> Was it for this the wild geese spread
> The grey wing upon every tide;
> For this that all that blood was shed,
> For this Edward Fitzgerald died,
> And Robert Emmet and Wolfe Tone,
> All that delirium of the brave?
> Romantic Ireland's dead and gone,
> It's with O'Leary in the grave.

It is difficult to read these lines without thinking that Yeats is recommending the blood sacrifice which had famously been at the heart of his play *Cathleen ni Houlihan*, set in 1798, the year of the uprising in which both Fitzgerald and Wolfe Tone died. When the play was performed at the Abbey in 1902 Cathleen, the spirit of Ireland, was played by Maud Gonne, and at one key moment in the play the heroine is made to say "They that have red cheeks will have pale cheeks for my sake, and for all that, think they are well paid." The words were greeted with ecstatic applause, as was the play's ending. A young man enters to announce the French have landed at Killala, come to help the rising. Has he seen an old woman—i.e. Cathleen—going down the path, he is asked. No, he answers, "but I saw a young girl, and she had the walk of a queen." Two years after the staging of *Cathleen ni Houlihan*, Yeats gave a lecture on Robert Emmet to an American audience, in the course of which he imagined Emmet going to his death

> full of a kind of ecstasy of self-sacrifice. . . . And out of his grave his ideal has risen incorruptible. His martyrdom has changed the whole temper of the Irish nation. . . . In Ireland we sing the men who fell nobly and thereby made an idea mighty. When Ireland is triumphant and free, there will be yet something in the character of the people, something lofty and strange, which shall have been put there by her years of suffering and by the memory of her martyrs. Her martyrs have married her forever to the ideal.

"September 1913" is written out of an angry despair, a voiced belief that memory of the martyrs no longer holds good. Yeats cherished memory. In the dedicatory verses to *Responsibilities* he spoke of one of his "fathers" who was "A hundred-year-old memory to the poor"; and his intense concern for the sanctity of such memory means that he lashes out against those who have "come to sense" and who merely "fumble in the greasy till" rather than murmur name upon name: of Wolfe Tone, Fitzgerald, Emmet, O'Leary. The phrase "murmur name upon name," however, appears in **"Easter 1916,"** and that poem is about the extraordinary moment where the power of memory has shown itself in the most devastating way possible. For the new martyrs have indeed "risen incorruptible." Yeats is brought to face the full implications of that memory which in **"September 1913"** he had wholly celebrated, which undoubtedly is essential to a nation's sense of its identity, but which may turn out to be curse as much as blessing. It is not so much the attack on those who add "the prayer to the shivering prayer" that concerns me about **"September 1913."** Rather, it is the endorsement of the dream of "Romantic Ireland." For such a dream may carry with it a responsibility to accept the blood sacrifice, for oneself and for others. Can such a responsibility be justified?

The short answer is, no. This is what **"The Second Coming"** is about. The blood-dimmed tide that has been loosed on the world is not merely sweeping over Russia and mainland Europe; it is threatening to engulf Ireland. Seeing this, Yeats comes to understand the full implications of what memory may mean, of what the ecstasy of self-sacrifice may entail; and these things cause him to redefine his sense of responsibilities. He does not become any less of an Irish patriot.

But the events of 1916 and the following years reveal the full horrors of entering history. It is a subject that preoccupies him in a number of great poems, including **"Easter 1916," "Meditations in Time of Civil War,"** **"Leda and the Swan"** and, more problematically, **"In Memory of Eva Gore-Booth and Con Markiewicz."**

"Easter 1916" has often been compared to Marvell's Horatian Ode, and the comparison is just. Both poems try to keep a difficult balance while exploring and weighing the terrible complexities of recent events; neither is merely evasive or rhetorical, although because they resist the chance to make final judgements both have been seen—perhaps unfairly—as evasive. As is well known, the events of Easter 1916 took Yeats entirely by surprise. He had not known what was in the offing and he makes that much clear in the poem's opening section, whose typically anapaestic trimeter line implies the trivia of a Dublin existence where all are thought to wear "motley." Only at the end of the section do the anapaests disappear, with the hammer-blow of "All changed, changed utterly," which, while it can be read as a pure iambic line has, in its forced, shocked utterance the feel of a molossus ("All chánged, chánged utterly"). Yeats names and honours those who resigned their part in the casual comedy, but it is the problematic nature of their heroism that most concerns him. Their strong certainty of purpose both rebukes the casual flux of human affairs lived for the moment and gives those same affairs an allure that is new in his poetry. The paltriness of fumbling in a greasy till is, as it were, transmuted by events into instinctive acceptance of the living moment. Or rather, what Yeats had seen as living by prudential values becomes redefined: the commonness of life is now seen in terms that make it natural, unselfconscious, glad with movement:

A shadow of cloud on the stream
Changes minute by minute;
A horse-hoof slides on the brim,
And a horse plashes within it;
The long-legged moor-hens dive,
And hens to moor-cocks call;
Minute by minute they live:
The stone's in the midst of all.

And then follows the grieving recognition that "Too long a sacrifice / Can make a stone of the heart." In **"September 1913"** Yeats had celebrated the "wasteful virtues" of Emmet and the others who had "weighed so lightly what they gave." But now?

In his marvellous autobiography, *An Only Child,* Frank O'Connor writes of the time during the Civil War in Ireland when he fought on the Republican side. Taken prisoner by the Free Staters he spent much of his time reading Goethe's *Faust.* He also came to be increasingly suspicious of the notions of heroism and martyrdom that sustained the fighters on both sides. One line from *Faust* so impressed him that he wrote it out and pinned it over his bed. "Grey is your theory, dear friend, and green is the golden tree of life." O'Connor had become sickened by the mystique of "dying for the cause." He tells of his revulsion at the song made up to celebrate the death of one young soldier whom O'Connor had seen, minutes before his execution, sobbing and screaming in abject terror at what was to happen to him. According to the song the soldier went to his death gladly. O'Connor protested at the horror of it all. "And did Pearse not want to die?" he was asked. "No," he replied, "He awoke too late."

Perhaps. Perhaps not. Yeats did not think so, but he did come to share O'Connor's fear of what sacrificial death might mean. In **"The Rose Tree,"** one of a group of poems written out of the Easter uprising, Yeats has Pearse and Connolly discuss how the Irish rose may bloom once more:

"But where can we draw water,"
Said Pearse to Connolly,
"When all the wells are parched away?
O plain as plain can be
There's nothing but our own red blood
Can make a right Rose Tree."

The blood sacrifice is beyond reason. Or rather it is an expression of commitment immune to all feeling: so at least Yeats believed, and it explains why he places Con Markiewicz at the head of those whose sacrifice he celebrates and, at the same time, questions. As woman she is most cruelly the victim of the historical moment at which she chooses to act. The original sweetness of her voice has become shrill in argument. Her mind has become a "bitter, an abstract thing" (the phrase comes from **"On a Political Prisoner"**). Like Maud Gonne, Con Markiewicz has destroyed herself for the cause. That, at least, is Yeats's view of the matter.

"O when may it suffice?" Yeats asks in the last section of **"Easter 1916,"** and answers, "That is heaven's part." I grant that to say this may seem evasive, but I do not think it is. What the phrase implicitly acknowledges is that once you have let violence loose you can't choose when to lock it up again. From the shocked awareness of this truth Yeats turns to the traditional role of poetry as consolation. The poet must

murmur name upon name
As a mother names her child
When sleep at last has come
On limbs that had run wild.
What is it but nightfall?

But the murmured cadences of those lines are cut off by the insistent "No, no, not night but death." The poet may not retreat from the actualities of what happened into the false consolation of lyricism. Yet these consolation seem to return with the litany of names:

MacDonagh and MacBride
And Connolly and Pearse

Now and in time to be,
Wherever green is worn,
Are changed, changed utterly;
A terrible beauty is born.

I have argued with more than one friend who thinks that these final lines are merely rhetorical and so constitute an evasion of responsibilities. Yeats, they say, is letting "poetry" win over hard thought. I can see the force of the argument but I cannot accept it. What else can he do? He has already explored the terrible beauty of the martyrs' act, of their being metamorphosed into stony certainty of purpose. To honour their achievement is not to underestimate its cost. Indeed, it seems to me that it is the cost which most engages him. Hence the importance of the poem's appearing in the same volume as **"The Second Coming"** and **"A Prayer for My Daughter,"** poems which brood on the terrors of history. Again, the contrast with English poets is instructive. There is only one English poet who even begins to approach Yeats's passionately intelligent concern with what he sees as the "mere anarchy" being loosed upon the twentieth-century world, and that is Auden.

Michael Robartes and the Dancer was published in 1921. By then Ireland had become, in Yeats's own phrase, "a whirlpool of hate," and worse was to follow with the outbreak of the Civil War. In a letter of the time Yeats commented gloomily, "Perhaps there is nothing so dangerous to a modern state, when politics take the place of theology, as a bunch of martyrs. A bunch of martyrs (1916) were the bomb and we are living in the explosion." In 1923 he wrote **"Meditations in Time of Civil War,"** and in the sixth section of that poem he speaks in anguish of how

We had fed the heart on fantasies,
The heart's grown brutal from the fare;
More substance in our enmities
Than in our love. . . .

"We" honestly admits to the shared dream of an heroic past—*Cathleen ni Houlihan,* **"September 1913"**—whose realization in the present has become terrifying.

The same year he composed his great sonnet **"Leda and the Swan."** This poem has been the subject of a great deal of commentary, not all of it to the point; but its central meaning is clear enough. Yeats is writing here about the violence of entering history, and about how all, even the most innocent, are caught up in it. The rape of Leda becomes, in his imagination, an instance of the ways in which violence is both intoxicating and terrible. Moreover, as in **"Easter 1916"** so here: once you let violence loose you cannot decide when to lock it up again; its consequences are further violence, unpredictable, appalling, cataclysmic. From the rape of Leda came Helen and Clytemnestra, Castor and Pollux.

Being so caught up,
So mastered by the brute blood of the air,
Did she put on his knowledge with his
    power,
Before the indifferent beak could let her
    drop?

That brilliant pun on "Being so caught up" makes it inevitable, I think, that the answer to the question in these lines is "yes."

And this explains why in **"Easter 1916"** Yeats sees Con Markiewicz as caught up by the events of her time and why in the elegy he composed for her and her sister he should see the girls as "dear shadows" who only in death come to "know it all, / All the folly of a fight / With a common wrong or right." But here we do come to a critical question. For all the tenderness with which Yeats here speaks of the girls, and for all the magnanimity he elsewhere displays toward Maud Gonne, the fact remains that he never swerves from his view of their "folly," he never thinks of them as other than victims, he never considers the possible justification of their "fight." Why not? The answer has to be that he is committed to a dream of Irish culture which W. H. Auden contemptuously called "the parish of rich women," and which, although it certainly amounts to more than that, is nevertheless not entirely or easily defensible. (Auden's phrase is more accurate about Yeats's image of Lady Gregory, and the Gore-Booth sisters, than it is about the women themselves.)

Yeats of course was too intelligent not to realize just how vulnerable was his dream of Anglo-Irish culture. In the first section of **"Meditations in Time of Civil War"** he writes magnificently about the failure of the country-house tradition in Ireland. It is not merely that "Maybe the great grandson of that house / For all its bronze and marble's but a mouse," where the angry splutter of the second line admits to a lost vitality of purpose. More radically, Yeats knows that violence and bitterness are inextricably present in the creation of the country-house tradition. For after all, the Anglo-Irish ascendancy got their houses by usurping the land. They ascended on the backs of others. Deep at the heart of the literature of the country house is and must be a sense of possible guilt. That is why Ben Jonson is so keen to insist that Penshurst is a model of social relations ("Thou art built with no man's ruin, no man's groan"); and it is why Jane Austen should wish to introduce Elizabeth Bennet and Fanny Price, among others, to the country house. Their marrying the heirs of such property will bring a much-needed flow of new blood as well as symbolizing those harmonious relationships which image social peace.

The Anglo-Irish poet faces even more acute problems when he comes to celebrate the country-house tradition. The taking of the land is not merely an act of appropriation by one class over another; it is imperialistic, the domination of one nation over another. Yet such houses, "where all's accustomed, ceremonious," symbolize Yeats's cultural, social and political ideal for Ireland. The ideal is most perfectly realized in Lady Gregory's house, Coole Park, and in two poems Yeats sets out his sense of its significance. As is well known, he had himself bought an old, broken-down tower on the edge of her estate. It became both the artist's tower, image of a lonely search for truth, and the indication of how he placed his art at the service of the landed gentry, or more particularly, of Lady Gregory.

Perhaps the first important poem to make use of the tower is **"In Memory of Major Robert Gregory,"** and we need to note that Yeats writes this poem not merely to celebrate Gregory's life and mourn his death, but to affirm his commitment to values that are, so it seems, to become time's victims. For Gregory's death is, after all, one of millions that contribute to the "blood-dimmed tide." This does not necessarily mean that "Our Sidney and our perfect man" has died prematurely. Yeats implies that Gregory knew his work to be finished in one brief flaring of creative intensity and that he therefore chose death rather than wasting into unprofitable old age. (At the time of writing the poem Yeats, in common with others, had been led to assume that Gregory had killed himself. Only later was it discovered that he had been accidentally shot down.) In **"An Irish Airman Foresees His Death"** Yeats presents Gregory in the act of balancing all, seeing himself poised between "this life, this death." In the Elegy, Gregory is more mysteriously presented as Renaissance man born out of time: "What made us dream that he could comb grey hair?" But this is alluded to rather than paraded as fact, for the simple reason that Yeats needs to proceed tactfully. To celebrate an act of suicide is not easy; but on the other hand, it will hardly do to suggest that Gregory behaved irresponsibly. The solution Yeats fashions is to imply that the values by which Gregory lived or with which he associated are edging towards extinction. Hence the importance of the tower, which Gregory helped to decorate. It is an image of a way of life—service to high art, to the country-house ideal—whose day is nearly done.

> Now that we're almost settled in our house
> I'll name the friends that cannot sup with us
> Beside a fire of turf in th'ancient Tower,
> And having talked to some late hour
> Climb up the narrow winding stair to bed:
> Discoverers of forgotten truth
> Or mere companions of my youth,
> All, all are in my thoughts tonight being dead.

The country-house ideal takes for granted sociability, and the token for such sociability is eating. But in Yeats's house friends "cannot sup with us." The sense of living on into the fag-end of a tradition is implicit, it seems to me, in that deliberate antiquated 'th'

tower." In other words, the tower is self-consciously maintained as a symbol of a disappearing world. (In **"Meditations in Time of Civil War"** Yeats says that he has taken Thor Ballylee "that after me / My bodily heirs may find, / To exalt a lonely mind / Befitting emblems of adversity"). At the end of the Elegy, the poet's attention is called to the "bitter . . . wind / That shakes the shutter"; and this is the apocalyptic "roof-levelling wind" of **"A Prayer for My Daughter."** It is Shelley's wind of revolutionary change blowing in from the Atlantic, but bringing for Yeats the deadly energy of democratic vistas.

It is in this context that we need to consider the two poems in which Yeats celebrates Lady Gregory and her house. The first of these, **"Coole Park, 1929"** is an extremely beautiful poem, both decorous and passionate in its affirmation of the values which Yeats associates with his great friend; and the amplitude of its cadences finely tells of his and fellow-writers' gratitude for all that she meant to them:

> They came like swallows and like swallows went,
> And yet a woman's powerful character
> Could keep a swallow to its first intent;
> And half a dozen in formation there,
> That seemed to whirl upon a compass-point,
> Found certainty upon the dreaming air,
> The intellectual sweetness of those lines
> That cut through time or cross it withershins.

But as that last line indicates, the house's accomplishments succeed almost in defiance of time; and time will have its way. The last stanza makes this abundantly clear:

> Here, traveller, scholar, poet, take your stand
> When all these rooms and passages are gone,
> When nettles wave upon a shapeless mound
> And saplings root among the broken stone. . . .

This is not empty fear. During the 1920s many great houses in Ireland were burnt down, others were abandoned; still others were falling into decay. Coole Park itself was no longer in Lady Gregory's ownership, although she continued to live there. But some years after her death in 1932 the house was pulled down.

It is Yeats's near certainty of the house's fate that makes him want to celebrate what it stands for. He is its elegist, and he returns to the role in **"Coole Park and Ballylee, 1931."** But here I am not so persuaded that all is as it should be. I baulk when I come to the insistent claim that Lady Gregory is "a last inheritor / Where none has reigned that lacked a name and fame / Or out of folly into folly came." What, *none?* And anyway, although the phrase "name and fame" may at first seem strikingly sonorous, isn't it rhetorical tat at best, and at worst shrilly snobbish? The same seems to me true of the moment where Yeats asks us to believe that "gardens rich in memory glorified / Marriages, alliances and families, / And every bride's ambition satisfied." Reading that, I recall Mr. Dombey reflecting that "a matrimonial alliance [with himself] *must,* in the nature of things, be gratifying and honourable to any woman of common sense. . . . That Mrs. Dombey must have been happy. That she couldn't help it." And what are we to make of the poem's conclusion?

> We were the last romantics—chose for theme
> Traditional sanctity and loveliness;
> Whatever's written in what poets name
> The book of the people; whatever most can bless
> The mind of man or elevate a rhyme;
> But all is changed, that high horse riderless,
> Though mounted in that saddle Homer rode
> Where the swan drifts upon a darkening flood.

I grant that the last line has a certain majesty in its dying fall, but the theme of "traditional sanctity and loveliness" which has on other occasions been treated with some scepticism (as in **"Ancestral Houses"**), is here made part of an uninflected threnody for past glories. Much the same thing happens in **"The Municipal Gallery Revisited,"** where Yeats announces of Lady Gregory, Synge and himself, that "We three alone in modern times had brought / Everything down to that sole test again, / Dream of the noble and the beggar man." You might say that Yeats is to be defended because he is speaking out of a proper deference to Lady Gregory's social standing. But when does such deference become servility? And yet even this isn't the point. For what Yeats ignores in these poems is Lady Gregory's own critical awareness of the culpability of the tradition in which he now uncritically places her. You have only to read her *Journals* of the 1920s to see how far he has mythicized her, just as he mythicized Hugh Lane, and in doing so has made a simplified and sentimentalized image out of someone who was far more complex than he wants to admit, since to do so would upset his own dream of the country-house ideal.

My own view is that Yeats, a man of passionate intensity, increasingly convinced himself that what he read into local and world affairs spelled death, not only for his ideal, but for any worthwhile dream of Ireland.

This is why, I think, he turned to Byzantium, as a refuge of art and artifice against the cruelties and inadequacies of life. In **"Sailing to Byzantium"** he speaks of wishing to leave a country where "Caught in that sensual music all neglect / Monuments of unageing intellect." The country is not Ireland, perhaps, and yet in a way it is. For the monuments of unageing intellect—Coole Park, Thor Ballylee?—are clearly of no appeal to young Ireland, or so Yeats has come to feel. The country might of course stand more generally for the postwar world. In his very interesting essay, "Barbarism and Decadence," Renato Poggioli suggests that decadence in Yeats's poem is represented by the "modern and changing West," and that Yeats willingly exchanges it for the "eternal East." The decadence Poggioli has in mind is "the sickness of youth." Certainly, the cultivated cynicism of the 1920s amounts to a kind of decadence. But the passionate tone of **"Sailing to Byzantium"** suggests Yeats's need to save himself. The poem concerns more his desire to make his soul than the country he has left behind, but at the end he is returned to the flux of history, to "What is past or passing or to come."

This, I think, is where Yeats's responsibilities always lead him, and it is not perhaps to be wondered at that on occasions he should seem to be petulant or arrogant or shrilly venomous when speaking of them or on behalf of those to whom he feels most responsible. Yeats can be extremely, tediously snobbish. He can also be offensively harsh. But his intemperate manners and speech arise out of the inevitable vulnerabilities of a poet who sees himself enacting or speaking for large responsibilities. As such, he is a potent force in a way that no English poet of the twentieth century can match. . . . (pp. 117-28)

John Lucas, "W. B. Yeats: The Responsibilities of the Poet," in his *Modern English Poetry—From Hardy to Hughes: A Critical Survey*, B. T. Batsford Ltd., 1986, pp. 103-29.

SOURCES FOR FURTHER STUDY

Ellmann, Richard. *Yeats: The Man and the Masks.* New York: Macmillan Co., 1948, 331 p.

Excellent biographical and critical study.

Hassett, Joseph M. *Yeats and the Poetics of Hate.* New York: St. Martin's Press, 1986, 189 p.

Considers "ways in which Yeats's preoccupation with hate illuminates particular poems and poetic themes."

Hone, Joseph. *W. B. Yeats: 1865-1939.* London: Macmillan and Co., 1943, 504 p.

Biography generally regarded as the finest available. Hone had the help of both Mrs. W. B. Yeats and Maud Gonne in preparing the text, as well as access to all of Yeats's unpublished papers.

Jeffares, A. Norman. *The Circus Animals: Essays on W. B. Yeats.* London and Basingstoke: Macmillan and Co., 1970, 183 p.

Contains essays on Yeats, his father, and his friend Oliver St. John Gogarty, including examinations of Yeats's "mask," Yeats as a critic, gyres, and women in Yeats's poetry.

Knowland, A. S. *W. B. Yeats: Dramatist of Vision.* Totowa, N.J.: Barnes and Noble Books, 1983, 256 p.

Chronological survey of Yeats's dramas in which the works are viewed, "not as appendages to or extensions of his poetry, or as expressions of his 'philosophy', but as viable theatrical experiences, offering insights to audiences with and without previous acquaintanceship with his work."

Webster, Brenda S. *Yeats: A Psychoanalytic Study.* Stanford: Stanford University Press, 1973, 246 p.

Argues that "the central thread of Yeats's life and work is his tireless, driven effort to 'remake' himself, to bring himself as man and artist into a satisfactory relationship both with his impulses and with a threatening reality. In this struggle, he was haunted by certain traumas from his childhood. He grappled with them in his everyday life as in his work, objectifying them in themes and symbols that he repeated obsessively in his writing."

Emile Zola

1840-1902

French novelist, short story writer, critic, essayist, dramatist, poet, and journalist.

INTRODUCTION

Zola was the founder and principal theorist of the Naturalist movement in nineteenth-century literature. Naturalism holds that all phenomena can be understood by scientific examination and that human beings are most accurately represented in fiction as creatures whose lives are determined by environmental and internal forces which they can neither control nor fully understand. In his most important series of novels, "Les Rougon-Macquart," Zola drew on current theories of hereditary determinism and demonstrated in his depictions of characters how various genetic and environmental factors determine human psychology and behavior. The novels *L'assommoir* (1877), *Nana* (1880), and *Germinal* (1885), generally regarded as the finest works in the series, are concerned with the misery and degradation of the French working class and have often been described as anatomies of disease, insanity, and perversion. While Zola did succeed in documenting a historical milieu with great detail and precision, commentators, nevertheless, find in the novels a highly personal vision expressed with emotion and artistry.

Born in Paris, Zola was raised in Aix-en-Provence, where his father was an engineer. When Zola was seven years old his father died, and, without his financial support, the family was plunged into poverty. Zola began his education at the local College Bourbon, where he became friends with Paul Cézanne. Considered a clever but indifferent student, Zola spent his leisure time wandering in the town and the countryside and reading and writing idyllic poetry. At eighteen he moved to Paris with his mother and attended the Lycée Saint-Louis; after twice failing his literature examinations, he left without a degree and for the next two years lived under financially straitened conditions. In 1864 he secured a position as a bookseller's clerk and the same year published *Contes à Ninon (Stories for Ninon),* a collection of short fiction which has more in common with medieval fables than with the strict realism of his later works. He also began developing his journalistic skills as a critic of art and music, and gained notoriety with the publication of an article supporting the artists of the then-controversial Impressionist school, to which his friend Cézanne belonged. His first novel, *La confession de Claude (Claude's Confession,* 1865), featured an unsentimentalized portrait of a prostitute, and when the book met with legal difficulties, Zola was accused of deliberately courting scandal. With *Thérèse Raquin (The Devil's Compact,* 1867) and *Madeleine Férat (Magdalen Férat,* 1868) he began to experiment with techniques that would lead to the Naturalism of the "Rougon Macquart" cycle.

In 1873 Zola entered the circle of Realist writers that included Gustave Flaubert, Alphonse Daudet, and Edmond de Goncourt. After *L'assommoir,* the seventh novel in the "Rougon-Macquart" series, brought him critical and financial success in 1877, Zola himself was surrounded by disciples. Guy de Maupassant, Paul Alexis, Joris-Karl Huysmans, and others met at Zola's home in Paris and his villa in Médan on the Seine. Together they published *Les soirées de Médan,* to which Zola and the others each contributed one short story. The group broke up shortly after Huysmans split with Zola in 1884 because Huysmans wanted to create works that were more personal and artistic than the Naturalist credo would allow. By then the analyses of hereditary degeneracy in the "Rougon-Macquart" novels had earned Zola a reputation among his contemporaries as a pessimistic determinist. Upon the publication of *La Terre (Earth)* in 1887, a group of young novelists writing in *Le figaro* denounced it as mercenary and pathogenic. Eventually Zola turned from the scientific analysis of the "Rougon-Macquart" cycle to the social pamphleteering of later novels such as *Fécondité (Fruitfulness,* 1899).

Zola's most famous example of social advocacy came in 1898 with his involvement in the notorious Dreyfus case. "J'accuse" ("The Dreyfus Case") is a vehement twenty-one page open letter to the president of the Republic that appeared in the journal *L'aurore.* The letter defended Alfred Dreyfus, a Jewish captain in the French army accused of treason and sentenced to life on Devil's Island, and charged that army officials had perjured themselves during the Dreyfus trial. As a result of his role in the scandal, Zola was twice charged for libel, suspended from the Legion d'Honneur, and, on the advice of legal counsel, fled to England. In 1899 the affair was reopened and Zola returned to Paris under a general amnesty. His actions in the case were considered instrumental in the eventual pardon of Dreyfus. In the next few years Zola published several more novels, including three volumes of the unfinished tetralogy "Les quatre évangiles." In 1902 he died during the night of asphyxiation caused by a faulty fireplace chimney.

In the "Rougon-Macquart" cycle Zola applied the methods of science to the novelist's art. F. W. J. Hemmings has remarked that "Zola reduced the craft of fiction to a mechanical technique," and this technique is visible in the author's *ébauches:* plot outlines, character sketches, and a general thesis to be worked out in each individual novel. An exhaustive researcher, Zola investigated the life of various social subgroups for the background of his works: he compiled a dictionary of slang to lend verisimilitude to the dialogue of the lower classes in *L'assommoir;* he learned about the theater and horse racing during the preparatory stages of *Nana;* and he studied a coal mining district during a workers' strike for *Germinal.* By his immersion in a particular milieu, Zola attempted to attain in his fiction the greatest possible fidelity to social fact. However, recent critics have questioned the extent to which Zola's novels actually reflect the guidelines of Naturalism. Brian Nicholas, for instance, has asserted that "the inclinations of the impressionist, the poet of humanity in the mass, presided at the conception of Zola's novels rather than any doctrinaire scientism."

Three of the most notable "Rougon-Macquart" novels—*L'assommoir, Nana,* and *Germinal*—have provided critics with evidence that Zola's work displays the concerns of both the scientist and the artist, as well as the conscience of the social reformer. *L'assommoir* traces the life of Gervaise, an industrious laundress with modest dreams whose kindness leads her to financial, moral, and physical ruin; *Nana* narrates the rise and fall of the precociously licentious daughter of Gervaise, who becomes the leading Parisian courtesan and symbolizes the ruin of Parisian society; *Germinal* features the son of Gervaise, Etienne, who becomes the socialist leader of an impoverished mining community. Despite scientific justifications for human behavior in these works, modern critics have emphasized their artistry and point out that Zola's novels evolved from a desire for social change as much as a scientific urge to compile a social record. Such critics find that Zola's genius as both artist and polemicist are especially evident in his rendering of crowd scenes, most notably the comical wedding party in *L'assommoir* and the horrifying spectacle of rioting strikers in *Germinal.* Other aspects of Zola's novels that have been closely examined are his complex narrative techniques, his allusions to classical mythology, and the implied religious or philosophical basis of his works. Many critics now agree that Zola's works, once considered simple documentations of the surface of human life, can be rewardingly studied from various and far more sophisticated perspectives.

With Naturalism Zola articulated a theory that affected the course of literature throughout the world. His literary precepts can be seen as an influence on the naturalistic dramas of Henrik Ibsen and Gerhart Hauptmann, on the Italian *verismo* movement, and on such American authors as Stephen Crane, Theodore Dreiser, and Ernest Hemingway. Although this conception of literature is no longer popular, or even plausible, the best of the "Rougon-Macquart" novels are regarded as masterpieces that transcend the strictly scientific aims of Naturalism.

(For further information about Zola's life and works, see *Contemporary Authors*, Vol. 104 and *Twentieth-Century Literary Criticism*, Vols. 1, 6, 21, 41.)

CRITICAL COMMENTARY

HENRY JAMES
(essay date 1902)

[An American-born novelist and critic, James has been lauded for his contributions to psychological realism and for exposing minutiae of thought and character through a subtle, mannered prose style. In the following excerpt from an essay written in 1902, he praises Zola's choice of style and subject, defending him against charges of crudity and prurience.]

[Thirty] years ago a young man of extraordinary brain and indomitable purpose, wishing to give the measure of these endowments in a piece of work supremely solid, conceived and sat down to *Les Rougon-Macquart* rather than to an equal task in physics, mathematics, politics or economics. He saw his undertaking, thanks to his patience and courage, practically to a close. . . . It expresses fully and directly the whole man, and big as he may be it can still be big enough for him without becoming false to its type. We see this truth made strong, from beginning to end, in Zola's work; we see the temperament, we see the whole man, with his size and all his marks, stored and packed away in the huge hold of *Les Rougon-Macquart* as a cargo is packed away on a ship. His personality is the thing that finally pervades and prevails, just as so often on a vessel the presence of the cargo makes itself felt for the assaulted senses. What has most come home to me in reading him over is that a scheme of fiction so conducted is in fact a capacious vessel. It can carry anything—with art and force in the stowage; nothing in this case will sink it. And it is the only form for which such a claim can be made. All others have to confess to a smaller scope—to selection, to exclusion, to the danger of distortion, explosion, combustion. The novel has nothing to fear but sailing too light. It will take aboard all we bring in good faith to the dock. (pp. 156-57)

It was the fortune, it was in a manner the doom, of *Les Rougon-Macquart* to deal with things almost always in gregarious form, to be a picture of *numbers*, of classes, crowds, confusions, movements, industries. . . . The individual life is, if not wholly absent, reflected in coarse and common, in generalized terms; whereby we arrive precisely at the oddity [of] the circumstance that, looking out somewhere, and often woefully athirst, for the taste of fineness, we find it not in the fruits of our author's fancy, but in a different matter altogether. We get it in the very history of his effort, the image itself of his lifelong process, comparatively so personal, so spiritual even, and, through all its patience and pain, of a quality so much more distinguished than the qualities he succeeds in attributing to his figures even when he most aims at distinction. There can be no question in these narrow limits of my taking the successive volumes one by one—all the more that our sense of the exhibition is as little as possible an impression of parts and books, of particular 'plots' and persons. It produces the effect of a mass of imagery in which shades are sacrificed, the effect of character and passion in the lump or by the ton. The fullest, the most characteristic episodes affect us like a sounding chorus or procession, as with a hubbub of voices and a multitudinous tread of feet. The setter of the mass into motion, he himself, in the crowd, figures best, with whatever queer idiosyncrasies, excrescences and gaps, a being of a substance akin to our own. Taking him as we must, I repeat, for quite heroic, the interest of detail in him is the interest of his struggle at every point with his problem.

The sense for crowds and processions, for the gross and the general, was largely the *result* of . . . the disproportion between his scheme and his material—though it was certainly also in part an effect of his particular turn of mind. . . . We feel that he *has* to improvise for his moral and social world, the world as to which vision and opportunity must come, if they are to come at all, unhurried and unhustled—must take their own time, helped undoubtedly more or less by bluebooks, reports and interviews, by inquiries 'on the spot,' but never wholly replaced by such substitutes without a general disfigurement. Vision and opportunity reside in a personal sense and a personal history, and

Principal Works

Contes à Ninon (short stories) 1864
   [Stories for Ninon, 1895]
Thérèse Raquin (novel) 1867
   [The Devil's Compact, 1892]
*La fortune des Rougon (novel) 1871
   [The Rougon-Macquart Family, 1879]
*La curée (novel) 1872
   [In the Whirlpool, 1882]
*Le ventre de Paris (novel) 1873
   [The Markets of Paris, 1879]
*La conquête de Plassans (novel) 1874
   [The Conquest of Plassans, 1879; also published as A
   Mad Love; or, The Abbé and His Court, 1882]
*La faute de l'abbé Mouret (novel) 1875
   [Albine; or, The Abbe's Temptation, 1882]
*Son excellence Eugène Rougon (novel) 1876
   [Eugene Rougon, 1876]
*L'assommoir (novel) 1877
   [Gervaise, 1879; also published as The "Assommoir,"
   1884]
*Une page d'amour (novel) 1878
   [Hélène, 1878]
*Nana (novel) 1880
   [Nana, 1880]
Le roman experimental (criticism) 1880
   [The Experimental Novel, 1880]
Les romanciers naturalistes (criticism) 1881
*Pot-bouille (novel) 1882
   [Piping Hot, 1889]
*Au bonheur des dames (novel) 1883
   [The Bonheur des Dames; or, The Shop Girls of Paris,
   1883; published in England as The Ladies' Paradise,
   1883]
*La joie de vivre (novel) 1884
   [Life's Joys, 1884]

*Germinal (novel) 1885
   [Germinal, 1885]
*L'oeuvre (novel) 1886
   [His Masterpiece, 1886]
*La terre (novel) 1887
   [The Soil, 1888; also published as Earth, 1954]
*La rêve (novel) 1888
   [The Dream, 1888]
*La bête humaine (novel) 1890
   [The Human Brutes, 1890; also published as The
   Human Animals, 1890]
*L'argent (novel) 1891
   [Money, 1891]
*La débâcle (novel) 1892
   [The Downfall, 1892]
*Le docteur Pascal (novel) 1893
   [Doctor Pascal, 1893]
†Lourdes (novel) 1894
   [Lourdes, 1896]
†Rome (novel) 1896
   [Rome, 1896]
"J'accuse" (letter) 1898
   ["The Dreyfus Case," 1898]
†Paris (novel) 1898
   [Paris, 1898]
‡Fécondité (novel) 1899
   [Fruitfulness, 1900]
‡Travail (novel) 1901
   [Labor, 1901]
‡Vérité (novel) 1903
   [Truth, 1903]

*These volumes comprise the series "Les Rougon-
   Macquart."
†These volumes comprise the trilogy "Les trois villes."
‡These volumes comprise the unfinished tetralogy "Les
   quatre evangiles."

no short cut to them in the interest of plausible fiction has ever been discovered. The short cut, it is not too much to say, was with Zola the subject of constant ingenious experiment, and it is largely to this source, I surmise, that we owe the celebrated element of his grossness. He was *obliged* to be gross, on his system, or neglect to his cost an invaluable aid to representation, as well as one that apparently struck him as lying close at hand; and I cannot withhold my frank admiration from the courage and consistency with which he faced his need.

His general subject in the last analysis was the na-

ture of man, in dealing with which he took up, obviously, the harp of most numerous strings. . . . [He] doubtless fell into extravagance—there was clearly so much to lead him on. The coarser side of his subject, based on the community of all the instincts, was for instance the more practicable side, a sphere the vision of which required but the general human, scarcely more than the plain physical, initiation, and dispensed thereby conveniently enough with special introductions or revelations. A free entry into this sphere was undoubtedly compatible with a youthful career as hampered right and left even as Zola's own. (pp. 160-62)

Taste as he knew it, taste as his own constitution supplied it, proved to have nothing to say to the matter. His own dose of the precious elixir had no perceptible regulating power. Paradoxical as the remark may sound, this accident was positively to operate as one of his greatest felicities. There are parts of his work, those dealing with romantic or poetic elements, in which the inactivity of the principle in question is sufficiently hurtful; but it surely should not be described as hurtful to such pictures as *Le ventre de Paris,* as *L'assommoir,* as *Germinal.* The conception on which each of these productions rests is that of a world with which taste has nothing to do, and though the act of representation may be justly held, as an artistic act, to involve its presence, the discrimination would probably have been in fact, given the particular illusion sought, more detrimental than the deficiency. There was a great outcry, as we all remember, over the rank materialism of *L'assommoir,* but who cannot see to-day how much a milder infusion of it would have told against the close embrace of the subject aimed at? *L'assommoir* is the nature of man—but not his finer, nobler, cleaner or more cultivated nature; it is the image of his free instincts, the better and the worse. . . . The whole handling makes for emphasis and scale, and it is not to be measured how, as a picture of conditions, the thing would have suffered from timidity. (pp. 162-63)

To make his characters swarm, and to make the great central thing they swarm about 'as large as life,' portentously, heroically big, that was the task he set himself very nearly from the first, that was the secret he triumphantly mastered. Add that the big central thing was always some highly representative institution or industry of the France of his time, some seated Moloch of custom, of commerce, of faith, lending itself to portrayal through its abuses and excesses, its idol-face and great devouring mouth, and we embrace the main lines of his attack. (pp. 165-66)

[The] singular doom of this genius . . . was to find, with life, at fifty, still rich in him, strength only to undermine all the 'authority' he had gathered. He had not grown old and he had not grown feeble; he had only grown all too wrongly insistent. . . . (p. 167)

There is simply no limit . . . to the misfortune of being tasteless; it does not merely disfigure the surface and the fringe of your performance—it eats back into the very heart and enfeebles the sources of life. When you have no taste you have no discretion, which is the conscience of taste, and when you have no discretion you perpetrate books like *Rome,* which are without intellectual modesty, books like *Fécondité,* which are without a sense of the ridiculous, books like *Vérité,* which are without the finer vision of human experience. (p. 170)

Nana is truly a monument to Zola's patience; the subject being so ungrateful, so formidably special,

that . . . the plunge into pestilent depths represents a kind of technical intrepidity.

There are other plunges, into different sorts of darkness; of which the esthetic, even the scientific, even the ironic motive fairly escapes us. . . . Our various senses, sight, smell, sound, touch, are, as with Zola always, more or less convinced; but . . . the mind still remains bewilderedly unconscious of any use for the total. I am not sure indeed that the case is in this respect better with [these] productions . . .—*La faute de l'Abbé Mouret, Une page d'amour, Le rêve, Le docteur Pascal*—in which the appeal is more directly, is in fact quite earnestly, to the moral vision; so much, on such ground, was to depend precisely on those discriminations in which the writer is least at home. The volumes whose names I have just quoted are his express tribute to the 'ideal,' to the select and the charming—fair fruits of invention intended to remove from the mouth so far as possible the bitterness of the ugly things in which so much of the rest of his work had been condemned to consist. The subjects in question then are 'idyllic' and the treatment poetic, concerned essentially to please on the largest lines and involving at every turn that salutary need. (pp. 171-72)

If you insist on the common you must submit to the common; if you discriminate, on the contrary, you must, however invidious your discriminations may be called, trust to them to see you through.

To the common then Zola, often with splendid results, inordinately sacrifices, and this fact of its overwhelming him is what I have called his paying for it. In *L'assommoir,* in *Germinal,* in *La débâcle,* productions in which he must most survive, the sacrifice is ordered and fruitful, for the subject and the treatment harmonize and work together. He describes what he best feels, and feels it more and more as it naturally comes to him—quite, if I may allow myself the image, as we zoologically see some mighty animal, a beast of a corrugated hide and a portentous snout, soaking with joy in the warm ooze of an African riverside. In these cases everything matches, and 'science,' we may be permitted to believe, has had little hand in the business. The author's perceptions go straight, and the subject, grateful and responsive, gives itself wholly up. It is no longer a case of an uncertain smoky torch, but of a personal vision, the vision of genius, springing from an inward source. Of this genius *L'assommoir* is the most extraordinary record. (p. 173)

The mystery . . . is the wonder of the scale and energy of Zola's assimilations. . . . How, all sedentary and 'scientific,' did he get so *near?* (p. 175)

Grant—and the generalization may be emphatic—that the shallow and the simple are *all* the population of his richest and most crowded pictures, and that his 'psychology,' in a psychologic age, remains thereby comparatively coarse, grant this and we but get another view of the miracle. We see enough of the superficial among novelists at large, assuredly, without deriving from it, as we derive from Zola at his best, the concomitant impression of the solid. It is in general—I mean among the novelists at large—the impression of the *cheap,* which the author of *Les Rougon-Macquart,* honest man, never faithless for a moment to his own stiff standard, manages to spare us even in the prolonged sandstorm of *Vérité.* The Common is another matter; it is one of the forms of the superficial—pervading and consecrating all things in such a book as *Germinal*—and it only adds to the number of our critical questions. How in the world is it made, this deplorable democratic malodorous Common, so strange and so interesting? How is it taught to receive into its loins the stuff of the epic and still, in spite of that association with poetry, never depart from its nature? It is in the great lusty game he plays with the shallow and the simple that Zola's mastery resides, and we see of course that when values are small it takes innumerable items and combinations to make up the sum. In *L'assommoir* and in *Germinal,* to some extent even in *La débâcle,* the values are all, morally, personally, of the lowest—the highest is poor Gervaise herself, richly human in her generosities and follies—yet each is as distinct as a brass-headed nail. (pp. 175-76)

When we others of the Anglo-Saxon race are vulgar we are, handsomely and with the best conscience in the world, vulgar all through, too vulgar to be in any degree literary, and too much so therefore to be critically reckoned with at all. The French are different—they separate their sympathies, multiply their possibilities, observe their shades, remain more or less outside of their worst disasters. They mostly contrive to get the *idea,* in however dead a faint, down into the lifeboat. (p. 176)

Henry James, "Emile Zola," in his *The Art of Fiction and Other Essays,* Oxford University Press, Inc. 1948, pp. 154-80.

GORHAM MUNSON

(essay date 1942)

[In the following excerpt, Munson discusses the effectiveness of Zola's essay "J'accuse" in the favorable outcome of the Alfred Dreyfus case.]

On the morning of January 13, 1898, the conscience of mankind, which had been outraged at the injustice visited upon Captain Alfred Dreyfus of the French Army's General Staff, found a stentorian voice in Emile Zola. Zola, nearing sixty, the battle for literary naturalism

won, was settling into the life of a worthy bourgeois when he was induced to interest himself in the Dreyfus Affair. He had become a Dreyfusard, but in this early January of 1898 Dreyfusard prospects were gloomy indeed. Then on the 13th on the front page of *L'Aurore,* the newspaper of Ernest Vaughan and Georges Clemenceau, appeared the headline-shout: "J'Accuse"; beneath was a long letter to Felix Faure, President of the French Republic, signed by Emile Zola. That day the circulation of *L'Aurore* leapt from a few score thousand to three hundred thousand, and the Dreyfus case was broken wide open again. (p. 141)

If I were to explain in three words the success, so far beyond Zola's hopes, of *J'accuse,* the three would be: surprise, audacity, challenge. The timing of the letter's release proved to be perfect. Zola's name was famous enough to ensure that *J'accuse* could not be greeted by the silence that kills without leaving a trace. And a daily newspaper was a prominent enough platform to reach a sufficient number of people to reopen the scandal. But the surprise lay in its form—a man-to-man appeal from one of France's literary giants, a leader in the profession of letters, to the political head of the nation. From his writer's eminence Zola spoke directly to the highest magistrate of the land. He spoke to President Faure with full mindfulness of official limitations placed upon that personage's actions but he detoured them by insisting upon the President's duty as a man.

Nothing at the time could have exceeded the breathtaking audacity of the letter's contents. Zola accused the War Ministry and the General Staff of the Army of a gross miscarriage of justice and of shocking efforts to conceal the miscarriage. He accused them collectively and singly by name. With the utmost courage he fired his accusations point-blank at high officials.

He then capitalized upon his surprising and audacious "break-through" of the anti-Dreyfusard defences by a ringing challenge. He dared the accused to bring him to trial for breaking the Libel Laws. This was the master-stroke. His taunting defiance stung the army into an unwise move—into putting Zola on trial in a civil court, exactly the step the Dreyfusards wanted to provoke.

Surprise, audacity, challenge—these were the tactics of the champion of truth. In executing them Zola employed a powerful rhetoric of indignation and a pulverizing ridicule. He marshalled facts and set them in a certain dramatic light so that their character of belonging in an "extravagant tragic serial romance" cannot be missed. His tone is adapted to his purpose—manly, open, frank, blunt, challenging, the tone of a man convinced of being right, of speaking by the dictates of conscience. Throughout there runs the strong current of his conviction that truth in the long run wins.

Most interesting of all, Zola spoke as an individual pure and simple and his letter was aimed at a single individual. He appealed to the pride and shame of Faure, to Faure's honor as a man, to Faure's qualities as an individual. Shall we not say, thinking of Paine, thinking of Paul, that the propagandist of truth is driven to speak from himself and that his appeal is to the individual heart and mind? (pp. 157-58)

Gorham Munson, "Zola's 'J'Accuse': The Moment When Zola Was the Conscience of Mankind," in his *12 Decisive Battles of the Mind: The Story of Propaganda During the Christian Era,* Greystone Press, 1942, pp. 141-59.

ANGUS WILSON
(essay date 1952)

[In the following essay, Wilson discusses the relationship between literary style and argumentative intent in Zola's novels.]

Zola has been declared not only obscene, but childishly so, and worse still, old-fashioned in his obscenity. To read his work seriously has been like facing the imputation of telling an old dirty joke. It is a charge which few have cared to incur. If we add to this the fact that the *Rougon-Macquart* has the misfortune to appear as a long family chronicle, although it is in fact a series of separate novels covered by the slenderest links, we can understand the oblivion to which it has been assigned. (p. 26)

Nothing perhaps can have seemed so serious a bar to achievement as his comparative lack of education. Education and taste were the two things he lacked to place him on a level with the classes he envied and despised. It is an ironic fact that it was ultimately to be in exactly these two spheres that the society he conquered was to be revenged upon him. (p. 27)

No nineteenth-century novelist, perhaps, succeeded so well in depicting the courage and honesty of the individual, aspiring workman of the century, and he does so with a lack of sentimentalism and a real understanding of the necessary limitations of such a life that is quite unique.

Such an exact class analysis if it had been rigidly adhered to, might well have produced novels that were text-books of political economy or social sermons rather than works of art. Zola, however, was too great an artist and too determinedly objective a writer to fall into this error more than occasionally. (pp. 35-6)

[Though] Zola needed the formal scheme of the [*Rougon-Macquart*] series to liberate his vast energies, and though he was often unaware himself of its secondary

nature, most of the novels of the series, and, certainly, the best, were carefully planned as separate units, and if they interfered with the whole, the whole had to be remoulded. Frequently the members of the Rougon-Macquart are only formally the central characters, the real emphasis of the novels being placed upon other social groups, of whom the adventurers and outcasts from Plassans form useful observers. . . . He made little attempt, beyond an occasional explanatory reference which almost always appears forced, to connect the members of the family in one book with those in another. Such characters as do reappear have little consistency, except for Nana whose future had probably already been planned in detail when she appeared as the vicious little girl of *L'assommoir. . . .* It was not the family heredity, nor even the theoretical class analysis that the family provided, with which Zola was concerned, however he may have wished to think so, but particular patterns of life which made immediate appeal to him. Nevertheless by establishing a broad general scheme and fulfilling it equally broadly, he insured that his artistic powers should be exercised over the widest possible field. (pp. 36-7)

Zola, like Dickens, mistrusted all the political parties. But whereas Dickens' political scepticism came from his view that all power was a corrupting influence on the will, Zola's contempt came largely from a general disbelief in the strength of the human will either for good or for evil. With his own abnormally developed will and energy, Zola was, perhaps, over-inclined to regard humanity as shifting, wind-swept sand whose apparent stability or direction was liable at any minute to be changed by some chance desire or momentary difficulty. (p. 40)

[For] Zola, as for Dickens, the picture of society which his analysis produced was too horrible to be passed over without some attempted solution. When the radical newspapers objected to his picture of the working classes in *L'assommoir,* Zola declared that as an artist he was concerned only with truth, not with opinions. This aesthetic creed of the naturalists was his constant sermon; but, nevertheless, it is possible to see a series of attempted solutions in the Rougon-Macquart novels which taken in conjunction with changes in his private life bridge the apparent gap between the objective novels of the family chronicle and the 'romans à thèse' and the propaganda novels of 1894 onwards. (p. 42)

Throughout his career Zola was attacked as a pornographic writer—a view which has since been increased in America by large numbers of illicit, hotted-up translations sold by book pedlars and in 'dirty' book shops. Nothing, in fact, could be less attractive than the squalor and disease which surround the sex life of his poor, the boredom and anxiety that beset his rich in their lovemaking. There are, however, certain romantic love episodes in Zola's work—though they are never cited by the smut salesman—about which an atmosphere of sensuality and excitement hangs that might be charged with the accusation of pornography. They are all of a very special kind: the innocent love of the very young, a sort of natural lovemaking of Adam and Eve before the fall. (pp. 47-8)

The answer to this sexual despair, the very core of his social pessimism, lies in Zola's own life. Nothing in Zola's early days in Paris had helped him to escape from his retrospective view of happiness, and his marriage seems to have proved to be no solution. Alexandrine was a good wife, ambitious, thoughtful for his needs, strong in character, emotionally profound. But she appears to have been only a supplement to his already deep mother-fixation. Had they been able to have children, all this might have been changed, but, unfortunately, this was not to be so. . . . [It] is only after his fruitful union with Jeanne Rozerat—a union which caused such misery to poor Alexandrine—that the picture changes. Already in *La débâcle,* more openly in *Le docteur Pascal,* and finally in *Paris,* the end of the long trilogy of Abbé Froment's road to a new faith, a note of hope appears—fecundity, work no longer as a drug but in happy knowledge that it will be carried on by posterity, a socialism gradual but sure because there is all the future in which to complete it—this was the faith which Jeanne Rozerat gave to Zola. It saved him from morbidity, and it ended his career as a great writer. (pp. 49-50)

The optimistic, cocksure bourgeois world of the 'forties and 'fifties was giving way to fin-de-siècle melancholy and ennui; all but the most obtuse felt the rotten boards creak beneath their feet, saw the scaffolding tremble above their heads. Zola, in his luxury and success, was seldom unconscious of these rumblings and groanings, and by his art, his force, his hatred, compassion and vulgarity, he drove the public to pile up his fortune as they queued to peer at the very hell they had spent most of their lives in avoiding. The peepshows were cleverly labelled—the Sanctity of the Family, the Honour of the Army, the Virtues of the Poor, the Ideals of the Artist, the Traditions of the Peasantry, the Splendour of the Church, the Soundness of Finance— and in each there lay a putrescent corpse, far more terrible than the skeleton the poor reader had shut away so carefully in the cupboard of his own guarded conscience. Even now, the greatest of the novels— *L'assommoir, La terre, Germinal*—have the quality of nightmares; how much more appalling must they have been for the contemporary reader. (pp. 52-3)

He saw each novel as a separate picture, planned the whole shape in advance as would a painter. We have already said that the *Rougon-Macquart* series as a whole with its science, its heredity, even its social analysis, was always subordinate to the needs of the individual novels, equally the internal considerations of each novel—characters, events, time, place—were all subject to the demands of the logic of the total book.

From the earliest notes made for the series, it is clear that Zola realized his need to ensure this air-tight quality in his novels if they were to succeed. He affirms his decision to avoid Balzac's methods of presenting more than one group of society in any particular book. It is only in the later books like *Paris* that the very poor and the very rich are shown together, and it is clear from the unsuccessfully crude contrast, with its obvious moralising flavour, that his earlier decision was a wise one. His cuts into society were, in general, horizontal and not vertical. Within these horizontal sections, he planned each succeeding chapter as a separate step in the progressive logic of the whole. . . . Logical steps fused into a whole by passion, and by another quality which he does not mention, acute atmospheric sensitivity. A solidly established formal scheme given movement by emotional force and life by shimmering atmosphere—an Impressionist painting of the highest order. It is not 'Naturalism' but impressionistic technique which explains Zola's greatness. (pp. 54-5)

If the nervous undercurrent in Zola's life was made manifest spasmodically by mental obsessions and delusions, it was evidenced throughout his life by a physical hyperaesthesia which, like his obsession with numbers, is another great corner-stone of his creative powers. He saw, heard and, above all, smelt his surroundings more intensely than the normal person. To judge from his work we would suspect it was many years before this excess of physical sensitivity was integrated with the rest of his personality. It was responsible for the development within him of a poet—not the derivative, Romantic imitator of his youth, but a poet whose detailed powers of natural description allied him more to the Parnassian school, and who converted the natural phenomena he felt so intensely into images and shapes that finally give this side of his work a close link with the Symbolists. (p. 57)

The whole history of the Rougon-Macquart is the development of a detailed, realistic canvas into a statement of a mood, an atmosphere of a certain place and time within the same limited confines. (p. 62)

It has been said more than once that Zola's great novels are the forerunners of the epic cinema—of D. W. Griffith, of Jean Duvivier or of Pabst—but excellent films though many of them would make, such a view ignores the fact that Zola's greatness lies in his use of words. He was a pictorial artist, but to say that his world would be better represented by the camera is the result of an age-old confusion of means and results in the arts. (p. 63)

If Zola's presentation of time and place supplies some key to the compulsion of his novels, his treatment of character gives the final answer. Zola was intensely interested in the physiological, medical approach to the human personality which the science of his youth propounded; one may well believe that the theories of Jeannet or Bergson would have attracted him as much as they did Proust, or that the views of Freud would have dominated him as they have later novelists. . . . As we have already noted, Zola began, like Dickens or Balzac, with characters that were largely humours. If he developed them, it was not by the enlargement of intellectual or emotional sympathy as George Eliot did, but by the unconscious infusion of his own personality into them. The Impressionist approach which he used could have led to a development of the interior monologue, as it did for Tolstoy, or to the tracking of memory as it did for Proust, but Zola's impressionism remained entirely fictional and external. Only one aspect of personal psychology really interested him deeply—the human will. It was probably this interest that attracted him to the works of Stendhal, at that time a neglected writer, and it is this interest that is predominant in his two 'psychological' horror stories, *Thérèse Raquin* and its later counterpart *La bête humaine.*

For the rest, character was for him merely a part of the general statement of his novels. Starting with a Balzacian realist approach, which was never entirely happy, he developed his humours in two directions; the central characters tended to be hardened into symbols, the others dissolved into 'humanity', crowds, groups. (pp. 66-7)

Central characters exist in all his novels, but they are a convention like the much advertised tenets of naturalism which he only supported one moment to deny the next. The approach to the scene is always external, and if that external viewpoint is sometimes for the sake of convenience labelled Gervaise or Étienne, the scenes in which they are present merge happily and easily into those in which they are not: the observer is always Zola's five senses. (p. 68)

With the publication of *L'assommoir* in 1877, Zola leapt from extraordinary talent to a mastery of his medium that can, without distortion, be labelled genius. The theme had been maturing in his mind since 1869, and the most striking feature of the book is its deeply felt quality. The heroine, Gervaise, is perhaps the most completely conceived character, belonging to that great class of submerged, unindividual figures that make up the very poor, to be found in all nineteenth-century fiction. The tragedy of her limited fight—limited by education and circumstances—to win a pathetic little vision of individual happiness from an uncomprehended and uninterested world is treated with the greatest pity and the least false sentiment. In a note, Zola says, 'I must show all the world trying to bring about her ruin, consciously or unconsciously', and so we see it. . . . [In] incidental figures we have the whole

world of strangers, of the educated, of the busybody and the official who beset and tyrannize and make small the submerged when they attempt to rise above the surface. The simple demands of Gervaise and Coupeau upon life, their capacity for gaiety, their childlike hopes and dreams are all attended by little incidents or remarks that foreshadow their futility. On second reading, perhaps, the careful interlocking of the present hope with its future foundering seems a little careful, a little arranged, but, at first encounter, the effect of gradual, yet inevitable descent is overpowering. The tragedy and the horror would be unbearable—indeed a mere recapitulation of the events would make them ludicrous—if it was not for the concept of limited, pitiable, yet complete human dignity which marks Gervaise. It is perhaps almost unbearable, almost inartistic, when events finally reduce her human dignity to animal squalor—reality has outrun art. We may despise the bourgeois critics who shouted against the outrageous horror of *L'assommoir,* but our special contempt must be reserved for those left-wing critics who did not find the picture of the submerged sufficiently noble. 'My characters', said Zola, 'are not bad, they are only ignorant and destroyed by the surroundings of crude need and misery in which they live.'

No account of *L'assommoir* is complete, however, without mention of the humour of the scenes of prosperity and gaiety which intersperse the descent of Gervaise. Such humour is abundant in many of his books, but nowhere so successfully as in *L'assommoir* and *La terre. . . .* The humours of ignorance and superstition, of the oddities of the simple have been surpassed only by Dickens. . . . (pp. 111-13)

If *L'assommoir* moves the reader's compassion for the submerged through the individual life of Gervaise, *Germinal . . .* uses the submerged community of the miners to compel his belief, if necessary, his hostile and frightened belief, in their right and their power to climb out of the hell to which indifference and greed have consigned them. If, in 1885, strike action was less rare than it had been when Dickens so sadly failed to grasp its necessity in *Hard Times,* it was still thought of by 'respectable' people as criminal violence. It was this aspect of bourgeois fear, this feeling that strikers were only collected criminals, violators of the sacred rights of property more vile than thieves because more dangerous, that Zola deliberately played upon. . . . *Germinal* is rightly regarded as one of the greatest novels of the masses. Nowhere perhaps have scenes of mass action been more deftly managed, nowhere the confused emotions and thoughts of simple people, treated like beasts and driven into self-defence that is often bestial, more directly made lucid without losing reality. Zola uses all his devices, and less obviously than in *L'assommoir.* The hero, Étienne Lantier, a stranger to the mining town, provides an observer for a community which has no self-consciousness. The building-up of that community through the lives of individuals makes a clear and detailed picture which later mass writers so often blurred by attempting to portray groups directly. Many left wing admirers, notably Barbusse, who have objected to the 'intrusion' of individuals, have failed to see that the force of compassion and anger which they praise rests exactly upon this method. Nowhere, too, is Zola's 'journalistic' approach—his visits to mines, his interviews with working men, his notes, his reading of reports—more truly vindicated than in the great imaginative scenes underground, the descents in the cages, the mining ponies, the flooded pits. (pp. 113-15)

L'assommoir is Zola's most compassionate work, *Germinal* his most angry, but *La terre* . . . is the most complete of all his novels. In it are brought together all the various strands of emotion which had competed for expression in the other Rougon-Macquart novels; in it Zola combines and blends more happily all the various methods of expression which had been individually perfected in its predecessors. It is a book of incidents and characters, that taken separately are the height of his exaggeration, his monstrous view of life, yet, united and fused, are the summit of his truth, his convincing projection of reality. (pp. 116-17)

But *La terre* achieves greatness, that is denied to many of the other novels as rich in horror and irony, by the truth, the simple nobility of the hero and heroine, Jean and Françoise, whose greater feeling and finer aspirations are so skilfully woven into the same pattern of external coarseness and callousness as the sunken, brutalized mass around them, that they give a final conviction of mankind's possible redemption in the most vile swamps. This sense of nobility in the lower depths of life can only be compared to the greatest successes of Dostoevsky in *The House of the Dead* or *The Idiot.* (p. 118)

Zola's artistic genius was the expression of emotional and intellectual conflict. Peace came to his spirit with Jeanne Rozerat and his children; intellectual solution followed more slowly but was no less complete. Though a lifetime of writing made it natural that he should seek to express this final solution in books, its true expression lay in action. The courage, the generosity and the force which he showed in his defence of Dreyfus are the monument of these last years of positive conviction, they have their place in the history of France and in the history of human freedom, but they can only form a brief appendix to a study of Zola as a writer. (pp. 120-21)

Angus Wilson, in his *Émile Zola: An Introductory Study of His Novels,* William Morrow, 1952, 148 p.

F. W. J. HEMMINGS
(essay date 1953)

[An English biographer and critic, Hemmings was one of the foremost authorities on Zola. In the following excerpt from his 1953 biography of the author, he offers an overview of Zola's novels.]

[*Thérèse Raquin* and *Madeleine Férat*] cannot be fully appreciated except . . . as experiments in a new realism—new, at all events, in the path of Zola's development, but one which leads back to Balzac and the positivist gospel. In these two works the young writer can be observed trying his hand at objective presentation of invented characters, the difficult feat that his other great forerunner, Flaubert, had toiled to achieve. Zola, of course, was far from succeeding at this first attempt. But he seems to have seen where and why he failed, and afterwards to have resolutely recast his method in order to come closer to grips with the problem. *Thérèse Raquin* and *Madeleine Férat* are not blind alleys from which Zola was obliged to retrace his steps; they are stages in the steady progression that led him up to the peaks of attainment, *L'assommoir* and *Germinal* and *La terre,* where the dispassionate objectivity of the artist is almost perfectly balanced by the passionate sincerity of his art.

The test by which we can most readily judge the objectivity of a work of fiction is a negative one: the reader should be unable, simply by studying the text in front of him, to draw any conclusions about the author's sympathies or antipathies, his creed or his philosophy. Flaubert, just about the time when Zola was meditating *Thérèse Raquin,* formularized this ideal when he wrote: 'A novelist, to my mind, *has no right* to give his opinion about the things of this world. He should, in his calling, imitate God in His, that is, create—and hold his peace (*faire et se taire*).' (pp. 23-4)

Measured against this standard of objectivity, neither *Thérèse Raquin* nor *Madeleine Férat* qualifies fully as a product of the 'new aesthetic'.

For a start, it cannot be said that, in the first of them, Zola 'never reveals himself in the turn of a sentence'. In little question-begging touches which will not escape the sensitive reader, Zola betrays the moral assumptions on which his book is based. The two central characters of *Thérèse Raquin* are a couple of villains; the pity is that they are considered in their villainy rather than their humanity. Zola cannot conceal the repugnance he feels for them, however scrupulously he analyses the attendant circumstances of their adultery and crime. (pp. 24-5)

What Zola wanted to demonstrate in *Thérèse Raquin*—in the main, that 'crime does not pay'—is, however, a moral truism, to which his readers might, on the whole, be supposed to subscribe without many misgivings. There was, therefore, little need for display of argument to persuade them to arrive at the conclusions Zola wished to lead up to. In *Madeleine Férat,* the case is different. Here Zola set out to wring consent to a belief by no means commonly accepted. *Thérèse Raquin* is a tract against homicide, and against adultery only incidentally. In *Madeleine Férat,* . . . the preoccupation with sexual infidelity in woman stands alone. It is abundantly evident that the author is himself preoccupied with the problem, that he interprets it along personal lines, and that, to all intents and purposes, he wrote the novel to phrase this interpretation. (p. 25)

Thérèse Raquin and *Madeleine Férat* are thus not true works of scientific realism as Zola had intended they should be; they are not objective presentations of

any recognizable reality. They are, in different degrees, stories with a high content of interpolated subjectivism; and their psychology, thickened into 'physiology', is engineered by unrealistic and unscientific postulates: Fate, and the all-powerful 'temperament', or the irresistible force of 'impregnation'. The books differ from the 'Gothic novel' of the eighteenth century only in that the supernatural, externalized as ghosts and bugaboos by Horace Walpole and Mrs. Radcliffe, is seated by Zola in his characters' nerves, in their blood, in their genital organs. (pp. 32-3)

For sheer determination and purposefulness there had been few events in recorded literature to match the twenty-volume series of *Les Rougon-Macquart,* and subsequently there has been perhaps nothing that can be put beside it except *À la Recherche du Temps perdu.* (pp. 35-6)

The innovation intended in *Les Rougon-Macquart* was to show the successive flowering of three, four, even five interlinked generations, to construct vertically down a genealogical line, not simply horizontally over a social superficies. As he promised his publisher, Lacroix, in the general plan he submitted in 1869, he would not only 'study the whole of the Second Empire, from the *coup d'état* down to the present day', but he would also 'study in a family the questions of common blood and environment'. In the first article, he would still be a historian; in the second, a student of embryology and physiology. (p. 38)

That heredity in some way influences individuality is . . . a truism: 'like father, like son' rates as one of the most commonplace of proverbs. To the artist in Zola, heredity was a substitute for old-fashioned Fate, the Spinner of the Homeric sagas. . . . (p. 40)

The hereditary streak is sometimes of hardly any practical account; environment seems all-powerful. Would Gervaise [Macquart in *L'assommoir*] have turned into a drunken old harridan without the misery of her life and the example of her husband?—surely the intemperance of her father and mother provided no more than an innate disposition to alcoholism which might just as well not have been there? Would her daughter have turned prostitute without the corrupting influences of the street and especially without the total disorganization of her home? Allowance must, of course, be made for the hereditary freak of exceptional sexual appeal and the hereditary thirst for enjoyment—but to these Zola attributes far less importance, in *L'assommoir* and in *Nana,* than he does to environmental factors. (pp. 43-4)

The new importance given to environment and experience was the means by which Zola insured himself against the danger of producing, as he had in *Thérèse Raquin* and *Madeleine Férat,* mere fatalist melodramas. Alone in the series, *La bête humaine* provides an example of a character entirely dominated by atavistic forces beyond his control. In the other novels, the influence of the family is not allowed to show itself too nakedly, its very presence remains shadowy. Each novel is primarily concerned, not with one or the other aspect of the legacy of evil in the Rougon-Macquart stock, but with one or another of the worlds which fit together as a panorama of the Second Empire. (pp. 44-5)

As far as possible, then, Zola reduced the craft of fiction to a mechanical technique; and his extraordinary thoroughness and patience will not fail to dismay many who imagine masterpieces to spring—as sometimes, undoubtedly, they do appear to—all complete from the brain of a great novelist. Through what hole in this tight-woven fabric could the wind of inspiration blow?—or is Zola's example one more piece of evidence in support of Carlyle's view that genius 'means transcendent capacity of taking trouble'? (p. 50)

La fortune des Rougon is a study in miniature of the passions and interests that conspired to overthrow the Second Republic. (p. 59)

It is an unsavoury story, and Zola's design is obvious: he wishes to show the inglorious origins of imperial rule. He does this firstly by exposing the pettiness, cruelty, and cowardice of the champions of Bonapartism, and secondly by throwing a halo of martyrdom round the heads of the militant republicans doomed to extinction. (p. 60)

On the whole, *La fortune des Rougon* reads as a satire of man's folly in ever hoping to establish, by violent political and revolutionary action, the ideal society. Save for the heroic but misled exceptions, men are too self-seeking to be effective agents of their own communal betterment.

The first book of the series is not one of the greatest. It has glaring faults of construction, due mainly to the huge amount of preparatory matter Zola felt it necessary to include as an introduction to the succeeding volumes. Like the last volume of all, *Le docteur Pascal*, it is a wall left unfinished, with the toothings projecting. (pp. 61-2)

Considered, however, as a prologue to the cycle, *La fortune des Rougon* is sometimes stirring; it is shot through with fitful prophetic gleams, when we seem, with Pascal Rougon, 'to glimpse for a moment, as in a flash of lightning, the future of the Rougon-Macquarts, a pack of ravening beasts unleashed and gorged, in a blaze of blood and gold'. It is a book that contributes to our understanding of the remaining nineteen novels, but it has few rewards to offer in itself. (p. 62)

[*Son excellence Eugene Rougon* is] the most truly political of [Zola's] novels until we come to [**La Ventre de Paris**]. (p. 69)

After *Son excellence* Zola began his 'novel of the working class', *L'assommoir.* Here the fact of social

suffering, evaded in the earlier books (except perhaps in *Le ventre de Paris*), is stated with an emphasis that leaves nothing to be desired. But *L'assommoir* is not a political novel, because there is no attempt to lay at anyone's door the blame for the degradation of the masses. The book demonstrated that the impartiality of the realist need not exclude a sense of social wrongs; but it also showed that, if the rules of realism were to be observed, and the artist were to refrain indefinitely from intervention and conclusion, then the social formula he reached would always be short of one term or the other. Either the oppressed would be shown without the oppressors, or the exploiters without the classes they exploit.

Zola overcame the difficulty once only in his career: in *Germinal.* There, the formula he evolved to avoid a crude siding against social tyrants was to exonerate them of the intention of tyranny, even though he could not overlook its reality. The *rentiers* in *Germinal* are naïvely unaware that their privileged comfort is founded on the blood and sweat of the miners; the manager class is a powerless agent of the abstract monster 'capital', which Zola relegates carefully to the shadows. By these means no one set of characters is shown to be unjust, though the fact of injustice is painfully evident; and so the appearance of impartiality is maintained, precariously but all the same convincingly.

This juggling feat was not repeated. Zola's logic eventually demanded that a verdict of Guilty should be returned against someone or something, even if only against a social system. Once he took it on himself to act the juryman, however, his artistic integrity was of necessity compromised, he found himself among the politicians, 'at the very bottom, in what is relative among human activities'. This is what happened in *Paris* and in the last three novels of his life; and it partly explains why *Paris* and the *Évangiles* rank increasingly lower as literature. (pp. 71-2)

L'assommoir was Zola's first unmistakable masterpiece. He was to write two or three books which might be considered more stirring, more moving, or more overwhelming, but he was never to compose a more perfect work of art. Sheer artistic perfection was not something Zola often came within reach of—perhaps he seldom even strove seriously after it; but among all his books *L'assommoir* alone is practically proof against the acid of purely formal criticism. (p. 94)

L'assommoir proved that Zola could, at his best, construct a novel as well as Flaubert and better than any other of his predecessors or contemporaries. None of the earlier novels had been to anything like the same degree so purposefully and economically built. By comparison, they sprawl and bulge; they do not sweep up to their culmination, they distract by subsidiary outgrowths. But *L'assommoir* has a classic simplicity of line which was not incompatible with the complexity and denseness of a work of realism. (p. 95)

There is nothing in the population of *L'assommoir* but what is redolent of human nature. For the first time Zola vaulted the forbidding walls of the 'prisons of clay'. Admittedly, it was human nature at its least polished and least subtle: this was perhaps why he managed it so well. His unlettered toilers, whose native spontaneity has not been trimmed or refined by any life of the mind or the spirit, were the ideal caryatids of the kind of monumental art which it was in him to construct. (p. 99)

[*Une page d'amour, Nana,* and *Au bonheur des dames*] all deal, in the last resort, with the same problem: the disruptive force of the passion of love. It was a subject which had hardly concerned Zola up till then. As a literary theme it has, of course, been common property since Helen's face launched the thousand ships, but there is, in Zola's treatment of it, a blend of horror and fascination, which suggests origins in a much nearer, in fact a private, conflict. (p. 138)

[In *Une page d'amour*] the intrinsic destructiveness of passion becomes, for the first time, the principal theme of a novel by Zola. . . .

There is a stuffiness in *Une page d'amour,* a muffling of echoes which represents a regression to the period before the *Rougon-Macquart* cycle was started. It is a closet drama of the same sort as *Thérèse Raquin,* with the difference that Zola tried to rise above the 'physiological' portrayal of character which had contented him in 1867. The result was a notable failure, unless Zola was serious in his declared intention of being 'flat and colourless'. (p. 146)

[*Une page d'amour* is] remarkable for a suddenly intensified exteriorization of Zola's latent dread of sexual passion, that incalculable and destructive outside force; and with it went, this time, a readiness to sound the alarm, to put his reader—and through him, society at large—on guard against the intruder. These are tendencies of which the first at least arose . . . from the recesses of Zola's personality. They display themselves far more strikingly in the next novel, *Nana.* (pp. 148-49)

Nana, the sequel to *L'assommoir,* is a coldly austere work, for all the licentiousness of many of the scenes. (p. 150)

To put his intentions beyond any doubt, Zola provided within the text of the novel the key to his symbolism, in the shape of a summarized article supposedly written by a journalist, Fauchery, under the heading "The Golden Fly". Here we read that Nana is the biological product of a diseased ancestral line and the social product of mean streets and stinking hovels. (p. 151)

While we may not doubt that Zola's intention was to issue a solemn warning against licensed prostitution and private vice among the leaders of a nation, we cannot doubt either that *Nana* mercifully exceeds this limited brief. The novel, as it develops, becomes a tremendous phantasmagoria in which an opulent and cultured civilization is shown sinking through vulgarity and debauchery to enervation and ultimate dissolution. (pp. 152-53)

Au bonheur des dames, in spite of its far sunnier treatment of the erotic theme, does not really represent any final abatement of this deep-seated disturbance. The story of the taming of Octave Mouret, now a millionaire, by the unambitious and instinctively virtuous Denise Baudu, a story which ends with the ringing of wedding-bells off-stage, has the innocent air of a prim mid-Victorian novel. (p. 160)

Au bonheur des dames was a transition novel, inaugurating the series of up-to-date economic or industrial studies which were to include *Germinal, La terre, La bête humaine, L'argent,* and, beyond the *Rougon-Macquart* series, *Paris* and *Travail.* The war between the sexes . . . pales before the death-struggle of a doomed commercial order. (pp. 160-61)

If Zola's novels are read, as he intended they should be read, straight through in the order in which he wrote them, a subtle change of texture will make itself felt somewhere halfway through the *Rougon-Macquart* cycle. Up to *Nana,* the books are *gratuitous,* almost, it might be said, decorative; they reflect, record, not always flatly and seldom unemotionally; but whatever intentions they have (political intentions in *La fortune des Rougon,* social ones in *L'assommoir*) are rudimentary, perhaps accidental. In the later phase, the works, while they never descend to pleading causes, are nevertheless *functional;* they serve to bring into prominence certain questions, certain problems: of a moral order in *Nana, Pot-bouille,* and *Au bonheur des Dames;* of an economic and social order in *Germinal, La terre,* and *L'argent;* of an aesthetic order in *L'oeuvre,* an international one in *La débâcle,* a religious one in *Le docteur Pascal.* This seems to be the characteristic quality and common denominator of the later books in the series. . . . (p. 164)

[As] we continue to consider Zola's literary career in terms of a gradual perfecting of the realist formula, we are bound to place *Germinal* in a class by itself. Here, the impersonal treatment of the theme is unexceptional: Flaubert's principle, *faire et se taire,* was observed to the letter, as it had already been in *L'assommoir.* But between *L'assommoir* and *Germinal* the balance tips slightly in favour of the second book. There is, in *L'assommoir,* a certain chilliness in the relentless march to catastrophe, which in *Germinal* is dissipated by the heat of dramatic friction. Gervaise has to fight her losing battle in desperate isolation and against forces many times too strong for her; Étienne and the miners, at least have the comfort of fellowship and the strength of their numbers, and they do not succumb without inflicting terrible damage on their adversary; their defeat, moreover, is anything but irrevocable. The generous fervour and the final—if deceptive—surge of optimism in *Germinal* humanize the austerely dispassionate handling of the subject. (pp. 175-76)

In another respect *Germinal* may be thought superior to *L'assommoir.* The merit of a work of art may up to a point be measured by the artist's skill in solving the difficulties set him by his subject. In a sense *L'assommoir* and *Germinal* deal with the same subject, or at any rate with the same problem—that of social injustice; and for a writer with even the dullest social conscience, the temptation to extract from that theme a momentarily successful but ephemeral *roman à thèse* [novel of ideas] is almost irresistible. In *L'assommoir,* as we have seen, the danger was met by suppressing the factor of social strife; in *Germinal,* however, Zola had the courage to give this factor full weight. In his preliminary notes he defined his novel as 'the struggle between capital and labour', adding that this question was 'the most important one the twentieth century will have to face'. Both the helots and their lords would be given equal place in the economy of the work, and none of the horrors of the class war would be glossed over. Zola's secret for preserving impartiality was to absolve both parties in the conflict from guilt: the root of the evil was to be left buried, and the author would refuse to point to scapegoats or to venture into any specific dialectical analysis of the situation. (p. 179)

In both *Au bonheur des dames* and *Germinal* (and later, in *La terre* also) the dilemma is the same: the path of free competition is the path of progress; but, since competition is simply the right of the stronger to devour the weaker, there will be stretched by the wayside the bodies of many an innocent victim. In *Au bonheur des dames* Zola was able to endorse this process, at least for its ends if not for its means; but when, turning from a purely internal struggle within the commercial class, he looked at the major clash between the possessors and the dispossessed, his complacency was shattered. (p. 181)

The most that can properly be claimed for *Germinal* is that its picture of social conditions was such that no reader save the most callous could remain complacent.

Yet even when so much is admitted, there remain the figures of Étienne Lantier and Hennebeau which cancel any over-optimistic estimations of the practicability and ultimate value of deliberately engineered social changes. *Germinal,* in short, is neither revolutionary nor counter-revolutionary; it is not primarily a vehicle for extra-literary concerns, and thus ought not to be judged, as too often it has been judged, by its accuracy as a social document, still less by its effectiveness

as a piece of propaganda. The only standards of evaluation which can properly be applied are aesthetic ones. (p. 197)

Although Zola understood them well enough for his purpose, he gave rather less place to economic questions in *La terre* than he had in *Germinal,* in which they are fundamental. (p. 205)

La terre was not the first novel of Zola's to deal with peasant life: there had been a forerunner, *La faute de l'abbé Mouret.* It is true that peasants play only a subsidiary part in this earlier book; but the little that is said of them is enough to show that Zola's conception of country life had changed little in the thirteen years' interval. In both books, the villagers' behaviour knows no moral restraints: rarely is a bride brought to church unless she is pregnant or perhaps already a mother. Their profligacy, however, is simply the brutish satisfaction of periodic appetites, their emotions being reserved for the earth. They farm their land with the passionate tenderness of a lover cherishing his first mistress, or, as Archangias puts it baldly: 'They love their plots of land so much, they would fornicate with them.' They are godless, but retain a certain respect for ministers of religion and a deep reserve of superstition. (pp. 205-06)

The passionate cleaving to the earth, amounting to an erotic frenzy—something that was only hinted at in *L'abbé Mouret*—is of primary importance in *La terre* and gives the book its overpowering odour of sweat and manure. In different degrees, the lust for land runs in the veins of most of the main characters in *La terre.* (p. 206)

Horrifying and yet strangely peaceful, ribald and grave in turns, *La terre* is a kind of *summa* of all that is characteristic of Zola. For this alone, perhaps, it has a better right to be styled epic than any other of his works. In contrast with *L'assommoir* and particularly with *Pot-bouille,* nearly all the action of *La terre* takes place out of doors. The freshness of the air blows away much of what would otherwise be sordid in Zola's invention. (pp. 214-15)

Nearer to hand and possessed of a more real existence than the 'god Capital' in *Germinal,* the earth had provided Zola with that impassive, indifferent antagonist which his dramatic instinct craved, to stand aloofly opposed to brawling humanity. He tried, but much less successfully, to use the same formula in *Le rêve,* where it is religion, in the shape of the cathedral, which fills the part. *La bête humaine,* his next work and the seventeenth of the series, was based on a similar dichotomy, but although far more impressive than *Le rêve,* it does not exhibit quite the same mastery as *La terre.* (p. 215)

La bête humaine is a good average specimen of Zola's art in its maturity. . . . It qualifies for the title 'epic' by the broad sweep of the author's vision. . . .

In particular, the rudimentary characterization Zola practised is nowhere easier to observe than in *La bête humaine* in which Zola was determined once more, as the preliminary notes indicate, to show 'psychology yielding to physiology'. He was reverting to his beginnings, in giving Jacques, Séverine, and Roubaud as little cerebral motivation as Thérèse and Laurent in *Thérèse Raquin*. (p. 216)

La bête humaine, with its theme of the underlying animalism of civilized man, is more rawly disillusioning than ever. (p. 222)

In *Le docteur Pascal* all the tried principles by the application of which Zola had achieved integrated and lofty works of art are rejected: objectivity, irony, the adherence to logical determinism, the refusal to philosophize and to read a sermon into 'the study of nature, just as it is'. The last novel of *Les Rougon-Macquart* makes a regrettably discordant coda.

It is not too much to say that it ends not only the 'Natural and Social History of a Family under the Second Empire' but also the period of Zola's specifically artistic production. If one reads on through the *Lourdes—Rome—Paris* trilogy, and if one still has the courage to trek through the 'deep desert sand' (the words are Henry James's) of the *Évangiles,* it can only be to mark the melancholy spectacle of an artist in gradual disintegration. (p. 239)

[Zola's] work has a living interest which it owes to the one significant innovation that his vision of the universe contained. Zola was the first writer to show a society in which the aggregate was greater than the separate unit. All through the novels of his maturity and decline runs this one fruitful and fundamental idea. It manifests itself artistically in his characteristic descriptions of crowds in which the individual founders and is lost to view; in the way his imagination was time and time again captivated by huge impersonal entities, factories and mines, bazaars and markets, battlefields and railways; in his evident incapacity to isolate, explore, and expound the self-sufficient character. It declares itself, too, in his thought, in the glorification of human fertility and productive labour, in the rapt fascination with which he brooded over ancestry and progeny; there is always the same idea, that the individual is negligible, that what matters is the whole, and the contribution the individual makes to the whole. . . . Zola was the prophet of a new age of mass-psychology, mass-analysis, mass-education, and mass-entertainment, an age in which the part is never greater than the whole. An age without fineness, almost certainly; without fire and without colour, perhaps; but an age, it may be, of greater strength and broader justice; on that no one can speak yet with finality, for this age that Zola wrote of is, without the least doubt, our own age. (pp. 290-91)

F. W. J. Hemmings, in his *Émile Zola,* Oxford at the Clarendon Press, 1953, 308 p.

ELIZABETH LANGLAND
(essay date 1984)

[In the following excerpt, Langland examines Zola's social and political ideals and objectives in *Germinal*.]

Germinal explores the relationship of workers and masters at Le Voreux mine during a crisis provoked by a disguised wage cut. Although society is focused in a particular place, that place is seen as paradigmatic of the larger world. This society is characterized by class divisions, which are represented as economic in nature; that is, *Germinal,* like other sociological novels, depicts society as a set of class relationships determined almost exclusively by wealth. Political systems reflect the economic structure. There exist rich and poor, workers and masters, the governors and the governed. The action of the novel revolves around class conflicts. The novel, in its structure and action, argues for social determinism and for the economic base of human relationships. This is the "reality" Zola wanted to stress, not an historical reality but a scientific one. He claims not to be writing a story about people who really existed but to be deriving true, general hypotheses about the behavior of human beings under certain conditions. By stressing the interdependence of individuals and environment, he is making social change a prerequisite to individual development.

Characters thus act by determinable laws. In characterization, then, the promptings of human hearts and souls are not represented. . . . Although most novelists do trace behavior at least partly to heredity and environment, they often assume there exists some larger motive or cause. Indeed, in many cases, characters ennoble themselves by transcending their heredity and environment. D. H. Lawrence tried to give this larger motive a name—"inhuman will"—and although his articulation of this concept was new, the belief in it was not. There is something more to character than inherited nature and nurture. . . . The naturalistic novelist, in contrast, concentrates on determinism by heredity and environment in order to make social reform an issue, in order to harry the social conscience. Since an individual cannot transcend his inherited nature, then it becomes imperative to alter his social environment. Only through social change can individuals grow.

In this logic, of course, morality is relative and must be seen as socially or hereditarily determined, rather than as an absolute expression of individuality and personal integrity. Moral absolutes interfere with a full revelation of the compulsion that social environment exerts on individuals. Moral behavior, rather than being a matter of social conscience, becomes a matter of social status, largely determined by material well-being. For example, in *Germinal,* La Mouquette is described as "an eighteen-year-old haulage girl. She was a strapping wench, with a bosom and buttocks that almost split her vest and breeches." A free and easy sexuality accompanies this physical endowment, but we, as readers, are not encouraged to judge or blame her for her promiscuity. In fact, her generous sexual nature is complemented by a very likable generosity in all other matters, both are simply an expression of heredity that is manifest physically. She even dies cheerfully, having shielded Catherine from bullets, but we do not see this act as a moral choice or as a complex psychological decision, a perception that would lend her character dignity. Her behavior is physiologically and socially determined.

Class and economic status also determine morality. No individual moral norms are absolute; they can shift as rapidly as social conditions shift. Until the strike at Le Voreux mine and the subsequent starvation, La Maheude violently opposes begging. Suddenly we learn that "neither Lénore nor Henri had come back from tramping the streets with Jeanlin, begging for coppers." . . . Étienne Lantier, the novel's protagonist, learns of this behavior "with aching heart. She used to threaten to kill them if they begged in the street. Now it was she who sent them out." . . . People will adopt whatever morality a situation demands. A great objection lodged against social or naturalistic novels is that they make character into mere mechanism. . . . The social novelist faces the difficult task of coupling stature and significance for his protagonists with social determinism. Zola's characters gain stature through their resentment; their moral flexibility does not prevent their bitterly resenting their subjugation and degradation. Individuals are aware of moral alternatives largely by contrast with a more dignified past. They are, after all, reflective beings, and their acute sense of degradation redeems in part their swift, amoral adjustment to new social conditions and their debasement within those conditions.

Because Zola is interested in art as well as social reform, he uses the resources of novelistic art to enhance his novel's examination of social process. In *Germinal,* Zola found the means to shape his work artistically—to create its beginning, middle, and end—without falsifying social reality. To do so, he conceived character and scene both metaphorically and objectively, and he conceived the action both in personal and in social/political terms. The novel thus has two complementary narratives.

We turn first to Zola's metaphoric conception of character. Although Zola binds most of his characters by heredity, environment, and the probabilities of the two, he also introduces various symbolic characters whose personalities and fates express the logic of his represented society. In this light, La Maheude and Maheu, with their larger concerns for justice and morality, are the matriarch and patriarch of the society. Their individual degradation charts for readers the larger degradation of society. Writers have difficulty in making readers identify with such an abstraction as society. When a fiction asks us to identify with individuals, its writer usually illustrates society's values in minor characters. Since the naturalistic novel's principal purpose is to reveal the nature of a particular society, even major characters are subsumed to that purpose. Personal development is subordinated to a desire to reveal flaws and limitations in society. For example, the patriarch Maheu—kind, considerate, and judicious—wins our sympathy through his concerned interest in Étienne and his unselfish desire to share what little meat he has with his children. As the strike progresses, Maheu fades further and further into the background. Suddenly he is shot down by the soldiers. We know little of his motives for being in the front lines except that La Maheude has goaded him on. When Maheu is killed, it is hard to feel the sympathy one would expect for such a likable character. It seems that the traits characterizing him neither explain why he is where he is nor do they provide sufficient psychological insight into his emotions at the moment. Zola distances us from his deliberately so that Maheu's experience can represent something outside himself. The system of symbolic structures—the use of red, of anger, of violence—suggests that Maheu, from a metaphorical standpoint, is consumed just as the society is consuming itself. We focus not on the loss of one sympathetic character but on a didactic point: society structured in this way will lead to senseless bloodshed and so destroy itself. (pp. 127-30)

Maheu, then, dramatizes one immediate end of social process. Zola employs other characters—Jeanlin, Bonnemort, and Cécile—to dramatize the ultimate end of this process. Bonnemort and Cécile, although very much products of heredity and environment, also represent a final confrontation between an overfed bourgeoisie and a starved working class: "They gazed at each other in fascination, she, buxom, plump, and pink from the days of well-fed idleness of her race, he blown out with dropsy, hideous and pathetic like some broken-down animal, ravaged by a century of toil and hunger passed down from father to son." . . . Bonnemort, a figure out of the past, the paradigmatic victim of social injustice, wreaks his vengeance on the flower of the bourgeoisie, Cécile.

Jeanlin, the other symbolic character, is first described as possessing a "face, like a small, frizzy-haired monkey's, with its green eyes and big ears." . . . The evolutionary implications of this description follow later: "Unhealthily precocious, he seemed to have the mysterious intelligence and bodily skill of a human foetus reverting to its animal origins," . . . and later: "[Étienne] contemplated this child, who, with his pointed muzzle, green eyes, long ears, resembled some degenerate with the instinctive intelligence and craftiness of a savage, gradually reverting to man's animal origins. The pit had made him what he was, and the pit had finished the job by breaking his legs." . . . In the last sentence Jeanlin's character is attributed to the pit, but he represents the end of a process that has been going on, a reduction of man to his animal instincts, a reversion back to his animal origins. We are to conclude that the ultimate effect of social determinism here is the dehumanization of man. Society, which is intended to humanize, becomes an agent to destroy him. Zola makes a powerful didactic point through this character; if society does not destroy itself, in perpetuating itself in its present form, it will destroy humanity.

Zola's strongest social criticism and his only social optimism—his vision of a new society—emerge through the structure of his novel: a paralleling of metaphor with fact, of personal experience with social experience. The novel opens at night when Étienne Lantier arrives at Le Voreux mine. The narrator describes the mine both as an evil beast and as an objective thing. . . . The first sentence personifies the mine. A literal description of the works follows, and the last sentences once again personify the mine, now as an evil beast. This metaphor makes us expect and fear certain events and desire alternative ones; it makes us feel the inevitability of destruction at this point. It allows us to anticipate the developing conflict. In short, it shapes Zola's objective presentation of society in novelistic ways. More important, in this juxtaposition of metaphor and fact, Zola remains faithful to the objective reality of the world he depicts. Part of the naturalistic novelist's effect depends on persuading readers to accept the fidelity of his vision of society. Implicit in Zola's theory of the novel lies a desire *not* to be seen as tampering with social conditions and represented society in the effort to suit larger artistic ends. Hence Zola insists that the novelist sets up his experiment and lets it run by itself; he does not prejudge the results. Zola's talent as artist, however, enabled him to discover means to shape events without falsifying social reality.

In addition to conceiving character and scene both metaphorically and objectively, Zola also conceives the action in two dimensions. *Germinal* entwines complementary narratives: a personal one, which focuses on the relationship between Étienne and Catherine and is resolved in their sexual consummation, and a social one, which depicts the larger class struggle and cannot

realistically be resolved since that resolution would dictate the dawn of a new era based on general equality. Unlike Thackeray's *Vanity Fair,* whose two narratives create conflicting social realities and therefore prevent the reader from arriving at a coherent set of social expectations, Zola's *Germinal* makes its two narratives share a social reality so that the expectations that shape one narrative can, by analogy, suggest a shaping to the other. The effect, then, of this intermingling of stories is that Étienne and Catherine's relationship shapes our expectations for society and ultimately allows us to anticipate another, better social reality that has its seeds in the destruction of the present one, although, in fact and realistically, society cannot change so quickly and dramatically, and our optimism is unwarranted.

Germinal begins with Étienne's arrival at Montsou. He almost decides to leave after one day in the mines, but two things detain him: "Suddenly Étienne made up his mind. Maybe he thought he saw Catherine's pale eyes up yonder, where the village began. Or perhaps it was some wind of revolt blowing from Le Voreux. He could not tell. But he wanted to go down the mine again to suffer and to fight." . . . He is attracted by a woman and a social situation. First he pursues Catherine, but, losing her to Chaval, he becomes interested in the political situation at the mines. He comes closer to Catherine for a while when he moves in with the Maheus, but she moves out to join Chaval, and her rupture with her family is mirrored by the miners' strike. Étienne becomes wholly involved in the strike, but love is also a factor in his political ambition. At the meeting in the woods, Étienne is spurred on by the thought of Catherine: "He had recognized Chaval among his friends in the front row, and the thought that Catherine must be there too had put new fire into him, and a desire to be applauded in front of her." . . . By this parallel structure, Zola has identified the romantic situation with the political one, a very important identification in the final effect of the novel.

The parallels continue. The miners seek violent retribution for injustice; Chaval and Étienne immediately thereafter come to blows over Catherine. The miners protest the importation of workers from Belgium and are shot. Catherine, too, is bloodied, but "it was the pent-up flood of her puberty released at last by the shock of that dreadful day." . . . Catherine's physical maturation suggests a maturity in the consciousness of the workers. The seeds now planted will grow to fruition. Finally, Étienne decides to return to the mine with Catherine. His love is at least a partial motive. Souvarine speculates, "When a man's heart was tied up with a woman he was finished and might as well die." . . . Étienne and Catherine have their consummation: he plants his seed in her womb in the bowels of the earth, a larger womb.

Although the workers return to work with seemingly no gains, we do not feel that *Germinal* is a pessimistic novel. The seed has been planted and will burst through the earth: "Men were springing up, a black avenging host was slowly germinating in the furrows, thrusting upwards for the harvests of future ages. And very soon their germination would crack the earth asunder." . . . Étienne's hopeful lyrical speculations on society would be unwarranted without the parallel love situation and its powerful consummation. In other words, our reaction to the novel has been precisely determined by the complex interrelationship between a personal situation and a social one.

Zola lays a social situation before us in great complexity, and he refuses to resolve it except by means of this parallel relationship between Étienne and Catherine described above. In a sense there are two resolutions in *Germinal:* a personal one and a social one. The personal one is resolved in the bowels of the earth; the social is actually never resolved. The workers return to work. We would like them, after all their suffering, to win their demands, but they do not, and to this extent we feel that we are in touch with the way things happen in the real world. Zola has, in short, enhanced his didactic ends; he affirms social determinism; he illuminates the inevitable consequences of class divisions in a capitalist society. Yet, at the same time, he has used parallel structures to achieve the power of resolution in anticipated social change without warping the social reality he wants to depict. As a result, Zola has created no simple social document but a novel with a strong element of reality that propounds a social theory and urges social change and that does so by engaging us with characters for whom we deeply care. (pp. 130-34)

Elizabeth Langland, "The Art of Sociological Naturalism in Zola and Dreiser," in her *Society in the Novel,* The University of North Carolina Press, 1984, pp. 124-46.

SOURCES FOR FURTHER STUDY

Bagauley, David, ed. *Critical Essays on Emile Zola.* Boston: G. K. Hall and Co., 1986, 198 p.

> Collects criticism on Zola, ranging from early reviews to contemporary scholarship.

Barbusse, Henri. *Zola.* Translated by Mary Balardie Green and Frederick C. Green. New York: E. P. Dutton, 1933, 279 p.

> Documents Zola's research and compositional methods.

Hemmings, F. W. J. *Emile Zola.* Rev. ed. Oxford: Clarendon Press, 1966, 329 p.

> The standard English biography, by a widely acknowledged authority on the author. Updates the 1953 edition of this work (see above excerpt dated 1953).

Parmée, Douglas. Introduction to *The Attack on the Mill, and Other Stories,* by Emile Zola, pp. vii-xxiv. Oxford: Oxford University Press, 1984.

> Emphasizes elements in Zola's short fiction that distinguish it from his novels, citing particularly the prevalence of irony.

Walker, Philip. *Zola.* London: Routledge & Kegan Paul, 1985, 257 p.

> Critical biography.

Warren, Jill. "Zola's View of Prostitution in *Nana.*" In *The Image of the Prostitute in Modern Literature,* edited by Pierre L. Horn and Mary Beth Pringle, pp. 29-41. New York: Frederick Unger Publishing Co., 1984.

> Concludes that Zola's depiction of the title character in *Nana* betrays misogyny and bourgeois attitudes toward sexuality on the part of the author.

WORLD LITERATURE CRITICISM

1500 to the Present

ACKNOWLEDGMENTS

ACKNOWLEDGMENTS

The editor wishes to thank the copyright holders of the excerpted criticism included in this volume, the permissions managers of many book and magazine publishing companies for assisting in securing reprint rights, and Anthony Bogucki for assistance with copyright research. The editor is also grateful to the staffs of the Detroit Public Library, Wayne State University Purdy/Kresge Library Complex, the University of Michigan Libraries, and the Library of Congress for making their resources available. Following is a list of the copyright holders who have granted permission to reprint material in *WLC*. Every effort has been made to trace copyright, but if omissions have been made, please let the editor know.

COPYRIGHTED EXCERPTS IN *WLC* WERE REPRINTED FROM THE FOLLOWING PERIODICALS:

for " 'Our Gatsby, Our Nick' " by Barry Gross; v. XIX, Spring, 1975 for "Anne Sexton: Somehow to Endure" by J. D. Mc-Clatchy; v. XX, Summer, 1976 for "Time, Uncertainty, and Kurt Vonnegut, Jr.: A Reading of 'Slaughterhouse-Five' " by Charles B. Harris. © 1970, 1975, 1976 by *The Centennial Review*. All reprinted by permission of the publisher and the respective authors.—*Chronicles: A Magazine of American Culture,* v. 15, May, 1991 for "A True Vindication of Edmund Burke" by Peter J. Stanlis. Copyright © 1991 by The Rockford Institute. All rights reserved. Reprinted by permission of the publisher and the author.—*CLA Journal,* v. 16, September, 1972; v. XXIX, December, 1985; v. XXXII, March, 1989. Copyright, 1972, 1985, 1989 by The College Language Association. All used by permission of The College Language Association.—*Claremont Quarterly,* v. 11, Winter, 1964 for "John Cheever: A Vision of the World" by Frederick Bracher. Copyright, Claremont Graduate School and University Center, 1964. Reprinted by permission of the author.—*College English,* v. 39, February, 1978 for "Ayn Rand and Feminism: An Unlikely Alliance" by Mimi R. Gladstein. Copyright © 1978 by the National Council of Teachers of English. Reprinted by permission of the publisher and the author.—*Columbia Library Columns,* v. 37, November, 1987. Reprinted by permission of the publisher.—*Commentary,* v. 54, December, 1972 for "Philip Roth Reconsidered" by Irving Howe; v. 70, November, 1980 for "The Posthumous Victory of Albert Camus" by Stephen Miller; v. 75, May, 1983 for "How Good Is Gabriel García Márquez?" by Joseph Epstein; v. 80, September, 1985 for "One Cheer for E. M. Forster" by Joseph Epstein; v. 81, May, 1986 for "Montezuma's Literary Revenge" by Fernanda Eberstadt; v. 82, December, 1986 for "Man of Letters" by George Sim Johnston; v. 92, November, 1991 for "Our Debt to I. B. Singer" by Joseph Epstein. Copyright © 1972, 1980, 1983, 1985, 1986, 1991 by the American Jewish Committee. All rights reserved. All reprinted by permission of the publisher and the respective authors.—*The Commonweal,* v. XLVIII, July 16, 1948; v. LVII, February 20, 1953, v. LXVIII, April 18, 1958. Copyright 1948, renewed 1976; copyright 1953, renewed 1981; copyright © 1958, renewed 1986 Commonweal Publishing Co., Inc. All reprinted by permission of Commonweal Foundation.—*Contemporary Literature,* v. 20, Spring, 1979. © 1979 by the Board of Regents of the University of Wisconsin System. Reprinted by permission of The University of Wisconsin Press.—*Critical Quarterly,* v. 17, Autumn, 1975. Reprinted by permission of the publisher.—*Criticism,* v. XXVIII, Fall, 1986 for "Thomas Gray: Drowning in Human Voices: by Wallace Jackson. Copyright, 1986, Wayne State University Press. Reprinted by permission of the publisher and the author.—*Critique: Studies in Modern Fiction,* v. XII, 1970; v. XIX, 1978. Copyright © 1970, 1978 Helen Dwight Reid Educational Foundation. Both reprinted with permission of the Helen Dwight Reid Educational Foundation, published by Heldref Publications, 1319 18th Street, N. W., Washington, DC 20036-1802.—*CSL: The Bulletin of the New York C. S. Lewis Society,* v. 21, May 1990. © 1990 New York C. S. Lewis Society. Reprinted by permission of the publisher.—*The Denver Quarterly,* v. 10, Winter, 1976 for "Bellow's Gift" by Seymour Epstein. Copyright © 1976 by the University of Denver. Reprinted by permission of the author.—*Diacritics,* v. II, Fall, 1972. Copyright © Diacritics, Inc., 1972. Reprinted by permission of the publisher.—*Dimension,* v. 3, 1970. © 1970 by *Dimension*. Reprinted by permission of the publisher.—*ELH,* v. 48, Summer, 1981. Copyright © 1981 by The Johns Hopkins University Press. All rights reserved. Reprinted by permission of the publisher.—*Encounter,* v. LVIII, May, 1982 for "The Fatality of Hatred" by Benedict Nightingale. © 1982 by Encounter Ltd. Reprinted by permission of the author.—*English Institute Essays,* 1946 for "Literary Criticism" by Cleanth Brooks. Copyright 1946, Columbia University Press, New York. Renewed 1975 by James L. Clifford. Reprinted by permission of the publisher and the author.—*English Journal,* v. XXII, November, 1933 for "The Case against Willa Cather" by Granville Hicks. Copyright 1933 by the National Council of Teachers of English. Renewed 1961 by Granville Hicks. Reprinted by permission of Russell & Volkening, Inc. as agents for the author./ v. 61, January, 1972 for "A Defense of Ken Kesey's 'One Flew Over the Cuckoo's Nest' " by Janet R. Sutherland; v. 61, December, 1972 for "Ray Bradbury and Fantasy" by Anita T. Sullivan. Copyright © 1972 by the National Council of Teachers of English. Both reprinted by permission of the publisher and the respective authors./ v. 61, October, 1972. Copyright © 1972 by the National Council of Teachers of English. Reprinted by permission of the publisher.—*English Studies,* Netherlands, v. 63, February, 1982. © 1982 by Swets & Zeitlinger B.V. Reprinted by permission of the publisher.—*Essays in Literature,* v. 4, Fall, 1977; v. VIII, Spring, 1981. Copyright 1977, 1981 by Western Illinois University. Both reprinted by permission of the publisher.—*Essays and Studies in English and Comparative Literature,* v. VIII, 1932. University of Michigan Press, 1932. Copyright, 1932, renewed 1960 by University of Michigan Press. Reprinted by permission of the publisher.—*Extrapolation,* v. 25, Fall, 1984. Copyright 1984 by The Kent State University Press. Reprinted by permission of the publisher.—*Field: Contemporary Poetry and Poetics,* n. 29, Fall, 1983. Copyright © 1983 by Oberlin College. Reprinted by permission of the publisher.—*The Georgia Review,* v. XXXII, Summer, 1978 for " 'Moonlight Dries No Mittens': Carl Sandburg Reconsidered" by Daniel Hoffman. Copyright, 1978, by the University of Georgia. Reprinted by permission of the author.—*Harper's,* v. 279, July 1989 for "On the Road to Nowhere:/ Kerouac, Re-Read and Regretted" by Sven Birkerts. Copyright © 1989 by *Harper's Magazine*. All rights reserved. Reprinted by special permission of the author.—*University of Hartford Studies in Literature,* v. 15, 1983. Copyright © 1983 by the University of Hartford. Reprinted by permission of the publisher.—*Hispania,* v. 55, May, 1972 for "The Poetry of Pablo Neruda" by Andrew P. Debicki. © 1972 The American Association of Teachers of Spanish and Portuguese, Inc. Reprinted by permission of the publisher and the author.—*The Hollins Critic,* v. XXI, June, 1984. Copyright 1984 by Hollins College. Reprinted by permission of the publisher.—*The Hudson Review,* v. XXI, Autumn, 1968; v. XLI, Summer, 1988. Copyright © 1968, 1988 by The Hudson Review, Inc. Both reprinted by permission of the publisher./ v. XI, Winter, 1958-59. Copyright © 1958, renewed 1986 by The Hudson Review, Inc. Reprinted by permission of the publisher.—*The International Fiction Review,* v. 7, Summer, 1980. © copyright 1980 International Fiction Association. Reprinted by permission of the publisher.—*The Iowa Review,* v. 8, Winter, 1977 for "Sylvia Plath and Confessional Poetry: A Reconsideration" by M. D. Uroff. Copyright © 1977 by The University of Iowa. Reprinted by permission of the publisher and the author.—*Italica,* v. XLIV, March, 1967. Reprinted by permission of the publisher.—*Journal of American Studies,* v. 2, October, 1968. © Cambridge University Press 1968. Reprinted with the permission of Cambridge University Press.—*The Journal of English and Germanic Philology,* v. LXIV, July, 1965 for "Thematic Unity in Lamb's Familiar Essays" by Donald H. Reiman. © 1965 by the Board of Trustees of the University of Illinois. Reprinted by permission of the publisher and the author.—*The Journal of Negro*

Education, v. XLIII, Summer, 1974 for "Analysis of Selected Poetry of Phillis Wheatley" by Angelene Jamison. Copyright © Howard University 1974. Reprinted by permission of the publisher and the author.—*Journal of Negro History,* January, 1967. Reprinted by permission of The Association for the Study of Afro-American Life and History, Inc. (ASALH).—*Journal of Popular Culture,* v. X, Spring, 1977. Copyright © 1977 by Ray B. Browne. Reprinted by permission of the publisher.—*Kansas Quarterly,* v. 7, Summer, 1975 for "Langston Hughes: A Kansas Poet in the Harlem Renaissance" by Cary D. Wintz; v. 16, Summer, 1984 for "Personal Fantasy in Andersen's Fairy Tales" by John Griffith. © copyright 1975, 1984 by the *Kansas Quarterly.* Both reprinted by permission of the publisher and the respective authors.—*London Magazine,* n.s. v. 8, July, 1968. © *London Magazine* 1968. Reprinted by permission of the publisher.—*London Review of Books,* v. 4, August 5-18, 1982 for "Falling in Love with Fanny" by V. S. Pritchett. Appears here by permission of the *London Review of Books* and the Peters, Fraser & Dunlop Group Ltd./ v. 11, May 1989 for "Spanish Practices" by Edwin Williamson. Appears here by permission of the *London Review of Books* and the author.—*Manchester Guardian Weekly,* April 8, 1990. First published in the Guardian. Copyright © 1990 by Guardian Publications Ltd. Reprinted by permission of Los Angeles Times-Washington Post News Service.—*The Massachusetts Review,* v. V. Autumn, 1963; v. IX, Winter, 1968. © 1963, 1968. Both reprinted from *The Massachusetts Review,* The Massachusetts Review, Inc. by permission.—*MELUS,* v. 9, Winter II, 1982; v. 10, Fall, 1983. Copyright, MELUS, The Society for the Study of Multi-Ethnic Literature of the United States, 1982, 1983. Both reprinted by permission of the publisher.—*Midstream,* v. XIV, August-September, 1968 for "Richard Wright and the Sixties" by Ronald Sanders; v. XXIII, December, 1977 for "Saul Bellow, on the Soul" by Alvin H. Rosenfeld. Copyright © 1968, 1977 by the Theodor Herzl Foundation, Inc. Both reprinted by permission of the publisher and the respective authors.—*The Midwest Quarterly,* v. IV, Summer, 1963; v. XXIX, Summer, 1988. Copyright, 1963, 1988, by *The Midwest Quarterly,* Pittsburg State University. Both reprinted by permission of the publisher.—*The Mississippi Quarterly,* v. 15, Fall, 1962. Reprinted by permission of the publisher.—*Modern Age,* v. 27, Winter, 1983. Copyright © 1983 by the Intercollegiate Studies Institute, Inc. Reprinted by permission of the publisher.—*Modern Drama,* v. XIV, September, 1971; v. XV, September, 1972; v. XVIII, March, 1975. Copyright 1971, 1972, 1975 *Modern Drama,* University of Toronto. All reprinted by permission of the publisher.—*Modern Fiction Studies,* v. VIII, Spring, 1962; v. 20, Summer, 1974; v. 25, Summer, 1979. Copyright © 1962, 1974, 1979 by Purdue Research Foundation, West Lafayette, IN 47907. All rights reserved. All reprinted with permission.—*The Modern Language Review,* v. 80, January, 1985. © Modern Humanities Research Association 1985. Reprinted by permission of the publisher.—*Mosaic: A Journal for the Comparative Study of Literature and Ideas,* v. XII, Fall, 1978. © *Mosaic* 1978. Acknowledgment of previous publication is herewith made.—*Mosaic: A Journal for the Comparative Study of Literature, New Views of the English and American Novel,* v. IV, Spring, 1971. © *Mosaic* 1971. Acknowledgment of previous publication is herewith made.—*The Nathaniel Hawthorne Journal,* 1976 for "Impaled Butterflies and the Misleading Moral in Hawthorne's Short Works" by James G. Janssen. Copyright © 1976 by Bruccoli Clark Publishers, Inc. Reprinted by permission of the author.—*The Nation,* New York, v. 205, September 25, 1967; v. 219, December 7, 1974; v. 222, May 22, 1976. Copyright 1967, 1974, 1976 *The Nation* magazine/ The Nation Company, Inc. All reprinted by permission of the publisher./ v. 184, March 9, 1957; v. 185, November 16, 1957. Copyright 1957, renewed 1985 *The Nation* magazine/ The Nation Company, Inc. Both reprinted by permission of the publisher.—*National Review,* New York, v. XXXVII, January 11, 1985. © 1985 by National Review, Inc., 150 East 35th Street, New York, NY 10016. Reprinted with permission of the publisher.—*Negro American Literature Forum,* v. 5, Winter, 1971 for "The Blues Poetry of Langston Hughes" by Edward E. Waldron. Copyright © Indiana State University 1971. Reprinted with the permission of *Black American Literature Forum* and the author.—*Negro History Bulletin,* v. 32, April, 1969. Reprinted by permission of The Association for the Study of Afro-American Life and History, Inc.—*The New Criterion,* v. IV, November, 1985 for "Is It All Right to Read Somerset Maugham?" by Joseph Epstein; v. V. October, 1986 for "Courtship in Congreve" by Louis Auchincloss; v. IX, May, 1991 for "Alexandre Dumas: Fact and Fiction" by Renee Winegarten. Copyright © 1985, 1986, 1991 by The Foundation for Cultural Review. All reprinted by permission of the respective authors.—*The New Leader,* v. LI, September 9, 1968. © 1968 by The American Labor Conference on International Affairs, Inc. Reprinted by permission of the publisher.—*New Orleans Review,* v. 12, Spring, 1985. © 1985 by Loyola University, New Orleans.—*The New Republic,* v. 114, March 18, 1946 for "Walt Whitman: The Miracle" by Malcolm Cowley. Copyright 1946 The New Republic, Inc. Renewed 1973 by Malcolm Cowley. Reprinted by permission of The Literary Estate of Malcolm Cowley./ v. 194, May 12, 1986. © 1986 The New Republic, Inc. Reprinted by permission of *The New Republic.*—*New Statesman,* v. LXVI, December 6, 1963; v. 85, May 11, 1973. © 1963, 1973 The Statesman & Nation Publishing Co., Ltd. Both reprinted by permission of the publisher.—*New York Herald Tribune Books,* August 23, 1936. Copyright 1936, renewed 1964 *The Washington Post.* Reprinted with permission of the publisher.—*The New York Review of Books,* v. XVII, November 18, 1971 for "The First Waste Land-I" by Richard Ellmann. Copyright © 1971 Nyrev, Inc. Reprinted by permission of Candida Donadio & Associates, Inc./ v. III, September 10, 1964; v. XXI, October 3, 1974; v. XXV, November 9, 1978; v. XXXI, June 14, 1984; v. XXXI, October, 11, 1984; v. XXXII, May 30, 1985; v. XXXIV, December 17, 1987; v. XXXIV, January 21, 1988; v. XXXV, March 3, 1988; v. XXXVI, April 13, 1989; v. XXXVII, February 1, 1990. Copyright © 1964, 1974, 1978, 1984, 1985, 1987, 1988, 1989, 1990 Nyrev, Inc. All reprinted with permission from *The New York Review of Books.*—*The New York Times,* December 5, 1971 for a letter to the Editor of The New York Times by Marcia L. Falk. Copyright © 1971 by The New York Times Company. Reprinted by permission of the author./ October 9, 1955, April 22, 1984; October 23, 1985. Copyright 1955, Copyright © 1984, 1985 by The New York Times Company. All reprinted by permission of the publisher.—*The New York Times Book Review,* March 21, 1982 for "Fistfuls of Masterpieces" by Cynthia Ozick; June 5, 1988 for "Time Has Been Kind to the Nymphet: 'Lolita' 30 Years Later" by Erica Jong. Copyright © 1982, 1988 by The New York Times Company. Both reprinted by permission of the respective authors./ October 24, 1920; December 3, 1939; April 13, 1952; June 15, 1952; September 7, 1958; September 20, 1959; September 29, 1968; October 23, 1977; December 23, 1979; November 8, 1981; October 10, 1982; October 16, 1983; April 15, 1984; May 19, 1985; July 13, 1986; September 13, 1987; December 20, 1987. Copyright 1920, 1939, 1952, Copyright © 1958, 1959, 1968, 1977, 1979, 1981, 1982, 1983, 1984, 1985, 1986, 1987 by The New York Times

Company. All reprinted by permission of the publisher.—*The New Yorker,* v. XXVII, August 11, 1951 for "The Vision of the Innocent" by S. N. Behrman. Copyright 1951, renewed 1979 by The New Yorker Magazine, Inc. Reprinted by permission of Brandt & Brandt Literary Agents, Inc./ v. XXVIII, May 31, 1952 for "Black Man's Burden" by Anthony West. Copyright 1952 by The New Yorker Magazine, Inc. Renewed 1980 by Anthony West. Reprinted by permission of the Wallace Literary Agency, Inc./ v. L. February 17, 1975 for "The Last Victorian" by George Steiner. © 1975 by George Steiner. Reprinted by permission of Georges Borchardt on behalf of George Steiner./ v. LIX, May 9, 1983 for "Reflections: Kafka's Short Stories" by John Updike. © 1983 by the author. Reprinted by permission of the publisher.—*Nineteenth-Century Fiction,* v. VII, December, 1952 for "The Window Figure and the Two-Children Figure in 'Wuthering Heights'" by Dorothy Van Ghent. Copyright 1952, renewed 1980 by The Regents of the University of California. Reprinted by permission of The Regents and the Literary Estate of Dorothy Van Ghent.—*Nineteenth-Century French Studies,* v. XI, Spring & Summer, 1983. © 1983 by T. H. Goetz. Reprinted by permission of the publisher.—*The Northwest Missouri State College Studies,* v. XXV, November 1, 1961. Copyright, 1961, by Committee on The Northwest Missouri State University Studies. Reprinted by permission of the publisher.—*Novel: A Forum on Fiction,* v. 7, Fall, 1973. Copyright © Novel Corp., 1973. Reprinted with permission of the publisher.—*Nyctalops,* v. 2, 1978 for "The Gothic Foundations of Ambrose Bierce's Fiction" by Philip M. Rubens. Copyright © 1978 by Harry O. Morris, Jr. and Edward P. Berglund. Reprinted by permission of the author.—*The Observer,* July 21, 1985. Reprinted by permission of The Observer Limited, London.—*Palantir,* v. 23, 1983 for "Allen Ginsberg's 'Howl': A Reading" by Gregory Stephenson. Reprinted by permission of the author.—*Papers on Language & Literature,* v. V, Spring, 1969. Copyright © 1969 by the Board of Trustees, Southern Illinois University at Edwardsville. Reprinted by permission of the publisher.—*The Paris Review,* v. 8 Summer-Fall, 1963 for an interview with Evelyn Waugh by Julian Jebb. © 1963 The Paris Review, Inc. Reprinted by permission of the Literary Estate of Evelyn Waugh./ v. 12, Winter, 1968 for an interview with John Updike by Charles Thomas Samuels. © 1968 The Paris Review, Inc. Reprinted by permission of John Updike and the Literary Estate of Charles Thomas Samuels./ v. 23, Fall, 1981 for "The Art of Theatre V" by Tennessee Williams. © 1981 The Paris Review, Inc. Reprinted by permission of the Literary Estate of Tennessee Williams.—*Parnassus: Poetry in Review,* vs. 12-13, 1985 for "Poets of Weird Abundance" by Diane Middlebrook; v. 14, 1987 for "Among Soft Particles and Charms" by Diane Ackerman. Copyright © 1985, 1987 Poetry in Review Foundation, NY. Both reprinted by permission of the respective authors./ v. 2, 1974; v. 8, 1980. Copyright © 1974, 1980 Poetry in Review Foundation, NY. Both reprinted by permission of the publisher.—*Partisan Review,* v. XVI, February, 1949 for "The Literary Dictatorship of T. S. Eliot" by Delmore Schwartz. Copyright 1949, renewed 1976 by *Partisan Review.* Reprinted by permission of the Literary Estate of Delmore Schwartz./ v. XXXII, Spring, 1965 for "The Eye of the Storm" by Geoffrey H. Hartman. Copyright © 1965 by *Partisan Review.* Reprinted by permission of the publisher and the author./ v. XVI, 1949 for "Everybody's Protest Novel" by James Baldwin; v. XVIII, January-February, 1951 for "The Book of the Grotesque" by Irving Howe; Copyright 1949, renewed 1976; copyright 1951, renewed 1978, by *Partisan Review.* Both reprinted by permission of the publisher and the respective authors.—*Philological Quarterly,* v. 62, Summer, 1983 for "Style and Rhetorical Intention in Wordsworth's 'Lyrical Ballads'" by Judith W. Page. Copyright 1983 by The University of Iowa. Reprinted by permission of the publisher and the author.—*PHYLON: The Atlanta University Review of Race and Culture,* v. XIV, second quarter (June), 1953. Copyright, 1953, renewed 1980, by Atlanta University. Reprinted by permission of *PHYLON.*—*PMLA,* v. 103, March, 1988. Copyright © 1988 by the Modern Language Association of America. Reprinted by permission of the Modern Language Association of America.—*Poetry,* v. XCVII, February, 1961 for a review of "To Bedlam and Part Way Back" by James Dickey. © 1961, renewed 1989 by the Modern Poetry Association. Reprinted by permission of the Editor of *Poetry* and the author.—*The Quarterly Review,* v. 304, October, 1966.—*The Review,* v. 8, August, 1963 for an interview with Robert Lowell by A. Alvarez. © *The Review.* Reprinted by permission of A. Alvarez.—*Romance Quarterly,* v. 37, February, 1990. Copyright © 1990 by The University Press of Kentucky. Reprinted by permission of the publisher.—*The Samuel Butler Newsletter,* v. III, Summer, 1980 for "Butler's 'Erewhon': The Machine as Object and Symbol" by Govind Narain Sharma. Reprinted by permission of the author.—*San Francisco Review of Books,* Spring, 1984. Copyright © by the San Francisco Review of Books 1984. Reprinted by permission of the publisher.—*Saturday Review,* v. XLVII, July 15, 1964. © 1964 *Saturday Review* magazine.—*The Saturday Review of Literature,* v. XXVI, April 24, 1943. Copyright 1943, renewed 1970 *Saturday Review* magazine.—*Saturday Review/World,* v. 2, October 19, 1974. © 1974 *Saturday Review* magazine.—*The Sewanee Review,* v. LXXIX, Autumn, 1971; v. LXXXIV, Spring, 1976; v. XCII, Summer, 1984. © 1971, 1976, 1984 by The University of the South. All reprinted by permission of the editor of *The Sewanee Review.*/ v. LV, Summer, 1947. Copyright 1947, renewed 1974 by The University of the South. Reprinted by permission of the editor of *The Sewanee Review.*—*South Atlantic Quarterly,* v. LXIX, Spring, 1970; v. 74, Winter, 1975. Copyright © 1970, 1975 by Duke University Press, Durham, NC. Both reprinted with permission of the publisher./ v. 59, 1960. Copyright © 1960, renewed 1988 by Duke University Press, Durham, NC. Reprinted with permission of the publisher.—*Southern Folklore Quarterly,* v. XL, March-June, 1976. Reprinted by permission of the publisher.—*The Southern Humanities Review,* v. XIV, Summer, 1980 for an interview with Eudora Welty by Jan Nordby Gretlund. Copyright 1980 by Auburn University. Reprinted by permission of Russell & Volkening as agents for Eudora Welty and by permission of Jan Nordby Gretlund./ v. XIV, Fall, 1980 for "Carson McCullers' Tomboys" by Louise Westling. Copyright 1980 by Auburn University. Reprinted by permission of the author.—*The Southern Quarterly,* v. XVI, January, 1978. Copyright © 1978 by the University of Southern Mississippi. Reprinted by permission of the publisher.—*The Southern Review,* Louisiana State University, v. VII, Autumn, 1941 for "Changes of Attitude and Rhetoric in Auden's Poetry" by Randall Jarrell. Copyright, 1941, by Louisiana State University. Renewed 1969 by Mrs. Randall Jarrell. Reprinted by permission of Mary Von S. Jarrell./ v. VIII, Summer, 1972 for "Mark Twain" by Robert Penn Warren. Copyright, 1972, by the author. Reprinted by permission of the William Morris Agency, Inc., on behalf of the Estate of the author./ v. IX, Winter, 1973 for "Dos Passos: The Learned Poggius" by Malcolm Cowley. Copyright, 1973, by the author. Reprinted by permission of the Literary Estate of Malcolm Cowley./ v. 17, Summer, 1981 for "The Poetry of Auden" by Austin Warren. Copyright, 1981, by the author. Reprinted by permission of the Literary Estate of Austin Warren./ v. IV,

Autumn, 1938. Copyright, 1938, renewed 1965, by Louisiana State University. Reprinted by permission of the publisher.—*Soviet Literature,* n. 3, 1968. © *Soviet Literature,* 1968.—*The Spectator,* v. 247, September 12, 1981. © 1981 by *The Spectator.* Reprinted by permission of *The Spectator.*—*Studies in Contemporary Satire,* 1974. © 1974. Reprinted by permission of the publisher.—*Studies in the Literary Imagination,* v. XII, Fall, 1979. Copyright 1979 Department of English, Georgia State University. Reprinted by permission of the publisher.—*Studies in the Novel,* v. IX, Winter, 1977. Copyright 1977 by North Texas State University. Reprinted by permission of the publisher.—*Studies in Romanticism,* v. VII, Winter, 1968. Copyright 1968 by the Trustees of Boston University. Reprinted by permission of the publisher.—*Studies in Short Fiction,* Fall, 1975; v. 18, Winter, 1981. Copyright 1975, 1981 by Newberry College. Both reprinted by permission of the publisher.—*The Texas Quarterly,* v. VII, Autumn, 1964 for "Turn Down an Empty Glass" by Janet Overmyer. © 1964 by The University of Texas at Austin. Reprinted by permission of the author.—*Texas Studies in Literature and Language,* v. VIII, Fall, 1966 for "The Early Poetry of Aldous Huxley" by Charles M. Holmes. Copyright © 1966 by the University of Texas Press. Reprinted by permission of the publisher and the author.—*Theoria,* Pietermaritzburg, v. LI, October, 1978. Reprinted by permission of the publisher.—*The Times Literary Supplement,* n. 4069, March 27, 1981; n. 4345, July 11, 1986; n. 4460, September 23-29, 1988. © The Times Supplements Limited 1981, 1986, 1988. All reproduced from *The Times Literary Supplement* by permission.—*The Transatlantic Review,* n. 41, Winter-Spring, 1972 for an interview with Eugene Ionesco by Ronald Hayman. © copyright Transatlantic Review, Inc. 1972. Reprinted by permission of Eugene Ionesco and the Peters, Fraser & Dunlop Group Ltd.—*Tri-Quarterly,* n. 5, Winter, 1965 for "The Novels of James Baldwin" by Robert A. Bone. © 1965 by *Tri-Quarterly,* Northwestern University. Reprinted by permission of the author.—*The Tulane Drama Review,* v. 8, Summer, 1964 for "Marlowe Today" by Harry Levine. Copyright © 1964, *The Tulane Drama Review.* Reprinted by permission of MIT Press and the author.—*Tulsa Studies in Women's Literature,* v. 7, Spring, 1988. © 1988, The University of Tulsa. Reprinted by permission of the publisher.—*Twentieth Century Literature,* v. 14, January, 1969; v. 18, January 1972; v. 21, October, 1975; v. 21, December, 1975; v. 23, December, 1977; v. 24, Winter, 1978; v. 25, Spring, 1979; v. 30, Spring, 1984. Copyright 1969, 1972, 1975, 1977, 1978, 1979, 1984, Hofstra University Press. All reprinted by permission of the publisher.—*Under the Sign of Pisces,* v. 11, Fall, 1980. Reprinted by permission of the publisher.—*Victorian Poetry,* v. II, December, 1964; v. 26, Spring-Summer, 1988. Both reprinted by permission of the publisher.—*The Village Voice,* v. XXVIII, October 4, 1983 for "The End of Irony" by Sean Wilentz. Copyright © News Group Publications, Inc., 1983. Reprinted by permission of *The Village Voice* and the author./ v. XXXIII, January, 1988 for an interview with James Baldwin by Quincy Troupe. Copyright © News Group Publications, Inc., 1988. Reprinted by permission of *The Village Voice* and Quincy Troupe.—*The Virginia Quarterly Review,* v. 53, Spring, 1977; v. 55, Spring, 1979; v. 62, Autumn, 1986. Copyright, 1977, 1979, 1986, by *The Virginia Quarterly Review,* The University of Virginia. All reprinted by permission of the publisher.—*West Virginia University Philological Papers,* v. 28, 1980. Reprinted by permission of the publisher.—*Western American Literature,* v. VIII, Fall, 1973. Copyright, 1973, by the Western Literature Association. Reprinted by permission of the publisher.—*The University of Windsor Review,* v. I, Spring, 1965 for "Joyce's Portrait-A Reconsideration" by Hugh Kenner. Reprinted by permission of the publisher and the author.—*Women & Literature,* v. 5, Fall, 1977. Copyright © 1977 by Janet M. Todd. Reprinted by permission of the publisher.—*Women's Studies International Quarterly,* v. 3, 1980 for "Views of Women and Men in the Work of Simone de Beauvoir" by Mary Evans. Copyright © 1980 Pergamon Press, Inc. Reprinted by permission of the publisher and the author.—*Women's Wear Daily,* January 6, 1984. Copyright 1984, Fairchild Publications. Reprinted by permission of the publisher.—*World Literature Today,* v. 56, Autumn, 1982; v. 57, Autumn, 1983. Copyright 1982, 1983 by the University of Oklahoma Press. Both reprinted by permission of the publisher.—*Yale French Studies,* n. 68, 1985. Copyright © *Yale French Studies* 1985. Reprinted by permission of the publisher.—*The Yale Review,* v. LIII, December, 1963; v. LXVII, Summer, 1978. Copyright 1963, 1978, by Yale University. Both reprinted by permission of the editors./ v. XXXII, Winter, 1943. Copyright 1942, renewed 1970 by Yale University. Reprinted by permission of the editors.—*A Yearbook of Studies in English Language and Literature,* v. 80, 1985-86 for " 'Their's Not to Reason Why': Alfred Lord Tennyson on the Human Condition" by Herbert Foltinek. © 1986 Wilhelm Braumüller. Reprinted by permission of the author.

COPYRIGHTED EXCERPTS IN *WLC* WERE REPRINTED FROM THE FOLLOWING BOOKS:

Aiken, Conrad. From "Virginia Woolf," in *Collected Criticism.* Oxford University Press, 1968. Copyright © 1927, 1929 by Conrad Aiken. Reprinted by permission of Brandt & Brandt Literary Agents, Inc.—Aiken, Conrad. From "William Faulkner," in *Collected Criticism.* Oxford University Press, 1968. Copyright © 1958 by Conrad Aiken. Reprinted by permission of Brandt & Brandt Literary Agents, Inc.—Aiken, Joan. From an introduction to *The Unbearable Bassington.* By Saki. The Folio Society Limited, 1978. Introduction © the Folio Society Limited 1978. All rights reserved. Reprinted by permission of the publisher.—Alazraki, Jaime. From *Jorge Luis Borges.* Essays on Modern Writers No. 57. Columbia University Press, 1971. Copyright © 1971 Columbia University Press. Used by permission of the publisher.—Alexander, Michael. From *The Poetic Achievement of Ezra Pound.* University of California Press, 1979. © Michael Alexander 1979. Reprinted by permission of the publisher.—Andresen, Kristen Wisloff. From "Woman's Place," in *Sigrid Undset.* Edited by Carl Henrik Grondahl. DYADE, 1983. Reprinted by permission of the publisher.—Auburn, Mark S. From *Sheridan's Comedies: Their Contexts and Achievements.* University of Nebraska, 1977. © 1977 by the University of Nebraska. Reprinted by permission of the publisher.—Auden, W. H. From "Don Juan," in *The Dyer's Hand and Other Essays.* Random House, 1962. Copyright © 1962 by W. H. Auden. Renewed 1990 by Edward Mendelson. All rights reserved. Reprinted by permission of Random House, Inc.—Auden, W. H. From *Forewords and Afterwords.* Edited by Edward Mendelson. Random House, 1973. Copyright © 1973 by W. H. Auden. Reprinted by permission of Random House, Inc.—Axelrod, Steven Gould. From *Robert Lowell: Life and Art.* Princeton University Press, 1978. Copyright © 1978 by Princeton University Press.

All rights reserved. Reprinted by permission of the publisher.—Balzac, Honoré de. From "Stendhal," in *Novelists on Novelists: An Anthology.* Edited by Louis Kronenberger. Doubleday & Company, 1962. Copyright © 1962 by Louis Kronenberger. Renewed 1990 by Mrs. Louis Kronenberger. All rights reserved. Reprinted by permission of the Literary Estate of Louis Kronenberger.—Barber, C. L. From *Shakespeare's Festive Comedy: A Study of Dramatic Form and Its Relation to Social Custom.* Princeton University Press, 1959. Copyright © 1959 by Princeton University Press. Renewed 1987 by C. Leo Barber. All rights reserved. Reprinted by permission of the publisher.—Barfield, Owen. From *Owen Barfield on C. S. Lewis.* Edited by G. B. Tennyson. Wesleyan University Press, 1989. Copyright © 1989 by Owen Barfield. All rights reserved. Reprinted by permission of the publisher.—Bart, Benjamin F. From *Flaubert.* Syracuse University Press, 1967. Copyright © 1967 by Syracuse University Press, Syracuse, N.Y. All rights reserved. Reprinted by permission of the publisher.—Battestin, Martin C. From *The Moral Basis of Fielding's Art: A Study of "Joseph Andrews."* Wesleyan University Press, 1959. Copyright © 1959 by Wesleyan University. Renewed 1987 by Martin C. Battestin. Reprinted by permission of University Press of New England.—Battiscombe, Georgina. From *Christina Rossetti: A Divided Life.* Holt, Rinehart and Winston, 1981. Copyright © 1981 by Georgina Battiscombe. All rights reserved. Reprinted by permission of Brandt & Brandt Literary Agents, Inc.—Baudelaire, Charles. From *Baudelaire as a Literary Critic.* Translated by Lois Boe Hyslop and Francis E. Hyslop, Jr. The Pennsylvania State University Press, 1964. Copyright © 1964, The Pennsylvania State University Press, University Park, PA.—Beach, Joseph Warren. From *American Fiction: 1920-1940.* The Macmillan Company, 1941. Copyright, 1941, renewed 1968, by Macmillan Publishing Company. All rights reserved. Reprinted by permission of the Literary Estate of Joseph Warren Beach.—Beaty, Frederick L. From *Byron the Satirist.* Northern Illinois University Press, 1985. Copyright © 1985 by Northern Illinois University Press. All rights reserved. Reprinted with permission of Northern Illinois University Press, DeKalb, Il.—Beaurline, L. A. From *Jonson and Elizabethan Comedy: Essays in Dramatic Rhetoric.* The Huntington Library, 1978. Copyright © 1978 Henry H. Huntington Library and Art Gallery. Reprinted by permission of the publisher.—Beauvoir, Simone de. From *The Second Sex.* Edited and translated by H. M. Parshley. Knopf, 1953. Copyright 1952, renewed 1980, by Alfred A. Knopf, Inc. Reprinted by permission of the publisher.—Becker, George J. From *John Dos Passos.* Ungar, 1974. Copyright © 1974 by The Ungar Publishing Company. Reprinted by permission of the publisher.—Bentley, Eric. From *The Playwright as Thinker: A Study of Drama in Modern Times.* Reynal & Hitchcock, 1946. Copyright 1946, renewed 1974 by Eric Bentley. Reprinted by permission of Harcourt Brace Jovanovich, Inc.—Bergonzi, Bernard. From *Heroes' Twilight: A Study of the Literature of the Great War.* Constable and Company Ltd., 1965. © 1965 by Bernard Bergonzi. All rights reserved. Reprinted by permission of the Peters, Fraser & Dunlop Group Ltd.—Berman, Russell A. From *The Rise of the Modern German Novel: Crisis and Charisma.* Cambridge, Mass.: Harvard University Press, 1986. Copyright © 1986 by the President and Fellows of Harvard College. All rights reserved. Excerpted by permission of the publishers and the author.—Berrigan, Ted. From "Jack Kerouac" in *Writers At Work,* Fourth Series. Edited by George A. Plimpton. Viking Penguin, 1976. Copyright © 1974, 1976 by The Paris Review. Used by permission of Viking Penguin, a division of Penguin Books USA Inc.—Berryman, John. From *The Freedom of the Poet.* Farrar, Straus and Giroux, 1976. Copyright © 1940, 1968, 1976 by Kate Berryman. Reprinted by permission of Farrar, Straus and Giroux, Inc.—Berrman, John. From *Stephen Crane: A Critical Biography.* William Sloane, 1950. Copyright 1950, renewed © 1977 by Kate Berryman. Reprinted by permission of the Literary Estate of John Berryman.—Bigsby, C. W. E. From an introduction to *Edward Albee: A Collection of Critical Essays.* Edited by C. W. E. Bigsby. Prentice-Hall, 1975. © 1975 by Prentice-Hall, Inc. Used by permission of Prentice-Hall/A Division of Simon & Schuster, Englewood Cliffs, NJ.—Birnbaum, Milton. From *Aldous Huxley's Quest for Values.* University of Tennessee Press, 1971. Copyright © 1971 by The University of Tennessee Press, Knoxville. Reprinted by permission of the publisher.—Birstein, Ann and Alfred Kazin. From an introduction to *The Works of Anne Frank.* Doubleday, 1959. Copyright 1952, © 1959 by Otto H. Frank. Renewed 1987 by Alfred Kazin and Anne Frank-Fonds Basel. All rights reserved. Used by permission of Doubleday, a division of Bantam Doubleday Dell Publishing Group, Inc.—Blansfield, Karen Charmaine. From *Cheap Rooms and Restless Hearts: A Study of Formula in the Urban Tales of William Sydney Porter.* Bowling Green State University Popular Press, 1988. Copyright © 1988 by Bowling Green State University Popular Press. Reprinted by permission of the publisher.—Bleikasten, André. From "The Heresy of Flannery O'Connor," in *Les Américanistes: New French Criticism on Modern American Fiction.* Edited by Ira D. Johnson and Christiane Johnson. Kennikat Press, 1978. Copyright © 1978 by Kennikat Press Corp. Reprinted by permission of the author.—Bleiler, E. F. From an introduction to *The Best Supernatural Tales of Arthur Conan Doyle.* By Arthur Conan Doyle, edited by E. F. Bleiler. Dover Publications, Inc., 1979. Copyright © 1979 by E. F. Bleiler. Reprinted by permission of the publisher.—Bloom, Harold. From *Agon: Towards a Theory of Revisionism.* Oxford University Press, 1982. Copyright © 1982 by Oxford University Press, Inc. Reprinted by permission of the publisher.—Bloom, Harold. From *The Ringers in the Tower: Studies in Romantic Tradition.* The University of Chicago Press, 1971. © 1971 by The University of Chicago. All rights reserved. Reprinted by permission of the publisher.—Boos, Florence Saunders. From *The Poetry of Dante G. Rossetti: A Critical Reading and Source Study.* Mouton, 1976. © copyright 1976 Mouton & Co., Publishers. Reprinted by permission of Mouton de Gruyter, a Division of Walter de Gruyter & Co.—Borges, Jorge Luis. From *Other Inquisitions: 1937-1952.* Translated by Ruth L. C. Simms. University of Texas Press, 1964. Copyright © 1964 by University of Texas Press. Reprinted by permission of the publisher and the author.—Borras, F. M. From *Maxim Gorky the Writer: An Interpretation.* Oxford at the Clarendon Press, 1967. © Oxford University Press 1967. Reprinted by permission of the publisher.—Bowen, Elizabeth. From "Katherine Mansfield," in *Seven Winters: Memories of a Dublin Childhood and Afterthoughts.* Alfred A. Knopf, 1962. Copyright © 1956, 1962 by Elizabeth Bowen. Renewed 1990 by Curtis Brown. Reprinted by permission of Curtis Brown Limited, London, as Literary Executors of Elizabeth Bowen.—Boyer, James. From *Thomas Wolfe: A Harvard Perspective.* Edited by Richard S. Kennedy. Croissant, 1983. Copyright © 1983 by Croissant & Company. Reprinted by permission of the author.—Boyers, Robert. From *Modern American Poetry: Essays in Criticism.* Edited by Jerome Mazzaro. McKay, 1970. Copyright © 1970 by the David McKay Company, Inc.—Bradbury, Malcolm. From *Saul Bellow.* Methuen, 1982. © 1982 Malcolm Bradbury. All rights reserved. Reprinted by permission of the publisher.—

Bradbury, Malcolm. From *What is a Novel?* Edward Arnold (Publishers) Ltd., 1969. © Malcolm Bradbury 1969. Reprinted by permission of the publisher.—Bradbury, Ray. From an interview in *Science Fiction Voices #2.* The Borgo Press, 1979. Copyright © 1979 by Jeffrey Elliot.—Bradford, Gamaliel. From *Daughters of Eve.* Houghton Mifflin, 1930. Copyright 1930 by Gamaliel Bradford. Copyright © renewed 1958 by Sarah Bradford Ross. Reprinted by permission of Houghton Mifflin Company.—Brady, Frank. From *James Boswell: The Later Years, 1769-1795.* McGraw-Hill, 1984. Copyright © 1984 by Frank Brady. All rights reserved. Reprinted by permission of the Literary Estate of Frank Brady.—Branden, Nathaniel. From *Who Is Ayn Rand? An Analysis of the Novels of Ayn Rand.* Random House, 1962. Copyright © 1962, renewed 1990 by Nathaniel Branden. All rights reserved. Reprinted by permission of the author.—Brander, Laurence. From *Aldous Huxley: A Critical Study.* Bucknell University Press, 1970. © Laurence Brander 1970. Reprinted by permission of the publisher.—Brassell, Tim. From *Tom Stoppard: An Assessment.* The Macmillan Press Ltd., 1985. © Tim Brassell 1985. All rights reserved. Used with permission of St. Martin's Press, Inc. In Canada by Macmillan, London and Basingstoke.—Brater, Enoch. From "Parody, Travesty, and Politics in the Plays of Tom Stoppard," in *Essays on Contemporary British Drama.* Edited by Hedwig Bock and Albert Wertheim. Hueber, 1981. © 1981 Max Hueber Verlag München. Reprinted by permission of the publisher.—Brée, Germaine and Margaret Guiton. From *An Age of Fiction: The French Novel from Gide to Camus.* Rutgers University Press, 1957. Copyright © 1957 by Rutgers, The State University. Renewed 1985 by Germaine Brée and Margaret Guiton. Reprinted by permission of the publisher.—Brennan, Elizabeth M. From an introduction to *The White Devil.* By John Webster, edited by Elizabeth M. Brennan. Ernest Benn Limited, 1966. © Ernest Benn Limited 1966. Reprinted by permission of A. & C. Black (Publishers) Ltd.—Brod, Max. From *Franz Kafka: A Biography.* Translated by G. Humphreys Roberts and Richard Winston. Second edition. Schocken Books, 1960. Copyright 1947, © 1960, renewed 1988, by Schocken Books Inc. Reprinted by permission of the publisher.—Brooks, Cleanth. From "Andrew Marvell: Puritan Austerity with Classical Grace," in *Poetic Traditions of the English Renaissance.* Edited by Maynard Mack and George deforest Lord. Yale University Press, 1982. Copyright © 1982 by Yale University. All rights reserved. Reprinted by permission of the publisher.—Brown, Frieda S. From *Religious and Political Conservatism in the "Essais" of Montaigne.* Librairie Droz, 1963. Copyright 1963 by Librairie Droz S. A., 8 rue Verdaine, Geneve. Reprinted by permission of the publisher.—Brown, John Mason. From *Dramatis Personae: A Retrospective Show.* The Viking Press, 1963. Copyright 1929, 1930, 1934, 1938, 1940, 1944, 1946, 1948-1955 inclusive, © 1957, 1958, 1962, 1963 by John Mason Brown. All rights reserved. Used by permission of Viking Penguin, a division of Penguin Books USA Inc.—Brown, John Russell. From an introduction to *Modern British Dramatists: A Collection of Critical Essays.* Edited by John Russell Brown. Prentice-Hall, 1968. © 1968 by Prentice-Hall, Inc.—Brownell, W. C. From *American Prose Master.* Charles Scribner's Sons, 1909. Copyright 1909 Charles Scribner's Sons, renewed 1937 by Gertrude Hall Brownell. Reprinted with the permission of Charles Scribner's Sons, an imprint of Macmillan Publishing Company.—Bruck, Peter. From "Langston Hughes: 'The Blues I'm Playing' (1934)," in *The Black American Short Story in the 20th Century: A Collection of Critical Essays.* Edited by Peter Bruck. B. R. Grüner Publishing Co., 1977. © by B. R. Grüner Publishing Co. Reprinted by permission of the publisher.—Bruss, Elizabeth W. From *Autobiographical Acts: The Changing Situation of a Literary Genre.* The Johns Hopkins University Press, 1976. Copyright © 1976 by The Johns Hopkins University Press. All rights reserved. Reprinted by permission of the publisher.—Brustien, Robert. From *The Theatre of Revolt: An Approach to the Modern Drama.* Little, Brown and Company, 1964. Copyright © 1962, 1963, 1964 by Robert Brustien. All rights reserved. Reprinted by permission of the author.—Bryant, Jerry J. From *The Open Decision: The Contemporary American Novel and Its Intellectual Background.* Free Press, 1970. Copyright © 1970 by The Free Press. All rights reserved. Reprinted with permission of Macmillan Publishing Company.—Bryer, Jackson R. From " 'Hell Is Other People': 'Long Day's Journey into Night'," in *The Fifties: Fiction, Poetry, Drama.* Edited by Warren French. Everett/Edwards, Inc., 1970. Copyright © 1970 by Warren French. All rights reserved. Reprinted by permission of the author.—Buckley, Jerome Hamilton. From *Tennyson: The Growth of a Poet.* Cambridge, Mass.: Harvard University Press, 1960. Copyright © 1960 by the President and Fellows of Harvard College. Renewed 1988 by Jerome Hamilton Buckley. All rights reserved. Excerpted by permission of the publishers and the author.—Bullitt, John M. From *Jonathan Swift and the Anatomy of Satire: A Study of Satiric Technique.* Cambridge, Mass.: Harvard University Press, 1963. Copyright 1963 by the President and Fellows of Harvard College. Excerpted by permission of the publishers and the author.—Burroughs, William S. and Daneil Odier. From an interview in *The Job: Interviews with William S. Burroughs.* By Daniel Odier. Revised edition. Grove Press, Inc., 1974. Copyright © 1969, 1970, 1974 by William S. Burroughs and Daniel Odier. All rights reserved. Reprinted by permission of Wylie, Aitken & Stone, Inc. and The Robert Lantz-Joy Harris Literary Agency.—Butterfield, Herbie. From "Ernest Hemingway," in *American Fiction: New Readings.* Edited by Richard Gray. London: Vision Press, 1983. © 1983 by Vision Press Ltd. All rights reserved. Reprinted by permission of the publisher.—Byron, Lord. From a letter in *"The Flesh is Frail": Byron's Letters and Journals, 1818-1819, Vol. 6.* Edited by Leslie A. Marchand. Cambridge, Mass.: Belknap Press of Harvard University Press, 1976. © Byron copyright material, John Murray 1976. All rights reserved. Excerpted by permission of the publishers. In Canada by John Murray (Publishers) Ltd.—Byron, William. From *Cervantes: A Biography.* Doubleday & Company, Inc., 1978. Copyright © 1978 by William Byron. All rights reserved. Reprinted by permission of Tessa Sayle Agency.—Cabell, James Branch. From *Some of Us: An Essay in Epitaphs.* Robert M. McBride & Company, 1930. Copyright, 1930, renewed 1958, by James Branch Cabell. Reprinted by permission of the Literary Estate of James Branch Cabell.—Callan, Edward. From *Auden: A Carnival of Intellect.* Oxford University Press, 1983. Copyright © 1983 by Edward Callan. Reprinted by permission of Oxford University Press, Inc.—Camus, Albert. From *Lyrical and Critical.* Edited and translated by Philip Thody. Hamilton, 1967. © 1967 by Hamish Hamilton, Ltd. Reprinted by permission of the publisher.—Camus, Albert. From *The Rebel.* Translated by Anthony Bower. Knopf, 1954. Copyright 1954, renewed 1984 by Alfred A. Knopf, Inc. Reprinted by permission of the publisher.—Canby, Henry Seidel. From *Classic Americans: A Study of Eminent American Writers from Irving to Whitman, with an Introductory Survey of the Colonial Background of Our National Literature.* Harcourt, Brace & Company, 1931. Copyright 1931, renewed 1958 by Henry Seidel Canby.—Carens, James F. From *The Satiric Art of Evelyn Waugh.* University of Washington Press, 1966. Copyright © 1966 by the University of Washington Press. Reprinted by permission of the publisher.—Carpenter, Lynette. From "Domestic Comedy, Black Comedy, and Real Life: Shirley Jackson, a Woman Writer," in *Faith of a (Woman) Writer.* Contributions in Women's Studies, No. 86. Edited by Alice Kessler-Harris and William McBrien. Greenwood Press, 1988. Copyright © 1988 by Hofstra University. All rights reserved. Reprinted by permission of Greenwood Publishing Group, Inc., Westport, CT.—Cash, Arthur Hill. From *Sterne's Comedy of Moral Sentiments: The Ethical Dimension of the "Journey."* Duquesne University Press, 1966. © 1966, by Duquesne University. All rights reserved. Reprinted by permission of the publisher.—Cecil, David. From *Early Victorian Novelists: Essays in Revaluation.* Constable, 1934, Bobbs-Merrill Company, Inc., 1935. Copyright 1935 by Macmillan Publishing Company. Renewed © 1962 by David Cecil. Reprinted with the permission of Macmillan Publishing Company. In Canada by the author.—Chesler, S. Alan. From "Tennessee Williams: Reassessment and Assessment," in *Tennessee Williams: A Tribute.* Edited by Jac Tharpe. University Press of Mississippi, 1977. Copyright © 1977 by the University Press of Mississippi. Reprinted by permission of the publisher.—Clark, Norris B. From "Gwendolyn Brooks and a Black Aesthetic," in *A Life Distilled: Gwendolyn Brooks, Her Poetry and Fiction.* Edited by Maria K. Mootry and Gary Smith. University of Illinois Press, 1987. © 1987 by the Board of Trustees of the University of Illinois. Reprinted by permission of the publisher and the author.—Clemen, Wolfgang. From *Shakespeare's Dramatic Art: Collected Essays.* Methuen, 1972. © 1972 Wolfgang Clemen. All rights reserved. Reprinted by permission of the publisher.—Clerc, Charles. From an introduction to *Approaches to "Gravity's Rainbow."* Edited by Charles Clerc. Ohio State University Press, 1983. © 1983 by the Ohio State University Press. All rights reserved. Reprinted with permission of the author.—Coale, Samuel Chase. From *In Hawthorne's Shadow: American Romance from Melville to Mailer.* University Press of Kentucky, 1985. Copyright © 1985 by The University of Kentucky. Reprinted by permission of the publisher.—Cohen, J. M. From *Poetry of This Age: 1908-1965.* Revised edition. Hutchinson University Library, 1966. © J. M. Cohen 1960 and 1966. Reprinted by permission of Unwin Hyman of HarperCollins Publishers Limited (London).—Cohn, Ruby. From *Edward Albee.* American Writers Pamphlet No. 77. University of Minnesota Press, 1969. © 1969, University of Minnesota. All rights reserved. Reprinted by permission of the publisher.—Commager, Henry Steele. From *The American Mind: An Interpretation of American Thought and Character since the 1880's.* Yale University Press, 1950. Copyright, 1950, by Yale University Press. Renewed 1978 by Henry Steele Commager. All rights reserved. Reprinted by permission of the publisher.—Conrad, Joseph. From *The Collected Letters of Joseph Conrad, Vol. I: 1867-1897.* Edited by Frederick R. Carl and Laurence Davies. Cambridge, 1983. Copyright © 1983 by Cambridge University Press. Reprinted by permission of the publisher.—Conrad, Joseph. From a letter in *Marcel Proust: An English Tribute.* Edited by C. K. Moncrieff. Thomas Seltzer, 1923.—Conrad, Joseph. From *Notes on Life and Letters.* Dent, 1921. Copyright 1921 by J. M. Dent & Sons. Renewed 1948 by John Alexander Conrad. Reprinted by permission of the publisher.—Corn, Alfred. From "Wallace Stevens: Pilgrim in Metaphor," in *The Metamorphosis of Metaphor.* Viking, 1982. Copyright © 1982 by Alfred Corn. Used by permission of Viking Penguin, a division of Penguin Books USA Inc.—Corrigan, Robert W. From *The Theatre in Search of a Fix.* Delacorte Press, 1973. Copyright © 1973 by Robert W. Corrigan. Used by permission of Delacorte Press, a division of Bantam Doubleday Dell Publishing Group, Inc.—Cowley, Malcolm. From *Exile's Return: A Literary Odyssey of the 1920's.* The Viking Press, 1951. Copyright © 1951, 1969 by Malcolm Cowley. All rights reserved.—Cowley, Malcolm. From *A Second Flowering: Works and Days of the Lost Generation.* Viking, 1973. Copyright © 1956, 1967, 1968, 1970, 1972, 1973 by Malcolm Cowley. Used by permission of Viking Penguin, a division of Penguin Books USA Inc.—Cowley, Malcolm. From *Think Back on Us: A Contemporary Chronicle of the 1930's.* Edited by Henry Dan Piper. Southern Illinois University Press, 1967. Reprinted by permission of the publisher.—Cowley, Malcolm. From an introduction to *Winesburg, Ohio.* By Sherwood Anderson. Revised edition. Viking Press, 1960. Copyright © 1960 by The Viking Press, Inc. Renewed 1988 by Malcolm Cowley. Used by permission of Viking Penguin, a division of Penguin Books USA Inc.—Crabbe, Katharyn F. From *J. R. R. Tolkien.* Ungar, 1981. Copyright © 1981 by The Ungar Publishing Company. Reprinted by permission of the publisher.—Crabbe, Katharyn W. From *Evelyn Waugh.* Continuum, 1988. Copyright © 1988 Katharyn W. Crabbe. All rights reserved. Reprinted by permission of the publisher.—Craig, Cairns. From *Yeats, Eliot, Pound and the Politics of Poetry: Richest to the Richest.* Croom Helm, 1982. © 1982 Cairns Craig. Reprinted by permission of the publisher.—Crawford, Thomas. From *Scott.* Revised edition. Scottish Academic Press, 1982. © 1982 Text and Bibliography Thomas Crawford. All rights reserved. Reprinted by permission of the author.—Crick, Bernard. From *George Orwell: A Life.* Atlantic-Little, Brown, 1980, Martin Secker and Warburg Ltd., 1980. Copyright © 1980 by Bernard Crick. All rights reserved. Reprinted by permission of Little, Brown and Company. In Canada by Martin Secker and Warburg Limited.—Crossley, Robert. From *H. G. Wells.* Starmont House, Inc., 1986. Copyright © 1986 by Starmont House, Inc. All rights reserved. Reprinted by permission of the publisher.—Curtius, E. R. From *Essays on European Literature.* Translated by Michael Kowal. Princeton University Press, 1973. Copyright © 1973 by Princeton University Press. Reprinted by permission of the publisher.—Daiches, David. From *Literary Essays.* Oliver & Boyd, 1956. All rights reserved. Reprinted by permission of the author.—Daiches, David. From *Robert Burns.* Rinehart & Company, 1950. Copyright 1950, renewed 1978, by David Daiches. All rights reserved. Reprinted by permission of Henry Holt and Company, Inc.—Daiches, David. From *Robert Louis Stevenson.* New Directions Books, 1947. Copyright 1947 by New Directions Publishing Corporation. Renewed 1975 by David Daiches. Reprinted by permission of David Higham Associates on behalf of David Daiches.—Daiches, David. From *Virginia Woolf.* Revised edition. New Directions, 1963. Copyright 1942, 1963 by New Directions Publishing Corporation. Reprinted by permission of the publisher.—Damrosch, Leopold, Jr. From *Symbol and Truth in Blake's Myth.* Princeton University Press, 1980. Copyright © 1980 by Princeton University Press. All rights reserved. Reprinted by permission of the publisher.—Dave, R. A. From "'To Kill a Mockingbird': Harper Lee's Tragic Vision," in *Indian Studies in American Fiction.* M. K. Naik, S. K. Desai, S. Mokashi-Punekar, eds. The Macmillan Company of India Limited, 1974. © Karnatak University Dharwar, 1974. Reprinted by permission of the publisher.—Davies, Horton. From *A Mirror of the Ministry in Modern Novels.* Oxford University Press, 1959. Copyright © 1959 by Oxford University Press, Inc. Renewed 1987 by Horton Davies. Reprinted by permission of the publisher.—Davis, Lennard J. From *Factual Fictions: The Origins of the English Novel.*

Reassessment. Third edition. Bowes and Bowes, 1975. © 1975 Douglas Hewitt. Reprinted by permission of the author.—Hibberd, Dominic. From *Wilfred Owen.* Edited by Ian Scott-Kilvert. British Council, 1975. © Dominic Hibberd 1975. Reprinted by permission of the publisher.—Hilfer, Anthony Channell. From *The Revolt from the Village: 1915-1930.* University of North Carolina Press, 1969. Copyright © 1969 by The University of North Carolina Press. Reprinted by permission of the publisher and the author.—Hipkiss, Robert A. From *Jack Kerouac: Prophet of the New Romanticism.* Regents Press of Kansas, 1976. © copyright 1976 by The Regents Press of Kansas. Reprinted by permission of the publisher.—Hirsch, Foster. From *A Portrait of the Artist: The Plays of Tennessee Williams.* Kennikat Press, 1979. Copyright © 1979 by Kennikat Press Corp. All rights reserved. Reprinted by permission of the author.—Hoffman, Frederick J. From *Freudianism and the Literary Mind.* Louisiana State University Press, 1945. Copyright 1945 by The Louisiana State University Press. Renewed 1972 by Caroline H. Bowser. Reprinted by permission of the publisher.—Holman, C. Hugh. From "Anodyne for the Village Virus," in *The Comic Imagination in American Literature.* Edited by Louis D. Rubin, Jr. Rutgers University Press, 1973. Reprinted by permission of the editor.—Holman, C. Hugh. From *The Loneliness at the Core: Studies in Thomas Wolfe.* Louisiana State University Press, 1975. Copyright © 1975 by Louisiana State University Press. Reprinted by permission of the publisher.—Honig, Edwin. From *García Lorca.* Revised edition. New Directions, 1963. Copyright 1944, 1963 by New Directions Publishing Corporation. Reprinted by permission of the author.—Howe, Irving. From an introduction to *Selected Short Stories of Isaac Bashevis Singer.* Edited by Irving Howe. The Modern Library, 1966. Copyright © 1966 by Random House, Inc. All rights reserved. Reprinted by permission of Random House, Inc.—Howe, Irving. From *Thomas Hardy.* Macmillan, 1967. Copyright © 1966 by Irving Howe. Copyright © 1967 by Macmillan Publishing Company. All rights reserved. Reprinted with permission of the publisher.—Hughes, Olga R. From *The Poetic World of Boris Pasternak.* Princeton University Press, 1974. Copyright © 1974 by Princeton University Press. Reprinted by permission of the publisher.—Huneker, James. From *Essays by James Huneker.* Charles Scribner's Sons, 1929. Copyright 1929, renewed 1957, Charles Scribner's Sons. Reprinted with the permission of the publisher.—Hussman, Lawrence E., Jr. From *Dreiser and His Fiction: A Twentieth-Century Quest.* University of Pennsylvania Press, 1983. Copyright © 1983 by the University of Pennsylvania Press. All rights reserved. Reprinted by permission of the author.—Hynes, Samuel. From *William Golding.* Essays on Modern Writers No. 2. Columbia University Press, 1968. Copyright © 1968 Columbia University Press. Used by permission of the publisher.—Isherwood, Christopher. From *Exhumations: Stories, Articles, Verses.* Methuen & Co. Ltd., 1966. Copyright © 1966 by Christopher Isherwood. Reprinted by permission of Candida Donadio & Associates, Inc.—Jarrell, Randall. From "Chekhov and the Play" and "The Acts," in *The Three Sisters.* By Anton Chekhov, edited and translated by Randall Jarrell. Macmillan, 1969. Copyright © 1969 by the Estate of Randall Jarrell. All rights reserved. Reprinted by permission of Mary Von S. Jarrell.—Jemie, Onwuchekwa. From *Langston Hughes: An Introduction to the Poetry.* Columbia University Press, 1976. Copyright © 1973, 1976 Columbia University Press. All rights reserved. Used by permission of the publisher.—Jenkins, Anthony. From *The Theatre of Tom Stoppard.* Second edition. Cambridge University Press, 1989. © Cambridge University Press 1987, 1989. Reprinted with the permission of the publisher.—Johnson, Greg. From *Understanding Joyce Carol Oates.* University of South Carolina Press, 1987. Copyright © University of South Carolina 1987. Reprinted by permission of the publisher.—Johnson, James Weldon. From "Preface to Original Edition," in *The Book of American Negro Poetry.* Edited by James Weldon Johnson. Revised edition. Harcourt Brace Jovanovich, 1931. Copyright 1931 by Harcourt Brace Jovanovich, Inc. Renewed 1959 by Grace Nail Johnson. Reprinted by permission of the publisher.—Johnson, Pamela Hansford. From *Hungry Gulliver.* Charles Scribner's Sons, 1948. Copyright 1948, renewed 1975 Charles Scribner's Sons. Reprinted by permission of Curtis Brown Ltd., London.—Johnson, W. Stacy. From *The Voices of Matthew Arnold: An Essay in Criticism.* Yale University Press, 1961. © 1961, renewed 1989 by Yale University Press, Inc. Reprinted by permission of the publisher.—Johnson, Wendell Stacy. From *Gerard Manley Hopkins: The Poet as Victorian.* Cornell University Press, 1968. Copyright © 1968 by Cornell University. All rights reserved. Used by permission of the publisher, Cornell University Press.—Johnston, John H. From *English Poetry of the First World War: A Study in the Evolution of Lyric and Narrative Form.* Princeton University Press, 1964. Copyright © 1964 by Princeton University Press. All rights reserved. Reprinted by permission of the publisher.—Jones, P. Mansell. From *Baudelaire.* Bowes & Bowes, 1952. Copyright 1952 by Yale University Press. Copyright renewed © 1980 by Richard Mansell Jones.—Joshi, S. T. From *The Weird Tale: Arthur Machen, Lord Dunsany, Algernon Blackwood, M. R. James, Ambrose Bierce, H. P. Lovecraft.* University of Texas Press, 1990. Copyright © 1990 by the University of Texas Press. All rights reserved. Reprinted by permission of the publisher and the author.—Jump, John D. From an introduction to *Alfred Tennyson: In Memorian, Maud, and Other Poems.* Edited by John D. Jump. J. M. Dent & Sons Limited, 1974. © introduction Everyman's Library Ltd., 1974. All rights reserved. Reprinted by permission of David Campbell Publishers.—Kaplan, Cora. From an introduction to *Aurora Leigh and Other Poems.* By Elizabeth Barrett Browning. The Women's Press Limited, 1978. Copyright © Cora Kaplan 1977. Reprinted by permission of Cora Kaplan.—Kar, Prafulla C. From "The Image of the Vanishing African in Chinua Achebe's Novels," in *The Colonial and the Neo-Colonial Encounters in Commonwealth Literature.* Edited by H. H. Anniah Gowda. Prasaranga, University of Mysore, 1983. Copyright Editor. Reprinted by permission of the editor.—Karl, Frederick R. From *A Reader's Guide to the Contemporary English Novel.* Revised edition. Farrar, Straus and Giroux, 1972. Copyright © 1961, 1962, 1971, 1972 by Frederick R. Karl. Reprinted by permission of Farrar, Straus and Giroux, Inc.—Karl, Frederick R. From *A Reader's Guide to Joseph Conrad.* Revised edition. Farrar, Straus and Giroux, 1969. Copyright © 1960, 1969 by Frederick R. Karl. Reprinted by permission of Farrar, Straus and Giroux, Inc.—Karl, Frederick R. From *American Fictions, 1940/1980: A Comprehensive History and Critical Evaluation.* Harper & Row, Publishers, 1983. Copyright © 1983 by Frederick R. Karl. All rights reserved. Reprinted by permission of the author.—Kawin, Bruce F. From *Telling It Again and Again: Repetition in Literature and Film.* University Press of Colorado, 1990. Copyright © 1972 by Bruce F. Kawin. All rights reserved. Reprinted by permission of the publisher.—Kazin, Alfred. From *Bright Book of Life: American Novelists & Storytellers from Hemingway to Mailer.* Atlantic-Little, Brown, 1973. Copyright © 1971, 1973 by Alfred Kazin. Reprinted by permission of the author.—Kazin, Alfred. From *The Inmost Leaf: A Selection of Essays.* Harcourt Brace Jovanovich,

1955. Copyright 1947, renewed 1975 by Alfred Kazin. Reprinted by permission of Harcourt Brace Jovanovich, Inc.—Kazin, Aflred. From *On Native Grounds: An Interpretation of Modern American Prose Literature.* Reynal & Hitchcock, 1942. Copyright 1942, renewed 1970, by Alfred Kazin. All rights reserved. Reprinted by permission of Harcourt Brace Jovanovich, Inc.—Kazin, Alfred. From an introduction to *The Stature of Theodore Dreiser: A Critical Survey of the Man and His Work.* Edited by Alfred Kazin and Charles Shapiro. Indiana University Press, 1955. Copyright © 1955 by the Indiana University Press. Renewed 1983 by Alfred Kazin and Charles Shapiro. Reprinted by permission of the publisher.—Kellogg, Gene. From *The Vital Tradition: The Catholic Novel in a Period of Convergence.* Loyola University Press, 1970. Reprinted by permission of the publisher.—Kelly, Katherine E. From *Tom Stoppard and the Craft of Comedy: Medium and Genre at Play.* The University of Michigan Press, 1991. Copyright © by the University of Michigan 1991. All rights reserved. Reprinted by permission of the publisher.—Kennard, Jean E. From *Number and Nightmare: Forms of Fantasy in Contemporary Fiction.* Archon Books, 1975. © 1975 by Jean E. Kennard. Reprinted by permission of Archon Books, an imprint of The Shoe String Press, Inc.—Kennedy, Andrew K. From *Six Dramatists in Search of a Language: Studies in Dramatic Language.* Cambridge University Press, 1975. © Cambridge University Press 1975. Reprinted with the permission of the publisher.—Kenner, Hugh. From *Samuel Beckett: A Critical Study.* Revised edition. University of California Press, 1968. Copyright © 1961, 1968 by Hugh Kenner. Reprinted by permission of the publisher.— Kent, George. From "Gwendolyn Books' Poetic Realism: A Developmental Survey," in *Black Women Writers (1950-1980): A Critical Evaluation.* Edited by Mari Evans. Anchor Books, 1984. Copyright © 1983 by Mari Evans. All rights reserved. Used by permission of Doubleday, a division of Bantam Doubleday Dell Publishing Group, Inc.—Kerjan, Liliane. From "Puro and Simplo: The Recent Plays of Edward Albee," in *New Essays on American Drama.* Edited by Gilbert Debusscher and Henry I. Schvey. © Editions Rodopi B. V., Amsterdam-Atlanta, GA 1989. Reprinted by permission of the publisher.—Kermode, Frank. From *D. H. Lawrence.* The Viking Press, 1973. Copyright © 1973 by Frank Kermode. All rights reserved. Used by permission of Viking Penguin, a division of Penguin Books USA Inc. In Canada by Frank Kermode.—Kerr, Elizabeth. From *William Faulkner's Gothic Domain.* Kennikat, 1979. Copyright © 1979 by Kennikat Press Corp. Reprinted by permission of the Literary Estate of Elizabeth Kerr.—Kidder, Rushworth M. From *E. E. Cummings: An Introduction to the Poetry.* Columbia University Press, 1979. Copyright 1979 Columbia University Press. Used by permission of the publisher.—Kiely, Robert. From *Robert Louis Stevenson and the Fiction of Adventure.* Cambridge, Mass.: Harvard University Press, 1964. Copyright © 1964 by the President and Fellows of Harvard College. All rights reserved. Excerpted by permission of the publishers and the author.—Kiely, Robert. From *The Romantic Novel in England.* Cambridge, Mass.: Harvard University Press, 1972. Copyright © 1972 by the President and Fellows of Harvard College. All rights reserved. Excerpted by permission of the publishers and the author.—Kinnamon, Keneth. From an introduction to *James Baldwin: A Collection of Critical Essays.* Edited by Keneth Kinnamon. Prentice-Hall, 1974. Copyright © 1974 by Prentice-Hall, Inc. Used by permission of Prentice-Hall/A Division of Simon & Schuster, Englewood Cliffs, NJ.—Kirk, Russell. From *Enemies of the Permanent Things: Observations of Abnormity in Literature and Politics.* Sherwood Sugden and Company, 1988. Copyright 1984 by Russell Kirk. Reprinted by permission of the author.—Kittredge, Mary. From "The Other Side of Magic: A Few Remarks About Shirley Jackson," in *Discovering Modern Horror Fiction.* Edited by Darrell Schweitzer. Starmont House, 1985. Copyright © 1985 by Starmont House, Inc. All rights reserved. Reprinted by permission of the publisher.—Klíma, Ivan. From "Capek's Modern Apocalypse," translated by Robert Streit, in *War with the Newts.* By Karel Capek. Northwestern University Press, 1985. Introduction copyright © 1985 by Ivan Klíma. Reprinted by permission of the publisher.—Klinck, Carl F. From *Robert Service: A Biography.* Dodd, Mead & Company, 1976. Copyright © Carl F. Klinck, 1976. All rights reserved. Reprinted by permission of the Literary Estate of Carl. F. Klinck.—Knapp, Bettina L. From *Edgar Allan Poe.* Frederick Ungar Publishing Co., 1984. Copyright © 1984 by The Ungar Publishing Company. Reprinted by permission of the publisher.—Knapp, Bettina L. From *Stephen Crane.* Ungar, 1987. Copyright © 1987 by The Ungar Publishing Company. Reprinted by permission of the publisher.—Knights, L. C. From *Some Shakespearean Themes.* Stanford University Press, 1960. © 1959, renewed 1987 by L. C. Knights. Reprinted with the permission of the publishers, Stanford University Press. Kreeft, Peter. From *C. S. Lewis: A Critical Essay.* W. B. Eerdmans, 1969. Copyright © 1969 by William B. Eerdmans Publishing Company. © 1988 by Christendom Educational Corporation. All rights reserved. Reprinted by permission of the publisher.—Kroll, Judith. From *Chapter in a Mythology: The Poetry of Sylvia Plath.* Harper & Row, 1976. Copyright © 1976 by Judith Kroll. Reprinted by permission of HarperCollins Publishers, Inc.—Kronenberger, Louis. From *The Polished Surface: Essays in the Literature of Worldliness.* Knopf, 1969. Copyright © 1969 by Louis Kronenberger. Reprinted by permission of Alfred A. Knopf, Inc.— Krutch, Joseph Wood. From *Five Masters: A Study in the Mutations of the Novel.* Jonathan Cape & Harrison Smith, 1930. Copyright 1930, renewed 1958 by The Trustees of Columbia University in the City of New York. Used by permission.—Krutch, Joseph Wood. From *Henry David Thoreau.* Sloane, 1948. Copyright 1948 by William Sloane Associates, Inc. Renewed 1975 by the Literary Estate of Joseph Wood Krutch. All rights reserved. Reprinted by permission of William Sloane Associates, Inc., a division of William Morrow and Company, Inc.—Kumin, Maxine. From "How It Was: Maxine Kumin on Anne Sexton," in *The Complete Poems.* By Anne Sexton. Houghton Mifflin, 1981. Foreword copyright © 1981 by Maxine Kumin. All rights reserved. Reprinted by permission of Houghton Mifflin Company.—Kunitz, Stanley. From *A Kind of Order, A Kind of Folly.* Atlantic-Little Brown, 1975. Copyright 1935, 1937, 1938, 1941, 1942, 1947, 1949, © 1957, 1963, 1964, 1965, 1967, 1970, 1971, 1972, 1973, 1974, 1975 by Stanley Kunitz. Reprinted by permission of the author.—Lagerkvist, Pär. From *Modern Theatre: Seven Plays and an Essay.* Translated by Thomas R. Buckman. University of Nebraska Press, 1966. © 1966 by Thomas R. Buckman. All rights reserved. Reprinted by permission of the translator.—Lamont, Rosette C. From an introduction to *Ionesco: A Collection of Critical Essays.* Edited by Rosette C. Lamont. Prentice-Hall, Inc., 1973. © 1973 by Prentice-Hall, Inc. All rights reserved. Used by permission of Prentice-Hall/A Division of Simon & Schuster, Englewood Cliffs, NJ.—Langland, Elizabeth. From *Society in the Novel.* University of North Carolina Press, 1984. © 1984 The University of North Carolina Press. All rights reserved. Reprinted by permission of the publisher and the author.—Lanham, Richard. From *"Tristram Shandy": The Games of Pleasure.* University of California Press,

Middleton Murry. Reprinted by permission of Julian Messner, Inc., a division of Simon & Schuster, Inc.—Nabokov, Vladimir. From *Lectures on Russian Literature.* Edited by Fredson Bowers. Harcourt Brace Jovanovich, 1981. Copyright © 1981 by the Estate of Vladimir Nabokov. Reprinted by permission of Harcourt Brace Jovanovich, Inc.—Nabokov, Vladimir. From *Nikolai Gogol.* New Directions Books, 1944. Copyright 1944 by New Directions Publishing Corporation. Reprinted by permission of the Estate of Vladimir Nabokov.—Nadeau, Maurice. From *The Greatness of Flaubert.* Translated by Barbara Bray. The Library Press, 1972. Copyright © 1972 by The Library Press. Reprinted by permission of Open Court Publishing Company, La Salle Illinois.—Nance, William L. From *The Worlds of Truman Capote.* Stein and Day, 1970. Copyright © 1970 by William L. Nance. All rights reserved. Reprinted by permission of Scarborough House Publishers.—Nathan, Leonard E. From *The Tragic Drama of William Butler Yeats: Figures in a Dance.* Columbia University Press, 1965. Copyright © 1965 Columbia University Press. Used by permission of the publisher.—Newton, K. M. From *George Eliot, Romantic Humanist: A Study of the Philosophical Structure of Her Novels.* Barnes & Noble Books, 1981. © K. M. Newton 1981. All rights reserved. Reprinted by permission of the publisher.—Oates, Joyce Carol. From *The Edge of Impossibility: Tragic Forms in Literature.* Vanguard Press, 1972. Copyright © 1972 by Joyce Carol Oates. Reprinted by permission of John Hawkins & Associates, Inc.-Oates, Joyce Carol. From *New Heaven, New Earth: The Visionary Experience in Literature.* Vanguard Press, 1974. Copyright © 1974 by Joyce Carol Oates. Reprinted by permission of John Hawkins & Associates, Inc.—O'Connor, Phillip F. From " 'Lolita': A Modern Classic in Spite of Its Readers," in *A Question of Quality: Seasoned "Authors" for a New Season, Vol. 2.* Edited by Louis Fuller. Bowling Green University Popular Press, 1980. Copyright © 1980 Bowling Green State University Popular Press. Reprinted by permission of the publisher.—Ornstein, Robert. From *The Moral Vision of Jacobean Tragedy.* University of Wisconsin Press, 1960. Copyright © 1960 by the Regents of the University of Wisconsin. Renewed 1988 by Robert Ornstein. Reprinted by permission of the publisher.—Ortega, Julio. From *Poetics of Change: The New Spanish-American Narrative.* Translated by Galen D. Greaser and Julio Ortega. University of Texas Press, 1984. Copyright © 1984 by the University of Texas Press. All rights reserved. Reprinted by permission of the publisher and the author.—Orwell, George. From *The Collected Essays, Journalism and Letters of George Orwell: In Front of Your Nose, 1945-1950, Vol. IV.* Edited by Sonia Orwell and Ian Angus. Harcourt Brace Jovanovich, 1968, Secker & Warburg, 1968. Copyright © 1968 by Sonia Brownell Orwell. Reprinted by permission of Harcourt Brace Jovanovich, Inc. In Canada by the Estate of the Late Sonia Brownell Orwell.—Pascal, Blaise. From *Pensées.* Translated by H. F. Stewart. Pantheon Books, 1950.—Patrides, C. A. From *Classic and Cavalier: Essays on Jonson and the Sons of Ben.* Edited by Claude J. Summers and Ted-Larry Pebworth. University of Pittsburgh Press, 1982. Copyright © 1982, University of Pittsburgh Press. All rights reserved. Reprinted by permission of the publisher.—Pattee, Fred Lewis. From *The Development of the American Short Story: An Historical Survey.* Harper & Brothers, 1923. Copyright 1923 by Harper & Row, Publishers, Inc. Renewed 1950 by Fred Lewis Pattee. Reprinted by permission of Harpercollins Publishers, Inc.—Peden, William. From *The American Short Story: Continuity and Change, 1940-1975.* Revised edition. Houghton Mifflin, 1975. Copyright © 1964, 1975 by William Peden. All rights reserved. Reprinted by permission of Houghton Mifflin Company.—Pell, Sarah-Warner J. From "Style Is the Man: Imagery in Bradbury's Fiction," in *Ray Bradbury.* Edited by Martin Harry Greenberg and Joseph D. Olander. Taplinger, 1980. Copyright © 1980 by Martin Harry Greenberg and Joseph D. Olander. All rights reserved. Reprinted by permission of the author.—Perry, Bliss. From *Emerson Today.* Princeton University Press, 1931. Copyright 1931 by Princeton University Press. Reprinted by permission of the publisher.—Peyre, Henri. From *What is Symbolism?* Translated by Emmett Parker. The University of Alabama Press, 1980. English translation copyright © 1980 by The University of Alabama Press. Reprinted by permission of the publisher.—Pinion, F. B. From *Hardy the Writer: Surveys and Assessments.* The Macmillan Press Ltd., 1990. © F. B. Pinion 1990. All rights reserved. Reprinted by permission of Macmillan, London and Basingstoke.—Pizer, Donald. From *Dos Passos' U.S.A.: A Critical Study.* University Press of Virginia, 1988. Copyright © 1988 by the Rector and Visitors of the University of Virginia. Reprinted by permission of the publisher.—Poggioli, Renato. From *The Poets of Russia: 1890-1930.* Cambridge, Mass.: Harvard University Press, 1960. Copyright © 1960 by the President and Fellows of Harvard College. Renewed © 1988 by Sylvia Poggioli. Excerpted by permission of the publishers and the author.—Porter, Katherine Anne. From an introduction to *A Curtain of Green and Other Stories.* By Eudora Welty. Harcourt Brace Jovanovich, 1941. Copyright, 1941, renewed 1968 by Eudora Welty. Reprinted by permission of William Morris Agency, Inc. on behalf of the author.—Pottle, Frederick A. From *James Boswell: The Earlier Years, 1740-1769.* McGraw-Hill, 1966. Copyright © 1966 by McGraw-Hill, Inc. All rights reserved. Reprinted by permission of the Literary Estate of Frederick A. Pottle.—Poulet, Georges. From *Proustian Space.* Translated by Elliott Coleman. The Johns Hopkins University Press, 1977. Translation copyright © 1977 by The Johns Hopkins University Press. Reprinted by permission of the publisher.—Prevost, Jean. From "Baudelairean Themes: Death, Evil, and Love," in *Baudelaire: A Collection of Critical Essays.* Edited by Henri Peyre. Prentice-Hall, 1962. © 1962 by Prentice-Hall, Inc. Renewed 1990 by Diana Festa Peyre. All rights reserved. Reprinted by permission of Mercure de France S. A.—Priestley, J. B. From *Literature and Western Man.* Harper & Brothers, 1960. Copyright © 1960 by J. B. Priestley. All rights reserved. Reprinted by permission of the Literary Estate of J. B. Priestley.—Pring-Mill, Robert. From a preface to *The Heights of Macchu Picchu.* By Pablo Neruda, translated by Nathaniel Tarn. Cape, 1966. Preface © 1966 by Robert Pring-Mill. All rights reserved. Reprinted by permission of Jonathan Cape Ltd.—Pritchett, V. S. From *The Living Novel & Later Appreciations.* Revised edition. Random House, 1964. Copyright © 1964, 1975 by V. S. Pritchett. All rights reserved. Reprinted by permission of the Peters, Fraser, & Dunlop Group Ltd.—Pritchett, V. S. From *The Myth Makers: Literary Essays.* Random House, 1979. Copyright © 1979 by V. S. Pritchett. All rights reserved. Reprinted by permission of Random House, Inc.—Proust, Marcel. From a letter in *Letters of Marcel Proust.* Edited and translated by Mina Curtiss. Random House, 1949. Copyright 1949 by Random House, Inc. Renewed 1976 by Mina Curtiss. Reprinted by permission of Mina Curtiss.—Quintana, Ricardo. From *Oliver Goldsmith: A Georgian Study.* Macmillan, 1967. Copyright © 1967 by Ricardo Quintana. All rights reserved. Reprinted with the permission of Macmillan Publishing Company.—Raby, Peter. From *Oscar Wilde.* Cambridge University Press, 1988. © Cambridge University Press 1988. Reprinted with the permission of the publisher and the author.—Rahv,

Philip. From *Image and Idea: Twenty Essays on Literary Themes.* Revised edition. J. Laughlin, 1957. Copyright © 1957 by Philip Rahv. Renewed 1983 by Betty T. Rahv. Reprinted by permission of the Literary Estate of Philip Rahv.—Raitt, A. W. From *Life and Letters in France: The Nineteenth Century.* Charles Scribner's Sons, 1965. Copyright © 1965 A. W. Raitt. Reprinted by permission of the author.—Rampersad, Arnold. From "Slavery and the Literary Imagination: Du Bois's 'The Souls of Black Folk'," in *Slavery and the Literary Imagination.* Edited by Deborah E. McDowell and Arnold Rampersad. The Johns Hopkins University Press, 1989. © 1989 The Johns Hopkins University Press. All rights reserved. Reprinted by permission of the publisher.—Reid, Alfred S. From *Style in the American Renaissance; a Symposium.* Edited by Carl F. Strauch. Transcendental Books, 1970. Reprinted by permission of the publisher.—Replogle, Justin. From *Auden's Poetry.* University of Washington Press, 1969. Copyright © 1969 by the University of Washington Press. Reprinted by permission of the publisher.—Rexroth, Kenneth. From *Classics Revisited.* Quadrangle Books, 1968, New Directions, 1986. Copyright © 1965, 1966, 1967, 1968 by Kenneth Rexroth. All rights reserved. Reprinted by permission of New Directions Publishing Corporation.—Rideout, Walter B. From *The Radical Novel in the United States, 1900-1954: Some Interrelations of Literature and Society.* Cambridge, Mass.: Harvard University Press, 1956. Copyright © 1956 by the President and Fellows of Harvard College. Excerpted by permission of the publishers and the author.—Rieger, James. From an introduction to *Frakenstein; or, The Modern Prometheus: The 1818 Text.* By Mary Wollstonecraft Shelley, edited by James Rieger. Bobbs-Merrill, 1974. University of Chicago Press, 1982. © 1974, 1982 by James Rieger. All rights reserved. Reprinted by permission of The University of Chicago Press.—Robbe-Grillet, Alain. From *For a New Novel: Essays on Fiction.* Translated by Richard Howard. Grove Press, 1966. Copyright © 1963 by Les Editions de Minuit. Copyright © 1965 by Grove Press, Inc. All rights reserved. Reprinted by permission of Georges Borchardt, Inc.—Romeln-Vershoor, Annle. From *A Tribute to Anne Frank.* Anne G. Steenmeijer, Otto Frank, and Henri van Praag, eds. Doubleday & Company, Inc., 1971. Translation copyright © 1970 by Doubleday, a division of Bantam Doubleday Dell Publishing Group, Inc.—Roscoe, Adrian A. From *Mother is Gold: A Study in West African Literature.* Cambridge at the University Press, 1971. © Cambridge University Press 1971. Reprinted by permission of the publisher and the author.—Rosenberg, John D. From an introduction to *Swinburne: Selected Poetry and Prose.* By Algernon Swinburne, edited by John D. Rosenberg. The Modern Library, 1968. © copyright 1967, 1968 by John D. Rosenberg. All rights reserved. Reprinted by permission of Random House, Inc.—Rosenthal, M. L. From *The New Poets: American and British Poetry Since World War II.* Oxford University Press, 1967. Copyright © 1967 by M. L. Rosenthal. Reprinted by permission of Oxford University Press, Inc.—Rosenthal, M. L. From "A Primer of Ezra Pound" in *Our Life in Poetry: Selected Essays and Reviews.* Persea Books, 1991. Copyright © 1991 by M. L. Rosenthal. Reprinted by permission of the publisher.—Rousseau, Jean-Jacques. From "Rousseau on 'Robinson Crusoe'," translated by Pat Rogers, in *Defoe: The Critical Heritage.* Edited by Pat Rogers. Routledge & Kegan Paul, 1972. © Pat Rogers 1972. Reprinted by permission of the publisher.—Rovit, Earl. From *Saul Bellow.* American Writers Pamphlet No. 65. University of Minnesota Press, 1967. © 1967, University of Minnesota. All rights reserved. Reprinted by permission of the publisher.—Rovit, Earl H. From "Ernest Hemingway: 'The Sun Also Rises'," in *Landmarks of American Writing.* Edited by Hennig Cohen. Basic Books, 1969. Copyright © 1969 by Basic Books, Inc., Publishers. Reprinted by permission of the author and the editor.—Rubin, Louis D., Jr. From an introduction to *Thomas Wolfe: A Collection of Critical Essays.* Edited by Louis D. Rubin, Jr. Prentice-Hall, Inc., 1973. © 1973 by Prentice-Hall, Inc. All rights reserved. Used by permission of Prentice-Hall/A Division of Simon & Schuster, Englewood Cliffs, NJ.—Russell, Bertrand. From *A History of Western Philosophy, and Its Connection with Political and Social Circumstances from the Earliest Times to the Present Day.* G. Allen and Unwin Ltd., 1946. Copyright 1945, renewed 1972 by Bertrand Russell. All rights reserved. Reprinted by permission of the Literary Estate of Bertrand Russell. In Canada by the publisher.—Russell, P. E. From *Cervantes.* Oxford University Press, Oxford, 1985. © P. E. Russell, 1985. All rights reserved. Reprinted by permission of Oxford University Press.—Sainte-Beuve, Charles Augustin. From *Selected Essays.* Edited by Francis Steegmuller, translated by Norbert Guterman. Doubleday, 1963. Copyright © 1963 by Doubleday, a division of Bantam Doubleday Dell Publishing Group, Inc. Used by permission of the publisher.—Sale, William M., Jr. From *The Age of Johnson: Essays Presented to Chauncey Brewster Tinker.* Edited by F. W. Hilles. Yale University Press, 1949. Copyright, 1949, by Yale University Press. Renewed © 1977 by Mrs. Frederick W. Hilles. Reprinted by permission of the publisher.—Sanders, Scott. From *D. H. Lawrence: The World of the Major Novels.* London: Vision Press, 1973. © 1973 by Scott Sanders. Reprinted by permission of the publisher.—Sanders, Wilbur. From *The Dramatist and the Received Idea: Studies in the Plays of Marlowe.* Cambridge University Press, 1968. © Cambridge University Press 1968. Reprinted by permission of the publisher and the author.—Sartre, Jean-Paul. From *Literary and Philosophical Essays of Jean-Paul Sartre.* Translated by Annette Michelson. Criterion Books, 1955. Copyright 1955 by S. G. Phillips, Inc. Renewed 1990 by Germaine Brée. Reprinted by permission of HarperCollins Publishers, Inc.—Schorer, Mark. From an introduction to *The Fortunes and Misfortunes of the Famous Moll Flanders & C.* By Daniel Defoe. Modern Library, 1950. Copyright 1950, renewed 1978 by Random House, Inc. Reprinted by permission of Random House, Inc.—Schorer, Mark. From "Sinclair Lewis: 'Babbitt'," in *Landmarks of American Writing.* Edited by Hennig Cohen. Basic Books, 1969. Copyright © 1969 by Basic Books, Inc., Publishers. Reprinted by permission of the editor and the Literary Estate of Mark Schorer.—Schorer, Mark. From *William Blake: The Politics of Vision.* Holt, 1946. Copyright, 1946, by Henry Holt and Company, Inc. Renewed 1974 by Mark Schorer. Reprinted by permission of the Literary Estate of Mark Schorer.—Schwarzer, Alice. From *Simone de Beauvoir Today: Conversations, 1972-1982.* Translated by Marianne Howarth. Chatto & Windus/The Hogarth Press, 1984. Copyright in the English translation © 1984 by Marianne Howarth. All rights reserved. Reprinted by permission of the author and Chatto & Windus/The Hogarth Press.—Scott-Kilvert, Ian. From *John Webster.* Longmans, Green & Co., 1964. © Ian Scott-Kilvert 1964. Reprinted by permission of the publisher.—Scott-Stokes, Henry. From *The Life and Death of Yukio Mishima.* Farrar, Straus and Giroux, 1974. Copyright © 1974 by Henry Scott-Stokes. All rights reserved. Reprinted by permission of Farrar, Straus and Giroux, Inc.—Seeley, F. F. From "Ivan Karamazov," in *New Essays on Dostoyevsky.* Edited by Malcolm V. Jones and Garth M. Terry. Cambridge University Press, 1983. © Cambridge University Press 1983. Reprinted with the permission of the publisher and the author.—Seltzer, Alvin J. from *Chaos in the Novel: The Novel in Chaos.* Schocken Books, 1974. Copyright © 1974 by Schocken Books, Inc. Reprinted by permission of Pantheon Books, Inc.—Setchkarev, Vsevolod. From *Gogol: His Life and Works.* Translated by Robert Kramer. New York University Press, 1965. Translation copyright © 1965 by New York University. Reprinted by permission of the publisher.—Shain, Charles E. From *F. Scott Fitzgerald.* American Writers Pamphlet No. 15. University of Minnesota Press, 1961. © 1961, University of Minnesota. Renewed 1989 by Charles E. Shain. Reprinted by permission of the publisher.—Shapiro, Karl. From *The Poetry Wreck: Selected Essays, 1950-70.* Random House, 1975. Copyright © 1953, 1955, 1960, 1968, 1970, 1975 by Karl Shapiro. Reprinted by permission of Random House, Inc.—Sharma, L. S. From *Coleridge: His Contribution to English Criticism.* Humanities Press, 1982. © L. S. Sharma 1982. Reprinted by permission of the author.—Sherwood, Terry G. From *Fulfilling the Circle: A Study of John Donne's Thought.* University of Toronto Press, 1984. © University of Toronto Press 1984. Reprinted by permission of the publisher.—Showalter, Elaine. From an introduction to *Alternative Alcott.* By Louisa May Alcott, edited by Elaine Showalter. Rutgers University Press, 1988. Copyright © 1988 by Rutgers, The State University. All rights reserved. Reprinted by permission of the publisher.—Sidney-Fryer, Donald. From *A Vision of Doom: Poems by Ambrose Bierce.* Edited by Donald Sidney-Fryer. Donald M. Grant, 1980. Copyright © 1980 by Donald Sidney-Fryer. Reprinted by permission of the publisher.—Sisson, C. H. From "H. D." in *The Avoidance of Literature: Collected Essays of C. H. Sisson.* Edited by Michael Schmidt. Carcanet New Press, 1978. Reprinted by permission of the author.—Slochower, Harry. From *Three Ways of Modern Man.* International Publishers, 1937. Copyright, 1937, renewed 1965 International Publishers Co., Inc. Reprinted by permission of the publisher.—Slonim, Marc. From *Epic of Russian Literature: From Its Origins through Tolstoy.* Oxford University Press, 1950. Copyright 1950 by Oxford University Press, Inc. Renewed 1977 by Tatiana Slonim. Reprinted by permission of the publisher.—Slonim, Marc. From *Modern Russian Literature: From Chekhov to the Present.* Oxford University Press, 1953. Copyright 1953 by Oxford University Press, Inc. Renewed 1981 by Tatiana Slonim. Reprinted by permission of the publisher.—Snow, C. P. From an introduction in *The Case-Book of Sherlock Holmes.* By Sir Arthur Conan Doyle. Jonathan Cape, 1974. © 1974 by C. P. Snow. All rights reserved. Reprinted by permission of the publisher.—Sokel, Walter Herbert. From "Perspective Dualism in the Novels of Böll," in *The Contemporary Novel in German: A Symposium.* Edited by Robert R. Heitner. University of Texas Press, 1967. Copyright © 1967 by the University of Texas Press. Reprinted by permission of the publisher and the author.—Solotaroff, Theodore. From "Philip Roth: A Personal View," in *The Red Hot Vacuum and Other Pieces on Writing in the Sixties.* Atheneum Publishers, 1970. Copyright © 1970 by Theodore Solotaroff. Reprinted by permission of Georges Borchardt, Inc. for the author.—Spitzer, Leo. From *Literary Masterpieces of the Western World.* Edited by Francis H. Horn. The Johns Hopkins University Press, 1953. Copyright 1953 by The Johns Hopkins Press. Renewed 1981 by Francis Horn. Reprinted by permission of the publisher.—Spurling, John. From *Graham Greene.* Methuen, 1983. © 1983 John Spurling. All rights reserved. Reprinted by permission of the publisher.—Stegner, Wallace. From *The Sound of Mountain Water.* Doubleday, 1969. Copyright © 1969 by Wallace Stegner. Used by permission of Doubleday, a division of Bantam Doubleday Dell Publishing Group, Inc.—Stewart, J. I. M. From *Rudyard Kipling.* Dodd, Mead & Company, 1966. Copyright © 1966 by J. I. M. Stewart. All rights reserved. Reprinted by permission of the author.—Stimpson, Catharine R. From *J. R. R. Tolkien.* Essays on Modern Writers No. 41. Columbia University Press, 1969. Copyright © 1969 by Columbia University Press. Reprinted by permission of the author.—Stouck, David. From *Major Canadian Authors: A Critical Introduction.* University of Nebraska Press, 1984. Copyright 1984 by the University of Nebraska Press. All rights reserved. Reprinted by permission of the publisher.—Stovall, Floyd. From an introduction to *The Poems of Edgar Allan Poe.* Edited by Floyd Stovall. The University Press of Virginia, 1965. Copyright © 1965 by the Rector and Visitors of the University of Virginia. Reprinted by permission of the publisher.—Strachey, Lytton. From *Books and Characters: French & English.* Harcourt Brace Jovanovich, 1922. Copyright, 1922, renewed 1950 by Harcourt Brace Jovanovich, Inc. Reprinted by permission of the publisher.—Stresau, Hermann. From *Thornton Wilder.* Translated by Frieda Schutze. Ungar, 1971. Copyright © 1971 by The Ungar Publishing Company. Reprinted by permission of the publisher.—Stupple, A. James. From "The Past, the Future, and Ray Bradbury," in *Voices for the Future: Essays on Major Science Fiction Writers, Vol. 1.* Edited by Thomas D. Clareson. Bowling Green University Popular Press, 1976. Copyright © 1976 by The Popular Press. Reprinted by permission of the publisher.—Styan, J. L. From *Chekhov in Performance: A Commentary on the Major Plays.* Cambridge at the University Press, 1971. © Cambridge University Press 1971. Reprinted with the permission of the publisher.—Suhl, Benjamin. From *Jean-Paul Sartre: The Philosopher as a Literary Critic.* Columbia University Press, 1970. Copyright © 1970 Columbia University Press. Used by permission of the publisher.—Sullivan, J. P. From "Pound's 'Homage to Propertius': The Structure of a Mask," in *Ezra Pound: A Collection of Critical Essays.* Edited by Walter Sutton. Prentice-Hall, 1963. © 1963 by Prentice-Hall, Inc. All rights reserved. Used by permission of Prentice-Hall/A Division of Simon & Schuster, Englewood Cliffs, NJ.—Swift, Jonathan. From *The Correspondence of Jonathan Swift: 1724-1731, Vol. III.* Edited by Harold Williams. Oxford at the Clarendon Press, 1963. © Oxford University Press, 1963. Reprinted by permission of the publisher.—Symons, Julian. From *Portrait of an Artist: Conan Doyle.* Whizzard Press, 1979. © Julian Symons 1979. Reprinted by permission of Andre Deutsch Ltd.—Tanner, Tony. *City of Words: American Fiction 1950-1970.* Harper & Row, 1971, Cape, 1971. Copyright © 1971 by Tony Tanner. Reprinted by permission of HarperCollins Publishers, Inc. In Canada by Jonathan Cape Ltd.—Tanner, Tony. From *The Reign of Wonder: Naivety and Reality in American Literature.* Cambridge at the University Press, 1965. © Cambridge University Press 1965. Reprinted with the permission of the publisher and the author.—Tate, Allen. From *Essays of Four Decades.* Swallow, 1968. Copyright © 1988 by Allen Tate. All rights reserved. Reprinted by permission of the Literary Estate of Allen Tate.—Taylor, John Russell. From *The Angry Theatre: New Drama.* Revised edition. Hill and Wang, 1969. Copyright © 1962, 1969 by John Russell Taylor. All rights reserved. Reprinted by permission of Hill and Wang, a division of Farrar, Straus and Giroux, Inc. In Canada by the Peters Fraser & Dunlop Group Ltd.—Thibaudet, Albert. From *Madame Bovary: Backgrounds and Sources, Essays in Criticism.* By Gustave Flaubert, edited and translated by Paul de Man. A Norton Critical Edition. W. W. Norton & Company, Inc., 1965. Copyright © 1964 by W. W. Norton & Company, Inc. Reprinted by permission of the publisher.—Thomas, Dylan. From *Quite Early One Morning.* New Directions, 1954. Copyright 1954 by New Directions Publishing Corporation. Renewed 1982 by Caitlin Thomas, Lleweyn Edouard Thomas, Aeronwy Bryn Thomas-Ellis and Colum Garn Thomas. Reprinted by permission of New Directions Publishing Corporation. In Canada by the Literary Estate of Dylan Thomas.—Thompson, Lee Briscoe. From "Minutes and Madness: Margaret Atwood's 'Dancing Girls'," in *The Art of Margaret Atwood: Essays in Criticism.* Edited by Arnold E. Davidson and Cathy N. Davidson. Toronto: House of Anansi Press, 1981. Copyright © 1981, House of Anansi Press Limited. All rights reserved. Reprinted by permission of the publisher.—Tilgher, Adriano. From "Life versus Form," translated by Glauco Cambon, in *Pirandello: A Collection of Critical Essays.* Edited by Glauco Cambon. Prentice-Hall, 1967. Copyright © 1967 by Prentice-Hall, Inc. All rights reserved. Used by permission of Prentice-Hall/A Division of Simon & Schuster, Englewood Cliffs, NJ.— Tolkien, J. R. R. From a letter to Stanley Unwin on March 4, 1938, in *The Letters of J. R. R. Tolkien.* Edited by Humphrey Carpenter with Christopher Tolkien. Houghton Mifflin, 1981. Allen & Unwin, 1981. Copyright © 1981 by George Allen & Unwin, now Unwin Hyman of HarperCollins Publishers Limited (London). All rights reserved. Reprinted by permission of Houghton Mifflin Company. In Canada by HarperCollins Publishers Limited (London).—Traugott, John. From *Tristram Shandy's World: Sterne's Philosophical Rhetoric.* University of California Press, 1954. Copyright 1954 by The Regents of the University of California. Renewed 1982 by John Lewis Traugott. Reprinted by permission of the publisher.—Trilling, Lionel. From *E. M. Forster.* New Directions Books, 1943. Copyright 1943 by New Directions. Renewed 1971 by Lionel Trilling. Reprinted by permission of New Directions Publishing Corporation.—Trilling, Lionel. From *Prefaces to the Experience of Literature.* Harcourt Brace Jovanovich, 1979. Copyright © 1967 by Lionel Trilling. Copyright © 1979 by Diana Trilling and James Trilling. Reprinted by permission of Harcourt Brace Jovanovich, Inc.—Unamuno, Miguel de. From *Selected Works of Miguel de Unamuno: Our Lord Don Quixote, Vol. 3.* Edited by Anthony Kerrigan and Martin Nozick, translated by Anthony Kerrigan. Bollingen Series LXXXV. Princeton University Press, 1967. © 1967 Princeton University Press. Reprinted by permission of the publisher.—Untermeyer, Louis. From *Makers of the Modern World: The Lives of Ninety-two Writers, Artists, Scientists, Statesmen, Inventors, Philosophers, Composers and Other Creators Who Formed the Pattern of Our Century.* Simon and Schuster, 1955. Copyright © 1955 by Louis Untermeyer. Renewed © 1983 by Bryna Ivens Untermeyer. All rights reserved. Reprinted by permission of Laurence S. Untermeyer.— Untermeyer, Louis. From *The New Era in American Poetry.* Holt, Rinehart and Winston, Publishers, 1919. Copyright 1919 by Henry Holt and Company. Renewed 1947 by Louis Untermeyer. Reprinted by permission of Laurence S. Untermeyer.—Updike, John. From "Reflections: Kafka's Short Stories" in *Odd Jobs.* Knopf, 1991. Copyright © 1991 by John Updike. Reprinted by permission of the Alfred A. Knopf, Inc.—Updike, John. From "Twisted Apples," in *Odd Jobs.* Knopf, 1991. Copyright © 1991 by John Updike. Reprinted by permission of Alfred A. Knopf, Inc.—Updike, John. From "The Author as Librarian," in *Picked-Up Pieces.* Knopf, 1975. Copyright © 1975 by John Updike. Reprinted by permission of Alfred A. Knopf, Inc.—Uphaus, Suzanne Henning. From *John Updike.* Frederick Ungar Publishing Co., 1980. Copyright © 1980 by The Ungar Publishing Company. Reprinted by permission of the publisher.—Urang, Gunnar. From *Shadows of Heaven: Religion and Fantasy in the Writing of C. S. Lewis, Charles Williams, and J. R. R. Tolkien.* Pilgrim Press, 1971. Copyright © 1971 United Church Press. Reprinted by permission of the publisher.—Uroff, M. D. From *Hart Crane: The Patterns of His Poetry.* University of Illinois Press, 1974. © 1974 by the Board of Trustees of the University of Illinois. Reprinted by permission of the publisher and the author.—Van Fossen, Richard W. From an introduction to *The Jew of Malta.* By Christopher Marlowe, edited by Richard W. Van Fossen. University of Nebraska Press, 1964. Copyright 1964 by the University of Nebraska Press. All rights reserved. Reprinted by permission of the publisher.—Van Ghent, Dorothy. From *The English Novel: Form and Function.* Holt, Rinehart and Winston, 1953. Copyright 1953, renewed 1981, by Dorothy Van Ghent. Reprinted by permission of the Literary Estate of Dorothy Van Ghent.—Vendler, Helen Hennessy. From *On Extended Wings: Wallace Stevens' Longer Poems.* Cambridge, Mass.: Harvard University Press, 1969. Copyright © 1969 by the President and Fellows of Harvard College. Excerpted by permission of the publishers and the author.— Vidal, Gore. From an introduction to *The Edith Wharton Omnibus.* By Edith Wharton. Charles Scribner's Sons, 1978. Copyright © 1978 Gore Vidal. Reprinted with the permission of Charles Scribner's Sons, an imprint of Macmillan Publishing Company.—Viereck, Peter. From "Vachel Lindsay: The Dante of the Fundamentalists," in *A Question of Quality: Popularity and Value in Modern Creative Writing.* Edited by Louis Filler. Bowling Green University Popular Press, 1976. Copyright © 1976 Bowling Green State University Popular Press. Reprinted by permission of the publisher.—Voltaire. From *Letters on England.* Translated by Leonard Tancock. Penguin, 1980. Copyright © Leonard Tancock, 1980. All rights reserved.—Wagenknecht, Edward. From *The Novels of Henry James.* Frederick Ungar Publishing Co., 1983. Copyright © 1983 by Edward Wagenknecht. Reprinted by permission of the publisher.—Wagenknecht, Edward. From an introduction to *The Stories and Fables of Ambrose Bierce.* Edited by Edward Wagenknecht. Stemmer House, 1977. Copyright © 1977 by Stemmer House Publishers, Inc. All rights reserved. Reprinted by permission of the publisher.— Wagenknecht, Edward. From *Washington Irving: Moderation Displayed.* Oxford University Press, 1962. Copyright © 1962 by Edward Wagenknecht. Reprinted by permission of the author.—Wagner, Linda W. From *American Modern: Essays in Fiction and Poetry.* Kennikat Press, 1980. Copyright © 1980 by Kennikat Press. All rights reserved. Reprinted by permission of the author.—Wagner, Jean. From *Black Poets of the United States: From Paul Laurence Dunbar to Langston Hughes.* Translated by Kenneth Douglas. University of Illinois Press, 1973. Translation copyright by The Board of Trustees of the University of Illinois. Reprinted by permission of the Literary Estate of Jean Wagner.—Wagner, Linda W. From "The Making of 'Selected Poems', the Process of Surfacing," in *The Art of Margaret Atwood: Essays in Criticism.* Edited by Arnold E. Davidson and Cathy N. Davidson. Toronto: House of Anansi Press, 1981. Copyright © 1981, House of Anansi Press Limited. All rights reserved. Reprinted by permission of the publisher.—Walker, Cheryl. From *The Nightingale's Burden: Women Poets and American Culture before 1900.* Indiana University Press, 1982. Copyright © 1982 by Cheryl Walker. All rights reserved. Reprinted by permission of the publisher.—Walker, Jayne L. From *The Making of a Modernist: Gertrude Stein from "Three Lives" to "Tender Buttons."* The University of Massachusetts Press, 1984. Copyright © 1976, 1984 by Jayne L. Walker. All rights reserved. Reprinted by permission of the publisher.—Wallace, Ronald. From *The Last Laugh: Form and Affirmation in the Contemporary American Comic Novel.* University of Missouri Press, 1979. Copyright © 1979 by the Curators of the University of Missouri. All rights reserved. Reprinted by permission of the publisher.—Waller, G. F. From *Dreaming America: Obsession and Transcendence in the Fiction of Joyce Carol Oates.* Louisiana State University Press, 1979. Copyright © 1979 by Louisiana State University Press. Reprinted by permission of the publisher.—Walsh, Jeffrey. From *American War Literature, 1914 to Vietnam.* St. Martin's Press, 1982, The Macmillan Press Limited, 1982. © Jeffrey Walsh 1982. All rights reserved. Reprinted by permission of St. Martin's Press, Inc. In Canada by Macmillan, London and Basingstoke.—Walton, Geoffrey. From *Edith Wharton: A Critical Interpretation.* Fairleigh Dickinson University Press, 1971. © 1970 by Geoffrey Walton. Reprinted by permission of the publisher.—Warren, Robert Penn. From "The Themes of Robert Frost," in *Selected Essays.* Random House, 1958. Copyright 1947, 1958, renewed 1986 by Robert Penn Warren. Reprinted by permission of Random House, Inc.—Watson, George. From *The Literary Critics: A Study of English Descriptive Criticism.* Second edition. The Woburn Press, 1973. Copyright © George Watson, 1962, 1964, 1973. All rights reserved. Reprinted by permission of the publisher.—Watt, Donald. From "Burning Bright: 'Fahrenheit 451' as Symbolic Dystopia," in *Ray Bradbury.* Edited by Martin Harry Greenberg and Joseph D. Olander. Taplinger, 1980. Copyright © 1980 by Martin Harry Greenberg and Joseph D. Olander. All rights reserved. Reprinted by permission of the author.—Watt, Ian. From *The Rise of the Novel: Studies in Defoe, Richardson and Fielding.* University of California Press, 1957.—Way, Brian. From *F. Scott Fitzgerald and the Art of Social Fiction.* St. Martin's, 1980, Edward Arnold, 1980. © 1980 Brian Way. Used with permission of St. Martin's Press, Inc. In Canada by Hodder & Stoughton Limited.—Welland, Dennis. From *Wilfred Owen: A Critical Study.* Revised edition. Chatto & Windus, 1978. © Dennis Welland 1960, 1978. Reprinted by permission of the author and Chatto & Windus.—Wellek, René. From *A History of Modern Criticism, 1750-1950: The Later Nineteenth Century.* Yale University Press, 1965. Copyright © Yale University. Reprinted by permission of the publisher.—Wellwarth, George. From *The Theater of Protest and Paradox: Developments in the Avant-Garde Drama.* New York University Press, 1964. Copyright © 1964 by New York University. Reprinted by permission of the publisher.—Weston, John C. From "Robert Burn's Satire," in *The Art of Robert Burns.* Edited by R. D. S. Jack and Andrew Noble. Barnes & Noble, 1982. © 1982 by Vision Press Ltd. All rights reserved. Reprinted by permission of the publisher.—Wilder, Amos N. From *The Spiritual Aspects of the New Poetry.* Harper & Brothers, 1940. Copyright, 1940, by Harper & Row Publishers, Inc. Renewed 1968 by Amos N. Wilder. All rights reserved. Reprinted by permission of HarperCollins Publishers, Inc.—Williams, Aubrey L. From *An Approach to Congreve.* Yale University Press, 1979. Copyright © 1979 by Yale University. All rights reserved. Reprinted by permission of the publisher.—Wilson, Christopher P. From *The Labor of Words: Literary Professionalism in the Progressive Era.* University of Georgia Press, 1985. © 1985 by the University of Georgia Press. All rights reserved. Reprinted by permission of the publisher.—Wilson, Colin. From *The Genius of Shaw: A Symposium.* Edited by Michael Holroyd. Holt, Rinehart and Winston, 1979, Rainbird, 1979. Copyright © 1979 by Colin Wilson; copyright © 1979 by George Rainbird Limited. Reprinted by permission of Henry Holt and Company, Inc. In Canada by Penguin Books Ltd.—Wilson, Edmund. From "James Joyce," in *Axel's Castle: A Study in the Imaginative Literature of 1870-1930.* Charles Scribner's Sons, 1931. Copyright 1931 Charles Scribner's Sons. Renewal copyright © 1959 Edmund Wilson. Reprinted by permission of Charles Scribner's Sons, an imprint of Macmillan Publishing Company.—Wilson, Edmund. From *Classics and Commercials: A Literary Chronicle of the Forties.* Farrar, Straus and Company, 1950. Copyright 1950 by Edmund Wilson. Renewed 1977 by Elena Wilson. All rights reserved. Reprinted by permission of Farrar, Straus and Giroux, Inc.—Wilson, Edmund. From *Patriotic Gore: Studies in the Literature of the American Civil War.* Oxford University Press, Inc., 1962. Copyright © 1962 by Edmund Wilson. Renewed 1990 by Helena Miranda Wilson. Reprinted by permission of Farrar, Straus and Giroux, Inc.—Wilson, Edmund. From *The Shores of Light: A Literary Chronicle of the Twenties and Thirties.* Farrar, Straus and Giroux, 1952. Copyright 1952 by Edmund Wilson. Renewed copyright © 1980 by Helen Miranda Wilson. All rights reserved. Reprinted by permission of Farrar, Straus and Giroux, Inc.—Wilson, Edmund. From *The Triple Thinkers: Twelve Essays on Literary Subjects.* Revised edition. Oxford University Press, Inc., 1948. Copyright 1938, 1948 by Edmund Wilson. Copyright renewed 1956, 1971 by Edmund Wilson and 1976 by Elena Wilson, Executrix of the Estate of Edmund Wilson. Reprinted by permission of Farrar, Straus and Giroux, Inc.—Wilson, Edmund. From "Pushkin," in *A Window on Russia: For the Use of Foreign Readers.* Farrar, Straus and Giroux, 1972. Copyright © 1943 by Edmund Wilson. All rights reserved. Reprinted by permission of Farrar, Straus and Giroux, Inc.—Wilson, Edmund. From *The Wound and the Bow: Seven Studies in Literature.* Houghton Mifflin Company, 1941. Copyright 1929, 1932, 1938, 1939, 1940, 1941 by Edmund Wilson. Copyright renewed © 1966, 1968, 1970, by Edmund Wilson. All rights reserved. Reprinted by permission of Farrar, Straus and Giroux, Inc.—Winters, Yvor. From *In Defense of Reason.* The Swallow Press Inc., 1947. Copyright 1937 by Yvor Winters. Copyright 1938, 1943 by New Directions. Copyright renewed © 1965 by Yvor Winters. Reprinted by permission of Ohio University Press/Swallow Press.—Woodcock, George. From *The Crystal Spirit: A Study of George Orwell.* Little, Brown, 1966. Copyright © 1966 by George Woodcock. All rights reserved. Reprinted by permission of the author.—Woodring, Carl. From *Wordsworth.* Houghton Mifflin, 1965. Copyright © 1965 by Carl Woodring. All rights reserved. Reprinted by permission of Houghton Mifflin Company.—Woodruff, Stuart C. From *The Short Stories of Ambrose Bierce: A Study in Polarity.* University of Pittsburgh Press, 1964. © 1964 by the University of Pittsburgh Press. Reprinted by permission of the publisher.—Wolf, Leonard. From *A Dream of Dracula: In Search of the Living Dead.* Little, Brown and Company, 1972. Copyright © 1972 by Leonard Wolf. Reprinted by permission of Little, Brown and Company.—Woolf, Virginia. From *"The Captain's Death Bed" and Other Essays.* Harcourt Brace Jovanovich, 1950, Hogarth Press, 1950. Copyright 1950, renewed 1978 by Harcourt Brace Jovanovich, Inc. Reprinted by permission of Harcourt Brace Jovanovich, Inc. In Canada by the Literary Estate of Virginia Woolf and The Hogarth Press.—Woolf, Virginia. From *The Common Reader.* Harcourt Brace Jovanovich, 1925. Copyright 1925 by Harcourt Brace Jovanovich. Renewed 1953 by Leonard Woolf. Reprinted by permission of Harcourt Brace Jovanovich, Inc.—Woolf, Virginia. From *The Death of the Moth and Other Essays.* Harcourt Brace Jovanovich, 1942, Hogarth Press, 1942. Copyright 1942 by Harcourt Brace Jovanovich, Inc. Renewed 1970 by Marjorie T. Parsons, Executrix. Reprinted by permission of Harcourt Brace Jovanovich, Inc. In Canada by the Literary Estate of Virginia Woolf and The Hogarth Press.—Woolf, Virginia. From *The Moment and Other Essays.* Hogarth Press, 1947, Harcourt Brace Jovanovich, 1948. Copyright 1948, renewed 1976 by Harcourt Brace Jovanovich and Marjorie T. Parsons. Reprinted by permission of Harcourt Brace Jovanovich, Inc. In Canada by the Literary Estate of Virginia Woolf and The Hogarth Press.—Woolf, Virginia. From *The Second Common Reader.* Harcourt Brace Jovanovich, 1932. Published in England as *The Common Reader.* Second series. L. & V. Woolf at the Hogarth Press, 1932. Copyright 1932 by Harcourt Brace Jovanovich, Inc. Renewed 1960 by Leonard Woolf. Reprinted by permission of Harcourt Brace Jovanovich, Inc.—Wright, Nathalia. From *Melville's Use of the Bible.* Duke University Press, 1949. Copyright 1949 by Duke University Press, Durham, North Carolina. Renewed 1976 by Nathalia Wright. Reprinted by permission of the author.—Wright, Richard. From a letter in *Dictionary of Literary Biography Documentary Series, Vol. 2.* Edited by Margaret A. Van Antwerp. Gale Research Company, 1982. Copyright © 1982 Gale Research Company. Reprinted by permission of Ellen Wright, the Literary Estate of Richard Wright.—Wright, Richard. From *Native Son.* Harper & Brothers, 1940. Copyright 1940 by Richard Wright. Renewed 1967 by Ellen Wright. Reprinted by permission of HarperCollins Publishers, Inc.—Yamanouchi, Hisaaki. From *The Search for Authenticity in Modern Japanese Literature.* Cambridge University Press, 1978. © Cambridge University Press 1978. Reprinted with the permission of the publisher and the author.—Yarborough, Richard. From *New Essays on Uncle Tom's Cabin.* Edited by Eric J. Sundquist. Cambridge University Press, 1986. © Cambridge University Press 1986. Reprinted with the permission of the publisher and the author.—Yates, W. Norris. From "Günter Grass," in *The Politics of Twentieth-Century Novelists.* Edited by George Panichas. Hawthorn, 1971. Copyright © 1971 by The University of Maryland. All rights reserved. Used by permission of the publisher, E. P. Dutton, an imprint of New American Library, a division of Penguin Books USA Inc.—Yermakov, Ivan. From "The Nose," in *Gogol from the Twentieth Century: Eleven Essays.* Edited and translated by Robert A. Maguire. Princeton University Press, 1974. Copyright © 1974 by Princeton University Press. All rights reserved. Reprinted by permission of the publisher.—Yourcenar, Marguerite. From "Humanism in Thomas Mann," translated by Grace Frick and the author, in *The Partisan Review Anthology.* Edited by William Phillips and Philip Rahv. Holt, Rinehart and Winston, 1962. Copyright © 1962 by Marguerite Yourcenar. Renewed 1990 Henry Holt and Company, Inc. Reprinted by permission of the author.—Yuill, W. E. From *Essays on Contemporary German Literature: German Men of Letters, Vol. IV.* Edited by Brian-Keith Smith. Wolff, 1966. © 1966 Oswald Wolff. Reprinted by permission of Berg Publishers Ltd.—Zabel, Morton Dauwen. From *Craft and Character: Texts, Method, and Vocation in Modern Fiction.* The Viking Press, 1957. Copyright 1943, 1956 by Morton Dauwen Zabel. Renewed 1985 by Viking Penguin Inc. Used by permission of Viking Penguin, a division of Penguin Books USA Inc.—Zamyatin, Yevgeny. From *A Soviet Heretic: Essays.* Edited and translated by Mirra Ginsburg. Northwestern University Press, 1992. Copyright © 1992 by Northwestern University Press. All rights reserved. Reprinted by permission of the publisher.—Zverev, A. From "A Lover's Quarrel with the World: Robert Frost," in *20th Century American Literature: A Soviet View.* Translated by Ronald Vroon. Progress Publishers, 1976. © Translation into English Progress Publishers 1976.

PHOTOGRAPHS AND ILLUSTRATIONS APPEARING IN *WLC* WERE RECEIVED FROM THE FOLLOWING SOURCES:

© Lutfi Ozkok: **pp. 1, 123, 2657, 3085;** Cover of *Things Fall Apart,* by Chinua Achebe. Reprinted by permission of Random House, Inc.: **p. 8;** © Alix Jeffry 1984: **p. 16;** Photograph by Greenberg-May Prod. Inc.: **p. 29;** The Bettmann Archive, Inc.: **pp. 52, 288, 539, 1185, 1373, 1417, 1528, 1610, 1652, 1939, 2096, 2280, 2713, 3049, 3818, 4114;** Culver Pictures, Inc.: **pp. 70, 443, 1664, 1774, 3496, 3712;** The Granger Collection, New York: **pp. 88, 159, 479, 582, 862, 969, 1426, 1517, 1661, 1738, 1751, 1923, 2556, 2814, 2897, 2906, 2927, 3184, 3409, 3539, 3608;** © Jerry Bauer: **pp. 106, 112, 1307, 2150, 2520, 2960, 3281, 3479;** Jacket of *The Handmaid's Tale,* by Margaret Atwood. Copyright © 1985 by O. W. Toad, Ltd. Jacket illustration/ design by Fred Marcellino © 1985. Used by permission of Houghton Mifflin Co. All rights reserved: **p. 117;** By permission of Margaret Atwood, courtesy of Thomas Fisher Rare Book Library, University of Toronto Library: **p. 113;** Hulton/Bettmann: **pp. 134, 195, 432, 883, 892, 4095;** AP/Wide World Photos: **pp. 170, 270, 1160, 3134, 3784;** Doisneau-Rapho: **p. 222;** Photograph copyright Foto Ilse Buhs: **p. 237;** © 1981 Thomas Victor: **p. 260;** Ullstein Bilderdienst, Berlin: **pp. 313, 380, 1499, 1683, 2192;** Photograph by Penny A. Wallace: **p. 330;** © Thomas Victor 1986: **pp. 362, 2171;** McCarter Theatre, Princeton N.J.: **p. 394;** UPI/Bettmann Newsphotos: **pp. 448, 2413, 2733, 3094;** Courtesy of the Afro-American Collection, Blockson Library, Temple University: **p. 457;** Photograph by Gerard Malanga: **pp. 531, 1990;** Collection of Mme. Catherine Camus: **p. 591;** East Photo: **p. 598;** Photograph by James Hamilton: **p. 615;** Photograph by Harold Halma: **p. 627;** Illustration by John Tenniel: **pp. 637, 639, 646;** Courtesy of the Cather Family: **p. 651;** © 1977 by Nancy Crampton: **p. 687;** © Nancy Crampton: **pp. 693, 1628;** Segalab: **p. 721;** Historical Pictures Service, Chicago: **pp. 749, 875, 1814, 2889;** Billy Rose Theatre Collection, The New York Public Library at Lincoln Center, Astor, Lenox and Tilden Foundations: **pp. 768, 2367, 3991;** Photograph by William Wright: **p. 793;** Photograph by J. Sibley Watson: **p. 829;** Copyright © 1968 by Columbia Pictures: **p. 902;** United Artists, 1951: **p. 909;** Drawing by Adolph Dehn: **p. 959;** Reproduced from *Crime and Punishment,* by Feodor Dostoevski, A Norton Critical Edition, edited by George Giban. Copyright © 1975, 1964 by W. W. Norton & Company, Inc. By permission of W. W. Norton & Company, Inc.: **p. 983;** Photograph by Carl Van Vechten, by permission of Joseph Solomon, the Estate of Carl Van Vechten: **pp. 1022, 2322, 3353;** Used with the permission of Liveright Publishing Corporation: **p. 1033;** Courtesy of the Hayward Collection, King's College Library, Cambridge: **p. 1133;** Durban Municipal Art Gallery, by permission of Omar Pound, © Estate of Mrs. G. A. Wyndham Lewis: **p. 1144;** © Photo by Bern Schwartz: **p. 1152;** © Eareckson: **p. 1231;** Courtesy of R. J. Buckingham: **p. 1256;** Jacket of *Maurice,* by E. M. Forster. W. W. Norton, 1971. Reprinted by permission of W. W. Norton & Company, Inc.: **p. 1268;** © ANNE FRANK- Fonds, Basle/Switzerland: **pp. 1272, 1280;** Prints and Photographs Division, Library of Congress: **p. 1286;** George Silk, *Life* Magazine © 1961 Time Warner Inc.: **p. 1298;** Photograph by Riess: **p. 1325;** Courtesy of the British Broadcasting Corporation: **p. 1334;** Courtesy of New Directions: **p. 1337;** Photograph by Layle Silbert: **p. 1390;** Courtesy of the German Information Center: **p. 1408;** Topham/The Image Works: **p. 1443;** Photograph by Howard Coster: **p. 1455;** Photograph by Isolde Ohlbaum, Munich: **p. 1512;** The National Portrait Gallery: **p. 1535;** Jacket of *Travels with My Aunt,* by Graham Greene. Bodley Head, 1969. Reprinted by permission of Random Century Group Ltd.: **p. 1549;** Sylvia Beach Collection, Princeton University Library: **p. 1621, 1934;** Photograph © by Jill Krementz: **p. 1637;** Malmberg/Black Star: **p. 1646;** Schiller-Nationalmuseum, Marbach am Neckar: **p. 1697;** Spinger/Bettmann Film Archive: **p. 1718;** Courtesy of Matthew Huxley: **p. 1756;** George Kramer, University of California, Los Angeles: **p. 1763;** Mary Evans Picture Library: **p. 1783;** Photograph by Beverly Pabst: **p. 1796;** Friedman-Abeles, New York: **p. 1806;** Lucas and Moore Studio: **p. 1833;** Courtesy of Barry Jackson: **p. 1846;** Photograph by Horace Lyon: **p. 1871;** Photograph by Maria Huxley: **p. 2051;** Photograph by G. D. Hackett: **p. 2059;** © 1962 by Universal Pictures: **p. 2068;** Photograph by Arthur Strong: **p. 2075;** Inset photograph by Malcolm Powell: **p. 2083;** Drawing by David Levine. Copyright © 1976 by NYREV, Inc.: **p. 2160;** Jacket of *The Fixer,* by Bernard Malamud. Farrar, Straus & Giroux, 1966. Reprinted by permission of Farrar, Straus & Giroux, Inc.: **p. 2184;** Thomas Mann-Archiv, Zurich: **p. 2201;** Photograph by Mark Gerson: **pp. 2268, 2590;** Courtesy of Clifton Waller Barrett Library, University of Virginia Library: **p. 2305;** Title page of *A Long Way From Home,* by Claude McKay. Lee Furman, Inc., 1937: **p. 2238;** Photograph by Fred W. McDarrah: **p. 2359;** The Humanities Research Center, University of Texas at Austin: **p. 2376;** Photograph by Robert Young, Jr.: **p. 2389;** © 1984 by Layle Silbert: **p. 2469;** Photograph by Graeme Gibson: **p. 2352;** Photograph by Joe McTyre: **p. 2539;** Collection of Mabel Fierz: **p. 2572;** Photograph by Vernon Richards: **p. 2580;** Cornell Capa-Magnum Photos Inc.: **p. 2621;** Ardis Publishers: **p. 2630;** Crown Studios: **p. 2640;** Copyright 1952 by London Films: **p. 2648;** Marie José Paz: **p. 2668;** Photograph by Sam Siegel: **p. 2695;** Photograph by Donald Cooper: **p. 2702;** Sylvia Beach Collection: **p. 2786;** Courtesy of Donald Gallup: **p. 2796;** Pictorial Parade, Inc.: **p. 2804;** Photograph by Phyllis Cerf Wagner: **p. 2874;** Jacket of *The Catcher in the Rye,* by J. D. Salinger. Little, Brown and Company, 1951. Reprinted by permission of Little, Brown and Company: **p. 3021;** Courtesy of the Library of Congress: **p. 3058;** Photograph by Richard Tolbert: **p. 3077;** University Library, Utrecht: **p. 3157;** The Museum of Modern Art/Film Stills Archive, courtesy of Paramount Pictures: **p. 3162;** The Museum of Modern Art/Film Stills Archives: **pp. 3166, 3172;** Copyright © Universal Pictures, a Division of Universal City Studios, Inc., courtesy of MCA Publishing, a Division of MCA Communications, Inc.: **p. 3212;** Copyright © 1974 by Twentieth Century-Fox Film Corp.: **p. 3218;** The Jewish Daily Forward: **p. 3294;** Hedrick Smith/NYT Pictures: **p. 3298;** Sevil: **p. 3306;** Photograph by W. G. Rogers, Yale Collection of American Literature, The Beinecke Rare Book and Manuscript Library, Yale University: **p. 3366;** Photograph by Martha Cox, courtesy of the Steinbeck Research Center/San Jose State University: **p. 3372;** Jacket of *The Grapes of Wrath,* by John Steinbeck. Copyright 1939, renewed © 1967 by John Steinbeck. Used by permission of Viking Penguin, a division of Penguin Books USA Inc.: **p. 3380;** The Metropolitan Museum of Art, Gift of I.N. Phelps Stokes, Edward S. Hawes, Alice Mary Hawes, Marion Augusta Hawes, 1937. (37.14.40): **p. 3505;** Popperfoto/Pictorial Parade: **p. 3531;** J. M. Dent & Sons Ltd: **p. 3618;** Reproduced by permission of George Allen & Unwin (Publishers) Ltd.: **p. 3642;** Drawing by E. W. Kemble: **p. 3722;** Photograph by Michael Chikiris: **p. 3747;** Jacket of *Bech is Back,* by John Updike. Alfred A. Knopf, 1982. Reprinted by permission of Alfred A. Knopf, Inc.: **p. 3757;** © Jill Krementz: **p. 3794;** Photograph by Robert A. Ballard, Jr.: **p. 3802;** Jacket of *Brideshead Revisited,* by Evelyn Waugh. Little, Brown and Company, 1945. Reprinted by permission of Little, Brown and Company: **p. 3831;** Copyright 1985 Thomas Victor: **p. 3878;** Poster drawing © 1986 by John Sokol: **p. 3886;** Courtesy of Eudora Welty: **p. 3890;** The Lilly Library, Indiana University: **p. 3906;** The Yale Collection of American Literature, Beinecke Rare Book and Manuscript Library, Yale University: **p. 3968, 3979;** © 1987 Thomas Victor: **p. 3987;** Photograph by Charles Sceeler, courtesy of William Eric Williams: **p. 4009;** Photograph by Sotheby Parke Bernet, 1982: **p. 4043;** Photograph by Harriet Crowder: **p. 4078;** Jacket of *Twelve Million Black Voices,* by Richard Wright Edwin Rosskam, Photo Direction. Copyright 1941 by Richard Wright. Used by permission of Viking Penguin, a division of Penguin Books USA Inc.: **p. 4083.**

WORLD LITERATURE CRITICISM

1500 to the Present

INDEXES

WLC Author Index

This index lists all author entries in *World Literature Criticism* and includes cross-references to other series published by Gale Research Inc. Authors who have used pseudonyms professionally are listed under their real names, with suitable cross-references. References in the index are identified as follows:

AAYA: *Authors & Artists for Young Adults*, Volumes 1-7
BLC: *Black Literature Criticism*, Volumes 1-3
BW: *Black Writers*
CA: *Contemporary Authors* (original series), Volumes 1-136
CAAS: *Contemporary Authors Autobiography Series*, Volumes 1-15
CABS: *Contemporary Authors Bibliographical Series*, Volumes 1-3
CANR: *Contemporary Authors New Revision Series*, Volumes 1-35
CAP: *Contemporary Authors Permanent Series*, Volumes 1-2
CA-R: *Contemporary Authors* (first revision), Volumes 1-44
CDALB: *Concise Dictionary of American Literary Biography*, Volumes 1-6
CLC: *Contemporary Literary Criticism*, Volumes 1-70
CLR: *Children's Literature Review*, Volumes 1-25
DC: *Drama Criticism*, Volume 1-2
DLB: *Dictionary of Literary Biography*, Volumes 1-114
DLB-DS: *Dictionary of Literary Biography Documentary Series*, Volumes 1-9
DLB-Y: *Dictionary of Literary Biography Yearbook*, Volumes 1980-1990
HW: *Hispanic Writers*
LC: *Literature Criticism from 1400 to 1800*, Volumes 1-19
MTCW: *Major 20th-Century Writers*
NCLC: *Nineteenth-Century Literature Criticism*, Volumes 1-35
PC: *Poetry Criticism*, Volumes 1-4
SAAS: *Something about the Author Autobiography Series*, Volumes 1-14
SATA: *Something about the Author*, Volumes 1-68
SSC: *Short Story Criticism*, Volumes 1-9
TCLC: *Twentieth-Century Literary Criticism*, Volumes 1-44
YABC: *Yesterday's Authors of Books for Children*, Volumes 1-2

Behn, Aphra
    1640?-1689 .... **1**:244-59
    See also DLB 39, 80; LC 1

Bellow, Saul
    1915- **1**:260-77
    See also CA 5-8R; CABS 1; CANR 29;
    CDALB 1941-1968; CLC 1, 2, 3, 6, 8,
    10, 13, 15, 25, 33, 34, 63; DLB 2, 28;
    DLB-DS 3; DLB-Y 82; MTCW

Bierce, Ambrose (Gwinett)
    1842-1914? **1**:278-94
    See also CA 104; CDALB 1865-1917;
    DLB 11, 12, 23, 71, 74; SSC 9; TCLC 1,
    7, 44

Blair, Eric Arthur
    1903-1950
    See Orwell, George
    See also CA 132; brief entry CA 104;
    MTCW; SATA 29

Blake, William
    1757-1827 .... **1**:295-312
    See also DLB 93; NCLC 13; SATA 30

Boell, Heinrich (Theodor)
    1917-1985
    See Boll, Heinrich
    See also CA 21-24R; CANR 24; MTCW

Boll, Heinrich (Theodor)
    1917-1985 .... **1**:313-29
    See also Boell, Heinrich (Theodor)
    See also CLC 2, 3, 6, 9, 11, 15, 27, 39;
    DLB 69; DLB-Y 85

Borges, Jorge Luis
    1899-1986 .... **1**:330-44
    See also CA 21-24R; CANR 19, 33;
    CLC 1, 2, 3, 4, 6, 8, 9, 10, 13, 19, 44,
    48; DLB-Y 86; HW; MTCW; SSC 4

Boswell, James
    1740-1795 .... **1**:345-61
    See also DLB 104; LC 4

Bradbury, Ray(mond Douglas)
    1920- **1**:362-79
    See also CA 1-4R; CANR 2, 30;
    CDALB 1968-1988; CLC 1, 3, 10, 15,
    42; DLB 2, 8; MTCW; SATA 11, 64

Brecht, (Eugen) Bertolt (Friedrich)
    1898-1956 .... **1**:380-96
    See also CA 133; brief entry CA 104;
    DLB 56; MTCW; TCLC 1, 6, 13, 35

Bronte, Charlotte
    1816-1855 .... **1**:397-413
    See also DLB 21; NCLC 3, 8, 33

Bronte, (Jane) Emily
    1818-1848 .... **1**:414-31
    See also DLB 21, 32; NCLC 16, 35

Brooke, Rupert (Chawner)
    1887-1915 .... **1**:432-47
    See also CA 132; brief entry CA 104;
    DLB 19; MTCW; TCLC 2, 7

Brooks, Gwendolyn
    1917- **1**:448-64
    See also BLC 1; BW; CA 1-4R; CANR 1,
    27; CDALB 1941-1968; CLC 1, 2, 4, 5,
    15, 49; DLB 5, 76; MTCW; SATA 6

Browning, Elizabeth Barrett
    1806-1861 .... **1**:465-78
    See also DLB 32; NCLC 1, 16

Bunyan, John
    1628-1688 .... **1**:479-94
    See also DLB 39; LC 4

Burke, Edmund
    1729-1797 .... **1**:495-513
    See also DLB 104; LC 7

Burns, Robert
    1759-1796 .... **1**:514-30
    See also DLB 109; LC 3

Burroughs, William S(eward)
    1914- **1**:531-47
    See also CA 9-12R; CANR 20; CLC 1, 2,
    5, 15, 22, 42; DLB 2, 8, 16; DLB-Y 81;
    MTCW

Butler, Samuel
    1835-1902 .... **1**:548-64
    See also brief entry CA 104; DLB 18, 57;
    TCLC 1, 33

Byron, George Gordon (Noel), Lord
    1788-1824 .... **1**:565-81
    See also DLB 96, 110; NCLC 2, 12

Camus, Albert
    1913-1960 .... **1**:582-97
    See also CA 89-92; CLC 1, 2, 4, 9, 11, 14,
    32, 63, 69; DC 2; DLB 72; MTCW;
    SSC 9

Capek, Karel
    1890-1938 .... **1**:598-614
    See also brief entry CA 104; DC 1;
    TCLC 6, 37

Capote, Truman
    1924-1984 .... **1**:615-32
    See also CA 5-8R; CANR 18;
    CDALB 1941-1968; CLC 1, 3, 8, 13, 19,
    34, 38, 58; DLB 2; DLB-Y 80, 84;
    MTCW; SSC 2

Carroll, Lewis
    1832-1898 .... **1**:633-50
    See also Dodgson, Charles Lutwidge
    See also CLR 2, 18; DLB 18; NCLC 2

Cather, Willa (Sibert)
    1873-1947 .... **1**:651-66
    See also CA 128; brief entry CA 104;
    CDALB 1865-1917; DLB 9, 54, 78;
    DLB-DS 1; MTCW; SATA 30; SSC 2;
    TCLC 1, 11, 31

Cervantes (Saavedra), Miguel de
    1547-1616 .... **2**:667-86
    See also LC 6

Cheever, John
    1912-1982 .... **2**:687-703
    See also CA 5-8R; CABS 1; CANR 5, 27;
    CDALB 1941-1968; CLC 3, 7, 8, 11, 15,
    25, 64; DLB 2, 102; DLB-Y 80, 82;
    MTCW; SSC 1

Chekhov, Anton (Pavlovich)
    1860-1904 .... **2**:704-20
    See also CA 124; brief entry CA 104;
    SSC 2; TCLC 3, 10, 31

Clemens, Samuel Langhorne
    1835-1910
    See Twain, Mark
    See also CA 135; brief entry CA 104;
    CDALB 1865-1917; DLB 11, 12, 23, 64,
    74; YABC 2

Cocteau, Jean (Maurice Eugene Clement)
    1889-1963 .... **2**:721-39
    See also CA 25-28; CAP 2; CLC 1, 8, 15,
    16, 43; DLB 65; MTCW

Coleridge, Samuel Taylor
    1772-1834 .... **2**:740-57
    See also DLB 93, 107; NCLC 9

Congreve, William
    1670-1729 .... **2**:758-76
    See also DC 2; DLB 39, 84; LC 5

Conrad, Joseph
    1857-1924 .... **2**:777-92
    See also CA 131; brief entry CA 104;
    DLB 10, 34, 98; MTCW; SATA 27;
    SSC 9; TCLC 1, 6, 13, 25, 43

Crane, (Harold) Hart
    1899-1932 .... **2**:793-810
    See also CA 127; brief entry CA 104;
    CDALB 1917-1929; DLB 4, 48; MTCW;
    PC 3; TCLC 2, 5

Crane, Stephen
    1871-1900 .... **2**:811-28
    See also brief entry CA 109;
    CDALB 1865-1917; DLB 12, 54, 78;
    SSC 7; TCLC 11, 17, 32; YABC 2

Cummings, E(dward) E(stlin)
    1894-1962 .... **2**:829-45
    See also CA 73-76; CANR 31;
    CDALB 1929-1941; CLC 1, 3, 8, 12, 15,
    68; DLB 4, 48; MTCW

Davies, (William) Robertson
    1913- **2**:846-61
    See also CA 33-36R; CANR 17; CLC 2, 7,
    13, 25, 42; DLB 68; MTCW

Defoe, Daniel
    1660?-1731 .... **2**:862-82
    See also DLB 39, 95, 101; LC 1; SATA 22

De la Mare, Walter (John)
    1873-1956 .... **2**:883-94
    See also brief entry CA 110; CLR 23;
    DLB 19; SATA 16; TCLC 4

Dickens, Charles
    1812-1870 .... **2**:895-912
    See also DLB 21, 55, 70; NCLC 3, 8, 18,
    26; SATA 15

Dickinson, Emily (Elizabeth)
    1830-1886 .... **2**:913-28
    See also CDALB 1865-1917; DLB 1;
    NCLC 21; PC 1; SATA 29

Dodgson, Charles Lutwidge
    1832-1898
    See Carroll, Lewis
    See also YABC 2

Donne, John
    1572-1631 .... **2**:929-48
    See also LC 10; PC 1

Doolittle, Hilda
    1886-1961
    See H(ilda) D(oolittle)
    See also CA 97-100; CANR 35; DLB 4,
    45; MTCW

Dos Passos, John (Roderigo)
    1896-1970 .... **2**:949-68
    See also CA 1-4R; CANR 3;
    CDALB 1929-1941; CLC 1, 4, 8, 11, 15,
    25, 34; DLB 4, 9; DLB-DS 1; MTCW

Dostoyevsky, Fyodor
1821-1881 .... 2:969-86
See also NCLC 2, 7, 21, 33; SSC 2

Douglass, Frederick
1817?-1895 .... 2:987-1003
See also BLC 1; CDALB 1640-1865;
DLB 1, 43, 50, 79; NCLC 7; SATA 29

Doyle, (Sir) Arthur Conan
1859-1930 .... 2:1004-21
See also CA 122; brief entry CA 104;
DLB 18, 70; MTCW; SATA 24; TCLC 7,
26

Dreiser, Theodore (Herman Albert)
1871-1945 .... 2:1022-39
See also CA 132; brief entry CA 106;
CDALB 1865-1917; DLB 9, 12, 102;
DLB-DS 1; MTCW; SATA 48; TCLC 10,
18, 35

Dryden, John
1631-1700 .... 2:1040-59
See also DLB 80, 101; LC 3

Du Bois, W(illiam) E(dward) B(urghardt)
1868-1963 .... 2:1060-76
See also BLC 1; BW; CA 85-88; CANR 34;
CDALB 1865-1917; CLC 1, 2, 13, 64;
DLB 47, 50, 91; MTCW; SATA 42

Dumas, Alexandre (Davy de la Pailleterie)
(pere)
1802-1870 .... 2:1077-95
See also NCLC 11; SATA 18

Dunbar, Paul Laurence
1872-1906 .... 2:1096-1114
See also BLC 1; BW; CA 124;
brief entry CA 104; CDALB 1865-1917;
DLB 50, 54, 78; SATA 34; SSC 8;
TCLC 2, 12

Eliot, George
1819-1880 .... 2:1115-32
See also DLB 21, 35, 55; NCLC 4, 13, 23

Eliot, T(homas) S(tearns)
1888-1965 .... 2:1133-51
See also CA 5-8R; CDALB 1929-1941;
CLC 1, 2, 3, 6, 9, 10, 13, 15, 24, 34, 41,
55, 57; DLB 7, 10, 45, 63; DLB-Y 88;
MTCW

Ellison, Ralph (Waldo)
1914- 2:1152-67
See also BLC 1; BW; CA 9-12R;
CANR 24; CDALB 1941-1968; CLC 1, 3,
11, 54; DLB 2, 76; MTCW

Emerson, Ralph Waldo
1803-1882 .... 2:1168-84
See also CDALB 1640-1865; DLB 1, 59,
73; NCLC 1

Faulkner, William (Cuthbert)
1897-1962 .... 2:1185-1200
See also AAYA 7; CA 81-84; CANR 33;
CDALB 1929-1941; CLC 1, 3, 6, 8, 9,
11, 14, 18, 28, 52, 68; DLB 9, 11, 44,
102; DLB-DS 2; DLB-Y 86; MTCW;
SSC 1

Fielding, Henry
1707-1754 .... 2:1201-18
See also DLB 39, 84, 101; LC 1

Fitzgerald, F(rancis) Scott (Key)
1896-1940 .... 2:1219-36
See also CA 123; brief entry CA 110;
CDALB 1917-1929; DLB 4, 9, 86;
DLB-DS 1; DLB-Y 81; MTCW; SSC 6;
TCLC 1, 6, 14, 28

Flaubert, Gustave
1821-1880 .... 2:1237-55
See also NCLC 2, 10, 19

Forster, E(dward) M(organ)
1879-1970 .... 2:1256-71
See also AAYA 2; CA 13-14; CAP 1;
CLC 1, 2, 3, 4, 9, 10, 13, 15, 22, 45;
DLB 34, 98; MTCW; SATA 57

Frank, Anne
1929-1945 .... 2:1272-85
See also CA 133; brief entry CA 113;
MTCW; SATA 42; TCLC 17

Frost, Robert (Lee)
1874-1963 .... 2:1286-1306
See also CA 89-92; CANR 33;
CDALB 1917-1929; CLC 1, 3, 4, 9, 10,
13, 15, 26, 34, 44; DLB 54; DLB-DS 7;
MTCW; PC 1; SATA 14

Fuentes, Carlos
1928- 2:1307-24
See also AAYA 4; CA 69-72; CANR 10,
32; CLC 3, 8, 10, 13, 22, 41, 60; HW;
MTCW

Galsworthy, John
1867-1933 .... 2:1325-36
See also brief entry CA 104; DLB 10, 34,
98; TCLC 1

Garcia Lorca, Federico
1898-1936 .... 2:1337-54
See also CA 131; brief entry CA 104;
DC 2; DLB 108; HW; MTCW; PC 3;
TCLC 1, 7

Garcia Marquez, Gabriel (Jose)
1928- 3:1355-72
See also AAYA 3; CA 33-36R; CANR 10,
28; CLC 2, 3, 8, 10, 15, 27, 47, 55, 68;
HW; MTCW; SSC 8

Gide, Andre (Paul Guillaume)
1869-1951 .... 3:1373-89
See also CA 124; brief entry CA 104;
DLB 65; MTCW; TCLC 5, 12, 36

Ginsberg, Allen
1926- 3:1390-1407
See also CA 1-4R; CANR 2;
CDALB 1941-1968; CLC 1, 2, 3, 4, 6,
13, 36, 69; DLB 5, 16; MTCW; PC 4

Goethe, Johann Wolfgang von
1749-1832 .... 3:1408-25
See also DLB 94; NCLC 4, 22, 34

Gogol, Nikolai (Vasilyevich)
1809-1852 .... 3:1426-42
See also DC 1; NCLC 5, 15, 31; SSC 4

Golding, William (Gerald)
1911-1991 .... 3:1443-60
See also AAYA 5; CA 5-8R; CANR 13, 33;
CLC 1, 2, 3, 8, 10, 17, 27, 58; DLB 15,
100; MTCW

Goldsmith, Oliver
1728?-1774 .... 3:1461-79
See also DLB 39, 89, 104, 109; LC 2;
SATA 26

Gorky, Maxim
1868-1936 .... 3:1480-98
See also Peshkov, Alexei Maximovich
See also TCLC 8

Grass, Gunter (Wilhelm)
1927- 3:1499-1516
See also CA 13-16R; CANR 20; CLC 1, 2,
4, 6, 11, 15, 22, 32, 49; DLB 75; MTCW

Gray, Thomas
1716-1771 .... 3:1517-34
See also DLB 109; LC 4; PC 2

Greene, Graham (Henry)
1904-1991 .... 3:1535-55
See also CA 13-16R; CANR 35; CLC 1, 3,
6, 9, 14, 18, 27, 37, 70; DLB 13, 15, 77,
100; DLB-Y 85; MTCW; SATA 20

Hardy, Thomas
1840-1928 .... 3:1556-73
See also CA 123; brief entry CA 104;
DLB 18, 19; MTCW; SATA 25; SSC 2;
TCLC 4, 10, 18, 32

Harte, (Francis) Bret(t)
1836?-1902 .... 3:1574-91
See also brief entry CA 104;
CDALB 1865-1917; DLB 12, 64, 74, 79;
SATA 26; SSC 8; TCLC 1, 25

Hawthorne, Nathaniel
1804-1864 .... 3:1592-1609
See also CDALB 1640-1865; DLB 1, 74;
NCLC 2, 10, 17, 23; SSC 3; YABC 2

H(ilda) D(oolittle)
1886-1961 .... 3:1610-27
See also Doolittle, Hilda
See also CLC 3, 8, 14, 31, 34

Heller, Joseph
1923- 3:1628-45
See also CA 5-8R; CABS 1; CANR 8;
CLC 1, 3, 5, 8, 11, 36, 63; DLB 2, 28;
DLB-Y 80; MTCW

Hemingway, Ernest (Miller)
1899-1961 .... 3:1646-63
See also CA 77-80; CANR 34;
CDALB 1917-1929; CLC 1, 3, 6, 8, 10,
13, 19, 30, 34, 39, 41, 44, 50, 61;
DLB 4, 9, 102; DLB-DS 1; DLB-Y 81,
87; MTCW; SSC 1

Henry, O.
1862-1910 .... 3:1664-82
See also Porter, William Sydney
See also SSC 5; TCLC 1, 19

Hesse, Hermann
1877-1962 .... 3:1683-1700
See also CA 17-18; CAP 2; CLC 1, 2, 3, 6,
11, 17, 25, 69; DLB 66; MTCW;
SATA 50; SSC 9

Hiraoka, Kimitake
1925-1970
See Mishima, Yukio
See also CA 97-100

Hopkins, Gerard Manley
1844-1889 .... 3:1701-17
See also DLB 35, 57; NCLC 17

Hughes, (James) Langston
1902-1967 .... 3:1718-37
See also BLC 2; BW; CA 1-4R; CANR 1,
34; CDALB 1929-1941; CLC 1, 5, 10,
15, 35, 44; CLR 17; DLB 4, 7, 48, 51,
86; MTCW; PC 1; SATA 4, 33; SSC 6

Hugo, Victor Marie
1802-1885 . . . . 3:1738-55
See also NCLC 3, 10, 21; SATA 47

Huxley, Aldous (Leonard)
1894-1963 . . . . 3:1756-73
See also CA 85-88; CLC 1, 3, 4, 5, 8, 11,
18, 35; DLB 36, 100; MTCW; SATA 63

Ibsen, Henrik (Johan)
1828-1906 . . . . 3:1774-95
See also brief entry CA 104; DC 2;
TCLC 2, 8, 16, 37

Ionesco, Eugene
1912- 3:1796-1813
See also CA 9-12R; CLC 1, 4, 6, 9, 11, 15,
41; MTCW; SATA 7

Irving, Washington
1783-1859 . . . . 3:1814-32
See also CDALB 1640-1865; DLB 3, 11,
30, 59, 73, 74; NCLC 2, 19; SSC 2;
YABC 2

Jackson, Shirley
1919-1965 . . . . 3:1833-52
See also CA 1-4R; CANR 4;
CDALB 1941-1968; CLC 11, 60; DLB 6;
SATA 2; SSC 9

James, Henry (Jr.)
1843-1916 . . . . 3:1853-70
See also CA 132; brief entry CA 104;
CDALB 1865-1917; DLB 12, 71, 74;
MTCW; SSC 8; TCLC 2, 11, 24, 40

Jeffers, (John) Robinson
1887-1962 . . . . 3:1871-85
See also CA 85-88; CANR 35;
CDALB 1917-1929; CLC 2, 3, 11, 15,
54; DLB 45; MTCW

Johnson, Samuel
1709-1784 . . . . 3:1886-1904
See also DLB 39, 95, 104; LC 15

Jonson, Ben(jamin)
1572?-1637 . . . . 3:1905-22
See also DLB 62; LC 6

Joyce, James (Augustine Aloysius)
1882-1941 . . . . 3:1923-38
See also CA 126; brief entry CA 104;
DLB 10, 19, 36; MTCW; SSC 3; TCLC 3,
8, 16, 26, 35

Kafka, Franz
1883-1924 . . . . 3:1939-52
See also CA 126; brief entry CA 105;
DLB 81; MTCW; SSC 5; TCLC 2, 6, 13,
29

Keats, John
1795-1821 . . . . 3:1953-70
See also DLB 96, 110; NCLC 8; PC 1

Kerouac, Jack
1922-1969 . . . . 3:1971-89
See also Kerouac, Jean-Louis Lebris de
See also CDALB 1941-1968; CLC 1, 2, 3,
5, 14, 29, 61; DLB 2, 16; DLB-DS 3

Kerouac, Jean-Louis Lebris de
1922-1969
See Kerouac, Jack
See also CA 5-8R, 25-28R; CANR 26;
MTCW

Kesey, Ken (Elton)
1935- 3:1990-2005
See also CA 1-4R; CANR 22;
CDALB 1968-1987; CLC 1, 3, 6, 11, 46,
64; DLB 2, 16; MTCW; SATA 66

Kipling, (Joseph) Rudyard
1865-1936 . . . . 3:2006-23
See also CA 120; brief entry CA 105;
CANR 33; DLB 19, 34; MTCW; PC 3;
SSC 5; TCLC 8, 17; YABC 2

Lamb, Charles
1775-1834 . . . . 3:2024-40
See also DLB 93, 107; NCLC 10;
SATA 17

Lawrence, D(avid) H(erbert)
1885-1930 . . . . 3:2041-57
See also CA 121; brief entry CA 104;
DLB 10, 19, 36, 98; MTCW; SSC 4;
TCLC 2, 9, 16, 33

Lee, (Nelle) Harper
1926- 4:2059-74
See also CA 13-16R; CDALB 1941-1968;
CLC 12, 60; DLB 6; MTCW; SATA 11

Lewis, C(live) S(taples)
1898-1963 . . . . 4:2075-95
See also AAYA 3; CA 81-84; CANR 33;
CLC 1, 3, 6, 14, 27; CLR 3; DLB 15,
100; MTCW; SATA 13

Lewis, (Harry) Sinclair
1885-1951 . . . . 4:2096-2114
See also CA 133; brief entry CA 104;
CDALB 1917-1929; DLB 9, 102;
DLB-DS 1; MTCW; TCLC 4, 13, 23, 39

Lindsay, (Nicholas) Vachel
1879-1931 . . . . 4:2115-32
See also CA 135; brief entry CA 114;
CDALB 1865-1917; DLB 54; SATA 40;
TCLC 17

London, Jack
1876-1916 . . . . 4:2133-49
See also London, John Griffith
See also CDALB 1865-1917; DLB 8, 12,
78; SATA 18; SSC 4; TCLC 9, 15, 39

London, John Griffith
1876-1916
See London, Jack
See also CA 119; brief entry CA 110;
MTCW

Lowell, Robert (Traill Spence, Jr.)
1917-1977 . . . . 4:2150-70
See also CA 9-10R; CABS 2; CANR 26;
CLC 1, 2, 3, 4, 5, 8, 9, 11, 15, 37;
DLB 5; MTCW; PC 3

Malamud, Bernard
1914-1986 . . . . 4:2171-91
See also CA 5-8R; CABS 1; CANR 28;
CDALB 1941-1968; CLC 1, 2, 3, 5, 8, 9,
11, 18, 27, 44; DLB 2, 28; DLB-Y 80,
86; MTCW

Mann, Thomas
1875-1955 . . . . 4:2192-2209
See also CA 128; brief entry CA 104;
DLB 66; MTCW; SSC 5; TCLC 2, 8, 14,
21, 35, 44

Mansfield, Katherine
1888-1923 . . . . 4:2210-28
See also Beauchamp, Kathleen Mansfield
See also SSC 9; TCLC 2, 8, 39

Marlowe, Christopher
1564-1593 . . . . 4:2229-47
See also DC 1; DLB 62

Marvell, Andrew
1621-1678 . . . . 4:2248-67
See also LC 4

Maugham, W(illiam) Somerset
1874-1965 . . . . 4:2268-86
See also CA 5-8R; CLC 1, 11, 15, 67;
DLB 10, 36, 77, 100; MTCW; SATA 54;
SSC 8

Maupassant, (Henri Rene Albert) Guy de
1850-1893 . . . . 4:2287-2304
See also NCLC 1; SSC 1

McCullers, (Lula) Carson (Smith)
1917-1967 . . . . 4:2305-21
See also CA 5-8R; CABS 1, 3; CANR 18;
CDALB 1941-1968; CLC 1, 4, 10, 12,
48; DLB 2, 7; MTCW; SATA 27; SSC 9

McKay, Claude
1889-1948 . . . . 4:2322-39
See also McKay, Festus Claudius
See also BLC 3; DLB 4, 45, 51; PC 2;
TCLC 7, 41

McKay, Festus Claudius
1889-1948
See McKay, Claude
See also BW; CA 124; brief entry CA 104;
MTCW

Melville, Herman
1819-1891 . . . . 4:2340-58
See also CDALB 1640-1865; DLB 3, 74;
NCLC 3, 12, 29; SATA 59; SSC 1

Miller, Arthur
1915- 4:2359-75
See also CA 1-4R; CABS 3; CANR 2, 30;
CDALB 1941-1968; CLC 1, 2, 6, 10, 15,
26, 47; DC 1; DLB 7; MTCW

Miller, Henry (Valentine)
1891-1980 . . . . 4:2376-93
See also CA 9-12R; CANR 33;
CDALB 1929-1941; CLC 1, 2, 4, 9, 14,
43; DLB 4, 9; DLB-Y 80; MTCW

Milton, John
1608-1674 . . . . 4:2394-2412
See also LC 9

Mishima, Yukio
1925-1970 . . . . 4:2413-31
See also Hiraoka, Kimitake
See also CLC 2, 4, 6, 9, 27; DC 1; SSC 4

Moliere
1622-1673 . . . . 4:2432-50
See also LC 10

Montaigne, Michel (Eyquem) de
1533-1592 . . . . 4:2451-68
See also LC 8

Morrison, Toni
1931- 4:2469-82
See also AAYA 1; BLC 3; BW; CA 29-32R;
CANR 27; CDALB 1968-1987; CLC 4,
10, 22, 55; DLB 6, 33; DLB-Y 81;
MTCW; SATA 57

Munro, H(ector) H(ugh)
1870-1916
See Saki
See also CA 130; brief entry CA 104;
DLB 34; MTCW

WLC Nationality Index

ALGERIAN
Camus, Albert **1**

AMERICAN
Albee, Edward **1**
Alcott, Louisa May **1**
Anderson, Sherwood **1**
Auden, W. H. **1**
Baldwin, James **1**
Bellow, Saul **1**
Bierce, Ambrose **1**
Bradbury, Ray **1**
Brooks, Gwendolyn **1**
Burroughs, William S. **1**
Capote, Truman **1**
Cather, Willa **1**
Cheever, John **2**
Crane, Hart **2**
Crane, Stephen **2**
Cummings, E. E. **2**
Dickinson, Emily **2**
Dos Passos, John **2**
Douglass, Frederick **2**
Dreiser, Theodore **2**
Du Bois, W. E. B. **2**
Dunbar, Paul Laurence **2**
Eliot, T. S. **2**
Ellison, Ralph **2**
Emerson, Ralph Waldo **2**
Faulkner, William **2**
Fitzgerald, F. Scott **2**
Frost, Robert **2**
Ginsberg, Allen **3**
H. D. **3**
Harte, Bret **3**
Hawthorne, Nathaniel **3**
Heller, Joseph **3**
Hemingway, Ernest **3**
Henry, O. **3**

Hughes, Langston **3**
Irving, Washington **3**
Jackson, Shirley **3**
James, Henry **3**
Jeffers, Robinson **3**
Kerouac, Jack **3**
Kesey, Ken **3**
Lee, Harper **4**
Lewis, Sinclair **4**
Lindsay, Vachel **4**
London, Jack **4**
Lowell, Robert **4**
Malamud, Bernard **4**
McCullers, Carson **4**
McKay, Claude **4**
Melville, Herman **4**
Miller, Arthur **4**
Miller, Henry **4**
Morrison, Toni **4**
Nabokov, Vladimir **4**
Oates, Joyce Carol **4**
O'Connor, Flannery **4**
O'Neill, Eugene **4**
Plath, Sylvia **4**
Poe, Edgar Allan **4**
Pound, Ezra **5**
Pynchon, Thomas **5**
Rand, Ayn **5**
Roth, Philip **5**
Salinger, J. D. **5**
Sandburg, Carl **5**
Saroyan, William **5**
Sexton, Anne **5**
Sinclair, Upton **5**
Singer, Isaac Bashevis **5**
Stein, Gertrude **5**
Steinbeck, John **5**
Stevens, Wallace **5**
Stowe, Harriet Beecher **6**

Thoreau, Henry David **6**
Twain, Mark **6**
Updike, John **6**
Vonnegut, Kurt, Jr. **6**
Warren, Robert Penn **6**
Welty, Eudora **6**
Wharton, Edith **6**
Wheatley, Phillis **6**
Whitman, Walt **6**
Wilder, Thornton **6**
Williams, Tennessee **6**
Williams, William Carlos **6**
Wolfe, Thomas **6**
Wright, Richard **6**

ARGENTINIAN
Borges, Jorge Luis **1**

AUSTRIAN
Kafka, Franz **3**

CANADIAN
Atwood, Margaret **1**
Davies, Robertson **2**
Service, Robert W. **5**

CHILEAN
Neruda, Pablo **4**

COLOMBIAN
García Márquez, Gabriel **3**

CZECHOSLOVAKIAN
Čapek, Karel **1**
Kafka, Franz **3**
Stoppard, Tom **6**

DANISH
Andersen, Hans Christian **1**

WLC Title Index

Homenaje y profanaciones (Paz) **4**:2661, 2663
L'homme aux quarante e'cus (Voltaire) **6**:3769, 3776, 3780
L'Homme qui Rit (Hugo) **3**:1742-43, 1745
The Honorary Consul (Greene) **3**:1550
A Hoosier Holiday (Dreiser) **2**:1029, 1037
Hopes and Impediments (Achebe) **1**:14
"Horae Canonicae" (Auden) **1**:137
"Horatian Ode on Cromwell's return from Ireland" (Marvell) **4**:2253, 2259, 2261, 2263-64
"The Horatians" (Auden) **1**:137
The Horatians and the Curiatians (Brecht) **1**:390
Hordubal (Čapek) **1**:603, 605-06
"Le horla" (Maupassant) **4**:2293
"L'Horreur sympathique" (Baudelaire) **1**:205
"A Horse Name" (Chekhov) **2**:708
"The Horse-Stealers" (Chekhov) **2**:709
"A Horseman in the Sky" (Bierce) **1**:288
Horses and Men (Anderson) **1**:79-80
"Horses--One Dash" (Crane) **2**:818, 824
"Hospital Barge" (Owen) **4**:2618
Hospital Sketches (Alcott) **1**:49-50
The Hot Gates (Golding) **3**:1455-56, 1458
Hotel in Amsterdam (Osborne) **4**:2598
The Hothouse (Pinter) **4**:2704, 2707
"The Hottest Coon in Dixie" (Dunbar) **2**:1111
The Hound of the Baskervilles (Doyle) **2**:1013, 1018-19
"The Hounds of Fate" (Saki) **5**:3001, 3005, 3007, 3009
"The Hour and the Ghost" (Rossetti) **5**:2937
"The House" (Sexton) **5**:3137
A House Not Meant to Stand (Williams) **6**:4006-07
The House of Bernarda Alba (García Lorca)
See *La Casa de Bernarda Alba*
"House of Flowers" (Capote) **1**:618
A House of Genllefolk (Turgenev) **6**:3701
"The House of Life" (Rossetti) **5**:2951-55, 2958
The House of Mirth (Wharton) **6**:3907, 3909-12
The House of the Seven Gables (Hawthorne) **3**:1595, 1598, 1601, 1607-08
"The House with the Maisonette" (Chekhov) **2**:710
The Housebreaker of Shady Hill (Cheever) **2**:690, 696
"How a Little Girl Danced" (Lindsay) **4**:2123
"How Bozo the Button Buster Busted All His Buttons when a Mouse Came" (Sandburg) **5**:3066
"How Brother Parker Fell from Grace" (Dunbar) **2**:1107
How He Lied to Her Husband (Shaw) **5**:3193
"How I Contemplated the World from the Detroit House of Correction and Began My Life Over Again" (Oates) **4**:2536
"How I Went to the Mines" (Harte) **3**:1585
"How It Strikes a Contemporary" (Woolf) **6**:4048
"How Lucy Backslid" (Dunbar) **2**:1112

"How oft when thou, my music, music play'st" (Shakespeare)
See "Sonnet 128"
"How Santa Claus Came to Simpson's Bar" (Harte) **3**:1589
"How Yesterday Looked" (Sandburg) **5**:3053
Howards End (Forster) **2**:1258-59, 1261, 1265, 1269-70
Howdy, Honey, Howdy (Dunbar) **2**:1114
"Howl" (Ginsberg) **3**:1396-98, 1404-07
Howl and Other Poems (Ginsberg) **3**:1399-1400, 1403
Huckleberry Finn (Twain) **6**:3716, 3718, 3721, 3726-28
Hudson River Bracketed (Wharton) **6**:3908, 3911
Hugh Selwyn Mauberley (*Mauberley*) (Pound) **5**:2789-93, 2795, 2797, 2803
Huis Clos (Sartre) **5**:3095-97
The Human Comedy (Balzac)
See *La Comédie Humaine: La Racherche de l'Absolu*
The Human Comedy (Saroyan) **5**:3075
The Human Drift (London) **4**:2140
The Human Factor (Greene) **3**:1550-51
"The Humble-Bee" (Emerson) **2**:1171
"A Humble Remonstrance" (Stevenson) **5**:3456
Humboldt's Gift (Bellow) **1**:265, 267, 271-72
"Humility" (Service) **5**:3131
"Hunchback Girl" (Brooks) **1**:454
Hunger and Thirst (Ionesco) **3**:1804-06, 1809
"The Hunger Artist" (Kafka) **3**:1950-51
The Hunted (O'Neill) **4**:2561
The Hunting of the Snark (Carroll) **1**:644
"Hurry Up Please It's Time" (Sexton) **5**:3138
"Hygeia at the Solito" (O. Henry) **3**:1677
Hymen (H. D.) **3**:1612, 1618, 1624
Hymenaei (Jonson) **3**:1920
"Hymn among the ruins" (Paz)
See "Himno entre ruinas"
Hymn in Honour of the Plague (Pushkin) **5**:2827
"Hymn of Apollo" (Shelley) **5**:3232, 3234
"Hymn of Man" (Swinburne) **6**:3563
"Hymn to Beauty" (Spenser) **5**:3339
"Hymn to Heavenly Beauty" (Spenser) **5**:3339
"An Hymn to Humanity" (Wheatley) **6**:3922-23, 3928, 3930
"Hymn to Ignorance" (Gray) **3**:1526, 1533
"Hymn to Intellectual Beauty" (Shelley) **5**:3233, 3238
"Hymn to Mercury" (Shelley) **5**:3236
"Hymn to Proserpine" (Swinburne) **6**:3562
"An Hymn to the Evening" (Wheatley) **6**:3918, 3924, 3927, 3930
"An Hymn to the Morning" (Wheatley) **6**:3918, 3927
"Hymne to God my God, in my sicknesse" (Donne) **2**:942
"A Hymne to God the Father" (Donne) **2**:942
Hymns (Spenser) **5**:3352
Hyperion (Keats) **3**:1956, 1958-59, 1967
"Hysteria" (Eliot) **2**:1146
I Cannot Be Silent (Tolstoy) **6**:3664
"I Didn't Get Over" (Fitzgerald) **2**:1235

"I do believe her though I know she lies" (Shakespeare)
See "Sonnet 138"
"I Have a Thing to Tell You" (Wolfe) **6**:4041
"I have longed to move away" (Thomas) **6**:3617
"I Heard Immanuel Singing" (Lindsay) **4**:2119
"I love those little booths at Benvenutie's" (Brooks) **1**:452
"I Must Have You" (Oates) **4**:2530
I Sing the Body Electric (Bradbury) **1**:371
"I Stood on Tiptoe" (Keats) **3**:1958
"i thank You God for most this amazing" (Cummings) **2**:842
"I think it Rains" (Soyinka) **5**:3319
"I Thought of Thee" (Wordsworth) **6**:4073
"I tie my Hat--I crease my Shawl" (Dickinson) **2**:927
I vecchi e i giovani (*The Old and the Young*) (Pirandello) **4**:2718
I Wanted to Write a Poem (Williams) **6**:4019
"The Ice Maiden" (Anderson) **1**:66
"The Ice Palace" (Fitzgerald) **2**:1232
The Iceman Cometh (O'Neill) **4**:2561-63, 2565-66, 2569
Ida Elisabeth (Undset) **6**:3738, 3741-42
"Ida M'Toy" (Welty) **6**:3889
Idanre and Other Poems (Soyinka) **5**:3319, 3320
"An Ideal Craftsman" (de la Mare) **2**:892
An Ideal Husband (Wilde) **6**:3957, 3965
The Ides of March (Wilder) **6**:3976, 3984
"The Idiot Boy" (Wordsworth) **6**:4076
L'Idiot de la famille (*The Family Idiot*) (Sartre) **5**:3093, 3099, 3101
Idiots First (Malamud) **4**:2176, 2181, 2183, 2186
Idler (Johnson) **3**:1894
"The Idyl of Red Gulch" (Harte) **3**:1580
"Une idylle" (Maupassant) **4**:2289
Idylls of the King (Tennyson) **6**:3575, 3579, 3584
"If" (Kipling) **3**:2014
"If" (Pirandello)
See "Se"
If Beale Street Could Talk (Baldwin) **1**:175
"if everything happens that can't be done" (Cummings) **2**:842
If Five Years Pass (García Lorca)
See *Así que pasan los Cinco Años*
"if i have made, my lady, intricate" (Cummings) **2**:840
"If my head hurt a hair's foot" (Thomas) **6**:3621
"If We Must Die" (McKay) **4**:2326, 2330, 2336-37
"Ignatius his Conclav" (Donne) **2**:939
Ile (O'Neill) **4**:2558
Illuminations (Rimbaud) **5**:2908, 2910-14, 2916, 2918-20
"Illusions" (Emerson) **2**:1174
Les Illusions Perdues (Balzac) **1**:183, 190
"The Illustrated Man" (Bradbury) **1**:366
"L'illustre estinto" ("The Illustrious Deceased") (Pirandello) **4**:2717
"The Illustrious Client" (Doyle) **2**:1016
"The Illustrious Deceased" (Pirandello)
See "L'illustre estinto"

Title Index

"There is mist on the mountain" (Scott)
5:3115

"There Was a Savior" (Thomas) 6:3619

"There Will Come Soft Rain" (Bradbury)
1:370

"There's Wisdom in Women" (Brooke)
1:434

Thérése Raquin (Zola) 6:4122-24, 4126,
4128

"Thermos Bottles" (Mishima) 4:2423

"These" (Williams) 6:4014, 4023

Things as They Are (Q.E.D.) (Stein) 5:3361,
3370

Things Fall Apart (Achebe) 1:3-10, 12

Think It Over, Giacomino! (Pirandello)
See *Pensaci, Giacomino!*

"The Third Expedition" (Bradbury) 1:370

"The Third Ingredient" (O. Henry) 3:1675,
1677

The Third Man (Greene) 3:1542, 1544,
1547, 1553

"The Third Resignation" (García Márquez)
See "La tercera regisnación"

The Third Violet (Crane) 2:814-15

Thirst and Other One-Act Plays (O'Neill)
4:2558

"This bread I break" (Thomas) 6:3617

This Gun for Hire (Greene)
See *Gun for Sale*

"This Is a Photograph of Me" (Atwood)
1:111

"This Is the Track" (Owen) 4:2618

This Side of Paradise (Fitzgerald) 2:1221-
24

"This Side of Truth" (Thomas) 6:3619

Thomas l'Imposteur (Cocteau) 2:726-27,
733, 736

"The Thorny Path of Honor" (Andersen)
1:57

Those Barren Leaves (Huxley) 3:1762,
1767-68

"Those lips that Love's own hand did make"
(Shakespeare)
See "Sonnet 145"

"Those Times" (Sexton) 5:3146

Thoughts and Details on Scarcity (Burke)
1:506, 509

"Thoughts on His Excellency Major General
Lee" (Wheatley) 6:3919

Thoughts on Religion (Swift) 6:3547

"Thoughts on the African Novel" (Achebe)
1:15

*Thoughts on the Cause of the Present
Discontents* (Burke) 1:506

*Thoughts on the late Transactions
respecting the Falkland Islands* (Johnson)
3:1895

"Thoughts on the Shape of the Human
Body" (Brooke) 1:439

"Thoughts on the Works of Providence"
(Wheatley) 6:3921, 3926, 3928, 3930

Thoughts on Various Subjects (Swift)
6:3535

"A Thousand Deaths" (London) 4:2141

Thrawn Janet (Stevenson) 5:3447

"Three" (Čapek) 1:601

The Three Clerks (Trollope) 6:3681, 3691

Three Deaths (Tolstoy) 6:3666

"Three Encounters" (Turgenev) 6:3708

"The Three Enemies" (Rossetti) 5:2931

Three Essays in Homage to John Dryden
(Eliot) 2:1137

"The Three Gables" (Doyle) 2:1013

"Three Hours Between Planes" (Fitzgerald)
2:1235

Three Lives (Stein) 5:3360-61, 3363, 3367-
70

"Three Meetings" (Turgenev) 6:3702

"The Three Million Yen" (Mishima) 4:2423

Three Musketeers (Dumas)
See *Les Trois Mousquetaires*

"Three Nuns" (Rossetti) 5:2942

The Three of Them (Gorky) 3:1490, 1492

Three Plays (Wilder) 6:3981, 3983

"Three Portraits" (Turgenev) 6:3697, 3702

Three Questions (Tolstoy) 6:3664

The Three Sisters: A Drama in Four Acts
(Chekhov) 708, 710, 713, 715-18, 720

Three Soldiers (Dos Passos) 2:955, 963

"The Three Strangers" (Hardy) 3:1566

"Three Vagabonds of Trinidad" (Harte)
3:1583, 1589

"The Three Voices" (Service) 5:3123

"Three Years" (Chekhov) 2:709

"The Threefold Destiny" (Hawthorne)
3:1605

Threepenny Opera (Brecht) 1:389-90

Threnodia Augustalis (Goldsmith) 3:1476

"Threnody" (Emerson) 2:1171-72, 1178

Thrones (Pound) 5:2801-02

"Through Death to Love" (Rossetti) 5:2951

"Through the Dutch Waterways" (Golding)
3:1456

Through the Looking Glass (Carroll) 1:637,
642-43, 647-49

"Thumbelina" (Andersen) 1:65

"Thumbling" (Andersen)
See "Poor Thumbling"

Thurso's Landing (Jeffers) 3:1874-75

"Thyrsis" (Arnold) 1:104

"Tiare Tahiti" (Brooke) 1:439, 443-44

The Ticket That Exploded (Burroughs)
1:535-37, 542

Tiempo mexicano (Fuentes) 2:1312-13

Tiers Livre (Rabelais) 5:2859-60, 2862-63,
2869

Till We Have Faces (Lewis) 4:2087, 2090,
2093-94

The Time Machine (Wells) 6:3859, 3861-
62, 3864-66, 3868-70, 3872, 3874

Time Must Have a Stop (Huxley) 3:1767-69

The Time of Your Life (Saroyan) 5:3070-
73, 3076-80

Time Present (Osborne) 4:2596, 2598,
2600-01

The Tin Drum (Grass) 3:1501-13

"The Tinder-Box" (Andersen) 1:57, 64-5,
67

"Tintern Abbey" (Wordsworth) 6:4076

Tiny Alice (Albee) 1:23-5, 27, 30-1

"Tiresias" (Swinburne) 6:3563

The Titan (Dreiser) 2:1025-30

*Los títeres de Cachiporra (Cachiporra's
Puppets)* (García Lorca) 2:1341

"Tithonus" (Tennyson) 6:3583

"The Titmouse" (Emerson) 2:1171

Tjodolf (Undset) 6:3741

"To a Contemporary Bunk-Shooter"
(Sandburg) 5:3054

"To a Foot, from its child" (Neruda) 4:2517

"To a Friend" (Arnold) 1:100

"To a Gipsy Child by the Sea-shore"
(Arnold) 1:101

To a God Unknown (Steinbeck) 5:3387

"To a Lady and Her Children, On the Death
of Her Son and Their Brother" (Wheatley)
6:3929

"To a Little Girl, One Year Old in a Ruined
Fortress" (Warren) 6:3814

"To a Louse" (Burns) 1:523

To a Magnate (Pushkin) 5:2832

"To a Republican Friend" (Arnold) 1:100

"To a Solitary Disciple" (Williams) 6:4012

"To a Wealthy Man" (Yeats) 6:4108

"To a Winter Squirrel" (Brooks) 1:457

"To Autumn" (Keats)
See "Ode to Autumn"

"To Be in Love" (Brooks) 1:456-57

*To Damascus (Toward Damascus; To
Damascus, Part III)* (Strindberg) 6:3517-
19, 3525, 3529

To Damascus, Part III (Strindberg)
See *To Damascus*

"To Delmore Schwartz" (Lowell) 4:2162,
2167

To Disembark (Brooks) 1:458

"To Dog" (Bierce) 1:292

"To Don at Salaam" (Brooks) 1:458

"To E. FitzGerald" (Tennyson) 6:3584

"To Fausta" (Arnold) 1:101

To Have and Have Not (Hemingway)
3:1658

"To Helen" (Poe) 4:2759

"To his Coy Mistress" ("The Coy Mistress")
(Marvell) 4:2253, 2255-56, 2258-59,
2264-66

"To His Excellency General George
Washington" (Wheatley) 6:3917, 3922,
3926

"To His Honor the Lieutenant Governor on
the Death of His Lady" (Wheatley)
6:3922

"To his Mistris Going to Bed" (Donne)
2:945

"To His Watch" (Hopkins) 3:1708

"To Imagination" (Brontë) 1:429

"To J. W." (Emerson) 2:1171

"To Jane: The Invitation" (Shelley) 5:3234

"To Keorapetse Kgositsile (Willie)" (Brooks)
1:458

To Kill a Mockingbird (Lee) 4:2062-63,
2065-68, 2070-74

To Kill Time (Gorky) 3:1485

To Let (Galsworthy) 2:1328

"To Maecenas" (Wheatley) 6:3922-23,
3928-29

"To Marguerite--Continued" ("Continued")
(Arnold) 1:100

"To Mr. R. W."If as mine is'" (Donne)
2:934

"To Negro Writers" (Hughes) 3:1731

"To Night" (Shelley) 5:3234

"To S. M., A Young African Painter, On
Seeing His Works" (Wheatley) 6:3929

"To Sir Edward Herbert, at Julyers" (Donne)
2:945

"To Speak of Woe That Is in Marriage"
(Lowell) 4:2165-66

"To the Countesse of Bedford."Madame,
reason is'" (Donne) 2:934

"To the Countesse of Bedford 'This twilight
of'" (Donne) 2:934

"To the Diaspora" (Brooks) 1:459

"To the Duke of Wellington" (Arnold) 1:100

To the Lighthouse (Woolf) 6:4046-47,
4052-53, 4056-58

Title Index